THE MAKING OF THE POPE OF THE MILLENNIUM

Kalendarium of the Life of Karol Wojtyła

THE MAKING OF THE POPE OF THE MILLENNIUM

Kalendarium of the Life of Karol Wojtyła

Adam Boniecki, MIC

MARIAN PRESS
MARIANS OF THE IMMACULATE CONCEPTION
&
ASSOCIATION OF MARIAN HELPERS
STOCKBRIDGE, MASSACHUSETTS 01263
2000

Library of Congress Cataloging in Publication Data
Number 00-102005
ISBN 0-944203-49-3

Expanded and Revised Edition of the original Polish Version *Kalendarium życia Karola Wojtyły* by Fr. Adam Boniecki, MIC Published by Wydawnictwo Znak-Kraków 1983.

Translated from the Polish by: *Irena & Thaddeus Mirecki et al. Maria Chrypinski, Andrew Chudzinski, Magdalena Konieczny-Pettey, Barbara Mirecki, Ewa & Paul St Jean, Maciej P. Talar.*

Editor of the English Edition: *Kazimierz Chwalek, MIC.*

Typesetting and Design by: *Patricia Menatti & Jessie Wolska.*

Cover Design by: *William Sosa.*
Cover Photo Credit: © *Adam Bujak.*

Project Manager & Photo Selection by: *Andrew R. Mączyński, MIC.*

FIRST ENGLISH EDITION

Stockbridge, Massachusetts

To His Holiness, Pope John Paul II
on the Occasion of His 80th Birthday
Grateful for His Life of Faith
and Dedication to Christ and His Church

Marians of the Immaculate Conception
and its
Association of Marian Helpers

May 18, 2000

Table of Contents

METROPOLITA KRAKOWSKI

A Word from Franciszek Cardinal Macharski
Archbishop Metropolitan of Krakow

It gives me great joy to welcome the English Edition of *The Making of the Pope of the Millennium: Kalendarium of the Life of Karol Wojtyla.*

Since its first printing in Poland, soon after the beginning of the Pontificate of the "Pope from Krakow," it has become the standard which no serious biographer can ignore. The proof of the lasting quality of the *Kalendarium* is that it can be enlarged upon and modified.

This splendid work was compiled by Fr. Adam Boniecki, a priest of the Congregation of Marians of the Immaculate Conception. He dedicated himself to this work with painstaking exactitude and devotion to every detail, coupled with his deeply respectful love of John Paul II and the Church. For this, I express my profound sincere gratitude to Fr. Adam, the author and a friend. I congratulate the Marian Community in Stockbridge, Massachusetts, for publishing the English edition of the *Kalendarium of the Life of Karol Wojtyla.* I eagerly look forward to my receiving the book in Krakow.

I pray that this work will help thousands of readers to know and love God, Merciful Love, who guided Karol Wojtyla on His path from Krakow to Rome.

+ Franciszek kard. Macharski

Krakow, February 22, 2000

A Word from the Provincial Superior

After several years of preparation, we are pleased to present to you a new publication entitled *The Making of the Pope of the Millennium, the Kalendarium of the Life of Karol Wojtyla.*

The value of this work is inestimable. Not only is it the best resource for exploring the early life of the man who became John Paul II, but it is also an excellent source of firsthand information on the life of the Church under the Communist regime.

From these writings we discover the foundation of what makes John Paul II the person he is. His holiness, his impact on the world, his powerful faith, his living for others, and his inexhaustible spiritual energy are made to stand out to inspire each and every reader.

Indeed, John Paul II is inspiring as a model of an academic priest who is also pastoral. There is no contradiction between the two. He is an eminently qualified theologian as well as an outstanding pastoral minister. In the same way, there is no contradiction in John Paul II as a priest who is faithful to the teaching of the Church and a priest who is willing to speak out on behalf of the poor, the politically marginalized, and the oppressed.

The intent of this book is to invite the reader to look beyond the simple entries of activities, summaries of homilies, reflections and talks to the real person behind these events. No one will leave this book, having read even a few short entries, without being touched and inspired by the life of this man whose faith in the Triune God is so alive, whose love of Mary, the Church and all people is so visible, and whose hope in eternal life is so unwavering.

Very Rev. Walter M. Dziordz, MIC
Provincial of St. Stanislaus Kostka Province
Congregation of Marians of the Immaculate Conception

INTRODUCTION TO THE ENGLISH EDITION

I do not know whether *Kalendarium* can be considered a biography. But frankly speaking, it is not so important. The book contains a chronological record of facts, documents, testimonies (verified), and statements by Karol Wojtyla himself, in which he spoke of his life on various occasions — all this without any "connective" narration or commentaries from the author. In this way *Kalendarium* is free from speculation or fabrication, which are usually inevitable in biographies. The format that I have adopted, that of a chronicle written *ex post,* prevents this from happening. The author of this work does not suggest anything. He provides elements necessary to compose a portrait and leaves it up to the reader to put these elements together. Thus, the reader, if he wants to, becomes a co-author of the biography. In this book he finds facts that are of great consequence and those that are quite minor, thus making it possible for the portrait to be painted in the full scale of colors: bright, dark and half-tones.

The introduction to the original Polish edition (*Kalendarium zycia Karola Wojtyly*, published by *ZNAK* 1983) tells the story of how this book came about. Here I wish to add a few pieces of information that were not included there.

My motive for undertaking the work on the *Kalendarium* was a deluge of nonsensical biographies about the new pope. I felt that fabricated biographies did no justice to the actual one; but, to tell the truth, I did not really know the actual one. I knew that Cardinal Wojtyla came from Wadowice, that he studied Polish Language and Literature at the Jagiellonian University, that he was a physical laborer during the war, that he was associated with the Rhapsodic Theater, that he studied at the Angelicum in Rome, that he was involved in pastoral ministry to university students, that he was a professor at the Catholic University of Lublin and one of the youngest bishops, that he was an active participant of the Second Vatican Council and, that he later led a retreat at the Vatican at the invitation of Pope Paul VI. I knew him from personal contacts and from his public activity as the Shepherd of the Archdiocese of Krakow.

I began my research. The process of uncovering the history of the life of the new Pope, whom I thought I knew quite well, proved to be a fascinating adventure, an adventure full of surprises.

I worked on the *Kalendarium* in 1978 and 1979 in a country under the conditions of strict Socialism. I had no technological tools at my disposal, not even a photocopier (the use of such devices was controlled by government censors), not to mention a computer. I had no access to a fax or telex. Long distance phone connections could be obtained only with the assistance of the post office and one always had to keep in mind that they could be monitored. I had a *Hermas-Baby* typewriter, a tape recorder which I used to record those documents that I could not copy (I would simply read them onto the tape), and a small Fiat 126 car by means of which I traveled from one corner of Poland to another. I made a lot of hand-written notes on sheets torn from notebooks. A few kind-hearted people assisted me in this effort.

After many months of work, when the typescript of the book was ready, the censors took it in their hands because every text intended for publication had to receive the permission of the Office of the Control of the Press. It turned out that the censors would not give permission for the *Kalendarium* to be published unless some fragments of the text were removed. Neither the publishing house *Znak* nor I myself could consent to this. Finally, as a result of heated discussions, appeals and pressure, the authorities agreed to allow the book to be published on the occasion of the Holy Father's second visit to Poland (1983). However, they did not allocate the necessary paper. I must explain here that I do not mean a free allocation of paper. In order to buy paper to have anything printed in Poland one had to obtain a special order of allocation. Nor were we permitted to sell the book in bookstores. We could only sell them through *"Church channels,"* that is outside the network of public distribution. The paper was donated by the Pier Giorgio Frassati Center of European Studies in Rome. The entire first edition — forty thousand copies — was sold out in a flash.

Although I prepared the *Kalendarium* during a time when everything intended for publication had to be written under the pressure of an *interior censor*, that is with the awareness that the text would have to pass through the hands of a government censor before it appeared in print — somehow I did not give in to this pressure. But there existed a certain obstacle. As I was writing, I was troubled by the question of what I could write without creating problems for the Church and, especially, for individual persons. Unfortunately, in spite of my caution, I was unable to avoid doing so. After the book had been published, I received a letter — fortunately the only one — with bitter reproaches. I had inadvertently revealed something that I should not have revealed. The reproaches were so vehement that I removed the piece of information in question from the current edition since it was not really essential to the entire text. There were also things about which I simply could not get any information. For example, in *The Chronicle of the Bishop's Activities* the future Pope was more than laconic with regard to his activities during his visits to Rome. I tried to respect his discretion.

Almost twenty years have passed since the first edition of the *Kalendarium*. Foreign publishers have made several attempts to have the book translated and published. In 1985 and 1986 attempts were made to publish the book in America. I am deeply grateful to all those who made efforts to that end. Ultimately, however, no one ventured to do so. The book was too extensive and, therefore, too expensive (translation!) and its form seemed too unusual.

Meanwhile, even without having been translated into foreign languages, the *Kalendarium* was fulfilling its purpose. It was intended to be a basis, a collection of factual material, a springboard for new biographies of the Pope. And, indeed, it has been. There are very few books about John Paul II, which are not based on the *Kalendarium* for those portions concerning his life before he was elected to the Chair of St. Peter. Many authors simply availed themselves of the book, but others would turn to me directly, asking for information. This gave me an opportunity to meet many excellent writers and engage in many interesting conversations about the Holy Father. However, what these authors later did with the information that they obtained from me is their business.

Of course, apart from the *Kalendarium*, many people have conducted and continue to conduct their own research. In 1980, *Libreria Editrice Vaticana* published an extensive bibliography of Karol Wojtyla's works through October 16, 1978, containing a list of his writings and works about him (Rev. Wiktor Gramatowski, SJ and Zofia Wilinska, *Karol Wojtyla negli scritti. Bibliografia*). At more or less the same time, in Krakow, Zofia Skwarnicka was compiling a bibliography of Karol Wojtyla's works as an appendix to the *Kalendarium*. It was the first attempt, at the time, to familiarize the reader with the scope of Karol Wojtyla's work on such a large scale.

Gradually other books began to appear — recollections by Karol Wojtyla's friends, elaborations of other documents, and new biographies of Karol Wojtyla. I could see with satisfaction that the *Kalendarium* was a useful tool for those authors. Particularly valuable among these works appears to be a monumental study entitled *Ks. Kardynal Karol Wojtyla Arcybiskup Metropolita Krakowski Nauczyciel i Pasterz. Listy pasterskie — Komunikaty — Zarzadzenia 1959-1978.* Wyd. Osrodek Dokumentacji Pontyfikatu Jana Pawla II. Rzym 1987 {*Karol Cardinal Wojtyla Metropolitan Archbishop of Krakow Teacher and Shepherd. Pastoral Letters — Communiqués — Ordinances 1959-1978.* Published: Center for the Documentation of the Pontificate of John Paul II. Rome 1987}. Under the direction of Rev. Michal Jagosz all episcopal letters, communiqués, and ordinances by the future Pope were gathered there and elaborated on. A working text prepared by Rev. Michal Jagosz, a kind of supplement and an errata to the *Kalendarium*, emerged as a "by-product" of this monumental work. When I began the work on the new edition, Rev. Jagosz generously made the fruit of his labor available to me. Because of this, many important additions and corrections could be introduced to the current edition. I credit some of the essential additions to the work of Rev. Jan Dyduch. In his book entitled *Kardynal Karol Wojtyla w sluzbie Kosciolowi Powszechnemu. Udzial w pracach Kurii Rzymskiej i Synodow Biskupich.* Wydawnictwo Sw. Stanislawa, Krakow 1998 {*Karol Cardinal Wojtyla in the Service of the Universal Church. Participation in the Works of the Roman Curia and the Synods of Bishops.* St. Stanislaw Publishing House, Krakow 1998}, the author presented Karol Wojtyla's participation in the work of the Holy See on the basis of documentation preserved in Krakow. These activities of Karol Wojtyla, which I am now able to mention in the current edition of the *Kalendarium*, allow the reader to understand how it was that he could be elected to the Chair of St. Peter. He was not an unknown, mysterious figure from behind the "Iron Curtain," but a man who had already played an important role in the work of the implementation of the teachings of the Second Vatican Council. His activity in this arena is little known, for there are few who see within the walls of the Roman dicasteries into the circles of the most competent representatives of the various nations, where the decisions and programs that change the face of the Church are made. Cardinal Wojtyla's participation in these works was very significant and highly appreciated.

I would like to mention several other books where I found valuable information to supplement the material I have gathered so far. These are: *Z ludzi wziety,* Oficyna Wydawnicza Papieskiej Akademii Teologicznej w Krakowie, Wydawnictwo "Czuwajmy" Krakow 1995 {*Taken From Among the People,* Publishing Office of the Pontifical Academy of Theology in Krakow, "Czuwajmy" Publishing House, Krakow 1995}, it is a collection of homilies and conferences on priesthood by Cardinal Karol Wojtyla, collected and compiled by Rev. Jan Dyduch; *Przez Podgorze na Watykan,* Marek Cholewa, Wydawnictwo "Czuwajmy", Krakow 1998 {*From Podgorze to the Vatican,* compiled by Marek Cholewa, "Czuwajmy" Publishing House, Krakow 1998}; Teresa Skawinska, *On rozda milosc. Wspomnienia,* Wyd. Polska Misja Katolicka we Francji, Paryz 1997 {Teresa Skawinska, *He Will Give Away Love. Recollections.* Published: Polish Catholic Mission in France, Paris 1997; *Zapis Drogi. Wspomnienia o nieznanym duszpasterstwie ksiedza Karola Wojtyly.* Wyd. Sw. Stanislawa, Krakow 1998 {*The Record of a Journey. Recollections of Rev. Karol Wojtyla's Unknown Ministry.* Published: Sw. Stanislaw Publishing House,

Krakow 1998}, recollections by the members of a group which Rev. Karol Wojtyla surrounded with special pastoral care in his first years as a priest. The members of the group were mostly university students. In time the students began professional work, many of them became academic workers and fathers and mothers of their own families. Gradually the children of the former participants would join the group. The group assumed the name *Srodowisko*[1] and that is how it has been referred to in the *Kalendarium*. Of course, the book is much richer in details than the *Kalendarium*. All of the camping trips, kayak trips, and other excursions organized under the leadership of Karol Wojtyla were listed and described there.

In a little note attached to the first edition of the *Kalendarium,* I asked readers to send in corrections and additions. I received many of them and they were a tremendous help to me in my work on the second edition. Among these materials, special mention should be made of the documentation provided by Mr. Czeslaw Domaradzki, regarding the young Karol Wojtyla's participation in a clandestine organization called *Unia.* I did not record this fact in the first edition of *Kalendarium* because I did not have adequate sources at my disposal. Moreover, Karol Wojtyla himself made no mention of the episode when he filled out a university questionnaire in 1951. To the question: "To what other [apart from those mentioned in a previous point of the questionnaire] political, social or military organizations do you belong?" Wojtyla answered: "No, I do not belong to any such organizations." Perhaps he thought that *Unia* was not a political, social, or military organization or perhaps, simply, such were the times and such were the rules of the game that you played with the authorities. Of the remaining correspondence which I received, one letter stands out — the one sent by Mr. Zdzislaw Szuba. It is twenty-eight pages of typescript containing detailed corrections and additions compiled with admirable laboriousness. In his letter the author correctly points out certain insufficiencies of the *Kalendarium* although, as it turned out following more thorough verification, some of his information was imprecise and some even untrue. Nonetheless, Mr. Szuba's contribution to the preparation of this edition was invaluable.

And, indeed, the contribution of all those who responded to my appeal and sent in both small and extensive corrections and information was equally invaluable. I thank them all from the bottom of my heart.

I should also like to thank all of the authors who decided to avail themselves of the first edition of the *Kalendarium* and who listed it in the bibliographies of their own works.

Finally, I express my gratitude to my religious brothers, the Marians

---

[1] See Glossary.

of the Immaculate Conception of the American Province of St. Stanislaus Kostka, especially the Marian Helpers Center in Stockbridge, Massachusetts. It is because of their efforts that the English edition of the *Kalendarium* is being published. I thank all those who undertook this initiative and then personally watched over its realization: Bro. Andrzej R. Mączyński, MIC, Fr. Kazimierz Chwalek, MIC, Mr. and Mrs. Thaddeus Mirecki for translating the text into English, Mrs. Ewa St Jean for her work *con amore* on the English text, and Dominika Schmid, who prepared the photographs for printing. The Marian Helpers Center in Stockbridge does an admirable job as it supports apostolic and social works conducted by the Congregation of Marians throughout the world, especially in the countries of the former socialist block. As a sign of my recognition and gratitude, I release all rights to the English edition to them.

Rev. Adam Boniecki, MIC

Easter Monday, 1999

INTRODUCTION TO
THE ORIGINAL POLISH EDITION

The idea of writing this book crystallized at a joint editorial meeting of *Tygodnik Powszechny*[1], the monthly *Znak* and Znak Publishers in November of 1978 — not quite a month after the election of the Archbishop of Krakow, Karol Wojtyla, to the Chair of Saint Peter. The necessity to prepare a chronicle of the life of the Holy Father was becoming evident even then, in light of the numerous biographies being published. It was becoming evident that there would be an ever-increasing number of those types of publications which, too often, have more to say about the author than about their subject and, too often, are geared more to satisfying public expectations than to relating the truth. These fears turned out to be justified.

The deadline for finishing the book was set for the end of February 1979. I estimated its length to be some 200 pages of typescript; however, as I begin writing this introduction, I have before me a manuscript of 1200 pages and the calendar reads August 31, 1979. Having submitted my manuscript for publication, I am by no means convinced that I have truly finished this work. The incompleteness of it is painfully obvious, but at some point one has to say "stop." I dare to presume, however, that the material collected on these pages contains the main elements that made up the day to day activities of Karol Wojtyla from his birth until October 16, 1978.

This *Kalendarium* is a kind of chronicle. Its purpose is to present facts without analyzing any causal relationships among them, without comments, and without evaluations. It is more source material for biographers that a biography in itself. Public interest in the person of Pope John Paul II seems to be constantly growing, as evidenced by the number of titles and print runs of books about him. Quite apart from the inherent merit of this printed material, its volume alone indicates the overwhelming need to understand who this man is who has so fascinated the Church and the world.

In presenting this book to the Holy Father, the content of which was written by his own life, I wish to express my gratitude for that which I encountered in the course of compiling this *Kalendarium* and which I have tried to express to the best of my ability. I am grateful as well for the type of life which is chronicled here and which cannot but influence the life of anyone who comes into contact with it.

---

[1] A Catholic weekly published in Krakow.

The materials which I have researched and collected are arranged chronologically. With the progression of years, the journal becomes more and more detailed. It is understandable that the documentation following Wojtyla's consecration as a bishop is much richer than that from earlier years. The differences between the respective sources dictated a decidedly different presentation of the facts of the earlier years as compared with later years. I used two types of sources: documentation and verbal accounts.

I was not successful in obtaining access to all of the documents which should form the basis of such a work. Thus, I was unable to acquire documents relating to the Holy Father's activities in the Main Committee of the Polish Episcopate, nor in the Plenary Conference. These documents are strictly confidential. I was, however, given (partial) access to documents of the Episcopal Committee for Pastoral Care and of the Committee for Education under the Episcopal Council for Education. The list of issues considered by the Episcopal Committee for the Apostolate of the Laity, under the chairmanship of Cardinal Wojtyla, and the schedule of the committee's meetings were provided by the former Secretary of the Committee, the present Archbishop of Krakow, Franciszek Cardinal Macharski.

Other documents from which I drew were found in the archives of the parishes in Czaniec, Lipnik, Biala, Wadowice and Niegowic; in the parishes of Sts. Peter and Paul and of St. Florian, both in Krakow; in the archives of the Krakow Curia, the Pontifical Theological Seminary, the Jagiellonian University, the Catholic University of Lublin, the Angelicum in Rome, and the Belgian College in Rome. I also had access to documents related to the Synod of the Archdiocese of Krakow and the Provincial Synod. A great help in organizing all of this documentation was provided by the "Chronicle of the Bishop's Activities." The three volumes of the "Chronicle" begun in 1958 are journals compiled by the Bishop {Wojtyla} recording his daily activities by date and time as is required of all bishops. In this case, a religious sister from the diocesan secretariat received from the Bishop, later the Archbishop and then the Cardinal, handwritten notes which she carefully transcribed into the chronicle. The "Chronicle of Activities," which at first had been compiled in a rather perfunctory manner, became more and more detailed with passing years. The last handwritten notes submitted for inclusion in the chronicle are those that Cardinal Wojtyla made during the period immediately preceding the conclave; and finally, the last entry in the volume is about his election to the papacy. A photocopy of that note is included in this book.

Often, these terse notations in the "Chronicle of Activities" were the only source of information, and they even made it possible to date other reports and documents. Some of the more terse notations in the "Chronicle" could not be corroborated by other sources; nevertheless I included them in this *Kalendarium* because I felt that, even though they were incomplete, they still contribute to the totality of the episcopal activities of the Holy Father.

Especially valuable sources of information for this journal were the transcriptions of his recorded homilies. Although this collection of some 7,000 typed pages (about 1,000 homilies) is but a partial documentation of the preaching activities of the Archbishop of Krakow. A prudent selection of fragments allows one to reconstruct a unique "spiritual journal" of the author. These homilies, for the most part spoken extemporaneously and not read, form a profound commentary on the bare facts compiled in this journal. I tried to select those fragments in particular where the speaker was "expressing himself," voicing his own personal outlook on various matters. The citations are often interrupted (indicated by ellipses in the text) to remove digressions and trains of thought relating to other parts of the homily. The intention was not to show the body of Christian doctrine expressed in the teachings of the Archbishop of Krakow, but to exhibit his own personality. Since all of these citations are dated (establishing dates was often quite difficult) and because these homilies will eventually be published in their entirety, it will then be possible to place the citations in their original contexts.

Here I must add an explanation of the entries in this *Kalendarium* regarding the activities of Bishop, later Archbishop, Karol Wojtyla at the Second Vatican Council. According to Fr. Prof. Stanislaw Nagy's account, Wojtyla himself claimed that the Council was for him a great study in theology (by this same account, the publications of Polish theologians, which he followed with close attention, were another source of his theological knowledge). These activities, however, could not be presented due to the terse nature of this chronicle. The documentation of the last Council is collected in the great edition of the Polyglotta Vaticana *Acta Synodalia*. It contains all of the texts proclaimed at the Council (whether orated or submitted in writing), and all of the commentaries submitted in writing by the Fathers of the Council. In this *Kalendarium* I have limited myself to noting the presentations of Bishop Karol Wojtyla before the Council, noting the subjects and dates. In the case of the texts submitted in writing, which in the *Acta Synodalia* are noted as occurring sometime between two specified dates, I have retained this dating convention, adding only an indication as to where the citations may be found in the *Acta*. His presentations, usually quite terse, could have been quoted here in their entirety, but it seemed to me that if they were removed from the context of the Council discussions and separated from the background in which they were presented, they might not be very understandable and could even be misleading. The activities of the present Holy Father at the Second Vatican Council have been fully documented in printed materials in the aforementioned collection and in other publications, and a full analysis would demand a separate, more thorough study.

I faced a difficult problem regarding the recording of the published writings of Father, Bishop, Archbishop, and, finally, Cardinal Wojtyla. The difficulties in establishing the dates of these publications and considerations regarding the readability of the *Kalendarium* led me to append a separate bibliography as a solution. Being a chronological record of writings, it forms, as it were, a parallel *Kalendarium* of his works. Including this information in the main text would have compromised readability, whereas the chronological organization of a bibliography allows the reader to relate each publication to its biographical context.

Besides documents, the most important of which I have just named, I have based this *Kalendarium* on the accounts of witnesses. Many of these I have collected and annotated myself; others I received in response to the appeal that appeared several times in *Tygodnik Powszechny*. Almost all of the accounts relating to his work at Solvay I obtained from a typed manuscript kept at the Krakow Curia entitled "The Nest from Which I Came." A meticulously bound copy, with a cover embossed with the title and the words "Krakow — Borek Falecki 1940-1944" was presented to the Archbishop by the workers of the Solvay factory on May 5, 1966. It contains accounts and recollections, transcribed from tape recordings, from the time when he worked at the factory as a laborer. His own recollections are found there among the others.

Other information that I received came from the records of various parishes and (primarily) convents and abbeys, from personal notes and accounts related from memory. I have tried to give the source of each account immediately after the citation, but due to editorial considerations this was not always possible. For example, in the accounts relating to his vacations and camping trips, I have not specified that this information was provided by the participants of these trips, who collectively recalled the dates, places, and some of the circumstances. This particular group, which was involved with Fr. Karol Wojtyla from the time of his pastoral work in the Parish of St. Florian, but which naturally underwent some changes in membership through the years, is identified in this *Kalendarium* as the *Srodowisko*. I found this term in the "Chronicle of the Bishop's Activities" and I have retained it herein.

The materials that I received almost always needed to be edited to conform to the rigorous style of the *Kalendarium*. Accordingly, I have excluded virtually all commentary, evaluations, and adjectives. In a word, excluded all which went beyond a strict recounting of the facts. Since the information needed to be arranged chronologically, some texts that were presented as integral whole had to be separated by date. On many occasions the information I received needed to be corrected, especially with respect to dates. Wherever I made a correction, I always sought unequivocal confirmation.

One example of such a correction is the story of an accident suffered by the worker Karol Wojtyla during the Nazi occupation. The person who found the injured man in the street recalled that the year was 1942; but the surviving admission records of the hospital where he was taken place this event beyond any doubt in 1944. Even so seemingly reliable a source as the headstone engraved with the date of the death of his brother turned out to be erroneous when compared to the cemetery records at Biala. Was every date successfully verified? I doubt it. Whenever there was any doubt as to accuracy, or whenever there was a discrepancy between sources, it became necessary to verify the information. In some cases, I happened upon a more accurate source, thereby allowing me to make the correction, but it was difficult to verify **every** piece of information, especially when the reliability of the source was not in question and the information was not contradicted by other facts.

As printed accounts of the life of the Holy Father multiplied, persons relating their own recollections tended more and more to repeat things they had read as if they themselves had been an eyewitness. When asked how he or she came to know a particular story, the witness would say, "But, it was written up in the papers." This happened to me right in Wadowice.

I was very skeptical of stories which seemed excessively uplifting, such as the one about how little Karol allegedly constructed sand figures of the saints. Such stories, even if true, seemed so entwined with age-old works of pious imaginations that it was not possible to evaluate them critically.

I omitted the account of only one witness who requested that his testimony remain confidential. It dealt with an incident from elementary school years. A friend of Karol's, playing with a revolver that had been left for safekeeping with Karol's father, not knowing that it was loaded, almost shot Karol when the gun unexpectedly fired. I am able to mention this now because a detailed account of this incident has already been published elsewhere.

I think it is significant that I did not receive a single account, whether true or false, that was unfavorable to the person of the Holy Father, even though a widely publicized appeal in the press should have easily provoked responses from malicious or unfriendly people. But there was not one report of this type, either signed or anonymous.

The need to "trim" the accounts to fit the style of the chronicle resulted in some regrettable losses. In removing all commentaries, especially those of a more general nature that could not be tied to specific facts, I had to omit, for example, the following reflections of a participant on one of the vacation trips. As an aside to a compilation of dates and places of some of these trips, he noted:

> **What did he need this for? In the first place, he was a priest, a shepherd of souls, and that is why he tried to be with people. He never imposed himself with lectures or sermons; quite to the contrary, he had to be provoked to enter into serious discussions. In the early years he observed us closely, he studied our characters, our reactions. He distinguished among us the characteristic traits of physicians, scholars, and engineers. The traits of each most likely contributed something to him, but he never attempted to combine those groups. It seemed that he also benefited from associating with us, that he discovered something about life as a result. If I were to sum it all up, it would be thus: the most important thing was that he *was there*, not that he spoke.**

The *Kalendarium* also omits those fragments of reports in which the authors spoke of their impressions, moods, or emotions. But I do wish to quote one such fragment because it has certain significance. Helena Merunowicz of Krakow writes:

> **On Sept. 8, I don't remember in which year (it could have been any year between 1954 and 1957) I went to Holy Mass at the Mariacki Church. Fr. Wojtyla ascended to the pulpit. I was very glad to have the opportunity to hear his sermon, which I expected to be given after a quick reading of the particular passage of the Gospel which priests usually read very hastily — sometimes skipping several generations. But when he began reading the "Genealogy of Jesus Christ" I forgot where I was and what I was listening to. Father Wojtyla read in such a way that we listened as if to an immensely interesting account of an important historical event, engaging in every detail. I don't remember the subject of the subsequent sermon, but I do remember and will never forget as long as I live how he read the "Genealogy of Jesus Christ."**

I cite here another account that is revealing but which could neither be accurately placed in time (it probably relates to events occurring between 1964 - 1968). It describes one of very many meetings of its type, in this case a meeting primarily of members of the Club of Catholic Intellectuals. This was related by Michal Marusienski, who was then an officer of the club.

> One day, the Archbishop invited to his home on Kanoniczna Street, to his very modest apartment, a small group of experts from a variety of disciplines. I took part in this meeting as a representative of the circle of engineers. There were lawyers, attorneys, agriculturists, scientists, and others. The aim of the meeting was to seek out moral criteria in the various professions and trades. The Archbishop wished to obtain actual information about the moral problems that arise in various professional environments … The Archbishop listened eagerly and perhaps, in some parts of the discussion, with some sadness to the presentations and the discussions that ensued. He posed very specific questions to each of us. He expressed his comments and opinions very carefully and thoughtfully, because he needed sincere, authentic information, but this information flowed in one direction only: these intellectuals were to present this information to their archpastor so that he could develop a proper outlook on the essence of the issue of morality in professional and scientific lines of work.

Often, terse extracts from the records of convents were preceded by introductory comments, as in this example from the Albertine Sisters:

> The nature of Bishop Wojtyla's contact with the Congregation of Albertine Sisters was quite varied. There were official pastoral visits, visits in response to invitations to attend celebrations of various anniversaries of the congregation, letters recommending various persons to the care of the sisters, and letters with seasonal greetings and good wishes. He would also come to visit unannounced, sometimes for a retreat, other times just to work in peace and quiet. He especially liked the house at Pradnik in Krakow. He would stay there in the guest quarters of the chaplain's house, the so-called "hut." He said that, after Laski, this is where he felt most comfortable. After the fence was removed at Pradnik and the grounds of the convent were exposed to the street, he would come to Rzaska. He stayed in Father Matlak's dining room (a long-time chaplain and confessor at the convent). There he wrote and prayed. The last time he was in Rzaska was in April of 1977, for a week of convalescence.
> In 1960 he himself proposed visitations of the houses and convents of the Albertine Congregation in Krakow. While still a seminarian and on the occasion of Fr. Jozef Matlak's patronal feast day, he brought a copy of his drama about Brother Albert for him to read. Fr. Matlak was then the pastor of the parish in Debniki.

The Congregation of the Sisters of Mercy {Daughters of Charity}, adds the following to the detailed information submitted from its convent records:

> Karol Wojtyla had contact with our congregation while he was still a student, especially with our house in Krakow on Warszawska {Warsaw} Street. During the Nazi occupation, the sisters of this house conducted charitable activities by feeding the poor, the prisoners (the prison on Montelupich Street), and the students. Ties with the congregation were strengthened when Fr. Karol Wojtyla worked as an assistant priest in the Parish of St. Florian in Krakow.

Similarly, the Sisters of the Congregation of Our Lady of Mercy write of the constant interest the Archbishop of Krakow showed in their work in "Zrodlo"[2] — a youth center run by the sisters — as well as in the beatification process of Sister Faustina Kowalska.

Information supplied by the "Light and Life movement" (a name used interchangeably with the term the "oasis movement" and the "living Church movement") is accompanied by the important commentary that the materials submitted pertain solely to direct meetings with him at retreats, conferences, and other activities, but do not include the many personal meetings the Cardinal had with Fr. Francis Blachnicki, the founder and director of the movement, nor do they include the Cardinal's many interventions in the cases of excesses committed by the authorities, especially in the province of Nowy Sacz. The "oasis movement" was incorporated by the Archbishop of Krakow into the overall archdiocesan pastoral plan. He became acquainted with the movement in 1969, which is to say, at its beginning.

Father Stefan Rozej, while submitting information based on the records of the abbey at Jasna Gora and other Pauline abbeys, adds:

> ... There developed a certain regularity, both recorded and reported by eyewitnesses, that while he was a student chaplain and, later, a bishop, he would come almost every year with a group of young people (often on bicycles) to pray at the Shrine of Jasna Gora.

Inz.[3] Jan Jackowski, remembering meetings with war veterans, writes:

> At an "oplatek,"[4] he met with Polish veterans, who served from 1914-1920 and 1939-1945. These meetings, held sporadically at first, became regular events: a Christmas get-together, an evening of carols, a Mass on the anniversary of the regaining of {Poland's} independence on November 11th. He approved of and supported the effort to renovate the memorial mound of Marshall Jozef Pilsudski at Sowiniec. He also intended personally to dedicate and bless within the Basilica of St. Mary in Krakow a memorial tablet dedicated to the fallen soldiers of the Krakow region. In April of 1978, the date of the dedication was set for the autumn of 1978.

Fr. Prof. Tadeusz Pieronek, an assistant in the work of the diocesan synod, told me, when he made the documents of the synod commissions available, that the Cardinal did not actually attend all the meetings. He would often go to Lasek Wolski near Krakow accompanied by his assistants, Fr. Prof. Marian Jaworski, Fr. Jerzy Chmiel, Fr. Prof. Adam Kubis, and Fr. Pieronek to stroll about for two or three hours and so to acquaint himself with the work of the synod, to offer his counsel, and to provide direction for further work. The *Kalendarium* does, of

---

[2] "The Source" or "The Well-spring"
[3] Professional title Engineer
[4] See Glossary.

course, note his presence at the "formal" meetings of the synod, but these informal strolls, which were no less important, were not documented anywhere.

I was also at a loss as to where to place the following information submitted by Fr. Eugeniusz Sliwka, a member of the Order of the Divine Word from Pieniezno:

> **The Cardinal paid many visits to our college on via dei Verbiti — Collegio del Verbo Divino in Rome — private visits for sport and recreation. Our college has a swimming pool which the Cardinal, presently the Holy Father, would use. It would be difficult to establish the dates of these visits, because nobody recorded them.**

Also not found in the *Kalendarium* are the common everyday activities that made up the life of the present Holy Father. For example, Fr. Tadeusz Matras, who was a student at the time when Fr. Karol Wojtyla was assigned to the Parish of St. Florian, told me of his discovery that every Friday afternoon, Fr. Wojtyla came for private adoration of the Blessed Sacrament and the Way of the Cross at the church of the Felician Sisters, where the Blessed Sacrament is continually exposed for adoration. According to a member of the Archbishop's household, he made the Way of the Cross every Tuesday and Friday. As a bishop, he would come to the Franciscan church in Krakow for prayers every morning at 6:30, kneeling in one of the back pews. Upon noticing this habit, the brothers installed a small lamp in the pew that he customarily used to facilitate his reading of the breviary. Soon after his election, the prayer habits of the Holy Father were described in *Tygodnik Powszechny* by Sister Jozefa Zofia Zdybicka, a member of the Grey Ursuline order, a colleague of his from the philosophy department of KUL[5] (TP 47/78).

> **At about the same time, Fr. Prof. Franciszek Tokarz was also commuting from Krakow to Lublin. He was a historian of Hindu philosophy, a "goral"[6] from Nowy Sacz, and a real character. After Fr. Wojtyla was nominated bishop in 1958, Fr. Tokarz said this to us at a lecture: "The Curia has finally listened to me. I often went there and told them: 'Make Wojtyla a bishop — he has piety, he has wisdom, he has goodness. The difference between him and me is that immediately upon waking (they were commuting together from Krakow by sleeper train), I go out for a smoke, but he kneels down by the window and prays, prays, prays without end ...'"**
>
> **As students, we would often see Fr. Prof. Wojtyla between lectures saying his breviary in an empty lecture hall or in the hallway. In June of 1958, when he found out about his nomination as bishop, he came straight from Miodowa Street to our house of the Grey Ursuline Sisters on Wislana Street without a word as to who he was and why he had come (he was dressed in civilian clothes, having been summoned from vacation), he went**

---

[5] Catholic University of Lublin
[6] Mountain person, inhabitant of Poland's mountainous southern region.

into the chapel and remained there in prayer for several hours. I realized just how much time he devoted to prayer when, already a Cardinal, he would come to Warsaw to our house on Wislana Street. Meditation, the Rosary, the breviary, the Way of the Cross, the Holy Mass — this was but the "morning dose." In the evening, after he returned from meetings at the Episcopate, he would speak with the various people who would be waiting to see him; at about 10:00 p.m. he would go to the chapel and pray for a long time.

Everyday activities included: Holy Mass at 7:00 a.m. (if there was no solemn celebration scheduled for later that day, but sometimes even then); time in the chapel until 11:00 a.m., where it was universally known that no one else should enter; then to the parlor which was always full of people waiting to see him. It was his custom first to greet everyone with a handshake, then to receive them each in turn, but sometimes he called someone "out of order." In those cases he would usually explain why he did so to the other people waiting. None of us, who were privileged to visit there, could ever forget the climate of those meetings. The Cardinal would seat himself at a table in the center of the parlor, the visitor would be seated to the left or right, so that the conversation was never held "across the desk." If there was a group of several people, they would all sit around the table. One always got the impression that all of the Cardinal's time and attention were given to the person before him, as anyone who has ever brought a matter to him would readily admit.

It often happened that, in the mornings when people came to see him, he also needed to preside over or participate in some meeting or symposium. He would then divide his time between the meeting and the receiving of those people. During intermissions, and sometimes even when the meeting had resumed, he would come to the parlor for a while, then return to his meeting. It was very easy to get to see the Archbishop of Krakow; one only needed patience and the time to wait for one's turn in line. He would go to lunch only after receiving all those who waited to see him. It was the duty of his chaplain, Fr. Stanislaw Dziwisz, to ensure that departures or other scheduled activities took place on time. He ate lunch together with the Curia workers in a room next to the kitchen, unless he was receiving someone in the dining room of the archbishop's apartments. He was not particular with regard to food. It was noticed that he scrupulously observed the rules of fast and abstinence, even those that were no longer binding, e.g. those preceding the feasts of Our Lady. When asked about this by one of the household help, he replied, "If a bishop doesn't fast, then who will?"

He usually worked on long automobile trips — he read, he prayed. He had a little lamp installed in the car. On some pastoral visits to parishes or to the sick he would need to go by horse-drawn cart, or if necessary, on foot. At first, his habit of reading on the road would also extend to his travels by cart. The late pastor of Jurgow, Fr. Jozef Wegrzyn, once told me about traveling with the young Bishop Wojtyla to some remote corner of the parish when the bishop engrossed himself in reading. The pastor asked if he could see the book. The bishop handed it over, whereupon the pastor calmly laid it down on the seat of the cart, sat on it and said, "Now, Your Excellency, will talk with me. After waiting for a visit for so many years, I'm not going to sit here and watch Your Excellency reading." And what did the bishop say to that, I asked. "What could he do, he talked with me" the pastor said proudly.

He would travel to his vacations with his friends by car. The driver would take him to the indicated place. The Cardinal would take a backpack and disappear into the forest. The driver would reappear at the same place on the designated day.

Just as he discussed matters of the diocesan synod during long walks in Lasek Wolski, he would often take a person on a walk in Krakow Park or some other outdoor area when he needed to talk to them at length — something that the citizens of Krakow remember well.

As a chaplain to university students, I invited the Archbishop to the student retreat to hear confessions every year. He would always accept this invitation with visible joy. Entering the Church of St. Anne in Krakow by the main entrance, dressed in a cassock and overcoat, with no visible insignia of his office except his Vatican Council ring, he would sit in an open confessional, cover his face with the end of his stole, and hear confessions for several hours.

I relate these several details to indicate that gaps undoubtedly occur frequently throughout this *Kalendarium*. There are gaps arising from the inability to describe everything, from the fallibility of human memory and from the difficulties of recording minor, fleeting episodes and encounters. Often, however, there is simply a lack of documentation. For example, it is known that the Archbishop of Krakow took part several times in the September pastoral meetings at KUL. Unfortunately, not all of these instances have been recorded in the documents of these conventions for priests.

Undoubtedly, some minor facts found their way "by chance" into this book. It was by chance that some people learned about the writing of this *Kalendarium* and others did not, that some agreed to write down their recollections and others did not. In this book, the descriptions of ordinary actions and encounters with ordinary people should be treated as examples. There were very many matrimonial blessings, visits, conversations, and encounters such as that found in the account sent in by Stanislaw Grzesiak of Poznan:

> **My mother Emilia established contact with Archbishop Karol Wojtyla by writing to him in 1964, asking him to pray for my intention. She was encouraged to do so when she found out that Karol Wojtyla was ordained to the priesthood on the day of my baptism, November 1, 1946. My mother sent the letter just before my graduation from high school, when I was having difficulty finding a direction for my life. The Archbishop replied that he would celebrate a Mass for my intention. For several years there was no other contact... My life took a variety of turns: post-secondary education, two years as a high school teacher, university studies. While I was at the university in Torun, my mother recalled to my mind the person of Karol Wojtyla, now a Cardinal. I then understood that what I had managed to achieve, I owed also to his prayers. So I began to write to him. Our correspondence, however, was quite sporadic...**

Further on, Grzesiak mentions various short greetings, a blessing sent on the occasion of his marriage, handwritten and typewritten notes signed by the Cardinal, and tells how dear to him these instances of the Cardinal's remembrance were. So as not to oblige the Cardinal to respond ("I didn't want to impose..."), he did not give his return address except in his first letter. Grzesiak saw the Cardinal only once from a distance, but the exchange of some dozen cards and letters played an undeniable role in his life.

***

In closing, I wish to thank all of those who made this book possible, especially the Znak Publishers and the editors of *Tygodnik Powszechny* for entrusting me with this fascinating work and making it possible for me to complete it. I thank Fr. Dr. Andrzej Szostek, MIC, for preparing materials relating to academic matters; Fr. Prof. Adam Kubis for materials relating to the synods of bishops; Prof. Danuta Michalowska for compiling a chronology of Karol Wojtyla's association with the theater; Tadeusz Szyma for preparing extracts from the "Chronicle of the Bishop's Activities"; Anna Turowicz and Krystyna Chmielecka for their help in selecting and preparing fragments of sermons. Anna Turowicz prepared fragments from the years 1969-1970 and 1973-1974, Krystyna Chmielecka from 1972, 1975 to June of 1977 and from 1978. I thank all those who came forward to help collect documents and accounts: Prof. Irena Bajerowa, who compiled the accounts of colleagues from his university years; Fr. Stanislaw Klimaszewski, MIC, who gathered information for the *Kalendarium* in Rome; Fr. Prof. Wojciech Feliks Bednarski OP, who provided materials from the Angelicum archives; Sister Jadwiga of the Sacred Heart of the Krakow

Curia, whose patient help in research was invaluable. I am grateful that I was given access to various archives. I am especially grateful to the Director of the Jagiellonian University archives, Prof. Leszek Hajdukiewicz and his staff; to the Pastor of Wadowice, Msgr. Edward Zacher, and all the pastors and assistant priests who made it possible for me to study various parish records. Special thanks to those, like Fr. Zacher; upon whose valuable time I imposed on many occasions.

The preparation of the *Kalendarium* would undoubtedly have taken much longer without the dedication, time and very effective work volunteered by Dr. Urszula Perkowska and Anna Chuda, M.A., in organizing the materials we collected. For this I hereby express my deep gratitude. I thank the author of the bibliography, Mrs. Zofia Skwarnicka. Finally, thanks go to Dr. Krzysztof Kozlowski, whose comments and thorough review prevented many errors and ambiguities, and to the editor Jozef Kozak, who was responsible for putting this work into a form allowing publication. I express my gratitude to the ladies who worked on typing the materials and text of the *Kalendarium*, especially Mrs. Janina Stolarczykowa, and Mrs. Felicja and Mrs. Barbara Podgorzec, who transcribed hundreds of pages of my not very readable manuscript.

The *Kalendarium* owes much to all those who provided illustrative material and valuable, often previously unknown, photographs. These materials were selected, classified, reproduced, and prepared for printing by Mr. Jerzy Kolataj and Mr. Rafal Kolataj, and I express my gratitude to them.

To all those who sent in accounts, documents, and photos and who gave verbal accounts and various information, who are too numerous to mention here, I express my sincere thanks and hereby recognize you as co-authors of this work. Without all of this wonderful help, which I enjoyed at every step of my work, this *Kalendarium* could not have been created.

Rev. Adam Boniecki, MIC

A Word from the Editor and the Project Manager of the English Edition

Many works have been written about John Paul II since his election as Pope over 21 years ago. Why another publication? *The Making of the Pope of the Millenium, Kalendarium of the Life of Karol Wojtyla* is not just another book about John Paul II. Since its original publication in Polish under the title *Kalendarium Zycia Karola Wojtyly* (Krakow: Znak 1983), it has been the primary source material and the most complete up-to-date documentary on the life and activities of John Paul II before his election as Pope. The biographers of John Paul II who took their task seriously recognized this and used the *Kalendarium* extensively.

Tad Szulc in his *Pope John Paul II: The Biography* stated: "For the pre-pontifical period, the most basic work is Father Adam Boniecki's *Kalendarium of the Life of Karol Wojtyla*, virtually a day-by-day account of his activities from birth on; it includes important texts and documents as well." Not only Tad Szulc, but others, such as Carl Berstein and Marco Politi (*His Holiness John Paul II and the History of Our Time*) and George Weigel, author of the excellent biography, *Witness to Hope, the Biography of Pope John Paul II*, have drawn materials for their works from this primary and authenticated source.

While the information about the future Pope is magnificent and inspiring, the value of this book goes beyond its usage as source material on the life of Karol Wojtyla. As a Bishop and Cardinal who was involved in the highest levels of the Church's pastoral ministry and its social affairs, the future Pope offers firsthand documentation on the life and activities of the Catholic Church in Poland under the Communist regime from the middle to the latter part of the 20th century. In this regard the *Kalendarium* is an unsurpassable source of historical data.

This book is written in the peculiar form or genre known as *kalendarium* or *calendarium* (a register of activities or transactions kept by a Church official). Many parts of the book are simple, very short, day-to-day entries of activities. This form of writing is the most compact way to record events, travel information, activities, and experiences. A scholar reading these entries will find an enormous amount of information and historical data about a particular activity, its setting, and the persons involved. In addition to the register of entries, the *Kalendarium* contains collections of primary source material, letters, homilies, and summaries of events written by Karol Wojtyla or by others who had firsthand knowledge or experience of that event.

The material found in the *Kalendarium* has been carefully translated into English. In our effort to retain the style and the authenticity of the original, the translation, at times, may appear to be cumbersome.

The Bibliography adds great value to the book. Several bibliographies of Karol Wojtyla's works have been published since the original publication of the *Kalendarium*. A noteworthy publication in this regard is *Karol Wojtyla negli scritti, Bibliografia* by Fr. Wiktor Gramatowski and Zofia Wilinska. However, we have included the bibliography prepared for the original edition by Zofia Skwarnicka. Its value lies in the descriptive quality of many entries.

This most complete, up-to-date documentary and the most reliable compendium on the life and activities of Karol Wojtyla, has not been available to the English speaking audience. *The Making of the Pope of the Millenium, Kalendarium of the Life of Karol Wojtyla* intends to fill this lacuna. It is our firm conviction that our publication will contribute deeper insights and knowledge of John Paul II and provide authentic information on the History of the Church in the 20th Century to the scholar and the interested reader alike.

Rev. Kazimierz Chwalek, MIC
Editor of the English Edition

Bro. Andrew R. Mączyński, MIC
Director of the Association of Marian Helpers
An Apostolic Ministry
of the Congregation of Marians of the Immaculate Conception

March 4, 2000

Translators' Note by Irena and Taddeus Mirecki

In addition to a faithful translation of Rev. Adam Boniecki's text, we have tried to add explanations of the significance of some of the events and utterances, especially those that need to be placed in the context of the Church-State struggle during the Communist era in Poland. The conventions we used are as follows:

- Text in parentheses (...) is as it appears in the original.
- Text in brackets [...] is as it appears in the original, usually designating Boniecki's comments or explanations.
- Text in braces {...} has been added by the translators.
- All footnotes have been added by the translators.

We have used notes in braces {...} in-line with the text where the explanation needs no more than several words. Longer explanations have been placed in footnotes.

Because this is primarily a reference work, we have repeated our notes and explanations every time an event or term is mentioned. In this way, the reader always has these elaborations at hand, regardless of the order of reading. We have made some minor exceptions to this, with a few terms which recur constantly throughout the text, we have placed them in a glossary at the end of the book. Still, there are frequent footnotes referring the reader to the glossary as glossary words occur in the text.

We wish to thank our collaborators in the work of translation: Maria Chrypinski, Andrew Chudzinski, Magdalena Konieczny-Pettey and Barbara Mirecki.

Acknowledgements

After the translation of the *Kalendarium* was made by Irena and Thaddeus Mirecki et al., and before this work was published, Fr. Boniecki expressed a desire to revise some parts, modify numerous entries as well as expand others. In the process, this edition of the *Kalendarium* is no longer a simple translation of the Polish Edition but a revised and expanded version. The translation of the modified and expanded parts was done by Ewa St Jean, who was also responsible for the comparative proofreading of the Polish and English texts. The coordinator of the translation, its guide and editor was Rev. Kazimierz Chwalek, MIC. Additional proofreading was done by: Sr. Isabel Bettwy, David Came, Rev. Richard Drabik, MIC, Mary Ellen McDonald, Rev. Martin Rzeszutek, MIC, and Paul St Jean. The Project Manager of the publication was Br. Andrew R. Mączyński, MIC.

FAMILY — SCHOOL YEARS

The Wojtyla family comes from the village of Czaniec near Kety. The oldest parish records reach back to the 18th century, while those that without a doubt relate to the forbears of the Pope, reach back to the 19th century.

CZANIEC is a village in the district of Biala, in Galicia {southern Poland}, near Kety. Area: 2,862 morgs, including 1,673 morgs of arable land and 730 morgs of forest;[1] (1,272 morgs of landed estate, 1,590 morgs owned by peasantry); 355 houses, population of 2,252. Parish in the deanery of Oswiecim (4,836 souls); parish church of St. Bartholomew, construction partly wooden and partly masonry, founded in 1650 and consecrated in 1839 by Bishop Zachariasiewicz of Tarnow; until 1560 a branch of the parish of Kety, single-room public schoolhouse, American-style mill, production of textiles. Czaniec is situated near the state highway to Vienna. The region around the manor house belongs to the estate of the Archduke Albrecht. The main occupation of the villagers is the production of canvas denim. At one time, the village was called "Grzanica." Cf. Bulowice.

BULOWICE, Upper and Lower, including Lesser Czaniec, district of Biala, in Galicia; area of 3,149 morgs including 2,233 morgs of arable land, 392 houses, population of 2,448, a filial parish of the deanery of Oswiecim with 2,570 Catholic souls. The old wooden church, tradition has it, was built by St. Adalbert, the Apostle of Poland; restored in 1540 by the co-owners of Bulowice, and burned down in 1814. On the basis of a decree issued by Emperor Francis I, a new filial parish attached to Kety was founded in 1817, and a new masonry church dedicated to St. Adalbert was erected. It was consecrated in 1822 by Grzegorz Ziegler, the Bishop of Tarnow. It has a public school with three classrooms. The villages of Bulowice are situated among the fertile hills alongside the state highway to Vienna. (*Geographic Dictionary of the Kingdom of Poland and other Slavonic Countries,* vol. I, Warsaw, 1880, pp. 731, 472.)

The oldest traces of the name Woytyla (also written as Wojtyla) are in a record pertaining to Maciej Wojtyla, born in 1765, married on July 22, 1800 to Marianna Kowalska. In the same period there are records of Franciszka Wojtyla, born in 1792, the wife of Wojciech Nanczyk; Jadwiga, the widow of Bartlomiej Wojtyla, who died on January 2, 1824 at the age of 65 (b. 1759); and Magdalena Woytyla, a widow, who died in Czaniec on February 10, 1787. It may be assumed that they were members of the same family, because the names Maciej, Franciszka and Bartlomiej also appear in this family later, when documentation is more complete. But these are only suppositions. The occupation of the Wojtylas of Czaniec is usually listed as "hortulanus," which in this context means a small farmer.

There are also many references to the name Wojtyla in the records

---

[1] A Polish morg was 0.56 hectares or about 1.4 acres.

of the parish of Biala. We find there, among others, Wojtyla the merchant, Wojtyla the vagabond, Wojtyla the beggar and others. It was not possible to establish whether there was any relationship to these Wojtylas.

A continuous genealogy may be established from BARTLOMIEJ WOJTYLA, married to ANNA HUDECKA (also written CHUDECKA[2]). They lived in Czaniec and had four children. This is the generation of the Pope's great-grandparents. The children of Bartlomiej and Anna were Franciszka, born March 25, 1826, the wife of Walenty Kowalczyk; Stanislaw, born April. 1, 1830, married to Julianna Madeja; FRANCISZEK, married to FRANCISZKA[3] GALUSZKA; Marianna, wife of Mateusz Ciezki.

In a record of sale no. 120 dated September 23, 1868, now kept in the museum in Zywiec, Franciszek and Stanislaw are referred to as "councilmen of the township," and on the birth certificate of his son Maciej, Franciszek is listed as "iudex communitatis."

FRANCISZEK and FRANCISZKA WOJTYLA also had four children: Jozef, born January 15, 1845; MACIEJ born January 1, 1852 (as recorded in the town records of Czaniec. In Lipnik, where Maciej is buried, the registry of deaths lists his date of birth as February 1st, and that is also the date on his headstone), married twice — first to ANNA PRZECZEK (not Przeczka, as was erroneously recorded in the Pope's birth certificate in Wadowice), then to Maria Zalewska; Jan, born October 9, 1854 and Pawel, born January 1, 1858, married to Franciszka Gasparo-Galuszka.

MACIEJ WOJTYLA, the Pope's grandfather, left Czaniec and moved to nearby Lipnik, where he is entered in the parish records as "sartor ex Czaniec" (a tailor from Czaniec) and "agricola" (farmer). In the memory of his relatives, he remained a guild master tailor. In Lipnik he lived in house no. 32. On September 3, 1878 he married ANNA PRZECZEK, the daughter of the baker Franciszek and his wife Maria, née Hess. Their son KAROL, the Pope's father, was born on July 18, 1879 in Lipnik (They were then living in house no. 31).

After the death of his first wife, Maciej married Maria, the daughter of the tailor Jozef Zalewski, born February 1, 1861, died October 6, 1917. With his second wife he had a daughter, Stefania Adelajda, born December 16, 1891 in Lipnik, died May 24, 1962 in Krakow.

Maciej Wojtyla died on September 23, 1923. He was buried in the

---

[2] The two spellings are pronounced equivalently.
[3] Franciszek and Franciszka are masculine and feminine forms, respectively, of the name Francis.

cemetery at the Parish of Divine Providence in Biala alongside his second wife.

Franciszek Wojtyla, the son of Maciej Wojtyla's brother Pawel, was a cantor in the parish of Czaniec. He led pilgrimages to Kalwaria, led the congregation in singing in the church, and was well respected in the parish. He died in 1968; Cardinal Wojtyla officiated at the funeral. It appears that the office of cantor had been associated with the Wojtyla family for a long time.

According to the personnel records of the military archives in Vienna, KAROL WOJTYLA (senior) was drafted into the Austrian army in 1900. Until that time he had worked as a tailor.

He was assigned to the 56th Infantry Regiment of Count Daun, stationed in Wadowice. After a year he was promoted to "gefreiter" (private second class) and transferred to Lwow. There he fulfilled the duties of a supervisor ("Aufsichtcharge") at a school of infantry cadets. In 1904, at the rank of "zugsfuhrer" (platoon leader) he was transferred back to his home unit in Wadowice, where he was promoted and served as a quartermaster's non-commissioned officer specializing in accounting. He then married EMILIA KACZOROWSKA.

These facts, extracted from the military records by Ernest Frost (*Der Papst aus einen fernen Land*,[4] Verlag Fritz Molden, Vienna) conflict with an account given by Stefania, the stepsister of Karol Wojtyla. According to her, the marriage occurred at a time when Karol was living in Krakow and assigned to quartermaster duties. After their marriage, the Wojtylas first lived on Felicjanek Street, then on Mazowiecka Street. It is certain that they were married in Krakow. No marriage record was found in any parish in Krakow; it may be assumed that it was recorded in the personnel books of a military parish. In 1939, some of these records were destroyed and others were moved to France. In any case, it was not possible to find the marriage record, nor the birth certificates of their first two children, nor the death certificate of their second child, a daughter who died in infancy. Karol and Emilia Wojtyla most likely moved to Wadowice in 1918 for it is only in this year that the name of their eldest son, Edmund Wojtyla, appears for the first time on the student roster (third grade) of the secondary school in Wadowice. A remark written by his name reads: "gifted, with distinction."

More information reconstructed from military records archived in Vienna: Their first son Edmund was born August 28, 1906 (August 27th, according to his headstone). At the time, Karol Wojtyla served in

---

[4] *The Pope from a Distant Land.*

the chancery of the Recruiting Board. His military record has entries indicating that he "is fluent in Polish and German, both spoken and written," his "outlines" are very well formulated, the final drafts of his reports are very correct, he "types quickly." Under the heading "Character and Personality Traits" (dated 1908): "Very well-developed, righteous, serious, well-mannered, modest, a man of honor, very responsible, very generous (gentle), tireless (hard-working)."

Several years later, Wojtyla's superior confirms this opinion: "Very proper in every respect, entirely trustworthy, a non-commissioned officer who fulfills his clerical duties perfectly, worthy of every distinction."

The regimental commander signed this opinion with the words "in agreement," and added: "An especially valuable, useful and brave non-commissioned officer." His "social demeanor" is described as "very pleasant, proper, well-mannered" and he is therefore said to have "all the traits of character that are desirable in a civil servant." After 12 years of military service, Wojtyla applied for a transfer to civilian government service. His application was supported by the regimental authorities, and he was given the highest recommendation. From his written application filed in this regard, it appears that the senior Wojtyla completed elementary school and three years of secondary education. His plans were dashed by the outbreak of World War I. In the days of mobilization and the weeks that followed, when the Russians first broke through the front and Krakow and Wadowice came within the range of artillery fire, Wojtyla must have made great contributions in his office, for he earned a commendation and was awarded the Iron Cross of Merit with a wreath (*mit Krone*). In 1915 he was advanced to the position of a clerical candidate for military records, thus becoming a commissioned officer. His nomination for promotion mentions, among other things, his "dignified conduct even outside of his professional service." The last mention of Wojtyla in the official records is dated 1916.

When Poland regained independence,[5] Karol Wojtyla {senior} transferred to the Polish army with the rank of lieutenant. Because of the state of his health, he retired not long after.

In a questionnaire of personal data for the Jagiellonian University, Karol Wojtyla entered: "Father — military official with the rank of lieutenant, office administrator (retired about 1927), deceased." ...

On the basis of *Officers' Annuals* from 1923, 1924, and 1928 it can be ascertained that Karol Wojtyla (senior) was a professional lieutenant employed in the chancery of the Recruitment Board for the District of

---

[5] At the end of hostilities in World War I, November 11, 1918.

Wadowice. In 1928 his name appears on the list of retired officers.

Those who knew him remember the senior Wojtyla as a collected, hard-working, courteous and good person. All accounts of him bear witness to his strong ties with his sons, especially with Karol, for whom he was both father and mother (his mother died on April 13, 1929 following a short illness). Those who knew him also recall his love of order and discipline, which characterized the upbringing of his youngest son.

Karol's father was a deeply religious man. There survive photographs of him with little Karol on pilgrimages to Kalwaria Zebrzydowska, and stories of his private pilgrimages to Czestochowa. Edward Gorlich, a laboratory technician at Solvay (today a professor) was astounded when Karol told him how they read the Holy Scriptures together at home.

In 1938, Karol Wojtyla moved with his son to Krakow, where they took up residence in a basement apartment of a house belonging to the Kaczorowski family. He survived the flight of 1939, the poverty of the first years of World War II. He died on February 18, 1942 in Krakow and is buried in the military cemetery at Rakowice.

The Pope's older brother, Edmund, is remembered by those who knew him as a very intelligent man, cheerful by nature and possessing great personal charm. He studied at the Jagiellonian University in 1924/25 through 1928/29. His responses at one examination, given in the presence of a large audience of fellow students, were rewarded with applause. On May 28, 1930 he earned the degree of Doctor of Medical Sciences (Archives of JU). All his acquaintances recall how close he was with his younger brother. There is a surviving photograph of a soccer team where Edmund Wojtyla, wearing a student's cap, is standing next to a very small Karol, who certainly did not then belong to the team. Another photo of young Karol amidst nurses in front of the hospital in Bielsko confirms reports that Karol would often visit his brother, the doctor. The inscription on his headstone, that he gave his young life in the service of his fellow man, is no exaggeration. During an epidemic of scarlet fever, according to eyewitness accounts, many doctors were afraid to minister to the sick. For his willingness to aid them, Edmund paid with his life.

There is no information about a sister who died in infancy. According to the account of Stefania Wojtyla, she was born and died in Krakow.

As to the family of the Pope's mother, the earliest ancestor, of whom there is a record in parish archives, is MIKOLAJ KAC-

ZOROWSKI, described in the same records as an "administrator" or "oeconomus," married to URSZULA MALINOWSKA, both from the parish of Biala (presently part of the city of Bielsko-Biala).

Mikolaj and Urszula were the parents of FELIKS KACZOROWS-KI, born June 26, 1849 in Biala. In the parish records of Biala, Feliks's profession is listed as "ephiparius" [saddler], "eccipiorum artifex", "ephippiorum opifex"{also saddler}; in the records of the parish of All Saints in Krakow, as "habenarius" [harness maker].

His first wife (they were married in 1875) was MARIA, née SCHOLZ, also called MARIANNA and MARIA ANNA (all these names were used interchangeably and refer to the same person). She was born in 1853, according to the inscription on her headstone in cemetery at Rakowice. But on the birth record of her daughter, Wiktoria Stefania born in 1885 and baptized in 1886 in the parish of All Saints in Krakow, the notation reads: "Maria Scholz, daughter of Jan and Zuzanna, 28 years of age," meaning she was born in 1858. Maria was the daughter of Jan Scholz, a cobbler, and Zuzanna née Rubicka.

Their children: Helena Augusta, born August 18, 1876, died July 10, 1905, married to the widower of her younger sister (Olga) Jozef Kuczmierczyk (the Pope's godfather) of Wilamowice near Bielsko; Olga Marianna, born January 7, 1879, died December 19, 1902, married to Jozef Kuczmierczyk (b. September 12, 1868, d. April 11, 1944); Maria Anna (the Pope's godmother), born in 1880, died November 27, 1959 in Krakow, married name Wiadrowska; Feliks Rudolf, born in 1881, died February 20, 1892 in Krakow; EMILIA (the Pope's mother), born March 26, 1884, died April 13, 1929 in Wadowice, married to Karol Wojtyla.

Around 1885 the Kaczorowski family moved to Krakow and took up residence at 17 Droga nad Rudawa. Here more children were born: Wiktoria Stefania, born December 19, 1885, died January 22, 1886; Robert, born April 26, 1887, died December 27, 1962; Rudolfina, born March 31, 1889, died June 30, 1948; Anna, born April 1, 1891, died December 17, 1962, married name Sanak.

The first wife of Feliks, Maria Anna Kaczorowska, died on April 12, 1897 (buried in the military cemetery at Rakowice in Krakow). In 1908, Feliks Kaczorowski married a second time; his wife's name was Joanna (it was not possible to determine her maiden name). According to the account given by Felicja Wiadrowska (the daughter of Maria Anna Wiadrowska, née Kaczorowska), they had three sons and a daughter, named Wanda. The only record in the parish of All Saints in Krakow is: "NN Kaczorowska 'non viva nata' 12 II 1908".[6]

The Kaczorowski family lived then in Krakow at 15 Smolensk Street. Feliks operated a saddlery, specializing in upholstering carriages.

Feliks Kaczorowski died on August 19, 1908 and he was buried in the family tomb in the military cemetery at Rakowice.

Robert took over the saddlery. He moved from Smolensk Street to Zwierzyniecka Street on the corner of Aleja Krasinskiego[7] (today the site of the "Jubilat" department store). The saddlery did not prosper and was eventually closed. During World War I, Robert is captured by the Russians; Rudolfina and Anna resided on Retoryka Street. After returning from captivity, Robert bought a lot in Debniki and with very little money, buying used brick, old windows, etc., he built a house in which he resided with his sisters until his death. In this house, in 1938, Karol Wojtyla took up residence with his son Karol, a student of the Jagiellonian University.

Today {1978}, the only living member of the Holy Father's immediate family from his mother's side is Felicja Wiadrowska, the daughter of Maria Anna Wiadrowska. The Holy Father wrote to Felicja after his election:

> **Dear Lusia, God has decreed that I remain in Rome. It is indeed an extraordinary edict of Divine Providence. These days I think a lot of my parents and of Mundek,[8] but I also think of your mother and father, who were always so good to me. I remember also our dearly departed Janina and Adam [Felicja's siblings], and our dearly departed Rudolfina, Anna and Robert. I commend their souls to God. They were all very good to me. I also pray for the soul of our dearly departed Stefania, my father's sister. Now you are the only one of my closest family ...**
>
> **John Paul II**
>
> **Vatican City, October 27, 1978.**

Fr. Karol Wojtyla looked after Marek, the son of Adam, during Marek's university studies. Marek Wiadrowski, born in 1939, married Kazimiera Passowicz. He died in 1978, leaving two daughters, Anna, born in 1972 and Maria, born in 1973. I give this information here because it relates to accounts later in the *Kalendarium*.

Regarding the siblings of the Pope's mother: Wiadrowski operated a shop for gilding picture frames at 7 Florianska Street in Krakow; Kuczmierczyk operated a restaurant on the corner of St. Ann and Wislna Streets (today the site of a department store). There he provided a site to his sister-in-law Anna Sanak, where she and her husband ran a religious goods store.

Emilia Wojtyla, née Kaczorowska, probably completed eight years

---

6 Unnamed Kaczorowska female stillborn Feb. 12, 1908.
7 Krasinski's Blvd. In Polish, the possessive form of names is used when streets are named after people.
8 Diminutive for Edmund.

at the school of the Daughters of Charity on Pedzichow Street in Krakow. She was of frail health, and spent her life taking care of the household and the children. People in Wadowice remember that she liked to chat with her neighbors, and to sit by the well in the courtyard of the house, where Lolek[9] played with his friends. She died after a short illness (myocarditis nephritis). The funeral was conducted by the Pastor of Wadowice, Fr. Prochownik.

May 18, 1920 — KAROL JOZEF WOJTYLA was born to Karol Wojtyla and Emilia, née Kaczorowska, while living in Wadowice at 2 Rynek {Market Square} apt. 4 (7 Koscielna Street, today), in a house owned by Chaim Balamuth.

May 20, 1920 — Baptized in the parish church of Wadowice by Fr. Franciszek Zak, a military chaplain. Godparents: Jozef Kuczmierczyk, his mother's brother-in-law, and Maria Wiadrowska, his mother's sister.

Actorum parochialis Ecclesia rom. cath. in Wadowice pro Wadowice destinata. TESTIMONIUM ORTUS ET BAPTISMI (T. IV Pag. 549 Nr. ser. 71 ...) Anno Domini millesimo nongentisimo vicesimo hoc est 1920 die duodevicesima 18 mensis Maii 5 natus sub Nro domus 2 et die 20 Junii eiusd. an. ab Adm. Rndo Dno Francisco Zak secundum ritum Romano-Catholicum baptisatus est Carolus Josephus binom. religio rom. Cath. sexus masculini, torus legitimi Pater —Wojtyla Carolus officialis milit. fil. Mathiae et Anne Przeczka Mater — Kaczorowska Aemilia fil. Felicis et Mariae Scholc. Patrini Josephus Kuczmierczyk, Maria Wiadrowska ux. Leonis.

(The above is a copy of the birth certificate from the archives of the Archdiocesan Curia of Krakow. In the parish archives, the name of the godmother was erroneously recorded as Wiatrowska.)

September 15, 1926 — Karol entered Marcin Wadowita Elementary School for Boys (grades 1 through 7) in Wadowice (registration no. 60). At the time Karol Wojtyla attended, the school was located in the city administration building on the Market Square. The offices of the city administration were on the ground floor, while the second floor and the annex were occupied by the school. During recess, the pupils spent their time in the square in front of the church. Working conditions for teachers were quite difficult; the class sizes were large. A branch of the school was opened on Mlynska {Mill} Street for pupils living near to and across the River Skawa. For example, in the academic year 1931/32, grade I-a (in the city hall) had 64 pupils, while I-b (on Mlynska Street) had 58. (As related by Tadeusz Bras, a teacher in Wadowice at the time.)

---

[9] Diminutive for Karol, Wojtyla's nickname in his youth.

January 31, 1927 — He finishes the first semester[10] of the 1st Grade. His grades: Conduct — Very Good;[11] Deportment — Good; Religion — Very Good; Polish — Good; Arithmetic — Good; Drawing — Very Good; Singing — Very Good; Games and Exercise — Very Good; number of days of excused absence - 20. (In the second semester — all his grades were Very Good).

January 30, 1928 — Karol Wojtyla, a student of the 2nd Grade, for the first semester of the academic year 1927/28, receives grades of "Very Good" in all subjects, except Handicrafts — Good. Excused absences - 36 class hours. Signed by the teacher, Krzyszlowski, and by the school principal.

May 28, 1928 — For the second semester of the year 1927/28 he receives grades of "Very Good" in all subjects. Excused absences — 4 class hours.

January 31, 1929 — For the first semester of the school year 1928/29 he receives grades of "Very Good" in all subjects. Teacher: Feliks Sponder

April 31, 1929 —- His mother dies. Entry in the book of the deceased of the Parish of Wadowice:

"Emilia Wojtyla died April 13, 1929. Funeral April 16th conducted by Fr. Leonard Prochownik. Myocarditis nephritis." Emilia Wojtyla died after a short illness. Later, her remains were moved to the family plot in the military cemetery in Krakow, where the father and brother of the Pope are also buried. The headstone bears an erroneous date of the mother's death: March 26th.

June 28, 1929 — He finishes the 3rd Grade of elementary school, with grades of "Very Good" in all subjects. Absent: 24 class hours (excused).

After the death of his mother, the rhythm of his life at home was very structured: school, dinner in the milk bar of Mrs. Maria Banas (4 Koscielna {Church} Street), two hours of play, homework, in the evening a walk with his father. Games: playing ball, running; on rainy days Ping-Pong in the Catholic Home. He did not take vacations away from home. The household was managed by his father, by then a retired military officer. Karol Wojtyla's (Senior) stepsister Stefania would come for the holidays and help to prepare the holiday celebrations. (As related by B. Banas of Wadowice.)

---

[10] Half-year
[11] Very Good is expressed by numeral 5 and is equivalent to a grade of A; Good - by numeral 4 and is equivalent to B.

January 30, 1930 — As a fourth grade elementary student he receives Very Good grades in all subjects for the first semester of the academic year 1929/30.

May 26, 1930 — He participates in a trip to Wieliczka {historic salt mines} with his father, teachers and classmates.

May 28, 1930 — Karol Wojtyla participates in the solemn ceremony of the conferment of a doctor's degree upon his brother at the Jagiellonian University (cf. the speech delivered by John Paul II as he received an honorary doctorate from the Jagiellonian University).

June 26, 1930 — For the academic year 1929/30 he receives grades of "Very Good" in all subjects. Absences in the second semester — 10 class hours (excused).

During his elementary school years, or perhaps early in his high-school years, he visited the Monastery of Jasna Gora in Czestochowa for the first time. He went there with his father and a small group of friends. (As related by B. Banas.)

SECONDARY SCHOOL

As a young priest, I fulfilled the duties of an assistant pastor in Wadowice for three years. In 1930, I was temporarily assigned to teach religion at the local secondary school. It appeared that the schedule of the regular religion teacher was overloaded and that he needed help. That is how I found myself teaching the first grade of secondary school, and that is how I began my long-time acquaintance with Karol Wojtyla, who was a student there. Anyone who met the current Holy Father when he was a young man remembers that he was of above average height, slender, with a thin, drawn face; and it would be hard to imagine how different the ten-year-old Karol Wojtyla's appearance was. He was quite tall as a boy, but also somewhat plump. He was a very lively boy, very talented, very sharp and very good. He was an optimist, but upon closer acquaintance one detected the effects of his being orphaned at an early age. I met him a short time after the death of his mother. I remember him for his great loyalty to his friends and for the lack of any conflict with the teachers. He got good grades. My contact with him in school lasted barely a year, but they did not end there. Our service at the altar drew us close together. Karol Wojtyla was a zealous altar boy. Later, we also drew close, I like to think, through the confessional, our personal talks and our visits with one another. That is how I met the father of my pupil and altar boy, Lieutenant Wojtyla, who had worked in the administration of the 12th Infantry Regiment stationed in Wadowice. I never saw him in uniform, but I did meet him after his retirement. He was a man of some years. He ran the household single-handedly and took great care in the upbringing of his son. I remember that father and son took their meals at the neighbors. They were just able to make ends meet. Their lifestyle was quite frugal ... After a short stay in Wadowice I was transferred to serve as an assistant pastor at Wawel Cathedral ... (Fr. Kazimierz Figlewicz, *Tygodnik Powszechny*, 44/1978).

January 31, 1931 — As a first year student at Marcin Wadowita State Secondary School (on Mickiewicza Street), he receives grades of "Very Good" in all subjects (except Physical Education — Good) for the first semester.

In that semester he begins the study of German, taught by his father. His father also prepared a Polish-German dictionary for him (as related by witnesses).

June 27, 1931 — He completes the first year of the classical curriculum of secondary education with grades of "Very Good" in all subjects. Excused absences: 7 class hours.

September 1931 — He begins his second year at Marcin Wadowita Secondary School. He receives grades of "Very Good" in all subjects for the first semester.

Information preserved in the school documents:

(The information listed below regarding Karol Wojtyla, a student of Marcin Wadowita Secondary School in Wadowice, as preserved in the school documents, was researched and compiled by Dr. Gustaw Studnicki of Wadowice. In 1984, he was kind enough to supply this information to the author of *Kalendarium* giving him a free hand as to how the information would be used in the preparation of the second edition of this book).

School Year 1931/32

Second year: The establishment of the classroom government and elections to the classroom board took place at the very beginning of the academic year. The members of the classroom board: President: Karol Wojtyla, Secretary: Wlodzimierz Piotrowski, Treasurer: Tadeusz Zieba (according to the proceedings of the School Board of Marcin Wadowita Secondary School 1931/32, p. 35).

The History Club. Readings and lectures on various subjects of history. Second year: from the collection of selected historical writings and materials, etc. Michal Gielas, Wiktor Kesek, Tadeusz Latko, Alexander Pawelski, Marian Wawrykiewicz, Karol Wojtyla ... Karol Wojtyla: Pulaski. Dabrowski's youth. The map of the Battle of Grochow was drawn by Karol Wojtyla (according to the proceedings of the School Board of Marcin Wadowita Secondary School 1931/32, p. 43).

Education in Economics: ... several students have been depositing money in the Community Bank in Wadowice and in P. K. O. {Polish Savings Bank}, Karol Wojtyla from the second year has saved up the most: 266.36 zloty (according to the proceedings of the School Board of

Marcin Wadowita Secondary School, 1931/32, p. 5).

An exhibition lesson on "Pulaski in America" was held in the second year class. After a review of the material from the previous lesson, student Karol Wojtyla delivered a brief report on an extract entitled "Pulaski in America" from a collection of selected historical writings by Gebert and Gebertowa ... (according to the proceedings of the School Board of Marcin Wadowita Secondary School, 1931/32, p. 30).

A report on the activities of the Parent Committee. ... A new committee was elected, including: ... Members: ... Dr. Przybylo. Lieut. Wojtyla. (According to the proceedings of the School Board of Marcin Wadowita Secondary School, 1931/32, p. 62).

June 1932 — He completes his second year with the grade of "Very Good" in all subjects. A note entered next to the grade for Polish Language reads: "exhibits special predilection."

Summer 1932 — participates in a parish pilgrimage to Jasna Gora.

September 1932 — he begins his third year at Marcin Wadowita Secondary School. He receives all grades of "Very Good" for the first semester.

Information preserved in the school documents:

School Year 1932/33

Third year: At the beginning of the school year, a new classroom government was established with Wojtyla as President (according to the proceedings of the School Board of Marcin Wadowita Secondary School, 1932/33, p. 33).

A committee was summoned to organize a special evening to promote abstinence from alcohol including a pledge ceremony. The committee prepared the program for the event. It took place on February 18th and the program was as follows: ... 3. Recitation by Wojtyla from Grade VIIIA (according to the proceedings of the School Board of Marcin Wadowita Secondary School, 1932/33, p. 49). N.B. The text should read: "from grade III." There was no other Wojtyla in this school at that time.

December 5, 1932 — The death of his brother, Edmund Wojtyla.

He died of scarlet fever, contracted from a patient during an epidemic of that disease. He was a physician, a resident at the Municipal Hospital in Bielsko. Karol used to visit his brother. According to Stefania, his father's stepsister, Karol would entertain the patients by putting on a "one man show." Entry in the cemetery record in Bielsko: "Wojtyla Edmund, physician, December 5, 1932 *(Todestag)*; temporary vault — November 10, 1934, *Krakau* Inscription on the headstone at the military cemetery in Krakow: "Dr. Edmund Wojtyla, resident physician of the Municipal Hospital in Bielsko, b. August 23, 1906, d. December 4, 1932 in the performance of his duties, sacrificing his young life in the service of suffering humanity." (Note the inconsistency of the dates!)

Minutes from the Thirty-First Ordinary Public Session of the Municipal Council of the City of Bielsko, December 22, 1932. Chairman: the Mayor, Dr. Kobiela, Secretary: Jozef Kopaczko. Point 5 of the Agenda: Condolences to Mr. Wojtyla, the father of the physician of the Municipal Community Hospital who died tragically. Before the council began the business of the day, the chairman spoke in honor of the deceased physician. Given below is the text of the speech quoted verbatim.

On December 4th, Dr. Edmund Wojtyla, a resident physician at the Municipal Community Hospital died after a severe, albeit only four days long, illness of septic scarlet fever. He contracted the deadly disease at the bedside of a severely ill patient whom he attempted to wrench from the claws of death, alas, in vain. For his dedication and extraordinary conscientiousness, he paid with his young life. The dearly departed Dr. Wojtyla was born in Krakow in 1906. He completed secondary school in Wadowice with perfect grades. He studied in Krakow, passed all his exams with distinction and, as one of the first in his class, received the degree of Doctor of Medicine in May of 1930. After a few months of internship at the pediatric hospital in Krakow he assumed the duties of a resident at the Municipal Community Hospital in Bielsko on April 1, 1931.

He was happy to have found there a place to further broaden his extensive knowledge and to practice his beloved profession. He was happy that his dreams were fulfilled, his dreams to be able to render support to his honorable father, whose pride he was, and, for his beloved younger brother, to fill the void that was created by the premature death of their mother. With enthusiasm and dedication he applied himself to the work entrusted to him until he was felled by this treacherous disease. The dearly departed Dr. Wojtyla always tried to assist his patients, not only by means of his profound knowledge which he continued to enhance by constant studies, but also by striving to be a compassionate brother to them — and this was recognized and appreciated by all. The community of Bielsko is loosing an extraordinary physician in the person of the prematurely deceased Dr. Wojtyla, one from whom humanity could have benefited yet more.

We shall forever remember his person, his generous work and the virtues of his noble character.

Peace to his memory!

The Members of the City Council, following the example of the chairman, rose from their seats and listened to this speech attentively.

(As recorded in the minutes from the sessions of the City Council of Bielsko. The text was found by Franciszek Jezak, published in *Kalendarz Beskidzki 1985* {the 1985 Beskidy Mountains Calendar} by the Society of the Lovers of the Bielsko-Biala Region, p. 83.)

December 22, 1932 — In the third year of secondary school, first semester: grades of "Very Good" in all subjects. Absent: 30 class hours (excused).

June 14, 1933 — For the entire third year, his grades are "Very Good" in all subjects. Absent: 51 class hours (all excused).

In the years 1932-1938 I attended secondary school with Karol Wojtyla; moreover, for most of those years, I shared a school desk with him, and we would do our homework together in Karol's home ... Karol had the habit, after completing the assignment in each subject, of going into the next room and returning after a few minutes. Once, the door to the next room was ajar, and I saw that Karol was on a prie-dieu praying... (Mgr. Inz.[12] Antoni Bohdanowicz, Sopot. School documents show that Antoni Bohdanowicz attended Marcin Wadowita Secondary School beginning in the third year).

August 10, 1933 — A farewell celebration for Rev. Kazimierz Figlewicz, curate and catechist, took place at the parish church in Wadowice. After the Holy Mass Lolek Wojtyla delivered a farewell address on behalf of the altar boys (cf. "Dzwonek" {"The Hand-Bell"}, no. 37/1933).

September 1933 — He begins his fourth year at Marcin Wadowita Secondary School. For the first semester he receives grades of "Very Good" in all subjects except for Polish and Latin for which his grades are "Good." This marks the beginning of his study of Latin. He also takes up drawing as an elective. Absences in the first semester: 12 hours.

Information preserved in the school documents:

School Year 1933/34:

At their meetings [of the school chapter of the Anti-Aircraft and Gas Weapons Defense League] the members participate in the training of rescue teams... The training was conducted by Boleslaw Drozdowski from the eighth year class. The training was preceded by a presentation and discussion which included: ... "Defending the City Against Gas Weapons" delivered by K. Wojtyla, February 12, 1934 (according to the proceedings of the School Board of Marcin Wadowita Secondary School, 1933/34, p. 18).

Other activities: ... 2/ During the LOPP {Anti-Aircraft and Gas Weapons Defense League} week from June 3 to June 10, 1934, the school chapter of the League organized a matinee with the following

---

[12] Master of Engineering

program: 1/ A medley of songs (performed by the school orchestra), 2/ An indoctrination lecture (given by W. Balon), 3/ School Choir, 4/ Poetry Recitation (K. Wojtyla), 5/ Chemical Warfare Defense Exercises in the school courtyard (according to the proceedings of the School Board of Marcin Wadowita Secondary School, 1933/34, p. 18).

June 15, 1934 — He completes his fourth year with the grade of "Very Good" in all subjects. A notation by the grade for Religion reads: "exhibits special predilection" Absences in the second semester: 14 class hours, all excused.

September 1934 — He begins his fifth year. For the first semester — grades of "Very Good" in all subjects including Greek, which studies he began this year. He no longer takes drawing as an elective.

Information preserved in the school documents:

School Year 1934/35

A collection for the *Fund for Polish Schools Abroad* will be opened by a reading for the students prepared by Karol Wojtyla from the fifth year. (According to the Book of Teachers' Council Minutes 1934-39, minutes of the February 12, 1935 meeting).

Professor Babinski will prepare Wojtyla, student of the fifth year, for a recitation (according to the Book of Teachers' Council Minutes 1934-39, minutes of an extraordinary meeting of the Teachers' Council regarding a tribute by the students on the day of the Marshal's {Marshal Pilsudski} funeral, May 16, 1935).

On February 18th, Wojtyla, a student of the fifth year (5a) delivered a reading to the entire student body on the subject of Polish schools abroad (according to the proceedings of the School Board of Marcin Wadowita Secondary School, 1934/35, p. 35).

An event was organized by the guard team on school premises [reference is made here to a school organization called the "Advance Guard"] ... The guard team also organized a May 3rd matinee {the anniversary of the first Polish Constitution} at which citizen Wojtyla delivered an address (according to the proceedings of the School Board of Marcin Wadowita Secondary School 1934/35, p. 17).

June 15, 1935 — He finishes his fifth year of secondary school with grades of "Very Good" in all subjects. Absences in the second semester: 1 class hour.

September 1935 — He begins his sixth year. In the first semester — grades of "Very Good" in all subjects. Absences: 4 class hours.

September 15, 1935 — Training with a unit of military cadets.

Information preserved in the school documents:

School Year 1935/36

On November 9, 1935 the school theater staged a production of *Antigone*. The performance for secondary school students took place in the morning and was preceded by a word of introduction from the Principal, Jan Krolikiewicz, and a poetry recitation by student Wojtyla. The performance was repeated that same evening for the general public. (According to the proceedings of the School Board of Marcin Wadowita Secondary School 1935/36, p. 5). The performance was prepared in conjunction with the Moscicka Secondary School for Girls. Karol Wojtyla played the part of Hajmon.

On February 29, 1936 the school theater presented *Sluby panienskie* {The Vows of Maidenhood}, Karol Wojtyla appeared in the role of Gucio. (As related by Halina Kwiatkowska née Krolikiewicz and by Professor Kazimierz Forys).

December 14, 1935 — He is accepted to the Sodality of Mary (entry in the *Golden Book* of the Marian Sodality of Marcin Wadowita Secondary School for Boys in Wadowice). According to a verbal account by Fr. Edward Zacher, Karol Wojtyla had been a candidate for the Sodality since 1933.

April 26, 1936 — He is elected President of the Marian Sodality of Students at the Marcin Wadowita Secondary School for Boys (as recorded in the *Golden Book* of the Sodality, preserved in the archives of the parish of Wadowice). He was President for two terms: from April 26, 1936 to April 18, 1937 and from April 18, 1937 to March 20, 1938.

June 20, 1936 — He completes his sixth year. He receives grades of "Very Good" in all subjects. He was absent three school days.

September 1936. He begins his seventh year. For the first semester — all grades of "Very Good." No absences.

This year he is a co-director of the production of *Nie-Boska Komedia* {*The Un-Divine Comedy* by Zygmunt Krasinski} staged at the Catholic Home. He plays the {protagonist's} part of Count Henry.

> I have many memories from Wadowice, where we would lend each other theatrical props and costumes. I was the manager of the amateur ensemble at the private secondary school in Wadowice, while he was the manager of the ensemble at the public school ... One time, we lent him a magnificent throne used by the celebrant on great feasts. The public secondary school was to put on a dramatization of the Apocalypse of St. John. Wojtyla played the part of St. John. The Abbot, Fr. Gabriel, upon seeing a young man unknown to him carrying this valuable piece of furniture on his head, thought that he was a thief and called after him: "Stop, fiend, where did you steal that!" (As told by Fr. Boguslaw Woznicki, Discalced Carmelite Friar).

[This report is probably inaccurate, because in 1937 the Apocalypse of St. John was presented in the Catholic Home under the auspices of Fr. Zacher.]

Information preserved in the school documents:

School Year 1936/37

In February 1937 a performance of *Balladyna* was staged. Karol Wojtyla played two parts: that of Kirkor and of von Kostryn. He assumed the latter role at the last minute, as the student originally assigned to play it was unable to participate in the performances.

In June of 1937 a performance of *Sobotka* by Jan Kochanowski was staged in the park in Wadowice.

An administration fee was paid by Karol Wojtyla, a student of the seventh year: first semester — 70zl, second semester — 50zl.

July 5, 1937 — Hermanowice. He completes the senior course of military training at a cadet camp. He merited the second rank, with an overall evaluation of "Good."

September 1937 — He begins his eighth year. For the first semester — grades of "Very Good" in all subjects except for the grade of "Good" in History and Physics/Chemistry. Absent: 5 class hours.

Information preserved in the school documents:

School Year 1937/38:

A play *Zygmunt August* by Stanislaw Wyspianski was performed on February 1, 1938, on the occasion of Ignacy Moscicki's (the President of the Polish Republic) name day. The students participated in a service at the parish church. After the service they all proceeded to "Sokol" to participate in a school-sponsored celebration which included ... and the performance of *Zygmunt August* ... This performance was repeated on February 2nd for the general public and was very well received. (According to the proceedings of the School Board of Marcin Wadowita Secondary School, 1937/38, p. 52).

Karol Wojtyla performed the leading role and, together with Kazimierz Forys, M. A., the mentor of the school's drama society, produced and directed the play.

On February 17, 1938, L.M.K. organized a matinee in "Sokol" to celebrate the occasion of Poland's "Betrothal to the Sea." The program included an address by Wojtyla from the eighth year, a choral poetry recitation by the students and a performance by the school orchestra. (According to the proceedings of the School Board of Marcin Wadowita Secondary School, 1937/38, p. 52).

Towards the end of this school period a poetry recitation contest was organized under the auspices of a renowned actress, Kazimiera Rychterowna, who was also a member of the judging panel. First place was awarded to Halina Krolikiewicz (later, Kwiatkowska, an actress); Second place — to Karol Wojtyla. Wojtyla chose the difficult text of *Promethidion* by C. K. Norwid for his presentation in the contest.

The school's troupe toured Andrychow and Kalwaria with their performances. The student-actors would travel to Krakow to see professional theatrical productions. (As related by Halina Kwiatkowska née Krolikiewicz and by Professor Kazimierz Forys).

May 6, 1938 — The Archbishop of Krakow, Prince Adam Stefan Sapieha visits Marcin Wadowita Secondary School in Wadowice. He signs the Golden Book of the Marian Sodality on that date. Welcoming addresses were given by Prof. Szeliski and by Wojtyla, a student of the eighth year.[13] (From the chronicles of Marcin Wadowita Secondary School.) The school's prefect and pastor of Wadowice, Fr. Zacher, related that the Prince Archbishop noticed the senior student who gave the welcoming address, and asked the prefect if Karol Wojtyla was considering entering the seminary. He was disappointed to hear that Wojtyla had chosen to pursue Polish studies.

May 1938 — He receives the sacrament of Confirmation. His sponsor is his friend's father, Mr. Silkowski.

At this time, Wojtyla met Mieczyslaw Kotlarczyk, a teacher in the private secondary school of the Carmelites. He was a frequent guest at his apartment situated across the street from the public secondary school. They would discuss theater, literature, and philosophy for hours on end. (As related by Mrs. Kotlarczyk.)

An administration fee paid by Karol Wojtyla, student of the eighth grade: first semester — 50 zl, second semester — 70 zl.

This is how he was remembered by people who knew him then:

> **I was his close friend throughout our secondary school years. He was far ahead of us in his way of thinking and in his interests. Although he gladly participated in school outings and in intramural soccer games, these were but small digressions for him, whereas for us such activities were the focus of our free time. He was greatly liked, admired and respected. He had a way of making us understand that it was a shame to waste our time on trifles ...**
>
> **His father was a charming man. He had great personal discipline and he demanded the same from Karol. He doted on his son. He tried to fill the void created by the death of Karol's mother. He took care of the washing and mending of their clothes. They bought their dinner out, but ate break-**

---

[13] The last year of secondary school.

fast and supper at home. Their financial situation was such that they had to live frugally, even though his father had quite a decent military pension. (As related by Zbigniew Silkowski, a secondary school friend from Wadowice. Cf. *Tygodnik Powszechny*, 43/1978.)

He was very reliable and possessed an undeniable literary talent. He could inspire his friends to work in the theater, which formed a large part of his own life. We appeared in the hall of the Catholic Home and we traveled to "the provinces," for example, to Andrychow. He was very religious, very pious. Every day before and after school he would step into the church. He was the president of the Marian Sodality in secondary school. Later, he would attend alumni reunions. (Secondary school teacher Kazimierz Forys. Cf. *Tygodnik Powszechny*, 44/1978.)

I remember when he used to eat breakfast here. He would be the cashier taking the money paid by other students for their meals. Sometimes they would ask, "Why him?" I would answer, "Because Karol is the most honest of all of you." (Zofia Warmuz, daughter of Jan Dudek, custodian at the secondary school in Wadowice. Cf. *Tygodnik Powszechny*, 43/1978.)

May 14, 1938 — Secondary school graduation examination.

... After finishing his studies at Marcin Wadowita State Secondary School in Wadowice, to which he was admitted in June of 1930, he took the standard final examination for neo-classical studies on May 14, 1938 ...

... He received the following final grades in the subjects under examination: Religion — Very Good, Polish — Very Good, Latin — Very Good, Greek — Very Good, German — Very Good. He also received the following final grades in these subjects studied in the years 6 through 8: History and Current Polish Affairs — Very Good, Introduction to Philosophy — Very Good; Physical Education — Very Good, Hygiene — Very Good. The State Examinations Commission has found Karol Wojtyla to be mature and adequately prepared to pursue higher {university} studies, and hereby confers upon him this Secondary School Diploma. Wadowice, May 14, 1938. Chairman of the Examinations Commission, Jan Krolikiewicz, Members of the Commission, Rev. Dr. Edward Zacher, Tadeusz Prelicki, Jozef Tik (German Language studies), Kazimierz Forys, MA (Polish Language studies), Zbigniew Czadrski (Latin Language studies).

This secondary school diploma, with seal, was presented upon registration at the Department of Philosophy of the Jagiellonian University on June 22, 1938. (The Archives of the Archdiocesan Curia in Krakow).

May 27, 1938 — Karol Wojtyla speaks on behalf of the graduating class, thanking the teachers and assuring them that they will live their lives guided by the principles that they learned here. (Archives of M. Wadowita Secondary School in Wadowice.)

June 20 to July 17, 1938 — "The draftee Wojtyla, Karol ... has fulfilled his service in the 9th Company of the 7th Youth Paramilitary Army Labor Battalion in Zubrzyca Gorna."

July 12, 1938 — He receives a certificate entitling him to wear the commemorative badge of the Youth Paramilitary Army Labor Battalion (certificate no. 62).

> When he was in Zubrzyca as an auxiliary bishop to Archbishop Baziak, Fr. Wojtyla administered the sacrament of Confirmation. At that time he mentioned that he knew Zubrzyca: "I worked here as a member of a youth labor battalion on the construction of the road between Zubrzyca and Krowiarki." I joked that maybe that was why the road was so bad. He answered that his job at the time was to peel potatoes. He was billeted in the house of a farmer by the {family} name of Misiniec. A picture survives from that time of Wojtyla serving as an acolyte at Holy Mass. (As related by Fr. Franciszek Skorupa.)

Summer 1938 — He moves to Krakow with his father into a house owned by the Kaczorowski family in the Debniki neighborhood, at 10 Tyniecka Street. They occupy a basement apartment of two rooms and a kitchen.

STUDIES IN THE DEPARTMENT OF
PHILOSOPHY OF JAGIELLONIAN UNIVERSITY
(POLISH STUDIES).

Karol Wojtyla, on the department's registration form, entered the following courses that he intends to take: Principles of Polish Etymology, Prof. K. Nitsch; Elements of Polish Descriptive Phonetics, Adjunct Prof. H. Oesterreicher; Polish Language Seminar, Asst. Lecturer S. Urbanczyk, MA; Theater and Drama in Poland Since the Middle of the 18th Century, Prof. S. Pigon; The Literature of "The Springtime of Nations" {The Revolution of 1848} — Analysis of Selected Works and Undergraduate Seminar, also Prof. Pigon; Analysis of the Theory of Drama, Prof. Dr. S. Kolaczkowski; Novels, Memoirs and Correspondence of Brzozowski, also Prof. Kolaczkowski; Polish Medieval Literature, Docent Dr. L. Kamykowski; Seminar in Old Polish Literature, also Docent Kamykowski; Interpretation of Dramaturgy (Wyspianski), Dr. W. Dobrowolski; Seminar in Bibliography, Asst. Lecturer J. Spytkowski; Introductory Russian, Instructor Dr. S. Bednarski; Interpretation of Contemporary Lyric Poetry, Instructor Dr. Dobrowolski.

In the second trimester: The History and Geography of Polish Inflection, Prof. Nitsch; continuation of the first trimester's studies with Prof. Pigon; The Role of Humor, Comedy and Irony in Literary Art, Prof. Kolaczkowski; Seminar in Old Polish Literature, Docent Dr. Kamykowski; Asst. Lecturer; Seminar in the History of Polish Literature, Asst. Lecturer K. Wyka; Exercises in the Grammar of Old Church Slavonic, Docent Dr. T. Milewski; Interpretations of Dramaturgy (Rostworowski), Instructor Dr. Dobrowolski; Introduction to Literature, Asst. Lecturer, Spytkowski; Introductory Russian, Instructor Dr. Bednarski; Interpretation of Lyric Poetry, Instructor Dr. Dobrowolski.

In the third trimester: Courses with Profs. Nitsch and Pigon and seminars with Asst. Lecturer Kazimierz Wyka, as in the second trimester; also Russian and Introduction to Literature. In addition, two hours per week with Prof. Dr. Mieczyslaw Malecki on The Character of Literary Antiquities. Approved for trimesters I, II, and III by Wladyslaw Konopczynski, the Dean of the Department of Philosophy. (Archives of JU: WF II 443).

To one of Prof. Pigon's first lectures at 20 Golebia Street, he {Wojtyla} came dressed in cotton drillcloth and sat in the first row next to Irena Klemensiewicz and myself, and that's how it remained ... During the year, Karol would sometimes leave the first row and sit in the back with his

friends Holuj, Zukrowski and Tadeusz Kwiatkowski.

While listening to the lectures, Karol Wojtyla had a habit of looking at the professor very intently (that was very characteristic of him), as if he wanted to absorb it all... In his social life, he did not avoid the company of us women, but neither did he seek us out. He came to lectures alone and he left alone. Even though we sat next to each other at the lectures, Irena Klemensiewicz, Karol Wojtyla and myself, we spoke little. In time, he formed his own circle of friends, which included Zukrowski, Tadeusz Kwiatkowski, and Holuj, these I remember. (Irena Orlewicz).

His friends considered him very talented and intelligent, although he never tried to shine and he did not create about himself the aura of "genius." Prof. Wyka thought very highly of him. (Maria Bobrownicka).

I remember that Karol Wojtyla often accompanied Anka Weber and played a particular role with regard to her. As I perceived it then, and as it still appears to me now, he protected her, a Jew, from potential aggression by members of the Pan-Polish Union. His attitude towards the Pan-Polish Union was negative, and he made no attempt to hide the fact.

I don't believe that he was particularly conspicuous among his circle of friends, except for the one fact, courageous for the time, that he protected his Jewish friend. Among his friends he was well liked and respected. He was modest, calm, always poorly dressed, giving the impression of a village boy, socially unpolished but of strong character. He stood in obvious contrast to his gregarious and self-assured friends. (Zofia Zarnecka).

His close friends from the university were Tadeusz Kwiatkowski, Juliusz Kydrynski, Jerzy Bober, Tadeusz Holuj, Wojciech Zukrowski, Janina Garycka, Halina Krolikiewicz (also from Wadowice), Krystyna Zbijewska. As a joke, they attached to the door of his dormitory room (in the building known as "Pigoniowka"[1] at 6 Garbarska Street) a plaque reading "Karol Wojtyla, Beginner Saint." (He must have lived there for at least some time, or perhaps this story told to me by my friends pertains to a practical joke associated with some other circumstances?) (Danuta Michalowska).

Others of his fellow students at that time: Maria Pachowna (now Przetacznik, a professor at J.U.), Anna Uhlowna, Maria Bobrownicka, Jerzy Lau, Marian Pankowski, Zdzislaw Wroblewski, Mieczyslaw Kieta, Irena Klemensiewicz. This was the last class that completed their eight-year secondary education according to the old program, i.e., before the reforms of Jedrzejewicz. This class had many remarkably talented people.

Residence

He lived in a dormitory near Blonie with Marian Pankowski. (K. Z.)

Academic Seminars

Seminar with Prof. Pigon at 20 Golebia Street, dealing with historical and literary themes.

---

[1] Colloquialism for "Pigon's Place" {after Prof. Stanislaw Pigon}

At one of the first sessions, the professor proposed the preparation and oral presentation of reports on assigned topics. The preparation and presentation of this report would bear on both the trimestral and final credits. As is usual in such situations, the academically weaker students kept silent, but the stronger, more accomplished ones did not rush to volunteer either. Eventually, several people, mostly second-year students, volunteered. But since the professor had also turned to the first-year students, Karol Wojtyla volunteered. The professor indicated that the assignment was not an easy one, that it would require a good knowledge of French. In subsequent sessions, Karol Wojtyla presented his report entitled Mme de Stael as a Theorist of Romanticism. The treatment was very comprehensive. The author continued to present it over several succeeding sessions. (Franciszek Kleszcz).

Seminar with Prof. Kamykowski —

Reports: *The Legend of St. Alexis and Conversations of Master Polycarp with Death.*

The lectures and seminars dealt with contemporary literature. They were held (probably) in the Collegium Maius. I remember the analysis of Andrzejewski's *Order of the Heart.* He took part in the discussion. These discussions would often continue in the hallways. They were heated, emotional. (Irena Orlewicz).

Classes with Prof. Kolaczkowski in the Collegium Physicum.

He recommended reading German authors who dealt with esthetics, such as Dilthey, Scheler.

(As related by Franciszek Kleszcz).

Classes in the Russian Language

... were taught by Stefan Bednarski, who later perished in Sachsenhausen. We read Krylow's fables. On one occasion, Karol Wojtyla corrected some errors in my written assignment. He had no difficulty with Russian, because he had an excellent ear and easily picked up accents. (Maria Bobrownicka)

He took part in the activities of "Studio 39" (a school of drama under the aegis of the Theatrical Confraternity of Krakow — Dr. Tadeusz Kudlinski, President; Wieslaw Gorecki, Secretary; Kazimierz Meyerhold, Musical Director.) (Danuta Michalowska)

From the beginning, he took part in the "Lectorate of the Living Word" conducted at J.U. by Wladyslaw Dobrowolski. (Halina Kwiatkowska).

September 27, 1938 — At the headquarters of the University Academic Legion he received a full summer uniform of the Legion: a four-cornered cap, a cloth coat, a cloth jacket, cloth infantry trousers, a pair of leather brogans, a pair of cloth puttees, a leather uniform belt, a trouser belt and two pairs of linen summer foot clouts.

September 27 — October 2, 1938 — A six-day introductory training course at the Academic Legion (his registration booklet shows no record of participation in training exercises).

September 27, 1938 — He receives a registration document issued by the National Headquarters of the Academic Legion (serial no. 10155), signed by Major Dr. Zdzislaw Szydlowski.

October 2, 1938 — The first Sunday in October, a Solemn Mass at St. Anne's Church marking the beginning of the academic year.

The solemn service gathered the Senate of the University and crowds of students. We were sitting in the first pew on the right aisle, Karol Wojtyla, Jerzy Lau, Stanislaw Pagaczewski and myself. When the ever elegant, distinguished and noble figure of Rev. Dr. Msgr. van Roy, an excellent speaker famous for his homilies, appeared on the pulpit, the entire congregation sort of held its breath. After a moment his sonorous voice and his words, chosen with meticulous expertise, filled the entire church. The homily was adorned with many Latin quotations. When his last words died away, Karol Wojtyla whispered to us: I would like to be able to speak like this, but how to achieve it? (As related by Mr. L. Petecki).

October 15, 1938 — Poster: "The Blue Room of the Catholic Home, Saturday October 15, 1938, *Our Road — The Poplar Tree Bridge,* an evening of literary readings by Jerzy Bober, Jerzy Kalamacki, Tadeusz Kwiatkowski, Karol Wojtyla. Recitations by K. Hajdys, L. Jablonska, H. Krolikiewicz, S. Sokolowski, J. Stwora. Students: 30 groszy, adults 49 groszy." (According to an account by H. Kwiatkowska, Karol Wojtyla recited his poetry himself.)

November 5, 1938 — A social get-together of the Polish Studies Club, with Professor Stefan Kolaczkowski in attendance, took place in an apartment located at Na Groblach Square across the street from the Nowodworski Secondary School. Janina Garycka, a student of the Polish Language and Literature was renting a room in this apartment. Karol (Wojtyla) was busy helping the hostess; he also took a few photographs (as related by Mr. Leslaw Petecki, a participant in this gathering, also a student of the Polish Language and Literature). At that time Wladyslaw Bodnicki was the president of the Polish Studies Club. There is no documentation of the club's activities. The only surviving records are a report of activities for the calendar year 1938, and a list of members, on which appears the name of Karol Wojtyla (later — the president was Tadeusz Ulewicz).

The literary section of the club organized evenings of readings for students of Polish, lectures and discussions on topics of current interest and evenings of poetry — for example, an evening devoted to the poetry of C. Norwid. The attendance would be about 20 to 30 people.

Other activities worthy of mention included a discussion on the reorganization of the teaching of Polish studies, and the participation of the club members in last year's action against *numerus nullus* {to prevent} Jews {from attending} the Jagiellonian University... (Archives of JU: S II 766, The Polish Studies Club)

I particularly recall how Karol Wojtyla took part in literary evenings

along with such colleagues as T. Kwiatkowski, W. Zukrowski, J. Han, and Marian Pankowski. Of course, at that time they all wrote poetry, and so did Karol.(Z. S.)

I don't remember the circumstances, but I am certain that he expressed a negative opinion about Zegadlowicz (Zmory), and had reservations about the elements of form and content of *Powsinogi Beskidzkie*. Claiming personal acquaintance with the folk sculptor Wowra, he questioned the way Zegadlowicz presented Wowra. In opposition to Zegadlowicz, he himself wrote *Ballady Beskidzkie* (I trust that I am recalling the title correctly). His colleagues, however, did not favorably receive this work. I think that these discussions took place during meetings of the Polish Studies Club. (Zofia Zarnecka)

November 28, 1938 — A letter from Dr. F. Grzesik, the Prefect of the District of Wadowice, exempting Karol Wojtyla from active military service because of his attendance at JU.

December 14, 1938 — He passed an examination in descriptive phonetics (according to a registration card deposited by Karol Wojtyla at JU in 1945, with the notation "I have the document." JUArchives, WT II 213).

January 26, 1939 — He paid annual dues in the amount of 4 zlote, as an ordinary member of the Society of Lovers of the Polish Language. Received by Urbanczyk.

I remember quite well two events in which Karol Wojtyla participated. The first was an author's soiree in the winter of the 1938/39 academic year, where he read his own poetry. They were ballads in the style of the poets of the "Skamander"[2] group with themes drawn mostly from folklore and legend; with one or two having Marian themes. They were well accepted, although there were some opinions that his forms were overly traditional. The second event was related to the "Days of Krakow" festival. (Maria Bobrownicka)

February 6, 1939 — He received a membership card of the Marian Sodality of the Students of JU. He joined the Eucharistic and Charity sections.

February 6, 1939 — He is granted an admission pass to the reading room of the Polish Academy of Sciences for 1939.

February 13, 1939 — A list of students of the first year, cadets of the Academic Legion, who are assigned to compulsory physical education. No. 18 on the list — Wojtylo (!), Karol. Sessions on Tuesdays and

---

[2] A group of Polish poets (among others, Julian Tuwim, Antoni Slonimski, Kazimierz Wierzynski, Jaroslaw Iwaszkiewicz, and Jan Lechon) gathered around a monthly by the same name, published from 1920 to 1928 and again from 1935 to 1939. The poets of "Skamander" opposed the excessive use of the theme of national martyrology and promoted instead the affirmation of life in its biological fullness and abundance. They believed that poetry should be natural and direct, come closer to the simple man and his daily concerns, understand his private world and his interests. They felt that poetry should embrace the colloquial language, "get out in the street" and capture the pulse of man's natural drives and passions.

Fridays from 8 to 9 PM, at the Gimnazjum Kupieckie[3] at 18 Loretanska Street. Sessions begin on February 23, 1939.

From March, he fulfills the duties of librarian of the Polish Studies Club. (Tadeusz Ulewicz)

April 6, 1939 (Holy Thursday):

> He attended the traditional Holy Thursday rite of the washing of feet by Archbishop Sapieha at Wawel Cathedral. Then he stood for quite a while, lost in thought, at the tomb of King Jagiello. He prayed for a long time in front of the Blessed Sacrament in the chapel of King Batory. This was in the morning. (Maria Bobrownicka)

May 18, 1939 — "He took part in a pilgrimage of university students to Czestochowa led by the academic chaplain, Rev. Tadeusz Kurowski. I don't remember any details." *(Maria Bobrownicka)* He will talk about this at the funeral of Prof. Antoni Kepinski (March 1972):

> My presence here may seem strange, but I made the acquaintance of the late Antoni Kepinski quite a long time ago. It was during a student pilgrimage to Jasna Gora. Both of us were students at the time; we rode together in the same railcar compartment and that young man caught my attention with his statements and his ideals, to which he remained faithful all his life.

Karol Kepinski, two years older than Karol Wojtyla, was then a second-year student of medicine at JU, and Karol Wojtyla was a newly registered student of Polish.

June 17, 1939 — He passes an examination in descriptive grammar with Prof. Kazimierz Nitsch, with a grade of "Good." On the same day, in Old Church Slavonic, with Prof. Mieczyslaw Malecki — a grade of "Satisfactory." (The archives of JU: WT II 213: Registration sheet plus "Subcommittee for holders of Master's degree.")

> After having earned the appropriate credits, at the end of the first year we could attempt two examinations: in descriptive grammar and either in Polish or in Old Church Slavonic. Passing two examinations was a prerequisite for admission to the course in historical grammar and the more diligent students tried to prepare themselves... (Franciszek Kleszcz)
>
> I have a more precise recollection only of my first university examination with Prof. Nitsch, taken together with Karol Wojtyla and a nun whose name escapes me ... The Professor summoned us to the examination room (the front one in the "Golebnik") after first noisily ejecting from this room a couple of miscreants who were followed by flying chalk, a sponge, and perhaps even a chair... I sat next to Karol. We were very scared. The professor began examining him first, calling on me to supplement the answers... We both got grades of "Good" and ran out happy and light as birds... (A female classmate)

---

[3] Merchants' High School

June 24, 1939 — He participates in a party to celebrate the passing of the examinations and successful completion of his first university year.

The party was held in the home of the parents of our classmate Anna Nawrocka (died in 1969), at 3 Siemiradzkiego Street. There was some wine and we danced to the gramophone. He danced along with the rest of us, but he was more interested in conversation than in dancing. Besides Karol Wojtyla, the hostess and the undersigned, present were Janina Garycka, Tadeusz Kwiatkowski, Marian Pankowski, and Wojciech Zukrowski. Many years later, when the late Anna Nawrocka was suffering from cancer, he came to visit her in the hospital and obtained for her some medications from the United States, which were unobtainable here. In his letter to me last year [1978 — ed.] he recalled her fondly. (Maria Bobrownicka)

Spring — summer 1939 — He writes the poem *David — A Renaissance Psalter* (Slavonic Volume) dedicated to his mother:

Above your white tomb
bloom the white flowers of life —
— O, how many years it has been
without you — winged spirit.[4]

June 1939

The Student Theater presented *The Cavalier of the Moon* by Nizinski in the courtyard of Collegium Maius. Karol played the role of Taurus in the Zodiac. Petecki played Twardowski; Kwiatkowski was Mefisto, Gemini {the twins} were played by Krolikiewicz and Czuprynowna. The production was quite popular. (Maria Bobrownicka)

July 1939 — He took part in the Social Action camp of the Academic Legion in Ozomla near Sadowa Wisznia (not far from Przemysl). One of the aims of the camp was to improve relations with the ethnic Ukrainians (hence the name "social action"). The commandant was Lieutenant (?) Miaczynski (or perhaps Maczynski). A participant of this camp, Adam Gatty-Kostyal remembers Karol Wojtyla as a great athlete who won praise from the camp athletic director Lt. Mroz. He played soccer enthusiastically, swam in the pond, etc. Towards the end of our time at camp, Zygmunt Nowakowski came to visit the students. (Adam Gatty-Kostyal related these facts; he also submitted photographs, which he had taken at the time. The camp participants did not know of these photographs which were developed and printed after the war. In the archives of JU, the documentation of the Academic Legion ends before the summer vacation of 1939).

From the beginning of his university days, Karol Wojtyla maintained a friendship with the family of Mr. and Mrs. Szkocki, at 55a

---

[4] Original in rhyming verse, rhyme scheme **abab**.

Ksiecia Jozefa Street (known as "Under the Lindens") in Krakow. Mrs.
Zofia Pozniakowa, a daughter of Mr. and Mrs. Szkocki, recalls:

> He was introduced by Juliusz Kydrynski, a student of my mother's, as
> his dearest friend. After that Karol, who had recently moved into the vicin-
> ity with his father, would take French lessons with Mrs. Jadwiga Lewaj,
> our tenant and a teacher who was very dedicated to her students. He called
> my mother [Irena Szkocka] "granny," and that is how he addressed her in
> the letters he wrote to her (which have survived). He was almost a daily
> guest "Under the Lindens." He invited us to see a play in which he was
> appearing; it was called *The Cavalier of the Moon*. After the outbreak of
> the war, he would come to us to listen to music. Here also we held read-
> through rehearsals of Zeromski's *Przepioreczka* {Little Quail}. One time he
> brought Osterwa with him. After the death of his father — just then the
> Germans had requisitioned our house — Karol suggested that we move in
> with him. I was then alone with two children, sick, my husband in a prison
> camp. His apartment, partly in a basement, was too small to accommodate
> all of us with our furniture. At that time, the Kotlarczyks moved in with
> him. Both of their daughters were born there.
>
> A friend of Mrs. Lewaj, Mr. Kulakowski, arranged for him to get a job
> at Solvay. (As related by Z. Pozniakowa; cf. TP, 44/1978)

August 30, 1939 — He returned the uniform to the Academic
Legion. (Per the archives of JU).

THE YEARS OF OCCUPATION

September 1, 1939:

> The war broke out. The day of September 1, 1939 is also associated in
> my memory with Karol Wojtyla. The morning air raids on Krakow caused
> a panic among the workers of the Cathedral, so I had no one to serve Mass
> for me. Karol came along just then, having walked from Debniki to Wawel
> to go to confession and Communion, because this was the first Friday of
> the month. This religious custom was scrupulously observed by this young
> student. I will never forget that first wartime Mass, at the altar of Christ
> Crucified, amid the howl of sirens and the blasts of explosions. Does our
> present Holy Father still remember that? ... (Fr. Kazimierz Figlewicz, TP 44/1978)

Mid-September 1939:

> Dear Mieciu,
>
> ... My expedition has reached almost to the San River. I traveled with
> my father. The trip tired him very much. Now he is feeling a little better.
> "Vita Cracoviensis." Just think, think! It consists of standing in line for
> bread, of (rare) expeditions to find sugar; also of morbid longing for coal
> and for reading. For us, life consisted of evenings on Dluga Street, of
> refined conversation, of dreams and longings. We dreamt away many an
> evening until midnight or beyond, but now...
>
> The theater is in operation. Maybe you already know about this,
> because supposedly you do get the "Courier." *The March Cavalier*
> (Karbowski), *Mrs. Dulska* (Korecka), now *Lobzowanie* and *By Domestic
> Drum*, also *Ladies and Hussars* and *Queen of the Suburb*. So vaudeville is
> well. I am not surprised. [Letter written after the war. The Germans
> allowed for the reopening of the Slowacki Theater. The last Polish-language

play was on Sept. 15, 1939]. I spoke with Woznik about some position in the theater, even as an extra. He was very gracious, even happy to see me in one piece, but of course he was not in the theater at the appointed time. I will have to go again. And again after bread.

Dobrowolski is here. He will conduct readings even though he was told that he would not get paid one cent; maybe I can arrange something with him. He's quite a decent chap and looks at these things from quite a different point of view, but then he also sees life quite distractedly and is forever running out of time. Well, now he has plenty of it. Czuprynowna and Danka are here. Only Kwiatkowski, after a long trek, has settled in Nadworna in the outer regions. Also, Kudlinski has returned.

Nitsch, like a specter who always returns to haunt the place to which fate ties him, has resumed pouring the nectar of Polish and Slavic literature into young minds (a minor seminar), and that 2 and 1/2 weeks before the official opening of the academic year. (Letter to Mieczyslaw Kotlarczyk)

October 1939 — A meeting at the home of the Kydrynskis, for the purpose of reading the classic Polish literature. Present are: Tadeusz Kwiatkowski, Danuta Michalowska, Juliusz Kydrynski, and Karol Wojtyla. They read, taking on various roles. From this develops the future Rhapsodic Theater. (As related by Juliusz Kydrynski)

November 2, 1939 — Karol Wojtyla registers for the second year of studies at the Department of Philosophy (in Polish Philology). A registration card filled out in 1945:

... In the second half of September 1939, I began my second year of studies at the Department of Philosophy of the Jagiellonian University (in Polish Philology). This lasted until November (the arrest of Polish professors in Krakow).

From March 1940, employed as a store messenger in the firm of J. Kuczmierczyk.

From October 11, 1940 as a laborer in the Solvay factory in Borek Falecki, a year in the quarry at Zakrzowek, then inside the factory. At the same time, since October 1, I attended the secret classes of theology at the Krakow Seminary. In August of 1944, without terminating my relationship with Solvay, I put on clerical garb. (Archives of JU: WT II 213)

Letter to Mieczyslaw Kotlarczyk:

To Brother Mieczyslaw in the Greek Theater
[address as on the envelope]
November 2, 1939
[In the middle of the second page of the letter] ... So this is Poland. I see her as you see her, but until now I did not see her in her full truth. I could not get the sense of the atmosphere of ideas that would be worthy of enveloping the nation of Mickiewicz, Slowacki, Norwid and Wyspianski... but still the market squares were full of petty merchants of the kind so despised by Kasprowicz. And today in my meditations I feel, I fully and consciously understand, it is obvious to me, that the idea of her lived in us just as it did in the generation of Romanticism. But it did not live in truth, because the peasant was beaten and imprisoned when he justly demanded his political rights, because he felt the approach of his hour of destiny,

because he was in the right. But the nation was deceived and lied to, and her sons, just as in the times of the partitions, were dispersed around the world, why, so they wouldn't rot in the jails of their own country. Did we really achieve liberation? I think that our liberation lies at the gate of Christ. I see an Athenian Poland, but more perfect than Athens by the boundless immensity of Christianity. That is the ideal envisioned by the bards, by the prophets of the Babylonian captivity. The nation has fallen like Israel, because it did not recognize the messianic ideal, its own ideal, which was raised like a glowing ember, but never realized! These are few reflections for you, my dearest friend, in response to your impassioned questioning ...

[On the last page of this extensive letter:] I take this opportunity to write about some matters, shall I say, more current in nature.

1) Miss Uhlowna, whose sister teaches in the same school as Mrs. Janina Obidowicz-Nowinska, told me at Nitsch's last seminar (October 31), that Mrs. Janka is very concerned because she has no news of her family in Wadowice. She doesn't know anything about the whereabouts of her husband and many other officers, either. Here is a way to provide her with the most comprehensive information.... [There follows a detailed discussion of how to get information to the interested parties.]

2) For two weeks now I've been going to a minor seminar on language conducted by Nitsch, who (tireless old man!) started this full three weeks before the beginning of the academic year. Registration ends on November 4 and there is a Mass. The academic year begins on November 6. Officially, that is.

3) In the theater, after *Mrs. Dulska, Lobzowianie* and *Drum,* there is *Ladies and Hussars* with Fabisiak, Woznik, Korecka, Rolinska, in a production by Frycz. I haven't been to the theater yet, first for lack of cash, secondly because such things are hardly on my mind, but maybe I'll go ...

I send you greetings in the name of Beauty, which is the profile of God, the cause of Christ, and the cause of Poland.

November 6, 1939 — The Germans arrest all professors of JU. Closing of the University.

I found out from Wladzia Wodzinska and from Mr. & Mrs. Bieglaski that you were returning to Wadowice via Krakow. I also evacuated, but my father and I returned from the Tarnobrzeg-Tarnow highway in the direction of Krakow. Father, no surprise, could not take any more of this hard trek.

I also heard from Danka Puklowna, who is supposed to deliver this letter to you, that she saw you in Wadowice. So evidently you survived. Thank God you managed to get there.

Aren't you thinking of returning to Sosnowiec? You can get there. The University is closed The theater is shut down. I commend you and yours to Divine Providence. Greetings and hugs. Also from my father ...

Letters to Mieczyslaw Kotlarczyk (provided by Mrs. Kotlarczyk):

December 28 (1939?)

Dear Mieciu,

Taking advantage of an unusual circumstance, I want to tell you of some details of my life over the past two months or so.

First and foremost, I must tell you that I am keeping very busy. Some people are currently dying of boredom, but not I. I have surrounded myself with books, dug in with Arts and Sciences. I am working. Would you believe that I am virtually running out of time! I read, I write, I study, I think, I pray, I struggle with myself. At times I feel great oppression, depression, despair, evil. At other times, as if I were seeing the dawn, the aurora, a great light. I wrote a drama or, more precisely, a dramatic poem, entitled *David*, in which he wears biblical robes and a linen shirt from the time of Piast[5] and a crimson cloak of a Polish nobleman. In it I have bared many things, many matters of my soul. I am very curious what you would say about it. I have already sent you these sonnets. I'm wondering how you find them. In any case, *David* is not one form; it is in prose and in verse, both bland and rhymed — sincere.

I am studying French very intensely. My teacher [Mrs. Lewaj] is an enthusiast of great, great Beauty; she is in love with Slowacki, Zeromski, and Conrad. So we have things to talk about.

Besides, I have met a new friend whose spiritual makeup is similar to ours. He is a fanatic "homo theatralis," a kindred spirit. We even put on small seminars where we read poetry, drama. He knows all of Norwid's *Bogumil* from memory, and many passages from {Wyspianski's} *Liberation*. He is my colleague from the Polish studies, but started somewhat later. Only now we drew so close. His name is Juliusz Kydrynski. His late father was a school inspector. Maybe you even knew him. How I miss our meetings on Dluga Street. We would have another brother.

[Explanation of Mrs. Kotlarczyk]: I lived in Krakow as a student. When he and his father moved to Krakow and Karol began his Polish studies, my husband would come to visit me. And every Saturday Lolek and his father would come to my house on Dluga. Then they would begin what they called an "analysis" of all the dramatic and non-dramatic literature. It would begin with "Well, Mieciu, let's cast roles." And they would play the roles of the great characters of poetry and prose. His father sat and listened. Those evenings on Dluga often lasted until late at night. [Mrs. K.]

I have read almost all of the mysticism of Slowacki, then much of Mickiewicz, now again Wyspianski *ab ovo*,[6] besides the Holy Scripture, the Old Testament. Yesterday was the feast of St. John the Evangelist; we read together the beautiful passages where Jesus bids farewell to his disciples in the room of the Last Supper. My Christmas was very sad, but whose was merry? Not yours, probably. But I am dazzled by the increased piety among the people, by this mystical strength.

I keep praying for Wicek...

In the winter of 1939/40, Kydrynski meets by chance Juliusz Osterwa in a used bookstore; he tells him of their group. Osterwa invites Kydrynski to come to his home on Basztowa Street in the spring of 1940. They go there together with Karol Wojtyla. From that time, they meet with Osterwa quite often. On Felicjanek Street they put on, especially for Osterwa, the second act of *The Little Quail*. Karol plays the role of Smugon. (As related by Juliusz Kydrynski)

February 1940 — He meets Jan Tyranowski. "With regards to my

---

[5] A Polish prince of the 9th century; he founded a dynasty whose decendants ruled Poland as crowned kings until the end of the 14th century.

[6] from the beginning

vocation to the priesthood, I owe very much to the late Jan Tyranowski, about whom I once wrote in *Tygodnik Powszechny*." (Archbishop Karol Wojtyla, *The Nest from Which I Came*; see also entry for September 1940).

Fragments of an article about Jan Tyranowski:

It was in the first year of the war. In February, the Salesian Fathers, who ran the parish of St. Stanislaw Kostka in Debniki in Krakow, organized a Lenten retreat, preparing with special care their sermons for young men. Having thus gained the attention of a large group, they announced that henceforth every Saturday there would be meetings for all those who are interested in religious issues. These meetings regularly attracted about 20 to 30 young people aged 16 to 25. The presenter, the well-known biblical scholar Fr. Jan Mazerski, a professor of JU (he perished in the Warsaw Uprising {1944}) was magnificent. The locale, a chapel, did not prevent him from calling upon the audience to participate in discussions and even to make presentations, which made the whole enterprise even more attractive.

It was then that the youth of Debniki first became acquainted with the man who is the subject of this recollection.

We will know him by the name of January

1

Remembering Jan seems to be necessary, we think, for several reasons. For one, to refresh the memory of this person for those who knew him; for another, to give others food for thought when considering the creative application of Catholic apostolic methods. For in that particular group, which for a variety of reasons had to disperse soon after, Jan played a very specific role: he became, in every sense of the word, an apostle. When he spoke for the first and then the second time at a meeting of the group of religious knowledge, all of the young people present had great reservations about him. This was caused in part by the obvious age difference (Jan's hair was then decidedly graying, even though he was barely forty), and much more so by his manner of formulating the issues, a manner that seemed overly pious, too much from the catechism, in no way original. So the first meetings with Jan created a certain distance between him and us. This was most acutely felt, it seems, by those who eventually would become closest to him. But it should not be surprising that our first meeting turned out, it appeared, so unfavorably. We approached each other from totally opposite poles, knowing nothing of each other. Besides, young people had no concept that in the sphere of religion, which each of us eagerly professed, there could be the possibilities that Jan revealed to us.

At this point, our recollections require some comments about the very methodology of expressing these memories about January Because it is not easy to remember this man, he cannot be understood as a mere compilation of the events of his life. For us, events did not define January External actions could never tell us everything about him. If every contact with a person leaves us with some general impression, so also our impressions and judgments of Jan were formed by our contact with him over the period of several years. Our impressions of Jan grew from regarding him as an aging, pious gentleman to a personal conviction that we were dealing with someone who was indeed a saint. So our internal experience of Jan overcame all of our resistance and reservations, and his personality became indelibly imprinted on us. It is this personality which is the subject of these reminiscences, as is his humanity which is so transfigured that his words and deeds were but a meager reflection of it. For his words and deeds must have seemed very ordinary to anyone who was not drawn into the orbit of Jan's interior life. No, Jan could not be known from the outside, he had to be experienced and tested from within.

Our road to knowing Jan was so much the harder because he brought with him a concept of life that was totally foreign to us. He wanted to draw his listeners to this new life. He was the apostle and teacher of this new concept. This is the essence of the matter: he was an apostle. With his very being, he gave witness to the truth he was proclaiming.

2

But was it really necessary to accept Jan himself before accepting what he brought to us? Jan simply proclaimed the truth about the full supernatural life of man, which is but the fulfillment of the riches of our Faith. These truths were well known from catechism, from books, from sermons. Did Jan really proclaim anything new? This is the very thing that Jan did not proclaim, did not teach, officially. Jan merely harvested souls, in the full meaning of that term. He wanted these souls to accept the truths of religion anew, but not as prohibitions and limitations. He wanted to elicit from the supernatural resources which he knew existed within all souls, the real form of the supernatural life of man; a life that, through the grace of God, becomes participation in the life of God.

That was the difficulty of his endeavor. Imagine, if you will, these young people who judged Jan quite skeptically, who carried within them an inflated concept of their own self-sufficiency and arrogance typical of their age. And each one of them asked: what does this man want of me? What is it that he finds lacking in me? For it became apparent very quickly that Jan was demanding something of them, of their lives, their convictions, their emotions, their attitudes. At first it was not easy to determine what it was that he demanded. The truth about the new, fuller interior life, a truth which Jan already possessed, was totally unknown to them. This was not a question of a lecture, of learning some new facts, but of reforming one's life and attitudes — a life which, until now, seemed quite good, virtually perfect, inviolable, impervious to all external influences, especially the influence of some overly pious old man. Each of us tenaciously challenged the truth of Jan's words and was reluctant to overcome his reservations, whether they sprang from reason, emotions or other sources. It was a long-lasting effort in which the processes of Grace were activated in young souls and fulfilled through contact with the interior life of this good, simple man. His inner life was like an anchor beyond his words; it explained his actions, it drew us to him despite all of our reservations and resistance. His words often offended us, not because they were inappropriate, but because they were so unoriginal, because our self-esteem was hurt by the realization of the gulf separating his inner life from ours. He showed us God much more immediately than any sermons or books; he proved to us that God could not only be studied, but also lived. But, above all, he surprised us with facts. Undoubtedly, there is a great difference between what is proclaimed by an apostle and what is proclaimed by anyone else. First of all, there is a difference in the attitude and capabilities of the listener. The apostle must be — and is — concerned with at least an incipient change in the listener. And this change is not a consequence of reasoned arguments, but the result of a Grace that transcends mere words. And how much harder is it to convince where the desired result is not only the acceptance of truth, but also the change of one's ego, the transcendence of the self.

That is what was special about Jan, something that made you feel that this man transcended the processes of grace. I repeat: he surprised us with the accomplished fact. Despite all the resistance, reservations and prejudice against his words, the way he expressed himself, or the thoughts that he wrote down about the interior life (which in reality consisted in copying passages from books on spirituality), there arose a certain necessity to give in to his internal truth and to imitate the life which he himself lived and of which he was the apostle. A theologian might say that such conclusions are not proper insofar as the apostolic influence of a person may arise from charisms, from graces freely given by God, which, in themselves, do not yet tell us anything about the holiness of a particular person. But Jan's apostolate was not for the masses. Jan did the most through personal conversations and consultations, when he would not lecture, would not teach, but accomplish everything through the kind of gravity that his internal life possessed.

3

So who was this Jan? It has been previously said that he was an apostle. Apostolate is perceived as an extension and expansion of one's contemplation into society in general, as transferring the effects of that inner contemplation onto others. Jan was a man very prone to contemplation, but he was not prone to be an activist, he was not a speaker. As a matter of fact, he considered the entire sphere of external action as a necessary obligation. His entire life, ever since early childhood, proved that he avoided direct action, contacts with people. That is why he changed his profession in his youth: by education he was an accountant, but he left his job, preferring to become a tailor in his father's workshop. In his later years, his father did not work any more; the tailor shop was taken over by his brother Edward. The family circle was completed by the aging mother. In these conditions, Jan found the necessary quiet and isolation from the world, and after a period of contemplation, he found this to be his true calling. What he wanted was isolation with God, the isolation whose social significance was understood only in Christianity. In Christianity, this significance is explained by the teachings of the Mystical Body of Christ.

Why didn't Jan simply enter a monastery? He was often asked about this. His answers were never fully satisfactory. It appears, however, that Jan imagined the monastic life to be very difficult and demanding, full of responsibilities. In any event, even while he isolated himself from the world, he remained within it. His life, however, became dedicated to profound asceticism, the details of which are impossible to discuss here. There is a wealth of information indicating that Jan used every means at his disposal to subjugate his body. It might be suspected that he even abused it. The main element of his interior life, however, was contemplation. For him, this did not mean a reasoned analysis of God's truths, a pure thought exercise. His aim was to become enamored of the subject under contemplation, he sought not a dry exercise of the mind, but a full exercising of the spirit.

To what extent these efforts (which in some periods reached up to four hours of contemplation per day) led Jan beyond the sphere of the tangible, to what degree he met within them the unknowable and unfathomable reality of God — that will forever remain his exclusive secret. Those who met him can judge this by the results, by the fruits of his work. For Jan, contemplation was a direct quest for God, not a gradual approach to the supernatural vision of the world as it was affected by the mystery of the Incarnation. This last aspect, it seems, was less well developed in Jan's internal life. A love for Jesus Christ, who was God, was for him more of a bridge to the transcendental reality of God, rather than a supernatural way of looking at the world. His going forth to meet God happened amid internal suffering. We can assume this on the basis of many of Jan's utterances. Whereas he did not like to speak about himself, he returned often to these matters. It was obvious that these were the most significant experiences of his life.

And now let us imagine that moment. Jan was summoned to the apostolate; he was summoned, because with his personality of a loner he himself would never have gone out to embrace it. He did not have the temperament of an activist, he did not imagine that he could ever influence anyone. (In general he was the type of person whose full measure of social worth could only be achieved within a guiding principle such as the Mystical Body.) He made excuses to his confessor — "But I don't know how to speak..." "Don't worry" he replied, "God will help you. Do not be afraid." And Jan dared. We must fully appreciate this to understand how much supernatural courage he needed for what he did. For he was so very different from the people to whom he was to minister. The road he traveled was so very different from theirs. He did not speak their language, think in their terms, and above all, there was this difference in the levels of interior life! He really needed to come down to their level and begin to learn things which he felt were superfluous and without value. But how can their interior life, their limited concept of God, meet the mature fruit of his contemplation? He realized, however, that what was needed was to introduce them to that very mystery. Before the war he was already a member of Catholic Action; he held the office of a secretary and fulfilled his duties with a conscientiousness that was apparent at every step. But then he was but an office worker of the apostolate. He had not yet matured to the apostolic revelation of what he had accumulated within himself; he had not yet dared to grasp a bold and personal apostolate.

This was to occur now. Jan understood that God was calling him to this. But for him it must have been a long and difficult leap...

He was an apostle of God's greatness, God's beauty, and God's transcendence. This he learned from his spiritual guide, St. John of the Cross. God exists within us not so we can stifle Him in the narrow confines of our human spirit; God is within us to tear us away from ourselves toward His supernatural transcendence. That was also the main goal of Jan's strivings. In this he was the strongest, the clearest, the most convincing, the most apostolic. God is within us. Jan knew this. One could often meet him along the banks of the Wisla {Vistula River}, or in his own home, explaining to some young listeners the essence of God's virtues, the methods of meditation or the mysteries of the gifts of the Holy Spirit. Theoretically these lectures were less than perfect, but we have described earlier in these musings the source of their power. If now we were to summarize Jan's apostolic style, we would have to say that he did not want to educate people merely to be good; he was not a moralist nor a psychologist. He was truly an educator and a theologian. He knew about the supernatural gifts deposited by Divine Grace in the depths of the human soul, and he wanted to bring forth this internal godliness in man. He wanted to discover it and make it apparent to each of his young companions. He wanted to help to develop this resource within man, the resource that we must continue to discover...

Our last experience of Jan for us was his illness and death. But first a few more details about his person.

This man was not a fiction or a symbol, but a real living person. His name was Tyranowski. Jan Tyranowski. He lived in Krakow, in Debniki, at 15 Rozana Street. He was born in 1900 and died in March of 1947... His family was of a typical suburban middle class. His father and brother Edward died before Jan did — and his mother died even as he lay on his own deathbed. It is worth noting that Jan's demeanor, for example the way he wore his watch, his expressions, all of the many details that reflect the social environment, were totally consistent with that environment. The entire difference was hidden within, and it was from within that all his external habits obtained their particular character. Jan guided his inner life according to the book *Mistyka* by Fr. Semenenko. Later, however, St. John of the Cross and St. Theresa of the Child Jesus became his chief spiritual masters. They were not only his masters, they led him to discover himself, they explained and justified his own life.

Jan's death was indeed a form of self-sacrifice. Jan approached it consciously; he wished it and prayed for it... (Karol Wojtyla, "The Apostle", TP, 5/1949)

February 21, 1940 — Karol Wojtyla was at the funeral of Prof. Stefan Kolaczkowski, who died shortly after returning from the prison camp in Sachsenhausen. (As related by Maria Bobrownicka)

From the diary of Juliusz Osterwa:

Krakow, March 9, 1940, Saturday — [1 Basztowa Street, 3rd floor, at the home of Matylda Sapieha, his mother-in-law]. It snowed again at night and there is a hard freeze ... I can hear and see how the Jews are digging with pick-axes at the hard, thick layer of ice on the road, the frozen mud. The sun peeks out from the fog now and then.... Two young men, Karol Wojtyla and my namesake Kydrynski. A reading about the Cossacks.

Krakow, March 16, 1940, Saturday. It's still white, the sun is somehow pale... Wojtyla and Kydrynski... A snowstorm — all is white. (Selected by Matylda Osterwina)

Lent 1940 — He is writing Job — *a Drama from the Old Testament.* Also in 1940 he creates Jeremiah — a National Drama in 3 Parts. (Typescripts saved by friends.)

Letters to the Kotlarczyks:

Here I am writing before Easter. I'm writing before the Feast of the Resurrection. Because I need to share with you, dear friend some words. "My lips speak from the abundance of my heart." How much could they say — how much? Here it is almost eight months that we haven't seen each other, where before we had a thousand things to discuss in a week.

... And now a little about me. I met Juliusz Osterwa. I met him at Kydrynski's, you know, that friend from the Polish studies. We went to visit him twice already. He is very cordial, he treats us very cordially, very sincerely, and he keeps inviting us. I told him about you — he said: a very interesting person, I just read his play... very interesting, very... He himself works very hard. He told us: "the concept of the theater is, in fact, no longer sufficient, we need something more." — "An actor is not a clown, but an activist fulfilling a mission." In any event, he is a man on a great, a very great, scale. And what is most impressive about him is the magnitude of his work, more work, and still more work. Presently he claims that his primary interest is language. He sees it as too sullied by foreign expressions, so that it loses its healthy roots. He showed us his notes. A theatrical calendar as we have imagined it: *Lilla Weneda* in May, *Balladyna* in July, Sulkowski in September, *The Wedding* in November, etc.

I myself have written a new drama. Greek in form, Christian in spirit, timeless in content, as is "any" Drama about suffering: Job. Some people here like it. It came about to some extent because I am immersing myself in the Old Testament. I've read the psalms of David, the Book of Job, the Book of Wisdom, now the prophets. Besides that, of the more important books: Slowacki and *the New Drama* (a wonderful book), and also *Lectures in Slavic Literature* by Mickiewicz. Prof. Kolaczkowski has died, Pigon is still living, and Nitsch I even ran into today. I am reaching into myself to develop myself. My Brother, how I would like to tell you more about the things which I am sure are of great interest to you. Regarding myself, I have two dramas: the first one — *Job* — a drama in Greek from, but with a chorus that's very loosely conceived and not very Greek. Each one in the chorus speaks for himself. The whole chorus speaks together only now and then. The starting point for the story is an event in the Old Testament. The story of Job, who very quickly lost his vast fortune, his sons and daughters, and then the Lord restored everything to him twice over. In my story it begins like this: Job's neighbors are gathering at his manor for a feast. Job greets them at the gate. But before he can lead them inside, messengers come one after another bringing terrible news. The revelers scatter, to return as a chorus of wailers. (They are convinced that the causes of Job's misfortunes are some secret vices of his, because they know of no public ones.) But before the wailers enter, Job recites a long monologue, covers his head with ashes and receives a visit from three of his friends. Already in the dialog with them the theme of the drama begins to form: that suffering is not always a punishment, that sometimes it may be (and often is) a prepayment. This idea is represented by Job, who after some initial rebellion, upon reflection comes to the realization of supreme justice, of a universal harmony. But despite all of this he cannot understand why he, a just man, is the subject of God's punishment. Here he is aided by the young prophet Elihu. Having found out about Job's misfortune (Job was his friend), he comes and in Job's presence has a prophetic vision: he sees the Passion of Christ, the Garden of Gethsemane, Calvary. Nobody understands him. But Job grasps it. Finally (if I may summarize), using the example of Christ's Passion, Elihu shows the developmental role of suffering (suffering as prepayment). Some fragments of his vision are represented on stage, so during the vision of the Garden we see an angel holding a chalice and descending in a shaft of light, at the end we see the outline of Calvary and the Cross at dawn. The drama opens with a prologue and ends with an epilogue.

People to whom I've read it liked it; some liked it a lot. It grabs you by the heart, it is eloquent, it is very dramatic and theatrical and quite concise (it is, after all, my debut).

My next accomplishment is a drama entitled *Jeremiah*, but will probably be called *The Monastery*. It was created very rapidly, as a revelation during the reading of the Book of Jeremiah. Story as follows:

Act I. A chapel by the gate of a temple (cathedral), the monastic cell of Fr. Piotr Skarga.[7] In the chapel an altar shrouded in purple (it's Lent). Fr. Piotr is praying. On the altar are angels holding up the shroud... At a certain moment, beyond the window of the chapel, some figures are seen passing (these are the "earthly gods") and going to a sermon at the Sejm {Polish Parliament}. Fr. Piotr has already noticed that these people have hardened their hearts. He begins to make associations with the story of Jeremiah, how the prophet struggled with the elders of Israel. Then the angels part the shroud. Beyond the shroud there is this scene: the statues on the altar come to life and there is the "Sermon of Jeremiah" to the elders of Judea. Fr. Piotr sees all of this, finds his purpose. The vision disappears. Fr. Piotr's monologue. During the entire act, a service is in progress in the adjacent church. Now it ends. Fr. Piotr goes out to preach.

Act II. The sermon. After the sermon a meeting with Zolkiewski (a ruler of souls, and a knight at arms). Together they must protect Jerusalem from defeat. They form an alliance. It is a long dialogue, which ends with the agreement that, after their deaths, they will return here for a final council. When they finish, a very young Br. Andrzej (St. Andrew Bobola) enters. Skarga, inspired, tells him to read from the book of prophecies. Andrzej reads about the suffering that will befall his own body in the future, and about the sufferings of the nation. At the end he gives them palms (it is a Sunday in April, a procession comes from the church, including three martyrs).

Act III. The year of the defeat at Cecora, 1620.[8] During the Tenebrae {early morning} service, a knight-messenger enters the church and brings news of the death of the Lord of Zolkiew. The king leaves the church. Later, during the service, Fr. Piotr appears, and then the triumphant Hetman Zolkiewski in magnificent silver armor. The final council. The Hetman is going before God for judgment. He speaks of the monastic order, of the communion of souls, of the nation. It ends with a speech to the Avengers. Here I develop the idea of Zolkiewski — may an avenger spring from my bones. Then two angels appear above, they blow on trumpets, summoning Zolkiewski to judgment. The end: Zolkiewski is seen ascending in a shaft of light, and Fr. Piotr takes up his last thought and utters into the empty church (full auditorium). So much for that. I just wanted to fill you in a little on what I'm doing here.

... As for Juliusz, yes, we are at his place every week, we feel almost at home there. He works here (you've got to hand it to him, he is a tireless worker). He's working on some of the dramas of his repertory. The entirety of the repertory looks just about like this: *Orestes, Oedipus, Antigone, Lilla Weneda, Midsummer Night's Dream, Balladyna, Forefather's Eve, The Undivine Comedy, The Wedding, Hamlet, Liberation*. He is concerned about the translations. I think we agree that the translations by Morawski and Butrymowicz are not only difficult to stage, but are hard for actors to play. Juliusz says, "I would like this to be fully understood even by the kitchen

---

[7] Skarga Piotr (1536-1612) a Jesuit, a royal homilist and confessor to King Sigismund III, an organizer and activist of counter-reformation, a prominent writer, the author of Kazania sejmowe {Parliamentary Sermons}, Kazania na niedziele i swieta {Sermons for Sundays and Every day}, Zywoty swietych {Lives of the Saints}.

[8] Polish-Turkish war

help" (he emphasizes the last words), so he is doing translations himself in a more dramatically appropriate vein. He has already translated *Antigone* and is now working on *Hamlet* (the soliloquies translated by Wyspianski). He charged us with working on others. I've already performed such an "Osterwian" revision of *Oedipus*. I translated it into "human" language. Juliusz was very satisfied but says that it is still not theatrical. He says that you have to learn the theater. Well, of course! (Don't take the non-theatrical result of my translation too seriously; Juliusz says the same thing about Kasprowicz's translations). In general, he got to like us quite a lot. We visit him every week (and I rarely miss "weeklies" of this type). In evaluating the entirety of his theatrical concepts, I see that he has given great thought and effort to the details (sometimes too great... sometimes his ideas are somewhat strange.) But with no flattery intended, you seem to suit me better. The theater is, after all, an atavistic burden for Osterwa... as are, unfortunately, his Warsaw origins. We are, if I may say so, more primitive. But sometimes he has some capital ideas. And besides, we are like brothers, and he is more like a little father (very friendly, but fatherly nevertheless). And as I have told you, he grew to like us. He says he would like to be close to us, very close. And oh, what is most important, it seems to me that you, my dear Lover of Art and Director, it seems to me, I suspect, that you aim higher and see further, and if not just yet, then I feel that your gaze will someday reach farther. Enough about Juliusz. This is the first time I've written so much. Well, now I have been able to sound him out, after so many "sessions." He really speaks fantastically! He must be some actor! And, of course, a director! What can I say. But... (but there is always a "but")...

... I know, Mieciu, that you were touched by misfortune. I am trying to sympathize with you. May God have mercy on them! You {plural} are always in our prayers. Of Wicek, of course, there is no word. Oh God! That we could meet again someday. All of us — as before — God willing! God willing! I would really like to see you, but, as far as I know, that is nearly impossible. Maybe someday.

One more matter. I know that you are hurting financially. So we — and please, take me very seriously and understand me — anyway, my father says that you can take advantage of our KKO Wadowice passbook, which Zosia took from us in November. You have it there; you could make use of it. The whole problem is with the unfortunate rule that the person making a withdrawal must show my father's identity document. But my father needs it here at all times, and it would be a great risk to be without it, but maybe you could manage in some other way. Think about it, you are closer there. The next time, hopefully as soon as possible, you could let us know. Here, Father is collecting 60 percent of his pension, so we can live, but you have nothing there...

A letter sent on another occasion:

Dear Mieciu,

I'm writing to you having heard of the terrible misfortune which befell your house [the arrest of Mieczyslaw Kotlarczyk's two brothers], that home so dear to me, a home where I was treated virtually as a brother. I realize that no words can mean anything at this moment, so I will refrain from uttering any. I will just say that now I feel even more as your {plural} brother. Will the pain close in upon itself, create a separate world? Or will it harden into the foundation of a new edifice? Will a new life grow from it? I believe that it will. I believe that no wave hits the shore without leaving upon it the signs of its flow. I believe that the surf is a creative force. My father sends his deepest expressions of sympathy.

Lolek

August 1940

We meet in the home of the Kydrynskis (10 Felicjanek Street). Talks of the theater. For Juliusz Osterwa, who is in contact with Karol Wojtyla, Juliusz Kydrynski and Tadeusz Kwiatkowski, we prepare a reading of Zeromski's play *My Little Quail Ran Off*[9]. Also involved is someone from the family of Pozniak-Szkocki.

Meeting with Osterwa in the home of the Pozniaks (Ksiecia Jozefa Street). We read fragments of Acts I and III. Karol Wojtyla reads the parts of all the professors — he impresses us with his acting inventiveness.

The three of us decide to prepare the staging of the entire second act of *Little Quail*: Karol Wojtyla plays Smugon, Juliusz Kydrynski — Przelecki, Danuta Michalowska — Dorota Smugon. Rehearsals are held every day (or almost every day?) in the evenings in the home of the Kydrynskis. (Danuta Michalowska)

September 1940

The presentation of the second act of *Little Quail* for invited guests (Osterwa did not come after all; perhaps he is not in Krakow). We take up work on Norwid's One Thousand and Second Night. Rehearsals in my home (10/1 Dunin Wasowicza Street, presently 36 Smolensk Street). Cast: Roger — Juliusz Kydrynski; a Lady — Danuta Michalowska; Doctor — Karol Wojtyla; Lucio — Tadeusz Kwiatkowski. Karol Wojtyla directs. The play is never shown.

At the same time, following Juliusz Osterwa's instructions, we are all working individually on Shakespeare's *Hamlet*. Osterwa told us to rewrite in our own words the parts that we were assigned. I don't know which part he assigned to Karol Wojtyla (Osterwa himself was working on Hamlet). Juliusz Kydrynski is writing a one-act play (in the style and under the influence of Szaniawski) entitled *The Pipe of Copernicus*. It is a poetic, allegorical transposition of a friendly agreement among three young people (having a parallel in the characters of the second act of *Little Quail*), entwined into a totally fictitious and satirical plot. (Danuta Michalowska)

"In September of 1940 I began working at the quarry in Zakrzowek." (Abp. Karol Wojtyla, *The Nest from Which I Came*)

To avoid being deported to forced labor, Karol registers as an employee of Kuczmierczyk, who ran a restaurant. Later, through the efforts of Mrs. Lewaj (a teacher of French, daughter of Wyspianski's teacher and a tenant in the house of Mr. & Mrs. Szkocki who taught Karol French), he is employed by Henryk Kulakowski, who was President of the "Solvay" Company in Poland (main office in Warsaw) before the war. He works initially in the factory's rock quarry several

---

[9] The title echoes words from a Polish folk song.

kilometers away from the plant. Juliusz Kydrynski and Wojciech Zukrowski work with him, among others. Limestone, which was necessary for the production of soda, was quarried by exploding charges of ammonium nitrate in holes drilled in the rock. The large blocks thus obtained had to be broken up and shoveled into the trams of a narrow-gauge railway. This was the work performed by Karol and his friends. He was temporarily assigned as a brakeman on the narrow-gauge trams. He worked in the quarry from September 1940 through the very severe winter (up to 30 degrees below zero Celsius {minus 22 Fahrenheit}). The work was very hard. From 8 a.m. until 4 p.m. He left the house about 7 a.m., on foot.

In the spring, the manager of the quarry, a Pole by the name Krauze, a very refined gentleman, assigns Karol as a helper to the blaster, the old man Labus. It was lighter work and represented a kind of promotion. The work consisted in carrying the ammonite charges to their appointed places, where Labus would set them. Later, the blaster and his helper sat in the barrack. (A description of the work in the quarry — according to an account by Juliusz Kydrynski.)

The following are accounts of Wojtyla's fellow workers at Solvay that were placed into an album entitled *The Nest from Which I Came* (typescript with photographs, collected and prepared by Karolina Biedrzycka). Three copies of the book were presented to the pastor of the parish, Rev. Wladyslaw Ryba on June 5, 1966 as a gift for the 50th anniversary of his ordination to the priesthood. One copy was addressed to him, the other two, to Archbishop Karol Wojtyla. Father Ryba passed the gift to the addressee on June 21st of the same year. One of the reasons for preparing this book was a desire to make reparations to the Archbishop for the open letter written by the workers of the Soda Works in Krakow (cf. *Kalendarium,* December 24, 1965). (This account comes from the author of the aforementioned book, Mrs. Karolina Biedrzycka). The book also contains a short text by Archbishop Wojtyla.

> I was working then on the tramway, as an engineer's assistant. The Archbishop worked on the tramway for perhaps three months. I saw how Karol Wojtyla... together with his friends coupled the cars. They worked on the track on which the trams traveled between the plant and the quarry...
>
> ... I met him once in the plant. It was 12 noon. The Angelus was sounding. He heard the bell, put down the buckets, crossed himself and prayed. Then he got up and went on. He was not ashamed of his actions before anyone. (Jozef Pachacz, assistant engineer)
>
> ... Several students had been hired into the plant. Mr. Wojciechowski (an engineer) and Krauze put them to work on the tracks. When they were assigned to me, manager Krauze told me to look after these people, that they could be useful, that I should not overtire them with hard work. I put them to work digging holes, filling in under the tracks, leveling the track

bed, filling under the crossties, stretching the track to a new layout. Karol Wojtyla, the present Archbishop, worked well, fulfilled his duties gladly; when he had a free moment at noon, he would read books. We talked about how we wanted the war to end, how we wanted to survive when it seemed we were to be crushed. He worked on the track for maybe 6 months, and then he went to the quarry... (Jan Zyla, track worker)

... I worked in the quarry at Zakrzowek. The present Archbishop worked with us from 1940 as a young laborer. Working conditions were very hard. Breaking up the rocks with a pickaxe and loading them into trams was not the easiest work... He was quiet, calm, industrious and friendly. He would gladly help everyone, even though he himself did not have an easy time of it. (Klemens Witkowski)

All of the workers in the quarry made an agreement that they would not help anyone in righting an overturned tramcar, because one person working at righting it lengthened the time the others had to rest and, as a result, the Germans had less work done "fur Sieg." All the workers obeyed this agreement — except the student Wojtyla, who could not stand the sight of a colleague's long struggle to right the cart, and he would help. The workers said to each other: "This Wojtyla will surely be a priest, if he has such compassion for his fellows." (This account was sent for *Kalendarium* by Mr. Marian Piwowarczyk, M.A., then a worker at Solvay)

I was the engineer of the steam locomotive. They were using this place to hide out. I saw Karol Wojtyla walking about the quarry with a shovel. I was overworked and in constant motion... I talked little with the Archbishop. (Blazej Trela)

He was so young when he came to work, I felt so sorry for him; he was not suited for anything. I thought to myself, the best thing for him would be to become a priest. He had such delicate small hands. I didn't let him work, but he worked. I was leaving the world, and he was just entering it. He helped me coil the wire; he followed me carrying the detonators. One time, as usual, I was setting the charges, and he was standing beside me. I said to him: it would be better for you to become a priest, and he just smiled. Later he mentioned to me, that he became that priest. (Franciszek Labus, a blaster at the quarry in Zakrzowek. This account was recorded when Labus was 90 years of age and very ill.)

Letter to the Kotlarczyks:

October 7, 1940 —

Dear friends, Halinka brought me your letter, which is so much the dearer because I have waited for it so long I am touched by it, as I am by the very fact of seeing a dear face from Wadowice. Deeply touched. I have close ties with the town of my childhood and early youth, a town that gave me much, very much. I think that it gave me more than Krakow could. The breath of the town and the breath of the land, a certain clarity of thought, and an undeniable foundation of culture.

First, I would like to tie in to what you said in your letter...

... Regarding that flame which has been kindled within me, I think that it depends most definitely on a higher power. It is not, I feel, a mere handicraft, but some sort of pull. I don't want to say: it's an act of Grace. But then everything is an act of Grace, or can be an act of Grace, you just have to know how and above all desire to cooperate with it, as we are taught by the parable of the talents. Now I believe that Grace must be accepted with humility, so in that respect the battle for Poetry will be a battle for humility. Besides, there is not as much of it as you think. I carry these things within me for a long time, and until they are internally complete, they don't allow themselves (literally) to be written. Of course it captivates me. Life rushes on and imposes certain haste. But *ars longa {art has long life}*, as one might say here in a slightly different meaning than usual. *Ars longa.* Maybe I will have a chance to read some of it to Halina. But I doubt it, because she is in a great hurry

I'll admit that I feel a greater attachment to the one I call, at least for the time being, *Jeremiah*. Although, Tadeusz, "Studio 39" does not intend this for the stage. But it seems to me that this is indeed something new. I am supported in this by my teacher [Mrs. Lewaj], the first person from whom I have experienced some maternal feelings. She believes in me. But I don't want to write anymore about that. I'm afraid I might get carried away ...

[Near the end of the letter] ... Currently I am a laborer. I do physical work in a quarry. Don't be alarmed! So far, I'm not splitting rocks. I'm just laying the tracks of the tramway, which runs between the quarry and the Solvay plant in Borek Falecki. The quarry is in Zakrzowek, quite near my house. I make good money (relatively speaking, of course), but the most valuable are the laborers' allowances. Besides, most of my friends work like I do. It's great for us. Hala[10] will give you details. Time flies when you're working. You become a fuller person.

Osterwianism has been temporarily suspended. The Director has left town. And besides, he does not impress me above everything else. Basically, I am more attracted to people with a mysterious interior, a great interior. This does not mean that the director does not possess that. But, believe me, I feel some resentment to these predestined celebrities. Maybe because we cannot, after all, speak on the same level. In any event, I don't feel any strong bonds, no, not at all...

October, November, December 1940

We are beginning to meet every Saturday in the home of Dr. Tadeusz Kudlinski (15 Sloneczna Street, presently 15 Boleslawa Prusa Street). The group has grown by the addition of several participants of the former "Studio 39"; besides the above-named, those regularly present are Krystyna Debowska, Boguslawa Czuprynowna, Emil Danko, and some non-actors: Wojciech Zukrowski, Tadeusz Ostaszewski (a young sculptor). Discussions on Wyspianski's *Wedding* (interpretation of the "visions" in act II), acting exercises (according to S. Wolkonski), rehearsals.

Karol Wojtyla and his father spend Christmas Eve at the Kydrynskis (according to information provided by J. Kydrynski). (Danuta Michalowska)

February 18, 1941 - The death of Karol Wojtyla, the father:

Karol Wojtyla, Sr. was a man of great delicacy, a deeply religious man.

---

10 Another form of the name Halina.

He felt great bonds of friendship with his son. During the war he occupied himself with running the household. On some occasions, he repaired his son's shoes. Karol, Jr. went to work, did the shopping, brought the food rations; most often this was dried peas. They lived very simply. On Sundays they went together to Mass at the Franciscan church. At this time Karol became a close friend of our family, of our mother, Aleksandra Kydrynska; he called her "mother." To her he offered the poem-drama *Job*, which he wrote in the apartment at Debniki. He and his father were with us at the Christmas Eve dinner in 1940.

Karol's father was ill that winter and Karol would come to us with tin dishes to get meals. On February 18, he left the dishes and went to the pharmacy on Batorego Street to get medicine. Then, together with Maria [sister of Juliusz Kydrynski, married name Michalowska] he went to Debniki. Maria was going to heat up the meal they brought. They found the father dead. Sobbing, Karol embraced Maria. Through his tears he said, "I was not at my mother's death, I was not at my brother's death, I was not at my father's death." Immediately he brought a priest. That day he moved in with the Kydrynskis, where he lived until September 1941.

He went to Mass every day, he prayed a lot in his room, and he lay prostrate.

One of the neighborhood women remembers how he and Juliusz shoveled coal into the cellar. (According to an account by Maria Michalowska and Juliusz Kydrynski)

February 22, 1941 — His father's funeral. Requiem Mass at 11:30 a.m. in the chapel of the Rakowice cemetery. Interred in the family tomb at the military cemetery. It was very cold that day. The headstone bears the inscription: "Karol Wojtyla, retired military, lived 62 years. After a short illness, having received the Holy Sacraments, fell asleep in the Lord..."

Around this time young Karol joined an underground organization called *Unia* and was sworn in by a member of the Main Committee of *Unia*, a "resident" of Krakow and Warsaw, Stanislaw Bukowski.

The underground movement *Unia* came into being in the first months of the Nazi occupation. Its founder and leader was Jerzy Braun, a philosopher and a poet. *Unia*, referring to the Polish traditions of freedom, personalism and federalism (the idea of federal union), adopted Christian principles as the basis for organizing social life. It was not a political organization striving for power in future Poland but a philosophical, ideological and educational movement with a Christian social program. Its aim was to reconstruct the way in which social life was organized in Poland and in the entire area described by the name of Christian civilization (cf. Jerzy Braun in *Czlowiek ze spizu* {Man of Bronze}, London 1981). *Unia* was in principle a federation of patriotic organizations (the first organizations to join *Unia* were *Warszawianka, Nowa Polska* {New Poland}, *Grunwald*, and later followed by others.

Stanislaw Bukowski, who swore the young Wojtyla in, was a prominent figure of *Unia*, an activist of Catholic Action before the war and an expert on scientific organization of work. During the Nazi occupation he fulfilled the duties of the manager of a big cigarette factory in Krakow. During his involvement with *Unia* he introduced there a division into a series of parallel bodies grouped together in the General Secretariat, such as *Unia Pracy* {Work Union}, *Unia Kultury* {Cultural Union}, *Unia Spoleczna* {Social Union}, *Unia Mlodziezy* {The Youth's Union}, *Unia Kobiet* {Women's Union}... Here also existed a combat organization of *Unia*, its members were, among others, Karol Wojtyla's friends — Wojciech Zukrowski and Tadeusz Kwiatkowski. In 1942 *Unia* was at its peak. In order not to break up the organized armed resistance in the country *Unia* transferred 20 thousand people under the command of Armia Krajowa {Home Army}. There was also a strongly developed civilian organization that numbered several thousand members in Warsaw, 1500 in Krakow, several hundred in Lvov, with strong groups in the Kielce, Krosno, Tarnow and Rzeszow regions. Its membership consisted of many professors, scientists, distinguished experts in various areas of knowledge. In 1942 *Unia* and another organization — Stronnictwo Pracy — {Labor Party} became united. Karol Wojtyla was active within "Unia Kultury" {Cultural Union} whose chairman was Artur Gorski, and vice-chairman Tadeusz Kudlinski, a writer and organizer of cultural life in Krakow. His contribution to the program of "Unia Kultury" was a concept of a political system called Norwid and expressed in his "Misterium sztuki pracy" {Mystery of the art of work}. Kudlinski was also a founder of the Rhapsodic Theater. One of the outposts of *Unia* was also the clandestine Rhapsodic Theater created by Tadeusz Kudlinski and Mieczyslaw Kotlarczyk and famous after the war for its magnificent productions of the masterpieces of literature. Among the students of this underground theater was young Karol Wojtyla who took the union oath before Stanislaw Bukowski and was released from this oath by him before he entered the Religious Seminary (Jerzy Braun, ibid. p. 153).

January (or maybe February?) 1941 — "A presentation of scenes from *Wesele {The Wedding}* in the Kydrynskis' apartment. I don't remember what part Karol Wojtyla played." (Danuta Michalowska)

February - June 1941

Regular meetings continue at the home of Dr. Kudlinski. We return to *The Pipe of Copernicus*, beginning rehearsals with 2 casts; one of them was according to the original idea of the author: Maria — Danuta Michalowska; the Poet — Juliusz Kydrynski; the Misanthrope — Karol Wojtyla.

Dr. Kudlinski establishes contact with Mr. Orzelski, the director of the city waterworks; there is a small theater in that area (at 4 Lowiecka Street) and the play is to be put on there. Soon, however, some employees of the waterworks are arrested, including Orzelski and the deputy director Tadeusz Kielanowski (he died in Auschwitz). We suspend the rehearsals of *The Pipe of Copernicus*.

At the Kudlinskis we work on *Wyzwolenie* {Liberation} by Wyspianski. Karol Wojtyla attempts the role of Konrad. The play was never shown.

We also try *Miguel Manara* by Oskar Milosz, (at the recommendation of Osterwa, who still shows interest in us by "remote control"), in several cast complements. Arrests of members of our group (Emil Danko, perished) interrupt this work.

After the death of his father (February) Karol maintains even closer contact with the Kydrynski family; he sleeps there, eats his meals. He works in the quarry with J. Kydrynski and W. Zukrowski.

In June, my mother and I receive an order evicting us from our apartment. My mother gets a job and a dwelling in Skawina; Karol offers me his apartment at 10 Tyniecka Street. We visit this apartment with T. Kwiatkowski and W. Zukrowski; they undertake to repaint it. For now, I'm leaving for vacation (July); my mother remains in touch with Karol, but rents me a room at some friends, where I move in after my return to Krakow. (Danuta Michalowska)

Letter to M. Kotlarczyk – undated:

... I'm sending you some fragments of the *Slavic Volume*. I read them here to Zosia and others as well, and to you I'm sending a written copy of this output of my spring longing, this cause dear to my heart and soul. I read these sonnets to Wicek back in June, but somehow I haven't had a chance to do it for you. We must express this idea which dwells within us more precisely, we have to reveal this current which drives the stream of our youth, but which thus far could not be revealed. This current has a common source within us: a deep love — a Slavic and Sarmatian[11] freedom, and not just a longing for beauty, but a demand for it. That of which we often spoke on Dluga — that art does not exist merely to be a realistic truth, merely a diversion, but, above all, it is a superstructure, a gaze forward and upward. It is the companion of religion and a guide on the road to God; it has the dimension of a romantic rainbow: from the earth and from the human heart towards the Infinite; it has the dimension of a romantic rainbow... Now in Poland, considering postwar poetry, it must be admitted, that it was mostly a diversion, mere form, and rarely was it imbued with the soul of the nation. And if it had any soul, it was that of the red banner and the easy but how insubstantial humanism of the {Communist} Internationale. It had nothing in common with Polishness except for its language...

May 23, 1941 — The SS arrests all the Salesian priests (the parish of St. Stanislaw Kostka, Debniki). Karol Wojtyla has close ties to this parish; he was often in this church, he belonged to the Living Rosary.

July 1941 — Mieczyslaw Kotlarczyk comes to Krakow.

---

[11] A name referring to the 17th and 18th century Polish gentry traditions and customs.

Karol organizes a meeting with Dr. Kudlinski, and also some sort of meeting of the entire "Kudlinski group" (I was then away from Krakow). (Danuta Michalowska)

September 1941

In early September Karol Wojtyla came to my office (I was working as a typist in the headquarters of "Spolem" then at 4 Mikolajska Street); he tells me of Kotlarczyk's arrival and recommends the reading of Slowacki's *King Spirit*, which we are to begin preparing. (Danuta Michalowska)

Also in September the Kotlarczyks move into the apartment at 10 Tyniecka Street, having been taken under Karol's wing.

August 22, 1941

In the afternoon we meet in the apartment of Mr. & Mrs. Debowski (7 Komorowskiego Street). Present were (I'm quoting from memory): Karol Wojtyla, Dr. Kotlarczyk and his wife, Halina Krolikiewicz (married name Kwiatkowska), Malgorzata Stanislawska, Anna Nawrocka, Juliusz Kydrynski, Tadeusz Kwiatkowski, Tadeusz Ostaszewski, Wojciech Zukrowski, and the hosts, Mrs. Debowska and her daughters Krystyna and Irena. Dr. Kotlarczyk presented his artistic program; the whole group will come under his management. This date is considered (and rightly so) to mark the origin of the Rhapsodic Theater. From then on, we meet regularly every Wednesday and Saturday at 6 p.m. (on those days, working hours were shorter in the German enterprises).

After several meetings, Kotlarczyk makes a selection of the group (under the pretext of making necessary cuts in the selected texts). The ones who remained were Karol Wojtyla, Krystyna Debowska, Halina Krolikiewicz and Danuta Michalowska. (That this was a proper selection is attested by the fact that these persons, and only these, with the exception of Karol Wojtyla, later made theater their profession). Tadeusz Ostaszewski, sculptor, fiancé of Krystyna Debowska, continued to attend most of the succeeding meetings. From 1945 to 1954 he was the regular art director of the Rhapsodic Theater. He designed the first production of *King Spirit*. (Danuta Michalowska)

We began to work immediately. The core of the ensemble consisted of: Karol Wojtyla (Polish major), Krystyna Debowska (student of the Advanced School of Business), Halina Krolikiewicz (Polish major), Danuta Michalowska (Polish major), and Tadeusz Ostaszewski (sculptor).

Never-to-be-forgotten Wednesdays and Saturdays, regardless of the terror and arrests. Regardless of the posters all over the city announcing more and more executions by firing squad, we held rehearsals of Slowacki, Kasprowicz, Wyspianski, Norwid and Mickiewicz. And often these rehearsals were in the cold, dark kitchen of our "catacomb" in Debniki, sometimes by candlelight when the power was turned off. Romantic rehearsals, deepening our Polish consciousness, our resolution to survive and reach the shores of freedom, faithful to our ideal of the theater.

This was the atmosphere in which we brought forth our premieres in locales on Komorowskiego, Kleparz, Potockiego, Szlak, Rekawka, Debniki, Retoryka, Siemiradzkiego and Sobieskiego.[12] Premieres in the dwellings of the Debowskis, Goreckis, Mrs. Ligocka and Mrs. Michalowska, the

---

12 Names of streets and districts.

Kudlinskis, Mrs. Schreder, the Szkockis, Stolfs and Bateks, and Miss Markiewicz. These premieres were always risky, even though they were secret and very clandestine.

These were the conditions in which we created a theater that, on an improvised stage, presented the utterance of a tormented Polish soul, an utterance that was brutally banished by a ruthless enemy "extra muros"[13] of any Polish theater. A whole scale of utterances: from the simplest folk song, through the rhapsodic songs of knightly troubadours, to the epics of national drama. The Rhapsodic Theater: as if something from the unrealized Theater of the Slavonic Spirit. As if a fragment of the dramatic program of Mickiewicz from his Parisian lectures.

We began with the rhapsodic verses of *King Spirit*. Hence the name of our theater...

From the outset, the conditions and circumstances of the occupation precluded any thought of a full theatrical staging, any thought of giving Slowacki's drama a theatrical setting. We resigned ourselves to a lack of scenery representing the Vistula and Popiel's[14] castle, of the scene depicting the Krakow Market Square, Wawel Castle and Skalka; there were no costumes from the Piast's era. Zorian did not have a waist-length beard, and Boleslaw the Bold did not have a catfish mustache and bushy eyebrows. There was no curtain, no spotlights, and no makeup. We were satisfied with the simplest scenic props: a dark background, a curtain with the death mask of the poet, on the piano a lighted candelabrum and a copy of the text of the play, and a rug on the floor. The ensemble, dressed in dark suits and dresses, recited the text with almost no gestures.

We also introduced music...

Among the participants of our clandestine presentations, besides those whose homes we used at the time, often were J. Osterwa, W. Woznik, Z. Mrozewski, Z. Kossak-Szczucka, J. Braun, T. Kwiatkowski, W. Zukrowski, W. Rowicki, K. Regamey, S. Pigon, K. Wyka, M. Ostrowska, S. W. Balicki, J. Turowicz and many others.

It became customary to hold discussions about artistic problems after our presentations...

The activities of the Rhapsodic Theater in the years 1941-45 included:

10 premieres, of which 7 were presented and 3 were prepared but not presented: excerpts from such novels as *Lalka* {The Doll by Prus}, *Quo Vadis* {Sienkiewicz}, *Ashes* {Zeromski}, *The Peasants* {Reymont}, *Prochno* {Rotting Wood} and *Zywe kamienie* {Living Stones} (1941- 42), Dante's *Divine Comedy* (1944) as well as *Milosierdzie* {Mercy} and *Straszne Dzieci* {Terrible Children} by Rostworowski (1944-45). The last premiere did not take place because of combat activity.

22 performances of plays: *King Spirit* — 4; *Beniowski* — 1; *Hymns* — 1; *Wyspianski* — 4; *Pan Tadeusz* — 3; *Samuel Zborowski* — 6.

Over 100 rehearsals or evening workshops in clandestine conditions...

On April 22, 1945, the opening of the Rhapsodic Theater was held in Krakow, in the hall of the "Freedom" {Wolnosc} Cinema on 18-ego Stycznia Street. The inaugural premiere consisted of fragments of *Grazyna and Konrad Wallenrod* by Mickiewicz, and *Zawisza Czarny* by Slowacki.

On that day the Rhapsodic Theater came out from underground to begin the next, overt phase of its activity, lasting (with a hiatus in the years

---

[13] outside the walls
[14] A mythical Polish king

1953-57) until today. (Mieczyslaw Kotlarczyk, *25 Years of the Rhapsodic Theater*, Krakow 1966. The Theater existed until 1967).

"In the summer of 1941 I was transferred to the factory for the so-called water purification near the boiler room." (Archbishop Karol Wojtyla, *The Nest from Which I Came*)

The following account was given by Prof. Edward Gorlich, then a graduate of chemistry and a student of geology at JU, a worker in the laboratory of Solvay (his accounts cover the period when Wojtyla transferred from the quarry to the plant, but do not specify dates more closely. Some details undoubtedly cover the autumn of 1942):

[Henryk] Kulakowski was the President of a European company "Solvay" in Poland. During the occupation, the director of the factory was the German Fohl; there was also a Polish director Mr. Walach. Kulakowski, who did not take active part in the management of the factory, hired many young people, thereby saving them from deportation.

Karol Wojtyla worked in the "purification," as that department was called. The water purification section was located next to the boiler room, on an upper floor; it was accessed by steel stairs covered with soda. You had to carry lime milk from the kilns (outside, about 100 meters) for softening the water. It was gathered in wooden buckets that were carried on yokes through the courtyard. Next you had to carry the sacks with phosphate and soda up the stairs to the tank. You mixed everything in the tank with a wooden paddle, and then you had to set it so the softening solution dripped out at the proper rate. Karol Wojtyla carried the wooden buckets (and this lodged in my memory) very quickly. The worker on duty was obliged to take samples to the lab, whose manager was Prof. Ernest Pischinger, and the lab technician (319) was Gorlich. I remember that the people in the laboratory felt that "when Wojtyla is in the boiler room, everything is surely going well."

Karol Wojtyla was happiest to take the night shift. It was quiet then. It was known that when he finished his assigned duties, he would kneel to read the breviary. In that period (1942-43!) he asked Gorlich to converse with him about the natural sciences. He explained that he had decided to become a priest, and that he needed to have these talks. They had several of these talks, in which Gorlich was the primary speaker, talking about the natural sciences, as he remembered, covering everything from the atom to the cosmos. As far as his choice of calling, Wojtyla explained that it was greatly influenced by a certain "hunchbacked tailor" and that his father was a religious man, that in his home they often read the Bible.

Karol Wojtyla distinguished himself by something that was hard to capture. Gorlich kept until today, as a memento of those times, a request by Wojtyla to withdraw his pay. Because Wojtyla worked the night shift, he could not get it himself. (The pay at that time was 80 — 90 grosze per hour. A laboratory technician earned 1.20 per hour.) Prof. Gorlich remembers until today one of the maxims that Karol Wojtyla liked to proclaim: "One must live life, but not overuse life."

One day Lolek came to work late, shaking from the cold (this was in winter). He did not have the fur-lined jacket that he usually wore. He explained to Dudek, after calling him aside, that at Mateczny he met an old man, slightly intoxicated, close to freezing. He gave him his coat, believing that it was easier for a young man to withstand the cold.

Mr. Dudek remembers a situation when Karol Wojtyla convinced his co-workers to forgo carrying out a verdict on a co-worker who had become a Volksdeutsch.[15] (According to an account by Jozef Dudek, 12 Zdunow Street, who had been a senior laboratory technician)

Accounts from the album *The Nest from Which I Came*:

Karol Wojtyla ... was assigned to work on purifying the water for the boilers. I was working in the factory as an electrician. I asked him, Sir, why did you come here? He answered that his school was closed, and he came to work here to avoid being deported to Germany... He left only the best impressions of himself... He was an emotional man ... he distinguished himself as a spiritual person and one who was sensitive to the misfortunes of others. There was no one else like him. He wore poor clothes. Foreman Czaja and I would often say: It would be a shame if such a good man were to perish among us... (Franciszek Pokuta, electrician)

We called him simply "the student" ... We worked on the same shift. He would pause while walking through the plant carrying a yoke with pails of the caustic liquor for softening the water. We would sit on the base of a machine and talk about various things. He was very religious. On the night shift, about 12 o'clock he would kneel in the middle of the purification room and pray. On many occasions I would come up to him and, in a soft voice, so as not to interrupt his prayer, I would tell him that the liquor was thickening. After a while he would finish his prayer and go back to work. But not all the workers respected his piety. There were those who would pelt him during his prayers with oakum or other jetsam, trying to interrupt him... (Wladyslaw Cieluch)

... I was charged with the care of the purification process, especially the chemical side. That's how I made contact with the Archbishop... As a worker who needed to know how much of each substance to carry in his pails, he would step into the lab to get that information... Often, coming into the lab after the night shift, he would meet Mankowski, a lab worker, and with Mankowski he would discuss religious subjects ... As Mankowski would later admit to me, these discussions would often end with Mankowski's defeat. He was a member of PPS {Polish Socialist Party}, an atheist ... I got the impression that after such discussions with the then laborer and now Archbishop, Mankowski felt renewed. Many times he stressed that he was outmatched in these discussions, and whether he liked it or not, he had to admit the superiority of this worker who became His Excellency Archbishop Karol Wojtyla. (Antoni Englot, laboratory technician)

I would go to the purification plant for water to wash the floors. I saw how he worked, how he carried the buckets. He worked on three shifts, I on one shift... In the purification room I saw him reading books, praying. We would bring milk from the kitchen and drink it together... (Franciszek Sojak)

We wondered who this was. We didn't ask much, because you really couldn't. I saw how he carried water on a yoke. I see him as if it were today, how he knelt on both knees during the May services, how he prayed. I won-

---

[15] Collaborator with the German invaders.

dered who this young man was. He seemed to be a pauper... (Stefania Burda, a worker in the cafeteria)

... I worked in the factory kitchen. Throughout the entire time that I worked there I never spoke with him. I only knew of him because he would come to the window where we gave out the meals for the workers. It was half a liter of soup and 10 decagrams[16] of bread. For a small additional fee, the workers could buy ration cards for meals for an entire month ... Meals were given out from 12 noon to 3 p.m., then from 9 to 10 p.m. I would also see him as he carried lime in buckets on a yoke. He would walk with his head bowed ... engrossed in thought. Many times I thought to myself that he was not a common laborer ... One time one of the young ladies, Irka Dabrowska, who worked in the kitchen as an assistant to the manager, said to me: "Mrs. Stenia, this pious boy (that's what we called him) is an educated person, very bright, he writes poetry, and now he is writing about St. Theresa." She told me that he didn't have a mother, just a father, that he lived in Debniki, that he was poor. One time she said to me: "Give him a larger slice of bread, because all he eats is what he gets here at work." ... When I worked in the afternoon, I would slice the bread myself for the evening, and I would always save him a larger piece from the end of the loaf; he himself would recall this later. Toward the end of the occupation I didn't see him anymore and I thought that he might have transferred to another factory. (Stefania Koscielniak)

October 11, 1972 — On the occasion of the dedication of a new polychromy in the Redemptorist church in Podgorze in Krakow, the Cardinal {Wojtyla}recalls:

I must make a special confession in front of these walls and in front of you. This church is tied with my life in an unusual way. You know well that during the occupation, I was a physical laborer working for four years in the Solvay factory in Borek Falecki. Many times, returning home from Solvay to Krakow I would step into this church, especially after the night shift, in the early morning hours, to be at the Holy Mass, to receive Communion. From here I drew great strength to last through the difficult times of the years of occupation. In those years, while I was a laborer, I also began my preparations for the priesthood in the clandestine Seminary of the Krakow Archdiocese. And that is why I recall your church with gratitude.

November 1, 1941 — The premiere of King Spirit in the same apartment (7 Komorowskiego Street). Among the invited guests are the actors Wladyslaw Woznik and Zdzislaw Mrozewski. Karol Wojtyla has a great artistic success in the role of Boleslaw Smialy {the Bold} (Fifth Rhapsody).

November 1941 — Repeat of *King Spirit* in the home of Wieslaw Gorecki (5 Kleparski Square). Karol Wojtyla changes his interpretation of Boleslaw Smialy in a manner that gives up on drama and tends more to reflection; he treats the text more like a recollection, like a confession. We are not happy with that, we attack him sharply, but he defends his "deepened" interpretation and will not give in.

November — December 1941 — We continue to meet at 7

---

[16] 3.5 ounces.

Komorowskiego Street. Two professional actors, Wladyslaw Woznik and Zdzislaw Mrozewski, join our group. We work on prose texts (relating to Christmas? from Reymont, Sienkiewicz, Prus, Berent). The presence of the actors changes the character of our meetings: there is more politics and storytelling, less concrete work.

There is an evening get-together of a social-artistic nature ("Oplatek"); also present are Tadeusz and Barbara Kudlinski, Wieslaw and Stefania Gorecki. We all begin addressing each other by our first names. Wladyslaw Woznik recites Wincenty Pol's Song of our Land and others. (Danuta Michalowska*)*

January 1942 — Kotlarczyk's next "reform" — he stops work on prose and without notifying the actors (i.e. Woznik and Mrozewski), we begin rehearsing *Beniowski* after the Christmas break.

February 14, 1942 — The premiere of *Beniowski* (at 7 Komorowskiego Street). Karol Wojtyla recites the so-called "appeal to Ludwika Sniadecka" (end of the 4th canto).

Wladyslaw Woznik sharply criticizes the selection of texts and the entire group's method of delivery of the verses.

February — March 1942 — Work on a new premiere — *Hymns* by J. Kasprowicz. March 28, 1942 — The premiere of *Hymns*. Karol Wojtyla leads the hymn *Holy God, Holy and Mighty* (group recitation), and performs the finale, *Hymn of St. Francis of Assisi*. (Danuta Michalowska)

Osterwa notes in his journal:

Krakow, April 17, Friday [1942] — The weather is hesitatingly getting better... Wojtyllo[!] Karol tells of Jul Kydrynski [probably about his arrest].

A pastoral letter. Sunshine...

May 2, 1942 — Osterwa writes, among other things: "Kydryn is set free" and no doubt he discussed this with

Wojtyla. (Noted by Matylda Osterwa)

April — May 1942. Work on *The Hour of Wyspianski* (without my involvement).

May 22, 1942 — Premiere (in my home, 21 Szlak Street). A magnificently staged ending of Act 3 of *Wesele {The Wedding}* for three players: Jasiek — Karol Wojtyla, Straw Man — Krystyna Debowska, Commentator — Halina Krolikiewicz. The performance was repeated three times.

September 1942 — Resumption of work after the summer break. Preparing works by Norwid. Rehearsals are held at 10 Tyniecka Street, in the apartment of Karol and the Kotlarczyks.

October 3, 1942 — The premiere of *Norwid's Portrait of an Artist,* in the home of Mrs. H. Ligocka, 2 Potockiego Street (presently Westerplatte Street). Juliusz Osterwa, present for the first time, lends his full support to the ensemble (despite the "opposition" of Woznik). *Portrait of an Artist* was performed twice. (Danuta Michalowska)

THEOLOGICAL STUDIES

In October of 1942 Karol began his studies by taking secret courses at the Theological Department of the Jagiellonian University [in Krakow], as a seminarian in the clandestine Seminary of the Archdiocese of Krakow. He lived and worked as before.

He obtained a release from his oath taken as a member of *Unia*:

1) **St. Bukowski took an oath and then released John Paul II from it. The Rhapsodic Theater was a creation of *Unia* and was directed by Tadeusz Kudlinski, residing at 15 Prusa Street, apt. # 9, Krakow. I wrote about it in *L'Osservatore Romano* immediately after the election of John Paul II — annotation my own — C.D., i. e. October 18 or 19.**
   1-12-83   Konrad Sieniewicz

2) **My colleague and friend from *Unia*, Stanislaw Bukowski informed me on one occasion during a conversation we had several years before his death, that as a chairman of the Krakow division of *Unia*, he was swearing in Karol Wojtyla, the present pope, as a member of *Unia* or (and I am adding this remark only now) that he witnessed this fact, and that he released him from the oath due to the fact that he (Karol Wojtyla) was entering the Religious Seminary.**
   Warsaw, October 17, 1983   Studentowicz

3) **I, hereby, testify that between the years 1960 and 1962, in Jerzy Braun's apartment in Warsaw, I heard Stanislaw Bukowski say that he was the one to release Karol Wojtyla from the oath, which he had taken upon joining the clandestine organization *Unia*, due to the fact that he was entering the Religious Seminary in Krakow.**
   Halina Adamowicz

The above documents were made available by Mr. Czeslaw Domaradzki.

Studies at the Theological Department of the Jagiellonian University during the German occupation:

The occupiers at first allowed the seminaries to teach, but tried to impose control over them through the Gestapo, to whom we had to present lists of lecturers (courses) and the subjects to be taught. It was emphasized that these lectures could not be conducted by university-level professors. Instruction could be given "on the level of a trade school" only in those subjects of a practical nature which were indispensable in the conducting of pastoral duties, but excluding any subjects of a purely academic nature. These dictates and prohibitions were ignored, and the lectures were regularly given by university personnel like the priests: Bishop Godlewski, Assistant Professor Krol, Associate Professor Marian Michalski, Florkowski, Mazerski, assistant lecturer Kurowski ... After it was forbidden to accept clergy into the seminary, the seminarians were typically placed as "parochial secretaries" in neighborhood parishes, from where they commuted to Krakow. Visits of the Gestapo to seminaries were by no means rare... Often the results of these visits were tragic, as in the Krakow semi-

nary, where five students of theology were arrested. All of them were either executed by firing squad or martyred in Auschwitz... Amid these difficult conditions, the professors of theology conducted studies for 100 students annually (fewer near the end of the war). (Report by the Dean of the Department of Theology, Fr. Tadeusz Glemma), (JU Archives, Sygnatura KHUW5)

Accounts of his colleagues:

It was my good fortune, thanks to the grace of God, to be close to the seminarian Karol Wojtyla in the Metropolitan Theological Seminary in Krakow from our first year of studies.

These were exceptionally difficult times, because the period of our preparation to the priesthood, at least in the early years, 1942 and 1943, coincided with the Second World War and the time of occupation. Our quest for the priesthood began during the Resistance. All of Poland was then deprived of its theological seminaries. There did exist at this time the Theological Seminary in Krakow, under the care of the unforgettable arch-pastor, Bishop, later Cardinal, Prince Adam Sapieha, but it was dying out, because it was forbidden to accept new candidates to the priesthood. Thus, year by year, the ranks of seminarians dwindled. In light of that situation, for the good of the Church in his archdiocese, Prince Bishop Adam Stefan Sapieha made the courageous decision to organize the education of seminarians in secret. Ten seminarians were accepted in the first year. Karol Wojtyla was one of those first ten.

After a week-long retreat we were given assignments appropriate to our vocations and issued books and writings for study. On assigned dates we reported for examinations by professors of Jagiellonian University. During vacations we made retreats in the strictest secrecy. We could not go about in clerical garb. Our colleagues lived with their parents or in various parishes, or held jobs, usually as physical laborers. In that way, our preparation to the priesthood combined our work in our lay careers — accidental, for the most part — with our new calling, resulting from our vocation, which was a great grace from God for all of us.

These were the circumstances in which we prepared ourselves for the priesthood, constantly unsure of surviving, never mind until next year, but until the next day. Some of our colleagues did not live to see that next day. One of our friends, after a search of his parents' home turned up books and notes from the first year of theology, was arrested and later executed by firing squad in Krakow. On the day of his execution, not knowing of his arrest, I came to Krakow to take my first examination in Holy Scripture. I was taking a shortcut to the professor's home through the Planty Park when I saw a broad stream of human blood on the ground. Nearby — a fresh group grave and a list of names of the executed. I read the name of our friend, the seminarian. The examination ended with a prayer for our friend who had given his life for the Church. These were the acts of terror that the Germans used to intimidate the entire Polish society. (Fr. Andrzej Bazinski) The author of this account prepared it partly on the basis of the recollections that Fr. Karol Wojtyla recorded on audiotape. It appears that the account refers to an execution in which no seminarian was killed, although reports were circulated that this was what had indeed happened. According to the documentation meticulously collected by Fr. Ryszard Wilczynski, pastor of the parish of the Holy Cross in Krakow, the only seminarian who was killed was Szczesny Zachuta. He was born about 1920 and was the high school classmate of Fr. Witold Kacz; during the occupation he worked in a small glass foundry, and he was a member of an underground resistance movement in which he went by the name of Feliks Mszanski. The assumed surname was that of his grandmother. Zachuta began his secret theological studies in 1942/43. He was constantly involved with helping the Jews, preparing them for baptism. He was arrested on April 13, 1944 and was killed in May of 1944. This account comes from the murdered seminarian's brother, Fr. Andrzej Zachuta (the diocese of Kielce), from Fr. K. Wojtyla, Fr. W. Kacz and Fr. M. Malinski. The latter one and Fr. Wojtyla knew Zachuta well, because he belonged to the group of Jan Tyranowski. He would go with Karol Wojtyla to serve at Mass for Prince Archbishop.

I was separated from Fr. Wojtyla only by the Market Square of Debniki, and we were joined by a common parish. In the parish of Debniki we both had opportunity to belong to the Bible Studies Circle led by Fr. Mazerski, and to the Living Rosary whose main mover was Jan Tyranowski. I often saw Karol strolling with him along the boulevards on the banks of the Vistula along Tyniecka Street. I know what such strolls meant from personal experience. They were the talks of a most involved lay spiritual leader with a potential apprentice of the spiritual life. But with the difference that Karol's association with him was most certainly not a one-way transfer, although it is hard to determine how much Master Jan benefited from what his "pupil" could impart to him even then. It seems that these were the talks of two charismatics. This period of meetings with Jan certainly must have crystallized his vocation to the priesthood, or at least to a more ideal monastic life (specifically with the Discalced Carmelites). So we met with Fr. Karol at the Salesian Fathers in the course of parish life, and at occasional social functions, on strolls. Our conversations dealt with theological matters. He posed questions; he talked about biblical and theological subjects. I will never forget the discussions we had on the subject of the presence of Jesus Christ in the Eucharist, and on many other subjects, especially with an eye to apologetics. This was a period when we weren't yet seminarians.

Later, despite our proximity, our frequent contacts and meetings, we did not know that we were both students of the Theological Seminary in Krakow (everything was highly clandestine). I was accepted to the Krakow Seminary while belonging to the diocese of Katowice. I didn't "discover" seminarian Wojtyla until 1942. Fr. Piwowarczyk, the former rector for whom I served Mass at the Mariacki Church, asked me if I would like to serve daily Mass for the Prince Archbishop in his private chapel. The next day I reported at 6:30 AM at the gate of the palace. They let me in and led me to the chapel, where to my amazement I found Karol Wojtyla.

"What are you doing here?" we both asked each other. It turned out that Karol was already the regular server and sexton. I assumed the role of assistant server. We served together that way until Sept. 10, 1944. From the day of the famous round up of captives (Sunday, August 8, in the afternoon), the Archbishop kept us all with him. The guys came from all over, not knowing one another.

Returning once more to the time when we served Mass, I must mention one other moment that was important to both of us. After Mass, we would get a breakfast, prepared by the incredibly kind Sisters of the Sacred Heart. So we went to work well nourished. (Fr. Franciszek Konieczny)

November 1, 1942 — On the anniversary of the premiere, a revival of

King Spirit in the home of Mrs. H. Ligocka. Osterwa was present again. Overall, *King Spirit* was performed 4 times. October - November 1942 — Work on *Pan Tadeusz* {by Mickiewicz}. Rehearsals in the home of Karol Wojtyla, 10 Tyniecka Street. (Danuta Michalowska)

November 21-23, 1942 (Krakow) — He takes part in the observances of the 400th anniversary of the birth of St. John of the Cross. At that time he also "invited himself" to a spiritual conference with the then mentor of our seminarians, Fr. Pawel Gut. From the student library, he takes out the works of St. John of the Cross. He came to love in a particular way the poetry of the Mystical Doctor. At that time he came to know the much older Fr. Jozef Prus, Provincial Superior of the Discalced Carmelites. In great secrecy, he confided to him his wish to enter our congregation... This was in 1942, the war had reached its apogee, the novitiate in Czerna was closed. There was also no possibility of getting a young, healthy man released from his place of employment. So, for this reason primarily, the induction of the novice Wojtyla was postponed until after the war.

At about this time they opened the clandestine Theological Seminary in Krakow, and Fr. Jan Piwowarczyk admitted Karol into the secret classes... (Fr. Boguslaw Woznicki, OCD)

November 28, 1942 — The premiere of *Pan Tadeusz* in the home of the Goreckis (5 Kleparski Square). Karol Wojtyla plays the role of Fr. Robak. During the scene known as the "confession of Soplica," the loudspeaker outside the window announces a war communiqué from the Wermacht. Karol does not interrupt the scene, but he is almost inaudible. *Osterwa*, who was present at the performance, later states that he should have waited and continued only after silence had returned. *Pan Tadeusz* was performed 3 times. (Danuta Michalowska)

... November 28 (1942) — *Pan Tadeusz* by Mickiewicz. I remember to this day an experience at one of the secret performances of the Rhapsodic Theater. It was an evening dedicated to *Pan Tadeusz*. One of the performers [Karol Wojtyla] recited slowly, with great concentration, fragments of the confession of Father Robak. Suddenly, in the silence, there sounded a speaker of the German radio installed across the street from the building where the performance was being held. "The headquarters of the Supreme Commander informs..." And we heard words about the victories that German arms were winning in Europe. The actor did not pause, did not change his tone of voice. He spoke quietly, calmly, as if he did not hear the strident tone of the loudspeaker. Mickiewicz did not take up the war of shouting. When the barker finished the glorification of German atrocities, Mickiewicz was announcing the reconciliation of Soplica with the Keymaster. I looked at the faces of the assembled guests. The same thought animated all of us. We all felt we were sons of this nation, a nation that over the course of centuries was often betrayed, but which will not succumb to terror. The moment was indeed singular. (Tadeusz Kwiatkowski, *Krakow's Underground Theater*, "Theatrical Journal," 1963, an issue dedicated to the Polish theater during the war.)

Further accounts of his fellow workers from Solvay (from the album *The Nest from Which I Came*):

He admitted to me that he was studying theology, and said that he will not turn back from this road. (Alojzy Slup)

It was Karol Wojtyla's duty, at the beginning of the shift, to bring about four buckets of lime, depending on the analyzed alkalinity of the water. If the water was hard, it was necessary to add lime. The lime was poured into a tank and dissolved in water. This solution was then let into a funnel. Then, Karol Wojtyla had to bring two buckets of soda or caustic. These were dissolved in a separate tank, depending on the instructions of the laboratory. The contents of this tank were to last four hours. The solution was then to drain through the valve into the decanter. The decanter was a round container which collected water and solutions of lime, caustic or soda, where all the hardness would be removed. Every two hours the waste would be released into the sewer. We had to watch the temperature of the water. From the decanter, the water went into the next tank, the so-called "harko." From that tank it went to the filter, and passed through it to the next container, from where the pump pulled it to feed the boilers. I saw many a time that Karol Wojtyla was praying. I didn't know whether he was a priest, or was to be one. We talked little. When he did his job, he would kneel in the corner and pray. He went about in wooden shoes and denims. He was always courteous and kind ... I saw him in the afternoon or on the night shift, as he would talk with Pokuta, a student of the Holy Scriptures. (Leon Hojda, a stoker in the boiler room)

I met the Archbishop at the time when he was a laborer, and transferred from the quarry to the purification plant. I was then working in the boiler room as a stoker. The Archbishop worked the longest in purification. He was poorly dressed, in denims and wooden shoes. He worked all three shifts, and carried buckets of soda or caustic.

One time, during the night shift, he went upstairs to the highest floor, where the solutions of soda and lime were controlled ... He was gone a long time. Maybe he fell asleep, I thought. I went upstairs and what do I see: he is kneeling and praying ... After several days, he comes to me and says: "Mr. Wilk, I would like to go to a religious service; maybe you could excuse me." ... The next day, he sat next to me and confided that he is studying to be a priest, that he is having difficulties and finds it hard to make ends meet. He asked that it would remain a secret, he did not want everyone to know.

He said that he was afraid to go out into the city, but that he has some clothes to sell. We had this friendly and confidential relationship for about two years. He was not ashamed, he prayed openly, he did not hide. He went to church as he was, in denims and wooden shoes.

I remember that Kulakowski took the students who were hiding out at Solvay under his care. He was the president of the stock company. (Jan Wilk)

1943

January — March 1943 — Work on preparing Slowacki's *Samuel Zborowski*. Rehearsals were initially held on Tyniecka Street, later, in the home of Wladyslawa Markiewicz, 6 Sobieskiego Street. She was a pianist and composer, and composed the music used in the production.

First half of March 1943 — The premiere of *Samuel Zborowski*. Cast: Samuel — Karol Wojtyla; Chancellor — Tadeusz Kwiatkowski; Lucifer — Mieczyslaw Kotlarczyk. Chorus — Krystyna Debowska, Halina Krolikiewcz, Danuta Michalowska. *Samuel Zborowski* had the greatest number of performances (6). One of the performances was attended by members of the Delegation of the National Government.

We knew that Karol Wojtyla had decided to become a priest and that he was studying theology, but he still participated regularly in our activities, so as not to disrupt the work of our team. *Samuel Zborowski* was the last production in which he took part, meaning that he was member of the theater until about the middle of 1943 (I am unable to give specific dates of subsequent performances of *Samuel*). Karol Wojtyla's subsequent cooperation with the Rhapsodic Theater was sporadic and of a different nature. In the autumn of 1943 (or was it in the winter of 1944?), together with Tadeusz Kwiatkowski, he served Mass in the Church of the Missionary Fathers on Czarna Wies, during which Krystyna Debowska and Tadeusz Ostaszewski were married. (Danuta Michalowska)

(He also published articles about the Rhapsodic Theater. They appeared in *Tygodnik Powszechny:* "Words about the theater" March 16, 1952 (no. 11) under the pen name Piotr Jasien; "Drama of word and gesture" April 7, 1957 (no. 14) under the pen name Andrzej Jawien; "Rhapsodies of the Millenium" January 19, 1958 (no. 3) — Andrzej Jawien; *"Forefathers' Eve* and the 20 years" October 1, 1961 (no. 40) — A. J.)

1944

Karol is a second year theology student at the clandestine Seminary. He continues to work at Solvay.

February 29 — Returning from Solvay after working a double shift, both day and night shifts (because of the distance of the plant from the city, the workers would trade shifts, so that they could make fewer long trips, and by working two successive shifts they would have more free time), he was struck by a German truck. This was near the end of the line of tramway route # 3. He was struck by a large truck, probably with the fender, as he walked along the curb.

According to the account given by Mrs. Jozefa Florek, an eyewitness to the accident, about 3 PM, on the street between Borek Falecki and Mateczny, she thought she saw something fall from a passing German truck. She got out of the streetcar and when she approached, she saw an unconscious man, dressed in work denims and wooden shoes, lying on the ground. She thought he was dead. She thought he had fallen out of the truck. She stood there helplessly, shielding the prone man from the passing cars. After a while, a passenger car stopped and a German officer, who got out of it, told her to bring some water from a roadside ditch. The water was muddy. The officer, having determined that the injured man was alive, stopped a truck loaded with lumber and ordered the driver to take the injured man to the hospital on Kopernika Street. There, in the book of admissions of the Surgical Clinic, this entry was made: "Wojtyla Karol, b. 1920, residing in Krakow at 40 Tyniecka Street [this was an error in the entry]. *Vulnersa lacer capitis. Commotio cerebri.*" He was discharged from the hospital on March 12, 1944. He convalesced in the home of his friends, the Szkockis. Jozefa Florek kept the letters he wrote to her, in which he tells her that she saved his life.

According to accounts by Mrs. Pozniakowa née Szkocka, he had not fallen out of a truck, but was struck by a passing vehicle. This is confirmed by a later account of a co-worker at Solvay:

> I did the same kind of work at Solvay as the Archbishop, but on a different shift. We would swap shifts with each other; one of us worked several successive shifts, then the other. I would spend my free time working in the house, and he needed the time for his studies. I visited him in the hospital when he was laid up by an accident. He was walking home from work when he was struck by a vehicle near Mateczny. After the hospital stay, he returned to work. His food was poor, all he had were some dry slices of bread. Later he would bring coffee from the kitchen and that's what he lived on. At that time the boiler room was under the supervision of foreman Czaja. I remember to this day that I owe the Archbishop one shift, which he worked for me... (Franciszek Wojcik, *The Nest from Which I Came*)

Further accounts of his co-workers:

> The work was hard and tedious. I saw him carrying by hand the buckets of lime liquor for purifying the water. He had to carry these heavy buckets up the stairs to the tanks... (Stanislaw Czaja)

> I was a stoker in the boiler room ... Karol Wojtyla was a worker in the purification of soda. He was very calm. In the mornings he prayed. He was a very good man. I felt sorry for him when he was struck by a car. I knew that he was studying, I saw how he read books, but I didn't look to see what he was reading. One time, having been to a reception, he brought cookies and gave them all away ... He would study at a table in the corner, where the water samples were analyzed. We were to make sure that nothing failed ... In the boiler room there were stairs leading up to the tanks; there amid the posts and pipes was a good spot for praying. It was the spot in the corner under the tank. Nobody bothered him there. (Tadeusz Sapek)

> I was a stoker in the boiler room. His work was not easy, but he did it conscientiously ... He was always courteous, helpful, I had a great deal of respect for him. I knew that he was studying and that he was satisfied with his chosen field of study. When we found a free moment, he would come down to the boiler room. We would sit on the bench and talk. As a memento of our talks he gave me a booklet entitled *The Gospels and Acts of the Apostles*. (Franciszek Lesniak)

> I often saw the Archbishop in the counting room ... I saw him kneeling and reading something. When I rolled out the carts of soda, he would jump up to help me. At once he would throw down the book and pretend he was doing something. I would try to calm him, saying that there were no bad people here, that he could go on reading in peace. He was always lost in thought but willing to help ... He would carry a liquid called bicarbonate in pails from the caustic section to the soda ash section. He wore wooden shoes over bare feet, short denim pants and a rubberized jacket. I often went out to town with him after work. He said little. He always knelt while reading in that counting room. (Jozef Trela)

Karol Wojtyla wore wooden shoes, if I remember correctly, over bare feet, without socks. He was dressed in an issue "verschalung" — denim work clothes. As he carried a yoke with two buckets filled with lime, his face was covered with sweat; he was gaunt and did not look healthy. (Andrzej Lempicki)

I really respected and valued him. My respect ... grew even more when once during the night shift he came and asked if he could pray in the manager's office, because the noise of the machines in the purification room was distracting him. I opened the room for him with pleasure. After the liberation, all of us who were in hiding went our separate ways ... My greatest joy was meeting him, after some dozen years, in my parish in Mogilany where he visited as a bishop. To my great fortune, our acquaintance has continued until the present time ... (Leon Niedbala)

He would come to us most often in the afternoon or at night; we would then discuss religion and other serious topics. We did not always agree in our views on certain subjects, at such times the discussions would get animated, but Lolek would always emerge victorious ... In the summer of 1944 he disappeared from our sight and we didn't know what happened to him... (Jozef Krasuski, laboratory technician)

I recall this little scene. I once met Karol Wojtyla at the purification plant, sitting on a bench with a book on his lap. He began to explain to me the arguments for the existence of God from the infinity of the universe. He spoke as if he were practicing for an exam. This must have been in connection with his studies at that time. (Andrzej Lempicki)

Summer of 1944 — Vacation at the parish in Raciborowice. The seminarian Karol Wojtyla stayed at the rectory, having been invited by the assistant pastor, Fr. Adam Biela, who came from Wadowice.

August 1944:

I left my job at the beginning of August 1944, having begun the 3rd year of studies at the Metropolitan Seminary (then clandestine, until the liberation in January of 1945), and simultaneously the same year at the Department of Theology at JU.

I attended the first two years of the Seminary and the Department of Theology in secret while working at the factory. Leaving my job precipitated a search and a possibility of an arrest by the occupying authorities, but thank God they were unable to find my trail.

In Krakow I lived in Debniki, at 10 Tyniecka Street, in the house of the late Robert Kaczorowski, my uncle. (Archbishop Karol Wojtyla, *The Nest from Which I Came*)

It wasn't until 1944 that he moved into the palace of Prince Archbishop Adam Stefan Sapieha. It happened like this. The Warsaw Uprising had broken out.[1] The Prince Archbishop, assuming that this would be the end of the war in Poland and that this marked the beginning of freedom for the country, ordered the seminarians to put on cassocks and to move into his residence. Karol Wojtyla was among them. But there were certain complications regarding this particular seminarian: he quit his job in a factory. The

---

[1] August 1, 1944

so-called "Labor Office" began to inquire into the whereabouts of the absent worker. They sent notices to his home threatening him with arrest. The young seminarian found himself in danger. And then one day the Prince Archbishop told me in the Curia: "The matter of Wojtyla has to be arranged in such a way that his name disappears from the list sent to the Arbeitsamt. You will go to Solvay and speak with director Kulakowski." To fulfill this assignment, I went to Solvay on foot. But director Kulakowski told me, "I am ready to jump into flames for the Prince Archbishop, but a German, not I, has been the real director here since the beginning of the war. This matter could prove to be difficult." He did not, however, refuse to help, and that he was effective is confirmed by the fact that the notices ceased. (Fr. Kazimierz Kiglewicz, TP 44/1978)

I can confirm that it was not easy to cover up the fact that Karol Wojtyla quit his job at Solvay. In a conversation between Ernest Pischinger, Wojtyla's supervisor at that time, and the German managing director Fohl, the latter expressed a suspicion that Wojtyla ran away to join the guerillas. (An account by Andrzej Lempicki who was also employed at Solvay at the time. Ernest Pischinger was his father-in-law).

September 4, 1944 — Karol petitions for admission to the tonsure and minor orders:

> To the Most Reverend Rector of the Prince Metropolitan's Theological Seminary in Krakow:
> The undersigned, a seminarian of the Prince Metropolitan's Theological Seminary in Krakow hereby petitions for admission to the tonsure and minor orders. He makes this petition with full cognizance of the duties and responsibilities, which he hereby assumes of his own free will.
> > Karol Wojtyla
> > (Archives of the Krakow Curia)

September 11, 1944 — Karol receives the tonsure from the Prince Archbishop. As required by canon law, his pastor submitted this reference:

> I know the seminarian Karol Wojtyla to be a young man who is exceptionally intelligent and passionate about learning and sacred doctrine. Matters of God are dear to him; he is drawn to the priesthood in all sincerity. Morally he is not only strong, but very well formed. This opinion is given on the basis of both personal observation and references. Fr. Matlak, Jozef, Parish Administrator.
> Chancery of St. Stanislaw Kostka Parish,
> Krakow, Debniki.   Krakow, November 14, 1945
> > (Archives of the Krakow Curia)

December 8, 1944 — The Feast of the Immaculate Conception of Mary.

> The Krakow seminary organized a Marian commemoration, at which seminarian Karol Wojtyla spoke. His appearance on our small seminary stage was an exceptional experience for us. He recited the *Litany to the Virgin Mary* by K. C. Norwid. The auditorium became perfectly quiet, the breathing was stilled. By the artistry of his spoken word he was not only showing us the beauty of Polish literature and poetry but, above all, he was expressing his deep love for Mary Immaculate. The day after the program

we found out from our professors that our colleague Karol Wojtyla had been a student of Juliusz Osterwa, we learned about his love of poetry and his active involvement in the clandestine Rhapsodic Theater in Krakow during the German occupation. (Fr. Andrzej Bazinski)

After the roundup of captives on August 8, 1944 [this was, in fact August 6, the co-called "black" Sunday], (I was then in the second year of theology, Karol Wojtyla in the third), the Prince Archbishop decided that the seminarians would take up residence in secret on Franciszkanska Street. At first we occupied the outbuildings of the palace, but after a short time we vacated those premises to free them for the Pauline Fathers from the Warsaw Uprising. To accommodate the seminarians, the Prince Archbishop gave up two parlors on the second floor. I took up residence there along with Karol Wojtyla and my other colleagues.

The inauguration of our stay in the Seminary took place in the Bishop's chapel. Although Rev. Prof. K. Klosak had been the acting Chancellor, at the first meeting the Prince Archbishop said. "We will not wait any longer for the Germans to permit the opening of the Seminary. From now on I am your Chancellor. We will put our trust in God's Providence. No harm will befall us." In this way he lifted our spirits and shielded Fr. Klosak from reprisals by the occupying authorities. The first retreat (unforgettable!) was conducted by the Rev. Prefect Turowicz, and thus we began the normal sequence of lectures in our curriculum. But various years were joined together. Living conditions were rather spartan. We had no furniture besides beds and a common table. All of our personal possessions were accommodated in small suitcases kept under the beds. But what a spirit of true communion and brotherhood. The realization that the Prince Archbishop himself was just beyond the door of our dwelling became for us a key factor that motivated and ordered our lives. By necessity we were bound to observe silence, to concentrate. We participated in daily Mass celebrated by the Prince Archbishop. Seminarian Karol Wojtyla distinguished himself in this whole group of seminarians. He was not a person who would impose himself upon others. For us, he was always Somebody. It is difficult for me to define what was so exceptional about him. I will try, as far as I can, to explain it:

His attitude at prayer: he could kneel for long hours. He was capable of excluding himself from other activities so that he could pray. And I think that what he was doing on his knees was both a prayer and a learning experience. For example, I once entered the Church of St. Joseph, possibly on Poselska Street (where there was perpetual adoration of the Blessed Sacrament) and there I found seminarian Wojtyla on his knees. His head was resting on the grille. In his hands he held a book. What could it be? Most certainly a text on asceticism. But nothing of the kind — it was a textbook of the history of the Church. He even studied the history of the Church on his knees coram Sanctissimo {in the presence of the Most Holy Eucharist}. It is therefore not surprising, that today he is writing this history. He never broke the silence. But then he was never annoyed when others would not observe the silence to the degree that they should have.

His depth of knowledge; he towered above all of us in his knowledge and his abilities. He always had the correct answer. He didn't use his knowledge to show off. Always focused, attentive at lectures, he would save the situation when a professor tried to stump the class with some more difficult issue. Even with the very demanding Rev. Prof. Ignacy Rozycki there was no situation where he didn't have an answer. It happened only once that when asked (he was our last hope for a correct answer), he said, "Please don't call on me today, I am indisposed. I didn't sleep today. I was at a meeting of the governing board of the Fraternity {Fraternal Aid Society} which dragged on until morning." It must be noted that by the wish of the Prince Archbishop, Fr. Wojtyla was vice-president of the Fraternity as a delegate of the Theological Department of JU.

He was always humbly dressed. Here I could say that he was inadequately dressed, especially in winter. He often shivered from the cold. He paid little attention to his external appearance (for the retreat he arrived in wooden shoes and denim shirt and pants. Everyone was immediately issued cassocks.)

He performed acts of mercy. This he learned from the great Prince Archbishop, who sold all his possessions so as to bring aid to "Mistress Poverty," as Brother Albert used to say. Each day we saw lines of paupers forming in front of the waiting room of Mr. Franciszek, wanting to gain "a hearing" with the Prince Archbishop. After a while, there would also form a group of Krakow's poor in front of the door to our dwelling — specifically, they asked for Fr. Wojtyla. I remember once, a man knocked on our door and asked to see Fr. Karol. He came to see the petitioner; he talked with him in the hallway. He went back to his bed, bent down, took out a sweater from the little suitcase under his bed and hid it under his cassock. He went out and soon returned, but without any visible bulge. He gave the poor man his brand new sweater, which he had just received the day before from Mr. Kotlarczyk. He himself was often cold and shivering. I don't know where he got what he would distribute. But people often came and asked for him. He shared with the poor whatever he could.

He was a very good comrade, and has remained so. Even after he became Archbishop. Once, as I was visiting Krakow, I decided to pay a visit to the Archbishop. There was a crowd of clients in the ground-floor waiting room. Also waiting was Rev. Prof. K. Klosak, who had already made it almost to the door. I came up to him and sat beside him. After a while, the Archbishop came out of his room and gazed around at all the assembled. Upon seeing me, he gave me a punch in my right shoulder (I can still remember how strong it was) as he went by, and said, "Hi, Franek. Wait until I see everyone else, then we can take our time talking." It was a very cordial gesture. Fr. Klosak said, "How great that he greeted you, his old colleague, so simply yet sincerely in front of everyone." Then we had a long, sincere talk. Afterwards, I accompanied the Archbishop as far as Kanoniczna Street, but I did not have time to stop in at his residence.

(According to an account by Fr. Franciszek Konieczny, a fellow student at the Seminary)

The seminarians of the 3rd and 4th year of Theology at JU were: Andrzej Bazinski, Kazimierz Borowy, Wladyslaw Majda, Kazimierz Suder, Jan Sidelko, Karol Targosz, Karol Wojtyla.

1945

The night from January 17 to 18, 1945 — The liberation of Krakow. Later, the work on returning the rooms of Collegium Maius to a usable state began. The windows in the Archbishop's palace were glazed. Then the seminary building, which had been occupied by the SS, was cleaned. (According to accounts by Fr. Mieczyslaw Malinski, *The Road to the Vatican*, Rome-London, 1979)

> **When the horrible war and occupation were over, we began a more normal existence in the seminary. Initially we lived in the residence of the Archbishop of Krakow, and later in the recovered and at least partially restored Krakow Theological Seminary at Podzamcze near Wawel.** (Fr. Andrzej Bazinski)
>
> **Seminarian Karol Wojtyla played the role of the "host."** (Fr. Kazimierz Suder)
>
> **I will never forget the impression that a conversation with a Soviet soldier made on me in 1945. It was shortly after the cessation of combat activities in the West. The soldier knocked on the gate of the seminary, which at that time was still partially in ruins. I asked him what he wanted, and when he asked if he could enter the seminary, I spent several hours talking to him. Although he didn't enter the seminary (besides, he had a very strange idea of what one might learn in a seminary), I learned a lot during our long talk about how God impresses Himself on human minds even in conditions that are systematically negative — as a truth which cannot be erased. This man had never in his life been in an Orthodox Church (although he mentioned that as a small child he was taken there by his mother, not since), and he heard at school and work that there was no God. "But anyway, I always knew," he repeated many times, "that there is a God. And now I want to find out more about Him..."** (From the Vatican recollections of Karol Cardinal Wojtyla. In the Polish edition, a typewritten note inserted in the printed copy on p. 19. Published by Edition du Dialogue, Paris 1980, pp. 26-27)

Studies:

Registration card submitted to the Dean of the Department of Theology

Academic year: 1944/45

Year of studies: 3rd

WOJTYLA, Karol Jozef is a regular student.

Residence: Franciszkanska Street, House No: 3

Military Draft Status: registered seminarian (Cert. No. 654)

List of courses for which he registered:

Tri-mester	Titles of Courses and Seminars	hrs/wk	Lecturer	Grade
I, II	De sacramentis in genere et de sacr. Eucharistiae in specie[1]	5	Rev. Dr. Eugeniusz Florkowski	excellent
I, II	Detailed Introduction to the Synoptic Gospels		Rev. Dr. Eugeniusz Krol	excellent
I, II	Virtutes theolog.[2]	4		excellent
I, II	Liturgy	2		excellent
I, II	Catechesis	2		v. good
II, III	Detailed Introduction to the Didactic and Prophetic Books of the Old Testament	2	Rev. Dr. Eugeniusz Krol	excellent
III	Poenitentia {Penance}	4	Rev. Dr. Wladyslaw Wicher	excellent
II, III	Exegesis of the Gospels	5	Rev. Dr. Jozef Kaczmarczyk	excellent
II, III	De Deo Uno et Trino[3]	5	Rev. Dr. Ignacy Rozycki	excellent
III	Proseminarium	1	Rev. Dr. Ignacy Rozycki	
I, II, III	Patristics	2	Rev. Dr. Marian Michalski	excellent
III	Church Art	2	Rev. Dr. Tadeusz Pomian-Kruszynski	excellent
III	Conservation of Monuments & Artifacts	1	Rev. Dr. Tadeusz Pomian-Kruszynski	{blank}
I, II	Hebrew	2	Fr. Efrem Glinski, OP	excellent
	Introduction to the Old Testament: the Historical Books and Cosm{ology}.			excellent
	Logic			v. good
	Metaphysics			excellent
	Theory of Knowledge			v. good
	Cosmology			v. good
	History of the Church, part I			v. good
	Apologetics			excellent
	General Introduction to the Holy Scriptures			v. good
	Inspiration in Canonical Texts			excellent
	Greek			excellent
	Hermeneutics			excellent
	Psychology			good
	History of Philosophy			v. good
	Moral Theology			excellent
	History of the Church, part II			excellent
	Apologetics			excellent

(Archives of JU: WT II 193)

... Karol Wojtyla would not leave the lecture hall and would use every free moment for studying Spanish. He wanted to read St. John of the Cross in the original language. He mastered this language quite quickly, because not long after, the assistant of the Spanish language class asked him for help in translating Spanish text that was supposed to be read on the Polish radio news a few hours hence.

Taking examinations together with our colleague Karol Wojtyla was not easy. There were only seven of us in our class, and we were often called

---

[1] On the sacraments in general and on the Sacrament of the Eucharist in particular.

[2] On theological virtues.

[3] Of the One and Triune God

into the examination room as a group. I answered first, because we were called on alphabetically by name. It was an examination in moral theology, and at the third question I began to doubt my knowledge. I took advantage of a break when the professor had to leave for a moment to go to the department office, and turned to my colleague Karol who was sitting next to me, asking for help with the answer. He told me: "Concentrate, be calm, I know you can answer" — but not a word in answer to the question. But I passed the exam with quite a good result. (Fr. Andrzej Bazinski)

At Rev. Prof. Ignacy Rozycki's seminar, he wrote a paper entitled *Faith according to St. John of the Cross*. He taught himself Spanish from a German-Spanish dictionary. (Fr. Kazimierz Suder)

Karol Wojtyla's answers to examination questions were somewhat different. Often he would answer with ideas that were neither in the lectures, nor in the professor's notes, nor in the recommended readings. The examining professor would smile benevolently, and we listened full of admiration, but also somewhat worried how this would affect our grades. He would explain to us that because he was especially interested in this subject, he sought out a more comprehensive treatment of it. The only thing was that there were more, many more such subjects that especially interested him, and for which he found such expanded treatments. (Fr. Andrzej Bazinski)

March 7, 1945 — During a seminar commemorating St. Thomas Aquinas he read a presentation entitled *The Personality of the Author of the Fourth Gospel on the Basis of the Gospel's Content.* (Fr. Mieczyslaw Turek, then a seminarian in his first year)

April 1, 1945 — He assumed the duties of a junior assistant at the Theological Department of JU.

L. 2057/46 — To Mr. Karol Wojtylo [error in the document] in Krakow: The Rector's Office of the Jagiellonian University hereby attests that in the period from April 1 until August 31, 1945, you fulfilled the duties of a junior assistant at the Theological Department of the Jagiellonian University, as provided by Art. 91 and 116 of the directive of the President of the Republic regarding the employment of professors by state institutions of higher education and the employment of the auxiliary academic personnel of such institutions ... Your salary for that period was paid according to group IX (nine).

Rector of the Jagiellonian University
(Archives of JU)

April 9, 1945 — He is elected Vice President of the Fraternal Aid Society of JU. The faculty moderator was then prof. Dr. Stanislaw Pigon, the President was Jozef Trojanowski, and then successively the Vice-Presidents were: Andrzej Wachulski and Jan Deszcz. Halina Messalska was also a Vice-President. Fr. Andrzej Deskur was the Director of the Legal Commission. Karol Wojtyla held the office of Vice-President until 1946. He attended no more meetings after the one on May 28, 1946. The offices of the Fraternal Aid Society were on the ground floor of the Rotunda, under the cafeteria. The second semester of the 1945/46 academic year was a period of particularly intense activity of the Society. (From the Archives of JU: BP 138, and from accounts given by Dr. Jan Deszcz)

> **Karol Wojtyla and W. Marian Traczynski CR were the representatives of the Department of Theology in "Bratniak" {the Fraternity} [the Students' Fraternal Aid Society] in the academic year 1945/46. We were members of the Fraternity's Board of Directors, and Cardinal Wojtyla was Vice-President. From the very beginning he was a voice of authority on the Board. He would often speak at board meetings, and propose many initiatives. His voice carried weight in the planning of the program of activities, in distribution of packages from America, in the assigning of living quarters. (Fr. Marian Traczynski, CR)**

May 26, 1945 — The rector of the Seminary presented a "transcript of grades received in examinations during the secret teaching in the years 1941-1945" to the administration of JU.

The secret teaching of theology (according to "collective protocols" presented on May 26, 1945 by Fr. Kozlowski, the Rector of the Prince Metropolitan's Seminary, to the administration of JU):

First year, 1942/43 — Students: Bazinski, Andrzej; Borowy, Kazimierz; Majda, Wladyslaw; Sidelko, Jan; Suder, Kazimierz; Targosz, Karol; Wojtyla, Karol; Konieczny, Franciszek; Koscielny, Stanislaw; Wilczynski, Ryszard; Starowieyski, Stanislaw.

Grades for Karol Wojtyla: Metaphysics, Apologetics part I, Greek, Hermeneutics, Introduction to Holy Scriptures part II (Inspiration): eminenter {excellent}; Logic, Theory of Cognition, Cosmology, Church History part I, Introduction to Holy Scriptures part I: valde bene {very good}.

Second year, 1943/44 — The same students, except for Stanislaw Starowieyski. Grades for Karol Wojtyla: Moral Theology, de principiis, Church History part II, Apologetics part II: eminenter {excellent}; History of Philosophy: valde bene {very good} ; Psychology — bene {good}.

Third year, 1944/45 — Grades for Karol Wojtyla: Introduction to the Old Testament, de Sacramentis, de Eucharistia, Liturgy, Moral Theology, Detailed Introduction to the Gospels: eminenter {excellent}; Catechesis: valde bene {very good}. (From the Archives of JU: KHUW5)

> **1945 — the fourth year of our studies. Together with him we were walking from the Seminary to Collegium Novum, the main building of JU, which also housed the Department of Theology. We were stopped by a poorly dressed woman who asked: "Which one of you is Father Wojtyla?" And then she explained the reason for stopping him. "During the occupation, Father, you worked with my husband in a factory in Krakow. At that time**

I gave birth to a child. My husband worked on the night shift. When you found out about the blessed event in our family, you, Father, after a full day of work, took on the night shift duties of a stoker so that my husband could be with me and our baby. You kept working these nights for him until I regained my strength. You never knew me, Father, yet you showed so much heart to me and my child. We will be grateful to you till the end of our lives, and we will cultivate this gratitude in our child. Please accept a small token of our gratitude — a pair of shoes." She said this with tears in her eyes. I remember that we walked the rest of the way to the Collegium in silence, I was so moved. The gift, a new pair of shoes, lasted only a few days in his locker. Unbeknown to his colleagues, he secretly gave them to a needy worker in Krakow, and continued to go about in the same well-worn shoes.

I don't remember seminarian Karol Wojtyla ever putting on a brand new cassock or coat. He could not do that, because in the circle of his many friends and acquaintances there were many families that were poor, people who were sick or otherwise needed help. (Fr. Andrzej Bazinski)

It was already in the summer of 1944 that seminarian Karol Wojtyla spent his vacation in Raciborowice.

When, after the war, Fr. Adam Biela was transferred to another parish, Karol Wojtyla, a student of theology, continued to spend vacations in Raciborowice, now as a guest of the then pastor, Fr. Jamroz. That's where we became acquainted. He met me one sunny day, when I was struggling with Latin in the shade of a tree. I was having difficulties with it. Our meeting began with the greeting, "May the name of Jesus Christ be praised." Then he asked about my studies, my difficulties, and offered to help me with my Latin. Thereafter we met almost every day in the afternoons. As a young man I had many doubts and many difficult questions, but Fr. Karol had answers to all of them, and he gladly shared them. I'll never forget our first wanderings about the countryside, to Mogila or Krakow. After the vacation, Karol would visit me at school on Krupnicza Street where I was attending adult classes. He usually brought something to eat. He would always say something kind and encourage me to study. I promised to visit him at the seminary, which he asked me to do, but I lacked the courage. When I finally went there, they told me that he was in retreat before his ordination. Eventually he found me. We agreed that the next day I would serve Mass for him at the Church of St. Andrew. He gave me his First Mass blessing; he blessed the Sisters at the gate of the cloister. During our breakfast together I learned that during the war the Church of St. Andrew was his favorite place of prayer. (Br. Romuald, a Cistercian from the Abbey in Szczyrzyc)

Vacation in Raciborowice. "General opinion is most favorable about his vocation to the priesthood... He is distinguished by a singular virtue of piety." (Testimonial from Fr. Jozef Jamroz, pastor of Raciborowice, about the seminarian Karol Wojtylo [!], relating to his conduct during Easter and summer vacations, issued December 4, 1945). (Archives of the Krakow Curia)

He enrolled in the 4th year of studies, 1945/46. On his registration form Karol Wojtyla, a student of the 4th year of the Department of Theology, entered the following courses and seminars: de Deo Creante et Elevante, de Verbo Incarnato, Mariology, de gratia, Dogmatic

Theology, Apostolic Sermons, The Sermons of the Fathers the Church, Polish Homilies of the 16th Century, Homiletics, Pastoral Theology, Structuring and Writing Sermons, Pastoral Work with Particular Age Groups, Various Types of Sermons, The Priest and the Sacrament of Baptism, Codex Juris Can.: Lib. III. de matrimonio, de processibus, de delictis, The Passion of Christ, The Life and Activity of St. Paul, The Acts of the Apostles, The History of Revelation, Exegesis of the Psalms, Catechesis, The Right to Life (a lecture in moral theology). (Archives of JU: WT II 194)

The seminarians of the clandestine seminary were now ordered to provide the missing documents, including a biography personally written by each student:

> Wojtyla, Karol Jozef (2 given names), was born in Wadowice (province of Krakow) and baptized in the parish church of that town where he absorbed the initial Grace of God. By the same Grace, he later completed his education, first the elementary grades, then the Marcin Wadowita Secondary School of the neoclassical type in the said Wadowice. Having passed his final {high school} examination in May of 1938, he was enrolled in September of that year in the student body of the Jagiellonian University, in the School of Philosophy, as a student of Polish philology. These studies were interrupted by the war in 1939, which also forced him to take on the job of a manual laborer in the "Solvay" factory. At this time he also lost his father, the last member of his immediate family; his mother died in his childhood, and his only brother, a physician in Bielsko, caught an infection and died a few years after his mother. At the same time the increased influence of God's Grace led him to a clear discernment of his vocation. Responding to that vocation, he began theological studies, first as a secret seminarian, then, from 1945, as a student of JU. (Archives of the Krakow Curia)

A letter from the Rector of the Jagiellonian University confirming {Wojtyla's} appointment to the post of junior assistant:

L. 3906/45 **Krakow, October 4, 1945.**
To the Dean's Office of the Department of Theology
Jagiellonian University
to L. 339/45
    I hereby confirm the appointment of Karol Wojtyla to the contractual post of junior assistant for the Seminars of the Department of Theology for the period from November 1, 1945 to August 31, 1946, with a scope of 15 hours per week, and I approve a remuneration as provided by the appropriate rulings.
    In light of the above, please conclude the requisite agreement with the above-named and forward it to the Rector's office, so that the payment of remuneration can be initiated. Also, please forward the missing questionnaire.
Signature on behalf of the Rector of the Jagiellonian University
Department of Theology: (m.p.) Lehr-Splawinski
Fr. Jan Krzemieniecki
                    (Archives of JU: S III 246 K. Wojtyla)

Seminar of Dogmatic Theology:

> October 24 — The first seminar meeting in the academic year 1945/46.

Those present: Dewera, Augustyn (Krakow Seminary); Br. Kosiak, Pawel (OP); Majda, Wladyslaw (Krakow Seminary); Sidelko, Jan (Krakow Seminary); Tyrala, Wladyslaw (Krakow Seminary); Wojtyla, Karol (Krakow Seminary). Rev. Dr. Rozycki submits a general plan of activities for the current academic year. It deals primarily with the origins of the Holy Spirit as described in the writings of Alexander of Hales, St. Bonaventure, John Duns Scotus, Ockham, Gabriel Biel, Wilhelm of Auxerre, St. Thomas Aquinas, Capreolus, Herveus from Nedellec, Cajetan.

First, they read the report by Wladyslaw Majda entitled *St. Hilary's Teachings about Original Sin.* (From the Archives of the Jagiellonian University (Z. 280), Chronicles of the Seminars in Dogmatic Theology since 1945 [until 1954])

Until the end of the academic year of 1945/46, the secretary of these seminars was — according to the notation made by Rev. Prof. I. Rozycki — "Wojtyla, Karol (Krakow Seminary)"

The minutes of the seminars, held every Thursday, are recorded in the hand of Karol Wojtyla. On the first page of the book of minutes, the secretary entered this title: "Academic year 1945/46. Seminar under the direction of Assistant Professor Rev. Dr. Ignacy Rozycki." Information about these seminars given in the following text is based on these minutes.

Seminar of dogmatic theology:

November 8 — Continuation of the reading of the work that was begun previously. The subject of analysis: *Comment in Matth.* (Migne P.L. vol. IX col. 976 no. 719) [There follows a quotation of the text under analysis].

November 15 — Continuation of work on the aforementioned text for the purpose of discovering the degree of applicability to a study of original sin according to the writings of St. Hilary of Poitiers.

November 22 — After a thorough analysis, it appears that the aforementioned text does not basically speak of original sin in the meaning of "peccatum originale originatum"...

November 29 — The text *Comment in Matth.* (Migne P.L. vol. IX col. 1020 nr. 758)... [There follows a quotation of the text under analysis] becomes the subject of group analysis.

December 3 — He passed an examination in dogmatic theology (administered by Rev. Prof. I. Rozycki) — *eminenter* {excellent}.

Seminar of Dogmatic Theology:

December 6 — Group analysis of the text *Tract. super Psalmos* {Treatise on Psalms} (Migne P.L. vol. IX col. 385 no. 155).

December 7 — He passed an examination in dogmatic theology (given by Rev. Prof. I. Rozycki) — *eminenter* {excellent}.[4]

December 12 — A regular meeting of the Council of the Department

---

[4] Either this entry is a duplication of December 3rd or examinations were given separately on materials covered by lectures and by seminars.

of Theology of JU. Upon a motion by Dean Fr. Jan Krzemieniecki, it was unanimously decided to restore full junior assistantships to Jozef Jurczyk and Karol Wojtyla.

Seal:
**Dean of the Department of Theology
of the Jagiellonian University
in Krakow**

CONTRACT
of employment, concluded in Krakow this 14th day of December 1945 between the Dean of the Department of Theology of the Jagiellonian University, acting on behalf of the Treasury of the Republic, as employer, and Mr. Karol WOJTYLA, as employee.
1. Mr. Karol Wojtyla, hereinafter called "the employee," agrees to fulfill, for the period from December 1, 1945 until August 31, 1946, the duties of junior assistant for the seminars of Dogmatics, Patristics and The History of Dogmatic Theology at the Jagiellonian University, to constitute a 30-hour week … (signature of employer: Rev. Dr. Jan Krzemieniecki, Dean; signature of employee: Karol Wojtyla).

Remuneration in 1945: base pay — 210 zl., wartime supplement — 370 zl.; adjustment for April, May, June 1945 — 945 zl — base and 1665 zl — supplement. Assistants named on this list: Rev. Dr. Piotr Bober, O. Glinski, M.A., Jozef Jurczyk, Zygmunt Siodmak, Karol Wojtyla. (From the Archives of JU)

December 13 — Seminar of Dogmatic Theology: Group analysis of further texts.

When a friend [of Karol Wojtyla's], Br. Leonard Kowalowka, was appointed Novice Master [of the Discalced Carmelites] in 1945, seminarian Wojtyla applied to the monastery at Czerna. Transferring from a theological seminary to a monastery required the permission of the bishop. Prince Adam Stefan Sapieha did not grant his "placet" {agreement} [telling the seminarian, that he should finish what he started], and Wojtyla remained in the Krakow Seminary. He continued to be Br. Jozef's (Prus) frequent guest … (As related by Br. Boguslaw Woznicki, OCD)

1946

Seminar of Dogmatic Theology:

January 17 — The seminar finished the discussion of the work *The Teachings of St. Hilary on Original Sin,* and Br. Pawel Kosiak (OP) began reading his work, *The Origins of the Holy Spirit according to Alexander of Hales.*

January 24 — Continuation of the reading of the work on the *Origins of the Holy Spirit according to Alexander of Hales.*

January 31 — The minutes list the current participants "who attend

regularly": Br. Pawel Kosiak OP, Fr. Feliks Schreder (Congregation of the Resurrection), Augustyn Dewera (Krakow Seminary), Wladyslaw Madeja (Krakow Seminary), Karol Wojtyla (Krakow Seminary). The seminar continued its reading of the work on the origins of the Holy Spirit according to Alexander of Hales.

February 7 — Continuation of the reading of the work on the origin of the Holy Spirit according to Alexander of Hales ... The seminar was also attended by Assistant Professor Rev. Dr. Rozycki, who began a lecture on scientific method in dogmatic theology.

February 14 — The entire session devoted to a lecture on academic method in the field of dogmatic theology and of theology in general. Rev. Dr. Rozycki spoke of the methods of research and bibliography, notetaking, and preparing academic studies.

At a gathering celebrating the elevation of the Prince Archbishop to the rank of Cardinal (February 18, 1946) [Karol Wojtyla] recited the *Sermon on the Love of Country* by Fr. Kajsiewicz. His colleagues recall that he "got stuck" and forgot his lines. After a fairly long period of silence, he resumed his recitation. (Fr. Kazimierz Suder)

In the periodical *Voice of Carmel* which was reactivated after the war (nos. 1, 2 and 3), he published a canticle "Song of the Hidden God." The text was submitted anonymously. The editor, Br. Woznicki, without the author's knowledge, signs the work "seminarian Karol Wojtyla," not realizing that at that time, seminarians were not allowed to publish anything. At Karol Wojtyla's request, the first pages with his name were removed, and the poem was printed again anonymously. The title page is decorated with a drawing by Giotto depicting St. Peter's boat. This is the first published work by Karol Wojtyla. In 1973, when the Discalced Carmelite Sisters from Kopernika Street recited for him a fragment of this poem about "the shores filled with silence," he interrupted them and said, "Yes, this is my work. But now, where are the shores filled with silence?" (According to an account by Br. Boguslaw Woznicki, OCD)

Seminar of Dogmatic Theology:

February 21 — Karol Wojtyla begins the reading of his work: *The Analysis of Faith according to St. John of the Cross.* Faith as a means of uniting the soul with God. He reads the introduction.

February 28 — The work [by Karol Wojtyla] presents Faith as a means of uniting the soul with God. According to St. John of the Cross, Faith constitutes a *medio proporcionado, proprio, proximo, legitimo y accomodato* for a union with God. The presenter begins an analysis of these properties.

March 7 — *Medio proporcionado* (proportionate {commensurate} means). The referenced texts are to be found in *Subida del monte Carmelo* (vol. II, cap. VIII, p. 6 ff... pub. Librerio de Sta Teresa C.D., Burgos 1929). The analysis presented by the author was faulty. As a result, the texts are assigned for group analysis.

March 14 — Group analysis of the aforementioned texts. They touch upon two separate problems: 1. What can we determine, from the writings of St. John of the Cross, about *medio proporcionado* (what does he mean by that term?); and 2. No created thing can be a proportionate {commensurate} means for uniting the soul with God because there exists no similarity in essence between God and creation, indeed, there is an infinite chasm (*distinctio infinita*) between the Being of God and creation. Homework assignment: recall how this question is treated by St. Thomas.

March 21 — Continuation of the analysis of the terms *medio proprio, medio acomodado, medio proximo* (a means that is proper, adequate, proximate), determining how these terms are defined in *Subida*. In this regard, there arises the question of *similitudo formalis aequivoca* (a one-time similarity of essence) and *similitudo formalis analogica* (a multiple similarity of essence). The group assignment will be to determine which of the texts analyzed so far contains the proportionate {commensurate} means of unification with God. Rev. Dr. Rozycki questions the accuracy of the analysis of the term *medio proximo*. The question remains for a subsequent group analysis and critique of the author's argument.

March 28 — A proportionate {commensurate} means of unification with God must possess the characteristic of multiple similarity of essence. Such a similarity, according to the universal teaching of theologians, is inherent in all created beings. However, by themselves, they still cannot be a commensurate means of unification with God, meaning that they cannot achieve such unification on the basis of their natures alone. Therefore, there must be a difference between other creatures and the commensurate means in the degree of multiple similarity of essence. This is the first issue submitted for group analysis. The second issue: what is the relationship between *medio proximo* and *proporcionado*. The thesis of the presenter is accepted, that there is no substantive difference, only *differentia virtualis minor*.

April 4 — Following the examination of homework assignments on the subject "How does St. John of the Cross understand Faith as related in *Subida II*, 9", the presenter continues the reading of his work: Faith as *medio legitimo* for the union of the soul with God. Homework assignment: once again, Faith as presented in *Subida II*, 9.

April 11 — The assignments do not provide an appropriate answer. The issue is, that according to *Subida II*, 9, God exists through Faith in the mind in an intentional manner, just as material objects exist in our mental concepts of them. The presenter continues to read his treatment. He begins to explain how St. John of the Cross understands the unification of the soul with God.

May 16 — The first seminar meeting after the Easter break. The presenter summarizes the discussions so far. Faith is a means of unification with God. The analysis continues: How does St. John of the Cross understand unification with God? The presenter has moved away from the text of *Subida I*, 5 and is now basing his argument on *Subida II*, 5. For homework: what are the similarities between God and Faith?

May 28 — Faith has all of the same properties as God, but ordered intentionally. An analysis to be performed by the presenter: What is the consequence of this in the role that Faith plays as a proportionate {commensurate} means of unification with God.

June 6 — The presenter responds: If faith, in its essence, is the same as the Essence of God but ordered intentionally, then it must be a proportionate {commensurate} means of uniting the intellect with God. By its very nature it unites the intellect with the Essence of God; for the purpose of uniting the intellect with God, it is sufficient to have Faith in intentional order.

This was then the first part of the issue: Faith as a proportionate {commensurate} means for the intellect to be united with God. The next issue: how is Faith a means of unifying man's soul with God. For the time being, the presenter is assigned to find support for his thesis in *Subida*.

June 13 — The last meeting of the seminar in the current academic year. The presenter, in fulfillment of his assignment, provides citations in support of his thesis. These are [here follows a long list of references to the work of St. John of the Cross]... The analysis of the texts is insufficient. Besides, some of them cannot in any way serve to demonstrate the truth of the thesis as stated.

From June 18th he is employed as an assistant for the seminar of Dogmatics at the Jagiellonian University:

To the Office of the Rector of the Jagiellonian University
The Council of the Department of Theology, at a meeting on June 7, 1946, unanimously decided to re-nominate Karol Wojtyla, the current junior assistant, to the post of junior assistant for the seminars of Dogmatics and of The History of Dogmatic Theology, for the academic year 1946/47.
I enclose the contract that we entered upon with him (etc.).

Dean - Jan Krzemieniecki

L. 316/46 CONTRACT — entered upon this 18th day of June 1946... accepts the duties of junior assistant for the seminars of Dogmatics, Patristics and The History of Dogmatic Theology for the period beginning September 1, 1946 through August 31, 1947. L. 349/46

Krakow, June 25, 1946.
(Archives of JU)

June 23 — Examination in Dogmatic Theology (Rev. Prof. I. Rozycki) — *eminenter* [excellent] * June 25 —Examination in Moral Theology (Rev. Prof. W. Wicher) — *eminenter* * June 26 — Examination in the Holy Scriptures (Rev. Prof. J. Kaczmarczyk) — *valde bene* * June 28 — Examination in Canon Law (Rev. Prof. J. Krzemieniecki) — *eminenter* * July 1 — Examination in the Holy Scriptures of the Old Testament (Rev. Prof. A. Klawek) — *eminenter* * July 3 — Examination in Catechetics (Rev. Prof. J. Rychlinski) – *eminenter*.

He spends the summer vacation in Raciborowice with Fr. Jozef Jamroz.

October 12 — He submitted a petition for admission to sub-diaconate * October 13 — Petition for admission to the diaconate. On the same day, in the chapel of the Archbishop's residence, he is ordained to the sub-diaconate by the Prince Archbishop * October 20 — In the chapel of the Archbishop's palace, he is ordained to the diaconate by the Prince Archbishop. On the same day he submitted a petition for ordination to the priesthood:

October 20, 1946
    To the Rector's Office of the Prince Metropolitan Theological Seminary in Krakow: I hereby petition for admission to the ordination to the Priesthood. I am fully aware of the obligations pertaining thereto, and I proclaim under oath in the attached document my complete awareness and full freedom of will in undertaking this step. Karol Wojtyla, Deacon, Seminarian (Archives of the Metropolitan Curia, Krakow)

October 28 — Feast of Christ the King

    The Metropolitan Seminary organized a commemorative meeting for three seminars, and seminarian Karol Wojtyla made a presentation, but I don't remember the subject. I was struck by the fact that the presentation was prepared in beautiful classical Latin and was spoken from memory, with no reference to notes. I thought: this is no average seminarian. (Fr. Brunon Magott, then a professor of the Czestochowa Seminary in Krakow)

October 31 — He took an oath, as prescribed by Canon law.

November 1, 1946 — ORDINATION TO THE PRIESTHOOD

    Cardinal Sapieha ordained him in his private chapel on November 1, 1946, on the Feast of All Saints. The ordination was performed separately {from the rest of the seminarians} and earlier, due to Fr. Wojtyla's imminent departure to Rome for further study. Thus his First Mass fell on All Souls' Day.[5] Fr. Wojtyla asked me to fill the role of *manuductor*[6] so I was a witness. The young celebrant said three "low" Masses, for the souls of his departed parents and brother, in an unusual place: at Wawel, in the Romanesque crypt of St. Leonard, amid the tombs of kings and national heroes. A solemn First High Mass was celebrated only a few days later in Wadowice. (Fr. Kazimierz Figlewicz, TP 44/1978)

At about this time he wrote to Mieczyslaw Kotlarczyk:

    Yesterday I went to see the performance of *The King Spirit*. But today I must apologize. Simply because I need to get well. In the morning I have to be at a Holy Mass at Debniki, and in the afternoon I must again wrap my throat, if I want to be able to speak at all at our Masses tomorrow.
    Maybe it is God's design that I can't come to this anniversary meeting. That is how I understand it — I should be present in your activity, just as a priest should be present in life in general, a hidden driving force. Yes, despite all appearances, that is the main duty of the priesthood. Hidden forces usually produce the strongest actions. So perhaps these First Mass and anniversary thoughts of mine will represent me. I commend all of you to God.   **Karol**

November 4 — First Mass at Wawel. "There was a large group of

---

[5] November 2nd
[6] Literally "guide of hands," an experienced priest who assists a newly-ordained one at his first Mass.

friends, including the entire Rhapsodic Theater." (Maria Bobrownicka)

A small post-First Mass reception was held in our home. (Initially he wanted to hold it in the home of his godmother, his aunt Wiadrowska, but she did not agree, feeling uneasy about the entrance through a run-down courtyard, about the apartment being too small — according to an account by her daughter F. Wiadrowska). Present at the reception were Fr. M. Malinski, Fr. S. Truszkowski and Fr. M. Kuczkowski. On the back of the First Mass holy cards, the new priest wrote by hand (because there was no means of getting them printed): "Fecit mihi magna... {"For He has done great things for me..."} Krakow, November 1, 1946" (According to an account by Z. Pozniakowa; see TP 44/1978)

On the same day, Juliusz Osterwa noted in his journal: "Krakow, November 4, 1946, Monday (already in the apartment at 5 Pijarska Street). Letter to Karol Wojtyla, a priest from this day." (Copied from Osterwa's journal by M.O.)

November 8 — Resignation from the post of junior assistant. At the regular meeting of the Council of the Department of Theology of JU, November 8, 1946:

In light of the resignation of the junior assistant, Fr. Karol Wojtyla (who is leaving for studies abroad) effective November 30, 1946, the Council unanimously decided to nominate Fr. Stanislaw Grzybek (M.A.) to the post of junior assistant. (Archives of JU)

November 11 — Administers the Sacrament of Baptism for the first time. He baptizes Monika Katarzyna, born October 20, 1946, the daughter of his friends Tadeusz Kwiatkowski and Halina née Krolikiewicz, at their home. The godparents are Zbigniew Wojciech Zurawski and Barbara Wanda Kudlinska. In the Registry of Baptisms of St. Anne Parish in Krakow, vol. III, p. 20, item 107, it is noted that the baptism was administered by "RD Carolus Wojtyla, Neopresbyter."[7]

November 15 — He departs for Rome for further studies.

On November 15, 1946 we left, Fr. Karol Wojtyla and I, sent by Archbishop Sapieha to study in Rome. We took a train from Krakow to Katowice, where we boarded an international train to Paris; from there we took another train to Rome.

Archbishop Sapieha wished for us to live at the Belgian College and asked Cardinal Hlond, who was in Rome at the time, to arrange this. These arrangements took a long time to complete, so we had to take up residence at the Pallottine Fathers, on Via Pettinari, where we were very cordially received by the then Council member, Fr. Turowski. Finally, in December, sometime before Christmas, we were accepted into the Belgian College at 26 via del Quirinale. We were received very cordially, and throughout our stay

---

[7] a new priest

(until 1948) we experienced much kindness from our Belgian superiors and colleagues. (Fr. Stanislaw Starowieyski)

At this time — there was a meeting with Cardinal August Hlond.[8]

I had the opportunity to meet Cardinal A. Hlond only once in my life. It was in 1946 (in the autumn), when I was sent for studies to Rome by Cardinal Adam Sapieha, who asked the Primate to facilitate my reception to the Belgian College in Rome. I owe it to Cardinal A. Hlond that I was accepted and that I could stay there for two years ... What really struck me at that time was great openness and cordiality in interpersonal relations... (From a letter by Cardinal Wojtyla to Abp. Antoni Baraniak, March 23, 1968)

The Belgian College in Rome

...was then located at 26 via del Quirinale, half a kilometer away from Angelicum. It was next to the Church of St. Andrew al Quirinale, a work of Bernini, which is the site of the tomb of St. Stanislaw Kostka. The church is separated from the College only by the Villa Pia Park, and one had to pass by this church when walking to Angelicum. The house, three stories from the street side, four stories from the garden side, was old, and was then sold by the Belgians. Since 1972 the College has been located at 35 via Gian Battista Pagano, in the building of the Belgian congregation of Fratelli di Carita.[9]

In 1946 the College had 16-17 students; in 1948 — 22. In the college there was a chapel served by Belgian nuns. (According to the information in Stanislaw Klimaszewski's letter)

Residency at the Belgian College and studies:

At the request of Cardinal Sapieha we began studies at the Pontifical Dominican University, known as Angelicum. Fr. Karol enrolled in the course "biennium ad lauream" {two year degree program} (he had completed a regular course of theology in Krakow), and I entered the first year of theology. From our first days in Rome we were learning to speak Italian and, of course, we had an excellent opportunity to perfect our French. Although our Belgian friends spoke Flemish among themselves, with us they spoke only French. There were about 20 of us in the College, mostly seminarians, but also several priests. In the second year of our stay, there were also several Americans. The rector was Fr. Maximilian de Furstenberg (today a cardinal). Most of our time, of course, we spent on our studies, but we also had time for spiritual exercises, well conducted liturgy and, of course, sightseeing in Rome. Together with the Rector and our colleagues we were at a special audience with the Holy Father Pius XII. I believe that we benefited much from our two-year stay at the foreign college; we mastered French quite well.

Our daily contact with colleagues whose characters were quite different from the Polish character taught us a lot. We frequently exchanged observations on this topic with Fr. Karol.

We had little contact with the Polish community in Rome, but we did not avoid it, either. We were in constant touch with the then pastoral leader of Poles living abroad, Bishop Gawlina. Sometimes we would visit the Polish Institute and College. We had good relations with the superiors of these

---

[8] Primate of Poland.
[9] Brothers of Charity

institutions, Rev. Rector Marian Strojny and Br. Francis Maczynski. We knew the Polish Jesuits who were staying in Rome at that time, and we had close contact with the Marian Fathers who, like us, studied at the Angelicum. (Fr. Stanislaw Starowieyski)

November 26 — He submitted a petition for admission to the Pontifical University, Angelicum. Transcript from the archives of Angelicum of a form filled out in Karol Wojtyla's hand:

> **Elenchus Auditorum facultatis theologicae: Vojtyla Carolus, dioecesis Cracovien.; commoratio: Coll. Belg.; natio: Polon. Ann.: B I Petitio inscriptionis [on the form]: habitat — Roma, via del Quirinale 26... petit inscribi ut alumnus ordinarius in Facultate S. Theologiae.**
>
> **Prima ascriptio in Facultatem Theologicam... num. matric. C 905 annus acad. 1946-1947. 26 Novembris**

November 27 — (A handwritten form filled out by Fr. Karol Wojtyla — archives of Angelicum):

> **27 Novembris 1946**
> **Disciplinae frequentandae — [subjects which will be studied] disciplinae principales: 1. Theol. dogm. — :qq selectae ex Summa a) de Deo Uno (I qu 1 - 26) de Verbo Incarnato (III, 1 - 59), b) de Deo Trino (I qu 27 - 43), c) de Sacramentis (III qu 62 - 83); 2. Theol. mor. — :qq selectae ex Summa. Disciplinae auxiliares: 1) Theol. asc. myst. De prefectione christiana sec. exigentias temporis nostris; 2) questiones theologiae Orientalium (I sem). Disciplinae specialis oblig.: 1) historia dogmatum. Exercitatio: De visione beatifica. Disc. oblig.: Institutiones gen. JC (II sem), Institutiones sepc. JC (I sem).**
> **Simplex auditor: De natura Theologiae sec. S. Thomam, De charitate quest. spec. subscriptio Decani: P. A. Ciappi OP**

This time was a golden age of the Angelicum in Rome. There were world-famous professors — F. Ceuppens, J. Voste, E. M. Toccafondi, L. B. Gillon, M. Browne (later a cardinal), P. Philippe (Cardinal, Prefect of the Sacred Congregation for the Oriental Churches) and R. Garrigou-Lagrange. The Dean of Theology was A. Ciappi — later a papal theologian during the pontificate of Paul VI and a cardinal from 1977. All of them were Dominicans.

1947

March 21 — A letter to Mrs. H. Szkocka in Krakow:

> ...We reside in the Belgian College. We study. I speak in the plural, not as *pluralis maiestaticus*, but rather because there are two of us doing all that is herein discussed. What then do we do? I believe there would be much to discuss with Madame Zofia regarding the Thomistic studies. This entire system is something beautiful, delightful, and still it bespeaks simplicity. It appears that thought and profoundness do not require many words. Perhaps even the more profound the thought, the fewer words are required.

The second essential thing — immersing oneself in Rome. This is a chapter which absolutely cannot be described in a few statements. This subject contains so many levels, so many aspects. One continually associates some details and feels constantly enriched. Yet I am still far from putting these experiences into some sort of order. Deo gratias...

March 25 (date of the Vatican Post Office postmark) — a letter to Mieczyslaw Kotlarczyk:

Dear Mieciu!
I have no news from you, although thanks to the *Tygodnik Powszechny* ... I have quite exhaustive information about your theater ... I realize well what difficulties you battle to maintain your family and your creation.

He visited S. Giovanni Rotondo and undertook other excursions.

Right after Easter, probably in 1947, we traveled, Father Karol and I, to S. Giovanni Rotondo, to meet the renowned Capuchin, Padre Pio.
During either the holidays or other free days we made other excursions, some lasting a few days, with our Belgian colleagues or just the two of us: into the environs of Rome, to monasteries, where St. Francis resided, to Monte Cassino, Naples, Capri and the area...
Once the two of us went to Subiaco, the cradle of the Benedictine order. With amazement we viewed the various tiers of the monasteries which arose around the famous grotto in which the young Benedict commenced his life for God. In the afternoon, as we were already departing, we paused to view again the "rocky nest" attached to the sharp slope, amid the mountains. Silence ruled; somewhere below a stream rustled. Father Karol then said only this: "One must arrange one's life, so that everything praises God, and the monks are adept at this." (Fr. Stanislaw Starowieyski)

May 18 — Prince Cardinal Adam Sapieha visited Father Karol Wojtyla and Father Stanislaw Starowieyski at the Belgian College.

July 3 — The licentiate exam. During the initial months in Rome, Father Wojtyla prepared for the licentiate exam, which he passed on July 3, 1947 summa cum laude, receiving 40 x 40, that is all the possible points from the four examiners. A written exam was not required.

July — from a letter to Mrs. Irena Szkocka:

...The last few weeks of the school year were a time of very intense work prior to the so-called licentiate, which is an exam from the entire theology. The exam, thank God, went well and now I have a freer mind. I am writing from Paris for a change, where I have managed to arrive, stopping at Marseilles and Lourdes. It is the Prince's will that I spend these holidays visiting France, Belgium, and perhaps Holland, observing methods of pastoral work. The latter is something very elusive. What is achieved depends on the Grace of God and one's perceptivity under the influence of the same Grace. Not only are the pastoral methods of interest to me. So are the monuments to be seen here. Northern France or Flanders with their Gothic... My current address is: until August 5, Paris, rue des Irlandais, and then until the end of the month, Brussels, Blvd. Poincare — Centre JOC. Toward the end of September, Rome again, via del Quirinale.

Summer 1947:

In the summer of 1947 we set off on a trip to visit France, Belgium, and Holland. First we traveled to Lourdes. We spent 2-3 weeks in Paris. We lived in the guesthouse of the Polish Seminary on La Rue Irlandais; for meals we went to the good Sisters of Nazareth. Of course, almost all of our time in this wonderful city was spent sightseeing.

From Paris we traveled to Belgium. As we had many invitations from our Belgian friends, we crossed the length and breadth of the country: we visited Flanders with its beautiful old cities, such as Gent and Bruges, as well as picturesque Wallonia. During this period we also became more closely acquainted with the JOC (Jeunesse Ouvriere Chretienne) and its founder, Father Cardijn, who had visited the Belgian College a few times.

From Belgium we went to Holland: for a week we traveled through the land of windmills and tulips. We entered somewhere near Bruges, stopped in Rotterdam, The Hague, and in Amsterdam we spent probably two days, looking at the "Venice of the North," as well as the famous masters of Dutch painting. We then drove through Hilversum, Maastricht and back to Belgium. I recall that throughout that week we did not spend a cent on lodging or meals. Here, as in Belgium, acquaintances and generous hospitality made our journey possible.

At the end of summer we separated for a few weeks: Father Karol wished to undertake pastoral duties among the Polish miners, somewhere in the region of Charleroi; I, being but a cleric, spent this time in a retreat house. I visited Father Karol towards the end of this period: in just a few weeks he had formed bonds with his "parishioners" and I remember that he was bid a warm farewell. We returned to Rome before the commencement of the academic year.

At various times during our stay in Rome we had opportunities to visit famous sanctuaries and the most beautiful of Italian cities; we thus became familiar with Assisi, Sienna, Florence, Milan, Venice and others. Primarily we visited the churches, but other monuments and museums as well, those endless galleries of Italian artists from the Middle Ages (early) up to the Renaissance.

During our stay of a few weeks in Paris we often utilized the Metro system for getting about that huge city. Most often it was crowded and the behavior of the French often left a lot to be desired. After a few days of such trips Father Karol says to me: you know, during these Metro rides one can superbly attend to one's inner life (contemplation). I must say that I was surprised by this observation on my friend's part... (Fr. Stanislaw Starowieyski)

October 5 — Letter to Mieczyslaw Kotlarczyk (written in Belgium. On the envelope — a postmark from Warsaw. Because of the high cost of postage, to this day letters are often given to persons heading for Poland with the request that they be posted there; alternatively, a few letters are sent in one envelope with the request that they be mailed to the respective addressees in Poland):

My Dear Mieciu,
Once again I have arrived at the conviction that you have a certain mission to fulfill in art, in the theater. What it might be, I do not know. I will admit that it is not even the one you have been fulfilling so far. That is what

> I think. This is interesting: I am always thinking of something — higher. You see, every day I read the Gospels in Polish. And often I read out loud. And often, when I am reading, especially St. John, I begin to read in a new way, as if in Franciscan chant — finding something and seeing and hearing. It then seems to me that I wish something within the field of your destiny — but I express this incorrectly, no one knows that — rather, your calling.

November 4 — Registers for classes in the new academic year: Lectiones frequentandae: 1. De prudentia — P. Lumbreras; 2. De psychologia religionis (2 sem) — P. Metodius Hudeczek; 3. De usu opinionis probabilis (1 sem) — P. Browne; 4. De obligatione eleemosynae (2 sem); 5. De unione sacerdotis cum Christo sacerdote et victima — P. Garrigou-Lagrange; 6. De contemplatione et de unione mystica cum Deo — P. Philippe.

Simplex auditor: De fine ultimo, de actibus hum. habit. et virtutibus — P. de Vito. Exercitio: Doctrina D. Thomae de Beatitudine — P. Gillon, metaphysica — P. D'Aurora.

At the bottom of the questionnaire, confirmation that Father Karol Wojtyla has license of his bishop ordinary: signed by the Rector of Collegium Belga, B. Fuerstenberg. (From the Angelicum Archives)

December 24, Christmas Eve:

> ...In the Green Salon, the Prefect extended the traditional greetings to the Monsignor. He responded in three languages, concluding in Polish.
> An international evening was held in the Hall: English singing and an excerpt from *Waar de ster bleff stille staan*, followed by one act from the play *Przyszedl na ziemie swiety*[10] by Adam Bunsch. It was directed by Father Karol Wojtyla. Bunsch's play is about Brother Albert. (From the chronicles of the Belgian College and the account by Father Stanislaw Starowieyski, a participant in the evening.)

1948

At the Belgian College two notebooks have been preserved in which the students entered by hand the loans of books from the College library. They were allowed to keep textbooks for 15 days, other books for a month. Thus, some entries are repeated numerous times. Fr. Karol Wojtyla: textbooks — Merckelbach *Summa Theologiae Moralis* — 13 renewals, Noldin *Summa Theologiae Moralis* — 7 renewals, repeated renewals of textbooks by the following authors: Voste, Billot, Pesch, *Summa Theologiae* by St. Thomas. Other reading: Mercier — *La Vie interieure* (a few times), S. Francois de Sales — *Traite de l'amour de Dieu* (a few times), S. Bernardus — *Opera omnia* (particular volumes a few

---

[10] There Came to Earth a Saint

times each), S. Alphonsus Liguori — *Opere spirituali* (a few times), Origiene — *Homilie sur la Genese*, Gregoire de Nysse — *Vie de Moise*, L. Grignion de Montfort — *La Vraie devotion a S. Vierge*, Benson–*L'amitie de Jesus Christ*, by the same author — *Le Christ dans l'Eglise* and others. Periodicals — *La Vie Spirituelle*.

February 25 — Letter to Mrs. I. Szkocka:

> ...Please believe me that my time flies by at great speed. I truly do not know how almost one and a half year has passed. Studies, observations, deliberations — it all has the effect of spurs on a horse. Thus each day is completely filled. It also gives me the feeling that I am serving God according to my abilities and according to His will, as designated by my superiors. Thus, all this activity is not only to take advantage of an unusual personal opportunity ... I maintain uninterrupted spiritual communion with my homeland–in thought, through prayer and reading, although I know very little of my close ones. About some, nothing...

June 14 — Doctoral examination, and on the same day, an evaluation of the thesis.

June 19 — Defense of the doctoral thesis. Pontificum Institutum Angelicum de Urbe. Sententia de examine scripti (retinenda): Infrascripti examinatores ab Adm. R. P. Regente designati attente perlegimus Dissertationen ad gradum Doctoratus in S. Theologia super materiam: Doctrina de Fide apud S. Joannem de Cruce et iudicamus eam approbandam esse cum nota 9/10 ... Romae 14 mensis Junii anni 48. Examinatores Fr R. Garrigou-Lagrange OP, Fr P. Philippe.

The Angelicum Book with entries of the students' grades:

> **Facultas theologiae–laurea, pn 59 Wojtyla Carolus cracovien., dies 14-16 examen praevium; vota 50/50. Dissertatio vota 18/20; defensio 19-6 vota 50/50. Nota complexiva 283/300/300, prof. fidei 23-3.49.**
> **Exitus examinis. Examen praevium; vota 50 ex 50, defensio dissertationis: vota 50 ex 50. Subscriptio praesidis examinis–p. Thomas Carde [Rector of Angelicum].** (Documents–Angelicum Archives)

For the formal announcement of the doctorate the thesis had to be published, which was beyond the means of the poor student from Poland.

Currently, the thesis has appeared in a few languages: La fede secondo S. Giovanni della Croce, Roma 1979 (Pontificia Universitas S. Tomaso–Herder); Prefazione del Card. Pierre-Paul Philippe O.P. Traduzione e note del P. Raimondo M. Sorgia O.P.

La Fe segum San Juan de la Cruz, traduccion e introduccion de Alvaro Huerga, Madrid 1979, Libreria Editrice Vaticana, Biblioteca de Autores Cristianos.

La foi selon saint Jean de la Croix, preface de Pierre-Paul Philippe O.P.

Pastoral activity during the period of study in Rome. Visiting the parish of Garbatello on December 3, 1978, as the first after his election, the Pope reminisced: "I came here almost each Sunday to assist in the pastoral duties during the time directly after the War when I was studying in Rome. Certain moments from that period are still vivid in my memory..." The parish was established in 1930 and was assigned to the jurisdiction of the diocese. In 1956 it counted 2,220 inhabitants, currently 18,500. It is located in the southern suburbs of Rome, neighboring the parish of St. Paul outside the Walls. Half of the population consisted of workers, in 1946 — very poor.

June 25 — Return to Poland from the studies.

July 8 — Receives a nominating decree, the so-called "aplikata," as Vicar[11] in Niegowic near Gdow.

July 18 — "On July 18 a reunion took place in Wadowice on the occasion of the tenth anniversary of the secondary school final examinations. The subsequent reunions took place in the years: 1953, 1958, 1963, 1968, 1973. The last reunion, moved from the year 1978, took place in September of 1979 ... in Rome!

We organized the first reunion together with the graduates of a parallel class of the Michalina Moscicka Secondary School for Girls. In the morning, as was customary in our school times, we went to participate in the Holy Mass which was said by Rev. Karol Wojtyla in the chapel of the Catholic Home at the parish church. During the Mass Rev. Karol Wojtyla delivered a sermon in which he reminisced that the place from which he was speaking as a priest was once a place of his performances as an actor of an amateur theater (before the war the chapel was a hall of the Catholic Home used for staging theatrical productions). After the Mass we proceeded to the school building and we took seats in the same classroom and in the same order as in our final year. I was sitting at Karol Wojtyla's left. J. Krolikiewicz, the school principal before the war, read the students' names from a list of attendance, which survived the war. Everyone present would share with others what had happened to him or her during those past ten years. With regard to our absent classmates —anyone who knew anything at all about any of them would share it with the rest of us gathered there. Out of the total of forty something students, about 13 of our colleagues fell during the war or simply died since 1938.

---

[11] curate, associate pastor

(The above account was sent by Antoni Bohdanowicz).

July 28 - Arrived at Niegowic (Elenchus sacerdotum par. Niegowic). Father Kazimierz Buzala was pastor there at the time, a priest highly esteemed by the Prince Archbishop Metropolitan Sapieha. Many notable priests of the diocese passed through Niegowic. Father Wojtyla resides at the vicarage. Co-vicar — Father Kazimierz Ciuba. Father Wojtyla taught at village schools in Wiatowice, Pierzchow, Cichawa, Nieznanowice. He is transported by horse and buggy, always absorbed in reading during the trip. (According to parish records and information provided by Mrs. Maria Trzaska, principal of the school at Niegowic)

> NIEGOWIC — village, county of Wieliczka, on a stream flowing from Szczyglow into the Raba, situated along the road from Marszowice to Krakuszowice. The area is hilly with fertile argillaceous[12] soil. At the northern edge of the village there stood a wooden church and the rectory buildings, to the south a large manor with outbuildings of a sizable estate. Except for a few Jews, the inhabitants are Roman Catholic. The area of the larger estate consists of 264 morgs[13] of fields, 30 morgs of meadow and gardens, and 3 morgs of pasture; the smaller estate consists of 172 morgs of fields, 36 morgs of meadow, and 3 morgs of pasture. Every fourth Wednes-day a market is held here. The Roman Catholic parish is one of the oldest, as it was established in 1049, and the original church burned down in 1761. Ten years later the current church was built, dedicated in 1788 by Bishop Janowski. Birth certificates have been preserved since 1717. According to Lib. Ben. by Dlugosz (I, 115 and II, 116) Niegowic had a parish church of the Assumption of the Blessed Virgin. The squire of the village was Jan Niewiarowski of the arms of Polkoza. The village had peasant land and a farm yielding tithe to the chapter of the Krakow cathedral, called Rzemiecicka, but actually to the vicar of the chapter. There is an elementary school and an institution for the poor here. The parish (Tarnow diocese, Wieliczka deanery) encompasses Krakuszowice, Nieznanowice, Niewiarow, Cichawa, Liplas, Wiatowice, Pierzchow, Pierzchowiec, Dabrowica with Wieniec, Podegrodzie, Jaroszowka, and Wolka, with a general count of 5,010 Roman Catholics. (Geographic Dictionary of the Polish Kingdom and other Slavic Countries, Warsaw, 1886, vol. VII, 1886, p. 75)
>
> "I went from Krakow to Gdow by bus, and from there a local man gave me a ride in his cart to the village of Marszowice; from there he advised me to take a shortcut through the fields on foot. I could already see the church in Niegowic in the distance. It was harvest time. I walked through the fields of grain with the crops in part already reaped, and in part still waving in the wind. When I finally reached the territory of the Niegowic parish, I knelt down and kissed the ground. It was a gesture I had learned from St. John Maria Vianney." (John Paul II, *Gift and Mystery*, New York: Doubleday 1996, pp. 61-62).

In Niegowic he led a Living Rosary together with Father Ciuba. He established a drama circle, which under his direction prepared and presented a play by Kossak-Szczucka *The Awaited Guest*, in the hall of the

---

[12] containing clay
[13] Morg is a land measure equivalent to 1.4 acres

Catholic House (currently the GS {Co-op}). He is remembered for his generosity in dealing with the poor. He cared for three underage children of a former estate employee who had passed away. He officiated at 13 marriages, the first of Stanislaw Substelny with Zofia Strojna — October 20, 1948, from Marszowice. He christened 48 children, the first on April 5, 1948 — Eugeniusz Wegrzyn, son of Antoni and Eleonora. In 1949 he participated in organizing a committee for the construction of a new church (the old one was transferred to Metkow–the belfry remained.)

August 1, Sunday — He celebrated his first High Mass at the parish church in Niegowic (cf. Archbishop Wojtyla's statement of March 14, 1968).

August 15 — *Odpust*[14] at the Niegowic parish. It was announced to the invited priests that the Vicar of Niegowic, Father Wojtyla, who recently returned from studies abroad, would speak after dinner about the situation of the religious youth in France and Belgium. Father Wojtyla was quite late for dinner, detained in the confessional by penitents, which the priests took badly, feeling offended by the young priest's absence. The lecture, however, completely altered the atmosphere, creating great interest and admiration. (According to an account by Father Jan Kosciolek, one of the participants)

November 10 (date of the Dean's Office stamp) — Application for admission to the doctoral examination:

> **To the Office of the Dean of the Department of Theology of the Jagiellonian University in Krakow. The undersigned, enclosing the dissertation entitled *De fide apud S. Joannem a Cruce*, requests admission to the doctoral examination. The dissertation was written during studies at the Pontifical University "Angelicum" in Rome, and defended during the summer examination session of the current year. However, the aforementioned thesis was already commenced during studies at the Department of Theology of the Jagiellonian University in Krakow. A master's degree has been conferred by this Department, certificate enclosed, together with documents confirming the results achieved at the "Angelicum." Rev. Karol Wojtyla (Niegowic, near Bochnia)**

The results achieved at the Angelicum (according to a note prepared by Rev. Karol Wojtyla for the Dean of the Department of Theology of the Jagiellonian University and enclosed with the application for admission to the doctoral examination):

> **pro examine praevio 50 pts. of 50 possible,**
> **pro defensionate dissertationis 50/50,**
> **general result 100/100, i.e. is summa cum laude.**

---

[14] See Glossary.

Resignation from the position of junior assistant:

L. 8434/46

Krakow, November 19, 1948

To the Office of the Dean of the Department of Theology of the Jagiellonian University:

In conjunction with his letter dated the 11th of this month, L. 594/46, I am informing you that, due to Rev. Karol Wojtyla's resignation from the position of junior assistant of the Department on November 30 of this year, I order that salary payments to him cease effective on that day.

(-) Franciszek Walter
Rector of the Jagiellonian University

November 24 — The date of issuance of the Diploma of Master of Theology of the Jagiellonian University:

Diploma of Master of Theology. Jagiellonian University in Krakow, Department of Theology. L. 284/48,

[Karol Wojtyla] completed the required philosophical and theological studies (clandestine) at the Theological Seminary in Krakow in the years 1942-1945, which, on the basis of the resolution by the Council of the Department of Theology of the Jagiellonian University, dated February 16, 1945, were credited by the Department of Theology of the Jagiellonian University, studies at the Department of Theology of the Jagiellonian University in 1945-1945/46, as well as at the "Angelicum" Institute in Rome in 1946/47 ... He passed the following examinations: Christian Philosophy and History of Philosophy with a grade of Very Good, Biblical Studies of the Old and the New Testament, the History of the Roman Catholic Church, Fundamental Theology, Dogmatic Theology, General and Particular Moral Theology, Canon Law, Pastoral Theology, including Liturgy and Homiletics, with grades of Excellent, Pedagogy, Catechetical Instruction, Methodology — with grades of Very Good; further he presented, and received a grade of Very Good for his Master's Thesis on the topic: *The Concept of the Means of Uniting the Soul with God in the Teaching of St. John of the Cross*. (Archives of the Jagiellonian University: WT II 2530)

An evaluation of the Doctoral Thesis by Rev. Karol Wojtyla (M.A.), by Father Wladyslaw Wicher:

...the thesis has two parts: analysis and synthesis. In the analysis the author dissects an entire sequence of texts from St. John of the Cross dispersed throughout his ascetic mystic works and juxtaposes them with scholastic teaching about faith ... The accomplishment of the author in this dissertation is the demonstration of the psychological experience of faith and of those states which evoke that faith in the soul, particularly through contemplation. The comparison of the perception of objects recognized naturally by the senses with the vision of God attained through faith both in His essential similitude and obscurity, is something completely novel and original in St. John {of the Cross}. Currently, the idea of religion as a psychic act in personal experience has been given more attention, and it is this very experience that is the subject of the author's inquiries based on the writings of St. John of the Cross.

The analysis demonstrates the inquiring and very precise mind of the

author — so precise that the reader frequently loses himself in the preponderance of details ... The Latin is generally correct, the terminology mostly scholastic. In the final analysis, the author is a bit too much of a dialectic, too little of a philologist...

A report on Rev. Karol Wojtyla's Doctoral Thesis. Rev. Ignacy Rozycki:

> ...In the analytic section [the author] exposes St. John's views on faith from the point of view of theology, psychology, and, above all, from the ascetic-mystical perspective. He points to the role of faith at various stages of mystic life as a source of union with God... The dissertation ... represents the first reflection on the entire question of faith and its role in the mystic teaching of St. John... (Archives, JU: WT II 273)

December 2 — Admission of Rev. Karol Wojtyla's Doctoral Dissertation: at its regular meeting, the Council of the Department of Theology decided unanimously to accept the doctoral dissertations by Rev. Grzybek and Rev. Wojtyla. (Archives JU: WT II 19)

December 16 — A regular meeting of the Council of the Department of Theology of the Jagiellonian University — "Father Wicher moved that a Doctorate in Theology be conferred upon Rev. Wojtyla and proposed a final grade of Very Good. It was unanimously seconded." (From the Council Minutes).

December 16 — Conferment of the Doctorate. In place of the Rector — Rev. Prof. Dr. Aleksy Klawek, Rev. Prof. Dr. Wadyslaw Wicher conferred the degree; the title of the dissertation: *Doctrina de fide apud S. Joannem de Cruce*.[15] (Archives of JU: WT II273)

---

[15] The Doctrine of Faith According to St. John of the Cross.

1949

March 17 — Recalled from Niegowic to St. Florian's Parish in Krakow. The Parish of St. Florian (an account by Rev. Czeslaw Obtulowicz, a vicar in this same parish at the time): in May of 1945 the parish was taken over by Msgr. Tadeusz Kurowski, who, until that time, was the academic chaplain at the Church of St. Anne. A group of students transferred with him. Father Wojtyla began visiting dormitories and student boarding houses, establishing active relations. A group to study St. Thomas *(Summa)* and a group to sing Gregorian chant (Joachim Gudel and the superb organist Franciszek Przystal) were established. The pastor himself was involved with the parents, the younger altar boys were under Father Obtulowicz's care, and the older ones under Father Wojtyla's. The liturgical education was based on the German edition by O. Parsch. The work with the parents and the self-education activities were characterized by not separating the intelligentsia from the simple people.

The Living Rosary — on the feast days of the Blessed Virgin the feast of each "rose" was celebrated. People of varying social status would gather at the home of one of the members belonging to the "rose" and all three priests would attend. This resulted in great closeness to people.

Koleda[1] — the entire parish was traversed, contact was made with the sick. The ill had been afraid to call the priest before, but now a continuous and lively rapport was established, with frequent visits from the priests. The Day of the Sick was celebrated very solemnly.

Father Wojtyla participated in one of the first pilgrimages to Kalwaria (Sept. 10, 1950). Afterwards he remarked: a priest does not have much to do there, everything is splendidly organized by the laity.

In this period he took Zdzislaw Skrzynski, a priest from the Lvov diocese, into his apartment (two rooms). The priest had no place to live; this was purely a gesture of good will. He was known for the ease with which he distributed money and things to the needy. Sometimes he would give Father Obtulowicz money for safekeeping.

August 20 — He administered the Sacrament of Baptism for the first time at St. Florian's parish, christening Barbara Anna, daughter of Tadeusz Pylko and Anna Matuszynska (till the end of his tenure, i.e. August 1951, he christened 229 children).

August 21 — For the first time, as a vicar of St. Florian's parish, he

---

[1] See Glossary.

officiates at the marriage of Zygmunt Stanislaw Szymoniak with Janina Gebica (as a vicar, he blessed 160 marriages in this parish).

In the summer season

As a vicar of the collegiate Church of St. Florian in Krakow, Rev. Wojtyla administered the archives, which contained much valuable material. On the suggestion of the Provost, Father Tadeusz Kurowski, he consulted with me several times, in my capacity as a historian experienced in professional archival work. (Prof. Dr. Jozef Mitkowski)

November 20 — Entry in the records of St. Florian parish announcing the start of conferences for university students to be delivered by Rev. Karol Wojtyla: "Beginning on Thursday — systematic lectures on the teachings of the faith. The first lecture: *Meditations on the Essence of Man.* Later, on the basis of handwritten-notes, these conferences were compiled into a typescript entitled *Meditations on the Essence of Man, In Our Image and Likeness,* Krakow 1951. (Teresa Skawinska, *He Will Give Away Love,* issued by the Polish Catholic Mission in France, Paris 1997, p. 26).

The students turned to us regarding the possibility of allowing their participation in religious conferences held specifically for them. Fulfilling this request, beginning Thursday and every week thereafter at 8:00 p.m., there will be lectures for the young people. Their topic will be a systematic exposition of the teachings of the faith (the conferences were conducted by Father Kurowski and Father Wojtyla.

December 18 — On Thursday, from 6 to 9 p.m., an "Evening of Contemplation" for young men. On Friday at 6:30 a.m., a "dialogue" Mass (recited) (led by Father K. Wojtyla)

In the academic year 1948/49, Professor Stefan Szuman conducted a seminar in the subject of ethology (in Krakow at 13 Manifestu Lipcowego Street, 2nd floor). Father Karol Wojtyla and Father Jozef Rozwadowski participated. (According to an account by a participant in the seminar). During the engagement at St. Florian's he studies English with Mrs. Adela Duninowa (at Pijarska Street, ground floor of the Czartoryski Museum).

As a young priest (vicar of St. Florian's parish) he sometimes attended the theater (at that time at 5 Warszawska Street) and would stay for the discussions following the performances. He blessed the marriage of our colleagues at the Church of St. Florian. He celebrated Mass for the company's intention on significant anniversaries of the theater. In 1950 he participated (praying silently) in a dedication ceremony wherein a box containing the documents of the Rhapsodic Theater was cemented into the foundation of an axis under the moving stage of a new theater being constructed at 21 Bohaterow Stalingradu[2] Street (currently "Teatr Kameralny"[3]). The entire

---

[2] Heroes of Stalingrad Street

[3] Chamber Theater

theater staff was present, as were the construction workers (in those times an official dedication would not have been possible). He wrote a review of the production of *King-Spirit* which, under the title of *Gold and Azure Legends,* was the premiere performance inaugurating the new period of the Rhapsodic Theater's activity after its restitution in 1957. ("TP", January 19, 1958, by-line Andrzej Jawien). (Danuta Michalowska)

1950

He fulfilled the function of a vicar at St. Florian's parish in Krakow, concerning himself with the student population, continued academic research.

January 1 — Became a regular member of the Theological Society in Krakow.

Winter 1950 — Organized courses for engaged couples at St. Florian's church. This was a complete novelty at the time. It was primarily student couples (Institute of Technology) who participated in the courses. The lectures were given by various invited speakers. (According to an account by H. Trojanowska).

March 13 — Conducted retreats for university students. In the May issue of *Tygodnik Powszechny* a poem entitled "Piesn o blasku wody"[4] appears, signed with the first use here of one of the three pen-names used by Father Karol Wojtyla, Andrzej Jawien. The surname Jawien, common in the parish of Niegowic, the author's first pastoral assignment, was borrowed from there. By coincidence, Jan Parandowski {the writer} named the hero of his book *Powrot do Zycia*[5] with that very name. Father Wojtyla, however, was not yet familiar with the book. (According to an account by Anna Turowicz)

June 29-July 2 — He organized and led a closed retreat for male students at the Monastery of the Camaldolese Fathers at Bielany. The matters concerning the outlook on the world were given special consideration. Concurrently, at the initiative of Father Wojtyla, a similar retreat was held for female students from the same milieu, in Czerna at the Carmelite Sisters, and in Trzebnia.

October 4 — He participated in the funeral of Kazimierz Rumian, former principal of the school in Raciborowice, whom he used to meet during summer vacations of 1945-46. As he told the children of the deceased, he learned of his death from an obituary in the newspaper.

From the records of St. Florian's Parish in Krakow:

As of May 10, 1945, Msgr. Tadeusz Kurowski became administra-

---

[4] Song of the Brightness of the Water
[5] *Return to Life*

tor of St. Florian's Parish. As of Sept. 29, 1944, Father Czeslaw Obtulowicz was the first vicar. In the organization of duties the primary emphasis was placed on the cooperation of the priests with the parishioners and on the apostolate of the laity. The Circle concentrates on the Living Rosary, on organizing groups to care for the church, the needy and the ailing. Beginning in 1948, three-day retreats for the sick are organized. The sick are attended to with constant pastoral care.

The meetings of the Living Rosary are slowly transformed into conferences at which Gasparri's Great Catechism is discussed. About 500 people participate in this. At smaller gatherings, the Holy Scriptures are read (interest in the Bible is the fruit of the Christmastime pastoral visits). Altar servers, numbering approximately 10 in 1946, approach 100 in 1952. The mission of the Circle — the systematic education of boys in the Eucharistic spirit. Acceptance to the Circle is celebrated on the feasts of the patron saints, St. Stanislaw and St. Aloysius and is preceded by days of recollection for the older servers and their parents.

> **It was the wish of the pastors to involve the parents, therefore, conferences for the parents of the altar servers were systematically organized. At these conferences they were introduced to the main principles of educational psychology, as well as to the Liturgy. An enormous service in this area was rendered by Father Karol Wojtyla, who, under the Monsignor's guidance, organized the effort.** {Quote not attributed}

Groups of 5 to 6 boys were created. Meetings, outings, etc. were organized. Parish catechesis dates from 1949/50. Initially it encompassed the older and younger youth, as well as university students. The students themselves applied for this. Their conferences were led by the Monsignor or by Rev. Dr. Karol Wojtyla (catechesis was introduced in the parish despite the fact that religious instruction was offered in the schools).

Catechesis: the young people were divided into three groups: beginners, intermediate and advanced. Each of these groups was composed of smaller ones, so that there were 12 groups in all, besides catechetical groups for university students and for adults. The groups for adults were led by each of the parish priests in turn. The basis was Gasparri's *Catechism*. The catechesis of university students was led by Father Wojtyla.

1951

He spent the last year working as a vicar at St. Florian's Parish in Krakow.

There he worked with the students on the preparation of a liturgical celebration for February 2 and then — the celebration of the Lord's Passion. At that time a group of people more actively involved in the student ministry is formed, the group will later assume the name of "Milieu" (cf. the list of participants in: Teresa Skawinska, *He Will Give Away Love*, published by Polish Catholic Mission in France, Paris 1997, p. 40). He introduces the students to St. Thomas's *Summa*. He initiates get-togethers to sing Christmas carols and outdoor Masses during trips and excursions. He organized the "little choir." Its members would meet at first at St. Anne's academic church. Joachim Guder, a music conservatory student was the choirmaster. The choir prepared Gregorian chants. Wojtyla introduces recited Masses (in Latin); he distributes and lends copies of the "Roman Missal" published by the Benedictines of Tyniec (Teresa Skawinska, *He Will Give Away Love*, p. 39 and subsequent pages).

January — At the request of Father Karol Wojtyla, a group of students is brought to the church by the female students active in pastoral ministry within the academic community, and practices singing carols in order to lead the faithful in song during the Feast of the Purification of Our Lady {Candlemas}.

February 1 — He officiates at the marriage of Stanislaw Balewicz and Maria Dik at St. Florian's Church. Both of them were associated with the Rhapsodic Theater at the time.

February 2 — The first performance of the "little choir" at St. Florian's Church. Fr. Karol Wojtyla suggests congregating at the Holy Mass on Wednesdays at 6 a.m. and making an attempt to learn Gregorian chant. Both suggestions are accepted by the youth and from then on, each Wednesday a group of students from the Institute of Technology and the female students from the Jagiellonian University will meet at the Church of St. Florian at 6 a.m. to participate in the Holy Mass celebrated by Father Karol Wojtyla and to listen to his brief lectures. After the transfer of Father Wojtyla to St. Catherine's Church, the same group, somewhat enlarged, participated in Wednesday Holy Mass at the same hour, singing the "Gregorian" (Missa de Angelis). At that time a paraliturgical service also took place — reading of the Gospels, singing of psalms, poetry. There were more such services. Actors from the Rhapsodic Theater and students participated. Numerous rehearsals were held at Father Wojtyla's apartment. The actors were particularly involved, among them Tadeusz Szybowski and Jan Adamski and among the students — Jacek Fedorowicz.

Father Karol Wojtyla maintained active contact with Kotlarczyk's theater, attended rehearsals at 5 Warszawska Street, participated in discussions. He was also a friend and advisor; he assisted in many difficult private matters of the theater's actors. He blessed their marriages. (According to an account by Jan Adamski).

Lent — Student retreat at St. Anne's Church in Krakow. Topic: resentments.

Passion Sunday — For the conclusion of the retreat for university students (March 5 to March 8) which he conducted, he organized Passion services at St. Florian's Church — a reading of the Passion of Christ by lectors, a male choir (students of the Institute of Technology and of the Jagiellonian University), and a female choir. The actors from the Rhapsodic Theater and Father Wojtyla himself participated in the services.

Autobiography (submitted at the Jagiellonian University)

I was born on May 18, 1920 in Wadowice (province of Krakow), son of Karol Wojtyla and Emilia, née Kaczorowska. I attended elementary school as well as high school (neo-classical type) at the place of my birth. There, too, I passed my final {high school} examination in May of 1938, and taking advantage of the postponement of the obligatory service in the army, commenced studies at the Humanities Department of the Jagiellonian University in Krakow (Polish philology). In 1939 the war interrupted these studies, and the conditions of living during the occupation forced me to work as a laborer in the "Solvay" works in Borek Falecki near Krakow from 1940 to 1944. This job saved me from being sent to forced labor in Germany and made it possible for me to begin studies at the clandestine courses at the Department of Theology of the Jagiellonian University in Krakow, beginning in October 1942. In this fashion, I completed the first two years of my theological studies working as a laborer. In August of 1944, as a result of the quick retreat of the occupying forces, it was possible to assemble the clandestine theology students at the Prince Metropolitan's Seminary in Krakow, where, after the liberation, I was able to continue my studies at the Department of Theology of the Jagiellonian University until 1946. In October and November of the same year, at the beginning of the last year of my studies, I received Holy Orders (ordination to the priesthood, November 1, 1946). Afterwards I went abroad at the request of Prince Adam Stefan Cardinal Sapieha, Archbishop of Krakow, and on the basis of a passport issued by the M.S.Z.[6], to undertake further theology studies in Rome. I studied at the "Angelicum" University from 1946 to 1948, and upon my return presented the dissertation entitled *Zagadnienia wiary w dzielach sw. Jana od Krzyza*[7] to the Department of Theology of the Jagiellonian University in Krakow, as a doctoral thesis. On its merits I was promoted in December of 1948, receiving the title of the Doctor of Theology at the Jagiellonian University in Krakow. Further, from July 30, 1948 through August 17, 1949, I was assigned to the parish of Niegowic near Bochnia, fulfilling the duties of a vicar. Effective August 17, 1949, I was transferred to the same position at St. Florian's Parish in Krakow, where I have remained to the present time.

[Rev. Karol Wojtyla as well as the entire biography handwritten]

Krakow, April 8, 1951   (Archives of the Jagiellonian University)

---

6 Ministry of Foreign Affairs
7 Problem of Faith in the Works of St. John of the Cross

May 4 — After a month-long preparation, the Gregorian Mass "de Angelis" was sung for the first time at St. Florian's Church. The male choir — students of the Institute of Technology and of the Jagiellonian University, the female choir — largely the students who were residents of the dormitory run by the Sisters of Nazareth. The choir was prepared by J. Gudel. Father Wojtyla, also engaged in the preparations, was the initiator of the whole undertaking.

June — He presided at the day of contemplation for the Congregation of the Children of Mary. The congregation was established by Roza Lubienska and was dissolved in 1960. The day of contemplation took place at the convent of the Sisters of the Presentation in Krakow.

On the Eve of Corpus Christi — Participation in the funeral of Emilia de Laveaux Karcz (one of the first seven women accepted to study at the Academy of Fine Arts in Krakow.) As told by the daughter of the deceased:

> I asked him to celebrate a requiem Mass at the cemetery and to conduct the funeral. Father Wojtyla said that, regrettably, he could not do so, as that day was the Eve of Corpus Christi, which demanded much time for the preparation of everything ... Father Wojtyla did consider it, but could not promise to fulfill my request ... The Carmelites of Rakowicka Street agreed to conduct the funeral. As I was kneeling ... with my family at the church during the Mass which had just started, I suddenly saw Father Wojtyla making his way through the congregation ... with a surplice under his arm ... He participated in the funeral service, and then led the procession to the gravesite. (Jozefina Pochwalska)

July 23 — Cardinal Adam Stefan Sapieha dies.

July 26 — The body of Prince Cardinal is transported to the Wawel Cathedral with the participation of the entire clergy of Krakow.

July 27 — Cardinal Adam Sapieha's funeral at Wawel. The Primate of Poland presided over the liturgy (cf. An address of April 17, 1976).

August 26 — The marriage of Stanislaw Swiatek and Zofia Zorek. The last one blessed by Father Wojtyla as a vicar.

August 27 — The baptism of Danuta Mordel — it is the last christening performed by Fr. Wojtyla as a vicar of St. Florian's Parish.

September 1 — Archbishop E. Baziak grants Father Wojtyla a sabbatical (until 1953) to write a post-doctoral work and prepare for the examination qualifying for assistant-professorship.

From this moment on all his pastoral duties must be coordinated with the Archbishop. At the express wish of the same, he moves to a house on Kanoniczna Street, where he shares an apartment with Rev.

Prof. Ignacy Rozycki. Over the next two years he celebrated Mass at St. Catherine's Church and later at the Mariacki Church.[8] He continued to work in the academic apostolate at St. Florian and assumed the apostolate of the health services (this was recommended to him by Archbishop Baziak during his ministry at St. Florian. It has not been possible to establish the date of this assignment.) The Gregorian choir moves to St. Catherine's Church.

> After leaving the position of vicar at St. Florian's Parish in Krakow, he remained the chaplain for the academic community at that church until 1958. Each Wednesday from 8:15 to 9:30 p.m., lectures and discussions on ethics were held throughout the entire academic year. Through all the years he led academic retreats at St. Florian (in the fourth week of Lent). On every First Friday of the month at 8:00 a.m., he said Mass with a homily for the academic group at St. Anne's collegiate church. In addition to the regular meetings, he willingly attended private meetings and gave individual consultations. (According to an account by Father T. Matras, participant of meetings — a student at the time.)

Sept. 25 — His name is written in the registry (pos. 2) of the house at 19 Kanonicza Street.

October 7 — Father Wojtyla baptized Anna Malgorzata at the Church of St. Szczepan {Stephen} in Krakow. On this occasion he visited the home of her parents, Edward and Izabela Owoc in the Second Dormitory at Blonia Krakowskie.

> I met Karol Wojtyla when he was not yet a priest, in the months just following the end of the war (1945). When later, after his return from Rome with a Master of Philosophy degree, I visited the vicarage at St. Florian, Rev. Doctor was interested in the philosophy of phenomenology as represented by Professor Roman Ingarden, who was my professor until the time when the department {of philosophy} was closed. At St. Florian's Church, not far from the Institute of Technology where I was a student, he organized lectures for engaged couples in 1950. I attended them with my future wife ... After the birth of our daughter ... our life's concern was finding an apartment in the overcrowded city. Rev. Doctor did not only minister to us, but also assisted me in the translations of foreign language texts, and found an apartment for us at that time. (Edward Owoc)

November 4 — His Patronal feast day on Kanonicza Street. Gift: a student's cap.

Advent — A day of recollection for the students (at St. Catherine's Church), topic: God's grace in specific sacraments. This year a text by Father Wojtyla, *Rozwazania o istocie czlowieka*,[9] was mimeographed:

> **I. (Introduction). The basis of our knowledge of man. Cognition. Experience as the basis of thought. The principle of causality.**

---

[8] Church of the Blessed Virgin Mary, in Market Square, one of the most famous of Krakow's churches, dating back to the 14th C.

[9] Reflections on the Essence of Man

II. Analysis. Overview of the subject. Inference from "culture." The spheres and levels of human experience. The senses. Cognition and sense perception. An analysis of the sphere of desire. Freedom of will.

III. Synthesis. An attempt to define the spiritual soul. The substantiality and immortality of the soul. The union of the soul with the body. A few remarks on the idea of the human person.

IV. Theology. In the light of Revelation. At the sources. The principle of new life. The first truth of Christian humanism.

Also (probably) this year — the text O poznawalnosci i poznaniu Boga:[10]

I. The concept of God: the idea of existence. Dogmatic teaching. Defining the parameters of the question. Toward the essence of God.

II. Supernatural knowledge.

Within the realm of the mystery of the Revelation. Infused knowledge. The problem of substantiation. "Motiva credibilatis." A theological analysis of faith: Faith is the result of supernatural grace.

Both texts comprised the summary of material discussed at the weekly meetings at the quarters of KSMM in Krakow (see January 1973).

In 1951, he describes his command of foreign languages in a personal questionnaire submitted at the Jagiellonian University: fluent in speech ("in writing" was crossed out by Father Wojtyla): French and Italian; weak: English, Spanish, German. (Archives, JU: S III 246)

---

[10] On God as Knowable and On the Cognition of God

1952

He began the second year of the sabbatical and worked on a post-doctoral disertation to qualify for assistant professorship. He continues the pastoral ministry to the students at St. Florian's, where the core of the group is based on the student Gregorian choir established in 1950. He celebrated Mass at St. Catherine's and resided with Rev. Prof. I. Rozycki on Kanonicza Street.

Lent — He conducted a student retreat at the Church of the Sisters of the Sacred Heart in Krakow on Garncarska Street.

Spring — Excursion with the choir into the environs of Krakow.

Palm Sunday — Went to Zakopane with the "little choir." Holy Mass at the "Ksiezowka." Visit with Mr. and Mrs. Skawinski, with the Albertine Brothers at Kalatowki. Viewing of crocuses.

May — Together with the "little choir" he visited the Camaldolese at Bielany, the Benedictines in Tyniec, Mr. and Mrs. Abrahamowicz in Kobierzyn.

June — An excursion with the students to Beskidy.[1] Arrival at Kozy, where the assistant pastor is Father Francis Macharski, a friend of Father K. Wojtyla (the pastor is Father Zygmunt Laczek.) The men spend the night in Kozy, the women in Bielsko. The next day (Sunday), the Holy Mass is at 6 a.m., followed by a hike into the mountains. (Excursions and days of contemplation with "the little choir" are also organized in later years — 1955, 1956)

June — He is invited again by the Congregation of Ladies Children of Mary to lead the Days of Contemplation (at the Convent of the Sisters of the Presentation in Krakow).

July 4 (5?) Czaniec – conducted the funeral of Franciszka Wojtyla, wife of Pawel (Pawel was the brother of Maciej, Father Wojtyla's grand-father).

From the record of the "little choir" at St. Catherine's Church in 1952/53:

> "In the Year of Our Lord 1952, October 14, or about that time, the chorus of St. Anne and the chorus of St. Florian fused and became the chorus of St. Catherine."
> At that time the chorus sang the permanent and variable parts of the Holy Mass. Fr. Wojtyla was in charge, referred to in the chronicle as "Benefactor of the Choir — the Spiritual Personage." He said daily Mass at St. Catherine's at 6 a.m., on Sundays and holidays at 7 a.m.

---

[1] An area of foothills of the Tatra mountains.

... It was a difficult task and a group of barely a few remained until the end of the Cardinal's stay in Krakow. (Maria Bucholc)

1953

This is the last year of the sabbatical (since 1951). He said Holy Mass at The Basilica of The Blessed Virgin Mary, remained involved in the ministry to the members of health service and continues to work with the students. The "little choir" established in 1949 still exists. A group of people which became known as the *Srodowisko*[2] is becoming more clearly defined.

Among other activities, at the quarters of the Catholic Society of Young Men, "Swit" {Dawn} (presently the home of the Krakow Philharmonic), he conducted Thomistic lectures/seminars attended by the students and a few assistants. The meetings took place weekly. They were based on the texts published in the monthly *Znak*.

He completes his thesis in preparation to the exam qualifying for assistant professorship.

> **It was in January 1953. One of us meant to organize a ski excursion of a few days to the Gorce Mountains, and suggested inviting Father Wojtyla to join us; we had known him from his pastoral work among the students – at this time we attended lectures and discussions which he led at the Catholic Society for Young Men located in the Philharmonic Building. We were, however, uncertain regarding Father Wojtyla's skiing skills and with this in mind, without declaring our actual intentions, we invited him on a two-day ski excursion to Bukowina and Zakopane. He accepted our invitation eagerly. We had to prepare skis for him as well as bindings to attach to the plain black shoes usually worn by the clergy. The fitting was done by one of us at the Institute of Physics of the Jagiellonian University on Golebia Street and then taken to Kanonicza Street where Father Wojtyla resided with Rev. Prof. Father Rozycki.**
> **The three of us (Karol Wojtyla, Andrzej Hrynkiewicz and Jacek Hennel) departed overnight on the train (this was around January 24, 1953) and by morning we found ourselves at Poronin, where after the Mass celebrated by Fr. Wojtyla, we were welcomed by the local pastor and invited to breakfast. From this excursion to Bukowina we remember good skiing conditions and a dinner at the home of an acquaintance of ours, farmer Jan Kramarz and his wife. Next we traveled to Zakopane, where Father Wojtyla spent the night at "Ksiezowka" {priests' place} in Kuznice. The next day the fourth participant (Stanislaw Szymczuk) joined us and together with Father Wojtyla, after Mass of course, we set out on a skiing excursion from Gubalowka through Koscielisko to Hala Pisana. From Kiry we returned by bus to Zakopane, and by evening we were already returning by train to Krakow.**

---

[2] See Glossary.

A small episode: upon the suggestion that we purchase first class tickets, Father Wojtyla protested saying: "No, no, we travel with the people!" During the excursion it became apparent that Father Wojtyla, who had not skied since high school, quickly regained his former skills and managed very well. Thus his test of skiing proved successful, and we could invite him without hesitation for the excursion to the Gorce Mountains, which initiated a whole series of further skiing trips. (Prof. Dr. Jacek Hennel, Prof. Dr. Andrzej Hrynkiewicz, Dr. Stanislaw Szymczuk–Institute of Nuclear Physics in Krakow)

End of February — Asked by Mrs. Helena Szkocka, he visited a former prisoner of Ravensbruck and a friend of Mrs. Szkocka, who was ill with cancer. The patient, not particularly religious, gave in to persuasion and agreed to a visit by the priest. Later (at the end of March of this year), already in the hospital, she asked for the same priest. Father Wojtyla came to the hospital, spoke with her at length and administered the sacraments. (According to an account by Helena Szkocka).

April 6 — Poraj. He officiates at the marriage of Jadwiga and Stanislaw Kozlowski. * April 7 — First joint pilgrimage of the group to Jasna Gora. * April 19 — Excursion (with the youth) to Jaworze, Blatnia, Bystra.

From the records of the "little choir" established at St. Florian's:

Around the Resurrection of Christ {Easter-time} in April of 1953, the Benefactor of our choir [Father Karol Wojtyla] and its conductor unexpectedly departed for a few days to the mountains. "Standing" on their boards {skis}, wound down the severe mountains. However, not being adept at the drollery of this type ... they were greatly battered and returned post haste to Krakow in a sorry state...

May — Excursion on foot (with the youth): Makow, Pcim, Myslenice.

May 17 — Excursion: Kozy, Magorka, Zywiec. In Zywiec — officiates at the marriage of a couple connected with the group * June 21-22 — Mountain excursion with the *Srodowisko* (ca. 10 people) Rabka, Lubon, Strzebel, Lubogoszcz, Snieznica, Cwilin, Kasina. * July 22-23 — Excursion with the youth: Zywiec, Romanka, Jelesnia, Huciska, Madahora, Leskowiec, Czartak.

July 22 — A letter from Father Karol Wojtyla to Prof. Stefan Swiezawski is dated this day:

Rev. Prof. Wicher has informed me that the Department of Theology of the Jagiellonian University has decided to turn to you for a critique of my dissertation to qualify for the assistant professorship ... In conjunction with this I allowed myself to deliver a copy of the dissertation to you and now further ask your kind consideration. I trust that your experienced judgment will assist the college of professors and the author of the dissertation to extract its real values as well as any actual drawbacks.

August 3-15 — Excursion to the Bieszczady Mountains — 17 people * August 3 — Arrival at Ustrzyki Dolne. The first outdoor Holy Mass * August 4 — Arrival at Ustrzyki Gorne * August 5 — Ustrzyki Gorne. Tarnica, Halicz, Ustrzyki Gorne * August — Ustrzyki Gorne, Polonina Carynska, Polonina Wetlinska, Smerek, Cisna. 16 hours of marching with a heavy backpack (20kg), which contained liturgical vessels, a chasuble and other vestments. The last 4 hours in the rain * August 8 — Cisna, Wolosan, Chryszczata, Duszatyn, Komancza; here a Mass in the church * August 10 — Komancza, Tarnawka * August 11 — Tarnawka, Rymanow, Lubatowka (hospitality provided by Father Domino) * August 12 — Lubatowa–Hyrowa * August 13 — The longest daytime trek, ca. 40 km: Hyrowa — Magura Watkowska. * August 14 — A High Mass was celebrated on the slope of Magura (Father Wojtyla explained to the participants of the excursion that, in the absence of the liturgical garb of the appropriate color, regulations required that the Mass be sung) — a hike to Hanczowa * August 15 — Hanczowa–Krynica.

This excursion was recalled by Father Wojtyla with special fondness. He had adequate time for meditation, for which he would lag behind alone apart from the group of wanderers. Here the custom of conversations with individual participants began. This form of ministry was practiced during all subsequent excursions. (According to accounts by the participants).

August 8 — A letter of Rev. Prof. Wicher to Prof. Swiezawski concerning the admission of Father Wojtyla to the assistant professorship:

> **On behalf of the colleagues in the Department of Theology at JU I turn to you, Highly Venerable Professor, with the respectful plea to accept the thesis and the evaluation of the dissertation by Rev. Dr. Karol Wojtyla entitled *An Evaluation of the Feasibility of Building a Christian Ethic on the Principles of Max Scheler*. It is clear that this evaluation and dissertation is in the character of private satisfaction for the author only, without any consequences in state law. Rev. Dr. Karol Wojtyla intends to be qualified by me in the area of moral theology. Publishing is currently impossible, even in part, and the ministry, where my colleagues in Warsaw have unofficially sought information, is not opposed to leaving doctorates and applications for assistant professorship in Departments of Theology under the former system, and thus we undertake such private and non-binding applications...**
> **(Prof. S. Swiezawski's archives)**

Turn of August to September — Kayak excursion on the Brda River — 5 days, 9 people. The first kayak excursion. Daily outdoor Masses. Daily long treks, great exertion. The rafts floating on the river are very disruptive. Interesting conversations and discussions by the campfire. At the end of the day — group prayer. (According to accounts by the participants)

September 15-25 — Excursion: from Sucha to Krynica (Babia Gora — Polica — Gorce)

Beginning in October — he lectures on Catholic social ethics to seminarians — students of the 4th and 5th year at JU (2 hours weekly).

November 29 — A day of recollection for the youth at the Ursuline Convent in Krakow. Topic: The liturgy of the first Sunday of Advent.

November 30 - December 3 — Completion of the proceedings for admission to assistant professorship at the Department of Theology of the Jagiellonian University * November 30 — Special meeting of the Council of the Department, voting on the acceptance of the dissertation *An Attempt at Formulating Christian Ethics According to Max Scheler's System* (175 pages of typed manuscript). Reviewers: S. Swiezawski from KUL (The Catholic University of Lublin}, Father A. Usowicz and Father W. Wicher from JU (all professors). Results of the vote: unanimously affirmative. All members of the Department Council were present * December 1 — An informal examination for admission to assistant professorship. Voting: all vote affirmatively * December 3 — A special meeting of the Council of the Department of Theology of the Jagiellonian Univesity: a lecture by Father Karol Wojtyla for the admission to assistant professorship, entitled *Analysis of the Act of Faith in View of the Philosophy of Values.* The lecture was unanimously approved. Then the entire process of application for admission to assistant professorship was voted upon (all voted for acceptance) and it was decided that K. Wojtyla be presented for approval by the Ministry of Higher Education as an Assistant Professor in Ethics and Moral Theology. "All members of the Department Council present. One Abstention." (The rest of the members: support for the decision). (According to the minutes of the meeting)

Reviews of the dissertation (fragments):

Prof. S. Swiezawski: [this thesis] sets the way for all other similar attempts to use various philosophies to interpret the many Christian teachings ... Superbly constructed methodical flow of deductions yields a comprehensive, clear and in-depth solution to the stated problem ... Besides this major achievement, it appears to me, the author was able to accomplish a second important thing, namely deduct the system of ethics contained therein solely from sources of Christian Revelation ... Further, the very presentation of Scheler's ethical views is not only a distillation of fragments of his writings, but an attempt to comprehend the vital connections within that system ... The author also emerges successfully from the difficult challenge presented by the exposition of Scheler's views, given most often by himself in a most complicated manner. It must be further emphasized that certain parts of the thesis are simply superb ..., that the author summons up good, original and well thought-out formulas ... The author's ideas expressed on the last pages of the conclusion of the dissertation are truly fruitful ... The

broadness of the author's perspective shows through these assertions, not yielding to the influence of the essentially negative conclusion regarding the usefulness of Scheler's system for scholarly discussion of Christian ethics... the thesis represents a valuable contribution to the Polish scholarly tradition ... I consider the thesis as very valuable and adequately meeting the requirements for acceptance to an assistant professorship. Krakow, November 11, 1953.

Rev. Prof. A. Usowicz: The positive aspects of the dissertation lie not so much in the analysis of Scheler's assumptions (that was done before) but rather in the comparative section, in which the author displayed a personal and original approach to the question, giving evidence of a great capacity for scholarly work ... The author ... is far from being a slave of literalness or philological pettiness. In his comparison he was able to grasp the central ideas ... Further, around these basic ideas, he capably concentrated derivative ideas, so that the thesis forms an organic whole ... Defects of the dissertation apply rather to the methodology ... Small defects, of an external nature, do not diminish the essential value of the thesis; it is completely appropriate as the basis of an application for acceptance to an assistant professorship. Krakow, November 10, 1953.

Rev. Prof. Wicher: The title ought to read "Usefulness of the System" ... as the author not only attempted to but did, in fact, present a penetrating analysis of Scheler's system in reference to sources of Christian morality ... In its entirety, this thesis is a good, reasoned, thorough analysis of Scheler's texts and of the texts of the revealed sources, particularly as it was not easy to present Scheler's terminology in the Polish language ... Since the thesis is an independent dissertation on the topic in this form, and fully indicates that the author is familiar with scholarly questions of philosophical ethics and moral theology, it is thus completely appropriate as the basis of an application for acceptance to an assistant professorship in moral theology. Krakow, November 22, 1953.

1954

January 24 — Skiing excursion from Huciska through Jalowiec to Sucha. (Father Wojtyla broke a ski and returned by sleigh).

February 25 — Letter from the Rector of the Jagiellonian University regarding the confirmation of the title for Rev. Dr. Karol Wojtyla:

Nr K 24/623/63/54   Krakow, February 25, 1954

Dean of the Department of Theology of the Jagiellonian University
Enclosed I am returning the files of Rev. Dr. Karol Wojtyla with the mention that, in accordance with point 5 of the ordinance by the Central Office of the Qualifying Committee for Employees of Institutes of Higher Learning of November 25, 1953, and until the announcement of appropriate regulations by the ministry, the Rector's Office has no authority to request the conferment of the degree of an assistant professor, an associate professor or a full professor upon persons not employed permanently at such an institute.

(Rector of JU, T. Marchlewski)

March 13-15 — A Lenten day of recollection for female teachers (at the Ursuline Sisters, Krakow.) Topic: Meditation on the work of redemption.

March 22-28 - Student retreat at St. Florian's Church.

Lesson I

...What is truth? This question was once asked by Pontius Pilate, this question is asked by man, this question is asked by the system. Truth is congruence with reality, congruence of thought, attitude toward the entire surrounding world. It demands subordination to reality, and not the reverse, reality cannot be subordinated to man...

The method of the Kingdom of God is the method of truth. Man must be prepared to accept reality in its totality. But contemporary man lives in only a part of reality, in the dimension of civilization's applications, not in the dimension of the person.

The parable of the treasure in which we sell everything in order to acquire the field where the treasure is buried, is perhaps the best rendition of our aspiration to the Kingdom of God.

"Cast your nets upon the deep." ...

The main ideas [of today's] contemplation: The first point: The Kingdom of God proclaimed by Christ. It is not merely a theory, an idea, a proposition, but a call to action. Action, above all interior action, is the method of the Kingdom of God. Christ views man interiorly, sees his spiritual side and knows that this side is open to the acceptance of the Kingdom of God. This is why Christ makes us aware of the soul's vulnerability to the acceptance of, to the action of the Divine. He makes us realize that this life is a gift. Man may participate in Divine Life because he has a mind and a will...

Lesson II

...Man is receptive to the Kingdom of God through his conscience. Conscience is an organ of the spiritual structure of man. Conscience is the judgment that evaluates good and evil. This is not an indifferent judgment. A practical judgment, which stimulates the impulse of the will, is voiced here. Thus it {conscience} has the character of a moral directive. And these directives have the character of concrete energy in man. Conscience is a concrete power, since it wields its own authority, which is able to reduce man to ashes. This reproach after Adam's sin manifested itself as shame, after the sin of Cain — as flight. The second sanction of conscience is contentment...

Earlier, one spoke of the purifying and unifying way, today one refers to the *mysterium tremendum* and the *mysterium luminosum*. It is the same thing. Man experiences the holiness of God and commences action, the act of elevating himself to God's holiness. The saints knew the way to purification — the way of purgatory. Purgatory is not something extraordinary. Before reaching God, man must pass through purgatory in order to be cleansed. The honest man does not recoil in the face of purgatory, for he wishes to reach God cleansed, without stain.

One man experienced the power of God's holiness. Jesus Christ. He bore the weight of man's guilt and stood with this burden before God. The awareness of sin on one hand and of God's holiness on the other drew Him to the sacrifice of self and to union with God. This explains the mystery of the Garden of Gethsemane and of Golgotha ...

Lesson III

The previous deliberations considered the Kingdom of God through the individual and in the life of the individual. At the same time, however, the Kingdom of God reaches society, which is not simply a loose gathering of human individuals. Some kind of relationship joins the individual to the whole. If the Kingdom of God is to reach life in a society, it must impress a mark on these relationships, on the relationships among people.

The Church does this — the Mystical Body of Christ. ...

Life is tied with giving birth. Our life comes from our parents. The act of conception carries the mark and image of God. Although it is an act of nature, it is a holy act, as it is inseparably tied with the spiritual birth of God. God marks us with His image, He creates our immortal soul. We must realize this, acknowledge this. And this must exert an influence on the life of the community ...

Sexual drive is a gift from God. Man may offer this drive to God exclusively through a vow of virginity. He may offer it to another human being with the awareness that he is offering it to a person. It must not be a matter of chance. On the other side there is another human being who must not be hurt, whom one must love. Only a person can love a person. To love means to wish for the other person's good, to offer oneself for the good of the other. When a new life is to come into being as the result of the act of giving oneself, this must be a gift of the person given out of love. In this area one must not separate love from the {sexual} drive. Love is not a fantasy, if it is tied to sexual drive, it guarantees through that drive an extension of love in a new, aroused life of a new person. If we respect the sexual drive within love, we will not violate love, we will not bring love to ruination ...

Lesson IV

At the beginning of Jesus' public teaching, one fact gave people much to think about. The temptation in the desert.

Satan's first temptation was: If you are the Son of God, command this stone to become bread.

Temptation — bread ...

Soon afterwards, Christ tested how much truth was hidden in the words of the Tempter. He taught in the region of Capernaum for some time. The crowd listened for a long time and was hungry. It was then that Christ employed the miraculous power of multiplying the five loaves. He then saw what power bread gives. They wanted to elect Him king. Christ escaped from the enthusiasm of the crowd. It was probably then that He arrived at the decision: "I will give to you bread which shall be my own body." He attempted to transfer their hunger into the realm of the Kingdom of God. But then His proposition met with disapproval. Almost everyone left Him. Only the Apostles remained — and they more out of habit. Christ decided to create and draw power for the Kingdom of God from this Bread-Body ...

To live in the Eucharist, one must be free of mortal sin. This is the first condition of not offending God gravely, in order to consume His Body. The second condition is to desire, and the third is to work on oneself ...

Lesson V

...The question of penance and the mystery of penance, namely, the sacrament...

Each of us carries two people within. One is who I am, the other who I should be. This is a very deep tenet of the human person and its inner life. It is not a deception, it is a reflection of reality. He who denies it either lies, or... is very deficient. This applies particularly to the young. Older people live in earned stabilization.

The second is a technical point. I cannot describe, nor understand with full insight who I am if I do not realize, if I do not view myself in light of who I should be. I must apply a measure of the ethical ideal to my actions. There is a constant tension between these two persons, or rather between these two images of a person. It is as if there were two poles, the negative and the positive. And this tension between them is the strongest current in human beings. The positive pole is my ideal; the negative, the person who I am. I must, therefore, constantly pull myself upward toward my ideal...

His Passion is especially conducive to the spirit of penance. Thus, without interrupting the lessons of the retreat, let us consider together His Way of the Cross.

First Station. Pilate condemns Jesus to death. Pilate says: Surely you know that it is in my power to crucify you or to release you? Christ says: You would have no power over me unless it had been given you from above. Therefore, he who had delivered me to you has the greater sin.

Second Station. Jesus takes up the cross. Jesus says: My yoke is easy, my burden is light. Jesus says: He who is not with me is against me, and he who does not gather behind me, disperses.

Third Station. Caiaphas said: I beseech you before all that is holy, that you say, are you the Christ? Jesus says: You have said it. The prophet Isaiah says: Like a sheep led to the slaughter or a sheep before the shearers, he was silent and opened not his mouth.

Fourth Station. Jesus meets his Mother. Jesus said: What will you from me Woman, my hour has not yet come. Jesus said: Did you not know that in these matters which are His, I must be at the side of my Father?

Fifth Station. Simon of Cyrene helps Jesus carry the cross. They forced Simon of Cyrene to help Him carry the cross. Jesus says: He who does not carry his cross with me, is not worthy of me.

Sixth Station. St. Veronica wipes Jesus's face. From the Gospel according to St. Matthew: Lord, when we saw you thirsty, hungry, naked, when we saw you as a guest or prisoner, did we not serve you? Jesus says: Truly I say unto you, what you have not done to the least of my brethren you have not done unto me.

Seventh Station. Jesus falls for the the second time. The prophet David: I am a worm, not a human being, ridiculed by others and held in common contempt. Jesus said to the Apostles: He who listens to you, listens to me, he who spurns you, spurns me.

Eighth Station. Jesus consoles the weeping women. Jesus says: do not weep for me, but for yourselves and for your children, for if this comes to pass with a living tree, what shall come to pass with a dry one? (The Gospel according to St. Luke.) Peter, departing from there, wept loudly.

Ninth Station. Jesus falls for the third time. If your sins be scarlet, they will become white as the snow. O Lord, leave me for I am a sinner, Lord I am not worthy that you enter under my roof, but only say the word and my soul shall be saved.

Tenth Station. Jesus is stripped of His garments. Jesus rose and touched a bier. And those carrying it stopped and He said: Young man, I say to you, arise. Jesus says: Could none of you stay awake but one hour with me? You, man, could you not stay awake but one hour with me? And you, woman, could you not stay awake but one hour with me?

Eleventh Station. Jesus is nailed to the cross. The prophet David: They pierced my hands and my feet. They counted all my bones. The prophet Isaiah: My body I gave to the floggers, my face I did not turn from those spitting upon me. Jesus says: My body is true nourishment and my blood true drink.

Twelfth Station. Jesus dies on the cross. Jesus says: Father, forgive them for they know not what they do. O Lord, remember me as you enter the Kingdom of Heaven. It is accomplished.

Thirteenth Station. Jesus is laid in the lap of His Blessed Mother. Simon's words: Here He lies for the rise and fall of many, and as the sign that many will oppose, and your own soul shall be pierced with a sword. Jesus says: Did you not know that I must be at the side of my Father?

Fourteenth Station. The body of Jesus is laid in the tomb. They sealed the tomb and went away. Man is to die once and then there is judgment. Jesus says: He who partakes of my Body and drinks my Blood has life everlasting, and he shall be raised up on the Last Day.

...This meditation brings to mind thoughts about the Church. We have become accustomed to thinking of the Church as an enormous tree grown from a tiny seed. But this is not all. In the Gospel, there is a parable of the gardener who prunes even those branches that bear fruit. The Church lives, but its life depends on sacrifice. Mortification and sacrifice {literally "death," i.e. the dying to self} are necessary to the life of the Church. By an overabundance of growth the tree would perish.

We need to understand this truth, especially today, when we consider the sacrament of penance. The sacrament of penance is inscribed in the very heart of the Church, in its mortification

There is death in the Church. Death because of sin. Perhaps it has been a number of years since your last confession. The time has come. Confession, cleansing and rebirth in God is one of the purposes of a retreat, one of the most important.

"If you do not do penance, you will perish."

Lesson VI — Marian Service

This is the last service of the retreat and the last conference dedicated to the Mother of God to remind us that this year is Her year. 100 years have passed since the solemn promulgation by the Church of the truth of Her Immaculate Conception. This compels us to close this meditation with the Marian truth...

Lesson VII

The conclusion of the retreat is the Holy Mass and Holy Communion which we celebrate together. This is a result of the initial premise of our retreat. An act is the first foundation, the method of the Kingdom of God. The Holy Mass is an interior act by Christ, in the fullest sense of the word. It is redemption...

Consequently, the topic of our retreat was the issue of an interior act which is the method of the Kingdom of God. The first function of the retreat is the function of truth, the final function of the retreat is the function of the Holy Communion, the interior union of our act with the act of Christ. And this union which began with the function of truth, must, through the Holy Communion, extend throughout our entire lives.

Christ said: "He who comes to me has everlasting life." Let us take life from Christ and let us take life fully.

(From a preserved typescript-stenograph by W.P.)

April 31-May 1 — The first excursion with the youth: Skawce, Leskowiec, Madohora, Kety.

June 25 - 29 — Student retreat concluded in discussion. (Topic: a woman's calling in life).

July 16-30 — Kayaking excursion (5 kayaks — 10 people) Czarna Hancza, Augustowski Canal to Augustow, Suwalki, Wigry, Jezioro Muliczne. Daily Holy Mass. Father Wojtyla gladly intones Marian hymns. Discussion at the campfires. During travel, he intones secular songs. Individual conversations, very intimate, retreat-like. The style and form worked out during this excursion endured for many years. Most of its participants continued until the last excursion in 1978. (According to accounts by the participants)

August 24-26 — Lublin, KUL {Catholic University of Lublin}. He led a retreat for priests. Two conferences on the subject: The Mother of God in the life of a priest.

...A priest calls Mary his Mother, in this word encompassing the complete relationship of an adult son. He must realize what Her Motherhood represents, and must therefore utter this word with complete interior concordance. This interior concordance of the priest's relationship with the Mother of Jesus Christ, who since Calvary became the Mother of all men, resolves itself into the following principles:

1) Since God's Only Begotten Son is the specific object of Mary's Motherhood and I, a human being, have a right to Her Motherhood only inasmuch as I find myself in the same state as this Son, I must, therefore, do everything to find myself in this state constantly. As this is a state of grace, I must therefore live in grace and through it continue to become like the Son of God. I may not demean Her Motherhood by being an unworthy son.

2) I must then, in accordance with the mandate of Jesus Christ, make Mary, the Mother of God's Grace within me, the Mother of my supernatural interior life. O, the supernatural life in man needs a mother, how much indeed! It leads to a new principle of existence, which is beyond nature.

Nature however is strong and wants to be independent, wants to exercise its own control over its faculties, inclinations, and desires. It succumbs only with resistance to life's new forces which are adjunct to grace. Moreover, the supernatural life requires that man remain in the state of a child. It is difficult for man to remain in the state of a child if he does not sense the mother. Without a mother, how easy it is to lose the awareness of being a son, and that is why He gave us a Mother, His own Mother.

3) And now, based on such an awareness of Mary's motherhood in relationship to us, we can and should allow her into everything that comprises the entirety of our priesthood. The more adult we are as sons, the easier it is for us to live with a constant awareness of Her Motherhood, perhaps even without many words. The entire interior attitude will determine Her Motherhood in relationship to us and our sonship in relationship to Her. I desire the same things that you do, Mother.

Thus, we must cast our attitude as priests towards Mary as Mother against the rich background of our being the sons of God. We must base our attitude on this very foundation. This is a tremendous mystery, the fact of being born of God through grace, a mystery incomparably greater than giving birth, giving life according to the order of nature. We must live according to this mystery. After all, we carry it within us, although its essence overwhelms our minds. And it is only this mystery of being the sons of God that places Mary's Motherhood on the appropriate plane in relation to us. At the moment when the redemption of the world was reaching its fulfillment, as it was reaching its zenith, Mary, Mother of Jesus, stood at the foot of the Cross together with a priest. Jesus said to His Mother: "This is your son" and then he said to the priest: "This is your Mother."

...A priest must possess a profound awareness of Mary's Motherhood of Grace, for it remains in a precise and deep relationship with his life's calling. A priest is a steward of the mysteries of God, a steward of grace. He knows the affairs of men from inside, from the perspective of those actions which are accompanied by efficacious grace, from the side of those actions in which man does not want to cooperate with grace, or, absorbed by some lesser goods becomes gradually insensitive to it. Thus knowing the affairs of man from the inside, a priest may not only examine them, but also act upon them. Because he is indeed a steward of grace, Christ, as well as the people, expect the priest to act within man, to accompany those actions which arise from grace, to avert collapse and to guard against spiritual insensitivity. This is the actual substance of his ministry.

This ministry allows the priest to live the breadth of Christ's mysteries, allows him to live in the realm of the Mystical Body. This ministry impresses a deep mark on the soul of the priest. It is, above all, the mark of Christ, but if we look more closely, we see that it also possesses common Marian qualities. Didn't St. Paul write to his brethren: "My children, to whom I give birth in pain"? This statement is like an outburst of the maternal self-awareness in the priest. And we could follow the ever new manifestations of this maternal pain of giving birth by traveling to Ars or to the hut of Father Beyzim in Madagascar, or to Bishop Lozinski's abode in Polesie and perhaps to many other living quarters and to many other lives of priests. And maybe also to my house and my life?

Thus the priesthood allows us to participate in the motherhood of grace, and to some extent in the Motherhood of Mary, the Mother of God's grace. And here, in this place, the awareness of the relationship of the priest to Mary runs somehow through the center of the priest's life. A priest is connected with the Mother of God because he is connected with Her Motherhood. He is connected with Her Motherhood through the very essence of his calling... (From a preserved typed manuscript by the author. W.P.)

August 10-14 — An excursion on foot: August 10 — Rabka, Turbacz * August 11 — Turbacz, Czorsztyn * August 12 — Czorsztyn, Szczawnica (via the Pieniny Mountains) * August 13 — Szczawnica, Przehyba * August 14 — Piwniczna, Hala Labowska, Krynica (11-12 participants.)

September — An excursion on foot to the High Tatra and Western Tatra Mountains.

September 12 — Conversation with Prof. Stefan Swiezawski:

At that time Father Wojtyla and I already knew each other in Krakow and we met often. During one of our one-day hikes to the Gorce Mountains, on the wonderful "walking path" between Turbacz and Luban that the three of us took (Fr. Wojtyla, my wife and I), we had a great, essential conversation regarding scientific research and the situation in Lublin. I fervently encouraged Fr. Wojtyla to give of his strengths and talents to our Department evolving in such difficult circumstances. It seems to me that this was the beginning of the Holy Father John Paul II's cooperation of many years, first as an assistant professor, later as a professor at KUL. From this point on we met even more frequently. We had many discussions, we often traveled together. A deep friendship was forming. Its telling expression and, in part, its starting point, was the fact that in November of 1953, I was invited to participate in the examination committee as the only lay reviewer of Father Wojtyla's thesis submitted as part his application for acceptance to the assistant professorship at the Department of Theology of the Jagiellonian University... (Stefan Swiezawski, *TP* 47/1978)

September 15 — Gubalowka, Kiry, Dolina Jarzabcza * September 19 — the Chocholowska shelter, Przyslop, Gronik * September 17 — Kuznice, Hala Gasienicowa, Koscielec * Sep 18 — Hala Gasienicowa, Kozia Przelecz, Zawrat, Kuznice * September 19 — Kuznice, Dolina Kondratowa.

October — After the elimination of the Department of Theology at JU, he gives lectures to the students of three seminaries (Krakow, Silesia and Czestochowa). The lectures were conducted according to the same system as at the Department. Fr. Wojtyla taught Catholic social ethics to fourth and fifth year auditors (2 hours weekly.)

October 9 — At the meeting of the Academic Senate at KUL[3], Dean Jerzy Kalinowski introduces a motion by the Council of the Department of Philosophy (the suggestion probably came from Prof. S. Swiezawski) to engage Rev. Dr. Karol Wojtyla as a contract employee to teach classes in philosophical ethics.

---

[3] Catholic University of Lublin

October 12 — Letter from the Vice-rector of KUL: "Herewith I entrust the following lectures in the Philosophy Department for the academic year 1954/55 to Rev. Dr. {Wojtyla}: 1 hr. weekly: History of Ethics Doctrines, 2 hrs. weekly, seminar. Vice-rector, Rev. S. Plodzien."

Within the scope of the History of Doctrines lectures — the topic: *Ethical act and experience* (Information from Rev. Styczen. Cf. Fr. Wojtyla's *The Problem of Will in the Analysis of Ethical Act...*, "Roczniki Filozoficzne" 5/1955-57, vol. 1, pp. 111-135)

> The first meetings took place within the framework of the metaphilosophical conversatorium, initiated under the direction of Jerzy Kalinowski during the academic year 1953/1954. Karol Wojtyla, a newly admitted docent {assistant professor}, began lectures in the Philosophy Department at KUL in 1954 and was immediately invited to participate in the meetings of the conversatorium. He commuted from Krakow overnight (there was no other train connection in those times) and had so many classes that he had great difficulty controlling his weariness and sleepiness in the evenings (when the conversatorium meetings took place). Despite this, he attempted to participate actively in the lively and penetrating discussions. Later, however, his responsibilities in Krakow and in Lublin increased, and he resigned from further participation in the metaphilosophical conversatorium. (Antoni B. Stepien, "TP" 47/1958)

November 19 — Tourist Karol Wojtyla was awarded the Bronze Badge for Hiking Tourism, category D, that is, for adults. Accompanying remarks by Janusz Andruskiewicz, MA, member of the PTTK,[4] who signed the certificate awarding the badge:

> Tourist Karol Wojtyla completed a certain number (a few, ten plus) of lowland excursions on foot totaling 166 km. More than one half, exactly 90 km., were completed in the so-called winter season, i.e. between November 1 and March 31 of the following year, according to the regulations of the OTP from those times ... The subcommittee of OTP, functioning within the framework of the Regional Committee for Tourism on Foot of PTTK in Krakow, and represented by me, verified (awarded), the Bronze Badge for Hiking Tourism, category "D" (for adults) to tourist Karol Wojtyla on November 19, 1954.

November 21 — A day of recollection for a group of students.

Lesson I:

> ...Man aspires toward God — He is his goal. Man aspires toward Him with his will, because God is love. Man approaches God primarily through love. The interior activity, of which man is capable, is the activity of love. For us, the physical activity of matter is usually most important, but this means remaining in one place, whereas progress, moving forward, occurs only in the spirit, in the aspiration toward God.

---

[4] Polish Govt. Tourism organization

This is the question which must be made the topic of today's recollection. Outwardly we head toward various goals, but interiorly, am I heading toward God through love or am I standing still? The Church is an organism of the greatest dynamics. It continually heads toward God, through love inculcated by Christ, instigated in God, the Holy Spirit...

Greatness lies in the spiritual realm. It is good to look into Psalm 8 about the greatness of man as God's creation. Pulling man below the standard —that is a horrible devaluation.

The first step to the awareness of the goal: to find one's place in the world, to believe in the richness of one's nature. This outlook cannot be separated from the issue of a journey. Man is great because he moves interiorly toward the living God, through love, while all of nature stands still.

Advent is not only a historical association, nor is it a time of awaiting the latest coming of the Savior, but it is a time which informs us that we are still on a journey. God wants to continue to come closer to man. He approached the physical world once by creating it. The physical world is somewhat closed to God, but the spiritual world can be opened to Him over and over again. The entire history of our souls consists in our opening and closing to God...

The day of recollection demands a transition from the material world to one's own inner world. Those who live too outwardly get lost. We must immerse ourselves in God, hear in ourselves the call of the Church: "Time to rise from sleep"...

Lesson II:

Am I proceeding, or am I standing still? Do I have love? Do I love more now than previously? — this is the second question to contemplate. There are periods of elation in life, especially in youth, periods of love. This often passes with age and what remains is routine. This is why it is so difficult to respond to the question: do I love more? The answers may be varied. The most important: to love more — that is to remain rooted more deeply and thoroughly in the blessings and graces assigned to me by God. Each blessing is not only given, but also assigned. The blessings exceed the assignment, but nevertheless God still demands ...

There is a difference between exalted love and tested love ...

Man, who is placed by God in the midst of such blessings must also be rooted more deeply and thoroughly in them. Each one of us has some assignment, condition, position, possessions in which he has a place. What does it mean to be rooted more deeply, for example, in your children, in your husband? It is related to your love for them. The ability to discover their humanity in them, to experience them deeply, to bring them up. To remain objective and sober about fellow human beings, in order to draw them where we are heading. Then those whom I am leading, they, too, will become rooted more deeply in themselves and in their blessings. Love is not bedazzlement, a sugary emotion; sometimes it is even anger — if necessary, opposition. To live more deeply in our professional duties, in the people with whom we live. There are people everywhere, preying on you, they are treacherous. But love prevails. St. John of the Cross said: "Where there is no love–there you should carry it, and there will be love"...

Mankind is not concerned only with great things, it is also concerned with small things because Christianity was not able to make them the best. Food for thought: how am I rooted in blessings and people. You need not necessarily and tangibly convert people, but you need to forge access for the living God in them.

Love is difficult, because it is subtle. It demands sensitivity to various situations. Love must be prudent. Prudence allows one to practice love in an effective manner. It tells one what more should be done, what should not be done any more and what should not be done yet...

In this light one must reach one's life:

1) through external elements to the interior element

2) reach God, who stands at the end of one's life, who awaits and constantly draws near to us, inasmuch as we clear the path for Him towards us. This is the thought for Advent...

Meditation:

To pray with mind, heart and will. Attune yourself to the fact that God is among us; find yourself in God's presence.

There are so many important matters about which man may converse only with God. Through these matters we become united with God Himself...

Theme: The epistle from the First Sunday of Advent:

"Brothers, you know it is full time now for you to wake from your sleep. For salvation is nearer to us now than when we first believed." The appropriateness of this statement is striking. The Apostle aims directly at the soul, draws a reaction from it. It is the hour to arise from sleep. Man must respond to this. The Apostle speaks through a metaphor, but through it he explains himself more clearly than if he spoke without the metaphor. This concerns the purpose of life. The letter is addressed to the Romans, but also to me; its connotation is not merely historical. These words speak to me. Thus I am the sleeping person. I acknowledged this too late myself...

Holy Mother, be an example for me, an example in a life of vigilance, service, love. I wish that my path through life be connected with yours. Not by words only, but by daily actions, resulting from my devotion.

Lesson III:

...We must now focus on hope. The need for hope in man's life emerges from the fact that man must have hope for daily things, for the small events, as well as hope on the grand scale, for all of life.

Regarding hope for today: we often arrive at resolutions: this is the new me, altered by an act of will. Resolutions can pertain to small things, but these can be ineffectual, these can fail to deal with the heart of the matter, creating the delusion that something has been decided. But the true resolution: that is the new me, that is the old persona struggling with the new one.

This process cannot succeed without hope...

Each self-analysis leads to conclusions, resolutions. They need not always be new things, one may stabilize the old ones. Excessive activity is not recommended. For instance, I may resolve to attend to what I already have...

Temptation despite hope: I am not able...

Second issue: that of tactics which are connected with the resolution. They rely on the method of behavior. They are in effect both when one tries to avoid sin and when one tries to do good. Tactics are limited to the knowledge of circumstances, and it is in our power to control circumstances, to remain silent, not to criticize, etc. Evil is like an avalanche, it starts with something small, and grows incredibly. We can diminish evil and enhance good. This is connected with being rooted in one's assigned blessings and graces. To have hope — is to live in the conviction that God loves me despite my weakness ... (From the stenograph by I.K.)

November 26-28 — Krakow, the monastery of the Sisters of St. Clare. Three conferences on the topic: "Are our vows necessary?" during the three days of recollection preceding the renovation of the religious vows by the sisters on November 29.

December 19 — A day of recollection for a youth group. Topic: the goodness of God, the mystery of God's love for man. * From December 19 — Advent retreat, or rather days of recollection before the Christmas holidays, three conferences (most likely) at St. Anne's academic church in Krakow.

1955

January (the semester break) — In Ochotnica Gorna skiing with a group of youth. Quartered in a highlander hut. In the evenings, discussions on philosophy and his outlook on life.

In February — A stay of a few days in Dolina Chocholowska. ("When we were climbing Jarzabczy on Saturday, he initiated the recitation of the rosary and the litany to the Mother of God.") * February 12-14 — Retreat for teachers (at the Ursuline Sisters) in Krakow. * February 26 — Skiing excursion to Leskowiec.

March 5-6 — Skiing excursion: Kroscienko, Dzwonkowka (overnight in a shanty), Przehyba, Rytro.

March 14-19 — Student retreat in Krakow * During this time a "Triduum Sacrum"[5] is held at the cloister of the Benedictine Fathers in Tyniec, together with other priests (Rev. Olejnik, Rev. Jankowski, the later Fr. Augustyn.) Participation in the liturgy and theological discussions.

March 25 — He became an assistant member of the Research Association at KUL (correspondent member of the Department of Philosophy TN KUL — December 21, 1955, active member — April 29, 1959)

April 12 — Skiing excursion to Zakopane.

May — Excursion: Krakow, Lubien, Szczebel.

May 28-30 — Fr. Karol's only participation in the International Kayak Rally on the Dunajec (his kayak was punctured at Sromowce Nizne, and sank at the finish line in Szczawnica. Only the breviary did not get soaked.)

---

[5] Three-day sacred observance

End of May or the beginning of June:

> **For the conclusion of the academic year at KUL, in the name of the seminarian's group led by Rev. Prof. Karol Wojtyla, I expressed gratitude for his effort and work with us and gave him a bunch of tulips. He hugged them to himself and immediately returned them to me suggesting I take them to the chapel. He accepted, but did not appropriate; he offered them to the Lord, from Whom I was very distant.**
> **This year we worked on St. Thomas' chapter of *Summa Teologica, De habitibus* — regarding habits — virtues, in the higher sense. This chapter is an introduction to the next, *De virtutibus* — about virtue, and it was the subject of a seminar in the following year. At that time Rev. Prof. particularly emphasized the fact that virtues determine the value of man, since they define him as a person.** (One of his students at the time)

June 26. Day of recollection at the Ursuline Sisters Convent in Krakow for a group of youth. Christ's conversation with St. Peter: "Enter onto the deep" and its continuation. "Do not fear, from henceforth you shall be the fisher of men." In this conversation Christ slowly enlightens Peter on what is significant in his life. Similarly, God slowly enlightens us through various occurrences in life. (From the notes of a participant.)

July 2-6 — A hike with the youth: July 2 — Kudowa, Karlow. * July 3 — Karlow, Wambierzyce. Holy Mass in the basilica * July 4 — Karlow, Duszniki * July 6 — Snieznik.

July 12-14 — Walking retreat in Pewel.

> **He came regularly to the evening meetings of a group of young people, which took place in my room in Lublin at 27 Szopena {Chopin} Street, to eat supper and participate in discussions aimed at deepening our knowledge of the Catholic doctrine. One year he discussed the encyclical *Mystici Corporis Christi*. He agreed to lead a retreat in the summer for a small group of female students from KUL. He gave it a specific form. Our gatherings took place not in the chapel, but outdoors, as we departed for the mountains for the day; the participants were to spend some time in prayer and meditation over certain texts from the Holy Scriptures: upon return in the evening, conference and prayer in the chapel (this took place in the Zywiec region, in Pewla Mala).** (Leokadia Malunowicz, *TP* 47/1978.)

July 17 - August 3 — A kayak excursion on the Drawa. Group reading: *The Screwtape Letters* by C.S. Lewis. 13 people: 6 double kayaks and a single.

August 19 — Letter by Father S. Plodzien, vice-rector of KUL: classes to be taught by Fr. Wojtyla in the academic year 1955/56: 2 hours weekly of lectures in the History of Ethical Doctrines for students of third and fourth year in practical specialization, as well as, for the same group of students, a seminar in the History of Ethical Doctrines: 2 hours weekly. Topic of the lectures: *Good and values* (typewritten).

September 22-25. — Pilgrimage with the *Srodowisko* to

Czestochowa — on bicycles: Krakow, Trzebinia, Olkusz, Wolbrom, Pilica, Ogrodzieniec, Siewierz, Czestochowa, 4-8 people. 20 others were met at Czestochowa. Holy Mass. Stations of the Cross.

October 2. Mountain trip with the *Srodowisko*: Bielsko, Biala, Gaiki, mountain pass Upanienki, Kozy.

October — He commences lectures on Catholic Social Ethic, in Krakow — 2 hours weekly. Also, a lecture on the Principles of Moral Theology for second year students (3 hours weekly.) "The Register of Examination Grades obtained by the Seminarians of the Czestochowa Theological Seminary No. 2 in Krakow" indicates the general improvement of grades under the professor. While in previous years the grade of "sufficienter" {satisfactory} was rare, this year there are many.

An account by the Rector of the Czestochowa Seminary:

> As a rector I often had the honor to host Fr. Karol Wojtyla within the walls of our Czestochowa Seminary. He lectured on the Principles of Moral Theology as the assistant to Rev. Prof. W. Wicher. The Department of Theology was no longer in existence and individual lectures were held at various Seminaries. One thing struck me: Rev. Prof. Wojtyla spent the breaks between lectures in the Seminary Chapel and not in our Seminary refectory where the professor priests would come for coffee or tea. (Fr. Bruno Magott, Rector of the Czestochowa Theological Seminary in Krakow in 1945/46 - 1955/56)

December 8 — Letter from the Rector of KUL to the Pallottinum publishing house regarding the publication of the thesis submitted by Rev. Dr. Karol Wojtyla as part of the requirements for acceptance to assistant professorship (It was already in 1953 that the thesis was sent to Pallottinum for publication):

> To the Editor of Pallottinum: L. dz. {No.} 3990/55/R
> Regarding Rev. Karol Wojtyla's thesis in application for admission to assistant professorship, submitted already in 1953.
> Rev. Prof. Wojtyla is an exceptionally good scholar; the publication of his thesis is very desirable not only from his point of view, but largely from the perspective of the scholarly interests of KUL.
> Rev. Iwanicki

Rev. Jozef Iwanicki was known to be demanding in his evaluation of the scholarly level of the employees at KUL, where he was Rector at the time.

December 10 — He led a day of recollection for a group of youth in Krakow. Topic: texts from the "Gaudete" Sunday.

Pallottinum's response:

> ...For my part I will endeavor to do everything so that Rev. Dr. Wojtyla's thesis *System etyczny M. Schelera jako srodek do opracowania etyki chrzesci-*

janskiej[6] appears in print as soon as possible. Reverend Rector must realize, however, that when it comes to publishing a work, not everything depends on the publishing house.

Rev. Leon Roman SAC

(The title of the thesis given in the letter from the publisher differs from the title given when it was presented as the basis of the process and the colloquium qualifying for admission to assistant professorship (Proba opracowania etyki chrzescijanskiej wedlug systemu Maxa Schelera[7]) The change probably comes from the author. The same title as given in the publisher's letter (System etyczny...) appears in an article in "Polonia Sacra" 6/1953/54, pp. 143-161, which presents a summary of the essential themes of the dissertation, however not its complete text. The dissertation published in 1959 by Towarzystwo Naukowe KUL has yet another title, namely: Ocena mozliwosci zbudowania etyki chrzescijanskiej przy zalozeniach systemu Maxa Schelera[8])

December 20 — Rev. Karol Wojtyla, member of the Towarzystwo Naukowe KUL[9], made a report on his thesis titled System etyczny Maxa Schelera jako narzedzie opracowania etyki chrzescijanskiej[10] (thesis published in "Polonia Sacra" 1955).

Classes of the Department of Theology, which was eliminated from the Jagiellonian University, continued in individual seminaries where clerics from Krakow, Silesia and Czestochowa gathered. Below, an account by one of the listeners, later a bishop, of lectures given by Rev. Prof. K. Wojtyla in the academic years 1955/56; 1956/57; 1957/58.

At the time I noted impressions related to his person in my clerical journal.

He would come to Aleje Mickiewicza 3 in an outfit not typical for a Krakow professor. Instead of a distinguished black hat he wore a leather cap, his cassock covered with a dark green coat made from a material most likely meant for a blanket. On spring and summer days, in the recreation hall (where the lectures were held), he would throw his trench coat over the back of a chair, a coat, which, as I managed to note, was of poorer quality than mine.

During the break, he would read his breviary in a corner or go one story up to the chapel, where he would kneel on the floor despite the great number of kneelers softened by cushions.

He lectured walking back and forth on the podium, and he did not so much lecture as proclaim a complex divine-human lesson. He was able to repeat particular issues in many versions. He would summarize everything again and then pause, looking at us, certainly wishing to convince himself that we had comprehended what he told us. Thanks to this I was able to record in a thick notebook almost all his lectures in Moral Theology and Social Ethics, from which I benefit to this day.

When he was examining us we had the feeling that he grew tired; he

---

6 M. Scheler's System of Ethics as a Means of Establishing a Christian Ethic.
7 An Attempt to Establish a Christian Ethic according to the System of Max Scheler.
8 An Evaluation of the Feasibility of Building a Christian Ethic on the Principles of Max Scheler.
9 Academic Association of the Catholic University of Lublin.
10 The Ethical System of Max Scheler as an Instrument for Establishing a Christian Ethic.

would remove his glasses, wipe his brow and ask a question and, when necessary, still another. He would give a grade after long deliberation. I was not able to find out if he "flunked" anyone.

The most interesting were the so called colloquia {colloquies}, which he held once a month. It was actually a recapitulation of the material already covered, during which he provoked us to express ourselves freely about what we had heard previously. Once I worked up the courage and spewed everything that was bothering me inside.

I was then a twenty-year old, stuffed with lectures heard at the Department of Law of the Jagiellonian University, as well as with "indexed" literature.[11] I was probably uttering nothing else but heresies or perhaps even blasphemies, since my colleague kept kicking me in the ankle and whispered with urgent concern: "Stop, or they will expel you." Colleagues from other seminaries (Krakow and Czestochowa) squirmed uncomfortably and some turned toward me with various expressions on their faces. This was exciting encouragement, especially since Fr. Professor was pacing the podium with his hands folded behind his back and his head hung. When I felt relieved, I sat down perspiring. Let happen what may, but I had to speak!

There was a tense and heavy silence in the room for awhile. Finally Fr. Professor stopped in the center of the podium and uttered a statement which no one expected and which surprised everybody: "Fathers, if you please, what your colleague has said here is evidence that he is beginning to think theologically..." after which he calmly began to straighten all of my skewed thinking, answering my questions and explaining my exclamations. The colloquium prolonged itself as others expressed their complaints against the world, mankind and God. With his cogent logic and suggestive argumentation, Fr. Professor resolved the doubts and problems of our hot heads.

At the end, he still suggested that we have an additional chat in the parlor. I must admit that after all these years I cannot recall exactly that private "spiritual conversation," but there is one thing has remained with me from that encounter. Now, when some of my rebellious and intractable listeners torment me with their "revolutionary" problems, I always recall Father Professor and try to be like him, at least in relationship to those entrusted to my care.

Not long afterwards we heard of the nomination of our Professor to Bishop. Many rejoiced in this promotion. Some of us worried. Pity to lose such a pedagogue and scholar to be a bishop. It turned out later that our apprehensions were unsubstantiated: Father Professor, the Bishop, remained as he was: a scholar and a priest.

His consecration at Wawel Castle is also fixed in my memory and imagination. Why? First, because the new auxiliary bishop wore an atypical, low miter. It seemed to me that it did not suit him, but evidently it was what he chose and humbly accepted. And one other thing surprised me. At the end of the ceremony, the Bishop blessed the people as he walked along the cathedral. When he approached the large, colorfully attired gathering of youth, he not only kissed the foreheads of the boys, but of the girls as well (most likely to the amazement of the older generation). He was incapable of cele-

---

[11] Books forbidden to Roman Catholics without the deletion or revision of certain passages.

brating his dignity. Once I managed to observe him when he was entering the Krakow seminary — now wearing a hat. In the corridor he was searching for something in his pockets. Then he pulled out a skullcap and placed it in its appropriate place.

I remember yet another little incident. At the door on Kanonicza Street (where the Bishop still lived in his humble room) two girls awaited their "chief." Their attire attested to the fact that they were students. He arrived with a quick step. One of them respectfully opens the door, suggesting precedence to the host. The Bishop does not take advantage of this politeness and pushes both students through the open door, as the *savoir vivre* fuss went on too long for him. (Fr. Romuald Waldera)

1956

January 7 — Skiing excursion: Zakopane, Bukowina, Roztoka, Zakopane (through Gesia Szyja) * The same winter — A short skiing trip in Krynica (a similar short trip in the following year).

Beginning of February — A retreat for the pupils of the Sisters of the Immaculate Conception in Szymanow.

...between grading and the dance — a visit of a few days from a renowned priest from Krakow, which the entire convent happily anticipated. His arrival was announced for 6:30 p.m. In the meantime, a great cold wave set in, causing great train delays. Even without this, Szymanow is accustomed to the sad reality that the horses find their way to the station on one schedule, while the guests arrive, or rather, walk, on another. So it was this time. The horses left the convent at 5:30 p.m. and returned at 11:00 p.m. with no one, and at 2:00 a.m., Father {Wojtyla} marched in the freezing darkness, in a temperature of minus 25 C degrees {-13 F}, from the station to the convent. In an athletic feat he attempted to conquer the entry gate, closed at that hour, and for half an hour he circled the house testing the resistance of all the doors one after another until, finally, Sister Idalia heard him from her cell. Since the door locks — perhaps as a result of the cold — went "on strike," it ended with Sister Amata leading the poor guest to his room at the chaplain's quarters through the attic. Fortunately, the amiable guest was not offended and everything else proceeded normally, even very positively. (From a letter of the then Superior of the Convent. The letter was written in 1956).

February 19 — Skiing excursion: Kasinka, Lubogoszcz, Mszana.

March 5-10 — Student retreat at St. Florian's Church in Krakow.

Period of Lent — Student retreat at the university church at KUL.

March 31 — Letter from the Vice President of KUL to Rev. Dr. Karol Wojtyla: "As of March 1, 1956, I entrust you, Rev. Doctor, with one hour weekly lectures in Ethics at the Department of Philosophy. Vice-rector, Rev. St. Plodzien."

Last week of March — Church of St. Florian: singing of the Holy Week matins with all the nocturnes, psalms, antiphons, and responsories. Fr. Wojtyla, Fr. Cz. Obtulowicz, Fr. M. Turek sat in the stalls on one side, and the choir on the other — all armed with the huge *Liber usualis.*

April 2-3 — Dolina Chocholowska — excursion to the summits of Grzes and Rakon.

Ca. April 3-4 — A lecture titled *Dwie koncepcje wolnosci* {Two Concepts of Freedom}within the program of a cycle of public lectures on "Ethical Issues" organized by the Academic Association at KUL March 28-April 6, 1956.

May 27 — An excursion on foot to the peak of Turbacz.

June 30 — A day of recollection. 4 teachings: Man's solitude before God and with God, God and man; Temptation; The problem of education. Mercy.

July 15-August 1 — Vacation. Kayak excursion on Czarna Woda (Wieprznickie Lake from Skorzew to Grudziadz).

> The excursion was very well organized and conducted according to regulations. 23 participants (11 "doubles," 1 "single"). Titles of books discussed during the excursion: *Bodies and Souls* by van der Meersch, *The Bells of Nagasaki* by K. Nagai, *The Ragpickers of Emmaus* by B. Simon, *Homeless Dogs* by G. Cesbron. Titles of films discussed: *Before the Deluge, The Next After God, The Comedians*. The topics for discussion were suggested by the participants of the excursions and always gladly undertaken, and often led and commented on by Fr. Karol. (T. Zyczowska)

September — Excursion on bicycles: Swieradow, Swidnica, with Mr. and Mrs. Janik (about 5 people)

September 16, 1956 — A mountain trip to Turbacz with the *Srodowisko* group returning from the Tatras.

September 28-30, 1956 — A pilgrimage with the *Srodowisko* to Czestochowa on bicycles: Jedrzejow, Szczekociny, Naglowice, Lelow, Janow,Olsztyn,Czestochowa; about 6 participants, in Czestochowa about 25 more people were met.

October — In the academic year 1956/57 he lectures on Propaedeutics of Theology and on Economic Ethics at the Krakow Seminary.

At the IWKR[12] in Lublin, he lectures on Moral Theology — Marital Ethics (he will continue these lectures in the following year).

October 24 — Father Wojtyla, as a member of the Academic Association at KUL, presented his thesis titled *O podstawach per-*

---

[12] Institute of Advanced Religious Culture

fekcjonizmu w etyce[13] at a meeting of the Association (Cf. *Roczniki Filozoficzne*[14] 5/1955-57 v. 4)

October 29 — Classes assigned to Fr. Karol Wojtyla in the Department of Christian Philosophy at KUL for the academic year 1956/57: 2 hours weekly — lectures in Moral Philosophy for students of the 1st and 2nd year, theoretical and practical specializations; 2 hours weekly — lectures on selected issues of Moral Philosophy for students of the 3rd and 4th year, practical specialization. (Norma i szczescie[15] typewritten); 2 hours weekly — exercises in Moral Philosophy for students of the 1st and 2nd year, practical specialization; 2 hours weekly — a seminar in Moral Philosophy for students of the 3rd and 4th year, practical specialization (the enlarged scope of duties and full employment at KUL was caused by the departure to Rome to Angelicum of Fr. Feliks Bednarski OP, professor and head of the Chair of Ethics).

Academic year 1956/57 — "Private lectures" on Thomism for students of English philology at KUL. These lectures conducted in a private residence were organized at the initiative of Prof. Przemyslaw Mroczkowski primarily for the sake of the assistants {junior lecturers}. (According to an account by Dr. Ewa Baranska)

November 16 — Motion by the Departmental Qualifying Committee as well as the Council of the Department of Philosophy to nominate Karol Wojtyla to the position of Assistant Professor in Ethics. The motion was made by Dean J. Kalinowski on November 21, 1956 before the Academic Senate of KUL.

November 27 — "At the meeting on November 27, 1956, the Academic Senate of KUL unanimously accepted the motion by the Department." Signed: Rev. Plodzien.

December 1 — From this day Rev. Dr. Karol Wojtyla is officially an assistant professor and a full employee at KUL (till now: assigned classes). From now on he also conducted post-graduate seminars (1 hour weekly.) Also in December: a motion to the Central Qualifying Committee for Employees of Institutes of Higher Learning to confirm him as an assistant professor.

Opinions about the value of his scientific research in connection with the motion for the title of assistant professor:

Rev. M. Rechowicz, Rector of KUL: Rev. Dr. Wojtyla is one of the most talented lecturers in the Department of Theology. Besides his studies in Krakow under the direction of Rev. Prof. Wicher, he also studied at the Angelicum for two years. Good preparation, deep scholarly interests, moral

---

[13] On the Foundation of Perfectionism in Ethics

[14] Philosophical Annals

[15] The Norm and Happiness

qualities and, finally, his loyalty to authority, completely justify the motion to confer the title and privileges of an assistant professor. Lublin, December 8, 1956.

Rev. W. Wicher from ATK: The entirety of scholarly achievement ... qualifies him completely as an assistant professor of ethics and as a conscientious, independent, inquiring scholar and as a fully qualified lecturer from a pedagogical point of view. Krakow, November 26, 1956.

Prof. A. Vetulani: The thesis on the Decree of Gracian (Cf. *Roczniki Teologiczno-Kanoniczne*[16], 4/1957 v. 1, pp. 31-71): earned a very positive evaluation by Rev. Lefebvre, former professor of the University of Lille, currently an auditor of the Roman Rota. Krakow, November 26, 1956.

Rev. I. Rozycki: The search for an individual outlook on the theological as well as philosophical set of problems in ethical issues characterizes Karol Wojtyla's scholarly activity. Since Karol Wojtyla is in fact an independent researcher in the full sense, it is right that the title of assistant professor sanction his status legally and officially. Krakow, December 3, 1956.

Karol Wojtyla's report on the entirety of his scholarly activity to date (also in connection with the proposed nomination to assistant professor):

[the research concentrates] on the basic issues of ethics, above all on the very philosophical principles of this field. They proceed in the direction of a certain synthesis, for which one prepares through thorough consideration of the elementary concepts of ethics and the issues of methodology.

December 2 — The first pilgrimage to Czestochowa by doctors from Krakow. Departure on a leased PKS bus at 4 a.m. Rev. Karol Wojtyla, chaplain to the health services in Krakow, said the Holy Mass at the miraculous icon of the Blessed Mother.

Stations of the Cross: each group with its pastor. Fr. Wojtyla led the group from Krakow (A casual participant asked if the leader is a bishop). (According to an account by Dr. Anna Starczewska)

December 10 — An Advent day of recollection for the youth.

December 16 — A day of recollection for friends who are engaged couples (topic: the religious aspect of marriage).

December 24 — Letter to Prof. Adam Vetulani:

Venerable Professor,
Today there are two traditional occasions which elicit congratulations: your patronal feast day[17] and Christmas Eve. This time, however, I wish not only to uphold this double tradition, but also honestly and sincerely thank you, Professor, for the offer to work on the Gdansk manuscript of the Decree, and for the direction and all your assistance in this work. Although a definite change in my scholarly interests has not occurred, please forgive me. Those matters are too deeply seated within me. Nonetheless, I owe very much to the work on the Gdansk manuscript. Since what I owe this work I

---

[16] Theological-Canonical Annuals
[17] Dec 24th is the Feast of Adam and Eve

also owe you, Professor, I wish to express my special gratitude today. A letter, a written word, may serve this purpose better than the spoken word. I will add that the Polish version of the thesis is to appear in the next issue of *Roczniki Teologiczno-Kanoniczne* probably sometime in the spring. Allow me further to extend, Dear Professor, sincere holiday wishes for your wife and sons. Rev. Karol Wojtyla (Archives of the Jagiellonian University: from the papers of A. Vetulani)

Since about 1957 until the time he became cardinal, he would stop in Lublin at the Convent of the Ursuline Sisters UR (10 Narutowicza Street). This convent was occupied by 56-70 sisters (the number varied from year to year), students at KUL, from various congregations. The Superior, Sister Angela (Wanda) Kurpisz, who earlier ran a boarding house for female students of the Jagiellonian University in Krakow, knew Fr. Wojtyla from his ministry among university students. She invited him to give spiritual conferences for the nun-students.

Father Wojtyla (later bishop) usually arrived early in the morning on the night train from Krakow, headed directly to the convent, prayed for a long time in front of the chapel in the corridor where there was a picture of the Blessed Mother, said the Holy Mass, ate breakfast and went to the university. He returned in the evening and then gave conferences to the student-nuns (at about 8:30 p.m.), the topics of which, according to the accounts given by some of the participants, were various aspects of the meaning of religious life. After the conference he ate supper. Students from KUL waited for him to walk him to the night train to Krakow. On some occasions he would remain in Lublin for a few days:

He lived in the guest room at the time, the so-called "green parlor" on the first floor by the chapel. He rose early for prayer. Before the Holy Mass he would pray the Way of the Cross in the corridor adjoining the chapel, before the picture of Our Lady of Czestochowa. I will always remember the silhouette of the bishop in his plain, black cassock, kneeling with his bent head hidden in his arms, absorbed in prayer. Sometimes the evening conferences would be replaced by the Stations of the Cross. The sisters would remain in the pews. Rev. Bishop would proceed from station to station and improvise a contemplation. {quote not attributed}

From the time he became cardinal, he would stop at the boarding house for priests at KUL. During that time, he would visit the Ursuline Convent, sometimes appearing unannounced, give a conference to the student-sisters, and lead the Stations of the Cross. "He demonstrated his gratitude to the sisters for every good turn. During the renovation of the convent kitchen in 1971/72, the Cardinal crossed the rubble to thank the sister who cooked dinner and to encourage her as she had to work under difficult conditions." (According to the accounts by Sister Natalia Rey and Sister Marta Ryk OSU.)

1957

March 31 — Bicycle trip with a group of the students of physics: Krakow, Tyniec, Bielany, Krakow.

June 9 — Bielsko, he blessed the marriage of friends.

June 15-16 — Walking trip (with a young couple) from Ptaszkowa to Krynica. On the way — meditations upon the mystery of the Holy Trinity and on holiness in marriage. On June 16 in the evening — a lecture-sermon (?) at the parish church in Krynica.

* July — Two excursions with the youth in the Bieszczady Mountains.

July 9-15 — Mountain trip with the *Srodowisko*: Komancza, Chryszczata, Cisna, Wielkie Jaslo, Mala Rawka, Ustrzyki Gorne, Halicz, Ustrzyki Gorne. One group (9 people) left, another group (6 people) arrived, he hiked with them for a few more days and left from Cisna.

July 27 - August 14 — Kayak excursion with the *Srodowisko* to Krutynia and Pisa (27 participants).

August 24-26 — Pastoral course at KUL — lecture (a subsequent typescript survived, undated): *The Propaedeutics of the Sacrament of Marriage*; in the remarks: "I gave a lecture of the same title at the pastoral course at KUL in August of 1957. The following paper, however, differs completely from the previous one." (Cf. Bibl. I, 30)

August 28 - September 5 — Pastoral course for women, at which he gives a conference: *Purity of Heart and Celibacy in the Light of Science*.

October — Academic year 1957/58: The same classes at KUL as last year. Topic of the monographic lecture: *Love and Responsibility*.

In the academic year 1957/58, lectures at the Krakow Seminary: Introduction to Theology and Economic Ethics.

October 4-5 — Pilgrimage to Czestochowa with a group of youth * October 6 — Excursion: Wadowice, Leskowiec, Skawce. A visit at Mr. and Mrs. Silkowski in Wadowice (with the group). Overnight at Ponikiew, a campfire was held.

October 23 — A pilgrimage of physicians to Jasna Gora {Czestochowa}.

November 1-2 — Meeting of psychologists and psychiatrists in Laski outside Warsaw. Lecture given by Rev. Karol Wojtyla on the topic: *Man in Various Aspects*.

November 15 — Letter from the Central Qualifying Committee for

Employees of Institutes of Higher Learning informing that the application submitted by the Academic Senate of KUL regarding the approval of Fr. Karol Wojtyla as assistant professor was considered favorably.

November 22 — Krakow, Church of the Felician Sisters. Conference for physicians.

> ...We spoke of the situation which is developing in the Church, namely that despite ideological, philosophical, and practical oppositions, the Church nonetheless continues to renew itself. This renewal manifests itself in the fact that the Church achieves an ever increasing awareness of the purpose of its existence. We also found that in this renewal of the Church there is a significant feature, namely, the role of the laity, who are given to fulfill their role independently, and this is because the Church is universal and lives in all areas of life. If we pay attention to the fact that, for instance, the Pope continually turns to the people, to those representing various specialties, speaks with them about the matters which concern him, attempting to be competent, it is because this side of God reaches all matters of mankind.
>
> Against this background we have outlined the current mission of the contemporary Catholic physician. (A summary given at the beginning of the next conference held on November 29)

November 29 — Church of the Felician Sisters. Subsequent conference for physicians.

> Today's conference will deal with the issue of our outlook on man. The point here is that there is a kind of view of man which constitutes some sort of specialty, a specific specialty of the Church and Christianity. There is also a view of man which, again, is specifically connected with the profession of a physician. The issue is whether these two outlooks overlap or, rather, whether they are related ...
>
> If we are now to answer the appeal of the Church, repeated so often these days, and do so from the point of view of our work, from the point of view of our calling: if we are to contribute something, from this point of view, to the work of building the Kingdom of God as it is in the spirit of today's Catholicism, then it is necessary that the physician's professional view of man be supplemented. "Help me to redeem man," the Church asks. To redeem man means to assist him in achieving the greatness he is meant to possess. It means to help him to mature to the union with God. This is what the Church means: "Help me to redeem man." ...

November 31— Official document from the Central Qualifying Committee containing the decision granting Karol Wojtyla the title of assistant professor (signature illegible, signed in proxy for Prof. Stefan Zolkiewski).

Henceforward he was an employee of KUL in the position of an assistant professor and director of the Chair of Ethics, and remained so until he was elected Pope, although shortly after becoming bishop he would work part-time, but as a full-fledged employee of the university. (Initially he taught assigned classes).

December 6 — Church of the Felician Sisters. Conference for physicians. Discussion of the pilgrimage of physicians from all over Poland:

I wish to devote today's conference to give an account of the pilgrimage to Czestochowa, as this was our joint action which has some meaning for us. Certainly, its underpinnings were not merely devotional. It was not out of particular piety that people of the same profession traveled to Jasna Gora for the second time (last year for the first time). It seems that these pilgrimages will become a tradition.

The main theme of this very large gathering of physicians from all over Poland at Jasna Gora was prayer. The starting point was a Holy Mass; group prayer made us aware that beside me, to my right, to my left, in front of me and behind me there is someone who thinks the way I do, feels like I do and aspires to what I do ...

The most interesting part of the pilgrimage was its conclusion, the discussion in the evening. In its course it became apparent what it is that the physicians who gathered there aspire to, what it is that they want. The evening discussion was led by the Bishop of Czestochowa who told them what the Church expects of them. This fact was clearly set before us. From the matters brought up there on that day, from all the discussions about what the medical circles want and what the Church wants from them, a postulate emerged: the physicians want to give and they want to take; of course, within the parameters of Catholic life in Poland, within the parameters of those tasks which the Catholic Church has to fulfill in Poland. The Church, which is apostolic in principle, sees today's Poland as a place of an apostolic mission. It sees the necessity of calling lay apostles, although not appointed, not clothed in habits. The Church exists precisely because there are apostles present everywhere within it ...

We stated that this circle of physicians, so numerous in Poland and so important in Poland, important in the life of the society and in the life of the Catholic Church, wishes to give and wishes to take. First then: what does it wish to take? It wishes, as it appeared from the declarations by representatives of some regions (e.g. the very telling declarations by physicians from the Gdansk region), to deepen its Catholic outlook on the world ...

All this, then, is underway among physicians: conferences, retreats, days of recollection, etc. The physicians perceive themselves not only as a professional group in the social sense, they perceive themselves as an operative group within the Church ...

The medical world wishes to give. What does it wish to give? It wishes to give what it can give from its profession. And here one heard of many initiatives. I will discuss the most characteristic ones. Above all, it wishes to give maximum care to suffering, ailing man ...

A doctor from a small town in Wielkopolska, a gynecologist, encountering cases of abortion in the course of his practice, describes how he tries with all his means to convince women who are a step away from this action not to go through with it. He employs all the arguments which are supplied by his medical knowledge, his human experience and, finally, his faith. Later, very humanely, he attempts to assist the woman on the path which can often be thorny after she had decided not to go through with this act. The need for organizing help was brought up. The doctor must cooperate with the local priest. They must then organize financial help for those mothers who want to take this step for the so called "social reasons." This is, of course, but a seed of an idea, but undoubtedly a question of the future...

The second task for physicians is to prepare young people for the Sacrament of Matrimony. We realize that trying to save a person in whom everything is already aflame or burned is too late. Therefore, one must prepare young people for their new responsibilities beforehand. The work performed by physicians in this area is extremely valuable; for example, conducting appropriate courses. Full assistance is provided by priests, by appropriate pastoral departments, but the doctors are at the helm. The priest cannot competently instruct young people in all areas of married life. This is another important element strongly emphasized there in Czestochowa. Beyond this, marital and premarital counseling is organized. And here in this area the physician's work enters directly onto the pastoral territory.

And further still, the care for the unhappy, abandoned, ailing person, who is not found in the hospital, but lives in frightful conditions somewhere alone in an apartment, which often does not appear fit for human habitation. This issue was brought to our attention by the nurses. On the basis of an article in *Tygodnik Powszechny,* this question, which aroused general interest, was discussed all over Poland. As a result, the nurses in some parishes have undertaken an action of such care for the ill, and are carrying it out. But this is a drop in the ocean; incomparably more is required here.

Physicians, then, wishing to give, enter the apostolic mission of the Church and fulfill it from their position. The meeting at Czestochowa made this evident beyond any doubt.

I am reporting, but in reporting I am also somehow appealing, speaking of things which are beginning and which must continue. We live in a big city and there are various needs in this city. Here our mind and our will must meet. They must meet because the salvation of man is always at issue. All that was discussed at Jasna Gora, all that was done and that is to be done in the future, all this is included in the program of putting the Jasna Gora Pledge into practice ...

As a result of what I have said today, it will be necessary to meet again during Advent. Should any desiderata evolve from today's thoughts, please make them known. One may not neglect a matter as important as the salvation of man.

December 7 — Letter to the Rector of KUL regarding a research trip. The reason given for the trip to Louvain (besides Belgium, he also planned to visit France and Switzerland) was the need to familiarize himself with materials on sexual ethics, which constituted the subject of his scholarly interest of the last few years: see lectures in 1957/58 and publications. On the recommendation of the Rector of KUL the ministry agreed to the trip; letter from the ministry dated January 8, 1958: "The Ministry of Higher Education supports the recommendation of the Rector of the Catholic University of Lublin regarding citizen Rev. Karol Wojtyla's travel to Belgium." (the document was addressed to the Department of Foreign Passports of the Provincial and City Command, Lublin). The trip fell through because Rev. Dr. Karol Wojtyla was not issued a passport.

December 13 - Church of the Felician Sisters, conference for physicians.

A week ago I was reporting on the physicians' pilgrimage to Jasna Gora and, as I spoke of everything that I heard there, above all from the physicians, I used this expression, that physicians increasingly feel as an operative group within the Church. This expression appears very bold and that is why I decided to return to it and justify it...

When a physician feels responsible for the entire person, the concept that he is an operative unit within the Church is already contained in this awareness. And if there is a group of 10, 20, 100 people with such awareness, then they all together feel as an operative group within the Church.

Around 2,000 physicians thought and expressed this at Jasna Gora. This is on the basis of the facts from Czestochowa...

Now a second justification, a more profound one, based on a truth about the Church which we know, or should know...

Thus a physician indeed encounters this dual legacy of man. For when he encounters death, he stands face to face with the heritage of Adam, if however, he meets with suffering, he encounters the legacy of Jesus Christ. Because Christ also suffered, and because Redemption was contained in His suffering. This double contact with man is the daily bread of a physician. We see then, that this is a contact not only with circumstance, but with various problems of man's fate and calling...

When a physician is at work, he is basically an operative unit of the Church. He does what the Church does within the scope of his activities. If 10, 20, 100 individuals of similar mind are found, that is, then, an operative group within the Church. This group only needs the awareness of what it is, what it can be and what it can accomplish. It accomplishes a great thing: it builds the Kingdom of God. But it could also destroy it. We know well that he who knows how to build, also knows, better than anyone else, how to destroy. The person who can best build the Kingdom of God is the priest; he is also the most capable of destroying it. Another who is capable of building Christ's Kingdom well is the physician, but he, too, is capable of destroying it.

The purpose of these weekly prayers is to help us not to destroy, but rather to build the Kingdom of God, for we surely are that operative group of the Church. We feel strongly bound with its destiny. We cannot be mere observers of what occurs within the Church. Christ describes his relationship with man in no uncertain terms: "He who is not with me, is against me," "He who does not gather with me, scatters." ...

December 14 — A day of recollection for the youth (on the topic of prayer.)

During this year, together with Msgr. Machay, Fr. Wojtyla considers a project of building housing for young married couples. There existed a potential construction site and the first steps were taken towards working out of the construction plans. (According to an account by Inz. {engineer} Stanislaw Rybicki.)

1958

January 1 — Krakow, Church of the Felician Sisters. Conference for physicians.

The Church is, after all, apostolic and missionary in its character. The Church's apostolic character conceals the dynamics of action, the need of action which arises from God's truth. The Church's apostolic character does not only have a quantitative meaning. The Church may never cease to be apostolic, not only in the sense that it proceeds from the apostles or that we constantly search its genealogy to establish whether the entire hierarchy proceeds from the apostles, but the Church is apostolic in the sense that it must enter into societies and areas of life which are not yet won. And if we look with the eyes of a true Christian sensing the apostolic character of the Church, our life continually presents this view with a succession of domains and areas not conquered, which must assimilate God's truth, must become permeated with it, must accept its light.

January 10 — Church of the Felician Sisters. Conference for physicians.

Many people cannot come to terms with Christian dogma. Yet, at the same time, they are willing to affirm Christian morality, which stands at the highest level, so high that mankind has never received a higher one from anywhere, nor can it expect to... The motive is the commandment to love contained in the moral program of the Gospels...The question arises: Man, for whom love is a need, why has love been assigned to such man? Placing love on the level of a commandment indicates that love does not equate itself with the need to love... The love Christ demands must be first elicited from man's inclination to love... The point here is that all these energies be directed, sent in the direction of the proper good. "Love God above all else, and love your neighbor as yourself." Thus, God, myself, and my neighbor.

January 13 — Church of the Felician Sisters. Conference for physicians.

Love is the main point of attraction because of which Christian ethics is a subject of interest even for non-believers. But it also serves as the main point of difficulty for man.

January 17 — Church of the Felician Sisters. Conference for physicians.

To begin deliberations on the topic of Christian Ethics, we have selected what lies at the very core of ethics and of the Gospels, namely the commandment of love. This is the issue which somehow must be dealt with first...

Had Christ said: feel God above all, more than you feel anything else, man would shrug his shoulders and say: that is impossible. But Christ said: you will love the Lord thy God above all. Feeling is probably a symptom of love, but not the most basic symptom of love. We are all convinced of this, although in everyday language we sometimes express it differently. When Christ said: *you shall love God above all else,* he addressed the whole man not his feelings only, but the whole, rational, spiritual nature. He addressed, of course, the need to love, but it is that need to love which exists in the

whole, spiritual, rational nature of man, and said: I place before you an absolute good. God is such a good. Could man comprehend this? ...

Sometimes people pose this question: When do I love God above all? There is a surprising answer to this question: when you avoid mortal sin. Let us agree that this answer encompasses the minimum of what it means to love God. Though indeed minimalist, still this is true love. In its style it does not agree with the essence of love, for love consists in doing something, creating something. But in this answer there is talk of not doing. Let us remember that for people, not doing is sometimes a very great act of love. From day to day man lives much more superficially, but man is also so very profound that this commandment, this demand could be set before him: You shall love the Lord your God... If God-Become-Man could tell man: love me above all else — this is a great honor, an unheard of advancement for the creature that man is. It bespeaks an enormous confidence in man's abilities.

January 24 — Church of the Felician Sisters. Conference for physicians.

More on the commandment of love ...

The most common complaint and difficulty which is advanced on this occasion is of this type: one can love man since, in some way, he demands love. Man is similar to us, we see him, hear him, experience him. How can we love God whom we do not experience? Moreover, the love of God interferes with the love of man: for if man engages himself in the love of God, there will be no room for the love of man. Man will not have the strength, the energy, or the heart left to still love man.

As a result, the first part of the commandment to love is tolerated by most people; but the second part, the love of neighbor, is acknowledged.

Man does not come out well in this. Something has to exist that can expand man's heart ...

God's commandment refers to the love of neighbor and the love of neighbor benefits incredibly from this association with the love of God. So let us assess and discuss this issue according to the proper models and not according to the inappropriate ones.

January 31 — Church of the Felician Sisters. Conference for physicians.

Let us consider certain thoughts on the topic of the love of neighbor. There is but one commandment of love: to love God and to love our neighbor. This is so because there is but one love — that which God pours into our hearts and which we embrace. There is but one love, and it is directed toward God and toward man. It flows from two sources: from the supernatural source of God's grace, and from our nature...

The love of neighbor: it is difficult to speak of it for it requires that we consider a long succession of situations, manifestations of life. There is yet another reason why it is difficult to speak of love for one's neighbor. This is a very lofty commandment. It places the whole issue of the relationship of man to man on a very high level. We all feel that there is something in this commandment which exceeds us, and which, at the same time, pinpoints what man's life is about ...

There are three elements which must be combined in our work in this area: the love of neighbor is the love of man ...

With this view of man's value one could remain a theorist, and that is why this view of man's value must be supplemented by the heart and by the will. From the perspective of the heart this view of man's value is supplemented by some kind of feeling, by establishing a connection, by putting oneself in his place, by entering his interior domain, by entering it with empathy. This feeling of empathy for another person is extremely important so that our understanding of man's value would not remain in the abstract. But, besides this, a third element is necessary, namely, one must desire the welfare of the other. This is most important. This is the ultimate proof of love for neighbor: to desire that good which is his good. And now a conflict can arise. To desire the good that is truly his good. Not the immediate good, influenced by the situation or the atmosphere. To assume responsibility for another person. To see what is to his benefit. To be him to the extent that one simply acts somewhat in his name. To understand what is good for him, sometimes better than he himself understands ...

The physician's calling is very closely connected with the commandment of the love of neighbor. This is probably the kind of calling and profession through which man approaches God by acts of love for his neighbor. Moreover, a physician has very intimate contact with actual people, not in the sphere of documents, files and things, but with actual persons. That is why a thorough consideration of these three elements which help us to put the love of neighbor into practice, is very necessary to this particular calling.

Around February 11 — Fr. Wojtyla participated in a week-long skiing course at Hala Lipowska. The instructor is Jerzy Ciesielski.

February 14 — Church of the Felician Sisters. Conference for physicians.

There are various human needs: closer ones and more distant ones; bodily needs, material ones — external and internal, spiritual and completely concrete. These needs beset me from every side. In all this I must somehow prove, verify my love. If I do not perceive these things, it is already evidence that I lack something. My love is not real ...

February 21 — Church of the Felician Sisters. Conference for physicians.

It is often said and heard that Christianity is a religion of mercy. Indeed, the words of the Gospels which refer to mercy for one's neighbor are deeply engraved in our memory ...

Basically, man carries within himself a resistance to mercy. However, since he recognizes mercy, he must acknowledge that he himself needs at least the help of other men. Meanwhile, each person carries within himself a strong need of self sufficiency: not to need! not to find oneself in a situation of need! And from this aspect mercy and a religion of mercy are not looked favorably upon by people. On the other hand, man needs mercy — herein lies the paradox.

We are not concerned here about the impression Christianity makes on Christians and non-Christians. What is of concern is the actual state of things. The actual state of things is that man needs mercy. And the scope of the need for mercy is much wider than we think ...

Each man stands at a point where he is needed by someone. And each man stands at a point where there are people all around him who need his help. Each one of us stands at such a point of always being needed by someone and being surrounded by those who need. This is why Christianity is real. The concept of a physician that excludes mercy is a contradiction. It would be hypocrisy. For in truth it is otherwise. We are at the very center of the program of mercy. This is the point from which we may best approach the Gospel, the truth about the Savior, about God, whom man has come to need because He continues to meet all the needs of man ... He uses us in order to bestow mercy upon all those in need.

February 28 — Church of the Felician Sisters. Conference for physicians.

One more matter deserves our attention in connection with the issue of the love of neighbor which we last discussed. It is the matter of compassion. Compassion is some kind of expression of kindness for a suffering person. As the suffering person is very closely connected with our profession, the issue of compassion is therefore a professional issue for us ...

I believe that all of us who often meet with human suffering must have the problem of compassion well thought out. Compassion which gives nothing to the person we sympathize with would be inadequate — if not harmful — if it were to demoralize the person we sympathize with; if it were, for instance, to assume the form of emotional dejection resulting from his suffering and thus oppress him even more.

This point must be deliberated. Undoubtedly, this is one of the tasks of the love of neighbor — a task of the highest order. The point is that our compassion should lift up and not deject. In order to elevate the suffering person, this compassion must depend on deeper energies within us which we have at our disposal: on the energy of will and mind. Therefore, we must see some purpose, we must cast our sight on man's life in its entirety. We must have a view, for instance, on the meaning of his death. After all, we are frequently the ones who are best aware of the fact that suffering gives death its beginning.

March 2 — A day of recollection for a group of young married couples (Deskur, Rybicki, Ciesielski) at the house of the Sisters of the Holy Family of Nazareth at Warszawska Street. Topic: the child.

March 7 — Church of the Felician Sisters. Conference for physicians.

A few more words tying in to what we have been considering for some time, namely the commandment of love.

It is formulated in this manner: "You will love the Lord your God with your whole heart and all your might, and love your neighbor as yourself."

The connection that exists between the love of neighbor and the love of oneself allows us to suppose that the emphasis here is placed on the fact that the measure of the love of neighbor is the love of self. This measure also goes the other way: the measure of our love of self is the love neighbor. This should be understood in such a way that there exists a constant factor limiting human egoism, and this factor is simply man's love of his neighbor, the love of another person ...

If a person has projected himself into all of this in the full context of the entire Gospel, then this commandment must appear to him as a principle ordering human life. There are difficulties, indeed. But the difficulty lies not in the principle, but in life. Man must struggle a lot to bring this principle into life. Human life is not conventional — it is turbulent, uneven. Man tipped the original balance and continues to live in it restlessly. And it is difficult for him to restore the tipped balance. It will not happen without struggle, one has to be prepared for it, one must even love it from the start.

This effort lies within man's capabilities. Besides, the commandment to love, given to man by God, is united with the act of God's love for man, namely with *grace*. This is why the balance and order described in God's commandment are possible to achieve.

These are the final statements on the topic of the love of God and neighbor before the retreat. Perhaps they will be most useful to us during the retreat in this very interpretation.

March 8-9 — Krakow, Chapel of the Ursuline Sisters. A day of recollection for the youth.

First Lesson: ... Contemporary life is disrupted, it has an excess of purposes which draw man in, use him up and leave him sterile. This wave of activities carries him, absorbs him, but the carried person does not have complete confidence in it. This surfeit of goals disperses the completeness and unity of life. Man needs homogeneity, he would feel much better if he had but one goal. We hear of this often, speak of it, and maybe consider it, but we do not see it. The contemporary man does not see it — the youth speak about it repeatedly. A surfeit of goals, an overproduction of sensations, we grab at them with our senses. But this one goal, embracing all functions, must be achieved with the mind.

Today one reads with embarrassment in Aristotle that the world has one goal and that this goal draws everything towards itself. This goal is God, who for Aristotle is beyond the world, self-contained — all creatures aspire toward Him for He draws them to Himself ...

Second Lesson: ... Our method is prayer. If we experience disappointment here it is simply because we do not know what prayer is. Here non-Christians put us to shame. We know what Aristotle said regarding prayer, what the Hindus say ... Prayer is the response to the mystery which this world carries within itself. When the contemporary man ceases to pray, he ceases to react correctly to the world ... The developing world is a kind of prayer and this process of development can be transformed into prayer. If the world diverts this process towards itself, it will perish under the achievements of technology and the so-called civilization. The point is that all of life, with its diverse activities, should become prayer. — "I can devote 3 minutes, half an hour to prayer," someone told me. That is too little. That is not an answer. The appropriate question should be: Does my prayer, such as it is — short or long — suffice for all of my life to be a prayer? How to discern this? I recognize this when God always prevails in my life. — Am I committed to God and to reason?

Here we must make an examination of conscience. This is the subject and texture of the Gospel: one must always pray. If we so pray, even if the prayer lasts three minutes, God will always prevail. This is the method of Christ and, at the same time, the method of realism ...

Third Lesson: The Holy Mass was something extraordinary for the first Christians. Special days were designated during Lent when they gathered and together meditated on the Gospels, on the words of Christ, on His

Passion and Death. The remainders of that are in the "Ember Days"[18] in the liturgy of the Church. In those times they experienced their faith and its meaning on their knees. We are now approaching this style. A sign of this is the evening Holy Mass. Let this day be a preparation for the evening Holy Mass ...

The topic of sin: Deep reflection on oneself leads to a sense of sin ...

An impulse of nature is not a sin, it is an impulse, an attribute of our corrupt nature. Sin originates in weakness, but it does not depend on weakness alone. The participation of the will is significant, not the impulse ...

An impulse often results from neglect, but not always. We possess the freedom of choice, we possess will, thus we have responsibility. There are opposite tendencies — to consider impulses as an indication of bad will. These are incorrect tendencies, in disagreement with the teachings of the Church and the Gospels. The first condition of the battle with sin is an integral view of oneself. When we make an examination of conscience we must analyze tendencies, temperament, since impulses are grounded in some foundation ... Going to confession does not mean you are rid of sin, but that the sins you have committed have been forgiven ... Let us name the sins committed against our neighbors today, let us make an examination of conscience about them, so that God does not surprise us with an examination one day ... We are often tempted not to enter the depth of our own conscience; let us reject this immediately and proceed into the depth. Man is a fickle creature. Do not rely on yourself. God wishes to be man's companion ...

Fourth Lesson: Penance ... A penitent man is an able man, who will not allow himself to be herded into the blind alley of the impulses of our nature tainted by original sin. A penitent man is an able man. The absence of penance — the absence of ability. The penitent man will always find a way, and this is related to joy. It is exactly this joy that the Gospel brought ...

The process of penance must commence not only with reflection, but also with prayer — on one's knees, in the spiritual sense. This is difficult, this takes effort. The subjective process of penance is difficult because it consists in carrying the cross.

The Way of the Cross serves as an illustration of our lives and of a particular part of the way of Christ's life. It is the highlight of man's life and of God's life ... We pray the Way of the Cross in order to confront our toil as we are confronted by Christ's toil. Contemplation leads to self assessment ...

We have one unique life, which is our talent granted by God and it must prove to be worthwhile to God. That is, at that moment we should have the awareness of having fulfilled our duty, which is expressed in Christ's words on the Cross — "It is accomplished." and "Father, into Your hands I commend my spirit." (Stenograph I.K.)

April 11 — Krakow. Church of the Felician Sisters. Conference for physicians.

The Resurrection of our Lord is the manifestation of Christ, the victory of good over evil, the victory of Christ over death. It is so understood by His followers and those who ponder the facts on which the Catholic faith is founded. For this is the victory of life over death, in some sense of the natural life. After all, Christ died a physical death and was resurrected to phys-

---

[18] Any of the days in the quarterly 3-day period of prayer and fasting, (the Wednesday, Friday, and Saturday after the First sunday of Lent, after Whitsunday, After Sep. 14, and after Dec. 13) observed in the R.C. Church and other Western Churches.

ical life ...

    These truths speak of something particular to the believing physician, that is to the person whose calling is the service to life, the defense of life against disease and death. These truths somehow speak about the meaning of the physician's calling and they affirm it in the light of Christ's death and Resurrection. Christ was often referred to as a physician and today He is still referred to in this manner, for example in the Litany to the Holy Name of Jesus.

    The fact of the Lord's Resurrection and the truth of Christ's death affirms the physician's calling, but also places this calling as if in a new perspective. For if my vocation is to defend life, the physical life, then, by reason of my faith, my allegiance to Christ, and my faith in the Risen Christ, it is also my vocation to defend this other life — God's life; to serve this other life as well — the supernatural life — in myself and in others. This would be the ideal: to combine the service to physical life with the service to spiritual life.

June 9 — He led a day of recollection at the KUL dormitory for female students at Poczekajka (Halina Wistuba in "Poslaniec warminski" {The Warmia Messenger} 1982, p. 175).

June 9/11 and 19/20 — A pastoral course for priests working in Krakow, in the building of the Major Religious Seminary in Krakow. Rev. K. Wojtyla's conference entitled *"Interior attitudes of the priest ministering to health professionals in light of the theological and ascetic principles of ministry to various professions"* (Aten. Kapl. 1958, vol. 56, no. 3; *Tygodnik Powszechny* 1958, no. 27).

June 26 — At KUL, the defense of the doctoral dissertation of Sister Maria Kasperkiewicz: *Friendship and its Place and Function in the Aristotelian System of Ethics*; professor conferring the degree, Rev. Dr. Karol Wojtyla. The first doctoral defense for which Rev. K. Wojtyla was the promoter.

June-July — Excursion to the Bieszczady Mountains.

July 4 — An official nomination is announced for the titular bishop *Antigon* (Cf. L' Osservatore Romano, August 31, 1958) and, at the same time, an auxiliary bishop to the Apostolic Administrator of the Archdiocese of Krakow, Archbishop Eugeniusz Baziak.

July 10 — The office of the Secretary of State sends a letter to Cardinal Primate Stefan Wyszynski informing him about the nomination of Rev. Karol Wojtyla to bishop, ordering him to accept the "canonical consent."

Around July 22 — Kayak excursion on the San with a youth group. (Route: Przemysl — Lezajsk)

August 1-4 — Private retreat at the abbey of the Benedictine Fathers in Tyniec.

August 3-20 — Kayak excursion on the Lyna River organized by a group of Fr. Wojtyla's friends, known as *Srodowisko*: August 3 — Waplewo — the Maroz Lake, August 4, 5, 6 — the Pluszcze Lake. On August 6 — Rev. Wojtyla left the group. He met with Cardinal Primate Wyszynski who notified him of the nomination to the auxiliary bishop of Krakow.

When he was nominated to the office of the auxiliary bishop of Krakow, I was ordered to receive from him the so-called "canonical consent", for the nominee is always asked whether he accepts the nomination, and to determine the time when his nomination should be announced in Poland. We found him on the Mazurian lakes at that time together with a group of young people, for he is a sportsman, you know (Cardinal Wyszynski, his address at the Warsaw Cathedral on November 6, 1978).

Cardinal Primate further recalled that when he asked the bishop nominee what he intended to do in the nearest future, Rev. Wojtyla replied that he was going to return to the lakes and continue his camp.

August 8 — The nomination of Rev. Karol Wojtyla to bishop is announced in Poland.

August 10 — he returns to the group and shares the news of his nomination. The kayak excursion continues till August 20. (Based on: *Zapis Drogi. Wspomnienia o nieznanym duszpasterstwie ksiedza Karola Wojtyly.* {A Record of a Journey. Memories of Rev. Karol Wojtyla's Unknown Ministry}, Krakow 1998.)

After the kayak excursion — a visit of a few days at the "philosophic holidays" organized by KUL:

I was on "philosophic holidays" organized by KUL in Swieta Lipka (August 1958). The majority of the participants were students, there were two high-school graduates and a few alumni. The youth gathered there came from Wroclaw, Warsaw, Bialystok, Lodz, and above all, Lublin, among them Bohdan Cywinski and Halina Bortnowska, as well as Rev. Prof. Stanislaw Kaminski. Toward the end of our stay, Rev. Prof. Karol Wojtyla, a young man in a sports shirt (it was a beautiful summer), came to Swieta Lipka for a few days. He brought with him a typewritten script of Love and Responsibility, distributed portions among us and later there was a discussion on the lawn, at the lake, at the wood's edge. (Ewa)

August 12 — From a letter to Prof. A. Vetulani:

Misery with the cleric-scholars; you educate him to become assistant professor and a "statesman" emerges. I struggle not to be too negative about this — research has already seized my mind too much. Another thing is how much room I will find for it in my life now. I have resolved to fight for it. The office of a bishop is an invaluable spiritual legacy from the Apostles, nonetheless, bishops must live in an era of "academic outlook."

All this began probably in the summer of 1958, when one day towards the evening, an unknown man dressed as a priest, hence a priest, knocked at the gate of the house of the sisters' convent. "Could I enter your chapel to

pray?" He was led into the chapel and left alone. When he did not emerge
for some time, they looked in on him. He lay prostrate on the ground. The
sister stepped back, filled with respect. "He must have an important matter,
perhaps he's a penitent." After another while, the sister looked into the
chapel again. The priest still lay prostrate. But the hour was late. The sister
went up to him and shyly asked: "Perhaps Father would be so kind to come
to supper?" — The stranger responded: "My train to Krakow isn't until
after midnight. Allow me to stay here. I have much to discuss with the Lord.
Do not disturb me." ... Today this man is called John Paul II, the Pope.
(Father Jan Zieja, "Pewien czlowiek,"[19] *Wiez*, no. 11, November 1978)

August 31 — As bishop nominee he baptizes Stanislaw Rybicki, son
of a couple belonging from the beginning to the group he worked and
traveled with.

September 1-4 — Jasna Gora. He participated in a retreat of the
Polish Episcopate (he occupies room no. 62 at the convent, is listed 43rd
in the register, after Bishop Andrzej Wronka, as Bishop Auxiliary of
Krakow).

September 4-6 — He participated in the works of the plenary conference of the Episcopate at Jasna Gora.

September 5 — "The Primate greeted the new bishops: Wronka,
Pluta, Drzazga, Blecharczyk and Wojtyla, then informed that bishops
Pluta and Wojtyla have been called to the Committee for General
Apostolate." (According to the minutes of the Conference of the Episcopate)

September 6-7 — Mountain trip to the summit of Pilsko. Holy Mass
for the *Srodowisko* group walking from Wisla to Piwniczna.

September 9-11 — The third post-war conference of professors of
theological institutes in Poland. Bishop K. Wojtyla is co-chairman of the
morality section (together with Bishop I. Swirski). On September 10,
under the auspices of the sociological section of this conference he
delivered a presentation entitled "The Program of Lectures on
Sociological Studies in Seminaries and at Theological Institutes in
Poland" (see *Roczniki Teologiczno-Kanoniczne* 8/1961, v. 3, pp. 65-66)

September 14 — He participated in a class reunion in Wadowice on
the 20th anniversary of the secondary school final exams.

September 20 — An account by an incidental person:

> I was in Krakow and went to confession at the Mariacki Church[20] An
> unknown priest, referring to what I had just told him about my son attend-
> ing the initiating retreat at the Seminary in Dolny Slask, told me of the
> retreat awaiting him prior to his consecration as Bishop, and asked for

---

[19] a Certain Man…
[20] The Basilica of the Blessed Virgin Mary, located in the Market Square, Krakow.

prayers for his intention, promising to pray for our son ... In May of 1959, as I was in Krakow again, I went to see Rev. Bishop, as my son was having doubts and difficulties, although he was managing with his studies very well. I was attentively listened to and then it was suggested that I come to the morning Holy Mass, which the Bishop wanted to offer for my son's intention. His own surprising initiative affected me deeply. During the Mass in the chapel adjacent to the sacristy at the Wawel Cathedral I saw and remembered the Bishop's long, supplicant gaze at the cross.

Subsequently, I met him, probably already as a cardinal, in the 1960s ... He immediately recognized the chance collocutor from Krakow. Similarly, at our next meeting in 1974 in Oswiecim {Auschwitz}. I received (in 1975) a letter with a blessing for my work, of which I had notified him.

September 21 — Procathedral in Lubaczow. Bishop nominee Wojtyla participated in the celebrations of the 25th anniversary of Archbishop E. Baziak's ordination.

September 25 — Bishop-nominee Wojtyla wanted explanations provided for the congregation during the ceremony of the consecration. Archbishop Baziak did not agree to this.

The only saving point is that there will be texts by Father Franciszek (Malaczynski OSB) which explain all the rubrics of the consecration and which many ladies are voluntarily transcribing.... The cassocks are ready, Mr. Bobrownicki will send them over to Kanonicza Street. The Bishop of Opole [Franciszek Jop] sent the chaplain with a gift for the day of consecration, asking that it (crosier, ring) be held in his hands during the ceremony in the cathedral ... The distinguished nominee awaits the celebrant together with the Capitulary at the entrance to the cathedral, therefore, it will be necessary to head for the Cathedral much earlier and wait first in the Treasury, in order to avoid the crowds. (From a private letter by Father Czeslaw Obtulowicz) (The bishop's cassock was a gift from Msgr. Ferdynand Machay)

September 23-27 — Retreat in Tyniec before the consecration as bishop. He participated in the liturgy, accepts and returns greetings.

September 26 — Two days before his consecration as bishop a letter (Record no. 7722/58) is sent from the Secretariate of State in the Vatican to Cardinal Stefan Wyszynski notifying him that the titular bishopry of *Antigon* mentioned in the previous letter (of July 10) was eliminated and, as of the year 1958, will no longer be listed in "Annuario Pontificio" (an official papal annual issued by the Secretariate od State, containing updated information on the condition/status of the Catholic Church). In view of this the Sacred Congregation of the Consistory designated *Ombi* to be Msgr. Karol Wojtyla's titular seat. The undersecretary who signed this letter asked Cardinal Wyszynski to pass this information on to the interested party.

September 28 — The Feast of St. Waclaw {Wenceslaus}. Consecration as Bishop at the Wawel Cathedral. Celebrants: Archbishop Eugeniusz Baziak (Krakow), Bishop Franciszek Jop (Opole), and

Bishop Boleslaw Kominek (Wroclaw).

He adopted the words *"Totus Tuus"* for his motto as bishop. The words come from the *"Treatise on true devotion to the Blessed Virgin Mary"* by St. Luis Maria Grignon de Monfort (cf. *Kalendarium*, May 20, 1965) — a work particularly close to his heart. The following is the fragment from which the motto *"Totus Tuus"* was borrowed: *At least once a year, on the anniversary of one's dedication, one should renew the pledge by fulfilling the same exercises for three weeks. One may also renew the pledge every month or even every week by means of these brief words: Here I am **all Yours** and everything that is mine is Yours, O my dearest Jesus, through Mary, Your Most Holy Mother* (Treatise..., 233).

He placed the letter "M" with a cross in his coat of arms. He retained the same coat of arms and motto as pope. The Vatican experts modified the design of the coat of arms a little so as to give it a look conforming to the requirements of heraldry.

> After receiving the consecration as bishop, he received wishes from the delegation of physicians, whom he looked after until now as chaplain for the health services. He said that he accepts their wishes and gift as a sign that in his service as bishop he should concern himself with matters of the medical profession. (According to an account by Dr. Anna Starczewska)

Prof. A. Vetulani's toast given at the reception on the occasion of the consecration:

> Your Excellency, Reverend Fathers, and Honorable Table Companions! Allow me to join in the toasts raised in the name of Bishop Docent Karol Wojtyla, Professor of the Catholic University of Lublin. Today's holy rites dignified Reverend Karol Wojtyla, elevated him to the ranks of the prelates, the heirs of the apostles, placed upon him honorable, though heavy and responsible duties, always difficult, and today probably more difficult than in those times to which our own memories reach. We are all in agreement in wishing him that God's assistance support him every step of the way in fulfilling these duties, which are now his. To these wishes allow me to add one thing only: may he have adequate strength and time to fulfill these obligations, which he has earlier taken upon himself and for which he has trained through strenuous work, the effort of many years, in order that he may further develop the discipline of study in which he independently treads as a professor of philosophy and ethics, as an immediate counselor to those who train for the battle for the victory of a scholarly Catholic world outlook in our society. My wish to you from the bottom of my heart, Reverend Bishop, is that your name engrave itself in the history of the Polish Church as well as in the history of the Polish academia and the Polish Christian culture. (Archives of JU, from the papers of A. Vetulani)

September 29 — in the morning (or perhaps still the evening of September 28). He turned his first steps as bishop to Czestochowa. He was accompanied by his young friends.

October 2 — In Bogaczowice Stare, a conference for the "active members" of the university student ministry.

From September 30 to October 5 — in Bogaczowice Stare (about 10 kilometers north of Walbrzych), in the buildings occupied at that time by the Grey Ursuline Nuns, a closed retreat was held for the so-called "active members" of the university student ministry from all over Poland. The retreat was organized by Rev. Canon Aleksander Oberc who fulfilled the duties of the diocesan director of the university student ministries in Wroclaw. The selection of the youth (and the entire organization of the retreat) was conducted in absolute confidentiality. I remember participants from Warsaw, Lublin, Poznan, Lodz, Krakow and Wroclaw, perhaps there were also some from other centers. I shared my room with a student of the 4th year of the Polish Studies — Bogdan Cywinski (a writer and publicist) and a student of the 5th year of the Institute of Technology in Krakow — Andrzej Pawica (engineer-designer). The high level of the retreat was guaranteed by the choice of lecturers — Rev. Bishop Boleslaw Kominek (2 lectures), Rev. Bishop Karol Wojtyla, Dr. Adam Stanowski, Assistant Professor Leokadia Malunowicz. Also participated: Rev. Rector Aleksander Zienkiewlcz, Fr. Joachim, a Dominican and priest from Poznan, Roman Kukulowicz and Rev. Oberc. Father Piotr Rostworowski, the prior of Tyniec at that time, delivered the retreat homilies.

Besides Fr. Piotr, it was Rev. Bishop Karol Wojtyla who particularly drew my attention. In very brief notes written in my pocket calendar I noted the topic of only his lecture and recorded my impression of him: "An extremely pleasant man, witty, sociable. He has a lecture on the freedom of man" (a remark added in parenthesis: "of the will").

Rev. Bishop Karol Wojtyla and Rev. Oberc arrived in Bogaczowice Stare on October 2, 1958 at about 11 a.m. His lecture and a discussion that followed took place after dinner in a little orchard by the Ursuline monastery (surrounded by a high wall which protected us from potential undesirable observers). Basking in beautiful sunny weather, we ate apples, listened to the lecture and discussed it with breaks for singing. Rev. Bishop taught us to sing, among others, "Zal, zal za dziewczyna, za zielona Ukraina"... {Longing, longing after the girl, after the green Ukraine...}. As I was not a student of humanities (I was at the 5th year of agricultural studies), I expressed an opinion in the discussion on free will, man's action and the protection of the Divine Providence, and I did so in an insufficiently precise manner. I was sharply criticized for it by assistant professor Malunowicz. Rev. Bishop Wojtyla came to my defense and explained what I wanted to express for which I was extremely grateful to him.

October 3 — In the morning after breakfast Rev. Bishop was supposed to leave for Krakow with Fr. Piotr Roztworowski. We did not want to let them go. First Fr. Piotr had to deliver a good-bye homily. And he did deliver, chiding us with the later famous words: "Don't be such pigs and don't give God this junk." Then Sylwia Nowakowska, a student of the first year of the University of Warsaw, hid his car keys. She returned them only after Rev. Bishop said: "Sylwia, give the keys back — I will officiate at your marriage." Prof. Dr. A.E. Waclaw Leszczynski

October 3 — 6 p.m. Pontifical Mass at the Wawel Cathedral *
October 5 —Sermon for the inauguration of the academic year — St. Anne's Church, Krakow * October 7 — Cathedral, inauguration of the

academic year. Krakow Seminary (sermon) * October 9 — Death of Pope Pius XII * October 12 — Skomielna Czarna, the blessing of a corner stone for the Church (sermon) * October 13 — Wawel Cathedral, Pontifical Mass following the death of Pius XII (deceased on October 9) * October 18 — (Feast of St. Luke) Church of the Felician Sisters, Krakow, Holy Mass and sermon for physicians * October 19 — 8 a.m. Bienczyce-Nowa Huta–Holy Mass and sermon * 5 p.m. — Krakow, St. Anne's Church — Holy Mass and sermon for lawyers * October 21 — Ursuline Sisters, visit to the Higher Institute of Catechesis (WIK) * October 23 — Church of St. Anne, lecture for students * October 20 — Franciscan Fathers, blessing of deacons and sub-deacons.

November 4 — Katowice. Meeting of the Pastoral Committee of the Episcopate * November 5 — Second day of the meeting of the Pastoral Committee of the Episcopate, dedicated to the participation of the religious in the 2nd and 3rd years of the Great Novena preparing the Church in Poland for the Millennium of Christianity. Lectures: Bishop Zdzislaw Golinski, Fr. Bonawentura Kadej and Fr. Wawryn. In the discussion, Bishop Wojtyla spoke of the program of the 3rd year of the Great Novena, of the academic strengthening of the pastorate, and of the problems of religious orders in the parishes * The same day — Krakow. Church of St. Mark — Holy Mass with a colloquium on educational themes * November 9 — 10 a.m., Pontifical Mass on the occasion of the coronation of John XXIII. The same day — chapel at Pedzichow — confirmation of deaf-mute children * November 11 — Zakopane, service and sermon at the parish church * November 16 — 7 a.m. Kozy, Holy Mass and sermon to conclude the mission * Same day —10 a.m. — Krakow, Pontifical Mass and sermon at St. Stanislaw Kostka parish * 6 p.m. — service and sermon for male youth at the parish of the Blessed Virgin Mary * 7 p.m. — Sermon for lawyers at the Dominican Fathers' Church * November 17 — 7:30 p.m., administration of tonsure[21] to six Reformed Franciscan clerics at the Church of the Capuchin Fathers in Krakow * November 20 — Requiem Mass for Rev. Prof. Tadeusz Glem * November 21 — 7 a.m. — Sisters of the Holy Family of Nazareth, Holy Mass and sermon * Same day — 10 a.m. — Ryczow, meeting of the Zatorski Deanery * 2 p.m. — Zywiec-Zablocie, meeting of the Zywiec Deanery * 6 p.m. — service and sermon in Zywiec-Zablocie * November 23 — Wadowice — solemn High Mass (on the occasion of the Bishop's nomination) and visitation at the convents of, among others, the Albertine Sisters. In response to the singing of "Ecce sacerdos magnus,"[22] with which he was greeted by the Albertine Sisters, he said "This great priest is Jesus Our Lord." This was his first visit to

---

[21] Shaving the crown of the head, a rite on the way to the priesthood.
[22] Behold the great priest

the Albertine House (Albertine Sisters) * After the consecration, Bishop Karol Wojtyla came on a visit to the then pastor, Msgr. Leonard Prochownik. He took the opportunity to visit his beloved convent Na Gorce.[23] (According to an account by Father Boguslaw Woznicki, a Carmelite)

Visiting the lower Carmelite seminary as an auxiliary Bishop, right after his consecration, he said: "I am glad that I may share with you my devotion to the Virgin Mary, Mother of the Scapular. I always wear the scapular I received from the hands of Fr. Sylvester on the day of my First Holy Communion and, although I lived in the shadow of the parish church, your church "na Gorce" has always been very dear to me. Among the many services which enchanted my soul as a child, I attended most eagerly the novena preceding the Feast of Our Lady of Mount Carmel. This was during summer vacation in the month of July. In those days one did not go away for vacation, like now. I spent the holidays in Wadowice, thus I never missed the afternoon services during the novena until the time of my departure from Wadowice. Sometimes it was difficult to leave friends, leave the refreshing waves of the beloved Skawa {river}, but the mellifluous sound of the Carmelite bells was so strong, so penetrating into the depths of the soul, that I went. Yes, indeed, I lived next to the parish church, but I grew up in the Church of St. Joseph." (From the chronicle of the Convent written by Fr. Konstanty Patecki who was director of the Private Secondary School of the Carmelite Fathers from 1957 to 1960)

The same day — 7 p.m. — Krakow, Church of the Discalced Carmelite Fathers — Holy Mass for the intention of the Beatification of Brother Albert, sermon. * November 30 — Confirmation of school children at the Church of the Redeemer in Krakow.

December 3 — Church of Sts. Peter and Paul in Krakow, Holy Mass with an educational conference by Rev. Dr. T. Rylko * December 4 — Church of St. Anne — Holy Mass for the deceased professors of JU * December 5 — A visit during the academic conference at the Church of Corpus Christi in Krakow * December 7 — 9 a.m. — the Church of St. Mark, Holy Mass for the editorial staff of *Tygodnik Powszechny*. Same day, in the evening — participation in a discussion with employees and sympathizers of *"TP"* * December 8 — For the first time as Bishop Auxiliary of Krakow, he ordains two deacons from the Congregation of the Friars Minor (Reformed) — Fr. Leszek Dudzinski and Fr. Tytus Kondys. This took place in Krakow at the Chapel of the Daughters of Charity on Warszawska Street. The Sisters renovated the chapel and asked the Bishop to consecrate it. He agreed, on the condition that he could confer holy orders there. (According to an account by Fr. Cherubin Kozera) * December 10 — Krakow, the Theological Seminary — meeting of the Polish Theological Society in memory of Pope Pius

---

[23] On the Hill

XII. Church of Our Lady of Lourdes — breaking of the wafer[24] with university students * December 17 — Oswiecim, parish of the Assumption of Our Lady — sermon during a student retreat * December 20 — Church of St. Anne in Krakow, conference and breaking of the wafer with students.

December 21 (Sunday), 5:30 p.m.

He confirmed a group of boys at St. Peter's Church in Krakow.

He spoke of the meaning of the sacrament and of the lasting union between those confirmed and their sponsors, who should remember those they sponsored on their name-days or on St. Nicholas Day. The speech, given in proximity to those confirmed, not from the lectern, was given in such a heartfelt tone that at its conclusion a crowd of boys threw itself toward the Bishop, surrounded him and would not let him go from among themselves for a long time. Among those confirmed was my son, Wojciech; I was sponsor to his colleague and friend. (Jozef Mitkowski)

December 22 — Rokiciny.

Passing through from Rabka, Karol Wojtyla, Bishop Auxiliary of Krakow, paid an unexpected visit. After supper he went to the chapel where the Congregation awaited. After a short prayer he spoke to us, emphasizing the meaning of Christmas. He thanked Mother Superior for her assistance in his work with students. He blessed us. The visit gave us much joy. (From the chronicle of the Convent of Roman Union Ursuline Nuns in Rokiciny)

December 24 — Tyniec, ordination to the Diaconate at the Benedictine abbey; Midnight, Pontifical Midnight Mass with a sermon.

December 29-30 — Tarnow — He participated in a Catechetical course and lecture, Moments of Apologia in Teaching.

Academic year 1958-59:

Because of the new duties resulting from his consecration as bishop, he is able to undertake responsibilities at the University (KUL) on a smaller scale than in the past years. The records of KUL lack detailed facts. It is known that his courses were taken over by several people: Fr. S. Olejnik, O. Szymanski OP, Fr. W. Piwowarski, A. Rodzinski. In 1963 Fr. T. Styczen received his doctorate and took over the basic responsibilities of the Chair of Ethics. In the personnel records, Bishop Wojtyla's so-called "engagements," i.e. the signed documents stating which courses are assigned to which employee in a given year, are missing. These documents are missing for the years 1958-59 and 1959-60. The situation is first rectified in the academic year 1960-61. Bishop Wojtyla is employed part time, he conducts a monographic lecture of one hour a week: Selected Issues from Ethics for the students of the 3rd and 4th year in theoretical specialization, and the students of the 4th and the 5th year in practical specialization; apart from this — two hours of seminars.

---

[24] A Christmas tradition of breaking the *Oplatek* wafer (recalling the breaking of bread of Christ with His Apostles at the Last Supper); a social gathering at which good wishes are exchanged.

In practice, he arrived a few times a year, as the time went by — less frequently, and then he conducted lectures for a few hours (2-5) concerning the problems he was currently working on, and held a seminar. There were years in which he found no time at all to come. In addition, a few times a year he would invite participants of the scholarly seminars to come to Krakow for meetings in which his past students would also take part. These seminars usually began around 3 p.m. and lasted until the departure of the train to Lublin, at 9 p.m. ; for those remaining in Krakow, they often lasted longer. Initially held over two days, eventually the seminars had to be limited to one day. In the final years, he invited only the faculty of the Department (without students) to these meetings and the seminar would be conducted during a four to five hour walk in the environs of Krakow. He treated this as his day of rest. Sometimes he would go skiing with Fr. T. Styczen. They would discuss scholarly matters. He liked this combination of the contact with nature and study, and he used this method not only with his collaborators from the Department of Ethics, but also with other scholars from Krakow and Lublin (especially). At the Krakow seminars, participants would inform him of important events in research (especially in ethics); he, however, continued to conduct — not as a fiction — a number of theses. So it continued until October 16, 1978. It may still be added that the aforementioned irregular, increasingly rare lectures and seminars in Lublin took place during his visits to KUL for various reasons, not directly connected with his function as head of the Chair of Ethics. (Rev. A Szostek)

In 1958 a mimeographed lecture on Catholic social ethics was published in Krakow, 218 typewritten pages:

Chapter I: Basic precepts of Catholic social ethics.
Proposition 1: Catholic social ethics is a theological study of a normative character. Proposition 2: Divine Revelation as the basis of Catholic social ethics allows for the support of its scholarly theses on the ethical law of nature. Proposition 3: The main assignment of Catholic social ethics is to bring justice and love into society.

Chapter II: The issue of the common good.
Proposition 1: The principle of the correlation between the common good of a society and that of an individual, which is accepted by Catholic social ethics, is based on the order of nature. Proposition 2: Individualism on one hand and totalitarianism on the other, together with the ethical systems established upon them, remain in conflict with the principle of the correlation between the individual good and the social good, which is recognized by the Catholic social ethics. Proposition 3: The principle of the common good demands, on the one hand, an honest collaboration among particular communities which exist within a given society and, on the other hand, respect for and attentiveness to their just rights. Proposition 4: Marxist social doctrine recognizes the great class struggle as a historical inevitability, and as an ethical imperative. Proposition 5: Catholic social ethics, recognizing cooperation for the common good as the prime ethical duty, admits that in many cases, struggle is the way to achieve these goods.

Chapter III. Ethical issues of family and nation.
Proposition 1: In order to achieve the ethical goal of the family, close cooperation between the married couple, the Church and the government

is required. Proposition 2: The nation, as a natural community, constitutes a specific good which must be taken into account by each individual and also by the community in its activity. Proposition 3: The common good demands of the individual a responsible love for one's country and loyalty to the nation, and the avoidance of extreme nationalism. Proposition 4: The moral stance of a nation lies in the delineation of the rights and duties of the nation in relations with other nations.

Chapter IV. The state and related ethical issues.

Proposition 1: By its nature, the state is instrumental as well as useful in establishing the society's common good. Proposition 2: The state achieves its goal through appropriate fulfillment of its duties in the areas of law, economics, and culture. Proposition 3: The authority, the power of the state comes directly from the society, indirectly from God. The political structure is good when it is suitable to the requirements of the common good. Proposition 4: Catholic social ethics delineate the rights and duties of citizens towards a legitimate and illegitimate government, the just and unjust one. Proposition 5: Assuming the sovereignty of the Church and the state in their respective spheres of activity, Catholic social ethics postulates cooperation between these perfect communities.

Chapter V. Principal ethical duties of international co-existence.

Proposition 1: Because all humanity comprises a natural and supernatural whole, which is composed of many nations and states, we should strive to arrange international life according to the principles of justice and love. Proposition 2: War is evil. Although it is allowed in international relations in principle — as a last resort for the restoration of justice among nations — it should be avoided as it can bring about even greater evil.

During this year he was one of the editors as well as the scientific editor of the second issue of *Roczniki Filozoficzne KUL* (v. VI). From here on, each year, the second issue of "Roczniki" was dedicated to the matters of ethics (until 1973.)

1959

January 5 — Krakow, He participated in the meeting of priests — catechists from outside Krakow.

January 7 — Zakopane, "Ksiezowka." Meeting of the Pastoral Committee of the Episcopate. Lectures and discussion: 9 a.m. — the situation of the Church from the pastoral point of view (lecturer, Bishop B. Kominek); the laity and laicization in 1957-58 (lecturer, Bishop Cz. Kaczmarek); In discussion, Bishop K. Wojtyla spoke of the situation at *TP* and *Znak*. 4 p.m. — the situation of the working class youth in the context of Polish secularity (lecturer, Bishop H. Bednorz); In discussion, Bishop K. Wojtyla spoke of the situation of the peasant and working class youth within the Krakow Archdiocese.

January 8 — The second day of meetings of the Pastoral Committee of the Episcopate. Bishop T. Wilczynski – the youth in the PGR[25]; Bishop K. Wojtyla — the pastoral problems of the university youth, among them — the ideological situation of the youth: three stages of the discussion of their outlook on the world and three levels of the intellectual make-up of the younger generation: materialism — positivism; independent ethics — liberalism; existentialism — situation(al) ethics … The university youth do not embrace the Church head-on, nor do they turn their back, they seem to stand alongside. One must search; the university youth need a new maximalism in pastoral activity and a comprehensive understanding in this matter. (From the minutes of the meeting.) Bishop W. Pluta — a lecture on preparing the youth for marriage; in the discussion Bp. K. Wojtyla presented the matter of organizing pre-marital courses for introduction to the Main Committee of the Episcopate.

January 9 — Third day of meetings of the Pastoral Committee of the Episcopate — lectures: Bp. Golinski on the subject of Catholic education for informed motherhood, Fr. J. Pawlik on the pastoral care for young women, and Fr. Malinowski on the pastoral care for young men. Bishop K. Wojtyla — participated in the discussion.

January 11 — Zakopane. Holy Mass at the parish church and a meeting with nuns at the Carmel of the Immaculate Heart of Mary and of St. Joseph. * Same day, at 4:30 p.m. — service and lecture for nurses in Zakopane * 6 p.m. — Holy Mass and a sermon for physicians.

January 15 — In the Mother House of the Albertine Sisters in Krakow, he spoke to the sisters on the occasion of the anniversary of the congregation: "We must make every effort to ensure that the great spirit of [Brother Albert], that wonderful idea, does not die away. This is your mission." He also said that he loves Brother Albert deeply and holds him in respect. He also understands what it meant for that man to abandon art, as he, himself had an inclination toward writing, for which there is no time now. This is a great sacrifice for him. This was the first visit to the house of the Albertine Sisters at Pradnik. (The Albertine Sisters)

January 15 — He participated in an *Oplatek*[26] hosted by the Ladies Congregation of the Children of Mary. In his address, he turned to those present with a plea for prayer for his intention and described himself as "the son of all the gathered ladies." (Zuzanna Kowalow)

January 16. Change of apartment and address. His departure from the house at 19 Kanonicza Street is recorded; he moves to 21 Kanonicza Street.

---

[25] Government-owned farms
[26] See Glossary.

January 19 — Nowy Targ a conference for the literati.

In addition, in January he attends a series of meetings in Krakow parishes preceding missions.

February 2 — Krakow, consecration of candles {Candlemas}, Holy Mass and sermon at the Church of St. Florian * February 3 — Pastoral Department of the Curia, meeting with parish priests of the archdiocese from cities outside Krakow * February 4 — Meeting of the Catechetic Circle * February 11 (Ash Wednesday) — Wawel Cathedral — consecration of ashes, Holy Mass.

February 14 — From the chronicle of the Ursuline Convent in Rokiciny: "During the absence of Mother Superior, Bp. Karol Wojtyla arrived. Upon hearing of her absence he wanted to leave but, as the car required repair, he stayed for supper."

February 19 — Lublin, lecture on "Human Nature as the Basis for the Ethical Formation of Man" presented during the 2nd Philosophy Week at KUL. The week was dedicated to the question of the awareness of God and the soul ("Deum et animam scire cupio") (Cf. the article by Bp. Wojtyla, *Znak* 11 (60) 1959)

February 21 — Krakow, Church of St. Barbara — conclusion of the retreat for the I and II Lyceum {secondary school} * February 22 — Church of the Bernardine Fathers — conclusion of a retreat for the Adam Mickiewicz Lyceum * February 23 — March 1 — Poznan, retreat for university students.

March 2-6 — The parish of Our Lady of Lourdes in Krakow, retreat for university students * March 7 (Feast of St. Thomas Aquinas) — 9:30 a.m., at the Dominican Fathers — Pontifical Mass and sermon * The same day at 4:00 p.m. — conclusion of the retreat for the Technical School of Mining * March 8 — Jedrzejow — sermon for the beginning of the Trenium in preparation for the celebration of the 800th anniversary of Blessed Wincenty Kadlubek's birthday * March 15 — Day of recollection for the editorial staff of *Tygodnik Powszechny* * March 16-19 — Retreat for nurses at St. Mark's Church in Krakow * March 16-20 — Church of St. Anne — retreat for academic workers.

March 19 — For the first time as a Bishop he visited the house of the Congregation of the Sisters of Our Lady of Mercy in Krakow (previously he gave sermons there a number of times on the third Sunday of the month.) He toured the institution, spoke with the students and, at 4:30 p.m. at the vespers, he gave a short homily to the girls from the pulpit. (Based on the entries in the chronicle of the "Jozefow" House, compiled by Sister Olga Abramczuk ZMBM)

March 22 — Beginning of the retreat for lawyers at the Church of the Dominican Fathers in Krakow * March 22-25 — Church of the Felician Sisters, retreat for physicians.

March. Illness. After a few days of illness, Dr. Stanislaw Kownacki was called in. A blood test indicated that he had mononucleosis. During the marrow biopsy, which was difficult to perform with the equipment of the day, he sympathized with the doctor that he {the doctor} had to exert himself so much in penetrating to the marrow through the truly hard bone.

April 1-3 — Days of Theological Studies in Krakow, with the participation of the professors of theology from all over Poland. Karol Wojtyla was the chairman of the organizing committee * April 1 — Krakow, Church of St. Peter — Holy Mass and a conference for educators * April 5-6 — Skiing excursion from Hala Gasienicowa through Zawrat to the Valley of Five Ponds to the path towards Morskie Oko * April 6 — Holy Mass and a conference for the literati in Nowy Targ * April 9 — Church of St. Anne in Krakow, conference for university students, *Community and Personality in the Church* * April 15 — Holy Mass for the intention of the beatification of Bishop Jozef Pelczar. The same day (the Feast of St. Joseph), in Wadowice, the Church of the Discalced Carmelites, he said the holiday High Mass during which he administered minor Holy Orders to about 70 clerics from various religious communities. In the sermon he spoke of St. Joseph who through the ages cares for Jesus Christ in His Mystical Body — the Church. During the dinner he spoke once more to the clerics and those assembled, expressing his joy at administering Holy Orders in the Church in which he liked to pray as a boy. (From the chronicle of the Convent of the Discalced Carmelites in Wadowice; compiled by Fr. Honorat Gil)

April 28 — Krakow, he participated in the meeting of the Catechetic Circle.

April 29 — The first service of the Novena to St. Stanislaw — celebration and a sermon.

May 3 — Borek Falecki — Holy Mass, sermon, participation in the renewal of the Jasna Gora vows, Confirmation, christening of a child * Kalwaria Zebrzydowska — he administered Holy Orders in the Kalwaria Shrine. He wrote in the guest book: "On the day of the Holy Orders under the gaze of Our Lady of Calvary" * May 8 — Krakow, Wawel Cathedral, celebration of the Feast of St. Stanislaw: sermon * May 10 — Krakow, 9 a.m. — procession to Skalka; 3:00 p.m. — initiation of altar boys * The same day at 6:00 p.m. — Pontifical Mass on the occasion of the 50th anniversary of the "Kopiec" works * May 11 —

Wawel Cathedral, 6:30 a.m. — Holy Orders administered at the altar of St. Stanislaw; 9:00 a.m. — participation in the celebration of the 13th anniversary of the consecration of the Primate of Poland * May 16 — June 8 — He visited the Deanery of Susk * May 24 — Lesna, Radziechowy parish — blessing of the cornerstone for the Church foundation * May — Excursion to Uklejna.

June 20 — The ceremony of awarding diplomas to the graduates at the Ursuline Sisters in Krakow (10:30 a.m.) * The same day, at 2:30 a.m. — participation in a meeting of the superiors of female religious orders, at the Jesuit Fathers * June 21 — Church of Sts. Peter and Paul in Krakow, confirmation of adults * The same day — Holy Mass and sermon for lawyers at the Dominican Fathers.

July 2 — Mountain excursion: Stroze — Maslana Gora — Szymbark together with the *Srodowisko* group en route to the Bieszczady Mountains.

July 5 — Czernichow Parish — blessing of the cornerstone for the Church foundation, sermon at Dabrowa Szlachecka * July 6-9 — Retreat for priests at the Theological Seminary in Wroclaw * July 10 — Krakow, Theological Seminary — Holy Mass and a speech for the conclusion of the retreat for priests (unio apostolica) * July 19 — Szczyrk — Holy Mass, sermon, blessing of the children, visit to "Gorka," consecration of the altar in the chapel at Salmopole * July 21-23 — Tyniec — short stay, recorded as follows in the chronicle of the convent: [Bishop Wojtyla] "who departed leaving in his wake irresistible charm, prayer, an interior glow."

July 29-August 15 — Kayak excursion to the Elblag-Ostroda Canal — Jeziorak — Ilawa (ca. 20 participants).

August 20 — Olsztyn — meeting of the Pastoral Committee of the Episcopate. Lectures: Rebirth of the Parish in Light of Papal Pronouncements and the Teachings of the Church (Bishop B. Kominek); The Role of the Liturgy and the Sacraments in the Spiritual Renewal of the Parish (Bishop Cz. Kaczmarek); Methods of Awakening the Awareness of the Value of the Sacraments and Sacramental Life in the Parish (Fr. Nawrocki); Bp. E. Nowicki, Bp. Wojtyla — participated in the discussion.

August 21 — Second day of the meeting of the Pastoral Committee of the Episcopate. Lectures pertaining to the Eucharist, Holy Mass, Sacrament of Penance, the sick, marriage in the parish ministry — Rev. Dr. H. Kocylowski. In the discussion after the last topic, Bp. Karol Wojtyla spoke up, among others. On this day pastoral ministry to particular social groups and professions were assigned. Bishop Karol

Wojtyla: pastoral care for male and female youth.

August 22 — Third day of the meeting of the Pastoral Committee of the Episcopate. Bp. Karol Wojtyla — lecture: Characteristic Difficulties and Tensions in Today's Parish Ministry. A discussion followed the lecture * August 30 — Krakow, Convent of the Daughters of Divine Charity — investiture and profession of vows.

September 1 — Participation in a retreat for bishops at Jasna Gora * September 5-29 — Visitation of the Wadowice Deanery * September 7 — While visiting the Parish of Wadowice he also visited the church, convent, and the Lower Theological Seminary of the Discalced Carmelites, located in the area. In an address to those gathered, he emphasized the necessity of cooperation with the diocesan clergy as well as the beauty of a life of prayer and penance. (From the records of the Convent of the Discalced Carmelites in Wadowice: compiled by Br. Honorat Gil) * September 11 — Confirmation in the parish of Witanowice, near Wadowice * September 21 —Wawel Cathedral — Holy Mass for the intention of the families of the clergy, sermon. For the first time in history he organized and celebrated a Holy Mass for the mothers and fathers of the priests of the Archdiocese of Krakow. After the Mass — a breakfast at the seminary and a service in the seminary chapel.

October 3 — As an Auxiliary Bishop (and titular "Ombitanus" {titular bishop of Ombi}) he sends "animadversiones" (remarks) in response to the questionnaire of the Pontifical Preparatory Commission for the Second Vatican Council. (*Acta et Documenta Concilio Oecumenico Vaticano II Apparendo* TPV 1960. Series I, vol. II, pars II "Antepreparatoria" pp. 741-748).

October 8-10 — He delivered a lecture during the days of prayer for the major superiors of women's congregations at Jasna Gora * October 11 —10:00 a.m. — Bishop Karol Wojtyla delivered a sermon at the collegiate Church of St. Anne in Krakow during the Holy Mass inaugurating the new academic year. It was not permitted to post any announcements besides a notice in the Church vestibule. In the places prepared for professors in the presbytery, the seats were taken in the following order, beginning at the entrance to the sacristy: Prof. Pigon, Prof. Vetulani, Prof. Bochnak, Prof. Plezia, and Assistant Prof. Mitkowski. The church was filled with young people. On behalf of the professors, Prof. Bochnak and Prof. Pigon went to thank the clergy for remembering the inauguration of the academic year. (According to an account by Jozef Mitkowski) * The same day, at the convent of the cloistered Dominican Sisters at Grodek (Mikolajska Street), he officiates at the investiture of postulant Waleria Mazurkiewicz (Sister Magdalena Maria), his former penitent. After the ceremony he stopped in the convent parlor (separated from the cloister by a grate).

October 11-12 — Together with Bishop B. Kominek he delivered conferences and lectures during the days of prayer for the Catholic literati at Jasna Gora * October 14 — Wroclaw — conference for university students * October 15 — Wawel Cathedral — Holy Mass for the intention of the beatification of Queen Jadwiga, sermon for young girls * October 18 — Holy Mass and sermon for physicians at the Felician Sisters in Krakow * October 24 — Sporysz — sermon for the conclusion of the parish missions * October 25 — 11:30 a.m. — blessing of a radiophonic system and a sermon at St. Kazimierz {Casimir} Church in Krakow * The same day, 3:00 p.m. — consecration of St. Szczepan {Stephen} Church, sermon * October 26 — Conference for the literati in Rabka * October 27 — Krakow, Church of Our Lady of Lourdes — conference for students * October 28 —Conference for students at St. Szczepan Church in Krakow * October 31 — Lodygowice — conclusion of a mission and a sermon.

November 4 — Katowice, Pastoral Department, meeting of the Pastoral Committee of the Episcopate. Lectures: Rev. Bishop B. Kominek: The Laity and Lay Apostolate; Bishop J. K. Lorek: The Polish Clergy in View of the Current Situation. In the discussion, Bishop Wojtyla spoke on the topic of deanery congregations. Bishop H. Bednor: Current Problems of the Youth. Bishop K. Wojtyla, participating in the ensuing discussion, spoke of what draws the youth away from the Church. For the next meeting he is to prepare one of the four lectures on the topic of students.

November 8 — Wawel Cathedral — sermon for the jubilee of the Coronation of the Holy Father * November 13 (Feast of St. Stanislaw Kostka) — Church of Corpus Christi in Krakow, sermon for youth * November 23 — Service at the Discalced Carmelites for the beatification of Brother Albert.

December 6 — He led days of recollection at the Ursuline Sisters in Krakow * December 8 — Sermon for young women at the Church of St. Anne * December 15 — Church of Our Lady of Lourdes — *Oplatek*[27] * December 16 — Conference for students prior to Christmas Eve at the Church of St. Szczepan {Stephen} in Krakow.

December 18 — Lublin, KUL — Defense of the doctoral thesis by Jan Bardan: An Evaluation of Sartre's Concept of Independent Ethics. Promoter: Bishop Karol Wojtyla.

---

[27] See Glossary.

December 20 — Day of recollection at the Ursuline Sisters in Krakow * December 24 — *Oplatek* at the social welfare establishment at 43 Krakowska Street run by the Albertine Brothers * The same day, at 12:00 a.m. — midnight Mass in Nowa Huta-Bienczyce * December 31 — Holy Mass for the end of the old year at the Franciscan Fathers church.

This year an article by Bishop Karol Wojtyla entitled *Le traite de "Penitentia" de Gratien dans l'abrege de Gdansk* appeared in the "Studia Gratiana" (7/1959, pp. 357-390). The correspondence between Prof. Adam Vetulani and Prof. Giuseppe Forchinelli on the topic of this publication survived. Prof. Vetulani wrote:

> **Tous les deux nous sommes infiniment chagrinés à cause du titre, qu'on a lui ajouté: il est l'evéque auxiliaire de Cracovie et rien de plus. Esperons qu'il n'aura pas des ennuis!... (Both of us are greatly troubled because of the title by which he [Bishop Wojtyla] has been called: he is only the auxiliary bishop of Krakow and nothing more. Let us hope this doesn't cause him difficulties...) (The publisher of the article had attributed to the author a position he did not in fact hold. Letter of July 12, 1960. Archives of JU)**

December 30. He sends his "opinion" to the commission preparing the {Second Vatican} Council/printed in: *Acta et Documenta...*/

1960

January 1 — Holy Mass and a New Year's sermon at the Basilica of the Franciscan Fathers in Krakow *

January 2 — During the funeral Mass at the Wawel Cathedral Bishop Wojtyla delivered the eulogy over the casket of Rev. Jan Piwowarczyk, the canon of the Krakow Chapter, writer and publicist, the first editor-in-chief of *Tygodnik Powszechny*. Rev. Monsignor Bohdan Niemczewski presided over the funeral service. He was assisted by Bishops: Herbert Bednorz of Katowice, Franciszek Jop of Opole, Karol Pekala of Tarnow, Stanislaw Czajka of Czestochowa and the Auxiliary Bishop of Krakow, Karol Wojtyla. In his report on the funeral Rev. Ferdynand Machay wrote that the eulogist *rightly applied to him* [i.e. Rev. Jan Piwowarczyk] *the words of the prophet: "For zeal of your house has consumed me and the insults of those who insult you have fallen on me (Ps 69,9). And these insults came not only from the enemies but also from those who should have understood his work"* (Notificationes, 1-4, 1960)

January 3 — Chapel of the Daughters of Charity in Krakow, Holy Mass with a sermon; after the Mass, he visited with the sick in the wards

January 6 — Nowa Huta — Bienczyce — Holy Mass inaugurating the novena to Our Lady of Perpetual Help. * Holy Mass and sermon at the Chapel of the Daughters of Charity, then a visit to the sick at the establishment at 2 Helclow Street in Krakow

January 13 — Holy Mass at the Sisters of the Presentation for the 300th anniversary of the Congregation in Poland.

January — The Academic Society of KUL {Catholic University of Lublin} published Fr. Karol Wojtyla's dissertation submitted in application for admittance to assistant professorship under the title *An Evaluation of the Possibility of Constructing Christian Ethics Based on the System of Max Scheler*, 136 pages ("Submitted for publication: June 15, 1958. Approved for publication: May 5, 1959. Publication completed in January, 1960"). Excerpts:

> Scheler's system attracted the attention of Catholic thinkers simply by its basic tendency to establish a concrete connection with the subject of human actions, and by referring to their moral values. However, there are certain aspects of the system, even more particular ones that evoke a direct association with Christian ethics, especially with the ethical content of the Gospels. In his system Scheler particularly emphasizes the meaning of love for a person, as well as the importance of imitating an ethical model to the entirety of moral life ... Having all these findings before us, we may ask with complete justification what connection there is between Scheler's system and Christian ethics. Does Scheler's system contain some complete treat-

ment of Christian ethics or at least of some of its issues? (p. 6) ... An overview of the basic theses of Max Scheler's system of ethics convinces us that the system can not be considered as a complete attempt to treat Christian ethics. We realize that Scheler's system of ethics is a philosophical system, built upon the principles of phenomenology and axiology, which is supposed to serve to encompass (formulate) and explain all moral facts and all ethical content, and not to be only a treatment of Christian ethics ... All of the givens stated above lead us then to the following statement of the main issue of this dissertation: since Scheler constructed a system of ethics in such a manner that it could serve to interpret all ethical facts and content, can this system also serve to treat the content of Christian ethics? In other words, can we, and to what extent, undertake the interpretation of Christian ethics with the help of Scheler's system? This question will constitute the main subject of our investigations in this dissertation. The actual subject, then, will not be Scheler's system itself or, and even less so, Christian ethics. The actual subject of this dissertation is to determine the level of suitability of Scheler's system for the interpretation of Christian ethics. In light of the question stated in this manner, we must ... still ask what we understand Christian ethics to be... In this dissertation we understand Christian ethics to be those ethical truths which were revealed by God and which the Church holds as principles of moral behavior. (pp. 25-26) ... In principle, the ethical system built by Max Scheler does not lend itself to a scholarly interpretation of Christian ethics. Although by defining ethical values as personal values, the system does establish a clear contact with the ethical content of the revealed sources, still, as a result of its phenomenological and emotional foundations, it does not suffice as a complete illustration and scholarly treatment of this subject. In particular, it does not suffice for the theological treatment, which is necessary in view of the fact that these are the revealed sources, which constitute the subject of supernatural faith. (p. 118) ... Although the ethical system created by Max Scheler is basically not suited to the interpretation of Christian ethics, it can nonetheless be incidentally (indirectly, occasionally) useful in scholarly work on Christian ethics as it simplifies the analysis of ethical facts on the phenomenological and experimental level. (p. 122)

From the review:

There has not been ... to our knowledge, neither in the literature of the West nor, certainly, in that of Poland, an attempt to show wherein lies the inadequacy of the basic principles of Scheler's ethical system for illustrating the ancient Christian ethical truths. Bishop Karol Wojtyla attempts to address this need ... (p.279) ... If one ignores certain, although infrequent, stylistic flaws, and the repetition which is sometimes tiring to the reader, but which results from the emotional premise burdening Scheler's system, it must be admitted that *An Evaluation of the Possibility of Constructing Christian Ethics Based on the System of Max Scheler* brings glory to the Department of Theology of the Jagiellonian University, which through its research contributed to its writing and which accepted it as a dissertation in application for acceptance to assistant professorship. (p.283) ... It seems, however, that the author of *Evaluation of the Possibility...* treated the positive side of the ethical principles of Max Scheler somewhat cursorily. As a tool of the system, the phenomenological method contributed many valuable and accurate observations, misleading Scheler only in their proper

interpretation. (p. 284) (Rev. W. Urmanowicz, *Ateneum Kaplanskie* 63/161, pp. 279-284)

January 25 — Meeting of the Pastoral Section of the Polish Theological Society. Lecture: Current ethical problems. /Bibl. I 681/.

February 1 — Myslenice — conference for the intelligentsia.

February 14 — He visited a hospice run by the Albertine Sisters in Krakow on Zielna Street. He made the rounds of all the wards. He approached each patient, blessed her, marked her forehead with a sign of the cross and squeezed her hands. He granted absolution to one who was then dying and prayed at her side for a long time. As a result of this visit, the sisters and the personnel had troubles with the authorities. (The Albertine Sisters)

February 21 — Krakow, Conference on the day of recollection for sisters who teach pre-school * February 25 — He visited the Albertine Sisters House at Pradnik in Krakow; hc spokc of thc role of the Congregation, which is to serve as a "leaven" in the community through the parish and the diocese. On the relevance of Brother Albert: "this spirit has not become obsolete, this spirit must be carried over to today's times" * February 28 — Chapel of the Albertine Sisters in Krakow, Holy Mass and a visit to the sick in the hospice.

March 6 — 4:30 p.m. — Meeting and discussion with physicians in his apartment at 21 Kanoniczna Street * March 7 — Convent of the cloistered Dominican Sisters at Grodek in Krakow, he invited himself to participate in the Feast of St. Thomas Aquinas. At 7 a.m. he said a low Mass, then, in the parlor, he delivered a brief lecture to the sisters * March 8-9 — Jasna Gora. He participated actively in the days of recollection for coordinators of pastoral ministry from all over Poland.

Lent (March 2-April 13) — For the first time he visited 35 of the sick in Krakow during Lent. From here on until the end of his bishop's tenure in Krakow, he faithfully adhered to this tradition. During visits to parishes he always visited the most gravely ill in their homes. (Alina Rumun)

March 11 — Krakow, He participated in the meeting of the Archconfraternity of Piotr Skarga. * March 15 — During High Mass at the Provincial House of the Daughters of Charity in Krakow at 8 Warszawska Street, he delivered a sermon on the occasion of the 300th anniversary of the death of the founder of the Congregation, St. Louise de Marillac. In the afternoon he said the solemn vespers thus concluding the anniversary celebrations. (Congrcgation of thc Daughtcrs of Charity)

March 19 — Chapel of the Sisters of the Sacred Heart of Jesus in Krakow, Holy Mass for intention of the beatification of Bishop Jozef

Pelczar * March 20 — Conclusion of the retreat for the Fifth Lyceum[1] at the Church of the Jesuit Fathers * March 23 — 8:45 a.m. — Church of the Bernardine Fathers — conclusion of the retreat for the Technical Lyceum * The same day — at 6:00 p.m. — at the Franciscan Fathers Church — Holy Mass and sermon for the conclusion of the retreat for young people from schools without religious instruction.

Around March 30 - April 2 — Lecture: *Remarks on the Inner Life of the Contemporary Youth and the Young Intelligentsia*, from the cycle of lectures organized by the Rector's office of KUL (later published in *Znak* no. 84/1961)

April 3 — Jasna Gora — He participated in the Mariological Committee of the Episcopate * April 5-7 — Church of Our Lady of Lourdes — sermons for married couples.

April 10-12 — He conducted a retreat in Lodz at the Church of the Jesuit Fathers (60 Sienkiewicza Street) for personnel of institutes of higher education.

> **He speaks plainly, concisely, each word thought out. The underlying thought of the retreat — there is no love without effort, and there is no effort without Love. I entered a few thoughts in my student journal: I should possess the Kingdom of God through Grace. Grace is the very joy of existence. What am I like? Ardent, tepid or cold? Tepidity equals indifference. The antidote is prayer, which leads to Love. You may not know how to pray. It suffices to want to pray, as prayer is an act of will ... We must beware of indifference, pray for the knowledge of Christ and the knowledge of self. Love without effort is a fiction. Without work on oneself, it expires. Also, a mutual effort of man and woman builds Love. Effort without love, for the sake of effort alone, is a fiction.**
>
> **The Church is not an organization of Christ; it is an organism of Christ. It is most difficult to offer one's sins to God ... It is easy to speak to Christ from the Pharisee's position, and yet Christ said that the publican was justified. It is not sufficient to cast off one's sins in the Sacrament of Penance, indeed one must offer them to God, one must offer oneself, too ... {like Simon of} Cyrene: ... God wishes that we assist Him. (Jolanta Modelska-Podlejska)**

During Lent he frequently participated in retreats for Lyceum {high school} students in Krakow (Holy Masses, homilies).

April 15 — He led the funeral procession for Sister Arnulfa (an Albertine Sister), Mother Superior of the House at Zielna in Krakow (he thus wished to compensate for the troubles with the authorities resulting from his visit on February 14). (The Albertine Sisters) * April 17 — 6:30 a.m. — Mogila — Resurrection procession, sermon * April 20 — Church of St. Anne in Warsaw — Holy Mass and the marriage of Janusz

---

[1] Secondary school

Rieger and Ewa Giedroyc * April 26 — Siersza — Chapel of the
Ursuline Sisters — Holy Mass and perpetual vows * April 27 — Riots
in Nowa Huta in response to the removal of the cross from the lot designated for the construction of a new church * May 5 — Meeting dedi-
cated to the matters of the apostolate for the literati of the arts * May 8-
8:30 a.m. — Holy Mass and confirmation of the youth at the altar of St.
Stanislaw at the Wawel Cathedral * Same day — 3:30 p.m. — conse-
cration of the Church in Lubien (sermon) * May 11 — Church of St.
Anne in Krakow, Holy Mass and a talk to the graduates of the IX and X
Lyceum * May 14 — Ordination of priests before the altar of St.
Stanislaw at Wawel Cathedral * May 15 — Procession to Skalka and a
Pontifical Mass * May 15-17 — Visitation of the Skawina deanery.
Within the framework of this visitation he paid a visit to the St.
Lawrence parish in Radziszow on June 6 * May 16 — 7:30 p.m. —
Church of St. Anne —Holy Mass and a talk to the high school graduates
from all of Krakow * Participated in the funeral of Rev. Jozef
Zastawniak (died May 15, 1960) * May 22 — Church of St. Mikolaj
{Nicholas} — First Holy Communion * May 29 — Kalwaria
Zebrzydowska. Visiting the parish church, he also participated in the
Holy Mass at the shrine. He spoke to the faithful emphasizing the mean-
ing of the shrine for the Archdiocese of Krakow.

In May he conducted a three-day retreat for the girls graduating from
the Joteyko Lyceum in Krakow, at the Church of the Carmelite Fathers
at Piasek.

June 5 — Jaworzno — Holy Mass for the intention of the high
school graduates, confirmation, and the distribution of awards for rell-
gious study * June 7 — Canonical visit at the parish of Tyniec.

June 15 — A letter: "Dear Ania {Anne}, from your letter I found out
that on June 12 you have made your First Holy Communion. I am very
glad that you have experienced this joy. I wish that you may be as close
as possible to Our Lord throughout your entire life, and that you may
often join with Him in the Holy Communion. Karol Wojtyla, who baptized you." (To: Ania Owoc; cf. October 7, 1951)

June 26. — Ordination to the priesthood of the Bernardine Friars in
Kalwaria Zebrzydowska.

End of June or beginning of July — a one-day trip with a pair of
friends: Myslenice, Uklejna, Lysina, Kasinka.

July 3 — Klaj, blessing of a cornerstone for a church * July 15 —
7:00 a.m. — chapel of the Theological Seminary in Krakow, a talk for

the conclusion of a retreat for organists * Same day — Pontifical Mass in Wawel Cathedral on the anniversary of the Battle of Grunwald[2] * July 17 — 10:00 a.m. — Church of St. Philip in Krakow, sermon for the Feast of St. Vincent * Same day — marriage of Wanda Wojtyla and Jozef Kajder in Czaniec * Same day — low Mass at Wawel for the intention of the beatification of Queen Jadwiga.

July 24-August 7 — Kayak excursion on the Obra * August 15 — Jasna Gora — 6:00 a.m. — after the Little Office of Our Lady, a sermon entitled "The Queen of the Polish custom" * August 23-25 — A lecture *Education for marriage* delivered as part of a summer cycle of lectures organized for the clergy by the Rector's office of KUL. (The theme of the entire cycle: Catholic marriage) * August 31 — Participation in a several-day retreat of the Polish Episcopate at Jasna Gora.

August 17-22 and August 24-30 — Mountain excursion with the *Srodowisko*: Komancza, Chryszczata, Gabry Wierch, Baligrod, a break for a trip to Lublin, Dolzyca, Falowa, the Otryt range, Smolnik.

In August, he granted an audience to Wanda Dynowska, also known under her Hindu name of Umadevi. She came to Poland for the first time after a 40-year stay in India. For many years she had studied and practiced the spiritual culture of Hinduism, mainly in southern India. She was the founder, interpreter and editor of the "Polish-Indian Library," which produced many volumes of the *Indian Anthology*. She offered these books to the Archbishop, and received his approval and blessing for her work.

September 11 (to October 2) — Visitation of the deanery of Niepolomice (excluding the parishes of Gdow and Tarnawa) * September 18 — Wawel Cathedral, consecration of Julian Groblicki as an auxiliary bishop of the Krakow Archdiocese. The main celebrant was Archbishop Eugeniusz Baziak; Bishop Karol Wojtyla was a concelebrant * September 26 — 9:00 a.m. — Nowa Huta — Bienczyce, Pontifical Mass * Same day — 2:30 p.m. — blessing of a cornerstone in Siepraw * September 27 — Church of the Missionary Fathers at Stradom in Krakow he participated in the jubilee celebrations of St. Vincent de Paul * Ordination of seminarians of the Archbishop's Theological Seminary at the Wawel Cathedral.

October 9 — 9:00 a.m. - sermon for the inauguration of the academic year at the Church of St. Szczepan {Stephen} in Krakow * Same day — 10:00 a.m., sermon at the Church of St. Anne * October 15-16 — Trip with a group of young people to Czestochowa. There, a Mass

---

[2] AD 1410, against the Order of Teutonic Knights; flags captured in this battle were removed from Wawel by the Nazis in 1939.

with sermon at the altar of Our Lady * October 23 — 11:00 a.m. -
Kalwaria Zebrzydowska: Mass and sermon for speech and hearing
impaired * Same day — 5:00 p.m. he participated in a traditional procession honoring St. John of Kety at St. Anne's Church in Krakow *
October 30 (Feast of Christ the King) — Conferment of the title of
"minor basilica" upon the church of the Jesuit Fathers on Kopernika
Street in Krakow and the blessing of the chapel of perpetual adoration
of the Eucharist. The chapel is the work of architect Luboslaw Dormus
and sculptor Jerzy Swiecimski. During dinner, there was a meeting with
these artists and Fr. Jan Popiel, the initiator of the construction.

November 6 — 10:00 a.m. - Pontifical Mass in Wawel Cathedral on
the anniversary of the coronation of Pope John XXIII * 2:00 p.m. —
Sacrament of Confirmation in the chapel on Pedzichow * 4:00 p.m. —
Theological Seminary he participated in a commemorative program
honoring the Pope * November 21 — Wawel Cathedral — Mass and
address to religious sisters on the occasion of Archbishop E. Baziak's
patronal feast day * November 22 — 8:30 a.m. - Zakopane - Mass for
the beginning of the activity of the newly-established deanery of
Zakopane * Same day — conference {sermon} for university youth at
the church of Our Lady of Lourdes in Krakow * November 23 — 6:00
p.m. — Church of the Carmelite Fathers in Krakow, a liturgical service
for the intention of the beatification of Brother Albert * 7:45 p.m. —
Church of St. Florian, Mass and sermon for educators * November 25
— Catechetical visitation at Lagiewniki (until the end of the year, several visitations[3] in Krakow and outside Krakow) * November 27 —
Conference for nurses at the Ursuline Sisters in Krakow.

December 11 — Church of the Bernardine Fathers in Krakow, ser-
mon for the Feast of the Immaculate Conception {December 8} *
December 13 —Conference for university students and *Oplatek*[4] at the
Church of Our Lady of Lourdes * December 19-21 — Church of St.
Anne, triduum[5] for engaged couples in preparation for marriage at
Christmas * December 24 — Midnight Mass in Nowa Huta —
Bienczyce * December 26 — Niegowic he participated in a caroling
service * December 31 — He participated in a service of expiation and
thanksgiving, and a sermon in Wawel Cathedral * Midnight, low New
Year Mass in the cathedral.

This year, the Institute of the Family began its activities, initially for lay
listeners {students}, and since 1965/66 also for priests. Until 1970 this was
an autonomous study group, since 1970 — a study group at the Pontifical
Department of Theology. The goals, character and functioning of the Institute

---

[3] A visit for purposes of religious instruction.
[4] See Glossary.
[5] Three-day observance

are presented in a later, undated document by Cardinal Carol Wojtyla (this information and the text of the document provided by Dr. Wanda Poltawska).

1. In the first point I wish to explain why I bless individual married couples during my episcopal visitations of the parishes. What is the purpose, and how can this be advantageously used in the totality of the parish ministry? Indeed, I consider meeting with married couples during visitations as a very important, even central, moment of the visitation. Marriage is a sacrament which binds two people; it is expressed by their union and is expressed by the family. Through this sacrament, the family is created within the Church, but, at the same time, the family in some measure creates the Church as a living community of the people of God. The meeting of the bishop with married couples during the visitation of a parish is like touching this very basic bond of the human community which is shaped in the Church and which in turn shapes the Church.

The meeting is conceived in such a way that it may serve as both a point of departure and an objective for local priests in their own ministry to families. Some priests try to take maximum advantage of this meeting with and blessing by the bishop, maybe even inviting individual married couples by letter, which serves to enliven this point of the visitation. It is undoubtedly useful if the maximum number of married couples from the parish takes part in this meeting, and receives again, from the hands of the bishop, the same blessing of the Church which they received on the threshold of their married life. And if children are also present at this blessing with their parents, then it becomes even more special (although children, and especially teenagers, meet with the bishop during the visitation in other circumstances as well).

However, the enlivening of the family ministry during the visitation cannot remain in isolation from the ordinary ministry in the parish. I stress "ordinary" ministry because the family ministry is deeply embedded in it and determines its form. In essence, a whole series, one could say the majority, of pastoral activities concerns families in a more or less direct manner, leads the family at various stages into the Church, and thereby shapes the Church. There cannot be, at the heart of the matter, any kind of separation of the family ministry — only a deepening of its individual elements, a more conscious emphasis in all pastoral activities on this basic reality called the family. There are many such elements: not only the Sacrament of Marriage, but the Sacrament of Baptism, and Confirmation, participation in the Eucharist (not only First Holy Communion), finally, the Sacrament of the Sick and Christian burial. In all of these pastoral activities, in most cases, the priest meets with the family, he molds the family, leads it into the Church, and impresses upon it, in the name of the Church, some mark of Christian life, awareness, and attitude. A good priest will always keep this in mind. The reality of the family will remain within his field of vision both with regard to the broad sphere of catechesis and, for example, with regard to charitable action. It is not sufficient merely to teach "someone else's" children, but it is necessary to continue to coordinate this religious teaching and upbringing with the apostolic calling of the spouses-parents themselves (this is the basic form of lay apostolate). It is not sufficient merely to visit the sick, this should be made into a "family" custom — but within the scope of the larger family of families which is the parish.

What was said here, was done by way of example, with the realization that such an example (from the area of catechesis or the charitable ministry) will engender ever more widespread practices in pastoral work. In the family ministry, the priest must not "extract" the family from its proper place in society and in the parish community, but he should consciously try to "reach" it, he should respect it and appeal to it, know of its apostolic capabilities and relate to them, he should fully implement those principles which were once expressed in the encyclical *Divini illius Magistri* and which, in our time, were recalled for us by the Vatican Council.

But, at the same time, some sort of "extraction" of the family and its vital concerns is very desirable in the entirety of the ordinary parish ministry. A matter which rises to the foreground in this regard is the *koleda*,[6] which is a widely-known and widely utilized means for the priest to meet with parishioners, especially the families of the parish. Koleda becomes difficult to carry out especially in urban environment, where it is most needed. Perhaps a new approach should be adopted where the starting point would be the parishioners' expectations towards, among others, this reality that every family in the parish is. And besides, it seems that the pastoral activities could refer to and relate to this reality more often and more directly than is now generally the case. For example, one could make note of certain anniversaries of marriage or baptism, thus expressing remembrance of individual families; one could sometimes assemble married couples in various groups for group prayer in those intentions which are most appropriate to the needs of their lives. Such prayer by married couples with and for other married couples, best done during a Holy Mass, can greatly enliven the family ministry. Of course, the matter has to be thought through and carried out according to the capabilities and needs of each parish. In any case, a fundamental method of the family ministry in the parish is to formulate the various pastoral issues in a way that will make the family recognize its place in the Church and help it to understand its responsibilities better. The priest's conduct must reveal the true love of the Church towards the family in a very sober and realistic manner, and conversely, it must awaken, maintain and deepen the trust of the family towards the Church. That is also the meaning of the blessing of married couples which takes place during the bishop's visitation of the parish, and that is what should be maintained and in some way renewed by the continuing family ministry.

This ministry, the details of which we will not explore here, at its fundamental level defines an appropriate climate, an appropriate level and direction of value judgment, which is expressed in the behavior of the priest. This is the climate and the behavior which give meaning and effectiveness to those activities which are discussed in great detail in the instructions of the Polish Episcopate regarding the matter of family ministry and preparation for marriage. The details of these instructions basically touch upon a single issue, namely responsible parenthood in the spirit of the teachings of the Church, particularly the encyclical *Humanae vitae*. It seems, however, that applying these instructions without the broader principles of family ministry in the everyday life of the parish, of which we speak here, might, and possibly even must, place the matter in some sort of isolation. This isolation has already been created, in the sense that the family ministry is understood to be, if not exclusively, then in the main, the set of activities aimed at responsible parenthood. In this area, the matter of the method or

---

[6] See Glossary.

technique of birth control sometimes exceeds in importance the matter of ethics and full awareness of all the issues involved.

This manner of understanding and conducting the family ministry is certainly inadequate. The problem of birth control, or even that of responsible parenthood, cannot be isolated, or the results may be the opposite of those desired. However, these important and difficult issues must be placed within the context of the entire family ministry — and where this ministry is lacking, the deficiencies must be corrected. Of course this does not mean that we can give up on family counseling (which is just beginning to take shape). It just means that we have to build these activities up very thoroughly within the entire framework of the parish pastoral work, which must be conducted with keener awareness — of and sensitivity to the family — and, in some way, together with the family. The fields of pastoral ministry and lay apostolate meet here at many points and complement each other.

2. Thoughts on the activities of the Institute of the Family.

The state of affairs which we see here and which we postulate for the parish ministry in the parishes has a clear bearing on the activities of the Institute of the Family. First of all, it appears to be quite appropriate that, being a resource for the parish ministry, its character is primarily educational. It will probably need to always maintain this character, since that points it in the direction of the ministry to the lay apostolate, which, simply stated, means a direction towards real life, and not merely knowledge about life. I also think that an Institute of the Family oriented in this fashion will not be replaced by "elitist" symposia or sessions, although these, too, have their meaning in shaping our knowledge of family life. Finally, I think that there should be several such Institutes of the Family in Poland, each working regionally for the benefit of several dioceses, gathering within them both the staff and students from these dioceses.

As far as the individual educational teams are concerned, they should probably continue to be teams of both clergy and lay people, as has been our practice until now. The issue of training lay people (and not only the so-called "women counselors") outside of Krakow requires some sort of consideration and solution. In addition, all the teams must be supported and replenished, infused with young blood, because the issue continues to be relevant in new ways. The overall goal of the training is to create a mature Christian view of marriage among the clergy and the laity, which in turn will provide guidance in both the parish ministry and the apostolate of the laity. It appears from this that the methods of training should be tailored to these ends — which means that we should proceed from a system of lectures and tests to seminars, discussion groups, or consultations. To support the training effort, a consulting group made up in large part of married couples should be established as part of the Institute of the Family. Consultation will also be necessary in order to give the entire family ministry a direction that stems both from the teaching of the Church and from the real-life experience of married couples and families.

At the present time, the Institute of the Family is a resource for the family ministry, a ministry directed toward responsible parenthood, and consequently directed towards counseling. Every effort is made to root this concept firmly in the Christian vision of marriage, both in the minds of the clergy and the laity. This is where the Institute sees its integral task.

It must be added that to fulfill this task, or rather the whole series of tasks, in areas of training, counseling and consulting, it is necessary to create a continuing scholarly workplace within the Institute, because it is well-known that teaching depends on scholarship. That is why the Institute of the Family is connected with the Department of Theology and not only with the individual departments of the Curia (although it is also connected with them, particularly with the Catechetic, Charity and Pastoral ones). It seems that in order to form this scholarly workplace, we must create departments dealing with specific topics. At the moment, the one with the greatest presence deals with ethical and pastoral issues, which encompass the theology of marriage and family. It would be useful to expand the department dealing with socio-pastoral issues, in the sense of a more thorough understanding, from this particular perspective, of the situation of marriages and families in Poland, and especially in our Archdiocese. All of this must be supported by a library and a card file. In addition to this, periodic meetings of the Institute could be held, not merely organizational ones, whose purpose is to provide direction for the work of the Institute, but scholarly and informational ones as well, whose purpose would be the mutual sharing of information about significant publications, events or initiatives in areas that interest the Institute.

The Institute of the Family, while continuing to maintain a lively contact with the entire family ministry, must gradually work out its liaison with the Department of Theology. In that regard, it has the status of a para-departmental study group at the moment. It must gradually seek to take root in the activities of the Department itself, especially with the chairs dealing with moral and pastoral theology. This is a slow and gradual process, but together we must plan the appropriate organizational and personal steps that will lead in that direction.

Karol Cardinal Wojtyla

This year saw the publication of the book *Love and Responsibility*, by the Academic Society of KUL.[7]

Also during this year, together with Fr. Jozef Majka he was the academic editor of the second book of Volume VIII of *Roczniki Filozoficzne KUL*.[8] From that point until 1973 he remained on the editorial team, each year preparing the issue dedicated to ethics.

In the 12th issue of *Znak* there appeared a text signed with the name Andrzej Jawien: *The Jeweler's Shop. Meditations on the Sacrament of Marriage, at times turning into drama.* In connection with the writing of this meditation, the author wrote to Mieczyslaw Kotlarczyk:

> I wish to inquire about two of your premieres, which I have not yet had occasion to see: *Dialogues of Love* and *A Letter to the Cannibals*. And besides that, I have to send you the fruit of my literary interests. For quite some time now, I have attempted the "rhapsodic style," which seems to me to be more conducive to meditation than to drama (maybe that is just my point of view). I send you the typescript for your consideration.
>
> **Karol**

(letter not dated)

---

[7] Catholic University of Lublin
[8] Philosophic Annals

December — Makow Podhalanski. Blessing of the church organ, sermon.

1961

January 6 — Stadniki, ordination at the Fathers of the Sacred Heart * January 8 — Czestochowa, 11:00 a.m. he participated in the consecration of Bishop Stefan Barela * Same day — 7:00 p.m. — at the Sisters of the Resurrection in Kety, low Mass and sermon.

Jan 13 — Rzaska: visit to the house of the Albertine Sisters, speech.

January 18-19 — Zakopane, "Ksiezowka" {priests residence}. Nation-wide conference of chaplains, among others, a presentation by Bishop B. Kominek, *The Laity in Polish Church Life* and reports from the national chaplains. Bishop Wojtyla, in place of the absent Fr. Roman Len SAC, the national chaplain of writers (in periodicals), informed the meeting of the situation in this area. Also, Bishop Wojtyla participated in the discussions on the reports, and he read comments on the issue of the apostolate of the sick.

January 24 — Low Mass at the Church of St. Anne. He preached a sermon and took part in *Oplatek*.

January 26 — Low Mass and sermon at the Church of St. Florian * January 27 (The Feast of St. Angela) — Low Mass and sermon in the chapel of Ursuline Sisters.

In January he visited the house of the Albertine Sisters in Rzaska for the first time (he was 3 hours late). He spoke of the spirit of poverty: "Be able to see, how God sees ... God needs your service, not only your visible service, but also the service of prayer, of penance. The world does not realize what good you bring into it..." (The Albertine Sisters)

February 2 — Church of St. Anne, participation in a procession, low Mass, sermon * February 17 — Lublin, a lecture "Thomist personalism" within the program of 4th Philosophical Week (February 13-17, topic: Philosophical bases of personalisms) (Cf. *Znak*, no. 83, pp. 664 - 675) * February 23 — In the Franciscan church in Krakow, Mass for the conclusion of a retreat for secondary-school students * February 26 — Sulkowice, consecration of a church, and the Sacrament of Confirmation.

March 4-7 — Bialystok: he conducted a retreat for intellectuals * March 8-11 — Lublin — a retreat for university students * March 12 — Convent of the cloistered Dominican Sisters at Grodek in Krakow, he conducted a liturgy during which Sr. Magdalena Mazurkiewicz made her temporary profession. Later, he met with the sisters in the parlor * Same day, in Hecznarowice (Bielsko county) — Mass and sermon for the end of a mission on the 50th anniversary of the founding of the parish

* March 17 — Krakow-Nowa Wies, Mass for the conclusion of an academic retreat * March 26-29 — Church of St. Joseph, he conducted a retreat for intellectuals.

April 21 — Kalwaria Zebrzydowska — participation in a regional conference of priests from 4 deaneries * April 28 — Mass at this conference * April 15 - 30 — Skiing in Zakopane (he stayed at "Ksiezowka").

May 4 — Mass and sermon at the Church of St. Florian in Krakow * May 7 — Wawel, conclusion of a novena to St. Stanislaw * May 8 — Pontifical High Mass * May 11 — Wawel, he baptized Malgorzata, daughter of Jerzy and Prof. Janina Janik * May 11-12 — Visitation of the deanery of Zakopane (Bialy Dunajec, Poronin, Zab, Nowe Bystre, Bukowina Tatrzanska, Brzegi, Jurgow, Rzepiska, Zakopane-Olcza, Zakopane, Koscielisko, Dzianisz, Chocholow) * May 25 — Wawel (the tomb of St. Stanislaw), ordination to the diaconate * Same day — canonical visitation of the house of the Ursuline Sisters at Jaszczurowka in Zakopane.

June 1(Corpus Christi) — 7:00 am — Mass in the chapel of the Carmelite Sisters in Zakopane. After Mass, during a conversation with the sisters, the bishop said, among other things, that during preparation for the Mass, he was struck by the words "Manna absconditum" and "desert," upon which he commented as follows: "In reality, Carmel is also a desert. To live in it is not only, as is sometimes thought, to taste God; Carmel is also the night and the desert ..." (According to an account by the Carmelite Sisters from Zakopane)

June 2 — He visited a hermitage on Kalatowki {Mts.}. He promised that he will come here "to get lost in meditation." (The Albertine Sisters)

June 3 — Krakow, he witnessed the marriage of a couple from the *Srodowisko*

June 10 — Witow, Mass, sermon, administered the sacrament of Confirmation. Afternoon: service in the chapel on Plazowka, then to Polana Chocholowska — festive train of horsemen, carriages, young people on bicycles. At Polana, greeted by "baca" and "juhasy,"[1] who offered him sheepmilk cheese. Speeches, prayers and singing in the chapel. He visited a mountain shelter. At the campfire, music, storytelling, mountaineers' dances.

June 13 — Sacrament of Confirmation at St. Florian's Church * June 17 — 3:30 p.m., conference to Mothers Superior in the chapel of the Ursulines * Same day — 4:30 p.m., Confirmation in the church at Wola

---

[1] Baca: head sheepherder; Juhasy: his assistants, among the mountain people of the southern Carpathian region of Poland.

Duchacka * June 18 — 8:30 am — sermon in the church at Wola Duchacka; at 10:00 am — Mass with sermon * June 24 — Chorzow, officiates at a marriage of a couple from the *Srodowisko* * June 25 — Chapel on Pedzichow Street — conference {retreat} for nurses.

July 2-5 — Czestochowa Seminary in Krakow: he led a retreat for priests * July 3 — In the chapel of the Felician Sisters on Mikolajska Street, Mass and sermon for the beginning of a catechetic course for the hearing and speech impaired * July 15 — Krakow, he witnessed at the mariage of a couple from the *Srodowisko* * July 24 — Wawel, Pontifical Mass for the 10th anniversary of the death of Cardinal A. Sapieha * July 31-August 16 —Kayak excursion with the *Srodowisko* on the Pilawa River: the Drawsko lake district, Pilawa, Pila.

August 11 — Letter to Prof. Adam Vetulani:

Esteemed Mr. Professor!
I can see that because of various vacation activities, the planned trek over Babia Gora {Mountain} to Osielec will not come about. For that reason permit me, by way of this letter, to express proof of my remembrance of your person, and of the academic attempt at Gratianology, which for the past several months has brought me closer to the academic workshop of the Esteemed Professor ...
                                                                    Rev. Karol Wojtyla

August 20 — Miedzygorze (diocese of Wroclaw), during the Marian days in Lower Silesia, he celebrated a Pontifical Mass and preached a sermon.

August 21 — Wroclaw, Theological Seminary, meeting of the Apostolic Committee of the Episcopate. Bishop B. Kominek gave the introduction and report; a discussion follows. Fr. Bernard Przybylski presented a pastoral program for the next year of the Great Novena. Animated discussion followed and Bishop Karol Wojtyla participated in it. As a result of the discussions, it was recommended that the subjects of sermons in the 6th year of the Great Novena be expanded. Next, a discussion took place (in which Bishop K. Wojtyla spoke) on the proposed instructions to the clergy regarding clerical garb.

August 24 — Theological Seminary in Krakow, Mass and sermon for the conclusion of the retreat for priests.

September 1-5 — Participation in the Episcopal Conference and in a retreat at Jasna Gora * Sept. 5-6 — Warsaw. Academic seminar for professors-theologians. [*Nasza Przyszlosc*, vol. 14: 1961, p. 311] * September 9 — Wawel Cathedral, Mass for the 20th anniversary of the Rhapsodic Theater. He participated in the celebration of the 20th anniversary of the Rhapsodic Theater (premiere of *Dziady*[2]). On this

---

[2] *Forefathers' Eve* by Adam Mickiewicz

occasion, he published the article *"Dziady" and the 20th anniversary*, signed by A. J. in *Tygodnik Powszechny*[3] of October 1, no. 40. (Danuta Michalowska)

October 1 — Jaroszowice, in the filial church of the parish of Wadowice, he blessed the tabernacle, said Mass and preached a sermon * October 4 — Church of St. Florian in Krakow, Mass and sermon for educators * October 8 — St. Anne's Church, sermon during a Mass for the inauguration of the academic year * October 9-11 — Canonical visitation of a part of the deanery of Wieliczka * October 9 — Official visit to the monastery church in Wieliczka: he said Mass and preached a sermon. Subsequently, invited by the order, he visited the monastery, the cell of the Servant of God Alojzy Kosiba, and the minor seminary. He participated in a meal in the refectory of the monastery. In the visitors' book he wrote: "As part of my visitation of the parish of Wieliczka, I visited the church and was hospitably received in the monastery. To my hosts I express a sincere 'May God bless.' I ask Brother Alojzy to pray for me. Bishop Karol Wojtyla, Vicar General"

October 15 — 9:00 am — Koscielisko, Chapel of the Pallotine Fathers — participation in the rosary procession, Mass and sermon. Same day — 5:00 p.m. — Wawel Cathedral, Mass with sermon * Same day — 7:00 p.m., Mass with sermon at the Church of St. Joseph * October 20 —Church of St. Anne: Mass for the Feast of St. John of Kanty * October 21 — With young people at Jasna Gora — he said Mass before the miraculous image and led the recitation of the rosary at the summit * October 22 — In the Church of St. Florian in Krakow, liturgical service and address to the families of altar servers on the occasion of an inaugural Mass * Same day — the Church of St. Anne, the conclusion of a devotion in honor of St. John of Kanty.

November 1 — Short stay in Tyniec * November 5 — Lublin, sermon during a Mass for the inauguration of the academic year at KUL[4] * November 1, 1961 — January 14, 1962 (with gaps) — he conducted a visitation of St. Anne's parish in Krakow * November 12 — At the parish church in Zakopane — a sermon for the 10th anniversary of the priesthood of those priests of the Archdiocese of Krakow who were ordained in 1951 * November 13 — Sermon in Zakopane * November 19 — In the Church of St. Norbert (The Missionaries of Our Lady of La Salette) sermon for the blind * November 23 — In the Church of the Discalced Carmelites, a liturgical service for the intention of the beatification of Brother Albert.

---

[3] A Catholic weekly published in Krakow, one of very few Catholic publications tolerated by the Communist government.
[4] Catholic University of Lublin

December 24 — He wrote to Prof. A. Vetulani: "...I have been sick for a month..."

December 31 — The Church of the Capuchin Fathers in Krakow, he participated in Masses at 8:15 a.m., 9:00 a.m., 10:00 a.m., 11:00 a.m., 12:00 noon; sermon at noon * Same day — in the Church of St. Anne, a sermon during vesper services.

1962

January 1 — While visiting St. Anne's parish, he came to the Church of the Capuchin Fathers. At 8:00 a.m. he celebrated Mass, at 12:00 noon he preached a sermon encouraging the faithful to persevere in the faith by observing the laws of God. (From the chronicle of the Capuchin monastery in Krakow, vol. II, compiled by Fr. Tytus Gorczyca) * January 3-4 — Visiting the sick of St. Anne's parish * January 5 — Celebrated Mass for the intention of the sick in the monastery of the Capuchin Fathers in Krakow. After the Mass, he spoke to the large gathering, encouraging them to endure the pain with patience and courage. (From the chronicle of the monastery) * January 6 — Church of the Capuchin Fathers. An evening Mass was celebrated by Fr. Provincial, during which Bishop Wojtyla, visiting St. Anne's parish within whose territory lies the Capuchin monastery, delivered an address to the third Order. After Mass, dedication of the three Franciscan Orders to the Most Sacred Heart of Jesus. (From the chronicles of the monastery) * January 7 — St. Anne's Church — blessing of children and infants * January 11 — St. Anne's Church, a conference on the topic of the encyclical Mater et Magistera * In the same church, Mass and sermon for single people.

January 15 — Zakopane, "Ksiezowka," meeting of the Pastoral Committee of the Episcopate. An attempt at the pastoral evaluation of the first half of the Great Novena — Bishop B. Kominek; Bishop K. Wojtyla — took part in the discussion (all participants stressed the extraordinary contribution of the Great Novena into the religious life of the nation). Later during the meeting, a report (Bishop Z. Golinski) on the convention of professors of homiletics in Krakow (January 28 and 29), dissolution of the homiletic subcommittee * January 16 — Zakopane, second day of meetings of the Pastoral Committee. A discussion of the program of the seventh year of the Great Novena ("charity and justice"); Bishop Wojtyla takes part in the discussion. Discussion of a proposed directive on clerical garb for the clergy, creation of a subcommittee that would be charged with working this directive out — subcommittee for ministry to priests. Presentation by Rev. T. Rylko, *Young candidates for the laity*. Rev. Bishop Wojtyla takes part in the discussion.

January 17 — Zakopane. A meeting of the Pastoral Committee of the Episcopate with the national priest directors of ministries to various social, professional and specialist groups. Rev. Bishop Wojtyla is the national director of the ministry to literati together with Rev. Len * Jan 18 — Second day of meetings of the Pastoral Committee with the national directors of ministries. Bishop B. Kominek presided, presented the actual situation of the Church in Poland. A committee to study morality (the moral situation) was established, the make-up of the committee: Rev. T. Rylko, Rev. Prof. K. Majdanski. A pastoral letter on the subject of demoralization is to be prepared over the next year by Bishop W. Pluta and Bishop K. Wojtyla. A summary of the discussions was given by Bishop Wojtyla * Same day — at the Church of St. Anne, Mass and *Oplatek*[5] for university students.

February 5 — At the residence at 21 Kanoniczna Street, a meeting of all the clergy of St. Anne's parish for the conclusion of the visitation * February 18 — At the parish church in Lipnik, Bishop Karol Wojtyla consecrated an altar and preached a sermon.

March 4 — The first morning Mass of the day {prymaria} for the beginning of a forty-hour devotion in the chapel of the Daughters of Charity in Krakow at 8 Warszawska Street * March 9 — April 28 — Visitation of the parish of Our Lady (the Mariacki Church) in Krakow * March 10 — He came to participate in Prof. Stanislaw Pigon's jubilee-celebrations at the auditorium of PAN[6] at 17 Slawkowska Street.

> He did not want to be seated in the first row among the "distinguished guests" and sat somewhere on the side. He thanked me for sending an invitation — at that time I was secretary of the Historical-Literary Commission of PAN, which had organized the celebration. (Maria Bobrownicka)

March 11 — As part of the visitation of the Mariacki Church parish, he visited the Church of St. Kazimierz (where the main house of the province of the Reformed Franciscans is located). He arrived at 8:00 a.m., and promptly celebrated Mass in the church filled with young people from trade schools. On this day the young people were receiving Holy Communion after the conclusion of a retreat. He preached a sermon for the young people. He participated in the subsequent Masses, and gave a blessing after each one; at the end, during the Mass at 1:00 p.m., he preached a sermon. After a noon meal with the Brothers in the refectory he gave a short talk. He was planning to stay for the "Gorzkie Zale" {Lamentations — a Lenten service}, but pressing matters did not allow him. He promised, however, to return one more time to the Franciscan Church of St. Kazimierz. And, indeed, he came the follow-

---

[5] See Glossary.
[6] Polish Academy of Arts and Sciences.

ing Sunday (March 18) when the Passion homily series had started; he listened to it in the sacristy, and stayed there for the rest of the Lenten service * March 15 — The make-up of the commissions of the Polish Episcopate was completed. Bishop Wojtyla was appointed to the Committee of Higher Education (according to the records of the Conference of the Polish Episcopate) * March 24 — In the parish Church of Biezanow, Mass and sermon for the conclusion of a retreat for men and male youth * March 29 — In the parish church in Jaworzno, he participated in a retreat for secondary-school students * March 30 — Mass and sermon for the conclusion of an academic retreat at the Church of Our Lady of Lourdes * March 31 — Rabka, participation in the conclusion of a retreat for high school students * Same day — Rokiciny — "In the evening, Bishop Karol Wojtyla arrived from Rabka with his ailing aunt (Stefania W.) and stayed for supper." (From the chronicles of the convent of the Ursulines)

April 5 — St. Anne's Church, Mass and sermon for the conclusion of a retreat for scientists * April 6 — Liszki, Mass for the conclusion of a retreat * April 9-14 — Retreat at the academic Church of St. Anne:

> **I. It would be best if we started from the most simple fact ... that we are here; what does it mean? II. Today I want to speak of the Gospel, that is means about Revelation ... The Gospel has a human content, a deeply human content ... III. What to do with this life which has been given to me? We find the answer to that question in the Gospel, we find it, looking at Christ. IV ... The Son of God became man to redeem us from sin. And that is why, in the Gospel, sin is found close to Christ ... V. Christ is God who converts us Himself — still ... He forms us today; in the Holy Communion, He wants to create us anew, to recreate us...**

April 16-18 — Retreat for artists at the Church of the Holy Cross.

> **The content of this retreat is contained in the title: "The Gospel and art." These associations [between the Gospel and art] come about primarily because God, of whom the Gospels speak, is Beauty (....) [from the introductory lesson]**
> **[About the resolutions of the retreat:] ... if we cannot manage anything else, and perhaps we cannot, maybe our resolutions are very shaky and we do not have confidence in their effectiveness — we must necessarily decide on one thing. Namely: on prayer ...**

April 18 — Convent of the cloistered Dominican Sisters in Krakow at Grodek. He visited the church in the name of Archbishop Baziak, accompanied by Msgr. Ferdynand Machay. He talked with the sisters in the parlor.

April 25 — In the cathedral in Katowice he participated in the jubilee celebrations of Bishop Juliusz Bieniek (he preached a sermon) * April 27 — In the Church of the Reformed Franciscans, Mass and sermon for the ailing of the parish of Our Lady * April 28 — Together with Archbishop E. Baziak and Bishop J. Groblicki, he participated in a ceremony of the dedication of the clergy of the archdiocese of Krakow to Our Lady, at the shrine in Kalwaria Zebrzydowska.

May 2-June 7 — (With interruptions) Visitation of the Makow deanery * May 13 — He participated in Marian Days in Kalisz * May 14-21 — Visitation of the Mszana deanery * June 9-10 — Visitation of the Azory parish * June 10 — During the visitation of the Parish of the Immaculate Conception in Krakow-Azory, after the High Mass, he paid a visit to the cloister of the Camaldolese Fathers at Bielany * June 11 — He led a funeral of Zofia Firley, former housekeeper of Bishop Stanislaw Rospond. She was laid to rest in the cemetery of the convent of the Sisters of Our Lady of Mercy; in the last years of her life she had stayed with them. (From the chronicles of the "Jozefow" {Josephinum} home)

June 12 — Siedlce, he participated in the funeral of Bishop Marian Jankowski and celebrated a low Mass at the altar of St. Anthony. He arrived a little bit late for the funeral by taxi from Warsaw. To Warsaw he had come by plane. (Rev. Zdzislaw Mlynarski)

June 14/15 — Death of the Archbishop Metropolitan of Krakow Eugeniusz Baziak * June 15 — Ordination of new priests * June 16 — He is elected Capitular Vicar by the Krakow Chapter * June 19 — He welcomed those who arrived for the funeral of the late archbishop of Krakow, Eugeniusz Baziak.

> **In order for us to look upon the Archbishop's life with deepest respect, even as we stand at his coffin, we must start from the Gospel parable of the shepherd. In the Gospel, this shepherd has a double representation. First we see him as he strides before his flock, as he watches, as he guards and defends. But we also see this shepherd of the Gospel ... as he searches ... for the lost sheep, and having found it, returns it to the flock and rejoices, is glad ... — [Further, about the connection between the cross and authority in the life of the late archbishop].**

June 21 — 9:00 a.m., High Mass at Wawel cathedral, Corpus Christi procession * 12:00 noon — procession at the Church of Corpus Christi * June 24 — Blessing of the children in Wieliczka * June 25 —Mass and sermon for the beginning of a study organized for pastoral vicars at the chapel of the Theological Seminary * June 26-27 — Gaszowice. A reunion.

> **Thanks to him, we could meet every year at social reunions, from which he would never be absent. He twice held such meetings at my place. In the case of the meeting in Gaszowice, he came straight from Warsaw. He was late, but only because, on the way, he said an evening Mass at a parish north of Krakow, where the priest had been arrested for saying Mass in temporary quarters and therefore supposedly illegally. I don't remember the**

name of the place. He stood at that altar at the moment when the parish community, and the priest-prisoner, needed encouragement.

After the reunion, the Bishop went to Bialystok, bypassing Krakow.
(Rev. Franciszek Konieczny)

June 27 — Chapel of the Ursuline Sisters, Mass and a talk for the conclusion of the school year of WIK.[7]

July 1 — He participated in Rev. F. Machay's jubilee at the Mariacki Church * July 2 — At the Church of the Felician Sisters — Mass for the beginning of the days of recollection for speech and hearing impaired * July 5 — Mass for the conclusion of a retreat for organists in the chapel of the Theological Seminary * July 15 — 10:00 a.m. — Mass for the jubilee of the chapel in Witow. Same day — a short visit at the Carmelite convent of the Immaculate Heart of Mary in Zakopane and at 5:00 p.m., vespers at the monastery of the Carmelite Fathers in Czerna * July 28-August 15 — A kayak outing on the Rega River. 5 kayaks, 10 persons. Discussion on the upcoming Vatican Council, anticipated course and its significance.

August 22-24 — Lecture for the clergy at KUL,[8] on the topic: The priest in the contemporary world. Presentation by Bishop Karol Wojtyla: *The Priest in light of contemporary changes* * August 24 — Sermon for the 400th anniversary of the reform of the order at the Church of the Discalced Carmelite Sisters in Krakow at 44 Kopernika Street * August 26 — Jasna Gora, he preached a sermon for the youth.

September 1 — A sermon about Blessed Bronislawa at the Church of the Most Blessed Savior * Same day — at 8:00 p.m. — he came unannounced to the Sisters of Our Lady of Mercy, whose institution was taken over by the state authorities on August 28th. He said that he is visiting religious congregations whose houses were confiscated in recent years and that he considers this congregation particularly wronged, because such actions strike at the very essence of its mission. He spoke of his desire to create psychological-pedagogical counseling centers in the parishes, and that the Sisters of Our Lady of Mercy, with their preparation and experience, are especially suited to this work. (From the chronicle of the "Jozefow" house)

September 8 — He participated in the coronation ceremony of the image of Our Lady in Okulice (Tarnow diocese) * September 11-14 — He participated in a retreat and a conference of the Polish Episcopate at Jasna Gora * September 17 — Zakopane, preliminary conference at the fourth session of the student ministry in Poland (September 17-19).

---

[7] Higher Catechetical Institute
[8] Catholic University of Lublin

General topic: Shaping the interior lives of the youth through the Sacraments.

About the 18th of September — Bishop Karol Wojtyla paid a visit to the Secretary of the Voivodship Committee of the Polish Communist Party regarding the seminary building at Manifestu Lipcowego Street. The authorities had tried to take over the building and turn it over to the Pedagogical College. After consultations with the Metropolitan Chapter, the Capitular Vicar, who had been recalled from the parish visitation in Maniowy, went to the Voivodship Committee and had a conversation with the Party Secretary. This was an unprecedented event. As a result of this conversation, a compromise was reached: The Pedagogical College took over the third floor, and the Seminary retained the rest of the building. The Pedagogical College left the seminary building at the end of 1978/79 academic year.

September 22 — In the Church of Sts. Peter and Paul in Krakow, a celebration in honor of Rev. Piotr Skarga: Mass and sermon, a visit to the crypt * September 30 — Nowa Huta-Ruszcza, Mass and sermon for the 700th anniversary of the parish.

In the academic year 1962/63, he resigned from lecturing at the Department of Theology in Krakow.

October 1 — The Capitular Vicar performs an act of dedication of the seminary buildings to the Blessed Mother. The first part of the act was recited in the seminary building on Podzamcze Street, whereupon the seminarians and professors under the leadership of the bishop proceeded in silence to the second building on Manifestu Lipcowego Street, where the second part of the dedication was recited. From then on, every year on October 1st, this act of dedication was renewed in a similar fashion.

October 3 — A sermon for the 400th anniversary of the Order at the Church of the Carmelite Sisters in Krakow on Lobzowska Street * October 4 — He participated in a Mass for the intention of the Holy Father John XXIII celebrated by Rev. Prelate B. Niemczewski at the Wawel Cathedral. [*Notificationes ...*] * October 5 — During a Mass celebrated by Bishop J. Groblicki, in the evening, one hour before departure for the Vatican Council he said:

> **And I must tell you, my dear brothers in the episcopate, in the priesthood, and brothers in the grace of baptism, that I set out on this trip, onto this great roadway from the tomb of St. Stanislaw to the tomb of St. Peter, with great personal emotion, with great trembling of the heart, in the full realization of the responsibility for everything that is happening at the tomb of St. Stanislaw and for everything that is to happen at the tomb of St. Peter in Rome.**

October 11-December 8 — Rome. Participation in the first session of the Vatican Council.

November 7 — He spoke during the 14th gathering of the first session of the Council regarding the 3rd chapter of the schema about the Liturgy. (*Acta Synodalia Sacrosanti Concilli Oecumenici Vaticani II* TPV 1970, vol. I, pars II, p. 314) * November 15 — Rome, the Church of St. Stanislaw, he preaches a sermon after the Mass for the late Archbishop E. Baziak.

November 17 — He wrote a letter (in Latin) to Padre Pio asking him to pray for a sick person: *Reverend Father, I ask you to pray for a woman about 40 years old, mother of four daughters, who spent five years in a concentration camp in Germany during the war. At present her life is threatened by a tumor. Ask God through the intercession of the Most Holy Virgin, to show His mercy to this woman and her family. Grateful in Christ. +Karol Wojtyla, titular bishop Ombi, Capitular Vicar of Krakow, Poland. Rome, Pontificio Collegio Polacco, Piazza Remuria 2A Roma.*

(The facsimile of the letter was published by the Italian press in the 1980s with the information that the person whom the Capitular Vicar of Krakow commended to Padre Pio was Dr.Wanda Poltawska)

* November 21 — He delivered a speech at the 14th gathering of the Council in relation to the 1st chapter of the schema about the sources of Revelation. (Acta Synodalia TPV 1971, vol. 1, pars III, p. 294) * November 23-27 — He delivered an opinion in writing relating to the schema on the mass media. (*Acta Synodalia* TPV, vol. I, pars III, p. 609)

November 24 — He delivered a speech on the Vatican Radio: "... above all, I would like to bring closer to the listener the spirit prevailing here [at the Council] ..." Later, he talked about St. Joseph, in connection with the introduction of St. Joseph's name to the prayers of the canon of the Holy Mass: "St. Joseph, being so close to the point where the human and the Divine meet, helps us first of all to interpret — the great concerns of human life: the first of these is family, and the second — work ..."

November 28 — A letter (in Latin) to Padre Pio with the information about the healing of a person who had been commended to the prayers of the famous Capuchin: *Reverend Father, the woman from Krakow was instantly healed on November 21 before the surgical intervention. I give thanks to God. I also thank You, Reverend Father, on behalf of this woman, her husband and family. In Christ +Karol Wojtyla, Capitular Vicar of Krakow.*

December 3-7 — He made a statement in writing regarding the schema of *De Ecclesia*. (*Acta Synodalia* TPV 1971 vol. I, pars IV, p. 598-599)

During the first session of the Second Vatican Council the poem(s), *The Church*, are written.

December 14 — Return from the Council. A welcome in Jaworzno, Holy Mass celebrated at the boundaries of the diocese (in the parish of Niwka) * December 16 — A conference on the topic of the Council at the Theological Seminary in Krakow * December 20 — Breaking of the Christmas wafer with the participants of the meeting at St. Anne's Church. Reflections from the Council — among others, at the outset, that the press transmitted information very well.

> **I would like to point out several facts, the first being — that the Council has brought the Church very close to us ... All of its activities shine with the spirit of Pope John XXIII — the tendency to show the truth, and to show it in such a fashion that it would captivate the contemporary man and find its way to him.**
> **... from the first day, the {participants of the} Council realized the importance of what is being carried into effect before the eyes of mankind, and from the very first day it established contact with all humanity.**

December 24 — Nowa Huta-Bienczyce, "Pasterka" {midnight Mass}, combined with the Sacrament of Confirmation * December 25 — Wawel Cathedral, Pontifical High Mass with a sermon on the topic of the Council and the papal blessing. A large part of the sermon was dedicated to the Holy Father John XXIII — "Do you love me? — to those words John XXIII seems to respond: I love You and through You I love all" * December 26 — the Church of St. Szczepan, Pontifical High Mass and a sermon about the Council:

> **In the thoughts of the Holy Father and in their implementation by all the bishops, this Council wants to be ... an act of love ... — an act which will weigh upon the history of the contemporary man and will, in some way, tear man away from hatred and push him in the direction of love.**

December 31 — 7:15 p.m., at the Mariacki Church: a Mass for the end of the year, a sermon about the Council, the conveying of the papal blessing * The same day — midnight, Mass with a homily for the beginning of the new year, in the Basilica of the Franciscan Fathers.

1963

January 11 — Lublin, KUL[1] — defense of the doctoral thesis by Fr. Tadeusz Styczen SDS: *The possibility of scientific ethics in J. Locke's writings.* Promoter: Rev. Prof. Bishop Karol Wojtyla. (He was the promoter of six, and the reader of 2 doctoral theses.) Rev. Dr. T. Styczen became an adjunct professor in the Chair of Ethics and the closest collaborator in Wojtyla's academic work. Already from 1963 T. Styczen took over most of the courses in ethics at KUL (T. Styczen had been a volunteer-assistant since 1957; a senior assistant since 1962, and an adjunct professor since 1963).

January 22 — Mass in Wawel Cathedral for the 100th anniversary of the January Uprising[2].

> **We owe them our gratitude because they gave us the precious gift of freedom. The gift of external freedom of our nation and the gift of internal freedom of man ..., and they gave us this gift of freedom in a new meaning. The inner freedom of man. Throughout our history, we Poles have often sinned against freedom by abusing it. And then, throughout long years of captivity, we would have to arduously win back what we had lost.**

January 25 — Church of St. Anne in Krakow, Mass with sermon for the end of a week of prayer for Christian unity:

> **The first thing we want is unity ... If all of us are praying for it, that means that in some sense we already have it ... I cannot forget certain meetings during the Council with the brothers from Taize, a Protestant monastery in France, whose entire life and activities are aimed exclusively at bringing about the unification of the Protestant world.**

January 28 — 5:30 p.m. — Zakopane — in the parish church, a sermon about the first session of the Second Vatican Council * Same day — 7:30 p.m. — sermon at the parish church of Nowy Targ * January 29 — Kalwaria Zebrzydowska — as the Vicar of the diocesan chapter after the death of Archbishop E. Baziak, he took part in an *Oplatek*[3] of priests from the regional deaneries, relaying to them the news from the Second Vatican Council.

February 1 — Social get-together at the home of Bishop Karol Wojtyla on Kanoniczna Street. About 30 invited guests discussed the Second Vatican Council. The host took this occasion to point out with satisfaction that the heretofore narrow circle of people in KIK (the Club of Catholic Intellectuals), *Znak* and *Tygodnik Powszechny* is being widened by the addition of new individuals and new chapters with a Catholic outlook. Docent Jozef Mitkowski, thanking the bishop in the

---

[1] Catholic University of Lublin
[2] 1863, against Russia during the partitions
[3] See Glossary.

name of the guests, used the expression that in our Bishop we see the successor of one of the apostles in unbroken apostolic succession. The Bishop smiled and said: Indeed, but I'm not sure of which apostle I am the successor. (On the basis of the notes by Jozef Mitkowski)

February 2 — Parish church in Wieliczka — sermon about the first session of the Second Vatican Council * February 3 — Biala, parish church of Divine Providence — sermon about first session of the Council * February 4 — Parish church in Zywiec — sermon about the first session of the Council * February 5 — Oswiecim, parish of the Assumption of the Virgin Mary — sermon about the first session of the Council * Same day — Oswiecim — Mass for the intention of Pope John XXIII.

> **After returning from the first session of the Council, I tried to meet with all the priests in various parts of the archdiocese — today, here in Oswiecim — and to relate to them what is contained, at least thus far, in this great event of the Church which is the Council.**
> **At the same time, at least here and there in the diocese, I also tried to relate that to the faithful.**
> **[Subsequently: About the attitude of Pope John XXIII to political matters; about the attitude of the Church to matters such as the {concentration} camp in Oswiecim {Auschwitz}.]**

February 19 — Notified of the death of architect Luboslaw Dormus, co-designer of the chapel of perpetual adoration in the Jesuit church in Krakow, he came to the funeral. He led the procession from the Church of the Most Sacred Savior to the cemetery and conducted the internment rites.

February 24 — "His Excellency Bishop Karol Wojtyla opened a 40-hour adoration with a Mass in the chapel of the Daughters of Charity of St. Vincent de Paul in Krakow, on Warszawska Street." (Congregation of the Daughters of Charity)

March 7 — The Dominican church — Pontifical High Mass for the Feast of St. Thomas Aquinas * March 8 — Mass and sermon on the Feast of St. John of God at the church of the Hospitaller Brothers of St. John of God in Krakow * March 10 — Parish church in Nowy Targ — Mass with sermon for the end of retreat for young people * March 17 — Mass with sermon for secondary-school youth in the Jesuit church in Krakow * March 19 — He preached a sermon during vesper services for the conclusion of the 40-hour adoration in honor of St. Joseph, patron of the chapel of the Sisters of Our Lady of Mercy. He was invited for that day by the Congregation. (From the chronicle of the Congregation of the Sisters of Our Lady of Mercy)

March 22 — Church of Our Lady of Lourdes — Mass with sermon

for the end of a retreat for university students * March 23 — Mass for the intention of the beatification of Bishop Jozef Pelczar, at the Sisters of the Sacred Heart in Krakow.

April 6 — Church of St. Anne — Mass and confirmation * April 7 — Church of the Dominican Sisters at Grodek, retreat for nurses — sermon * April 11 — Homily for the conclusion of a closed retreat for graduating high-school students, at the Church of the Congregation of the Resurrection * April 13 — Easter Saturday in the evening — Resurrection {Easter} Mass in the Wawel Cathedral * April 15 — The cathedral — consecration of Jan Pietraszko, pastor of the academic Church of St. Anne in Krakow, as auxiliary bishop of the Krakow Archdiocese. Cardinal Wyszynski was the main celebrant, Bishop Wojtyla concelebrated.

April 17 — Sermon for the beginning of a pilgrimage of priests of the Archdiocese of Krakow to Jasna Gora. Bishop K. Wojtyla led the pilgrimage of clergy from the Archdiocese of Krakow. During the night vigil he renewed his act of dedication to the Blessed Mother, he celebrated the Eucharist before the image of Our Lady of Czestochowa at 5:30 a.m. during which he said, among other things:

> **There are many of us here at Jasna Gora. People of various states, various professions, pray at Jasna Gora; it is fitting that we should have our own days of prayer at Jasna Gors; that we, as priests of every archdiocese, of every congregation may experience our own priesthood more deeply and discover our bond of unity.**

April 23 — Jasna Gora — pilgrimage and vigil of a second group of priests from the Archdiocese of Krakow.

> **We usually come here, to Jasna Gora, as the leaders of pilgrimages, with our parishioners, with groups of young people. This time we come here not as leaders of pilgrimages, but as pilgrims and penitents ourselves ... When the late Archbishop first confided in me his thought of dedicating all the priests of the Krakow Archdiocese to the Blessed Mother, I told him: Your Excellency, first in Kalwaria. And that thought was realized last year. Kalwaria is our home shrine, to which we owe so much ... Today ... we are to re-affirm our dedication of a year ago. [He spoke further about the societal character of this pilgrimage.] At the same time, each of us in this society brings his own personal relationship to the Blessed Virgin. And I ask that each one of us now reaches back into the past and consider how your personal relationship to the Blessed Virgin has been shaped over the years, from pre-school years, through childhood and youth — and how does it appear today? ... [Further on the relationship of priests to the Blessed Mother, on priestly responsibility, with references to the Vatican Council]**

April 24 — Jasna Gora, the end of the pilgrimage, sermon. In all, over 80% of the priests of the archdiocese took part in this pilgrimage and the prayers at Jasna Gora.

We will be grateful in our actions, in our pastoral and priestly duties, which we pledge to conduct with gratitude and great humility for Your Son, O Blessed Virgin.

April 27-May 5 — Canonical visitation of the parish of Christ the Good Shepherd at Pradnik Czerwony in Krakow.

May — Meditations written by Bishop Karol Wojtyla are read in all the churches of the Archdiocese of Krakow throughout the entire month during the evening services.

May 3[4] — He participated in a solemn High Mass at Jasna Gora. The main celebrant was Stefan Barela, the bishop of Czestochowa.

May 5 — Wawel Cathedral — renewal of vows and the beginning of the 7th year of the Great Novena * May 6 — As part of the visitation of the parish at Pradnik, he visited the Albertine Sisters in their house on Woronicza Street and promised to undertake the matter of the beatification of Brother Albert in Rome. He delivered a conference on the unity within the Church through the parishes. The Albertine Sisters assist very productively in the work of the Good Shepherd Parish at Pradnik. * May 7 — the Mariacki Church — celebration of the nomination of the church to the status of a basilica * May 8 — Sermon for the Feast of St. Stanislaw in Wawel Cathedral. Reference to the preparations for the Millennium of Poland's Christianity.

— What kind of reality is Baptism?
— The Sacrament of the Priesthood.
— The role of St. Stanislaw: There are too many attempts to reduce the whole matter between Bishop Stanislaw and King Boleslaw to the sphere of politics alone. But the basis of St. Stanislaw's position was his supernatural episcopal responsibility for the people of God, to which the king also belonged, as a baptized person.

May 11 — Due to the Bishop's efforts, a tombstone was erected in the convent cemetery on the grave of Zofia Firley, a longtime housekeeper on Kanoniczna Street. There were several proposed designs. The final choice of the design was left to the Congregation, "...so it will be consistent with the style of your cemetery," as Bishop Karol Wojtyla said. (From the chronicle of the Congregation of Sisters of Our Lady of Mercy)

May 12 — 9:00 am — procession from Wawel to Skalka * Same day — 6:30 p.m. — sermon on the occasion of the mounting of a memorial tablet to Fr. Rafal Kalinowski and Br. Albert Chmielowski, participants of the Uprising of 1863,[5] in the church of the Discalced Carmelites, on Rakowicka Street in Krakow:

---

[4] See Glossary.
[5] against Russian occupation during the 125-year partition of Poland.

It will be worthwhile to imagine them [today], as they appeared in 1863, at the outbreak of the January Uprising, when they were deciding whether to take part in it. [In later parts of the sermon he spoke of the way of life and the way to sainthood of both.] ... Let us ask God that conspirators, members of underground resistance movements, may be elevated to the honors of the altar, since in our history we often had to break through to freedom from the underground. Let us pray that all conspirators, all heroes of the underground may find in them {Kalinowski and Chmielowski} their patrons, so that these two can become the spokesmen of the freedom of man and the freedom of nations — a matter so human yet, at the same time, so Christian, so evangelical, so divine.[6]

May 13. — In his capacity as Vicar of the diocesan chapter and ordinary judge, he headed the first session of the tribunal opening the informational process into the life and sanctity of the Servant of God Br. Alojzy Kosiba of the province of the Reformed Franciscans. He convened the tribunal by a document dated May 9, 1963, under the authority of a dispensation from the Apostolic See granted to him as a Vicar of the Chapter. The session was held in the audience hall of the residence of the Krakow Archbishops * May 15 — 5:00 p.m. — on his way to a visitation, he stopped at the little convent cemetery of the Sisters of Our Lady of Mercy, in order to pray at the grave of Zofia Firley. (From the chronicle of the Congregation of the Sisters of Our Lady of Mercy) * May 15 -June 15 — Canonical visitation of parishes in Glogoczow, Rudawa, Zabierzow, Modlnica, Korzkiew, Wawrzenczyce, Gorka Koscielnicka, Luborzyca, Krzeszowice.

May 16 — Mass in the house of the Sisters of the Holy Spirit at 12 Szpitalna Street in Krakow. For the first time as a bishop.

May 26 — Ploki. Marian days of the Krakow Archdiocese.

I welcome His Excellency Bishop Pawel from Wroclaw; I welcome here all their Excellencies — bishops from various parts of Poland, who today, on this Sunday, are visiting the various Marian sanctuaries within our archdiocese. I will be hurrying to these other places, so that I can greet there our guests, our pilgrims in the rank of bishop. From here I go to Oswiecim, then to Bielsko-Biala, from there to Makow Podhalanski, to Wadowice and Inwald, further to Dziekanowice near Wieliczka and to Wieliczka itself, then I will return to Gaj on the road between Krakow and Myslenice. Yesterday I already greeted two bishops, one of whom is going to Gdow and Niegowic today, and the other to Liszki near Krakow, to venerate the Blessed Mother with us during the Marian Days of the Archdiocese of Krakow.

May 29 — The welcome of Cardinal Francis Konig {of Vienna , Austria} on the border bridge in Cieszyn,[7] later the Cardinal visited the archbishop's palace in Krakow.

---

[6] Significance: The communist government did not acknowledge the bravery of the non-communist anti-German underground resistance of WWII, treating many of its fighters as crinimals.

[7] On the border with Czechoslovakia

May 31 — Krakow. Chapel of the Congregation of the Sisters of the Most Holy Soul of Christ the Lord [general house]. Eulogy at the casket of Mother Paula Zofia Tajber, the foundress of the Congregation.

June 3 —— Death of Pope John XXIII * June 6 — Wawel — Pontifical requiem Mass for Pope John XXIII * June 8 — Ordination of priests in the Church of the Congregation of the Resurrection in Krakow * June 11 — Visit to the house of the Daugthers of Charity of St. Vincent dePaul at 59 Nowa Wies Street in Krzeszowice, in the company of the pastor, Fr. Rudolf Schmidt. (Congregation of the Daughters of Charity) * June 21 — Wawel Cathedral, adoration {of the Blessed Sacrament} by priests; address about the election of Pope Paul VI * June 26 — Mariacki Church — rites of mourning in the crypts * June 27 — 4:00 p.m. — arrived for the conclusion of the kindergarten year at the Augustinian Sisters (at 12 Skaleczna Street, Krakow). At that point the kindergarten was taken away from the sisters and came under secular jurisdiction. The meeting was prolonged to the extent that the bishop telephoned the Curia telling them to start a scheduled conference without him, that he would arrive somewhat later. (Sr. Aleksandra Trojan OSA) * June 30 —Czestochowa, Jasna Gora. A pilgrimage of men and male youth from all over Poland, under the motto: "Fathers of families help the Father of Christianity." At 9:00 a.m., Bishop Karol Wojtyla was the main celebrant in a Mass and preached a sermon on the subject, "Fathers of families help the Father of Christianity to introduce love, peace and justice in the world" * Same day — 6:00 p.m. — Wawel — Pontifical Mass and sermon on the occasion of the coronation of Pope Paul VI.

First week of July — Three-day vacation trip with friends, former students, on the tenth anniversary of the first trip to the Bieszczady Mountains. Travel by cars to Ustrzyki Gorne. Hike to Poloniny. Return by car. For the first time, the participation of a representative of the next generation of his students, eight-year-old Andrzej K.

July 3 — Sermon commemorating Pope John XXIII given from the altar of Queen Jadwiga at Wawel * July 9 — Czestochowa. He participated in the funeral of Bishop Z. Golinski * August 11 — Nowy Sacz —coronation of the image of Our Lady of Consolation * August 15 — Coronation of the statue of Our Lady Queen of Podhale[8] in Ludzmierz. Bishop Wojtyla: "On the head of Our Lady of Ludzmierz we have placed the papal crown, the crown of Pope John XXIII. That crown allows us to call her, now more than ever, the Queen of Podhale." He asked Cardinal Wyszynski to perform the coronation. Words about the

---

[8] The mountainous Carpathian region in the south of Poland, just south of Wadowice where Wojtyla was born.

role of the Primate: "God has given you the immense grace of your office, a grace which we admire, for which we thank God, which is one of the sources of our collective might." The coronation of the statue was performed by Cardinal Wyszynski. As the Primate was performing the coronation, the scepter slipped out of the Blessed Mother's hand. Bishop Wojtyla caught it in flight.

August 16 — Monastery of the Bernardine Fathers in Kalwaria Zebrzydowska. Returning from the coronation of Our Lady at Ludzmierz, he stopped, together with 15 bishops, at the shrine in Kalwaria; there they participated in the "funeral of Our Lady" and he spoke to the pilgrims: "The purpose of our coming here is that we want to experience the Marian observances with the people of faith." * August 18 — He preached a sermon for the end of the great *Odpust* of the Assumption. Address during Marian Days in Kalwaria Zebrzydowska * August 28 — Participation in the Episcopal Conference at Jasna Gora * August 29-30 — Catechetical course at the Theological Seminary in Krakow.

August — Czestochowa. Days of the ministry for priests. Lecture on the subject: The Church in the world and in Poland.

Summer. Kayak trip on Lake Sasek and neighboring lakes.

Sept. 1 — Krakow, the Church of the Norbertine nuns. Holy Mass for the conclusion of the triduum in honor of Blessed Bronislawa. Rev. Bishop spoke from the altar. He was accompanied by Rev. Wladyslaw Dlugosz and pastor Rev. Malecki.

First half of September 1963:

> He came to the building of the City Council to take part in a social get-together organized by the then first secretary of the Council, Jan Antoniszczak, who intended to hold a solemn convention of the former students of Polish philology from our academic year to celebrate the 600th anniversary of the Jagiellonian University, under the patronage of rector Kazimierz Lepszy. Those invited by Antoniszczak were supposed to form an organizing committee of this convention. Present were — besides the Bishop and Antoniszczak — Tadeusz Holuj, Mieczyslaw Kieta, probably Krystyna Zbijewska (but I am not sure of this) and myself. After leaving the Council building, the Bishop talked with me at some length at a tram stop on the subject of the Vatican Council. As usual, he mostly listened, he tried to elicit what we expected from the Council, how we saw the *aggiornamento*, what our awareness of these matters was. (Maria Bobrownicka)

September 17 — The authorities of the city of Krakow decided to take over one wing of the building of the Silesian Seminary in Krakow. There was to be an eviction. On September 17, 1963 the rector of the Seminary, the vice-rector and the procurator went to the head of the City Council demanding a reversal of this decision — to no avail. On their way back they went to see Bishop Wojtyla, who telephoned the director of the City Council. The call was taken by the vice-director. The Bishop said that as a citizen of Krakow and as a Pole he is ashamed of this decision. He also telephoned L. Motyka, the first secretary of the Party. He assured the priests from the seminary that on the day of the eviction he would come to be with them and to protest the action. Some time later the director of the City Council telephoned the Seminary and asked for the rector, whom he told that he had thought about the matter more. The decision was reversed, the wing of the building was not taken over. (According to an account by the then Father Procurator)

September 21 — The parish of Our Lady of Lourdes — dedication of a little classroom for religious instruction.

October 6 — Church of the Dominicans in Krakow, on the day of departure for the second session of the Second Vatican Council (via Warsaw), sermon on the Feast of Our Lady of the Rosary, in the presence of Bishop Piotr Dudziec of Plock. 23 Polish bishops had already left on September 25th. "I could not leave with the other bishops because of illness ... I can leave tomorrow by plane from Warsaw, so I need to leave Krakow today ... I wish to take this opportunity to say good-bye to you." In subsequent parts of this sermon: about the Vatican Council, a plea for prayer. "Our cause is progressing. Our common cause. The common cause of the entire Church." He also spoke of the fact that Bishop Julian Groblicki was denied a passport — he expressed hope that the appeal will have an effect. Further, about the rosary, about the necessity of praying the rosary. At the conclusion, about the Council's Act of Goodness which was promoted in the letter from the Episcopate which had just been read.

October 7 — Departure by plane from Warsaw for the second session of the Second Vatican Council in Rome. October 19 — Program on Radio Vatican: the 600th anniversary of the Jagiellonian University — St. John of Kanty (about the role of the University, the history of JU, its ties with the Church in Krakow and the universal Church).

> **Over the period of more than 500 years that it has been a living part of the organism of the Jagiellonian University, it [the Department of Theology] has undoubtedly earned the right to be a full participant. It is all the more painful that it cannot take part in the University's great jubilee. I say this first of all as a former student of the Jagiellonian University. I was connected with two of its departments: first — the Department of Philosophy, then — the Department of Theology. At this point I would like to recall with reverence the memories of all the professors and theologians, many of whom were claimed by the last war. To the living I convey sincere wishes and expressions of mutual joy at this great jubilee of our Alma Mater.**

November 25 — Vatican Radio — program on the role of the laity in the Church.

The people of God — and above all the lay people — have the most immediate obligation here. The world was entrusted primarily to them, so that they could bring into it, into all the facets of its existence, all that which is in the Son of God ... truth and love ... If someone were to ask me, what the role of the laity in the Church is, I will answer that it consists in completing the work of Christ, the Son of God, in the world and with the world's help. It consists in regaining the world, in all of its facets and manifestations, for the Eternal Father. On the road to this, however, lies an even higher aim: to regain man himself, in his humanity, for the Eternal Father...

The close connection between the clergy and the laity in the Church is a charismatic property of the People of God. Its beginning lies in Christ our Priest. Catholics living in the world today must in great measure regain the awareness of their participation in the Priesthood of Christ — this means to fundamentally reconsider the fact of their Baptism and Confirmation.

October — November — Second session of the Vatican Council. Expresses opinion with regard to the declaration on religious freedom. ["Collegium Polonorum" 1964, p. 105-6].

December 1 — Parish of Seregno (archdiocese of Milan) — Mass, sermon, he thanked for the bells for the Church of St. Florian in Krakow * December 2 — End of the second session of the Second Vatican Council * December 5-15 — Pilgrimage to the Holy Land. Letter to the priests of the archdiocese in which he describes this voyage:

In the current year, after the close of the second session of the Council, I had the good fortune to participate, along with dozens of bishops from various countries, in a pilgrimage to the Holy Land. We feel that in working on the renewal of the Church at the Council, we must turn directly to Christ Himself, whose Church is His Mystical Body. And hence the desire to visit these places where He was born, lived, taught, acted, and finally suffered, died on the cross, rose from the dead and ascended into heaven. This desire was expressed on the day of the close of the second session of the Council, on December 4th, by the Holy Father himself, Pope Paul VI. He announced that next month he would go on a pilgrimage to Our Lord's native land. This announcement has become reality in recent days.

The Holy Father's pilgrimage lent an even higher meaning to the pilgrimages made by the Fathers of the Council to the Holy Land, including the one in which I had the good fortune to participate from December 5 to 15 of 1963, together with over a dozen other bishops from Poland. I did not treat this participation as a personal or private privilege, but as a grace granted me by Providence to be shared with others. And that is why, shortly after returning from the Council session and from the Holy Land, I wish to share my still fresh memories of this pilgrimage first of all with you, my brothers in the priesthood. Maybe this concise collection of memories will be useful to you in your pastoral work, maybe you can use it for preparing catechism lessons or sermons for Christmas, Lent or Easter. In any case, I wish that your eyes could, at least by means of this letter, look on what I was given to see — and I wish that you, too, could see it with your own eyes one day. This does much to enliven faith ...

In my letter I will try to follow at least somewhat the chronology of the life of Our Lord, departing from the chronology of our visit to the Holy Land ... The voyage to Our Lord's native land began in Egypt. So we were first on the trail of that Exodus to the Promised Land which the Chosen People traveled in the Old Testament. In beautiful sunny weather, we could plainly see this trail from the air: the deserts of Egypt up to the shore of the Red Sea, then the mountains of Sinai and again the desert, with virtually no signs of vegetation. We approached Jerusalem in a wide arc, and landed at the airport (on the Arabian side) ...

We spent the night from December 8th to the 9th in the shrine of the Nativity, celebrating Masses from midnight until 5:30 a.m. At 5:30 a.m., the Orthodox begin their services. The altar which commemorates the moment of Christ's birth belongs to them, while the neighboring altar, commemorating the laying of the Newborn in the manger, belongs to the Catholics. We adored the Mystery of the Nativity of God, and kissed the ground at the place where God came into the world; we celebrated Masses at the altar of "Praesepe." We were in a stone grotto which at one time gave shelter to the Holy Virgin and St. Joseph ... I must add that the Polish bishops sang a few Polish carols in the grotto, having been asked for this by the aging Fr. Borkowski — a Polish Franciscan who has been working in the Holy Land for decades.

The history of the Nativity led us also from Bethlehem to Jerusalem, namely to the temple — on the fortieth day after the Nativity. The distance from Bethlehem to Jerusalem is not great — it can be traversed there and back within a day ... Bethlehem itself was the witness — albeit unknowingly — of the first days and weeks of Christ's life. There also were spent the first days and weeks of the maternity of Mary. A particular commemoration of this maternity is the *Grota Lactis*. According to tradition, on this spot the Blessed Mother nursed Jesus with the milk of her breast, and a drop of her maternal milk fell on the ground. The tradition is alive and well: from time immemorial, women who suffer from a lack of maternal milk make pilgrimages to this spot — both Christian and Muslim women — to beg for Mary's help ...

During a brief stopover in Egypt, in Cairo, we did not visit the place where the Holy Family stayed until the death of Herod, before returning to Nazareth. From Nazareth, the 12-year-old Jesus went with Mary and Joseph to the temple in Jerusalem and stayed there, while the two of them, not knowing of this, were already on their way back. To this day people point out the spot where, according to tradition, the Blessed Mother and St. Joseph realized that Jesus had remained in the temple. The road leads from Jerusalem to Galilee, to Nazareth, through Samaria. This is the road used by Galilean pilgrims on their trips to the temple of Jerusalem for the holy days.

The temple itself ceased to exist in the year 70 after Christ. We move about on a great square, where the temple stood since the time of Solomon, surrounded by a series of courtyards ...

The site of the temple of the Old Testament is a holy place for us, Christians, first of all because it was the temple of the True God, which Our Lord plainly called "the house of my Father," secondly, because our Redeemer visited this temple many times during His lifetime ...

On December 9 we could not reach the place where, according to tradition, the baptism of Jesus took place, because after a rain lasting all day and all night, the last section of the road was flooded. Similar circumstances — when we reached the Dead Sea — prevented us from reaching Qumran ...

The Lake of Gennesaret still possesses the same charm that we read about in the pages of the Gospels. It is still full of fish, and many fishing boats still sail on it, and the fishermen still pull their nets as in the times of Jesus. The traces of the Savior's presence around the lake, and memories of the Gospels, are very numerous ...

Nearby is Capernaum Bethsaida (Julias) — the shrine where St. Peter was given primacy. It is right by the shore of the lake. Our Lord said to Peter: "Feed my lambs, feed my sheep." We stop on the shore and pick up stones from the water as souvenirs.

On December 13 we spend many hours by Lake Gennesaret. We stop at the point where the River Jordan flows out of the lake. The banks, in contrast to what we had seen at the river's mouth, are covered with trees and dense vegetation. In general, Galilee, the native land of Our Lord, is different from the stony and desert-like Judea. We are struck by the beauty of the landscape, gently rolling, with mountain ranges stretching in different directions. The land is fertile; we are watching it in winter, but it is most beautiful in spring, when it is covered with fresh greenery and flowers. We looked at Galilee, the native land of Our Lord, mainly from Mount Tabor. We went up the mountain in the evening, and after nightfall, and in the morning before sunrise, and again and again, in order to look at this land, the land sanctified once and for all by the presence of the Son of God. We spent the evening of December 12 and the night from the 12th to the 13th on Mount Tabor, in the monastery of the Franciscans, and on the morning of the 13th we said Mass in the shrine on the mountain. The mountain, which is the site of the Transfiguration of Christ, has a commanding view of the countryside and provides an overlook far to the north, where the snow-covered peaks of Hermon are visible ("Tabor et Hermon de nomine Tuo exsultant").

Among the traces and memories of the presence of Our Lord from the period of His public life, we visit Jacob's well in Samaria, which exists to this day and to this day provides water for pilgrims. Jesus Christ referred to this very water in his conversation with the Samaritan woman, mentioning to her "the water of life" (John 4, 10) ...

Let us come back again to Judea and approach Jerusalem with the thought of recalling the Passion, Death and Resurrection of Our Lord in the holy places ...

Above Bethany, on the slopes of the Mount of Olives we find Bethphage — the place from which Our Lord set off for Jerusalem amid triumphal hymns, welcomed with palm branches ... At a church connected to a Franciscan monastery, we see the "litostratos" which is mentioned in the Gospel of St. John as the place where Jesus was condemned. From the chapel of the "de Sion" Sisters we descend to the underground chambers which were the places of imprisonment, scourging and crowning with thorns. These chambers make an indelible impression. A similar impression is left by the image of the scourged Jesus in the chapel of the sisters. Above the main altar was the balcony where Pilate showed Jesus, scourged and crowned with thorns, to the Jews, saying, "Ecce homo." When we go outside, we find ourselves on the Way of the Cross; its first stations remain within the fortress of Antonia.

At first we go downhill. The Way of the Cross descends until about the 7th station. The 3rd station (the first fall under the weight of the cross) and the 4th (meeting with His Mother) deserve mention because they were both renovated by Poles after the last war. This was the work of Msgr. Pietruszka who has worked many years in Jerusalem, and who created a small "Polish" museum of an archeological-biblical character at the 3rd station of the Way of the Cross. The Sisters of St. Elizabeth run two Polish homes in the Arabian and Israeli sectors of Jerusalem ... The last stations (10, 11, 12, 13, 14) are found within the basilica of Calvary and the Holy Sepulcher.

We enter this basilica and go first to the chapel on the upper level, the chapel of Golgotha. We kiss with great devotion the place where the Cross stood, we place upon it our episcopal insignia and devotional items we wish to take back to Poland for our dear ones ...

We leave the basilica, which has made a tremendous impression on us. This impression is not diminished by the fact that the outside and inside walls of the basilica are covered with scaffolding. There is a coexistence of denominations: Roman Catholics (Franciscans), Orthodox Greeks and Armenians conduct their services here — and this does not seem scandalous, although we know that what lies behind this, is the breakup of Christianity, so very opposite to the wish of Jesus "that they may be one" ...

We are at the end of our stay in the Holy Land. It was short, but it led us to what is most essential and most holy in this land. We are very grateful to our Holy Father that he is planning a pilgrimage to the native land of Our Lord, of whom he is the visible representative on earth. We are also grateful that he directed us there ... Some places which we know from the Scriptures we simply passed by in our journey, for example, Naim, Arimethea, and Megiddo. Others were not on our route, for example Cesarea Philippi, where Our Lord foretold the primacy of St. Peter. But two other places should be mentioned at the end of this description.

One of these was Joppa, with the Church of St. Peter, who experienced a strange vision here, in Joppa, and set off from that spot to baptize Cornelius. It should be added that the church in Joppa has a chapel of Our Lady of Czestochowa, and the local Franciscan, a Pole, preaches sermons in our language, because that is the primary language of most of the faithful. The second place I wish to mention is the Areopagus in Athens. It is a place near the Acropolis, with its magnificent temples, where St. Paul spoke to the Athenians about the God unknown to them. Both of these places which I mention here lead us out of the world of the Gospels into the world of the Acts of the Apostles — into the beginnings of the history of the Church ...

December 10 — He submitted an opinion in writing in the discussion of the Council decree on ecumenism. The opinion concerned the problems of *De Libertate religiosa*[9] * December 16 — During his stay in Rome, he presented a postulating letter, signed by all of the Polish bishops present at the Council, to Fr. Naruszewicz, the postulator of the beatification process of Brother Albert. Together with the postulator (accompanied by Mr. Dante, a lawyer), he appeared before Cardinal Larraona, the prefect of the Congregation of Rites, with new documents. After his return, he would tell the Albertine Sisters that he did a lot of chasing about in the matter of Brother Albert. (An account by the Albertine Sisters, a letter by Fr. Naruszewicz)

---

[9] On religious freedom

December 17-18 — Rome — Warsaw * December 25 — Midnight Mass in Nowa Huta. He spoke of this during a sermon at Wawel the same day:

> **The parish in Nowa Huta has not had a church for so many years! Masses are said in a little chapel. There is an altar on the exterior wall of this chapel, and throughout the whole year people participate in Mass standing under the open sky. On feast days they must stand in the sleet and rain. The Midnight Mass which I just said was celebrated in a great freeze. Several thousand people participated … What a closeness between this Midnight Mass in Nowa Huta, and what I had seen in Bethlehem: a humble grotto open to the elements …**

December 25 — Sermon at Wawel — he made reference to his trip to the Holy Land (as a backdrop for the reading of the Gospel) and to the Holy Father's pilgrimage planned for January. Christmas wishes:

> **… not only to you, my dear brethren, present here at this moment, but to everyone in the archdiocese, to all the faithful, to all the unfaithful. I want to tell them from the depth of our joy, from the depth of the Mystery of the Birth of the Lord, that there is no more magnificent fate for man, than to be born with Christ in the Lord …**

December 26 (Feast of St. Stephen). In the Church of St. Stephen in Krakow, sermon on the subject of the diaconate, a matter that had just been discussed at the Council.

> **The diaconate is needed everywhere … and not only in its ritualistic sense, as a degree of ordination, for the stewardship of certain sacraments — in places the priest cannot reach, for the teaching of religion — in places the priest cannot reach, but for the performing of so many acts of Christian love! Acts of mercy towards the soul and towards the body, towards all who need them … The diaconate is needed everywhere in the world. A diaconate of people of good will …**
>
> **We will be praying that there will be enough priests, but, following the thoughts of the Council …, we will have to think of a wider diaconate, of one that is an all-encompassing, social, familial, parochial complement of the pastoral work of bishops and priests, through service and even through the service of the word {preaching}, and especially through the service of good deeds by all people of good will …**

December 30 — Nominated as Archbishop Metropolitan of Krakow * Class reunion on the occasion of the 25th anniversary of the final exams in Secondary School. The reunion took place in Krakow in the house at Kanonicza Street where Bishop Wojtyla lived. There, in the house chapel, a Holy Mass was celebrated, during which some of Karol Wojtyla's friends served as altar boys; one of them was Zbigniew Silkowski. (As related by A. Bohdanowicz) * Same day: "A group of the Sisters of Our Lady of Mercy went to the Ursuline Sisters, where His Excellency Bishop Wojtyla was speaking of his pilgrimage to the Holy Land." (From the chronicle of the Congregation of the Sisters of Our Lady of Mercy)

December 31 — Midnight, Church of the Franciscan Fathers — a sermon summarizing the major events of the year: the death of Pope John XXIII, matters discussed at the Council; in the archdiocese: Marian Days, prayers for the intention of the Council, preparations for the Millenium of Christianity, the new auxiliary bishop Jan Pietraszko, the year of waiting for the nomination of the Archbishop Metropolitan "for whom we have all been praying and, in the meantime, we, the bishops working in Krakow and in the Archdiocese have been trying, as best as we can, to meet the needs of human souls ..." * Same day — a pastoral letter in connection with the closing of the second session of the Vatican Council and the pilgrimage of the Holy Father to the Holy Land.

1964

January 6 — Three church bells arrived in Krakow for St. Florian, the Collegiate Church on the order of Pope Paul VI, as a gift of the Milan archdiocese. They were named: Panna Maria {Virgin Mary}, Ambrose, Charles Borromeo and Florian. The bells were hung on May 4 , 1964, after difficult dealings with the authorities to get them exempted from customs duties as "musical instruments" (70,000 zl. + 20 zl. per day "storage fees").[1]

> **The initiator of obtaining the bells for the collegiate church was its provost, Rev. Dr. Tadeusz Kurowski, who brought the matter of purchase or acquisition to the interest of Cardinal Montini, then the Archbishop of Milan. An intermediary in these matters was the former curate of St. Florian's, and now the auxiliary bishop of Krakow, Rev. Karol Wojtyla. During the first session of the Second Vatican Council, Bishop Wojtyla thanked Cardinal Montini for his decision to make such a generous and valuable gift. Montini mentioned that he could still remember his first visit in Poland after the First World War, and the moving sight of Polish parishioners, simple people, perseveringly searching for the bells from their parish churches in the yards that held scrap metal requisitioned for the war effort but then abandoned by the Germans. He said about the Poles, that this is a "popolo santo,"[2] to which Wojtyla protested humbly but in real earnest. He did not, however, convince Montini. So, again, we have a Pope who is very sympathetic to Poles, and at the same time a very distinguished Pope.** (Note by Jozef Mitkowski, written ca. the middle of January, 1964 on the basis of a conversation with the provost, Fr. Tadeusz Kurowski)

January 6 — Cathedral — "today's celebration is a celebration of faith in a very unique way..." He spoke of the pilgrimage to the Holy Land by Pope Paul VI, that ended on this day: "The Pope goes to seek the unity of Christianity at its roots..." * January 10 — A letter to the priests *Two weeks in the Holy Land with the bishops of many nations* — (12 typed pages) with the description of the pilgrimage and own reflections. (See entry for December 5, 1963)

Jananuary 12 — Krakow, St. Anne's Church. He spoke about his participation in the second session of the Vatican Council: on the Church.

January 18 — The official nomination of Bishop Karol Wojtyla to the post of the Archbishop of Krakow * Same day — visitation of the parish of the Piarist Fathers at Rakowice in Krakow. He also visited the chapel of the Sisters of the Holy Spirit for Mass at 10:00 a.m. * Same day — Zakopane — a meeting of the Pastoral Committee of the Polish Episcopate. Bishop Karol Wojtyla: a presentation entitled *De-Christianization and Re-Christianization as a Problem of Contemporary*

---

[1] Average monthly pay at that time was about 2500 zl.
[2] holy people

Man (with consideration of counter-measures). In it he talked about atheism and secularism, and the perceptions and directions connected with them (liberalism, totalitarianism, Communism, nationalism and internationalism, agnosticism and indifferentism — "indifference without negation"). Processes leading to de-Christianization — the modern system of tempting contemporary man. Chances for re-Christianization: the Holy Spirit, the humility of contemporary man; the exceptional character of the Gospels and the Church in the face of the proposals offered by "competitive" ideologies. Re-Christianization as a challenge. (13 typed pages)

January 19 — The announcement was made of the nomination of Rev. Dr. Karol Wojtyla, currently capitular Vicar of Krakow, to the post of Archbishop ordinary of Krakow. Date of nomination: January 18, 1964. The Papal decision, with a request for indication of acceptance of the office was dated December 30, 1963. Not counting Aron in the 11th century, who was the Archbishop for all of Poland, residing in Krakow, and Archbishop Baziak, whose nomination to the Krakow Metropolitan See was never officially announced, Karol Wojtyla is the second Archbishop of Krakow; the first being Adam Stefan Sapieha, to be nominated on the basis of the Concordat of 1925. * Same day — 6:00 p.m. — in the palace of the Archbishop – *Oplatek*[3] for the youth of Orawa * 8 p.m. — Krakow, St. Anne's Church. A conciliar conference on the subject: Episcopal ministry as a concern of the People of God * Jan 23 — Kalwaria Zebrzydowska — the cloister of the Bernardine Fathers. Participation in a convention of priests from four deaneries. Notation in the visitors' book: "Regional conference. A heartfelt thank you for your hospitality, and I pray that this hospitable place may be a rich artery of faith and grace for the archdiocese."

Jan 23 — Kalwaria Zebrzydowska, a convention of the deanery of Susk. In reference to the nomination of the Archbishop of Krakow Msgr. Jozef Motyka said:

> **Everyone who accepts a leadership role is concerned about finding support, about gaining the hearts of his followers. Please accept our declaration that we congratulate you most sincerely, we are filled with joy and we wish you all the blessings of God ... Please love us, as we were loved by Cardinal Adam Stefan, and you can be sure that we will love you in return ... and please do not think that you will be alone. The hearts of so many priests — all of them are loving hearts, sincere hearts.**

In response, Msgr. Motyka, the pastor of Mucharz became his *manuductor*[4] in the bishop's ministry:

> **The first deanery where I came for a visitation was that of Susk, and the**

---

[3] See Glossary.
[4] "guider of hands," an experienced priest who assists a newly-ordained one at his first Mass.

first parish — that of Mucharz. And the Rev. Monsignor taught me how to do that, because I knew nothing of those things ... I realize that I am in a very favorable position. At this moment I am as if born into the world, and my mother is the entire Holy Church, but especially this Church of Krakow, to which I have belonged since birth and since the beginning of my priesthood. And when today, by the will of God and the will of the Holy Father, I become Archbishop Metropolitan of Krakow, I experience this as a birth from the womb of my Mother.

In the continuation of his address, he elaborated on the issues from the second session of the Second Vatican Council — later, responded to the questions posed by the priests on the subjects of worker priests, collegiality, the Roman Curia ("the Roman Curia does not govern the Bishops, they are governed by the Pope, who uses the Curia in the administration of the Church..."), press information, *Tygodnik Powszechny*, the Orthodox churches * Same day — *Oplatek*[5] for the mentally handicapped children at the Carmelites {Calced} in Krakow * January 25 — Pontifical Mass for the conclusion of the octave of prayers for the unity of Christians: "I would like to explain how the issue of ecumenism and the issue of the unification of Christians presents itself at the Vatican Council ... All of us, we Christians, we Catholics, our separated brothers in the East and the West, must come together just as we are at the present time ... This is the actual state of affairs". Further, about the perspectives of ecumenism, "that are in God's hands".

January 26 — St. Anne's Church — conference: "Laity as the issue of the people of God" * Pastoral letter for the first Sunday of Lent — to the faithful (there was a separate letter to the priests): "On the 30th of December 1963, the Holy Father Paul VI called me to be the Metropolitan Archbishop of Krakow..." * January 27 — Bielsko-Biala — a sermon about Vatican II, at the parish church * January 30 — Zakopane, the chapel of the Carmelite Sisters at 8 Koscielna Street — a meeting with the religious sisters of Zakopane. Conversations about the Vatican Council, impressions from the pilgrimage to the Holy Land * Same day — 6:00 p.m. — a sermon about Vatican II at a parish church in Zakopane.

February 8 — Post Vatican Council conference in the chapel of the Albertine Sisters in Krakow.

February 11 — Krakow, Theological Seminary — he is present at an accordion concert by two blind performers: Henryk Przelozynski and Jozef Glowacki.

February 12 — A solemn meeting of the Council of the Pontifical Department of Theology with the newly-nominated Archbishop Karol

---

[5] See Glossary.

Wojtyla.

> I came not only from within your group, but from under your guidance. That is the reality. My professors were Rev. Rector E. Florkowski, Rev. Prof. W. Wicher, Rev. Prof. M. Michalski, Rev. Prof. K. Klosak; Rev. Prof. I. Rozycki taught me the methods of scholarly research, while Prof. Fr. S. Smolenski was my spiritual director. My attitude toward academics was shaped by the professors of Krakow ... We can base our future on the same principles as before ...

In reference to the academic milieu, the Archbishop expressed the following wishes: "To find people willing to perform academic research, to renew the team of professors, to publish to the full extent of possibilities."[6] (From the minutes of the Council)

February 14 — Krakow-Ludwinow. Institution of the Way of The Cross in St. Bartholomew chapel.

February 28 — Church of the Carmelites {Calced} in Krakow, Holy Mass with sermon for the conclusion of a retreat for single women.

March 1 — Myslenice — Lenten devotions {Gorzkie Zale — Lamentations}, sermon about the Vatican II Council.

> Before his ingress, the Archbishop of Krakow came to Jedrzejow to offer the Most Holy Sacrifice {of Mass}at the feet of his great predecessor. He had a great devotion to Blessed Vincent, whose earthly remains are laid to rest in a silver casket there in the Church of the Cistercian Fathers. When he was a young man, the present Holy Father was an altar server for the then diocesan priest, today a Cistercian, Fr. Klemens Swizek. His respect for Fr. Swizek was striking. Usually he would not announce his arrival at Jedrzejow. He would come quietly, unnoticed, as if to friends and to a place where he could pray in peace about the great matters of the Church. He would pray for a long time at the altar of Blessed Vincent before all of his more significant undertakings. (Sr. Kazimiera, a Dominican nun)

March 7 — Tyniec — a day of recollection before his ingress as the Archbishop at Wawel * March 8 — Wawel — ingress to the archdiocesan cathedral; a welcoming address by Msgr. Bohdan Niemczewski. A speech by the newly nominated Metropolitan Archbishop:

> I think that to be a shepherd means to be able to accept everything that others contribute. To be able to accept means, in large measure, to be able to give — to be able to somehow coordinate and integrate everything, so that the common good may grow from it, and that this common good incorporate the good of each because each one of us has his own place in the work of Redemption, has his own place in God's plan. Each one of us is a great treasure.

In the afternoon, in the auditorium of the Seminary — a get-togeth-

---

[6] Significance: the communist regime limited the possibilities for publication of non-socialist literature.

er with the priests and lay friends. "… in moments of candor one can speak of oneself, and since those assembled here influenced in some way the course of my life … and are a part of the mystery of my birth from the womb of my Mother the Church..." He spoke of assuming the responsibilities of the Metropolitan See, of his deceased parents and brother, a doctor, whom God took at the age of twenty-six. "He caught an infection — there was no earthly way to save his life." He then reminisced about the entire milieu of priests:

> … I regret that Fr. Pawela, my religion teacher from elementary school, is not here with us. The deceased should be remembered before God, so I recall Fr. Leonard Prochownik, Fr. Canon Rospond, Fr. Canon Tadeusz Wlodyga … All of them are priests of Wadowice, who by their priestly lives, by their attitudes, in some way instilled in me the beginnings of my calling.
>
> I also wish to mention Msgr. Kazimierz Figlewicz, who in those times — at the beginning of the 8-year secondary school … was my religion teacher, and more than a teacher, because he was the director of my young and rather difficult soul. May God bless my high school catechist Rev. Dr. Edward Zacher, who remained faithful to Wadowice.
>
> … the 25 years which separates us from our high school graduation has not changed us very much, although shortly after graduation we went through a great historic experience — many of my school friends are heroes of the war of 1939, many died at the front, many went through the great frontlines … When after 25 years we came together for a reunion last year, I had the impression that this war did not destroy us so much as built us up …
>
> I found myself in Krakow in the autumn of 1938 as a student of the Department of Philosophy at the Jagiellonian University, in the Department of Polish Philology. I am really sorry that my venerable professor, the Nestor of Polish Studies, Prof. Stanislaw Pigon is prevented from being here today by the state of his health. His presence would have been an expression of liaison with this short, but so important period in my life …
>
> In 1939 my studies of Polish Philology were interrupted by the war, by the arrests of the professors. That started a period in my life that was a trial, but one — I often think upon this — that was much, much easier than the trials of many of my colleagues …
>
> I recall this with pride and gratitude toward God — it befell me to work for 4 years as a physical laborer. It was at this time that the most important matters in my life were awakened and crystallized in me, and the path of my vocation was decided.
>
> I worked in the factory which was called Solvay before the war, … in the quarry in Zakrzowek and especially in the boiler room, where I worked for 3 years. I recall those years with emotion and with deep gratitude towards the people there, the good, simple people, who were so warm to me, an educated person (they knew I was a university student), who would say to me: "Sir, if you've done your work, please take up your books." And when I worked on the night shift, they would say to me, "Sir, you've done your work, go take a nap, we will take care of things here." And when it was necessary to stay for a second or a third shift, these good and simple people came and brought their bread and milk and said, "Sir, if you are staying here, then have something to eat, so you will last." These are very small

things, but one never forgets such things.

It was at that time, when I was a laborer, that the deepest issues of my life, my interest in the humanities, in the Polish language and literature, and in theater crystallized. I had been closely connected, from even before the war, with Mieczyslaw Kotlarczyk (we come from the same town), and we cooperated during the time of occupation ... in creating a theater, a new theater. When my vocation called me away from the stage, the theater continued to establish itself, and Mr. Kotlarczyk became the director.

Literary interests, dramatic interests — all of this filtered in some way through my soul and resulted in a vocation to the priesthood. I would be remiss if I failed to mention ... Jan Tyranowski here. An intellectual, but also a tradesman — a man who chose his profession so that he could better commune with God, a man who could exert a tremendous influence on the young. I don't know if I owe my vocation to him, but in any case, my vocation came in the climate that he engendered, in that climate of the mystery of supernatural life which he brought in his dealings with us. He did not hesitate to have discussions with us, even on the subject of St. John of the Cross.

I began the clandestine seminary, meaning I began studies at the clandestine Department of Theology of JU, in 1942. I must recall my teachers: first of all, the late Rev. Rector Jan Piwowarczyk. Later, after the end of the occupation, Msgr. Karol Kozlowski, canon of the Metropolitan Chapter, Msgr. Stanislaw Smolenski; the Rev. Prefects, especially Rev. Prof. Kazimierz Klosak. Actually, he was the only professor who brought me close to philosophy during my seminary days. For the case with this philosophy was very special indeed ... I am indeed a professor at the Department of Philosophy, but I hardly ever heard any lectures about philosophy, so I am a self-taught philosopher. Then came theology. I must say that both philosophy and theology fascinated me very much. Here at the Department of Theology of the Jagiellonian University, I found professors with great reputations and a great love for these subjects ...

Here I wish to remember in a special way Msgr. Wladyslaw Wicher, a professor of moral theology, who accepted me into his department, and Rev. Prof. Ignacy Rozycki, to whom I owe so much at this stage of my life. I am grateful to him first of all for showing me how to conduct academic research in theology ... To Fr. Ignacy Rozycki I owe one other thing. When, after several years of pastoral work, I was assigned solely to academic endeavors, to prepare my dissertation for admission to assistant professorship, Rev. Prof. Rozycki invited me to come to live with him, which I did for 7 years ...

My service as a Vicar and the pastoral ministry in Krakow opened wide perspectives for me: working with university students somehow became natural. That was when we began meeting with Bishop Jan [Pietraszko], who helped me take the first steps in this area, and with many other chaplains of the academic community.

In 1951, when I left the parish to devote myself solely to my studies and to preparing my dissertation for admission to assistant professorship, I still maintained the ministry to university youth, and especially the ministry to individuals. What I achieved during these years in this specialized academic workplace of intellectuals was expressed in the book *Love and Responsibility*. I wish to thank these young friends of mine with whom we created this book, analyzing the very profound, difficult, but also beautiful, problems of human life ... I also wish to thank them for bringing me into the lifestyle of contemporary man. And for bringing me close to nature again; with them I began to experience mountaineering, skiing, kayaking, cycling ...

Gradually our spheres widen: to the milieu of the Krakow university, to our beloved Department, which received such a blow in 1954: it was abolished. It had existed for almost 600 years (just a little less than the entire University). Its abolition was a blow to the interests of our entire culture ... I am the last docent formally accepted into the faculty of the Department of Theology of JU ... Philosophy led me, perhaps mostly with Prof. Swiezawski's help, to the Department of Philosophy at KUL and to its young, vibrant milieu. During many discussions outside the lecture hall, at various tea parties (it turns out that they, too, are important) we were able to talk about many issues from the perspective of merits and method. Because of these discussions I saw my scholarly task anew ...

Prof. Vetulani wanted to make a canonist of me, or at least a theologian cooperating with canonists, especially in studies of the great Gratian ... But my love of philosophy and theology proved stronger. The only publication in this area appeared, thanks to the Professor, in Studia Gratiana in French, my only foreign publication, ...

In 1958 I was consecrated an auxiliary bishop of Krakow by the late Archbishop Baziak. And this brought me to a new workshop, a new milieu: into the milieu of priests. Because a bishop, more so than an individual priest, is in contact with the priests of the whole archdiocese. In the course of five and a half years, these contacts have multiplied significantly ...

A year and a half as the Vicar of the Metropolitan Chapter. I wish to thank very sincerely those who chose me to administer them. When I think of Monsignor [Niemczewski], I wish to say (the Monsignor will forgive me): "You have what you wished for." ... Nothing in this world is ready-made. Each of us is born, then learns to crawl, then attends the first grade, then matures ...

Surely all of the great pastors at the Krakow Metropolitan See, our predecessors, matured during their terms of office. They were brought up by our Mother the Church. When She becomes the Bride, She remains the Mother, She brings us up.

March 15 — Makow Podhalanski — Lenten Devotions, sermon about the Second Vatican Council, a get-together with young people. In Makow this visit was dubbed a "minor ingress" * Same day Archbishop Karol Wojtyla celebrated Mass in the chapel of the Daughters of Charity of St. Vincent de Paul in Krakow and preached a sermon, fragments of which are quoted below:

"My Dear Sisters: What I want to say to you flows from the words of your Sister Visitator, who told me about the storm of prayer you sent to heaven upon learning of my nomination to head the orphaned Metropolitan See. Immediately I was reminded of the words of Our Lord: "the kingdom of heaven has been subjected to violence, and the violent are taking it by storm." We must be those violent ones. In this day and age we experience many difficulties. Before, 50 years ago, when Cardinal Sapieha could tend to hundreds of poor people in your house, could serve them personally — those were different times. Everyone accepted us with joy; our work was so much easier. Today our work is made difficult; our hands are tied; doors are not opened for us; we must storm heaven violently to gain it for ourselves and for the souls entrusted to our care.

I felt this storm of your prayers — and not only yours, because it was a call of the entire Archdiocese for a shepherd to the See of St. Stanislaw which had been vacant for 12 years. I myself encouraged prayers for this intention, of course not thinking of myself. That storm echoed in heaven — and heaven will always answer earth. "La Charite" means love, and this is what you have emblazoned on your cornets. That is why a person feels so much better seeing that cornet. Today you are being removed from hospitals and this too is some sort of a cross, and the cross is always fertile and fruitful. Dear Sisters of St. Vincent and of St. Louise, although your work in hospitals and pre-schools has been taken from you, do not cease to fulfill your mission of charity. Visit homes where they need you, where they await your service so full of love and sacrifice, your kind words; in this way you gain the favor of society, and you gain souls for the Church. I don't know how to thank you, Sisters, for your prayers of day and night; maybe I shouldn't thank you — may Our Lord thank you. I ask your continued prayers and I trust that aided by these prayers, the Archdiocese of Krakow will slowly, step by step, attain the Kingdom of God."

Today, on the Feast of our foundress St. Louise de Marillac, after Mass, he went to the seminary (novitiate), and then to see the sick and aged sisters in the infirmary. He thanked the sick sisters for their prayers and asked for further prayers. Then he spoke to them of the great value of suffering and of the treasures which the ill sisters earn for the Congregation, for the Church, and for the Shepherd of the Diocese. He said then, "Although I am young and strong, although I fly in airplanes, climb mountains, ski, I still turn to the weakest, so that by the riches of their suffering they may bring down the strength and power of the Holy Spirit and the blessing of God upon my work in the Archdiocese." After the blessing, he left the Mother House. (Chronicle of the Dauthers of Charity)

March 17 — Church of Sts. Peter and Paul in Krakow, a Mass for the hearing and speech impaired * March 18 — Cloistered convent of the Dominican Sisters in Krakow at Grodek. For the conclusion of a retreat for nurses, he celebrated an evening Mass and preached a homily. Later he talked with the Sisters in the parlor * March 21 — Sermon for the conclusion of an academic retreat at St. Anne's Church in Krakow * March 22 — Palm Sunday — introduction to the retreat for physicians at the Church of the Felician Sisters in Krakow. About the Church in the context of the teachings of the Second Vatican Council — the issue of lay people in the Church — an outlook on the world: "Among the goods deposited by God in the visible, material world, there is one very, very basic good, namely the good of life … Further, about the vocation of a physician, a bond between the physician and the Creator, about who the physician is. * Same day — at the cloistered convent of the Dominican Sisters in Krakow at Grodek. He presided over a solemn ceremony of the profession of vows by Sister Magdalena Mazurkiewicz. In the parlor, the prioress and Sister Magdalena thanked the Archbishop * March 24 — A speech for the conclusion of a retreat for lawyers in St. Joseph Church: a matter of freedom of conscience in light of the continuing deliberations of the Second Vatican Council:

> **The issue here is of the basic right of the interior person ...**
> **Christianity, which always proclaims that the spirit takes priority over the**
> **body, must very plainly and decisively declare the rights of the interior per-**
> **son, the person's free space within the interior life. [Further — about con-**
> **science:] ... in society, man must be able to form a true and sure conscience**
> **... [About tolerance. Besides information from the Council, a reflection for**
> **the retreat, mainly about confession, about who the confessor is:] ... and**
> **even if you should feel offended by something he says, remember that he**
> **kneels ... although he passes judgment, just as you do in your court — he**
> **kneels before the great cause of God.**

March 25 — During a retreat for artists at the Holy Cross Church, he delivered a lecture on the understanding of liturgy as a reflection of the Church in its own Mystery * March 31 — Church of St. Anne — for the conclusion of a retreat for university students on the topic of the Church: "Last autumn, during the second session of the Second Vatican Council, I have experienced the Church very deeply, first of all as the truth of faith, but also as a reality ..." About the Vatican Council: "This is a great undertaking; these are not merely superficial changes or reforms ..."

April 4-18 — Canonical visitation of the parish of St. Joseph in Krakow * April 4 — Mass at the home of ailing Mrs. Bartek * April 14 — In the framework of the 4th Week of Social Consciousness (April 13-16; topic: social education), a presentation entitled *The Role of a Christian Community in the Social Education of Man.*

April 19 — A meeting of groups from *Tygodnik Powszechny* and *Znak.* The session was dedicated to the matter of pastoral culture. It lasted three days; on the suggestion of the Archbishop, the session was held at the house of the Albertine Sisters at Pradnik in Krakow. The Archbishop was present for most of the time, and spoke at the conclusion. The major topic of his speech: the layman — creator of Christian culture — believer, apostle, shepherd. For the conclusion, he suggested to have a Mass celebrated in the meeting room: "it will at once put everything that we have talked about in the last three days — although it sometimes did not sound quite right — on the proper plane upon which it all stood from the very beginning or, at least, upon which we wanted to place it ..."

April 22 — Funeral of Msgr. Tadeusz Kurowski, who died on April 20. He was a long-time chaplain-secretary to Prince Cardinal Adam Sapieha, involved in ministry to university students at St. Anne's Church. He was administrative director of the Curia, canon of the Metropolitan Chapter and pastor of St. Florian's parish in Krakow, where Karol Wojtyla had served as Vicar.

> [The deceased] not only knew how to assign tasks from the outside, but he also knew how to respect the initiatives of others; I myself experienced this very deeply. [Further in the sermon, about the activities, the priestly life and the faith of the deceased, and about what he had gone through in prison.] I wish to tell you here that I learned very much from him, not only when I was his co-worker here; I learned much more later ... from his experiences and from the faith with which he bore his experiences ... For me he became *forma gregis* by his faith.

At 12:00 noon he led a funeral procession to the tomb of the cathedral canons of Krakow at the Rakowicki cemetery.

Over 3000 people came to the funeral, old, young and children. Noteworthy was the fact that the entire group was deeply engrossed in prayer and a great sense of sadness was very evident. (Notes by Jozef Mitkowski, April 23, 1964)

April 29 — Kalwaria Zebrzydowska — cloister of the Benedictines. Presided at a conference of priests of the four deaneries; the topic pertained to the Second Vatican Council.

May 2 — Chapel of the Archbishop — Mass for religious sisters and nurses * May 3[7] — High Mass and a renewal of the Jasna Gora pledge at Wawel * May 4-7 — Canonical visitation in Wilkowice * May 8 — Pontifical High Mass for the Feast of St. Stanislaw at Wawel Cathedral * May 10 — St. Anne's Church, sermon for the 600th anniversary of the Jagiellonian University.

> ... this is, after all, 600 years of seeking the truth, seeking among the natural potentials of man. The natural talents by which man strives toward the truth have their source in the Spirit of Truth ... There are also other talents ... there is also another Truth ... The Truth of the supernatural order ... [Further: the history of the founding of the University, mention of prominent professors, ties with the Church.] ... I speak also by virtue of being the successor of Zbigniew Olesnicki[8] and the many Bishops of Krakow who were grand chancellors of JU, and also because I am the last person to have been admitted to the faculty of the Department of Theology at JU in December of 1953 ... I speak in the name of all those who were bypassed in this observance of the jubilee ... We cannot accept the thought that this, our Alma Mater, could reject us. We were her faithful children ... I say this with deep conviction of the reality that is man ... striving for the full knowledge of truth, who cannot pass indifferently over a matter so important as is the reality of God and man's relation to it. This relation, which is religion, is the deepest reality of man and connected with it is the deepest right of the human person ... the right to know God and to give Him appropriate worship.

May 18 — A meeting with the Sisters on Szpitalna Street — Mass at 7:00 a.m. (birthday of the Archbishop) * Same day — Mass and

---

[7] See Glossary.
[8] Bishop of Krakow in the early 15th century

homily to the graduating high school class in Kety * May 20-26 — Bielsko-Biala, canonical visitation of the parish of Divine Providence * Before the 21st of May. He presented his motion in writing on the proposed document on ecumenism. It pertains to section IV (10 lines of print). (*Acta Synodalia* TPV 1974 vol. III pars II pp. 838-839) * May 25-26 — Bielsko-Biala — Leszczyny, visitation of the parish of Christ the King * May 28 — 9:00 a.m. — Wawel Cathedral, High Mass and Corpus Christi procession * May 25-31 — Zywiec, visitation of Our Lady Parish * May 31-June 2 — Zywiec, Zablocie visitation.

June 2 — Kielce, conclusion of visitation. A farewell to the image of Our Lady — sermon * June 2-4 — Zywiec, visitation of Christ the King Parish * June 5-7 — Plaszow, visitation.

Before June 10 — He submitted a statement in writing, in the name of the bishops of Poland — comments pertaining to the draft of "De Ecclesia". (The text is also signed by Bishop Jan Jaroszewicz, Apostolic Administrator of Kielce.) (*Acta Synodalia* TPV 1973 vol. III, pars I pp. 613 - 617)

June 8-10 — Canonical visitation in Rychwald and Pewel Slemienska * June 10-11 — Lipowa, visitation of St. Bartholomew parish * June 13 — 3:50 p.m. — conclusion of days of recollection for the high school graduates at the Church of the Carmelites {Calced} in Krakow * Same day — 5:00 p.m. — Mass with sermon, blessing for the sick at St. Joseph Church in Krakow at Podgorze * June 14 — In Parczew: participated in the celebration of the 400th anniversary of the acceptance of the resolutions of the Council of Trent by King Zygmunt Augustus at a seym {assembly of delegates, parliament} in Parczew (in 1564). Cardinal Stefan Wyszynski presided over the celebrations, assisted by Archbishop Boleslaw Kominek and nine bishops * June 21 — 8:00 a.m. — Wawel Cathedral — ordination of new priests * 6:00 p.m. — Cathedral — Pontifical High Mass on the anniversary of the election of Pope Paul VI * June 24 — Wawel — installation of new members of the Metropolitan Chapter, Holy Mass * June 27 — Jasna Gora. A speech during days of prayer of an organization of Catholic Intellectuals known as "Odrodzenie" {Rebirth}: "The work of the Polish bishops at the Second Vatican Council" * June 28 — Tyniec — presence at the solemn vespers and sermon for the 25th anniversary of the return of the Benedictines to Tyniec.

July 1 — Tyniec — He ordained Father Michal Bigosz OSB * July 7 — Presided over a funeral of Sister Izydora Konigsmann from the Congregation of the Daughters of Charity, at the Rakowicki cemetery in Krakow. He was assisted by monsignors, canons of the cathedral and numerous clergy. (Congregation of the Daughters of Charity)

July 9 — Private chapel at 3 Franciszkanska Street, Mass for the late Sisters Izydora Konigsmann and Aniela Brudlo. After Mass he talked with the Daughters of Charity for a while. (Congregation of the Daughters of Charity)

July 11 — Stryszawa. He visited Cardinal Primate Stefan Wyszynski at Siwcowka — a house of the Sisters of the Resurrection. Siwcowka was the Primate's summer retreat.

"The Most Venerable Rev. Archbishop Metropolitan Karol Wojtyla arrived to greet the Most Reverend Dignitary of the Holy Church, His Eminence Cardinal Stefan Wyszynski, as a guest in his Archdiocese." (From the records of the religious house in Stryszawa)

July — A kayak outing on the Slupia river.

August 15 — Kalwaria Zebrzydowska — sermon for the Feast of the Assumption. The Primate of Poland, Cardinal Stefan Wyszynski also participated and wrote a note in the commemorative book: "In remembrance of our common observance of the Feast of the Assumption, with a heartfelt 'God Bless You'" * August 16 — Sermon for the celebration of the Assumption in Ludzmierz. About the coronation of a year ago:

> **Behind this coronation are whole centuries ... millions of people, centuries of people ... who in various parts of this hard land believed in Christ [Further on he speaks about] this atmosphere, which is being propagated very forcefully, rudely, by all available means, this atmosphere which tries to convince us that man lives only for this world and for temporal things, for economic production, etc. — We need Our Lady of Ludzmierz and Her coronation.**

August 26 — Presided during a Pontifical High Mass near the summit of Jasna Gora.

August 27-29 — KUL — in a series of lectures for the clergy, entitled *Ethos of the Polish Character,* he delivered a lecture *On the Upbringing to Truth and Freedom.*

August 29 — 4:00 p.m. — 200th anniversary of the beatification of Wincenty Kadlubek. Solemn commemorative meeting at the Theological Seminary in Krakow at 8 Podzamcze Street, under the leadership of Archbishop Wojtyla in the presence of other bishops. Lectures were given by: Prof. Marian Plezia, *Kadlubek in Light of His Times* and Prof. Jozef Mitkowski, *Master Wincent, the Father of Polish Letters.*

> **The speakers — and in those times it was an act of courage to speak at a meeting of that type — were invited to supper by the Archbishop, who kissed them warmly upon their departure. So how could one refuse such a man, regardless of the consequences, the participation in this church event?** ... (Jozef Mitkowski)

End of August or beginning of September — He participated in the Bishops' retreat at Jasna Gora. The notes of the monastery reflect a new regularity: the name of Archbishop Karol Wojtyla immediately follows the name of the Primate {Cardinal Wyszynski}. (O. Rozej)

September 5 — 3:30 p.m. — Wawel Cathedral, a celebration on the occasion of the 600th anniversary of the approbation of the university in Krakow by the Pope (September 1 and 13, 1364), i.e. its effective founding.

The celebrations were opened by Archbishop Wojtyla. Lectures were delivered by Rev. Bishop Prof. Dr. Piotr Kalwa and Prof. Dr. Adam Vetulani. Those participating were: Cardinal Wyszynski, Archbishops Kominek and Baraniak, 33 bishops, invited professors of JU {Jagiellonian University}, representatives of KUL.[9] The celebration started with the singing of *Gaude Mater Polonia*. After the lectures, there was a word of thanks. There was a request made to all assembled to sing the *Bogurodzica*[10] and to pray for the founders of JU: King Kazimierz, servant of God Queen Jadwiga and King Wladyslaw Jagiello. * 6:30 p.m. — St. Anne's Church, remarks for the opening of the celebration:

> ... which is in fact a pilgrimage to the tomb of St. John of Kanty ... We wish to repay a debt, to fulfill our obligation in the face of a great historical fact, and at the same time to show the role of the Church of those times in creating our Polish culture, equal to the highest level of European civilization.

Later, the Bishop of Wroclaw Boleslaw Kominek delivered a lecture, the Primate — a sermon, and *Te Deum* was sung at the tomb of St. John of Kanty.

September 9 — A letter to the priests of the Archdiocese was addressed before his departure for the third session of the Second Vatican Council. In it, he presented the issues that are to be discussed at the Council. He informed that he was going to the Council with Bishop Jan Pietraszko. He asks for prayers and promised more detailed information * Same day — at the Mariacki church, after a Pontifical Mass for the dead in two World Wars — before the prayers by a symbolic coffin (50 years from the beginning of World War I and 25 years since World War II), in his sermon he made a reference to *Pacem in terris* by Pope John XXIII.

September 10 — Wawel Cathedral — a speech on the day of departure for the third session of the Council in Rome:

> I will admit that as I am leaving for this session with a certain — I

---

[9] Catholic University in Lublin
[10] A hymn to the Blessed Virgin dating from the 14th Century; a battle hymn of Polish knights and effectively the first Polish national anthem.

would say — suspense, I expect discussions on the subject of the draft of *De Ecclesia in mundo huius temporis,* i.e. on the Church in the modern world ... Let us all be together in this great unity of the people of God.

September 14 — He submited a motion in writing pertaining to the draft of a Decree on the apostolate of the laity (among others, a role of the apostolate of writers). (Acta Synodalia TPV 1974, vol. III, p. IV, pp. 788-789) * September 23-28 — He submited in writing his observations on the draft of the Declaration on the freedom of religion. (*Acta Synodalia* TPV 1977, vol. IV, p. II, pp. 292-293) * September 25 — He took the floor at the 88th general congregation of the Vatican Council during the discussion of the draft of the Decree on Ecumenism. Spoke on the chapter *De libertate religiosa* — on religious freedom. (*Acta Synodalia* TPV 1974 vol. III, p. II, pp. 530-532) * September 28 — A speech on Vatican Radio: "The Church in the contemporary world". "... you, who love the Church, and you, who love the world, pray that our words be simple, convincing, and that people have enough good will to understand and accept ..."

October 8 — At the 107th congregation of the Council he spoke on the issue of the apostolate of the laity (about dialog). He was the only speaker who began his speech: *Venerabiles Patres, Fratres et Sorores*[11] thereby recognizing the presence of women auditors. (*Acta Synodalia* TPV 1974 vol. III, p. IV, pgs. 69-70) * October 11 — While still at the Council, he wrote a letter to the priests of the Archdiocese: words of thanks for prayers, information about the activities of the Council and this information: "during this session I have received a pallium for Krakow ..., along with me 40 archbishops from all parts of the world and many countries in Europe have received it ..." (he lists all the sees because "this might provide a certain insight into the universality of the Church. From this one can draw a lesson in religion, as well as geography"). He explained the meaning of the pallium — asked for prayers for the intention of the Vatican Council * October 13-15 — He submited in writing his comments pertaining to the draft of the decree *De Ministerio et Vita Presbyterorum*[12] (among others, that priests must minister not only to the laity, but to one another as well). (Acta Synodalia TPV vol. IV, p. V, p. 519)

October 19 — Radio Vatican, he delivered a speech about the dignity of the human person.

The human person is one of the elements of the doctrine of the Second Vatican Council. Although none of the prepared constitutions or decrees deal with the human person directly, still, the human person is deeply embedded in the entire teaching of this Council, a teaching which is beginning to emerge from our labor of several years ... To respect the dignity of

[11] Honored Fathers, Brothers, and Sisters
[12] On the ministry and life of priests

man means to place him above everything that derives from him in the visible world …

[In the continuation, he shows why the issue of human dignity is one of the fundamental elements of the thought of Vatican II.]

October 20-November 5 — In the name of the Polish bishops, he submitted comments in writing relative to the text of the 4th chapter of the draft of the document on the Church in the contemporary world. (Acta Synodalia TPV 1975 vol. III, p. VII, pp. 380-382) * October 20-November 5 — He submitted in writing comments pertaining to the draft of the document on the Church in the contemporary world: part 2 in general, and chapter 1 (on the issues of marriage). (Acta Synodalia TPV 1977 vol. IV p. III, pg. 242) * October 20-November 5 — In the name of the Polish Episcopate, he submitted in writing detailed comments on the draft of the document on the Church in the contemporary world, pertaining to the introduction and first three chapters. (Acta Synodalia TPV 1975 vol. III, p. V, pp. 680-683) * October 21 — 108th general congregation of the Council, he spoke in the name of the Polish Episcopate, presenting proposed corrections to schema 13 (On the Church in the modern world). This was a more precise text of material presented earlier in written proposals. (*Acta Synodalia* TPV 1975 vol. III, p. V, pp. 298-300 and 300-314)

In November he was nominated to *Subcommissio Centralis*, initially composed of eight bishops, later of several dozen experts, including laymen; this commission was responsible for the preparation of the 13th schema of the Council's *De Ecclesia in mundo huius temporis* (On the Church in the modern world).

November 21 — Conclusion of the third session of the Vatican Council. Afterwards, a pilgrimage to the Holy Land with the other bishops.

It was to these places that Abraham, the man of the great encounter (*tres vidit et unum adoravit*) journeyed. He brought within him the internal place of encounter to these external places where the entire earth became the LAND, the DWELLING. Abraham, the visible sign of the new Adam. One must approach these places through the desert … (A. J., "Travels to Holy Places," *Znak* 132/1965, pg. 773-777)

November 30 — An audience with Pope Paul VI. He spoke about the audience to the priests of the Krakow deanery during a meeting on January 13, 1965.

… I wish … to tell you about an audience that I had with the Holy Father Paul VI on November 30 [1964], where the atmosphere was such that it is better described in a verbal account than a written report … The Holy Father received me virtually on the eve of his departure for Bombay … He greeted me by expressing his satisfaction at the opportunity to make my acquaintance, although I had the fortune of knowing him when he was still a cardinal, during the first session, but this was the first time we were meeting in the new circumstances.

Immediately the Holy Father began reminiscing about the Prince Cardinal {Sapieha}. This is indeed a great thing — wherever one goes in Rome, whomever one speaks with, when that person hears the word "Krakow," he remembers the Prince Cardinal... Then the Holy Father talked about Krakow... that it is such a beautiful city, and he asked, "what is happening in your Krakow?" I thanked him for the church bells [a gift of the Milanese parish of Seregno, which on the initiative of then Archbishop Montini[13] donated bells to the parish of St. Florian in Krakow.[14] Next the archbishop {Wojtyla} talked about the jubilee of the University, its history and its connections with the Church, that] ... obviously, the church aspect has been totally brushed aside... The Pope asked about the church celebration, and said with emotion: "Because, dear brother, today we must take great care of our studying youth" ... Then he said: "The principal challenges of our ministry as bishops are the priests, the workers and the students." I told him ... that before I became a student of theology, I was a student in a secular department, and as far as workers — I was also a worker for several years. I noticed that the Pope seemed pleased that I had been a worker. Later, I presented albums from the coronation of Our Lady of Ludzmierz; with deep emotion he began blessing those pictures and said to his secretary: ... "this is Poland, only there is this possible ..."

[About the Pope himself:] He radiates much love, but also suffering ... In the course of these two years he changed much, he became somehow very warm ... He is tired ... The style which he initiated is costing him quite a bit ... This is a man of great depth. Sometimes he is spoken of as the Pope of humility. Undoubtedly this is true ... He senses the contemporary world with all of its problems and he somehow carries that world ...

He looked through everything to the end ... I tried to somehow prevent him from doing that, because it seemed to me that it wasn't necessary to peruse all of these pictures so scrupulously, but he looked at them ..., and it wasn't only a formality ...

December 6 — He returned from Rome * December 8 — The Mariacki Basilica in Krakow, a sermon after his return from the third session of the Vatican Council. He informed about the works of the Council, about Pope Paul VI:

> If you had seen this Pope how I saw him a week ago at my audience, from up close, if you could look at his face so profound, fatigued with love, this face so deeply moved with difficult matters of the Church and of contemporary humanity — then in that face you would see everything that gave rise to the Vatican Council, and everything that this Council undertakes, until its conclusion.

He spoke of the emotion with which Pope Paul VI recalled Poland, and looked at the large crowds in the photographs in the album given to him. In connection with the mystery of the Immaculate Conception — he spoke about the Church, about the work of the Council, about ecumenism and

---

[13] Later to become Pope Paul VI.
[14] See entry for Jan. 6, 1964.

about the work on the proposed document on the Church in the contemporary world. * The same day, at the Albertine Sisters at Pradnik, he reported on the status of the {beatification} process of Brother Albert. Among others, he spoke of the great fondness for the person of Brother Albert felt in Rome — "the spirit of Brother Albert is very close to the spirit of the Vatican Council, to the spirit of today's Church." (The Albertine Sisters)

December 11 — Meeting of the Council of the Pontifical Department of Theology in Krakow

> **After the part of the meeting dealing with organizational and administrative matters, the meeting was honored by the presence of Archbishop Dr. Karol Wojtyla, who informed those present of his audience with the Holy Father, and shared his thoughts on the progress of the third session of the Vatican Council ... He also made some general suggestions regarding our milieu, concerning the celebration of the 1000th anniversary of Polish Christianization.**
>
> **He also presented the status of works undertaken to bring about the beatification of Queen Jadwiga.** (From the minutes of the Council)

December 13 — Church of the Dominicans — academic *Oplatek*[15] * December 14 — Theological Seminary in Krakow, He participated in a meeting of professor priests * December 15-18 — Warsaw, a conference of the Polish Episcopate * December 19 — Krakow, a meeting with the Pastoral Department * December 20 — He participated in a Mass, reading of a decree about the division of the parish, an address at a chapel in Rabka * December 21 — 10:30 a.m. — Chapel of the Ursulines in Krakow, Mass , an address regarding the third session of the Council * Same day — 5:00 p.m. — a meeting of Krakow priests * December 24 — 4:00 p.m. — Wawel, he participated in matins * 11:00 p.m. — Mogila * December 25 — Pontifical High Mass at Wawel — his first since he received his pallium [a homily on this subject was delivered by Bishop Jan Pietraszko] * December 26 — Church of St. Szczepan in Krakow. In the context of life and death of St. Szczepan, as revealed in the Acts of the Apostles, he talked about "what is a true meaning of what we call freedom of religion". "I speak of it , because the issue of freedom of religion was one of the main topics of the third session of the Vatican Council". Further, the analysis of what religion is, and finally the conclusion:

> **So that man may give this response to God, there must be an atmosphere of religious freedom in society, that means ... an atmosphere of respect for the human conscience, for people's convictions, for the internal person, for the inner personal depths in which this response is to be born, to be formed. An atmosphere of respect. And beyond that, when it comes to**

---

[15] See Glossary.

the Church, there must be conditions in which the Church can assist man in the formation and expression of this response ... The undertaking and the consideration of the issue of religious freedom is also a sign of progress.

December 28 — 10:00 a.m. — *Oplatek*[16] of young priests at the Theological Seminary in Krakow, and at 3:00 pm, a conference * December 31 — 6:00 pm — St. Florian Church — sermon during vespers for the end of the old year * 12:00 midnight — Mass and homily for the New Year at the Church of St. Francis in Krakow.

---

[16] See Glossary.

1965

January 1-4 — Zakopane-Jaszczurowka — ski trip, he stopped at Jaszczurowka at the Ursuline Sisters SJK * January 6 — Pontifical Holy Mass at Wawel * January 7 — Mass at the Church of St. Szczepan {Stephen} celebrating fifty years of academic work of Prof. Ludwik Ehrlich * January 9 — *Oplatek* at KIK

January 13 — He spoke to the priests of the Krakow deanery at the Theological Seminary in Krakow. Part I — pertaining to the Pope: about the audience held on November 30, 1964, and the presentation of papal distinctions. Part II — pertaining to the Council: the work of the Council until now and its consequences for theology and pastoral work; the Constitutions *on the Church* and *on Liturgy*. Announcement about the introduction of the new ritual of celebrating Mass, about "the ways of disseminating thought" (this matter demands our careful reflection here), about ecumenism and about other documents still not completed. (Here I will try to summarize from memory). Further on — in great detail about the work of the Council (Wroclaw and Krakow presented comments/projects in reference to schema XIII)

January 14 — Rokiciny, convent of the Ursuline Sisters: "While returning from Zakopane, Archbishop Karol Wojtyla dropped in for a short visit to Archbishop Kominek and stayed for dinner" * January 15 — He chaired a meeting of priests from four dioceses at Kalwaria Zebrzydowska and held discussion on the Constitution on Liturgy * The same day — a meeting of the Pontifical Department of Theology in Krakow. The Dean informed about the opening of the licentiate studies for priests (70 students).

[The Archbishop] underscored the importance of academic work. Krakow is, after all, recognized as one of three centers of theological thought in Poland. This community is concentrated first and foremost in the Seminaries. A very important postulate is to maintain a proper academic center and to keep infusing this place of work with life and energy. The premier task ... is to encourage and assist those working on their theses to be submitted as partial fulfillment of the requirements for acceptance to assistant professorship ... Young theologians have been relieved of their pastoral duties and can concentrate on academic work and on the preparation of their works for publication, moreover, their work, just as the published work of the reverend professors will be rewarded in material terms, as well as in other ways ... The completion of the ranks of this group is being accomplished to the best of our ability...

The second theological center is the Theological Society, whose work should increasingly take on the form of seminars (rather than, as it has up to this point, of lectures) ...

The main emphasis in the work of the whole community is first and foremost on the questions put forth by the Second Vatican Council which opens enormous possibilities for all theological specialties, and then, on the issues associated with the celebration of a thousand years of Christianity in Poland. Other signs of activity are publications, very limited in Krakow, hence, there is a need to publish in other centers ... (From the minutes of the Departmental Council)

January 16 — A low Mass with a sermon at a chapel on 21 Kanoniczna Street * January 17 — A sermon at St. Joseph Church, Krakow-Podgorze — dedicated to the Vatican Council.

> There is a need to talk about the Council. Although we know everything about it ... the information still does not form an integrated whole ... It is necessary for us, bishops, who are eyewitnesses {to the Council} ... to talk about it, so that the entirety of the Council can be formed in the consciousness of the whole Church, all the faithful, and all people of good will ...

January 23 — Speech at the Church of the Missionary Fathers in Krakow-Nowa Wies: "The purpose of my visit and the purpose of my sermon is to inform you about the Council ... in order to bring us into the reality, of ... the Church as determined by the Council..."

January 24 and 25 — A Mass and sermon at the Church of the Dominican Fathers within the octave of prayer for Christian unity. "The Council which speaks about freedom of conscience and of religion speaks about an ecumenical {universal} examination of conscience... Subordination of freedom to truth means that there is a road in front of us, a common road of searching for the single truth..."

January 26 — in Warsaw — the Main Committee of the Conference of the Polish Episcopate * January 27 — the plenary conference of the Polish Episcopate * January 28 — Caroling at WIK in Krakow.

January 31 to April 6 — participation in the work on the schema XIII on the Church in the modern world, in Ariccia and Rome * January 31 to February 6 — Ariccia — in work groups — preparation of the *Constitution on the Church in the modern world*. He participated in the group whose members are, among others, Father J. Danielou, H. de Lubac.

> The great years of the Second Vatican Council have arrived. Once again we are given the opportunity to find ourselves among those, who worked on the text of the constitution *Gaudium et spes*. Although we did not belong to the same work group, we still met at the meetings organized for the numerous groups preparing the text of this memorable document about the presence of the Church in the modern world. There were many memories I cherish to this day, the week-long meeting in Ariccia near Rome and the customary walks there, two of them with Archbishop Wojtyla, at which time we touched upon the most fundamental questions concerning the role of the Church towards culture and its correct interpretation. These were unforgettable moments — and that was when I started to realize, that my exquisite friend and colleague has very much to say on the subject of matters deci-

sive for the future of the Church. (Stefan Swiezawski, "TP" 47/1978)

Letter to Professor Stefan Swiezawski of April 16, 1977 (regarding the text of the lecture delivered at Milan and sent as an article to be included in the commemorative book prepared by KUL for the professor's seventieth birthday), about the work being done on the preparation of schema XIII:

> I am now offering to you, Honorable Professor, a work in which there certainly resound the echoes of analyses carried out at the time on the borderline of eternal philosophy and modern phenomenology. Above all, I am hopeful that the echoes of your own convictions and concerns will also resound in this work, my Dear Professor Stefan, the convictions and concerns, which you expressed as the auditor of the Second Vatican Council, during the period of the preparation of the famous Constitution on the Church in the modern world. We both remember well that working session, which took place near Rome in February of 1965, and all the conversations that took place outside the discussions that were carried out in the various groups — and above all the content, the weighty content, which found its proper place in the document of the Council itself.
>
> My present pronouncement ties in precisely with that content, and originates from similar convictions and concerns ...

February 12 — Speech aired on the Vatican Radio, in which he talks about the work of the *Subcommissio Centralis*. The *Subcommissio Centralis* is preparing schema XIII. He mentioned the people with whom he was collaborating on this subcommission: "many names that are well known in Poland, for example, Fr. Y. Congar, J. Danielou, Lebret, B. Haring, Thiels, Houtart, Mr. Folliet, Rev. Philips of Louvain, Fr. Tromp, of the Poles — Prof. S. Swiezawski and Dr. M. Habicht, the auditors of the Council." * The Vatican Radio, on the twentieth anniversary of the liberation of the concentration camp in Oswiecim {Auschwitz}: "... Apart from the painful memories, there arises in us a desire, a strong desire: that for the price of this Calvary, the modern man regain his humanity appropriate for the times in which he happens to live ..."

February 25 — Krakow, the residence chapel, Mass for the late Iwon Gall, director and scenography designer.

March 3 — Ash Wednesday — Mass at Wawel * March 6 — Celebrations at St. Anne's Church (in the morning the bishops of Czestochowa, Silesia, and Krakow participated) attended by students and teachers of theological seminaries to commemorate the 400th anniversary of the founding of the first theological seminary in Krakow and in Poland.

> If there is a lack of vocations to the priesthood in a Christian community, if they are not born, if they do not come to the seminaries, if they do

not reach priesthood, then the community bears a negative witness of itself as a Christian community, revealing its inner weakness, proving to be a poor soil.

March 7 — 12:00 noon — address on the topic of the Council at St. Mikolaj {Nicholas} Church in Krakow, dedicated to the implementation of the liturgical constitution (the first Sunday of Lent, i.e. this very day, was the first stage of introducing the constitution in Poland) * Same day at 4:45 p.m. — at the Basilica of the Dominican Fathers, during the ceremonies in honor of St. Thomas Aquinas, an address after the Pontifical Mass:

> ... Let today's ceremonies be a fulfillment of yesterday's. May the theological seminaries in Krakow, which survived for so many centuries and which, after all these years and in today's difficult conditions, have expanded so much, for apart from the three diocesan seminaries, there are ten religious seminaries, always find in St. Thomas the strong, solid ground of faith and holiness.

March 8 — Mass in Jedrzejow (at the Cistercian Fathers) on the anniversary of his ingress * March 9 — At KUL within the framework of the 8th Philosophical Week (March 8-12) devoted to the subject: "From the borderline between ethics and the philosophy of values," a presentation by Archbishop Wojtyla *On Some of the Cultural Implications of the Modern Interpretations of Ethics* * March 14 — 12:45 p.m. — in Plaszow, sermon about the Council * 7:00 p.m. — a meeting at his residence with *Tygodnik Powszechny* and *Znak* * March 15 — Pontifical Mass at Wawel for the victims of Oswiecim {Auschwitz} * March 16 — 5:00 p.m. — at his residence — a meeting with historians regarding the observance of the Millennium * March 21 — speech at the conclusion of a retreat for high school students at St. Anne's Church in Krakow — what is the Council and, in particular, about religious freedom in the context of the vital problems of secondary school youth * March 22 — 3:00 p.m. — at his residence — meeting with the national directors of ministries to artists * March 23 — 5:30 p.m. — meeting at his residence with artists * March 24 — 5:00 p.m. — meeting at his residence with professors * The same day at 7:00 p.m., a low Mass for *Tygodnik Powszechny* * March 25 — Meeting at his residence at 5:00 p.m. with writers * March 26 — At KUL — two defenses of doctoral theses, whose promoter was Karol Wojtyla. Stanislaw Grygiel: *Moral Consciousness in the Philosophy of Sartre*; Sister Hildegarda A. Szymeczko: *Teleology or Exemplariness in the Ethics of St. Thomas Aquinas.*

March 29-April 6 — In Rome, at a session of the working group preparing the *Constitution on the Church in the modern world* * April 11-17 — ordination to the priesthood at Wawel (April 11) and observances of the Holy Week * April 18 — 6:00 am — Resurrection Mass in Bienczyce * April 21 — Mass at Wawel for the opening of the session of professors of philosophy * April 24 — 6:00 p.m. — in a chapel at the palace of the Archbishop, a session regarding the beatification of Mother Celina Borzecka * The same day — 8:30 p.m. — Easter repast at KIK * April 25 — In Gniezno, participation in the celebrations commemorating St. Wojciech {Adalbert} * April 26-28 — the Chapel of the Ursuline Sisters in Krakow, present at a course for sisters superior (delivered an address) * April 28 — 8:00 p.m. — Easter repast at the Dominicans.

May 1 — At the Jasna Gora monastery in Czestochowa, he participated in the observances of the Feast of the Queen of Poland. He led the procession along the ramparts of Jasna Gora * May 2 — 10:00 a.m., at Wawel — renewal of the Jasna Gora promises * Also on May 2 — Participation in the celebrations of the 25th anniversary of the existence of the parish associated with the monastery Church of the Immaculate Conception of the Blessed Virgin Mary in Krakow at Azory, administered by the Reformed Franciscans. After the Gospel, he administered the Sacrament of Confirmation to about 200 children * May 3[1] — Sermon at the Mariacki Basilica — about the meaning of baptism. Also reflections on the last year of the novena in preparation of the first millennium of Christianity in Poland and on the entering into the next millennium * May 4-5 — Canonical visitation of the Kobiernice parish * May 7 — Meeting of the Pontifical Council of the Department of Theology in Krakow.

> **The Archbishop proposes that, in addition to the regular meetings of the Departmental Council, special meetings should also be organized, at which the academic works of lecturers and professors would be discussed, particularly the works by those who are preparing for exams for acceptance to assistant professorship ... that he should be informed on the matter of likely candidates for strictly academic work, the purpose of which is to educate future cadres of academic researchers for the Department. (From the minutes of the Departmental Council)**

May 8 — 3:00 p.m. — At his residence, a conference discussing the findings of the inquiry regarding the remains of St. Stanislaw (the Archives *Our Future* nr. 75 Res) * The same day — 6:00 p.m. — High Mass at Wawel * May 9 — 9:00 am — a procession from Wawel to Skalka. In Krakow, at the church on Skalka — the coronation of the image of Our Lady of St. John of Matha; the Holy Mother of Captives: "... the Mother of freedom, whom we call the Mother of Captives, because you always restored freedom to prisoners ..." (from the sermon) * The same day — a sermon in Szczepanow * May 10-12 —

---

[1] See Glossary.

Canonical visitation of the Zator and Oswiecim parishes * May 13-16 — Canonical visitation of the parish of the Assumption of the Virgin Mary * May 15 — Mass and a sermon for secondary school graduates at St. Anne's church in Krakow.

> ... more important than knowledge is the point in the development of one's entire humanity, which one is supposed to reach or cross at the time of this exam ... Matura[2] opens the period of work on one's own humanity.

May 16-18 — Canonical visitation of the parish of Our Lady Help of Christians.

May 20 — At the meeting of the priests of Krakow.

> When I was preparing for the priesthood — and I prepared myself for the priesthood for a few years while I was a worker — I received from the then Holy Father a well known, famous (although at that time it was not so famous yet) book by Saint (at that time not yet a saint but blessed) Louis Grignon de Montfort entitled *A Treatise on the Perfect Devotion to the Most Blessed Virgin Mary*.
>
> I must admit that this was a moment, when I was experiencing great difficulties as I reflected upon the matter of the devotion to the Most Blessed Virgin Mary and the relation of this devotion to the devotion for Christ our Lord. And thus, I struggled for quite a long time with this treatise that had fallen into my hands as if by Providence. I studied it over and over again in various directions, you could say, there and back. I returned to many of its fragments over and over (I got the paper rather dirty at that).
>
> But I must say, that after a few months of this kind of study, something began to take shape inside of me on this matter. And what I am going to share today, comes specifically and totally from that time.
>
> I would like to try and share with you, dear priests, how this took shape in me (some twenty years ago).
>
> I understood then, first of all, that the true devotion to the Blessed Mother results from a deep understanding of the Mystery of Redemption. In order to have a deep relationship with the Blessed Mother (not just outward piety, not just a cult rooted in sentiment, but a deep relationship) — St. Louis de Montfort is distinctly concerned with this profound relationship — I would say: this commitment.
>
> In order then to have this deep relationship with the Blessed Mother, it is necessary to refer to Her in the full context of the Mystery of our Redemption. In any case, the Mystery of Redemption is here in the foreground; a little further in the background would be the whole Mystery of the Trinity, and specifically that, which St. Thomas's theology refers to as *missiones divinarum personarum*. Thus, we are speaking here about these mysteries of God, from which the *Constitution on the Church* is also derived (if you, dear priests, have already had it in your hands, then you can be convinced of it). This is one side of the issue. The true devotion to the Blessed Mother results from the understanding of the Mystery of Redemption. But there is also a second side to the issue: this devotion introduces us to the

---

[2] Secondary school graduation examination

Mystery of Incarnation.
That was my personal experience.

May 21-24 — Canonical visitation of the Kety parish * May 24 — he sent a reprimand to the faithful of the parish in Nowa-Biala where brawls between Poles and Slovaks erupted (instigated by political circles). Since his order of January 30, 1965 has not been obeyed, he reminded the parishioners that songs in Polish should be sung at two Sunday Masses and songs in Slovak at the other two Sunday Masses. He warned that should the scandalous brawls continue, the parish will be punished with an interdict (a ban on celebrating the Holy Mass) * May 25 — regional conference of the priests from Bielsko-Biala.

May 25 — Addressed congratulatory letters with blessings on the occasion of the 50th anniversary of the ordination to the priesthood to: Fr. Anatol Pytlik OFM, commissary of the Holy Land, and Jan Kety Grabowski OFM, a long time catechist, a former provincial, from the Reformed Franciscans province * May 26 — Presided over the regional convention of priests at the shrine of Kalwaria Zebrzydowska. The subject of the meeting were matters relating to the Council * May 27 — Participation in the Marian Days at the cathedral in Przemysl. High Mass, a procession, closing address * May 28 — 7:45 am — Mass in Lezajsk on the occasion of the Marian Days. * The same day, a lecture at KUL * May 31 — Zakopane — "Ksiezowka" — a conference (25 typed pages) "(..) what is the relationship of baptism, or the anniversary of baptism, with a dedication to the Blessed Mother."

June 1 — Myslenice, regional conference of priests * June 2 — Regional conference in Trzebinia * June 3 — In Trzebinia, visiting the sick on retreat * The same day — 6:00 p.m. — Pontifical Mass at Wawel for the repose of the soul of Pope John XXIII. * June 5-12 — Canonical visitation of the parish at Borek Falecki * June 7 — On Monday after Pentecost, Mass at the Sisters of the Holy Spirit at St. Thomas's Church on Szpitalna Street.

June 8 — Regional conference in Oswiecim — the morning session devoted to the topic of the 9th year of the Great Novena (baptism and dedication to the Blessed Mother) and the second part devoted to the discussion of the canonical visitation for "… both deaneries which are participating in today's meeting, underwent "a visitation storm" not so long ago — and so, it is necessary that they now experience a post-visitation tranquillity …"

June 9 — In Czestochowa — on a day of recollection for diocesan representatives dealing with matters of Marian devotion: 7:00 am — Mass and homily; 9:00 am — a report, *Historical Perspectives of*

Surrendering Poland into the Maternal Bondage of the Blessed Mother *
June 13 — In Piekary Slaskie — Pontifical High Mass with a sermon, at
the coronation (re-coronation) ceremony of Our Lady of Piekary. The ceremony of re-coronation was performed by Cardinal Wyszynski Primate of
Poland * June 14 — Mass and sermon on the occasion of a social gathering in Radlin (Silesian diocese) * June 15 — 10: 00 am — at his residence,
a meeting of catechists for the conclusion of the school year * 6:30 p.m. —
Nowa Huta-Bienczyce, a Mass with a sermon in memory of those murdered in Krzeslawice during the years of the occupation * June 17 — 9:00
am — Wawel, High Mass and procession for the Feast of Corpus Christi *
3:00 p.m. — A Corpus Christi procession in Krakow-Nowa Wies * June
18 — a gathering of the deaneries of the city of Krakow. He assessed his
own presentation as "largely doctrinal." It is followed by two other presentations — more pastoral, more practical (The Millennium of Christianity
and dedication to the Blessed Virgin Mary) * June 20 — In Olsztyn — participation in the ceremonies marking the 20th anniversary of the reactiva-
tion of the Polish church administration in the Warmia region. After the
Mass he delivered a brief speech on the relations between Krakow and
Warmia. (The sermon during the Mass was delivered by Cardinal Boleslaw
Kominek) * June 21 — 8:00 am — at his residence, Mass with sermon at
the coffin of the late Jan Vetulani.

> **Amidst all of this that each of us must give of himself, we would like to
> offer you, Janek, up to Christ, so that he would take you and accept you.
> This Christ, to whom it was once said "You have the words of eternal life".
> We are giving you up to Him. This is the final act of both our faith and your
> faith. And if we do this in pain, we also do it in hope. In the hope to which
> your life and your death inspired us. Your life and your death. Life and
> death make up man's complete destiny on earth. How quickly did they
> shape the entirety of your destiny! How quickly you matured to your meet-
> ing with God! May He accept you and bestow upon you everlasting life and
> light which surpasses our sight. (Archives of JU, correspondence of A. Vetulani 212)**

On the same day, at 2:00 p.m. — the funeral of J. Vetulani at the
cemetery in Rakowice * June 21 — at the meeting of the Departmental
Council — (in Karol Wojtyla's absence) "according to the wishes of His
Excellency the Archbishop, candidates for higher studies ought to work
at a parish for at least a year..." (From the minutes of the Departmental
Council)

June 22-23 — Conference of the Polish Episcopate in Warsaw *
June 25 — At his residence — meeting with biblical scholars * June 29
— At the parish church in Bolechowice, Mass with a sermon in con-
nection with the transferring of holy relics.

July 1 — Meditations and a concelebrated Mass with the class of
1952 in the chapel of the Theological Seminary * July 5 — Mass with

a sermon for Poles from Canada, at the altar of St. Stanislaw at Wawel Cathedral * July 6-19 — Kayak trip on the Radew and Parseta rivers with an excursion to Kolobrzeg (about twenty people).

July 18 — Coronation of the image Our Lady of Rychwald. The coronation was performed by the Primate, Stefan Cardinal Wyszynski — the participants were the Archbishop of Wroclaw, the Bishop of Tarnow, the Bishops from Katowice, Czestochowa, Opole, Wloclawek, as well as the Superior General of the Dominican Order. An address by Archbishop Wojtyla and, after the coronation — by the Primate. The ceremony took place in a downpour.

July 25 — Wrote a decree regarding the writings of the Servant of God Br. Alojzy Kosiba (Reformed Franciscan).

July 30 — Stryszawa. He visited the Primate, Cardinal Stefan Wyszynski at Siwcowka.

August 13 — Participated in the conclusion of the ceremony known as "the funeral of the Blessed Virgin" at Kalwaria Zebrzydowska, delivered a sermon * August 15 — In Kety, at the Sisters of the Resurrection.

On August 15th, at about 5 p.m., a pleasant visit by His Excellency Archbishop Wojtyla and {his} secretary Rev. Canon Dowsilas. After a welcome His Excellency proceeded to the chapel where he delivered a brief conference to the sisters gathered there. He took supper in the big parlor in the company of several priests with Father Dean at the head. He returned to Krakow with his chauffeur. Rev. Canon Dowsilas remained to participate in tomorrow's celebrations (Based on the diary of the then Superior General of the Sisters of the Resurrection, Mother Teresa Kalkstein; this fragment was sent by Sister Klaudia Luszczkiewicz CR).

On August 16th, at the monastery of the Sisters of the Resurrection, a committee consisting of the Judges of the Tribunal, priests and a medical doctor, in the presence of the sisters, opened the sarcophagi of the Servants of God Celina Borzecka and Jadwiga Borzecka, the foundresses of the Congregation. The Archbishop visited the monastery in connection with this event.

* Personal retreat at Tyniec — towards the end he visited a seriously ill grave-digger and met with a group of children (about 60) in the church.

August 21 — "Rev. Dr. Michal Sopocko, who stayed a few hours at the Congregation of the Sisters of Our Lady of Mercy, had an audience with the archbishop. To the question of the possible diocesan process for the beatification of Sister Faustina, His Excellency replied: This matter is foremost on my mind, maybe we will still be able to begin it this year." (From the chronicle of the Congregation of the Sisters of Our Lady of Mercy)

August 22 — Service, with sermon, at the Discalced Carmelites in Czerna for the intention of the beatification of Servant of God Br. Rafal Kalinowski * August 23-25 — Symposium at the Catholic University of Lublin. He delivered a lecture entitled *The Idea of the People of God and the Mission of the Laity* * August 26 — 9:00 am — Mass before the Miraculous Image at Jasna Gora; 10:30 am — He participated in a Pontifical High Mass and in the dedication of women to the Blessed Mother * The same day, Sister Imelda Wrobel and Sister Hieronima Grobicka were at an audience with Archbishop K. Wojtyla, inquiring into the possibility of starting an inquiry regarding Sister Faustina Kowalska. His Excellency the Archbishop declared: "They are bombarding me with requests to begin the process, hence, I handed down the whole matter to the Auxiliary Bishop Julian Groblicki." The Sisters immediately proceeded to Bishop Groblicki, from whom they found out, that he had received the order to take care of this matter. (From the chronicle of the Sisters of Our Lady of Mercy) * August 28 — Pastoral Committee of the Episcopate in Trzebnica * He sent another reprimand to the parishioners in Nowa-Biala.

September 1 — Wroclaw, Session of the Episcopate of Poland within the framework of nationwide celebrations of the 20th anniversary of the establishment of church life in the Western and Northern Territories. A speech on the mutual ties between the Diocese of Krakow and the Diocese of Wroclaw over the period of a millennium and on the role of the Church in preserving the Polish language and culture in Silesia in the 19th and 20th century * A pastoral letter to the diocese for the opening of the school year — including an announcement that he will celebrate Mass on this day "offering up to the One Holy Triune God our year-long effort of catechesis" (2 typewritten pages) * September 3 — Mass with sermon at the Sisters of St. Norbert, during the Triduum in honor of Blessed Bronislawa. * On the same day — a conference at his residence on matters dealing with the celebrations of the Millennium * September 4 — Mother General Szczesna Wlostowska and Sister Beata Piekut (who had been commissioned since April to handle the matter of Sister Faustina) pay a visit to Archbishop Karol Wojtyla. He is very interested in the matter and is very favorably disposed towards Sister Faustina's message. (From the chronicle of The Congregation of the Sisters of Our Lady of Mercy)

September 5 — A ceremony of the dedication of the Archdiocese of Krakow to the Blessed Mother, at Wawel Cathedral. A short speech: "I thank the clergy and the faithful of the archdiocese for being together with me on this day ... that together we dedicated our past to the Blessed Mother, and that you prepared yourselves to dedicate our vows of

Baptism and our future to her" — also a farewell before his departure for the 4th session of the Council.

September 7 — Sent a congratulatory letter with a blessing to Father Wincenty Rejmer from the province of the Reformed Franciscans on the occasion of the 60th anniversary of his ordination to the priesthood. At first, Fr. Rejmer was a missionary in the Franciscan Guardianship of the Holy Land, and then the superior of the monastic houses in Poland. * The same day — at his residence, the beatification process of the Servant of God, Jadwiga Borzecka * September 8 — Mass with a sermon during the Marian Days at Wislica * On the same day — a sermon at St. Anne's Church in Krakow, before departing for the 4th session of the Council (with Bishop Jan Pietraszko, pastor of this church):

> **"...it is more difficult now to speak of the Council. The time has already passed, when the Council was the central experience of the Church, and maybe even of all mankind ... After all, that is the internal rhythm of a human being, that from experiences he crosses over into reflection, into thought, into the depth."**

September 14 - December 8 — Rome, the Fourth Session of the Council.

September 19-22 — As the Archbishop of Krakow, he submited in writing his opinion in the discussion on the seventh chapter of the plan *De Ecclesia* (Acta Synodalia TPV. 1974 vol. III, p. II, pages 178-179) * September 15-22 — He submited in writing his opinion in connection with the discussion on the chapter IV of *De Ecclesia* (Acta Synodalia TPV 1972 vol. II, p. III, p. 340) * September 22 — At the 133rd general of the Council, he participated in a discussion on religious freedom *(De libertate religiosa)*. He spoke in the name of the bishops of Poland *(Acta Synodalia TPV 1977 vol. IV, p. II, pp. 11-13)* * September 28 — At the 137th general of the Council, he participated in a discussion on the first part of the document on the Church in the modern world (among other things, on the subject of atheism). *(Acta Synodalia TPV 1977 vol. IV, p. II, pp. 660-663)*

September 19 — The Vatican Radio broadcasts fragments of {his} statement on the subject: *The Problem of Atheism*. [Print.]

October 17 — Paray-Le-Monial, France — Pontifical High Mass for the Feast of St. Margaret Mary, in the afternoon — a procession and sermon. On the same day — Monceau Les Mines — participated in the celebration of the blessing of the banner of the Fraternity of the Mothers of the Rosary. A speech during a meeting of the participants. *(Glos Katolicki* 1989, no. 45)

October 20 — Vatican Radio — "Elucidation of the declaration on religious freedom". The main aspects of the declaration being prepared by the Council — with reference to Pawel Wlodkowic and his activity at the Council of Constance, and to St. John of Kanty (the feast day of this saint).

October 21 — His Excellency Archbishop Karol Wojtyla, the Metropolitan of the church of Krakow, issued a decision to begin the information process of the Servant of God, Sister Faustina Kowalska, and because he left for Rome to attend the Second Vatican Council, he instructed the Auxiliary Bishop Julian Groblicki to initiate this process. The process was initiated on October 21, 1965. (From the chronicles of the Congregation of the Sisters of Our Lady of Mercy) * October 24 — Mission Sunday in Mantua, a Mass with sermon, in the afternoon — a concelebrated Mass in the cathedral with bishops from all the continents * October 31 — Mass with a sermon at Ferrara, on the occasion of the fraternization (gemellaggio) of the universities of Ferrara and Turin, in addition, a Mass with a sermon at the seminary.

November 1 — At the invitation of Bishop Czeslaw Sipowicz {Ceslaus Sipovic}, Superior General of the Marian Fathers, he participated in a dinner at the general house of the Congregation (Rome, via Corsica 1). Along with Cardinal Wojtyla there arrived other Polish bishops, Fathers of the Council (Archbishop B. Kominek and bishops: W. Skomorucha, S. Barela, P. Kalwa, J. Fondalinski, J. Krupas, J. Oblak, F. Jop, J. Jaroszewicz, Cz. Falkowski, J.K. Kowalski, W. Majewski, H. Grzadziel, M. Modzelewski and Fr. Tomzinski, Superior General of the Pauline Fathers. Speeches were delivered by Archbishop Kominek and Bishop Majewski).

In November (after November 20) Rome. Archbishop Karol Wojtyla is reunited with Jerzy Kluger, his schoolfriend, son of the then leader of the Jewish community in Wadowice. (The reunion and the history of this friendship were depicted in a book by Gian Franco Svidercoschi *Letter To My Jewish Friend*, Publishing House "m", Krakow, 1995)

December 8 — The conclusion of the Second Vatican Council.

Between December 1-8 — he spoke about the Nowa Huta parish on the Vatican Radio:

> **I came to Nowa Huta many times, in order to experience personally the two realities within it: the reality of Christ, who comes down to the people, and the reality of the People of God living with Christ and bearing His outward sign, which is the cross ... For a few years now I have been celebrating [Christmas Midnight Mass] there, under the open sky, in temperatures twenty degrees below freezing (-4 degrees F) and among ice covered trees; at other times in the snow, and at still other times, in rain driven by December winds, with wet ground under one's feet, directly in the mud. The**

people always gathered by the thousands, regardless of the weather ...
Maybe nowhere else but here ... do Christians give that kind of witness to
the mystery of the birth of the Son of God. There is a striking similarity in
the external conditions.

[Further on, more about the history of the Nowa Huta parish and the cornerstone
offered by Pope Paul VI.]

December 17 — Mass with a sermon at the academic chapel in
Vienna * December 18 — Arrival at 6:40 am in Katowice, later a Mass
with a sermon at Dabrowa Narodowa. The same day, a greeting homily
at Jaworzno * December 19 — Ordination of deacons in Chrzanow *
December 20 — Best wishes extended by religious Sisters. During the
greetings, he addresses the Mother Superior of the Albertine Sisters:

What I went through there [in Rome] on account of you! I brought back
for you the decree of approval, I defended your habit. They wanted to
change it, but I mentioned, that your habit was so simple, that in Krakow it
reminded us of Brother Albert — and they relented. (The Albertine Sisters)

The Polish Bishops attending the Council disseminated 56 letters to
the Episcopal Conferences of various countries, inviting the bishops to
take part in the celebrations of the Millennium of Christianity in Poland.
Among these letters was also a message to the German Episcopate. Two
thirds of the message was dedicated to a discussion of the painful history of the relationship between Germany and Poland. In the message, the
bishops also expressed an understanding for the suffering experienced
by the Germans. The message ends with these words: "We forgive you
and ask your forgiveness". The text of the letter was not published in the
Polish press. Immediately, though, the Party carried out a violent campaign against the bishops using the motto: "We will not forget and we
will not forgive". It was made known, among other things, that Polish
and German bishops took part in the preparation of the text, dated
November 18, 1965; that from the Polish side, Archbishop B. Kominek,
Archbishop K. Wojtyla and Bishop J. Stroba participated. One of the
effects of the campaign against the bishops was this text was published
in a party-run daily newspaper of Krakow:

An open letter from the workers of the soda plant in Krakow to
Archbishop Karol Wojtyla.

His Excellency Archbishop Karol Wojtyla of Krakow
The workers of the soda plant in Krakow were deeply shocked by the
content of "the Message" delivered by the Polish bishops to the German
bishops.
The tragic history of our nation during the Nazi occupation is well
known to your Excellency, who as a laborer in the "Solvay" factory lived in
our environment during the occupation and felt its tragic results.
It is therefore with great indignation, as well as with astonishment, that
we received the news of your participation, Rev. Archbishop, in the initial

discussions with the German bishops, and your participation in drawing up and signing "the Message," in which authoritarian decisions were made on matters of vital interest to our nation. No one gave the Polish bishops a mandate to take a position on matters which are obvious for the majority of the citizens, and belonging to the competence of other bodies. For it should be clear even to the bishops, that the only one entitled to make pronouncements in the name of the Polish nation is the government of the Polish People's Republic. We are not asking whether His Excellency forgot about Oswiecim {Auschwitz}, where, among others, thousands of Polish priests perished by the hands of the German henchmen, or whether His Excellency forgot about the expulsion of the children of Zamosc and the nightmarish conditions of this expulsion, as well as other bestial methods of biological extermination. These things cannot be forgotten. That is why we declare, that the license which the bishops took in drawing up of "the Message," where, among other things, mention is made of the alleged guilt of Poles towards Germans, offends our sense of national identity. There is nothing that the Germans have to forgive us, since the direct guilt for the outbreak of the Second World War and its bestial course falls exclusively on German imperialism and fascism, and its successor, the German Federal Republic. — Knowing His Excellency as a former worker of our plant during the time of the Nazi occupation, we must express the deep disappointment that filled us upon learning of your actions, Rev. Archbishop, that were not like those of a good citizen at all.

Once again, we resolutely protest against the views and the actions represented by a part of the Polish Episcopate in the course of preparing and in the actual text of "the Message".

(signatures follow)

Krakow, December, 1965

(*Gazeta Krakowska {The Krakow Gazette}*, December 22, 1965 no. 303/5550)

December 24 — The Archbishop's response. (Since the letter could not be published in the Polish press, it was read in the churches. Perhaps it was for this reason that on January 13, 1966 the letter did appear in the columns of the Krakow daily *Dziennik Polski* along with a malicious commentary in the fashion of "*our society reacted with indignation...*"

To the workers of the "Solvay" plant

I received your letter on the 22nd of December, a letter whose text was already known to me. It was published as an open letter in the pages of Krakow's press.

In the first sentences of the letter, you remind me of the German occupation, when I was just like you, a laborer in the "Solvay" plant; first at the quarries in Zakrzowek, later in the boiler room at Borek Falecki. This terribly difficult period for all of us, became a priceless and vital experience for me, precisely because I was able to experience it as a worker together with and among you. I value this particularly and consider it the best school of life and the best preparation for my present tasks.

Nevertheless, reading the subsequent words of your open letter, I realized with pain that it is not only a grave public accusation against me, but more seriously, a sort of verdict reached "in absentia."

Furthermore, the reading of your letter convinced me that you are not familiar with all of the facts to which you refer as you bring in such a harsh verdict against me and the Polish bishops.

The first words of your letter immediately attest to this. It follows from them that you did not check what was the actual contribution of myself and the other bishops to the correspondence between the Polish Episcopate and the Episcopates of the entire world on the topic of the Millennium, but you blindly repeat the reports of the German press, which are then echoed by the Polish press.

Upon careful reading of your letter, I must contend that you couldn't have written it, if you had honestly acquainted yourselves with the actual text of the letter of the Polish bishops to the German bishops and with the German bishops' response to this letter. Then, you would have had to perceive the following:

1 — that these letters remain closely connected with the religious observance, which is the Millennium of Poland's Christianity. They are based on the deepest principles of Christian ethics contained in the Gospel, and they follow these principles consistently.

2 — that, in their letter, the Polish bishops presented, first of all, a long and emphatic compilation of the wrongs which our nation experienced from the Germans throughout history, particularly in the recent period of the horrible occupation. The German Bishops accept this accusation in its full extent, asking first God Himself, and then us, to forgive the guilt of their nation. It is necessary to compare both letters exactly in order to determine that against the background of their request, our request of forgiveness maintains its proportions in accordance with the Gospel. Never has it been so in the relations between people, especially over such a long period of time, that people would not have something for which to ask mutual forgiveness.

3 — that, in their letter, the Polish bishops affirmed most emphatically the right of the Polish nation to the Western Territories with the border on the Odra and the Nysa, although they did this in a different manner than politicians do. By reason of their pastoral mission, they based the rights of the Polish nation to the Western Territories on the fundamental principle of morality. This principle is the right of a nation to exist. The letter of the Polish Episcopate expresses our right to life as a nation, in the light of the historical as well as recent facts. This type of argumentation must have swayed the convictions of both the German bishops and all other Fathers of the Council, who were acquainted with our letter. This also bears great implications for our national interest. And that is why the German bishops clearly state in their response that the Germans who were resettled from the Western Territories must and "want to realize for themselves that a new, young generation (a Polish one) is growing up there, in those lands that were handed over to their fathers, and that this Polish generation considers these lands to be their native region".

It is hard to continue with this exposition. I tried to touch upon the most essential things. I maintain once again, that an honest reading of the entire content of both letters would have led you to the conclusions stated above, and not in the direction of such hurtful judgments which you expressed in your letter against me and the other Polish bishops.

I respond to this letter, above all, as an individual who has been wronged. Wronged, because I was accused and defamed publicly, without any attempt to honestly look at the facts and the essential motives. When we worked together during the occupation, a lot of things united us — and among these, the first and foremost was a respect for the human being, for conscience, individuality, and social dignity. This is what I learned in large measure from the workers at "Solvay" — but I am unable to find this fundamental principle in your open letter.

As I write and publish this with great pain, I must state that not only do I have the right to my own good name, but all of the people whom I represent and for whom I am a Shepherd as the Archbishop of Krakow also have a right to my good name. The only thing that motivates me is a respect for truth and for the good manners of our public life. I hope that you will make efforts to place my response to your letter in the pages of our press, so that those who have already read your letter could also acquaint themselves with my reply.

(-) Rev. Karol Wojtyla
Archbishop Metropolitan of Krakow

Krakow, December 24, 1965

December 24 — 7:00 am — Mass in the cathedral at the grave of Cardinal Adam Stefan Sapieha * 4:00 p.m. — Vespers in the cathedral * 12:00 midnight — Christmas Midnight Mass with sermon at Nowa Huta-Bienczyce * December 25 — Low Mass in the residence chapel for former working companions from Solvay and their families * The same day, at Wawel Cathedral — sermon during a Holy Mass concelebrated with the Fathers of the Council from the Archdiocese of Krakow: Bishop J. Pietraszko, Bishop J. Groblicki and the Abbot of the Cistercians from Mogila. The topic of the sermon: the deeper meaning of this concelebrated Mass — the essence of the Church — the Church in the contemporary world — the principle of dialogue — the dialogue of the Church — from the tomb of St. Stanislaw to the tomb of St. Peter, the communion of Christ's Church — the correspondence of the Polish Episcopate regarding the Millennium (reference to the letters to the German bishops and the reactions to them) — the renewal of the Church in Poland — the announcement of the Jubilee Year, invitation to a pilgrimage to the Wawel Cathedral.

December 26 — A sermon at St. Szczepan Church in Krakow, dedicated to the matter of the letters of the Polish Episcopate to the German Episcopate, which became the cause of a violent campaign against the Polish bishops. In the sermon — reference to the lack of familiarity with the correspondence, or even the texts of both letters — analysis of the notions of "forgiveness" and "forgetting" — analysis of the letter of the Polish Episcopate — analysis of the letter of the German bishops — "this matter is passing through our conscience" — the responsibility of the bishops and the people of God for the divine truth of the Gospels — the good and the strength of forgiveness.

December 31 — Sermon at the Mariacki Church for the end of the year; the need for a religious retrospective: a year in which the Second Vatican Council concluded its deliberations. This Council was an ecumenical Council, "it took up once again the great task of Christ, that of uniting Christianity and of uniting the Church. This task is without precedent" — The unification of Christianity and the history of the Church in Poland: "a situation on the boundary of Western and Eastern Christianity" — a testament of Christian faith and morality expressed in the correspondence of the Polish Episcopate in the matter of the Millennium — the moral right of the nation to exist — do we remain within the mystery of Providence and within the mysteries of modern history: "we do not want to turn back the course of history" — a current matter: the church in Nowa Huta:

> ... it was supposed to have been built after 1956. Nevertheless, the building of this church never came to pass ... The efforts of the parishioners and the clergy, and my efforts, led to this, that this year, in the summer, we received permission to expand the existing chapel at the parish in Nowa Huta. The chapel is very small, the parish numbers about twenty thousand souls (..) the Holy Father blessed a stone from the grave of St. Peter the Apostle ... he blessed this stone so that it would be the cornerstone of the church which is supposed to stand in Nowa Huta.

The same day, 12:00 midnight — a Mass at the Franciscans and a sermon for the New Year.

1966

January 3 — Mass with sermon for the opening of the regional conference in Zakopane at "Ksiezowka" (deaneries: Zakopane, Nowy Targ, Spisz and Orawa) * January 4 — Led the regional convention of priests at the shrine in Kalwaria Zebrzydowska: the preparation of the archdiocese for the Millennial Jubilee of Poland's Christianity (deaneries: Makow, Sucha, Wadowice, Skawina). * January 5 — Mass with sermon for the opening of the regional conference in Krakow at the seminary chapel (deaneries: Myslenice, Mszana, Bolechowice, Mogila, Czernichow, Niepolomice) * January 6 — Solemn Mass with sermon for Krakow altar servers at the Wawel * The same day — A meeting with doctors in the residence at 21 Kanoniczna Street and a post-Vatican II discussion * January 7 — A Mass with sermon for physicians at the Felician Sisters Church.

January 8 — 7:00 p.m. — An observance of *Oplatek*[1] was held in Krakow at the hall of the Archconfraternity of Mercy, a hall handed over for the use of the Club of Catholic Intellectuals (5 Sienna Street). President Stefan Wilkanowicz greeted the guests. Archbishop Karol Wojtyla spoke. Those present were: an Orthodox bishop and an Evangelical minister, Rev. Msgr. Dr. Ferdynand Machay, representing the dissolved Archconfraternity of Mercy; Adam Bochnak and Ludwik Ehrlich, professors of the Jagiellonian University; assistant professors: Franciszek Bielak, Przemyslaw Mroczkowski and Jozef Mitkowski. Candles were lit and Christmas carols were sung. (According to an account by Jozef Mitkowski)

January 9 — A sermon in the cathedral on the Feast of the Holy Family. According to the Holy Father's wish, the celebrations of the Jubilee, which he had announced, are to be concentrated at cathedrals: "that is why I invited you to the cathedral today". In the sermon: the truth about marriage and the family, as stated in the documents of the Second Vatican Council — the eternal teaching about marriage — the community of persons — not only to give birth, but also to bring up — the mission of the Redeemer was fulfilled largely due to the fact that He was a member of a Family * The same day in Oswiecim {Auschwitz} — a sermon celebrating the baptisms administer at the beginning of A.D. 1966 * On the same day, the Vatican Radio broadcast Cardinal Wojtyla's conference entitled *Creation and Redemption* * January 10 — Mass with sermon, for the opening of the regional conference (deaneries: Biala, Zywiec-South, Zywiec-North) held at the chapel of the

---

[1] See Glossary.

Daughters of Divine Charity in Bielsko-Biala * January 11 — Mass with sermon for the opening of the regional conference (deaneries: Oswiecim, Zator, Jaworzno, Chrzanow) in Oswiecim, at the chapel of the Salesian Fathers * January 15 — Residence chapel on Franciszkanska Street, thanksgiving service on the occasion of the 75th anniversary of the foundation of the Congregation of the Albertine Sisters * On the same day — a lecture at the plenary session of the Polish Theological Society: *The Work of Theologians during and after the Second Vatican Council* * January 16 —Wawel, participation in a High Mass and a sermon to the sisters of various religious orders on: the place of religious sisters in the Church on the basis of the *Constitution on the Church* (Chapter 4) and the *Decree on the appropriate renewal of religious life* * January 18 — The Vatican Radio broadcast the conference: "*Communio Ecclesiarum* or the celebration of the Millennium of the Church in Poland in relation to the rapprochement of the Churches at the Vatican Council" * January 20 — He blessed the single-family home of Mr. & Mrs. Radlinski (Ewa Radlinska — a colleague from his student days at the Jagiellonian University).

January 25 — Concelebrated Mass and homily in Krakow at the Basilica of the Dominican Fathers for the conclusion of the octave of prayers for Christian unity:

> ... the way to unite Christians is very simple ... today, we already know that the unity among Christians means, above all, the conversion of all Christians without exception to Christ, who said: "Father, make it so that they will be one" ... — When we all pray, then the prayer of us all comes down to the one prayer of Christ and to the one Christ, who also prays ...

January 26-27 — Conference of the Pastoral Committee * January 27 — Residence chapel, Mass and homily for the deceased bishops and priests together with the Bishops' Pastoral Committee.

January 28 — A session of the Council of the Pontifical Department of Theology "... the Archbishop spoke. He stressed the necessity of conducting studies on the theological thought of the Second Vatican Council. After the Archbishop's declaration, a discussion slowly ensued ..." (From the minutes of the Departmental Council)

January 29 —

> His Excellency Archbishop Karol Wojtyla monitored the progress of the case of the Servant of God, Sister Faustina. He communicated through Fr. Izydor Borkiewicz OFM, the postulator, that it was his wish to suspend the Masses that had begun to be celebrated every Thursday at the altar of Mercy, in order to prevent any appearance of spreading the cult in the form proposed by Sr. Faustina. This could harm the matter. "We are presently treading as if on glass" was the way the archbishop put it. He also said that if it should be demonstrated that the Diary of Sr. Faustina had been incor-

rectly translated into Italian, then the Holy Office would consider withdrawing the so-called "prohibition" of 1959 of the propagation of the cult of God in His Mercy in the form proposed by Sr. Faustina. (From the chronicle of the Congregation of the Sisters of Our Lady of Mercy)

January 31 — In the residence chapel, the conclusion of the information process of Celina and Jadwiga Borzecka.

February 2 — Mass with sermon, and the blessing of candles, at Borek Falecki. On February 2, Archbishop Karol Wojtyla arrived at the Church of Our Lady of Victory in Borek Falecki. In his sermon he said that he is offering this Holy Mass both for those workers of "Solvay" who did not sign the letter and for those who did and whom he has forgiven. He said that he could not find consolation for a long time until an image stood before his eyes — that of Jesus who, while at Annas, was struck by one of the servants. Jesus asked him: "If I have spoken wrongly, bear witness to the wrong; but if I have spoken rightly, why do you strike me?" During this sermon, full of pain and grief, the Archbishop said this about the "Solvay" soda works: "it is a nest from which I came." Reference is made here to the letter signed by the workers of the Soda Works in Krakow published within the framework of a {political} campaign which followed the exchange of letters between the Polish and German bishops. Cf. *Kalendarium*, December 24, 1965. (The account comes from Karolina Biedrzycka, author of the book-album entitled *The Nest From Which I Came, cf. Kalendarium*, September 1940 entry) *
February 5 — Mass with sermon at the residence chapel, for sisters who work as nurses in the parishes * February 6 — Mass with sermon for the 75th anniversary of the Congregation of the Sisters of the Resurrection, at their mother house in Kety.

February 12 —

Saturday. Although this was not a day of audiences, His Excellency Archbishop Wojtyla received Mother General Szczesna Wlostowska. The Mother General submitted to him a petition seeking permission to exhume the remains of the Servant of God, Sr. Faustina. The Archbishop promised to respond to the request after he conferred with the postulator, Father I. Borkiewicz OFM. The Mother General, likewise, invited His Eminence to "Jozefow", the house of the Congregation, for dinner on the 14th of February. The whole tribunal of judges would also be invited to the dinner, in connection with the second solemn session in the matter of the Servant of God, Sr. Faustina. The Archbishop could not accept the invitation, for the reason that he would be busy after the session, and that it would not be possible for him to participate. He did say, however, that he could visit the sisters on that Sunday evening, the 13th of February. And indeed, the Archbishop came to "Jozefow" after 7:00 p.m. on the 13th, directly from Nowa Wies, where he had been celebrating with the Missionary Fathers the solemn Feast of the Apparition of the Blessed Virgin Mary in Lourdes.
After dinner, a meeting took place in the main hall of the Congregation

with His Eminence and all the sisters of the Congregation. He asked them about, among other things, their methods, their system of upbringing and its results. Sister Kazimiera Twarowska answered his queries.

Towards the end of the discussion, the Archbishop joked, turning to the chaplain, Fr. Jan Stosur, that he, himself, would like to be in the Father's position. This precipitated a storm of applause. In closing, the Sisters sang the Jasna Gora promises, before the image of Our Lady of Czestochowa, and then the Archbishop left amid the resonant singing of *Ad multos annos*
(From the Chronicle of the Congregation of the Sisters of Our Lady of Mercy)

February 13 — Mass with sermon for the seminarians at the Theological Seminary (at 4 Manifestu Lipcowego Street) * The same day — Feast of the parish patron saint at the Missionary Fathers, in the Church of Our Lady of Lourdes in Krakow at Nowa Wies. * February 14 — 10:00 a.m. —pre-retreat conference for priests; 4:00 p.m. — in the chapel at his residence, the opening of the process *de non cultu* (of the non-existence of a public cult) in the matter of the Servant of God, Brother Alojzy Kosiba, a Reformed Franciscan; in addition, the session: *super scriptis* pertaining to Sr. Faustina * The same day — 6:30 p.m. — Kalwaria Zebrzydowska, monastery of the Bernardine Fathers (chapel of the Blessed Virgin) — Mass with sermon for the inauguration of the retreat for priests with twenty-five years of service * February 15 — He signed a decree regarding the writings of Sister Faustina * February 15-16 — Academic session at his residence: "The Diocese of Krakow in the Middle Ages" * February 20 — Solemn Mass with sermon at the Wawel Cathedral, for parishes arriving in pilgrimage on the occasion of the Jubilee * February 25-26 — Academic session at his residence: "The Diocese of Krakow from the 16th to the 18th century."

February 25 —

After his return from Rome, His Excellency Archbishop Karol Wojtyla, announced that in order to get to know the religious congregations and establish closer contacts with them, he would be inviting the congregations in succession, once a week, to a Mass celebrated by him in the chapel of the Curia. The turn of the Sisters of Our Lady of Mercy fell on the 25th of February. Virtually all of the sisters attended this Mass. The Mass was recited and interwoven with the songs by the Sisters. The Archbishop gave a speech in which he stressed that the purpose of our Congregation, apostolic through and through, was very dear to him, that it suited his thoughts and desires, and that it was especially appropriate for today's times. He also expressed his conviction that God Himself would repay us for this work.
(The chronicles of the Congregation of the Sisters of Our Lady of Mercy)

February 27 — Mass with sermon at the Wawel Cathedral for parishes arriving in pilgrimage in connection with the Jubilee. The same day — St. Anne's Church — sermon on the Church and the modern world, in connection with the Second Vatican Council * February 28 — 7:00 a.m. — Mass with sermon at the residence chapel, for the Sisters of the Holy Spirit.

The end of February — He visited Professor Tadeusz Milewski, a linguist, at the neurological clinic in Krakow. The professor was very ill and died shortly thereafter, on the 5th of March. (According to an account by Prof. Stanislaw Urbanczyk)

March 2 — At the residence chapel — Mass with sermon for the Congregation of the Daughters of Divine Charity * March 6 — Solemn Mass with sermon at the Wawel on the occasion of the Jubilee * March 7 — Wawel — seminary celebrations combined with the postconciliar Jubilee * The same day — Pontifical High Mass at the Church of the Dominicans on the Feast of St. Thomas Aquinas.

March 8 — 6:00 a.m. — at the Cistercians, Mass at the grave of Blessed Wincenty Kadlubek. The Archbishop often came here to pray in private at the grave of the Blessed, a predecessor in the See of Krakow (According to an account by Sister Kazimiera, a Dominican nun and a sacristan of the church in Jedrzejow) * March 9 — 10:00 a.m., St. Anne's Church — Mass for the late Prof. T. Milewski; 12:00 noon, Rakowice — he presided over the professor's funeral * March 10 — Mass with sermon at the Church of St. Peter and St. Paul for the conclusion of a retreat for the speech and hearing impaired * March 12 — Residence chapel, Mass with sermon for the Augustinian Sisters * March 13 — (Sunday) At St. Anne's Church in Krakow, a commentary (continuation) on the *Constitution on the Church in the modern world*; also a description of the situation of man in the modern world: on vocation and a person's response to it. * The same day — commemorative Masses with sermons at the Wawel Cathedral, at 12:00 noon and 5:00 p.m., on the occasion of the Jubilee Year * March 17 — 7:00 a.m. — the residence chapel, Mass with sermon for the Sisters of the Presentation.

March 17 — Session of the Council of the Pontifical Department of Theology

Archbishop Karol Wojtyla called attention to the necessity of making changes in the program of theological studies in accordance with the decisions of the Second Vatican Council and the Decree of the Congregation of Catholic Education. The decree ... permits specific Episcopal conferences a voice in the matter. On the basis of these postulates, it becomes necessary to re-analyze the obligatory "ratio studiorum".

After the Archbishop's presentation there was a lively exchange of opinions and proposals. No proposals were decided on. (From the minutes of the Departmental Council)

March 20 — Mass with sermon at the Wawel Cathedral, on the occasion of the Jubilee Year * The same day — in Kety — Mass with sermon, baptism and dedication of a baptismal font * March 27 — 7:00 a.m. — in Nowa Huta-Czyzyny, Mass with sermon, dedication of a baptismal font * 10:00 a.m. — St. Anne's Church in Krakow, a sermon (continuation of the commentary) on the *Constitution on the Church in the modern world* — more specifically: about dialogue. "...And this is a great proposal made by the Church of our times: to arrange the relations between people according to the principles of dialogue, and not according to the principles of conflict and war ..." Reflections based to a large degree on the texts of Pope Paul VI's encyclical *Ecclesiam suam* * 12 noon —Wawel Cathedral, solemn Mass with sermon on the occasion of the Jubilee * 6:00 p.m. — St. Anne's Church, sermon for secondary school students * March 28 — Mass for the beatification of Bishop Jozef Pelczar at the Church of the Sisters of the Sacred Heart * March 30 — At the Dominicans, visitation of the relics of the Holy Cross from Lublin, Mass with sermon * March 31 — Chapel at 21 Kanoniczna Street, Mass for *Tygodnik Powszechny* and *Znak*, meeting with the editorial staff of both periodicals.

April 1 — Service at the Franciscan Fathers in Krakow * April 2 — Chapel at the residence, Mass with sermon for the Sisters of Nazareth.

April 2 — Krakow, residence of the Archbishop — a session of the subcommittee formed by The Bishops' Pastoral Committee for the purpose of preparing a program of sermons for the year 1967: consisting of Archbishop Wojtyla, Bishop J. Groblicki and Bishop J. Pietraszko, Rev, H. Kocylowski, Rev. A. Bardecki, Fr. S. Nawrocki, Fr. M. Lisowski. Before the start of the deliberations on the proposed program, Archbishop Wojtyla presented the difficulties of fitting all of the lessons of the Vatican Council ("the elaboration of the logic of the Second Vatican Council") into the sermons of one year. After the discussions, an outline draft of the program was accepted (for further elaboration). It was resolved that the article *The Internal Logic of the Second Vatican Council* written by Archbishop Karol Wojtyla will be printed in the diocesan monthly publications and in the "Library of Preaching." The task of gathering a team to prepare the actual texts of the sermons was entrusted to the Archbishop with the cooperation of his auxiliary bishops. (From the minutes of the Pastoral Committee)

April 3 — 9:00 a.m. — at the cathedral, the blessing of palms and the ordination of priests * 7:30 p.m. — St. Joseph's Church (Bernardine Sisters), Mass and a retreat for lawyers * April 4 — Monday of the Holy Week — Makow Podhalanski, ordination to the priesthood of three men from Makow and one deacon from elsewhere. Participated in the receptions at the homes of the newly-ordained priests * April 6 — Wednesday of the Holy Week, Mass with sermon at the Church of the Felician Sisters for the conclusion of the retreat for physicians * April 8 — Good Friday, 10:00 a.m. — Stations of the Cross at the Theological Seminary

* 3:00 p.m. — at the cathedral, prayers at the crucifix of Queen Jadwiga *
April 9 — Holy Saturday — Easter vigil Mass at the cathedral — reflection on the first Millennium of Christianity in Poland and an appeal:

> **This evening, on the eve of Easter 1966, let us renew our [baptismal] promises in a different way, more deeply, more powerfully, in a way that requires all of our spiritual strength. Let us renew these promises, everyone for themselves, and let us renew them, everyone for everyone else ... for our entire past, so that we may proclaim our faith in the Resurrection of those who have died. And let us renew these promises for our entire future, so that we may inspire faith in the generations that will follow...**

April 11 — Easter Monday — in the chapel at the Bishop's residence, witnessed the marriage of Maria Pawicowna and Ireneusz Kania, graduates of the Jagiellonian University, who were involved in the academic apostolate {Campus ministry}. (Maria Bobrownicka)

April 14 — 3:15 p.m. — at the cathedral in Gniezno, a solemn High Mass and a conference on the Millennium * April 15, 7:30 p.m. — at the cathedral in Gniezno — participation in a session on "emigration" * April 16 — 7:00 a.m. — in Gniezno — Mass at the tomb of St. Wojciech {Adalbert}; 5:00 p.m. — Vespers for the conclusion of the Millennium celebrations * The same day — in Poznan, at the Rectoral parish, a Pontifical High Mass * April 17 — 10:00 a.m. — at the cathedral in Poznan, participation in the services to celebrate the Millennium, 4:30 p.m. — participation in a session on the subject of the Millennium. * April 18 — Kokoszyce — Mass with sermon for the priests of the diocese of Katowice on the 10th anniversary of their ordination to the priesthood * April 19 — 7:00 a.m. — Mass with sermon in the residence chapel, for the Little Sisters Servants of Mary Immaculate from the province of Stara Wies * April 20 — 7:00 a.m. — in the residence chapel, Mass with sermon for the Franciscan Sisters of the Family of Mary * April 21 — Wawel Cathedral, promulgation of the documents of the Vatican Council to religious orders of men; Mass with sermon. * April 23, 1:00 p.m. — Church of the Franciscan Fathers — a conference pertaining to the Vatican Council for the Mothers Superior of religious orders * 8:00 p.m. — Easter repast at the Club of Catholic Intellectuals.

April 24 — Wroclaw — a report delivered at a solemn celebration of the 400th anniversary of the Seminary in Wroclaw. A discussion of the decree *De institutione sacerdotali*:

> **The document maintains a very moderate character, rather non-reformatory. A reformatory act was the Tridentinum initiative. Vatican II, in turn, upholds this great reform, which consisted in the introduction of theological seminaries into the Church ... The Second Vatican Council feels the need for certain changes, but ... hopes that the seminaries will also develop**

and accommodate according to their new position within the Church and will follow along the process of universal accommodation ... {the Council} counts on the fundamental maturity of the institutions ...

[A detailed analysis of the documents follows, chapter by chapter] (Cf. *Wroclawskie Wiadomosci Koscielne*[2] 21/1966)

April 26 — Krakow, Participation in the session of the Polish Theological Society dedicated to the Millennium {of Christianity in Poland} * April 28 — 10:00 a.m. — Zembrzyce — the funeral of Rev. Stanislaw Wilk * 6:30 p.m. — the parish of the Assumption of the Blessed Virgin Mary in Krakow, service for graduating secondary school students * April 29 — 6:00 p.m. — the beginning of the novena to St. Stanislaw at Wawel Cathedral.

May 2 — 7:00 a.m. — residence chapel, Mass with sermon for the Sisters of St. Joseph * The same day — Czestochowa, participation in the celebrations at Jasna Gora. * May 3[3] — 6:00 a.m. — in Czestochowa, the sermon *The Baptism of the Nation and the Surrender of Poland into the Maternal Bondage of the Virgin Mary* * 11:00 a.m. — celebrated an outdoor High Mass.

May 6 — Wawel — He greeted the itinerant image of Our Lady of Czestochowa. The procession stopped for a moment in front of the cathedral, where, in a downpour, a crowd was waiting. Here, a short welcome speech ("I had to stop here for at least a moment, so that you could glance at it [the image of the Blessed Virgin]"). Sermon at Wawel Cathedral:

> Now, we are about to enter the second millennium, and behold, Mary has arrived at the Wawel Cathedral to lead us there ... This is exactly how she has led the entire Polish nation, the entire Church of Poland, step by step ... into the new millennium of faith and Christian life ... We welcome You to the Wawel Cathedral, O Handmaid of the Lord, Queen of Poland...

May 7 — A public session of the Polish Episcopate at the Wawel Castle, dedicated to the history of the Church of Krakow. Welcoming remarks to the participants of the academic session: the Primate, the bishops, the rectors, the professors, etc. Five short addresses (the result of the work of the academic session in February). A Mass, celebrated by the Archbishop of Poznan, Antoni Baraniak, inaugurates the session; the last presentation — Archbishop Karol Wojtyla: *Adam Stefan Cardinal Sapieha, the Archbishop of Krakow, and the Clergy of the Archdiocese of Krakow during the Dark Night of the Occupation* * The same day — 4:30 p.m. — at the Dominicans, a solemn session of the Polish

---

[2] Church News of Wroclaw
[3] See Glossary.

Episcopate, examining the life of religious orders in the archdiocese of Krakow.

May 8 — A sermon at Skalka in Krakow, after the procession from the Wawel. Carried in the procession, along with the holy relics of St. Stanislaw, St. John of Kanty and St. Jacek {Hyacinth}, were the holy relics of St. Adalbert — a gift of the Primate to Krakow. The Archbishop read two telegrams from the Holy Father. During the sermon, the crowd repeated the profession of faith recited by the Archbishop: "You are the Rock, and on this rock, I will build my Church", "You are Jesus Christ, the Son of Mary". From the sermon: "... my dear brother bishops, priests — when hard blows fall upon us, we always feel that these blows reach back through the past all the way to the head of St. Stanislaw and to the heart of St. Adalbert ... but I mention the blows only briefly ..." The sermon was interrupted repeatedly by applause and outcries * The same day — 7:00 p.m. — at the Wawel, a farewell ceremony for the image of Our Lady of Czestochowa:

> ... You were at home, every step, every minute, every second ..., you are at home here in this Cathedral, with everything it contains that connects us with our past (..) You are at home, together with us in the present. This was proven by all those who came here constantly, day and night, to be with you ... This is our inner reality, our Christian, Polish inner reality. You fill it for us, so very completely ...

* On the same day (May 8) — a letter to the editorial office of *Tygodnik Powszechny*: "The religious experience of the Millennium". Krakow, the Church of St. John: a sermon on the first anniversary of the coronation of the image *

April 10 — 3 Franciszkanska Street, Krakow, participation in the session closing the canonical process on the life and sanctity, on the nonexistence of a public cult, and on the writings of the Servant of God, Br. Alojzy Kosiba OFM. * May 12 — 7:00 a.m. — in the residence chapel, Mass with sermon at the coffin of an infant; and at 3:00 p.m., a funeral at Rakowice * May 13 — 7:00 a.m. — in the residence chapel, Mass with sermon for the Felician Sisters; 5:00 p.m. — in the same chapel, the opening of the beatification process of the Servant of God, Fr. Pawel Smolikowski CR * May 14 — Mass and sermon in Myslenice, for graduating secondary school students.

May 15 — Szczepanow — the conclusion of the observances of the Millennium in the diocese of Tarnow.

> The road into the past runs within us, and when we follow it, it becomes a surging river in us ... I, the Bishop of Krakow, the most unworthy successor of your fellow countryman St. Stanislaw, Bishop and Martyr, came here to Szczepanow, in order to be reborn... There are many of these places

in our country — this is one of the first.

May 19 — In Kety, in the chapel of St. John of Kanty, a Mass with sermon for graduating secondary school students.

May 20 —

> The Archbishop of Krakow, Karol Wojtyla, celebrated a Holy Mass for our congregation in the chapel at the palace of the Archbishop. The sisters who attended the Mass were: those participating in a retreat before the profession, the novices and the postulants. Afterwards, the Reverend Archbishop met with the sisters in one of the halls of the palace and cordially spoke to them. (The Congregation of the Daughters of Charity)

May 21 — In Katowice, at the Church of St. Peter and St. Paul, Mass with sermon in observance of the Millennium.

May 22 — 10:00 a.m. — in Czestochowa — Jasna Gora, the Day of Prayer for the Health Service, Mass with sermon on the dedication of the members of the medical profession to the maternal bondage of the Blessed Virgin: service or mission to people as a calling flowing from Holy Baptism and the baptismal promises.

> What do we dedicate and why do we dedicate it? ... this is a priceless calling; we are dedicating our service to people ... which is simultaneously the foundation of your Christian mission and your resemblance to Christ ... The more it embraces us, the more our calling, our life, our destiny becomes similar to that of Christ's.

The same day — 2:30 p.m., in Piekary Slaskie, where the millennial celebrations with the participation of the Polish Episcopate were taking place, a sermon for men * On the same day at 5:30 p.m. in Zywiec-Zablocie, the blessing of the banner of the Millennium, Mass with sermon * May 23 — A meeting at the editorial offices of "Nasza Przeszlosc"[4] in connection with the 100th anniversary of the birth of Cardinal A. S. Sapieha (in attendance, among others, Prof. A. Vetulani) * May 28-29 — Observances of the Millennium in Gdansk and Gdansk-Wrzeszcz, participation in a service for the youth * May 29 — In Bydgoszcz — participation in the coronation of the image of Our Lady Mother of Beautiful Love * May 31 — In the residence chapel, Mass with sermon for novice mistresses of various religious orders * The same day — 7:00 p.m. — celebrations on the occasion of the 300th anniversary of the present Church of St. Casimir in Krakow, one belonging to the Reformed Franciscans (they were the first in the Kingdom to build a place of worship under this patron, in Krakow in 1625, at the end of St. Anne Street. The church was destroyed during the Swedish inva-

---

4 "Our Past"

sion, and the building of the present church on Reformacka Street was begun in 1666). A Mass with sermon and a procession.

June 3 — at the Wawel Cathedral — Mass on the anniversary of the death of Pope John XXIII.

> **We did this in the past years, but this year we are doing it for different reasons ... In the past years, this was a Mass of mourning. This year it is a Mass in the octave of the Pentecost: a Mass for the intention of his elevation to the honors of the altar[5] ...**

June 4 — Participated in a session of the Council of the Pontifical Department of Theology in Krakow * June 5-6 — Observances of the Millennium in Lublin. A sermon during the Mass concelebrated by the professors of KUL; participation in the academic session at KUL * June 7 — In the residence chapel — Mass with sermon for the Little Sisters of the Immaculate Heart of Mary * June 8 — In the residence chapel — Mass with sermon for the Sisters of the Resurrection of Our Lord * June 11 — Trzebinia, visiting the sick during a retreat * June 12 — a sermon in Alwernia, for the 350th anniversary of the monastery; a procession in the octave of the Feast of Corpus Christi * June 14 — Lubien, Mass and sermon for priests meeting at a social reunion of the class of 1964 * June 17 — Wawel — adoration of the Blessed Sacrament by priests * The same day — participation in the session of the Council of the Pontifical Department of Theology in Krakow on the subject of modifying the program of studies. A special committee presented some proposals. Resolutions were undertaken * June 18 — a Mass to celebrate the Millennium in Olsztyn * June 19 — Participation in the observances of the Millennium in Frombork * June 21 — He issued an order which gives permission to take photographs of family celebrations in the church * June 29 — Pontifical Mass with sermon at Wawel, on the 3rd anniversary of the coronation of Pope Paul VI.

During the 1965/66 academic year, he was invited to give a lecture on the Second Vatican Council to the students' club of the Agricultural College. He accepted the invitation. Due to the opposition of the secretary of the school's party organization, the invitation was withdrawn, and the lecture never took place. (According to an account by Piotr Iwanski, the student who originally extended the invitation)

The summer of 1966 — A trip of a few days on the Brda River.

July 2 — Wadowice — Mass with sermon for the 100th anniversary of the local secondary school * On the same day — Halcnow. The Feast

---

5 making him a saint

of the Visitation of the Blessed Virgin Mary, Millennial celebrations. A speech to the youth about fulfilling God's Commandments * July 4 — Wawel Cathedral, a solemn Mass with sermon for sextons * July 8 — in the residence chapel, a Mass for the late Zofia Starowieyska-Morstinowa * July 14 — Kamien Slaski, Pontifical Mass with sermon at the birthplace of St. Jacek {Hyacinth}, Bl. Czeslaw, Bl. Bronislawa * July 15 —Oswiecim {Auschwitz}, parish of the Assumption of the Virgin Mary, sermon on the twenty-fifth anniversary of the death of Maximilian Kolbe * July 16 — Arrived at Sidzina near Jordanow, for *Odpust*[6]. Celebrated Mass and delivered a sermon. Heart-felt welcome from the "gorale"[7] * July 17 — Mass with sermon at the Dominican Fathers, honoring St. Jacek {Hyacinth} * The same day — observances of the Millennium in Wislica (diocese of Kielce), Pontifical High Mass and the coronation of Our Lady of Lokietek * The same day, in the evening — a sermon in Tropie at the hermitage of St. Swierad.

> **This is one of the places where Christian life in Poland began and became deeply rooted ... This is not the only root, but one of the roots from which the tree grew, without that root this tree would not be here, this thousand-year old tree.**

July 22 — Celebrations of the Millennium at the Church of the Felician Sisters in Krakow. A sermon: *Te Deum* of the Millennium — a short history of the congregation — the Felician Sisters in the entire world — the fruits of Baptism — Felician service — demands of charity — the mystery of the Heart of Mary — trust in the Mother of God * July 23 — Celebrations in connection with the Millennium in Tarnow — Holy Mass.

July 24 — Celebrations of the Millennium in Stary Sacz. A sermon on the Feast of Blessed Kinga {Kunegunda} and in her honor:

> **We look from here in the direction of Wawel, the home of saints; and from the perspective of the beginning of the second Millennium of Christianity, we pray to God that every Polish home in some way resemble the Wawel — the home of saints. May those saints be present everywhere.**

August 7 — Celebration of the Millennium in Lomza, Mass with sermon for young people * August 14 — Participation in the celebrations of the Millennium in Opole * August 15 — Participation in the "*Odpust* of the Millennium" in Kalwaria Zebrzydowska * The same day, in Ludzmierz — the observance of the Ascension. Sermon:

> **The "Magnificat" of the Mother of God - the beginning and the end of Mary's road - the vision of God in His mysteries: "... This teaching tells us**

---

[6] See glossary.
[7] Mountaineers of the Carpathian region in the south of Poland.

to transcend the boundaries of earth". It is the calling of a human being to Unity with God. "... Although we live on earth, and are absorbed very much by its purposes and tasks ... we must tell ourselves, as we confess our faith ...that we are journeying across the earth not just towards death. Death is not the crowning event of our lives, because what kind of crowning would that be? — But, we are also heading ... towards the immortality of the soul, towards the unification, the Resurrection of the body, towards glory. [At the coronation of Our Lady of Ludzmiersk, in preparation for the 1000th anniversary of Poland's Christianity — thanksgiving for the fruits of the Holy Baptism — a prayer for future Polish generations.]

August 17 — Cathedral in Katowice, participation in the transfer of the holy relics of St. Jacek {Hyacinth} * August 19 — Participation in the ceremonies of "the funeral of the Blessed Mother" in Kalwaria, Mass in the chapel and a concluding sermon at the Little Grave * August 20 — Millennium at the diocese of Przemysl. A solemn Mass celebrated by Archbishop Karol Wojtyla in front of the basilica. The sermon was delivered by Cardinal Wyszynski; Archbishop Wojtyla spoke after the Mass. (Summary of the address in the *"Chronicle of the Diocese of Przemysl"* 1966, vol. 6, p. 129) * The same day — 8:00 p.m. — Millennium Mass in Krasiczyn * August 21 — at the Dominican Fathers in Krakow, the conclusion of the ceremonies honoring St. Jacek, sermon * August 22 — Krakow, the Church of the Felician Sisters. Mass and sermon on the patronal Feast of the Immaculate Heart of the Blessed Virgin Mary. [KW 40] * August 22 — 9:00 a.m. — in the cathedral, Mass with sermon for the 25th anniversary of the Rhapsodic Theater * 5:00 p.m. — In Chocholow, a sermon at the ceremony on the occasion of the 100th anniversary of the death of Father Wojciech Blaszynski * August 26 — Participation with the Primate in a Pontifical High Mass at Jasna Gora. Archbishop Karol Wojtyla led a ceremonial procession around the ramparts of Jasna Gora * August 28 — Czestochowa, a key-note speech, at the basilica of Jasna Gora, during the National Day of Prayer for men and male youth * August 31 — he is nominated chairman of the Committee for the Apostolate of Laity which was appointed by the Conference of the Polish Bishops. The Committee participated in the drafting of the pastoral instruction *On Family Ministry* and prepared a *Directory of the Apostolate of Lity*. The last document met with high praise from the Council for the Laity; the Council printed the text in its official information periodical.

September 2 — The opening of the exhibition of the Millennium, at the gallery of the Carmelite Fathers (at Piasek) in Krakow. Sermon: the achievements of the Carmelite Fathers — the past serves the future.

September 3 — Krakow, the Church of the Norbertine Sisters: Holy Mass and sermon for the conclusion of the triduum on the Feast of Blessed Bronislawa [KW 19].

September 4 — Katowice, the inauguration of the peregrination of the image of Our Lady of Czestochowa around the diocese of Katowice. On September 2 — the copy of the image of the Mother of God that was to travel across Poland was being transported from Warsaw to Katowice. In the area of Bedzin the car was stopped by the functionaries of the militia {police} and from there returned, under escort, to Jasna Gora. The image was accompanied by Jozef Kurpas, Auxiliary Bishop of the diocese of Katowice, two priests working in the Katowice Curia and a Pauline father. The image, guarded by the militia, remained at Jasna Gora [till June 13, 1972 when it removed without permission by Rev. Jozef Wojcik and, beginning in Radom, resumed its national pilgrimage]. The peregrination in the diocese of Katowice — without the image — began on September 4 at the Katowice cathedral. Present at the commencement of the peregrination was the Metropolitan of Krakow (as related by Rev. Henryk Piech). On his way to Katowice, he was stopped by a group of people in a provocative manner. The fragment of the sermon quoted below refers to the conversation with these people:

After the First World War, when a new church hierarchy was organized, a new diocese was established in Katowice. This diocese was made part of the metropolitan see of Krakow. It was a confirmation of the historical ties that bound the two areas together. A specific expression of these historical ties and the ties that still bind the two today, is the Theological Seminary of the diocese of Katowice, which is located in Krakow. It was established there because of the efforts of the great Silesian, the first Bishop of Czestochowa, Fr. Teodor Kubina. The seminary is an expression of the spirit of Silesia and of a profound need for unity; the unity of the nation and, at the same time, the unity of Christians.

At the invitation of Reverend Bishop Coadjutor, I hurried here for today's celebration, so that I could take part in it — for the inauguration of the peregrination in the diocese of Katowice is, at the same time, the inauguration of the peregrination in the province, i.e. the metropolitan see of Krakow, as noted in the opening remarks of the Reverend Bishop. As I was hurrying here, I was stopped on the road by a group of people. They were lay people: a few men, a few women. These people pointed to the land, which I was entering. And they told me this: look at the land (I am unable to repeat word for word what they said; I wasn't prepared for it; I was surprised. I wasn't able to record this conversation on a tape recorder, nor was I able to write it down on a stenograph. Consequently, I am only repeating the sense of what they said). They said: Look at the land which you are entering. It is a land that owes its wealth to hard work, the hard work of our nation. And then, they addressed me directly in this manner: Be careful not to harm the unity of our nation. I replied: My dear brothers, none of the bishops will harm the unity of our nation. Every bishop takes pains to work for our national unity.

After all, the reason we have all come here is to look at the sign of our unity; of our Christian unity but also our national unity; this unity, which has been shaped in our Polish souls over the centuries; this unity, whose shaping has been watched over by the image of Our Lady of Czestochowa.

A visible painting, and not an invisible one!

We are only the servants of this unifying mission, the source of which is Christ, and She is the handmaid, the first handmaid.

When I think of the journey of the image of Our Lady of Czestochowa, which begins in the diocese of Katowice; when I think of these parishes, which are waiting for the arrival of this image, and which, perhaps, will not get to see its arrival — and on the other hand when I think of those parishes in the diocese of Opole, who recently had this symbol of our spiritual unity in their homes — I think, I reflect and then I ask:

– will its presence there, and absence here, give rise to a feeling of some sort of difference?

– will it not remind us of a border, which we should not be reminded of?

I think, I reflect, and I look for arguments!

The Reverend Bishop Coadjutor has aptly said, that due to the Second Vatican Council, the actions of Pope John XXIII and Pope Paul VI, the Church has entered into a period of dialogue with all people of good will, without exception. And dialogue depends on the presentation of arguments. We are searching for these arguments in history!

We are searching for these arguments in the Constitution!

We are searching for the arguments for our unity!

This unity is very deep. On the Polish soil it has lasted a thousand years.

September 8 — The Feasts of the Birth of the Mother of God at the Church of the Carmelite Fathers at Piasek in Krakow. Sermon: the mystery of the birth of the Virgin Mary in the liturgy of the word — the birth of man through the grace of Baptism — the history of the image of Our Lady of Piasek in the Millennium (links with Polish history — Sobieski — the partitions — Cardinal Dunajewski) — Baptism: birth from God — the Thousand Years of Christianity set against the backdrop of the Vatican Council — the Blessed Mother as the prototype of our birth from God.

September 11 — Millennial celebrations in the diocese of Tarnow and the coronation of the statue of Our Lady of Limanowa. Sermon:

The mystery of the Birth of the Most Holy Virgin Mary — the second birth: the Annunciation, the third: as our Mother — Our Lady of Limanowa: "the Mother of the thousands of people, who, in the year of the Lord 1966 ... will surround Your statue". We have come to repay a debt of a thousand years — the Church in the newly born, modern world: "... we ask ... where is the place of a human being in this progress, whose direction and goal Jesus Christ set for us, because if we rejected it, we would then betray the cause of humanity" — the sign of today's coronation — entering into the new Millennium.

The same day, in Myslenice — participated in the Millennium Mass — *Odpust* * September 12-13 — The Archbishop participated in the funeral of Rev. Karol Kozlowski * September 13 — Lublin, KUL. A report at the academic session of Polish theologians: *The Importance of the Pastoral Constitution "Ecclesia in mundo huius temporis" for*

Pastoral Work * September 15 — Celebrations of the Millennium in Orawka * September 17 — A sermon in Radomsko in connection with the 700th anniversary of the parish of St. Lambert * September 18 — Participation in the observances of the Millennium at Siedlce — he celebrated the main Mass at an outdoor altar in front of the cathedral. In a short speech after the Mass, he reminded the faithful that the documents pertaining to the Uniates of Podlasie are stored at the Church of the Holy Cross in Krakow. (Father Zdzislaw Mlynarski)

September 19 — A letter to the editor of *Nasza Przeszlosc*[8], Rev. Prof. Alfons Schletz, in connection with the publication of the 25th volume of the periodical:

> **I would like to express my profound happiness that these volumes saw the light of day in Krakow by the Wawel. They have become for us the beacon of our common past; a difficult, yet great past. The Reverend Editor was able to gather around himself a number of historians, both clerical and secular, who filled the pages of *Nasza Przeszlosc* with their valuable work ... I would like to express in this letter the conviction that is surely dear to the Reverend Editor and your co-workers, because it is one that stands in affirmation of your efforts. I would like to stress that your efforts fulfill an important social function, that they respond to the real needs of life and learning. I am happy that I can say this to the Reverend Editor in the year of the Millennium, when our entire past takes on such a special meaning and expression for all Poles. We are particularly grateful this year to those who live with the problems of our past, so that we may thoroughly know the truth about the past, and make that truth the solid foundation for our future, our progress and development. The human spirit lives for truth and that is why it is always searching for it.** (From the Archives of *Nasza Przeszlosc*, no. 75 Res)

September 20 — Mass at Wawel Cathedral, in connection with the 700th anniversary of the Servant of God, Prandota * The same day — a sermon in Rabka, during the millennial observances in the deanery of Makow * September 23 — the Church of the Carmelite Fathers on Rakowicka Street in Krakow, a sermon at the grave of Brother Albert, during a Holy Mass on the 50th anniversary of his death: a profile of Brother Albert, a prayer for his elevation to the honors of the altar ("saintly by the crown of the People of God") — a model of Christian charity * September 24 — the Church of the Sisters of the Presentation — celebrations of the Feast of Our Lady of St. John de Matha (the Holy Mother of Captives). "In the course of the last hundred years, the Mother of God became the most prominent Patroness of freedom" — The rest of the speech refers to the document of the Second Vatican Council *On Religious Liberty* * September 25 — Celebrations of the Millennium at

---

[8] "Our Past"

the Church of the Cistercian Fathers in Nowa Huta-Mogila. Sermon: the Divine Providence in the Millennium of Christianity in Poland — the meaning of the Cross: the truth about man's labor — Yesterday and today — Stara and Nowa Huta[9] — the national past in the chronicles of the abbey — Pope John XXIII and Pope Paul VI, and the church in Nowa Huta — *Te Deum* of the People of God * September 25 — The observances of the 750th anniversary of the abbey in Staniatki (Benedictine Sisters). Sermon: Dialogue from two sides of the cloister — the history of the Monastery (the history of the Polish Monastery) — the Apostolate of the Benedictine Sisters — "Stabat Mater" — reference to the image of Our Lady of Sorrows, crowned by Rev. Archbishop Sapieha * September 27 — 9:00 a.m. — at Jasna Gora in Czestochowa, participation in the pilgrimage of the "captive image". A sermon in the chapel before the miraculous image * The same day, at 7:00 p.m. — the Church of St. Peter and St. Paul in Krakow, observances in honor of Piotr Skarga — sermon * September 29 —Celebrations of the Millennium in Mszana Dolna, a concelebrated Mass with sermon * The same day — a session of the Council of the Pontifical Department of Theology in Krakow. A discussion of the further motions by the Committee dealing with issues of the changes in *ratio studiorum.* During the discussion "Rev. Prof. T. Dlugosz refers a question to His Excellency Archbishop — what is the intellectual and moral level of the graduates of the department..." The Archbishop remarks, that "it is difficult to answer ... because it is difficult to compare. Nonetheless, the last few class years represent a great level of value. The average is decidedly favorable..." With regard to the further reform of study, "it is necessary to base it on specific instructions. I suggest that the Committee deliberate on this during the whole year." (From the minutes of the Council of the Department of Theology)

September 30 — at the Church of the Franciscan Fathers in Krakow, celebrations in connection with the Feast of Our Lady of Sorrows. Sermon: St. Francis: bringing God closer to people — the path to God through man — the meaning of the suffering of Our Lady of Sorrows — the significance of the visitation of the image of the Blessed Mother.

October 1, Saturday — Drohiczyn, Most Rev. Archbishop Karol Wojtyla began the millenial celebrations with the rosary service (Sister Leonia Sewartowska OSB) * October 2, Sunday — Most Rev. Archbishop of Krakow celebrated a Holy Mass with a homily for high school and university students from the entire diocese at the Church of the Franciscan Fathers. The young people were completely enchanted by his

---

[9] Stara Huta: Old Steel Mill; Nowa Huta: New Steel Mill

person and often recalled his homily. Before his departure the Archbishop visited the Church of the Benedictine Sisters (in ruins at the time). After a few days an engineer sent by the Archbishop arrived to calculate how many shingles would be needed to cover the roof of the church. Unfortunately, the Most Reverend Metropolitan was later unable to obtain permission for the shingles to be sent to the church (Sister Leonia Sewartowska OSB) * October 3-4 — Krakow, Silesian Religious Seminary. He participated in a symposium dedicated to the history of the Church in the diocese of Katowice. [Bibl. I 910 and *Tygodnik Powszechny*, October 23, 1966] * October 4 — 5:30 p.m. — in the residence chapel, a sermon for nurses * The same day — 7:00 p.m. — the Church of the Dominicans — the rosary and a Mass with sermon * October 6 — 7:00 a.m. — the residence chapel, a Mass with sermon for the Higher Institute of Catechesis * October 7 — He issued a decree allowing for one Mass to be celebrated in the afternoon or evening hours in all churches of the archdiocese (based on *Motu Proprio* by Pope Paul VI of November 30, 1963) * October 9 — Celebrations of the Millennium in Wloclawek. A sermon for the youth: "to you, who are able to come here and listen to these words — and I know that many could not be here, that they were forcibly detained ... — to you belong the answers of the future..." * October 15 — Wroclaw, a solemn Mass at the grave of Blessed Czeslaw * October 16 — Trzebnica, within the framework of the celebrations of the Millennium, a sermon at the holy relics of St. Jadwiga {Hedwig} * October 18 — In the Church of the Felician Sisters — to the workers of the health service: "the Christian mission of a doctor is a humanitarian mission." Further on, about the *Constitution on the Church in the modern world* and, in connection with this document, on the dignity of man and on the sacrament of Baptism * October 20 — A millennial gathering of the deanery of Wieliczka, a concelebrated Mass with sermon; the tour of the salt-mine and the chapel of Blessed Kinga * The same day — 5:00 p.m. — at the Theological Seminary, the inauguration of the academic year, and at 7:30 p.m. at St. Anne's Church —celebrations in honor of St. John of Kanty with the participation of the alumni, rectors of the seminaries, representatives of KUL and ATK[10], and the bishops of Czestochowa and Silesia. Sermon: the meaning of dates — John of Kanty lived at the time of the 500th anniversary of Christianity in Poland, "a significant and characteristic point ... was that we already had a university" — John of Kanty, professor, theologian, saint — the patron saint of the Department of Theology of the Jagiellonian University ("we are standing at the roots of theology in Poland") — the first academic year of the second Millennium — the responsibility connected with the Christian testimony.

---

[10] Akademia Teologii Katolickiej {Academy of Catholic Theology} in Warsaw.

October 21 — A sermon at the chapel of the Ursuline Sisters in Krakow, on the Ursuline vocation * The same day, in Lublin: within the framework of the Second Ecclesiological Week (KUL, October 21-28, theme: "The Church in the Modern World") — a presentation by Karol Wojtyla *The Human Community in the Eyes of the Second Vatican Council* * October 23 — In Lubaczow, within the framework of the celebrations of the Millennium, a Pontifical High Mass with sermon * The same day — St. Anne's Church in Krakow, academic procession honoring St. John of Kanty * October 25 — in Poronin, a solemn millennial gathering of the deanery of Zakopane, a concelebrated Mass with sermon * October 26 —Maniowy — the millennial celebrations of the deanery of Spisz, a concelebrated Mass with sermon * October 27 — Zator, a solemn millennial gathering of the deanery of Zator, a concelebrated Mass with sermon * October 28 — At the Church of the Carmelite Fathers at Piasek in Krakow, on the Feast of St. Jude Thaddeus, Mass and sermon: the importance of the saints for contemporary times — we grow in appreciation of the humanity of the saints * October 30 — Wawel Cathedral, the Feast of Christ the King. Sermon: the interpretation of authority (a function of service) — Christ as King — the Kingdom of God on earth — the thirst of humanity — our trial * A note written by Cardinal Wojtyla in the chronicle of *Rorantysci* — a cathedral choir at the Cathedral of St. Waclaw {Wenceslaus}in Krakow: "In the Year 1966 of Our Lord, on the Millennium of Christianity in Poland, on the Feast of Christ the King, the cathedral choir of the Wawel Basilica celebrated the 20th anniversary of resuming its work at the Royal Archcathedral. On this occasion, I wish, from the bottom of my heart, God's blessings upon the Dear Heirs of the tradition of *Rorantysci* and their Choirmaster (Michal Jan Wozny) as they cherish and nurture the great treasure of the beauty of music — the treasure of the nation and the Church, which should be particularly cultivated and nourished in this first and foremost Shrine of Poland in the new Millennium of Faith. Rev. Karol Wojtyla, Archbishop Metropolitan of Krakow.

November 2, All Souls Day — 8:00 a.m., in the crypt of St. Leonard at Wawel, the second and the third Mass for the deceased; 9:00 a.m. — after the Pontifical Mass, a procession and descent to the royal tombs * On the same day — 5:00 p.m. — in the chapel near the concentration camp in Oswiecim {Auschwitz}, a solemn Mass and a procession into the camp * November 4 — Patronal Feast day Mass at the Wawel * November 5 — a sermon during the celebrations of the Millennium in Zielona Gora (diocese of Gorzow) * November 6 — Mass with sermon for the Millennium in Gorzow * November 9 — Liszki, a solemn millennial gathering of the deanery of Czernichow * November 10 — In Skawina, a solemn millennial gathering of the deanery of Skawina * November 12 — A Mass for the opening of the celebrations of the Millennium in Plock * November 13 — Participation in the High Mass in Plock to celebrate the Millennium. * November 14 — Niegowic, a solemn millennial gathering of the deanery of Niepolomice, a concelebrated Mass with sermon * November 15 — in Czerna at the Carmelite Fathers, a sermon during the Mass for the beatification of Fr. Rafal {Kalinowski} * 3:00 p.m. — Chrzanow, a solemn millennial gathering of the deanery of Chrzanow, a concelebrated Mass with sermon * November 16 —Modlnica, a solemn millennial gathering * November 17 — the Church of the Franciscan Fathers, a Mass with sermon at the holy remains of Bl. Salomea * November 19 — Mass in Bialystok, during the celebrations of the Millennium * November 23 — in Lublin at KUL, Adam Rodzinski's thesis and defense qualifying for assistant-professorship, *At the Roots of Moral Culture* (reviewer — Karol Wojtyla) * Sermon during the Holy Mass at the Church of the Discalced Carmelites in Krakow on the 50th anniversary of Brother Albert's (Adam Chmielowski) death. The Mass was celebrated by Bishop Julian Groblicki * November 24 — Zywiec, the parish of the Birth of the Blessed Virgin Mary, a solemn millennial gathering of the deanery of Zywiec-North, a concelebrated Mass, closing remarks * November 25 — Rajcza, a solemn millennial gathering of the deanery of Zywiec-South, a Mass with sermon * November 27 — 10:00 a.m. — Wadowice, the celebrations of the Millennium for the deanery of Wadowice * The same day — 5:00 p.m. — Jaworzno, celebrations for the deanery of Jaworzno * November 29 — Dobczyce, a solemn millennial gathering for the deanery of Myslenice, a Mass with sermon * November 30 — Celebrations of the Millennium in Osiek — the deanery of Oswiecim —a Mass with sermon.

December 3 — At the cloistered convent of the Dominican Sisters at Grodek: "In order to make it possible for the sisters to obtain the indulgence on the occasion of the Jubilee, Archbishop Wojtyla celebrated a morning Mass for the nuns. The Archbishop brought the Eucharist to the sisters who are ill. He stopped for breakfast at the meeting area of the convent." (From the chronicle of the convent) * December 5 — He issued an order regarding the distribution of the Eucharist in the afternoon hours * December 7 — Nowy Targ, a solemn millennial gathering of the deanery of Nowy Targ, a Mass with sermon * December 9 — A meeting of the Council of the Pontifical Department of Theology. "Summing up, he made suggestions regarding the report to the Sacred Congregation and regarding the organization of lectures at the department." (From the minutes of the Departmental Council) * December 10 — At the Church of the Capuchin Fathers in Krakow, *Odpust* on the Feast of Our Lady of Loretto:

His Excellency Reverend Archbishop Karol Wojtyla was greeted at the gates of the Church of the Capuchin Fathers at 6:00 p.m. He did not want to prolong the welcome, because immediately after visiting us he was to travel to Makow Podhalanski. Many others had come to greet him; including invited guests, canons of the chapter, professors at the seminary, and higher and local superiors of the Order.

During the Mass, H. E. the Archbishop delivered a sermon on the subject of the Catholic family. He reminded us of the vows of Thaddeus Kosciuszko and the deeds of Brother Albert, which had as their goals the defense of the family. The former, the defense of the family of our nation, and the latter, Brother Albert, wanted to create a family for the homeless, something that they had been deprived of. The Loretto House is a shrine of the Catholic family, reminding us of the House of the Holy Family, a model for families throughout history.

After the solemn Mass, the Archbishop made his way to the refectory of the monastery for a moment, and then he left for Makow Podhalanski (From the chronicle of the monastery of the Capuchin Fathers, recorded by Fr. Roman Dudak)

December 11 — Celebrations of the Millennium at the Church of the Bernardine Fathers in Krakow, a procession and sermon * The same day in Makow Podhalanski — the *Odpust* on the Feast of Our Lady of Makow. Consecration of the altar, the dedication of the Stations of the Cross, the blessing of the polychromy painted by Prof. Maciej Makarewicz * December 12 — a solemn millennial ceremonial gathering in Bielsko-Biala, at the parish of Divine Providence, a concelebrated Mass with concluding remarks * December 16 — in the evening, at the cloistered convent of the Dominican Sisters at Grodek in Krakow. Participation in a retreat meeting for nurses. Then, he visited the meeting hall of the convent, and talked with the Sisters * December 18 — A sermon at the celebration of the 750th anniversary of the Dominicans * December 22 — He made his private retreat at the Albertine Sisters, in the house at Czerwony Pradnik in Krakow. On the same day — the conclusion of the retreat and words to the Sisters: "You have no idea what it means to see this Albertine habit on the streets of Krakow, or for that matter anywhere in Poland. This is the symbol of that extraordinary person (Brother Albert), the symbol of the Gospel ... A symbol of service, of service to people mostly ... abandoned and disinherited." (The Albertine Sisters) * December 23 — 7:00 a.m., at the residence chapel, a Mass with sermon for Mothers Superior and the sharing of the Christmas Eve *Oplatek*[11] * December 24 — 8:00 a.m., in the cathedral, participation in the "roraty" {early morning Advent service}, 12:00 midnight — Christmas Midnight Mass in Bienczyce.

December 25 — Sermon at the Jesuit Fathers in Krakow, in the church next to the seminary of the Order. The sermon relates to the com-

---

[11] See Glossary.

munique of the Polish Episcopate "on the threat to six theological seminaries":

> **Each theological seminary represents the most vital concern for the People of God ... Its existence, its inviolability and authenticity is our common concern ... Each priest is worth his weight in gold, because he is the guarantee of the continued existence of the life of God in churches, in dioceses, in us.**

The same day — in the chapel of the Albertine Brothers in Krakow, on the 50th anniversary of Brother Albert's death: "He died on Christmas day, as if our Eternal Father wanted to give everyone a sign: here a new saint is born for the heavens. For this is the kind of opinion that has surrounded Brother Albert for many years in Krakow and in Poland, despite the fact that the beatification process has just recently been put into motion". Then, he visited the cell of Brother Albert. He stood in silence, and upon leaving, said: "When you look at his photographs from when he was a boy up until when he was a young man —you see what love does to a person". Descending the stairs he said to an older sister: "I celebrate this anniversary with you, as no one else's". In the hall of the ill: "Brother Albert had a shelter, and I had Solvay". (The Albertine Sisters)

December 26 — Mass with homily for the Millennium, at the Church of St. Szczepan {Stephen} * December 27 — Mass with homily during the millennial celebrations in Mucharz * December 29 — At the Theological Seminary, Mass with homily for the conclusion of a closed retreat for high school graduates * December 29-30 — Committee for the Apostolate of the Laity. The first meeting: the concept of the apostolate of lay people in Vatican II; specific goals: completing the committee's membership (initially 5 bishops plus 4 priests) * December 30 — In the residence chapel, Mass with homily, with the participation of the members of the Committee of the Apostolate of the Laity and of religious sisters * December 31 — Homily at the Mariacki Basilica in Krakow: a look at the past Millennium — The presence of Christ in the past Millennium — Freedom and dialog — The Mother of God connects the past with the future... * The same day, at midnight — Mass with homily, singing of *Unto Your Protection*,[12] in the Basilica of the Franciscan Fathers.

---

[12] It is either an ancient Marian hymn and prayer or a hymn to God the Father that begins with the same words.

1967

January 2 — He wrote to Mieczyslaw Kotlarczyk:

I am very happy to hear of your successes, which are even more valuable, because they were gained through much effort and suffering. I wish you the most fulfilling integration of your workshop and the blossoming of your style of theatrical art, one which I also consider my own.

Karol

January 6 — At the Cathedral, a solemn Mass with a sermon for altar boys * Pope Paul VI established the Council for the Laity (*Consilium de Laicis*). At the very beginning of its existence, the Archbishop of Krakow was appointed as one of its consultants. His term lasted 5 years: he remained in the Council till 1976 — the time when it became the Pontifical Council for the Laity * January 10 — Residence chapel, a solemn act in connection with the diocesan process in the beatification cause of Father Pawel Smolikowski CR * Jan 11 — Krakow, the residence of the Archbishop. He opened an academic session for moral theologians. Subject: The Foundations of the Catholic Ethics of Marriage * January 13 — St. Florian's Church, Mass and sermon dedicated to the triptych of St. John the Baptist, which was recovered after the occupation * January 15 — Spends about two hours at the *Oplatek* organized by the Rosary Circle in Tyniec * On the same day: Krakow-Pradnik Czerwony: participated in the celebration of the 76th anniversary of the foundation of the Congregation of the Albertine Sisters (Print. *The Testimony of Total Dedication*. Krakow 1984) * January 16 — presided over the funeral ceremonies of Rev. Msgr. Michal Krzywicki, apostolic administrator in Drohiczyn. The Apostolic Administrator died on Friday, January 13. The severe winter and bad weather made it difficult to obtain the telephone connection. It was only on Sunday, January 15, in the evening that a telephone connection with Rev. Metropolitan was made. On that same evening he immediately left for Drohiczyn. The night was freezing cold and they (together with Rev. chaplain and their chauffeur) had to dig through snowdrifts 6 or 7 times. On Monday, January 16 at 10 a.m. Rev. Metropolitan arrived at the church in Drohiczyn. He began the Holy Mass immediately, presided over the ceremonies and led the funeral procession to a rather remote (considering the wintry season) cemetery. (Sister Leonia Sewartowska OSB) * January 17 — the Church of the Sisters of the Sacred Heart, a Mass in honor of the 125th anniversary of the birth of Jozef Pelczar * January 20 — at St. Andrew's Church, the announcement of the Primate's decree.

January 21 — Dominican Church in Krakow, an octave of prayer for unity among Christians.

"My Dear Brothers and Sisters in Christ — with these words, I turn to all of you, who are joined in the unity of the Catholic Church, as well as to you, dear Brothers and Sisters, who are still separated from it..." Further on — referring to the fragment of the Gospel about the centurion: "the power of humility is truly amazing ... The mystery of Christ coming to each of us ... to the community, to the Church ..." Christ's prayer for unity, which "we probably understand better now than any of the Apostles at the Last Supper ... When we are — still — the witnesses of our separation: Father, I am not worthy ... The Church, the whole of Christianity, took on the attitude of the publican ... on this humility is founded the hope of future unity.."

January 22 — A sermon during the millennial celebrations in Igolomia, with reference to Brother Albert, who was born here 120 years ago: "It is very good that we have you, Servant of God Adam-Albert; what a wonderful way you are showing us, not only in the past — but also into the future, because humility and love are never outdated."

January 24 — A *koleda* visit at the residential co-op of the former post office employees, in Krakow at Soltyka Street. Among them lived some ladies whom he knew from Wadowice, now retired postal workers. The Cardinal signed the visitors' book in the common room of the house (the material sent by Mr. Zdzislaw Ryn from Krakow): Dear Ladies, I have "discovered" your home with great joy and I am grateful for your invitation and reception. May the Lord bless all the tenants and members of the co-op. May the same spirit of love, peace and solidarity always dwell among you. + Karol Wojtyla, Archbishop Metropolitan of Krakow.

January 25 — At the Dominican Church in Krakow, the conclusion of the octave of prayer for unity among Christians — referring to the liturgy of the Word {Scripture readings}: "A great brightness dazzled him (St. Paul)." The bedazzlement with the truth of Redemption is the "basis of ecumenical prayer". Searching for the Church in every person; common prayer — the meeting point.

January 31 — At the cathedral in Lodz, a sermon at the coffin of the Bishop of Lodz, Michal Klepacz:

The shepherd of the diocese, its third bishop: rebuilt the seminary, rebuilt churches, took care of parishes; a person, who loved the truth — a scholar, focused on human problems; participated in the work of the Second Vatican Council; work in the Episcopate: he headed the Committee for Higher Education and Seminaries, he was a member of the mixed committee (talked with the representatives of the government), a person of dialogue, "it matters very much to all of us, my Brothers and Sisters, that this responsible and also very creative part of the activity of the late Bishop Michal Klepacz be well understood, that it will never be falsely interpreted by anyone."

February 21-23 — Lublin, the Tenth Week of Philosophy at KUL[1]: "Philosophy and Theology". A presentation by Karol Wojtyla inaugurating the Week: *Ethics and Polish Theology* (See *Znak*, no. 159/1967) * February 19-26 — Canonical visitation of the Nowa Huta-Bienczyce parish. * February 24 — Visiting the Bienczyce parish with the Papal envoy, Msgr. Agostino Casaroli, and Msgr. Andrzej Deskur.

March 2 — Mass at 3 Franciszkanska Street at 7:00 a.m. Later, a short meeting with the Sisters of the Holy Spirit * March 5-26 — Canonical visitation of the Nowa Huta-Pleszow parish.

March 24 — Participation in Good Friday services at the mountain of the Crucifixion in Kalwaria Zebrzydowska, a sermon * March 25 — Krakow, Wawel Cathedral. Holy Saturday: Mass and sermon * March 26 — Resurrection Mass in Nowa Huta:

> **Many a time since those days, people have "decreed" the death of Christ ... many a time, they have announced the death of God, saying: "there is no God", but they did not realize that then man and his intellect must fall into nonsense ... We who are gathered here today, we came in order to proclaim to this great new city — Nowa Huta — to these splendid blast furnaces and magnificent factory chimneys, and to these new residential blocks, that God lives — that Christ lives ... Once upon a time, three weak women gave testimony to this; today, there are probably over ten thousand men and women here, and all of us, following in the foot-steps of the three women, are giving the same testimony to the resurrection of Christ.**

The same day, Easter Sunday, at the Wawel Cathedral, the parishioners from Nowa Huta-Pleszow and Lubocza assembled to celebrate the conclusion of the visitations of Nowa Huta: "I would like to bid my farewells to you [after the period of visitations], and to tell you in leaving; those of you who do not have your own church, that is you from Pleszow, and you, too, from Bienczyce — that, behold, here is your church."

March — Various conferences for the opening or for the conclusion of retreats, for nurses, university students, secondary school students, doctors, lawyers, and others; also at the parish of Bienczyce.

April 2 — Mass with sermon at the Missionary Fathers at Stradom (the residence chapel), on the occasion of the jubilee of *Nasza Przeszlosc*[2] * April 5 — A day of recollection for priests at Jasna Gora (about 500 people). "We are celebrating today's Mass, in order to ask our Blessed Mother, the Queen of Poland, to visit the parishes of the

---

[1] Catholic University of Lublin
[2] "Our Past"

Archdiocese of Krakow in the guise of Her exquisite image of Jasna Gora." Through Mary, we are inviting Christ: "this is a joint invitation … Our wine jars are empty."[3] The same day — according to an account by Father Leon Knabit OSB — the Archbishop walked around the altar of the miraculous image, as is the custom of pilgrims. The surprised priests followed him. In the afternoon, he led the Stations of the Cross. The same day, at 8:00 p.m. at the Dominican Fathers in Krakow, a Mass with a sermon and an Easter repast for university students.

April 6 — A meeting of the Committee for the Apostolate of the Laity: the preparation of the participation of lay people in the Third Congress of the Apostolate of the Laity in Rome (Fall 1967), and a questionnaire before the Congress. The chairman (the Archbishop) is appointed as a consultant of the Consilium pro Laicis (for a term of nine years), and Prof. Swiezawski, a consultant of the committee "Iustitia et Pax." Four lay people are co-opted into the commission. * April 13-20 —He participated in the first session of the Council for the Laity. In his address he suggested that the program of work of the Council be adapted to the situation of those countries where the apostolate of lay people continued to develop despite the lack of organizational forms. He was an advocate of close cooperation with the Conferences of local Episcopates and informed {the Council} about the establishment of the Committee for the Apostolate of the Laity by the Conference of the Polish Episcopate * April 16 — participation in the concelebrated Mass together-er with the bishops from Consilium de Laicis, at the chapel of St. Martha in Rome. * April 18 — The committee "Iustitia et Pax" began its deliberations * April 20 — an audience with Pope Paul VI * April 22 — Mass in Rome, at the chapel of the Sisters of the Resurrection * April 23 — Mass with sermon at the chapel of the Felician Sisters in Rome * April 24 — the Vatican Radio, a chat on the subject of Consilium de Laicis * April 28 — Krakow, Mass with sermon at the residence chapel, for the Sisters of Our Lady of Mercy * April 29 — Mass with sermon at the residence chapel, for the Felician Sisters * The same day — at Wawel, the beginning of a novena before the Feast of St. Stanislaw. Sermon:

> **The testimony of St. Stanislaw told our countrymen, our ancestors once and for all — and it also tells us — that God's truth and God's laws are above man; that man has to make an effort to measure up to this truth and to these laws, even at the cost of his own life.**

April 30 — Jaworzno, anticipation of the visitation.

May 1 — At the Church of the Dominican Fathers — a sermon at

---

[3] Reference to Gospel account of the wedding feast at Cana.

the morning Mass: on praying the rosary, also on the 70th anniversary of the birth of Pope Paul VI — On the Synod of Bishops, which began without the Polish delegation ("The Primate did not receive a passport; two delegates, among them the Archbishop of Krakow, could not leave — the Polish Episcopate has the right and the obligation to be represented at the Synod by only these three representatives") — about the youth: "The young people have a very difficult spiritual road ahead of them" — about the visit of the image in the Archdiocese — about the seminary:

> This morning, I inaugurated a new school year at the Archbishop's Seminary in Krakow ... the number of seminarians exceeds 180 ... there are 45 in the first year of studies ... During the prayer of the rosary, please remember the intention of the seminarians called up for military service. According to existing legislation, they have a right to be released from this service ... nevertheless, the seminarians are still drafted during their time of studies at the seminary. Surely this is some sort of a test of their vocation ... Fortunately, a large majority comes through this test, but they do need support. [He recommends all of these matters as intentions for the prayers of the rosary.]

May 3[4] — Participated with the entire Polish Episcopate in the celebrations of the Feast of Our Lady Queen of Poland, in Czestochowa. Led the Eucharistic Liturgy at 7:00 p.m.

May 4 — At the Church of St. Florian in Krakow, a sermon during the observances of the patronal feast and the Feast of the Ascension:

> ...St. Florian was a witness of Christ. Ascending into Heaven, Our Lord said to his Apostles: "You will be my witnesses" — through them, in some measure, he said those words to all people ... In our times, which attempt to suggest so forcibly to man that his fate and calling is only mundane, that everything is temporal and ends with death, we read the testimony of St. Florian. We do so in order that ... we can make it our own.

May 6-10 — Visitation of the parish of St. Nicholas in Chrzanow. During the visit, on May 8 and May 10 — hearing of confessions.

May 8 — A session of the Council of the Pontifical Department of Theology. The Archbishop informs the members of the Council of the decision of the Congregation concerning the College (letter of April 27).

> It may be accepted that there are no obstacles or reservations as to doctorates; that the organization of studies should be worked out with the local Episcopate; the document of the Congregation assumes that doctorates are or will be conferred. The faculty already possesses the fundamental set of legal documents, as well as the basic team of professors... (From the minutes of the Departmental Council)

---

[4] See Glossary.

May 11 — At the Church of St. Anne, he spoke to university students on the subject of *Consilium de Laicis:* "...to the existing congregations [an explanation, what in reality the Roman congregations are: 'not so much departments, as profiles of the activity of the Church'] new organizations have been added." He introduced these organizations, and specifically the Council for the Laity: "For me, someone from a country where Catholic organizations have been virtually non-existent for twenty years, everything that was said there, and the entire way of thinking about the apostolate through organizations, was a way of thinking that was rooted in the past ... But for me there is no doubt that the lay apostolate is alive and exists." Further, about the apostolic calling of Christians, on the basis of the document of the Vatican Council on the apostolate of lay people.

May 12 — Participation in the opening of an exhibit dedicated to Brother Albert, organized by Rev. Prof. Schletz, in the house of the Missionary Fathers at Stradom in Krakow. "... All of Poland is interested in the person of Brother Albert, and they regard him as their own particular treasure. They are waiting for the moment when they will be able to talk of this Father of the destitute with the addition of 'Blessed and Saint' " (The Albertine Sisters)

May 12 — A sermon at St. Anne's Church for graduating secondary school students: the analogy between the Last Supper and the present congregation. "... life on this earth is given to each one of us as a test, an examination. Each of us is tested on the entirety of our life. 'I will not leave you orphaned'." * May 12 — The Vatican Radio broadcasts an interview with Archbishop Karol Wojtyla on the occasion of the 100th anniversary of the birth of Cardinal Adam Stefan Sapieha * May 13 — a meeting at his residence of "Nasza Przeszlosc"[5], dedicated to Cardinal Sapieha; at 6:00 p.m. in the cathedral — a Mass for the 100th anniversary of the birth of Cardinal Sapieha * May 14 — Procession from Wawel to Skalka. A sermon at Skalka: the history of Christianity — of the great holy bishops, including St. Stanislaw; and, against this historical backdrop, a reference to the 100th anniversary of the birth of Prince Cardinal Adam Stefan Sapieha. The sermon dedicated to the late Metropolitan was delivered during the celebration by Bishop Jerzy Ablewicz, Bishop Ordinary of Tarnow * The same day, at 5:15 p.m. — Holy Mass at the church on Szpitalna Street. Then, a meeting with the Sisters (an evening of religious songs) * May 17 — He headed the regional conference of priests, at the shrine in Kalwaria Zebrzydowska. The topic of deliberations was liturgical renewal. * May 18 — At the

---

[5] "Our Past".

Theological Seminary, after the adoration of the Blessed Sacrament by priests, a conference on the topic of the Council * May 20-21 — Participation in the millennial celebrations in Sosnowiec. * May 21 — at 4:00 p.m., the beginning of the canonical visitation in Jaworzno-Niedzieliska, Confirmation * May 25-31 — Canonical visitation of the parishes of St. Catherine and St. Adalbert in Jaworzno * May 25 - Jaworzno, the procession of Corpus Christi * May 28 — Piekary, a sermon for husbands * May 29 — Pope Paul VI announces the summoning of the consistory. Among the names of the new cardinals is the name of Archbishop Wojtyla.

May — regional conferences.

June 1 — At the residence chapel, at 7:00 a.m. — Holy Mass, then a short meeting with the Sisters of the Holy Spirit * The same day — Mass in the chapel, with the participation of the superiors of the religious orders of women; greetings after the Mass * June 1-4 — Visitation of the parish of St. Peter and St. Paul in Trzebinia * June 7 — At the residence chapel, Mass with sermon for the laity * June 9 — At the residence chapel, Mass with sermon for WIK.[6]

June 9 — A letter to the minister of culture, Lucjan Motyka, in connection with the liquidation of the Rhapsodic Theater:

Honorable Mister Minister!
I am writing to you, Honorable Minister, in connection with the announced liquidation of the Rhapsodic Theater in Krakow. The news of this has troubled many people, for whom the activity of the Theater is very dear; especially those who are aware of its difficult past, and its conspiratorial beginnings during the period of the Nazi occupation. It is precisely during this time that I was collaborating with this Theater. The Theater — under the direction of Dr. Mieczyslaw Kotlarczyk — played an important role in the service of Polish culture. It wants to keep performing this service, as indicated by its entire activity, both before 1953, and after 1956, when the Theater was reactivated after a few years of darkness. It is worth noting, that the few years during which the Theater was inoperative were perceived by society as a wrong inflicted against Polish culture. When the Theater was again reactivated, it was judged by society as a proper correction of this wrong.
This is exactly why I turn to you, Honorable Minister, because I am deeply troubled by the announcement of this second closing of the Rhapsodic Theater. I am also troubled by the removal of its deserving and meritorious founder and director. I consider this my utmost responsibility because I was involved in the founding of this theater during the difficult days of the occupation. This is why I maintain the conviction, that you,

---

[6] Higher Institute for Cathechesis

Honorable Minister, will also consider my voice in this matter and repeal the decision of the authorities of Krakow.

+ Karol Wojtyla
Archbishop Metropolitan

(A copy of the above letter was sent to director Kotlarczyk, with a short letter of explanation from Fr. Kuczkowski, the chancellor of the Curia).

June 10 — "Cardinal Karol Wojtyla celebrated Mass at the chapel of the Daughters of Charity of St. Vincent de Paul, in Krakow on Warszawska Street, on the occasion of the visit in Poland by Sister Suzannne Louise Guillemin, the Superior General of the Congregation of Daughters of Charity. In his sermon, the Archbishop stressed that native languages play an extremely important role in the liturgy. After Mass, he met with Mother General and then visited the sisters in the infirmary, where he spoke with the elderly and ill and gave them his blessing." (The Congregation of the Daughters of Charity) * June 10-11 — Participation in the millennial celebrations — at the cathedral in Lodz * June 11 — Pontifical Mass in Tum-Leczyca. * June 12 — Holy Mass at Jasna Gora * June 13 — a meeting of the Committee for the Apostolate of the Laity — a report on the work of the Roman bodies of the apostolate of the laity — *Consilium de Laicis, Iustitia et Pax* — the tasks of the committee — participation in the Congress of the Apostolate of the Laity * June 13 — Defense of the doctoral dissertation by Jerzy Galkowski *An Analysis of Moral Norms in John Duns Scott*. Promoter: Rev. Archbishop Karol Wojtyla. Galkowski — since 1962, an assistant professor in the Chair of Ethics at KUL * The same day, at 12:00 noon, in the auditorium of KUL, the academic community offers its congratulations to Archbishop Karol Wojtyla, on the occasion of his nomination as Cardinal * June 14-16 — Mass with sermon in Warsaw, at the chapel of the Ursuline Sisters SJK * June 17 — Krakow, at the residence chapel, Mass with sermon for the *Srodowisko*[7] (a name adopted by a group of former students, with whom he maintained friendship, contact and collaboration until the end. The Archbishop traveled with them on vacation excursions) * June 18 — Blessing of the church in Klaj, sermon * June 19 — at the residence chapel, a concelebrated Mass with sermon for the conclusion of the academic year of the Liturgical Study.

June 21 — A sermon at the Wawel Cathedral before the departure for the consistory, where "the Holy Father will accept the Archbishop of Krakow into the select company of the Cardinals of the Holy Roman Church".

About the predecessors — the Cardinals of the See of Krakow: "This is

---

[7] See Glossary.

therefore a tradition, albeit not an uninterrupted tradition, but one of the oldest traditions in Poland ... The Holy Father, Paul VI, did this certainly in consideration of the thousand years of Poland's Christianity ... Though this decision of the Holy Father fills me with gratitude and joy, I also accept it — please forgive me — with some fear. It is the fear of responsibility." Further, about the greatness of Cardinal Adam Stefan Sapieha, and about the Cardinal Primate. "The concept, the term of Cardinal, must evoke specific associations, it must be related to feelings of the greatest responsibility ... Will I be up to it?" Further, a request for prayer and for trust, a trust which "I base upon God (if I based it upon myself, I would be mad). I base this trust particularly upon the Mother of Christ ... into whose hands we totally submit ourselves ... so that She might use us, direct us, and permit us to rise to the challenge." A request for remaining united in prayer, particularly on June 29; about the other Cardinals, especially about Archbishop John Krol of Philadelphia. In conclusion: "Thus, my dear Brothers and Sisters, I undertake my pilgrimage from the grave of St. Stanislaw to the grave of St. Peter and — God willing, back from the grave of St. Peter to the grave of St. Stanislaw."

June 22 — Before his departure to Rome to receive his Cardinal's hat, the Archbishop went through a day of recollection at the shrine in Kalwaria Zebrzydowska. He wrote these words in the chronicle of the monastery of the Bernardine Fathers:

Before my departure for Rome for the observances of the 1900th anniversary of the martyrdom of the holy apostles Peter and Paul, the observances of which the Holy Father, Paul VI has connected with the consistory and the appointment of new Cardinals, I came to visit Our Lady of Kalwaria, with whom I have been connected since childhood. I came to entrust everything to her once again and anew.

June 23 — Departure for Rome, farewells * June 24 — Vienna, Mass at the residential chapel of Cardinal Konig * June 25 — Sunday, a small group of the Sisters of the Resurrection welcomed Cardinal — nominee Wojtyla at Roma-Termini. Sister Laura handed him a bouquet of red roses grown by Sister Margeryta from Balucki (from Warsaw) and brought by Mother Teresa. (From the diary of Mother Teresa Kalkstein, Superior General of the Sisters of the Resurrection) * Holy Mass at the Church of St. Stanislaw in Rome * June 26 — 7:00 a.m. — Mass at the Polish College in Rome; 9:30 a.m. — in the Aula Pia, the conferral of the nomination as Cardinal * June 27 — 7:00 a.m., Mass with sermon, at the chapel of the Felician Sisters in Rome * June 28 — 7:00 a.m., Mass with sermon at the chapel of the Ursuline Sisters in Rome * 5:00 p.m. — in the Sistine Chapel, the investiture of cardinals by Pope Paul VI * June 29 — 6:40 p.m. — at St. Peter's Square in Rome, concelebrated Mass with Pope Paul VI. In front of the Basilica the Holy Father announces the Year of Faith * As a newly created cardinal, he is appointed by Pope Paul VI member of the Congregation of the Council (dealing with matters of discipline of the diocesan clergy and the lay faithful) which was transformed into the Sacred Congregation for the Clergy on August 15th. Cardinal Wojtyla participated in the preparation of the document on the formation of the clergy. His proposals regarding the formation in the early years of priesthood were included in the *Circular Addressed to the Chairmen of the Conferences of Bishops Regarding the Permanent Formation of the Clergy, Especially Young Clergy*, dated November 4, 1969. The situation was similar with regard to Catechecal Directory published in 1971. His proposal to begin work on the preparation of the catechism of the Church, which he made at that time, was not taken into consideration. He actively participated in the works on the subsequent documents regarding councils of priests, parish ministry, associations of priests and the proper allocation of clergy (Cf. Rev. Jan Dyduch, *Kardynal Karol Wojtyla w sluzbie Kosciolowi Powszechnemu* {Karol Cardinal Wojtyla in the Service of the Universal Church}, Krakow 1998). At the same time he was appointed member of the Sacred Congregation for the Oriental Churches (Cf. Rev. Jan Dyduch, ibid., p.44) * June 30 — 6:30 p.m. — St. Paul's Basilica in Rome — Capella Papalis * On the same day at the Generalate of the Congregation of the Sisters of the Resurrection of Our Lord, the Holy Mass was celebrated by His Eminence Cardinal Wojtyla. Later — a cordial conversation with the Dignitary and his attendants. (From the diary of Mother Teresa Kalkstein, Superior General of the Sisters of the Resurrection)

July 2 — Rome, St. Stanislaw Church, a sermon after his nomination as Cardinal. He refered to a parable about the verification of human spiritual values: "a good tree cannot bear bad fruit".

But allow me today to speak and think of this calling as if it were my own. I am fully aware that each one of us must demonstrate his worth as he follows the path of his calling (this will determine whether he wins or loses his life). I know that I must prove myself in a specific way while I follow the path of my new calling, and that I must demonstrate my worth anew: this will determine whether I win or lose my life.

Today's Gospel speaks of the testing of man's worth; for man is continually faced with such a test. Each one of us has a certain calling and a certain task in life. A calling and a life's task are very important: each of them is the stage where the test of man's worth is performed. I must also go through the test of my worth as a person, and walk to the end of the path of my calling. This, my dear friends, is the reason why we have gathered here today ...

We are to pray together today, my dear Brothers and Sisters, so that the test of the worth of each one of us — and specifically the test of the worth of the new Polish cardinal — turns out well: that he fulfills his new calling just as Our Lord said in today's Gospel. And so, this is the theme of our prayer: this is what we came here for; and I sincerely ask for such a collective prayer from all of you.

As I ask you for such a prayer, I will at the same time try to identify the sources that make our prayer so effective. My dear Friends, the Lord Jesus used the analogy of a tree. We know this analogy very well: a tree always grows from some soil. The secret of a tree bearing fruit lies in the particular relationship that exists between the tree and the soil from which it grows. It is necessary then, to consider this comparative element in our contemplation.

July 3 — 12:45 p.m. — an audience at the Vatican with the Holy Father Paul VI for the entire Polish community in Rome and for the pilgrims led by His Eminence Cardinal Wojtyla. The Pope exhibited great cordiality for the new cardinal and for the entire nation. (From the diary of Mother Teresa Kalkstein, Superior General of the Sisters of the Resurrection) * July 7 — Holy Mass at Osjak * July 8 — Vienna, Kahlenberg, Holy Mass with sermon. * July 9 — The return of Archbishop Karol Wojtyla from Rome after receiving the title of Cardinal from Pope Paul VI.

July 9 — a welcoming sermon delivered in front of the Wawel Cathedral during his ingress, after his return from Rome:

Praised be Jesus Christ!
My dear Cracovians! I welcome you and bring you greetings and blessings from the Holy Father. I also bring back his gift with me: this gift I wear. And though, my dear friends, I wear this gift, this gift is not for me, but for the entire Church of Christ in Poland, and particularly for the Church of Krakow. (Applause)
It is a gift for the Church of St. Stanislaw, bishop and martyr, who — through his blood, was the first to identify the color red with the Bishops of Krakow. It is a gift for the Church of Adam Stefan Cardinal Sapieha and for all of the bishops and cardinals of the See of St. Stanislaw, where I am the tenth in line.
And, my dear Friends, it is a gift for you, for the Church of Krakow. I am happy that by the will of the Holy Father, I am able to use this gift to bring you joy and to serve you. Because from now on, I am supposed to serve you even more; I am to look even more to Christ, who came to this earth "not to be served, but to serve." Therefore, I will serve you even more; I will serve the entire Church in Poland; and also serve the entire Church of Christ on earth; but, in a most distinct way, I will serve — You.
That is why I ask you now very fervently, my dear Brothers and Sisters in the grace of the Sacrament of Baptism, my Brothers and Sisters in the grace of the religious calling and in the grace of the Sacrament of the Priesthood; my Brothers in the grace of the episcopacy, I ask you now to join me in the Most Holy Sacrifice of Christ. This will be the fullest expression of the unity that exists between us always, but especially on this day.
This is my plea: enter the Cathedral, surround it, so that we may pray together and offer ourselves together to Our Lord Jesus, near the altar of St. Stanislaw, the Bishop of Krakow and martyr. I cordially invite you into the Cathedral!
Praised be Jesus Christ!

July 9 — A sermon at the Wawel Cathedral during the celebrations of the ingress — a word of thanks for participation in the Mass; a word of thanks to the Bishop of Tarnow for celebrating it; a homage to the Primate:

> I come from the grave of St. Peter to the grave of St. Stanislaw with new duties, with new responsibilities. By placing a Cardinal's red biretta on my head, the Holy Father wanted to tell me that I should place an even greater value on blood. Above all, that I should value the Blood of my Redeemer; that for the price of Our Redeemer's Blood I should take a stand in the Church of God even if I have to spill my own blood ... A new ring: a union not only with my own Church of Krakow (a fear gathers inside me when I utter the words: "my own"), but also a union with the Universal Church ... I take on this new responsibility with a deep sense of humility. I know that I am a Zacchaeus ... Everyone must climb onto the wayside tree, meaning that he must wager everything on Grace — wager your whole soul on Grace!

The same day, a lunch for the cardinal. There, a toast from Prof. A. Vetulani:

> Somewhat intimidated, yet deeply touched, I raise this glass {toast} into the hands of Your Eminence, our respected and beloved Archshepherd. I am somewhat intimidated by the high honor, the highest in the church hierarchy, with which Your Eminence returned to Krakow today, to the Wawel hill, and by this so distinguished group of guests and table companions. I am touched, that of the representatives of the laity here assembled, I am the first one to speak to express my joy on the occasion of this great honor, which was bestowed by the great Pope Paul VI, and which through the person of His Eminence was bestowed upon the entire Polish nation.
>
> The fact that I was asked to speak, I owe to the friendship which Your Eminence has shared with me until now, and I hope that I will not put it at risk. This friendship goes back a long way, strengthened by the departure of him, who from all of my closest relatives, particularly loved Your Eminence. Our friendship is old, because our paths have been crossing for a long time, first, when Your Eminence, as a very young priest, led your profound retreats at the Church of St. Anne or at the Felician Sisters; next, when under the direction of the venerable Rev. Prof. Wicher and then Prof. Ingarden, you probed the secrets of philosophy, attaining in time the position of a docent and then of a university professor.
>
> As your much older friend, I spoke in this same hall after the celebrations of the consecration of Your Eminence to the rank of bishop, nine years ago. The late Archbishop Baziak shook his head, when upon delivering my congratulations I added an appeal that Your Eminence, even with your new duties, find time to continue educating a young generation of Polish, Catholic philosophers. The then Archshepherd of our diocese shook his head at that time, because he was aware that in time, Your Eminence would be charged with duties that are ever more honorable, but at the same time ever more difficult. And yet, once a thoroughbred scholar, and Your Eminence certainly was and is one, has tasted from the fount of learning, he will always remain faithful to it. A great professor is not one who writes voluminous works. In the history of Polish academics we have examples that no less important for the development of our culture are those who inspire our youth, who initiate enterprises of research, and who are the protectors of science. Even today, the study of the history of the Polish Church

is reaping the benefits of the important initiatives of Your Eminence. I will mention only one, an academic session organized with the participation of the scholars from the Catholic University of Lublin, and dedicated to the role of the Church of Krakow in the thousand-year history of our country. In this way, Your Eminence has been continuing the beautiful tradition, going back many centuries, of the heads of the diocese of Krakow, a recently renewed *Studium Generale* of the chancellors of the university in Krakow. Many shine among them, but one who shines particularly brightly is the great predecessor of Your Eminence, the watchful protector of university studies and the guardian of the purity of the faith, the first Polish Cardinal, Zbigniew Olesnicki. And although today, after the thorough laicization of our university, after the exclusion of the Department of Theology from within its walls, there remains not a trace of the official influence of the ordinaries of Krakow on the direction of knowledge nursed in this first, and for a long time the only, source of Polish learning, one does not have to hold an official position in order to be the mentor of minds searching for the truth. I wish Your Eminence from the bottom of my heart, and I believe in the possibility of realizing these wishes, that Your Eminence, despite all of the existing adversity, may reap the richest harvest from your academic activity, as an inspirer and protector of Polish Catholic learning; and that you may rejoice in its many-sided development, for the good of the Polish nation, which is ever faithful to the Church, today and in generations to come. (Archives of the Jagiellonian University)

July 10 — 7:30 a.m. – The chapel at 21 Kanoniczna Street, Mass with sermon, First Communion and Confirmation * July 11 — At the residence chapel, a Mass for Sisters of religious orders * July 25 — Przemysl, a session of the Pastoral Committee of the Episcopate, the topic: "Renewal according to the Vatican Council" — the chairman, Archbishop Boleslaw Kominek welcomed the newly created Cardinal Karol Wojtyla, who "was for many years our theologian, who, in the framework of the Committee, worked out the issue of dialogue within the Church." (From the minutes) * July 26 — Mass with sermon in Krasiczyn, the birthplace of Cardinal Adam Sapieha.

July 30 — Stryszawa. The Most Reverend Mother and His Excellency Rev. Archbishop Wojtyla, who came to visit His Eminence Cardinal Wyszynski, entered the refectory … In a very unaffected manner, standing all the time, he tasted some of the dishes offered by the Most Reverend Mother and, after a brief, pleasant conversation, left the refectory. It was a very moving experience when, after Benediction, in which both Dignitaries participated, they both stood on either side of the altar and simultaneously gave us their pastoral blessing. (From the chronicle of the religious house in Stryszawa).

July — a few days on the Drawa River.

August 1 — Bachledowka. (From 1965 to 1973, Stefan Cardinal Wyszynski spent a period of time in July-August of every year at the rest house of the Pauline Fathers in Bachledowka, not far from Zakopane, in the parish of Nowe Bystre. Cardinal Wojtyla always paid a visit to the Primate, once at the beginning of his stay — a welcoming one — and then, towards the end, on the occasion of his name-day {August 16}.)

"Reverend Cardinal Wojtyla arrived late at night, creating a family atmosphere. During dinner, he expressed his name-day greetings to the Cardinal Primate. Then there was an evening of songs. Following a service in the chapel and the singing of the Jasna Gora appeal — the Cardinal departed." {quote unattributed}

August 2 — a sermon at the Mariacki basilica, at the coffin of Rev. Msgr Ferdinand Machay:

The testament of the deceased, his portrait, his life, which "will become a subject of penetrating biographical analysis for future generations" — The road to Poland — The road to Poland through Christ — Participation in the history of Poland — Relationship to man — A pioneer of cultural life — A heart sensitive to any human misery — A pastor of the Mariacki basilica — A prayer, "that this great priest, this wonderful person, this great person (and this also refers to his physical stature), be taken by Mary by the hand and, like a small child (these werehis wishes), be led by her to her Son and to the Eternal Father."

August 13 — In Lesniow (diocese of Czestochowa), at the novitiate of the Pauline Fathers, the Cardinal led a Eucharistic Liturgy and delivers a sermon, in connection with the coronation of the statue of Our Lady of Lesniow; the coronation was performed by Cardinal Primate * August 14 — Holy Mass at the residence chapel, for the intentions of the Sisters. After Mass, in one of the halls of the palace, he spoke with the nuns * August 15 — At Ludzmierz, a young girl greeting the Cardinal recited a poem, whose final words express the expectation that he would now become Pope. This aroused general amusement. The Cardinal did not laugh — he bent down with dignity and kissed the little girl on the forehead (Antoni Mackowski) * August 15 — The Sacred Congregation called for by the Vatican Council became the Sacred Congregation for the Clergy. The make-up of the new Congregation remained unchanged * He participated in the *Odpust* for the Feast of the Ascension and for the first time entered the shrine in Kalwaria Zebrzydowska as a cardinal, in the new attire * The same day, at the Mariacki Basilica — A reminiscence of how, twenty-two years ago, Prince Cardinal Adam Stefan Sapieha, upon his return after having received a Cardinal's hat, came to the Mariacki Church:

"I can see this clearly before my eyes. I was then just a seminarian and I participated as a seminarian in the solemn service — and meeting. At that time the Wawel Cathedral was still closed. And right after I arrived at the Wawel Cathedral, I proceeded to the now-deceased Rev. Msgr. Ferdynand

Machay, the archpastor of the Mariacki basilica ... He invited me to the celebrations of the feast of the Ascension." Further on in the sermon, reflections on the mystery of the feast; this mystery says that "every person is called by God to the greatest glory ... This glory consists, above all, in the highest recognition of the dignity of man, the recognition by God the Creator." Still further, on the encyclical *Populorum progressio*. In the last part of the sermon, about the visitation of the image of the Mother of God: "this visitation is closely connected with the mystery of the sign: Mary is the sign of the Grace of God and is simultaneously the sign of our collaboration with the Grace of God."

August 18 — Kalwaria Zebrzydowska, "the funeral of the Mother of God".

I drove here for the funeral of the Mother of God, and when I keep hearing the shouts: Long live! Long live! — then I know the reason why the Mother of God could not have died, that she had to be taken up into heaven ... that her beloved Son had to perform this miracle ... Maybe this thought is not wholly and strictly theological, but it just came to me, so I am sharing it with you at the outset ... I would like to thank you and salute all of you very cordially, dear pilgrims — for I, too, am a pilgrim. I am pleased that we have met here year after year.

[Further on — about the pilgrimage of Pope Paul VI to Ephesus — The renewal of the Church is in the hands of Mary — The social encyclicals — *The Church in the modern world* — Perspectives — Inviting the Mother of God to the archdiocese. (The sermon was received with applause and with song.)]

August 19 — Kalwaria (Saturday, 7:00 a.m.), a Mass for the intention of the visitation of the archdiocese, announced in the previous day's sermon. "I came here today specifically to ask the Mother of God to come ... because I know from the experiences of many of the dioceses in Poland, that such a visitation is of great benefit for the souls." * The same day, at the cathedral in Plock, a Pontifical Mass with a sermon in honor of St. Stanislaw Kostka * August 20 — Plock-Rostkowo — Observances of the 400th anniversary of St. Stanislaw Kostka * August 22 — In Lublin, at the chapel at KUL, a sermon for the opening of lectures for the clergy * August 22-25 — A retreat for priests at the Theological Seminary in Krakow * August 25 — At the Church of the Capuchin Fathers, a visit in connection with the presence there, of the Superior General of the order, Father Clement of Vlissingen. Notes of the chronicler:

On the following day, Father General and Father Provincial went to visit Archbishop Cardinal Karol Wojtyla. Because August 21, 1967 was the 80th anniversary of the religious profession by the Servant of God, Brother Albert Chmielowski, in our church (at the Loretto chapel), it was decided that Father General would celebrate the Mass, and the Cardinal would deliver the sermon. The celebrations took place in the evening at 6:30 p.m., with a large turnout including the Albertine Sisters, the diocesan and the religious clergy, as well as the members of the Krakow chapter. In his sermon, His Eminence presented the profile of "the Apostle of the paupers of Krakow", comparing him to Father Damian, the apostle of lepers. A portion of his sermon was dedicated to the person of Father General. The Cardinal spoke for the second time during dinner, in the refectory of the order. At the end of his address, Father Provincial spoke up. He cordially thanked His Eminence, Father General, and the clergy for their participation in the holy ceremonies. (From the chronicle of the Krakow monastery of the Capuchin Fathers, Volume 5, copied by Father Andrzej Zebik)

A sermon relating to the parable on talents:

He did not bury his talents ... he discovered some deeper layer of truth, he arrived at a greater good, he found the greatest love — and he followed that ... Personally, I try to take advantage of every visit in Rome, in order to look after the matter of the beatification process of Brother Albert ... We would like to offer the Church and mankind something of great value.

August 26 — Jasna Gora, a sermon during the Pontifical High Mass: The human family — The activity of Pope Paul VI for the cause of peace — The intention of the Pope to visit Jasna Gora and the importance of this intention: "this is to stress that our family of a thousand years of history and Christianity, has a particular significance". Words to the Primate of Poland: "After the Second World War, and after the horrible occupation, we particularly needed the awareness that we were a family. Those were times of contempt and times of migration..." – The visitation in the archdiocese of Krakow ("the image of Our Lady of Czestochowa was not allowed to come ... and yet the visitation continues").

August 28 — Krakow, the Church of the Sisters of the Visitation. Mass and sermon on the Feast of St. Augustine.

August 29 — September 1 — The retreat of the Episcopate at Jasna Gora * August 31 — The liquidation of the Rhapsodic Theater. A letter to Mieczyslaw Kotlarczyk relates to this fact (undated):

For the past few days I was away at a visitation near Chrzanow. This is why I was unable to write sooner. I would like to tell you, nevertheless, that I consider what happened to the Rhapsodic Theater a great wrong done to the Polish culture. The motivation, which supposedly appeared in the press — that it was necessary to liquidate the Rhapsodic Theater because of the lack of room for Groteska {theater} — is inconsequential. Calling up an ideological rationalization proves — not for the first time, after all — that there is a lack of freedom in the sphere of ideology.

There is also a concern about you and your health, recently seriously threatened. I know you were prepared for this blow, but a blow is always a blow. I will try to call on you next week. I handed your letter over to the Primate. I include very sincere greetings and I commend all of you to God.

Karol

September 1 — Krakow, the Church of the Norbertine Sisters. The Feast of Blessed Bronislawa. After his return from Czestochowa, in the evening, Rev. Cardinal celebrated a Holy Mass and delivered a sermon.

September 2 — In Bienczyce, participation in a Mass for the opening of the school year * September 3 — A sermon in Bulowicc on the occasion of the 150th anniversary of the church, and the pastor's 30th anniversary of priesthood * September 4 — At the Augustinian Sisters in Krakow; the observances at the convent on the Feast of Our Lady of Consolation. The Cardinal visited the oratorium and talked individually with each sister. He agreed to a group picture in the oratorium. (Sister Alexandra Trojan OSA, the archivist of the Congregation) * September 10 — Pontifical High Mass in Gietrzwald, during which Cardinal Wyszynski performed the coronation of the image of Our Lady of Gietrzwald * September 13-14 — A meeting of the Committee for the Apostolate of the Laity. A probe on the topic of the first implementations of the Second Vatican Council — an overview of the duties of the apostolate of the laity in Poland; against this background, refining the plans of the Committee * September 15 — Holy Mass in the morning, with the participation of the Albertine Sisters (at the residence), and at 6:00 p.m. the opening of the apostolic process for Brother Albert Chmielowski: "... his person continues to give great testimony" * September 16 — Jasna Gora, a lecture for Catholic intellectuals on the topic of the theology of the laity (the participation of the Cardinal Primate and the Bishop of Czestochowa). The lecture is based on the documents of the Second Vatican Council, and refers to the work of the Committee of the Polish Episcopate for the Apostolate of the Laity, as well as to the approaching Congress of the Apostolate of the Laity in Rome. "... Every lay person becomes a witness by the power of the gifts which he received. He also becomes a living instrument of the mission of the Church; to the extent of Christ's gift" * September 16-18 — Visitation of the parish of Sucha. * September 16-24 — Participation in the Conciliar Week of Prayer in Bydgoszcz. During his stay in this city, he visited a Carmelite Convent on Spacerowa Street. He talked with the sisters about the joy of the Carmelite calling; and blessed a new foundation, so that it will fully develop (Sister Maria Jozefa of the Incarnation OCD) * September 17 — The celebrations connected with the Feast of the Exaltation of the Cross in Nowa Huta-Mogila.

> ...that is why we are all hurrying to the Feast of the Exaltation of the Cross — all of Nowa Huta, the tens of thousands of people, who carry their own crosses daily — because when we look at the cross, then we find ourselves in it; we find the deep truth about ourselves, about our spiritual elevation, which is in God.
> [Further on, about the need for giving individual witness to the eleva-

tion of man.]

September 19 — At St. Florian's church, Holy Mass with sermon for the opening of the retreat for the ill.

September 20 — The conclusion of the diocesan process of the Servant of God, Sister Faustina Kowalska:

> It began with a Mass by His Eminence Cardinal Karol Wojtyla at the Archbishop's chapel, for the intention of the Congregation of the Sisters of Our Lady of Mercy. In attendance were the sisters of the Krakow house, and the sisters from other houses of the Congregation.
>
> After the Mass, His Eminence invited Mother General and all of the sisters to his drawing-room; and at the request of Mother General, Szczesna Wlostowska, promised, that he would come today to "Jozefowo" for a moment after the conclusion of the session on the matter of the Servant of God, Sister Faustina.
>
> At 6:00 p.m., in this chapel, the information process on the life and virtues of the Servant of God, Sister Faustina, was solemnly concluded. The acts were signed by His Eminence Karol Cardinal Wojtyla and forwarded promptly to the Congregation in Rome.
>
> At 7:30 p.m., the priests — members of the Tribunal, came to "Jozefowo" for a moment of prayer at the grave of the Servant of God, Sister Faustina. His Eminence the Cardinal arrived a few minutes after 9:00 p.m. He prayed for a longer moment at the grave of the Servant of God, and then, in the company of the sisters, headed to the main hall of the Congregation. He talked with the sisters for several minutes, blessed them, and then departed. The goodness and the grace of the Cardinal was touching, the more so, that even though he was inundated with work, at a time just before his scheduled departure for the Synod in Rome, he found a moment to come to our house. (From the chronicle of the Congregation of the Sisters of Our Lady of Mercy)

The same day — a summing up of the meeting with missionaries at the Krakow Seminary. He pointed out the issues touched upon in the Primate's letter — the act of dedication at Jasna Gora and the renewal of the baptismal promises.

> [On the visitation of the image: it must be] a very deep religious act, not only externally, in the social dimension ... but also in our own, personal, internal dimension ... A person will not be able to give himself up to the Blessed Virgin as her own, unless he, himself, accepts it and makes it happen. In pastoral care, a person is never the object, but the conscious subject.
>
> [The second element: the union with the Post-Vatican II Church in the world. People] sense what the Spirit is saying to the Church ... Not only the intellectuals of a few of the superintellectual parishes in Krakow are awaiting it, but the simple folk are, too. The simple people are the ones who possess an even greater *sensus catholicus*: thus, they have an even better sense of what the Church in the modern world is.

September 24 — Holy Mass with sermon for the conclusion of the Vatican Council Week at the Church of the Missionary Fathers in Bydgoszcz at Szwederow. * September 25 — At the chapel of the Grey

Ursuline Sisters in Warsaw, Holy Mass with sermon for the participants of the Congress of the Apostolate of the Laity * September 2 - October 29 — the first ordinary session of the Synod of Bishops in Rome. The delegation of the Polish Episcopate to the conference was to have included: Cardinal Stefan Wyszynski, the Primate of Poland; Karol Wojtyla, Archbishop Metropolitan of Krakow; and Bishop Piotr Kalwa, the Ordinary of Lublin. Cardinal Karol Wojtyla did not leave for Rome. His action was taken to show solidarity with Cardinal Stefan Wyszynski, who was refused his passport by the civil authorities * September 30 — Referring to this incident, the Holy Father, Paul VI, declared in his speech inaugurating the work of the Synod: "We are sending special, heartfelt greetings to Cardinal Wyszynski, Cardinal Wojtyla, and the Polish bishops, who did not make their way to Rome, because they were in solidarity with their Primate. We are not hiding, either, our bitterness at this refusal, for no apparent reason. This is the same bitterness we feel at the harmful conditions that have been forced upon the Church in several countries, where its due freedom is denied; where the Church is the object of unjustified suspicion, moral and legal pressure, and anti-religious opposition". The same day, Bishop Wladyslaw Rubin read to the bishops in the Synod hall the letters, signed by the Holy Father, sent to both Cardinals: Stefan Wyszynski and Karol Wojtyla.

October 1 — 7:00 a.m., at the chapel of the Theological Seminary, a concelebrated Mass for the opening of the school year, a sermon about the Rosary, referring to the 70th birthday of the Pope * The same day, a sermon during the Mass for the intention of the Holy Father, Paul VI, on his 70th birthday — at the basilica of the Dominican Fathers in Krakow:

> [The Bishop of Rome is the head of the community of love:] If the essence of the Church is to perpetuate Christ, then his calling is, above all, to spread love, and to serve love.
> [The presence of Paul VI in the modern world:] ... He is present in all places where the most difficult human matters are being decided ... He is leading the actions which flow from the Vatican Council ... the great work of the renewal of the Church ... Let us think, what it means to be attentive to the inspirations of the Holy Spirit, to stand as he does in the center of all the matters regarding the Church and the world, to hold his hands on their pulse and to have an enormous, by human standards, responsibility for the matters of God and his people — just as he does.

October 3 — In the residence chapel, a concelebrated Mass for the opening of the Liturgical Study * October 3-4 — Canonical visitation of the Krzeszow parish * October 3 — The funeral of Col. Dr. Jan Cialowicz * October 4 — Rakowice, the funeral of Prof. Alexander Birkenmajer * October 8 — St. Anne's Church, a sermon for the inauguration of the academic year * October 11 — In the residence chapel, a Mass with a sermon for the Little Sisters Servants (the 5th anniversary of Vatican II and the Feast of the Motherhood of the Blessed Virgin) The Sisters of the Holy Spirit were also invited to attend the Mass * October 14 — Bienczyce, a Mass and a sermon for the inception of the construction of the church * October 15 — At Trzebnica, participation in a Pontifical Mass and closing remarks on the 700th anniversary of the canonization of St. Jadwiga * October 16 — a Pontifical Mass at the Wawel Cathedral on the 150th anniversary of the death of Tadeusz Kosciuszko; descent into the crypts.

October 17 — a sermon at the Church of the Sisters of the Visitation in Krakow, during the ceremonies honoring St. Mary Margaret Alacoque.

> **The road to understanding ["of the mystery hidden in God from the beginning through all eternity"] leads through love ... Love presumes understanding: we can only love that which we know. But at the same time, love frees our understanding and helps us to know better, deeper, more interiorly ... love, if it is to lead to a better understanding of God, to an entering into His mysteries, must be full of humility.**

October 18 — To the health service workers at the Church of the Felician Sisters in Krakow: "The harvest is great, but there are few workers". Progress, culture, civilization — "the maturing of the world through humanity". The maturity "from God", "due to the fact that God became a human being", "the great need of the people to discover that maturity — which the world has received from God — to also recognize it and realize it ... There are far too few ... people, in general, who can fully understand what value the world has, not solely of itself; but what value the world has because it was created by God, and because God became a human being." The apostolate of the laity understood by the Vatican Council as an extension of the mission of Christ. "To meet with suffering, that is a specific type of harvest." A calling.

October 18 — In response to the letters received from the Fathers of the Synod, three Polish bishops, among them Cardinal Karol Wojtyla, sent a proclamation in which, among others things, we read:

> **Joyful at the opportunity given to you by our Lord Jesus to collaborate with the Representative of Christ, for the good of the Holy Church, we, the delegates of the bishops of Poland, humbly send you our kiss of peace and unity. At the same time, we are convinced that even though we are absent in body, we are with you in spirit, and we are effectively helping in your work, by the grace of our suffering.**

October 20 — A sermon during the celebrations in honor of St. John of Kanty, at the academic Church of St. Anne — inauguration of the academic year of the theological schools in Krakow. In his sermon, he moved from the person of Rev. John of Kanty, professor and saint, to the reflections of today — The Vatican Council, in which we find "full affirmation of values and the world" and of "man in the world". Further on, about the Synod of bishops, which dealt with this matter, with "the truth about man and the truth about the world — ... the world and man cannot define themselves without reference to God". On the significance of theology in connection with the model of St. John of Kanty:

> it is necessary ... that we know well, what the value of our work is; the value of that workplace where, taking up the heritage of so many generations, so many centuries, we still labor to know the truth, to deepen the faith; to learn the truth, which is in the service of love; so that we, too, may be in the service of that love in this age, which like all ages, needs love above all else.

The same day, at 5:00 p.m., in the hall of the Metropolitan Seminary, the inauguration of the academic year * 7:30 p.m., at St. Anne's Church, the inauguration of the academic year for the theological institutions, a sermon * October 22 — 3:30 p.m., in Bronowice Male, the consecration of the enlarged parish chapel, a procession, the rosary * 6:30 p.m. — At St. Anne's Church, procession and veneration of the holy remains of St. John of Kanty * October 29 — 10:00 a.m., Wawel Cathedral, High Mass and sermon during the observances of the Feast of Christ the King: The conversation between Christ and Pilate — The truth about the Kingdom of God — The interpretation of the truth about this Kingdom, in terms of the Second Vatican Council, particularly in terms of the constitutions *on the Church* and *on the Church in the modern world* — The Apostolate of the Laity — The Synod of Bishops and the 4th World Congress of the Apostolate of the Laity — The Apostolate of the Laity as a need for Christian action * The same day, at 3:00 p.m., in Panewniki-Katowice. The diocese of Krakow accepts the visitation of our Lady — with the participation and sermon by Cardinal Primate. Sermon by Cardinal Karol Wojtyla: "Today, the diocese of Katowice is not passing the image on to us, it cannot pass it on. What it is passing on to us — after a test of will that lasted more than a year — are the fruits of spiritual victory; the victory of faith."

October 30 — Kalwaria Zebrzydowska. The Cardinal presided over the convention of priests from the entire archdiocese. Over 500 of them attended. This is what the Cardinal said to them:

> We are coming to the shrine in Kalwaria Zebrzydowska in anticipation of the peregrination of Our Lady through our archdiocese. We are anxious to fulfill this very pleasant obligation. We are starting from this place, where our faithful meet and where we meet with them. From here, we invite our Blessed Mother to come to visit all of our churches.

The same day. His first autograph as Cardinal, in Kalwaria Zebrzydowska:

On the 30th of October, in the company of several hundred priests of the Archdiocese of Krakow, we came on a pilgrimage to the Shrine in Kalwaria Zebrzydowska, to the altar of the Blessed Virgin, to commence the Visitation in the parishes and churches of the Archdiocese. The Icon of Our Lady of Czestochowa, which in the form of its Millennium copy has already visited half of the Polish dioceses, was not allowed to enter the diocese of Katowice more than a year ago (September 4, 1966). And this is why, yesterday (October 29, the Feast of Christ the King), this diocese, our neighboring one and one that is like a sister to us, was unable to pass this same image of the Visitation on to us. What it did pass on to us, however, was its spiritual gain from the year-long Visitation of Mary. This is what we receive today at the Shrine of Kalwaria Zebrzydowska — we, the priests and bishops of the archdiocese. We will begin next Saturday, November 4th, in the parish of Nowy Targ, together with all of the People of God.

May Our Lady of Kalwaria support us in this great deed.

A sermon to the priests and ministers in Kalwaria Zebrzydowska:

It might appear to some, that our celebrations of the Millennium were overly triumphal. In reality, hidden below the surface, was first and foremost a deep sense of responsibility for the future; a profound calling — from the bottom of our souls — that the future generations of the People of God living on our Polish soil may be worthy of the grace of baptism: that man would not fail in this *admirabile commertium*. So that those who are still young and callow today, those who are still in the cradle or under the heart of their mother, would not fail in the future.

Yesterday, in the presence of many tens of thousand of Silesians, at the parish of Panewniki-Katowice, we took over the visitation. The act of taking over was performed under the direction of Cardinal Primate himself, at the spacious Church of the Franciscan Fathers. It is a wonderful task, passed on to us by our neighboring, brotherly diocese of Katowice.

It was a very special transfer. Neither the diocese of Katowice, nor its Archshepherd, could pass the actual painting on to us. This painting which failed to arrive at the cathedral of Katowice more than a year ago (we know well under what circumstances), despite continuing efforts, requests, our insistence, and constant petitions from the clergy and the community of the diocese of Katowice; it did not reach any of the churches during more than a year-long visitation.

As far as we are concerned, we, too, have already been given a negative response in this matter. At the appropriate time I submitted a request delineating the proper reasons; reasons that, moreover, were very profound and fundamental, and flowed just as much from the sense of our religious freedom and its principles, as from the sense of well-understood patriotism. After all, it certainly is not beneficial, from the point of view of our nation, that the image of Our Lady of Czestochowa, the image of the visitation, cannot be freely seen by the faithful, with all due considerations of orderly assembly, in individual parishes; that it cannot be given its due respect by the faithful in individual parishes, but that it is kept "guarded" at Jasna Gora. In coming forward to the authorities, I had this circumstance chiefly in mind; that this state of affairs is like a painful wound for the entire society, and that we would like to contribute to the healing of this painful wound, to remove the inexpressibly sad state of affairs, which we view as a clear insult to things we hold holy, and in which, also, there is some sort of violation, some injury to the religious feelings of the people of faith — a huge majority in our nation — which is surely not in compliance with the premises of the constitution, nor with the premises of an authentic rule of law. In petitioning in this matter, I categorically stressed that the image of Our Lady of Czestochowa will be transported in a closed vehicle to the respective churches, that the greeting and farewell of the image will take place within church grounds and places of worship. I also mentioned that permitting the image to come to our archdiocese, and releasing it from Jasna Gora, will be for us a proof and a gauge of the religious freedom in our country, the freedom of which we wish to partake with full respect for public order.

I said all of this; I said it in your name and in the name of more than one and a half million faithful in the archdiocese. All of my efforts failed to meet with any understanding. The response, which I received last week on Thursday was signed by both of the heads of the People's Provincial Council and the city of Krakow. It was negative.

Nevertheless I turned again to the Chairman of the Council of Ministers {the Cabinet} in this matter, presenting even more thoroughly these rights, the rights of a moral and a social nature...

When it comes to that side of the problem, my Dear Brothers, I must say that the diocese of Silesia went through a very difficult test, and that from the very beginning it passed the test admirably. From the beginning, the bishops of Silesia, and later the priests, came forward in every deanery with requests for returning the painting to peregrination.

But I would like to repeat again what I said yesterday, while receiving the image in Katowice, that, first and foremost, our brotherly diocese of Silesia is for us a lesson for another reason: They taught us, in the span of more than a year, a new "style" of visitation. They discovered, moreover, its deepest content and its deepest meaning. When the visitations began without the image, as the Bishop-coadjutor of Katowice mentioned yesterday in his speech, the first days of the visitation seemed somehow dramatic. It is precisely they, who lived through those dramatic days. But with the passage of time, they realized that the visitation, in spite of the empty frame, still continues: The Mother of God is present!

The living faith of the people of God was victorious; the true content of that faith was manifested. It turned out that faith seeks its proper object in the *PERSON*. If faith venerates an image, then this is only a *cultus relativus*; above all faith venerates the *Person*, goes out to meet with the *Person*, associates with the *Person* of Mary; and through this association with her *Person* faith fulfills that *admirabile commertium*, which, as we conclude from yesterday's report by the Bishop of Katowice, took place so splendidly in our neighboring and brotherly diocese; because after all, we belong to the same Archdiocese of Krakow. The participation of the people of God by day and by night, and particularly the participation of men, as we heard, was huge. In some of the smaller parishes, the number of Holy Communions during the missions preceding the visitations was three times the number of parishioners. And, in all of the parishes, the number of Holy Communions exceeded to some degree the number of parishioners: *admirabile commertium....*

October — Participation in the jubilee celebrations in honor of St. John of Kanty, in Olkusz.

November 1 — 7:00 a.m., in Bolechowice. A High Mass and sermon for the conclusion of the visitation by the Blessed Mother at the parish * 3:30 p.m., Mass and homily, in the chapel at the Rakowicki cemetery in Krakow:

> When we come to every cemetery with faith, my Dear Friends, and we stand at the graves of our loved ones, both close and distant, then our eyes see a different picture of this above-ground city that descends into the graves and grows under the ground into piles of skeletons, grows with the dust of the earth, confirming the truth of these words: "Thou art dust, and unto dust thou shalt return". In the light of our faith, this picture changes into the picture of the Church, which here on this earth has its temporal form; it also has its temporal limits.

November 2 — 7:00 a.m., at the crypt of St. Leonard at Wawel — two Masses; 9:00 a.m. at the cathedral, participation in a Holy Mass, a solemn procession and the descent to the royal tombs * 4:00 p.m., in the chapel at the concentration camp in Oswiecim {Auschwitz}, a High Mass and sermon. Then, a procession through the camp to the cell of Maximilian Kolbe * November 4 — The first visitation of a parish — Nowy Targ — with the participation of Cardinal Primate and Cardinal Archbishop of Krakow. Greeting — The meaning of the empty frame — A reference to the mystery of Baptism — The visitation as a lesson of motherhood. "No one is excluded from this love, no one is pushed away — we all are visited and invited to the visitation."

November 6-11 — Participation in the visitation ceremonies at these localities: Odrowaz Podhalanski, Raba Wyzna, Czarny Dunajec, Waksmund, Ostrowsko, Lopuszna, Klikuszowa * November 12 — At the cathedral in Krakow, a Mass and a prayer for the beatification of Queen Jadwiga, and a sermon for male youth on the occasion of the celebrations in honor of St. Stanislaw Kostka, on the eve of the 400th anniversary of his death. "It is very significant, that we have two Stanislaws among the Polish saints, and one of them is the patron of the other ... For both of these saints, the glory of God was their goal of life." Reflection on the future of the assembled youth: "Remember St. Stanislaw, my young countrymen; remember, that he left all of you a particular spiritual heritage — 'I have been created for higher things'." November 11 — 7:30 p.m., a conference at the basilica of the Jesuit Fathers in Krakow.

"What does the hierarchy expect from the lay people, and what does it promise in return? ... It expects, above all, a new, mature and deep unity in Christ ... in three areas, corresponding to the triple character and mission of Christ." The prophetic mission — lay people are the first teachers of faith — the need for constant deepening. The priestly mission: the priestly character of marriage — of the family — social services — creating a climate of love. The kingly mission — The Christian style of work. What does it promise in return? — a deepening of community, service and assistance in acquainting the faithful with Christ, service in the sacraments, love for the life and labor of lay people.

November 13 — The Silesian Seminary. A commemorative meeting in honor of St. Stanislaw Kostka * November 16 — Krakow, residence of the Archbishop. Symposium on ecumenism in theological teaching * November 16 — Katowice, participation in the funeral of Bishop Stanislaw Adamski * November 17 — At the Franciscans in Krakow, a Mass with sermon in honor of Blessed Salomea * November 18-26 — Visitation of the parish of St. Szczepan * November 25 — Poronin — sermon during the visitation of the Mother of God * November 29 — Mass in the cathedral, a procession of mourning to the graves of the most recently departed archshepherds (Dunajewski, Puzyna, Sapieha, Baziak) * At 8:00 p.m., in the Church of St. Szczepan, a conference for students.

The last decade of November — Ingress of the Cardinal in Wadowice.

Fragment of a sermon, delivered in November:

> **For the past few days, I was unable to participate in the visitations of the parishes by Our Lady of Czestochowa, because of several days of meetings of bishops in Warsaw. Therefore, the Reverend Bishops from Krakow were unable to participate in the visitations ...**
> **We are establishing here the foundations of a new Millennium of faith. In establishing the foundations, we are already thinking about the house which will be built upon these foundations by future generations. We are thinking of building a house, the house of God, from which He will not be evicted: as it sometimes happens in the new houses of the people, where there is no room for God.**

December 1 — Participation in the celebrations connected with the visitation in Maruszyna and Ludzmierz * December 2 — Visitation in Makow Podhalanski * December 5 — Holy Mass for Jozef Pilsudski, at the crypt of St. Leonard * December 8 — Siekierczyna — the ancestral home of Cardinal Jan Krol {of Philadelphia} (Cardinal Karol Wojtyla arrived with the Bishop of Tarnow, Jerzy Ablewicz):

> **Once upon a time, tens of years ago, the ancestors, the parents of Cardinal Jan Krol, departed from this country to a new world ... In leaving this place and going to seek bread across the ocean, they brought to their new homeland something even more valuable than bread. Namely, they brought with them their healthy souls and unblemished blood ... they brought these values in dowry to their new homeland, a place which gave them bread in return.**

> **One day I told the representatives of Polonia[8]: Your Cardinal Krol will be unable to make his ingress to his familial parish — I will do it for him … I celebrated my ingress at my familial parish in Wadowice less than two weeks ago … I have arrived here, today, in his place.**

December 12 — At the Church of St. Sczczepan, Holy Mass with sermon for the deceased professors of the Jagiellonian University * December 13 — At St. Anne's Church, a concelebrated Holy Mass with academic chaplains, during the celebrations of the 200th anniversary of the canonization of St. John of Kanty * December 14 — At the Church of St. Szczepan, a meeting with pre-schoolers * December 15 — At the convent of the cloistered Dominican Sisters in Krakow at Grodek. The Cardinal arrived at the gate of the convent in order to participate in the conclusion of the retreat for nurses. He was unable to get in for some time, because he could neither get a response when he knocked at the gate, nor when he rang the bell. The Sisters were not expecting him and so they were at choir. The Cardinal stayed briefly after Mass. The Sisters were embarrassed and the conversation did not flow well. The Cardinal was in a hurry and he did not touch his prepared dinner. (From the chronicle of the convent) * December 17 — At Wawel Cathedral, the opening remarks at a Mass celebrated by Cardinal Primate. A day of recollection for the national chaplains of various social, professional and specialist groups — Krakow, at the residence of the Cardinal — with the participation of Cardinal Primate and the bishops * December 19 — Participation in the celebrations of the visitation of the image of Our Lady of Czestochowa in Gronie * December 20 — Church of St. Szczepan, 6:00 p.m., Mass for single people; 8:00 p.m., *Oplatek[9]* for university students * December 23 — Participation in the visitation celebrations in the parishes of Mietustwo and Nowe Bystre * December 24 — Bienczyce, Christmas Midnight Mass and sermon * December 27 — At the chapel of the Theological Seminary, a concelebrated Holy Mass with the representatives of the most recent graduating classes of priests * December 29 — At the residence chapel, Holy Mass with sermon for married couples * The same day, a meeting of the Committee for the Apostolate of the Laity. The co-opting of new members (married couples). A report of the Polish delegation at the Congress of the Apostolate of the Laity in Rome, delivered by Father Stanislaw Rylko — Report from the Congress — The plan of action (for several years). The first meeting of the Committee with the Pastoral Committee. A meeting of the participants of the Congress * December 30 — In the chapel of the Theological Seminary, Holy Mass with sermon at the retreat for graduating secondary school students.

---

[8] A Polish community outside of Poland
[9] See Glossary.

December 31 — At the Carmelite Fathers at Piasek — participation in a service, sermon:

We are also the witnesses of an attack on faith, of the formation of other tendencies, other attitudes; of the position that faith and religion are unworthy of a human being; that faith and religion are contrary to a person's reason and, above all, to his social, mundane involvement. We are witnesses, at every step, of the so-called process of secularization, which in large part is calculated, and forced upon people of faith. They are still being given the right to profess their faith, but in a way that forces them to keep their religious convictions in the depths of their souls, within the four walls of their homes, or in church. But anywhere else — no. Public life will be overtaken by the process of secularization; and so: not in schools, not in hospitals, not in summer camps — and all this in spite of the fact that there are believers everywhere; that children who go to summer camps are children of believers and are religious themselves.

Today, the concept of the bastion of Christianity belongs in the past, it is a historical concept. Today, it is necessary to transform that concept into a conscious maturity of faith, into its mature profession, into witnesses for Christ everywhere. This bastion certainly exists in all of us: it is the heritage of a thousand years. I speak about this, my Dear Friends, in the first year of the new Millennium, which the Holy Father, Paul VI, has labeled the Year of Faith.

December 31 — At the Church of the Franciscan Fathers — Holy Mass and sermon. "Just a moment ago the clocks struck midnight ... this was the first moment of the year that has just begun." The name Jesus means Savior. "This name — according to the words of the prophet Isaiah ... also means the Master of Peace." The 1st day of January, by the will of Pope Paul VI — The Day of Prayer for Peace.

1968

Beginning of January. As he was skiing down the Kasprowy Mountain, the Cardinal lost his commemorative breviary. A search over several days by many people did not produce results. The breviary was found by Maria Chalubinska, who upon learning about Cardinal's distress, set out next day at dawn on her own search. She turned in the lost article to the GOPR {Volunteer Mountain Rescue Service}, with the request that it be returned to the owner. (An account by Prof. Dr. Aniela Chalubinska)

January 5 — 7:00 a.m., Holy Mass with homily in the chapel of the Grey Ursuline Sisters in Zakopane * January 7 — Krakow, 11:15 a.m., Residence chapel, Mass and sermon for the participants of the Congress of the Apostolate of the Laity in Rome * January 9 — Wadowice, Holy Mass with sermon and the funeral of Rev. Canon Jan Pawela * January 10-11 — Krakow, residence of the Archbishop. A symposium dedicated to the analysis of the starting point of the kinetic and theological argument for the existence of God * January 14 — Visitation of the Blessed Mother at the church in Staniatki. Homily pertaining to the carol "Wesola Nowina"[1] and to the reading about Cana of Galilee: "Our Holy Mother is concerned about our needs, so ordinarily and simply ... The Church is concerned about the temporal good of humankind: Pope Paul VI established the New Year's Day as the Day of Peace, he desires that justice and peace would prevail in the lives of men. He is also concerned about the hungry whose number in the world is increasing * Same day — 2:00 p.m., in the residence at 3 Franciszkanska Street, *koleda*,[2] the Cardinal visited all the tenants of the Archbishop's residence * 5:00 p.m., visitation of the image in Komorowice * Jan 15 — 6:00 p.m., Mass at the Wawel Cathedral for the repose of the soul of Andrzej Malkowski, founder of Polish Scouting * Jan 21 — 8:00 a.m., Mass in the Chapel of the Sisters of the Holy Spirit at 6 Lotnicza Street in Krakow. Afterwards, a meeting with professors, engineers and doctors frequenting this chapel * 12:00 noon — Nowa Huta-Pleszow — blessing of the restored interior of the church, sermon * Same day — 7:00 p.m., at the basilica of the Dominicans during the week of prayers for unity among Christians, a homily in reference to the words of the Centurion: "Father, I am not worthy ...":

> **Even here, in this church in Krakow, we are witnesses, still, of a division. Father, I am not worthy, I am still not worthy, I still have not matured! Thus speaks the Church of Christ in the 20th century. Thus speaks the**

---

[1] "Joyful News"
[2] See Glossary.

Church in the words of its supreme Pontiff and all of its most eminent shepherds in all Christian communities. However, simultaneously, these words of the Centurion from Capernaum awaken our hope for maturing and for maturity. For Jesus Christ entered under the roof of this man precisely because he said "I am not worthy ..."

Jan 27 — 11:00 a.m., a celebration at the seminary of the Missionary Fathers * 6:00 p.m., St. Anne's Church, a funeral Mass for the soul of prof. Jan Olbrycht. * Jan 28 — 10:00 a.m., Residence chapel, Mass with sermon for marriage counselors. * January 30 — Participation in visitation celebrations in Spytkowice near Zator * January 31 — 7:00 a.m., Residence chapel, Mass for the intention of Stas Rybicki.

In addition, during this time, Masses with homilies at the residence chapel for nuns of various religious orders.

February 3 - 7:00 a.m., Residence chapel, Mass for the intention of Marysia Ciesielska * 10:00 a.m. — at the residence, a conference of priest-deans * Visitation — 4:30 p.m. in Piotrowice, 6:00 p.m. — in Przeciszow * February 5 — 8:00 p.m., departure for Rome. * February 6 — 8:00 a.m., Mass at the nunciature[3] in Vienna * February 7 — Mass at the Polish College in Rome * February 8 — 12 - Masses at the nuns' convent * February 13 — Mass in the chapel of the Palazzo S. Calisto for members of *Consilium de Laicis*. * February 14 — 4:30 p.m., at the Institute of Church Studies, participated in the lecture given by F. Bednarski OP, subject: The dynamic formulation of the law of nature by St. Thomas Aquinas * February 17 — Holy Mass at the Polish College for Cardinal Pierre Veuillot * February 18 — 11:00 a.m., at the Polish College, concelebrated Mass with student priests. Homily.

February 18 — Rome, assumption of the duties of the titular bishop of the Church of San Cesareo in Palatio. The oldest information about this church (an ancient diaconate) reaches back to the 7th century. The church was neglected and abandoned in the Middle Ages and consecrated anew ca. 1600 during the pontificate of Pope Clement VIII. The election of Pope St. Sergius I was held here in 687 and Eugene III in 1145. The rector of the church, at the time when Cardinal Wojtyla assumed his duties of the titular bishop, was Msgr. Orlandi of the Sacred Congregation for the Sacraments. He was the one to greet the Cardinal at the entrance to the church on February 18th, at 5:00 p.m. The homily by the Cardinal: St. Peter and St. Paul — faith — gratitude for the gift of faith. The thousand year long sowing of the seeds of faith on the Polish soil ("I unite myself with my beloved homeland, my beloved Krakow"), Mother of God: "It is such a strange coincidence that today

---

[3] Vatican diplomatic mission

is also the day when she [the Blessed Mother] is visiting the parish where I was born and baptized, where I received the gift of faith." The second part of the speech — in Italian, was not preserved * On the same day — a dated, congratulatory letter to Fr. Wladyslaw Skwirczynski of the Reformed Franciscan Province, on the occasion of the 50th anniversary of his religious life * February 19 — 10:45 a.m., Rome — Mass at Basilica Vaticana ad Caput St. Pietri. * 11:45 a.m. — an audience with Pope Paul VI * In the afternoon — a visit and tour of the Institute of Church Studies in Rome, Via Mecenate 37, a note in the guest book: "I thank God for the work that has already been done here, which I admire, and ask His blessing upon the further development of this work through the intercession of the Seat of Wisdom" * February 20-27 — Rome, Felician Sisters chapel, Masses and sermons * February 28 — 7:00 a.m., Mass at the Polish College, blessing of ashes * 10:00 p.m. — Departure for Krakow * February 29 — Mass at the nunciature in Vienna.

March 1 — Mass at the nunciature in Vienna * March 2 — Beginning of the visitation of the parish of All Saints in Krakow, Mass and sermon for the intention of the deceased parishioners * March 4 — 7:30 a.m., Mass at the Wawel — at the tomb of St. Stanislaw * March 3-4 — Visitation of the Virgin Mary at St. Kazimierz parish in Krakow.

March 4 — Sermon at St. Kazimierz church during the visitation of the Virgin Mary in the first Krakow parish. Before Mass, the Holy Father's benediction was read. "When I asked the Holy Father for His blessing, I heard: 'Write it in Polish and we will send it.' That is why I received the text in Polish, which the Bishop-celebrant was kind enough to read here before the Mass." Sermon pertaining to St. Kazimierz:

> It is not sufficient to say: he had a devotion to the Holy Mother; he burned with it, and his devotion was faith and love ...
> It is necessary to raise the level of faith very high ... it must be mature, responsible and alive ... It is necessary to raise the level of hope, because modern man is often near despair ... And it is necessary to raise the level of love in human souls. For there is too much indifference in our lives, too much alienation, hostility, hatred ... That is why She comes to visit the parish.

March 5 — 8:00 a.m., Mass at the Wawel on the 850th anniversary of the death of bishop Maurus (the bishop of Krakow in the years 1109-1118); descent to St. Leonard's crypt * March 7 — (the Feast of St. Thomas Aquinas), 6:00 p.m., Mass and sermon at the Dominicans * March 8 — Anniversary of the ingress, Mass in the residence chapel * 8:30 p.m., youth retreat at the chapel of the Ursuline Sisters * March 9 —4:30 p.m., Nowa Gora, conclusion of the visitation * 6:00 p.m. in Trzebinia — commencement of the visitation * March 10 — Tarnow, in the morning, participated in the celebrations of Bishop Jerzy Ablewicz's

25th anniversary of the ordination to the priesthood * On the same day — Lamentations {Lenten services} at St. Peter and St. Paul Church, a speech to the Living Rosary group and a visit at the Sisters of St. Clare * March 11 — 5:00 p.m., conclusion of the visitation in Chrzanow-Koscielec * 6:00 p.m. — Commencement of the visitation in Byczyna. * March 13 — 9:00 a.m., A regional conference of priests in Rabka * March 14 — Zakopane, "Ksiezowka", 9:00 a.m., regional conference * March 15 — At St. Joseph's Church (convent of the Bernardine Sisters) in Krakow, on the occasion of the canonical visitation at All Saints Parish and the Feast of St. Joseph. The Provincial Superior of the Bernardine Fathers was present. From the homily by the Cardinal:

> I must state that I often visit this church. It has some special climate. I would say it is the climate of St. Joseph's reverie about God. I do not know, my dear Brothers and Sisters who so often come to this church, whether you also experience the same sensation... However I always depart from this church with this feeling. It may not fulfill special pastoral functions ... however, it fulfills a particular pastoral function, very necessary in Krakow, that is — it gives the faithful from all of Krakow the opportunity to pray, to visit Jesus Christ in the Blessed Sacrament ... I think that the Bernardine Sisters, who live and pray behind these walls, contribute to this. We do not see their faces, but we hear their prayers ... we think about their lives ... that they have given up everything else in order to gaze upon the Lord through their faith, to reflect upon the mysteries of God.

March 16 — 5:00 p.m., conclusion of the visitation in Siersza * 6:00 p.m., commencement of the visitation in Szczakowa * 8:00 p.m., Mass at St. Anne's Church in Krakow for the conclusion of a student's retreat, sermon on the topic of the parable of the prodigal son — "Jesus Christ surely told this parable only in order to forbid us, humankind, once and for all to think and speak about ourselves as wastrel children, as wastrel sons."

March 17 — 11:45 a.m., at the Franciscans, homily for the blind * On the same day, participation in an academic retreat at the Dominican church * March 18 — 6:30 p.m., Franciscans — retreat for secondary school students * 8:20 p.m., sermon for the commencement of an academic retreat at the Church of Our Lady of Lourdes in Krakow: "Why did I come here? ... because I always come to academic retreats ... I came in order to pray with you, because you came here to pray and in order to pray for academic youth — for you." * March 19 — A visit at the Bernardine Sisters in Krakow * March 23 — 4:30 p.m., participation in the celebrations concluding the visitation in Szczyrk * 6:00 p.m., commencement of the visitation in Bielsko-Biala at The Divine Providence parish * March 26 — 4:30 p.m., conclusion of the visitation in Filipowice * 6:00 p.m., commencement of the visitation in Jelen * March 28 —Siedlce. He participated in the funeral of Bishop Ignacy

Swirski * 7:15 p.m., at St. Anne's Church, participation in a retreat for scholars * March 29 — 7:30 p.m., at the Franciscans, homily during a retreat for single people * 8:15 p.m., at the Jesuits' Church, participation in an academic retreat * March 30 — Visitation celebrations in Chrzanow. * March 31 —visitation celebrations in Dabrowa Narodowa * On the same day, at the Church of St. Peter and St. Paul, blessing of small children * 4:00 p.m., in the chapel of the Ursuline Sisters, a retreat for literati — a conference.

April 3 - Homily during a retreat for speech and hearing impaired at St. Peter and St. Paul Church * April 5 — Tarnow, Holy Mass and sermon during a celebration of the 25th anniversary of Bishop Jerzy Ablewicz's ordination to the priesthood. (KW 46) * April 6 — 11:00 a.m., at the residence, scholastic session devoted to Edith Stein, with a presentation read by Prof. R. Ingarden * 7:30 p.m., participation in a student retreat at St. Anne's Church * April 7 — He ordained 22 deacons — alumni of the Theological Seminary in Krakow * 8:00 p.m., the Church of St. Joseph (the Church of the Bernardine Sisters), a retreat for lawyers * April 8 —5:30 p.m., visitation at the Church of the Redemptorists * April 9 — 6:00 p.m., visitation of the parish in Prokocim * At 7:30 p.m., participation in a retreat for young people at St. Peter and St. Paul Church * April 10 —7:30 p.m., retreat for doctors at the Church of the Felician Sisters at Smolensk.

April 11 — Holy Thursday, morning Mass, blessing of oils. Homily:

We are here as a community of the Church of the Krakow Archdiocese, we are reliving your departure, Lord Jesus, through torment and death, through participation in our human death; we await Your Resurrection ... We are all preparing jointly — as the Catholic Church, a part of Your Church — to participate in Your Resurrection; in this spiritual power, with which You, the Lord's anointed One, wish to bestow on us all. You wish to anoint Your people gathered in Your Church. Amen.

April 13 — Krakow, Rev. Cardinal Wojtyla visited the monastery of the Sisters of St. Clare.

April 14 — The Sunday of the Lord's Resurrection {Easter} — concelebrated Mass at the Wawel Cathedral, in the presence of representatives of all Krakow parishes. Homily: the mystery of the empty tomb, the mystery of life:

"Do not be surprised that I invite you here, that I urge you to come here frequently, because in this Cathedral a profession of faith in the Resurrection has a particular meaning ... It was already centuries ago that our forefathers built their faith in rebirth, in the reunion of everything that was divided: our Country was then divided ... The Church ... continues to work so that humanity should become our leaven.

4:30 p.m., blessing of a cornerstone for a new church under the patronage of St. Nicholas in Witanowice near Wadowice, sermon * April 15 — 7:00 p.m., participation in the celebrations of the visitation in Miedzybrodzie Bialskie * April 17 — 7:00 p.m., visitation in Czaniec * April 20 — 6:00 p.m., visitation in Witkowice * 7:00 p.m. — in Kety * April 21 — The cathedral in Tarnow, he consecrates bishop Piotr Bednarczyk * April 24 — 9:00 a.m., Zywiec-Zablocie, interdeanery conference * 6:00 p.m., solemn visitation in Grojec * 7:00 p.m. — in Poreba Wielka * April 26 — 9:00 a.m., Nowy Targ — interdeanery conference, Mass with sermon for its commencement * April 28 — 9:00 a.m., Gniezno, Pontifical High Mass and a concluding address for the Feast of St. Wojciech {Adalbert} * Same day — 7:00 p.m., academic conference at the Jesuit Fathers in Torun: *The Apostolate of the Laity* (see "Ateneum Kaplanskie" 71/1968) * April 29 — 7:00 a.m., the Church of the Sisters of St. Elizabeth, Mass with sermon * Same day — Krakow, Wawel — beginning of a novena before the Feast of St. Stanislaw:

> **As your Bishop, I feel particularly responsible for having St. Stanislaw venerated in Krakow and in Poland ... I welcome the representatives of St. Anne's Parish, St. Nicholas's Parish and the parish of Przegorzaly, and shall humbly beg that they venerate St. Stanislaw as he deserves to be. That he be venerated all the more, as he meets with more affronts {hurled at him} during the last decades.**

May 1 — 8 a.m., administered the Sacrament of Confirmation to the extremely ill 9-year-old Marcin Sikorski at his home, at 2 Bracka Street in Krakow * On the same day at 7 p.m., in Kety-Podlesie, he participated in the visitation celebrations * May 2 — 8 p.m., visitation in Brzeszcze * May 3 — Jasna Gora, homily delivered on the ramparts: The greeting of Jesus Christ and of the Virgin Mary — The presence of Mary in the history of the People of God on the Polish soil — The significance of the date of May 3[4] — "In order for the transformations taking place in the history of societies and in the history of our nation to bring about some good, it is necessary that man be physically strong and spiritually healthy; that man remain sober, capable of love ... and capable of meeting the living God" — Thanksgiving for the visitation of the archdiocese — Trust — Maternal bondage — The closing of the image ("the removal of the image does not signify Your absence") — the Mother.

May 4 — 5:00 p.m., celebrations of the visitation in Jawiszowice * May 5 — Visitation of the Blessed Mother at the Church of St. Florian; from the sermon:

---

[4] See Glossary.

In Her — such is our faith and our hope — God returns to the world, even though He is rejected by man and by the world, God comes to man, enters the world in order to bring new value to everything that He has created.

May 6 — In Wadowice, Mass with homily for the commencement of a deanery conference * Same day — Borek Falecki, Krakow, visitation of the Virgin Mary:

This great factory — this chemical plant — was also my workplace during the four years of the Nazi occupation. During these years of occupation, it was here that my priestly calling was formed. First, my calling was shaped at the stone quarry, and later, finally, here, at the soda plant, within reach of this church. I say, "this", but I really mean "that one" ... It was an old, small, wooden church, really a barrack (...) Always, when I pass by this factory, especially near the boiler room of this factory, I am reminded of this path of my life and the deciding moments of my life. At such times I recall a small book in a blue cover. As a worker of Solvay, I took it along with a slice of bread for the afternoon or the night shift (it was more difficult to read on the morning shift). On the afternoon shift, I often read this book. It was titled, *Treatise on the Perfect Devotion to the Blessed Virgin Mary*; the author was Louis Maria Grignon de Montfort, a blessed at that time, later elevated to the honors of the altar as saint (...) I read it so much that it was entirely stained with soda on the covers and inside. I remember these soda stains well, because they are an important element of my entire inner life. From this book I learned the real meaning of the devotion to Our Lady. I had this devotion as a child, and as a high school student and at the university — but this book, which I read here, taught me the true essence and depth of this devotion.

May 7 — Received in audience Maria Felicja Pastoors OSU, Mother General of the Order of the Ursuline Sisters of the Roman Union * On the same day — celebrations of the visitation of the image in Skotniki * May 9 — 6:00 p.m., Tyniec. He took part in the visitation of the Blessed Mother. He concelebrated a Mass and preached a sermon. He visited a seriously ill man.

May 10 — The Visitation of Our Lady at the Good Shepherd Parish at Pradnik in Krakow:

This parish, located at the crossing of important roads, toils and agonizes, because although it has a roof overhead, it may well be said that this roof is more like that of a shack than of a place of worship. Even a flock of sheep has a right to a roof overhead ... Mother of God ... look at this church. Mother of the Good Shepherd and Mother of the Parish of the Good Shepherd, obtain for us a church that the parishioners have for so long desired, for which they have strived, and to which they have a right ... Forgive me, Blessed Mother, for burdening You with this plea, but you are accustomed to this.

The same day, he visited Mother General at the convent of the Ursuline Sisters.

May 11 — Czestochowa, day of prayer for university students. In the evening, a key-note address for the opening of the celebration.

May 12 — Krakow, Procession from Wawel to Skalka. Homily at Skalka — Reading of the telegram from the Primate — Welcome of bishops and pilgrims: the moral unity of the People of God, the jubilee year of faith; "this retreat is especially dear to me, because at that moment, on the 29th of June last year, when Pope Paul VI announced the Year of Faith to the Church, I was in Rome and together with the Holy Father I concelebrated the Holy Mass in front of St. Peter's Basilica" — Analysis of the attributes of faith — Threats to faith —

> **Here before these relics of St. Stanislaw, I wish to say that all the hardships and perils to which our living faith is exposed produce ... a special opportunity to shape that faith. We must all tell this to ourselves and not be afraid. God is more powerful than people! If someone really wishes to live his faith (...) he will be equal to the task! ... May the knowledge of who we are accompany us everywhere; let us not lower our heads — let us look everyone in the eye.**

Same day — 5:00 p.m., participation in the conclusion of the visitation of the parish of St. Catherine in Krakow * 6:00 p.m., Mass at Plaszow for the beginning of the visitation * May 13. Visitation of Our Lady in Nowa Huta-Bienczyce * May 14 — At the Parish of the Immaculate Conception in Krakow-Azory (led by the Reformed Franciscans), during the celebrations of the visitation, the Cardinal said a Holy Mass and preached a sermon. The parishioners experienced the visitation very deeply — there were many conversions, in some cases — after many years of being away from the Church. About 10 thousand faithful participated * May 16 — Celebrations of the visitation in Rajcza * May 17 — Sermon for the beginning of a deanery conference in Bielsko-Biala * Same day — participation in the visitation in Ujsoly * May 19 — Dabrowa Gornicza, a speech for the conclusion of the ceremony of the coronation of the statue of Our Lady of the Angels * On the same day — 7:00 p.m., celebrations of the visitation in Zwardon * May 25 — Participation in the visitation in Ciecina.

May 26 — 9:30 a.m., a sermon in Piekary Slaskie during the pilgrimage of men and male youth: Greeting of the pilgrims — Thanks for the welcome. Closeness:

> **I feel most deeply a pilgrim's bond with you. Physical labor is not unknown to me. I understand you well, dear Brothers...**
>
> **I cannot refrain from confessing to you my special secret. Last year I spoke here during a retreat for husbands ... I am a little embarrassed to say this — but it is difficult not to admit this. Well, it so happened that when I returned to Krakow on the next day, I found a letter from the Holy Father on my desk, appointing the Metropolitan Archbishop of Krakow to the**

College of Cardinals ... I consider Our Lady of Piekary the special patroness of my new appointment.

In the continuation of the homily: The Lord's Ascension and the Descent of the Holy Spirit — Faith is the continuation of Christ's presence — A day dedicated to mass media ("we will ask that, through the mass media, the word of truth (...) contribute to the advancement of mankind and the enlightenment of souls (...) so that these media not serve exclusively for the infiltration of slander and accusations against religion and the Church" — Mediation by Mary; the visitation — also about the ties between Silesia and Krakow.

On the same day — 6:30 p.m., participation in the visitation celebrations in Radziechowice * May 29 — 7 p.m., concluding remarks in Debniki at the observance of the 400th anniversary of St. Francis de Sales * May 30 — In Czestochowa, a day of prayer for priests from the Institute of Interior Life — he talked about the life of priests in the Church and for the Church.

May 31 — The visitation of Our Lady in Zywiec-Zablocie parish. Homily: The truth about the Kingdom of Christ and the Kingdom of Mary —

Therefore, if we are spiritually mature people, mature Christians, then no captivity threatens us. The source of man's subordination is his surrender to material things, to that which is transitory; subjugation to the external conditions, economic and material. These are surely the conditions of human life, but they cannot restrict a person internally. The source of freedom is the spirit, this spirit is awakened in us by Christ, and His Mother molds it in her maternal way.

June 2 — Descent of the Holy Spirit {Pentecost}. Wawel Cathedral — concelebrated Mass with the priests of the deaneries of Chrzanow and Jaworzno (in conjunction with the visitation).

In our times especially, it is necessary for us to beseech for joy. For we get the impression that joy has vanished from our lives: that sadness has increased, that despair has intensified. Today we sense a certain anxiety in the younger generation of all of mankind because youth is eager for joy — and joy goes hand in hand with truth and purity of heart.

At 12 noon — Mass on Szpitalna Street. Later, a meeting with the Sisters of the Holy Spirit (a midday meal, photographs) * Same day — 5:30 p.m., participation in the celebrations of the visitation in Zywiec * 7:00 p.m., visitation in Miedzybrodzie Bialskie.

June 3 — Wawel — Holy Mass on the 5th anniversary of the death of Pope John XXIII:

We ask ... that his true legacy may survive ... he was the Pope of peace; ... he began in the Church ... the era of ecumenism; ... he prayed that unity

and harmony among all people of good will draw nearer and become reality.

Same day — 8:00 p.m., participation in the visitation celebrations in Lekawica near Zywiec * June 5 — 7:00 p.m., visitation in Rychwald * June 6 — 3:00 p.m., Trzebinia, a visit during a retreat for the sick * Same day — 7:00 p.m., visitation in Lodygowice * June 7 — 7:00 p.m., visitation in Zarzecze.

June 8 — Sandomierz, sermon at the celebrations of the 150th anniversary of the Sandomierz diocese. He spoke referring to the beginning of the Sandomierz diocese during the partitions:[5]

> During this difficult period — as attested to by unbiased works and textbooks on history — the Catholic Church played an important role on the Polish soil, when it comes to maintaining unity with the nation ... The bishops and priests never allowed the Church to become Russified ... The unity of the Church with the nation possessed and still possesses a fundamental significance both for the Polish nation and for the Church.

June 9 — 8:00 a.m. Sandomierz, a sermon for children and a homily during a High Mass celebrated by Bishop Franciszek Jop * June 10 — Meeting of the Council of the Pontifical Department of Theology. During the opening of the meeting, he introduces several issues to be resolved:

> More explicit specification of the relationship of the Department to the Krakow Theological Seminary. This relationship should be formulated more precisely and more flexibly ... up to the separation of the personal union of the rector of the seminary and the dean of the Department ... Closer designation of conditions and progress of studies "ad gradum", not only for the licentiate, but also for the doctorate ... Closer association of the professors and theology students of other theological institutes in Krakow with our Department, especially through academic sessions, combined lectures etc ... The studies and additional training of priests involved in pastoral work should be connected with the department ... (From the minutes of the Council of the Department)

June 11 — The Church of St. Florian in Krakow, Cardinal Wojtyla administered the Sacrament of Confirmation to the children, students of the 6th grade. On the same day Rev. Kazimierz Orzechowski (a former actor of Warsaw theaters) celebrated his first Holy Mass. A photograph of the Cardinal and the kneeling newly ordained priest survived (Cf. The chronicle of St. Florian parish).

June 12 — 3:00 p.m.. Franciscan Fathers monastery — meeting for the conclusion of catechization.

---

[5] Poland was partitioned by Austria, Prussia and Russia from 1772 until 1918, and from 1795 lost its political, but not its cultural or national, identity.

June 13 — Feast of Corpus Christi, Wawel Cathedral:

It is also the concern and obligation of every bishop to care for the public worship of the Blessed Sacrament. Therefore, ever since I became the Archbishop Metropolitan of Krakow, and it is already my fifth year — I have striven and made attempts that everywhere in the diocese, in all parishes, Eucharistic processions could be organized. I also make efforts to ensure that they be held with dignity in Krakow, for this is after all the fruit of our spiritual attitude, our spiritual attitude towards the Blessed Sacrament.

Since these matters require the permission of the secular authorities, as well as coordination with them, we try — when coordinating the route of the procession of the Blessed Sacrament in the various parishes — to ensure that the route is over roads that are decent, not over the worst roads, uneven and potholed, but over normal streets. We ask for this everywhere, because we feel a close connection even between the external appearance of the road or street on which the procession walks, and what we feel internally towards Our Lord Jesus concealed in the Eucharist. If there is anything unsuitable, if these are inappropriate roads, we ask that the processions not be held on them. There are enough roads and enough streets to find appropriate ones for this one day. This is how it is, as far as parish processions in various churches are concerned. A parish procession is also held at Wawel, around the cathedral on the Wawel hill.

But a special obligation of a bishop in the seat of his see is to lead the central procession — not only the parish ones. Such a central procession was always led by my late most esteemed predecessor, Prince Adam Cardinal Sapieha, from Wawel along Grodzka Street to the Market Square, and from the Market Square along Grodzka Street back to Wawel. He led it as long as he could and as long as his strength permitted.

We know that after his death in 1951 there was a hiatus: there was a vacancy in the Metropolitan See. Ever since — by the will of God and by the appointment of the Holy Father — I took over that see, I have been petitioning every year to be able to lead, as the Metropolitan Archbishop of Krakow, that central procession. I petition the authorities and present to them strictly religious arguments in support of this. If you could see, my dear brothers and sisters, the stacks of documents and letters in the Metropolitan Curia which have been sent in this matter! And I did not stop at writing; I also suggested meetings and I did talk with them — I am convinced that among people of good will, matters should be arranged and can be arranged on the basis of dialogue.

However, when all of this had no effect, I appealed to the central {national} authorities last year. In the current year I reminded the central authorities of my appeal, and I also sent representatives of the Metropolitan Chapter. They returned with the opinion and conviction that "the Archbishop of Krakow — and it was additionally said, especially since he became a Cardinal — should not encounter any obstacles in leading the procession beyond the precincts of the Wawel hill" (the procession on Wawel hill, of course, is only a parochial procession). On the basis of this — as we judged — assurance, a communique was read in the churches of Krakow last Sunday that the central procession, led by the Archbishop of Krakow, will not encounter obstacles in going beyond the precincts of the Wawel hill. Of course, there still remained the matter of the route for the procession. I mentioned that the traditional road of this principal cathedral procession had led from the Wawel to the Market Square and back to the cathedral. But whenever I proposed the itinerary of the cathedral procession, I always added, that I am willing to negotiate on the subject of the route. Arguments were presented, however, that there are "impediments to transportation." To be sure, according to our deep conviction, there are no impediments to transportation. It is difficult for us to understand such arguments when we see that on days that are not holidays such as Corpus Christi, but on ordinary days, there are various marches on these same streets and on the Market Square: it is sufficient to mention the traditional Krakow "Lajkonik".[6] It is strange that this is not considered an impediment to transportation. However, in order to express our good will, I presented the possibility of an alternate route for the Wawel procession which I would lead. Unfortunately, in the last few days, already after the Sunday when the communique was announced, all of my proposals were turned down. Because of this today's central procession will not take place.

I tell you this, my dear Brothers and Sisters, dear inhabitants of Krakow, with great sadness. I beg your pardon for this — that we exposed you to this disappointment, but believe me — ever since I became bishop, I have done everything I could in order that a public expression of the Devotion of the Blessed Sacrament could be celebrated in our town. I did everything and I intend to continue to do so.

I apologize to all here who are disappointed that this procession will not take place. Yesterday evening, we notified all the churches with a new communique about the cancellation of the procession, however, the communication, sent at such a late time, naturally could not reach everyone and inform them effectively. Only some learned about it.

I trust that you will forgive me; I trust also that if time allows, you will be able to take part in processions in other parishes to which you belong (after all, the Wawel parish is small, with only a hundred and several score souls), since some processions — as I have been informed, take place in the afternoon. However, I want to promise you here that I shall continue all endeavors in order for this act of the Eucharistic cult, i.e. the Corpus Christi procession, led by the bishop in his diocesan see, to take place in Krakow. We are certain that in striving to achieve this, along the ways that are available to us, we really do strive for the common good. It is for the common good, after all, that people have a sense of freedom of worship, and also of public worship.

Same day — 5:30 p.m., Pewel Slemienska — participation in the celebrations of the visitation * June 16 — 6:30 a.m. — visitation of the parish of Zywiec — Sporysz * On the same day, at the cathedral in Katowice — delivered a speech at the celebration of Bishop Juliusz Bieniek's 50th anniversary of the ordination to the priesthood * June 17 — Kokoszyce (diocese of Katowice), meeting of the Pastoral Committee of the Polish Episcopate: Archbishop Boleslaw Kominek, *Signs of the Times for the Contemporary Church;* Bishop Ignacy Tokarczuk, *Contemporary Secularization — Manifestations and*

---

[6] "Lajkonik" is a man in Tatar dress riding a hobby horse through the streets, during a crowd-drawing festival commemorating the repulsion of the invading Tatars in the 13th century.

Evaluation; discussion followed; Bishop Jerzy Modzelewski, *The Pastoral Model of the Diocesan Curia*; Bishop Wilhelm Pluta, *The Pastoral Minimum and Maximum of the Contemporary Parish*; discussion followed * On the same day — 6:00 p.m., participation in the celebrations of the visitation in Piaski Wielkie * 7:00 p.m., visitation in Biezanow * June 1 — Second day of meetings of the Pastoral Committee of the Polish Episcopate. The program of preaching — the pastoral plan, a draft of a pastoral letter (sent back for revision). In the afternoon, Cardinal Karol Wojtyla talked to the participants about the work of the Committee of the Apostolate of the Laity — many points in common, the need of cooperation * June 19 — 12:00 noon, address for the end of the academic year at the Liturgical Institute * On the same day, Krakow, the parish of Corpus Christi. A visitation of Our Lady * June 21 — 5:00 p.m., participation in the celebrations of the visitation in Lagiewniki * At 12:00 noon, in the Church of St. Anne, a Mass with sermon to secondary school students for the end of the school year * June 22 — 7:00 a.m., in the chapel of the Ursuline Sisters, a Mass with sermon for the Higher Catechetic Institute for the end of the academic year * June 22 —After the scandalous incident in the parish of Nowa Biala which led to turmoil during the Corpus Christi procession, he addressed a letter to the parish, in which he announced that the people who pushed the priest carrying a monstrance with the Holy Eucharist are being punished with excommunication. In his letter he also quoted the code of penal law which provided for the punishment of persons disturbing religious services and ordered that propitiatory services be held.

June 22-27 — Social Week at KUL and a presentation: *Social Function of Catholic Universities*; in print: "A Catholic University. Concept and Postulates" (for the 50th anniversary of KUL), ZN KUL 11 (1968) 3-4, 13-16.

June 24-25 - Meeting of the Committee for the Apostolate of the Laity — analysis of comments on the subject of the Congress — program of work on the *Directory of the Apostolate of the Laity* in Poland, on the aspects of the apostolate of the Sacrament of Confirmation, on contacts with the diocese, on pastoral councils with the participation of the laity.

June 27 — 8 a.m., Sluzewo (Wroclaw diocese), concelebrated Holy Mass with priests — colleagues from the same year of ordination, on the 20th anniversary of the ordination. Homily:

> **Please allow, dear parishioners of Sluzewo, that first we introduce ourselves. Today we came to visit the pastor of your parish on the 20th anniversary of priesthood, and when we visit the pastor, we visit the parish at the same time. We came because we are colleagues. This bond began for us at**

the Theological Seminary in Krakow, first as seminarians, later as priests, and today we would like to express it in this parish ... You see that there is not a large group of us, because we come from very difficult times. And there were not many vocations at that time, and not many possibilities of realizing your calling to the priesthood at a seminary, but for this reason we appreciate this vocation all the more and thank God for the priesthood which we were able to achieve (...) We are happy that our comradely and priestly celebration at the parish church in Sluzewo will take place before the image of Our Lady of Perpetual Help. This image reminds us of the one upon which we gazed in the seminary chapel, as it hung on the main pillar. It can be said that Mary looked at our preparations for the priesthood, that she assisted all of our endeavors, which brought us closer to our ministry. We experienced then her Mystery of Perpetual Help. This is how the picture of Our Lady of Perpetual Help spoke to us at the seminary. (Fr. Andrzej Bazinski, colleague from studies, pastor in Sluzewo)

June 28 — Gniezno, 109th plenary conference of the Polish Episcopate, 7:00 p.m. — Mass at the tomb of St. Wojciech {Adalbert} * 7:00 p.m., participation in group prayer at the tomb of St. Wojciech * June 29 — 6:00 p.m. in Poznan, Pontifical Mass and coronation of the image of the Blessed Mother (performed by Cardinal Wyszynski) * June 30 — 8:00 a.m., in Sroda Wielkopolska, Mass with sermon * 10:30 a.m. in Poznan, participation in the celebrations of the 1000th anniversary of the diocese.

In addition, during the month of June — 2 baptisms, a marriage, jubilees of priesthood, concelebrated Mass with priests of the class of 1966/67, Confirmation.

During the summer of this year, kayak trip on the Sasek Lake.

July 2 — 5:30 p.m., participation in celebrations of the visitation in Budzow * 7:00 p.m., visitation in Tarnawa Dolna * July 4 — 10:30 a.m., sermon at Wawel for the sextons of the Archdiocese of Krakow * Same day — 5:30 p.m., participation in the visitation at Huciska * 7:00 p.m., celebrations of the visitation in Palcza * July 5 — At the chapel of the Ursuline Sisters, Mass with sermon on the occasion of the meeting of the provincial chapter.

July 5. On August 20, the Congregation of the Sisters of Our Lady of Mercy will celebrate the 100th anniversary of the founding of its house in Krakow, called "Jozefow" {Josephinum}. Today Mother Superior, Jolanta Wozniak, with her assistant, Sr. Matea Slowinska, invited His Eminence the Cardinal to celebrate a Mass in the chapel of the sisters for the intention of the Congregation on the day of its anniversary. His Eminence accepted the invitation. (From the chronicle of the Congregation)

July 6 — 6:30 p.m., the Mariacki Church, participation in a Mass on the 25th anniversary of the death of Gen. Wladyslaw Sikorski[7] * Same day — 7:30 p.m., Zembrzyce, visitation of the Blessed Mother.

May our trust be greater than our own needs: may it be wider than our human hearts ... may it resemble the great apostolic trust of the two courageous men Cyril and Methodius — the holy apostles of the Slavic peoples.

July 7 — Installation of the miraculous image of Our Lady of Ruda in Jasien near Ustrzyki Dolne (Bieszczady, Przemysl diocese). Cardinal Wojtyla led the solemn concelebrated Mass in front of the church and spoke after the Mass. (Synopsis of his speech in "Chronicle of the Przemysl Diocese" 1968, Bk. 6, p. 165). The same day at 7:00 p.m., participation in the visitation celebrations in Trybsz * July 11 — 7:00 p.m., visitation in Kacwin * July 11-27 — Kayak excursion with the *Srodowisko*: the Sasek lake - Wielbark, private Masses, sometimes with sermons * July 25 — Promulgation of the encyclical *Humanae Vitae* * July 27 — 6:00 p.m., commencement of the visitation in Mszana Dolna * July 31 — Bachledowka — he offered his best wishes to Cardinal Wyszynski on the occasion of the feast of his patron saint.

August 11 — Pontifical Holy Mass and coronation of the image of Our Lady in Swieta Lipka (performed by Cardinal Wyszynski) * August 12 — Conclusion of the visitation celebrations in Jablonka, 6:00 p.m., beginning of the visitation in Gdow * August 13 — 7:00 a.m., participation in the celebrations of the 300th anniversary of the shrine in Kalwaria Paclawska * August 14 — Niegowic — visitation of Our Lady. "Having once arrived here as a Vicar, I celebrated my first High Mass. I am happy that today I am able to repeat this as your bishop."

August 15 — The Mariacki Basilica in Krakow, sermon: How the Second Vatican Council looks at Our Lady — She is a witness of the meeting of God and humanity — the reaffirmation of the value of human life in the encyclical *Humanae vitae*:

The evidence of God's truth and the evidence of the truth about man on the subject of the beginning of human life, the transmission of life, which, in human terms, is a difficult one ... This matter cannot be diminished. But if it appears to be difficult, if it creates great demands for man in the realm of morality, it is necessary to answer these demands ... The Church, being acutely aware — of the weakness and sinfulness of man, never rejects the truth about the greatness of man.

On this day — visitation of Our Lady of Ludzmierz (5th anniversary of the coronation of the image), sermon: two images in the liturgy: the Visitation of St. Elizabeth and the Assumption of Our Lady. "These two

---

[7] Chief of staff of the Polish armed forces fighting with the Allies during WWII, later the premier of the Polish government in exile, died in a plane crash under suspicious circumstances; the British government was long suspected of having a hand in his death. See the 1970's British drama entitled *The Soldiers*.

images become as one: one arises from the other." Further, the analysis of the first verses of the *Magnificat*:

> **Always at the beginning of one's endeavors, thoughts and words, it is necessary to seek the glory of God and the worship of God. Such a sentiment seems to be foreign to people of the present day and to the contemporary civilization — we see this in our homeland ... This is why our civilization is sad, it becomes more and more often some totality without a beginning ... it becomes as if a hollow trunk without start or finish ... The human spirit will always seek an ultimate joy, consolation and rest: but this can be found only in God.**

August 16 — Kalwaria Zebrzydowska, "The Funeral of Our Lady" (the Cardinal is greeted with applause and the singing of "Sto lat."[8] His speech consists of extended prayer intentions, offered to the faithful, and joint prayers: for the Holy Father — Hail Mary...; for the Church in Poland — Hail Mary...; for ourselves and all pilgrims — Hail Mary...; thanksgiving for the visitation of the archdiocese — Hail Mary...; for the young people — Hail Mary...; for the church in Nowa Huta — Hail Mary...; for the deceased — Hail Mary...; Eternal rest grant unto them... Benediction — the Promises of Jasna Gora * August 17 — 7:00 a.m. Private Mass in Kalwaria Zebrzydowska.

August 17 — 6:00 p.m., Skarzysko-Kamienna, on the way to Studzianna for the celebrations of the coronation of the Image of Our Lady:

> **I was very happy today when at the place where one passes Skarzysko, there stood Rev. Monsignor, the pastor of your parish, who stopped my vehicle and invited me: "please come to visit us." [Regarding the celebrations in honor of Our Lady, in which he participated]: It would be difficult for me to list all the places — shrines, all the celebrations and coronations, in which I as bishop have participated ... we go north, south, east and west, seeking places, which for many generations and centuries were centers of special worship and love for the Mother of God. [In continuation — about the apostolic work of St. Jacek {Hyacinth} — about the Mother of God in the constitution of the Vatican Council on the Church, and about the concern for Christ's legacy]: We are convinced, and in the course of life's experiences we are all the more persuaded, that this path of salvation and this method of salvation, which Christ taught us, of the salvation which He constantly accomplishes, cannot be replaced with anything else.**

August 18 — 11:00 a.m., in Studzianna, Pontifical High Mass and coronation of the image of Our Lady of the Holy Family * 7:00 p.m., at the Church of the Dominican Fathers in Krakow, Pontifical Holy Mass with procession and blessing with the relics of St. Jacek * August 19 —

---

[8] May you live 100 years

5:00 p.m., visitation celebrations in Podleze * 6:00 p.m., Lazany — visitation of Our Lady.

> **When I say the Krakow Church, I want to say by this that it is also a part of the Universal Church ... when we receive the Body of Christ under the form of bread, we must think about His Mother. After all, this Eucharistic Body would not be ours to share, would not be a sacrament, if a humble, simple and pure Galilean Girl had not once answered God: "Let it be done to me according to your word" ...We desire to nourish ourselves with the Body of Christ in order to be the Body of Christ. For this is the most magnificent essence that mankind can possess: to be Christ, nourishing ourselves with Christ's Body.**

August 20 - Krakow-Lagiewniki, "Jozefow", 100th anniversary of the house of the Sisters of Our Lady of Mercy — concelebrated Holy Mass. Homily:

> **There are such situations in the life of a person, when one needs God's mercy. These are as if the nadirs of one's very life, to which one sometimes sinks — a man, a woman, a young lad, a young girl. These are the times of greatest depression to which a person sinks, though not always completely through his or her own fault, and then stays there through force of habit, and then finds that it is difficult to rise from that pit by one's own will power ... at these times such a person needs ... a good maternal or sisterly hand; a hand which then becomes the tool of God's mercy. It must be full of goodness. The word and the heart, which are to become the living instruments of God's mercy, must be very subtle and mature, in order to uplift another person, not to belittle him, but to show him God as Father, in His incarnate mercy.**
>
> **I was a witness of how you were deprived — humble evangelical workers — of your workplace ... However, He, who is mercy incarnate, did not cease to be necessary, ... and so you are also needed ... there is a huge workplace hidden, or perhaps also a visible one – in our town, where there are many young people who are non-conforming or difficult ... we wish, together with you, to pray that you may find a way ... I have watched, for many years, how you struggle in order to adapt to possibilities and necessities.**

Following the celebration and dinner, the Cardinal returned to the hall again and for a long time conversed with the sisters who surrounded him, then he blessed them and left. (From the chronicle of the Congregation of the Sisters of Our Lady of Mercy)

August 21 — 7:00 a.m., Chapel on Pedzichow Street, Holy Mass with homily, investiture, profession. * August 24 — 7:30 a.m., At the Wawel Cathedral, ordination of deacons, homily * On the same day he sends a letter to the Bishop of Plock on the occasion of the celebrations associated with the devotion to the Blessed Virgin Mary in Czerwinsk and on the occasion of the conferment of the title of minor basilica upon the church there * August 25 — 11:00 a.m., Jedrzejow, at the Cistercians, participation in the celebration of the 750th anniversary of the arrival of Blessed Vincent to Jedrzejow. Same day — 4:00 p.m.,

Skala (Kielce diocese) — 700th anniversary of the death of Blessed Salomea. Concelebrated High Mass with the bishop of Kielce — homily: "I come here not only as bishop, but also as a pilgrim … to this place, where once came the Piast Princess Salomea, in order to spend the remaining years of her life here, near Wawel, to spend them in prayer, in God's service." * August 26 — Jasna Gora, 11:00 a.m., led the procession and celebrated a Pontifical Holy Mass. Same day — 5:00 p.m., visitation in Lapanow * 6:00 p.m. — visitation in Droginia:

> I came directly from Jasna Gora, where this morning, in the presence of the throngs of pilgrims from various parts of Poland, the bishops celebrated the festive name-day of Our Lady of Jasna Gora. I had the good fortune today to celebrate the Most Holy Sacrifice of Mass on the ramparts of Jasna Gora, during which the homily was proclaimed by the Cardinal Primate … I gazed at the countenance of Our Lady in her visitation image. It can be found today at the summit … I thought … what is displayed at the summit of Jasna Gora, should be here in this empty frame … But it is not! … There is some kind of affront in the fact that the visitation image of Our Lady is imprisoned. Our Lady of Jasna Gora will not escape, nor will we take Her away by force. She has the right to leave from there and to come visit here. We continue to wait for the acknowledgment of and the respect for our rights. What I am saying here, I say with a feeling of great pain. I do not wish to accuse anyone … I speak with a sense of righteousness. We have the right to express our veneration and respect for the Mother of God, before Her image, not before the empty frame.

August 28 — 7:00 p.m., Participation in the visitation celebrations in Pcim * August 31 — 7:00 p.m., visitation of Our Lady in Dobczyce.

September 1 — Jasna Gora, 10:00 a.m., Holy Mass, 11:00 a.m., homily for the participants of the pilgrimage for men and boys:

> Not long ago, the Gospel according to St. Matthew was filmed in Rome. The author of the film was a great Italian director, an atheist. The creator of the film showed in his work this gaze of a Mother at her husband, at his heart, when he was full of apprehension and later when thanks to the Holy Spirit, he understood the mystery which had taken place in Her. This film perfectly renders the gaze of Mary at her Husband's soul … We, Poles, know this date [September 1, 1939] in a special way … It meant for us the shattering of border barriers, the aggression of invaders. We still carry this bad date within us, in our entire existence as a nation. At that time we experienced the painful awareness of what it means to be a weaker nation, which a more powerful nation can trample … Although it so happened that we fell at our defensive ramparts, yet we remain with the consciousness that it is necessary to defend every just cause … We shall pray to God for nations who are close to us and for our own, that a mutual trust be established: the trust of the weaker in the stronger … We constantly carry the responsibility for the great cause of religious freedom, of the spiritual freedom of mankind …
> [About the matter of responsible parenthood]: We, men, must openly say: this is our matter. This is, after all, in accordance with the deepest bio-

logical truth. Neither a husband nor any young man can hide his masculine responsibility behind a girl, behind a woman, behind his wife... [About alcoholism]: Sometimes it takes a greater hero to refuse a destructive drink, than to stand with a bayonet eye to eye with the enemy.

The same day at 6:00 p.m. — Participation in the visitation in Trzemesnia * September 2 — At the Church of the Norbertine Sisters, Mass with homily for the Feast of Blessed Bronislawa (as recorded in the Book of Activities. The chronicle of the monastery records this Mass under the date of September 1: "an outdoor Mass with sermon") * Same day — 6:00 p.m., visitation celebrations in Krzyszkowice * September 3 — Participated in the funeral of Bishop K. Pekala in Tarnow. He eulogized the deceased on behalf of the Polish Episcopate * September 4 — 7:00 a.m., Seminary chapel, concelebrated Mass with the clergy, homily on the occasion of a nationwide conference * September 5 — 5:30 p.m., Participation in the visitation celebrations in Jawornik * 6:00 p.m., visitation in Rudnik * September 6 — 7:00 p.m., Visitation celebrations in Harbutowice * September 8 — Piaseczno near Gniew (Chelm diocese), performed the coronation of the statue of Our Lady, Pontifical High Mass, homily.

September 9 — Theological Seminary (Krakow, Manifestu Lipcowego Street), 12:30 p.m., Mass and lecture inaugurating the 1968/69 year of the Institute of the Family:

My dear brothers and sisters, we are inaugurating this study group, whose title perhaps will gradually be defined, but which at present we call the Family Institute. A study group which, in light of our pastoral obligations, in light of the responsibility of the Church for God's truth, in light of life — the human life, the interior life of our brothers and sisters, spouses and parents — seems to be a necessity ... We must turn to the Holy Spirit because we must serve the truth in this entire matter. The last encyclical of our Holy Father Paul VI, beginning with the words *Humanae vitae*, is the expression of this truth. An unchanging truth, which the Church has always proclaimed, concerning the morality of marital life, of family life, and where, in this framework of the morality of married life and family life, lies the special matter of responsibility for the conception of life. All of this found its expression in the encyclical *Humanae vitae*, and was prepared in a special manner by the work of the Second Vatican Council ... It is necessary that these matters, which you are to deal with, my dear friends, take on for you this deep meaning; that you deeply feel these problems, which will occupy you here during your year-long study; that you pray about them intently. Perhaps we must create a great spiritual front in this matter, ... We must combine this study with prayer, because through prayer God's Truth finds its way into the human intellect, into the human heart, and to our own heart, to the minds and hearts of those to whom we are sent.

Same day — 5:00 p.m., celebrations of the visitation in Sulkowice * 6:00 p.m., visitation in Krzywaczka * September 10 — 10:30 a.m., at the Church of St. Florian in Krakow, sermon and benediction during a retreat for the sick * September 11 — 4:30 p.m., celebrations of the visitation of Our Lady in Glogoczow * 6:00 p.m., visitation in Zielonki * September 11-14 — Personal retreat at the Benedictine abbey in Tyniec * September 14 — 5:00 p.m., celebrations of the visitation in Giebultow * 6:00 p.m., visitation in Modlnica * September 15 — 11:00 a.m., Pontifical High Mass with thanksgiving on the 50th anniversary of regaining independence[9] * Same day — 6:00 p.m., Pontifical High Mass at the Cathedral of the Holy Cross in Opole * September 16-17 — The Episcopal Conference in Opole. Participation in the funeral of Antoni Pawlowski, Bishop Ordinary of Wloclawek: on September 17 —in Opole — where the Bishop died, and on September 19 — in Wloclawek — where he was buried * September 18 — 6:00 p.m., visitation of Our Lady in Zabierzow * September 20 — 6:00 p.m., celebrations of the visitation in Przegorzaly * September 21 — At the residence chapel, Mass with sermon, the blessing of a banner for the parishioners from Andrychow * Same day — 6:00 p.m., participation in the celebrations of the visitation at the parish of St. Nicholas in Krakow * September 22 — He celebrated a Mass and preached a sermon at a convention of the Living Rosary in Kalwaria Zebrzydowska * 4:00 p.m., Poreba Wielka — sermon on the anniversary of the consecration of the churches in the Krakow Archdiocese. "Just as once, in the house of Zacchaeus, various invited people met with Christ, so we meet with each other and with Christ..." * 6:00 p.m., participation in the celebrations of the visitation in Wawrzenczyce * September 24 — Krakow, the Church of St. John of the Sisters of the Presentation. Holy Mass and sermon to the faithful and the students of the High School. * On the same day — meeting of the Council of the Pontifical Department of Theology. Organizational matters. "The Cardinal spoke in the matter of the classes taught by assistants, indicating the need to organize them into a team and to establish ongoing contact with them through the Council of the Department." (From the minutes of the Council) * Same day, 6:00 p.m., celebrations of the visitation in Pobiednik Maly * September 25 —Departure for Rome for an "ad limina" visit * September 26 — Private Mass at the nunciature[10] in Vienna * September 27 — 6:30 p.m., private Mass at the Polish College in Rome * September 28 — 12:00 noon, concelebrated Mass with sermon for Consilium de Laicis at the Church of St. Calixtus in Rome * September 29 — 9:00 a.m., Mass with sermon at the Basilica of St. Peter, in the chapel of Our Lady of Czestochowa.

October 3 — 5:00 p.m., Church of St. Stanislaw in Rome, Holy Hour for priests * October 5 — 7:30 a.m., Mass at the Basilica of St.

---

[9] At the end of WW I, after more than 120 years of partitions
[10] Vatican diplomatic mission

Paul outside the Walls * October 6 — 10:00 a.m., at his titular Church of St. Cesarius, celebrated a Mass with a sermon and witnessed a marriage * 1:00 p.m., meal with Cardinal Franjo Seper at the Yugoslavian College * 5:00 p.m., at the Basilica of St. Peter, participation in the beatification of Korean martyrs * October 7 — 10:00 a.m., "ad limina" audience in Congregazione dei Vescovi * October 8 — an "ad limina" Mass at the Basilica in Rome, at the tomb of St. Peter * October 10 — participated in the plenary session of the Sacred Congregation for the Clergy. Participated in the works on the preparation of the document on the councils of priests * October 12 — Mass with sermon for the beginning of the academic year at the College of the Sons of Divine Providence * October 13 — Paris, the Polish church, Mass with sermon. He is accompanied on his trip by Bishop Jerzy Stroba and Msgr. E. Lubowiecki, episcopal visitator of Poles in Germany * October 14 — 7:00 a.m., Paris. Mass with sermon at the Polish Seminary * Same day — Taize, a visit to the congregation, participation in choral prayer. This was his second visit. The date of the first visit to Taize could not be established precisely (around the year 1964). Br. Roger Schutz wrote of his visit to Cardinal Wojtyla in May of 1973. Together they went on a pilgrimage to Piekary. Br. Roger went to Piekary with the Cardinal for the second time in 1975.

During the prayers of the congregation of Taize, the name of Cardinal Wojtyla had been mentioned for a long time as one of the friends for whom the congregation prayed.

October 15 — Rome, private Mass in the evening * October 16 — 4:30 p.m., at the Institute of Church Studies, participation in a lecture by Rev. J. Chmiel, subject: *The Concept of Love in the First Letter of St. John the Apostle* * October 17 — 10:30 a.m., Rome, blessing of the grave of Andrzej Langman, at the cemetery * October 18 — Vienna, private Mass * October 19 — Return to Krakow.

(Fragments of an interview granted by Cardinal Wojtyla to Rev. Alojzy Orszulik on October 19, 1968, *Tygodnik Powszechny*, no. 2. 1969):

We were giving a report according to a particular directive: our task was to provide main statistical data and, first of all, to characterize the religiousor spiritual life {in Poland} and the directions in pastoral ministry.

Such a report is submitted to the Congregation of Bishops. Cardinal Confalonieri is the Prefect of this Congregation. The conversation that we had with him on this subject suggested that the Congregation will gradually become acquainted with our report and will send us their comments.

Another copy of this report — delivered to Archbishop Casaroli — reached the Holy Father, so that during the audience the Holy Father already knew about it and was familiar with its content. Essentially, the opinion that he expressed about our report was very positive but this was

not the main subject of our conversation with the Holy Father.

About two thirds of this conversation, which lasted 45 minutes, concerned the encyclical *Humanae Vitae*, certainly due to the fact that the Holy Father himself cares very deeply about this issue and also because I have already had several earlier mandates from the Polish Episcopate to present the opinion of the Polish Church and the Polish theologians on this encyclical to the Holy Father. Thus the matter had already been prepared during the previous audiences. In short, I can say that the Holy Father was very pleased with our position and cooperation with regard to this matter and that, at the same time, he called for, asked for further cooperation. This cooperation is necessary and its direction emerges after the publication of the encyclical. The Holy Father realizes that theology, especially moral theology faces very serious tasks — in the area of casuistry and spiritual direction. These tasks also stand before pastoral ministry and lay apostolate. When I told the Holy Father that there is a separate family ministry in Poland and a Committee for Family Ministry at the Polish Episcopate, he expressed his deep satisfaction at this fact.

The matter of our involvement in the work concerning the encyclical — especially the participation of moral theologians from Krakow — is a separate and extensive issue and it is difficult to discuss it *in extenso* here in this interview. I am only mentioning it briefly.

Now, with regard to the other subjects of the audience, I want to say that a very important and a very timely subject for all of us, for the Church in Poland, is the Holy Father's interest in the matters of beatification and canonization. It can be concluded from our conversation that the Holy Father himself sees the need to have a Pole beatified or canonized in the near future. He is interested in such figures as: Fr. Kolbe, Queen Jadwiga {Hedwig} and Brother Albert. I think that, based on this, we can make very optimistic prognosis for the nearest future.

Naturally these matters are of interest to the congregations, the last matter in particular is of interest to the Sacred Congregation of Rites where I held conversations on the subject of the beatification, especially of Queen Jadwiga, because it is this matter that we have been working on particularly hard here in Krakow.

I would like to mention two other congregations that I visited in connection with my *visitatio liminum,* namely the Congregation of the Doctrine of the Faith where, again, the issues connected with the response to *Humanae Vitae* were the subject of our conversation and where I submitted my report on the matters of our Archdiocese, and the Congregation of Higher Education which at present bears the name of Congregatio pro Institutione Catholica. The interests of this second congregation are directed primarily at the seminaries, institutes of higher learning and departments of theology. It is in the congregation pro Institutione Catholica, whose Prefect, Cardinal Garrone, I know well from the Second Vatican Council and with whose Secretary, Archbishop Schroeffer, I am also acquainted due to our work together at the Council, that I always discuss the matters of the Department of Theology in Krakow as well as the general matters of the Church's teaching in Poland. All this is subject to the Holy See.

So much with regard to the first purpose of my visit — the visiting of the apostolic thresholds. The visiting of the apostolic thresholds itself is expressed in such a way that the visiting bishop celebrates Holy Masses at the Basilica of St. Peter, at the Basilica of St. Paul, at the graves of the

Apostles ...

During my last stay in Rome I was invited by Cardinal Seper to visit the Jugoslavian College and I talked to him about essential matters, not for the first time, by the way. Cardinal Seper is of the opinion that when it comes to the sense of faith and the theological correctness, his homeland and our homeland, the Church in Yugoslavia and the Church in Poland can contribute a lot to the universal church in this respect, particularly with regard to the western Church where a certain loosening of the theological thought can be observed.

To be more specific, since the question regarding Fr. Schillebeeckx was posed and since I knew that many different interpretations have already been put on this issue in Poland, I asked Archbishop Philippe, the secretary of the congregation, about the state of this matter. Essentially his answer confirms what we have already read in *Tygodnik Powszechny* as a kind of repetition of the press conference at the Vatican. What is most important is the fact that there is no disciplinary process in the Schillebeeckx matter. According to its new statute adopted towards the end of the Council, the Congregation for the Doctrine of the Faith considers it its duty to become acquainted with theological doctrines. In order to do so the congregation turns to either the authors of these doctrines or to the experts. In Fr. Schillebeeckx's case it turned to his professor, Fr. Rahner. And it was probably this fact that prompted a lot of guess work among journalists who are always curious and in this case began to speculate about some alleged disciplinary process. Meanwhile, nothing of the kind is taking place...

- ... " Consilium de Laicis" which holds its plenary sessions twice a year held one this time in the last days of September and the first days of October. I participated in this session. It was an interesting experience insofar as "Consilium de Laicis," a new post-conciliar body of the Holy See, gathers the representatives of virtually all continents, especially among its lay members.

With regard to the clergy, the bishops and priests — they fulfill the role of consultants there. I am one of the consultants. It seems to me that the last meeting of "Consilium de Laicis" was very rich and fruitful. What contributed to this was the presence of new members from Asia, Japan, the Philippines, Brazil and Canada who brought in certain new, in fact, very positive, trends, which is very important in connection with the discussion on the encyclical *Humanae Vitae* ...

In short, I can say that during this session "Consilium de Laicis" has indeed turned towards the problems of the Church, particularly towards the problems of laity. It is sufficient to list the tasks which "Consilium de Laicis" set forth at this session for the future, namely the problem of dialogue within the Church, which is of unparalleled importance to the cooperation between the religious, their hierarchy and the laity, and between the laity and the religious and their hierarchy. Another problem — the youth; the Council for the Laity approaches this issue from the point of view of discernment and apostolic possibilities.

In connection with the encyclical *Humanae Vitae* attention was called to the need for an in-depth study of the problems of married couples and families in order to be able to handle the tasks set before the laity by the Holy Father in his encyclical.

Yet another issue are the problems that Latin America brings to the Council for the Laity. We must remember that the session of "Consilium de

Laicis" was held soon after the Eucharistic Congress in Bogota as well as after such an historic event as was the continental meeting of the Conference of the South-American Episcopate. According to the opinions which I heard and the texts which I had the opportunity to read in Rome, this Conference raises great hopes. It is evident that the Church in Latin America is aware of its real problems and has adopted an appropriate position with regard to solving these problems. The so-called ethics of revolution is a matter of particular importance from the doctrinal and pastoral point of view in countries where there exists tremendous social and economic inequality. The Church in Latin America, both the hierarchy and the laity, seems to have an appropriate outlook upon this matter and seeks its own way.

Finally, in its further work, "Consilium de Laicis" focuses its great interest on the issue of the spirituality of the contemporary lay Catholic, the issue with which we will be dealing more and more as time goes by. In accordance with motu proprio by which it was called to life by Pope Paul VI, "Consilium de Laicis" continues to strive to develop an apostolate of international dimensions and, at the same time, to remain in touch with the lay apostolate on the level of particular countries. With regard to this very level, I am its representative as I preside over the Committee for Lay Apostolate at the Polish Episcopate and I feel particularly connected with this area of activity by "Consilium de Laicis." ...

* October 19 — In the morning, the Vatican Radio broadcast a program by Cardinal Wojtyla on the occasion of the celebrations of the 50th anniversary of the Catholic University of Lublin:

> The university is a special place of work. To someone coming from outside, it is more apparent as a place of didactic occupation ... But as we observe the internal dynamics of the university, we come to realize that the centers of its life lie deeper, that they are determined by scholarly work of both an investigative and a creative character ...
>
> [About Catholic universities such as, for example, Louvain, which] contain all possible "secular" departments ... including medicine and engineering ... In each of these departments, the endeavor of the mind seeking the truth in a relevant area, albeit the most secular, the most physical, may and should be combined with faith, which throughout all of these areas seeks its affirmation and deepening. *Intellectus quaerens fidem*. Such is the profile of the contemporary Church and contemporary Catholicism ... Simultaneously, a Catholic university forms a sort of living argument against all those who tend to assert a sign of equality between religion and irrationalism.

October 20 — Naleczow, a private Mass * Lublin, participation in the 50th anniversary of KUL[11] * Same day — 6:00 p.m., St. Anne's Church in Krakow, Mass with the participation of the theological schools of Krakow. "In comparison with the 50th anniversary of the Lublin school, our Krakow theological tradition is so much longer. It can be said that it created the theological tradition in all of Poland, that all theological schools, theological studies, milieus, in some sense emerged

---

[11] Catholic University of Lublin

from it."

October 21 — 7:00 a.m., Wawel Cathedral, tomb of St. Stanislaw, Mass and sermon to seminarians upon returning from the trip to Rome * October 22 — 6:00 p.m., the cathedral in Warsaw, participation in the celebrations of the 20th anniversary of Cardinal A. Hlond's death * October 24 — 5:00 p.m., participation in the visitation celebrations in Biskupice * October 27 — Krakow, Wawel Cathedral, Feast of Christ the King.

> I invited you along with the distinguished Metropolitan Chapter. You have come here so that the Wawel Cathedral would resound with the glory of Christ the King. It is royal in its past, from its foundations to its summit. May it be royal today, Anno Domini 1968, when it is filled with the People of God ..., which is the royal priesthood of Christ.

Same day — 1:00 p.m., Pisarzowice — blessing of a cornerstone. About the building of a new church in place of the old one that burned down:

> We are happy that this matter has met with the understanding on the part of those who in the course of their administrative duties decide these things. We are happy and wish that all similar matters, so numerous, all similar necessities — so many in number, would find similar understanding ... so that wherever people need a church, that church would rise.

Same day — 5:00 p.m., participation in the visitation celebrations in Mogilany * October 30 — 4:30 p.m., celebrations of the visitation of the Blessed Mother in Izdebnik.

October 31 — Lanckorona — visitation of the Blessed Mother.

> To welcome Her in an image unavailable to our eyes ... Our eyes have the right to see Her, since her likeness is the property of the Catholic Church in Poland, it is also the property of the Episcopate, and was blessed by the Holy Father, so that it would visit parishes and churches on the Polish soil ... For this reason we are constantly reminding those who should be reminded, we are constantly demanding and entreating that the image of Our Lady of Jasna Gora return to its visitation route.

On the same day the Cardinal sent an article to *L'Osservatore Romano* entitled: "The Seminary Experience: Obedience and the Spirit of Independence." (According to a note made by Rev. Director M.J.). The article was published under the title: "Experiences de nos grands seminaires". *Seminarium* 1969, no. 1.

November 1 — 7:30 a.m., visitation ceremony in Skawinki * Same day — Chapel at the Rakowicki cemetery in Krakow, Mass with homily, funeral procession. "Christ walks through Krakow cemeteries and constantly speaks to us about those who left us: I have led them across..." * Same day — At the Dominicans in Krakow, conclusion of the rosary prayer services. "Although October has ended and we are escorting the image of Our Lady back to her chapel, may the rosary, my dear friends, remain with us, and we with the rosary. To the end..."

November 2 – 9:00 a.m., Wawel Cathedral, participation in a solemn Mass and a funeral procession to the royal crypts * Same day in Zywiec — funeral of Rev. Msgr. Stanislaw Meus — pastor, ... "It is the duty of every priest to bear witness to Christ, the priest must bear this witness with his life, and also with his death ..." * 4:00 p.m., Oswiecim {Auschwitz}, chapel on the grounds of the former concentration camp — Mass with sermon and procession to the wall of death (for the past several years the Cardinal has always come here for All Souls Day).

> **Not long ago I was received in audience by the Holy Father Paul VI. After a lengthy conversation, the Holy Father asked me: "What could I do for the Polish Church and the Polish nation?" I answered: Holy Father, we, Poles, are waiting for the beatification or canonization of one of our countrymen — candidates to be raised to the honors of the altar. "Who are they?" I told the Pope: There are 50 of these candidates for canonization or beatification from the Polish nation. The Polish nation is probably waiting the most for the beatification of Father Maximilian Kolbe. The Pope listened to my words, ordered that the names be noted — besides, they were familiar to him — and announced: "I know that this is very necessary for you, that it is very necessary that some Pole should be soon raised to the honors of the altar ..."**

On the same day — 9:00 p.m., visitation celebrations in Zebrzydowice.

November 4 — Cardinal Karol Wojtyla's name-day. Wawel, solemn Holy Mass * On the same day — a visit in the parish of Radziszow where a "visitation by Our Lady" was taking place. It consisted in transferring a symbolic lit candle from parish to parish after the copy of the miraculous image was detained by the security police. The Mass was celebrated by Bishop Julian Groblicki. Cardinal Wojtyla arrived during the Mass and delivered a speech after the Mass ended (Cf. The chronicle of the Radziszow parish) * November 5 — Krakow, Rakowicki cemetery, he celebrated a funeral Mass and led a funeral procession for the late Ludwik Ehrlich, law professor at the Jagiellonian University (deceased October 31).

November 7 — Meeting of the Council of the Pontifical Department of Theology in Krakow: "the Cardinal presented a project of forming 4 studies at the department, i.e. liturgical, family, catechetical and the study of dialogue. The Council concerned itself with the Liturgical Institute ...

It was agreed that solemn meetings of the Council of the Department, in observance of the jubilees of Rev. Prof. W. Wicher and

Rev. Prof. T. Dlugosz, will be held in the second half of January and the second half of February 1969." (From the minutes of the Council)

November 9 — 6:00 p.m., Skawina, visitation of the Blessed Mother. Sermon about the miracle at Cana of Galilee: "This first miracle was performed because of the material needs of the couple of newlyweds and their family ... The power of God was shown in a fashion that was sudden and not subject to any laws of nature."

November 10 — 5:00 p.m., Marcyporeba, visitation of the Blessed Mother — 50th anniversary of the regaining of independence.[12] From the sermon:

> In the soul of a Pole two emotions are paired: a deep religious piety, and a patriotic love of the Homeland. The religious emotion — the love of God and the love of neighbor which flows from it — leads us to our eternal homeland, but it also espouses our ardent relationship to our temporal homeland, it feeds and deepens this relationship. These two emotions have united in our souls especially because of our experiences through history — the suffering and misfortunes of our nation. It was in times such as those that we experienced what a great source of strength our religion is.

November 11 — 10:00 a.m., at Wawel, participation in a High Mass, the concluding prayers for the 50th anniversary of independence * 6:00 p.m., Requiem Mass for countrymen on the occasion of the 50th anniversary of regaining independence * Same day — 7:00 p.m., at the Dominican Church, sermon and prayer on the occasion of the 50th anniversary * November 12 — Celebrations of the visitation in Kalwaria Zebrzydowska * November 13 — 5:00 p.m., visitation at the parish of St. Stanislaw Kostka in Krakow * November 14 — Krakow - Bronowice, visitation of the Blessed Mother:

> There is a spontaneous expression of the radiance by the arrival, by the visitation, by the presence, which is an expression of a strong, living faith which transcends this empty frame. As if the image itself became unimportant: what is important is the arrival of Someone — just as then, to the house of Zacharia and Elizabeth.

November 16 — Krakow, parish of Our Lady of Lourdes — visitation of the Blessed Mother.

> The weather is unpleasant, it is autumnal, Polish, inclement. Can we imagine Our Lady visiting our country without such rainy autumn weather? Rainy weather — such as Reymont describes in his novel *The Peasants*.[13] If this rainy, autumnal, November weather was no more, could it be said that Our Lady really visited the Polish land?

November 17 — 12:00 noon, Biskupice, Mass with sermon, bless-

---

[12] At the end of WW I, after more than 120 years of partitions

[13] It was for this novel that Wladyslaw Reymont was awarded the Nobel prize for literature at the turn of the 20th century.

ing of the construction work around the church * Same day — 5:00 p.m., Wawel, homily to young people during the observances of the Feast of St. Stanislaw Kostka:

> The vast current of the history of our nation: from the first Stanislaw, who lies here, to the second Stanislaw, whom we honor today, down to us. The relay race of history (...) You dream sometimes of fame, you envy the various people who have achieved it. Never envy trivial things, but seek true glory. Sometimes this true glory is not renowned or boisterous — it is hidden. Sometimes it arrives only after death ... It is most important, however, that this be true glory arising from a real good.

Same day — 6:00 p.m. in Krakow, the Basilica of the Franciscan Fathers, solemn Mass and homily on the 700th anniversary of the death of Blessed Salomea. In attendance: members of the Metropolitan Chapter, the Department of Theology, pastors of parishes and the Franciscans. In the sermon, reflections on the meaning of Blessed Salomea's life for the contemporary times * November 19 — 5:00 p.m., celebrations of the visitation in Bronowice Male * November 20 — 5:00 p.m., participation in the visitation of the parish of the Holy Cross in Krakow * November 21 — Krakow, the Church of St. John, Mass with sermon on the Feast of the Presentation of the Blessed Virgin Mary * November 22 — 12:00 noon, private Mass at the chapel of the KUL boarding school. Same day — opening address (together with Fr. T. Styczen) in a discussion on the relationship of ethics and metaphysics, within the framework of a symposium organized by the participants of the specialization seminar in theoretical philosophy, November 22-23. The title of the Cardinal's lecture: *The Attitude of a Metaphysicist* * November 23 — 5:00 p.m., celebrations of the visitation in Raclawice * Same day — Wieliczka, sermon for the Feast of St. Clement. About the audience with the Holy Father:

> At that time I heard some very encouraging words about our nation from him. Perhaps I had reasons to think otherwise. But the Pope, as if guessing my thoughts, said to me: "I know what I should think of Poles, I know how to judge them ... For me the symbol of Poland will always be Christ, who carries his cross [referring to the statue in front of the Church of the Holy Cross at Krakowskie Przedmiescie in Warsaw]". The Pope told me who we are — that we are the people of hope. If we are not to disappoint mankind and if we are not to disappoint ourselves, we will be the people of hope!

November 24 — 10:00 a.m., Jasna Gora, the consecration of the Bishop of Lodz, Jozef Rozwadowski. Cardinal Wojtyla was the main consecrator: "In the year of her visitation, the Our Lady of Jasna Gora, performs some special exchange of values in the Church of God between us [Krakow] and you [Lodz]..." Same day — 5:00 p.m., participation in the visitation celebrations in Czernichow * November 24-25 -

Scholarly symposium of the Polish Theological Society on the subject *"Professio fidei* of the Holy Father Paul VI." Initiator: Cardinal Wojtyla, he also performs the function of a host, participated in the discussion and recapitulated the entire symposium. (Cf. *Ateneum Kaplanskie* 74/1970, pp. 142-144) * November 26 — 5:00 p.m., visitation celebrations in Kamien * 6:00 p.m. — in Nowa Wies Szlachecka * November 28 — 9:00 a.m., Mass for priests and clergy of the Krakow archdiocese with the participation of deans * 5:00 p.m., participation in the visitation celebration in Poreba-Zegoty * Same day — 6:30 p.m., farewell to Bishop Jozef Rozwadowski at St. Florian's Parish in Krakow, where the Bishop was pastor.

> The Holy Spirit himself calls the Bishops of the Church. Of course, their nomination does take place through human agency; to be sure, people participate in it, in some measure the entire People of God, especially the bishops are called to this. The Holy See participates in this nomination through its representatives. To some extent, even secular agents take part, expressing their "nihil obstat" regarding the person of the candidate. However, the unchanging truth remains that through all of these human factors, the bishop is called from the midst of the People of God and shaped by the Holy Spirit ...
>
> A new responsibility, an unknown path, a new diocese, a new, huge industrial city. And simultaneously an unknown territory. Because there are such ways of God that lead all humanity and each of us to the promised land and to the unknown land as well.

November 29 — 5:00 p.m., visitation in Rybna * November 30-31 — visitation of St. Kazimierz Parish at Grzegorzki. Sermon for the beginning of the visitation:

> It is difficult not to refer to the very beginnings of the tradition of the canonical visitation. These beginnings are connected with the beginnings of the Church and of Christianity. There was no canon law at the time, but there was the Gospel, there were the Apostles ... who knew Jesus and who accepted their mission from Him. And it was precisely in the spirit of this mission, taken from the Redeemer, that these Apostles were constantly on the road and constantly hastened to people in order to preach the Gospel to them. Once they have proclaimed the Gospel and established a Christian community, they kept returning to this community. A community was an assembly of the faithful, a prototype of today's parish ... The purpose of an apostolic visitation was to maintain a living connection with the One who is the beginning and the end of everything in the Church — with Jesus Christ ... That was their mission. They fulfilled this mission to the end of their days, often sealing it with a martyr's death ... It is the wish of every bishop as well as mine that this visitation have in it something of the apostolic visitations ... I intend to conduct this visitation which begins today, very slowly, step by step, without haste. Because this is not merely a formality ... I intend to devote the entire period of Advent to this visitation ... and to visit your church many times, and primarily to visit the community of the faithful ... I wish this visitation to be a series of meetings, through which you can

draw closer to the community of the Church of Krakow of which I am the bishop ... and through the bishop — to the community of the universal Church.

December 1 (First Sunday of Advent) — 10:00 a.m., residence chapel, Mass for marriage counselors from the entire Archdiocese * Parish of St. Kazimierz — visitation.

So many people do not go forth to meet God, so many people seem to avoid Him, forget Him. So many people proclaim an agenda that He does not exist. And indirectly, by way of contrast, this wandering of man points to the truth. Why do they shout so loudly that there is no God? Do they by chance want to drown out something within themselves?

Same day — 4:00 p.m., participation in the celebrations of the visitation in Krzeszowice; 5:00 p.m. — visitation in Zalasie * December 2 — He pays a visit to observe religion classes in grades 1, 6, and 7 at the Parish of St. Kazimierz * 5:00 p.m., celebrations of the visitation in Tenczynek * December 3 — Participation in religion classes in grade 6 and in grades 1 and 2 of secondary school at the Parish of St. Kazimierz * 5:00 p.m., participation in the celebrations of the visitation in Sanka * 6:00 p.m. — visitation in Paczoltowice * December 4 — Participation in religion classes in grade 8 at the Parish of St. Kazimierz * December 5 — Participation in religion classes in grades 6 and 8 * 5:00 p.m., participation in the celebrations of the visitation in Morawica * December 6 — 6 a.m. - 8:00 a.m., he heard confessions (the first Friday of the month) at the Parish of St. Kazimierz, paid a visit to religion classes in grades 3 and 4 of the technical secondary school — including boarding school students at the Parish of St. Kazimierz * 4:00 p.m., blessing of young children * December 8 — 11:00 a.m., participation in a Holy Mass for pre-school children celebrated by Msgr. Jan Mac * 5:00 p.m., visitation celebrations at Salwator * Same day — Czaniec, presided at the funeral of Franciszek Wojtyla, paternal cousin of his father, who was a parish cantor and a guide of pilgrimages to Kalwaria * December 9 — 4:00 p.m., residence chapel, conclusion of the (apostolic) beatification process of Brother Albert * 5:00 p.m., celebrations of the visitation in Czyzyny —Nowa Huta * Same day — meeting with university students at the hall of St. Kazimierz Parish * December 10 — 5:00 p.m., participation in the visitation celebrations in Ruszcza * Same day — at the Parish of St. Kazimierz, he visited the sick in their homes * December 11 — He visited the sick of St. Kazimierz Parish, participated in religion classes of grade 6 * 5:00 p.m., participation in the visitation celebrations in Mogila * 8:00 p.m., at the Church of Our Lady of Lourdes in Krakow, participation in an *Oplatek*[14] for university students.

---

[14] See Glossary.

December 12 — Meeting of the Council of the Pontifical Department of Theology at the residence of H. E. Cardinal Karol Wojtyla — Metropolitan Archbishop of Krakow, chancellor of the Department [this title will henceforth be used in the minutes of meetings of the Council of the Department]. Among others, information about the reply from the Secretariat of State to the letter sent to the Holy Father in connection with the encyclical *Humanae vitae*, and the announcement of a solemn commemorative assembly for the 50th anniversary of regaining independence by Poland. (From the minutes of the Council) * Same day — celebrations of the visitation at the Parish of the Blessed Virgin Mary in Krakow.

December 13 — The Mariacki Basilica in Krakow, blessing of a memorial plaque dedicated to the priests who were victims of the Second World War:

> **They spiritually confirmed the law of Christ and the Church in our nation. With their blood and death they earned the right for Christ and His Church to be recognized in our nation. Subsequently, no one could say, and no one will ever be able to say, that Catholic priests did not participate in the fate of their nation, especially, in a cruel fate ... that in the most difficult moments of the nation's history, they isolated themselves. We know that the percentage of those who went to prisons, to camps, who met their deaths, is in proportion. They shared proportionally in the martyrdom of the Polish nation.**

December 15 — 12:00 noon, Krakow, the Mariacki Basilica, solemn conclusion of the peregrination in the Archdiocese of Krakow. Coronation of the Mariacki image of the Blessed Virgin, and transfer of the visitation to the diocese of Tarnow. The Primate, the Archbishop of Poznan, the Bishop of Tarnow and other bishops participated with a crowd of faithful. Addresses were delivered by Cardinal Wojtyla, the Primate, Bishop Jerzy Ablewicz * Same day — 5:00 p.m., at the Church of the Sacred Heart of Jesus in Tarnow, solemn handing over of the image of the Blessed Virgin to the Diocese of Tarnow, Mass with sermon * December 16 — 6:00 p.m., at the Wawel Cathedral, votive service for the beatification of Queen Jadwiga, Brother Albert and other Polish candidates for sainthood, with the participation of the Primate and the Episcopate. Introductory address * December 18 — A visit to the sick, blessing of married couples (10 years of marriage) at the Parish of St. Kazimierz in Krakow * December 19 — 7:00 a.m., residence chapel, Mass with sermon for the Higher Catechetic Institute, Christmas greetings * 6:00 p.m., St. Kazimierz Parish, Mass with sermon for married couples; individual benedictions.

> **During the past days, many married couples, and thereby many families of this parish received the blessing of the bishop ... I ask for your**

patience, there are many of you in church, therefore, it must take a while. I shall gladly bestow this blessing upon you so as to somehow meet with each person, and especially with each family, through this sign. Priests visit families "po koledzie"[15] and bless each house. Unfortunately, I cannot visit each parish to that extent, but wish at least to meet with the families and in this manner to perform my *koleda* as a bishop.

December 20 — 4:00 p.m., blessing of and participation in the Stations of the Cross * 6:00 p.m., Mass and benediction for married couples (over 25 years) at the Parish of St. Kazimierz * Same day — at the convent of the cloistered Dominican Sisters in Krakow at Grodek, participated in the conclusion of a retreat for nurses.

December 21 — Funeral of Prof. Stanislaw Pigon. The Cardinal celebrated Mass by the coffin at the Church of St. Anne and preached a sermon. He led the funeral from the cemetery gate at Rakowice * Same day — 5:00 p.m., in Mogila, performed the benediction of Abbot Bogumil Salwicki * December 22 — 7:00 a.m., bestowed tonsure and minor holy orders * Same day — Rokiciny:

> On his return trip from the ceremony of the blessing of the {church} bells in Raba Wyzna, Cardinal Karol Wojtyla stopped to visit us. He entered the chapel by way of the new addition, where, after a short prayer, he gave his blessing to the Congregation. Next, at the request of Mother Superior, he blessed the catechetical room, named after St. Angela Merici. Black coffee was served in the parlor over which the Cardinal conversed with the Sisters, took interest in the house and in the work of the Sisters. (From the chronicle of the convent of the Ursuline Sisters)

Same day — 5:30 p.m., St. Kazimierz Parish, Mass and sermon during the exchange of the mysteries of the Living Rosary * 6:30 p.m., Mass with sermon and blessing of single people * December 23 — 12:00 noon at the academic Church of St. Anne, funeral Mass for Prof. Niewodniczanski, 2:00 p.m., funeral at the Rakowicki cemetery.

> After the death of my husband, Prof. Henryk Niewodniczanski, I went to my parish [of St. Szczepan] early in the morning on December 21, in order to notify them about his death and discuss the details of the funeral. To my great surprise I was told that there had already been a telephone call from the Curia, from the Cardinal, who "takes everything upon himself", that in three days at twelve o'clock, there will be a Holy Mass at the academic Church of St. Anne, and at 2:00 p.m., the funeral at the Rakowicki cemetery ... He celebrated the Mass in Latin, and when I gave him my special thanks for this at the cemetery, he smiled and whispered to me: I wanted to please him, I was familiar with his eccentricities... (Irena Niewodniczanska)

December 24 — 8:00 a.m., Wawel Cathedral, participation in "roraty".[16] * Same day — Krakow-Nowa Huta, Pasterka:[17]

---

[15] See *Koleda* in Glossary
[16] Early morning Mass celebrated in Advent, the 4 weeks before Christmas.
[17] Midnight Mass on Christmas Eve.

The Church, which is already emerging here, is rising because at this place you stood for it, you knelt for it, and here at this place you suffered for it; it was obtained by your prayers — by your faith, your fervent, steadfast attitude ... I would like to say to Jesus Christ: See, how You have become enriched. How many there were of those, who came to visit You at midnight on the day of your birth in Bethlehem, and how many there are of those, who came here, in Nowa Huta, in order to surround Your Polish Bethlehem ...

I celebrate the second Mass of the day at my residence chapel at 3 Franciszkanska Street. This Mass has always been attended by the families of the employees, laborers, my former fellow workers at Borek Falecki ... and the third, which carries the title of royal, I celebrate at the royal Wawel Cathedral at 10:00 a.m.

December 25 — 10:00 a.m., Wawel Cathedral, Mass and sermon:

While I am speaking these words ... at this very moment, there are people, although not very many, who are circling the moon. An event which is exceptional in the history of human knowledge and technology... For the first time man has left the Earth in the full sense of the word. He has gone beyond the Earth's atmosphere, the Earth's gravity: he has found himself in the orbit of another heavenly body ... Will they return? Will they succeed in once again crossing the Earth's orbit? ... Man is a creature who constantly seeks and constantly surpasses the threshold of his previous accomplishments ... Man ... is more and more the master of creation, in accordance with the plan of His Creator ...

And so God was born ... He Himself went forth to meet these aspirations which are inherent in man, the aspirations to surpass himself: to obtain more, achieve more, to be someone greater still ... In becoming man, He showed man the ultimate end of possibilities, which is not in creation, not in the visible universe, but in God Himself ... Man may transcend himself by becoming a "Son of God."

December 26 — 7:30 a.m. at the residence chapel, Holy Mass on the occasion of the "golden wedding" of Jan and Anicla Dultz * 4:30 p.m., in Myslenice, Mass with sermon and the blessing of an altar and the renovated church * December 29 — 8:00 a.m., Krakow, Mass with sermon at the chapel of the Theological Seminary for graduating secondary school students on retreat: "The Gospel must be read with your life, otherwise you cannot read it" * On the same day — at the residence at 3 Franciszkanska Street, a reunion on the 30th anniversary of the Secondary School final exams {matura}.[18] At 10:30 a.m., at the residence chapel — Holy Mass with homily (his friends were altar servers). After the Mass, in the parlor — sharing of memories and a dinner (Antoni Bohdanowicz) * Same day — Warsaw, 5:00 p.m., participation in the funeral of Bishop Zygmunt Choromanski * December 31 — Krakow, a visit to Fr. Jan Mac, a deserving builder of the church, celebrating a jubilee; a ride along the perimeter of the Parish of St.

---

[18] Secondary school graduation

Kazimierz; in the evening — a liturgical service for the end of the year.
Sermon:

> ...The service for the old year is a service of thanksgiving and concilia-
> tion. Every person feels the need for such a service at the end of the old year
> and on the threshold of a new one, because it is particularly this day and
> night, and the morning of the next day, that make us aware of the tempo-
> rary nature of all creation. They make us aware of the burden of time to
> which we are unforgivingly subject, they make us aware of the arbitrariness
> of our temporal life, and at the same time, of the great responsibility to live
> that life in goodness, so that one day we may stand before God with our
> entire life, with all of its years, weeks and hours, because He alone is eternal.
> [In the continuation of the sermon, a discussion of the events of 1968:
> the Eucharistic Congress in South America, the encyclical *Humanae vitae*,
> the visitation of the Blessed Mother in the Krakow Archdiocese, the coro-
> nation of the image at the Mariacki Basilica.]

December 31 — midnight, the Basilica of the Franciscan Fathers;
sermon:

> The name of Jesus Christ marks and begins the history of human
> redemption. History is a temporal matter: history is man and time. And
> behold, into time came a Man who was the Son of God, and He saturated
> time with God's Salvation.

In 1968 he prepared a lecture (unpublished): *Man in the Area of
Responsibility (A Study on the Concepts and Methodology of Ethics)*, p. 74.
Excerpts:

> This study of the concepts and methodology of ethics is the fruit of ear-
> lier research and ongoing discussions within the Lublin community ... It is
> also appropriate to explain the title of this work. It forms, to some extent, a
> continuation of the study entitled *Person and Act*. This experience (of man)
> ... contains within itself the experience of morality as an integral element,
> without which it is not possible to construct a theory of the person ... To
> some extent what we call the experience of morality is, from the onset, an
> understanding of morality. In this way morality becomes the proper realm
> of ethics. Ethics is nothing other than the process of understanding the
> question of morality, taken "to the ultimate." The proper moment of moral-
> ity is embodied in the experience of obligation. To a certain extent, obliga-
> tion and its experience is embodied in causation and its experience ... One
> might say that the experience of one's moral obligation constitutes an essen-
> tial moment of the experience of morality ... Nonetheless, the two are not
> simply identical ... The experience of morality possesses, as it were, differ-
> ent layers and different aspects (axiological, praxiological, deontological). It
> seems that it is possible to ascertain the two following divergences, which
> delimit the area of contention over the interpretation of morality. 1. In the
> area of metaphysical reduction, man is ultimately left as a being, which is
> — and becomes — either good or evil, whereas in the field of phenomeno-
> logical reduction we stop at experiencing a particular value as "good —
> evil." 2. The second subject of contention in the interpretation of morality is
> the problem of attempting to tie moral obligation with purposefulness ...
> This dispute is taking place on a foundation of a basic understanding of

morality that is common to the representatives of both of these diverse interpretations. Only the positivistic and the neopositivistic mentalities place us beyond the boundaries of this area ... Since "moral good" = to be good as a human being and "moral evil" = to be bad as a human being, therefore, morality entails the specific union of axiology and ontology (pp.1-20).

[Part II, Normative ethics and personal responsibility; here, among others, a dispute about utilitarianism, norm and patterns. Part III, The natural law and the personalistic norm (explanation of norms and the normative character of ethics in light of the ultimate causes, the transcendental character of the law of nature.]

His position on the concept of ethics is also expressed in articles which by their subject matter are related to this lecture: "The Problem of Experience in Ethics", *"The Philosophical Annals"* 17/1969, bk. 2, pp. 5-24, and "The Problem of the Theory of Morality" *in: In the Current of Post-Conciliar Issues,* vol. 3, Warsaw, 1969, pp. 217-250. He thought about the concept of ethics from the beginning of his scholarly work, as was manifested by the subject matter of his first articles in *"The Philosophical Annals,"* 1955-57. He thought about writing a book devoted to the subject of the foundation of ethics. He was unable to realize this intention before 1978; Rev. Prof. Tadeusz Styczen, his successor in the Chair of Ethics at KUL {Catholic University of Lublin} undertook it and is trying to accomplish it. (Compiled by Rev. Andrzej Szostek)

1969

January 2 — Funeral of Matylda Sapieha at the cemetery at Salwator
* January 5 — An article by Cardinal K. Wojtyla, *The Truth of the Encyclical Humanae vitae* was published in *L'Osservatore Romano* (no. 1/1969). In Poland it was reprinted by the journal "Za i Przeciw"[1] (without the knowledge or consent of the author).

January 6 — The Feast of the Epiphany at the cathedral, also — dedication of the heating system funded by the American Polonia. Homily:

> **The Three Wise Men stood eye to eye with a Gift, and received God's gift that became Man. A poor infant, in a stable, alone. (But they) knew, that to a God who gives of Himself, you must give of yourself: a gift for a Gift ... Today's event: the arrival of the Three Wise Men in Bethlehem is not a closed event: it is open to each of us. [In this homily he also thanked the American Polonia.]**

January 7 — *Oplatek*[2] in Borek Falecki * January 8 — 5:00 p.m., *koleda*[3] — pastoral visit at the residence and at the editorial office of *Tygodnik Powszechny*[4] at 12 Wislna Street * January 10 — Registered as a permanent resident of the Archbishop's Residence at 3 Franciszkanska Street. Until then he resided at 22 Kanonicza Street. In reality his possessions were moved earlier while the Cardinal was abroad. Until the time of his nomination to auxiliary bishop, he lived with Rev. Prof. Ignacy Rozycki at 19 Kanonicza Street * January 11 — 7:00 p.m., *Oplatek* — Club of Catholic Intellectuals on Sienna Street.

January 12 — Zakopane, dedication of a rectory, solemn Holy Mass on the occasion of the Feast of The Holy Family, patronal feast of the parish; homily:

> **[It is in a family] that man becomes man. [Married love] must always test itself, and by its nature must be focused on the child ... It is our desire that our Polish families ... have a love that does not flee from the child, but is totally committed to the child, but wisely ... That man should grow to become our hope on earth, but also the hope and the future of the Kingdom of God ... Through what can we be fulfilled in our life and in our life's calling ... if not through your children, through new mature people to whom we can, in turn, entrust our future and our hopes?**

Same day — Zakopane, meeting with religious sisters, the speech and hearing impaired and the laity.

January 12 — 9:00 a.m., to the ailing and their care-givers at the parish church in Zakopane: Suffering and loneliness of the sick "is not theirs exclusively, it belongs to the entire parish, to the entire Church! ...

---

[1] "For and against"
[2] See Glossary.
[3] See Glossary.
[4] A Catholic weekly published in Kracow; one of the very few Catholic publications allowed by the Communists.

I firmly believe in this truth. This truth guides me in my personal life, I use it to the fullest in my pastoral and episcopal work." * 7:00 p.m., Zakopane — meeting with priests * January 14-16 — Krakow, 3 Franciszkanska Street, meeting of the Pastoral Committee of the Polish Episcopate.

January 14 — After his return from Rome, Archbishop Kominek shared his perception of the Church in the West. Among others, on the crisis (according to the minutes): "There is no crisis in the Church in the sense given by the article by Turowicz in *Tygodnik Powszechny*. In the long discussion that ensued, Cardinal Wojtyla expressed his opinion (according to the minutes): "Card. Wojtyla acknowledged that the archbishop's presentation agreed in general with the article by Mr. Turowicz, but maintained that the archbishop's analysis was deeper and more supernatural, full of faith and hope..." Presentations and discussions: by Bishop I. Tokarczuk — *The Issue of Religious Freedom in Light of the Documents of the Second Vatican Council from the Point of View of Polish Reality*; the matter of the Theological and Pastoral Institute at KUL.

January 15 — Concelebrated Mass at the residence chapel for the participants of the Pastoral Committee meeting * January 16 — 9:30 a.m., 3 Franciszkanska Street, Pastoral Committee meeting including chairmen of all committees of the Polish Episcopate. Introduction by Archbishop B. Kominek. The topic of the meeting: *Problems of Implementing the Vatican Council in Poland*, presented by Cardinal Wojtyla (1.5 hours of text). Second part of the meeting: proposals regarding a pastoral plan for implementing the principles of the Second Vatican Council in Poland; third — presentation of a *modus procedendi* — sketching a plan for developing subjects that should be taught. All motions from the discussion (according to the minutes) were summed up by Cardinal Wojtyla: the Polish Episcopate, including the Primate, must be fully and comprehensively informed by means of a report prepared by Cardinal Wojtyla. During this meeting the conference must decide whether it should continue the plan of the implementation of the Second Vatican Council by itself or create special subcommittees. In his presentation and summation he raised, among others items, the issue of preparing a new catechism ("a totally new approach"). The second part of the meeting dealt with "pastoral actions." (According to the minutes of the Committee meeting)

January 17 — St. Anne's Church, memorial Mass for Andrzej Malkowski, founder of Polish Scouting. The church was filled with older scouts; for the recessional they sang a scouting hymn: *O Lord God, our Father, keep us in Your care.* * January 18 — 7:30 a.m., Wawel

Cathedral, private Mass, 5th anniversary of his elevation to the rank of the archbishop * 8:00 a.m., he participated in a solemn anniversary Mass for this occasion * Same day — 7:30 p.m., Mass with a homily for the *Srodowisko* * January 19 — 4:00 p.m., Church of the Sisters of St. Norbert, *Oplatek*[5] for school girls * 6:00 p.m., at the residence — *Oplatek* for catechists * 8:00 p.m., St. Joseph's Parish, *Oplatek* for university students * January 22 — he addressed an edifying letter to the parish of Nowa Biala in which he listed the criteria which every true Catholic should meet. The tone of this letter was softer than that of his previous letters. The Cardinal expressed hope that the appointment of a new pastor will help to restore peace in the parish * January 23-25 — Krakow, A session for theologians from all of Poland on the subject of the encyclical *Humanae vitae* (Sources: "Analecta Cracoviensia" 1/1968; cf. also "Notificationes" 1969 pp. 1-70). Strong support for the position of Pope Paul VI. Cardinal Wojtyla was chairman of the session and gave a presentation: *The Teachings of the Encyclical on Love* ("Analecta Cracoviensia" 1/1968; cf. also *L'Osservatore Romano* 109/1969 no.1) v January 25 — 7:00 p.m., at the Dominicans, conclusion of the week of prayers for unity among Christians, concelebrated Mass and parting remarks * January 29 — Church of the Sisters of the Visitation, Feast of St. Francis de Sales, patron of Catholic writers. Homily:

> **A pen ... can be used to both build and destroy ... If people who refer to themselves as Catholic writers wish to use their pens to build, then they must posses a very deep sense of faith. If all they want to do is not to use their pens to destroy, then they at least need a well-grounded sense of faith.**

February 1 — Chapel at 3 Franciszkanska Street — Holy Mass. The Sisters of the Holy Spirit were invited to participate. Later, a visit with the sisters — blessing of Sister Gertuda Soltys on the 50th anniversary of religious life * February 1-2 — Meeting of the Committee for the Apostolate of the Laity. Report pertaining to the apostolate of the laity in the universal Church in light of *Consilium de Laicis* — issue: the dialogue within the Church.

February 2 — A pilgrimage of the Archdiocese of Krakow to Jasna Gora {Czestochowa} (800 priests and 4000 faithful). Night vigil, profession of faith, — *Credo* of Pope Paul VI, prayers for a papal visit. Cardinal K. Wojtyla was the main celebrant and homilist. In stating the purpose of this particular pilgrimage the Cardinal said, among other things:

---

[5] See Glossary.

I wish to explain ... those purposes. But in order to explain, my dear friends, I must reach into history. I must remind you, my dear brother priests, of a similar evening in April 1967, when we came here, not for the first time, on our priestly pilgrimage. We came then to Jasna Gora, to invite the Mother of God to the Krakow archdiocese, to invite her in the glory of her image which was traveling all over the country. We have prayed with the full ardor of our priestly souls, we have prayed on our knees, walked around her image on our knees: to obtain the grace of her visitation. And although we were not graced with the arrival of her image, we must remember that we were graced with her spiritual visitation.

February 3 — The Church of the Franciscans, conference for the superiors of religious orders of men: *A Role for Religious Orders in the Church and the World* * February 4 — At the residence chapel, Mass and homily at 1:00 p.m. for the archdiocesan study group for family ministry * February 7 — Chapel of the Sisters of St. Seraphim, Mass and homily for diocesan female instructors * February 8 — Residence chapel, Mass and homily for the participants of a course for nurses * February 9 — 12:00 noon, Our Lady of Lourdes parish church, Mass and homily, meeting with the students of KUL and with physicians * February 10 — Kalwaria Zebrzydowska, main celebrant at a Mass of thanksgiving from archdiocesan priests for the visitation by the Blessed Mother. Homily:

We must pray thoroughly about everything that we do to implement the Second Vatican Council's directives. The realization of the Council is not a collection of superficial changes. Let us not fall into that trap. It must come from within, it must come from the depths of faith. It must be motivated by charity, not a desire to criticize.

February 14-15 — Presided over the elections of the abbot of the Benedictine monastery in Tyniec (Fr. Placyd Galinski was elected abbot at that time). The Benedictine monastery in Tyniec was dissolved by the Austrian authorities in 1816, the last abbot died in 1801. After nearly 120 years of absence, the Benedictines returned to the ruined Tyniec abbey on July 30, 1939. The monastery gradually developed and obtained the rank of a priory. On February 10, 1969 Cardinal Karol Wojtyla raised the priory to the status of an abbey * February 15 — Pastoral Committee of the Polish Episcopate, second day of deliberations. The Cardinal was the main celebrant of a concelebrated Mass, and participated in the meeting. Presentations: Rev. Weron — *Theology of the Laity*; Rev. Zienkiewicz — *The Moral and Religious Situation of the Polish Youth* 1968/69. Discussion; announcements * February 16 — 4:00 p.m., Silesian Seminary, the unveiling of a portrait of the late rector, Rev. K. Michalski, concluding remarks * February 18 — 9:00 a.m., Residence chapel, concelebrated Mass for participants of a symposium on Canon law * February 20 — 10:00 a.m., conference of priests who are deans * 5:30 p.m., Council of the Pontifical Department of Theology in Krakow. The minutes do not show any remarks * February 22 — April 6 — Visitation of the Corpus Christi Parish in Krakow.

February 28 — Visit at a Jewish Synagogue on Szeroka Street in Krakow. During a canonical visit to the Corpus Christi Parish at the Kazimierz district of Krakow, the Cardinal expressed a desire to visit a Jewish community. The pastor of the parish, in consultation with Mr. Maciej Jakubowicz, the leader of the community, established a time and place for the visit. Mr. Jakubowicz asked that the rule to cover one's head when entering a synagogue be observed. Accompanied by the pastor, the Cardinal, dressed in a black cassock and coat, proceeded to Szeroka Street. It was Friday and the Jews were gathering for prayers. Mr. Jakubowicz greeted the Cardinal in front of the synagogue. After a fairly long conversation, the Cardinal entered the synagogue and remained there a long time, standing in the back. Later, he went with the pastor to another active synagogue, where they found only one Jew at prayer. The Cardinal recalled later how he received greetings every year from Mr. Jakubowicz, but didn't know who the sender was. (According to the accounts by the then pastor, and entries in the book of visitations)

March 3 — Krakow — The Church of Corpus Christi, Mass at the tomb of Blessed Stanislaw Kazimierczyk — during the visitation (KW 5). * March 9 — 6:00 a.m., hospital run by the Brothers of the Order of St. John of God, Mass and homily, he brought Holy Communion to the sick in the hospital wards; at 8:00, 9:30 and 11:30 a.m. — he participated in Masses at the Church of the Brothers of the Order of St. John of God, at 3:00 p.m. in Lenten services {Lamentations} * Same day — 9:00 p.m., left for Rome via Vienna for a symposium in the Pontifical Commission for Dialogue with Unbelievers * March 11-12 — Rome — at a session of the Council for the Laity he undertook the matter of the theological status of lay people in the Church and the need for dialogue with the laity. A doctrinal committee was appointed, Cardinal Wojtyla became its member * March 15 — Audience with pope Paul VI at the Vatican * Same day — approval of the statutes of the Conference of the Episcopate. Formally became Deputy Director of the Conference * March 18 — Rome, chapel of the Polish College, concelebrated Mass with Msgr. Edward Lubowiecki and other priests from Krakow * March 19 — St. Peter's Basilica in Rome, participated in a Holy Mass celebrated by the Holy Father * 4:30 p. m., Institute of the Church Studies, participation in the lecture by F. Bednarski OP, subject: *Deduction of the General Theological Moral Norms from the Principles of Natural Law.*

March 23 — At the Polish Church of St. Stanislaw in Rome —

homily referring to the topic of the symposium:

> Striving to make the reality of the cross newly desirable, understandable and effective — as the Vatican Council and all of the post-Council activities of the Church indicate — is a broad opening to all people and to all peoples, an opening leading also to a dialogue ... with those people who simply don't accept any religion, but who, as I had opportunity to experience yesterday, do not wish to be called unbelievers, because that name has a negative connotation. And they, too, feel the great riches, the unique heritage which is hidden in the Gospels and in the cross.

March 25 — St. Peter's Basilica in Rome, concelebrated Mass with the priests of the Krakow Archdiocese studying in Rome.

March 26 — The Vatican Radio, interview with Cardinal K. Wojtyla:

> My personal work in the *Consilium de Laicis*[6] is in the role of a consultant. For that is the only role that the clergy can play there, to be consultants. I appreciate that I can fill this role, that thanks to the five meetings held to date ..., thanks to the contact with the people who represent the Church on all continents, in so many different places on earth, I myself could learn so much. And for my part, I could bring in certain values, a certain meaning, ... a special experience of the Church in Poland.

Same day — Mass at the nunciature in Vienna.

March 26 — Return to Poland * After the return — an interview on the subject of the work associated with the 5th session of Consilium de Laicis. Interviewed by Rev. Stanislaw Malysiak (Pismo okolne {Circular letter} no. 18/69) * March 28 — Took part in a Mass of the Passion of Our Lord at the Franciscan Church in Krakow * March 29 — St. Anne's Church, concelebrated Mass with homily for the conclusion of a student retreat * March 30 — 2:30 p.m., ordination of new priests at the Cathedral:

> You are to be priests and ministers; learn to love all the paths by which people come to Jesus Christ, on which they sometimes get lost, lose their footing; sometimes they don't know if they are making progress or not; and they fall, and they lift themselves up. Be for them what a priest must be: another Christ, "alter Christus."

* 8:00 p.m., Church of St. Joseph, beginning of a retreat for lawyers.

March — Canonical visitation at the Corpus Christi Parish in Krakow.

> During Lent, the Cardinal visited the Parish of Corpus Christi.

---

[6] Council of the Laity.

It was already in the first few days of the visitation that he informed the pastor of his desire to visit the sick of the parish who were in private homes. At that time I was working in the Parish Social Care office run by Mrs. Hanna Chrzanowska for all of Krakow and the diocese. I had in my care the sick who were most needy, most of them living alone. I was asked to come to a meeting. His Eminence the Cardinal planned two days of visits and asked me to be his guide. We went by car from house to house, street by street. The Cardinal was alone, without his chaplain, with only his driver. We visited all the houses whose addresses I knew; many were humble, neglected, some not prepared for such a visit; we went into courtyards, basement apartments, upper stories, garrets, wherever there were sick people who were bedridden or otherwise unable to leave their homes.

The Cardinal would sit very close to the bed of each sick person and talked to them with paternal kindness. The sick, I noticed, were not flustered, they spoke freely of things which were close to their hearts. The Cardinal carefully listened to everything, sometimes wrote down an address, asked questions, kissed them on the head or the forehead, blessed them and asked for their prayers for the intention of the Church. One sick woman asked with great simplicity for intervention in arranging a summer convalescence outside of the city. The Cardinal ordered me to remind him of this matter at the appropriate time. Thanks to his intervention, the sick woman spent a vacation at a convent near the mountains.

It so happened that it was near the end of our visits that we came upon a sick 42-year-old woman, the mother of two daughters. She had had an operation for a brain tumor; that day she felt weaker and did not have the strength to sit up. The Cardinal leaned over her bed and with great compassion listened as she told him of her suffering. The situation was very grim. Her husband was an addicted alcoholic, her younger daughter mentally retarded and crippled by polio. Throughout her married life, and even now, she said, she often had to run away from her husband with her children and mother, afraid for their lives. She also talked about her brain operation. The Cardinal was extremely concerned and moved by the suffering and the situation of this woman. I noticed that his brow was covered with beads of sweat and his veins bulged. With his hand he wiped the tears from her face, and kissed her several times on the forehead. He also spoke with the crippled daughter.

In almost every house, the Cardinal asked the sick if they were satisfied with how I took care of them, and how often I came to visit them. He also asked these questions in this house, but also assured this woman that I would come to see her more often. After we left that apartment, he said to me, "That woman is the most sick and the most needy of all whom we have visited." He also asked me to come here more often and to give her my special attention and care.

At the home of one sick grandmother, there were many other younger members of the household who were waiting for the visit. Everyone brought their own troubles there. After a lengthy conversation with the old woman and with the other ailing people who had come there, the Cardinal was invited to the table. He did not refuse. There was a sincere atmosphere of love and mutual understanding.

Every person was important to him, for everyone he had a kind word or some gesture of compassion. In between visits he talked with me not only about the patients in my care, but also about my calling to this work. He also asked if I ran to the sick every day in the same way as today. I said yes — everyone is waiting for me.

We visited over 20 sick people. (Sr. Irena Odoy, OSA, parish caretaker of the sick)

March — April. During the visitation at the Corpus Christi Church; to single people:

> Human life, even in the single state, is not empty, if it is filled with God. It becomes full, it can be very full. Some of you know perfectly well, from your own experience, what I am speaking of. You could say more about this subject than I ... No person is ever useless; each of us is always needed for something.

April 1 — Sermon in Dziekanowice; the funeral of the pastor, Fr. Szczepan Muniak.

> I will never forget this, because in more than ten years of my service as a bishop, I have only once heard such an opinion from an assistant priest about his pastor: "Archbishop, I have a saint for a pastor." I hesitate to repeat this opinion here, I was afraid to say it, but I have already said it. I also remember ... a conversation with him when he talked about all his assistants. He spoke of them all with such love, with such striking respect for the individuality of each one of them. He told me how he tried to find a common language with each one of them and how, with God's help, he did find it with each one of them.

April 2 — At the Church of the Felician Sisters, Mass with sermon for the close of a retreat for physicians.

April 3 — At the Cathedral on Holy Thursday (on the blessing of the oil of the Holy Chrism, the oil used to anoint catechumens and the sick):

> We are to touch the sources of these strengths, we are to bless them and offer them to the Church of Krakow. But when we do that, we do so filled with awe, because we know that in touching the matter of the sacraments, which will be administered throughout the next year in the Krakow Church, we also touch the internal meaning of the sacraments: the grace of God and this supernatural strength, which is imparted to us through the sacraments.

April 5 — At the Wawel Cathedral, at 5 p.m., the rites of Holy Saturday, a concelebrated Mass, the Resurrection Mass.

April 6 — At the Church of Corpus Christi, for the conclusion of the visitation of the parish, during the Resurrection Mass:

> To end the visitation of your parish and to emphasize the special bond which exists between every parish, every church, and the Cathedral, I sincerely invite your parish to a Mass at the Cathedral today, on the day of the Lord's Resurrection, at 10 a.m. I will be celebrating this Mass together with the priests of your parish, and I ask for your participation. In this way, may

the Parish of Corpus Christi once again thank its great past, its ancestors, in the Cathedral at the tomb of its founder, King Casimir the Great {14th Century}.

The same day — Easter Sunday — at the Wawel Cathedral:

Resurrection is always about death. Man carries within him the seed of death, both a biological death, and an even deeper one, a spiritual death. Resurrection is always about death, but about a death vanquished... Jesus Christ was victorious over his own death, so that He could show us how to overcome death in man.

April 7 — Dedication of the church bells in Siepraw.

Every epoch had its own creativity ... But these works belong already to the past ... Human thought and human imagination and artistic value are always going forward, are always seeking new means of expression, to be able to say that they are alive, active, making progress. That is why we have new styles, new works of art, new churches, new in their architectural expressions.

April 8 — 11 a.m., Mass and sermon at the Church of St. Anne, at the coffin of Prof. Zenon Klemensiewicz, one of the victims of an airplane crash.

When we stand by this coffin, we have the feeling that this man did not merely leave us, but was snatched from us, torn from our midst. Torn unexpectedly, violently; torn in tragic circumstances; we all know the circumstances ... We recall his enormous contribution to the annals of Polish culture ... His enormous contribution to the knowledge of what we hold especially dear, what expresses our humanity, what gives expression to our national community both in the past and now: of language, of the word which was spoken by Poles, of the word which is still spoken by Poles.

The same day — 4 p.m., at Rakowice, the funeral of Prof. Klemensiewicz.

April 9 — Radziszow near Krakow. Funeral of Anna Haller, sister of Gen. Jozef Haller, a long-time teacher of Polish at the teacher's college in Myslowice; a catechist, organizer of Polish and religious life in the western provinces * Same day — pilgrimage of priests and faithful of the Krakow archdiocese to Jasna Gora. Night vigil. Communion with the Holy Father, who wanted to be present:

Anywhere else he wants to go, he can go. And wherever he wants to go, all roads immediately open before him. But he could not come here for our Millennium. What did we do to deserve this? And what did he do to deserve this, that he could not come here for the millennium of our baptism? ... [But he is present here in spirit] He knows what our Jasna Gora is, he knows, what the meaning of the prayers spoken here is, he knows the meaning of our vigils, of all of our sacrifices: what a rock they are for the Rock of Ages.

April 10 — Jasna Gora, concelebrated Mass with newly ordained priests for the intention of Pope Paul VI, during the pilgrimage of priests and faithful from the archdiocese of Krakow (in the presence of Bishop Stefan Barela).

As the Archdiocesan Church of Krakow, a small part of the Universal Church, we want to be a part that is healthy, alive and growing, receiving those thoughts which flow from the Head, the invisible Head, Jesus Christ, and from the visible Head, who is His Vicar. And, under the influence of these impulses, to become a part that actively works for the good of the whole.

Also — the rosary was recited on the fortifications.

April 11 — Lublin, a presentation entitled *The Human Person and Natural Law,* for the 50th anniversary of KUL. (April 10-12 — *Natural Law: Theory vs. Practice*) (Cf. *Philosophical Annals* 18/1970, vol. 2, pp. 53-59) * Same day — 7 p.m., the Mariacki Church, Mass for the intention of those killed in the airplane crash.

April 12 — At the Church of the Salesian Fathers at Debniki — reference to the Gospel account of how St. Peter and St. John ran to Christ's tomb.

I want to relate these thoughts to the effort which the contemporary Church makes in order to run to the place of the contemporary resurrection of Jesus ... That is how we might imagine the enormous task of implementing the directives of the Second Vatican Council. It is an effort, it is a spiritual run, it is even some kind of haste, although that haste must not result in superficiality ... The entire Church must "spring to its feet" and run to the site of Christ's contemporary resurrection.

April 13 — In Tyniec, a Mass with the first, in the last 150 years, benediction by an abbot, Fr. Placyd Galinski OSB.

Wherever on this earth, within the last 2000 years, there arose an authentic community of the disciples of Jesus, there He was among them. And such a place could always be called a place of the Last Supper {the Cenacle} ... And it so happens that this place where we meet today, is also a place of the Lord's Supper ... A place that is singular because of its great past stretching almost a thousand years, a place of great significance in the history of our nation, a place of great significance throughout the history of the people of God on Polish soil ... We are suffused with tremendous gratitude for the great past of Tyniec and the Benedictines of Tyniec, ... but we are also grateful for the resurrection of this Benedictine Tyniec.

April 13 — 3 p.m., the chapel of the Theological Seminary; sermon during the days of recollection for graduating high school students {boys} * 4 p.m., chapel of the Ursuline Sisters, sermon during the days of recollection for graduating high school students {girls} * April 14 — 10 a.m., concelebrated Mass for the 25th anniversary of priesthood.

April 15 — At the Church of the Sisters of the Sacred Heart, on the 75th anniversary of the founding of the order:

> **We, especially those of us who can watch their [the Sisters'] lives very closely — and I can say this for myself, because I see the lives of the Sacred Heart Sisters every day; they work both at the Metropolitan Curia and at the Bishop's residence in Krakow — we see that they are servants, that they serve in the spirit of charity, and that always, at every moment, their service flows from the Sacred Heart of Jesus.**

April 18 — Makow Podhalanski, concelebrated Mass for the opening of a regional conference * 8 p.m., Krakow — Nowa Wies, conclusion of catechesis in grade 11 * April 19 — 4 p.m., at the church in Krakow — Rakowice, confirmation of about 700 young people, sermon * April 20 — 12 noon, convent in Kalwaria Zebrzydowska, Mass with sermon for the conclusion of the training of those involved in family ministry * April 20 — sermon in Czestochowa for the 25th anniversary of the priesthood of Stefan Barela, the Bishop of Czestochowa:

> **Being a bishop is like discovering yet another and different aspect of the priesthood. It happens in the same way. It happens first of all by turning towards Jesus Christ, the only Shepherd, the only Shepherd and Bishop of our souls. This turn {on the part of the bishop} is even deeper, more ardent, more demanding. It is also a turn towards the souls, towards the souls which have been redeemed by the Blood of Christ. Perhaps the turn to individual souls is not as immediate as in the work of a parish priest, a pastor or an assistant, but it is more comprehensive, because a bishop has a broader view of the community of the Church. And if a priest discovers and realizes his mission in the community of the Church, then the bishop does even more so … This is the Church in our awareness, in us, the bishops of Vatican II, the Church that is a place where the entire human family meets, a place of reconciliation, of closeness, of a coming together for a shared dialogue and a shared suffering. Maybe for us, the Polish bishops of the era of the Second Vatican Council, it is more for a shared suffering than a dialogue.**

April 21 — 9 a.m., at the Franciscans, a sermon to Mothers Superior * 10 a.m., conference of the Committee for Priestly Vocations * Noon — regional conference in Nowy Targ, deaneries: Nowy Targ, Spisz and Orawa * April 22 — 10 a.m., regional conference at the residence, deaneries: Bolechowice, Czernichow, Niepolomice * The same day — Kalwaria Zebrzydowska — he participated in a convention of curators of shrines from all of Poland; he preached a sermon on the meaning of the shrine in Kalwaria, analyzing the common elements between the "little paths" of Jesus Christ and the Blessed Mother * 6 p.m., at the

Parish of the Good Shepherd in Krakow, Mass with homily for high school graduates * April 23 — Bielsko-Biala, chapel of the Daughters of Divine Charity, concelebrated Mass and sermon for the opening of a regional conference for the deaneries of Biala and Zywiec.

April 24 — Meeting of the Council of the Pontifical Department of Theology in Krakow. Among others, a discussion of the proposed statutes of the Department in connection with the rules contained in *Norma quaedam*. The Cardinal presented the matter related to the departure of Rev. T. Rakoczy and Rev. T. Chmura for studies abroad. He also broached the subject of nominating junior assistants at the Department, some of whom could be selected from among the students of the Department... (From the minutes).

April 26 — At the Cathedral in Gniezno, for the celebration of the Feast of St. Adalbert (in the presence of the Primate, Archbishop Baraniak and other bishops):

> From here, as we know, St. Adalbert set off for Prussia, on the shores of the Baltic sea, where he found a martyr's death ... Then, "the seed died." Jesus Christ, speaking of His own Death and Resurrection, compared Himself to a seed which must die if it is to bear fruit. Saying this, Christ was referring primarily to Himself, He was referring to His greatest mystery, which the Church continues to rediscover, which is rediscovered anew by every Christian: to the great mystery which we call the mystery of Easter, which is made up of death and resurrection. The seed dies and bears fruit.

April 27 — Gniezno, the Cathedral, Mass by the tomb of St. Adalbert. 9 a.m., a procession with the relics of St. Adalbert, sermon * April 28 — 8 a.m., Wawel Cathedral, Mass for the intention of the beatification of Queen Jadwiga, sermon * 10 a.m., a regional conference at the residence, Krakow deaneries: III, IV, V * April 29 — 10 a.m., regional conference at the residence, Krakow deaneries: I and II * 5 p.m., at the residence chapel, the conclusion of the beatification process of Pawel Smolikowski * 6 p.m., Wawel Cathedral, participation in the beginning of a novena to St. Stanislaw.

April 30 — At the Mariacki Church, during the installation of Msgr. Teofil Kurowski as Pastor:

> We are well aware that the mission which you are accepting here is not solely a parochial mission. The Parish of the Mariacki Church, despite its great wealth in terms of structures and religious congregations, is one of the smaller ones in Krakow in terms of the number of the faithful. Perhaps all of the parishioners taken together could fit without difficulty in this venerable church. But this parish, and specifically the Mariacki Basilica, is the church of the whole of Krakow, and often the Archbishop of Krakow looks to this church, especially on Marian feasts, as a place to meet with all of the

faithful of Krakow.

May 1 — The Church of St. Joseph in Podgorze; sermon for the Feast of the parish patron:

> **On this day, the whole world celebrates human labor — in a secular vein, let us say, as a temporal good which has a fundamental meaning in human civilization, culture, economy, social life, political systems ... [However] man works not only externally, but also internally; he works not only on created things, on the world which God has entrusted to him, but also works on himself, on his soul. Without this internal spiritual labor, it is impossible to obtain salvation.**

May 3[7] — Jasna Gora, 11 a.m., Pontifical High Mass with the recitation of Pope Paul VI's "Creed" * Same day — the Main Committee of the Polish Episcopate * May 4-5 — Conference of the Polish Episcopate at Jasna Gora * May 5 — Meeting of the subcommittee for implementation of the decisions of the Second Vatican Council in Poland. Cardinal K. Wojtyla, Archbishop B. Kominek, Bishop I. Tokarczuk, Bishop J. Stroba, Bishop K. Majdanski, Rev. Dr. H. Kocylowski. The meeting was opened by Cardinal Wojtyla, who presented the opinion of experts, whom he has called to review the writings on the subject of implementing the decisions of the Council in Poland and on the subject of a pastoral plan (Rev. Prof. Majka, Rev. Prof. Jaworski, Rev. Prof. Macharski, Rev. Prof. Nagy). Copresentation by Bishop Tokarczuk: "We need a concrete plan, practical actions. We need to better define the areas of action, attitudes, direction of our work, goals to be attained" (according to the minutes). A working meeting was scheduled for June 30 in Krakow. (From the minutes of the Pastoral Committee)

May 6 — 10 a.m., regional conference in Krakow, deaneries: Krakow VI, Mogila, Wieliczka * 5 p.m., at the Church of the Jesuit Fathers, Mass and sermon for married couples * May 7 — Church of St. Stanislaw Kostka, Mass with sermon for married couples * May 8 — At the residence, first session of the Council of Priests * May 9 — In Mogila, conclusion of the instruction for young people in the crypts under the church (so-called catacombs). The Cardinal liked to go there *incognito*. He would often arrive unannounced (as recounted by the Cistercians of Mogila) * On the same day — Krakow, St. John's Church of the Sisters of the Presentation. Sermon on the anniversary of the coronation of the image of Our Lady of St. John * May 10 — Church of St. Anne, Mass with sermon for graduating high school students * May 11 — At Skalka, on the Feast of St. Stanislaw (in the presence of the

---

[7] See Glossary.

Primate, Archbishop Baraniak, and other bishops):

> We are here on a great pilgrimage, a pilgrimage which leads through all of our history, through all of the last millennium, and is never interrupted. And if the pilgrimage was interrupted externally, as during the partitions or the occupation, it was never interrupted internally; even when separated by the cordons of the partitions, the Polish people always came to these holy places, to this great triptych (Our Lady of Czestochowa, St. Adalbert, St. Stanislaw).

May 11-18 — Visitation of the parish in Andrychow * May 11 — First sermon in Andrychow during the visitation:

> Perhaps, at times, you are afraid that a climate of unbelief, of laiciza-tion, of atheization is forming around you, that all of public life, official life, is imbued with this climate, that in this public life there is a silence about God, that you are not permitted to speak of Him there, that a believer is sometimes afraid to admit his belief!
>
> If that is the case, then this situation presents us with a formidable task and a challenge! A challenge for our faith to become mature, deeper, to become more mature, more aware and interacting with others. Perhaps also more courageous.

May 14 — Sermon for school children during the visitation in Andrychow:

> Each person will be faced with a struggle in life. Not a physical struggle, not some "fight" of the kind that boys are known to get into among them-selves. Each person will be faced with a spiritual struggle. A struggle — and I will now tell you a strange thing — do you know with whom? – mostly with yourself. Each person must struggle with himself for his[8] own self.

Same day — to the sick of the parish in Andrychow:

> Remember, that you fulfill a special mission in the parish, in the diocese, and in the whole Church. You are especially close to Jesus Christ. And besides that, you are teaching us love, you demand love from us. And we must continually find that social love, through you and for you. And you rec-iprocate with your sacrifice and your prayers.

May 15 — Sermon for the conclusion of the visitation in Andrychow:

> The visitation by a bishop is nothing other than a mutual administering of the various Graces of God. There comes to you a bishop, who by nature of his ordination, of his consecration, is a steward of Grace: one who brings this Grace, who distributes it. But this bishop, as a steward of Grace, is in various ways himself blessed with the Grace of God. And we were witness-es of this during this past week.

May 17-8 — 9 a.m., at the residence, received the Superior General

---

[8] In Polish, these terms are gender-neutral.

of the Order of Friars Minor, Fr. Konstantyn Koser who was visiting the brothers of his congregation in four Polish provinces.

May 18 — Sermon at the setting of the cornerstone of the church in Nowa Huta-Bienczyce:

Today everyone is looking at Nowa Huta ... They look with the eyes of the soul, with the eyes of faith, the eyes of hope and love. Because what is happening in Nowa Huta today deserves such a glance, such a communion of faith, hope and love ... A moment ago I placed a cornerstone into the foundation of the church in Nowa Huta. I just placed it there, because it had been blessed by the Holy Father himself. I remember that day, near the end of the Second Vatican Council, when together with your pastor, through the offices of the Primate, we turned to the Holy Father Paul VI asking him for a cornerstone for a church to be built in Nowa Huta. The Holy Father answered our plea in a most telling manner. He ordered for a stone be removed from the ancient Basilica of St. Peter, not the one which now stands on the Vatican Hill, but the older one, from the times of Emperor Constantine. And it was that stone, taken from that Basilica, that he blessed in our presence as the cornerstone of the church in Nowa Huta.

It is a fact that says so much. A cornerstone is that element of a structure which unites it and integrates it, and this element for your new church is a stone from the Basilica of St. Peter, a stone blessed personally by the successor of St. Peter. And just consider the historical significance of the fact that the structure from which the cornerstone for the church in Nowa Huta came, was the basilica of Constantine. This is a basilica that looks into the first era of Christianity, into the era of the martyrs, the era of those who shed their blood for Christ and for His cross.

The stones from that ancient structure are witnesses of those times: early Christian times, heroic times, times of the highest testimonials of faith, testimonials which were given not only in word and deed, but also in life and death.

And it is from such a church, from such foundations, that the holy stone for the building of the church in Nowa Huta comes. My dear brothers and sisters, when we were placing this stone in the foundation of your church today, I had the impression that it was not I alone who was placing this stone, not I alone who was performing this sacred liturgical rite, but that through my hands this was being done here by the Successor of St. Peter himself. Because such is the purpose of this gift. He wished to express that he is building this church with all of us who have been building it here for over a dozen years: because the history of the construction of this church is long — long and very eventful.

Before the construction even started, from the very beginning, we gave witness {to Christ}: by our petitions, our applications, our efforts, and when necessary — by sacrifice, and, above all, by our tenacity and patience. We stood here on the spot where there was a tiny chapel that could not accommodate the parish of many thousands of faithful, we stood the year round under God's sky! With no roof over our heads for us or for our Christ!

This, my brethren, is the history of the building of the church in Nowa Huta. It is fitting that this history will be witnessed by the stone from the basilica of Constantine, a stone which has witnessed the same faith, perseverance and patience of the first Christians around the hills of Vatican.

On behalf of the Holy Father, I have placed the cornerstone in its appointed place, where it will bear witness to our communion with the Church of Christ throughout the world, to our communion with the Church of Christ and of St. Peter, the Church of the first centuries of Christianity, the Church of the Apostles and the martyrs. We remain in that Church and grow out of it, and put our roots into it! Just as the stone, taken from the Basilica of Constantine on the Vatican Hill in Rome, has become rooted in this our structure ...

This church in this place speaks for us, and it speaks of us. It says — it should say — to God Himself: "These, the sons of this land, the sons of the Polish land, gathered at their new place of work, in a gigantic industrial city near Krakow, say to You, Eternal Father, who art in heaven, that You are also here, on earth! Once you came to us, and since then have allowed Yourself to be brought down to earth in the person of Your Son! The sons of this land want to bring you down here, Eternal Father, in the person of Your Son! They want to bring You here so that you can share their life, their hard labor."

It is indeed significant that the cornerstone for the church in Nowa Huta comes from the basilica of Constantine. The name of that great Roman emperor recalls the times when Christianity found its appropriate recognition from the civil authorities of the Roman state. That is why this stone says so much to us in so many ways. We Christians, we who profess Christ, who want to create the presence of God by erecting a temple for Him, we also want to create things of this world. It is not true, my dear brothers and sisters, that we do not want to create the things of this world! Or that the Church will hinder us in doing that! The Church is an inspiration for us, an inspiration to create a new world! To create Nowa Huta! And if that inspiration were lacking, we would also lack a powerful factor required for building this tremendous workshop of contemporary civilization and industry!

Gathered today by the sign of the Cross, we ask of all: that the building of the church in Nowa Huta might proceed properly, that it not encounter obstacles and stoppages. We speak here with full respect for authority, but also with a full realization of our rights as citizens, the rights which we continue to earn by our conscientious day-to-day work. We say this, my dear brothers and sisters, here by this sign of the cross, by which Constantine once received a different sign, a sign of victory: "In this sign you will be victorious!"

The same day — 9 p.m., in Lodz, Mass at the Salesian Fathers for the conclusion of Sacrosong.

May 19-21 — Canonical visitation in the parish of Klikuszowa * May 22 — Departure for Zakopane * May 23-31 —Private Masses at the Ursuline Sisters.

End of May — In Jaszczurowka he accepts the visit of Fr. Pedro Arrupe, Superior General of the Jesuits.

June 1 — Mass with sermon, at the Ursuline Sisters in Zakopane * June 2 — Meeting of the Committee for the Apostolate of the Laity. Philosophical aspects of dialogue for the purpose of preparing for a symposium in Rome (participation of the Committee in preparatory meetings). Final editing the *Directory* — "pro memoria" for pastoral ministers on the subject of the lay apostolate * June 2-8 — Canonical visitation of the parish of Skawina * June 5 — In Trzebinia, Mass with sermon during a retreat for the sick * June 8-15 — Canonical visitation of the parish of Nowy Targ. Sermon to married couples, with blessing, during the visitation:

> When I give you my episcopal blessing, I wish that it first of all encompass the two of you, just as it did when you stood on the steps of the altar to exchange vows with each other and to offer your vows to God. But I also wish for my blessing to encompass all those whom you wish to include: your children, your families, the families of your children, your grandchildren — everyone, all those who make up the family of families that forms every parish and also your parish.

Meeting with graduating high school students and working youth:

> Whatever you shall be in life, whichever calling you choose, remember, that the fundamental calling of a human being is to have humanity. And you must always realize that fundamental calling, always and everywhere I fulfill my calling to the extent that I have true humanity ... Only one who is truly human is truly a child of God.

Confirmation during the visitation in Nowy Targ:

> A person who is confirmed still maintains in the depths of his soul the characteristics of a child, of a child of God. Because man never stops being a child of God; the more he matures, the more he is a child of God. The more mature in faith, the more a child of God. "I mark you with the sign of the Cross." Is that anything new? You were already marked with this sign of the cross at your baptism, then your parents taught you the sign of the cross. But today the bishop brings that cross to the surface, upon your forehead. There, on your forehead, it is written that you are a Christian. You must not erase it, you must not hide it: you must give witness, you must profess.

June 9-10 — At the residence: Committee for Family Ministry * June 15-17 — Canonical visitation at the parish of Czarny Dunajec * June 16 — 7:00 p.m., Zywiec, concelebrated Mass with homily, 10th anniversary of priesthood (reunion of the seminary class of 1959) * June 17 — 9:00 a.m., Skomielna Biala, homily for the reunion of the class of 1966 * June 18 — 9:00 a.m., concelebrated Mass with homily at the residence chapel for the conclusion of the courses at the Family Study group * 2:00 p.m., Myslenice, homily for the conclusion of the pilgrimage of the sick from the deanery * June 19 — Warsaw, the Secretariate of the Primate, Main Committee of the Polish Episcopate * Evening — in the galleries of St. Anthony's Church (the Reformed Franciscans) in Warsaw, dedicates a tablet honoring Wladyslaw Pener, a soldier decorated for heroism in two wars, prisoner of Auschwitz and Buchenwald, tortured to death at the Dora concentration camp (stepfather of E. Owoc —

cf. October 7, 1951) * June 20 — Warsaw, plenary conference of the Episcopate * June 21 — Krakow, private Mass at the residence chapel * June 22 — Kodyn on the Bug River, celebrations of 150th anniversary of the diocese of Siedlce. Cardinal Karol Wojtyla celebrated Mass and addressed the faithful at Calvary in front of the Church of the Holy Spirit. (According to an account by Fr. Zdzislaw Mlynarski) * June 23 — 7 a.m., residence chapel, Mass with homily for the conclusion of the beatification process of the Servant of God, Mother Angela Truszkowska * 10:00 a.m., Extraordinary meeting of the Council of Priests * June 23-24 — Canonical visitation at the parish of Mietustwo * June 26 — Trzebnica, Mass at the altar of St. Jadwiga {Hedwig}.

June 26 — Trzebnica, convent of the Missionary Sisters of St. Charles Borromeo, meeting of the Pastoral Committee of the Episcopate. The meeting started on June 25 — first day: issues of ecumenism, in the afternoon — discernment of the religious situation in Poland. Cardinal Wojtyla arrived on the second day of the meetings * A reading of a letter from the Primate (a reply to the minutes from prior meetings that were sent to him) calling the attention of the Committee to the **Polish** pastoral programs — the Great Novena, the Millennium, surrender to the maternal bondage of the Blessed Mother, prevention of social problems, crusade of charity and love ... In the opinion of one of the participants, "the performance of the Pastoral Committee was rather weak, lacking form, with no communication with local communities. Unlike — the Marian Commission..." Discussion of methodology: Cardinal Wojtyla stated that the implementation of the directives of the Second Vatican Council is the most important issue for the Committee. During the last year he himself was working on a specific concept of implementing the directives of the Second Vatican Council. (From the minutes of the Committee)

June 27 — 8:00 a.m., Krakow, at the Ursuline Sisters, took part in the closing of the school year at the Higher Catechetic Institute * 7:15 p.m. — the Mariacki Church, Mass for the late Jerzy Zawieyski * June 29 — Men's pilgrimage to Kalwaria; Mass and parting remarks: "Because the Church is now expanding and rebuilding, the bedrock on which the Church of Christ is continually being rebuilt must be all the stronger, must form a stronger foundation for the entire edifice which God, through the signs of the times, is demanding of the contemporary Church." * Same day — 5:00, Rudnik, the beginning of a social get together; blessing of an image of Our Lady of Perpetual Help, homily * 7:30 p.m., Krakow, procession at the Church of St. Peter and St. Paul for the Feast of the patrons of the parish * June 30 — 7:00 a.m., Rudnik , social get together — concelebrated Mass * 10:00 a.m., at the residence, subcommittee meeting for implementation of the directives of the Second Vatican Council.

July 1 — 7:30 a.m., Residence chapel, Mass and homily for the candidates for the first year of studies at the Seminary * July 4 — Wawel Cathedral, Mass and homily for sextons on the anniversary of the consecration of the Cathedral * July 6 — Rajcza, Mass and homily on the 300th anniversary of the image of the Blessed Mother * July 7-19 — Zawoja, three private Masses with homilies * July 20 — Return to Krakow * July 21-August 4 — Private Masses, often with homilies * August 5 — Bialka Tatrzanska, funeral Mass and procession for the late Rev. Canon Jerzy Czartoryski, closing remarks * August 6-9 — Private Masses * August 9-19. Bachledowka, personal retreat * August 15 — Ludzmierz, solemn Holy Mass, procession, closing remarks * 4:00 p.m., participated in the rites of "the funeral of the Mother of God" in Kalwaria Zebrzydowska — despite the rain he walked with the pilgrims — homily * Same day — 7:10 p.m., at the Mariacki Church:

> The horizontal time line of human progress is marked by death. Man progresses and develops the world in which he lives, but does not escape his own death. He progresses along the particular path that has been given to him, then he departs ... The vertical progress of man towards God is spiritual. And its prime characteristic is that it is not subject to death ... There is something in the very nature of that spiritual progress towards God, of this unification with God, that transcends the limitations of death. We realize that if the [horizontal] direction of the progress of humankind were the only dimension, it would ultimately represent a defeat. Death. A erasing of each of us. And that is what materialism, in fact, teaches us. It is a dismal doctrine, but ultimately, it teaches the truth about death. [Today's feast] is, shall I say, a thoroughly humanistic feast! Because it speaks of the greatness of man. It opens the ultimate perspectives of that greatness in unity with God...

August 22 (?) — Sermon for the Feast of Our Lady {Queenship of Mary}:

> The overall plan of God's love includes fertility. God is fertile in His love, through which from all time he generates His Son, who is one in substance with Him. And human love, conjugal love, bears particular similarity to God's love because it is also fertile: it gives beginning to new human beings. And giving the beginning to new human beings, it gives the beginning to new images of God. We could say that not only is the new life multiplying, but the Divine element is multiplying in the world, through this wonderful work of parents, the work of giving birth.

The same day — 6:00 p.m., at the Seminary, Mass for the conclusion of a retreat.

August 24 — Coronation of the image of Our Lady in Myslenice (in the presence of Archbishop Baraniak and other bishops).

Through this coronation, as through many other coronations of the
Blessed Mother, our entire nation thanks her for her thousand-year-long
pilgrimage with us. You walked with us, you were in hiding, you were in
secret (or: discreet), many did not know of your presence, but we knew and
felt that you were walking with us.

August 25 — 7:00 a.m., Wawel Cathedral, Mass at the altar of St.
Stanislaw * 4:00 p.m., visit to Jasna Gora {Czestochowa} before his trip
to Canada and the USA * August 26 — Departure from Warsaw to
Rome * August 27 — Rome, concelebrated Mass at the chapel of the
Polish College * August 28 — 7:00 a.m., Rome, concelebrated Mass at
the chapel of the Polish College.

The Cardinal's stay in Montreal from August 28 to September 1,
1969, according to the program sent by Artur Tarnowski from Montreal
(Cf. also: Rev. Franciszek Macharski *"Relacja z podrozy"* (*Tygodnik
Powszechny* 5 (1969) and the *Chronicle of the Bishop's Activities*.

The trip was occasioned by the 25th anniversary of the Polish
Canadian Congress. The Cardinal, invited as the representative of the
Polish Episcopate, visited the main Polish centers with Toronto at the
head. The culminating point of the jubilee celebrations was a great ban-
quet on September 13th and a Mass on September 14th which gathered
over eight thousand people. The visit was not limited to meetings with
Polish compatriots. Because of many meetings held with the Canadian
bishops, *the visit became (on the level of hierarchy) a meeting of the
Churches: the Church in Poland and the Church in Canada* — wrote
Rev. Franciszek Macharski who accompanied Cardinal Wojtyla.

August 28 (Thursday) — 3:35 p.m., Montreal, arrival at Dorval air-
port, Air-Canada, flight 871 from Paris: Cardinal K. Wojtyla, Bishop Sz.
Wesoly, Rev. Prof. F. Macharski and Rev. S. Dziwisz. Greeting of guests
at the airport lounge by the representative of the Archbishop of
Montreal, Auxiliary Bishop Leo Blais; by the representative of the
Mayor of the City of Montreal, councilman Jean Guilett; by the repre-
sentatives of the Polish Canadian Congress: Mr. W.Z. Jarmicki,
President of the National Directorate; Mr. Kogler and Mr. Brodzki from
Toronto; Z. Celichowski, President of the PCC Council; M. Taras,
President of the Montreal Region; by members of the Montreal reception committee: Prof. T. Romer, chairman, A. Tarnowski and Stepien; by
pastors of the Polish parishes in Montreal, Fr. Bambol, Fr. Mazur and Fr.
Miller. Departure of the Cardinal in an archdiocesan car with municipal
police escort to the palace of Archbishop Paul Gregorire * 8:10 p.m.,
arrival of the Cardinal with an accompanying priest and President
Celichowski at the headquarters of the Polish Mutual Help Society
located in the Mikolaj Kopernik building on Rue Jolicoeur 2721, where

they were welcomed by the hosts: president Januszkiewicz, president Olszewski, representatives of the Congress who were organizing the reception: M. Taras, regional president, and board members, guests from Toronto: Jarmicki, Kogler and Brodzki, and the entire Montreal reception committee. All were presented to the Cardinal and short welcoming speeches were given by president Taras on behalf of the Montreal Polonia, and president Jarmicki on behalf of the Polish Canadian Congress, followed by Cardinal Wojtyla's speech. The official part of the program was ended with the singing of *Boze cos Polske*.[9] There followed a meal and conversation.

August 29 (Friday) — 7:00 am, private Mass at the chapel of Archbishop Paul Gregorire; 9:45 a.m., departure in a limousine under municipal police escort to the City Hall * 10:00 a.m., visit of his Eminence with his entourage, the representatives of the Polish Canadian Congress and members of the Montreal reception committee with the Mayor of Montreal, M. Drapeau, esq. The Cardinal signed a book of distinguished guests of the city * 10:30 a.m., left the City Hall with city representatives to visit the exhibit *Man and His World*. Tour of the exhibit area, viewing of a film about Canada * 12:00 noon, group photo by the statue of M. Kopernik at the exhibit * 1:00 p.m., lunch on the Island of St. Helena at the Helene de Champlain Pavilion, hosted by the City of Montreal for the Polish Canadian Congress on the occasion of the visit by Cardinal K. Wojtyla. Speech in French by Mayor Drapeau, a word of thanks, also in French, by the Cardinal * 2:30 p.m., short press conference at the pavilion with French, English and Polish-language press * 3:15 p.m., arrival of the Cardinal and his entourage, accompanied by Fr. Bambol, pastor, to Our Lady of Czestochowa parish. Visit to the church, guided by artist Jan Katski, whose beautiful works decorate the church; he was one of the curators of the Wawel treasures while they were stored for safekeeping in Canada.[10] After the presentation of the Parish Committee, a short dance program presented by two parish youth groups dressed in Polish folk costumes * 5:00 p.m., In the company of Fr. Bambol — a short visit with Mr. Kazimierz Stanczykowski at the CFMB radio station to tape an appeal to the Montreal Polonia, inviting them to attend a concelebrated Mass at the Cathedral on Sunday * 6:00 p.m., visitation of the Church and the Parish of St. Michael the Archangel, supper at the rectory with pastor Miller.

August 30 (Saturday) — 8:50 a.m., Cardinal Wojtyla departs for Dorval airport in a limo provided by the Congress * 9:55 a.m., the Cardinal and the accompanying Polish Church dignitaries depart for

9 God Protect Poland
10 During WW II.

Quebec, landing there at 10:30 a.m.. Quebec, visit with Cardinal Maurice Roy, the Primate of Canada, concelebrated Mass and homily at the Seminary chapel * 6:20 p.m., departs from Quebec to Montreal by Air Canada * 6:55 p.m., arrived at Dorval airport, was met by Mr. Tarnowski and Mr. Stepien. Meeting of the Cardinal with orphans, who were celebrating the 20th anniversary of their arrival in Canada under the guardianship of Fr. Krolikowski. Next, the Cardinal and Bishop Wesoly went to supper at the residence of Mr. & Mrs. Taras.

August 31 (Sunday) — The day of the main celebration in Montreal. 8:30 a.m., a car of Polish Canadian Welfare Society in Montreal took Cardinal to Maria Sklodowska-Curie Center * 9:00 a.m., low Mass celebrated by the Cardinal for the elderly at the Center, short speeches in Polish and French. Tour of the Center, a visit with the residents, breakfast hosted by the administration * 12:00 noon, arrived at the residence of the archbishop and received Fr. Edmund Szymkiewicz, Provincial Superior of the Franciscans, from Baltimore * 1:00 p.m., lunch at the archbishop's residence for Church dignitaries from Poland, Rome and Fr. Provincial Szymkiewicz, hosted by Archbishop P. Gregorire * 3:00 p.m., High Mass in Polish at the Cathedral at Dominion Square concelebrated by Cardinal Wojtyla, Fr. Provincial and the Polish clergy in Montreal. During Mass, the Archbishop formally greeted his distinguished guest from Poland. Cardinal Wojtyla thanked him in French, than gave a homily in Polish, presented the relics of St. Stanislaw and, at the conclusion, blessed the faithful. 6:00 p.m., supper at the rectory of Our Lady of Czestochowa, the taping of an interview for the Polish section of Radio Canada, for the listeners in Poland, about the Cardinal's first impressions of his visit to Montreal and Quebec.

September 1 (Monday) — 7:30 a.m., the Cardinal celebrated a Holy Mass, afterwards — he visited a home run by the Polish Sisters of the Resurrection, caring for children up to age 13 * 9:30 a.m., a short visit to a Polish Library of the Canadian division of the Polish Institute of Sciences at McGill University. The Cardinal was accompanied by the members of the reception committee Mr. Tarnowski and Mr. Stepien, who bid him farewell at the Institute. At 10:15 a.m., the Cardinal left for St. Wojciech {Adalbert} Mission at the Parish of the Holy Trinity where he was awaited by Fr. Mazur, the pastor, Fr. Zuchowski, the Mission director, and a Polish Committee * 11:15 a.m., visitation at the Holy Trinity Church and blessing with the Blessed Sacrament, afterwards breakfast at the parish rectory * 1:30 p.m., return to the residence in preparation for departure * 2:30 p.m., departure for Ottawa in two private automobiles, belonging to Mr. Adam Zurowski of Ottawa and to the District of the Polish Canadian Congress, from in front of the archdiocesan building. In further travels, the Cardinal was accompanied by Mr. W. Z. Jarmicki.

September 2 — 5:00 p.m., Ottawa, the Parish of St. Jacek {Hyacinth}, concelebrated Mass with homily, presentation of the relics of St. Jacek * September 3 — 6:00 p.m., Calgary, Parish of Our Lady of Czestochowa, solemn Holy Mass with homily; presentation of the relics of St. Stanislaw * September 4 — 7:00 a.m., Calgary, Parish of Our Lady of Czestochowa, baptism, concelebrated Mass with homily * Same day — 6:00 p.m., Edmonton, the Parish of Our Lady of the Rosary, greeting, homily * Sept. 5 — 8:00 a.m., Edmonton, visit to St. Albert, the grave of the Servant of God Br. A. Kowalczyk * 10:00 a.m., sanitarium in Scavo * 12:00 noon, Vylmo, meeting with Polish clergy * 6:00 p.m., Edmonton, Cathedral, concelebrated Mass and homily, presentation of the relics of St. Stanislaw * September 6 — 10:00 a.m., Winnipeg, welcome * Sept. 7 — 10:00 a.m., Winnipeg, visit at St. Andrew Bobola Parish and St. John of Kanty Parish * 4:30 p.m., the cathedral in Winnipeg, solemn Holy Mass and homily, presentation of the relics of St. John of Kanty * Sept. 8 — 9:00 a.m., Winnipeg, Parish of the Holy Spirit, concelebrated Mass and homily * 3:00 p.m., Toronto, Port Credit, arrival, greeting * September 9 — Toronto, visit * 4:00 p.m., a meeting with the Polish clergy of the Province of Ontario * 8:00 p.m., St. Stanislaw Parish in Toronto, concelebrated Mass and homily, meeting with parishioners * September 10 — 1:00 p.m., departure for Hamilton, visit at St. Gabriel Parish in Burlington and with Bishop Joseph Ryan * 7:30 p.m., Hamilton, St. Stanislaw Kostka parish, Novena to the Blessed Mother of Perpetual Help, a word of greeting, meeting with parishioners * September 11 — 8:30 a.m., Hamilton, St. Stanislaw Parish, concelebrated Mass and presentation of the relics of St. Stanislaw * 11:00 a.m., departure for London {Ontario}, visit with Msgr. Pluta, meeting with the Polish clergy at Bishop Emmett Carter's * 8:00 p.m., Our Lady of Czestochowa Parish in London, a Mass of welcome with Bishop E. Carter * September 12 — 10:00 a.m., London, Our Lady of Czestochowa Parish, concelebrated Mass and homily, visit * 1:30 p.m., Woodstock, Holy Cross mission, blessing of the crucifix, a speech * September 13 — 10:00 a.m., Toronto, St. Casimir parish, Mass and homily for the beginning of a school year * 2:00 p.m., a speech at the Mother of God Parish * September 14 — 4:00 p.m., Toronto, at the so-called Coliseum, the main celebration, concelebrated Mass and homily, later in Port Credit — a meeting with the committee responsible for organizing the celebration * Fragment of the speech in Toronto:

"My Dear Compatriots, we are all repaying a great debt similar to the debt that children owe to their parents. What I want to express as the prin-

cipal conclusion from my more than two weeks' long visit to Canada, is this very conviction that you, Dear Compatriots, try to and do repay this debt to Poland. You are repaying it here in Canada. And I am convinced that yours is a good repayment because we do live in a great family of nations and the thing that also testifies to the value of each nation is this nation's participation in the life of others, in the life of the entire humankind. I think that your participation in the life of Canada, in the life of humankind is very valuable and that your new homeland highly estimates this participation."

* Sept. 15 — 10:00 a.m., Oshawa, St. Jadwiga {Hedwig} Parish, Mass and homily * 6:00 p.m., Oshawa — St. Catharines, the Mother of God Parish, concelebrated Mass and homily * September 16 — A visit to the Niagara peninsula and the falls, a visit to the Polish cemetery * Same day — he crosses the border to the USA * 6:00 p.m., Buffalo, St. Stanislaw Church, Mass and homily * September 17 — 8:00 a.m., Chapel of the Felician Sisters, concelebrated Mass and homily * 4:00 p.m., blessing of a Polish hall at the college library of the Franciscan Sisters in Buffalo * 5:00 p.m., the Parish of the Assumption of the Blessed Virgin Mary, speech to the parishioners * September 18 — 12:00 noon, Hartford — New Britain, greetings, an address * 3:00 p.m., Hartford — New Britain, cemetery, blessing and prayers for the departed pioneers at the grave of Msgr. L. Bojanowski * 6:00 p.m., New Britain, the Sacred Heart of Jesus Church, concelebrated Mass and homily * September 19 — Cleveland, welcome by Polonia at the airport * 12:30 p.m., Chapel of Our Lady of Czestochowa at the Franciscan Sisters of St. Joseph (Jozefitki), greeting and blessing * St. Peter and St. Paul Church, greeting and blessing * 7:30 p.m., St. Stanislaw Church in Cleveland, concelebrated Mass and homily * September 20 — 7:30 a.m., the Church of St. Peter and St. Paul, concelebrated Holy Mass with homily * Same day — 12:00 noon, Pittsburgh, university, unveiling of Maria Sklodowska-Curie memorial plaque, an address to the countrymen and university representatives, supper at the residence of the Bishop of Pittsburgh, tour of the city * September 21 — 12:00 noon, Pittsburgh, visit with the Sisters of the Holy Family of Nazareth * 4:00 p.m., at the cathedral — concelebrated Mass and homily * September 22 — 12:00 noon, Detroit, welcome at the airport by Cardinal John F. Dearden, Primate of the USA, the Archbishop of Detroit * 6:00 p.m., visit to Polish parishes (St. Ladislaus, Our Lady Queen of the Apostles and St. Florian), prayers at the grave site of Polish priests (Fr. Jozef Dabrowski) * 6:00 p.m., Detroit — Hamtramck, "Polish town", Church of St. Florian, concelebrated Mass and homily * 11:00 p.m., Orchard Lake, Seminary chapel, first speech * September 23 — 10:00 a.m., seminary chapel in Orchard Lake, concelebrated Mass and homily * September 24 — welcome at the airport in Boston * 7:00 p.m., St. Wojciech {Adalbert} Church in Boston, Mass in Polish, Cardinal Richard

Cushing participating, remarks after Mass * September 25 — 7:00 a.m., Boston, orphanage run by the Bernardine Sisters, Mass and homily * Same day — welcome at the airport in Washington D.C., tour of the Arlington cemetery, prayers at the tomb of the unknown soldier, grave sites of: John Kennedy and his brother Robert, Paderewski, a monument to Gen. Wlodzimierz Krzyzanowski; later — St. Matthew's Cathedral * Visit to the seat of the National Catholic Bishops Conference and to the main office of the Organization of Catholic Husbands (Mr. Worth, president) * 6:00 p.m., Washington D.C., National Shrine of the Immaculate Conception, concelebrated Mass and homily * September 26 — 7:00 a.m., Washington, private concelebrated Mass at the Apostolic Delegation * Same day — tour of the new cathedral in Baltimore * St. Louis (at the airport, Cardinal John Carberry), tour of the old and the new cathedral, of the Curia, etc. * 7:00 p.m., St. Stanislaw Parish in St. Louis, Eucharistic service and homily, a meeting with countrymen, departure for Chicago * September 27 — 10:00 a.m., Chicago, the Parish of the Holy Polish Martyrs, concelebrated Mass and homily * 1:00 p.m., dedication of the Millennium monument at the cemetery of the Resurrection of Our Lord * 4:30 p.m., St. Jacek {Hyacinth} Parish, participated in a Eucharistic service, homily, departure * September 28 — 10:00 a.m., Philadelphia, Seminary, a word to seminarians * 11:00 a.m., Doylestown (American Czestochowa), concelebrated Mass with Cardinal John Krol, homily, meal, commemorative program * 5:00 p.m., Eucharistic service * September 29 — 9:00 a.m., Doylestown, meeting with priests, departure * Same day — 7:00 p.m., Brooklyn, St. Stanislaw Kostka Parish, concelebrated Mass and homily * September 30 — 10:00 a.m., Brooklyn, Holy Cross Parish, homily during Mass, departure * Same day — 7:00 p.m., New York, St. Patrick's Cathedral, concelebrated Mass and homily.

October 1 — Lodi, Chapel of the Felician Sisters, concelebrated Mass and homily, farewell, departure from the Kennedy airport at 8:30 p.m.

October 2 — 1:00 p.m., Rome, private concelebrated Mass at the Polish College chapel * October 3-8 — Rome, Polish college, privates Masses * October 9 — 12:30 p.m., Consilium de Laicis chapel, Mass and homily * October 10 — 7:30 a.m. - Rome, Polish College chapel, private concelebrated Mass * Participated in the plenary session of the Sacred Congregation for the Clergy dedicated to the issue of the councils of priests.

October 11-28 — First extraordinary session of the Synod of Bishops in Rome. Topic: closer communication between the conferences of bishops and the Apostolic See and among the conferences themselves. Cardinal K. Wojtyla took part in the Synod on the basis of his appointment by the Pope. He was part of the second French-language group * October 11 — 7:30 a.m., Rome, Chapel of the Polish College, private Mass * 9:00 a.m., Sistine Chapel, participation in a concelebrated Papal Mass, with a homily by the Pope for the opening of the Synod * October 12 — 12 noon, Monte Cassino, private concelebrated Mass at the tomb of St. Benedict, visit to the Polish cemetery * October 13-28 — usually at 7:00 a.m., at the chapel of the Polish College, private concelebrated Masses.

October 15 — Speaking in a discussion on the schema governing the deliberations of the Synod, Cardinal Wojtyla said:

> The schema quite rightly emphasizes the concept of communion (communio), which is something more than the concept of community (communitas) or group activity. The idea of communion stresses inter-personal relations, of one individual with another, both in an interchange of external values and in an interior participation of the persons. That is why the idea of "communion" is central to the collegiality of bishops.

October 24 — In the Synod hall, Cardinal K. Wojtyla presented the following proposal:

> It would be good if, before the conclusion, the Synod prepared a sincere and faithful account of the authentic spirit of these deliberations. The current session was closely observed, and is the subject of significant expectations both within and outside the Church. Sometimes the opinions and commentaries were quite remote from the real spirit of this assembly. Therefore, it becomes necessary to publicize a declaration which will shed light on the spirit and purpose of our work: a real communion and mutual exchange by which we asked how the Church could better fulfill its mission, both internal and external, in accordance with the dictates of Vatican II. To this end we must conserve and strengthen the energies of the Church, and also to add to them the energies which derive from collegiality.

October 25 — The designated leader, Cardinal Angelo Rossi, announced to the assembled Fathers of the Synod that a special committee was called to prepare a final declaration on the work of the Synod. Cardinal K. Wojtyla was appointed member of this committee * The same day — 5:00 p.m., Rome, Basilica of Santa Maria Maggiore, present at a concelebrated Papal Mass.

October 27 — Cardinal K. Wojtyla read the text of the declaration of fidelity of the Synod of Bishops. The declaration was greeted with applause. It includes these significant words:

> The Fathers of the Synod wish to express their respect and love to the Supreme Bishop, the Vicar of Christ and the Shepherd of the Universal Church... They thank him for his constant teaching in times when many feel that their faith is in danger. They ask him not to relinquish his authority of the universal Shepherd and, from the bottom of their hearts, they declare their assistance in his mission... Having entrusted the care and the govern-

ment of the Church to the Apostles and their successors with Peter at their head, it is necessary, first of all, to maintain and strengthen those energies which find their vivifying source and basis either in the primacy of the Supreme Pontiff or in the collegiality of bishops... The unity within the Church, so highly desired by the Christian faithful, depends in large measure either on the cooperation between the Supreme Pontiff and the conferences of bishops, or on the cooperation among the conferences themselves.

October 29 — 7:00 a.m., Rome, Chapel of the Sisters of the Resurrection, Mass with homily * October 30 — 7:00 a.m., private concelebrated Mass at the Chapel of the Polish College * October 31 — 7:00 a.m., Rome, Chapel of the Felician Sisters, Mass with homily.

November 1 — 1:00 p.m., private concelebrated Mass * Same day - the Vatican Radio broadcast an interview about his trip to Canada:

As far as the contacts with my countrymen in Canada are concerned, the laity played the most important role. It was they who took the initiative to organize this visit.

My visit was of an ecclesiastical and religious nature but it also emphasized what is so significant for Poles, for the Polish soul, and what remains a spiritual value for Poles, even those far away from the homeland. Our countrymen in Canada find their spiritual link with Poland mainly through the Church.

[About the old rural emigration:] The oldest group of immigrants is found in an area known as Kaszuby ... These first Polish immigrants came to Canada as a sign of protest against the German Kulturkampf. This is very telling: the Canadian Kaszuby testify to the Polishness of the Kaszuby people in Poland. This old rural group of immigrants has great accomplishments in maintaining their native Polish language. I spoke with people who have never been to Poland, who have never been taught Polish in any school, and yet they spoke beautiful Polish, and that with the characteristic accent of the region from which their parents came, for example, with the accents of Lwow or Poznan. The young people whom I met often speak Polish poorly, but with some deepest layer of the soul they are tied to Poland and to Polishness.

November 2 — 10:00 a.m., Polish military cemetery in Bologna, Holy Mass with homily * The same day — on the Vatican Radio, about his trip to the United States:

This was somewhat different than in Canada, because the trip was organized by the Polish Seminary in Orchard Lake.[11] Throughout our trip we had constant contact with the American Church hierarchy, and the cardinals and bishops were very hospitable, nowhere did I feel any lack of interest in the cause that I represent. Indeed, in many places I was surprised by the reception, but in the sense that it exceeded my expectations.

[About Cardinal Krol of Philadelphia] who is, shall we say, my contemporary in terms of the elevation to the rank of cardinal: we came to

---

[11] Near Detroit, Michigan

Doylestown, the American Czestochowa, together by helicopter; in Poland one does not yet go to Czestochowa by helicopter. After his nomination [Cardinal Krol] could not go to the parish of his ancestors [Siekierczyna near Limanowa] to perform the customary ingress, so I filled in for him. It is difficult to provide the exact statistics of how many of our countrymen have already become a part of the American society. But it is known that the numbers are in the millions ... Social and cultural progress came gradually, in the second or even the third generation. One gets the feeling, however, that our countrymen appreciate the place they have earned in the American society, and are thinking of further advances.

November 3 — All Souls' Day (this year observed on the 3rd of November), 6:45 a.m., Rome, Polish College, the Sisters' chapel, three private concelebrated Masses * November 4 — 6:00 p.m., Rome, Church of St. Stanislaw, Mass with homily * November 5-8 — Rome, Polish College, private concelebrated Masses * Assisi, Basilica of St. Francis, Mass * November 10-11 — Rome, Polish College, private concelebrated Masses, return to Krakow * November 11 — Warsaw — the Okecie airport. Interview given to Rev. A. Orszulik after the return from the Extraordinary Synod of Bishops.

November 12 — 7:00 a.m., Krakow, the residence chapel, Mass * November 13 — 7:00 a.m., Wawel Cathedral, at the Confession of St. Stanislaw {shrine with the saint's relics}, Mass with homily * 8:00 a.m., Cathedral, participation in a conventual Mass.

Shortly after his return he again received Wanda Dynowska-Umadevi on her second trip to Poland. Most recently, Wanda Dynowska had been living in northern India and was completely dedicated to organizing aid for the Tibetan refugees, primarily for children. She worked very closely with the Dalai Lama. During her conversation with the Cardinal she described the desperate plight of the Tibetan people. The Cardinal expressed his great sympathy and promised to say a Mass for the intention of both the murdered and the living Tibetans.

November 16 — 9:00 a.m., the Dominican Church, Mass with homily for university students * 5:00 p.m., Cathedral, at the Confession of St. Stanislaw, sermon to young people * 7:45 p.m., at the Mariacki Church, after the return from Canada and the United States:

The gospel about the tree, which is like the Kingdom of God ... When I was visiting our countrymen overseas, I often saw that tree with the eyes of my soul. Man lives by the laws of nature, but differently than the rest of nature. The tree does not ask about its roots, but it has them. It does not ask about the mustard seed from which it grew, but it did grow from that seed. But man must ask about such things. That is why there is a bond between us, living here on the banks of the Vistula, and our countrymen, living across the ocean: a bond of common roots, from which there grows this common tree, although it grows in different parts of our globe. We [the

Polish Church] grow and spread from the mustard seed which is Christ Crucified and Resurrected. And through our works, through our suffering, through our spiritual accomplishments, through our history, through our witness, through our culture, we bring a new life, new content and new values to the great tree of the spirit. And this ... is our place in the family of man. It is more than just a spot on the globe, a geographic locale assigned to us by Providence. While I was visiting with our countrymen, thousands of kilometers from here, I came to realize in a very special way, that, indeed, this is not just a geographic locale. It is a place in the spiritual communion of the great family of man, in which we, Poles, have our own special place, in which to be Polish means to bring in certain special values. I came to realize this, when I heard what the Canadian and the American bishops had to say about this, how they spoke about what Poles brought to the Church living on the American soil, in Canada and the United States: what they brought and what they continue to bring. This is a fundamental truth which I have experienced firsthand.

They welcomed me as a visible symbol of the bond between them and us. Despite all the distances in time and space, there is a bond between us. And this bond does not loosen, even if, with the passage of time, they depart from our language — their children forget how to speak Polish, they know the language poorly or not at all — but still the bond remains.

They welcomed me then as a sign of this spiritual bond — not a material bond, not a political one, but spiritual, a bond which exists among all of us, which connects us through time and space. The bond which connects us in the Church, throughout our entire thousand-year heritage of faith and Christian life, this is the bond that is most meaningful. It becomes immediately apparent: I did not have to explain anything to them, I did not have to make any excuses before them. I was immediately accepted as one of them, in the name of that bond.

We can see what are the truths, what are the values that unite us. It follows from this that we must uphold this Christian truth, this Gospel which has been so deeply ingrained in the Polish soul, which in its own way forms the value of that soul. The Gospel, which is forever renewed and which, in our times, too, gives life to the entire human family — to every people, every nation of this great human family, which creates prospects, which forms the foundation of life and determines its purpose.

November 17 — 7:00 a.m., Mass with homily at the Church of the Franciscan Fathers, for the Feast of Blessed Salomea * November 18 — 7:00 a.m., residence chapel, Mass with homily for the opening of a special chapter of the Congregation of the Sisters of the Sacred Heart * November 21 — Krakow — the Church of St. John, of the Sisters of the Presentation. Sermon on the Feast of the Presentation of Our Lady * November 23 — Wieliczka, Church of St. Klemens (Feast of the parish patron):

A bishop, who expresses the communion of the People of God, must also concern himself with the care for the Universal Church ... He may be the Shepherd of some local Church but, as the Vatican Council teaches, he cannot shut himself in this Church ... The experience of all the (local) Churches, through their shepherds, must be shared, must be exchanged.

This leads to a greater richness of the Universal Church.

The same day — 6:30 p.m., at the Church of the Discalced Carmelites, during a service for the intention of the beatification of Brother Albert Chmielowski:

> I am often in Rome and I see how the issue of the Church of the poor is maturing. I see this at various gatherings, to mention only the last Synod, I see this in the importance given to the bishops and the episcopates of the so-called Third World, the world of the poor. I see how particular attention is paid to their voice, and how the problems presented by them take on a special significance ... The cause of this beatification is not only — as one might say from a strictly human perspective — one of our Polish ambition, but also a great cause of the entire contemporary Church, which is proceeding today in the same direction as was Brother Albert ...
>
> We would like to say: Holy Father, here in Poland we have a man who was a living incarnation of the Church of the poor. He was a living incarnation of the cause which is so important to the Church of today, so important to you personally. Bestow upon this our countryman, the Servant of God, Brother Albert Chmielowski, the title of Blessed, the title of Saint, so that under this title he can continue to proclaim the great cause of the Church of the poor, both in our land and in the entire universal Church of Christ. (The Albertine Sisters)

November 25 — At the chapel on Franciszkanska Street, on the occasion of the opening of a General Chapter of the Sisters of the Sacred Heart: "Now this great work [of the Vatican Council] belongs to all of the People of God. It has been divided among all the congregations that exist on earth within the rich and varied community of the People of God." * 11 a.m., the Church of St. Anne, requiem Mass for the late Rev. Prof. Aleksy Klawek, funeral * November 26 — 11a.m., Jasna Gora, the Chapel of Our Lady, Mass with homily for seminarians making a retreat after their return from military service (impressions from the trip to Canada and USA, and from the Synod of Bishops in Rome) * November 27 — 10 a.m., Wawel Cathedral, Mass for the souls of deceased bishops and priests * At the residence, conference of priests — deans * Same day — 8:00 p.m., St. Anne's Church, conference on the subject of the Synod:

> There is a complementary relationship between collegiality and the primacy. These two authorities complement and complete each other. This is by no means an antithetical relationship. These two highest forms of authority in the Church do not exclude each other nor do they compete. The Synod has taught us, bishops, to be together, it taught us to exchange views, communicate our experiences to one another, share our concerns ... A Synod is more concise than a Council, but mutual communication is what makes up its basic context. Communicating in a common faith was a great experience for us: the communion of faith, the primacy of Peter, but also the unity of the episcopal, i.e. the apostolic, mission of all the bishops in the world, collegially.

November 28 — 10:35 a.m., Krakow, 3 Franciszkanska Street, meeting of the subcommittee for the implementation of the directives of the Second Vatican Council in Poland: Cardinal Karol Wojtyla, Bishops: Tokarczuk, Stroba, Pietraszko; priests: Rev. Dean J. Majka, H. Kocylowski. Presentations: Bishop J. Stroba, Bishop I. Tokarczuk, Rev. Prof. Majka, Rev. Krucina.

November 29-31 — Canonical visitation of the Parish of Our Lady of Lourdes, Krakow — Nowa Wies.

November 30 — Krakow, the Church of St. Andrew. Holy Mass with sermon.

December 3 — Meeting in an auditorium at KUL[12] with the university community on the subject of the Second Extraordinary Synod of Bishops * Same day — at KUL, during a symposium (December 1-3) dedicated to Christian culture, a presentation by K. Wojtyla entitled *Education to the Fullness of Human Culture*. * December 4 — Lublin, KUL, chapel at a boarding school of student priests, concelebrated Mass.

December 5 — Meeting of the Council of the Pontifical Department of Theology in Krakow.

The Cardinal, who during his stay in Rome participated in the Synod of Bishops, in the work of Consilium de Laicis, the Congregation for the Oriental Churches, the Congregation for the Clergy and the Congregation for the Doctrine of the Faith (where Rev. Prof. Rozycki cooperated with him), made his observations: There is a need for the Polish theological milieu to take part in the work of the Apostolic See; there is a great need in Rome for this kind of work. In order to facilitate the spread of Polish theological thought to an international forum, the Cardinal submitted a "pro memoria" in that regard to Cardinal Garrone, suggesting, among others, that- a list of theological works appearing in all, especially the less known, languages be maintained and that a proper policy of publicizing the less known works be adopted, he suggested that efforts should be made to bring about "gemellagio" (coupling into twins) of universities... He also spoke of the possibility of cooperation with the Seminary in Orchard Lake in the United States... Organizational and personnel matters were discussed. The Cardinal expressed a view that pastoral medicine should be a subject taught at the Department. He also suggested that a memorial book to honor the late Rev. Dr. Aleksy Klawek be put together. (From the minutes of the Council of the Department)

December 7 — Katowice, conference for priests involved in pastoral ministry to university students * December 8 — After his return from the Synod, the Cardinal came to the shrine in Kalwaria to spend a personal day of recollection there. Despite the deep snow, he traversed the

Way of the Cross, using ski poles to navigate. After this devotion, which lasted several hours, he did not seem tired, but radiated good cheer and energy * The same day — at the Church of Our Lady in Myslenice:

In retracing her steps down the trail of our redemption from Calvary ... the Immaculate Mother of Christ ... always and everywhere strives to assist all of us to overcome the effects of the Original Sin which are in every one of us. In this way she repays that singular debt that she incurred through her Son in the work of Redemption, the debt for the grace of the Immaculate Conception.

December 14 — The Mariacki Church, on the first anniversary of the coronation of a copy of the image of Our Lady of Czestochowa (in the presence of Bishop Jerzy Ablewicz):

Mary was, is and shall always remain the most important witness of the closeness of God. In her the Word was made Flesh, God became Man. The unbounded took on bounds, found a created and human dimension for all time: in her, eternity meets time. All the definitions of the truth, which was fulfilled in her, can be expressed in the simple sentence of today's liturgy: "The Lord is near:" in her, the Lord is near, and thanks to her, He is near to us.

The same day — at the inauguration of an ordinary meeting of the Archdiocesan Council of Priests in Krakow:

In essence, collegiality is nothing other than a common responsibility, with the Holy Father, for the entire Church; it does not eclipse his unique responsibility. Collegiality complements it, makes it more apparent ... It provides a richer base of experience, a new view upon the Church, through as many eyes and as many hearts as there were bishops at the Council and now at the Synod.
The truth about communion, whether of bishops with the Pope, or of priests with their bishop, is magnificent. This is the most Christ-like truth, which He gave to His Apostles.

The same day — 4:30 p.m., at the Franciscans, Mass with homily for charity workers * December 20 — 9:00 a.m., residence chapel, Mass with homily for WIK {Higher Catechetic Institute} * December 22 — Christmas greetings from all religious congregations in Krakow * December 24 — 8 a.m., Wawel Cathedral, participation in the morning services {roraty}; at midnight — Holy Mass in Nowa Huta:

It is a law of nature that a woman giving birth should find a room, a roof over her head ... Here [in Nowa Huta] we come to the new-born Christ with a feeling that there is a special analogy between the stable of Bethlehem, the events of Bethlehem, and the events here. Because here also, for many years, there was no room for You, Lord, no roof over Your head. And we all felt, and all of Poland felt, and the whole world felt, that room should be found...
On this night, all of us, awed by the great love of God which has entered humanity, entered the history of the human soul, compare His great love

with our tiny, human love ... May our love remain unbroken, especially in our families, in our marriages, in the mutual relationship of parents and children, between generations. May our love remain unbroken in our Christian nation. May it be reborn, may it go out into society, despite everything that is trying to destroy and undermine it.

On the same day — Krakow, the Religious Seminary of Krakow. He opened a meeting dedicated to the Second Synod of Bishops.

December 25 — 10:00 a.m., Mass at the Cathedral:

Today, on Christmas Day, all believers — and even those who stand apart — live through some inexpressible experience. We come face to face with a mystery which confirms all of creation, and especially man. God, the Creator, put aside His creation, especially man, because of sin, because man has sinned. That God accepts his creation, and especially man, anew. [The Word of God] became a very rich and creative leaven for our Polish culture ... This leaven of the Word of God, which has entered the history of the Polish soul, continues beyond Poland: it serves other societies, it serves the whole great family of man.

December 26 — The Church of St. Szczepan:

Sometimes we wonder, when we meet people who do not believe, who doubt, why we are so helpless, why we can't advise them, why we can't justify our faith, why we can't show them the way which we, and the entire Church, are traveling ... This weakness surely comes from the fact that our dialogue with God is so infrequent.

December 27 — 4:00 p.m., chapel of the Theological Seminary, sermon for the beginning of a retreat for graduating high school students * Same day — sermon to the youngest priests of the Krakow archdiocese:

What is the state of my awareness during the Holy Mass? Am I only concerned with the proprieties of offering Christ's Sacrifice ... Or am I aware that it is Christ who is offering it through me, that He is entrusting Himself, His own deed, to me. To so entrust oneself, one's own deed, to so many people, is evidence of great trust. The deed which He performed and which is still being performed in Him: the giving of Himself to the Father, encompassing everyone and everything: that is the deed of Christ. He offers it to me, entrusts me with that deed. Am I fully aware of that? Does that awareness go with me everywhere? When I proclaim the Word of God, again, He entrusts me with His thoughts, with His Word. When I grant absolution... I know, dear brothers, that listening and judging can be tiring, because man has his limits. And still, thank God, we have those long lines at the confessionals, especially at certain times ... But is there anywhere in my awareness as a priest this thought that it is again He who entrusts me, a priest, with His power to forgive sins, and thereby, as it were, entrusts me with His Cross, through which He paid for the sins of every man and of all mankind?

December 28 — Zakopane, Feast of the Holy Family, to the families of Polish-Americans from all of Podhale:[13]

> During my trip to North America, your compatriots from here, from Podhale ... greeted me cordially and entertained me with song. They try to sing in the same way you sing here, but no one anywhere knows how to sing the way you sing here. They also entertained me with dances; they try to dance the way you dance here, but no one anywhere knows how to dance "krzesany"[14] the way you dance it here. In any case, they do everything to maintain the bond with their native land, especially with Podhale. That is why they received me as one of their own. I was not a stranger, but one of them ...
>
> "Lift your hand, O Child of God, and bless our dear land"[15] — we ask this for our country, knowing that the strength of our country, as for every nation and for every society, is in the family. We do much too little to strengthen that strength... Too much was done to weaken the bonds of marriage and family! We must help people, we must help marriages, we must help families: that is why there is a state, that is why there is a strong society, to help families.

* 6:00 p.m., Nowy Targ, *Oplatek*[16] with university students * December 31 — Parish of Our Lady of Lourdes, for the conclusion of the visitation and the end of the year:

> [On meeting with the poor, the sick:] These are often shattering meetings, shattering in their human tragedy, deeply moving, because they show what a great treasure our faith is, what strength it gives to man, and how this strength becomes most apparent in infirmity ... I think that the most precious element in the life of your parish is the strong direction toward the future: that is why you make so much room for the young ... This testifies to the fact that the parish is looking to the future, is shaping the People of God in the perspective of time.

Same day — at the Franciscans, Mass for the end of the year (midnight), sermon:

> It is my wish to you all and to myself that whatever this new year, the beginning of the eighth decade of this century, brings to us, that it would be within the Sacrifice of Christ ... Everything is already within it. But what I mean is for us to take everything in this new year and to be able to place it within the Sacrifice of Christ ... May everything, by being part of His Sacrifice, have a full meaning, and be for us a source of grace and a source of good.

December 1969. The third book by Cardinal K. Wojtyla appears: *Person and Act,* PPT, Krakow 1969. He had worked on it for several years and fragments of it had appeared before its publication:

> *"Person and Act* as an aspect of awareness" in *Pastori et Magistro* — a collective work published for the 50th anniversary of the priesthood of Bishop P. Kalwa, Lublin 1966, pp. 292-305. *"Person and Act.* The reflexive

---

[13] The mountainous Carpathian region in the south of Poland.

[14] A Polish mountaineer's dance

[15] Words of a Christmas carol

[16] See Glossary.

functioning of awareness and its emotionalization" in: *Stud. Theol. Vars*. VI (1968) no. 1 pp. 101-119. *"Person and Act* in the context of man's dynamic nature" in: *Of God and Man, Philosophical Issues* — a collective work edited by Bohdan Bejze, Warsaw 1968, pp. 204-226.

Fragments of the book *Person and Act*:

This treatise arises from a need to provide an objective look at the great process of discovery which might be called the experience of man. It is the richest of all of man's experiences, and also the most complex ... This experience arises from all of the other experiences, it is their sum, or rather their result ... However, other persons, besides myself, become the subject of experience. Man's experience is formed by his experience of himself and of all those people who have some direct contact with him ... But I experience others in a different way than I experience myself (pp. 5-7) ... In a way, each experience is also an understanding of what I am experiencing... We hold the position that an act is a particular moment when we gain insight into — and thus experience — a person ... In its full experiential content, the fact "man acts" ... can be understood ... as the act of a person. (p. 13) ... This treatise has a reductive character ... On the way to the interpretation of the of concepts of person and act, there arises the problem of the proper integration of the two kinds of understanding which arise from the differences in the experience of [self and others — AS]. The solution to this problem is one of the main goals of this treatise. Attaining this goal is all the more difficult insofar as we are dealing with that current of philosophical tradition which for centuries has shown a decided dichotomy...

In this work, we attempt to resolve that dichotomy... in the very concept of man. It is to the philosophy of consciousness that we owe, indirectly, the more thorough knowledge of man from the point of view of his consciousness — and this certainly leads to an enrichment of the vision of person and act. We would still like to take advantage of this enrichment, even while remaining in the area of the philosophy of existence. An attempt to properly integrate the two kinds of understanding, which arise from both aspects of man's experience, into the concept of person and act, must become an attempt at integrating two philosophical orientations, or even two philosophies. (pp. 20-23) ... In citing this sentence [citation from *Gaudium et Spes* as a motto of the book[17] — A. Szostek], the author wishes to refer to the time when the study on person and act was in its early stage. He also wishes to recall the particular intellectual climate of the time when he was pondering the issues discussed in this treatise. It was the climate of the Second Vatican Council and, in particular, of the team which, at the Council, undertook the task of writing the constitution on the Church in the modern world. (p. 23) ... Man must not lose sight of his proper place in the world which he himself has shaped — and that is the world of culture and civilization, i.e. the "contemporary world" that we considered with such care while preparing the constitution *Gaudium et Spes*. In some measure, this treatise also refers to the book *Love and Responsibility* published seven years ago ... *Person and Act* has its roots in that earlier treatise. It was also that work that gave rise to the need to study the person in greater detail ... Above all, we are striving to reach an understanding of the human person for its own sake. We

---

[17] "The Church by reason of her role and competence, is not identified with any political community nor bound by ties to any political sysytem. It is at once the sign and the safeguard of the transcendental dimension of the human person." *Gaudium et Spes*, Pastoral Constitution on the Church in the Modern World, 76.

need to touch upon the human reality at the most appropriate point — at the point indicated by human experience, at the point from which man cannot retreat without the sense of losing himself. (pp. 25 - 26) (Compiled by Fr. A. Szostek)

1970

January 2-6 — Zakopane. Ski trip. He lived and said Holy Masses at the Ursuline Sisters at Jaszczurowka.

January 6 — Wawel Cathedral: "Faith is the most interior matter for each of us; it is a personal encounter with God Himself" * January 7-10 — Private Masses at the residence chapel * January 9-10 — Krakow, the palace of the Archbishop. Scientific conference dedicated to the issues on the division between physics and the philosophy of nature * January 10 — 8:00 p.m., *Oplatek*[1] with the Club of Catholic Intellectuals * January 11 —9:00 a.m., chapel of the Ursulines, conference of teachers; explanation of the changes in the liturgy of the Holy Mass * 4:00 p.m., *Oplatek* for catechists * January 12 — At the Jesuit Fathers, a word to the brothers attending a course * January 14-17 — Warsaw, chapel of the Ursuline Sisters, private Masses * January 18 — 8:00 a.m., Krzyzowa, Mass with homily, dedication of the church organ * January 18-19 — Ski trip: Zlatna — Lipowska — Ujsoly * January 19-25 — Private Masses at the residence chapel * January 20 — "At the invitation of His Eminence the Cardinal, a large group of Sisters of Our Lady of Mercy took part in a symposium dedicated to the issues of the Second Vatican Council" (From the chronicles of the Congregation) * January 20 — Krakow, 3 Franciszkanska Street, meeting of the Episcopal Committee for Pastoral Ministry; 9:00 a.m., concelebrated Mass at the chapel * 10:30 a.m., At the beginning the Cardinal announces that the agenda of the meeting was prepared by the subcommittee for the implementation of the decisions of the Second Vatican Council in Poland, during the meetings on: May 3, June 30, and November 29, 1969. The meeting was chaired by Archbishop B. Kominek. Report by the chairman: *Pastoral Work in Poland in the Context of the Religiousness of the West.* Further in the meeting, an analysis of the specific situation in Poland (Bishop I. Tokarczuk and Rev. J. Majka) — on the self-realization of the Church according to the directives of the Vatican Council. * January 21 — Second day of deliberations of the Episcopal Committee for Pastoral Ministry. The Cardinal took part in the discussions of the presentation by Bishop J. Stroba, *The Proclamation of the Good News in Light of the Vatican Council.* He[2] spoke of the need for integrating everything that the Church has said at the Council with what was said before, the need of preparing a new catechism, and of issues arising from the new missal readings. Summing up the deliberations, Cardinal Wojtyla said: "the sociological-religious study of the Church in Poland has been complet-

---

[1] See Glossary.
[2] unclear whether Stroba or Wojtyla

ed" — now we must "work out a plan for the future and present it at the plenary session of the Episcopate." He also spoke about the need to integrate the teaching of religion with preaching, and about the need for the Committee to tackle ethical issues:

> ...lay ethics is making progress, and we must examine that progress ... to determine if the solutions offered by lay ethics are congruent in some measure with Christian ethics: ... how lay ethics influences the Christian character of the family. We must discuss the issue of Christian attitude, for example, discuss the fact of breaking with penance. We must pay attention to the internal matters of the Church, including the issue of the clergy...

A team (including Cardinal Wojtyla) was selected to prepare the subjects of presentations for the Committee's June meeting. (From the minutes of the Committee)

January 22 — Krakow, 3 Franciszkanska Street, days of reflection for national directors of pastoral ministry to various social, professional and specialist groups * Same day — meeting at the residence on the subject of the apostolate of families * January 23 — Second day of reflection for national directors of pastoral ministry, together with the Committee for the Apostolate of the Laity. The first part of the day was dedicated to presentations on the role of small groups, informal groups, and the theological basis of their activities (Rev. E. Weron and Rev. J. Majka). After the intermission, there were discussions and sharing of experiences in this area * January 23-24 — Meeting of the Committee for the Apostolate of the Laity. Meeting with national directors of pastoral ministry to various social, professional and specialist groups. Issues of the culture of pastoral ministry — publicizing and utilizing the *Directory* — the Committee's methods of action.

January 25 — Church of the Missionary Fathers at Stradom (after the nomination of Rev. Albin Malysiak to the rank of bishop):

> We look into that great light, in which Christ the Priest comes to us: the Son of God, Incarnate, Crucified and Risen from the dead ... And as He once said to Saul-Paul so powerfully, on the road to Damascus: "Come, follow me", so He says it to us. Let us follow Him! Let us pray that we may all know how to follow Him ... And let us pray for this especially for the priests, let us pray for the bishops, who are to lead us in following Christ into the Kingdom of God.

Same day — 7:00 p.m., at the Church of the Dominicans, for the conclusion of an octave of prayers for the unification of Christendom:

> St. Paul says, "we are," and we understand this to mean: "let us be the helpers of God." That means, let us seek the unity which makes us one in Christ; let us seek it despite our differences. That is how we understand it, we, the Christians of the 20th century, we, the Catholics of the era of the Second Vatican Council. We know that it is unity which we still lack. And

we believe that we must mature into creating it.

On the same day there was a get-together (there were many of them) with his former university colleagues at the home of Mrs. Irena Kijakowa, mother of Ewa Radlinska. At the parting, the hostess wishes the Cardinal that he ascend to the Chair of Peter one day... The Cardinal burst out laughing at that, and said, "Granny, thank you very much; nobody has ever wished me that." (According to an account by Ewa Radlinska) Present at the gathering were: Irena Kijakowa, Ewa Radlinska, Irena Bajerowa, Maria Bobrownicka, Janina Garycka, Krystyna Zbijewska, Halina and Tadeusz Kwiatkowski, Tadeusz Ulewicz. (According to an account by Maria Bobrownicka)

January 26 — 9:00 a.m., Bielsko-Biala, concelebrated Mass with homily for the opening of a regional conference * On the same day — Krakow, Pradnik Czerwony. The chapel of the Albertine Sisters. A speech on the anniversary of the establishment of the Congregation * January 29 — 5:00 p.m., *Oplatek*[3] in the refectory of the Dominicans * Same day — at the Sisters of the Visitation, on the Feast of St. Francis de Sales:

> The word "bishop" means guardian. A guardian: he who watches and cares for the highest good, which in every person is his immortal soul ... And for the good of immortal souls, the bishop guards the great, magnificent heritage of God's truth ... I can still see before me all my brother bishops, of different races, different nations, as they were gathered, a few years ago, at the Council, and as they were, just a few months ago, gathered at an extraordinary Synod of Bishops in Rome. All of these bishops of the world, of the Catholic Church, I commend to your prayers.

January 30 — At the bishop's palace, he received a group of scholars from the Jagiellonian University, the University of Silesia and the Academy of Agriculture in Krakow, who were concerned about the slow pace of implementing the decisions of the Second Vatican Council.

> The reservations concerned the attitude of the clergy towards the laity (paternalism), the forms of parish work, preaching, teaching of religion, etc. The Cardinal listened carefully, explained, spoke of the difficulties, often he agreed with them, asked for their patience. The conversation lasted a long time. Present were: Irena Bajerowa, Urszula Dambska-Prokop, Ryszard Luzny, Wieslaw Witkowski, Prof. Franciszek Nowotny and the undersigned. The Cardinal remembered the details of this conversation very well, because on May 8, 1977, during a session of the synod in Mogila, he said that what the synod is now working on, is the realization of our desiderata and the response to our concerns expressed then. (Maria Bobrownicka)

Same day - 8:00 p.m., *Oplatek* for lawyers.

---

[3] See Glossary.

January 31 — Meeting of the Council of the Pontifical Department of Theology in Krakow.

> **In the agenda item devoted to "current business," the Cardinal suggested that courses of theology for lay people be organized at the Department of Theology. Enrollment for such courses could be done through parishes... (From the minutes of the Council)**

February 1 — 8:00 a.m., Chapel of the Sisters of the Holy Family of Nazareth, Mass with homily (50th anniversary) * 2:00 p.m., the residence, visit with all residents and singing of carols * 7:00 p.m., Mass and get-together with physicians (*Oplatek*) * February 2 — 5:00 p.m., Godziszka, Mass with homily, dedication of the church organ * February 3 — 7:00 residence chapel, Mass with homily for the conclusion of a course for nurses * 9:30 a.m., chapter house at the Dominicans, sermon for the beginning of a course for missionaries * February 4 — Zakopane, concelebrated Mass with homily for the beginning of a regional conference * On the same day the Cardinal sent the text of his report: *Suggestions Regarding Dialogue in the Church* to Primate Wyszynski * February 6-8 — Zakopane — Jaszczurowka, skiing * February 7 — He delivered (through Bishop Julian Groblicki) the renovated statutes of the Department of Theology in Krakow (approved in June of 1974, after corrections had been introduced) to the Sacred Congregation for Catholic Education * February 8 — 2:50 p.m., residence chapel, baptizes a child of a family of friends * Same day — 6:30 p.m., Church of St. Joseph at Podgorze (on the occasion of dedicating of the central heating system):

> **[The Son of God] became, and continues to become, a Gift for all of us, so that we could also become a gift for others. So that we could share with one another a good word, a noble deed and a climate of true humanity for which we have to struggle with some other, antihuman, climate which attempts to impose itself on our lives.**

February 9 — 5:00 p.m., Olpiny (diocese of Tarnow), participation in the celebrations of the Visitation by the Blessed Mother * February 11 — Wawel Cathedral, Mass with the blessing of ashes * February 12-14 — Residence chapel, private Masses * Krakow — the Palace of the Archbishop, scientific session dedicated to the issues of the research on Christian antiquity. Cardinal Wojtyla: opening remarks. (The session lasted two days: February 13-14) * February 14-29 — Canonical visitation of the Parish of St. Florian * February 15 — 3:00 p.m., the Parish Church of St. Mikolaj {Nicholas}, sermon to invalids * February 16 — Church of St. Florian, at a meeting with single persons:

> **In a sense, a single person does not live within the strictures [of a family], but in the evening [of his life] that person must also give an accounting**

of his activity in love and service for others. [The parish] must show the way, must show the need, issue the call ... This is social charity; it is made up of such small services; this is how Jesus Christ sees it.

February 18 — 11:00 a.m., Warsaw, participation in the funeral of the late Stanislaw Wyszynski, father of the Primate * February 19 — Mass at the Chapel of the Daughters of Charity, at 2 Helclow Street in Krakow, for the conclusion of a retreat for the sick. He preached a sermon, and then met with the sisters and the sick (Congregation of the Sisters of Our Lady of Mercy) * February 20 — 6:00 p.m., Stations of the Cross with the faithful at St. Florian's Church * February 22 — Sunday, 6:30 a.m., Narutowicz Hospital, Mass with homily for patients.

That day he came to the provincial house of the Daughters of Charity in Krakow, on Warszawska Street, to preach a sermon for the close of the annual retreat. He was asked to do this by the Missionary Fathers (19 Sw. Filipa Street). He said to them: "It was not in the program that I should speak here; I was abducted by the Missionary Fathers who are your brothers — because you have one father, St. Vincent, and one Mother. They are also your spiritual directors. I will come to see the sisters on Friday; today I was asked to say a word for the close of the retreat. Your retreat master has already done that. I just want to add, in connection with today's Gospel about the Transfiguration of Our Lord, that this retreat should transfigure you for Christ. We must continually be transfigured, and turn our intentions into deeds, so that our life will bear fruit. When you, sisters, disperse and return to your respective houses, just as the apostles dispersed into the world, may you spread the Word of the Lord, just as the apostles did, may you continue to be transfigured in Christ, as we must continue to be transfigured until we close our earthly eyes and open the ones which will see Christ in the brightness of eternity. These are my wishes for you, sisters. And now, please, return me to the Missionary Fathers." After giving his blessing, he left the chapel and returned to the Missionaries. *(Congregation of the Daughters of Charity).*

February 25 — 12 noon, the residence, meeting of priests who head the deaneries * February 26 — 12 noon, auditorium of the Theological Seminary, a memorial get-together for the deceased professors, Rev. Wladyslaw Wicher and Rev. Aleksy Klawek.

February 27 — Friday. During the visitation of St. Florian Parish, 6:20 p.m., he came to the house of the Daughters of Charity (8 Warszawska Street). He said Mass at the chapel and preached a homily:

"As I visit the various parish organizations, such as rosary groups, catechists, and private groups, I also visit religious congregations. There are 3 of them in this parish: Daughters of Divine Charity, Sisters of the Holy Family of Nazareth, and Daughters of Charity. They form the wealth of the parish, they are a help in maintaining the religious spirit." In his homily, he made reference to the Gospel about the landowner who rented out his vineyard to the workers ...
Applying the lesson of the Gospel to the Daughters of Charity, he said

that our Heavenly Father sent His Son to us trusting that we will pay Him appropriate respect. He sent His Son as the deposit of Grace which we are to use to enrich ourselves and to carry to our neighbors. The trust that the Father placed in us obligates us to make reparations for the sins of those who, just as they did years ago, sin by killing, by crucifying Jesus in their souls, by mocking Him, by not believing in His eternal existence. The trust that God the Father placed in us also requires us to give witness to Him and His Son by our love of Him, by a love that permeates our whole being, by a life of sacrifice for our neighbors who live in poverty, by our conduct worthy of the brides of Christ.

After the Mass, he bestowed his blessing upon those gathered in the chapel: the Missionary Fathers, the Sisters of the Holy Family of Nazareth and the Daughters of Charity. Then, as usual, he went to the infirmary to visit the aged and sick sisters; he spent a few moments to talk to each one of them and to bestow his blessing. Then he spoke to the remaining sisters gathered in one of the rooms, and bestowed his blessing. The sisters presented the Cardinal with a bouquet of roses. Upon leaving, he asked for their prayers.

After meeting with the sisters in the infirmary, the Cardinal went to a room in the provincial house, where all the sisters were gathered. After greeting the Cardinal, Mother Visitator presented him with the relics of St. Vincent and a small cross. Then she presented a report on the population of the convents in the Krakow province of the order. After a short speech, the Cardinal visited with the novice sisters (at the seminary) and the student sisters at a junior institute. After dinner, he went to the house at 11 Warszawska Street. The Cardinal was accompanied by, among others: the chaplain and the pastor, Rev. Broszkiewicz, along with several of the Missionary Fathers.

In the commemorative book, for the date of February 27, 1970, he entered these words:

"On the day of visitation, conducted during the visitation of St. Florian Parish, when I again had occasion to visit your houses on Warszawska Street, with a sincere blessing for the aged and sick sisters, for the junior institute, for the novitiate, for all the sisters, for Mother Visitator. Father Karol Wojtyla, Metropolitan Archbishop of Krakow." (Daughters of Charity)

February 28-March 3 — Visitation of the parish in Olszanica.

March 4 — 10:00 a.m., celebration of the feast of the parish patron saint — St. Kazimierz {Casimir} at the Church of the Reformed Franciscans in Krakow. On the third day of a 40-hour devotion, he said Mass and delivered a homily to a very large group of faithful * March 5 — 2:00 p.m., Lublin, Chapel of the Ursuline Sisters (?), private concelebrated Mass * Same day — defense of a thesis by Rev. Tadeusz Styczen, entitled *The Issue of Ethics as an Empirically Validated and Generally Applicable Theory of Morality* — in fulfillment of the requirements for acceptance to assistant professorship. The reviewer of the thesis was Cardinal Prof. K. Wojtyla * March 6 — 8:15 p.m., Church of St. Anne in Krakow, Mass for the end of a retreat for university students * March 7 — 6:00 p.m., Dominican Fathers, Mass with homily for the

Feast of St. Thomas Aquinas * March 8 — 11 a.m., Gorlice, Pontifical High Mass with sermon for the conclusion of the visitation by the Blessed Mother in the Tarnow diocese * 5:00 p.m., a sermon for the beginning of the visitation in the Przemysl diocese * 9:00 p.m., departure for Katowice, from there, departure for Rome * March 9 — 8:00 a.m., Vienna, private Mass at the chapel of the nunciature[4] * March 10-14 — Rome; he lived at the Polish College. Participated in the 4th plenary session of the Council for the Laity. Delivered a report entitled *Apostolate of the Laity in Abnormal Situations.*

March 10 — Delivered his comments and remarks on the outline of the document regarding the location and cooperation between Church-run universities and faculties (within the framework of works on the reform of the Church academic legislation) to the Sacred Congregation for Catholic Education. Cardinal Wojtyla particularly emphasizes the necessity of cooperation and assistance by the stronger centers to the weaker ones. He also suggests that religious seminaries be affiliated with departments of theology. As a chairman of the Committee for Catholic Education of the Conference of the Polish Episcopate, he successfully inspires the introduction of this practice in Poland. The work on the new regulation of the matters of the Church-run institutes of higher learning was concluded with the constitution *Sapientia Christiana* issued by John Paul II on April 15, 1979.

March 15, Rome, at the Polish Church of St. Stanislaw:

The life of God, which has been imparted and is continually being imparted to man, allows man to surpass himself, allows him to transcend the limits of death with the hope of life. And from that point of death, which is the limit of every human life, the life of God returns into the temporal life of man. It enters into the whole fabric of human life and forms its chief framework. Man continually transcends himself by accepting the life of God.

March 16 — 7:00 a.m., Rome, Chapel of the Polish College, private concelebrated Mass * March 17 — 7:00 a.m., the College, chapel of the sisters, private concelebrated Mass * March 18 — 5:00 p.m., Vienna, Mass in the chapel of the nunciature.

March 19 — Warsaw, the Primate's chapel, private Mass * March 21 — 5:00 p.m., Tyniec, concelebrated Mass with sermon, later participation in a meeting of the parish council. From the parishioners of Tyniec he received the gift of a sweater * March 22 — 7:00 a.m., Krakow, Church of St. Florian, address for the conclusion of a parish retreat * 9:00 a.m., Wawel Cathedral, ordination of priests, sermon * 4:30 p.m., Jablonka, ordination of priests, sermon * March 23 — 8:00 p.m.,

---

[4] Vatican diplomatic mission

Krakow, Church of St. Joseph, Mass with sermon during a retreat for
lawyers * March 24 — 4:00 p.m., Wawel Cathedral, Tenebrae * 7:30
p.m., Church of the Felician Sisters, Mass with homily for the end of a
retreat for physicians * March 26-28 — Wawel Cathedral, the rites of
the Holy Week * March 29 — 5:45 a.m., St. Florian's Church,
Resurrection Mass, sermon for the conclusion of the visitation of the
parish * March 31-April 4 — ski trip, Zakopane — Jaszczurowka.

April 4 — 4:00 p.m., Krakow — Borek Falecki, Mass with sermon,
Confirmation, parish Easter repast * He wrote a letter to *Tygodnik
Powszechny* on the occasion of its 25th anniversary. The letter dated
April 4, 1979 was published in the issue no. 16/1970 dated April 19,
1970:

> Throughout its 25 years of existence and activity *Tygodnik Powszechny*
> has covered this very period in the history of Polish Catholicism which
> required of us a particular kind of self-understanding - a self-understand-
> ing of a different, we might say, greater degree - than that of the Catholicism
> in many western countries. We must not think that this process is over. This
> basic cultural process still continues, still begins anew and takes new forms.
> Nevertheless, everything that we have accomplished in the sphere of cre-
> ative self-definition during the last quarter of a century must be treated as
> our own possession and, at the same time, an equally important contribu-
> tion to the Christian culture of all nations participating in the life of the
> Church. And it is from this point that we must continue to begin anew.
> My wish for you is that you should be able to continue to make such
> beginnings and I ask God to help you in this work.

April 5 — Wawel Cathedral, consecration of Bishop Stanislaw
Smolenski and Bishop Albin Malysiak:

> "As the Father has sent me, even so I send you. Receive the Holy Spirit."
> Surely one might stagger under the weight of those words. And surely the
> Apostles staggered in the Upper Room. But, inspired by these words, we
> must stand up straight and look to where Christ is pointing: "So I send you"
> ... Upon your shoulders we will put the weight of the Gospels, about which
> Jesus said: "My burden is sweet and my yoke is light." May you take up that
> Gospel, so light and sweet, yet still a burden, a yoke, and proclaim it to all
> the people ...
> We turn our gaze to this Cathedral, to the Upper Room here in Krakow.
> The past of a thousand years, as old as the history of our fatherland, as old
> as the history of Christianity in this land. From that past the future takes it
> beginning, from generation to generation.

April 7 — Blessing of the Chapel of the Daughters of Charity at the
nursing home (2 Helclow Street) after its repainting, followed by a Mass
and sermon. He was warmly greeted by the sisters and the sick. After
Mass, he met with the sisters * April 10 — Residence chapel, Mass with
sermon on the occasion of the special chapter of the Albertine Sisters *
April 11-30 — Canonical visitation of the parish of Wieliczka * April 14

— 10 a.m., the residence, Council of Priests * April 16 — 4:00 p.m., residence, adoration of the Blessed Sacrament by the priests.

April 19 — At Jasna Gora, in the chapel of Our Lady of Czestochowa, at a day of prayer for Catholic intellectuals, a homily relating to the Gospel account of the miracle at the marriage feast at Cana:

> We sense some sort of symbolism and allegory in these vessels which were first empty and became full ... The other element of this allegory is man. One element is an object, the vessel; the other element is each one of us. Christ, who is seen and presented by St. Paul as complete and full, can and will fill each of us ... I ask that you become a community of thought and a community of hearts, and I ask that you receive Christ into your community again, so that He can enter us and fill us anew, and complete us. He is the fullness from which we take, and He is the fulfillment for which we all strive ... We expect that by praying to and with the Mother of God, we will become participants in the Holy Spirit, and by His power can also become the extensions of the first Apostles and disciples of Christ who came out of the room of the Last Supper. They came out, and entered people's lives, and tied the Gospel to those lives. And they experienced God's might, which is called Grace, in all the paths of human life. We expect the same things; that is why we come here...

April 20 — 9:00 a.m., Krakow, Church of St. Peter and St. Paul, Mass with homily for the opening of a conference dedicated to the Second Vatican Council * He does not participate in the plenary session of the Sacred Congregation for the Clergy which took place on that day, but sends his written elaboration on the subject of the associations of priests * April 22 — 9:00 a.m., residence chapel, Mass for the opening of a training course for the apostolate of families * April 23 — 7:00 a.m., Church of St. Adalbert, Mass with homily * Same day — 2:00 p.m., Wicliczka. With the clergy and representatives of the laity he visited the salt mine and the chapel of Blessed Kinga; then he came to the monastery of the Reformed Franciscans, to a tumultuous welcome by the friars and the students of the minor seminary. He participated in an assembly called in his honor, then he was greeted by the faithful at the church. At 5:00 p.m. he said Mass and preached a sermon. He took part in a meeting with the friars and with representatives of the friends and benefactors of the monastery. He visited the cell of the Servant of God Alojzy Kosiba. He entered these words in the chronicle of the monastery: "In memory of a visit which was a part of the visitation of the parish of Wieliczka, with a heartfelt blessing and a request for remembrance in prayer at the grave of Servant of God Alojzy. Cardinal Karol Wojtyla."

April 25 — 7:00 a.m., Chapel of the Little Sisters Servants of Mary Immaculate, Mass with homily * Same day — 7:00 p.m., Gniezno, during the observance of the Feast of St. Adalbert:

> How telling are these, the processions in Gniezno and in Krakow [in honor of St. Stanislaw]. They speak of the continuing journey of the People of God on the Polish soil. The road on which we travel through this world, working, suffering, rejoicing, fulfilling our various vocations, the road of the People of God on the Polish soil leads to God.
>
> [Let us not make excuses about bad conditions, about the lack of Catholic organizations:] Organizations are not the most important. The most important is faith — definitely! Organizations can become an empty framework, if this framework is not filled with the living faith. On the other hand, the living faith can never become an empty framework: it will always be creative, it will always express itself in life, fulfill itself in love, because that is its nature.

April 26 — Participated in the celebrations in honor of St. Adalbert in Gdansk: participated in the service on St. Adalbert's Forest Hill, led the procession with the Most Holy Eucharist and blessed the pilgrims. After the High Mass — a speech.

> [Baptism — a grafting into Christ, and therefore into His mission] To participate in salvation does not mean only that we have the right and the duty to take from salvation. It also means that we have the right and the duty to contribute to the work of salvation ... we are all included in this work from the beginning of our existence as Christians. We are all tied to Him, but the single mission of Christ is realized by each of us in a different series of realities: situations, issues, concerns and callings. My place in life, my obligation, my calling, are the fruit and the consequence of my relation to the mission of Christ, and are therefore unique.

Same day — 6:00 p.m., a meeting with university students at the Basilica of the Blessed Virgin Mary[5] in Gdansk (conference for the youth) and Holy Mass. After the Mass — a visit to the "priestly chapel" and prayers for the priests murdered during World War II * April 27 — 7:00 a.m., Oliwa, the cathedral, Mass with homily about the role of the laity in the Church * 10:00 a.m., conference for the clergy and sisters of the Gdansk diocese about the role of a cathedral church * April 28 — Celebrated a Holy Mass at the chapel of the Bishop's Seminary in Oliwa and spoke to the alumni. He left Gdansk in the afternoon * 7:00 p.m., Kalisz, the collegiate Church of St. Joseph, participation in the consecration of a memorial chapel dedicated to the priests of Dachau * April 29 — 4:30 p.m., the collegiate Church of St. Joseph, a concelebrated Holy Mass for the 25th anniversary of the liberation of the priests from the concentration camp in Dachau.

May 1 — Church of St. Joseph in Krakow, at the Bernardine Sisters:

> [The contemporaries of Jesus were amazed and perhaps scandalized by

---

5 Church of Our Lady, Market Square, Krakow

Jesus, "the son of a carpenter"] We, on the other hand, are amazed and give thanks; we glorify the One Triune God for the plan of salvation which ... ran through the heart, the hands and the whole life of a simple man, Joseph the carpenter; that the Savior of the World grew up in his home, that He who is the eternal Creator, learned to work — as Man — from the man who was His foster father on earth.

Let us love our work, let us perform it as well as possible, let us strive to excel in our work ... But let us be guided in this by God's perspective. Let us realize that we, too, are fulfilling God's plan of salvation which runs through our hearts and our hands, through our trials, through our care for our loved ones whom God has entrusted to us. Let this be our pride, let us be guided by this, live for this.

Same day — at the Church of St. Joseph at Podgorze:

[Mentions his participation in the 25th anniversary of the liberation of the Polish priests from the Dachau concentration camp, observed at the Church of St. Joseph in Kalisz:] This confidence in the care of St. Joseph is something that is very evangelical. [At its source] stands the trust which the Heavenly Father showed to St. Joseph by calling him to be the adoptive earthly father of the Son of God, our Redeemer.

May 3[6] — Czestochowa, pilgrimage of seminarians from higher diocesan and religious seminaries on the occasion of the 50th anniversary of the priesthood of Pope Paul VI. 11:00 a.m., led the celebration of a solemn High Mass * Same day — 7:00 p.m., the cathedral in Wroclaw, participation in a jubilee Holy Mass * May 3-6 — Wroclaw * May 4 — At the Wroclaw cathedral, on the occasion of the 25th anniversary of the establishment of the Polish church administration in the western and northern provinces, an address to university students:

The awareness of the dual birth of man: a birth from the parents, the father and mother; and a birth from God. This second birth is a great mystery ... This unseen reality corresponds to the unseen reality of God Himself. That is why we find ourselves in the confines of a mystery here ... A man — even an evil one — feels the need to repent, to return to the norm, to the standard, which, along with Grace, is instilled in us at Baptism by the living, visible Christ. We know that God does not give up on any person, and especially not on a baptized person ...

Christianity is ambitious, and this basic Christian ambition, concentrated on man, explains all of the demands made by Christ Himself. Christ is demanding, and He Himself is the measure of how His demands should be met ...

In his drive to take dominion over the earth, man can strive so hard as to lose himself, such that he seems to lose the sense of his own importance, that his primary focus switches to various civilizations, various works, various products, and his life allows no room or time for mankind.

May 8 — Feast of St. Stanislaw, 8:00 a.m., Krakow, Wawel

---

[6] See Glossary.

Cathedral, ordination of sub-deacons, sermon * 1:00 p.m., the residence, Council of Priests * 6:00 p.m., Wawel Cathedral, Mass concelebrated with the Council of Priests, sermon:

> **900 years separate us from his life, his office of bishop, from his pastoral care and from his death. How different were the times, how much has changed. But one thing has remained unchanged: our faith is unchanged, his faith and our faith, the faith of his epoch and of ours. Faith as reality and faith as responsibility.**

May 10 — 9:00 a.m., Wawel — Skalka, procession in honor of St. Stanislaw, opening remarks * May 11 — Meeting of the Committee for the Apostolate of the Laity. Issues regarding the theology of the stewardship of the laity for the world — analysis of the degree of implementation of the decisions of the Second Vatican Council in Poland * May 12-13 Franciszkanska Street, meeting of the Committee of the Polish Episcopate for Catholic Education.

> **Subject of deliberations: issues and conditions of accrediting academic departments, qualifications of academic staff, degree requirements and nomenclature, issues of cooperation between the departments and theological seminaries, structure of the departments and issues of the regionalization of the studies of theology. Present at the meeting, besides the members of the Committee, are the rectors and deans of academic institutions in Poland. The Cardinal pointed out that the goal of today's meeting is not only to standardize the theological sciences in Poland, but also to align them more closely to the Church and to popularize them. In summation: "The Church has a fundamental and undeniable right to make its own decisions in matters of church education, and must defend that right ... The Church must take advantage of the constitutional principle of universal access to education ..." He stated the fact that the Church had limits imposed on its academic activities ... "We must adopt a dynamic stance, and strive to increase academic cadres ... but at the same time, we must apply consistent standards for awarding the degree of assistant professor ..." (From the minutes)**

May 13 — Meeting of the Committee for Catholic Education. The Cardinal informed everyone present about the transformation of the Subcommittee for University Studies into the Committee for Catholic Education, and the addition of two new members: Bishop Kazimierz Majdanski and Bishop Walenty Wojcik.

May 15 — Olszanica, Confirmation.

> **During the visitation (February 28 to March 3), the Cardinal so impressed the faithful of this small parish (1000 souls) near Krakow that they kept asking their pastor when they might be graced by another visit. He suggested that they invite him for the celebration of the Sacrament of Confirmation — the visitation in February had come on too short of a notice to allow the candidates to prepare for the sacrament. But how to reach the Cardinal? His chaplain is ever watchful and will direct the request to someone else once he finds out what it is. After a Mass at Wawel — dur-**

ing which the Cardinal greeted the faithful from the parishes which he had visited — the Olszanica contingent went to see him and told the chaplain that they wanted to thank the Cardinal personally for his greeting. When they were admitted, they announced their petition — successfully. They organized a commemorative gathering, because the Cardinal's 50th birthday was on May 18th. He was presented with a medallion created by Prof. Bronislaw Chromy from Wola Justowska (obverse: the Good Shepherd, reverse: Wawel Castle, Tatra Mountains and inscription.) (According to an account by a participant of this gathering)

May 16 — Meeting of the Council of the Pontifical Department of Theology in Krakow, dedicated to the organization of special institutes at the Department — the creation of a Liturgical Institute (2-year course) and a Pastoral Institute of Dialogue. (From the minutes of the Council) * Same day — 6:00 p.m., Rogoznik, Mass with homily, dedication of a church organ * May 17-24 — Canonical visitation of the parish of Gdow * May 18 — 12 noon, Mass with homily in Kalwaria Zebrzydowska, at the shrine of the Blessed Mother * Same day — at the Church of Our Lady of Perpetual Help in Wadowice, on his 50th birthday:

[The parish as a Christian community which, in our times, takes the place of the catechumenate:] Your parish had the right — even the duty — to call me here on this day or in this time period, to demand my coming here to worship the One Triune God, to give public thanks for the grace of Baptism which was bestowed upon me here. And I ... do it with great joy ... I wish to honor this baptismal font where I was accepted as a child of God and a member of the Church, to honor it as we all honored it during the millennium of Poland's Christianity. Today I do it for personal reasons ... To you, my dear brothers and sisters, to you, dear brothers in priesthood, sons of this land, to you, dear Reverend Professor, to the entire Church of God, to the parish of Wadowice, I express my sincerest, my warmest filial thanks and "May God bless."

May 19 - Leskowiec * May 20 (Tuesday after Pentecost) — 7:00 a.m., Mass at the church on Szpitalna Street. Afterwards, breakfast meeting with the Sisters of the Holy Spirit and children. The sisters offer their greetings for his 50th birthday * May 23 — 7:00 a.m., residence chapel, Mass and sermon for children after their First Communion * May 23 —He signed the statute of the Liturgical Committee of the Archdiocese of Krakow * May 24 — 5:00 p.m., Nowy Targ, Mass with homily, confirmation, blessing of lectors * May 26 — 6:15 a.m., Warsaw, chapel of the Grey Ursuline Sisters, private concelebrated Mass * May 27-June 2 — Pilgrimage of 220 priests — former prisoners {of concentration camps} — to Rome * May 27 — Monte Cassino, at the graves of Polish soldiers, with a pilgrimage of priests, former prisoners:

The testament of the truth, given by our countrymen through many generations, the truth that "Poland is not yet lost!"[7] And also the testament of "for your freedom and ours", this common testament of the soldiers and of the captives is somehow united by one stem, from which they both grew as if two equal branches ... The Polish priest has always tried to be one who, above all else, united our earthly homeland with our heavenly Homeland. That is why he was so close to his earthly homeland, that is why his roots there were so strong, so that he could lead all and lift them up to the heavenly Homeland.

May 28 — 7:00 p.m., Rome, participation in a Mass with Pope Paul VI * May 29 — At the Basilica of St. Peter in Rome, during a solemn concelebrated Mass on the occasion of the 50th anniversary of Paul VI's ordination to the priesthood, with a pilgrimage of Polish priests and former prisoners:

> We come here [to the Confession of St. Peter] to bear witness in a particular context of our history: first, in the context ... of the millennium {of Poland's Christianity} ... But we also come to bear this witness in the perspective of our generation, which in a very specific way has gone through fire and blood ... We come then to bear our humble witness to the Successor of Peter, who is the Shepherd of the entire Church, on whose shoulders Christ has placed a special cross, a special responsibility, to whom he entrusted his ship sailing through the ages, at a time of extraordinary experiences and storms. We there, in Poland, see it, and we who come from there, from the country on the Vistula River, feel it very strongly. And that is why we are constantly with Peter.

May 30 — An audience with the Holy Father Paul VI for the group of pilgrims — priests, former prisoners of concentration camps. A speech by Cardinal Wojtyla (KW 51). Rome — a speech during a social gathering of the priests — pilgrims * On the same day — at the Church of St. Andrew at Quirinal in Rome, at the tomb of St. Stanislaw Kostka:

> Let us pray that we may know how to be the shepherds of that [Polish] youth, that we may know how to hear them, and to hear them to the utmost, to hear what comes from the very depths of their souls. And that, having heard and understood, we may know how to lead them, how to show the way...
> There was something in this saint (Stanislaw Kostka), something very close to us: the great inner tenderness, a Slavic and Polish emotionality, and at the same time an unstoppable rush to everything that is good and true.

May 31 — 9:30 a.m., Rome, Basilica of St. Peter, participation in the canonization ceremonies of St. John d'Avila.

June 1 — 7:30 a.m., Rome, Chapel of the Sisters of the Resurrection, concelebrated Mass, sermon * June 2 — chapel of the Polish College, concelebrated Mass, sermon * The same day, the Vatican Radio broadcast a speech about the pilgrimage of priests, former prisoners of con-

---

[7] Opening words of the Polish National Anthem

centration camps: "Our pilgrims stressed that they, the living, wanted to bear witness on behalf of all of those who perished ... The living must bear witness to the dead, and give life to those truths and those values for which they died." * Same day — return to Krakow * June 6 — 7:00 a.m., residence chapel, Mass with sermon and First Holy Communion * June 6-8 — Canonical visitation of the parish of Kacwin * June 6 — Sermon in Kacwin for the beginning of the visitation of the deanery of Spisz:

> Only in these parts of the country do parishioners greet their bishop in this way. From the boundaries of the parish, all parishioners take part in this welcome: the young people turn out in great numbers, the parishioners send a carriage for me, they do not want to hear about travel by car ... Before me rode a group on horseback, behind me — walked a group of girls carrying a wreath — that's how ceremoniously I was escorted here ...
>
> [Reminiscence of the visit to Rome and the audience with the Holy Father; further, about the bond among all bishops, and through them of all the churches with the Pope, the Successor of Peter:] We all find ourselves in this Church and we deeply feel these bonds. It is particularly during a visitation that these bonds come to life anew. The presence of a bishop in a parish — such as my presence in your parish now — is, first of all, to help you to feel that bond with the Apostolic Church again ... to help you feel that you are a living part of the Church.

June 7 — Kacwin, sermon and blessing of young married couples:

> Christian life is made of various works, various obligations, various joys, various sorrows, various disappointments, various professions, various callings — but it all comes together at one point, namely, in the fact that we meet with God in our common Sacrifice. [I came here] to tell you ... of this great unity which exists among us in the Church. To all of you, to you parents, I turn to you as to my co-workers. After all, all parents who bring up their children in the Catholic faith are indeed the co-workers of the bishops, the shepherds and apostles of the Church.

The same day — sermon and blessing of widows, widowers and older married couples in Kacwin : "...A solitary life is often a hard life, but it gives opportunity to open your heart to God, and also, in your solitude, to discern the various needs of your neighbors" * Same day — Nowy Targ, participation in a convention of priests observing the 10th anniversary of their ordination * June 8 — For the conclusion of the visitation of the parish of Kacwin:

> [Three words spoken in front of the tabernacle before leaving the parish: thank you, I beg your pardon, I leave:] I thank Jesus Christ, I thank His Blessed Mother and I thank you; I thank your pastor.
>
> I beg your pardon. I beg the pardon of all those for whom I did not fulfill all the expectations they had of me.
>
> I leave: I must go from here. My duties call me elsewhere, to other obligations. So I say: I am leaving. But I am also leaving something behind, something for all of you, for your good will and for your hearts.

Same day — 7:00 p.m., Zawoja, sermon during a concelebrated Mass of the class of 1968 * June 9 — At the parish of Rudawa, during a social gathering of young priests (class of 1967):

> This gathering, which is a custom, a tradition of generations of priests in our archdiocese ... is important for you, is important for me as your bishop, is important for all of society, for all of God's people in the Archdiocese of Krakow.
> The priesthood is an interior mystery of each priest ... This interior mystery deserves the greatest respect, both with regard to the man who was called, who answered the call, and with regard to Him who does the calling. This is a mystery between man and God, between a priest and Christ.

The same day — in the parish of Liszki, during a social gathering of young priests (class of 1966):

> The priesthood was given to you and assigned to you ... Its integration with the human identity is never fully completed ... My foremost wish for you, as your bishop who gave birth to you as priests, who laid hands on you, so that you might become priests, so that you might accept your priesthood, who have assigned this priesthood to you ... My wish for you is that you identify with your priesthood as fully as possible, that year by year you become more mature priests.

June 10 — residence chapel, Mass with homily for the Ursuline Sisters * June 11 — 7:00 a.m., Siedlce, chapel in the residence of the Bishop of Siedlce, private concelebrated Mass * Same day — Lesna Podlaska, monastery of the Pauline Fathers, meeting of the Episcopal Committee for Pastoral Ministry. Presentation by the chairman, Archbishop B. Kominek: *Objectives of the Committee in Light of its Legacy of 25 years.* Discussion followed. After intermission, at 3:00 p.m., presentations by Rev. Prof. S. Olejnik, *Current Moral Problems;* Rev. Prof. T. Slipko, *What does Marxism Contribute to the Cause of Morality?*; Fr. K. Meissner, Moral Issues of Marriage and Family; Fr. Orszulik, on the standards of sexual ethics as reflected in Polish publications. Rev. Prof. J. Majka presented the final version of the pastoral program for 1970/71.

June 12 — Second day of deliberations of the Episcopal Committee for Pastoral Ministry. Discussion of the programs for the coming year, issues relating to the coordination of the particular committees. * Same day — Krakow, residence chapel, Mass with homily for those involved in family ministry * June 13, 4:00 p.m., residence chapel, two baptisms * 6:00 p.m., marriage of Witold and Katarzyna Herman * June 14 — 7:00 a.m., the Church of St. Anthony in Bronowice Male:

> From our own experiences we know just how much it costs to build this interior Church within us: we must pay for it. That is the law of the Gospel.

It is not possible to build the interior Church in comfort, with ease — it is just not possible.

And that is also how we build our external temples to God, our churches, just as we build our faith — in hardship.

Same day — 9:00 a.m., Church of St. Szczepan in Krakow, he dedicates a memorial plaque in honor of those who were murdered and died in the Ravensbruck concentration camp. When asked to attend this ceremony, he at first declined, because he was scheduled to take part in a men's pilgrimage to Kalwaria on that day. But when he saw the disappointment of the women survivors who asked him, he assured them that he would come to dedicate the plaque. About 200 women who had been prisoners of Ravensbruck attended the ceremony. (Accounts by: Dr. Zofia Patkaniowska, Elzbieta Orkanowa, Jozefa Strusiowa, Maria Piotrowska) From the sermon:

> And the awareness that the camp is also an altar, the awareness that the camp is a Gehenna, the lowest pit, but somewhere there is an altar which holds dominion over that pit — that awareness lived in the souls and that awareness helped to survive ... and today that awareness demands to be commemorated.
>
> The camp was a cry not only to men, but to God: a participation in the Cross of Christ, in his Sacrifice.

The same day — 11:30 a.m., in Kalwaria Zebrzydowska, during a pilgrimage of young men, with the participation of Bishop I. Tokarczuk, on the 20th anniversary of the placement of the cross on Kalwaria:

> Our times are the times of men, of bearing witness by men, the times of the Cyrenian, who perhaps is not eager to go and take up the cross, who is perhaps ashamed ... to take up this cross with Christ, but who, upon realizing what is at stake, does take up the cross, walks with Christ, accompanies Him, is his confidant — and bears witness to Him everywhere.

Same day — 5:00 p.m., beginning of the visitation in Lipnica Mala; Confirmation * June 15 — 8:00 a.m.: "I heard confessions during a Mass for parents and young children, then I spoke and blessed the youngest parishioners..." (From the Chronicle of the Bishop's Activities) * Continuation and conclusion of the visitation in Lipnica Mala * June 16 — 7:00 a.m., Warsaw, private Mass at the Ursuline Sisters * June 17 — Participated in the opening of an Albertine exhibition in Warsaw. The opening was performed by the Primate. * The same day — 7:00 p.m., Warsaw cathedral, Mass for the intention of the beatification of Brother Albert * June 18 — 7:00 a.m., Mass at the Ursuline Sisters * June 19 — 10:30 a.m., Church of St. Anne in Krakow, requiem Mass for the soul of Prof. Roman Ingarden (mention of Rev. Konstanty Michalski and his term of "heroic thinking"):

> It is necessary to think heroically, in order to think reality through to

the end. This has always been the calling of philosophers. And this kind of thinking about reality becomes more difficult as time progresses — if it is to be consistent, if it is to allow for all of the complications of human knowledge and all of the paths by which it advances ...

We ask that the earthly path of heroic thinking, the earthly path of man, might end in eternity with this one word: "Father!"; with this one word which transcends all words, which subsumes everything and in which everything is fulfilled.

3:00 p.m., the funeral of Prof. R. Ingarden at Rakowice Cemetery * Same day — a meeting of the Council of the Pontifical Department of Theology in Krakow: Presentation to the Council of the rules and regulations of specialized academic sections as approved by the Episcopal Conference; other administrative matters of the Department, including the affiliation of the Higher Catechetical Institute. The Cardinal informed the Council that he had obtained the permission of the bishop of Tarnow for lectures by Fr. Michal Heller (from that diocese) * June 20-22 — Canonical visitation of the parish in Zubrzyca Gorna * June 21 — During the visitation in Zubrzyca Gorna, to parents, with a blessing:

> [On parenthood as a God-given power to transmit life:] We, the believers, have always regarded it a miracle: how glorious it is and how wondrous, how close to God it puts mankind ... The Christian dignity of parents arises from the fact that they are co-workers of the Creator Himself ... Nobody, no matter how great an orator, could tell you more about who you are ... This I ask of you, that you never think of yourselves anything less than this.

Same day — in Zubrzyca Gorna, during a visit with young people, speaking about what the Church demands from young people and what She gives in return. Of confession, comparing it to a handhold which might be found by someone falling from a height:

> Confession is just such a lifeline, such a handhold ... Confession is that brake: I must stop my fall! You cannot hold on to it by your own strength. You cannot manage on your own. But with the help of the grace of the good, forgiving and healing Christ, you will find it easier to deal with yourself.

June 22 — In Zubrzyca Gorna during confirmation:

> We know very well, that through Baptism we become children of God. Children, just like the children of our parents, who are carried about in the arms of the father or mother, so we become children of God ... And I will add: we never stop being these children. We are to be children of the Lord even in our oldest years.

June 22-24 — Canonical visitation of the parish in Podwilk.

June, undated, in Jablonka:

> We need to see — with our eyes open more widely — the truth about priesthood, how it appears in all its reality: how profound it is, how mag-

nificent, how close to Christ! How much that truth, that reality, is within you! And also how, in a very special way, it is within us, priests and bishops, how it is in us, for you, but before that it was in you, for us! Because a priest is taken from the people. Every priest, every bishop, and even the Holy Father. Just as, ages ago, were the Apostles!

June 23 — 8:00 a.m., Bogucice, diocese of Opole, concelebrated Mass with homily at a social convention * June 25 — 10 a.m., Warsaw, church at Bielany, Mass with homily for the inauguration of a convention of biblical scholars * June 26 — 7:00 p.m., Krakow, residence chapel, Mass for the repose of the soul of J. Vetulani * June 28 — 7:00 a.m., Wawel Cathedral, ordination to the diaconate * Same day — 11:30 a.m., Wadowice, parish church, Mass and closing remarks on the anniversary of his baptism * June 29 — 7:00 p.m., Church of St. Peter and St. Paul in Krakow, Mass, closing remarks and procession * June 30 — 7:30 a.m., concelebrated Mass with priests observing the 25th anniversary of their ordination to the priesthood.

June. To family counselors:

> The salvation of the family, its sanctification, must come from the family itself, from the married couples. They are called to the apostolate in milieus their own ... We, priests, realize that in seeking your help, we also want to offer our help to you. However, the initiative and competence lie primarily in your hands.

Beginning of July — The Cardinal received a group of six students from the Technical University of Krakow, who, as part of their summer apprenticeship, conducted surveys of the bishop's palace. During that time, the Cardinal on several occasions demonstrated his cordial interest in the students' work, he talked with the ones he happened to meet, to one of them he sent a torte for his name-day. This emboldened the students to ask for a meeting with the cardinal. They talked for about an hour, speaking of common, everyday matters. (According to an account of a participant of this meeting)

July 2 — 5:00 p.m., private Mass in Kalwaria Zebrzydowska * July 4 — 5:00 p.m., residence chapel, baptism * July 5 — 7:30 a.m., Facimiech, the parish of Krzecin, Mass with homily * July 6-August 1 — tourist trek, private Masses, two of them with sermons.

August 1 — Bachledowka. By way of exception, because of illness, Cardinal Wojtyla did not come to convey greetings to the Primate. He sent his chauffeur with a letter * August 2-13 — Muszyna, sisters' chapel, private Masses, twice with sermons * August 14 — In Kalwaria Zebrzydowska, the ceremony of "the burial of the Blessed Mother":

> This part [of the observance] which we are now beginning ... reminds us of Her parting with this earth and, at the same time, reminds us of our

parting with the earth, which will take place some day ... The Feast of the Assumption reminds us of the ultimate truth of our faith: we are called to everlasting life ... to unity with God ... to heaven.

August 15 — 11:00 a.m., Jasna Gora, Chapel of the Blessed Mother, low Mass, participation in High Mass by the summit * The same day — Krakow, the Basilica of our Lady (the celebrant was Bishop Jean Sauvage, bishop ordinary of Annecy in France), sermon by Cardinal Wojtyla about the "Magnificat" and thanksgiving for miracles:

> Miracles indicate the intervention of God in the matters of this earth, in temporal matters ... But, at the same time, all of this {i.e. the miracles}, while revealing God to us by the manner in which it "happens," is not as far-reaching as Grace. Grace goes further than a miracle ... grace carries something that might be called "divinization." Here, God does not express Himself in the manner in which He takes action, but is present in the very essence of the action ... Grace is not as visible, not as striking, as a miracle. It is discrete, it is hidden deep in the human soul, but in essence it is much higher than any miracle.

August 16 — Kalwaria Zebrzydowska, on the Feast of the Assumption of the Virgin Mary:

> [About the "little paths" of Jesus Christ:] Here, on this Kalwaria, on this hill, the paths of Jesus break off ... by the tomb, as if the ones who traveled these paths did not wish to say the last word. But this last word, unspoken by them, became spoken even more fully. This end was served by the "little paths" of Our Lady. We see how her paths seem to cross those of Our Lord, how they intertwine ... We know that the Blessed Mother was assumed into heaven body and soul, because She was immaculately conceived. Here, on Kalwaria, we see clearly that this happened because of the merits of Jesus Christ, our Savior.

The same day — 5:00 p.m., Michalowice, on the occasion of the blessing of an altar:

> The center of the altar's *mensa*[8] has within it the relics of saints. That is the witness of the truth of this altar, on which Christ's Sacrifice will be fulfilled. A witness — because the saints, whose relics we have placed in this altar, gave witness to the Sacrifice of Christ with their lives.

August 17 — Krakow, at the basilica of the Dominican Fathers on the Feast of St. Jacek {Hyacinth}:

> As He became flesh, as he became Man, the Son, God-the Word, took on our human speech along with a human body and soul. And in that human speech He uttered to us the inexpressible truth, God's truth ... And we witnessed how, in various nations, that Word of God became the property of these nations, shaping the cultures of these nations ... But beyond all of the works which expressed the Word of God in the human language of our

---

[8] tabletop

nation, the Word was expressed, above all, in our souls. For it is the soul, the soul of every one of us, that forms the basis and the very essence of culture.

August 19 — Residence chapel, Mass with homily, Confirmation * August 20 — Kroscienko, in front of the Chapel of the Good Shepherd. The first direct meeting of the Cardinal with the "Oasis" movement. In a talk and interview, the Cardinal became acquainted with the principles, the program and the life of the "Oasis of the Living Church."

August 23 — At Jasna Gora during a pilgrimage of men (the celebrant was Bishop Jozef Rozwadowski, Bishop of Lodz):

All of us enter into the sphere of this interaction [of God with man], all of us encounter it; and all of us are affected, as if anew, by what Christ said so simply at the wedding feast of Cana: ... "Draw some out..." And all of us, led by the Church into the mystery of the sacramental action of Christ, continue to draw from the Lord ...

We are witnessing that a greater number of men are drawing ever closer to Christ and to the Church ... It seems that men have understood, have come to realize that, in our times, religion is above all a matter of conviction.

Same day - Myslenice, on the anniversary of the coronation of the image of Our Lady of Myslenice:

I ask ... that through Him, through Christ, you find yourselves in the Church, that you define your place there, and that by so doing you might find the meaning of your life and a great joy: for it is a great joy to be a part of the People of God. Because it is a great joy to live in Christ.

August 26 — 11:00 a.m., Jasna Gora, he was the principal celebrant during a Holy Mass by the summit * August 27 — Krakow — Extraordinary Chapter of the Sisters of the Sacred Heart. Homily * August 28 — 11:00 a.m., residence chapel, Mass with homily, Confirmation.

During the summer vacation, a group of Polish children from Lwow were visiting Poland at the invitation of a group of scouts. These children (and some young people) were confirmed in Krakow by Cardinal Wojtyla. Among them were my niece and nephew, Jan and Malgorzata Nikodemowicz. Due to some family-related reason, they were late for the day of general confirmation. When the Cardinal was asked, he very graciously agreed to administer the Sacrament of Confirmation to the two in his private chapel. He spoke with them very cordially, and presented them with little missals and rosaries. (Eugeniusz Nikodemowicz)

August 29 — Opole. He participated in the celebrations of Bishop Franciszek Jop's 50th anniversary of the ordination to the priesthood. Delivered a homily during the Mass celebrated by the Bishop (later Bishop Jop played the tape with the recording of this homily to the members of his family). Earlier (August 18th), in a special announcement, Cardinal Wojtyla wrote about the jubilee of a bishop to whom *"the Archdiocese of Krakow owes a very special debt of gratitude"* and announced that he himself and a delegation of clergy from Krakow would participate in the jubilee celebrations.

August 30 — 10:30 a.m., Nowy Sacz, the Church of the Jesuits, High Mass, closing remarks * 6:00 p.m., Kety, blessing of the altar, sermon. A brief visit at the house of the Sisters of the Resurrection.

September 1 — Krakow, Church of the Sisters of St. Norbert, on the Feast of Blessed Bronislawa:

> **All of us ... accept the truth of Christ's words about choosing the better part; all of us try in some way to choose this better part ... We know that we must find in ourselves, in man, some room, some interior space for that better part. We realize that if we were to lack this interior space in us, humans, the space for what is better, for what is Divine, we would make ourselves a lot poorer.**

September 2-4 — Warsaw, Chapel of the Ursuline Sisters, concelebrated Mass * September 5-9 — Krakow, residence chapel, private Masses * September 8 — Sister Maria Hlond had the first talk with H.E. Cardinal K. Wojtyla on the subject of organizing a new center run by the Sisters of Our Lady of Mercy for the young people of Nowa Huta * September 10-11 — Residence chapel, requiem Masses * September 13 — Zawada (diocese of Tarnow), on the occasion of the 50th anniversary of the coronation of the image of Our Lady of Zawada, Pontifical High Mass with sermon:

> **[We would like] to be able to see Mary as we see her today ... as that holy place of the first meeting with God. And that, as we look at that place of the first meeting with God, at that most holy place, we might be able to say that we, too, are a place where God dwells.**

Same day — 5:00 p.m., Medyka (diocese of Przemysl), sermon during the celebrations of the Visitation by Our Lady * September 15 — 10:00 a.m., residence chapel, Mass with homily for the beginning of the Catechetical Institute * September 16 — 1:00 p.m., residence chapel, Mass for diocesan representatives dealing with matters of liturgy * September 17 — 10:00 a.m., the residence, conference of priests — heads of deaneries * September 19 — 12:30 p.m., residence chapel, Mass with homily, blessing of an image for the Mission of St. Adalbert in Montreal * September 19-22 — Visitation of the parish in Niedzwiedz and the rectorate in Mszana Gorna.

September 20 — Mogila, during the celebration of elevating the Church of the Cistercian Fathers to the rank of a minor basilica:

> **We can surely point out many people, and maybe we can even point to ourselves, as to those who found that the Cross was and is the only answer in their suffering. We think: yes, I am suffering, but God who became man**

also suffered. As I suffer, I look at Him, I see His Cross ... The Cross contains the highest measure of all human affairs, a measure so great that it surpasses all human scale. That is a consequence of our original greatness. It is a consequence of the fact that we are created in the image and likeness of God, and that our actions are measured not only by a human standard, but also a divine one. And God, who created us, has not and will not withdraw from that. He measured us once by that standard and He always wants to bring us up to it. But, since we, especially we who have sinned, and we have all sinned, cannot measure up to that standard, it took the Cross, on which the Son of God was hung, to give back to us, humans, the Divine standard by which to measure our lives and actions.

September 24 —12:30 p.m., Mass for priests from the deaneries of Krakow, celebrated in the chapel at 3 Franciszkanska Street. Meeting related to the introduction of the Polish language into the liturgy. The Sisters of the Holy Spirit were invited to participate in this Mass * Same day — 2:00 p.m., meeting of the Council of the Pontifical Department of Theology in Krakow.

The Cardinal referred once again to the problems of the academic milieu of Krakow, and pointed to the need for establishing closer ties with that milieu, and for a more effective planning of the academic activities of the whole milieu ... A very pressing issue is the number of junior assistants and assistant lecturers, of which the College has too few ... (From the minutes)

September 25 — Mass for priests from other deaneries, in the chapel of the Archbishop's palace * September 26-28 — Canonical visitation of the parish of Wisniowa * September 26-28 — During the visitation at the parish of Wisniowa, to the young people:

Defend your humanity. This is the great heritage of Christianity, the great heritage of our faith: that we think highly of mankind and we set high standards for mankind. This is the only way to attain high regard for mankind.

September 29 — 9:00 p.m., departure for Rome * September 30 — 7:00 a.m., Eisenstadt, private concelebrated Mass, visit with Bishop Stefan Laszlo.

October 1-4 — Rome, Polish College * October 4 — 9:30 a.m., Rome, Basilica of St. Peter, participation in the pronouncement of St. Catherine as Doctor of the Church * October 5-10 — Rome, Masses successively at the Polish College, S. Calisto, at the Sisters of the Holy Family of Nazareth, at the Sisters of the Resurrection * October 7 — Pontifical Institute of Church Studies, 4:30 p.m., participation in a lecture by Rev. A. Haas SAC, subject: *The Confraternity of the Divine Mercy* * October 11 — 8:30 a.m., Basilica of St. Clare, concelebrated Mass * October 12-13 — 7:30 a.m., Rome, Chapel of the Polish College, private concelebrated Mass * October 14 — 8:00 a.m., Terminillo, private concelebrated Mass * October 15 — 7:30 a.m.,

Rome, Polish College, Holy Mass * October 16 — 7:30 p.m., Vienna, chapel of the nunciature[9], Holy Mass * October 17 — 9:00 a.m., residence chapel, private concelebrated Mass * October 18 — 7:00 a.m., Naleczow, at the Salvatorian Fathers * 9:00 a.m., Lublin, chapel of KUL, participation in the inauguration of the academic year, address * October 20 — 5:00 p.m., Krakow, Theological Seminary, inauguration of the academic year at the Department of Theology * 7:30 p.m., Church of St. Anne, sermon for the inauguration of the academic year at the Pontifical Department of Theology * October 21 — 10:00 a.m., residence chapel, Mass with homily for the inauguration of the academic year at the Institute of the Family * October 24-26 — Canonical visitation of the parish of Bronowice Wielkie.

October 24-26 — During the visitation in Bronowice Wielkie, to young married couples:

> In today's liturgy of the Word ... Christ stands before us truly alive: Christ as He was among people, when He did good things for them, bringing them life, health, comfort, grace. And that is the Christ that remains in the Church. The Church not only believes that Christ is in Her, but that the Church itself is the extension, the continuation of the life of Christ on earth. And Christ continues to act in this extension of His life in earth, as realized in the Church. He acts as He did then, among people ... It may not be the touch of His hand. It may not be the sound of His voice. But the Church, in its actions, wants to repeat and continue the touch of His hand, the sound of His voice.

October 25 — 7:00 p.m., Church of St. Anne, participation in the observance of the Feast of St. John of Kanty * October 27 — 7:00 a.m., Jasna Gora, Chapel of Our Lady, Mass with a sermon to seminarians returning from military service * Same day — 10:00 a.m., Parish of Our Lady of Lourdes, Krakow — Nowa Wies, sermon to young people * October 29 — 7:30 p.m., residence chapel, Mass with homily for the intention of the late Jerzy, Kasia and Piotrus Ciesielski and for the intention of Danuta and Marysia * October 31 — 4:30 p.m., Pisarzowice, Mass, blessing of the crucifix and sharing of the blessing from the Holy Father * Same day — sermon at the basilica of the Dominican Fathers in Krakow:

> Through the scores of rosaries prayed [in the churches] and in various, sometimes very strange, locations: through these decades of the rosary, how many human pleas and how much true love for one's fellow man, whom we try to help by our prayer. Through prayer we bring God to man, and also through prayer we lift man up to God.

November 1 — 5:00 p.m., Rudawa, sermon for the beginning of a

---

[9] Vatican diplomatic mission

novena for the 900th anniversary of the parish * Same day — Church of St. Peter and St. Paul, dedication of the organ:

> **In human terms, in temporal terms, each person is stamped with the sign of death. Each of us is born into this world with this stamp and with this destiny: we must die. But Christ tells us that each person is stamped with a different sign. He or she is enveloped in God's love, and love does not allow death.**
>
> **Today, in a very special, universal way, we celebrate God's presence in man.**

Same day — 3:00 p.m., at the Rakowice Cemetery in Krakow:

> **How particularly significant are these words today, on the eve of tomorrow's feast:[10] "What we are to be in the future has not yet been revealed; when it is revealed, we shall be like Him because we shall see him as He really is." People who have passed away are remembered by their actions, monuments, fame, which often lasts for centuries after their passing. But we wish, first of all, to commend our deceased to Christ. Because we care not only about the trail that their lives, sometimes very rich lives, left after them — we care primarily about them ... We have no other way of reaching them and we are separated from them by this boundary. Jesus Christ alone stands on this boundary between life and death. He alone is the Lord of life, through His death.**

November 2 — 9:00 a.m., Wawel Cathedral, participation in Holy Mass, procession to the tombs of the kings * Same day — 4:00 p.m., Oswiecim {Auschwitz} and Brzezinka, laying of a wreath in the camp chapel, Mass with homily, procession to the wall of death and to Block XI. From the sermon:

> **Here, too, was a Calvary. More than a quarter of a century has passed, only traces remain of this Calvary, it has become a monument, but before it became a monument, it was a reality. And the reality was different from a monument: it was horrible, it was inhuman. Just as inhuman as was the Calvary of Christ ... When the camp was here, there was no priest who could sacramentally express the sacrifice made in the souls of the prisoners, at least not openly. There were those who did that in secret; their secret Masses had tremendous gravity. They were saturated with human sacrifice, with the human Calvary to an extreme degree. Through this, they came extremely close to that Calvary of Christ.**

November 4 — The Cardinal's name-day. Mass at Wawel Cathedral at 7:00 a.m. Greetings from religious congregations * November 4-7 — At the abbey of the Benedictine Fathers in Tyniec, personal retreat before departure for Rome * November 6 — 6:00 p.m., Mariacki Church, prayers for the 25th anniversary of the death of Wincenty

---

[10] All Soul's Day

410 *Kalendarium*

Witos[11] * November 7 — Homily during a marriage ceremony:

> **It is possible for that bond between two people to reach such fullness as the Creator intended for marriage: "They shall be two in one flesh." Nevertheless, one person cannot become the owner of another, he and she must always remain a gift for each other ... Fidelity is the future of love, it is the sign of its fulfillment. It is what man can and must attain in the face of such a gift.**

Same day — departure for Katowice and Rome * November 8 — 8:30 a.m., Vienna, nunciature,[12] private Mass * November 9 — 10:00 a.m., Vatican, audience with the Holy Father * November 10-13 — Participated in the plenary session of the Sacred Congregation for Divine Worship. At the session he presented his remarks regarding the reform of the so-called minor orders. The Cardinal postulated that consultations with all the Conferences of Bishops in the Church be conducted. In February of 1971 the Congregation informed the Cardinal that such consultations had been initiated. The issue of close cooperation with the local episcopates in the work of the reform of the liturgy was one of the keynotes in other interventions by Cardinal Wojtyla. (Cf. Rev. Jan Dyduch, *Kardynal Karol Wojtyla w sluzbie Kosciolowi Powszechnemu* {Karol Cardinal Wojtyla in the Service of the Universal Church}, Krakow 1998) * November 13 — 6:00 p.m., Rome, Church of St. Andrew at Quirinal, Mass with sermon at the tomb of St. Stanislaw Kostka[13] * November 14 — Rome, Church of St. Louis, participation in a Holy Mass for General Charles de Gaulle * November 16 — 8:00 a.m., Louvain * November 17 — 8:00 a.m., Luxembourg, Mass at the cathedral * November 18 — 8:00 a.m., Ludau near Strasbourg, chapel, concelebrated Mass with sermon * November 19-20 — Fribourg, Switzerland.

November 21 — 7:00 p.m., Krakow, Church of the Felician Sisters, sermon for the 100th anniversary of the house * November 21-30 — Canonical visitation of St. Mikolaj {Nicholas} Parish * November 22 — Feast of Christ the King, 10:00 a.m., at Wawel Cathedral, Mass concelebrated with priests from Spisz, Orawa and Mszana, sermon:

> **We must build the Kingdom of God, the Kingdom of Christ in our times, too. It is always possible to build it, even when it seems that the whole world is conspiring against it! God writes His simple, great truths on the winding paths of human life. Oftentimes, everything that opposes God, helps to make the Kingdom of God on earth a more conspicuous, more profound reality.**

The same day — to young married couples in Wisniowa:

> **Children are the fruit ... of love, but not merely by the fact that they**

---

[11] A Prime Minister in Poland in the 1930's

[12] Vatican diplomatic mission

[13] Nov. 13 is the Feast of St. Stanislaw Kostka

exist, that they were conceived, that they came into the world. They are the fruit of our love because through them we express our humanity, our human maturity, which we are to instill in them — day after day and year after year, as if drop by drop — until they are shaped into mature humans, in our image. And all of us, they and us, parents and children — in the image of Jesus Christ, the Son of God.

Same day — evening, a meeting with the sick at the Parish of St. Mikolaj in Krakow. Mass for the sick was said by Rev. Witold Kacz, the chaplain of the sick, later: a get-together in the religious education room, where the Cardinal was present * November 23 — in the morning, at the Church of St. Anne in Krakow, Mass over the urn containing the ashes of Jerzy Ciesielski and his children Kasia (9 years old) and Piotrus (8 years old). Assistant Professor, Doctor, engineer Jerzy Ciesielski — a scientific worker of the Krakow Institute of Technology — was one of Rev. Karol Wojtyla's closest friends. In the 1950s they organized and developed the tourist ministry. Jerzy Ciesielski and his children died in a catastrophe of a ship on the Nile near Khartoum where the deceased was a lecturer at the time. The funeral took place in the afternoon at the cemetery in Podgorze {a district of Krakow}. A fragment of the eulogy:

> "Jurek {Jerzy Ciesielski} carried God's witness in himself. And he shared this witness ... He knew that this witness of God which he carried in his soul must not be hidden under the bushel basket, that it is a light: therefore he bore witness. We are fully aware that the man who left us, was a man who bore witness. I dare say: he bore exceptional witness. It was exceptional also for this reason that he never said: I bear witness. And yet everyone knew that he did bear witness. He never said: I strive for holiness. And everyone knew that he strove for holiness."

November 28 — 10:00 a.m., Wawel Cathedral, Mass concelebrated with the pastors and rectors of St. Mikolaj's Parish * November 24-26 — Warsaw * November 29 — Krakow — Lagiewniki. Meeting with the young people who came to the recreation room run by Sister Klawera Wolska from the Congregation of the Sisters of Our Lady of Mercy and by a Salesian priest, Fr. Henryk Skorski. "At first the young people were shy. We sang songs together, there was some conversation ... After visiting for over an hour, and after prayers in the chapel, His Eminence left." (From the chronicles of the Congregation of the Sisters of Our Lady of Mercy)

December 1 — 10:00 a.m., at the residence chapel, Mass for the intention of bishops and priests for the opening of a conference of deans * December 4 — Meeting of the Council of the Pontifical Department of Theology in Krakow. He {the Cardinal} was among the speakers; he supported the idea of making pastoral medicine an academic subject * December 5 — Meeting of the Committee for the Apostolate of the Laity: dialogue within the Church following the symposium in Rome —

pastoral councils, both at the diocesan and parish level; meeting with national directors of pastoral ministry on the subject of the *Directory* and small communities in relation to professional ethics * 1:00 p.m., residence chapel, requiem Mass as part of the session of the Committee for the Apostolate of the Laity * December 6 — Residence chapel, during a Mass for the participants of the meeting of the Committee for the Apostolate of the Laity:

> **It could be said that man is predisposed to Advent, that waiting for something is deeply ingrained in his psyche. This is very significant; it means that man, as he is, is not self-sufficient and does not fully find himself in whatever he does. This also means that man, following the calling of his innermost heart, feels a need to transcend himself.**

Same day — Krakow, during the visitation of the Church of St. Mikolaj:[14]

> **[We bear witness to Christ by the gift of goodness:] Indeed in our public life and in public institutions, we are forbidden to speak of God openly, to speak of Christ openly, but even if our lips are silent about Christ, if our lips are silent about God, if we bear witness to Him by our actions, everyone will recognize this.**

December 8 — 7:30 a.m., Chapel of the Sisters of the Sacred Heart, Mass and sermon for the 75th anniversary of Sister Weronika's perpetual profession * Same day — during the visitation in the Church of St. Mikolaj, to the altar servers at the Church of the Jesuits:

> **When a boy, a young man or an adult man finds himself close to the altar, Jesus Christ ... tells him many things in his soul, as if prompting him. Prompting is not always a nice thing to do: as you well know, in school it gets you a rap on the knuckles from the teacher. But when Our Lord prompts you, it is a most wonderful thing. You must only pay attention to what it is that Our Lord, who is so close, is saying to you. And listen in such a way that what you hear will remain with you through later years, and throughout your life.**

December 10 — 9:00 a.m., residence chapel, Mass concelebrated with the Council of Priests, a sermon * Same day — during the visitation of St. Mikolaj's Church, to the physicians:

> **Let us pray that man become the central focus of your work; that you always see and feel with him, that you experience him in all of his truth — as you are called to do by your profession. But even more, that you experience man within the dimensions of Christ, because, after all, this is a man who needs help, who is suffering, who comes to seek your assistance – how easy it is to identify him with Christ, just as He — Christ — identified Himself: "Whatever you did... {for the least of my brethren}"**

---

[14] December 6 is the Feast of St. Nicholas

December 12 — during the visitation in the Church of St. Mikolaj, Mass for professionals in the humanities and sciences:

> **Everything that the Book of Genesis has assigned to man, the Creator assigned to him with the words of that Book: "Take dominion over the Earth." This whole process of shaping the face of the earth to the measure of man, to his needs, the whole process of shaping the earth as the home of man, is the result of man's labor. You play your part in that process.**

December 13 — 9:00 a.m., Lodz, Church of the Jesuits, sermon to university students * December 13 — At the cathedral of Lodz, for the 50th anniversary of the diocese:

> **[The external mission of the Church, on distant continents] ...but besides this external mission, the Church also has an internal mission. She turns toward ever new times and generations, to ever new societies, to ever new facts. She interprets all of them as signs of the times, the signs of Divine Providence, and bases her mission on them.**

December 14 — 7:00 p.m., residence chapel, Mass for the intention of Prof. Marian Miesowicz, who was gravely ill at the time * December 16 — Lublin * December 17 — 10:45 a.m.. Krakow — Nowa Wies, Church of Our Lady of Lourdes, Mass with sermon, an *Oplatek*[15] with university students.

December 20 —

> **At 7:30 p.m. Cardinal Wojtyla visited me at the neurological clinic in Krakow, where I was convalescing after an operation of a tumor. Half an hour earlier, the radio gave the news of the changes in the government (the resignation by Gomulka and the selection of Edward Gierek as First Secretary[16], in connection with the events on the Gdansk Coast). Since I had heard that bulletin with the other patients and the Cardinal had not yet heard anything, I related what happened. The Cardinal listened in silence with the utmost attention. At the end, his comment was: "Indeed, God acts in mysterious ways." His visit lasted about half an hour. Then the Cardinal talked with the staff and the patients, and also went for a while to the neuro-surgical ward to see a priest whose condition did not permit a long conversation.**
>
> **I have the honor of knowing Cardinal Wojtyla personally since 1949 (the Church of St. Florian in Krakow). Later we maintained contact at conventions of professors of ethics and moral theology, and subsequently, when he became bishop and cardinal, more sporadically, on the occasion of various solemn observances. (Fr. Jan Jakubczyk)**

December 21 — 7:30 a.m., chapel of the Theological Seminary, tonsure, ordination to minor orders and diaconate, sermon * December 24 — He wanted to celebrate a solemn Midnight Mass on Christmas night, outdoors, in front of the chapel of the Parish the Immaculate Conception

---

15 See Glossary
16 of the Communist Party

in Krakow — Azory (Reformed Franciscans). In an address delivered on that occasion, he said that for a number of years he celebrated Masses under the starry skies in the parish of Nowa Huta-Bienczyce, praying with the parishioners for the permission to build a parish church. Their common prayer was answered; the construction of that church has begun and is proceeding. This year he came to the parish at Azory to ask God, just as in Nowa Huta, to grant the same grace — the construction of a larger church at Azory is a pressing matter. This prayer, too, was answered. The Department of Religions of the Presidium of the National Council for the City of Krakow, by a decision of January 28, 1971, granted permission for the enlargement of the church at Azory.

December 25. Wawel Cathedral:

We thank Thee, Lord Jesus, that you came and became Man, to lift us up, to summon us, humankind, to something that is greater than us ... And maybe, because of our weakness, we would like to decline Your summons, decline the love to which You call us. But you do not allow it. How? Through your own weakness, through the fact that you are a Child. A defenseless Child, lying in the hay — that is how You prevent us, through Your own weakness, from closing our human hearts to love.

Same day — at the chapel of the Rakowice Cemetery in Krakow, as part of the visitation of the Parish of St. Mikolaj:

On this day, may our participation in the Eucharist and our common prayer become an extraordinary witness to the Birth of Christ. That Birth of Christ which takes place eternally in those who have left us, in those who live in God.

December 26 — At the Church of St. Szczepan in Krakow:

"You will bear me witness." May these words be taken up by each one of us, by each disciple of Christ. Let us not be afraid to call ourselves by that name. It is not a negotiable category; being a Christian is not merely an entry in my identity papers, it is a very profound reality within me. I am a Christian, that means I bear witness to Christ with my own life, in the dimension, and in the scope, in which that life is realized.

December 27 — On the Feast of the Holy Family, at the Church of the Carmelite Sisters in Krakow:

The love of two people ... becomes mature when it can give of itself to new persons, when it can bend over them with total dedication and caring, when it can express itself through them, even to the point of forgetting itself.

The same day — at the parish church in Zakopane:

The family stands at the root of all the values of every nation. In a way, the nation expresses itself through the family, because the family shapes people, new generations, in the spirit of the nation. The family transmits the culture of the nation. (First, the language.) After language come all the elements and values which make up the mosaic of the culture of each nation. Thus, the nation lives through the family, and owes its biological and spiritual existence to the family.

December 28 — The Cardinal's chapel, 10:30 a.m., Mass concelebrated with about 70 priests ordained in the three most recent years. Later, *Oplatek*[17] and an artistic program prepared by the Sisters of the Holy Spirit * December 29 — Warsaw * December 30 — 10:30 a.m., the residence chapel, concelebrated Mass with priests ordained several years before. *Oplatek* * December 31 — 7:30 a.m., Mass with sermon at the chapel of the Ursuline Sisters, for the opening of their provincial chapter * Same day — at St. Mikolaj's Church, an address for the conclusion of the visitation and the year:

> [Mention of the events on the Gdansk Coast:[18]] ...these were tragic events. The measure of the tragedy which played itself out in these days is that Polish blood was shed by Poles! [Examination of conscience — the right to food, the right to freedom:] ...an atmosphere of genuine freedom, untrammeled and not questioned or threatened in any practical sense; an atmosphere of inner freedom, the freedom from the fear of what may befall me, if I act this way or go to that place, or appear somewhere. These are very important values, which contribute to the common good, the values which must be respected, if the life of society is to run properly, in peace.

December 31 — At a Mass celebrated at midnight in the Basilica of the Franciscans in Krakow:

> This past year, especially in its final stages, was a difficult and painful one for us. Behind us are the hard experiences of the last few weeks, and these just before Christmas. They will be recorded as a bloody page in the annals of our national history — written with Polish blood spilled by Poles. This awareness has accompanied us throughout the past few weeks, during the Feast of Christmas, and it surely accompanies us tonight. This night has a different character than usual, and only very few could spend this time looking for entertainment. Instead, we feel the need for expiation, for recollection before God, for an examination of conscience, prayer for the dead, and for those suffering there, far from us, in the cities of the Coast.

---

[17] See Glossary
[18] Workers in the shipyards of Gdansk and Gdynia rioted in early December to protest rising food prices.

1971

A book dedicated to Cardinal Karol Wojtyla was published to commemorate the 25th anniversary of his ordination to the priesthood: *Logos and Ethos. Philosophical Treatises,* PTT Krakow 1971. Dedication: *Eminentissimo CAROLO CARDINALI WOJTYLA Archiepiscopo Metropoliae Cracoviensis, Commissionis Episcopatus Poloniae, pro causis doctrinae catholicae promovendae Praesidi, Cracoviensium studiorum Philosophiae atque Theologiae Protectori eximio hoc anno quinque sacerdotii lustra celebranti professores Philosophiae Cracoviae.*

January 1 — Post-visitation conference with all clergy conducting pastoral work at St. Mikolaj {Nicholas} Parish (including the Jesuits and the Carmelites) * January 2-6 — Zakopane-Jaszczurowka, Chapel of the Ursuline Sisters, concelebrated Masses * January 6 — 6:00 p.m., Wawel Cathedral, High Mass, meeting with representatives of visited parishes, homily:

> For this man, this Child, to be revealed as God to the three Wise Men from the East, it was necessary that a new light shine in their minds. Revelation always takes place between God and man. God reveals Himself, but man must accept the revelation of his God ... It was this inner light, more than the light of the star, that drew them to the encounter with God who revealed Himself in human flesh: for He was born as the child of Mary ... And similarly, we, too, are on the road to Bethlehem year after year...
>
> The Church is forever in a state of mission ... abroad, but also, constantly, in a state of mission within, into the inner depths ... Nations and individuals who have already become Christian must continue to become Christians anew.
>
> Today we think of missionaries ... I remember meetings [during the Council] with many bishops of the Dark Continent. I remember the first one of them I met, from Guinea ... We found out that all white missionaries had been expelled from this African Guinea. For racial reasons? Political ones? And recently..., that this only remaining native archbishop, a Black African, was imprisoned ... Today at the altar I think of my black fellow bishop and brother, who is in prison because he accepted the Word of God, he accepted the Revelation, and in response — dedicated himself completely to Christ ... The Church is a missionary Church ... she has always been that; ... if the Church ceased to be a missionary Church, if she stopped in one place, if she contented herself with thanking for the gift she received, then the Church would cease to be true to Christ, who continues to be born, continues to die, continues to be raised from the dead and who continues to send ...
>
> "They offered Him gifts" ... Today, at this historic altar at Wawel, when we think of the gifts we should offer to our Savior, in emulation of the Magi, we think of myrrh first. Because myrrh denotes suffering. And we cannot forget the events of the past few weeks, which, perhaps, were not as violent here, not so painful, but in other parts of our country, in other large cities, they were very painful and resulted in the deaths of Poles at the hands of other Poles. Myrrh ... suffering ... I offer this suffering up to Christ, I offer

today's Mass for the intention of those who died, whose number and names are unknown to us. They deserve this from us, so we offer this gift — myrrh — to Christ, along with the gifts of the Magi, at the altar of St. Stanislaw, the martyr.

January 8 — appoints a Preparatory Committee for the Synod of the Archdiocese of Krakow * Same day — 6:30 p.m., Chapel of the Sisters of the Holy Family of Nazareth, Mass and homily * Jan 9 — 8:00 p.m., *Oplatek*,[1] Club of Catholic Intellectuals * Jan 10 — Krakow, Chapel of the Sisters of the Holy Family of Nazareth, Mass and homily for teachers:

> God, as the supreme educator, shows us how to combine fatherhood with service, Divinity with service. In the human order, the father or the educator or the teacher is the one who imparts humanity. And their service must be like Christ's service, full of concern and care for everything that is in man, so that "the bent reed is not broken" ... Full of concern and care for all of man's weaknesses, which must be healed, not broken, and for all the seeds of good which are within man, so as not to "extinguish the glowing wick," the first spark ... Being an educator is very costly. It costs one one's very own person. It is the most authentic gift of man: It costs one one's very own person.
>
> [Today] we are witnessing a separation of education from upbringing. Knowledge is imparted. However, knowledge, even if very deep, very valuable, can be still separated from upbringing: from the gift of a person ... We are witnessing a flight away from man — both on the part of the educator, and on the part of the one being educated. This creates a vacuum. People no longer meet, generations do not meet. And if they do meet, it is on some plane of knowledge. But they do not meet in the communion of humanity...

January 11 — St. Anne's Church in Krakow, Mass for the late Prof. Wladyslaw Szafer, former rector of the Jagiellonian University.

> Here I must remember my last conversation with the deceased a few weeks before his death. The main topic of that conversation was our Homeland, the future of our nation. A great educator, a great scholar, and also a great son of the Polish nation was speaking. We must frequently recall this great son of the Church, who gave so much evidence of understanding the mission of the Church, especially in Poland...

January 12 — 7:30 p.m. Krakow, home of Mrs. Pozniak: Mass and homily at Mrs. Irena Szkocka's, 93 years old at the time. With reference to the Gospel just read, about the finding of Jesus, he said that it was his wish to her: "to multiply in years. Yes — he repeated — because with her ardent and faithful prayers she obtains many graces for us all..." (According to an account by Helena Szkocka)

January 13 — Krakow, 3 Franciszkanska Street, meeting of the

---

[1] See Glossary.

Episcopal Committee for Pastoral Ministry. 10:30 a.m., presentation by the chairman of the Committee, Archbishop B. Kominek: *The Parish, Its Sanctification, Elite Groups, Apostolate of the Laity*; discussion. 3:00 p.m., proposal of the "pastoral Vademecum" — presented by Bishop W. Pluta; discussion. After the break:

> **Cardinal Wojtyla read a presentation entitled *A Positive Discussion of the Moral and Religious Condition of Our Society* ... Citing passages from Schaff's book *Marxism and the Individual*, he juxtaposed them with his treatment of the issue in the book *Person and Act*. Schaff ... represents a trend which, in some measure, affects our society. [Conclusion:] Social life is not based on healthy principles; there are attitudes in our society that are not authentic and therefore a serious threat to the common good. The pragmatic materialism of the West is not yet a dominant force here; in our society it has a different form — the pursuit of scarce material goods, and the overvaluing of such goods. We need a close liaison of the Church with society; the Church should understand the aspirations and tendencies in our society and should guide them. (From the minutes)**

January 14 — Second day of meetings of the Episcopal Committee for Pastoral Ministry. Presentation by Bishop I. Tokarczuk — the same topic as Cardinal Wojtyla * Same day — 8:15 p.m., Dominican church, *Oplatek*[2] for university students * January 15 — 5:30 p.m., Chapel of the Daughters of Charity, Mass and homily, "Jaselka",[3] *Oplatek* for young people * January 16 — 7:30 p.m., St. Anne's Church, Mass for the late Andrzej Malkowski[4] * January 17 — 9:00 a.m., residence chapel, Mass and homily for the Family Apostolate, *Oplatek* * 12:30 p.m., at the Franciscans, *Oplatek* for the blind * 2:00 p.m., *Oplatek* for female youth at the house of the Albertine Sisters * 7:00 p.m., residence, *Oplatek* for a student group, the builders of the church in Kurow * January 19 — 6:30 p.m., residence chapel, Mass and homily, *Oplatek* for a charity group from St. Szczepan Parish * January 20-23 — private Masses at the residence chapel * January 22 — meeting of the Council of the Pontifical Department of Theology. He gives a report on the number of students at Catholic institutions of higher learning in Poland. (From the council minutes) * January 23 — Residence, 7:00 p.m., *Oplatek* for physicians * January 24 — Church of the Missionary Fathers at Stradom, Mass and homily for "Oasis" groups {charismatics} * 4:00 p.m., about 700 parishioners from Makow Podhalanski came to visit with the Cardinal at his residence * Same day — 7:00 p.m., the Dominican Basilica, Mass and homily, closing of an octave of prayers for unity among Christians:

> **We ask ourselves this question: where are we? At which point on that**

---

2 See Glossary
3 Christmas play
4 Founder of Polish Scouting

road which is supposed to lead us to full unity, to the unity of the Church? ... What to answer? ... In the last decade a very decisive step was made on the road toward the unification of Christians ... the course of history has been reversed. For we were in separation, and that was, to some extent, a principle guiding our thinking and our actions. Since the Second Vatican Council, a desire for unity and the efforts to accomplish it have become the guiding principles of our thinking and actions ...

We began to think about the Church, taking God, not man, as our starting point. God, our Father, who in His eternal love wants to save all of us.

At the same time we are well aware of what separates us and, with the passage of time, we realize that what had divided us, what still divides us Christians, is, after all, quite deep, that it has entered deep into the history ... of the Church, ... of society ... of human souls, and that it has created a certain state of affairs, a political state of affairs ... We are also aware of the intellectual changes that took place throughout the history of the Church, of the differences and divisions in the realm of theology, in the realm of understanding the revealed truth, and those in points which are very essential, critical ...

We are realists, and Christians must be realists with a full appreciation of the action of the Divine Grace ... The journey towards unity must go on, we must all undertake it ... There are impatient ecumenists in the Church, ardent and impatient. Everyone must be reminded of these words once said by Jesus Christ: "In your patience you will possess your souls" ...

Patience is the virtue which, according to the teachings of St. Thomas Aquinas, is the closest to fortitude. Fortitude prompts us to undertake difficult obligations and to remain strong in the face of adversity. Patience teaches us to maintain difficult positions. It teaches us to persevere even when that involves suffering ... It always provides the ability to look ahead, it provides persistence in achieving great aims ... It is a virtue which we are all in great need of as we walk along the road towards the unification of Christians.

January 26 — Warsaw, the Main Committee of the Polish Episcopate * January 27-28 — Warsaw, plenary conference of the Polish Episcopate * January 29 — 5:00 p.m., at the Dominicans, *Oplatek*[5] for veterans * January 30 — 5:00 p.m., residence, *Oplatek* for artists * 7:00 p.m., residence chapel, Mass and homily, *Oplatek* for lawyers * January 31 — Mass for the intention of Stanislaw R., a day before a very difficult operation * Same day — 4:00 p.m., *koleda*[6] at the Seminary * 5:00 p.m., Wieliczka, Mass, homily and a blessing of lectors * 7:30 p.m., *Oplatek* at the Seminary.

February — A skiing trip to Przehyba * February 1 — 5:00 p.m., *koleda* at the Higher Cathechetic Institute * 6:30 p.m., residence chapel, Mass and homily for the *Srodowisko* * February 2 — 12 noon, *koleda* at the residence * February 3 — 10:00 a.m., residence, conference of priests — heads of deaneries * 6:00 p.m., residence chapel, Mass and

---

[5] See Glossary.
[6] See Glossary.

homily for *Tygodnik Powszechny* and *Znak*, then a social get-together * February 4 — 6:30 p.m., residence chapel, Mass and homily for the conclusion of a nursing course for parish assistants.

February 6 — Presided over the funeral of Edmund Bobrownicki. "At 11:00 a.m. he said a Holy Mass at the casket at the Rakowice cemetery chapel, than led a funeral procession to the grave." (Maria Bobrownicka)

February 14 — 10:00 a.m., residence, Mass on the 50th wedding anniversary of Antoni and Wanda Starczewski. Mr. Starczewski did not want to agree to this celebration, claiming that "since he is not a prince, a cardinal should not celebrate this Mass for him." The Cardinal, in turn, asked that it be relayed to Mr. Starczewski, that he also presided over the marriages of workers, and a 50th anniversary is not only a celebration for the couple, but for the entire family. (According to an account by Dr. Anna Starczewska) * Same day — 4:00 p.m., Nowa Huta-Bienczyce, participated in a service for the Homeland * February 15-18 — residence chapel, private Masses * February 19 — 6:30 p.m., residence chapel, Mass and homily for nurses * February 20-March 1 — canonical visitation of the Holy Cross Parish in Krakow * February 21 — homily during the visitation at the Holy Cross Parish:

> ...two poles of the potential which lies dormant in man: the pole of hate, that hate which Saul felt towards David ... and the other pole — the pole of goodness. Christ, as if responding to the Old-Testament passion and hate of Saul, says: "Love your enemies" ...
> It is very easy to say "I love," but it is very difficult to invest that word with all of the meaning it should have. In seeking the truth about love within himself, man must tear through the shallow quest for pleasure, selfishness, profit. He must break through to that selflessness which underlies true friendship. What is more, even with selflessness, man sometimes does not earn the right to friendship. And then love must be stronger than that lack of friendship, which is enmity, as Christ taught us with His word and with His life.

Same day — Church of the Holy Cross, 9:00 p.m., participated in a Holy Mass for tourists * February 22 — Church of the Holy Cross in Krakow, a homily to married couples:

> We know that in our times, starting out in life is not easy for young couples, that you must often begin without your own place to live, without adequate means to start a family ...
> Love is never ready-made, we must continually learn it, we must continually mature in it — and the life that married couples begin together is always a school of love.
> We live in an age of great temptation in that regard. What kind of temptation? The temptation to substitute something else for this genuine love, and to call that "something else" love, too ... By its very nature, married

love ... is oriented toward giving birth ... Here, the temptations of contemporary mankind, of contemporary marriage, approach the boundaries of crime. But our civilization, our media, have for a long time blurred these boundaries, calling this evil — a good! The crime was called — a right! ... The upbringing of a new person. Your child lives with you and it demands from you many attitudes, many values, many virtues. The child demands a whole climate, a climate that only a family can provide.

February 24 — Ash Wednesday. A meeting of the personnel of all departments of the Curia. A presentation by the Archbishop *On the Work of the Metropolitan Curia.* Later on, all employees of the Curia received a copy of the text. After the presentation there was a discussion, or rather questions were taken pertaining to the issues presented.

On the Work of the Metropolitan Curia

I. Practical and detailed comments about the activities of our Metropolitan Curia should be preceded by at least a short reflection of a theological nature. For in order to understand clearly — what the Curia is, we must look into the theology of the local Church. The teachings of the Second Vatican Council allow us to form a certain outlook on this subject. The local Church is an organic part of the Universal Church, and is to some degree patterned after the Universal Church. It is not only a subordinate part, but also a part that is homogenous (of a single kind). This homogeneity is determined by the identity of the People of God, and also by the position of the Bishop, who is a full member of the College of Bishops which remains under the dominion of the successors of Peter.

The Bishop is the head of the local Church. He heads it as a priest, teacher and shepherd. The Curia is an institution which is supposed to make it possible for the Bishop to fulfill his role of the leader of the local Church and to facilitate his work. It is an office (i.e. institution) tied most closely to the Bishop's office (i.e. ministry) in the Church.

What does this leadership or ministry of the Bishop in his Church consist in? It consists in fulfilling the mission of a priest, teacher and shepherd in such a way as to shape the community of the local Church, made up of many communities. The Second Vatican Council has taught us convincingly that the mission of the Bishops in the Church implies the mission of the entire People of God, i.e. Christian life which is the fruit of Divine Grace - the fruit of the Holy Spirit sent by the Father by virtue of Christ's Redemption. The mission of the Bishop as priest, teacher and shepherd in the diocesan Church implies the reality of the People of God, and is meant to serve the shaping of the people in the community of that Church.

The Curia, as an institution tied to the office (i.e. ministry) of the Bishop, is meant to help in that. The structure of the Curia and its activities must be such that the underlying goal of the Bishop's mission in the Church is more easily and more effectively accomplished. The individual departments of the Curia form specialized entities which strive to discern the various facets of life in the diocesan Church, from the point of view of the Bishop's mission. These entities participate more closely, we could say more "centrally," in his authority. And Bishops exercise authority in the Church by the will of Christ.

Regarding the exercise of authority itself, according to Catholic social ethics, all authority, and especially that within the Church, should have a dual character: of leadership, but at the same time of service. This dual character is tied very closely with the principle of subsidiarity, which holds that the primary goal of authority is to assist its subordinate entities in fulfilling their own tasks. Wherever the entities are self-sufficient in fulfilling their tasks, the superior entity should leave them in their self-sufficiency, and not do the things which they are capable of doing themselves.

The times in which we live, the times after the Second Vatican Council, in conjunction with the particular situation of the Church in Poland, require that the Bishops undertake a number of initiatives which will renew the Church and simultaneously maintain and strengthen her assets and presence in our society. It is from this point of view that we should examine the work of our Metropolitan Curia. It is also from this point of view that we should consider the observations presented herein.

II. These observations are not meant to encompass the entirety of the diverse subject which is the work of the Metropolitan Curia. The scope of this work is defined both by Canon Law and by long experience. Here we mean only to point out several aspects of the Metropolitan Curia's activities — specifically those that arise from the reorganization of this central institution in the archdiocese, and those connected with the creation of new entities representing the clergy or even the laity, as prescribed by the Second Vatican Council. These observations are made in response to the current situation, and they follow the developing situation in the hope of ensuring the proper course of this development.

Basically, the observations touch upon two matters: 1) internal coordination; 2) external coordination.

Re 1). Given the current growth of the Curia, especially of its pastoral departments, it is essential that these departments not work only for themselves and in isolation, but that they interact very closely with one another. How is this interaction to be organized, and who is to initiate it? Obviously, the initiative may come from the Ordinary Bishop or any of the individual Bishops — but it may also come from the directors of the departments or from those responsible for the various pastoral ministries within the archdiocese. Any such initiative can and should always be based on some concrete reason. Having such a reason, it is always possible to assemble a meeting of an appropriate team of those workers of the Curia or of those priests who are needed to discuss the relevant matter.

Re 2). External coordination is to be understood as the entirety of actions of the organs of the Curia "in the field." How are these actions to be characterized, especially the actions of the pastoral departments, organs and centers? These departments, organs and centers not only direct the various areas of pastoral activity in the archdiocese, but also conduct some very specific activities in their sphere of specialization and can provide a basic analysis of needs and some appropriate suggestions. We must clearly understand that this specialization is the basis of effective activity "in the field." Whether and how the parishes and deaneries accept the activities of the various departments and organs of the Curia depends, in great measure, on what these departments and organs have to offer, what they bring.

In any case, the work of each department and organ of the Curia should be geared not only towards the handling of immediate matters, but should have an overall plan of action, a plan arising from a fundamental discernment of issues, a realistic plan whose implementation can be, in turn, monitored by the appropriate departments and organs of the Curia.

Episcopal visitations which we are conducting in a five-year cycle (for Krakow, in a cycle longer than 5 years) constitute a very special form of support for the coordination of the work of the Curia.

This coordination should encompass the following activities:

a) The departments and organs of the Curia prepare the visitation, or alternately conduct their own preliminary visitation. This pertains particularly to the Department of Catechesis, and also to the Department of Economics.

b) The departments and organs of the Curia — each in its own area of competence — will provide the visiting Bishops with information about the parishes to be visited, and will also submit their desiderata. It is desirable to present these in writing, and possibly also to talk over the pertinent matters with the visiting Bishops.

c) After the visitation, the departments and organs of the Curia will receive information from the visiting Bishops on the state of the parish in relation to their particular areas of interest, along with recommendations for further direction of activities. Here it is desirable to establish and utilize standardized reports and surveys of visitation.

These observations are submitted for consideration and comment by all interested parties.

February 24 — inter-deanery conference devoted to matters of the Apostolate of the Laity:

In this regard [the issues of the laity and their apostolate], the Church in Poland finds itself in a particular situation. I speak of this with some authority, because as a member of Consilium de Laicis, the Council of the Laity at the Apostolic See, I am familiar with this issue as it manifests itself all over the world, in the entire Church. This issue presents itself differently in the world at large than it does with us and our neighboring countries.

The goal of [this] working conference is a better assessment of the situation, an assessment of how the apostolate of the laity is being built and implemented, among us. Not in the whole Church, not even in the whole Church in Poland, but here among us ... in this actual case of the group of parishes represented here ... The goal is, first of all, to see the role of the lay people in our Polish context ... The removal of the laity from participation in the life of the Church through Catholic organizations has produced an atrophy of the understanding of the role to be played by the laity in the Church. Or if not an atrophy of this understanding in general, then at least a dislocation, a deformation. It could be that this deformation also contains some sort of new formation, I am certain of that, we just have to elicit it ... We will not be able to change the external situation ... to bring about the sudden appearance of Catholic Action organizations in one form or another. Besides, we know what kind of consequences that would bring about. We can already observe the vegetative state of the few authorized organizations of Catholic laymen which exist here ... At meetings in Rome I say: there are no organizations of the lay apostolate in Poland — but there is the apostolate of the laity ...

If it is (insufficiently) expressed, wherein lies the reason? In part, it lies on the side of the laity, in their so-called intimidation, in their incompetence: they don't know how, they don't know what to do? ... But, in part, it lies on our side ... we have grown accustomed to the lack of participation by the lay people in the activities of the Church ever since the Catholic Action organizations were dissolved, forcibly disbanded. A certain attitude formed among us priests which makes it difficult for us to see the role and the mission of the laity in the Church.

The first step ... is to sharpen our priestly awareness, within our own circle. It is the attitude of the priests that determines whether the apostolate of the laity does or does not exist.

Same day — 6:00 p.m., Theological Seminary, installation of the Stations of the Cross, conference of deacons * February 25 — 9:00 a.m., Zakopane, parish church, homily before a regional conference * February 26 — Krakow, 7:00 a.m., residence chapel, private Mass * February 27 — Zakopane, 7:00 a.m., Chapel of the Ursuline Sisters, Mass * February 28 — During visitation of the Holy Cross Parish in Krakow, he visited the Chapel of the Sisters of the Most Holy Soul of Jesus at Pradnik Bialy — preached a homily to married couples who are parents:

The chapel of this house has served as the base for the parish pastoral ministry, which was so necessary here, in this part of Krakow ...

Today I would like you to recall the day of your marriage, and that blessing. And I myself will remind you of it, and will bestow that blessing again upon each married couple here present ... May the blessing return to you at this new stage of your life as a married couple and as a family ... I ask you to come up to the altar one couple after another to receive this blessing from your bishop. And if it should so happen — as there are various circumstances — that a couple could not be here together, then let the one who is here — the husband or the wife — kneel here and receive that blessing for the spouse and for the whole family.

March 4 — Warsaw, Mass at the Ursuline Sisters * March 5-7 — private Masses, residence chapel in Krakow.

March 6 — Meeting of the Council of the Pontifical Department of Theology in Krakow. It was decided, among others, that a book should be published on the occasion of the 900th anniversary of the death of St. Stanislaw (1979); Rev. Prof. B. Przybyszewski was asked to be the editor, a decision was also made to organize an academic session in 1972, to determine the topics to be covered in the book. There were also discussions on the future legal status of the Department. The cardinal shared information about conferences and planned writings on this topic. (From the minutes of the Council meetings)

March 7 — 4:00 p.m., the parish church in Borek Falecki, Mass and homily, blessing of church bells * On the same day — concelebrated Mass and homily in honor of St. Thomas Aquinas at the Dominican basilica in Krakow:

We shall pray that theology will always remain the wisdom of the

Church. The Church is blessed with the gift of wisdom; it is the first of the gifts of the Holy Spirit. It is necessary that theology serve the wisdom of the Church and be its expression ...

We shall pray, as we keep before our eyes the variety of societies, cultures and civilizations in which the contemporary Church lives, for the strength to find, through the creative work of the theologians, an expression, a contemporary expression, for the Word of God in all those societies, cultures and civilizations. An expression which can inspire minds as well as hearts, an expression which is the particular gift of the Holy Spirit to the people of our times, an expression which serves the Gospel of our generation. We shall pray for this for all the theologians of the Church, of whom St. Thomas remains the prince ...

We shall pray that the Church, which is lumen gentium, the light of the people, may possess that light and possess it in such a way that it might shine before the people of our times.

March 11-12 — He heads the delegation of the Committee for the Apostolate of the Laity to the symposium of *Concilium de Laicis* in Rome. Cardinal Wojtyla prepared a report *On Dialogue within the Church* * March 11 — He submitted a letter to the Sacred Congregation for Divine Worship requesting that Polish saints be included in the calendar of the universal Church. The request had a positive result (Cf. Rev. Jan Dyduch, *Kardynal Karol Wojtyla w sluzbie Kosciolowi Powszechnemu* {Karol Cardinal Wojtyla in the Service of the Universal Church}, Krakow 1998) * March 13 — Vienna, chapel at the nunciature,[7] private concelebrated Mass * March 14-15 — Rome, Polish College, private concelebrated Masses * March 16 — 6:00 p.m., Rome, St. Stanislaw Church, Mass and homily for the intention of Edmund Nowicki, Bishop of Gdansk * March 17-20 — concelebrated Masses and homilies at the chapels of Felician Sisters, Sisters of the Resurrection and Ursuline Sisters * March 21 — 4:00 p.m., a conference for nuns * Same day — Mass and homily at St. Stanislaw Church in Rome. The homily based on a gospel reading about the prodigal son:

Let us begin with an analysis of the deep hungers experienced by the prodigal son ... A hunger for bread: ... Today, a hunger for bread is the lot shared by many people ... A dramatic division of contemporary mankind into a minority of wealthy nations, possessing a surplus of goods, and the majority of poor, hungry nations... This is a veritable chasm which is difficult to fill, difficult to cross, although it seems so simple. It would seem sufficient that they {the rich} see themselves as the prodigal sons, that they go the Father and, before this their Father, become aware of all the obligations that they have with regard to their brothers ...

A hunger for reconciliation ... a hunger for unity ... We hope that whatever separates us, antagonizes us, defeats us, is not the stronger element. We want everything that unites us, that brings peace to be the stronger element ...

---

[7] Vatican diplomatic mission

What I say here is a reflection of the work which we have done here in the past week, within the framework of the session of Consilium de Laicis. The council of the laity has summoned many people from the whole world to come and think over and discuss the issue of dialogue within the Church

...

[Of matters pertaining to Poland:] During the events of last December and the subsequent weeks, the Polish Episcopate tried, above all, to become a messenger of peace, of interior peace. We called to mind everything that is required for such interior peace. But, above all, we called all the sons of our Homeland to prayer, we asked them to show their good will, to be ready to do everything necessary in order to counteract the evil already perpetrated, or any unknown evil which should be avoided...

March 22 —7:00 a.m., Polish College chapel, concelebrated Mass * March 23 — Rome, Chapel of the Norbertine Sisters, concelebrated Mass and homily * March 24-25 — Rome, Polish College, concelebrated Masses * March 25 — 11:00 a.m., Vatican , an audience with Pope Paul VI * Same day — 6:30, Vienna, Mass at the nunciature * March 27 — 7:00, arrival in Krakow.

March 27-April 4 —Canonical visitation of the parish of Kobierzyn. "In the morning I returned from Rome, and at 5:00 p.m. I went to the parish church in Kobierzyn" (From the visitation report). The visitation was continued by Bishop Jan Pietraszko and Bishop Stanislaw Smolenski. * March 27 — 7:00 p.m., the parish of Kobierzyn, a discussion on the subject of marital ethics * March 28 (Passion Sunday) — Kobierzyn, homily during the visitation (the church in Kobierzyn is located on the grounds of a psychiatric hospital):

I know that I find myself at that place within our Greater Krakow which is a place of particular suffering. As if a separate city of human suffering. It is indeed at this place that the presence of Christ, who carries all of our sufferings, is so very clear. From the very moment that I entered the hospital church, that thought has been with me, that thought has penetrated me very deeply: the thought of how clearly Christ is present here, through all of the suffering...

March 29 — Departure for Warsaw * March 30-April 1 — Warsaw, conference of the Polish Episcopate.

April 2 — 5:00 p.m., celebrated the Stations of the Cross with parishioners during the visitation in Kobierzyn * April 3 — Visited some of the wards of the psychiatric hospital, especially some priests undergoing treatment * April 3 — Conclusion of the canonical visitation of Kobierzyn:

Your parish ... also has hundreds of the sick, and, indeed, the most seriously sick — not only the physically ill, but also mentally ill patients who fill your hospital known throughout Poland ... And I could be there, and I could be part of the communion that the sick and the well, the ones who take care of them, form around Christ the Lord. And I could visit the sick, at least some of them. Especially dear to me were the children at the hospital of Kobierzyn whom I could visit yesterday...

Same day — 7:30 p.m., Mass for the conclusion a retreat for university students at the Church of St. Anne in Krakow. Sermon:

> We have grown accustomed to looking at the cross, whereas in truth, the cross is a reality which shakes the foundations of our human existence. This reality keeps telling us, so imaginatively, it keeps showing us what redemption is; it says that the initiative came and continues to come from God, and it says that God pays with Himself for the reconciliation with man, with me.

April 4 — 9:00 a.m., Wawel Cathedral, ordination of new priests, homily * Same day — 5:00 p.m., Jordanow, Chapel of the Ursuline Sisters, ordination of new priests, homily * April 5 — 7:00 a.m., Zakopane, private Mass * April 6 — 8:00 p.m., St. Joseph's Church, Mass during a retreat for lawyers * April 7 — 11:00 a.m., Lapanow, funeral of Rev. Dean Tadeusz Siepak * Same day — 7:30 p.m., Krakow, Church of the Felician Sisters, Mass and homily for the conclusion of a retreat for physicians * April 7-10 — Wawel Cathedral, liturgy of the Holy Week * April 11 — 6:00 a.m., Nowa Huta-Bienczyce, Resurrection Mass, homily:

> Wawel may be regarded as a magnificent testimony to the past, but here is a testimony to the present and to the future. We bear witness to the Resurrection here, at this place where a new city and a new, gigantic place of human labor, of Polish labor, is being built! ... There is a particular significance to your witness. It did not begin today, it has lasted for twenty years, ever since they started to build Nowa Huta near Old Krakow ... We know very well how much that witness has cost ... The witness borne by us, Christians of the latter half of the 20th century, on Polish soil, and especially here, in Nowa Huta, for over 25 years ... although it has met with opposition, it must eventually meet with recognition ... In the last few months there was talk of the contributions made by the Church ... of the contributions made by believers, not only nonbelievers, to the cause of the Homeland, to the common good. And there was talk of the rights of the people of faith in the common Homeland — and that is the way it should be!

Same day — Resurrection Sunday — Mass at Wawel Cathedral. To this Mass he invited in "a very special way those parishes of the old and new Krakow, which were visited by the bishops in the recent period, especially during Lent" (Holy Cross, Bialy Pradnik, Prokocim, Piaski Wielkie, Kobierzyn).

> It is necessary for us to meet here, in this center which is not only an archive of the past, to meet at the tomb of St. Stanislaw, to take up the message of Easter and to integrate it into the content of our times ...
> We, who are convinced that the cause of Christ and our cause with Him are just, wish to convey that conviction to the young generation. We want

the youth to get to know the Gospel, to live a life of grace; we wish that Mass could be said at the hospital in Prokocim! Because it was our countrymen from the United States who funded this hospital and wanted it guaranteed that the hospital should have full spiritual care. And that is why they built a chapel. The purpose of the chapel is that Holy Masses could be said in it, and not to hold some other kinds of meetings...

April 11 — The Sacred Congregation for the Clergy publishes *Directorium Catechisticum;* Cardinal Wojtyla participated in the work on this document (Cf. Rev. Jan Dyduch, op. cit.)

April 12 — Easter Monday, Church of the Congregation of the Resurrection in Krakow:

I will refer to a conversation I once had with a Marxist, a Marxist by conviction. It is difficult at this time to recall his name, but it is also difficult to doubt his conviction. In that conversation he himself started talking about the immortality of man. And he said that there is an opposition towards death in man. Man wants to transcend his life, which has an end. But he cannot transcend it. Or maybe he can, but only through history, through other people, through society, through his work ... If we take into consideration what he said in the first part, we are almost at the same point described first by the prophet David, and later by St. Peter in his lesson on the resurrection ... In Christ ... is the fulfillment of the deepest, most elementary longing of the human spirit ...

What do we demand? We demand that in our social life, in our public life, these profound human matters be given the attention and the treatment that they deserve. So that there are no attempts - as there once were, after the resurrection of Christ — to buy with money those who would be silent...

April 14 — Zakopane, an illness (*sine missa* {no Mass}) * April 15-16 — Krakow, 1·00 p.m., residence chapel, private Mass * April 15 — "at the request of Cardinal K. Wojtyla we had to take care of Kazia and accept her into our House ... she found herself in very difficult living conditions." (From the chronicle of the Sisters of Our Lady of Mercy) * April 17-18 — Meeting of the Committee for the Apostolate of the Laity: enlargement of the committee membership; *Directory* in the life of the Church, meeting with a lay representative of the diocese — on the subject of dialogue; meeting with *Iustitia et Pax*[8] * April 20 — 1:00 p.m., residence chapel, Mass with homily for mothers superior * April 21 — Mass and homily for the beginning of the construction of a church in Jaworzno:

As we look at our Polish land, at everything that was left on it by the centuries and the generations in the realm of church architecture, we read this dimension of mankind and relate it to our era, because we believe in man, in his full dimension! That is why we ask persistently and patiently, that wherever there are people, there could also be a place for God to meet

---

with people, for people to meet with God. And we have thus asked, persistently and patiently, in Nowa Huta, we have thus asked, persistently and patiently, in Jaworzno, we are and we will continue to ask, persistently and patiently, in Pisarzowice and many other places in the archdiocese ... where there is a need. Wherever our persistent, patient plea is met with understanding — we are grateful; wherever such understanding is lacking, our persistence and our patience will continue. For that persistence and patience regarding the houses of God flow from within us! From each and every one of us. This is the dimension of man, and we will conform our desires and our persistent and patient, but unshakable, efforts to this dimension of man on Polish soil...

April 22 — Extraordinary meeting of the Council of the Pontifical Department of Theology — the doctorate of Rev. Tomasz Chmura * April 23 — At the Church of St. Wojciech {Adalbert} in Krakow: "If we associate St. Adalbert with the era of the nation's baptism, then St. Stanislaw might, in the history of our Christian nation, represent the moment of confirmation..." * April 24 — Gniezno, the cathedral, procession in honor of St. Adalbert, closing address * April 25 — 9:15 a.m., Gniezno, the cathedral, Pontifical High Mass with the procession for the Feast of St. Adalbert * Same day — Chorzow, Church of St. Andrew, Sacrosong (festival of religious song):

It is some sort of wonderful searching; in that searching there is a certainty that the Church, Christ, Christianity and everything that is an expression of contemporary times — a secular expression — have very much to say to each other, that they can meet. In every sacrosong there is a confirmation that the contemporary form is waiting to be infused with this singular content. The content which is from Christ, the content which helps us, through Christ, to reveal the truth of creation — the beauty of creation, the goodness of creation — in ourselves, around ourselves, among us...

April 29 - 6:00 p.m., Wawel Cathedral, participation in the beginning of a novena to St. Stanislaw * April 30 (Feast of St. Catherine of Sienna) - Convent of the cloistered Dominican Sisters in Krakow at Grodek. He celebrated a solemn Mass and spoke a sermon entitled *The Development of the Kingdom of God in the Soul of St. Catherine*. He entered the refectory along with his entourage to take breakfast, he walked about the entire convent, visited the sick sisters. Upon leaving he said: "You have a very beautiful convent and good conditions for contemplation." From the sermon about St. Catherine:

It was a short life, lasting only 33 years, but it was a life rich with interior treasures: the action of the Spirit of Wisdom, of God's love and of some unusual strength ... She owes her title of the Doctor of the Church to the wonderful combination of her interior life with the Spirit of Wisdom and her mission in the Church.

April 30-May 2 — Canonical visitation of the parish of Osielec * April 30 — Osielec, Confirmation of about 260 people.

Spring — In a report entitled *The Matter of the 900th Anniversary of St. Stanislaw and the Provincial Synod*, the cardinal formulated the proposal of calling the First Synod of the Krakow Province.

He makes reference to the historical anniversary of the pastoral work of St. Stanislaw (1072-1079) and wishes to point out the force which the figure of this saint brings to the history of Christianity in Poland, in particular to the history of the salvation of Polish society. The Synod is to be a connection, after nine centuries, to the person of the saint through "working on the enrichment and deepening of our faith as is required in our times." Having outlined the canonical framework of the Synod, the Cardinal formulated some proposals in the nature of an orientation. The provincial Synod could be composed of the pastoral synods of the individual dioceses. The starting point for such a pastoral synod must be the appropriate identification of the teachings of Vatican II, from the point of view of their gradual introduction into the totality of teaching and pastoral work. The work of the pastoral synods would take place in a series of working groups. Each group would first perform a study, and only then put forth proposals of an organizational nature ...

The provincial Synod would have to be based initially on the activities of a single preparatory committee and, subsequently, on the activities of several, as required. The task of the first committee would be to notify every diocese represented in the Synod of post-Council activities in other dioceses. The work of the other preparatory committees would be based on this factual material. If the goal of the Synod is to tighten the bonds and strengthen the sense of community in the metropolitan see, then each diocese must in advance reserve the right of conducting the work according to its own needs and experiences ...

The decisions of the Synod would reflect the common consideration of a variety of matters, and would therefore expand our base of experience.

Because of the historical circumstances — the 900th anniversary of the death of St. Stanislaw — we could invite participants from other dioceses as guests.

The Plenary of the Episcopal Conference would be informed about the deliberations and progress of the Synod.

(The Metropolitan See {= Province} of Krakow includes the dioceses of Czestochowa, Katowice, Kielce and Tarnow.) (From the minutes of the Synod)

May 3[9] — 10:00 a.m., Jasna Gora {Czestochowa}, Pontifical High Mass with procession * Same day — 6:30 p.m., solemn Holy Mass for Cardinal Primate on the occasion of the 25th anniversary of his consecration as bishop. Sermon by Cardinal Wojtyla:

I now wish to address you, Your Eminence, Most Esteemed Cardinal Primate. We all know that on May 12 of this year it will be 25 years since your consecration as bishop, a consecration which took place here, on Jasna Gora, and which began the pastoral work of Your Eminence. We all know, and we, your brother bishops, know this best, that you wish to observe this anniversary quietly, in meditation, and we understand. We understand that

---

[9] See Glossary.

it would be difficult to speak of this other than with Christ and His Mother, and we wish to honor your will, but we ask just one thing, that tonight Your Eminence accept this Holy Mass which is being celebrated by your proven brother bishop, the Archbishop of Poznan, as a gift from the entire Polish Episcopate.

Tomorrow, here at Jasna Gora, a conference of the Episcopate will be held. We are here together so that by this one gesture — with which Your Eminence also agrees — to express what Your Eminence, and what each of us, wants to simply say to Jesus Christ and to His Mother ...

It is all that we can offer, but it is truly everything ...

May 4 — Jasna Gora, plenary conference of the Polish Episcopate *
May 7 — Krakow, Church of St. Anne, Mass and homily to high school graduates:

There is a fear which is morally positive, appropriate. Man needs this kind of fear; a fear which flows from the sense of responsibility, which to some extent defines that sense. Then in my consciousness I can properly tie it into cause and effect. So I know that in order to achieve certain effects, I have to attempt to influence certain causes, and in order to avoid certain effects, I have to remove, exclude, certain causes. The sense of fear which accompanies such thinking, such an attitude, is a creative force ... If Jesus Christ said that His disciples are responsible people, then it is not necessary to teach them to fear and to educate them in fear: the fear of the effects ... A responsible person should be at peace with his conscience ...

We are called to glory. All of the evaluations we receive, all of the grades of very good or excellent at the final high school examination or university examinations are but minor details, mere insignificant dust on this calling to glory. I, a human person, am to prove myself ultimately in the eyes of God: this is the ultimate maturity to which I am called.

May 8 — The appointment of the Preparatory Committee for the Synod of the Archdiocese of Krakow. Members: Msgr. Dr. Eugeniusz Florkowski, chairman; Msgr. Czeslaw Obtulowicz; Fr. Provincial Stanislaw Nawrocki; Rev. Dr. Franciszek Macharski, chancellor of the Theological Seminary; Rev. Prof. Tadeusz Pieronek, secretary; Rev. Dr. Stanislaw Kosowski, pastor of Trzebinia; Rev. Marian Jakubiec, pastor of the Most Holy Redeemer Parish in Krakow; Rev. Stanislaw Gorecki, vicar from Krakow; Rev. Bronislaw Fidelus, vicar from Krakow; Sr. Karolina Kasperkiewicz, representative for matters pertaining to congregations of women; Mr. Janusz Bogdanowicz; Mr. Stefan Wilkanowicz, editor. Purpose: during the entire year of 1972 to "prepare a comprehensive plan of action for the Synod ... study the opinions among clergy and the laity" * Same day — 8:00 a.m., Wawel Cathedral, ordination of subdeacons, sermon * 6:00 p.m., Mass at the Cathedral concelebrated with the Council of Priests * May 9 — 9:00 a.m., procession to Skalka, a word of greeting. Same day — in Nowa Huta-Bienczyce, a service commemorating encyclicals on social issues, on the 80th anniversary of Rerum Novarum. Celebration led by the Primate,

Cardinal Stefan Wyszynski, main address by Ignacy Tokarczuk, the Bishop of Przemysl. Participating: Antoni Baraniak, the Archbishop of Poznan and the bishops of the Opole region. Cardinal Wojtyla — introductory address: "Almost all the successors of Pope Leo XIII touched upon the same new issues, new problems: the problems of social justice and social peace ... The Church has followed the development of these new issues step by step..."

May 10 — 10:00 a.m., the residence, Council of Priests * May 11 — 8:00 p.m., Wroclaw, conference on the subject of *Rerum Novarum* * May 12 — 10:00 a.m., Czestochowa, Jasna Gora, introductory address during the observance of the 25th anniversary of the Primate's consecration as bishop * Same day — 6:00 p.m., Church of St. Catherine in Krakow, symposium on the 500th anniversary of the death of the Servant of God Izajasz {Isaiah}Boner, professor of the Jagiellonian University, with the participation of the parishioners, the Chapter, and the Department of Theology; sermon * May 13 — Chapel of the Daughters of Our Lady of Sorrows, Mass, address to the General Chapter: "...it is important who will guide this [religious] family and who will be the first servant of the common good, and who will inspire you, sisters, to seek out this good, to remain in the congregation, in the unity of the family, serving God as your community is supposed to serve..." * Same day — 4:00 p.m., residence chapel, adoration of the Blessed Sacrament by priests * May 14-21 — Canonical visitation of the parish in Makow Podhalanski * May 14 — 6:00 p.m., for the opening of the canonical visitation in Makow Podhalanski:

> **I am grateful for your invitation. I must confess that until now no other parish has invited me in the way that the parish of Makow did. It was a great experience, and remains famous in Krakow, how you came in such unusual numbers, because there were as many as 600 of you, to the bishop's residence at 3 Franciszkanska Street, you sang your beautiful Christmas carols, you toured that house, you were satisfied with a very poor snack, all for the purpose of inviting your bishop to your parish.[10]**

During the visitation he delivered the following homilies:

Confirmation.

A sermon for elderly couples.

A sermon for younger couples.

A sermon for the single.

Blessing of married couples.

---

10 See entry for January 24, 1971

May 15 — 6:30 a.m., Makow, hospital chapel, Mass with sermon, distribution of communion in the chapel and to the sick in the wards * May 16 — 3:00 p.m., Makow, an address during the blessing of motor vehicles * May 18 — 9:00 p.m., group prayer at the grotto of the Blessed Mother on Zrodlana Street * May 19 — 10:30 a.m., Bialka, group prayer by a wayside chapel * Same day — in Makow, Mass concelebrated with priests from the Makow parish * May 20 — evening, Makow Podhalanski, visit in the house at 102 Wolnosci Street, where the Blessed Sacrament is kept (in the home of Mrs. Rutowska) * May 22 — Meeting of the Council of the Pontifical Department of Theology in Krakow. Among other matters, the Cardinal described the program of the all-Polish theological convention in Lublin and indicated the need to show interest in its activities. He also presented a letter which he intends to send to the Premier of the Polish People's Republic in the matter of the Department of Theology. The letter recalls historical facts and demands that the wrong done to the Polish culture and to the theological community by abolishing the Department in 1954 be rectified. The Council expressed its support. Plans regarding the observances of the 25th anniversary of the Cardinal's priesthood were also made. (From the minutes of the Council)

May 22-25 — Canonical visitation of the parish of Liszki * May 24 — 3:00 p.m., Piekary, visit to a branch of the Kobierzyn psychiatric hospital. In the chapel, an address to the patients and the medical staff, prayer * May 25 — 6:00 p.m., Liszki, sermon closing the visitation, during a May service:

> **I was told much about how your children constantly sit in front of the television, that they get much of their information from there, much of what shapes their imagination. But perhaps they also get a certain anxiety from there, because this is very superficial knowledge ... The common sense of the parents, of the older generation, still has its meaning. We just have to make sure that the generations meet, that the fundamental obligation of man on earth and, especially ... of a Christian community, continues to be fulfilled; the obligation of bringing up new people, bringing them up in the spirit of Christ ... For, indeed, the Kingdom of God suffers violence in our times, suffers violence on our earth. And that is why we need people of action, who will take it away from this violence by force.**

May 26 — The first session of the Preparatory Committee of the Synod. The cardinal presented his report *The Matter of the 900th Anniversary of St. Stanislaw and the Provincial Synod* (text: *Notificationes* No. 6-8, 1972). The Committee was to prepare a reasonably detailed concept of the Synod on the basis of the available publications, of the materials concerning post-Vatican II synods in various countries, and of its own opinions. The Committee is also to tap all possible formal and informal communities. It is also to prepare the structures of the Synod. The character of the Synod will be pastoral, it should involve everyone as far a possible, it should be an opportunity to study the Vatican Council, especially in smaller study groups, it is to become a pastoral action and lead to practical conclusions. The Synod is to complete its work in 1979. "We must also think through and discuss the concrete form of the Synod of the Church Province of Krakow."

May 27 — 8:00 a.m., residence chapel, concelebrated Mass with sermon for professors of patristics[11] * May 28 — 7:00 p.m., Church of the Jesuits on Kopernika Street, concelebrated Mass with sermon on the 50th anniversary of the dedication of the church * May 30 — 9:30 a.m., Piekary Slaskie, sermon during a pilgrimage of men (in the year of prayer for the life of the nation—sermon on that topic):

> There is a sort of hierarchy among living creatures; there are creatures that are increasingly more perfect ... Man has, among the creatures on this earth, the fullest measure of life; man is the most perfect of the creatures. And man transmits this fullness, this life, to new persons. And how very significant it is that when two young people, a man and a woman, a bride and a groom, kneel on the steps of an altar to enter into marriage — to celebrate the sacrament of marriage — the Church prays to the Holy Spirit and sings the very same words which we proclaim here today: "Send down your Holy Spirit, and new life will arise! And You will renew the face of the earth!" For it is in that life which arises out of two people, in marriage, that the face of the earth is renewed. This is our Christian way of thinking. We do not think only in terms of quantity — we think of quality, and we say: the face of the earth is renewed in every human being, who comes from the womb of a mother, as if the whole work of creation were starting anew, as if God the Creator were acting again, God -the Holy Spirit to whom we call out and whom we ask: may new life arise...

May 30 — 5:00 p.m., Feast of Pentecost, Wawel — Holy Mass and sermon for members of the parishes visited during the spring:

> This cathedral — we believe — is the Cenacle of our Church ... The tombs of kings, leaders, poets, saints ... this is a place where the bishops of Krakow have been laid to eternal rest beginning with St. Stanislaw ... Here, year after year, the bishop extends his hands over the deacons and tells them what Christ told the Apostles: "Receive the Holy Spirit," and he sends them to the various parishes and churches of our diocese ... Here, as well, we lay hands on the priests who are to become bishops ... That is why this place, from which the life of our Church emanates, deserves to be the place where we meet, especially on the day of the descent of the Holy Spirit ... That is why I invite you, that is why I even urge you, to come to this place ... And it has become a custom that when the bishops visit the parishes in the spring, the parishes return the visit at the Wawel Cathedral on the day of Pentecost ... At a meeting like today's, we relive that deep bond that exists between us.

---

[11] Study of the Fathers of the Church

The expression of that bond is the fact that your esteemed pastors, the pastors of your parishes here present, are offering with me this Most Holy Sacrifice. Many of us are offering one Sacrifice.

June 1 — At the Sisters of the Holy Spirit in Krakow, on Szpitalna Street:

When the priest kisses the altar at the beginning of the Most Holy Sacrifice, he wants to express in his own name and in the name of all who participate in the Mass, that, in spirit, he is trying to encompass Christ and all of His work. For, according to an ancient liturgical tradition, the altar represents Jesus Christ and his work: the work of our redemption ... When we come to participate in the Holy Mass, we come to bring to it and then to take from it the unique and irreplaceable portion which each of us shares in Christ's work of redemption ... It is fitting that such a telling gesture occurs at the very beginning of the liturgy of the Holy Mass.

After Mass — a supper and a meeting with the sisters * June 2 — 10:00 a.m., residence chapel, concelebrated Mass with priests during days of recollection, homily * June 3-11 — Canonical visitation of the parish of Myslenice * June 3 — First Friday of the month. First day of the visitation:

This morning I had opportunity to witness how the parishioners here honor the Sacred Heart of Jesus, how many of them go to confession and Holy Communion ... I had an opportunity to spend some time with the ill, those that were capable of coming to church ... and, in the afternoon, to visit at least some of the sick in their homes ... Today I managed to visit one part of the parish of Myslenice, the village of Polanka ... Now, at my request, your pastor has invited married couples to the evening Mass ...

It is not enough for me to visit the parish as an anonymous entity. I wish to meet the people of the parish, especially the married couples.

To young people:

[Prayer:] If on one hand we can say that prayer flows from faith, then on the other we can say that faith flows from prayer. A person who abandons prayer may not only weaken, but even lose his faith.

[Work:] Work is necessary for man not only to help him to earn a living, but also to help him to be a person, to be somebody.

[Prayer and work:] The Christian program is made up of these two factors.

[Respect for parents:] The relationship you have with your parents in the years of your youth will go with you and will return to you: it will return in your own children.

[Life's calling:] The majority of the people are called to a life of marriage and family. This calling is also a holy one.

June 5 — At noon, the blessing of a wayside chapel of Our Lady of Czestochowa in Chelm * June 6 — Myslenice, hospital, 6:00 a.m., Holy Communion for about 100 patients and the confirmation of one female high school student * Same day — 4:00 p.m., parish church in Myslenice, meeting with the speech and hearing impaired * June 7 —

Warsaw, Main Council of the Polish Episcopate * June 8 — 9:30 a.m., Murzasichle — concelebrated Mass and sermon for the 10th anniversary of the ordination to the priesthood of several priests. He came late, and explains himself:

> Yesterday I returned late from Warsaw, and today from early morning I had to take care of very pressing business relating to the procession of Corpus Christi in Krakow ... We must struggle hard for this fundamental right, the right to publicly demonstrate our devotion to the Blessed Sacrament on the day of Corpus Christi in Krakow. These struggles take up time and strength ... I came here having stolen myself away from the parish of Myslenice, where a visitation is in progress.

June 9 — 9:00 a.m., Zakopane, Mass concelebrated with the priests of the class of 1963; sermon * Same day — parish church in Myslenice, meeting with representatives of the laity.

June 10 — Corpus Christi. For the first time since 1939, a procession sets out beyond the walls of Wawel. Sermon at the fourth altar:

> From the beginning of my pastoral duties at this great, historical seat of the metropolitan bishops of Krakow, i.e. since 1964, I have turned to the authorities year after year for permission to hold a procession from Wawel to the Market Square. I have done this more or less under your eyes, informing you of every step which I took in this regard, because I believed that this was our common cause. Today, in the eighth year of my pastoral duties at the seat of the metropolitan bishops of Krakow, for the first time after so many years, a procession from Wawel ventures outside the confines of the walls of Wawel. We rejoice in this, but I must admit that it is a joy through pain. I cannot, and we cannot, forget at this moment that it took such terrible sacrifices, far from here, on the coast of the Baltic sea, for the longtime pleas of the People of God in Krakow to be understood ... The pleas for this public procession on the Feast of Corpus Christi ... Our hearts turn to those who lost their lives, so that their sacrifice could pave the way for certain changes. One of those changes is today's procession from Wawel, from the cathedral and beyond the walls. [But] we know well that the central procession of Corpus Christi in Krakow, always walked from Wawel to the Market Square. It was that way until 1939. This has its historical meaning ... It is a route full of historical content. The nation has its identity through its awareness of history, and this awareness must not be undermined and destroyed. The nation owes its identity to history just as it does to language, just as it does to culture; all of these contexts and values are intertwined. And that is why a procession from Wawel to the Market Square is one of those elements which build historical awareness, and not only in us, citizens of Krakow, but in all of Poland. I could not accept [the route of today's procession], it was designated for us. I, the Metropolitan Archbishop of Krakow could not accept it and I made it known not only to the authorities of Krakow, but also the highest authorities of our country — I made my appeals all the way there, to the premier and vice premier, because together with you I am guided by the same awareness, the awareness of history, which is a refuge for our society, so grievously tested by history ... We are the citizens of our country, the citizens of our city, but we are also a People of God who has its own Christian sensibility, and it must hurt

us that various events are allowed to take place on the Market Square, but the Bishop of Krakow carrying the Blessed Sacrament cannot set foot on Market Square! We will continue to demand our rights. They are obvious, just as our presence here is obvious. We will demand!...

June 11 — Borzeta. Holy Mass, afterwards — a procession to the cemetery, prayer for the dead (as part of the visitation of the parish of Myslenice) * On the same day — a sermon for the conclusion of the visitation * June 12-14 — Trzemesnia — visitation. Sermon during confirmation:

> A person who believes, is not someone who has just an abstract idea of God, a vague, general notion that God is some kind of force, or even someone, some personal wisdom directing the world. A person who believes, is someone who has contact with God, the Creator and our Father ... And the proof of this contact, this union with the living God as our Father, is the believer's readiness for remorse, for penance, for conversion.
>
> If you consider what lies at the bottom of the whole materialistic outlook which is in various ways forcing itself into the mind and soul of contemporary man, it is just this false promise: "You will be like gods..."

June 14 — 7:30 p.m., Wieliczka, concelebrated Mass with priests from the class of 1967, sermon * June 15 — 7:00 p.m., Morawica, concelebrated Mass with priests from the class of 1968, sermon * June 16 — 11:00 a.m., Gilowice, concelebrated Mass with priests from the class of 1969 * Same day — 6:30 p.m., Jaworzno, concelebrated Mass with priests from the class of 1966 * June 17 — 5:30 p.m., residence chapel, concelebrated Mass with sermon for sisters from Czechoslovakia * June 18-21 — Canonical visitation of the parish of Jawornik * June 19 — Meeting of the Council of the Pontifical Department of Theology in Krakow. Report on the activities of the Department — "ratio studiorum" for the year 1971/72, other organizational matters. The cardinal participated and took part in the discussions. (From the minutes of the Council) * Same day — 8:30 p.m., residence chapel, Mass on the 6th anniversary of the death of J. Vetulani * June 20 — 7:30 a.m., dedication of an enlarged church at the parish of Rakowice in Krakow (this is the fourth parish after Nowa Huta, Mogila and St. Szczepan Parish, in an area of large apartment buildings, with 30,000 parishioners):

> Very often when speaking with our authorities about the needs for church construction, we are told, and not only in Krakow: but there are so many churches. It is true that there are many churches in the center of Krakow. This should be some sort of a lesson, a voice of history to those now in power. If, at one time, when the number of inhabitants was only a tenth, or even less, of what it is today, if, at that time, there were so many churches, what is the appropriate conclusion? ...
>
> Church construction must be tailored — especially in this day and age, when we speak of the importance of society and community — to the places where parish congregations are being formed. When these congregations were formed in the center of Krakow, that is where many churches were

established ... Today, there is a significant move to the outskirts, to new housing. Here is where new congregations are forming, and they want to have their own churches, their own places of Christian community, where they can truly meet without crowding ...

When I blessed this church, I sprinkled its walls inside and outside with holy water. Then I sprinkled the altar, then the floor, in the shape of a cross: one line from the altar to the door, then another line, across the first one, in front of the great altar. The people parted and freed up space in the shape of a cross, then they came back to stand on the spot where your bishop had sprinkled the floor. This is significant. We not only look at the cross, we not only kneel before the cross, we also stand on the cross. This is the solid ground from which our human life, our Christian life, grows. (From a sermon preached on the same day to men at Kalwaria. He spoke to them about the blessing of the church at Rakowice.)

Same day — in Kalwaria Zebrzydowska, sermon to a pilgrimage of husbands and young men:

In 1949, at the call and under the direction of Archbishop Sapieha, men from all of the parishes of the Krakow archdiocese came here in pilgrimage and erected a new cross. Afterwards, the pilgrimage was forgotten. It was renewed three years ago, in 1968 ...

The cross put up so many years ago is still waiting and calling you. And it turns out that the calling bears fruit ... Our numbers have at least doubled ... I hope that soon our numbers here in Kalwaria will equal the crowds of the other pilgrimage, the Silesian one from Piekary ...

We come to confirm that the way of Jesus Christ is our way ... that His Cross is our cross, that we stand around that Cross, that we carry it in our hearts, that we build our lives upon it ... Today, you brought a new cross, not only to replace the old one, which is damaged, but also to express continuity. Twenty-two years is almost a generation ... Today, a new generation comes here, a generation of sons ...

It is good that here, in Kalwaria, it is not only priests who speak. Laymen also speak and talk of their matters, of their place in the Church, of the responsibility of the laity ... Although Catholic organizations have been forbidden, there remain lay Catholic men and women, and this cannot be hidden, this cannot be trampled into the ground.

Catholic lay people in the entire Church, not only in Europe or in America ... have the freedom to associate in Catholic organizations of the laity, and to interact with the apostolate of the hierarchy ... But we are here! We are here. And by the very fact that we are here, we bear witness.

June 22 — 8:00 a.m., Gniezno, the Primate's Basilica, Mass at the altar of St. Wojciech {Adalbert}, later — a meeting of the Main Committee of the Polish Episcopate * June 23 — 8:00 a.m., the Primate's private chapel, private concelebrated Mass, plenary conference of the Polish Episcopate * The same day — in Krakow — the second meeting of the Preparatory Committee of the Synod of the Archdiocese of Krakow was held.

Contrary to prevailing tradition, the Synod cannot have a purely legalistic (juridical) character ... That would confirm the impressions of some people that the Church is just one of the many organizations on this earth, and one enveloped in an ironclad legalistic framework. One of the fruits of the last Council is the "different self-awareness" of the Church, which, besides the indispensable legal aspect, emphasizes its character as a community ... The Synod should become a gathering of all who will undertake a serious, teamwork effort to discover the state of the Church in the archdiocese, to understand the mission of that Church in light of the teachings of the Council, and to take up initiatives to fulfill that mission ... Besides theoretical deliberations, we must find effective means of bringing the teachings of the Council to life. (As related by the secretary of the Preparatory Committee, *Notificationes* 6-8, 1972)

June 24 — 7:00 a.m., Paradyz, plenary conference of the Polish Episcopate.

June 24 — Gorzow Theological Seminary in Goscikowo-Paradyz, conference of the Episcopal Committee for Pastoral Ministry. Acceptance of the final edition of the program of preaching. Cardinal Wojtyla "supports the program as presented, because it is practical, related to the liturgy, it includes the explanation of the new missal readings, it is based on doctrine, its aim is to implement the teachings of the Council ... for that reason it returns to the fundamental principles of pastoral work." (From the minutes)

June 27 — 11:30 a.m., Jasna Gora, participation in the 25th anniversary of the priesthood of Bishop Wladyslaw Rubin, closing address * Same day — 5:00 p.m., Kurow, the parish of Slemien, blessing of the cornerstone for a new church, homily * June 28 — Residence chapel, participation in the Holy Mass for the 25th anniversary of Bishop W. Rubin * 9:00 a.m., Theological Seminary (4 Manifestu Lipcowego Street), sermon to priests on the 15th anniversary of their ordination * 3:00 p.m., Chapel of the Ursuline Sisters, Mass with sermon, conference for the 20th anniversary of the Higher Institute of Catechesis. From that date, on the basis of a decision by the Congregation for Catholic Education, the Institute became tied with the Pontifical Department of Theology * June 29 — 5:30 p.m., Skomielna Biala, move into a new church, sermon * June 30 — 9:00 a.m., Zytniow (diocese of Czestochowa), concelebrated Mass with sermon at a social gathering of priests from his seminary year.

July 1 — 11:00 a.m., led the liturgy at a teachers' day of prayer at Jasna Gora * Same day — 6:00 p.m., Krakow, Church of the Bernardines, Mass with sermon at the tomb of Blessed Szymon {Simon} of Lipnica * July 7 — 8:00 a.m., Bachledowka, private Mass * July 8 — 7:00 a.m., Krakow, residence chapel, private Mass * July 9-10 — Rest * July 11 — Jaroslaw. The end of the celebrations of the visitation of Our Lady in the diocese of Przemysl; transferring of the symbols of the visitation to the archdiocese of Lubaczow. He led a solemn concelebrated Mass. The sermon is preached by Cardinal Primate * July 12-13 — Kalwaria Zebrzydowska, Chapel of the Blessed Mother, Holy Mass * July 13 — "Taking advantage of the presence in our house of Cardinal Karol Wojtyla and his guests, Mother Provincial invited him to supper. During the meal, the sisters sang religious songs, accompanied by six guitars. The Cardinal bestowed his blessing and left around 9:00 p.m.." (From the chronicle of the convent of the Ursuline Sisters in Rokiciny) * July 23 — 6:00 p.m., Wawel Cathedral, Mass for the 20th anniversary of the death of Cardinal A. S. Sapieha.

July 31 — August 3. Lake Ostrowiec.

August 1 — Jasna Gora, concelebrated Mass for the 750th anniversary of the Tertiary Orders. At the midday meal he presented name-day wishes to the Primate * August 7 — 10:00 a.m., Belzec, concelebrated Mass for the conclusion of the peregrination in the archdiocese of Lubaczow * Same day — 5:00 p.m., Tomaszow Lubelski, concelebrated Mass for the beginning of the visitation of Our Lady in the diocese of Lublin * August 13-14 — Kalwaria Zebrzydowska, participation in the observances of "the funeral of the Blessed Mother." Mass with sermon by the "little grave."

August 15 — He is appointed member of the Sacred Congregation for Divine Worship (later the name was changed to Sacred Congregation for Sacraments and Divine Worship) dealing, among other things, with the preparation of the new liturgical norms. He remained its member until the time of his election to the Holy See (Cf. Rev. Jan Dyduch, op. cit., p. 65) * The Mariacki Church in Krakow. Sermon: "Marian geography" — the sanctuaries where Poles pay homage to the Blessed Virgin on the Feast of the Assumption today; among the more important: Kalwaria Zebrzydowska and the Mariacki Church in Krakow. Kalwaria: "...and what is most significant, the majority of those pilgrims are young people..." Mariacki Church: "...the image of the Blessed Virgin and above all, the artwork of Wit Stwosz." Referring to the scenes depicted in the altar,[12] he spoke of God coming down to man, of God's mysteries in Mary, also of Father Kolbe, whose life ended at the very center of dehumanization {Auschwitz}. Of coming to God. "Let us think [today] how the Mother of God came to God — let us pray that each of us comes to God, that each of us, with His help, fulfill what is the mission of man, what is man's ultimate calling and goal." * Same day — Ludzmierz * August 17 — 10:00 a.m., residence chapel, funeral Mass for Dr. Janina

---

[12] The falling asleep of the Virgin Mary among the Apostles prior to her Assumption.

Wiadrowska, 12:00 noon, funeral at the cemetery at Salwator. Dr. Janina Wiadrowska, daughter of Leon and Maria nee Kaczorowska — a maternal first cousin of the Cardinal * August 21 — Krakow — Pradnik Czerwony. Homily at the chapel of the Albertine Sisters * August 22 — 6:30 a.m., Chapel of the Felician Sisters (16 Batorego Street), Mass with sermon for the 50th anniversary of the vows of the Mother Superior General * Same day — Jasna Gora, at the summit, day of prayer for men and male youth:

> The family takes shape within marriage and becomes a very special community. A community that is special because its central concern is the human person. You may ask which person? I will tell you: every person. The husband-father. And the wife-mother. And also the child, every child. Each one of them is the central concern of the family. Each one them individually and all of them together. That is what is special about the family, that every person within it is important. Important because he or she is a human, he or she is one of us. The husband is important to the wife, because he is the object of her love, her chosen one, just as she is his chosen one. The child is important to both of them the first one, the second one, every one. Every one, because each one of them is the fruit of their love. For this reason, the family is the affirmation of man. We think about this too little, we reflect on it too little, and we do too little to make it a part of the social program of our lives. But it is the family that is a condition of the affirmation of man. When a person goes outside of the family, no matter where, say to work — especially in those gigantic contemporary workplaces, in industry — or even in school, or in a place of entertainment — that person becomes an anonymous being. But when the person returns to the family fold, he regains his individual value. The person is someone unique and unrepeatable, someone to love, someone we know, for whom we wish the highest good. And that is why the family is indispensable for shaping the truly human, the truly humanistic model of society …
>
> When the father of the family works, he does so with the thought of his family in mind. He works to give his family bread, to support it. We know, we see that in our times the work of the father is often insufficient to support the family. So the mother also works. The wife works. This is a universal phenomenon. It has become so common that, in many cases, the woman who is a wife and a mother wants to work. It becomes her personal ambition. Undoubtedly, there is some measure of good in that but, as I said a moment ago, all good must be considered according to some order, some hierarchy.
>
> So, the work of a woman, who is a wife and mother, is a good to the extent that it does not affect the good of the family, the communion of marriage, the indissolubility of marriage and, above all, the transmission of life and the upbringing of children. Under these conditions, the work of a woman is good …

Same day — 5:40 p.m., Krakow, Dominican Church, service in honor of St. Jacek {Hyacinth} * August 24 — This is the date that appears on a letter to Dr. Andrzej Rozmarynowicz informing him that he was awarded the decoration of Knight Commander of the Order of St. Sylvester the Pope by the Vatican (the presentation was made in

December of this year) * August 26 — 11:00 a.m., Siersza, Mass with sermon on the occasion of the 25th anniversary of the parish, dedication of the remodeled church * Same day — 5:00 p.m., Staniatki, concelebrated Mass, benediction of the Mother Abbess of the Benedictine Sisters.

September 1 — 6:30 a.m., Krakow, Church of the Most Holy Redeemer, Mass with sermon in honor of Blessed Bronislawa * Same day — 7:30 p.m., Jasna Gora, retreat for the Episcopate * September 2 — 7:00 p.m., Chapel of the Blessed Mother, Mass for the intention of the Synod * September 3-4 — Jasna Gora, retreat for the Episcopate * September 5 — 11:00 a.m., Jasna Gora, led a solemn concelebrated High Mass by the summit, offering the whole world to the Blessed Mother * Same day — 5:00 p.m., Wielun, High Mass with sermon, coronation of the image of the Blessed Mother * September 6 — The third meeting of the Preparatory Committee of the Synod of the Archdiocese of Krakow. Analysis of suggested topics. Discussion of the system and meaning of the work in study groups; the work of these groups will be the basis for drafting the documents of the Synod * September 7 — 4:00 p.m., Trzebunia, concelebrated Mass with sermon for the 20th anniversary of the ordination of priests from the class of 1951 * September 10 — 1:00 p.m., residence chapel, Mass concelebrated with Seminario Romano (for a tour group of priests and seminarians from Seminario Romano) * September 11 — Torun, the parish of the Redemptorists, Mass and marriage of Marek Wiadrowski — son of Karol Wojtyla's maternal first cousin, Adam, son of Maria Wiadrowska nee Kaczorowska, Karol's godmother. Marek died in 1978. During his studies in Krakow, while the house in which he was living with his mother (on Florianska Street) was being renovated, he was taken in by his uncle, Rev. Karol Wojtyla, and lived with him on Kanonicza Street. He took part in kayak outings with the young people. Besides Felicja Wiadrowska, the maternal first cousin of the Pope, Marek's daughters, Anna Wiadrowska and Maria Wiadrowska, are the only relatives from his mother's side. An account by Kazimiera, Marek's wife:

My first personal contact with Cardinal Wojtyla was on the last Sunday of May or the first Sunday of June 1971. I came to Krakow to visit Marek. Uncle {Karol} found me a place to stay for the night at the Sisters of the Sacred Heart. He himself was busy, as usual, but he told Mr. Franciszek to give us breakfast, and he agreed to meet with Marek in Myslenice, where he had gone for a visitation. I was quite nervous traveling there to be presented as the fiancee. I was in no way calmed by Marek's comments: "He will probably like you 'and' He is really quite a normal person." The introduction took place in the sacristy of the church in Myslenice. And right from the first glance, from the first smile, always so full of goodness, there was a great sense of relief — indeed he was "normal." He started conversing with

us quite normally, asking about what I did, how old I was (at the time I still looked quite immature), what our plans for vacation were, when we intended to get married. Because there was a dinner waiting for him, he just told Marek what he was to show me in Myslenice, he kissed us, gave his blessing, and as we were leaving, he said, "Drop by again to see me sometime, I will always find a bit of time."

Our next meeting was in sad circumstances. The sister of Marek's father and of aunt Luska, Janina Wiadrowska, died on August 18th of this year. Marek and I came to the funeral. Again, I felt uneasy in this situation — as I was not Marek's wife yet, I did not want to "elbow" my way into the family, but Marek insisted on my coming with him to Krakow. I will always be grateful to Uncle Karol for his tact and ability to guess the frame of mind and the feelings of others. When the funeral procession was forming, he "placed" me next to Aunt Wiadrowska, saying, "but of course if the two of you are to be married, you are already in the family."

Our wedding took place on September 11, 1971 in Torun. We did not postpone the wedding because of the aunt's death, for we were not planning a wedding dance anyway, and the dates had been set earlier (in the office of the civil registry for August 31). Knowing that punctuality was Uncle's weak point, we told him that the marriage ceremony would take place at 1:00 p.m., but the invitations were printed to read 1:30 p.m. Besides, we agreed that if Uncle should arrive early, he would stop at my parents' house, and if there was no time, he would go straight to the church and telephone us from there so that we could leave for the church. 1:00 p.m. came and Uncle did not show up, and the telephone was silent. 1:30 p.m. — the same. 2:00 p.m. — dead silence, and the impatient guests are already in church. At the house, we were agitated, hungry (because of Holy Communion {at the time a period of fast beginning the previous midnight was required before the reception of the Eucharist}), cold, because the weather was cool and my father had not lit the central heating, so that it wouldn't be too warm when the house filled. At 2:30 p.m. our pastor called and told us to quit fooling around because no cardinal is going to show up, and he has another wedding at 4:00 p.m. Somehow we mollified him and agreed that if the Cardinal does not arrive by 3:00 p.m., we will give up and have the pastor officiate at our marriage. We went to church with a great sense of disappointment, in such bad humor, that I answered to my aunt, who was whispering words of encouragement to me: "I don't care how, I don't care who, just let's get it over with." At the moment when we stood ready "to go" under the choir loft, there was a commotion at the entrance and the Cardinal burst in, in an unbuttoned cape, literally at the last minute, because the pastor was just finishing vesting for Mass. During the marriage ceremony itself there was also an amusing incident. In his haste, Uncle did not look at our documents. From the day of my birth, everyone has called me Kaya, even though my given name was Kazimiera. At the moment when Uncle was to ask "Kazimiera, do you take...," he realized that he did not know my name. Without covering the microphone, he whispered, "And just what is your real name?"

Later, there were our trips to Krakow (always together — Marek and I). Each time, very short visits with Uncle — Fr. Stanislaw would call him out from his activities — always very cordial, always with thoughtful questions about our domestic matters, often at very strange hours of the day.

The first such visit — on the Feast of Christ the King, on the 25th anniversary of the Cardinal's ordination to the priesthood … The next visit was in January of 1972. We went to tell him that we were expecting a child in August. After a momentary silence at this news, his first question was — do you need anything. At the time we were in need. We lived in Katowice in a single rented room, although the apartment left by Marek's parents stood locked and empty in Torun (Marek was a mining engineer and there was no work for him in Torun). We found a separate room with a kitchen in a tenement, but the lease cost 30 thousand. Uncle loaned us the money. Three years later, when I came to repay the loan, I saw the pain he felt at the necessity of taking the money from me. He explained to me, "My dear child, this was not my money. I borrowed it from the funds, and now I am going to return it; I don't have my own money." I felt very badly then, because we understood that very well. The most important thing for us was that we could turn to him for help in any difficult situation, and there were many of these, that he always found time and understanding for us. Next time we saw Uncle at the end of June 1972. He put off other meetings so he could talk with Marek, who needed that very much at that time. After such visits we received letters — how are you, how are things at home, when will the baby be born. Always accompanied by warm words of encouragement and a blessing.

My first letters from the hospital after the birth of my daughter (August 24, 1972) were to my mother and to Uncle, while Marek's telephones were in the reverse sequence. In his reply, Uncle expressed great joy that the child is alive, healthy and, again, he sent his blessing for the little one and her parents.

Uncle wanted to baptize Ania in Krakow, but I, still overly cautious at the time, was afraid of taking the child on a trip, because that was a disruption in her routine, there were problems with feedings, etc.

Uncle saw Ania for the first time in August of 1973. It was a week before her first birthday, so it must have been August 17th. I remember that it was an awfully hot day. We waited for Uncle for quite a long time, because he had returned from a trip "to the field." When we came back, Uncle was resting, and this was probably one of the few days when he did not have any obligations in the afternoon. His eyes followed the impish child, who was running around as lively as a spark, he gave her fruit, took her on his shoulders, asked very knowingly about weights, sizes, etc. He couldn't get over how quickly she was becoming "grown up." I was pregnant again, so he was asking how I will manage, whether I had a difficult time with the first birth. This was probably our longest visit, and it was so relaxed and familial, without a ticking clock before our eyes.

Marysia was born on November 8, 1973 — and again there was his letter expressing relief that this little one also arrived safely into the world.

This time we took Marysia to Krakow to be baptized. At the beginning of January 1974 I went to make definite plans with Uncle. I was amused by his lack of practicality, because he set the date for the next Sunday. When I asked him timidly, "But can we do that, without godparents?…", he was surprised — "Why?" He did not consider that the godmother, being from Gdansk, the godfather from Torun, had to arrange time off from work to be able to come. I was there with Ania at that time, and he made sure that I and the child were given lunch. When Mrs. Marysia was running around setting the table, he dropped in again to see if we were eating.

On January 27th Uncle baptized Marysia at the chapel. After the baptism, he put on a reception — the sisters prepared delicious food, tea, coffee. All of this took place during a pause in his normal Sunday duties, because he was busy before the baptism, and immediately after Fr. Stanislaw was pressing that "they are waiting." And again there were letters — about domestic matters, joyous ones (we obtained an apartment) and sad ones.

With two small children and a job, even a trip to Krakow was a major undertaking. In this period Marek alone would visit his uncle, and I probably wasn't in Krakow through the end of 1974. In February of 1975 there was another family catastrophe, and again Uncle was our mainstay. There were telegrams, telephone calls, conversations in Krakow — always with an eye on the clock, because he was "stealing time" from meetings, conferences, etc.

Then again peace and quiet, and letters with greetings, with current news; Marek and Ania would go to Krakow to convey name-day greetings. In February of 1976 Ania was invited for the first time to a party for children. She went with her father and both came back delighted, because Marek met his friends from the kayak trips.

At the end of July or maybe at the beginning of August 1976 there was another matter in which we needed Uncle's help. He told me to meet him in the evening, "...because now I'm going to the seminary, then I have to meet with so-and-so, at 9:00 p.m. with another group, but come at 8:30 p.m. and we will have time to talk calmly."

Around December 15, 1976, in a similar fashion, leaving an ongoing conference, he could "calmly" give me half an hour of conversation. In February of 1977, I took both girls to the children's party. But because the train was very late, we arrived at Franciszkanska Street after the other children had already left. Uncle felt very sorry that the girls were so disappointed, so in place of playtime he took them through all the rooms of the residence (in that kind of space, children reach a state of euphoria), he talked with them over tea and cookies, and then, because he was going out for an evening drive, he drove us to the station in his car.

On the first free Saturday of 1978 (January 7), Uncle fulfilled his longstanding promise and visited our home. Year after year Uncle would postpone the visit because of lack of time, and whenever he was returning from the May pilgrimage to Piekary, he was always traveling with some important personage and it was not appropriate for him to stop by. In his Christmas letter he promised to come, but he did not specify when that would be. Suddenly, on Saturday evening, a young man sent from a meeting of Uncle's former pupils came to warn us that in half an hour the Cardinal would come to visit. The house was a mess (on free Saturdays I worked at the school), Marek was already asleep, because he was ailing; at least we had some tea (often, on Saturdays, after the stores closed, it would turn out that we ran out of it). Uncle stayed a short time, maybe an hour, because, I think, Mr. Turowicz, with whom he was returning to Krakow, was waiting for him in the car in front of the house. Uncle's first steps were to the room to see the children, who were already asleep, then to see the rest of the apartment, then "better let's just talk, instead of wasting time to prepare tea." On leaving, he promised that "the next time, I will stay longer." I joked that given his lack of time, the next time might be when the girls are getting married. Laughing, he assured us that it would be sooner, certainly no later than the girls' First Communion. Both of our estimates were wrong.

In April of 1978 I went again for a long talk with Uncle. And again Fr. Stanislaw fit me into a break in his appointments.

Then there was that terrible visit at Corpus Christi, to make arrangements for the funeral. Marek died on May 24. Uncle could not come to the funeral in Torun, because as you know well, Father, he had guests from abroad at the time. Fr. Stanislaw Dziwisz, Fr. Wladyslaw Fidelus and two other priests whose names I don't remember came in his place. Fr. Stanislaw brought me a letter from Uncle, the only one that was handwritten ...

Our last meeting was also related to Marek's death. Uncle said a Mass for the repose of his soul, then invited my aunt and me for a short talk. This was on the 8th or the 15th of June.

In a letter of September 28, 1978 he wrote: "...and I ask you, drop in to see me when you are in Krakow." And it hurts today just as much as it did that first day when the results of the conclave were announced, that this will never happen. (Kazimiera Wiadrowska, Torun)

September 11 — 7:30 p.m., address to the clergy and faithful of Plock, before the celebration of the first anniversary of the coronation of the image of the Our Lady of Czerwinsk. At the request of the Bishop of Plock he spoke about the approaching Synod of Bishops. Near the end of his address:

We know well how Christ acted. Christ preached, proclaimed the word, but in doing so, He remembered that his listeners were hungry and He asked the apostles: where shall we get bread? In every age, the Church cannot merely stop with the proclamation of the Word, but must also ask the apostles: where shall we get bread?

The contemporary Church, Pope Paul VI, the Council, and now the Synod, must utter these very words which, in the name of the needy and the poor, we will address to God anew. Perhaps [in Poland] this issue has different dimensions than in the First and the Third World — the rich world and the poor world. But even in our land, do we not witness how human life becomes inhuman? Do we not witness various manifestations of dehumanization, lack of respect, lack of justice, lack of love, especially in the social sphere? In this age and in these conditions, which claim to be socially progressive, do we not see something quite to the contrary? Instead of social commitment, do we not witness the loosening, the weakening of the most fundamental social bonds?...

September 12 — Czerwinsk, Marian shrine of the diocese of Plock, on the anniversary of the coronation of the image:

We pray to you, O Blessed Mother of Czerwinsk, for a victory for our young people, for all of the Polish youth and for the youth of the world. The future of the world lies in their hands. They must achieve a true victory, if all of the victories of the human race are not to turn into one great calamity: greater still than the calamity of the last war. We turn to you, Father Maximilian Kolbe, whom in 5 weeks we will call with the name of Blessed. You, the first martyr of the concentration camps to be raised to the honors of the altar, you, the first victor, whose victory was won amidst the greatest weakness, please become the patron of our generation, of our times, and in accordance with the truth proclaimed by your whole life, proclaim always and everywhere that your victory was won through Mary Immaculate!

Same day — 5:00 p.m., visit to Niepokalanow[13] * September 15 — Tarnow, the cathedral, sermon for the 150th anniversary of the Theological Seminary in Tarnow * September 17-19 — Visitation of the parish of Czulice * September 18 — 11:00 a.m., days of prayer for "Odrodzenie." He presented an address to the participants: *Apostolic Formations of the Laity* * Same day — 7:00 p.m., Krakow, Church of the Missionary Fathers (Stradom), Mass for priests, co-workers of "Our Past."

September 21 — 8:00 a.m., Lublin, academic church, homily for the opening of the Congress of Polish Theologians * September 21-23 — Lublin, KUL, Congress of Polish Theologians on the subject: *Theology and Christian Anthropology.* Cardinal Karol Wojtyla chaired the entire Congress and delivered a report *The Mission of Theologians in the Post-Conciliar Church* * September 24-25 — Warsaw * September 26 — Kielce, the cathedral, concelebrated High Mass with sermon for the 800th anniversary of the cathedral * Same day — 5:30 p.m., Andrychow, consecration of the altar, sermon * September 27 — Fourth meeting of the Preparatory Committee of the Synod. Work on the submitted synodal topics and on the text of information regarding the preparatory activities, to be read in the circles of clergy and laity * Same day — 9:00 p.m., departure from Krakow to Rome for the second session of the Synod of Bishops (September 30-November 6) * September 28 — 7:00 a.m., Vienna, chapel of the nunciature,[14] concelebrated Mass * September 29 — Arrival in Rome * September 30 — 10:00 a.m., opening of the Synod; 5:00 p.m., first meeting of the second ordinary session of the Synod of Bishops, on the topic of the priesthood and justice in the world. Cardinal K. Wojtyla took part as a representative of the Conference of the Polish Episcopate. He was assigned to the French language group C

September 30-October 16 — Rome, private concelebrated Masses.

October 2 — Rome, Synod of Bishops. In the debate on the schema on the priesthood, Cardinal Karol Wojtyla stated:

It will be very useful not only for the spirituality of the priesthood, but also for the study of the priesthood, to consider the personal calling by which one answers Christ's invitation to leave everything and follow Him. In this sincere giving of his own self, the priest may find his personal identity and his place in contemporary society. The call to follow the Redeemer more perfectly is closely related to the bond between the sacrament of priesthood and celibacy, which, as in the past, should remain untouched. Being grafted unto Christ, each priest, with the help of his calling, participates no less in chastity than in obedience and poverty. Church law should

13 Home monastery of St. Maximilian Kolbe.
14 Vatican diplomatic mission

be added to the personal and spontaneous obligation of the priest; these two things do not contradict nor preclude each other.

October 5 — Rome, the Vatican Radio. Speech: Before the beatification of Fr. Maximilian Kolbe.

October 8 — Synod of Bishops. After the reports from the language groups, Cardinal Karol Wojtyla said:

> Considering the work accomplished in the main auditorium and in smaller groups, the Synod should give testimony of the Church's faith in the ministerial priesthood. This is justified by the need to allay the present fears and uncertainties; as a result of this testimony, theological elaboration will certainly follow. The Synod cannot fail to give this proof, which should be done, first of all, by the Bishops. It is obvious that the proof should be formulated on the basis of doctrine, and must express the intention to present doctrinal elements according to the directives of the Fathers...

October 13 — Synod of Bishops. Speaking in discussion before the section on the practical problems of the priesthood, Cardinal Karol Wojtyla said on behalf of the Polish Episcopate:

> The mission of the Church, the apostolate, the various callings within the community of the People of God, etc. should be considered in light of the clear and binding teachings of the Second Vatican Council, also when it pertains to the service and the life of priests on one hand, and the obligations and activities of the laity on the other ... In addition, there is another topic with regard to which the preparatory document exhibits certain flaws: namely the importance of the Sacrament of Penance in the spiritual life and service of the priest.

October 14 — Cardinal Karol Wojtyla held a press conference in connection with the beatification of Fr. Maximilian Kolbe * October 16 — 7:00 p.m., Rome, chapel of "Domus Pacis," concelebrated Mass with pilgrims from Poland * October 17 — 10:00 a.m., Rome, Basilica of St. Peter, beatification of Maximilian Kolbe, Mass concelebrated with the Holy Father * October 18 — 6:00 p.m., Rome, Basilica of the Twelve Apostles, concelebrated Mass after the beatification with the participation of Primate Wyszynski and Cardinal Krol {of Philadelphia} * October 19 — 7:00 p.m., chapel of Seminario Romano, concelebrated Mass with sermon * October 20 — Program on the Vatican Radio about the beatification of Maximilian Kolbe:

> In the consciousness of all people of our time, he [Fr. Kolbe] first became a symbol of the suffering dealt to people by people out of hate. But, in turn, he is now becoming the symbol of love which is more powerful than hate. Thanks to love, even the suffering dealt to people becomes a sort of creative force, a force which helps to discover humanity more fully ... We know the meaning that the graves of martyrs had for the first Christians from the times of the persecutions, we know what respect and veneration they exhibited towards their earthly remains ... This is the reason why the Church in Poland, ever since the end of the war, has seen the need for such

a place commemorating the sacrifice, the need for an altar and temple particularly in Oswiecim {Auschwitz}. The beatification of Fr. Maximilian Kolbe has deepened this need.

Same day — 7:00 p.m., Rome, Germanicum chapel, Mass concelebrated with Cardinal Julius Dopfner, sermon * October 22 — Second session of the Synod of Bishops in Rome. His statement presented in writing: De iustitia in mundo * October 22-24 — 7:00 a.m., chapel of the Polish College, private concelebrated Masses * October 24 — 10:00 a.m., Rome, Basilica of St. Peter, Cappella Papale for the Day of Missions * October 25 — 6:00 p.m., Rome, Angelicum, defense of the doctoral thesis by Fr. Michal Bednarz from the diocese of Tarnow: *Les elements parenetique dans la description de la Passion chez Synoptiques.* The Cardinal was present due to his connection with Angelicum and with the diocese of Tarnow, which after all, he pointed out, belongs to the Metropolitan See of Krakow. * October 25-28 — 7:00 a.m., chapel of the Polish College, private concelebrated Masses * October 27 — 4:30 p.m., Pontifical Institute of Church Studies, participation in the lecture by A. Vetulani, subject: Rev. A. Cardinal Sapieha, the Metropolitan of Krakow, During the Last War * October 30 — 5:30 p.m., participation in the dedication of a church under the appellation of Our Lady Queen of Poland * Same day — at the Synod of Bishops, as part of a series of presentations in sede responsionum, Cardinal K. Wojtyla raised certain issues, which he had previously presented in writing, during the debate on justice in the world:

> The Synod cannot devote less attention to those aspects of justice that touch upon freedom, conscience and religion than it does to those that touch upon poverty and social needs. The importance of culture should be emphasized, so that it is recognized as a fundamental good for human dignity, in the life and development of every nation and in the justice that is due to immigrants. We must also conduct a more thorough study of how to relate the teachings about justice to the teachings about "community" within the Church. These teachings state that each particular Church is not an entity unto itself, but must allow for the existence of other Churches ... We will not be able to solve the problems related to justice within the Church without true community, truly realized.

October 31 — Pilgrimage to La Verna.

November 1 — 8:30 a.m., La Verna, the chapel of the Stigmata of St. Francis, concelebrated Mass on the 25th anniversary of his priesthood * November 2 — 9:00 a.m., Bologna, Polish cemetery, Mass with sermon. Lecture at the university * November 3 — Return to Rome * November 4 — Rome, the Vatican Grottoes. At the Chapel of Our Lady of Czestochowa — he celebrated a Holy Mass on the occasion of his name-day {the feast of his patron saint} and the 25th anniversary of his ordination to the priesthood (cf. Notiziario Diocesano) * November 5 —

Synod of Bishops. Cardinal K. Wojtyla was elected as a candidate from Europe to the Council of the Secretariate of the Synod of Bishops, along with Cardinal Vicente Enrique y Tarancon and Cardinal Joseph Hoffner * On this day he gave a written response to the questions contained in the letter of Prof. Donald R. Shandor, Graduate School of Journalism. Columbia University NY * November 7 — 10:00 a.m., Rome, Seminario Romano, ordination of deacons, homily * Basilica Santa Maria in Trastevere. Present at the Holy Mass celebrated by the Primate. Also present: Bishop Wladyslaw Rubin, Bishop Antoni Baraniak and Bishop Boleslaw Filipiak (cf. Notiziario Diocesano) * November 8 — 4:30 p.m., at the Pontifical Institute of Church Studies, he delivered a conference on the subject: *Alcuni problemi del sacerdozio ministeriale alla luce della terza sessione del Sinodo dei Vescovi* (Notiziario Diocesano, Bibl. I 1008) * November 9 — Departure from Rome for Krakow * November 10 — 6:30 p.m., Vienna, chapel of the nunciature, private concelebrated Mass * On this day the Vatican Radio broadcast Cardinal Wojtyla's speech: *After the Conclusion of the Synod of Bishops* * November 11 — 9:00 a.m., residence chapel, private concelebrated Mass * November 13 — At the parish church in Krakow — Plaszow, at the Priests of the Sacred Heart, Mass, sermon, consecration of the new altar.

> The altars are now turned, as we say it, "to face the people" ... to better express what [the priest] means when he says these words during the Holy Mass: "...my sacrifice and yours", to emphasize that he offers up this Sacrifice together with the People of God, with the whole congregation gathered at the liturgy, and that, as a priest and as the steward of the Holy Eucharist, ... he is the servant of the People of God...

November 14 — "Osservatore della Domenica" publishes Cardinal K. Wojtyla's statement on the subject of the Synod of Bishops in 1971 * Same day — 8:00 a.m., Libiaz, blessing of church bells, sermon * 10:30 a.m., Wadowice, Mass with sermon on the occasion of the 25th anniversary of his ordination to the priesthood:

> The deepest law of the heart and of life demands that I thank the Holy Trinity here at my parish: first for the gift of spiritual birth in the Sacrament of Baptism ... for the Sacrament of the Priesthood, for the grace of the calling to serve at the altar ... because although I arrived at the priesthood after having left the parish of Wadowice, it is certain that this parish prepared me for the priesthood ... first through my parents and my Christian upbringing in the family, next through the parish, its atmosphere, its spirit, its life ... Here, I saw luminous examples of the Christian life of my teachers, high school professors, my countrymen of the older generation ... and my contemporaries ... In thanking my mother parish, I must also thank the Mother of the Church; it was here, in this sanctuary, that she first revealed herself to me spiritually in her motherhood as the one in whom we must have boundless trust ... It was here, to this chapel, that we came, the

schoolboys and high school students of Wadowice, to confide in her the cares of our boyhood, of our student days, and to draw her into, make Her a party to those youthful cares, which in their own way seemed so difficult.

Same day — 4:00 p.m., Greboszow, Mass with sermon, solemn dedication of commemorative plaques for the 25th anniversary of the death of Fr. Piotr Halak and Major Henryk Sucharski, commander of the defense of Westerplatte[15] * November 17 — 7:00 p.m., Church of the Franciscan Fathers, concelebrated Mass with sermon in honor of Blessed Salomea * November 18 — Poznan. At the parish church, an address during Days of Social Action on the occasion of the 80th anniversary of *Rerum novarum*:

> [The letter of Pope Paul VI Octogesima adveniens] gathers the entirety of the Church's teachings and action [on social matters] into a very concise and strong whole. The Synod which was convened at just such a time, at the request of the Holy Father, also concerned itself with the matter of justice in the contemporary world ... The words of the Pope endow this matter with a primary importance in the spiritual {literally, "vertical"} dimension while the statements of the Synod give it importance in the political {literally, "horizontal} dimension. In the Synod, all the local Churches express their opinion through their bishops. In a sense, the episcopate of the entire world expresses its opinion through its representatives.
>
> How is it expressed, what kind of tone does this social teaching and the involvement of the Church in the issue of justice have in the modern world? The problem of justice continues to exist in the entire world ... the problem is unresolved, it continues to reemerge and to reemerge in many different ways. Injustice is felt by individuals, by nations, by societies, by particular social groups within nations and states. There are many such instances of injustice, there are many calls for justice ... The world is becoming more sensitive to what is just and what is unjust ... a greater sensitivity to all the phenomena known as neocolonialism — which means the tendency to take advantage of nations by nations, the poor by the rich, or the weak by the strong ...
>
> The Church realizes that bringing justice to the world does not depend solely on the Church, but the Church also realizes its duties and responsibilities in this area ... This realization arises from Revelation ... The Synod reminded us once again of the strong connection that exists between justice and the love of God and the love of neighbor, that connection which is established by the Gospel ... Around this altar we must gather workers and university professors — representatives of all kinds of human work. For work is that sphere where human justice or injustice manifest themselves most clearly ... in work, we must see man, we must see man first of all! Man is not for work: work is for man ... Man cannot be reduced to the level of a mere tool — he must be a person.

November 19 — Poznan, Days of Social Action * November 20 — Krakow, solemn session of the Council of the Department of Theology

---

[15] A fort near Gdansk {Danzig}, on Gdansk Bay. Beginning on the morning of September 1, 1939, it was bombarded from the air and from off-shore (by a german war ship "Schlezwig-Holstein", and was defended heroically by a small contigent under the command of Major Henryk Sucharski until September 7th, when they were forced to surrender.

on the occasion of the 25th anniversary of the ordination to the priesthood of His Eminence Cardinal Karol Wojtyla, Grand Chancellor of the Department, with the participation of invited guests from KUL and Krakow * 5:00 p.m., Mass concelebrated with 16 participants of the anniversary celebration. The Cardinal delivered a sermon on the subject of sacrifice * 6:00 p.m., wishes (conveyed by Rev. Dean Stanislaw Grzybek) and presentation of commemorative volumes signed by the group: *Guiding Concepts of the Council's Constitution on the Church* and *Logos and Ethos*; wishes by Rev. Stanislaw Kaminski, Dean of the Department of Philosophy at KUL,. A lecture by Rev. Prof. Marian Jaworski about the academic work of the Cardinal (mainly about his book *Person and Act*). The honoree presented his academic curriculum vitae, emphasizing the role played by various professors along the way. The celebrations were concluded with a dinner and the wishes conveyed by Rev. Prof. Wladyslaw Smereka, President of the Polish Theological Society in Krakow * November 21 — 10:00 a.m., Wawel Cathedral, address at the end of the Holy Mass (the sermon was preached by Bishop Jerzy Ablewicz of Tarnow) celebrating his 25th anniversary:

> **I had the opportunity to prepare for my anniversary at the Synod of Bishops in Rome, where the first subject of deliberation was the priesthood. On the day of the anniversary of my ordination, God's Providence directed me to the shrine of La Verna, the place of the stigmata of St. Francis of Assisi. However, by the will of the Church of Krakow, I commemorate this anniversary also at the Wawel Cathedral, at the place where the earthly remains of the unforgettable Prince Cardinal rest, of the one, who ordained me, and where, in the crypt of St. Leonard, on November 2, 1946, I celebrated my first Holy Mass … I am the first servant of the Church of Krakow, the first servant of our common good and our common salvation in Jesus Christ and in the Church.**

November 23 — 9:30 a.m., residence chapel, Veni Creator for the opening of a meeting of priests who are deans * St. Anne's Collegiate Church in Krakow, 7:30 p.m. — Holy Mass with the blessing of a plaque commemorating Jerzy Ciesielski. Fragment of the inscription on the plaque: *A Christian of the 20th century. With his life he gave witness to his love of God and neighbor* * November 25 — Meeting (a course) for deans * November 26-30 — Rome * November 29 — 4:30 p.m., Pontifical Institute of Church Studies. Participation in the lecture by Rev. J. Langman, subject: *The Last Canonization and Beatification of Poles.*

December 1-3 — Warsaw * December 3-4 — Canonical visitation of the parish of the Piarist Fathers at Rakowice * December 5 — 11:00 a.m., 12:00 noon and 1:00 p.m., participation in the observance of the Feast of St. Nicholas for the youngest parishioners of Rakowice * 3:00

p.m., participation in a Holy Mass for young people from boarding schools, homily * December 8 — Lublin — Homily and speech at a solemn session of the Council of the Department of Christian Philosophy of the Catholic University of Lublin — on the occasion of the 25th anniversary of the establishment of the Department (per Rev. Director) * 7:00 p.m., the Basilica of the Franciscan Fathers, solemn Holy Mass for the conclusion of a novena to Blessed Maximilian Kolbe. Sermon:

> **The first man, the first people, did not follow God, but followed themselves or, rather, followed the evil spirit which had already rejected the saving will of the Creator and Father. And, in this way, the first humans, our first parents, closed themselves to God ...**
>
> **Sin cannot be overcome only by a negative approach — by not doing evil; the best method of overcoming evil is to do good.**

December 11-12 — The residence, Committee for the Apostolate of the Laity * December 12 — Residence, Committee for Family Ministry * Same day — Mass with sermon at the chapel on Wieczysta Street in connection with the visitation of the parish of Rakowice * December 12 — On the anniversary of the coronation of the image of the Blessed Mother at the Mariacki Basilica in Krakow:

> **I mention the beatification of Maximilian Maria Kolbe, because this event has particular meaning in the history of the Church on Polish soil and in the history of Polish Catholics. He is the first blessed of the second millennium, at its very beginning. He is a blessed who, in a very particular way, expresses our times, our age, all of its difficulties, sufferings and humiliations, but also all of its dynamism. Truly, a blessed of our times ...**
>
> **The Church in Poland, with its attention set so intently on the figure of Mary Immaculate, is at the same time struggling with a variety of difficulties: it is fighting for human souls, it is fighting for the soul of the nation, it is fighting for its moral fiber. It is continually fighting for the moral health of the family, and for the health of our youth, and for the future of society, and it is struggling with so many other difficulties. And against that background of the moral struggles of our time, the background of the struggles of the Church in our native land, comes the beatification of our countryman, a prisoner of Auschwitz, and it says to us, as the prophet Isaiah said: "Courage, o ye of timid soul!", as the Apostle James said: "Have patience and perseverance."**

December 14 — 9:00 a.m., residence chapel, concelebrated Mass for the beginning of the Council of Priests * 10:00 a.m., concelebrated Mass for the beginning of days of recollection for priests of the class of 1971 * December 15 — 10:00 a.m., at the Dominicans', *Oplatek*[16] for university students * December 16 — 4:00 p.m., residence chapel, adoration of the Blessed Sacrament by priests * 8:00 p.m., Church of Our

---

[16] See Glossary.

Lady of Lourdes, Krakow-Nowa Wies, Mass with sermon, *Oplatek* for university students * December 17 — 8:00 p.m., at the Jesuits', *Oplatek* for university students * December 18 — Mass, homily and address at a solemn meeting of the Council of the Department of Christian Philosophy at KUL[17], on the 25th anniversary of the establishment of the Department * Same day — participation in an *Oplatek* for the entire university * December 1 — Visitation at Rakowice. Participation in a Mass at 8:00 a.m. at the Church of the Sisters of the Holy Spirit. At 10:00 a.m. he celebrated a Mass, at 9:30 p.m., he met with the Sisters on Szpitalna Street, participated in an artistic program which the Sisters had prepared * Same day — 3:00 p.m., at the Franciscans', *Oplatek* with charity workers * Same day — participation in a Mass at the chapel on Wieczysta Street (visitation of Rakowice).

December 21 — To the deacons and subdeacons of the Theological Seminary in Krakow:

> **On the road to our priesthood, the Church points out to us the various fundamental elements of the future edifice which is to denote our future life. One such element is the total and exclusive submission to God: I give Him all of my heritage, I care for nothing else, I want nothing else, I choose Him alone. Another element ... is the love for the Church in its visible form ... Just as the priest is entrusted with the keys to the chapel and the church, to the sanctuary which he will protect, so also he is to be entrusted with the secrets that the human soul shares with God. The measure of his maturity is the extent to which these secrets are laid open before him. You have been entrusted with the Word of God, which is the fullness- of wisdom, and it is your calling to exert all your strength to know this Word ever more profoundly ... And the most fundamental element is: service.**

December 22 — Meeting of the Preparatory Committee of the Archdiocesan Synod. After a series of meetings (October, November, December) in the deaneries and with the laity, an analysis of the conclusions drawn from these meetings. The proposed topics were often considered "too theoretical, authoritarian and clerical." There is a need for an opinion survey.

December 24 — 12:00 noon, *Oplatek* at the residence * December 24 — Krakow, Nowa Huta-Bienczyce. An address before the Midnight Mass, preceded by the wishes for the anniversary of his priesthood:

> **During the course of these years we witnessed the difficult struggle which these parishioners waged to get their church ... Each Christmas night, like today's, united us anew in this community of struggle, in this community of tireless struggle. We stood here on those nights of Christmas Eve, during Midnight Mass, in the rain, in the snow, in the cold. And thus,**

---

[17] Catholic University of Lublin.

gradually, by our perseverance and our patience, our presence here and our prayers have borne fruit in the form of this wonderful church of Nowa Huta which is rising ... It is our common joy, we feel it especially tonight. Because on this night, as on no other, we feel that we are one family which wants to have one common house of prayer ... On this night of Christmas Eve I will not be celebrating the Midnight Mass for you here, at this place, but I will go nearby, to celebrate the Midnight Mass at Mistrzejowice, at the place where a new group of Nowa Huta's People of God is forming around their priests. And just as you did here, for years praying under the open sky, so are they now, praying to God and man for a roof over their heads, for the human right to a place of worship, to a parish: a human right! Forgive me, my dear brothers and sisters, that on this night I will not be here. (..) I go there, where my duty calls me. I am, as your pastor said, the bishop of the entire Church of Krakow, and I must be filled with concern for all the churches, all the parishes, especially the poorest ones. You are no longer the poorest, you have already achieved something. There are parishioners in Nowa Huta who are poorer than you. So you will understand, that on this night I want to be with them. Christ was born in the greatest poverty, and I want to seek Him there amidst the greatest poverty, where there is not yet a roof over the head, where troubles keep mounting, where we have to explain ourselves and where we continually fail to find understanding. But we hope that the great lesson of patience and perseverance given by the faithful, the entire People of God together with their priests in the parish of Nowa Huta-Bienczyce, will be emulated and will bear fruit. Your parish, according to some approximate estimates, has 70 thousand Catholics. The settlement of Mistrzejowice will have 45 thousand Catholics, or at least that many inhabitants. How can this be thought to be one single parish! ...

You gave me here your wishes for my anniversary ... The greatest gift for the anniversary of a bishop are churches and parishes in which the People of God can freely praise Jesus Christ and be united with Him ... Let us pray to Jesus, who is being born on this night, to help your brothers and neighbors to create a parish and build a church.

December 24 — Krakow, Nowa Huta — Mistrzejowice, Midnight Mass, thousands of people in the open. The Mass was said under a small roof; the authorities levied fines for its construction.

When Christ was born, the shepherds came to Him at once and surrounded Him. A community of the People of God was formed around Christ. And this is repeated here: a community of the People of God is forming around Christ. Christ is represented by His priest, who has the power to offer His Sacrifice and transform bread into His Body and wine into His Blood. The community congregates around this priest. This is a fact of this society, and we speak here in its name ...

We are applying for a parish for this settlement, we carry our petitions to the authorities, because this has be agreed upon with them, but we also reason thus: true social facts find understanding and approval among those who control society.

The more so, that this social fact, by all measures, serves a useful purpose. The priest who shepherds your flock here under the open sky, who has nothing save your good will and your solidarity, is not pursuing any personal goals, is not seeking any personal gain. What does he want? He wants to teach the Gospel, God's truth, but, at the same time, the deepest truth of humanity, he wants to teach the principles of morality, he wants to teach God's commandments. Is this not in the best interest of this new city, Nowa Huta — that the people who live here observe the moral law? That personal, family and social morality should blossom here? Is this not in the best interest of the nation, of the state? Surely this priest does not deserve punishment for this! Surely he deserves only praise ...

We will pray by singing, as we always sing at Christmastime: "Lift your hand, O Child of God, bless our dear country! With good counsel and prosperity, support its strength with Your strength." Because we want true strength for our earthly homeland. And we are witnesses to the fact that such strength flows from faith, flows from Christ newly born into our souls. We can then take that strength into our personal lives, our family lives, into our workplaces, into the splendid workplace of Nowa Huta, and into all the facets of our lives ...

December 25 — At the Wawel Cathedral, the third Mass for Christmas:

Our homeland has a history of a thousand years, and it existed even before that, in prehistoric times. And in the course of that thousand years, several scores of generations have passed by. And the older generation has always thought about the younger one, how will it create, build, how will it love our country. And we think today: who will be the Poles of tomorrow? You my children, the youth of today, are the Poles of tomorrow ... Our Lord Jesus Christ, who Yourself became a child and a boy, embrace our Polish youth with Your light.

December 27 — 10:00 a.m., residence chapel, concelebrated Mass with sermon for a Christmas get-together of priests from the class of 1970/71 * December 28 — Concelebrated Mass, with sermon, for priests of the classes of 1967, 1968, 1969 * Same day — 4:00 p.m., visit at retreats for high school seniors (girls) organized at the Albertine Sisters, Sisters of St. Joseph and the Norbertine Sisters * December 28-January 6, 1972 — Zakopane — Jaszczurowka * December 29 — He visited high school seniors on retreat at the shrine of Kalwaria Zebrzydowska, spoke to them very cordially during a Holy Mass at the Chapel of Our Lady * December 30 — He wrote a short introduction to the *Kalwaria Prayer Book* being published by "Verum" * December 31 — The conclusion of the canonical visitation of the Rakowice parish in Krakow:

This change in the date makes us consider the beginning and the end of our earthly existence ... We think of those whose earthly existence, or to put it in Christian terms, whose earthly pilgrimage was ended, was closed this year ... That is how it is with every human existence on this earth. Time is the measure of the passing of everything that is created ... The reflection on passing, the passing which marks the beginning and the end of our lives, leads us back through all the generations of humanity, through the history of our planet to the beginning of all creatures, and directs us to Him, who gave beginning to it all. To Him, who was beyond the beginning and who gave beginning to all that was created ...

He who is eternal, who is beyond time, beyond passing, subjected Himself to time — God allowed Himself to be encompassed by human history: He Himself became Man.

We, the people of faith, always connect the mystery of time and the law of our passing with this view of God, who does not pass, but who came into time, into our history, and is leading man, each of us, all of mankind, towards the eternal divine destination ...

Same day — midnight, at the Basilica of the Franciscan Fathers in Krakow:

We, who pray together here in Krakow, join our prayer with that of the Holy Father, we pray for the unity of the body which has one Head. We pray that we may, at the beginning of this new year, draw all blessings and all graces, in every possible measure, from this one Head, from Christ — the Beginning. For each of us, for every person: the person of our times, the person of our year, the person of our city, the person of our Church. For each one who is in this world, for each one, who is yet to be born — for every person ... We will spend this New Year night under the patronage of the great son of St. Francis on our Polish soil, whom the Holy Father raised to the honors of the altar a few months ago: Blessed Maximilian Maria Kolbe.

1972

January 2-5 — Zakopane. He lived and said Masses at the house of the Ursuline Sisters in Jaszczurowka. Skiing.

January 6 — Feast of the Epiphany. Pontifical Mass at Wawel Cathedral.

Just as Herod stood in the way of the three Wise Men, so do various impediments stand in the way of the faith of our generation, of the faith of our brothers. There is a concerted effort, a whole body of work whose goal is that people not believe. That the light of the guiding star should be extinguished. That it should be extinguished especially for new generations, for future generations. We then ask this question: What star, in the place of this one, will you show us? But we are gathered here first of all to pray and, as we pray, we share a wish that we may find the way of faith; that all people of good will in our city may find this way ... and especially our youth ... This is our wish for one another here, at the Wawel Cathedral, at the threshold of the year 1972. It is a very important year in the history of the Church of Krakow. It was 900 years ago, in 1072 ... that Stanislaw from Szczepanow took over the Episcopal See of Krakow ... The short, but fruitful, seven-year apostolate of Bishop Stanislaw served to enrich the faith here in the Church of Krakow ... He also rendered very important service to our nation, especially in the times of the Piast dynasty, because his elevation to the honors of the altar became a symbol of the unification of Poland ... As a bishop, your bishop, I take this opportunity to tell you that we will use the seven years from 1972 to 1979 to try to deepen our faith. Where will we find the light to do that? We will find it in what has become a great source for the entire Church, namely the Second Vatican Council ... We will get to know the thoughts, the truths, the directions of the Council, first of all at the Synod of the Archdiocese of Krakow, which is just beginning and which, God willing, will become the Synod of the Metropolitan See of Krakow, on this great 900th anniversary of St. Stanislaw ... May the Star of Bethlehem shine for us, the people of the middle of the 20th century, and become a beacon for our times.

January 9 — 11:00 a.m., Pietrzykowice, concelebrated Mass with sermon (for the 25th anniversary) * 4:30 p.m., Giebultow, sermon * 6:30 p.m., Lagiewniki. A short mention in the chronicle of the Sisters of Our Lady of Mercy: "Today our young people hosted H. E. Cardinal Karol Wojtyla" * 8:00 p.m., *Oplatek*[1] at the Club of Catholic Intellectuals * January 11 — 10:30 a.m., meeting with the bishops of the Krakow Metropolitan See.

January 12 — Krakow, 3 Franciszkanska Street, meeting of the Episcopal Committee for Pastoral Ministry. A report by the Committee chairman, Archbishop B. Kominek, *Principles of the Program of the Committee for Pastoral Ministry*: "to take the teachings of the Council

---

[1] See Glossary.

and the Polish patrimony as the basis." (From the minutes). A report based on the discussions of the presidium (Katowice, December 16, 1971) and on the work by Cardinal Wojtyla entitled *The Issues of Implementing the Teachings of the Council in Poland and the Pastoral Plan of Implementing the Teachings of the Council in Poland* (January 1970). A report by Cardinal Wojtyla on the subject of the five-year activities of Consilium de Laicis; among others: "there is a pressing need to prepare the clergy for cooperation with the laity; due to external circumstances, the clergy has forgotten how to work with the laity. The forms of the lay apostolate that we develop, can be used as models in the universal Church, because many countries are experiencing a crisis of catholic organizations." (From the minutes). In the ensuing discussion — a motion to establish a Directory for the apostolate of the laity. The proposed rules and regulations of the Committee were discussed * Participation of the Committee in a service at the Mariacki Basilica, "With the youth for the youth" — participation of several thousand young people. Cardinal Wojtyla greeted the participants * January 13 — Second day of deliberations of the Committee for Pastoral Ministry. Discussion of the schedule of sermons for 1972/73. An outline of the social Crusade of Charity presented at the direction of Bishop Bronislaw Dabrowski.

January 14 — 6:30 p.m., residence chapel, concelebrated Mass for university students from the student ministry run by the Jesuits; *Oplatek* * January 15 — Participation in a meeting of the Council of the Pontifical Department of Theology in Krakow * On the same day he issues an order by the power of which the Archdiocesan Museum of Religious Art will be established * January 16 — 8:00 a.m., Chapel of the Ursuline Sisters, Mass with sermon, *Oplatek* for teachers * 12:00 noon, Tluczan, dedication, sermon * 4:00 p.m., Mszana Dolna, Mass with sermon, *koleda*[2] * January 17 — Expanded meeting of the Preparatory Committee of the Archdiocesan Synod, with the participation of sociologists. Beginning of the preparation of the structure of the Synod. Subcommittee for preparing the statutes and the rules and regulations of the Synod * Same day — 7:30 p.m., Church of St. Anne, Mass for the repose of the soul of Andrzej Malkowski[3] * January 18 — 8:00 a.m., Wawel Cathedral, Mass on the occasion of the anniversary of the nomination to the rank of the archbishop, participation in the Chapter's *Cantata* * January 21 — Krakow — Chapel at the Palace of the Archbishop. Funeral Mass and sermon at the casket of the late Sister Agnieszka Wegrzyniak — Sisters of the Sacred Heart * January 22 —

---

[2] See Glossary
[3] The founder of Polish Scouting.

4:30 p.m., the residence, *koleda* with priests who are catechists * January 23 — 9:00 a.m., residence, *koleda* for members of the family ministry, sermon * Mass of Thanksgiving and sermon at the Church of St. Mark in Krakow on the occasion of the successful completion of the work on the preservation and renovation of the church * Afternoon — Chapel of the Ursuline Sisters, he spent an hour at a symposium of the Higher Catechetic Institute on the subject of education to prayer, delivered an address to the participants * 4:30 p.m., Borek Falecki, *koleda* * 7:00 p.m., residence chapel, Mass with sermon for lawyers, *koleda* * January 24 — 7:00 p.m., at the Dominican Fathers, Mass with sermon for the conclusion of an octave of prayer for the unification of Christians, agape * January 26 — 6:00 p.m., 4 Soltyka Street, house of female postal workers, *koleda*. A note in the visitors' book: "I thought that it has been only two years since our last *koleda* together — and it has been five years already. Time flies very fast. Only the co-op at Soltyka Street is always young with the youth of the spirit which is formed everywhere by human nobleness and the love of neighbor. God bless in the New Year. Signed: Karol Cardinal Wojtyla, the Metropolitan of Krakow, Rev. Stanislaw Dziwisz, S. Grodecki, pastor * January 28 — Higher Catechetic Institute, singing of carols.

January 29 — Krakow-Debniki, Church of St. Stanislaw Kostka, Holy Mass, blessing of the Stations of the Cross.

As we experience this day together at the parish of Debniki, as I experience this day with the parish of Debniki, my memories and yours must go back to those years long ago. To those dark years, difficult years, the years of terror, the years of occupation; because it was here that I lived through those years, in this parish, in this part of Krakow; I lived through those years among the people of Debniki, among these parishioners, these young people and these pastors. I will never forget that day when we parishioners, especially we young parishioners, gathered around our priests, found out that all or almost all of the priests of the parish of Debniki and the Salesian inspectorate had been arrested, and shortly thereafter taken to concentration camps. Just as Fr. Maximilian Kolbe. Most of them did not return from there. We remember and honor their names; some of them left this world in the opinion of sanctity. In any case, those horrible, inhuman times left a unique testament in our memories, and in my memory as one of the parishioners here. Undoubtedly, the parish of that time of German occupation, 30 and 25 years ago, experienced very deeply the sacrifices made by various parishioners ... I also recall those times in a very personal way. And I am convinced that my priestly vocation, to which I came at that time and here, in this parish, was helped by the prayers and sacrifices of my brothers and sisters, and of those priests of that time, who paid for the Christian life of every parishioner, and especially of every young parishioner — at that time I belonged to the young people of the parish — not only with words, not only with the shining example of their lives, but also with the sacrifice of their blood ...

The way traveled by the priests of the parish of Debniki — and not only by them, but also by the parishioners themselves — and here I am thinking particularly of one whose personal heroism of life always remains in my memory — that is the road we must also travel, if we are to arrive.

Same day — 6:00 p.m., at the Dominicans', *Oplatek* for students * 7:00 p.m., the Palace of the Archbishop, Holy Mass for the workers of health services. *Oplatek* after Mass * January 31 — Extraordinary meeting of the Preparatory Committee of the Archdiocesan Synod (incomplete membership). They discussed the issue of the procedures for forming study groups and committees, the issues of the relationships among these groups. The cardinal on the subject of the inauguration: it may be more in the character of a definitive announcement of the Synod than the actual inauguration of the work of the Synod * Same day — 7:00 p.m., residence chapel, Mass with homily * February 1 — 12:00 noon, Bielsko-Biala, Chapel of the Daughters of Divine Charity, concelebrated Mass and sermon during a regional conference * February 2 — 12:00 noon, the residence, *koleda* with the household staff * 5:00 p.m., sermon at Wzgorza Krzeslawickie (Nowa Huta) on the Feast of the Presentation of Our Lord (Candlemas):

> Today is the feast of the Presentation Our Lord in the Temple, and on this feast all of us gathered here, the inhabitants of Wzgorza and Stoki, members of the ancient parish of Pleszow, turn to all people to see how Our Lord does not have a temple here. We turn especially to the authorities of our country and our city, so that this temple, so desired, so needed according to all human rights, could finally stand here ... There is no trackless wasteland from which a person could not return to the straight path of salvation to which Jesus Christ leads every one of us. Today we proclaim this with the entire Church ... as we hold these blessed candles in our hands. We bring our faith into our daily lives. This faith is the basis for our desire that a church should stand here, at Wzgorza Krzeslawickie and Stoki ... As your bishop, who meets with you like this, at a Mass, for the first time, I wish to convey to you my deepest respect and admiration for your faith. I wish to express my deepest respect and admiration for your priests, for the pastor of your parish and his co-workers, who with such perseverance and patience are shaping the souls of this part of the parish of Pleszow and who, so humbly but firmly — ignoring all the humiliations, all the unjust fines: why should a priest be fined for teaching moral truths? for teaching others how to be people of noble character, how to be good citizens — should a priest be fined for that? In spite of all of this, your pastors are creating a church here ... I wish to tell you that, for my part, I will do everything that leads to that end. I am mindful of what these Wzgorza Krzeslawickie[4] were some scores of years ago. I also remember that here, on these hills, our countrymen died, were executed by firing squad, for loving their homeland. We are their heirs and we accept their legacy. We also wish that a church may rise at this place where so many people bore wit-

---

[4] Hills of Krzeslawice

ness to their love of the country, the love which was based on the love of God, the love of the Gospel and of the Church. It is our desire that a church may rise here so that the new generations can truly, with complete freedom, with a sense of complete freedom, shape their characters and set out on that certain, bright road which leads through our life to God.

Same day — *koleda* at the Theological Seminary * February 5 — 6:30 p.m., the residence, conclusion of a nursing course * February 6 — 12:00-3:00 p.m., he visited the Church of the Stigmata of St. Francis in Wieliczka, under the care of the Reformed Franciscans. He said a solemn Mass, and gave a sermon appropriate for the occasion. Then he blessed the new catechetic classrooms and the newly-built pavilion for the parish pastoral center, erected at the monastery of Wieliczka on August 27, 1971. From the sermon:

> Because the creation of new parishes has been, in practice, reduced to zero — during the past year, most of our petitions were denied ... because the formation of new parishes has been made so difficult by the secular and administrative agencies, we must seek other solutions. We must share our pastoral duties better, to the extent that conditions permit.
> And it is here, in Wieliczka, that such favorable conditions are present to some degree ... and, as a result of a canonical visitation of over two years ago, a division was made and accepted. I express my joy at this. [The pastoral situation in Wieliczka has created] a particular opportunity for a better division of pastoral responsibilities between diocesan and religious priests ... The pastoral care given by religious priests can bear unique fruit and become a source of unique blessings from God ...

The same day he received a delegation of the faithful from the village of Czarnochowice asking him to join their village to the parish at the monastery * February 7-15 — The residence, private Masses at 4:00 p.m., 12:00 noon, 11:00 a.m., 7:00 p.m., 10:00 a.m. — probably an illness * February 16 — 12 noon, residence chapel, Mass with sermon, Ash Wednesday * 7:00 p.m., residence chapel, the closing of the apostolic process of the Servant of God Urszula Ledochowska * February 18-19 — Residence chapel, private Masses * February 20-April 3 — Continuation of the visitation of the Parish of the Most Sacred Savior (begun by Bishop S. Smolenski), interrupted by a trip to Rome (February 26-March 17) * Interview entitled: *Il sacerdozio et le aspettative della Chiesa* — conducted by Flavio Capucci. (Print. CRIS April 6, 1962) * Visit to 27 bedridden patients and Msgr. Juliusz Malysiak * February 20 — Visitation of the Parish of the Most Sacred Savior in Krakow. First sermon:

> The Most Reverend Bishop, who began the visitation of this parish in my place, because of my illness, ... met with a group of the youngest married couples of this parish. As I meet with you today, I wish to extend my sincere greetings ... My obligations in this period of Lent require that I stay in Rome for almost three weeks, to take up various duties at the

Apostolic See. For this reason, there will necessarily be gaps in my visit to your parish.

Second sermon — before the blessing of married couples:

The divine foundations of the Church, of the community of the People of God, are set deep in man, in human nature, in the human soul, in the human heart. And it is necessary that man be true to this thought of God which is expressed in him, that he not distort it, not change it in his own way. Then both the individual and the social face of the earth, that human face of the earth, will be shaped in a way that is most human and most divine.

February 21 — 12:00 noon, Kalwaria Zebrzydowska, the monastery, Holy Mass with sermon during a regional conference of priests from 7 deaneries * February 22 — 12:00 noon, Oswiecim {Auschwitz}, the Salesian Fathers, Mass with sermon during a regional conference * February 26 — Departure for Rome * February 27-March 5 — Rome, Polish College, private concelebrated Masses * March 6 — Terminillo, parish church, private concelebrated Mass * March 7 — Polish College, private concelebrated Mass * March 10 — Rome, Chapel of the Sisters of the Holy Family of Nazareth, concelebrated Mass with sermon during a retreat * March 13-14 — Terminillo, parish church, private concelebrated Masses * March 15 — He is a *relator* {the key speaker} at a plenary session of the Sacred Congregation for the Clergy dedicated to the matters of the Councils of Priests. The *Circular on the Councils of Priests* issued by the Congregation in 1973 includes all the postulates made by Cardinal Wojtyla (Cf. Rev. Jan Dyduch, *Kardynal Wojtyla w sluzbie Kosciolowi Powszechnemu {Karol Cardinal Wojtyla in the Service of the Universal Church}*, Krakow 1998)

In 1972 he obtained from the Congregation for Catholic Education the approval for the practice of affiliating (by means of an agreement) religious seminaries with departments of theology, which ensured that seminary studies enjoyed the same status as university studies. This was later included among the norms contained in the Apostolic Constitution entitled *Sapientia Christiana* of April 15, 1979.

March 17 — Return to Poland * March 18 — The Feast of St. Joseph at the Church of the Bernardine Sisters in Krakow:

If the matters of God and the matters of man, the most ordinary ones, could be so splendidly concentrated in the person of St. Joseph, then every person, and especially every man, every father of a family, every worker, can in some way find himself in him ... He is a model which is so easy to imitate, because it is so human.

The same day — 9:00 p.m., residence chapel, concelebrated Mass with sermon for the conclusion of a day of recollection * March 19 — Visitation of the Parish of the Most Holy Redeemer, Mass for the sick:

I often have occasion to speak with the Holy Father, Pope Paul VI, during my visits in Rome, as I did in the past few weeks. I will never forget one conversation from a few years ago, when the Holy Father, facing some very grave decisions relating to his office as teacher said to me: "I ask that people who are suffering, especially pray for this intention. If you know of people who are willing to offer up all their suffering for this matter, please ask them to do so." I remember that, at the time, there were many people in Krakow and in the Krakow archdiocese, who immediately offered up all of their sufferings for this difficult matter which Pope Paul VI was facing in his office and responsibility as teacher.

March 20 — 7:30 p.m., Church of St. Anne, Mass with sermon for the beginning of a retreat for university students, after his return from the funeral of Msgr. Franciszek Baradziej at the parish of Niedzwiedz.

March 21-25 — Retreat meditations at the Church of St. Anne in Krakow:

At the outset, I wish to pose a very simple question. I pose it to everyone and also to myself, even though I ask it in the second person: Do you pray? ... To exit from distraction, to take one's life away from distraction, requires concentration ... A person is a conscience ... And finally those commandments, in which all the others are contained ... the commandments of the love of God and of our neighbor, which Christ gave us as the last word expressing His care, as Judge and Father, for our human conscience ... And that is why we must, during this retreat, direct all of our attention to this matter, remembering that here we touch a core in each of us, we touch what determines our own "self," our human dignity, our very person ...

I remember a letter that I once received from a great scientist, a naturalist; a letter which touched me deeply. The author wrote (I will quote from memory, because the original of the letter is long lost, but I will remember it, I think, for the rest of my days) — the author wrote this: For the most part, I do not find God on the paths of my science. But there are moments — most often in the face of the majesty of nature, for example, the beauty of the mountains — that a strange thing happens: I, who do not find God on the paths of my science, at such moments I feel that He is! And then I begin to pray.

From the years before the war I remember a conversation with an author whose creative paths were very intricate. It was difficult to tell, on the basis of his work, whether he was a believer or a non-believer. Nevertheless, in that conversation, this man, several score years older than myself, began to speak about confession. If I remember correctly after all these years, he said something like this: confession — what a magnificent institution. If it did not exist, we would have to invent it — it is that necessary for people.

March 26 — Visit to a rheumatological hospital at Puszkina Street, Mass with sermon * Same day — 2:00 p.m., house of the Sisters of the

Tertiary Order of St. Francis on Lelewela Street, visit to the house and the Chapel of the Blessed Sacrament * March 27 — 8:00 p.m., Church of St. Joseph, Mass with sermon during a retreat of lawyers * March 28 — 8:00 p.m., Church of the Holy Cross, retreat for artists * March 29 — 1:30 p.m., Church of the Felician Sisters, participation in the conclusion of a retreat for doctors * March 29-April 1 — Wawel Cathedral, liturgy of the Holy Week.

April 1 — Holy Saturday, Resurrection Mass at Wawel Cathedral. A short sermon before the renewal of the baptismal promises:

> When we hold the lighted candles, the sign of faith, in our hands ... let us turn our eyes to the altar on which rest the holy relics of St. Stanislaw, Bishop and Martyr. And in their presence, let us, as his descendants in faith, the children of the same Church of Krakow and of the same nation, renew the baptismal promises with special reverence ...

Sermon during the Mass:

> Just as once Paul told the Corinthians, so did Bishop Stanislaw from Szczepanow tell our ancestors: "If you have risen from the dead with Christ, then seek what is on high." And he said this consistently. He said it to everybody. He said it to the king. He said it at the price of his life and his words, bathed in martyr's blood, remained in the tradition of our nation. And when these words were quieted, the nation was in decline. 200 years ago was the first partition of Poland. At that time, no one sought what was on high — they looked low! But there was an awakening. The words of Paul and the words of Stanislaw were heard again, they were taken up by Polish minds and Polish hearts. This is proven by the fact that the heroes of the struggle for independence and the bards of our nation lie here, next to his relics! That is the language of history, of the past generations. That is the well-proven truth. Today we return to this truth ... in order to examine our own lives.

April 2 — Feast of the Resurrection of Our Lord {Easter}, Nowa Huta-Mistrzejowice:

> And I am also here to bear witness with you, dear brothers and sisters, to bear witness with your tireless pastor, that all of us here together, at Mistrzejowice, believe in the Crucified and Risen Christ, and that we want to form a Christian community, a parish, at His side ... We have spoken and written of this quite plainly. We have written to everyone, because, after all, we do respect the authorities. We turn to these authorities with the plea that they recognize what is taking place here, what it is that we are all witnessing, and give it appropriate attention. For the time being, we have this poor, miserable classroom in which we cannot fit. The neighboring parish of Nowa Huta-Biencyce has 70 thousand souls now. Not long ago, it was written in *Tygodnik Powszechny* that it was the biggest parish in Europe ... So we keep issuing our pleas. If you were to come to the Metropolitan Curia in Krakow, you would see the pile of letters written in the matter of Mistrzejowice. These are the petitions which we submit, so that everything that is taking place here would be recognized and allowed

to continue in decent conditions ... I think that what we ask for is a just and good cause. Recently, so much has been said about respecting the needs of the society. I think that what we represent here is an important need.

The same day — visit to the Helcel Sanitarium for chronically ill patients in Krakow: "My wish for you is that the Resurrection of Our Lord bring bountiful gifts to your souls. May it be the source of spiritual strength: when the body is weak, exhausted by the difficulties of life, it is all the more important that the spirit be strong."

April 3 — Easter Monday, Church of the Congregation of the Resurrection in Krakow, Holy Mass.

I think that Fr. Maximilian is, first of all, a contemporary witness of Christ. But he is not the only one: he is a witness to the life, Passion and Resurrection of Christ to the degree of heroism. We are all witnesses to Christ's Resurrection. That is the character of our faith ... we find ourselves at the extension of everything that happened at the time of Christ's Resurrection, among its first witnesses ... and, in our times, we create the same things and we struggle for the same truth about resurrection that they did in those times ... Those who founded your congregation in the 19th century wanted to be, in a very special way, witnesses to the Resurrection for the Polish nation and for other Slavic nations. They understood very well that the Resurrection is not only a historical fact, but a fact of tremendous spiritual significance. That it is a fact which can transform man, give him faith in life. A fact that can lift both man and society up from the lowest fall.

April 3 — *Odpust* of Emmaus, visit to the Chapel of Blessed Bronislawa at the Kosciuszko Mound (Holy Masses are said there several times a year) * Apr 5, — 9:00 a.m., Salesian Church (parish of St. Stanislaw Kostka), concelebrated Mass with sermon for the beginning of the Congress of Vocations. At the Congress he delivered a report entitled *The Theology of Priesthood* * April 7 — 8:00 a.m., Wawel Cathedral, participation in a Holy Mass celebrated by Msgr. Annibale Bugnini * April 9 — Komorowice, Mass for married couples.

The role of Christian marriages is to maintain an appropriate level of Christian dignity, of Christian love, a level of responsibility for the life which you beget: the life to which you give a beginning and which you are then to lead by the hand towards a full and mature society.

The same day — Komorowice, Confirmation. "The beginning of the loss of faith is always connected with a neglect of the personal relationship with Our Lord." * Same day — Komorowice, visit to the hospital, group prayer at the Chapel of the Blessed Sacrament, address to the patients and sisters * April 12 — Warsaw, Main Committee of the Polish Episcopate * April 13 — Wroclaw, meeting of the Episcopal Committee for Pastoral Ministry. Reports: Archbishop B. Kominek:

The Parish as a Form of the Fulfillment of the Church; Bishop H. Bednorz: *The Situation of Urban Parishes*; Bishop I. Tokarczuk: *A Portrait of Rural Parishes in Light of Current Changes*; discussion followed. Report by Rev. Rector J. Majka: T*he Future of Parishes in Poland*. Service at the cathedral "With the youth for the youth," sermon by Cardinal Wojtyla * April 14 — Second day of the meeting of the Episcopal Committee for Pastoral Ministry. The program of preaching for 1972/73 and of pastoral work 1972/73 * Same day — Wroclaw, chapel of the Theological Seminary, concelebrated Mass with sermon.

April 15-19 — Visitation in Lodygowice. Sermon during Confirmation: "Do I strengthen you? No — my child — I, a man, cannot strengthen you ... the Holy Spirit strengthens you."

To the elderly and the sick:

> **You are not only to be taken care of, but you should also take care ... You can do very much by your prayer and your sacrifice, your suffering ... you can obtain much from Jesus Christ for those who may not need physical help, but who often are in terrible need of spiritual help ... Your role in the parish is not merely passive.**

To the members of the Third Order and the Living Rosary:

> **Today again is a time of those followers of St. Francis of Assisi who live in various parishes, who work in various professions, fulfill family obligations ... We must ask, through the intercession of St. Francis, that Christ give us the wide-open eyes of faith and love, which will allow us to notice all the needs of our neighbors. The Marian way, the way of Mary, is the way that the Church in Poland has been following for entire centuries ... the prayer of the Living Rosary, in particular, is a form of group prayer.**

The last day of the visitation:

> **While in Upper Lodygowice, I spoke of the great need of building a church in that part of the parish. I spoke with the parishioners and explained what the Metropolitan Curia is also doing in this matter ... Many priests have come from your parish. And vocations continue to be generated here ... All of them speak of your community, of your parish.**

April 20 — 10:00 a.m., conference of priests — heads of deaneries * 8:00 p.m., Club of Catholic Intellectuals, Easter repast * April 22 — 7:30 p.m., Gniezno, the cathedral, vespers and procession with the holy relics of St. Adalbert. Sermon in front of St. Michael's Church in Gniezno: "Just as Adalbert came to Gniezno only to go on, so the mission of the Church has come to our generation, to the Millennium of Christianity — and the Millennium of Poland — only to go on further. To pass onto our generation..." * April 23 — 9:30 a.m., Gniezno, the cathedral, Pontifical High Mass at the altar of St. Adalbert, sermon:

> **Into the whole program of progress, the progress of civilization, we**

must introduce the most essential element: we must introduce the progress of man. The Church comes to you with that program ... The mission of the Church in our age, in the contemporary world ... is nothing other than the evangelical leaven from which the true dignity of man arises. And just as St. Adalbert came with the leaven from the Hill and went to the shores of the Baltic, so also we take the same leaven and carry it across the whole Polish land.

April 28 — A meeting of the Council of the Pontifical Department of Theology in Krakow. The Cardinal performs a review of the entirety of problems currently affecting the Department. He discusses his correspondence with the Prime Minister (a response to his letter of June 1971 came in the form of an acknowledgment of receipt from vice-premier Wincenty Krasko); correspondence with the Head Office of the Control of the Press and Presentations relating to the recognition of the name of the Department; correspondence with the Vatican. Speaking of the future: "Presently we seek a specific character for our Department ... It will be first of all a history, a history of art." Tasks: "ad intra {internal} — education of qualified academic personnel; ad extra {external} — academic symposia and publications." (From the minutes of the Council of the Department)

April 29-May 2 — Visitation in Bolechowice, eight sermons.

[Welcome:] I wish to get to know these brothers and sisters of mine whom Divine Providence has entrusted to my care as the Bishop of Krakow. And I wish that you would get to know me better...

April 30 — 3:30 p.m., Confirmation:

Yesterday evening, in one of the local parishes, in Brzez, I participated in a very beautiful meeting with young people, during which I did not say that much ... The youth of this parish wants to proclaim Jesus Christ, wants to proclaim His Gospel in word and song. But we must also proclaim the Gospel with actions, deeds...

To young married couples:

We know what it means to tear one body apart. It means to take away life, to destroy life. We must not destroy the life of a person! We must not destroy the life of a marriage...

To older married couples:

Human parenting, human fatherhood, human motherhood, cannot relate only to the body: it must also relate to the soul... [From the second sermon to older married couples:] We are united from top to bottom, and in the horizontal plane, among ourselves; and that is how we constitute the Church...

April 30 — 6:00 p.m., meeting with members of the Living Rosary and the Third Order, the beginning of May devotions:

... so that this month may allow you and help you to come to love the Mother of God anew ... because she is ours, she is the Queen of Poland, in her we have placed all our hopes! As we face these difficult times, these great conflicts, the struggle of the human spirit over the Kingdom of God...

May 1 — Address to the sick and to the Albertine Sisters after a Mass at an institution for the terminally ill in Wieckowice:

Although this house is a place of suffering, we are convinced that it is a place of great good, that here the whole Divine economy of salvation is revealed and shines forth on the parish of Bolechowice and the entire Church of Krakow.

May 1 — Sermon at the Church of St. Joseph in Podgorze:

All human labor is based on the work of creation ... The Son of God standing in the workshop of St. Joseph teaches us, humans, that work is the road to God ... Human labor cannot be measured solely in the categories of temporal gain, it cannot be encompassed solely in the framework of the laws of economics ... These are not supreme, man must be above them ... Jesus Christ, standing at the workshop of human labor, tells us that we also need to show justice to the human spirit; that man, at the workshops of labor, cannot become anyone's slave. And the hardest slavery is that of the spirit ... St. Joseph, the carpenter, but also a father in the human sense, the breadwinner for the Holy Family, tells us and will continue to tell us for all time that labor must be subordinated to the laws of the human family.

May 2 — Sermon for the end of the visitation in Bolechowice:

In the course of this visitation I came to realize how much can be accomplished for the development of the community of the People of God in a relatively short time ... Many a time I was a guest of your church and your rectory, in the days when the dearly departed Msgr. Rajski was still living ... and I must note that a great work has been done here ... I am leaving with great joy even though this joy was clouded by the news that this visitation was interfered with, that there were various threats ... I say this here, so that it may be known that I am aware of this; threats to persons who wanted to meet with their bishop, to young people, to persons who wanted to decorate places of worship for the visit of their bishop ...

May 3[5] — 10:30 a.m., Jasna Gora, the summit, Pontifical Mass for a day of prayer for the Polish youth * 6:00 p.m., Jasna Gora, participation in a Holy Mass * May 4-6 — Jasna Gora, Plenary Conference of the Polish Episcopate * May 6 — 7:00 a.m., Jasna Gora, inauguration of a pilgrimage of university students, rosary on the ramparts; at 11:00 p.m. a sermon to the students at the Chapel of Our Lady, during a Holy Mass concelebrated with bishops and priests:

The symbol of water changed into wine. But all of us who come here want to change this symbol into reality. We want to change it into our own

---

[5] See Glossary.

reality. That is what brings us here. Before us, it brought here whole generations of students, from all of Poland.

That is what brought us here. Surely — a religious tradition; surely — a piety, the Catholicism of our country; but at the bottom of all of that was a desire to ennoble man. To transform man ...

In our times, in these times of particular tension and trial, it is all the more necessary that human life be touched by wisdom and love, it is all the more necessary that every person, especially every young person, extricate himself from the climate of pessimism and doubt, and believe in the possibility of making oneself better and making the world better.

The beginning of this miracle was performed by Christ in Cana of Galilee ...

May 7 — 10:00 a.m., Jasna Gora, the summit, concelebrated Mass for the student pilgrimage * Same day — 6:00 p.m., sermon in Szczepanow[6] before the observances of the Feast of St. Stanislaw, Bishop and Martyr:

He [St. Stanislaw] took up, with great heroism, the battle of his time. May we, following his example, be able to take up the battle of our time, and give to the time in which we live the same expression of faith, hope and charity that he, Stanislaw from Szczepanow, gave to his own time of nine centuries ago.

May 8 — Wawel Cathedral, ordination of subdeacons:

The Synod of Bishops which was held in the autumn of last year in Rome, expressed this thought in its final document, that the priesthood, being a gift from Christ to the Church, indicates that Christ meant this gift to be definitive: irrevocable and irreversible. And this is precisely the nature of the decision for the priesthood.

Same day — inauguration of the Synod of the Archdiocese of Krakow. Keynote address (cf. *Notificationes* August 6, 1972):

We undertake a basic goal of enriching and deepening our faith, of making it aware and mature, adapted to our time; we want this faith to also manifest itself in mature Christian responsibility. We want it to have influence on life, to shape our morality, to lift morality from those perils and dangers which threaten it ever more clearly.

This date also appears on a letter to Msgr. Eugeniusz Florkowski — a letter of thanks to the Preparatory Committee of the Synod, which finished its work on May 8, 1972 — the day of the inauguration of the Synod.

May 9 — 6:00 p.m., Mariacki Church, Mass for graduating high school students, closing address * May 10 — 9:00 a.m., residence chapel, Holy Mass concelebrated with the Council of Priests, homily

---

[6] Birthplace of St. Stanislaw

May 12 — 10:00 a.m., Pelplin, funeral of Bishop Kazimierz J. Kowalski, solemn concelebrated requiem Mass * May 14 — 9:00 a.m., Feast of St. Stanislaw, Bishop and Martyr, at Skalka in Krakow: "We wish to express our fidelity, through Stanislaw, to Christ. To Christ, who is the light of the world; and He has led us, Poles, in this light for a thousand years. We trust that He will continue to lead us" * Same day — Cistercian abbey in Nowa Huta-Mogila — 750th anniversary.

On the site of the old forge, a new forge was built, on the site of a small one, rises a great Nowa Huta[7]. And the people who live here are the Polish people, and the People of God. And that great need of combining matters of the people with matters of God, of combining prayer with work and work with prayer, is a primary need here ... In order to be faithful to the heritage of Iwon Odrowaz, who first led the Cistercians here, to the old forge, the Bishop of Krakow stands with the People of God, he stands by this brave pastor, who now does in Mistrzejowice what another pastor once did in Bienczyce — serves the People of God under the open sky because that is what his priestly conscience prompts him to do, just as the bishop's conscience prompts the bishop to stand by his priests. Even though some may not like it, even though some said "the Cardinal should not come here." He comes here and he will continue to come here, because that is the will of God, and God's word must be heard before that of man. And that is also the will of the People of God, and the will of the People of God must be heard!

May 15-16 — Krakow, Committee for Catholic Education * May 17 — 4:00 p.m., Theological Seminary, conference with heads of deaneries * May 19 — Kety, funeral of Msgr. Jozef Swiader. Sermon:

There probably was no other priest in the Archdiocese of Krakow, who had such a great sense of humor. But we felt that under that surface was a great depth of humanity; an integrity which expressed a particular humanity shaped by a Christian calling, and then a priestly calling. To some extent he hid this depth under an external guise of humor and witty words. But we felt that these words, even when witty and light, had their specific gravity: they served the truth. The human truth and God's truth ... He was a man of community. He was a man who united, and did not divide ... It is especially significant that as we escort this priest to his place of eternal rest ... in two days the bishop will lay hands on newly-ordained priests, just as 50 years ago a bishop laid hands on this then newly-ordained priest.

May 21 — 9:00 a.m., ordination of priests at Wawel Cathedral. "I have just one plea to you: that you take this great trust which the Church and the People of God place in you, and use it as the measure of what is expected of you." * Same day — 4:00 p.m., ordination of priests at the shrine of Myslenice. "Before I lay my hands on your heads to con-

---

[7] Nowa = new; Huta = steel forge or mill.

fer the Holy Spirit upon you, I will ask the Blessed Mother, whom I crowned here in this courtyard three years ago, to be the Mother of your priesthood, and to be the Mother of many, many vocations in the region of Myslenice."

May 22 — Meeting of the Council of the Pontifical Department of Theology in Krakow. Organizational matters, among others — the affiliation of the Institute of the Documents of the Second Vatican Council in Czestochowa. The Cardinal "indicated the need for appointing a special committee that would provide a thorough examination of the problems of institutes, and especially their relation to and association with the Department of Theology." (From the minutes) * Same day — 6:00 p.m., Parish of the Good Shepherd in Krakow, blessing of a cornerstone: "...whoever rejects Jesus Christ, be it a person, a society, or a nation, rejects the cornerstone that ensures the stability of spiritual growth."

May 23 — Dedication of a new home and chapel of the Sisters of the Holy Spirit at the parish of Rakowice (on Lotnicza Street):

> **In very many parishes, there are religious sisters alongside the priests. This creates a new element of parish life. It is a very valuable element. I say this as a bishop who sees the life of many parishes ... The sisters bring into the parish an element that is feminine, motherly, sisterly — different from the one brought in by the priests, pastors, men: a closeness to human life and to its everyday concerns such as sickness, children, family.**

Holy Mass, participation in an evening of poetry, recitation of the works by Andrzej Jawien * May 24 — Kalwaria Zebrzydowska, participation in a pilgrimage of priests from the whole archdiocese. The pilgrimage had an expiatory character because six priests had left the ministry this year. There were also other difficult problems * May 26 — Meeting of the Council of the Pontifical Department of Theology in Krakow. Reports on the subjects of doctoral dissertations presented by Rev. Dr. Jerzy Chmiel and Rev. Dr. Stanislaw Nowak. The Cardinal congratulated the presenters. (From the minutes of the Council of the Department)

May 27-29 — Rycerka Gorna, canonical visitation * May 27 — after Confirmation:

> **...you brought me ... a gift; a gift so human, so Polish, and at the same time so very evangelical, namely a gift of bread: a loaf of bread ... I come to you not with my own gift, but with the gift of the Holy Spirit.**

May 28 — 9:30 a.m., Piekary Slaskie, participation in the pilgrimage of men, closing address * Same day — evening, Rycerka Gorna, meeting with young people who are out of school and working *

May 29 — Sermon for the end of the visitation in Rycerka:

> Today as I traveled about the farthest reaches of this parish, the fathers and mothers said to me: Could you bless us here, on this spot, because it will be difficult for us to get to church. But in the end you came to church in such great numbers...

May 31-June 2 — Canonical visitation of the parish of Giebultow.

June 1 — Wawel, procession of Corpus Christi. Sermon at the first altar:

> The procession of Corpus Christi, the one that leaves from Wawel, the one always led by the Bishop of Krakow, has its ancient traditions. It is a procession ... of our city, of our whole history ... It always left from Wawel and went to the Market Square ... This year we made every effort to keep this ancient tradition and to fulfill the expectations of the Catholic community of Krakow. They were not fulfilled ... I express here the wishes of the entire Church of Krakow, the entire Catholic community of Krakow, when I say: we are waiting ... We attach great importance to this matter.

Sermon at the fourth altar near the Theological Seminary of Krakow: "...at this last, so important a station of the procession of Corpus Christi, let us pray for priestly vocations in our Church, in our country and in the whole world." * Same day — 4:00 p.m., Giebultow, meeting with the young people from the boarding house of the Agricultural Technical School * June 2 — Following the motion by the Main Committee he approves the statute of the Pastoral Synod of the Archdiocese of Krakow and the institutions of the Synod * 4:00 p.m., the parish of St. Casimir, funeral of Msgr. Jan Mac * June 3-6 — Canonical visitation of the parish of Ciecina * June 4 — Ciecina, meeting with physicians at a midday meal; at 7:00 p.m., meeting with a parish youth group in the catechetic classroom; 8:00 p.m., meeting with intellectuals * June 5 — Ciecina, Mass, Confirmation of an infirm parishioner * June 6 — 9:00 a.m., residence chapel, Mass with sermon for the beginning of the Congress of Biblical Scholars. Cardinal Wojtyla sent also a letter of welcome to the participants of the Congress * Same day — 5:00 p.m., Ciecina, meeting with the representatives of a committee for the construction of the church, meeting with and address to members of the Living Rosary and the Family Rosary, prayer. Sermon:

> The matter of the construction of the church in Ciecina, put forward many years ago by the parish of Ciecina and by the Metropolitan Curia, is still waiting for resolution ... You continue to bring this matter up, and you are right in doing so ... In short, I want to tell you that since 1957, the authorities have granted almost no permissions for building churches in our archdiocese. Whatever permissions were granted, they were either for the rebuilding of burned churches, or the expansion of existing small

churches-chapels, such as the famous case of the church in Nowa Huta, or, most recently, the one at Azory in Krakow, the expansion of which is now in progress after the first permission was obtained. As a result, it is easy to see that great needs have accumulated over the course of 15 years. Every year we present the authorities with a list of several score required church buildings ... We are convinced that, given the good will of the authorities, if three such buildings were allowed per year, the matter could be solved in — let us say — 20 years. We are still waiting for that good will. We are all waiting, the whole society, and this parish. We wait with patience and perseverance, but we will not give up.

Same day — 8:00 p.m., Jelesnia, social get-together with priests from the class of 1967 * June 7-8 — The residence, Congress of Biblical Scholars * June 7 — 10:00 a.m., Jordanow, social get-together with priests from the class of 1969, sermon:

It is a beautiful tradition that the priests of our archdiocese who were ordained in the same year, meet year after year in their social groups. And to this meeting they usually invite their bishop to be with them.

Same day — at the residence, Congress of Biblical Scholars * 5:00 p.m., Mistrzejowice, Confirmation, sermon:

As I was testing your children on the catechism before their Confirmation — and they had learned these truths very well — I placed great emphasis on the Sacrament of Reconciliation, because it is an indispensable element of our Christian life...

June 9 — The Feast of the Sacred Heart of Jesus, at the Sisters of the Sacred Heart. "This feast is celebrated by the Church in order to engender charity in us, to form it within us. And should this charity be misshapen, to reshape it anew."

June 10 — 10:00 a.m., concelebrated Mass with sermon for the 100th anniversary of the Publishing House of the Apostolate of Prayer:

... we are not gathered here by chance. The 100th anniversary of the Publishing House unites us at one workshop, on one plane of obligation: the social obligations of the Church which we want to represent here.

Same day — 12:00 noon, cemetery at Salwator, funeral of Prof. Antoni Kepinski, psychiatrist. Sermon during the requiem Mass:

We wish to pray for the dearly departed Antoni. He asked us that his departure from this earth and his funeral be as simple as possible, free from speeches. And we tried to fulfill his wishes ... Let us pray for such an enrapturing vision, the vision of God face to face ... for the soul of this man who, in life, gave so much attention to the matters of the soul, to the healing of human souls. In this he saw his vocation.

June 10-12 — Canonical visitation of the parish of Straconka * June 11 — Pilgrimage of female youth from all of Poland in Czestochowa:

So much depends on you when it comes to purity, when it comes to respect for the dignity of a person ... This begins already in the life of teenagers ... The calling of a woman is to unite people through the heart ... That is why it is so necessary to cultivate the virtues of the heart. It is necessary to fight against its faults.

Same day — 11:00 a.m., Kalwaria Zebrzydowska, concelebrated Mass with sermon during a pilgrimage of men from the Archdiocese of Krakow * June 12 — 7:30 p.m., Leszczyny, social get-together with the class of 1955 * June 13 — 10:00 a.m., Zakopane, "Ksiezowka," concelebrated Mass with sermon to priests on the 20th anniversary of their priesthood * Same day — 12:30 p.m., Raba Wyzna, meeting with priests ordained in 1970 * June 14 — 6:00 p.m., Jawiszowice, concelebrated Mass with sermon during a meeting with the class of 1968 * June 15 — 6:00 p.m., Wawel Cathedral, Mass for the 10th anniversary of the death of Archbishop E. Baziak * June 18 — Visitation of the Blessed Mother in the parish of Pulawy (diocese of Lublin), High Mass at 10:00 a.m. celebrated by Cardinal Karol Wojtyla, with a sermon by the Primate. Later — in Radom, participated in a concelebrated Mass at the Mariacki Church during the celebrations of the Visitation by the image of Our Lady of Czestochowa. The first Mass at the image after it had been released * June 19 — Tyniec, participation in a meeting of priests from the Archdiocese of Krakow, Czestochowa and Silesia who are alumni of the Department of Theology of the Jagiellonian University, on the 40th anniversary of their priesthood. He concelebrated a Holy Mass (with Bishop Bednorz and Bishop Rozwadowski), spoke, participated in a dinner and a social get-together * Same day — 6:00 p.m., Zubrzyca, meeting with priests ordained 10 years ago. Concelebrated Mass.

I wish to recall the beginning of this decade, which was so significant for all of us ... You can surely remember ... that ten years ago, on the 15th of June, the Lord God called to Himself the late Archbishop Eugeniusz. And almost the very next morning, the Metropolitan Chapter ... entrusted me temporarily with the responsibility for the entire Church of Krakow. One of my first acts in that post was your ordination ... In some cases I already know a great deal about your charisms, in others, I am still seeking, as your bishop, their final form.

June 21 — 7:00 p.m., residence chapel, Mass with sermon for the end of the first year of theological studies * June 22 — 10:00 a.m., Zakopane — "Ksiezowka", concelebrated Mass with sermon to priests who were celebrating the 15th anniversary of their priesthood * June 23 — 6:00 p.m., Krakow, Ursuline Sisters, end of the academic year at the Higher Catechetic Institute; presentation of diplomas * 8:00 p.m., residence chapel, Mass for the repose of the soul of Prof. A. Kepinski.

June 25 — Niepokalanow,[8] celebrations in honor of Blessed Maximilian Kolbe, Mass for young people.

> **This poor son of St. Francis decided — led, no doubt, by the calling of God — to dedicate his apostolic activities towards the dissemination of ideas by using modern means of communication ... He knew that for his apostolate to be effective, he would have to use all the modern technical means at his disposal; he was a man of his time ... In the victory of our countryman at Auschwitz, the whole world sees a sign of hope, a sign of the superiority of love over hate ...**
>
> **Niepokalanow is a modern place of work upon man ... We trust ... that love will turn out to be stronger than hate, that by the intercession of Mary Immaculate, Jesus Christ will gain a victory in the souls of this youth, for whom and with whom we pray so ardently, so that they may fully understand the message of Niepokalanow and Auschwitz.**

June 26 — 11:00 a.m., the residence, Main Council of the Polish Episcopate * June 27 — 10:00 a.m., the 131st plenary conference of the Polish Episcopate * June 27 — 4:00 p.m., Wawel Cathedral, meeting in the chapter house, at 5:00 p.m. a public session, concelebrated Mass at the confession of St. Stanislaw, homily:

> **And all of us, heirs and inheritors of Bishop Stanislaw from Szczepanow, are known by the general term of the appellation: pastores et traditores. We are not afraid to be called "traditores" if we are "pastores" {shepherds} ... And a "pastor" is called upon to "tradere", that is, to give up his life for his sheep.**

June 28 — The 131st conference of the Polish Episcopate approves the statutes of the newly-constituted Educational Council of the Polish Episcopate. Art. 3 Par. 1 of the statutes reads that the chairman of the Episcopal Committee for Catholic Education is the chairman of the Educational Council. From this date on, the records of the Rector's office at KUL[9] holds documents from (and to) Karol Wojtyla as the chairman of the Educational Council * June 29 — 7:00 p.m., Church of St. Peter and St. Paul, sermon during a Mass before a procession * June 30 — 7:30 a.m., residence chapel, Mass pro Summo Pontifice.[10]

July 2 — 9:00 a.m., Jasna Gora, concelebrated Mass with 15 priests; sermon to the pilgrims: teachers and educators; Cardinal Karol Wojtyla led an act of surrender into the maternal bondage of the Blessed Virgin Mary * July 4 — 9:00 a.m., Wawel Cathedral, Mass with sermon for sextons of the Archdiocese of Krakow * July 5 — 7:30 a.m., residence chapel, private Mass * July 6 — Bachledowka. Cardinal K. Wojtyla arrived with Msgr. Andrzej Deskur, and left the next day at 6:00 p.m. * July 7-9 — Residence chapel, private Masses * July 10 —

---

[8] Home monastery of St. Maksymilian Kolbe.
[9] Catholic University of Lublin
[10] For the intention of the Supreme Pontiff.

8:00 a.m., Kalwaria Zebrzydowska, Mass * July 11-13 — Vacation, private Masses * July 14-17 — Kalwaria Zebrzydowska, the monastery, retreat * July 17 — Wawel Cathedral, Mass with sermon on the anniversary of Blessed Queen Jadwiga * July 18 — 8:00 a.m., Church of the Bernardine Fathers, Mass with sermon for the Feast of Blessed Szymon from Lipnica * July 19-24 — Trip to the Plesno Lake * July 25-28 — Krakow; Mass at the residence chapel at 7:30 a.m. * July 29 — 8:00 a.m., Zawoja-Wilczna, private Mass * July 29 — Bachledowka, Cardinal Wojtyla arrived in the morning, went on walks and conversed with the Primate; he played ball with the young people and took active part in an evening of singing. In the evening, he and the Primate listened to a concert of an amateur ensemble of gorale {mountain folk} from Ratulow * July 30 — Bachledowka, private concelebrated Mass * Same day — 5:00 p.m., Debica, sermon for the 100th anniversary of the death of the Servant of God Edmund Bojanowski.

August 1-12 — Tourist outing, Holy Masses with homilies * August 13 — Niepokalanow, 10:00 a.m., sermon during Mass; 11:30 a.m., Pontifical Mass.

August 14 — Oswiecim {Auschwitz}, wall of death (block XI), concelebrated Mass with sermon:

> ...today we come for the first time on the day which the Church has designated as his [Fr. Maximilian Kolbe's] feast to pray to him who has been raised to the honors of the altar ... We experience very deeply the mystery of the communion of saints; with all of our being we touch the saint who was "born" here.

August 15 — Feast of the Assumption of the Blessed Virgin Mary, Ludzmierz:

> Let us recall the day of the coronation of Our Lady of Ludzmierz: it was 9 years ago ... and the weather was quite different than today: there was a torrential rain in the morning, and in the afternoon, during the coronation itself, the rain stopped, but the skies did not clear ... Today, there are no torrents of rain, only torrents of sunlight coming down on our celebration. We are very happy at this, for it is a sign of heaven's grace towards our fields and towards our human bodies ... For us Poles, the 15th of August has always been associated with the ripening of the fruits of nature; from all directions people come to church bearing the crops of the earth: sheaves of grain, ripe herbs; we should also bring the ripe fruits of human labor.

Same day — Krakow, the Mariacki Basilica, ordination of deacons:

> The Church prays for priestly vocations. And the Church feels its identity — as we were told by the recent Synod of Bishops in Rome, and before that, by the Second Vatican Council — when these priests are found ... The priest, and even more so a bishop, is expected to serve.

August 16 — 7:30 a.m., residence chapel, Mass for the intention of Dr. J. Wiadrowska * Same day — Tylmanowa and the Blyszcz Mountain.

On that day the Cardinal participated, as a pilgrim, together with others, in a program of the day of communion among the various "Oasis" groups. The day of communion is treated as a day of pilgrimage, and a mountain summit is the designated place of meeting of the various "Oasis" groups.

At that time, the designated meeting place was the summit of the Blyszcz Mountain near Tylmanowa, called "Mount Tabor" by the "Oasis" groups. In the morning, when all the groups set out, the weather was fine, but as they approached the summit, the sounds of an approaching storm were becoming more and more clear.

The Eucharistic service was begun at the summit by several score concelebrants and about 700 faithful. The Cardinal managed to deliver a homily, and then, until the end of the Mass, there was a torrential rain. Two umbrellas were available to shield a part of the stone field altar.

On the way back to Tylmanowa, the warm air allowed everyone to dry off. In an address to all gathered, the Cardinal said that he felt personally close to this lifestyle. He was speaking both of the activities of the "Oasis" groups and of praising God on the mountaintops. It was his first Eucharist celebrated on a mountain summit.

From this first meeting until the last ones, a frequent subject of his homilies and addresses was the connection between the program of renewal proclaimed by the Second Vatican Council and the realization of this program in the methodology of the "Oasis" movement.

In the final part he said: "I think that if there is an oasis, then there must be, unfortunately, a desert, because an oasis only has meaning in a desert. But the existence of a desert cannot discourage us, it should encourage us to form as many oases as possible. A desert is a threat only if there is no oasis. We are threatened by a desert. Or let me say it another way: we would be threatened by a desert, if we did not create oases."[11]

August 17 — 7:00 p.m., Dominican church, Mass with homily on the Feast of St. Jacek {Hyacinth} August 18 — 4:00 p.m., Kalwaria Zebrzydowska, the "funeral of Our Lady." "I wish to welcome in a special way the pilgrims from beyond the Tatra Mountains, to whom we want to say here in Kalwaria, that we never stop praying for you."

August 20 — Kalwaria Zebrzydowska, the Feast of the Assumption:

I think that we here, at our Polish Calvary, experience some small tests of our faith, like today ... the Feast of the Assumption, moved to the nearest Sunday — we observe it in the rain ... This Kalwaria is not a comfortable shrine. There are not many places to lodge, nor good provision for food, and the roads are not good ... That is how it is here, and we wouldn't want it any other way ... This is what Kalwaria reveals to us: just as the

---

[11] Quotation not attributed.

Blessed Mother follows Christ, so we grow close to Christ here, we overcome various obstacles — both internal and external — and here we find ourselves in the state that our Father wants us, that is in the state of children of God, brothers of Christ ... It is a source of great joy to us that young people come here in such great numbers for these celebrations in Kalwaria at the time of the Assumption. We see these young faces, so tanned, sometimes appearing strange to the older generation ... they bring with them the instruments which they are so fond of, they put on their hats, which suit them so well — that's the way they are. We were different. But what is important is that however they are, they find their way here.

Same day — Podstolice, Confirmation. Sermon after Confirmation:

I come to you from Kalwaria, from the shrine of the Blessed Mother to which your parish often makes pilgrimages. It is a custom that on the Sunday after the Feast of the Assumption, the pilgrims return to their parishes. So I come here with them ... When I come to a parish, I fulfill my mission as a bishop, my mission which is a heritage of the mission of the apostles ... I come to this parish with special emotions. Two years ago your parish was visited by Bishop Albin [Malysiak], my co-worker ... He told me much about the religious life, the zeal ... that enlivens this parish ... I am glad ... that I could stand next to your priests, including the former pastor, the current pastor, to embrace your parish in my heart and in my prayers.

August 21 — 4:00 p.m., Olszowka, concelebrated Mass with sermon for the end of an "Oasis" session * August 22 — Presentation entitled *The Priesthood from the Aspect of Service* as part of the summer session for clergy at KUL[12] (August 22-24, overall subject: "Priesthood as Service") * August 24 — The residence, conference of the heads of deaneries * August 25 — 5:30 p.m., chapel of the Theological Seminary, concelebrated Mass for the conclusion of a retreat for priests, sermon * August 26 — 10:30 a.m., Czestochowa, Pontifical High Mass; 6:00 p.m., participation in a Mass of Thanksgiving for the canonical regulation of the Church administration on the western and northern territories, participation in the procession.

August 27 — 11:00 a.m., Smardzowice (in the diocese of Kielce), Pontifical High Mass with a closing word, coronation of the image of the Blessed Virgin (the coronation was performed by the Primate) * Same day — 5:00 p.m., Bujakow, blessing of a cornerstone, Mass with sermon * August 28 — At the Chapel of the Sisters of St. Augustine in Krakow, he said a Holy Mass dedicated to the person of St. Augustine. He met with the children who are under the care of the sisters. (Sr. Aleksandra Trojan OSA) * August 29 — 8:00 a.m., Wroclaw, presentation at a course for priests * August 30 — 8:00 a.m., residence chapel,

---

12 Catholic University of Lublin

concelebrated Mass with sermon for the Polish Seminary from Paris.

September 1 — At the Norbertine Sisters in Krakow, the Feast of Blessed Bronislawa:[13]

> **In every name — especially in our Slavic names — there is a particular exhortation ... We keep calling to her, with her name — defend the honor! ... We can never forget the day of September 1, 1939 ... 33 years ago we gathered here like today. And on that day, in apprehension of the drama which was then beginning, we called out: defend the honor! ... We know how our nation was humiliated, trampled, made to suffer. But it defended its honor.**

September 2 — 8:00 a.m., 1 Bracka Street, Apartment # 3, Mass in the home of an ill woman * Same day — evening, at the Ursuline Sisters in Rokociny * September 4 — 10:00 a.m., Main Council of the Polish Episcopate * September 5 — Poznan-Zabikowo, blessing of the place dedicated to the victims of World War II, solemn Mass for the intention of the beatification of Edmund Bojanowski * September 7— 7:00 p.m., Mass for the repose of the soul of Anna Morawska * September 8 — 6:00 p.m., Biezanow, Mass with sermon for the beginning of the observances of the 550th anniversary of the parish, blessing of stained-glass windows.

September 10 —10:00 a.m., Miejsce Piastowe, Pontifical concelebrated Mass on the occasion of the 50th anniversary of the founding of the Congregation of St. Michael the Archangel * Same day — 5:00 p.m., Okulice, vesper service, closing address on the occasion of the 10th anniversary of the coronation of the image of the Blessed Mother * September 13 — 10:00 a.m., Krakow, the residence, conference of heads of deaneries * September 14 — 11:00 a.m., the residence, meeting of the Educational Committee together with the deans of the Theological College * September 15 — He sends a letter offering his condolences and consolation to the Augustinian Sisters after a tragic automobile accident (one sister died, two seriously injured). (Sr. Aleksandra Trojan) * Same day — meeting of the Council of the Pontifical Department of Theology in Krakow. At the outset, the Cardinal took up several departmental matters dealing with three subjects: fixing the attention of the clergy and the laity upon the matter of the Department of Theology; problems associated with the establishment of a degree of Master of Theology; matters relating to the organization of work in the Department (ratio studiorum, academic seminars, publications — also abroad): a proposal of cooperation from the Polish Seminary in Orchard Lake.[14] (From the minutes of the Council of the Department)

---

[13] The name means "defender of honor"
[14] Near Detroit, Michigan.

September 15-18 — Visitation of the parish of Ujsoly.

When a parish gathers around its bishop, then he wishes to bestow a particular blessing on the married couples. By doing so, he reaches, as it were, to the very foundation of social life, of Christian society, which exists in the parish.

[The day of families who dedicated themselves to the Sacred Heart of Jesus:] It is necessary that the family live in an atmosphere of charity ...

[To the suffering, the lonely, the elderly:] The subject of today's group prayer is the grace of suffering. Because everything in human life is a grace and is connected with grace ... The grace of suffering is a great blessing to society ...

[To the members of the Living Rosary:] If you believe in God, if you remain in touch with Him, then you pray. If you do not pray, then there is some sort of breach in your faith ... The generosity of the heart is lacking: you must communicate with God with a generous heart.

[Last concelebrated Mass:] There is a need for a large community of the People of God, as we have been taught ... by the Second Vatican Council ... That is why we are undertaking a great effort in the entire Church of Krakow ... it is a pastoral synod whose goal is, first of all, to bring to our Church, to our consciousness, to our lives, the great teachings of the Second Vatican Council, which are like the Gospels translated to address the needs of man and Christians of our time.

September 20 — Poronin, meeting with priests who lead "Oasis" {charismatic} groups.

We live in an age in which, by following the particular lead of the Holy Spirit, we are to rediscover and deepen our faith in the Church. [This] lies at the basis of the movement which is represented here today by the priests ... and the laity present here ... To believe in the Church means to discover man, ... it also means to discover the community, to discover God within man ... It is characteristic of your communities that you are rediscovering the Church primarily in the people of the future, in the young ...

[Words during a group meal:] On the basis of my experience, which I've gained over the five years of my participation in the Council of the Laity, I can tell you that much is being said in the West ... about how we are faced with a crisis of lay organizations; of that form of organization which we attempted and which we ended over a dozen years ago ... not because we abandoned it, not because we closed it, but because it was forbidden to us ...

I am very happy that this movement ["Oasis"] began, ... that it is maturing and maintaining its identity ... I had nothing against it from the very beginning, because I felt a need ... and was waiting for something to come and fill it. When I first discussed the summer "Oasis" in Kroscienko, I thought that priests — or at least some of them — also felt this need. And since that talk, which took place 3 or 4 years ago ... I have become better acquainted with this movement and with its methods, with the living "oases" themselves — and I think that this is a movement which deserves our best wishes for further growth ... I wish it for all the priests, and I wish it for myself, that more and more priests in the Church of Krakow ... discover their calling to the youth ministry ...

This is a special movement ... Its program does not destroy spontaneity ... The method of "open eyes" consists in experiencing the beauty of nature as a wonderful expression of the Creator ... we experience it with our eyes, our minds, our hearts ... I am very pleased with that.

September 22 — 9:00 a.m., residence chapel, concelebrated Mass with a sermon for university students * September 23-25 — Visitation in Gilowice. During Confirmation:

...it is necessary that the response you give to God through your faith be a response through your actions... your living...your behavior... your attitude — not only on holidays but every day.

September 24 — Blessing of families:

A blessing is a prayer; but at the same time it is like a response from God to whom we pray. He says to us ... Father, Son and Holy Spirit, that He wants good things for us ... Accept this blessing from my hands today, from the hands of your bishop, who can come to visit a parish only once in a while, but who wants to tell you and share with you as much as possible during such a visit.

September 25 — Feast of Blessed Wladyslaw from Gielniow:

Through his apostolic action, through his life and death, the Blessed, became associated with the capital city of Warsaw, and is the patron saint of the capital of Poland ... Prayer is a great reserve of strength for the Church ... We need a great campaign of prayer directed at heaven, the campaign whose results will come back to earth.

I know that there are members of the Franciscan Tertiary Order in this parish, perhaps not too many of them, because, unfortunately, due to administrative pressures, the tertiary movement has been weakened in the post-war period — although it should not allow itself to be weakened. The contemporary times are full of opportunities and needs which are very appropriately met by the spirit of St. Francis. We need ... a special love of neighbor in these times — times which are not only rife with human labor and economic struggle, but also with many kinds of egoism.

September 27 — 7:30 a.m., Gorzow Wielkopolski, chapel at the Bishop's residence, private concelebrated Mass * September 28 — 8:00 a.m., Pleszew Wielkopolski, mother house of the Little Sisters Servants of Mary Immaculate, concelebrated Mass with sermon * Same day — 6:00 p.m., Wawel Cathedral, Feast of St. Waclaw {Wenceslaus}:

Our Mother the Church gave to this temple ... two patrons ... This cathedral is not only a great shrine of our Polish history, but ... a shrine of the Slavic world, of all the Slavic peoples ... By the tomb of St. Stanislaw and the relics of St. Waclaw ... we begin the days during which we will sing and speak, pray and meditate, on what it means to build the Church.

Same day — evening, the Mariacki Basilica, introductory address for the beginning of Sacrosong[15] * September 29 — 7:00 p.m., at the Franciscans, participation in Sacrosong * On the same day — Krakow, speech to the members of the Secretariate of the Synod * September 30 -October 2 — Visitation of parishes in Bielsko-Biala and Lipnik.

October 1 — 4:00 p.m., Lipnik, group prayer at the funeral of a woman of the parish * Same day — 7:30 p.m., Nowa Huta-Bienczyce, conclusion of Sacrosong:

> Here in Nowa Huta, where a new church is rising, we sang today about building the Church within us, among us and in the world ... I have been involved with Sacrosong from the beginning, that is, from 1969, when Sacrosong first appeared in Lodz, so it is appropriate to also look into the future.
>
> I was told that I should bestow some additional prize from me personally upon the last group, and the last soloist for their call for peace. I think that it should be done. And I would like ... to take what was sung by the other groups, those rewarded with the highest prizes — about Blessed Maximilian, and that litany about the Way of the Cross — to take it in my ears and my heart to Auschwitz.

October 3 — Krakow, at the Discalced Carmelites. 50th anniversary of the Carmelite Sisters of the Child Jesus: "...we wish upon you the spirit of childhood which is so needed by contemporary humanity, humanity which is so entangled in its apparent glories." * October 4 (Feast of St. Francis of Assisi) — Theological Seminary in Krakow, beginning of a new academic year: "You must be very simple, but at the same time you must progress in knowledge, in education, in forming your character. You must be so simple that the mysteries of the Kingdom of God may reveal themselves more fully to your young souls, your hearts and your personalities." * Same day — 11:00 a.m., Opole, he visited Bishop Franciszek Jop * 5:00 p.m., Czestochowa, inauguration of the Institute for the Decrees of the Second Vatican Council, participation in a Mass, address in an auditorium * October 5-6 — Residence chapel, private Masses * October 7 — 8:30 p.m., Czestochowa, Jasna Gora evening prayer service * October 8 — 6:30 a.m., Jasna Gora, Way of the Cross * Same day — 10:00 a.m., Church of St. Anne in Krakow, beginning of the academic year. "Never, in the course of human history, have any cultures been created by might ... Man the creator, especially the creator of culture, science, spiritual values, must be internally free." * 11:00 a.m., Nowa Huta-Mistrzejowice, an address after a Mass: "...in the current year, the civil authorities of Krakow recognized the need to build a church in Mistrzejowice. We receive this news with great satisfaction. At the same time we wish to

---

[15] Festival of sacred song

point out that the Metropolitan Curia in Krakow has long before petitioned for the creation of a new parish in Mistrzejowice ... We will continue our efforts because we feel that our demands are right and just." * 12:30 p.m., private chapel, meeting with priests and young people from "Oasis 1972." "And may this song of the young generation become a good introduction to the renewal of the Church of Krakow through the Synod ... And may this meeting in my home, at which I am very glad, serve to advance the great work of our personal and communal renewal in Jesus Christ." * 3:00 p.m., Lanckorona, sermon for the 100th anniversary of the birth of Father Marszalek.

October 10 — Meeting with the directors of synodal work groups * October 11 — Krakow-Podgorze, at the Redemptorist Fathers, opening of an independent apostolate at the church; blessing of a new polychrome * October 13 — 6:00 p.m., Nowa Huta-Bienczyce, service of Our Lady of Fatima on the eve of observances in Auschwitz.

> As I join you in our common prayer, I wish to invite all of Nowa Huta, all of Krakow, again, to take part in Sunday's observances in Oswiecim {Auschwitz} ... I don't think there will be any impediments. We have received many indications that the importance of this moment is understood, and I believe that we will not experience any difficulties or obstacles in making this pilgrimage to Oswiecim.

October 15 — Oswiecim, observances in honor of Blessed Maximilian Kolbe on the anniversary of his beatification. Present: Cardinal John Joseph Krol {of Philadelphia}- head of the Episcopate of the United States; Cardinal Paolo Bertoli, Prefect of the Congregation for Causes of Saints, who conducted the beatification process until the end; Cardinal John Wright, Prefect of the Congregation for the Clergy.

> We wish to greet everyone in this Eucharistic community made up of tens of thousands ... Today's gathering is a meeting of Poles from all of Poland and Poles from abroad ... with the representatives of other nations ... The Church of Poland comes here under the guidance of its bishops and the leadership of its Primate ... We ask him for his words, for his nourishing and strong words from his authority as Primate.

11:00 a.m., Brzezinka, participation in a Mass with Cardinal Krol and introductory address; 3:00 p.m., Auschwitz, laying of wreaths in the cell and at the wall of death, prayer for the victims of murder (with Cardinal Krol and the bishops) * 6:00 p.m., Wawel Cathedral, Mass and prayer for the beatification of Queen Jadwiga, led by Cardinal John Krol. Sermon:

> Let me recall here the moment when together with Your Eminence we were called by His Holiness Pope Paul VI into the College of Cardinals. It was in May of 1967, and the consistory took place in June. I set out for Rome right from here, from the confession of St. Stanislaw; and from here

I addressed the people of Krakow ... expressing the great joy that a year after the Millennium of Christianity, Poland has two new cardinals: one in Krakow, the other in Philadelphia. Your Eminence expressed similar sentiments from the United States.

October 16 — 9:00 a.m., Siekierczyna, participation in the ingress of Cardinal Krol, concluding address * 12:00 noon, in Limanowa with Cardinal Krol * Tarnow — speech for the conclusion of Cardinal Krol's visit * October 17 — 9:00 a.m., Zakopane, regional conference * 8:00 p.m., Krakow, Church of Our Lady of Lourdes, Mass with sermon for the beginning of the academic year * October 18 — Kalwaria Zebrzydowska, regional conference of priests from 7 deaneries. He presented the issues related to the Synod of the Archdiocese of Krakow * Same day — 7:30 p.m., Krakow, Church of the Felician Sisters, Mass with sermon for health workers, on the Feast of St. Luke, patron saint of physicians * October 19 — 10:15 a.m., auditorium of the Pontifical Department of Theology, participation in the lecture of Rev. Prof. P. Siwek * A ceremony of presenting Rev. Prof. Wincenty Urban with a commemorative book on the occasion of the 25th anniversary of his scientific work — Krakow, the editorial office of "Nasza Przyszlosc" {Our Future} * 7:30 p.m., Church of St. Anne in Krakow, Feast of St. John of Kanty, Mass for teachers and educators.

The education of a person is not equivalent to merely teaching ... This process must allow for both cognitive truth ... and the interior truth of the person: the truth of conscience, which consists in the correspondence of actions with convictions ... We must not educate in a debased hierarchy of goals and values.

Would that the educator did not have to hide his convictions, because of the threat of dire consequences to follow. I don't know, maybe there is no threat, maybe it is just a fiction which people have invented for their own use, to defend their own weakness. But if there really is the threat of such consequences ... then this threat works against the education of the person.

Tomorrow, the Department of Theology — the Pontifical Department of Theology in Krakow — will gather around the tomb of St. John of Kanty. At the beginning of the academic year, this group numbers 1054 persons ... It has been excluded from the ancient community of the Jagiellonian University, but continues to work as a Church institution — and, as we can see, there are plenty of people to work for.

October 20 — 8:00 a.m., Church of St. Anne, Mass by the tomb of St. John of Kanty * 5:00 p.m., meeting of the Council of the Pontifical Department of Theology in Krakow, with the participation of guests: Prof. Izydora Dambska and Assistant Professor Wladyslaw Strozewski. In the first part of the meeting, Rev. Dr. Jozef Tischner presented a report on the results of his doctoral research in a presentation entitled *Philosophy and the Human Issues of Man* * 7:30 p.m., Church of St. Anne in Krakow, inauguration of the academic year, introductory remarks:

What the declaration of the Second Vatican Council says about freedom of religion is the declaration of the entire Church, and of all the circles of the academic apostolate in Poland.

The more mature a person is, the more aware in his faith, the more he should — and the more he does — realize what a great good God is. And this is a blessing, this is a grace.

October 22 — Catholic University of Lublin, inauguration of the academic year:

The community of the Catholic University of Lublin is a great workshop in which Jesus Christ, who lives within the Church, and in which the Church of Jesus Christ, the Church on our own Polish soil, wish to carry out, year after year, the mission of salvation, which is manifested through learning the truth for the sake of love, through the unceasing pursuit of the truth for the sake of love.

Same day — departure for Rome * October 23-28 — Rome, Polish College, private concelebrated Masses.

October 26 — Rome, the Vatican Radio broadcast an interview with Cardinal Wojtyla: The Celebrations in Oswiecim-Brzezinka {Auschwitz-Birkenau} on the first anniversary of the beatification of Fr. Maximilian Kolbe.

October 29 — At the Dominicans' in Krakow, on the 750th anniversary of the establishment of this religious order in Poland. A short sermon at the end of the Mass:

As I conclude this Sacrifice, I wish to say that the Church of Krakow keeps and venerates the head of St. Jacek, just as it keeps the heads of St. Stanislaw and St. John of Kanty. All of these holy relics are a sign of sainthood, and at the same time a sign into the future.

October 30-31 — Wroclaw, plenary conference of the Polish Episcopate.

October 30 — In the Wroclaw cathedral — presided over a Holy Mass concelebrated by the bishops from the western and northern territories; the Mass was celebrated on the occasion of the establishment of dioceses on these territories.

November 1-5 -Visitation of St. Catherine Parish in Krakow.

[Greeting:] ... As a priest, I was associated with the Church of St. Catherine for a few years.

The Church of St. Catherine is not only a work of art ... it is a legacy, it is a tradition of the human spirit ... an acknowledgment that God is great, that God is the exaltation of the human heart ... Let us not allow ourselves to be diminished — this is a danger for contemporary man.

[The hospital:] I feel very close to all the ones who suffer in the Church of Krakow, I continually seek contact with them, I turn to them, because I know how great the power of the sacrifice of human suffering is ... And that is why I often ask you, the sick, for help.

[To a congregation of Eastern Rite Catholics:] Your Church was a pioneer, it began the unification of Christians of the East and West, the unification of the Church around its one common shepherd. And this can be, should be, a source of pride for you.

[Blessing of married couples:] The pastoral activities of the Church have greatly increased in the area of marriage and family life. Do not be surprised ... rather, you yourselves must undertake this with us. We need a great Christian effort ... so that Poland will not die out ... that a spiritual love be present in all of society ... Because after years of terrible birth control propaganda, dictated by economic considerations, this ethical foundation has been shaken in public opinion.

November 1 — Rakowice Cemetery, sermon for the Feast of All Saints:

If ,on one hand, our contemplation of the fate of man ends at the door of death, if it ends at each grave, how very significant it is, then, that we worship the Risen Christ among these graves of the Rakowice Cemetery. He is the Patron of this chapel, so that we may find support not only in our contemplation but also in our prayer.

Same day — Skalka, the crypt of the notables, meeting with the Pauline Fathers * November 2 — Wawel Cathedral, requiem Mass and procession to the royal tombs * November 3 — Institution run by the Albertine Sisters at Krakowska Street. Visiting the sick. * Participated in an evening organized by the student ministry at the Church of the Pauline Fathers at Skalka in Krakow * November 4 — Church of St. Catherine in Krakow, Feast of St. Charles Borromeo:

Who is this St. Charles,[16] who is my patron, to me? ... He is a constant reminder of my particular bond with Jesus Christ, of my belonging to Him ... And from the time when His name became my name, I also took on the full meaning of these splendid words: "Jesus Christ is my life."

On his name-day he accepts wishes (after Mass at 7:00 a.m.). He visited religion classes conducted by the Sisters of St. Augustine, he visited the sisters, among them — the one injured in an automobile accident, he spoke with each one separately. He visited the cloister garden and the sisters' refectory. (Sr. Aleksandra Trojan OSA) * The same day he visited the Daughters of Charity on Piekarska Street (chapel, meeting room, laundry, workshop).

November 5 — 8:00 p.m., departure for Rome via Katowice and Vienna; return — November 24 — via Vienna. In Rome, concelebrated Masses, usually in the morning at the Polish College * November 9 — 12:00 noon, the Vatican, audience with the Holy Father (delegation)

---

[16] Karol is Polish for Charles

* November 11 — 8:00 a.m., Terminillo, concelebrated Mass * November 12 — 12:30 p.m., Grecio, concelebrated Mass * November 13[17] — Rome — the Polish College. Speech at a dinner * 4:00 p.m., Rome, Church of St. Andrew at Quirinal, concelebrated Mass at the tomb of St. Stanislaw Kostka.

November 14 — In the Congregation he appeals for the beatification process of Brother Albert to be expedited. This was not his only appeal in this matter. (From the correspondence of Fr. Naruszewicz with a Sister Superior of the Albertine Sisters)

November 19 — 10:00 a.m., Rome, Church of St. Stanislaw, Mass; sermon by the Primate * November 20 — 8:00 p.m., private audience with the Holy Father * November 25 — 10:00 a.m., Krakow, residence chapel, private concelebrated Mass.

November 26-December 31 — Visitation of the Parish of St. Stanislaw Kostka.

November 26 — Feast of Christ the King, Wawel Cathedral, with the participation of delegations from recently visited parishes:

As I was visiting your parishes, I always invited you to come with a return visit to this Cathedral. It is the Mother of all the churches, all the parishes, in our archdiocese ... Yesterday I came back from Rome and immediately upon my return I learned that there is a complaint, from your area, from around Zywiec, that a chapel was built illegally. But I ask: how much did these people do, how much did all of us do and continue to do, so that churches and chapels can be built legally?

November 29-30 — He hosted an academic conference on the subject of the history of the Church in Poland and Krakow in the 11th century. The conference was held at the archbishop's residence in Krakow, in a group of about 50 experts-historians. They discussed the times when St. Stanislaw lived * November 29 — 7:30 p.m., residence chapel, Mass for the repose of the soul of the late Stefania Poltawska.

December 1 — 8:00 p.m., Church of the Jesuits, First Friday of the month, concelebrated Mass with sermon for academic youth * December 2-4 — Meeting of the Committee for the Apostolate of the Laity. The beginning of work on a directory concerning dialogue within the Church — a document about lay people in parish pastoral councils, and on participation in the European Forum. Meeting with the Committee for the Academic Apostolate {Campus Ministry}, subject: "The Youth and the Apostolate" * December 4-6 — The residence,

---

[17] Nov. 13 is the Feast of St. Stanislaw Kostka.

Committee for the Academic Apostolate * December 5 — Participation in a "St. Nicholas" celebration for altar servers at the Parish of St. Stanislaw Kostka * December 6[18] — Participation in a "St. Nicholas" celebration for kindergarten children * Same day — Metropolitan Curia, a symposium for priests involved in ministry to university students, organized by the Archdiocesan Institute of the Family. Summary: extensive discussion of the encyclical *Humanae vitae.*

> **I spoke with the Pope many times, both before the publication of the encyclical, and even more often afterwards — and at every conversation we returned to this subject, because he knows my interest — and that of our entire community here — in the problem. Several years after the encyclical had been promulgated, I heard him say: "If I were to write it now, after the this whole wave, I could not write anything else."**

December 8 — 7:00 p.m., Jordanow, dedication of the parish church, homily * December 9 — Meeting of the Council of the Pontifical Department of Theology in Krakow. The Cardinal informs the Council of the comments of the Sacred Congregation for Catholic Education regarding the proposed statutes of the Department. The proposal was not definitively approved, but it was recognized as a basis for the practical activity of the Department. Also, information about the preliminary steps towards the affiliation of the diocesan seminaries in Czestochowa and Tarnow with the Department. (From the minutes of the Council) * Same day — 8:00 p.m., a get-together with the student group "Spes" {Hope}, *Oplatek,*[19] address.

December 11 — Lublin, KUL, closing address at a memorial ceremony dedicated to Rev. Idzi Radziszewski on the 50th anniversary of his death * Same day — participation in *Oplatek* for the entire university * December 12 — 9:00 a.m., residence chapel, Mass with sermon for the beginning of a meeting of the Council of Priests * December 14 — 6:00 p.m., residence chapel, Mass with sermon for a group of sisters who take care of the sick (Ms. H. Chrzanowska) * December 15 — 8:30 p.m., the Jesuit church, *Oplatek* for university students * December 16-19 — Visitation of the parish of Mydlniki * December 17 — 7:00 p.m., Mariacki Church, sermon on the anniversary of the coronation of the image of the Blessed Mother * December 18 — 10:00 a.m., the residence, conference of priests — heads of deaneries * December 19 — 8:00 p.m., Church of Our Lady of Lourdes, Mass with sermon, *Oplatek* for university students * December 20 — 7:00 a.m., residence chapel, Mass with sermon for seminarians of the first year of the Krakow Theological Seminary * Same day — a visit to an "Oasis" group at the

---

[18] December 6 is the Feast of St. Nicholas
[19] See Glossary.

Parish of St. Stanislaw Kostka, an address * December 23 — Visit to a nursing home at 41 Zielna Street, Mass with sermon in the chapel of the home, visit with the sick, blessing of the home of one of the staff, visit to the Albertine Sisters.

December 24 — Nowa Huta-Mistrzejowice, before Midnight Mass:

> **I am constantly here in my thoughts and in my heart. Mistrzejowice has become as important and as prominent an issue for the Church of Krakow as Bienczyce once was. Earlier, I always said Midnight Mass there, but now a church is being built there. But here, Jesus Christ ... is being born under the open sky ... I wish you all perseverance, so that the church in Mistrzejowice, for which we have approval, could begin to rise. Now I am going to your brothers and sisters at Wzgorza Krzeslawickie, and I will convey your greetings to them.**

The same day Nowa Huta-Wzgorza Krzeslawickie, Midnight Mass:

> **And we stand here, at this place, where the new-born Christ does not have a roof over His head ... All of us gathered here invite him and plead that here ... where God is being born, unto these people, unto these many thousands of people, new people, people of hard work, people of great accomplishment — that God may be born here, in accordance with the traditions of our Polish culture: under a roof! ... We think that this is in accordance with the traditions of our Polish culture. We have always invited God under our roof.**

December 25 — 8:30 a.m., residence chapel, Mass with sermon for the families of his co-workers from Solvay at Borek Falecki * Same day — 10:00 a.m., Wawel Cathedral, concelebrated Mass with the participation of the deanery that he visited most recently. Sermon: "This House of God is the place of eternal rest for the most eminent persons of our Polish land ... It is truly a great Polish Bethlehem." * December 26 — The Feast of St. Szczepan {Stephen}, the Church of St. Szczepan in Krakow:

> **[History and needs of the parish — "a subject not for a sermon"] The parish has 65 thousand souls ... the second as to size in today's Krakow, after the famous Nowa Huta ... When I visited the parish 5 years ago, the pastor and I decided that we needed to apply for the permission to build a new church in the section of the parish where the settlement of Azory is located ... We did submit an application to this end in the first months of 1968 — and we are still waiting for a decision in this matter.**
>
> **All of this ... constitutes a problem ... of our Church of Krakow, of our archdiocese ... Believe me, there are many problems like this, they keep mounting. I say this, so that the needs of this parish community, of the whole Church, may be understood by those who make administrative decisions.**

December 28 — 5:00 p.m., Theological Seminary (at 3 Manifestu Lipcowego Street), concelebrated Mass with sermon during a retreat for high-school seniors (boys) * 6:00 p.m., Chapel of the Daughters of

Divine Charity (14/16 Pedzichow Street), concelebrated Mass with sermon during a retreat for high-school seniors (girls) * December 30 — 7:30 a.m., Carmelite Sisters (44 Kopernika Street), Mass with sermon in the cloister.

December 31 — 12:00 noon, Zakopane, Church of the Holy Family: "One of the primary tasks, which I set for myself in my ministry as bishop, is the apostolate of the family." * Same day — midnight, at the Franciscan Fathers in Krakow:

> And the fact that we begin the New Year with the Blessed Mother, is for us a source of particular hope. Because we have learned to trust Her and to entrust everything to Her, ... because for centuries we have called her the Queen of Poland ... because she is the Mother of the Church.

This year his book, *Sources of Renewal: A Study of the Implementation of Vatican II*, PTT Krakow 1972, was published. Fragments from the book:

> This work is intended as an attempt at "initiation." It is not a commentary on the documents of Vatican II, because that is the work of theologians; that work is gradually being done, also in Poland. This work could rather be seen as a "vademecum," leading up to various documents of Vatican II, but always from the point of view of integrating them into the life and faith of the Church. (p. 7) ... At the basis of the implementation of Vatican II, or rather, at the basis of renewal as envisioned by the Council, is the principle of the enrichment of faith. (p. 11) ... The enrichment of faith, which we take to be the central postulate of the implementation of Vatican II, should be understood in two ways. It should be understood not only as an enrichment per se, but as an enrichment of the entire existence of a believer in the Church — enrichment flowing from the teachings of the Council. So, this enrichment of faith, in its objective sense, which marks a new stage in the Church's effort "to achieve a fullness of God's truth," is also an enrichment in the subjective, human, existential, sense. And it is this aspect that needs to be given most attention. This "pastoral" Council has opened a new chapter in the pastoral work of the Church. (p. 14) ... The very concept of the implementation of the {teachings of the} Council, as expressed in the title, could lead the reader to expect a series of detailed descriptions of how the Second Vatican Council is — or at least how it should be — implemented in our Church. And this "how" could be expected to include specific practical methods, ways or techniques of organizing our activity in order to ensure the implementation of the plans presented by the Council ... However — all considerations of "how to implement the Council" must be preceded by some statements of a more fundamental nature. The key point is: what exactly is meant by: "to implement the Council." So, the point is to decide what is to be implemented. In this study on the implementation of Vatican II we tried to concern ourselves not so much with the "how" as with the "what." This second topic is more fundamental. (pp. 357-358) ... The deep awareness of the greatness of the gift that faith represents in the soul of every man and in the life of society, has given rise to the need to entrust that faith to the Mother of God and Mother of the Church ... The enrichment of the faith in the teachings of

the Council are: thought and direction. The enrichment of the faith in the Church consists in: full initiation, the maturity of understanding and attitudes of all of the members of the People of God. Christ clearly pointed to the "leaven which raises the entire loaf" (Mt. 13:33) (p. 360)

1973

January 1-5 — Zakopane, skiing; stayed at Jaszczurowka at the Ursuline Sisters * January 6 — 6:00 p.m., Wawel Cathedral, Pontifical High Mass and sermon, greetings to Krakow parishes * January 7 — 10:00 a.m., Cisiec, Mass and sermon * Same day — 5:00 p.m., visited with the youth in a meeting room run by the Sisters of Our Lady of Mercy.

From the time the meeting room for young people was created, Cardinal Karol Wojtyla was notified of this work, because he was very interested in the initiation and development of this type of activity. At meetings with Sr. Klawera Wolska, the instructor at the meeting room, he would often repeat: "Only you, Sisters, can conduct this type of activity, because God called you to that and provided you with a particular charism in that regard." The proof of his care and interest in this endeavor were the Cardinal's annual meetings with the youth of "The Source." Beginning in 1970, until the time when God called him to the Chair of St. Peter, every year, on the Sunday after the Feast of the Epiphany, he would spend an afternoon at "The Source" at 3/9 Wronia Street. The first such meeting, on November 29, 1970, had the character of a name-day observance, because of the recent (November 4) name-day of the Cardinal. The next visit at the meeting room took place on January 9, 1972.[1]

Same day — 7:30 p.m., *Oplatek*[2] at KIK {Club of Catholic Intellectuals} * January 8 — 10:00 a.m., at the residence, annual meeting of bishops of the Krakow Metropolitan See.

January 9-10 — Krakow, 3 Franciszkanska Street, meeting of the Episcopal Committee for Pastoral Ministry. Presentation: *A Polish Priest in light of Current Dangers* — Archbishop B. Kominek; Bishop W. Miziolek — outline of the pastoral program for 1973/74; program of preaching — Rev. Prof. Leszek Kuc. A subcommitee was elected for the preparation of a six-year pastoral program (for the period after 1975): Cardinal Wojtyla, Bishop Stroba, Bishop Tokarczuk, Bishop Etter, Rev. Prof. Majka and Rev. Prof. Kuc. A discussion was held on the topic of parish pastoral vademecum (Rev. Kocylowski). (From the minutes of the Committee)

January 11 — 2:00 p.m., Chelmek, adoration of the Blessed Sacrament and *Oplatek* with young priests * January 12 — 7:15 p.m., residence chapel, concelebrated Mass and sermon, Christmas carols sung by university students from the youth ministry group at the Jesuit church * January 13 — "Participated in a social get-together of former students of Polish language and literature, from his class, at the apart-

---

[1] Source not attributed.
[2] See Glossary.

ment of Halina and Tadeusz Kwiatkowski at 3 Batorego Street in Krakow. Present were: Irena Bajerowa, Janina Garycka, Ewa Radlinska. Krystyna Zbijewska, Tadeusz Ulewicz and I. Stanislaw Urbanczyk was also present, he was an assistant when we were students (he conducted classes in descriptive grammar)." (Maria Bobrownicka) * Same day — 7:00 p.m., *Oplatek* for physicians, at the residence chapel * Jan 14 — Chapel of the Ursuline Sisters in Krakow, an address to teachers: "We must discover some time in our life — the sooner, the better — … God's calling which is hidden behind this human vocation: an order to work, an assignment to work, a profession..." * Same day — 3:00 p.m., Libiaz, Christmas carols, homily * 7:00 p.m., residence chapel, *Oplatek* for lawyers * January 15 — 2:00 p.m., St. Florian Parish, *Oplatek* with priests ordained in 1971 * January 17 — 6:00 p.m., St. Anne's Church, Mass in memory of Andrzej Malkowski[3] * January 18 — 8:00 a.m., Wawel Cathedral, participated in a Holy Mass on the anniversary of his nomination as archbishop * Same day — 2:00 p.m., Rajcza, post-visitation conference * On the same day the Vatican Radio broadcast an interview with Cardinal Wojtyla: *500th Anniversary of the Birth of Nicholas Copernicus* * January 19 — evening, residence, Administrative Council * January 19-20 — Visitation of the Parish of the Sacred Heart of Jesus in Trzebinia (Society of the Divine Savior — Salvatorian Fathers and Brothers) * January 21 — Trzebinia, to married couples:

A bishop arrives to visit a parish not only superficially, not only in the administrative sense. He comes to enter the whole community of the People of God and to touch, as it were, those central points of Christian life of the parish community. He does it through many meetings with the faithful.

[About the day of marriage, a reminder of the significance of that day in the life of each couple, but also in the life of the Church and the parish:] A society, nation or country which weakens the role of the family in the upbringing of children, which tears parents away from children or children away from parents, acts to its own injury!

Our Mass ends with an individual blessing for each couple. I wish … to express in this blessing all my concern as well as all my confidence, that all the Christian marriages in this parish will live up to their calling.

[For the end of the visitation:] You are working here for our times, for our Homeland and Church. You are building it here, in this industrial area among a petroleum refinery, steel mills and mines. You are creating the Mystical Body of Christ. You bind all of it, all of your human labor and effort, your considerable effort; you bind it, by mystical ties, with the Holy Spirit … We cannot see it with our eyes, even the eyes of the visiting bishop cannot see it. But it becomes visible to the eyes of faith.

January 23 — Warsaw, Main Council of the Polish Episcopate *

---

[3] Founder of Polish Scouting.

January 24-25, Warsaw, plenary conference of the Polish Episcopate. The Conference appointed a Church committee to commemorate the 500th anniversary of the birth of Mikolaj Kopernik {Nicholas Copernicus}, Chairman — Cardinal Karol Wojtyla * January 26 — 10:00 a.m., residence, a synodal meeting with religious sisters, WIK[4] ; Christmas carols * January 28 — 12:00 noon, sermon for the beginning of the visitation of the Mariacki Church * Same day — 5:00 p.m., chapel of the Theological Seminary, *admissio inter candidates* (formerly: minor orders), lecture * January 30 — 2:00 p.m., Church of the Sisters of the Visitation in Krakow, Mass and sermon, post-visitation conference:

> The Council wrote: "Christ has revealed Man to mankind." This says so very much. We know that Christ has revealed God to us ... But the Council says that Christ revealed Man to us, and that the mystery of Man is fully revealed only in the mystery of Jesus Christ. So man, too, is a mystery, and must be understood in the light of the Revelation and the historical reality of Jesus Christ, a reality that is still relevant to every person, to every age.

Same day — 5:00 p.m., Zywiec, concelebrated Mass.

January 1973 — Presentation entitled *The Teaching About Love, Which Should Be Adopted as the Basis of the Preparation of University Students for Marriage:*

> Young people want to listen and read about love. It is obvious that this is the subject closely connected with their lives ... I know this primarily from my experiences in the academic apostolate at the time when I was still able to be personally involved in such an apostolate. And I can confide in you, if that is still any secret, that my book *Love and Responsibility* was written on the basis of all these contacts, this apostolate. It arose from the needs ... from reflections ... from the exchange of ideas. Of course, later, all of this was somehow transformed, and the book took on the shape that it did ... I would like to make reference to this book right at the outset — despite all of its deficiencies which, as time goes by, I can see ever more clearly and which, I feel, need rectifying. I feel the need of some kind of sui *generis retractationes* in this matter; still, for the time being, I have nothing else from my own workshop other than this book, to which I can make reference.
>
> (About the perversions of love, about contraception:) In Rome I examined the huge documentation of the opposition to *Humanae vitae.* I read the proclamations of bishops and episcopates from all over the world ... and I came to realize that the sphere of the Atlantic culture, the one with which we are closely associated, is the only sphere contesting *Humanae vitae.* We have witnessed how the concepts and practices of love, of responsible parenthood, were warped in our society. And today, the same people who contributed to this, are suddenly raising the alarm ... Birth control was pic-

---

[4] Higher Institute of Catechesis

tured as some sort of social imperative. After 15 years, there are calls for an increase in birth rates. Those people who were being persuaded to avoid children in marriage, who were told that children were not the proper purpose of marriage in this social structure, are now being urged to have children and more children ... And now, after all this, how audacious it is to speak of human values! Pardon me for getting carried away.

Two fundamental thoughts about love from the Holy Scriptures: "God is love" and "The love of God is poured into our hearts by the Holy Spirit who has been given to us." So, when we, theologians, speak about love — whether we speak of it with the voice of our lips, or with our entire attitude, with our awareness, with an inner voice of our thoughts and hearts — we must always understand love as real participation in God's love. Great, true, human love is just such a participation ...

I will never forget my young friends, one of them is no longer living, and he was a great individual. Whenever we met — in our student days, and later, when he was an independent man, an academic worker, and still later, when he was a husband and father, whenever we met, this matter was the center of his interest: how we continue to create, to build our love in our marriages, in our families ...

In our pastoral work, we must teach, in every way possible, that love is not only a matter between two young people, but that it is also their matter with Him, with God ... It is necessary that, right from the start, love begin to seek its affirmation and guarantee in its ultimate source, in its fullness — because by itself it is incomplete ... What is needed is nothing other than the communion of that human love with the great Love, i.e. with the all-encompassing God acting through Jesus Christ.

February 1 — Departure for Australia via Rome. February 2 — At the Okecie Airport in Warsaw, meeting the B. family.

At that time Mr. & Mrs. B. were taking their seriously ill son to Italy, in the faint hope of finding medical help there. The child was completely immobile and had to be carried. "He came up to us, tactfully asked about everything, then he blessed our child, making a sign of the cross on his forehead, and assured us that he would remember him in his prayers..." In Rome, at the airport, he notified the Ursuline Sisters who were waiting for the arrival of the couple with their sick child, and relayed the message that the same day he would say a Mass for their intention. Later, there was a telephone call and... financial aid for the purpose of saving the child. After several months, when it turned out that another trip was necessary to continue the treatment, he offered his assistance again. "At that time we were already writing to him, 'Dearest Father.' The news of the death of our dear son came to him late. He wrote then: 'Dear Mr. & Mrs. B., with all my heart I join with you in your pain at the loss of your beloved son Mirus. It is difficult for us now to understand the verdicts of God's Providence ... May the Blessed Mother be your refuge in these difficult moments.' ... Later I wrote to the Cardinal revealing the state of my soul before him; I said that he would be justified if he chose to turn away from a person who no longer believes in anything. An answer came immediately: 'Madam, I know well that in this suffering, which you are now experiencing ... all expressions of sympathy would be insufficient. From your last letter I can tell how much you are suffering. I just want to assure you that I remember ... before God, just as when your son Mirus was alive. If you should happen to be in Krakow some time, please come visit me.'"

On the first Christmas after the death of our child, he sent greetings and wrote in his letter: "...I continue to commend you, Madam, to the care of the Blessed Mother, and I keep hoping that we will have occasion to talk in person." Much later, convinced by a religious sister of her acquaintance, she decided to call on the Cardinal: "When we came (I went with this sister), several clergymen were already waiting. He greeted everyone, walking up to them and shaking hands. He walked up to us, said a few warm words and asked us in for a talk. I saw that I was unnecessarily afraid of hearing trite phrases which only further wound the heart. Many would have wanted to quickly get rid of a guest as inconvenient as I was, but he gave his precious and very limited time to a mother crushed with grief, without letting on by even the smallest gesture, that behind the door there waited clergymen with problems that were more important to the Church than one suffering person. He spoke warmly, as if shyly: 'The mystery of suffering, the mystery of the cross, cannot be explained... I certainly cannot explain it... I assure you that I will remember you in my prayers, in my Masses. And please come again. Please write. We must somehow support each other...' For a long time he was the only one who provided strength and support. In my long breakdown of faith I was often strengthened by the thought that if a man like the Cardinal believes in God, and believes so strongly, then maybe He does exist. He did not know that he played a great role in my return to God."

On June 1, 1974, in the afternoon, he found time to confer the Sacrament of Confirmation on our other son in his private chapel. During the Mass he delivered a special sermon to this boy and his parents, in which he remembered the departed little brother, spoke about the pain of the parents, and about what the only remaining son should now become for those parents. After the official ceremony, he went up to them and embraced everyone warmly. Subsequently he maintained correspondence with the parents and with Wladus. On his own initiative he offered a place in his chapel for the deposit of an urn with the ashes of a relative who died abroad, while formalities for its permanent disposition were being conducted. He wrote then (September 17, 1974): "May the light of the Holy Spirit allow you to understand the unseen grace of God which is given through the visible signs of suffering, and may the Sorrowful Mother give you strength to bear these crosses. It was she who stood at the foot of Christ's Cross, she who held His dead body in her arms and laid it in the grave, and she who had the prophecy of Simeon before her eyes throughout Her life. Could there be greater pain than this?..."

In response to name-day wishes and a note about a Mass for his intention ordered in Czestochowa, he wrote back with a thank-you (also for a handmade bookmark —a gift from Jawus), ending with these words: "Our roles are reversing. Now I will be obliged to you for the gift of prayer and the cordiality which you have shown me." (According to an account by B. B. written for the *Kalendarium*, which it was necessary to abridge)

February 2-6 — Rome, the Polish College * February 6 — Interview on the Vatican Radio before the trip to Australia for the Eucharistic Congress:

Participation in this Congress is particularly valuable to me also for this reason that I am a novice here. I have never participated in a Eucharistic Congress, so I am acting like a novice. I am going towards something unknown, something that is yet to be revealed, yet to be experienced, lived. Experienced — not for myself, but for the entire Church in Poland. After all, I will participate in this Australian Congress because of a mandate that I was given. I am going there as the representative of the Polish Episcopate.

February 6 — Rome — Manila. Until March 1 —the text of Cardinal Wojtyla's journal of the trip was printed in several publications. Here is the complete text, made available by the Krakow Curia:

February 6. I made the long trip from Rome to Manila in the Philippines in an airplane of the Dutch airline KLM, which departed from Fiumicino at 8:45 p.m. on February 6. (I came from Krakow to Rome a few days earlier, arriving on the Feast of Our Lady of Candles, also known as the Feast of the Presentation in the Temple.) The plane stopped in Karachi and Bangkok, and arrived in Manila on February 7, at 7:00 p.m. — when our watches showed 12:00 noon Rome time. We still had time, around 8:00 p.m., to concelebrate a Mass in Manila at the Church of the Redemptorist Fathers, who came to take us from the airport. When I write "we" and "us" I am speaking of Bishop Szczepan Wesoly from Rome (unfortunately, Bishop Wladyslaw Rubin could not come because of his duties at the Synod), and Fr. Stanislaw Dziwisz, my chaplain.

February 7. It was very good that we had a 5-hour layover in Manila, because that gave me a chance to see the city that was once visited by the unforgettable Archbishop of Krakow, Cardinal Adam Stefan Sapieha, when he took part in a previous Eucharistic Congress. That was in 1937. His whole trip by ship, in both directions, lasted almost half a year. Today, by jetliner, 13 hours in one direction. So it was very good that I could stop in Manila —also because I said Mass at the Church of the Redemptorist Fathers on the day of the so-called perpetual novena (Wednesday). This devotion of both petition and thanksgiving to Our Lady of Perpetual Help, practiced also in some churches in Poland, gathers, in the capital of the Philippines, several score thousand people at several Masses during the day, and especially in the evening. Even during our Mass — and it was the last one and unscheduled — the church was filled and many people came to the Table of the Lord {received Communion}. I was struck at first sight by the piety of the Filipinos; many people proceeded on their knees in the aisle of the main nave, like they do in Poland around the image of Jasna Gora; there were many candles lit in colored lamps.

Through conversations with our hosts, we quickly became aware of the issues of Catholicism and Philippine society. Because of the late hour I did not ask for an audience with Cardinal Rufino Santos, the archbishop of the Philippine capital of 4 million inhabitants; I just telephoned the Papal Nuncio to tell him that on the way to Australia I had stopped for a few hours to say Mass, taking advantage of the hospitality of the Redemptorist Fathers. The flight was leaving at 11:55 p.m. (4:55 p.m. in Rome).

February 8. At the Polish missionaries in New Guinea. The second night aboard the plane brought us closer to Australia, but we still did not reach that continent. We stopped in New Guinea, landing at Port Moresby, which is the capital of that part of the island which is, for now, still under

Australian administration; next year it is to receive its political independence. This is the eastern part of the island; the western part remains under Indonesian rule.

The visit to New Guinea was arranged by the missionaries from the Society of the Divine Word who work here, and among whom are many Poles. In the spring of last year the ordinary bishop of Goroka, John Edward Cohill, an American, came to Krakow with two missionaries, one of whom was Polish, the other Slovak; all were from the Society of the Divine Word (SVD). When they found out about my planned trip to Australia, they came to invite me to visit their mission in New Guinea. And so from February 8 to February 10, I could take advantage of their invitation, whose purpose must be considered in the context of the increasing presence of Polish missionaries in the missionary work of the whole Church.

In Port Moresby we were met at the airport by the fellow priests of our Polish missionaries; they are working at the local major seminary. It is an inter-diocesan seminary and also an inter-congregational one. Several score native seminarians are being prepared for the priesthood. So far, there is only one native among the teaching staff, and only one native among the members of the Episcopate of this country, whose official name is Papua and New Guinea. Around noon we flew by local plane to Goroka, where we were awaited at the airport by the missionaries of the Society of the Divine Word and three religious sisters, Poles from the Congregation of the Servants of the Holy Spirit, along with the Vicar General of the diocese. Bishop Ordinary had gone to Australia for a conference of the Episcopate. We enjoyed the hospitality of his house, where the diocesan Curia and the pastoral institute are also located. The purpose of this institute is to study the situation in the missions, and to provide orientation for missionaries arriving in New Guinea. Their numbers are still insufficient. It is enough to mention that in the Goroka diocese, 70 thousand Catholics are served by a mere 30 plus priests. The Vicar General (a Black man from the United States) was surely expressing the opinion of his bishop, and of the whole body of priests, when he expressed hope that their guest from Poland would consider augmenting these ranks in the future. Especially, that our countrymen working here won a great deal of respect — as evidenced by the letter that the regional superior of the Society of the Divine Word sent to me.

The Church is by nature a missionary Church, and it is so everywhere, not only in the missions. Nevertheless, its missionary character is particularly evident in the missions. These thoughts guided all our contacts, at the altar and at meals, and in visits to various mission outposts — as many as could be visited in so short a time. After Mass, which we concelebrated in Polish for our countrymen, the entire population of the mission, made up of natives and representatives of other nationalities, and headed by the aforementioned Vicar General, came together for a meal. We became acquainted and exchanged speeches, and then we saw a film about the life of a missionary made by Fr. Jozef Jurczyga. It should be noted that this film was already seen in many Polish parishes when Fr. Jurczyga and his bishop visited Poland, as was mentioned previously.

It was necessary to rest after two sleepless nights. For now, fatigue turned out to be stronger than the watch, which — although it was night in Goroka — indicated early morning hours in Europe. This memory of European daily rhythms would come back again. Because of the significant altitude (over 1600 m {5300 ft} above sea level), the tropical climate was not evident.

February 9. The following day we started our visits in the morning. I concelebrated Mass with Bishop Szczepan, the local Vicar General and all the priests, in the chapel of the school for catechists, whose director, Fr. Antoni Bulla, is a Pole. This was a unique liturgy: the Eucharistic prayer in Latin, my homily in Polish (immediately translated into a language understood by everyone), the entire liturgy of the word in the native language. Besides their own dialects, they speak a language called Pidgin English, which is something of an official language. The singing by the group of catechists, in the native language, was splendid; their appearance totally authentic according to local customs. It is difficult to describe; you should look at it in photographs. In any case, the Melanesians have a dif-ferent outlook on clothing than we do, although the presence of many Europeans has caused a certain conformity, especially in the city of Goroka itself, which is not only the seat of the diocese, but also, speaking in our own terms, of the voyevodship.[5]

After the Mass and a meal, the natives honored us with their dancing and a kind of pantomime depicting the arrival and killing of the first white missionary on the island. They spoke in their own language and handed us gifts according to their customs.

At this stage of missionary work, the school for catechists seems more fundamental than a theological seminary. Catechists fulfill a basic role in their communities, i.e. in the villages, where a missionary priest can come only from time to time. It was very appropriate, then, that this is what they showed us first. Next we went to a mission outpost located relatively close to Goroka. This village was called Namta. Fr. Ernest Ferdlej, a missionary from the Society of the Divine Word, born in Bielsko, is a German who speaks Polish poorly. With the help of lay assistants, he organized his outpost splendidly: the church, the school, the living quarters, the outbuildings — all in all, an excellent base for pastoral work. A great part of this work is the school operated by the mission. We visited two classes where young parishioners of Namta (grades 3 and 4) were being taught by a native male teacher and a woman teacher, a lay missionary from Europe.

Before we left for Namta, we were received in Goroka itself, in a large elementary school operated by the Sisters Servants of the Holy Spirit, but the teaching staff is almost all native. Our greeting was ceremonial and cordial, the children sang beautifully in their language — and then with great enthusiasm pressed forward to receive pictures of Our Lady of Czestochowa. I took the same gifts to the children of Namta. Under the guidance of a very hospitable pastor, who first treated us to a meal in his home, we visited the whole village, and even looked into the houses of natives. Doing that, and along the way, we learned a great deal about their life, customs and religiosity — but these would require a separate detailed report. We traveled by an all-terrain vehicle. However, the missionaries cannot use it to get everywhere. They have to walk to many places, often many kilometers through thick brush. The terrain is mountainous and full of beautiful vistas. On the way, in many places, we crossed streams which were very similar to the streams in our Polish mountains.

After returning to Goroka we visited a large youth center (administra-

---

[5] An administrative division in Poland; it, in turn, is divided into counties.

tive center, sports facilities, etc.) and the house of the Sisters Servants of the Holy Spirit, with its beautiful chapel; we were received very hospitably by them.

The entire evening after the meal, we talked with the Poles only, again in the school for catechists. The priests told much about their work, they spoke spontaneously and drew on their vast experience. It was evident how deeply they had entered into their missionary calling and how completely they had dedicated themselves to it. They also listened to what we had to say about Poland. But overall, missionary subjects were in the majority. Almost all of them took part in this get-together, telling us that this was an exceptional opportunity. Working in far-flung posts and in various dioceses, of which there are 17 in New Guinea, they get together only once a year for a retreat.

February 10. Once again we concelebrated Mass in Polish in the bishop's chapel, and the words of the homily directed everyone's hearts and thoughts to the Church in Poland and to Our Lady of Czestochowa visiting the parishes in our native land. Then a meal, farewells, and departure by plane for Port Moresby, from there departure for Brisbane in Australia at about 1:00 p.m.. The secretary of the Papal Delegate to New Guinea (the Delegate himself was at the Episcopal Conference in Sydney) took advantage of the time between our arrival and departure for Australia to show us the city and to tell us many interesting things about the situation and the work of the Church in this very original country. I must admit, it is still very exotic — but in a year it is supposed to become an independent state. The UN is monitoring the transition to independence.

Brisbane

We took our first steps on the Australian continent, which was the goal of our voyage, in Brisbane. At the airport we were greeted by Fr. Kasjan Wolak, a Capuchin and local pastor, with his co-worker, Fr. Zbigniew Pajdak, of the Society of Christ, and lay representatives of the local Polonia [6] Also present was the Vicar General of the archdiocese, in the absence of Archbishop Patrick M. O'Donnell. There are representatives of the press, which spread current news of the visit.[7] We went to Browen Hills, where our countrymen have their church. It is a parish church, where Fr. Kasjan was the pastor and Fr. Zbigniew the assistant, but there are few Anglo-Saxon parishioners, and the Poles received the full measure of pastoral care from this church.

We could see this immediately at our liturgical welcome, to which our countrymen came in large numbers, despite the fact that it was a Saturday. Fr. Kasjan gave a very cordial address, we sang the litany to the Blessed Virgin, and at the end I spoke, making reference to the fact that the same litany is sung to the same melody in so many churches and chapels of our native land.

At 5:00 p.m., Mr. Peterson, the Premier of Queensland (that is the name of the state here), came to the rectory. He could not participate in the evening reception, but wanted to greet the cardinal from Poland personally. The reception itself took place at 7:30 p.m. at the Polish Home, which is the seat of all the Polish organizations and the entire Polonia of Brisbane. In the greater city area it numbers about 3000 persons. About 200 invited

---

[6] Polish community
[7] Significance: the press in Poland would carefully avoid reporting any news related to the Church.

guests gathered on this occasion, among them representatives of local civil and church authorities (including the Archbishop of the Anglican Church, the rector of the university[8]). Receptions of this type have their own particular protocol. At this one, the President of Polonia, Mr. Inz. Sudol, opened by greeting us with bread and salt.[9] Speeches at table were limited to three: Fr. Kasjan, a minister of the state government (Mr. Sullivan) representing the absent premier, and the last word was given to the guest from Poland, who spoke of the meaning of the term "Polish home" in multiple contexts. He thanked the representatives of Australian society that they made it possible for our countrymen to create many such "Polish homes" here — and at the same time he outlined the importance of every Polish home, in Poland and abroad, against the background of our time. The meeting was concluded by a group singing of "Idzie Noc,"[10] as at a scout campfire. We returned to the rectory at about 11:15 p.m.

February 11. Sunday. A well-publicized Mass for Polonia at 10:00 a.m.. We concelebrated it with Bishop Szczepan and Msgr. Jaroszka from Melbourne. Polonia turned out in large numbers: scouting, organizations, color guards. In my homily I made reference to the purifying force which flows from Christ, shapes man and builds his culture, infusing it with values that are fundamental and irreplaceable. In this context I also mentioned Blessed Maximilian Kolbe. The blessing of a new monstrance after the Mass and the procession with the Blessed Sacrament were a kind of further preparation for the Eucharistic Congress, which was the main goal of our trip to Australia and the central event this year in the life of Polonia. I should add that the priests worked in the confessionals without pause on Saturday and on Sunday morning. A large part of the Eucharistic gathering received Holy Communion.

After the High Mass, the first meetings and group photos took place in front of the church, especially with the large group of altar servers. But the main meeting with Polonia was set for 5:00 p.m.. It is unfortunate that Fr. Kasjan could not take part in it. Through many years of pastoral work, he earned the respect and loyalty of his countrymen. He had been ill for some time, and that afternoon the doctor took him to the hospital. So the meeting with Polonia had to take place without the pastor. It was partly outdoors in front of an open stage, from where we could hear the Polish language in poetry and song from the mouths of the young generation. The children of our countrymen spoke, sang, and above all danced (magnificently!) the polka, krakowiak and polonaise. The foundation of their education and upbringing in the spirit of their native culture and tradition are the Saturday Polish schools and youth organizations, above all scouting. So from the depth of my heart I thanked all who contribute to this work — it is difficult to name them all here, but each of them has made invaluable contributions to the shaping of the Polish spirit in these young people, who are being carried away by the currents of everyday life beyond the reach of that life that is the very beat of their parents' hearts.

After the first part, which was a display of the valuable heritage and achievements of the entire Polish community in Brisbane, the second part was more social: snacks, conversation, group photographs (not only with large groups, but also with individual families). All of this so that the trace of our meeting would be left not only in the heart...

---

8 Unclear whether the archbishop and chancellor are the same person or two people.
9 An ancient Polish tradition dating back over a thousand years.
10 *Night is Nigh*, "Taps"

New Zealand

February 12. After a very hot day in Brisbane, a tropical rain fell in the evening and the air became more bearable. At 6:00 a.m. we flew off to New Zealand, stopping at Sydney for several hours. We were accompanied to Sydney by Msgr. Jaroszka. At the airport we were awaited by priests of the Society of Christ with their Australian Provincial, Fr. Jozcf Kolodzicj. Wc concelebrated a Holy Mass in a church close to the airport, thanks to the kind hospitality of the pastor and his assistant.

We arrived in Wellington about 3:00 p.m. (4 a.m. European time). At the airport we were met by Msgr. William J. Heavey, Vicar General of Cardinal McKeefrey, who was absent because of the Episcopal Conference, by Polish consul general Mr. Czapiga with his wife (he was also present at the farewell on February 14), and Mr. Mikolaj Polaczuk, director of the Polonia pastoral council. In the waiting room, children were singing "Plynie Wisla, plynie {The Vistula flows},"[11] and immediately, at this first meeting, a family atmosphere had been created. For a moment we were occupied by television and the press, which published news of our visit in the next editions.

Our countrymen prepared lodging in a hotel called "The Lodge," and from there, in the evening (at 7:30 p.m.), we went to a truly familial gathering at the Polish Home. The Church in Wellington was represented by the aforementioned Msgr. Heavey, who, my countrymen said, was their sincere friend. He spoke in the first group of speakers, which also included the president of the local Association of Poles, the president of the Polish Combatants {Veterans} Association, and Fr. Wladyslaw Lisik, of the Society of Christ, the local pastor of Polonia. I was asked to speak after dinner; before that, the Polish youth gave a splendid demonstration of national dances, and a men's chorus (the president called them the "nightingales of Wellington") created an appropriate atmosphere among the assembled guests.

Then I spoke, relating my remarks to the prayer in which we ask "bless this meal" — and I spoke of everything that our emigrants suffered in the past, on their trek through Siberia and Persia, on all the wartime fronts, in German labor camps. I also spoke of what a spiritual meal it was, is and will be to maintain contact with our Polish heritage, with Poland and her thousand-year bond with Christianity. My preparation for this meeting and this address was provided by my conversations with Sr. Monika Aleksandrowicz, a Grey Ursuline in Warsaw, who had worked in New Zealand for over a dozen years, and by the interesting book by Krystyna Skwarko titled *The Settlement of Polish Youth in New Zealand in 1944* (the author herself was present at this meeting at the Polish Home). The fortunes of these orphans were indeed unique, and now they form the basis of the Polish community. From their group comes Fr. Bronislaw Wegrzyn, a priest in the Wellington archdiocese, who helps Fr. Lisik in the pastoral care of Polonia. After the speeches, we established a series of individual contacts and conversations. The people recalled their native land, their families in Poland, and asked me to relay greetings to them, etc.

February 13. In the morning we paid a visit to the Mayor of Wellington, Mr. Francis Kitts; in the afternoon we saw the Premier of the

---

[11] A Polish folk song

New Zealand government, Mr. Norman Kirk, at the parliament buildings. I took the opportunity to present to him a medallion for the 900th anniversary of St. Stanislaw, while in return I received a symbolic shepherd's staff, a work of folk art crafted by the local inhabitants. Concerning these inhabitants, the ancient Maoris have intermingled with the newcomers from Europe, mostly Anglo-Saxons. Catholics make up about 20% of the population; this includes the Polish community, which is taken to be around 3000. The majority of them came after the Second World War. However, an earlier wave of immigration, primarily from Pomorze[12] arrived here back in the times of Kulturkampf.[13] In actuality, Polonia is made up primarily of those who came after 1944, and their children. They strive to bring these children up in the traditions of their homeland, and they take care to teach the Polish language, as I could ascertain during an afternoon visit to the Polish Home where I met a group of youth from the Saturday Polish schools of Wellington and Petone. The meeting was organized by the parents' committee and the teachers. The program was truly moving: recitations, enactments, a Christmas pageant. Young mouths correctly, although with some difficulty, pronounce Polish words and sing Polish melodies. I spoke briefly, and then we talked in small groups, we had a snack, we took pictures which the people wish to keep or to send to their relatives in Poland as souvenirs of this meeting.

At 7:30 p.m., the most important meeting with the Polonia of New Zealand took place, at a Mass at the Church of Our Lady on Boulcott Street. It should be stressed that the local clergy and religious sisters turned out in large numbers to participate in a concelebrated Mass in Polish. Msgr. Heavey led the liturgical greeting, and then he spoke, to which I answered with a few words of English before the homily. My homily was tailored to the liturgical texts for the Feast of Our Lady Queen of Poland. It touched upon the most crucial moments of our Christian spirituality, through which we meet and recognize our communion despite the distances of space and time that separate us.

After the Mass, our New Zealand hosts received us at the rectory. Conversation with all the participants of a get-together proceeded much better at a stand-up meal.

February 14. Wednesday. At 9:00 a.m. I said a Mass (concelebrated) at the Church of St. Joseph, where Polonia normally gathers for liturgy. In my homily I tried to point out the fundamental meaning of faith and its apostolic propagation. At the same time, Bishop Szczepan said a Mass at another Polish center, at the Church of St. Peter and St. Paul in Lower Hutt.

Then we went to visit the sick: first to the hospital, where Polish veterans of World War II are being treated, then to private homes. Here I met the deserving long-time teachers of Polish, to whom Poland and Polonia owes a debt no smaller than that owed to the heroic soldiers. I told them so — and I wish to bring back to Poland the memories of these moving encounters. Thank God that the personnel of the hospital and the charity section of the Pastoral Council maintains such constant care over these Polish men and women who are so worn out by life and hard work.

The farewell dinner at the Polish Home at 1:00 p.m., gathered together not only the most active group of Polonia, but also distinguished guests,

---

12 Pomerania, on the Baltic coast
13 Kulturkampf — in the 19th C., Bismarck's forced germanization of Polish territories occupied by Prussia in the partitions of Poland.

both secular and clerical (among others, Bishop John Patrick Kavanagh), who have been connected with our immigrants for a long time and have shown them much good will. It was pleasant to hear that they hold the Polish nation in high regard. It was pleasant to learn that in order to better understand the Polish spirit, they read the words of Mickiewicz in English translation. I thanked them once again and promised to take all of this back to Poland, and repeat it there. We ended with song, taking turn singing in Polish and English. The last group photo was taken with the deserving hostesses of the dinner.

The time had come to say farewell to this beautiful mountainous land at the antipode of Europe. The plane for Sydney was leaving at 4:45 p.m. New Zealand time. With this stage of the journey, we are starting to get closer to Europe, to Rome and to Krakow, although this is but the first small step (still, about 2500 km). New Zealand is the farthest from Poland — it makes no difference if we were to come here going east or west. Maybe that is why the Poles here experienced this visit so warmly. They gave evidence of this throughout the whole stay, and it was even more evident at the farewell at the airport. During the boarding of the plane, and later, until the departure, they never left the roof of the airport building, and bade us farewell by waving their arms. In closing, it is necessary to express special gratitude to all of the organizers of this visit, especially the Polish Pastoral Council headed by Mr. Mikolaj Polaczuk. Detailed information in this matter is contained in a special communique which is being submitted for the records.

Sydney

February 14. At about 7:00 p.m. (9:00 a.m. European time) we land in Sydney — the largest city in Australia, with about 2.6 million inhabitants. It is also the seat of an archdiocese of about 750 thousand Catholics. Archbishop James Darcy Freeman, who is to be made cardinal at the next consistory on March 5, waited for us at the airport. With him is a group of Australian and Polish priests, including Msgr. Witold Dzieciol, Rector of the Polish mission, and Fr. Jozef Kolodziej, the Provincial in Australia of the Society of Christ. There is also Mr. Malczyk, Consul General, and Consul Janusz Chomeniuk. This official greeting is followed by the mandatory press conference, and only then — a meeting with the large group of our countrymen. The hallways are lined with ranks of scouts, and the reception hall has room for several hundred people. Msgr. Dzieciol speaks, the children present flowers, I respond by bringing greetings from Poland and I propose that we sing something together. Everyone spontaneously begins the hymn "God, who hath protected Poland." Then various groups and individuals approach to establish closer contact or to ask about someone they know. Slowly we leave the airport.

Cardinal Freeman invited us to live at his home, so we prepared to stay the night, but first we spent the time before bedtime on conversation with our hospitable host. Our schedule for the following day called for beginning our activities at about 10:30 a.m., and we had meetings in several different points of the very extensive city. Most of our time will be spent on getting around.

February 15. First we went to the house of the Sisters who take care of the aged. Among others, we met a woman who was 97 years old, and who had last been to Poland in 1905. There was a separate house for retired priests. Here also, in separate quarters, lives Cardinal Thomas Norman

Gilroy, the former Archbishop of Sydney. At that time, however, the Cardinal had to go to the hospital, so the planned visit could not take place. But, again, some time was spent at a press conference.

From the Sisters' house we went to the priests of the Society of Christ, who occupy a small house in the Bankstown district. From there, a good hour of driving to the most important meeting of the day, in Marayong. There, the Sisters of the Holy Family of Nazareth had for a long time operated an orphanage. A Polish church of original design, under the title of Our Lady Queen of Poland, was built on their land during the year of the Millennium. It was dedicated by Cardinal Gilroy in 1966. The image of the Blessed Virgin is a gift of the Primate of Poland, and it was blessed by Pope John XXIII. In this church, located just outside of the city, the Poles from Sydney and the whole state meet for their celebrations. They also met on this day, coming not only from the various parts of this great city, but also from other cities of New South Wales. That is the name of this state on the Australian continent.

The concelebrated Mass began at 6:00 p.m., after a liturgical greeting and the customary words of welcome from the children and from Fr. W. Michalski, a priest from the congregation of Sons of Divine Providence. The sermon after the Mass, on the subject "man lives not by bread alone, but by every word that comes from the mouth of God," emphasized the primacy of God's wisdom and God's law in the life of nations, in the face of materialism spreading under various guises. Coming from the Cathedral of Wawel, I also made reference to the 900th anniversary of St. Stanislaw. The effort to ensure that spiritual values are given appropriate importance in our lives is dedicated, by both the Polish Church and our countrymen in Australia, to the Mother of the Word Incarnate, whom we venerate as the Queen of Poland.

The meeting in Marayong had a second part, in which there were two speeches and a series of songs sung by choirs of adults and children. Because it had been raining, this part of the program was held inside the church, but then everyone went outside to see the folk dances splendidly performed by the local youth. In this fashion, our get-together lasted until 10:00 p.m.. We ended by singing the hymns "All Our Matters of Today" and the "Promises of Jasna Gora." The atmosphere was very warm and intimate. On our way out, we were obliged to exchange words and memories with many of our countrymen.

February 16. In the morning, after a concelebrated Mass at the residence of the Archbishop of Sydney, we went to visit Polish Homes in three different cities which lie within the area of greater Sydney. The first was Parramatta, the second Bankstown, the third Ashfield. All of these homes are centers of Polish culture. Polish social and religious organizations are located there, and children and the youth come to learn the language and history in so-called "Saturday schools." The priests maintain close contact with these centers. They provide their countrymen not only with pastoral care, but also help to maintain the spirit of Polish nationality. On Sundays they say Masses at their respective parish churches. In free moments they hear confessions and visit the sick in homes and hospitals. They systematically visit all of the faithful in their parishes, and they teach the children the truths of the faith and Christian morals in the Saturday schools.

All the meetings were very cordial, although each one had a somewhat different character because of the different social contexts. In Parramatta, the pastor of the Australian parish came to the meeting. In Bankstown, the meeting was very official. It began in the chamber of the city council, where the local mayor spoke, emphasizing the merits of Poles as citizens of his city, where they represent about 10% of the population. Then we all went to the Polish Home for its opening and blessing. In Ashfield — which was the first settlement of Poles in Sydney — I visited both the Polish Home and a club, also accompanied by the mayor. Everywhere, of course, there were speeches of welcome, to which I tried to respond in Polish or English, as appropriate.

At 2:00 p.m. it was necessary to fly from Sydney to Canberra. Before leaving Sydney, however, I would like to give the names of all the Polish priests who participated in the meetings and, above all, who celebrated the evening Mass at Marayong with me. They are the ones who tirelessly fulfill their pastoral duties among our countrymen, helping to maintain faith and the Polish language and culture. The group of priests working in the area of Sydney (New South Wales) is made up, first of all, of the priests of the Society of Christ: Fr. Jozef Kolodziej, the Australian provincial; Fr. Stanislaw Marut, Fr. Andrzej Duczkowski, Fr. Miroslaw Chlebowicz and Fr. Jan Westfal from Newcastle; also the priests from the congregation of Sons of Divine Providence: Fr. Wlodzimierz Michalski, Fr. Stanislaw Antoniewicz, and Fr. Artur Staroborski, a Franciscan.

During my visit on Australian soil, beginning with my arrival in Sydney, I was accompanied by Msgr. Witold Dzieciol, who is the rector of the Polish mission in Australia.

Canberra

Canberra owes its rapid growth in recent years (up to 160 thousand inhabitants) to the fact that it was chosen to be the capital of the nation and the federal government. It is a city beautifully situated against the mountains, on a lake, amid rich greenery. It is modern and dynamic, but at the same time very peaceful. Archbishop Thomas Cahill, whom I knew personally from the Synod of Bishops, especially as a member of the Council of the General Secretariat to which we were both elected in 1971, hosted us very warmly in his see, from the moment of our arrival until the end. Here, too, we were guests at the Archbishop's house, where Fr. Miroslaw Gebicki of the Society of Christ, the pastor of Polonia in Canberra, has been living for a year.

Besides this, the federal government was plainly trying to make its presence felt during the Polish celebration, receiving us with a dinner at the parliament building. The following day, Saturday, February 17, a solemn session was to be held in Melbourne, with the participation of the Prime Minister of Australia and numerous representatives of the scientific community, to observe the 500th anniversary of the birth of Mikolaj Kopernik {Nicholas Copernicus}. Bishop Szczepan Wesoly went to the session in Melbourne, where Prof. Jerzy Zubrzycki and Prof. Przybylski of the University of Canberra were to make presentations, but I remained in Canberra to continue my meeting with my countrymen, because the meeting could not be rescheduled.

The course of the meeting was as follows: After the ceremonial greeting at the airport where an address was given by the aforementioned Prof. Zubrzycki (a native of Krakow), and where children, in the company of their parents, recited poems, sang songs and presented flowers, we went to the archbishop's residence. Then we partook of the hospitality at the

Parliament buildings after which we participated in the ceremonial opening and dedication of the Polish Home, which was named by the local White Eagle Club as Mikolaj Kopernik Home. In this fashion, the Polish celebrations in Canberra tied into the all-Australian celebrations in honor of our countryman. I blessed the house in the presence of Archbishop Cahill and representatives of the civil authorities. I integrated my address into the program of the evening, which included many other speeches, choral performances, and piano music. Toward the end, a more familiar and friendly atmosphere prevailed, and we — the whole assemblage — began to sing patriotic and religious songs, and to get to know one another better.

February 17. Saturday. At 9:00 a.m., I said Mass at the new cathedral of St. Christopher. The cathedral had been consecrated 2 weeks before, and the Archdiocese of Canberra has existed for only 25 years. Poles came in great numbers with their color guards, scouts, the youth and children in national costumes. In my homily I tried to emphasize the meaning of faith in human life, both individual and social. After all, faith carries with it a conviction that our existence has a meaning and purpose, that there is ultimate order in the world, that good conquers evil, regardless of how powerful that evil might seem to be in the temporal world. I made reference to Blessed Maximilian, our countryman, and I stressed that the Church, which provides her children with the gift of faith, gives them, like a good mother, a fundamental treasure, even if she could not give anything else. In this, the Church imitates the Mother of God. Our Motherland, where Mary has been venerated for so many centuries, has integrated its earthly maternal role with the whole tradition of Christian culture, which also accompanies its children when they emigrate.

Before noon of the same day we were received in the home of the SPK (Polish Combatants {Veterans} Association), where after a speech by the president, the scouts presented their artistic program. In response, I emphasized the contributions of Polish soldiers during the last war, and in reference to the activities of the local scout troop, I mentioned the contributions that scouting makes to the patriotic and religious upbringing of our youth. Then there were meetings and conversations with individual participants, photographs and group singing. A special memento of this meeting was a statue of the Blessed Mother for the church in Nowa Huta. "We have chewed on a lot of steel in our day, and some of us still carry it inside," said the president. "May this statue, cast from those fragments, be our gift for the church in Nowa Huta."

After lunch in the hospitable home of Archbishop Cahill, I visited one more Polish center in Queanbeyan. The course of this visit was similar to that in Canberra. Our countrymen have almost finished their Polish Home, where they gather for social activities aimed at maintaining their Polish heritage through organizations, a Saturday school of Polish, and various events. Fr. Gebicki helps them in this, commuting in to say Mass and provide other pastoral services.

From there we went directly to the airport to fly to Melbourne. The archbishop and numerous countrymen came also. We made farewells very warmly.

February 17. At 6:30 p.m. I arrived in Melbourne, the city of the 40th International Eucharistic Congress on the Australian continent. The host of the Congress, Archbishop James Robert Knox, who is to be made cardinal at the next consistory, was waiting at the airport. Besides, there was a large contingent of local Polonia with their pastors; boy scouts and girl scouts form a guard of honor. First we go to the reception salon, then to the car, which is being driven by Mr. Zarzycki. It was he who organized the trip to Australia and made all of the airline connections. Our place of residence in Melbourne during the Congress is the Polish Pastoral Center headed by Fr. Jozef Janus S.J. Here we will live and from here we will participate in the various activities of the Congress which have been planned out to the smallest detail. The full documentation is waiting on the desk in my room. The program of the Congress is very rich and varied.

February 18. Sunday. The solemn inauguration of the Congress takes place at the Cathedral of St. Patrick at 3:00 p.m.. I participate with the other cardinals and bishops; we take our places in the sanctuary. The majority are representatives of the Church from this geographic region, but there are also Europeans. Cardinal Slipyj, Cardinal Willebrands, Cardinal Oddi are here. The second group is formed by the American cardinals: Cardinal Cody from Chicago, Cardinal Cooke from New York (who came only for the end of the Congress), there is, of course, Cardinal Shehan as the Papal legate, and also Cardinal Wright, although he came from Rome as the Prefect of the Congregation for the Clergy. As far as the cardinals from the Far East, those taking part in the Congress were: Cardinal Cooray of Ceylon, Cardinal Darmojuwono from Indonesia, Cardinal Kim from Korea (Seoul), and Cardinal Yu Pin from Taiwan; Cardinal Rosales came from the Philippines (Cebu), Cardinal McKeefry from New Zealand; from Africa: Cardinal Rugambwa and the Cardinal-elect from Kenya, Archbishop Otunga of Nairobi. And, of course, both Cardinals-elect from Australia, Archbishop Freeman of Sydney and Archbishop Knox of Melbourne. The previous Archbishop of Sydney, Cardinal Gilroy, could not attend the Congress because of illness. I have named just the cardinals; the archbishops and bishops formed a much more numerous group. In any case, as one from Poland, I was an unusual guest. Nevertheless, my presence with Bishop Szczepan Wesoly in Australia finds full justification if one considers the Polish community in Australia, which I am concurrently visiting.

The opening ceremony itself was quite brief. After the salvos and fanfares of the military, Cardinal Lawrence Shehan, the Archbishop of Baltimore, USA, the special legate of the Holy Father, entered the cathedral accompanied by the Archbishop of Melbourne. After a short adoration of the Blessed Sacrament, they took their seats. The notary of the Archdiocesan Curia read the letter of the Holy Father to Cardinal Shehan naming him the legate to the Congress. Then Archbishop Knox gave a short address welcoming the legate, the representatives of the Australian authorities, and the guests. The Papal legate spoke third, pointing out the significance of the Eucharistic Congress which was beginning.

After the speeches, the assembly sang *Veni Creator* and the deacon solemnly read the Gospel of St. John 15:5-12, in which the words: "Love one another, as I have loved you" can be found. These words were chosen as the motto of the Congress. Then the assembly led by the Cardinal-legate, sang the beautiful prayer of the faithful, ending with the words of the Our Father. We shared the kiss of peace, and the legate blessed us all. The cardinals and bishops left the church singing a Eucharistic hymn, as in Rome, to the applause of the congregation.

That same day I said two Masses for our countrymen, tying the subject of the homilies to the opening of the Congress. I said the first Mass at 12:00 noon at the Church of St. Ignatius, connected directly with the Polish Pastoral Center run by the Jesuits (Fr. J. Janus). I said the second Mass at the parish church in the district of Yarraville at 7:00 p.m., for our countrymen living in that district and the neighboring parishes. The pastor at this second location is Fr. Marcin Chrostowski, a Dominican. After Mass I participated in a meeting which took place in the Polish Home. The program consisted of speeches by the President of the Polish Alliance and by Fr. Chrostowski, and of some very good singing by the children of the Saturday school. This reminded me of the expression by one of the poets about the heart that beats, and in which there is Poland — and I made a reference to this in my address. The conclusion was a walk around the room to engage in conversation, and then a get-together at the table.

Visit to Poles in Tasmania —Hobart

February 19. One day of the Congress week, namely Monday, February 19, was dedicated to a visit to Poles in Hobart, the capital of Tasmania. The history of the Polish community on this island south of Australia began after the Second World War, when soldiers of the Carpathian Brigade came to Tasmania. Here, after demobilization, they had to begin a new hard life. Later, other Poles came from Germany, and from the East.[14] Slowly they established themselves, and thanks to excellent organization, cooperation and solidarity, they achieved their present state of ownership. Here I speak not so much of the ownership by individuals or families, but of the entire Polonia. Extremely well-organized, the Polonia not only maintains a Polish school that has a significant enrollment of children and youth, not only has bought its third home for its social activities, but also serves its community members by a well-functioning credit union through which many people have been able to purchase property or to rebuild. (It should be noted that several years ago a forest fire destroyed a series of houses belonging to our countrymen near Hobart.) There is close cooperation between the organizations and the pastoral work of the Church, which for several years has been led by Fr. Franciszek Feruga, of the Society of Christ, who has earned the full respect of his countrymen.

From Melbourne I traveled by plane to Hobart and arrived there at about 10:30 a.m. At the airport I was greeted by a large number of Poles, among whom a group of scouts was most prominent. After the initial presentations and greetings, I had to dedicate a few minutes to the local television, after which we went to the rectory of St. Theresa Parish, where we were to stay. Dinner at 2:00 p.m. was an opportunity to get to know the main representatives of the Polish organizations. An extensive speech, from which I learned the most about the life of the Poles here, was given by Mr. Kowaluk, the current President of the Polish Alliance in Hobart. Other speakers supplemented his information, especially with regards to the Polonia of Launceston. In response, I told them how much the accomplishments of Polonia here tell me about the characteristics and abilities of our nation.

After dinner we had an opportunity to drive to the summit of Mt.

---

[14] "The East" — a common euphemism for the Soviet Union, since it was not advisable to mention by name the place that so many wanted to leave.

Wellington by car (!), to talk with the local Australian pastor and with the Pastoral Council. Archbishop Young, who was away at the Eucharistic Congress, has gained a reputation among the Poles of a pastor who is sympathetic and dedicated to them.

During a concelebrated Mass at 7:30 p.m., I had an opportunity to confer the Sacrament of Confirmation on 34 young members of the Polish community. My homily was on that subject. Participation in the Eucharist was full; probably the whole church came to the Table of the Lord {received Communion}.

After Mass, another meeting in the Polish Home. The program included not only the performance of a choir, but also a well-acted play especially written for this occasion by Ms. Jackiewicz. It appears that our countrymen in Hobart have not only organizational talents, but artistic ones as well. Unfortunately it was late, and we had to part although there was so much more to say. The plane for Melbourne was leaving at 7:00 the next morning; the night of rest would not be very long. Still, the next morning a sizable group of our countrymen assembled at the airport. I left Hobart (February 20) with the most favorable memories.

February 20. On this day at 10:40 a.m., I attended the solemn meeting organized for the guests of the Congress by the Australian authorities, the authorities of both the State of Victoria and the City of Melbourne, at the National Gallery of Victoria. Speeches were given by the Premier, the Mayor, the Cardinal - legate and, in the name of the pilgrims, a woman representing the laity from outside of Australia. After the speeches, there was half an hour for socializing. The event was concluded by fanfares and a performance by the Sistine Choir from St. Peter's Basilica in Rome.

In the evening, at 8:00 p.m., we concelebrated a Mass with the Cardinal-legate at the great stadium, the Melbourne Cricket Ground. This Mass was intended for the various ethnic groups that live in Australia, among them the Poles. To get an idea of the origins of these groups, it is sufficient to say that the first liturgical reading was in Italian, the second in Polish, the responsorial psalm in Dutch, French, Croatian and Maltese, while the prayer of the faithful was said in: Chinese, German, Maronite, Melkhite, Lithuanian, Latvian, Czech, Russian, Slovak, Slovenian, Ukrainian, Spanish, Hungarian, Irish and Portuguese. Australia is a huge country of immigrants. Accordingly, the celebrating bishops came from various countries and various continents, and the homilist, Bishop Thomas, touched upon the fundamental problems, not only of a spiritual and pastoral nature, but also of a social one, that are related to the rights of immigrants on Australian soil.

At the offertory, representatives of various groups, in their national costumes, presented gifts to the celebrant. It was, at the same time, a wonderful esthetic experience.

The same day at 3:00 p.m. there was a concelebrated Mass for the youth at the Church of St. Ignatius. The main celebrant was Bishop Szczepan Wesoly, while I gave the sermon touching upon the Eucharistic Congress and the anniversary of Copernicus. After Mass we went to the parish hall for a meeting with the teachers and children of the Polish schools. Elementary and secondary grades teach about 700 students, many of whom are the children of the second generation outside of Poland. They will build the future of Polonia. Just as was the case many times before, here again, a group of scouts participated very actively in the meeting.

February 21. Wednesday. After a private concelebrated morning Mass at the Church of St. Ignatius, I made my way to the Cathedral of St. Patrick. We were invited to participate in the consecration of three new auxiliary bishops of the Archdiocese of Melbourne. The main celebrant was Cardinal-elect, Archbishop Knox. The entire Episcopate of Australia and the Papal Delegate, Archbishop Gino Paro, participated in the consecration. Everyone concelebrated and everyone participated in the laying on of hands. A very exalted and profound liturgy.

In the evening of the same day, at 8:00 p.m., I led a paraliturgical service at the Parish of St. Albans on the outskirts of the city. The service had the character of the liturgy of the word (or what we call a biblical hour); the main accent was on the need for renewal in the spirit of social charity (renewal of Christian life). Services of this type took place at the same time in various parishes of Melbourne (as "ecumenical services"). My presence at St. Albans was due to the fact that a large portion of the parish community is made up of Poles, and their pastoral director is Fr. Marian Laban, is a priest of the Society of the Divine Word. That is why, in addition to the English texts prescribed by the formula of the liturgy, I spoke to them in Polish, and at the end, the local pastor himself invoked the singing of the hymn "God, who hath protected Poland." I should add that this liturgy, which, like the Holy Mass, consists of three readings interwoven with singing, was concluded by a blessing with the Blessed Sacrament in a monstrance.

After the service I met with my countrymen in the parish hall. There was much singing. As in many other places, they asked me to convey greetings to the Primate and the whole Episcopate.

February 22. Thursday. We went to St. Patrick's Cathedral for 10:30 a.m. to concelebrate a Mass with the Cardinal-legate for the intention of priests (clergy renewal). The Mass was concelebrated by the cardinals, bishops and several hundred priests. After the homily, delivered by the Archbishop of Melbourne, there was a renewal of the vows of priesthood. During the canon I stood between Cardinal Wright and Cardinal Kim of Korea and I pronounced the words of the prayer for the deceased. I must repeat my observations from yesterday's consecration of the new bishops: a profound liturgy, the experience of the Eucharist as an offering and a repast, as a gift and a source of priestly responsibility.

At 8:00 p.m. we gathered at the Cricket Ground to participate in an ecumenical service. The leaders were the Cardinal-legate, Cardinal Knox, the Archbishop of Melbourne, Cardinal Willebrands, representatives of other Christian churches and communities, including — the Anglican Archbishop of Melbourne, who is the Primate of the Anglican Church in Australia. The content of this service, which was not only a prayer for the unification of Christians but also a kind of paraphrase of a Christian supper (agape), celebrated in mindful memory of those who are hungry and in need, deserves its own detailed analysis. In any case, we recited the Apostle's Creed together, having first renewed our baptismal promises. The homily, or rather a commentary, was given twice; the first speaker was Lukas Visher, the second, Cardinal Willebrands.

On the same day, at 6:00 p.m., I was a guest at the Polish Home where representatives of Polish organizations gathered in great numbers. Unfortunately, because of the ecumenical service planned for 8:00 p.m., the meeting and dinner had to be kept brief. As I delivered my address with those constraints in mind. I tried to characterize our common relationship to our homeland which must unite all of us Poles no matter where we find ourselves.

February 23. Friday. In the program of the Congress, this was a day of the youth. We did not go to the morning Mass at the Cricket Ground held for the boys and girls who are students of Catholic schools (There were, reportedly, 150 thousand). After a morning concelebrated Mass at St. Ignatius, we drove out of the city to visit a place that serves as a summer camp for the Polish youth and the children of Melbourne. This place is called "Polana."[15] Nearby there is a so-called Sanctuary, i.e. a large park, where one can encounter free-ranging animals (especially kangaroos) and birds of Australia. You can even have your picture taken with them. The hospitable Fr. Janus and Mr. Zarzycki made this visit possible for us, too.

At 8:30 p.m. we participated in a Mass at Meyer's Music Bowl. Before Mass, there were performances by groups which, in our terms, would be called beat groups, but of a different variety than in Poland. Those who know such things could compare this Mass to the Polish Mass by Katarzyna Gartner. In any case, this youthful style is well-known to us from our academic apostolate and from sacrosongs.[16] It appears that contemporary youth share a common language which transcends latitude and longitude. I noticed that during this Mass for the youth, Communion was given as we do, on the tongue, not in the hand. The homily was carefully calculated to establish contact with this very particular auditorium.

February 24. Saturday. Blessing of the shrine of Our Lady Queen of Poland in Essendon, Melbourne. This celebration drew Poles not only from Melbourne but also from other cities and communities. Many Polish priests and sisters came. The shrine is located on grounds neighboring the house of the Sisters of the Resurrection, who run a school here. The Archdiocese of Melbourne was represented by Bishop John Cullinane, while the City of Essendon by its Mayor (Essendon is a separate city but also a part of Melbourne).

The Poles in Australia decided to build the shrine of Our Lady Queen of Poland in Melbourne, just as they built the church in Marayong (Sydney)for the Millennium, i.e. in commemoration of the visitation of the Blessed Mother which united them spiritually. A committee was formed, our countrymen pitched in, Msgr. L. Jaroszka brought a copy of the image of Jasna Gora from Rome. It was blessed by Pope Paul VI during an audience in 1970 for Polish priests who were prisoners of concentration camps. At the moment the shrine is unfinished. It will take much effort and sacrifices to be completed. Our countrymen, however, are full of zeal and energy.

I celebrated the Mass during the dedication of the church together with Bishop Szczepan and Msgr. Dzieciol. During the Mass I preached a sermon in which I spoke about how their work to build this church should be accompanied by work to build their own spiritual interior. After the ceremony in the church and a meal at the Sisters', there was a get-together with a solemn program (a choir from Geelong sang) and speeches. And after this program, an unscheduled series of encounters, conversations, autographing of paintings, pictures and books. An atmosphere of true community.

---

[15] "Forest clearing"
[16] Festivals of sacred song

The meeting in Essendon stretched out so much that we did not make it to the aborigine Mass scheduled for 3:00 p.m.. Bishop Szczepan and the priests went to the Mass in the Byzantine rite at 8:00 p.m.

February 25. Sunday. Ordination of priests and conclusion of the Congress.

The celebration which we experienced in Essendon on Saturday February 24 was complemented by the ordination of priests at the Church of St. Ignatius (Richmond) on Sunday. On that day, at 12:00 noon, Fr. Wieslaw Slowik and Fr. Leonard Kiesch, two deacons from the Society of Jesus, were ordained to the priesthood. They entered the order in Poland and belonged to the Malopolska province of SJ. Upon the petition of Fr. Jozef Janus, a priest who made great contributions to Polish pastoral ministry in Melbourne (he came here shortly after the end of the war), they were both sent from Poland to Australia as seminarians. Here they continued their studies, here they were ordained to the diaconate, and, at the same time, entered the Polish community and became familiar with its problems. In this way, they were prepared for their pastoral work among the people here.

The ordination drew a large number of Poles to St. Ignatius Church. Also present were representatives of the order, the local provincial of The Society of Jesus, a Jesuit bishop who was a native of Slovakia, a Pallotine bishop (a German born in Wroclaw and working in the missions) and many other confreres of the newly-ordained. We celebrated the Mass in Polish, and the ordination was also conducted in our native tongue. I preached a sermon during the Mass, and the two new priests spoke before the final blessing, one in Polish, the other in English.

The priesthood is intimately tied to the Eucharist. That is why this ordination, on the day of the closing of the Eucharistic Congress in Melbourne, was so timely.

The same day, at 6:00 p.m., at the great stadium of the Melbourne Cricket Ground, the last Mass of the Congress was celebrated. All of the cardinals present at the Congress concelebrated it with the Papal legate, who gave the homily. Before the blessing, we heard the voice of the Holy Father, who spoke to the participants from Rome, stressing the great importance of the Congress in view of the problems of the modern world. On that day, the crowd at Cricket Ground was larger than at any other celebration so far. This last Eucharistic meeting of the Congress of Melbourne was given the name "Statio orbis."

After the end of the celebration there was a short visit in the home of the Archbishop of Melbourne to thank, congratulate and bid farewell to the host of the Congress. It was 9:00 p.m., on Sunday February 25, when we left his home in Racheen.

February 26. Monday. All the Polish priests gathered in Essendon, taking advantage of the hospitality of the Sisters of the Resurrection. We celebrated a Holy Mass in the chapel (it was not possible to do it in the church, because further construction started right after the dedication). I gave a homily during this Mass, which was attended by the Sisters and a large number of our countrymen. After Mass and a few photographs together, we began a pastoral conference. Msgr. Dzieciol, rector of the Polish mission (the recognition of this institution by the Australian Episcopate is pending), presented the state of pastoral work as conducted by Polish priests in Australia. A several hour-long discussion ensued, during which I tried to present the activities of the Church in Poland, while Bishop Szczepan Wesoly formulated the main issues of pastoral work among Poles abroad. After the conference I was still able to spend some time with the hospitable Sisters of the Resurrection.

At 7:20 p.m. we went to Geelong. This is an industrial city (population about 100 thousand) within the Archdiocese of Melbourne, located on the shore of the ocean, and is home to about 3000 Poles. Their pastoral minister is Msgr. Lucjan Jaroszka, a priest from the Diocese of Lodz, who came to Australia after release from a concentration camp. Our countrymen are guests in a large Church of Our Lady. Here, every Sunday, they participate in a Mass in their native language, and hold other liturgies like the Way of the Cross and "Gorzkie Zale" services {Lamentations} during Lent. There is a copy of the image of Our Lady of Czestochowa here (earlier, there was an image of Our Lady of Perpetual Help) before which the Poles most often pray.

Bishop Szczepan celebrated a solemn Mass, while I preached a sermon, in which I referred to the Eucharistic Congress and the dedication of the shrine of Our Lady in Essendon. Before Mass, an address was given by Msgr. Leo Morris Clarke, the local pastor, who is also dean and Vicar General, very friendly to Poles. After Mass I stopped in front of the church for a while for conversation with my countrymen. Children recited poems and presented flowers, and veteran soldiers asked me to bless their colors. Besides Msgr. Jaroszka, two other retired priests, Fr. Karol Warzecha and Fr. Feliks Wozniczak, live here in the home of the Wojcik family. Their hosts asked me to dinner. It was one more chance to meet my countrymen here. Around 11:00 p.m. we returned to our lodgings on Richmond in Melbourne.

A look at the entire Congress.

In ending these notes, it should be mentioned that they do not exhaust the entirety of the Eucharistic Congress in Melbourne nor do they give the full picture of this event. Personally, I could participate in only a small part of the extensive and multi-faceted program of the Congress, because, at the same time, I was intent on fulfilling the duties to my countrymen and to the Polish apostolate, connected with my stay in Australia. That is why I feel the need to supplement these notes and to give a more complete look at the entirety of the Eucharistic Congress in Melbourne.

By its nature, a Eucharistic Congress is a unique experience of the Eucharist, which expresses the faith and love of the entire Church, but which is also saturated with the local elements typical for the place and society in which the Congress is held. That is how it must have been at all the previous congresses, and that is how it was in Melbourne. Many times I thought to myself, that if a Eucharistic Congress took place in Poland, it would have to have a different mode of expression than the Australian one.

If we look at the entire program, even if it was not possible to participate in all of it, we see what guiding principles the organizers adopted and what leading thoughts they wanted to get across. The Catholic Church in Australia congregates about 3 million inhabitants of that country or, on average, 25% of the population. This ratio varies in the different states and different dioceses, but overall that is the average. The majority of the population are Christians belonging to churches and denominations which came out of the Reformation, with Anglicans in the forefront. There are also several hundred thousand natives. If we follow the program of the

Congress, we must notice a very strong ecumenical accent. This accent was already visible in the week of preparation (February 11 to 18), and even more strongly during the week of the Congress itself. The Aboriginal Mass, meaning the liturgy celebrated in the language and style of the first Australians, was the part of the program tailored to this segment of society.

This ecumenical theme of the Congress, which was very strongly emphasized, was connected with a second theme, also very prominent, which contained several topics and issues of importance to the Church in Australia. These topics could be related to the constitution on the Church in the modern world promulgated by the Second Vatican Council and to the activities of the committee Iustitia et Pax. We must not forget that Australian society is an affluent society, but it lives in close proximity to the third world, especially India. Therefore, the presence of Mother Teresa of Calcutta was very significant; her congregation is actively involved in the problems of the poverty of that society. The program of the Eucharistic Congress included such topics as the Church in the face of change and the future; action for world development, population and ecology; the theology of liberation. These were the topics of conferences and symposia (among others, one on "St. Thomas and the Eucharist"), seminars and meetings. But these same topics were also clearly emphasized during the individual liturgical and paraliturgical gatherings. Thus, for example, the gifts at the offertory were presented with the most needy in mind.

It appears that this theme, along with the theme of ecumenism, made up the primary content of the renewal of the Melbourne Archdiocese in the individual parishes and communities of the Church there. The idea of renewal is taken from the Vatican Council. The organizers made reference primarily to the documents on ecumenism and the contemporary world. It was evident that the Congress took place within the first and the third circle of dialogue conducted by the contemporary Church, as we read in Pope Paul VI's encyclical *Ecclesiam suam*.

While not ignoring this opening to the outside (ad extra), even giving it wide exposure in the program of the Congress, the organizers also concentrated sufficient attention upon the Eucharist as a sacrament which shapes the Church internally (ad intra). In this regard, the Eucharistic Congress in Melbourne gave us a thorough look at the life of the Church in Melbourne, and indirectly, in Australia. There was a place in the Congress for the aged, the sick, the unfortunate, and also children and the youth. A special service was held for the speech and hearing impaireds. Special consideration was given to women and mothers. Among the professions, nurses were distinguished. Among apostolic groups and societies, special mention should be made of the Legion of Mary, the tertiary orders (whose conference took place under the meaningful title "Christian leadership"), the Society of St. Vincent de Paul, and the Cursillo movement. Also participating in the Congress was a very specific form of apostolate, apostolatus marus[17] (not surprising, because Australia is surrounded by the ocean). Our family apostolate and family counseling would find its equivalent in the "family-centered health care" part of the Congress. There was also a special place in the program of the Congress for scouting (scouts and guides). Activities dealing with works of charity were represented in many

---

[17] Apostolate of the Sea.

ways, also in the ecumenical sense ("carrying Christian unity").

Obviously, the program of the Eucharistic Congress had to include those who stand closest to the Eucharist. There was an item in the program dedicated to ministry at the altar (altar servers, lectors). Religious sisters and brothers were gathered in turn around the Eucharist. But, above all, much time and space was given to priests, and also future priests. During the Congress a new seminary was opened, there were ordinations of priests, priests celebrated their Eucharistic hours, and the central point of the program was the great concelebrated Mass on Thursday, as was mentioned in these notes. There was also the consecration of three bishops, which is also mentioned in this journal.

The program of the Eucharistic Congress. In its variety of themes, societies, organizations, and artistic presentations (one could see a series of exhibits, stage productions and films, hear splendid choirs, including the Sistine Choir from Rome) — tried to focus the contents of these varied elements around certain principal ideas which were expressed in a motto for each day. And so, the opening Sunday of February 18 was under the motto *The People of God*, Monday, under the motto *The Life of Christ*; Tuesday, *Personal love of Christ*. The central ideas for the following days were: Wednesday, *The compassion of Christ;* Thursday, *Unity in Christ;* Friday, *The suffering of Christ*; Saturday, *The Mother of Christ* (Mary's day); and Sunday February 25, *The peace of Christ*, with its *prayer for peace*.

As we can see, the organizers of the Congress wished that Christ, living in the Eucharist, would affect all the various areas and matters of human life. The Eucharist stood before the participants of the Congress in Melbourne as a sacrament by which the Church lives on a daily basis, through all ages; a sacrament through which the Church continues to rediscover itself, its relationship to the family of man and to all the problems afflicting that family. It could even be said that this "ecclesiastical" sense of the Eucharist (by which this Congress clearly made reference to Vatican II) somewhat outweighed its "christological" sense, i.e. the truth of Christ's presence in the Eucharist as the greatest good of the Church. It could be said that the attention of the Congress in Melbourne focused more on the Church which is seeking itself through the Eucharist, seeking the meaning of its mission, both ad intra and ad extra — and finds itself. This seemed to get more emphasis than the fact that in the Eucharist, the Church is continually finding Christ, lives in Him and surrounds Him with the highest adoration. For example, there was an almost total lack of moments of adoration of the Blessed Sacrament, which has a central significance in the tradition of Eucharistic Congresses and generally in the whole Catholic cult of the Mystery of the Altar.

The Melbourne Congress presented the Eucharist as a sacrament which shapes the Church, a sacrament which is for the Church an unceasing call to love ("Love one another as I have loved you," John 15:12 — this was the central motto of the whole Congress). The Congress told us to seek Christ primarily in this exhortation, even more than in the contemplation of His sacramental Presence.

The Church is a Missionary Church. It is everywhere and always on a mission. This was another theme of the Congress and seems to have been thoroughly incorporated into its concept. The mission of the Church was brought to the Australian continent by the representatives of older nations which had embraced Christianity for centuries. Among them are also

Poles, numbering about 100 thousand. The Church in Australia exists both in its Western, Roman form, and in the Eastern, Byzantine rite (Catholics of this rite are primarily Ukrainians, numbering about 20 thousand).

The goal is to ensure that the People of God on the fifth continent more fully participate in the love whose everyday source is the Eucharist. This certainly was the goal of the Church of Melbourne and of its pastor who invited us to the 40th International Eucharistic Congress in his city. The organizers of the Congress passed their test with high marks. We will all continue to pray for its spiritual fruits. "Because the Eucharist is the entire good of the Church..." (a quotation from the decree on the ministry and life of priests, as in my word on the Eucharist)

Adelaide
February 27. After the conclusion of the Eucharistic Congress there was one more meeting with the Polish priests in Essendon, after which, on February 27, we flew to Adelaide. We arrived after 2:00 p.m., and were met at the airport by Archbishop James William Gleeson, the local ordinary, and a large contingent of our countrymen. I know Archbishop Gleeson well from the Vatican Council; we sat close to each other. At the time he was still coadjutor *cum iure successionis* of his predecessor, Archbishop Beovich (who was from a Yugoslavian family). After greetings at the airport we went to see the Mayor of the city, where after a short conversation we signed the visitors' book. We were then received at the house of the archbishop, from where we left at about 4:30 p.m. and went to the newly-built Mikolaj Kopernik Home. We were to open and dedicate it. Present at this ceremony were representatives of the state government and the Mayor of Ottawa (that is the name of the city, which is also part of Adelaide). This beautiful home, built by the local Polonia with great sacrifices and input of their own labor, is to serve to maintain the Polish spirit, especially in the next generation.

Among several other speakers, I also gave an address, emphasizing the bond between the first and the second generation of Poles in Adelaide. The first generation arrived here carrying the experiences of war, camps and fronts (I have in mind, among others, Rev. Canon Jozef Kuczmanski from the Diocese of Wloclawek, a prisoner of the concentration camp in Dachau, who began pastoral work among Poles in Australia, initially working as a laborer). There is a need for mutual respect between the generations; the second is building upon the foundations established by the first. The representative of the state government emphasized the significant contribution of the Poles to the life of Australian society. He also unveiled the memorial tablet. Prof. Marian Szczepanowski spoke on behalf of the Polish Historical Society and presented us with books published by that Society.

From the Kopernik Home we went to the cathedral for a solemn concelebrated Mass. Archbishop Gleeson spoke first; I responded to his words at the beginning of my sermon. The Mass was in honor of Blessed Maximilian Kolbe, and I referred to his person in my sermon. At the end, an address was given by Rev. Canon Kuczmanski, who is the dean of the Polish priests working in the state of South Australia. Besides him, the following priests are working here: Fr. Gracjan Kolodziejczyk and Fr. Szczepan Krajewski, Conventual Franciscans (the latter came recently from Poland); Fr. Lukasz Huzarski, a Dominican; and Fr. Tadeusz Miksa, from the Congregation of the Passion, who is particularly active in Adelaide. Also helping in pastoral work for Poles is Fr. Leon Czechowicz, a son of Polish immigrants, born in Australia, who was ordained to the priesthood in this archdiocese. In addition, two other sons of Polish immigrants, from the Archdiocese of Perth, are preparing for the priesthood in Adelaide. They also took part in this meeting.

The solemn Mass was ended, as always, by the singing of the hymn "God, who hath protected Poland." Our countrymen participated in great numbers. There were also the Sisters of the Resurrection, whom I did not have time to visit; I only met with them by the church. After the Mass, we made two visits. The first was to the Polish Home, where the ladies greeted me with bread and salt. The presidents of organizations gave very interesting addresses, introducing all those assembled. I tried to respond as cordially as possible. A second such meeting at the Kopernik Home meant that I could not remain at the Polish Home as long as I and the hosts wanted. Also, considerations for Archbishop Gleeson dictated that the visit not be prolonged. At the Kopernik Home, the youth put on a beautiful show of national dances, to which I made reference in my address. We ended with group singing.

February 28. The next day in the morning I flew to Perth, with a farewell at the airport by the archbishop and a sizable group of our countrymen, among them a woman representing a committee for the reconstruction of the oldest Polish church in the area, and a young lady representing Polish university students, who have their own organization in Adelaide. In Adelaide, I also parted with Bishop Szczepan Wesoly, who remained in Australia and New Zealand until March 25. I owe him a tremendous debt of gratitude for assisting me during this trip, no less than during my trip to North America in 1969.

Perth

The last place on the schedule of my visit to Australia is the city of Perth, lying on the coast of the Indian Ocean, the capital of a state and the seat of an archdiocese. The plane arrived from Adelaide an hour earlier than called for in the timetable. At the airport we were awaited by Archbishop John Goody and Msgr. Witold Dzieciol, for whom Perth is the home base, and Fr. Zenon Grodz of the Society of the Divine Word, who works with the Monsignor in pastoral ministry to Poles in Perth and all of Western Australia. The third Polish priest working here, Fr. Jan Gajkowski, is in poor health. Because of the early arrival, not all of my countrymen from Perth could come to greet us, but there was an opportunity later to explain this and make up for it.

Archbishop Goody invited us to his residence next to the cathedral, where a liturgical meeting of local Polonia was to take place that evening. At dinner I met Cardinal Willebrands, who also stopped in Perth on his way back from the Eucharistic Congress. Then we went with the priests to a hospital, to visit a paralyzed countryman from Poznan. There, this person, Mr. Slabolepszy, presented me with a picture which he painted using his mouth, because he has completely lost the use of his hands.

Next we visited the Brothers of St. Joseph, where Msgr. Dzieciol acts as chaplain, which also allows him to minister to the Poles. Similarly, Fr. Grodz is a chaplain at a Sisters' convent in another part of the city. The two priests divide the pastoral work, traveling to individual locations in Western Australia, some of them a considerable distance from Perth. Besides this, they attach great importance to visiting families, especially to visiting the sick.

After returning to the residence, I met with Mr. and Mrs. Haller in the matter of mementos of their father, the late General Jozef Haller.[18] The Haller family is associated with the village of Jurczyce, parish of Radziszow, in the Archdiocese of Krakow.

At 7:00 p.m. I concelebrated a Holy Mass at the Perth cathedral, together with Msgr. Dzieciol and Fr. Z. Grodz. Archbishop Goody also participated; he greeted me at the beginning, saying warm words about Poland and the Church in Poland. Msgr. Dzieciol also spoke. In my sermon I referred to the words of the Archbishop, I explained the meaning of the Millennial Act of Jasna Gora, and I addressed the youth in a special way. According to the archbishop, there were about 1500 people in the cathedral.

We didn't get to the Polish Home until 9:00 p.m. (in Rome and Krakow it is then 2:00 p.m.). About 600 of our countrymen gathered in a huge hall, among them many young people and children. After the greeting with bread and salt, we began the program and meal. There was a performance by a choir, then speeches, recitations (a girl recited the *Ode to Youth*[19] in beautiful Polish), and, of course, national dances in various interpretations: first children, then the youth, all of whom danced with unusual verve. Msgr. Dzieciol spoke. Although his words were brief, it is well known that he is one of the pioneers of pastoral ministry in Australia. He came here on the contract of a physical laborer to provide his countrymen with pastoral care in the most difficult period. Today they have their own society, their organizations, their houses, their property. The social action of Polonia has been systematically developed in cooperation with priests and pastors. The presidents of Polish organizations in Perth speak of this, just as in other places throughout my whole trip.

Archbishop Goody speaks, then it is my turn. My address is a sort of summation of my entire trip on the eve of my departure from Australia. I present the Archbishop with a commemorative medallion of the 900th anniversary of St. Stanislaw. Since, at one time, he spent a year in Yugoslavia, he knows a little Croatian, so Slavic etymologies are not totally foreign to him. Sometimes, when he notices that certain Polish expressions sound familiar, he checks their meaning, and often correctly guesses that meaning. We return from the Polish Home at about midnight (in Melbourne it is 3:00 a.m.). Tomorrow (or, in fact, today) will bring several more visits with representatives of the Australian authorities, with the Sisters of the Holy Family of Nazareth, and then the flight to Rome.

March 1. Together with Cardinal Willebrands and Archbishop Goody, we pay official visits to the Governor, to the Prime Minister of the state of Western Australia and to the Perth City Council. From our conversations, the most interesting for me was the one with the Governor (the Governor is the representative of the Queen of England, whose rule extends to Australia as well).

At the house of the Sisters of the Holy Family of Nazareth we celebrated a farewell Mass together with the chaplain. Rev. Peter Quinn, Bishop Auxiliary of the Archdiocese of Perth, and local Australian clergy, were present at the dinner.

The farewell at the airport was particularly warm this time. A great number of our countrymen came, including children and the youth. They were constantly singing songs, asked for a blessing and mutual remem-

---

[18] A great Polish hero; at the end of WW I, he led a legion of Polish Americans and Polish Canadians in a fight to free Poland from the partitioning powers.

[19] By Adam Mickiewicz

brance. At about 3:45 p.m. (8:45 a.m. European time) we departed for Rome via Singapore, Kuala Lumpur and Bahrain on the Arabian Peninsula.

March 1 — His active participation in the work of the Sacred Congregation for the Clergy results in his membership in the Congregation being extended for the next five years. He is also appointed a member of the Congregation for Catholic Education.

March 2-3 — Rome * March 3 — 10:00 a.m., Vatican, an audience with the Holy Father * March 4 — 10:00 a.m., Rome, St. Stanislaw Church, Mass and sermon with the participation of Cardinal-nominee B. Kominek and bishops from Poland * March 5 — 10:00 a.m., Vatican, secret consistory; 12:00 noon, public consistory; 6:00 p.m., St. Peter's Basilica, he participated in a Mass concelebrated by the Holy Father and the new cardinals * March 6 — 10:00 a.m., Rome, Congregation pro Clero * March 7 — 7:00 a.m., Polish College, sprinkling of heads with ashes {Ash Wednesday} * March 8 — 6:00 p.m., St. Stanislaw Church, participated in a Mass celebrated by Cardinal B. Kominek, sermon * March 9 — 7:00 a.m., Polish College, private concelebration * At 11:00 a.m., he returns to Krakow by plane.

March 10-11 — Visitation of the parish of Bielany near Kety * March 11 — On the first Sunday of Lent, a pastoral letter from the Archbishop entitled *About the First and Greatest of God's Commandments* is read in all churches of the archdiocese * March 12 -13 — Zakopane * March 14 — 10:30 a.m., residence, Council of Priests * March 15 — 6:00 p.m., Theological Seminary, concelebrated Mass and sermon, a get-together after the Eucharistic Congress.

March 16 — 11:00 a.m., residence, Committee for the celebrations of the 500th anniversary of Copernicus * Same day — 5:00 p.m., meeting of the Council of the Pontifical Department of Theology in Krakow. Among others, a discussion of the proposed agreement of cooperation between the Department and the Theological Institute of the Missionary Fathers in Krakow. The Cardinal read a letter from Cardinal G. M. Garrone addressed to the Episcopal Committee for Catholic Education regarding a request by the Superior General of the Jesuits for granting the Jesuit Department of Philosophy the status of an open department (during discussion a number of complications were pointed out). Cardinal Wojtyla informs the Council about the discussions between Bishop Bronislaw Dabrowski, Secretary of the Episcopal Conference and Aleksander Skarzynski (Director of the government Office of Religions) on the subject of the local Department. (Minutes of the Council of the Department)

March 17-18 — Visitation of the parish of Wilamowice * March 20

— departure by plane for Rome for a meeting of the Council of the Secretariat of the Synod of Bishops * March 24 — 12:00 noon, Vatican, an audience with the Holy Father * March 25 — 7:30 a.m., Rome, titular Church of St. Caesarius, concelebrated Mass * 10:00 a.m., St. Stanislaw Church in Rome, during a Holy Mass for the 50th anniversary of the death of Archbishop Jozef Bilczewski (celebrant — Bishop Rubin) —sermon:

> We ask for glory for every person who leaves this world with the sign of Christ's Passion and Resurrection. But in this instance, we ask for glory in yet another sense. In this sense, in which the Church expresses, in certain of her servants here on earth, the glory of eternal life, the glory of sainthood, the glory of participation in the Paschal Mystery to the end.

Same day — in Rome (probably at the hall next to the Church of St. Stanislaw), an account of the trip to Australia:

> Whenever I hear the word "Australia," ... I look at my watch. That is what I got used to in Australia. While I was there, I also kept looking at my watch, which kept European time ... This became a conditioned reflex: I did it there, to calculate the time here, and now I do it here, for the same purpose, to calculate ... what is the time there. This has always interested me ... As far as Melbourne ... it is now 9:30 p.m. there, and in New Zealand it's already 10:30 p.m. and they are going to bed. And what are we doing? And that is what followed me for several days after my arrival there and then after my return here, because I didn't know what to do about this change of time. These are the antipodes ... about which I previously spoke in a carefree manner, but now with a greater sense of responsibility, because I know what that means in practice ...
>
> Bishop Wesoly is still in Australia and is still walking "upside down" ... Unfortunately, I will not see him in Rome and I will not be able ... to exchange and validate my experiences with him, because he has gained more of them, being there longer. I wish to express my particular gratitude to him, because this is the second time he has accompanied me on a trip to our emigrants ...
>
> As far as the state of the Polish spirit — here I speak of Australia and New Zealand, because there are no Poles in New Guinea. They are there only incidentally. They are primarily missionaries, and it was the goal of my journey there to meet with the missionaries and to become acquainted with the missionary activity of the Church, conducted by our countrymen, primarily the Polish priests of the Society of the Divine Word. The state of the Polish spirit on this continent is good. I would even say that it is better than in the United States and even in Canada ... First of all, the Polish community is young ...; these are primarily our countrymen who came there as a result of the Second World War, by various routes ... They are ardently committed to the spirit of Poland ... this whole wave of emigration lives for Poland, although it lives so far away from Poland ... Poland has provided the content of their young lives and their mature lives. Poland became the object of the sacrifices they made on the front lines of battle, in concentration camps, etc. and that is why, by the price of this suffering and these experiences, Poland is written very deeply in their souls. That is the first generation ...

The second generation keeps the Polish spirit and the attachment to the homeland of their parents relatively well, even though they already consider themselves Australians ... It seems that when it comes to maintaining the knowledge of the Polish language, the situation there, in Australia and New Zealand is probably better than ... in the United States or even in Canada ... The family home is still very influential in this regard ... Our countrymen make an effort to maintain the Polish Saturday schools ... As far as the youth are concerned, the scouting organization, present everywhere in these two countries, does much good in maintaining the Polish heritage ...

At every airport, meeting hall and church, the boy scouts and girl scouts were always in the foreground ... I think it was in Tasmania that I told them: you remind me most of firemen ... In Poland, when we bishops come to visit a parish, then, most often, the organized and uniformed group that greets us is the group of firemen. Since these are volunteer firemen, they earned this right to greet the bishop and to be their own representatives. And so, this is what I said to these boy scouts and girl scouts ...: you remind me of firemen, not because your uniforms are similar, but because, just as they are in Poland, here you are everywhere the honor guard for the bishop ...

These youth organizations, of course, educate by entertaining. That is a well-proven method of education ... As far as entertainment is concerned, the strongest element is that of national folk dance. The Polish spirit expresses itself through the feet. I said this in America and I must repeat this a fortiori[20] in Australia. Indeed, the dances are the best testimony of the Polish spirit of this second generation. The first generation no longer has the strong feet to jump around in krakowiaks, mountaineer dances, kuyawiaks or others. So, the younger generation does it for them ...

This Polish spirit ... is maintained well, the second generation knows the Polish language sufficiently, so much so that one can ... speak in Polish to the children, to the youth, and they can always answer ... If not immediately, then after a while, with the help of their mother, but they will answer ...

As far as the future of the pastoral ministry to Polonia, a factor which bodes well is the presence of many young priests ... It is they ... who give this pastoral ministry its Polish authenticity ... We in Poland ... had to learn a new style of pastoral care, a style that is less institutional, more missionary ... It seems that the style brought by the young priests from Poland is very much needed in Australia ...

[Bishop Rubin remembers that during his stay in Australia, he took part in scout camps.] [Cardinal Karol Wojtyla:] The Polish experience of pastoral care, and especially the experience of pastors, is often expressed in this kind of talk: "Well you see, there was this one pastor, he did this and that, but then when his successor came after him, he couldn't manage" ... But getting back to these scouts: Bishop Rubin was there for two months, he went with them to camp, slept with them in tents; and now they come to me, as if this was a trip from Krakow to Myslenice: "Come here to camp with us." So that's how it sometimes is in this world, that's how it can be with scouts, and also with pastors, and even with bishops.

---

[20] more strongly

March 27 — Return to Krakow * March 30 — 6:00 p.m., St. Kazimierz {Casimir} Church, Mass and sermon during a retreat for the youth * Same day — 11th meeting of the Main Committee of the Pastoral Synod of the Krakow Archdiocese (The first meeting took place on May 25, 1972, Bishop Stanislaw Smolenski — chairman, Rev. Tadeusz Pieronek — secretary, Rev. Stanislaw Malysiak, Rev. Kazimierz Gorny). "The Cardinal assessed the Committee's year of work very positively and presented plans for future years: it is important to create parish pastoral councils, because study teams can't guarantee everyone's involvement. The Synod should not be left on the periphery of matters. The councils will incorporate existing study teams into their ranks, they will also become representatives of the diocese. Committees of experts must be called to put the thoughts and accomplishments of the study teams in order. It is important to start work on the *Catechism of the Council and Synod*; this must be a contemporary synthesis of Catholic teachings, a positive exposition, not just a textbook to teach religion in school. The matter of the provincial synod — the bishops have decided to create a small inter-diocesan committee for the provincial synod. The topic of the upcoming Synod of Bishops — Evangelization in Today's World, should be the motivation to further work." (From the minutes)

March 31-April 1 — Visitation of the parish of Pychowice. During the visitation in Pychowice to married couples:

As many times as a human being fulfills his calling to love thoroughly, with dedication and sacrifice, so many times he is closer to God. Because God is love; and a man that truly loves, shows by his actions that he was created in God's image. Thus he also shows that God exists.

April 1 — Pychowice, a speech after the Mass (celebrated by the chaplain Rev. Dziwisz) to people who are alone, of ill health; to the elderly; to the members of the Living Rosary * Issues an announcement about the first pilgrimage of women and girls (on Sunday, September 9) to Kalwaria Zebrzydowska * April 4 — 7:00 p.m., residence, a meeting with *Znak* and *Tygodnik Powszechny* * April 5 — 6:30 p.m., St. Joseph's Church, Mass and sermon during a retreat for high school students * April 6 — 7:00 p.m., residence chapel, Mass for *Tygodnik Powszechny* and *Znak* * April 7-11 — Visitation of St. Bartholomew Church at Debniki. St. Bartholomew Chapel, capacity 20 -30, became a center of a new parish from the time of the development of a large new subdivision. During many Sunday Masses, people participating in the Mass stood outside in the elements. In the tiny St. Bartholomew Church, during the visitation:

This is not the first time I am visiting a parish in Krakow, a big-city

parish, that has no roof over its head. And not for the first time we are making efforts, very patient and persistent efforts, to provide a roof over its head ... Because, after all, this is ... a human and a civic right.

When we stand here like this, and I begin my talk to you, then I want to tell you, or rather ask all of you here assembled, do you at least have good shoes? Because you have to stand under the bare sky and you have to stand on the bare ground. And if the shoes are poor and the soles are thin, then you can catch a cold. And I feel a discomfort, an urge not to prolong my words and my service, because indeed someone could pay for it with the loss of health ... I am a member of the Council for the Apostolate of the Laity at the Vatican, but this type of apostolate of lay people is unknown to them. And when I tell them about it, they open their eyes wide at the possibility of an apostolate that consists in standing for years under the bare sky and on the bare ground in order to participate in the service of God; and thus, through patience, faith, persistence to win a roof over the heads of our parish community.

[To married couples, on the gift of oneself through all the efforts of family life:] You, who are spouses and parents, could at this moment say: "We know this better than you do." I admit it. That is your calling. That is why I do not get into the details of your life as parents, but I state and remind you of one thing: this altar is a great lesson of family life ... May this lesson, so often repeated, bear its fruit in the lives of your families.

[Second sermon to married couples, with a blessing:] Love, as we well know from experience, is not only wonderful and attractive, it is also difficult. And it proves itself the most, when it becomes difficult ... A society which does not support the community of marriage, the community of the family, prepares a bad future for itself. And that is why sometimes we look with fear upon our Polish society which does not sufficiently support community and unity, and the permanence of marriage and the family. We are afraid that we may be preparing a bad future for ourselves.

[After confirmation:] Whenever a new bishop is consecrated (and when I was consecrated as a bishop at the Wawel Cathedral almost fifteen years ago), the bishop who performs the consecration places the book of the Gospels on the shoulders of the priest who is becoming a bishop. They open the book and thus opened, with both wings as it were, they place it on his shoulders, as a sign that he is to carry the Gospel, as it were, on his shoulders; that the Gospel will be the burden and the mission of his whole life ...

Faith: to see your life in the light of God. Then you live differently. I heard from a non-believer who often speaks at meetings, that he knows when believers are listening to him. They listen differently; they have a different vision of their lives.

April 8 — 9:00 a.m., at the Dominicans, sermon to young people for the conclusion of a retreat * 3:00 p.m., the Bernardine Fathers, sermon for charity volunteers * April 9 — 8:00 p.m., a meeting with representatives of the engineering profession in the apartment of the pastor (parish at the Church of St. Bartholomew) * April 10 — 6:30 p.m., a meeting with teachers * Same day — 8:00 p.m., a meeting with a synodal study team (in reference to the visitation of the parish at St. Bartholomew Church) * April 11 — At the tiny St. Bartholomew

Church, for the conclusion of the visitation, during the blessing of the smallest children:

> The visit to your parish will remain in my heart as a very dear and significant event ... And that is because you are a Christian community which is being formed anew. At one time, there was a parish at the Church of St. Bartholomew. Then all traces of it were lost. Today, when a new settlement is growing here, near Wawel, and the parish is coming to life again, it indicates how deeply the Gospel, Christ and the Church, are written in the hearts of the inhabitants of the settlement. How much they want to be the People of God, gathering around Christ in His Church ... This visitation has made it obvious to me, your bishop. I have resolved in my heart and in my will to take your efforts and the efforts of your pastor, as my own, and to work with you until their successful conclusion ... It could be that we will have to continue these efforts for many years and through many disappointments, but we have had a lot of experience with this in Krakow and we will not be discouraged.

April 11-13 — Zakopane-Jaszczurowka. Skiing * Same place — April 12 —A seminar on ethics. Participating in this seminar were Cardinal Karol Wojtyla; Rev. Dr. Tadeusz Styczen SDS, chairman; Rev. Andrzej Szostek, MIC. The meeting in Zakopane was dedicated to a discussion of the *Elements of Ethics,* which after the *Elements of Metaethics* will become the second part of a textbook on ethics, prepared by Rev. Styczen. The discussion focused on the definition of morality. *Elements of Ethics* was discussed in great detail. It was noted that it would not be wise to retreat from the set of problems that was described as educational ethics. The third part of Elements was also analyzed (an approach to the Absolute). The meeting lasted 200 minutes. (Information based on the minutes prepared for the Kalendarium by Rev. Andrzej Szostek. There were many more seminars of this kind, but since the minutes are not available, this one is presented as an example).

April 14 — Ordination of deacons, sermon:

> Always, before the eyes of your soul, you should see the image of Christ who serves: who serves with His whole self. Because the fact that He died, that He was crucified, is the fullness of Christ's service. Christ serves with His whole self, he pays with His whole self. And that is why He redeems, that is why He sanctifies ... man, sanctifies Israel, or the chosen People of God ... If you always act to see Christ who serves with His whole self and who thereby redeems us ... then it will be easy for you to serve. You will understand what it means to serve, and what the joy of that service is; the service, which is spoken of throughout the entire tradition of the Church, as being the same as reigning.

April 15 — At the Mariacki Basilica, during a visitation:

> [To married couples:] I wish to bestow this blessing upon you in the same way I, and all the bishops, bestow it during the visitation of individ-

ual parishes. We always do this with a clear emphasis. We emphasize the place of every marriage and of every family in the Church. Not only the physical place but, above all, the moral place, i.e. the mission and meaning of every marriage and every family in the Church. I ask you then, that you come here, in couples, husband and wife, to the steps of the great altar, to this solemn spot in front of the altar of {sculpted by} Wit Stwosz {Weit Stoss}. I will bestow the blessing on individual couples. If there are children — and I see that there are — then have them come up with you. Let this be a blessing of the families.

[To the young people:] "The son of God took on the form of a servant" ... and "Glory to You, King of eternal glory." On the one hand, a servant, on the other — a King ... Man is called to service. Human life cannot be understood in any other way. It is service. And only then, when it serves great causes, true values appropriate goals, only then is this life worth anything and only then is it worth living.

[To children:] You know well that at every Mass, before the consecration, we repeat: "Blessed is He, who comes in the name of the Lord." But today these words take on a special, historical meaning. Because it was today that they were uttered. And those who ... thus proclaimed the coming of the Son of David, meaning the Messiah, Christ, were the boys and girls of Jerusalem. And it has thus remained. In the souls of children there remains this particular fervor, this enthusiasm for Our Lord ...

Same day — 8:00 p.m., at the Mariacki Basilica, the end of the visitation (Mass for craft guilds):

I thank you also for coming here to meet with your bishop. Because there is a great tradition in Krakow in that regard. Close contacts were maintained between the craft guilds and the unforgettable late Prince Cardinal Adam Stefan Sapieha. I know about this very well. These traditions were passed on to me. I bemoan the fact that I cannot maintain these contacts with the craft guilds to the same extent. Although it is made difficult externally, you can rest assured that internally it is the same bishop who has the same relationship with you, to your work, to your guilds and communities, as all of his predecessors, and especially that last great one whom I mentioned.

Retreat for university students at the Church of Our Lady of Lourdes:

First Conference: The method. "With all of our humanity we must stop by Jesus Christ" (From the liturgy of the Holy Week). From the letter to the Philippians: "Jesus Christ ... though he was in the form of God, did not count equality with God a thing to be grasped, but emptied himself, taking the form of a servant ... and became obedient unto death." The history of man's attitude towards God: "It could be said that, from the beginning, man has lost the perspective of existence ... Jesus Christ teaches us to find that perspective of existence anew ... What are you, mere man, what are you and what is all of creation in the face of Him who is the Creator? ... Jesus Christ taught us that to serve means to have dominion. First of all, to have dominion over oneself, to mature to such a degree, to have so much within you, that you can give of it to others."

Second conference: The Gospel of the anointing in Bethany. Christ speaks of the "essence" of being, hence of "metaphysics, but in His own language. So, if He speaks of God, then not of the 'Absolute' but of the 'Father.' Christ touches upon these fundamental matters as He looks in the eyes of death, His own and ours, and always connects it with the resurrection. The human existence on earth is of various lengths. But we know for certain that this existence is limited, temporal ... I think that in the perspective of Christ's truth about man, this existence is some sort of a test. There are various criteria of the worth of person: work, social utility. But there is also the criterion of humanity ... What kind of human are you? ... And that is the only way to judge matters of human morality, both personal and social, i.e. by beginning with man, with his values ... Because God, who created man in His image and likeness ... seeks that image and likeness in man."

Reference to Mary's gesture and Judas's criticism, and the response of Jesus, who knows the motives of one and the other, who judges their actions. The purpose of the retreat is to provide an opportunity to examine your own actions and failures and to judge them. "When man poses all these questions to himself together with Christ, then they bring him into a state of grace, of repentance."

Third conference: The Gospel about the events in the Upper Room, during the time before the Last Supper, in an atmosphere of fellowship, with intimations of Judas's betrayal and Peter's denial. The contrast between the attitudes of these two apostles: the spiritual abandonment on the part of Judas, his entanglement in betrayal, and the temporary abandonment on the part of Peter. "Peter did not leave Jesus spiritually, and that is why he later returned to Him; to some extent, he returned all the more closely, because he had denied Him." A consideration of these two approaches to life and a consideration of God's friendship which is offered to every person. Sin as the antithesis of this friendship. Friendship as the kind of love depicted in the "hymn to love" from the Letter to the Corinthians. "It is a pact between two individual beings where we can say objectively that they are "by" each other. The love of two people must be, above all, a friendship; distortions: "and you must make sure that they speak of your dormitories with respect. I say this to you as your bishop, because I often have to defend the honor of those houses."

God offers His friendship and that is why He respects freedom.

Of the sensitivity of conscience and the visibility of our actions to God: "What joy it is that in an examination of conscience I always encounter God's judgment of me. And, to some extent, God always accepts the judgment of my conscience, despite the infinite truth which He is ... And that is how He ultimately judges me."

On confession: "Confession expresses a love which is never exhausted. No human weakness, no human sin, no human crime — not even that! — can exhaust the love that is in God ... The Sacrament of Penance is the sacrament of hope — each time. Love is greater than sin. Good is greater than evil."

Fourth conference: "The Gospel differs from all other knowledge of man, because all this knowledge is above all ... derived from the past. But all of the knowledge of man that is contained in the Gospel is directed at the future of man, is derived from the future of man" — It deals with the full communion with God. Hence the meaning of prayer as an attempt at this communion within the relationship of creature to Creator. "... The richness of prayer, apart from our subjective emotions, consists in the fact that prayer is this communion, already here, already now."

April 15 — 7:00 p.m., St. Mikolaj {Nicholas} Church, oratorio, parting remarks * April 16 — the Cardinal's chapel, beginning of an apostolic process regarding the second miracle performed by God through the intercession of Mother Ursula Ledochowska. (From the chronicles of the Ursuline Sisters in Krakow) * April 17 — Biala, after a regional conference of priests, about a resolution on educational reform:

> Parents in every society have the right that their children be raised and educated according to their beliefs and not against them. Catholic parents have the right that their children, their baptized and believing children, be brought up and educated in the spirit of their faith, their world outlook, and not in the spirit of atheism ... And that is why our children can't be held in schools all day, because it eliminates the time available to catechize them in our parishes ... We want to be good citizens of our country, of the land in which we live. Many times, especially in times of hardship, all citizens, believers and non-believers alike, were asked for cooperation and help. And now, the people who believe are asking those who once asked and continue to ask them for help: respect our rights!

Same day — 3:00 p.m., Krakow, Our Lady of Lourdes Church, Haydn's oratorio *The Seven Last Words of Christ on the Cross* * April 18-21 — Wawel Cathedral, participation in the liturgy of the Holy Week * April 19 — Wawel Cathedral on Holy Thursday, in commemoration of the 40th anniversary of Bishop J. Groblicki's ordination to the priesthood and the 10th anniversary of Bishop J. Pietraszko's consecration as a bishop, and the renewal of priestly vows for all diocesan clergy:

> Pray for your priests, so that God would pour forth His gifts upon them, so they would become faithful servants of Christ ... Please pray for me as well, so I would be true to the apostolic task that was bestowed upon my unworthy person. May my everyday presence among you make me become a living and more perfect picture of Christ the Priest, the Good Shepherd, Teacher and servant for all.

Same day — 9:00 p.m., the Mariacki Basilica, Holy Hour with the clerics * April 21 — Holy Saturday, Wawel Cathedral, sermon on the topic of the Resurrection as an historical fact and our participation in the Resurrection through Baptism:

> I wish to offer today's Holy Saturday Mass for the intention of our countrymen who live on the farthest continent, in Australia ... During my visit there and when I was leaving them, I promised that after my return I would pray for them by the holy remains of St. Stanislaw, together with the distinguished Metropolitan Chapter and all of you. And today I wish to keep that promise to them ... Through the Church, it is so much easier for them to find their way back to their native land, even though they are so far ... That is why I invite you today, dear brothers and sisters, our coun-

trymen in distant Australia, to our Paschal congregation of Holy Saturday. We are united by our common homeland, a common language, a common history. We are united by the horrible experiences of the times in which we have lived and continue to live. But, at the same time, we are united by the same faith, the same light of Christ and the same hope which will never let us fall into despair.

April 22 — Mistrzejowice — during Resurrection Mass:

When the bishop of the Church of Krakow stands among you, not in the Cathedral, although he will be going there later to celebrate the Resurrection, it is because, at this place, the example given by the Risen Christ, is especially eloquent. I have heard of your splendid participation from the priest who conducted the Holy Week retreat. I've heard how, in the rain, ignoring the weather, priests have heard confessions, and the faithful waited in long lines for the Sacrament of Penance. Because, "He is given to us as an example, that we must rise from the dead."

April 22, Wawel Cathedral, the day of the Resurrection:

There is but one place in the history of humanity, one such day, from which we can see the history of mankind, the sense of man's existence on earth from beginning to end. That is the day of the Resurrection of Christ. This day is engraved in our hearts and our souls, engraved in history, engraved in this Wawel temple. This is not a graveyard of history. This is a grand testimony of Resurrection. And we know, this day and this mystery could never be erased, at any price, from the Polish soul, because then that soul would become blind.

April 23 — At the Church of the Congregation of the Resurrection:

The Apostles have preached Christ's work... His mission, His Messianic mission, His work of Redemption without consideration of the consequences. No arguments, no human means, no persecutions could deter them from that.

April 26 — 9:00 a.m., concelebrated Mass and sermon for the beginning of a session of theologians dedicated to new interpretations of dogmas * April 28 — 8:00 a.m., residence chapel, concelebrated Mass on the occasion of the session of theologians * Same day — 7:00 p.m., Gniezno, Feast of St. Wojciech {Adalbert} * April 29 — Gniezno, Feast of St. Wojciech, meeting with the youth * April 30 — 12:00 noon, a get-together with the Club of Catholic Intellectuals in Krakow.

May 1 — 6:30 a.m. Krakow, private Mass * Same day — Wroclaw 11:00 a.m., meeting of the Episcopal Committee for Pastoral Ministry, chaired by Cardinal B. Kominek. Presentation by Bishop I. Tokarczuk: *Theology of Labor*. Discussion of the Warsaw project: "Program of pastoral activities for 1973/74," the Committee accepted the program of preaching. Cardinal Wojtyla presented the outline of the pastoral program for 1974/75 to the participants. The topic is the apostolate of lay people — in Poland it is shaped by the parish organization — about the triple mission of Christ, the theology of the laity, the role of lay people, different forms of community action in the parish, especially in pastoral councils. The program is being prepared by the Krakow community. (From the minutes)

May 2 — Second day of meetings of the Committee. Introduction to planning for years 1975/76. Cardinal Wojtyla: "A direction to our planning was given by the Second Vatican Council and we must remember that". In presentation; analysis of the signs of the time; Poland's place in geography and history; the crisis of Atlantic culture; Poland's own heritage; fear of the West ("The Polish Church, in spite of all criticism, is becoming more interesting to the West"); alliances with the East; the Church in a secular state. At the center of attention of the planning: man, his integral liberation and salvation. Discussion follows. (From the minutes) * Same day — Church of the Carmelite Sisters (in Krakow), Mass by the coffin of the late Hanna Chrzanowska, Rakowicki cemetery, funeral. Hanna Chrzanowska established a parochial nursing service in Krakow for patients in their homes. Along with the nurses and nuns she involved university students. During his speech at the Carmelite Sisters Church, the Cardinal read a fragment from the letter of the deceased. Later on he said:

> If I may be allowed to say: Thank You, Madame Hanna, for being among us, for being the way you were. You are being thanked by the caretakers of the sick, by religious sisters, nurses, university students, by the entire Church of Krakow. I thank you as a Bishop of the Church of Krakow. You were a great help and support for me. But rather, we would like to thank the Lord that you were among us such as you were, with your great simplicity, your inner peace, but at the same time with your inner ardor; that you were among us an incarnation of Christ's beatitudes from the Sermon on the Mount, especially the one that says: "Blessed are the merciful..." ... We thank God for your life which was so eloquent, which left us a testament so clear, so unequivocal.

May 3[21] through 5 — Jasna Gora, presided over the liturgy of the Holy Mass at 11:00 a.m. * May 5 — during the 136th plenary conference of the Polish Episcopate, a clarification in the matter of university degrees in theology and other church studies was accepted, and signed by Cardinal S. Wyszynski and Cardinal K. Wojtyla * Same day — 5:00 p.m., Wieruszow, former Church of the Pauline Fathers, he participated in the observances of the 300th anniversary of the death of Fr. Augustyn Kordecki:[22]

> We bishops come here straight from Jasna Gora, where we celebrated

---

[21] See Glossary.
[22] Prior of the Pauline Abbey at Jasna Gora during the successful defense of Czestochowa against the Swedish invasion in 1656.

the Feast of Our Lady Queen of Poland on May 3. We remember that this title was bestowed on the Blessed Mother after the miraculous defense of Jasna Gora, whose main hero was Fr. Augustyn Kordecki ...

The historical moment when Fr. Augustyn Kordecki appears, when he makes the heroic decision to defend Jasna Gora when all of Poland is submerged in the deluge.[23] This historical moment indicates that his genius was the beginning of a new time, of new historical enterprises and of a new Polish spirit ... There is no place in Poland that is independent, and what is worse, there is widespread bribery and treason. And against that background the prior makes his decision. We will not surrender Jasna Gora, we will defend it to the last. A military decision, but made by a monk, a priest. Such a great decision required not only the courage of a warrior leader, but the sacrifice and humility of a religious. And we know that Fr. Augustyn Kordecki was victorious. Jasna Gora astonished the whole nation. It alone managed to withstand the deluge, the last island of independent existence and independent spirit. This fact said very much to its contemporaries, but this fact says even more to subsequent generations.

The Polish Episcopate comes here from Jasna Gora, where we were working together. The Conference of the Polish Episcopate studied the weighty government documents of the last few days with particular attention and particular anxiety. These documents are a report on the state of education and an act of the sejm {parliament} in the matter of educating the young generation ... We studied these documents and we determined to our horror that they formulate everything in such a way as if the entire past of Polish history did not exist; as if the Polish spirit, whose magnificent example is Fr. Augustyn Kordecki, did not exist; as if the Church were absent from the history of the Polish nation and Polish upbringing, as if the Church, that is Christians, Catholics, people of faith were absent from the contemporary life of our country, as if we didn't exist. We are studying the voluminous documents dealing with the upbringing of our nation, the youth of our country, where the vast majority is Catholic, and there is nothing in these documents that would express respect for the Catholic principles of upbringing, for the Christian heritage of upbringing. There is nothing which would ensure that the upbringing given to our youth will be consistent with our common convictions.

I said that we read this with the greatest horror. Because who do they think we are, really? What do they take us for? There are rights that are acquired, there are rights that are strictly limited, but there are the rights of the human person. To these belongs the right to freedom of conscience, the right of freedom of religion. These rights determine indirectly the whole direction of upbringing. So we must speak of this ... We came here to learn from him that brave stance again, that heroism that led to the decision: we will defend Jasna Gora. We came here to learn from him that faith, that hope which transcends everything, that rises above all threats; that faith and hope which writes the history of the Church and the history of Poland.

May 6-7 — Visitation of the parish of Miedzybrodzie Bialskie *
May 8 — 8:00 a.m., at the Wawel Cathedral, ordination of deacons:

There may be a kind of inner death, a trace of martyrdom in your deci-

---

[23] The Swedish invasion of the mid-17th c. is commonly called "the Deluge."

sion, in your readiness. You offer up your life and stand here ready to give up what is to be given to so many of your contemporaries, the calling to family life. But you are fully aware of why you are doing this, because you know that you can open your hearts even wider, you can serve even more and you can embrace many people in spiritual fatherhood. You know that it is possible to give your soul for your sheep in a different way than the fathers and mothers do in their families. This is the form given to the pastoral ministry of the Church by Christ!

Same day — second plenary pastoral meeting of the Krakow Archdiocesan Synod, presided over by Cardinal Karol Wojtyla at Wawel Cathedral. Participants: members of synodal committees, representatives of 325 synodal study groups, other accredited persons and guests for a total of 1150 people. The cardinal greeted those present: "We want to be aware how far the work of the Synod, begun a year ago, has progressed ... we also want to look into the future of our work and dedicate it to our Patron Saint on his Feast day." Speech for the beginning of the second year of the Synod's work:

It is necessary that this [what the Second Vatican Council has accomplished] be now transplanted to our particular Church. In the second year, it will be necessary that work committees first of all, but also, gradually, the committees of experts, help the study groups as generously as possible ... We will have to wait for the thoughts, comments, questions or suggestions from these groups which are to reach our committees and help them in drafting the documents of our Synod; first proposals, and then, gradually, resolutions ... The pastoral character of the Synod of the Archdiocese of Krakow, its uniqueness and originality, is demonstrated by the fact that it does not rely only on work committees and committees of experts, but seeks a possibly broad contact with the entire community of the People of God of the Archdiocese of Krakow ... The Second Vatican Council has shown us that all of us are the Church. And it ordered us to stop making such distinctions as were used until recently, where we talked and heard about, on the one hand, the teaching Church as an active agent in the Church, and on the other, the listening Church as the passive agent.

May 9 — 10:00 a.m., residence chapel, concelebrated Mass for the beginning of the Council of Priests * Same day — 6:30 p.m., Rajcza, concelebrated Mass and a social get-together with priests ordained in 1971 * May 10 — 9:00 a.m., residence, session dedicated to Nicholas Copernicus * 6:00 p.m., St. Florian Church, Mass and sermon, May service, a get-together with the academic apostolate * Same day — a meeting of the Committee for the Apostolate of the Laity. Work on dialogue, on the apostolic aspect of Confirmation, the issue of ministries in preparation for the priesthood and in the apostolate of lay people (lectors, acolytes) * May 11 — 1:00 p.m., Kalwaria Zebrzydowska, private Mass * May 12 — In Nowa Huta (in the presence of Cardinal Artur Tabera, Bishop Franciszek Hengsbach from Essen and Bishop Andre Rousset from Pontoise):

The building of the church in Nowa Huta, the Church of your parish, is an especially expressive symbol of the Church of Christ which is constantly being built, not only through its visible foundations and walls, but it is also being built through the invisible foundations and walls in the hearts and the souls of the people ... The Church is first and foremost in the souls and the hearts of the people. Those people create a community, a society. They give it expression, and this builds the Church.

May 13 — Procession St. Stanislaw from Wawel Cathedral to Skalka with the participation by: Cardinal Karol Wojtyla; Cardinal Artur Tabera, Prefect of the Roman Congregation for Divine Worship; Cardinal Stefan Wyszynski and Cardinal Boleslaw Kominek, the Polish bishops and Bishop Rousset, Auxiliary Bishop of the Pontoise diocese, chairman of the Committee of the French Episcopate for immigration, Bishop Hengsbach from Essen; Bishop Jozef Buchkremer from Aachen.[24] Cardinal Tabera presided during a concelebrated Mass at Skalka. Introductory remarks by Cardinal Wojtyla at Skalka:

Walking along the streets of Krakow we gave a particular testimony of our spiritual identity which we do not want to or intend to lose under any circumstances. We do not want and we will not allow our Polish and Christian identity, marked by a thousand years of Christianity, marked by the mission of St. Stanislaw, Bishop and Martyr, to be taken away ... This is the same city, the same university, the same past and the same direction for the future! ... The presence of university youth is especially significant and dear to us. It testifies to the fact that the testament, the evidence of identity left at the beginnings of our history by St. Stanislaw as the holy relic for the Church and the nation, this evidence of the identity of our history, of our past, is also the evidence of the identity of our times and of our future.

Same day — 5:30 p.m., St. Anne's Church in Krakow, a solemn open session on the occasion of the 500th anniversary of Mikolaj Kopernik with the participation of Polish bishops, professors, seminarians, and citizens of Krakow. The Primate of Poland presided over the session. * May 14 — 6:00 p.m., concelebrated Mass and sermon during a get-together with priests ordained in 1970 * May 15 — 10:00 a.m., first meeting of the Educational Council of the Polish Episcopate at the residence of the Archbishop at 3 Franciszkanska Street in Krakow. Cardinal Karol Wojtyla, chairman of the Episcopal Committee for Catholic Education and chairman of the Educational Council, delivered an inaugural address and presented new statutes of the Council that were approved by the plenary conference of the Episcopate. The participants of this meeting are members of the Council and other individuals who are to cooperate with the Council. A presentation (penned

---

[24] Essen, Aachen — cities in West Germany

by the Author) informs that the Educational Council was established by the resolution of the 134th the Episcopal Conference on January 24, 1973. The statutes leave it up to the Council to establish its own operating procedures

> **The Polish Episcopate sees the need for an Educational Council as a body that can render opinions on the matters which I have tried to outline here. It is counting on the competence and the dedication of all members to the cause of Catholic education. But, at the same time, the Polish Episcopate sees the Council as a body that represents Catholic education. It is probably difficult to speak at this time of an Academy of Church Studies in Poland, but on the basis of the recommendations of the Vatican Council, on the basis of the suggestions contained in the documents of the Apostolic See, and also the traditions of Catholic education in Poland, the establishment and activities of such a representative body seem entirely justified.[25]**

In light of the new statutes, the discussion touched upon the matter of academic degrees in theology and other church studies. Organizational matters were discussed, a statutes committee was established, a secretariat was formed, a vice-chairman was elected (Rev. Prof. Marian Rechowicz). A discussion was held on the topic of proposed programs for the Year of Polish Learning. * May 16 — 9:00 a.m., residence, Committee of the Episcopate for Education * May 17 — 2:00 p.m., Biala, regional conference * May 18 — Presentation during the spring regional conference of priests from the deaneries of Krakow. He spoke about the resolution on educational reform:

> **The rights of citizens are not meant to be manipulated at will; they are meant to give the citizens some sense of protection in the scope of their essential freedoms ... Krakow is especially endangered, because it is in these huge parishes that catechetic instruction reaches several hundred hours per week ... Catechesis in the family ... It could be that this is a time when we have to prepare for this, but we cannot do this totally.**

Same day — 5:00 p.m., a meeting of the Council of the Pontifical Department of Theology in Krakow. The Cardinal informed about the establishment of the Educational Council of the Episcopate. He presented a draft of a letter of agreement to grant an open status to the Philosophy Department of the Jesuit Fathers. Forms of cooperation were discussed (excluding the possibility of institutional merger). The Council accepted proposals of the Department's cooperation with the Institute of the Missionary Fathers in Krakow and the theological seminaries of Tarnow, Silesia, and Czestochowa. (From the minutes) * Same day — residence chapel, Confirmation * May 19 — 8:30 a.m., the

---

[25] Quote not attributed; probably Wojtyla.

Kalendarium

opening of the tomb of Kazimierz Jagiellonczyk * May 20 — 7:30 p.m., at Wawel Cathedral during ordination:

> You are entering here through the Church, that means through its sacraments. You are entering here through the Church, that means through your Christian families. Through your overworked fathers, and your mothers full of dedication. You are entering here through the Church, that means through your parishes, where God's soil is being tilled, and the fruits from the Lord's vineyards are constantly being harvested.

Same day — In Nowa Huta during the ordination of one of the parishioners:

> I have been to your parish many times, as it was being born. And it was born — we all know it well — in very difficult circumstances, in great pain. We have met here most often on Christmas Eve, during Midnight Mass ... I used to visit here on many different occasions. I don't think there is another parish in this diocese where I have been more often as your bishop than in this parish of Nowa Huta-Bienczyce ... Today I come here with particular emotion, to ordain one of you to the priesthood, a child of this parish, who grew up here and prepared for the priesthood amid all of the struggles which this community of the People of God has been through.

May 21 — In Bulowice, during a get-together for young priests:

> A priest is from God, but a priest is of the people. A priest is of the people, he is a man, but he is and must be a man of God ... The priesthood is a toil and the priesthood is difficult, but it is a blessed toil.

May 23 — 7:00 p.m., Silesian Seminary, a get-together with superiors and seminarians, a talk about his trip to Australia * On the same day — the Palace of the Archbishop. Meeting and discussion on St. Stanislaw, Bishop and Martyr, and a presentation by Prof. Labuda * May 24 — 10:00 a.m., Wadowice, regional conference; 6:00 p.m. parish church, Mass and sermon * May 25 — Krakow, 10:00 a.m., Theological Seminary, regional conference * May 26 — 9:00 a.m., Wagrowiec, an address for the opening of the Third Congress of Polish Biblical Scholars. At first Cardinal Wojtyla sent a letter (dated April 6) to the participants of the Congress, later, he probably delivered a speech at the opening of the Congress (see: Bibl. I 1137. Kal. p. 524).

May 27 — Piekary Slaskie, during the annual pilgrimage for men (in the presence of Cardinal Kominek, Silesian ordinary and auxiliary bishops):

> Faith is the Word of the Living God spoken to man. Is that all? No, this is only the source. Faith is the response of a living man given to the Living God; given with the mind, given with the heart, given with the entire life. Living man responds to the Living God in faith ... Faith begins in God's Word, and faith is expressed in man's word, and through faith man becomes great, not small! And through faith man is in truth, and not in

falsehood. And through faith man is in love, not in hate ...

We have the right to have more space in this homeland where we are the majority! We have a right to have more roofs over our heads when we pray! We have the right, in all of these planned programs of upbringing and education, about which there is so much talk and discussion, we have the right to have more room for teaching religion, for catechesis in the parishes! And this right is not aimed against anybody. It is for the good of all! It is for peace! So we ask that these rights be recognized and respected.

May 28 — 7:00 a.m. residence chapel, concelebrated Mass with Brothers from Taize (prior Roger Schutz) participating * May 29 — Warsaw, 10:00 a.m., departs for Belgium via Frankfurt at the invitation of Bishop Emil De Smedt from Bruges * May 30 — 8:00 a.m., Louvain, private chapel, private concelebrated Mass * May 31 — 11:00 a.m., Bruges, Cathedral of the Holy Redeemer, concelebrated Mass, he delivered a sermon in Flemish * 6:00 p.m., led the famous procession in honor of the Most Precious Blood of Jesus.

June 1 — 11:00 a.m., Louvain, visits a Polish Mission * Same day — 6:00 p.m., Brussels, chapel of the Polish Catholic Mission, concelebrated Mass and sermon * June 2 — 10:00 a.m., Frankfurt, private concelebrated Mass at the chapel in the residence of the Apostolic Inspector for Poles in Germany * Same day — 6:00 p.m., Suchedniow (Sandomierz diocese), sermon during the visitation of the image of Our Lady * June 3 — Wawel Cathedral, before the cross of Queen Jadwiga {i.e. the crucifix before which she used to pray}, 10th anniversary of the death of Pope John XXIII:

> This successor of St. Peter, this Roman Pope, was so simple, was so full of love. One might say that the prayer of Christ, our archpriest, found its daily expression in him... This prayer was expressed in him. He lived it constantly and tried to unite everyone. He wished to unite the Church internally and to unite all of Christianity. He also wished to unite humanity. He turned to all the separated brethren, to all people of good faith.

Same day — 11:00 a.m., in Kalwaria, during a pilgrimage of men from the Archdiocese of Krakow — the day, on which a pastoral letter about reforms in education was read in all parishes of Poland:

> Prayers rise up to the Lord, but they also burrow deeply into the conscience of man, into his soul. Prayers go up to God, but they also deeply shape the human community ... We yearn for God![26] We yearn not only for bread, we yearn not only for material goods, temporal goods, the progress of civilization and the development of industry: we yearn for God! ... Sing this everywhere, and let this be the cry of all those who live on Polish soil and believe — an unceasing cry. If we cannot cry out in any other way, then at least we will cry out in this fashion!

---

[26] Words of a Polish religious hymn.

June 3-4 -Visitation of the parish of Graboszyce * June 4 — 11:00 a.m., Milowka, parish church, concelebrated Mass and sermon, a get-together for priests ordained in 1967 * June 5 — 4:00 p.m., seminar on ethics * June 6 — 12:00 noon, Zakopane, during a regional conference of priests:

> **The Lord Jesus imposed upon his disciples the obligation to profess the faith for all time. From Him to us flows the obligation to know the faith. We must know our faith. To know it, we must learn it. And that is the fundamental duty of the family and the Church ... It is our common cause; our generation will answer before God and the history of our nation for the great heritage of faith, morality and Christian culture. This heritage has lasted a thousand years, it is well tested. It gave us much strength. Our history was not easy, it was very difficult. We went through partitions, we went through occupations. Our native language was taken away from us. In all these experiences, the faith, the Gospel and the Church were our support ...**
>
> **The cause of man's spiritual freedom is the most important. Man can sometimes be in material poverty, but as long as his spirit is free, then man is still free. The worst thing is when man loses the freedom of his spirit! The worst thing is when man loses the freedom of his spirit for temporal goods, for material gain; when, for the price of these gains he endangers or forgets matters of the spirit, matters of conscience, matters of faith and religion.**

June 6 — Nowy Targ, 7 p.m. , Mass, remarks after the regional conference.

June 7 — In Oswiecim {Auschwitz}, after a regional conference of priests:

> **Atheism means godlessness, or upbringing without God. It is claimed that this is an expression of progress. We have fundamental doubts in the matter ... I cannot keep them hidden when I speak at Auschwitz, the place of the horrible concentration camp, which is also — let us not forget — the fruit of an atheistic upbringing. Without God and against God. We know from the experience of our newest history that without God and against God, one does not bring up people of value. Very often, though, one brings up the kind of people who created Auschwitz ...**
>
> **The time has come to own up to Christ. You can no longer pretend, you can no longer serve two masters. If someone wants to serve mammon, let him. But those who want to serve God must profess that clearly ... You must profess, you must not be afraid. There are many millions of us, we have all of our history behind us, we have the law behind us. We need only muster the courage, the determination and the will and profess Christ.**

On the same day — Nowy Targ, 7:00 p.m., Holy Mass, an address after a regional conference.

June 8 — A meeting of the Council of the Pontifical Department of Theology in Krakow. Lecture by Rev. Dr. Michal Heller given in fulfillment of the requirements for admission to assistant professorship. In the second part of the meeting, Cardinal Wojtyla informed everyone gathered that Cardinal G. M. Garrone, Prefect of the Congregation for Catholic Education, will be attending the celebrations connected with the anniversary of Copernicus. He also presented matters pertaining to Rev. Jan Kracik's return from studies abroad and his possible employment by the Department. (From the minutes of the Council) * Same day — 5:00 p.m., Trzebinia, retreat house, he visits the sick during their retreat * June 10 — 10:00 a.m., Skarzysko-Kamienna, Pontifical Mass for the conclusion of the pilgrimage of the image of Our Lady in the Diocese of Sandomierz * Same day — 4:00 p.m., Kielce, beginning of the pilgrimage of the image of Our Lady at the Holy Cross Parish * June 11 — 12:00 noon, Kroscienko. It was the shortest, but very significant visit in Kroscienko, a center of the oasis movement {charismatics}. From a historical perspective, the movement considers this date as the beginning of its intensive growth. The main event of this celebration, which took place on the Feast of Mary, Mother of the Church, was the dedication of a statue of the Blessed Virgin on Kopia Gorka, and the dedication of the whole movement to the Immaculate Mother of the Church. The act of dedication was performed by the Cardinal. Then he delivered a short address. Due to many obligations, he had at first called his visit to Kroscienko off. However, he still came, even though he was not expected, because, as he explained "he opened a small window" through which "he left Krakow, and through which he must return very quickly". From early morning he had this "internal imperative of the heart," "this inner need," to participate in this celebration so important to the movement. "By my presence here ... I would like to emphasize the importance of this apostolic initiative, which has found its nest or rather its source here, and from which it is trying to radiate." (According to an account by Rev. F. Blachnicki) * Same day — 6:00 p.m., Piaski Wielkie, 50th anniversary of the parish:

We are a community of the People of God which, as a whole, as well as through its individual members, is filled with one concern: the concern for salvation, the concern for grace, for truth, for repentance. The concern of the pastor must somehow divide itself into very many concerns. The concern of the pastor is made up of the concerns of all the parents. The concern of the pastor is made up of the concerns of all the sick. And conversely, his concern is their concern. In this they meet ... My wish for you is that you might feel the whole responsibility which Christ has put upon you; by His redemption of us, by stretching out His arms on the Cross for us, for all of us, for small children and for dying old men. For the sober, the honest, the upright, and for the drunkards, the hooligans, for everyone. He paid the price of His Blood for everyone . May you feel this ever more completely, more deeply.

June 12 — 10:00 a.m., Krakow, Holy Cross Parish, social get-together * June 13 — 8:00 a.m., Piaski Wielkie, concelebrated Mass and sermon during a social get-together * Same day — 6:00 p.m., St. Anne's Church, concelebrated Mass with Bishop Johannes Degenhardt and priests from the Diocese of Paderborn * June 14 — Zakopane, three concelebrated Masses with priests ordained in years 1972, 1966, 1963, sermon * June 15 — Warsaw, Main Council of the Polish Episcopate, private Mass at the Primate's chapel * June 16 — Pieniezno, house of the Society of the Divine Word, plenary conference of the Polish Episcopate, 7:00 p.m., commemorative program on the occasion of the 50th anniversary of the Society of the Divine Word in Poland * June 17 — 9:00 a.m.. Frombork, Copernican session, 12:00 noon, concelebrated Mass for the 500th anniversary of Mikolaj Kopernik's birthday * 5:00 p.m., Olsztyn, private Mass * June 18 — Warsaw * June 20-21, visitation of the parish of Glebowice * June 21 — on the Feast of Corpus Christi, the Cardinal led a Eucharistic procession from the Wawel Cathedral to the streets of Krakow * Same day — at the Jesuit church, the Feast of Corpus Christi: "Any upbringing that tries to tear a child away from the heart of the mother and father, can't produce truly humane results. Maybe it is possible to bring up some rank and file kind of people in this fashion, I don't want to use the term "robots." People cannot be raised without nurturing by the father and mother." * June 22 — Wawel Cathedral, Holy Mass on the 10th anniversary of Pope Paul VI's pontificate:

> **With our hearts and our intentions we surround the Peter of our times in the person of Pope Paul VI, forming with him the closest community of faith ... From its first days, the Church has not only professed faith in Peter, but it has also prayed for Peter. The Church supports him with prayer, just as the Church of Jerusalem supported Peter when he was put in prison by Herod ... He is after all a man, but a man whom God, whom Christ, endowed with a superhuman authority: "Whatever you shall bind..."**

Same day — 12:00 noon. Residence, arrival of Bishop W. Rubin * Same day — meeting of the Council of the Pontifical Department of Theology in Krakow; among others, a matter of the agreement of cooperation with the Ecclesiastical Institute in Czestochowa. The Cardinal participated in the discussion. (From the minutes) * June 23-24 — Visitation of the parish of Palczowice * June 24-25 — A visit by Archbishop Emmanuele Clarizio from Rome * June 26 — 7:30 p.m., residence chapel, a Mass for J. Vetulani * June 27 — 12:00 noon — end of the school year at the Higher Catechetic Institute. Later, dinner for the faculty and female students at the refectory. (From the chronicle of the Ursuline Sisters in Krakow) * June 29 — 10:00 a.m., Rdzawka, concelebrated Mass and sermon on the 300th anniversary of the Marian Fathers. Rev. Witold Nieciecki, MIC, the Superior of the Polish Province of the

Congregation welcomed the guest. Fragment of the sermon delivered by Cardinal Wojtyla in Rdzawka:

We are meeting in Rdzawka, where the Marian Fathers have been ministering for several years, so that we may together recall the beginning of their religious Congregation 300 years ago on the Polish soil. Father Provincial has already mentioned that this was the first Congregation, the first religious order founded in Poland and by a Pole. Therefore, the fact that this Congregation is Marian in its character, that it is connected with Mary Immaculate, is so very meaningful. It is as if a great bridge connected this initiative of Father Papczynski, Servant of God and founder of the Marians 300 years ago with a contemporary figure that is so close to our hearts, that of Blessed Maximilian Maria Kolbe who called himself a "knight of Mary Immaculate" but others referred to him as a "fool for Mary Immaculate." It is obviously a certain heritage, a certain law of our spiritual history. And it is this law that found expression in the establishment, in the existence and in the mission of the religious order founded by the Servant of God, Fr. Stanislaus Papczynski, 300 years ago and developed by his followers.

* Same day — Mass and sermon at St. Peter's Church in Krakow for the intention of Pope Paul VI, for the 10th anniversary of his election to the Chair of St. Peter.

June 30 — Krakow, the residence. First meeting of the Committee of Experts of the Provincial Synod (Cardinal Karol Wojtyla presided). Based on a study prepared by the Cardinal (see the undated entry after the dates April 30-May 2, 1971), the Committee of Experts completes a preliminary research into the needs and possibilities of holding a Provincial Synod. The make-up of the Committee was established on the basis of consultations with the bishops, and in accordance with the suggestions of ordinary bishops from the dioceses constituting the province.

July 1 — Visitation of the parish of Piotrowice * July 2 — 9:00 a.m., Jasna Gora, concelebrated Mass and sermon for a pilgrimage of teachers and educators (about 2500 participants) * July 3 — The Cardinal nominated a new director of the Higher Catechetic Institute, Sr. Scholastyka Knapczyk OSU. A congratulatory letter of thanks for a job well done was sent to the previous director, Sr. Angela Kurpisz. (From the chronicles of the Ursuline Sisters in Krakow) * July 4 — 9:00 a.m., Wawel Cathedral, solemn Mass on the anniversary of consecration (with the participation of sextons) * Same day — 3:00 p.m., Rajcza, Mass and sermon for a pilgrimage of the sick * July 8-20 — Cisiec, private Masses * July 8 — Cisiec, at a church constructed illegally:

Civil laws demand to be respected. If, in the course of more than a dozen years, the Metropolitan Curia has gathered over 50 petitions for the construction of various churches and chapels, and these petitions have not

been acted upon for so many years, then it is not surprising that people have lost faith in the laws, and the rights[27] to which they are entitled. It is in our best interest, one might say, that churches be built with the permission of the authorities and not without such permission. That is what we strive for with all our might. That is how we have always presented this matter ... Given that what happened here in November has already happened, we are trying and I, as the Bishop of the Church of Krakow and the whole Metropolitan Curia — to handle these matters in such a manner that we may reach agreement with the authorities, so that you may obtain appropriate permission of the authorities for building the church here, on this spot where it has already been built, and taking advantage of what has already been done. That is our position. I think that it is proper, just, and takes your labor, your generosity and your sacrifice into account. I also think that it is proper in relation to the authorities, because we do not want to diminish respect for the authorities. We wish to establish a respect for the authorities just as we expect them to respect citizens' rights. That is our stance; that is my direction of action.

July 21-28 — Zawoja, Masses and sermons at the chapel on Wilczna * July 29 — Kroscienko, Chapel of the Good Shepherd. The Cardinal delivered a speech at the end of a Mass in which members of the Oasis movement {on retreat there} and local parishioners participated. In this address he indicated the connection between the renewal of the Church, as envisioned by the Vatican Council, and the renewal of a Christian and the renewal of the liturgy. He emphasized that the Oasis movement is working out the shape of the renewal of the Church, because it bases and concentrates the renewal of the life of the faithful on the liturgy, especially on the correct formation of Eucharistic gatherings. After the Mass, he met with individual Oasis groups in Kroscienko. He met with the young people, university students, priests, seminarians, religious sisters, and a group of adults. Everywhere, he asked them to do the talking; he wanted to listen. In the evening, all the Oasis groups met in the so-called Tent of Light on Kopia Gorka. There, he asked to hear their opinions and, above all, he wanted to listen to singing, and he sang along with everyone. In summarizing his all-day stay in Kroscienko, he pointed out the issue of the formation of lay apostles: "In this epoch in the life of the Church in Poland, Christ demands certain extraordinary efforts and extraordinary attitudes. For this reason, additional formation is necessary, since the ordinary pastoral ministry in the parishes produces only ordinary effects." (An account submitted by Fr. F. Blachnicki) * July 30-31 — 7:00 a.m., residence chapel, private Masses.

In July — a few days at Lake Jeziorak.

---

[27] In Polish, the same word means both "law" and "right".

August 1 — Bachledowka and Rokiciny, convent of the Ursuline Sisters. From the chronicles: "August 1. Today, Cardinal Karol Wojtyla was with us for dinner. Later, he blessed the mothers and their children who were staying at our place". * August 9 — Bachledowka, he began a three day retreat. He spent a lot of time praying at the chapel, said the Way of the Cross, said the rosary and breviary. During those three days he took pains to remain in complete isolation, he did not maintain contact with anyone. On August 12, for the conclusion of his retreat, he celebrated the Eucharist at 8:00 a.m. and delivered a sermon to a large group of gorale {mountaineers} based on the theme of *Kiedy ranne*[28] * August 12 — Boleslaw (Kielce diocese), Mass and sermon during visitation * August 13 — Rdzawka, Mass and sermon during a meeting of the Oasis groups from the Archdiocese of Krakow * August 14 — 12:00 noon, Oswiecim, Mass and sermon during a day of recollection for altar servers of the entire diocese * Same day — Oswiecim, Mass and sermon at the place of the death of Blessed Maximilian Kolbe * Also on the same day — Kalwaria Zebrzydowska — on the eve of the Assumption of the Blessed Virgin Mary, a sermon to the youth. (KW 9) * August 15 — Ludzmierz, High Mass and sermon * Same day — Cardinal Antonio Samore, Prefect of the Roman Congregation for the Sacraments, arrived in Krakow; with Cardinal Wojtyla, Bishop Groblicki and Bishop Smolenski, he took part in the liturgical service for a *Odpust* at the Mariacki Basilica. The next day, Cardinal Samore departed for Oswiecim and Kalwaria * August 16 — 8:00 a.m., concelebrated Mass with Cardinal Samore by the tomb of St. Stanislaw, meeting with the youth from England * Same day — Siepraw, during the funeral of pastor Jan Przytocki:

> **He was gentle, he was loved by his brothers in the priesthood ... The reason he was loved was because he in turn loved his brothers in the priesthood, his contemporaries, his co-workers. Young priests, straight from the seminaries would come to him. Under his eye they would make their first steps, gain their best experiences, the best formation of their characters.**

August 17 — A word at the grave of the late Bishop Jan Nowicki, Apostolic Administrator for the Archdiocese in Lubaczow.

August 18 — 11:00 a.m., Jedrzejow, concelebrated Mass and sermon for the 750th anniversary of Blessed Wincenty Kadlubek * Same day — 5:00 p.m., Krakow, Church of the Dominican Fathers, sermon, procession during a service in honor of St. Jacek {Hyacinth} * August 20-25 — 7:00 a.m., residence chapel, private Masses * August 25 — Rokiciny, a notation in the chronicles of the Ursuline convent: "While

---

[28] "When the dawn rises", a morning hymn of prayer.

visiting his friends, Cardinal Karol Wojtyla stopped also at our house. In the evening, at 6:30 p.m., he went with the assistant pastor from Raba Wyzna and our Sister to Bielanka with a pastoral visit to a sick person, ... 18 year old Krzys {Christopher} Chmielarczyk. This boy had been prepared by us for First Holy Communion. After his return, the Cardinal had supper with us." * August 26 — Jasna Gora. At 11:00 a.m., Pontifical High Mass for the Feast of Our Lady of Czestochowa, a sermon at 7:00 p.m.:

This new act of covenant, which, as I have said, goes deeper into and binds more strongly with the heart of the Mother of God, is the fruit of the experiences of the entire millennium. It is the result of the test which the covenant of 300 years ago — the vows of King Jan Kazimierz — was put to. It has been our experience over the course of these three centuries, that although we Poles have not kept our vows in every respect, she, Mary, has kept hers. She proved to us that she is with us not only as the Queen of the Crown of Poland (for in the meantime, the crown fell from the heads of Polish kings), but she is with us as the Mother of the People of God who inhabit our land. The new act of covenant with the Mother of God goes further and says more, but in the context of our times, these which are now and those which are to come. These times are going in the direction set for the entire Church by the Second Vatican Council. In gifting us with the magnificent teaching on the Church and on the Church in the contemporary world, the Council has particularly emphasized the meaning of religious freedom. Our millennial dedication to Mary arose from the background of the teachings of the Council. Our surrender to the maternal bondage of Mary for the freedom of the Church in Poland and in the world ... Our concern for the freedom of the Polish spirit. This concern has been awakened in us due to the announced reform of education. This reform says not a word about our Christian society, about the contribution of Christ, the Church, Christianity to the upbringing of the Polish nation. Nor does it say a word about the rights of Christian parents, who make up the vast majority of this nation, to raise their children according to their own convictions. It says nothing about religious education, about the primacy of the family in the task of upbringing. While a lot is being said about the family and its obligations in upbringing, the reality is that the family is expected to help the school in the implementation of a program — which arises from atheistic principles — which the school is propagating. But, in the meantime, the rights of man and the family demand that the school assist the parents and the family in the upbringing of children according to their convictions ... In the name of the principles enumerated here, in the name of the conventions signed by our government against discrimination in education, we demand that there be complete freedom for the teaching of religion, that the opportunity for catechization, to which families have a definite right, not be taken away under false pretenses. We also demand that no methods of intimidation be used against the majority of parents who wish their children to learn the truths of Christian faith and morals in centers of religious education, according to the pastoral and the teaching mission of the Church.

August 27-30 — The Silesian Seminary, catechetic course. During the days of recollection for the catechists of the Archdiocese of Krakow at the Silesian Theological Seminary, he delivered a lecture *Catechization in the Light of the Reform of Education* to grade school teachers and later to teachers of the youth * August 27 — Cardinal Raimondi, Prefect of the Roman Congregation for Canonization and Beatification Causes, and the secretary of the said Congregation, Archbishop Giuseppe Casoria, arrived in Krakow. He concelebrated a Mass at the Wawel Cathedral at the altar of St. Stanislaw for a favorable outcome of the beatification and canonization causes undertaken by the Church of Krakow. Later, at the archbishop's residence, he met with the postulators, vice-postulators and the tribunals * August 28 — 8:00 a.m., Church of the Felician Sisters, participated in a Mass celebrated by Cardinal Raimondi, prayers at the tomb of the Servant of God Aniela Truszkowska * Proceeds to Tarnow with Cardinal Raimondi * August 29 — Wroclaw, Theological Seminary (Wroclaw Pastoral Days attended by priests from all over Poland), a lecture entitled *Foundations of the Pastoral Mission of Priests.*

September 1-2 — Miedzybrodzie Zywiecke, parish visitation * September 3 — 7:00 p.m., Krakow, Church of the Most Holy Redeemer, Mass and sermon during the triduum {three day celebration} in honor of Blessed Bronislawa * September 8 — Celebrated a service for the beginning of a new school year in the largest pastoral center in Krakow, the parish of Nowa Huta-Bienczyce. Preached a sermon and blessed a statue of Our Lady of Canberra[29] * September 9 — Kalwaria Zebrzydowska, the 1st Women's Day, under the motto: "A Woman in the Service of the Gospel." Delivered a sermon to 80,000 participants on the topic: woman's prayer * Same day — took part in the 5th Men's Day and preached a sermon stressing the right of citizens to teach religion to their children * September 10 — At the residence, a meeting of the superiors of the religious orders of women, dedicated to the topic of the education of nuns * September 12-14 — Warsaw * September 15 — Lodz * Same day — 2:00 p.m., Zdunska Wola, sermon on the 50th anniversary of the congregation of the Sons of Divine Providence in Poland:

> In some measure, even these great "fools" for Divine Providence — and there were many of them in our Polish land — fundamentally rejected all means of wealth. They depended on that power which obligates the heart of the Father to open in love in the direction from which comes the testament of the poverty of the Sons of Providence.

September 16 — The parish of Bujakow, blessing of a cross for the

---

[29] Australia; see entry for February 17, 1973.

summit of a church built within a year:

> **Let this Cross speak of our faith. Just as all crosses speak of our faith through the centuries. Crosses that mark the history of our Homeland. A difficult history, one which would not be possible, we must say, without the sign of the Cross! It would be most difficult to survive in this place in Europe, under the pressures from the East and from the West, were it not for Christ's Cross which has kept us standing straight! Crosses are the witnesses of times; they are the witness of centuries. They speak about who we are. One more cross is joining all of the crosses on this Polish soil, on the soil of the Diocese of Krakow ..., the summit cross of your church.**

September 16-17 — Canonical visitation of the parish of Wlosienica and a visit to the house of a deserving old woman * September 19 — 6:00 p.m., Mogila, at the Cistercian Fathers, at the Basilica of the Lord's Cross:

> **If we look at the Cross with the perseverance of faith, if we do not turn away from it, then at the end of our questions and our perseverance we must always discover that its meaning is how much is man worth? Man must be worth a lot, he must have an enormously high price, if God pays for man with His own death on the Cross ... In the name of this truth, man's life becomes worth living. It becomes worth living even if, in human terms, it becomes unlivable.**

September 12-24 — Canonical visitation of the parish of Jawiszowice. A meeting with the Living Rosary and groups of Reparative Communion. A meeting in a catechetical room with a congregation of the Third Order of St. Francis * At this time, a Mass and sermon at the Chapel of the Daughters of Charity at 2 Helclow Street. After breakfast he visited the sick ward. He conversed with the sick and blessed them. (From the chronicles of the Daughters of Charity) * September 24 evening — he departs for Rome, ad limina apostolorum[30] * September 25 — Vienna * September 26-October 5 — Rome, concelebrated Masses with sermons * September 28 — Rome, St. Peter's Basilica, at the altar of Our Lady Queen of Poland, a concelebrated Mass and sermon (on the anniversary of the consecration of the Basilica) * Same day — 15th anniversary of Karol Wojtyla's consecration as a bishop. On this day, on the Feast of St. Wenceslaus, the entire archdiocese prayed for the intention of its shepherd, and a special Mass was celebrated at the Wawel Cathedral * September 29 — the abbey of Valombrosa, concelebrated Mass and sermon * September 30 — Milan — Seregno, St. Joseph's Parish, concelebrated Mass and sermon (this parish donated church bells to St. Florian's Parish in Krakow).

October 5 — 12:00 noon, audience with the Holy Father * October

---

[30] "To the apostolic thresholds", a phrase used to describe the periodic visits of every Bishop to the Holy See.

6-8 — Paris, Polish Seminary, concelebrated private Masses * October 9 — Chamonix, concelebrated private Mass * October 10 — Annecy, Shrine of St. Francis de Sales and St. Jane Frances de Chantal, a visit to the Sisters of the Visitation * October 11 — Paris, 7:30 a.m., Polish Seminary, a private concelebrated Mass * Same day — 5:00 p.m., Krakow-Lagiewniki. In Lagiewniki at the blessing of a cornerstone for a church under construction:

> My tardiness was caused by my long journey ... Only this morning, I was celebrating Mass in the capital of France. As you can see, my journey was a long one, and I could come here for your celebration only thanks to modern means of locomotion ... When I was in Rome, I told the Holy Father that in Poland, in this archdiocese, living people are building living churches. And although we really need churches built of stone, concrete and brick, the churches built of these inanimate materials are rising only because there are living people who are building these living churches. These people represent an important social fact which cannot be opposed or denied. This social fact requires recognition and respect ... How eloquent your faith is to me. This sacrifice of the inhabitants of Lagiewniki, so closely tied with the place of my work and my calling. The sacrifice of my brothers and sisters with whom I once shared the hardship of physical labor during the occupation ... How dear to me is the fact that I can bless the cornerstone for the structure of your common sacrifice.

October 13 — 5:00 p.m.. Olkusz, Mass and sermon on the Feast of the Visitation of the Blessed Mother * October 14 — St. Anne's Church, at the opening of the 1973/74 academic year:

> This year, the prayers of the Church at the academic shrine of St. Anne take on a special dimension and a special meaning. Not only because this is the 500th anniversary of the birth of Mikolaj Kopernik {Nicholas Copernicus}. As we know, he was a student of the university in Krakow; it was here — as he himself stated — that he obtained his knowledge of astronomy. This year, too, is the 500th anniversary of the death of St. John of Kanty. The year 1973 is, as we can see, connected with the year 1473 in many ways. And I think that we should first congratulate the Jagiellonian University, that during the course of its history it has produced the brilliant scientist, by whose discovery of the truth about the physical world mankind still lives, and that at approximately the same time it has produced a saint from the ranks of its professors. I think that there are few universities in the world which, after centuries of existence, can boast such accomplishments ...
> Following the light of today's liturgy of the Word, we pray that this learning at the University may flow from wisdom and lead to wisdom; that it not remain merely subservient to one or another kind of utilitarianism, because then the greatness of man will be lost to it. And it must serve the greatness of man, of every person... And today we must pray ... that everyone in this great academic center of ancient Krakow may freely, freely and without fear, ask Christ the question which is asked by the young man in today's Gospel: "Master, what should I do to gain eternal life?" That is a question which takes the measure of man.

Same day — 4:00 p.m., in Kety at the parish of St. John of Kanty, with a pilgrimage on the Sunday preceding the feast, in the presence of Bishop Pietraszko:

> **Before this great pilgrimage of the Polish Church, represented by its bishops and by its scientists, sets off to the tomb of the sainted Professor in Krakow, we come here to you, to Kety, to this parish ... in which the life of St. John had its beginning. Both his human life, which was given to him by his parents, and his spiritual and supernatural life, which was given by our Holy Mother the Church through Baptism ... 580 years ago, John's family, his parents, deeply rooted in the Church, in this parish, gave life to their child and brought that child up in the spirit of faith and morals drawn from the Gospel. They shaped a man who, through his family, made his mark in the Church and made his mark in the history of his nation, in the history of the family of man, in the history of the salvation of humankind. He made his mark with great letters. And that is what we want to emphasize by our coming to Kety, to this church and this parish.**

After the celebrations in the parish he was invited by the Sisters of the Resurrection to stop at their house for a moment. After a short conversation regarding the emblem of Kety (... half an eagle and three eggs. The conversation centered around a question who {i.e. what other saint} will hatch from the third egg, as the two previous eggs yielded St. John of Kanty and St. Ludowika of Kety. The Cardinal expressed hope that these will be the foundresses of the Congregation.) When the Cardinal seemed to be ready to leave, Sister Superior of the house asked him to stop by the cell of a blind sister Klemensa (Sikora) who was not well that day and stayed in bed. He went with great joy, exchanged a few warm words, made the sign of the cross and kissed her on the forehead ... Finally, the Cardinal went to the crypt, stood there in silence a long while, afterwards, "Our Father" ... Rev. Stanislaw (Dziwisz) whispered to Sister Superior that everything that regards the Mothers as well as this prayer in the crypt should be recorded in their chronicle because it is important in the beatification processes (From the chronicle of the religious house of the Sisters of the Resurrection of Our Lord Jesus Christ in Kety).

October 16 — 8:15 p.m.. Church of Our Lady of Lourdes, Mass and sermon for the new academic year * October 17 — 7:00 a.m.. Theological Seminary, Mass and sermon during the first meeting in a new academic year * Same day — 6:00 p.m., With the Primate of Poland and other members of the Main Council of the Polish Episcopate, he participated in the ceremonies of a second internment of King Kazimierz Jagiellonczyk and his wife Elzbieta in Wawel Cathedral * October 19 — Krakow, 3 Franciszkanska Street, 2nd meeting of the Educational Council of the Polish Episcopate. A report on the status of academic cadres in Poland was given for years 1972/73. Cardinal Wojtyla: "It should be added that a professor must be basically affiliated with only one institution." A proposal of the Council's rules and regulations was discussed, a creation of a new body of the Educational Council was considered, the issue of interdisciplinary seminars was mentioned. The second part of the meeting was at 3:15 p.m., together with the Episcopal Conference and in the presence of Cardinal Gabriel Maria Garrone, Prefect of the Sacred Congregation Pro Institutione Catholica. Cardinal Wojtyla delivered an account in French on the status of Catholic education in Poland. He said:

> **The Poles have remained faithful to the culture of the West, just as they have remained faithful to the Church and the Successor of St. Peter, whose seat is in Rome. The activities of the Catholic Church in Poland had a fundamental significance for the formation and development of learning and national culture. It is sufficient to remind ... that in the new conditions it is unavoidable that the Church in Poland, removed from cooperating with the government in the realm of education, teaching and upbringing, should itself take up the obligations which arise from its age-old mission. (From the minutes)**

Same day — 6:00 p.m.. Public session of the Episcopal Conference at St. Anne's Church in Krakow, by the tomb of St. John of Kanty. Cardinal Wojtyla participated together with Cardinal Garrone, Prefect of the Congregation Pro Institutione Catholica, the Primate of Poland, Polish bishops, members of the Educational Council of the Polish Episcopate, clergy, and representatives of Krakow communities. Cardinal Wojtyla delivered a homily.

October 20 — 10:00 a.m.. Auditorium of the Department of Theology, inauguration of the new academic year 1973/74, with the participation of Cardinal Garrone * Same day — 7:30 p.m., St. Anne's Church, celebration in honor of St. John of Kanty, Mass concelebrated with academic chaplains * October 21 — 11:00 a.m., Lublin, an address for the inauguration of the academic year at the Catholic University * Same day — 7:00 p.m.. St. Anne's Church in Krakow, at the conclusion of the celebrations of the 500th anniversary of St. John of Kanty {John Cantius}:

> **St. John of Kanty was a professor and a priest. In his time, he was what we would call an academic chaplain today. He might be called the patron of academic chaplains all over the world. I doubt whether he would have many competitors in that respect, meaning that there are not many people who would so closely combine the duties of a professor with the mission of a priest. For this reason, these holy relics, this church, should form a center of the academic apostolate in Krakow, if not in the material sense, then at least in the moral sense.**

October 22 — 4:00 p.m.. Gniezno, participated in the celebrations of the 25th anniversary of the death of Primate A. Hlond

October 23 — The Church of the Carmelite Sisters (Kopernika Street), Mass and sermon for the sisters for the intention of the missions (100th anniversary of the birth of St. Theresa of the Infant Jesus):

> **Two times in today's liturgy of the Word, we are reminded of this statement by Jesus: "Unless you turn and become like children..." ... At the same time, the *History of the Soul* shows what it means to become like a child and thoroughly experience the fatherhood of God, to experience one's small journey which leads to the greatest of things. All of this was shown to us by St. Theresa of the Infant Jesus, by her life, her calling, her life as a religious sister. And this has become permanently imprinted on the fabric of the contemporary Church.**

October 25 — 9:00 a.m., Silesian Seminary, Krakow, a day of meditation for clerics drafted into the military service.[31] * Same day — Cardinal Julius Dopfner, chairman of the West German Episcopate, arrived in Krakow. On his way to Krakow, in the company of Cardinal Wojtyla, he paid a visit to Oswiecim {Auschwitz} and the camp at Brzezinka {Birkenau}. * October 27-30 — the parish of Brzeszcze, canonical visitation * October 28 — At the institute of the Salesian Fathers in Oswiecim, on the first anniversary of the beatification of Blessed Michal Rua, first student and successor of St. John Bosco:

> **Today you do not have your institutions, you do not have your schools, your dormitories. But you still have a numerous religious family, the largest in Poland. Think about, pray for a way to enter upon the road traveled by Polish youth, by the new generation; how you might influence it, without schools, without institutions? Solely through apostolic ardor? How might you help the youth to hear the voice of Christ, to understand His call, to follow Him?**

October 31-November 1 — Canonical visitation in Psary, the parish of Ploki * October 31 — In Ploki, during the visitation, to the members of the Living Rosary:

> **The Kingdom of God is won by patience, by perseverance. It is not flashy, it does not depend on sudden outward success, on massive propaganda. The Kingdom of God is won by patience, by humility, by perseverance. And those are the conquests we make through prayer ... In the Kingdom of God, we can never say: Enough, now you can rest, my soul. The Kingdom of God on this earth means constant movement, constant striving, but a peaceful, deep, patient striving. Prayer is the best expression of that.**

Same day in the evening — a get-together with the parishioners who helped with the work on the enlargement of the chapel.

In October — Cardinal Wojtyla presented further plans for the

---

[31] Clergy did not have a deferment from military service in Poland.

enlargement of library facilities of the Theological Seminary.

October-November — During October and November he appointed directors of the particular areas of pastoral ministry in the deaneries, i.e. family ministry, youth ministry, liturgical service ministry.

November 1 — During a visitation in the parish of Ploki, to married couples:

> **As we contemplate the holiness of men, of God Himself, on the Feast of All Saints, we who are here on earth must become aware of the order of sanctification ... Saints are not created at the moment of their departure from this earth. Saints do not live only in heaven. Saints mature here on earth. And the passing into heaven is but the ending of a long process of preparation during the earthly pilgrimage.**

Same day — cemetery in Bodzianow:

> **As the bishop of the Church of Krakow I come together with you to this cemetery and I stop at this grave here before us. It is the grave of a priest from your area. From here he came, and here he returned, the late Msgr. Kazimierz Buzala. But I stop at this grave because I am tied by special bonds of love and gratitude to this priest. He was my first pastor. As a young priest, I began my pastoral ministry by his side, and I have kept a grateful memory of his person, his priestly individuality. And when I stop at his grave, I am joined with my spiritual mentor in the communion of faith, which for him has already turned into the happiness of seeing God. I am joined with him in the communion of hope, which for him has turned into the union with God for whom he strove. And for me, for all of us gathered here, this faith is still a striving, this hope is still a direction of our journey.**

The same day — The Basilica of the Dominican Fathers in Krakow, the return of an image of Our Lady of the Rosary to the chapel (the image had been displayed in the basilica during the month of October). Sermon about the rosary:

> **This is the crown of the Blessed Mother, the Queen of All Saints. These are the expressions in her visage and in her crown, of the history of human souls, the history of all the holiness which is known only to God, which is continually being shaped and formed anew, in which we all participate, and in which she extends her maternal help.**

November 2 — 8:00 a.m., Rakowice, cemetery chapel, Mass and sermon, 9:00 a.m., Wawel Cathedral, Mass and procession to the royal tombs * 4:00 p.m., Oswiecim, the wall of death, the bunker of Father Maximilian Kolbe, Mass, opening remarks * November 3 — Krakow —Metropolitan Curia, Theological Seminary, his name-day celebrations * November 4 — Raciborowice, 500th anniversary of the consecration of the church:

> **The territory of the parish of Raciborowice included the village of**

> Bienczyce. I remember very well this village of Bienczyce as one of the
> localities of this parish, where the pastor or his assistant would come to say
> Mass on Sunday in that small chapel ... where the religious sisters worked.
> And so this small chapel of Bienczyce became the beginning of a great
> church for a new parish ... It is the parish of Nowa Huta — Bienczyce ...
> But that is not the end of the story ... After several years, the parish turned
> out to be too small ... So we had to think of a new place, of beginning a new
> parish, and again this was done within the territory of the old parish of
> Raciborowice, in a place you know well, a place known as Mistrzejowice ...
> Just look, what came about as the result of the consecration of your church
> 500 years ago! ... Through the Providence of God, it was erected here and
> consecrated here five centuries ago, so that when the time was right, new
> churches and a new parish might emerge from it.

Same day in Niepolomice:

> I wish to extend my heartfelt thanks to the parish of Niepolomice ...
> for inviting me to the celebrations of the Feast of St. Karol {Charles}, who
> is the second patron saint of your parish, and my first patron saint since
> the day of my Baptism ... Reverend Pastor of Niepolomice invites me here
> every year, but I cannot come every year, because of various other obliga-
> tions. This year it fortunately turns out that, together with you, I can pay
> homage to our common patron ... When a saint, for example St. Charles,
> stands over the crib of a baby, he takes that child's life, which continues to
> develop, into the reality of his personality ... And gradually, even if the per-
> son in question is not very perceptive, gradually, this great truth of the holy
> personality seeps into his consciousness, into his soul, into his life ... I come
> here, indeed, as a pilgrim, in order to hear once again what St. Charles
> professed: "I love You, my God, my strength!" I come here so that I may
> take his profession into my heart to overcome my weakness, to find in it a
> program for my life from this point forward, a program of further service.
> Divine Providence has decreed that, like my patron, I, too, am a bishop and
> a cardinal, and I, too, was a Father of the Council which took place 400
> years after the Council of Trent, of the Council of our times, namely the
> Second Vatican Council.

November 5 — For this day, the cardinal invited the priests of the
Archdiocese of Krakow to the shrine of the Blessed Mother in
Kalwaria, so as to begin the Holy Year there, in the community of
priests. More than 600 priests came. Almost all of them concelebrated
Mass with the Cardinal and the bishops. During the Mass the Cardinal
led a contemplation on the topic of the Holy Year. A special mention of
the Primate of Poland, who at that time was celebrating the 25th
anniversary of his primacy, was made in the petitions, as well as in the
homily. A special letter was sent to the Primate from the participants.
(According to *Notificationes* m. 11. R. 1973) From the sermon:

> In the intentions of the Holy Father, and in our own plans, the Holy
> Year is not merely an addition to the ordinary life and pastoral work of the
> Church. It is a celebration of that life, a more concrete realization, a spe-
> cific enlivening and deepening of that life. Therefore, we will continue to

work in the same fields of endeavor as we normally do, but we will work within that dimension which is imparted to these endeavors, especially the pastoral and apostolic ones, by this Holy Year, this Year of the special inspiration of the Holy Spirit.

Same day — 8:00 p.m., Residence chapel, concelebrated Mass for the academic apostolate * November 6 — 11:00 a.m., Residence, a meeting with priests interested in matters of church construction * November 8-9 Tyniec, private retreat * November 9 — 7:00 a.m., residence chapel, a Mass for the intention of the Polish Language Institute * On the same day — Krakow, the Archbishop's Curia. A speech to the newly nominated priests in charge of the youth ministry and the ministry of the liturgical servants * November 10-11 — visitation of the parish of Pisarzowice * November 10 — 4:30 p.m., Pisarzowice, consecration of a new church, 650th anniversary of the parish * November 11 — in the evening, Pisarzowice, a get-together with the parishioners most involved in the construction of the new church * November 12 — 8:00 a.m., at the Wawel Cathedral (25th anniversary of the primacy of Cardinal Stefan Wyszynski):

> Twenty-five years ago, Bishop Stefan Wyszynski, then the Bishop of Lublin, accepted the will of God the Most High, as given by the Holy Father, and delivered by the then Metropolitan of Krakow, venerable Prince Cardinal {Sapieha}. He accepted it with the thought which is so well expressed in today's liturgy: "Lead me, O Lord, on Your eternal path." In his obedience to the will of the Holy Father, he was guided by the deepest faith; that faith has always accompanied him. He knew that he was taking a path into the unknown, and that what he was taking up would be unspeakably difficult — beyond human strength; that perhaps no Primate ever had such a difficult role to fill in the history of the Church in Poland.

Same day — 6:00 p.m., Warsaw, the cathedral, participated in the celebrations of the Primate's 25th anniversary * November 13 — 5:30 p.m., Krakow, St. Florian's Church, Mass and sermon, ordination of lectors and acolytes:

> The liturgy of the Word reminded us of the meaning of the Word of God, its miraculous way of uniting man with God. First and foremost, this Word of God unites God with man. And having borne fruit in the soul of man, it returns, as it were, to God. My wish for you, dear Lectors, is that your service of the Word will also bear fruit. Start with the living faith that the Word which you read, which you proclaim, is the Word of the Living God, which must not return empty to the throne of God.

Same day — 8:00 p.m., the Basilica of the Jesuit Fathers, concelebrated Mass and sermon, blessing of books, an agape with the university students. About vocation and quest for perfection:

I think that you who are now listening to me ... somehow carry that quest within you. There may be different measures of it. Admittedly, the measure of St. Stanislaw Kostka[32] is the measure of a saint. There may be different measures, but ultimately, in each of these measures there is one single measure: it is called the quest for perfection, for holiness. And this — as we were reminded by the Second Vatican Council — is the everyday calling of Christians. All of us are called to holiness.

November 14 — 11:00 a.m.. Zakopane, regional conference * November 15 — 10:00 a.m.. Biala, regional conference * November 17-19 — Ploki, canonical visitation of the parish. During visitation, a Mass for married couples:

A person cannot be formed except by looking at people. He or she must have an example of humanity. The first and most important examples are those of the father and mother. That is the example that a child sees every day and according to which he or she is formed ...

It is well known that the people of this parish work very hard. With your work, you have made great contributions to your neighbors, to society, to the nation. These contributions must also be made to God. So that your work might have the highest value in the eyes of God. That is why you need Christ in your families. Let Him be present. He was, after all, a man of work, a man of physical work. May He shine the great light of God upon your labor; the light which does not pass away, even though "heaven and earth shall pass away;" everything that man creates will pass away, but the Word of God will not pass away, the Light of God will not pass away. And the man who walks in this light will not pass away, either.

November 18 — Chapel in Ploki-Lgota. Visitation:

As I come to Lgota today, I see many faces of the people whom I met yesterday and this morning. First of all, the young people whom I confirmed yesterday, and whom I questioned about the truths of the faith, are here again today. Evidently I did not distress them too much with my examination, or they would be afraid to come today... But I see them here in great numbers and I recognize them, because at Confirmation there is the opportunity to get a closer look at these young faces and to remember them ...

Your community here must be especially close to the heart of your bishop. I am visiting Ploki for the first time, and for the first time I find myself on this spot by the chapel in Lgota, where you have built this humble shelter ... while you stand there in the field next to the chapel. I must tell you that a bishop in Poland, and especially a bishop of the Church of Krakow, has many places like this where people stand under the open sky the whole year round, as you do here ... There are such places in Krakow and near Krakow ... And I must tell you that these places are especially dear to my heart. I visit them most often and I gladly offer the Sacrifice of the Holy Mass there ...

We will also bless this room for religious education. The property of the local pastor, which has been sealed shut and for reasons unknown, cannot

---

[32] November 13 is the feast day of St. Stanislaw Kostka.

be used for religious education. As if the parish in Ploki had too much space under a roof: it is enough to come here and see how it is on Sundays, how people stand out in the open ... And I ask that someone see this, that you not be denied these few extra square feet of floor area for the children who are to learn religion. And that is why we will bless this sealed room from the outside, singing, as does all of Poland, the hymn "We yearn for God." And we hope that our singing will be heard both by God and by men.

Same day — 12:00 noon. Cardinal Wojtyla is the principal celebrant during a Mass at the Mariacki Basilica concelebrated by the Superior General of the Congregation of the Resurrection and 40 superiors of religious orders — during the solemn celebration of the 100th anniversary of the death of the Servant of God Rev. Hieronim Kajsiewicz organized by the Congregation of the Resurrection. A sermon was preached by the Bishop Ordinary of Przemysl, Ignacy Tokarczuk. The Cardinal spoke at the end of the Mass:

> The Polish land is passing away. People on it, our ancestors, are passing away. But all of those I have mentioned: Wincenty Kadlubek, St. John of Kanty, Mikolaj Kopernik {Nicholas Copernicus}, Augustyn Kordecki, Fr. Hieronim Kajsiewicz, those who have passed away, call out with one voice: Your Word will not pass away. That is how they call out to Christ, that is how they call out to the Father, Son, and Holy Spirit.

November 20-21 — At the residence of the Cardinal, another scientific session was held on the topic of the imageography of St. Stanislaw, with the participation of scientists: priests and laity * November 20 — 12:00 noon. Krakow regional conference, 8:00 p.m., St. Anne's Church, conference for university students on the subject of authority * November 21 — in Wadowice, on the solemnity of the Presentation of Our Lady, Mass and benedictions for young lectors, for a *schola* for girl singers, and for a church renovated by the parishioners:

> Every time I come to the church in Wadowice, I am again made aware that my dedication to God began here, at this baptismal font ... Today, a few minutes from now, when your sons, who have been prepared for liturgical service as lectors, approach the altar ... then, in this blessing that I shall bestow on each of them, accepting their readiness for this service, there will be some portion of the Presentation in the temple, when the Mother of God herself was offered.

* On the same day — Krakow, the Church of St. John of the Sisters of the Presentation of the BVM, sermon.

November 22 — Oswiecim, regional conference * November 23 — 10:00 a.m., Krakow, regional conference of the deanery of the immediate vicinity of Krakow * November 23 — At the Church of the Discalced Carmelites, during an observance in honor of Brother Albert:

Each sainthood is a kind of victory of God in man. Each sainthood is a new life which comes through death, through spiritual death ...

"I thank You Father, that you have hidden these things from the mighty, and revealed them to the small." This is so appropriate, this is so like Brother Albert. This expresses the entire truth of his life so concisely. Indeed he became small, ever smaller, ever poorer, ever more humble, completely divested of self, ever more a brother to those who were the most needy. And as a result, those great matters of God which the Father hides from the mighty and reveals to the small were opened up to him.

When, after a few days, the senior Sister came to thank him for participating in the service, the Cardinal said: "I could constantly talk about Brother Albert." He also told her of a letter which he had sent to Cardinal Raimondi, Prefect of the Congregation for the Causes of the Saints, in which he wrote that in connection with the Holy Year, he sees Brother Albert as the first among the Polish candidates to the honors of the altar. (The Albertine Sisters)

November 24 — At the Basilica of Franciscan Fathers for the 50th anniversary of the choir of St. Cecilia:

God is the source of all existence and of all life, and life is a very rich reality. This reality is very rich in the realm of nature, and so much richer in the realm of man ... The life of humankind is composed of every person, of various nations, various cultures, of the entire family of man which is made up of the common heritage of all people and of all nations for so many ages of history, for so many generations.

November 25 — Wawel Cathedral:

The Creator rules in one fashion in the rest of creation, but rules differently in man, in families, in communities, in nations, in humanity, in the Church and through the Church. Differently and in conformance with what He Himself has decreed from the beginning. God, the Creator and Lord, wishes to rule in man according to the law of Grace. By the power of this law, we were admitted from the beginning to participation in the Kingdom of God. Christ made us the Kingdom and the priesthood, upholding what the Father decreed from the beginning when He said to the first humans: "Have dominion" ... You came here from the various parishes of the Archdiocese of Krakow which have been visited during the course of this year by the bishops of the Church of Krakow, by me and my brother bishops.

Same day — 6:00 p.m., the Dominican church in Wroclaw, on the 750th anniversary of the Dominican Order, by the relics of Blessed Czeslaw. For the conclusion of the jubilee started in October 1972 by the tomb of St. Jacek {Hyacinth} in Krakow:

The Kingdom of God is within you, Christ said, and this is a fundamental truth. It is indeed within each of us, but in various ages of history there have been people in whom the Kingdom of God was realized much more perfectly, much more fully, much more abundantly. These people were the apostles of their times. They read the Gospel not only with their eyes, not only with their minds and their hearts, but with their whole being, their whole genius. These were people to whom the Church owed its renewal in various ages ...

Today, all of us in the 20th century carry the responsibility for the Kingdom of God in our times. This is a different assignment. Maybe these times are, in a way, more difficult, or maybe it only seems so to us. The finger of God writes the story of the salvation of man, of nations, of humanity on everything, and He is constantly building His Kingdom, His true Kingdom, the cornerstone of which was laid by Christ standing before of Pilate as one condemned. The Kingdom of God is within us and that is why our plea must be ardent. Our times demand it. If it was necessary for the likes of Francis, Dominick, Jacek and Czeslaw, and Thomas Aquinas to struggle for the Gospel in the 13th century, then we, too, have to struggle for the Gospel in our century.

November 26 — 10:00 a.m.. Wadowice, regional conference * November 28 — 10:00 a.m., Residence chapel, concelebrated Mass with the participants of a course for assistant pastors (1st year) * Same day — 6:00 p.m., St. Mark's Church in Krakow, symposium of the Liturgical Institute in honor of the Servant of God, Archbishop J. Bilczewski:

> May the participation in the Eucharist, which is the reason for our gathering here, allow us to tear through all of the veils of this temporal world in which all of us are entangled, which determines in a variety of ways how we penetrate with our faith into that Kingdom which is not only to come but which is already here. The Kingdom which was at the beginning, the Kingdom which is the Alpha, and which will be at the end, which is the Omega. The Eucharist always places us at the very center of this Kingdom, the Kingdom of the Living God shrouded in mystery.

November 30 — Krakow, Church of St. Andrew, he celebrated a Holy Mass according to the new Sacramentary.

December 1 — Mistrzejowice, a blessing of temporary church facilities, a cross and a plot for the church, beginning of the Holy Year, Mass and sermon:

> And so a community grew up; it showed the world, by its faith and perseverance, that it exists ... By your perseverance you bore witness to your faith and to the presence of the Church. In this new part of Nowa Huta, called Mistrzejowice.
>
> This witness became eloquent and convincing. It became especially eloquent and convincing ... on that night of Christmas Eve, the first time I came to you as a bishop, to stand with your pastor and with you, to bear witness together with you that your cause is our common cause, the cause of the entire Church of Krakow, of the entire Church of God in Poland. Because the cardinal and the bishop of the Church of Krakow express the cause of the Church in the Krakow Archdiocese and in all of Poland ... I wish to thank all the parishioners who in so short a time, while the settlement is still being built, have achieved this full awareness of parish membership. This is usually not easy to achieve in new settlements.

Same day — 9:00 p.m.,Theological Seminary, a conference for the beginning of the Holy Year * December 2 — Stalowa Wola, the Diocese of Przemysl, consecration of a new Church of Our Lady Queen of Poland. The church is consecrated and a solemn Mass is celebrated by Cardinal Wojtyla, who addressed the congregation after the Mass. Same day in the evening, the Cardinal, in the company of Bishop Boleslaw Taborski and Bishop Tadeusz Blaszkiewicz (the auxiliary bishops of the Diocese of Przemysl), went to Babica near Rzeszow and celebrated a second Mass in memory of Rev. J. Mac, a priest of the Archdiocese of Krakow, martyred in Oswiecim {Auschwitz}.

December 4 — 3:00 p.m.. A meeting of the Main Committee of the Synod. The Cardinal offers a positive assessment of the development of the Synod's organization, of how the study groups have been constituted, and of the participation of the youth. He proposes that the Committee begin preparing outlines for the final documents. There should be one main document, with detailed documents based on it. The guiding principle in preparing the documents: the nature and essence of the particular Church (the theology of the Church of Krakow and historical elements). There must be also a document analogous to Chapter V of Lumen gentium, because Krakow is a city of saints. Also: eschatology, Marian elements, the cult of the Sacred Heart of Jesus. A separate issue is the freedom of religion and the field of academics, specifically the Department of Theology. (The text of his address is in the acts of the Synod.)

December 8-10 — Visitation of the parish of Wodna-Krystynow, Confirmation of two bedridden boys, for the conclusion, a supper with a group of parishioners * December 8 — in Rychwald:

> We will pray that the spiritual fruits of the Holy Year may be more powerful than all of the activities of the Spirit of Darkness, the spirit of the temporal world, the spirit of materialism and atheism, that these fruits be stronger in you. That all of us may pass this historic examination of faith and Christian life which our generation has been called upon to take.

December 9 — In the Wodna-Krystynow parish, a Mass for married couples and a blessing:

> As He joined a man and a woman in this close union ... God said to the first humans: "Be fruitful and multiply!" This means: transmit life to new creatures in your image; and because in your image, then also in My image, because if you are created in the image and likeness of God, then your children, your issue, the children to whom you give life, are also created in the image and likeness of God. You don't have to read far in the Holy Scriptures to find this entire truth: it's right on the first pages ...
> As I bless each married couple, remember that this blessing is also an expression of the communion which you have, through the priests and

bishops, through the successors of the Apostles, with Jesus Christ Himself. We are all the People of God, we are building the Kingdom of God, we are building the living Church, we shape it in the souls of our children, our youth. That is our calling, and of this we will have to give an accounting before God.

December 10. In Wodna-Krystynow parish to the children: Mass and a blessing.

> For a bishop, the visitation of a parish is always a great joy. It is a deeply moving experience. Because as the Bishop of the Church of Krakow I am the pastor of all the parishes ... And because I can't be here constantly like your local pastors, this day or two or three that I can be with you is so dear to me. To be here with you, to meet with you, to serve you with the sacraments, to bless you, to strengthen your faith, especially with the Sacrament of Confirmation, and to encounter, in a variety of ways, everything that the Holy Spirit constantly accomplishes in your Christian souls.

Same day — a meeting of the Council of the Pontifical Department of Theology in Krakow. The Cardinal made reference to the 500th anniversary of the death of St. John of Kanty and the 600th anniversary of Queen Jadwiga, the foundress of the Department of Theology, as an occasion for further intervention, also by way of the Apostolic See, in the matter of reinstatement of due rights to this institution. Also, about raising the demands made on the Department by the academic community and the clergy. About initiatives awaiting action: establishing the status of pastoral institutes, development of cooperation with the Department of Philosophy of the Jesuit Fathers, working out the concepts of strictly academic institutes, matters of the museum, the archives and the library, developing and improving publications. (From the minutes of the Council of the Department)

December 11 — 9:00 a.m., Residence chapel, concelebrated Mass for the beginning of the Council of Priests * Same day — cemetery in Kaniow, during the funeral of Rev. W. Kanczuga (a young priest, ordained in the Millennium year of 1966):

> It is my ardent wish that this sign of your departure, departure in the priesthood, departure in Christ, speaks to all of us in the same way as would the departure of a man to his brothers. Because after all, death is also an annunciation. It is also the annunciation of the hope of eternal life, a hope which we proclaim, which we live, by which we guide ourselves through this vale of tears to our eternal Homeland. Death is the annunciation of renewal, the annunciation of the Kingdom, the annunciation of fulfillment, the annunciation of the House of the Father. And all of this after a pilgrimage, after hardship, after exhaustion, after suffering.

December 12 — 8:00 p.m., Church of the Dominican Fathers,

---

[33] See Glossary.

Oplatek[33] for university students * December 13 — 10:00 a.m., Warsaw, Main Council of the Polish Episcopate * December 14 — 8:00 p.m.. *Oplatek* with the university youth at the Parish of Our Lady of Lourdes in Krakow-Nowa Wies:

> The meetings of the early Christians, in their second part, had a familial character. They were called feasts of love, agape. And our Polish tradition of *Wigilia*[34] descends in a direct line from those proto-Christian feasts of love. It is a feast during which we share bread, the bread of temporal life. But this bread has a singular similarity to the Bread of the Eucharist ... This *Oplatek* {Christmas wafer}, broken and shared by Poles at the *Wigilia* supper, emphasizes that this is a Feast of love ...
>
> If we read properly from the depth of our souls ... then on that Christmas Eve, in the face of the Mystery of God's Nativity, every person takes on a particular value. Every one without exception. Because each one is illuminated by the light of God Incarnate. That means of God, who became Man. To each person — every one without exception — He applies His own measure, His own dimension, the dimension of His Divinity. Through this, each person takes on the highest value...

December 15-17 — Visitation of the parish of Wola Justowska, Mass and sermon in a hospital, the Holy Communion in the sick wards * December 15 — 8:30 p.m., Church of the Jesuit Fathers, *Oplatek* for university students * December 16 — At the Mariacki Basilica, 5th anniversary of the coronation of the image of the Blessed Mother and the conclusion of the visitation of the image of Our Lady of Jasna Gora {Czestochowa} in the archdiocese:

> Because we have to give thanks for goodness received, every year we wish to give thanks to the Blessed Mother for the year of peregrination which ended with the coronation at the Mariacki Basilica. At the same time, thanksgiving opens the heart of the one to whom we give thanks. A new bond is established, a new path for the exchange of gifts is opened. And, certainly, it is so in our communion with Mary the Mother of God, with Her Son, and with God Himself.

December 17 — 1:00 p.m., a visit to the convent of the Sisters of St. Clare * Same day — 3:00 p.m., Lanckorona, during the funeral of Msgr. Jan Marszalek, a priest who died at the age of 101:

> I know that our people know how to show gratitude, and how to show gratitude to priests. They have such a sense of faith, that they often pray for their priests. As if you sensed ... that we especially need your prayers; not only here on earth, when we have a particular responsibility for the salvation of every soul, but also after death, when we depart from here to face God's judgment, carrying with us this greater responsibility for the Church, for the salvation of men. And for that reason it is truly uplifting, when I hear, during my visits to various parishes, that the faithful ... often

---

[34] Christmas Eve dinner, the central celebration of the Polish observance of Christmas.

offer prayers for deceased priests and offer Mass intentions for their departed pastors. It is a beautiful gesture.

December 19 — Tyniec, he is the main celebrant of a parish Mass for the Holy Year. He preaches a sermon * December 20 — Krakow. Residence, a second meeting of the Committee of Experts of the Provincial Synod, Cardinal Wojtyla presided * December 21 — St. Anne's Church, in anticipation of the actual day of the 500th anniversary of the death of St. John of Kanty, in the presence of the Bishop of Czestochowa:

> This anniversary is especially meaningful to us, to the Church of Krakow, ... to the academic community, to the Department of Theology which has existed in Krakow since the end of the 14th century, to the theological seminaries which are present in Krakow in numbers not seen in any other city of Poland, because there is more than a dozen of them: 3 large diocesan seminaries and about 10 religious ones with a range of student populations.

December 22 — Our Lady of Lourdes Parish, on the occasion of the 50th anniversary of the parish:

> Today, in this act of thanksgiving, we should remember certain people. Fifty years ago, the Bishop of the Church of Krakow was the unforgettable Adam Stefan Sapieha, a prince by birth and a prince of the Church ... but, above all, a great man, a man of Providence, a man of God for our Homeland in our most horrible time, the time of occupation ... It was he who created parishes. In places where there was yet no city, in places where a city was yet to rise. He created them with foresight. This ancient, historic Krakow is surrounded by 500 such new parishes ... wherever they could arise, which was not always easy ... How grateful we must be to that bishop who had the foresight to create a parish here at the appropriate time. He created a second ring. Thank God that we have this second ring of churches and parishes within old Krakow. Because of this, we can now think about and fight for a third ring which is a requirement of our times. For places like Nowa Huta, Azory, Krowodrza, Bronowice, and other districts. We all have so much to be grateful for. We are grateful to the generation of our fathers and grandfathers, and we, fathers, are grateful to the young generation. Because it has turned out that this parish became, in a particular way, a parish of the youth. I come here several times a year, because the young, the students from all over Poland, don't give me peace, they want to have a bishop among them. I was here several days ago and they were here, standing as you are now. The church was packed, shoulder to shoulder. There was no room for a pin — all university students.
>
> Christian life is created by every Christian. What would we be if it weren't for our parents who brought their children up as Catholics. What would we be, it weren't for the teachers who, despite obstacles, support that upbringing ... if it weren't for our neighbors. What would we be, if it weren't for all these good people — sometimes nobody knows about them, only God knows.

December 23 — Malec, the family environs of St. John of Kanty:

> I have heard much about you and about the concern you have shown for your parish and Christian community, which you have demonstrated by enlarging this old chapel which could no longer suffice for your growing town and community. You wanted to have a roof over your heads ... and you arranged for it. I come to you today to emphasize that the Bishop of the Church of Krakow knows about what you did here and he expresses his appreciation and thanks for your concern shown here. Because this is our common cause and our common concern.

Same day — in Dabrowa Narodowa, for the conclusion of the mission in preparation for the Holy Year:

> I appeal here from this altar to the authorities, that the matter of the center of religious education for this community be settled! Not partially, not by halfway measures! But in the fashion which the Catholic population of our city deserves! Which it has earned by its labor! It cannot be that people, who by their hard labor upon the earth and beneath the surface of the earth make daily contributions to building the welfare of our homeland, should be deprived of a roof over the heads of their children, where these children can peacefully learn religion! We have a right to that; the law is on our side. And what I say now, I say in full awareness of the responsibility for the rule of law which exists and should exist in our state!

* On the same day — Glebowice — the celebration of the blessing of the new altar.

December 24 — Residence, breaking and sharing of *Oplatek* {Christmas wafer} with: the sisters, the priests, the staff of *Tygodnik Powszechny*, staff of the Curia; 6:00 p.m., "Wigilia" supper with the seminarians * Same day — a "Wigilia" address at Wzgorza Krzeslawickie before "Pasterka" {Midnight Mass}:

> We come here together with Bishop Julian, who will celebrate Midnight Mass here with you. I celebrated it last year. I am going to Mistrzejowice. We have to rotate year by year. But from the longing of my heart I come here to tell you the words of my warmest Christmas greetings ... We are convinced that justice will be served. And that we won't have to experience this Midnight Mass year after year, and all the other Sundays and feasts of the entire year, in the cold and the rain; that we will find that longed-for roof over our heads, so that we may properly commune with our God and with one another.

Mistrzejowice — 12:00 midnight. " Pasterka," sermon * December 25 — Christmas Day, Wawel Cathedral:

> Today I wish to welcome you here at the Cathedral of Wawel in a very special way, because this Christmas is particularly festive for us, for the Church of Krakow. It is the first Christmas which we celebrate in the Holy Year. You know well that our Holy Father Paul VI, following the centuries-old tradition of the Church, has announced a Holy Year, a great Jubilee of Jesus Christ ... The Holy Father wants the entire People of God to gather around their bishops, so that together we may experience the great Jubilee of Jesus Christ as a Feast of the Church. We are to discover His mysteries,

we are to deepen our awareness of Him. From this awareness we are to develop an attitude of life appropriate to the People of God, appropriate to Christians and Catholics of our time ... We are one family of God, we sit at one "wigilia" table. In truth this table is not set here, in the Cathedral of Wawel. We have left the "wigilia" table in our homes. But here, in the Wawel Cathedral, there is an altar on which we will break bread, the Body of Christ, and we will eat the bread, the Body of Christ, and drink the wine, the Blood of Christ. All of our wigilia get-togethers, those tables where we broke the *Oplatek*[35] and will continue to do so, are the extension of this Feast of love which the Son of God has prepared for us.

Dear brothers and sisters, partakers in this Feast of love, I greet you, I break with you this Bread of the Lord, I break the *Oplatek* with you ... And as at Baptism, and as at Confirmation, I ask each one of you:

"Do you believe in God, the Father Almighty, Creator of heaven and earth?"

I do believe!"

"Do you believe in Jesus Christ, the only-begotten Son of God?...

On the special invitation of the Cardinal, a large number of religious sisters take part in this Mass * December 26 — Gorzow, cathedral, consecration of Bishop Pawel Socha CM, sermon:

The Holy Spirit's choice precedes our consciousness, our discernment. In the consciousness of the community of the Church of Gorzow, in the consciousness of your bishop and shepherd, in the consciousness of the Polish Episcopate and the Primate, this choice took shape only recently. But how much earlier the Holy Spirit must have made the choice, and by what roads He had to lead our bishop-elect up to the moment when he stands here before this altar, so that we may lay hands on him to transmit to him the apostolic succession. For all of this we must thank the Holy Spirit, who Himself calls up bishops, with us as intermediaries.

The choice is completed by people. The Apostolic See has the last word. A moment ago we heard the notification of the will of the Holy Father. The bishop-elect enters the college of the Episcopate of the Universal Church, he enters into a special bond with the Successor of Peter himself. That is the human dimension of this event, but this human dimension is permeated with Divine mystery. The Holy Spirit calls bishops up. And we, who gather here for this consecration, wish to bow our heads and our hearts in a spirit of faith, to fall on our knees before that unseen Maker of sanctity, the Sanctifying Spirit. Before that unseen inviter to the ministry — to every ministry, that of Christians, priests, bishops. And while so kneeling, while bowing our heads and our hearts before the Holy Spirit, we wish to receive from Him all of the power with which He endows the new bishop of the Church today, your auxiliary bishop, so that he may serve the people of God in the Church of Gorzow.

And as the Primate of Poland has already said, we wish to dedicate him in a particular way to Mary, the Mother of the Church, because she was at the creation of all the bishops, when she was present at the descent of the Holy Spirit. Today may she also be the maternal Intermediary in trans-

---

mitting the power of the Holy Spirit to our nominee ...

... Dear Brother, this is our wish for you, a bishop: When you speak, may those to whom you speak be unable to resist the Spirit who will be speaking through you. Regardless of whether you speak to the faithful, in fulfillment of your duties as bishop, or to brother priests at various meetings of the clergy, or to religious sisters, who especially need the concern of a bishop, or whether you speak to small children, or to gray-haired older people, whether you speak to the sick or to the healthy, whether you speak to married couples, or whether you speak to the authorities, may all those to whom you speak be unable to resist the Spirit who will be speaking through you. May you be always filled with the Spirit which Christ gave to the Apostles, and through the Apostles to the entire Church. The Spirit which we, through our unworthy ministries, in continuation of the Apostolic succession, transmit to you.

May this Spirit be strong within you. You yourself may be weak, but may He be strong within you, so that the eloquence of your words and the eloquence of your life may be as effective as was the eloquence of St. Stephen, the first witness to Christ, who bore this witness even unto death.

December 27 — At the cathedral in Wroclaw, the consecration of Bishop Jozef Marek, with the participation of Cardinal Kominek and numerous other bishops. Sermon:

The liturgy of the Church has woven the figure of John the Apostle into the octave of Christmas, into the mystery of Divine Nativity, ... This has a very deep justification. St. John the Apostle and Evangelist was the one who most concisely and most meaningfully defined the mystery of the Birth of Christ: "And the Word was made Flesh and dwelt among us." These words, which we all know by heart, define the mystery. And we must see not just an event, but a mystery in Christmas. Otherwise, we cannot participate in it. And that is why St. John ... earned his place in the liturgy of the octave of Christmas.

December 28 — 6:30 p.m.. Theological Seminary, Mass and a sermon during a retreat for graduating high school students and a get-together with them * December 29 — 9:00 a.m.. Kalwaria Zebrzydowska, concelebrated Mass and sermon for the conclusion of the retreat for graduating high school students * December 30 — 12:00 noon, residence chapel, Mass and sermon for the 35th anniversary of his final high-school examination * Same day — in Zakopane, on the Feast of the Holy Family, in the presence of the Bishop of Lomza, a sermon:

In the commandment to honor your father and mother, there is also a commandment to the father and mother, that they be worthy of honor. This is the moral authority of parents, of parenting, an external authority within the family ... This fundamental value must not be taken away from any child. No child can lose confidence in his or her own parents ... They are often so conditioned, so dependent on various attitudes, on various modes of behavior, ... that it is not possible to omit anything, to bypass anything, to leave any slack. Marriage and the family are the smallest social unit, but also the most precise one. And that is why it is the easiest to break. Just as it is easiest to break a small, precise mechanism ...

In all of this there is a cry, there is a humble plea, which I direct today, through the intercession of the Holy Family, through the mystery of the Birth of Christ, to the Heavenly Father Himself ... Believe me, your bishop, that this cry never leaves my heart. It is a cry for the salvation of our Polish families, it is a cry for the salvation of our Homeland through the family, through Christian families.

December 31 — Krakow, 6:00 p.m., St. Szczepan Church, a service and a sermon for the end of the old year * Same day at midnight — at the Franciscan Fathers church, Mass and sermon:

So in this new year, may Mary be the beginning of a better world for us. Even if the world is difficult, even if it has much evil, but if it has Christ, if it has Mary, and it will have Her, it has Christ, then that world always carries within it the beginning and the seed of a better world...

December — jubilee Masses for the inauguration of the Holy Year in Krakow and beyond * The Church of St. Catherine in Krakow — a word to the participants {female} of the apostolic retreat for the animators of apostolic communities.

Sometime during the year of 1973 (a precise date could not be established), a visit to ailing Tadeusz Zajaczkowski residing on Krolowej Jadwigi Street. Tadeusz Zajaczkowski — (1880-1974) — during World War II was associated with the Delegation of the Polish Government in exile. He made great contributions during the 20-year period of Poland's pre-war independence; a man of deep faith, quiet, humble. The conversation lasted for about an hour. (Irena Jezewska)

1974

January 1-5 — Zakopane-Jaszczurowka — skiing * January 1 —
9:00 p.m., Zakopane, sermon for the beginning of the Holy Year *
January 2-5 — Zakopane, private Masses and a concelebrated requiem
Mass * January 6 — Wawel Cathedral, concelebrated High Mass with
sermon, a service for the Holy Year:

**Our entire ministry for the Holy Year is geared towards the family and
the youth — so that we would see in our Christian family communities, in
our parish communities, how great God's gift is, so we would never allow
it to be taken away from us at any price.**

Same day — 3:00 p.m., Halcnow, participated in "Jaselka"
{Christmas play} * Same day — 7:00 p.m., *Oplatek*[1] at the "Zrodlo"
{Source}. "His Eminence Cardinal Karol Wojtyla attended this
Christmas-time celebration on the invitation of the Congregation. The
youth came in great numbers to this meeting with the Cardinal. This
evening was recorded in pictures." (From the chronicles of the
Congregation of the Sisters of Our Lady of Mercy) * Same day — 8:00 p.m.,
Oplatek of the Club of Catholic Intellectuals.

January 8-9 — Krakow, 3 Franciszkanska Street, meeting of the
Episcopal Committee for Pastoral Ministry on the subject of pastoral
and preaching programs. Cardinal B. Kominek was absent due to recu-
peration. Bishop Wladyslaw Miziolek presided. Cardinal Wojtyla presented (on January 9) the pastoral program for the years after 1975;
additional comments on the subject were offered by: Rev. Rector Majka
and Father Nawrocki. (From the minutes of the Committee)

January 12-13. Meeting of the Committee for the Apostolate of the
Laity. Work on dialogue (third edition of part I), continued work on the
text pertaining to councils; preparation of a pastoral program for the
years 1974/75. A discussion with invited guests: the apostolate of the
adult laity and the Sacrament of Confirmation * January 12 — 7:30
p.m., residence chapel, Mass and sermon for the *Srodowisko*[2] * January
14 — 11:00 a.m. Residence, a New Year's meeting of Bishops of the
Krakow Metropolitan See.

January 15 — 8:00 a.m.-1:30 p.m., Krakow (3 Franciszkanska
Street) meeting of the Committee of the Polish Episcopate appointed
for the purpose of preparing a resolution of the Conference of the
Polish Episcopate for the Synod of Bishops of 1974, on the topic of
evangelization of the contemporary world. Members of the Committee

---

[1] See Glossary.
[2] See Glossary.

were: Cardinal Wojtyla, Archbishop A. Baraniak, Bishop J. Ablewicz
and Bishop I. Tokarczuk. The editor of the proposed resolution — Rev.
Dr. Adam Kubis from Krakow * January 16 — Residence, a meeting
of the Committee for the Year of Mikolaj Kopernik * January 17 —
1:00 p.m., Lipnik, adoration of the Blessed Sacrament and *Oplatek*[3]
with priests ordained in 1971 * 5:00 p.m., Witkowice, a get-together
with priests ordained in 1972. He spoke about the Christmas Vigil supper and the breaking of the wafer:

> **We gather together. It is a family gathering. Although our family of
> priests has a different character, a different appearance, it is a family — it
> is nonetheless a family. And it is a family because we all have one Father.
> And, in a particular way, our priesthood reminds us and all people of this
> Father; because it has its origin in Him, because He sent His Son to us into
> the world. And, by becoming Man, the Son of God at once entered the his-
> tory of mankind as a priest. For He immediately turned everyone's
> thoughts and hearts to the Father.**

January 18 — Wawel Cathedral, 10:00 a.m., 10th anniversary of his
nomination as the Archbishop of Krakow, ordination of acolytes and
deacons. "I direct my remarks especially to your families. I thank the
Christian parents for giving us their sons, so they would support the service of deacons, and later of priests, of bishops and of the Bishop of the
Church of Krakow." * January 19 — 4:00 p.m., residence, *Oplatek* with
artists * 6:30 p.m., residence chapel, Mass and sermon for the alumnae
of Sacre Coeur.

Jan 20 — 9:30 a.m., sermon for the Study Group on Family and
Marriage, *Oplatek* * 10:30 a.m., Metropolitan chapel, Mass with sermon and blessing of the banner of Bractwo Kurkowe.[4]

> **This might be a good time to thank Bractwo Kurkowe for their
> upholding of Eucharistic traditions in Krakow for so many centuries. And
> that they are upholding those traditions today, by participating in the
> Corpus Christi procession, giving today's twentieth-century procession a
> connection with the centuries, connecting that which is with that which has
> gone before; showing to the entire Krakow community that it has grown
> from the same root, that it is a continuation, a living extension of that soci-
> ety which began in the times of the Piasts, in the times of the Jagiellons[5], in
> the times when Bractwo Kurkowe was being founded. And that the Polish
> society and the community of Krakow venerates the Body of Christ today
> just as it did throughout the centuries, and just as it did throughout the
> centuries, so it does today.**

Same day — 11:30, the Franciscan church, *Oplatek* for the blind *
4:00 p.m., Metropolitan chapel, Mass with sermon and *Oplatek* for
teachers.

---

[3] See Glossary.
[4] Krakow marksman's society.
[5] Piast dynasty, Jagiellonian dynasty: dynasties of Polish kings

May we never lose the understanding that man is a great work, a holy work. And he is a great and holy work because God entered humanity. By becoming Man, He set out the full measure of every man. And we, who believe in Jesus Christ, must never forget about that measure, must never limit it, must never retreat from it in the education of man ...

To educate means to shape humanity at its deepest level ... that level which defines man. To educate, you must be a mature human being yourself. Education is more difficult than teaching. Because information, facts, the content of teaching in this or that field, can be transmitted in an impersonal manner. Facts can stand alone. But it is not possible to educate without inner truth. To educate, you must share your inner truth, the truth of your humanity. And you must transfer that truth of your mature humanity onto the one who needs to mature in humanity.

Same day — 7:00 p.m., Metropolitan chapel, concelebrated Mass and sermon, *Oplatek* for lawyers.

I would like to wish you from the bottom of my heart that you may be animated by the Holy Spirit; that the matters which form your calling, my dear guests of this evening, be animated anew by the Holy Spirit this year; and that each interpreter of the law, defender of the law and spokesman of the law receive all the gifts of the Holy Spirit mentioned today by St. Paul ... including the gift of piety. That means not only a deep reverence for God Himself, but for all of God's creation, especially for every man, who as a special creature demands special reverence and special renewal.

January 22 — Warsaw, Main Council of the Polish Episcopate * Jan 23-24 — Warsaw, 140th plenary conference of the Polish Episcopate * January 25 — 7:15 p.m., the Mariacki Church, Mass for the 100th anniversary of the birth of Wincenty Witos[6] * January 26 — 6:00 p.m., the Dominican church, *Oplatek*[7] for veterans * 7:00 p.m., Metropolitan chapel, *Oplatek* for physicians:

I think that every one of you ... can fairly easily come to realize that what lies at the heart of your work, your calling, is the work of salvation. For, indeed, salvation encompasses the entire person. Maybe sometimes we tend to narrow this reality, the vision of salvation, when we think of the salvation of the soul as if in isolation.

January 27 — Metropolitan chapel, *Oplatek* for those involved in family ministry:

My wish for you is ... that you, that your love may radiate inwards. For I believe this is the essence of the marital communion of husband and wife — that their love, that these two personalities, which have both been created in the image and likeness of God, radiate inwards. Each of them is unique; each is embraced by Eternal Love and each is called to eternal marriage, to eternal communion ... But besides radiating inwards, from heart to heart, from person to person, from husband to wife, from parents

---

6 Polish Prime Minister in the 1930's
7 See Glossary.

to children; besides this radiating inwards, which gives shape to the family, an authentic Christian shape, may your love also radiate outwards. May the love of your Christian marriages and families radiate outwards and, by your example, demonstrate, bear witness, attract.

Same day — Church of the Missionary Fathers on Stradom, sermon on the occasion the patronal feast of the Church, i.e. the Conversion of St. Paul:

> It might be said [about St. Paul] that his was a belated calling into the group of the Apostles, just as there are belated vocations to the priesthood ... Nevertheless, it is an authentic calling; it comes directly from Christ Himself ... Christ summons him personally, but summons him as His persecutor, turns him around on his way; gives his journey a new direction. Therefore, it can be said that a vocation is a conversion ... The one who once went against Christ, now turns to follow Christ and to go forth into the world with Christ.

Same day — 7:00 p.m., the Dominican Basilica, concelebrated Mass for the conclusion of the octave of prayers for unity among Christians:

> All those baptized in the name of Jesus Christ, even if they are separated by historical differences, have the right to hope that the Holy Spirit, the unifying principle, is acting within them and is leading everyone to a single communion in the Church of Christ ... [The Church of Krakow] ardently desires the fulfillment of what Christ Our Lord prayed for so intently at the Last Supper, thinking of His disciples and all of His followers throughout the ages: "Father, that they may all be one." We take up that prayer here. It is a reproach to us, that we do not have the unity that was desired by Christ. But it is also a call full of hope, a hope that we can gradually achieve such unity.

January 28 — 5:00 p.m., the Ursuline Sisters chapel, Mass with sermon, an evening of Christmas carols with the Higher Catechetic Institute * January 30 — 10:00 a.m., residence, conference of priests — heads of deaneries. Subject: The Holy Year, 600th anniversary of the birth of Queen Jadwiga {Hedwig} * 7:30 p.m., Theological Seminary, an evening of Christmas carols * Jan 31 — 6:00 p.m., Chapel of the Salesian Fathers — Losiowka, concelebrated Mass with sermon for the 75th anniversary of the Salesian Fathers in Poland.

January — At the Dominicans', opening remarks for the inauguration of the days of recollection for the religious preachers of missions and retreats:

> The pastoral ministry is always regular, it always concentrates on age-old issues and truths. Because the human soul is always the same, it has the same needs, the problem of sin and repentance is the same, and the ways of God's Grace are the same, or at least very similar.
> But there is an overload of talk in society, expectations are different,

demands are higher. Long ago, people heard the priest from the pulpit. Today, besides the speaker on the radio, they hear the speaker on television, they hear, they see, and maybe even inadvertently, they compare ... There is a tremendous battle over the morality of our society, the morality of married life, of family life, the morality of the young generation. And you must realize that when you go up to a pulpit during a mission or retreat, you are going into the thick of that battle.

In January — Krakow, the Basilica of the Dominican Fathers. Sermon on the Feast of St. Thomas.

January — 50th anniversary of Rev. Karol Sadlik's and Rev. Wladyslaw Matyszkiewicz's ordination to the priesthood. Sermon:

The work of the honorees, their service to the People of God, has borne bountiful fruit. It is difficult even to count these fruits, difficult to give any sort of statistics. And there is no need for that, and you yourselves would not wish it. Because, as we all know very well, the fruits of the priest's labor, its effectiveness, are known to God alone; the effectiveness resides deep in the souls of men, and, by this reckoning, it is immeasurable.

February 2 — 4:00 p.m.. Wiktorowki, Chapel of the Queen of Tatry[8], concelebrated Mass with sermon * February 3 — 4:00 p.m., Theological Seminary in Krakow, blessing of a new part of the building, *koleda*[9] * February 5 — 6:00 p.m., residence chapel, Mass and sermon for the conclusion of a course for nurses * February 6 — A visit by Archbishop Luigi Poggi and Rev. Msgr. Andrzej Deskur. It was officially announced that *the Archbishop was interested in the conditions of the apostolic work of the Church of Krakow and in the problems of the construction of new churches* (*Notificationes*, 11-12, 1975) * February 7 — 9:00 a.m., Wawel Cathedral, introductory remarks during a concelebrated Mass with Archbishop Poggi, Bishop Groblicki and Msgr. Deskur * February 8 — 10:30 a.m., Theological Seminary, regional conference of the deaneries of Podhale[10] * February 10 — 9:00 a.m., Mogila, Church of the Cistersian Fathers, homily about Queen Jadwiga {Hedwig}:

Her [Queen Jadwiga's] greatness, the greatness of the human heart, is never out of date ... [From her] we need to learn especially that inner law of sacrifice, we need to learn the intensity of prayer by which man grows spiritually. We need to learn that not everything in life depends on more possessions, and this is so typical of people in our time: the drive to possess as much as possible. The greatness of a person depends on being somebody. And a person becomes somebody through the offerings made from the depths of one's heart.

---

8 Tatry—the highest part of the Carpathian Mountain range, in south-central Poland on the border with the Czech Republic.

9 See glossary.

10 Podhale—the high foothills region of the Carpathians and Tatra Mountains where the gorale (mountain folk) live.

The same day — at 10:00 a.m., at the metropolitan chapel, to nurses:

The meaning that the Church gives to the work of humans, to their professional calling, is an ultimate meaning ... After all, by performing the work of our profession day after day, year after year, we are supposed to earn not only a retirement pension for ourselves, but we are to earn eternal life ... In the secular world, they tell us only of years of service, of professional obligations. The Church tells us that this service, this work, is connected with the highest calling of man: the calling to communion with God; that man clears a path to this unity by his work, by choosing a lifelong profession ...

Your magnificent profession, which is so closely connected with the good of mankind, with the care of people, as if taken from a journal of love, this magnificent profession can be deformed, can be made shallow ... It can be said that your entire profession is taken from the Gospel. If you wanted to look for the deepest roots of your calling, you will find those roots in Christ, in Him who bent over suffering people.

The events, sufferings, deaths which you find in your workplace have their tragic meaning. I think that the greatest tragedy of our society, of our nation, is the death of people who have not yet been born: those who are conceived but not born. And I do not know how we shall pay in the judgement of history for this horrible crime. But it is obvious that this cannot pass without consequences. Just as the terrible sins of our nation in the 18th century did not pass without consequences — we paid for that — so also there will be consequences of the sins of our century, sins which are committed so thoughtlessly and so prevalently.

Same day — 12:00 noon, the Mariacki Basilica, about Queen Jadwiga on the 600th anniversary of her birth:

She taught us about the mission of history. Before, we were fighting for our unity, for our statehood: that was the work of the Piast dynasty, ended with Kazimierz the Great[11]. Jadwiga taught us and our brother nations the mission of history. This remained in our consciousness. We know that it is not sufficient to fight for one's existence, it is necessary to have an awareness of one's obligations and one's mission in the course of human history ...

February 11 — 10:00 a.m., Wadowice, regional conference * Same day — a sermon at the Church of Our Lady of Lourdes:

The Holy Year reminds us of the holiness of time, and calls us to holiness of soul, of conscience and of person ... We are convinced that it is ultimately only the Living God who can establish contact with living man. And it is only through this contact, through this dialogue, that living man can truly discover himself!

February 12 — 10:30 a.m., Theological Seminary, a conference of Krakow deaneries: III, IV, V, VI * February 13 — 8:30 a.m., residence chapel, concelebrated Mass and sermon for a meeting of archeologists

---

[11] King Casimir (ruled: 1333-1370), last of the Piast dynasty. Queen Jadwiga's (ruled: 1384-1399) marriage to Jagiello (ruled: 1386-1434), Grand Duke of Lithuania, began the Jagiellonian dynasty.

and professors of patristics[12] * 10:30 a.m., Theological Seminary, regional conference of Krakow deaneries: I, II * February 14 — 9:00 a.m., Nowy Targ, regional conference * 3:00 p.m., Zakopane, regional conference * Same day — 7:30 p.m., Mass and sermon in honor of the Blessed Sacrament at a convent of the Carmelite Sisters in Zakopane: "...the most difficult issue of our time, which has become a daily concern for us, is this great test of faith: the test of faith of a whole generation, the test of faith of all of society, the old and the young..."

February 15 — 10:00 p.m., Oswiecim, regional conference * February 17 — 10:00 a.m., Wawel Cathedral, concelebrated Mass with sermon on the occasion of the 600th anniversary of the birth of Queen Jadwiga.

> This anniversary is being celebrated by all of Poland. But Krakow has first rights to that celebration. The celebration is the right and the duty of the Church of Krakow, because she was a beloved daughter of that Church. It is the right and the duty of the Bishop of the Church of Krakow, who to this day wears on his robes the rational[13] embroidered by her ...
>
> God has told us Poles the entire truth of our history through the life of this young queen, whom He called back to Himself from this earth, from here, from Wawel. But she told us everything that needed to be said. She told this to us, to the nation that lives between the West and the East, to the nation that must shape its life, its mission, its responsibility here in this place in Europe. It was through Jadwiga that the King of kings and the Lord of history established the measure of that responsibility and pointed out the direction ... We pray here, at the place of her eternal rest, at her tomb, for our homeland, for the Polish nation. But we also pray for all those nations and peoples for which she was a mother, just as she was a mother for us. We pray for Lithuania and Ruthenia[14], we pray for all of Europe.

Same day — 6:00 p.m., Wawel Cathedral, archdiocesan pilgrimage of the youth for the Holy Year and the 600th anniversary of the birth of Queen Jadwiga, Mass and homily:

> That Jadwiga was up to [the making of the sacrifice] ... was above all the fruit of prayer, of conversation with the Crucified Jesus Christ, who loved so much, that He has the right to dictate to the human heart! And what He dictates, what He inspires, will never violate the human heart, will never break it. For it is at the price of sacrifice that the heart matures and develops.

February 18 — Wawel Cathedral, on the actual day of Queen Jadwiga's birth, solemn Mass with the participation of the Theological Seminary and the Metropolitan Chapter. A reference made to the celebrations on the day before:

---

[12] Scholars who study the (writings of) the Fathers of the Church.

[13] An imitation of the pallium

[14] Today's Belarus

We still have yesterday's pilgrimage in our memory: the Cathedral filled to the last pew with young faces and young hearts; and again as many young pilgrims outside the basilica ... May Jadwiga be an inspiration for us, may she pray with us, here, in this Cathedral, where for so many centuries her personal prayer has been present: that attentive, ardent prayer flowing from her suffering heart. Here, in this Cathedral, may her presence be repeated in our time, in the Holy Year which falls on the 600th anniversary of her birth.

February 19-20 — 11:00 a.m., residence, a meeting with co-authors of *Theology of the Family*. "Besides encouraging new initiatives in the pastoral care of families and marriages, the Cardinal undertook the task of preparing a co-authored work on the subject of the theology of the family. This work was almost finished when the Cardinal left for the Chair of Peter." (Bishop Stanislaw Smolenski). In that group work Cardinal Wojtyla penned an extensive introduction explaining the concept of the "theology of the family," as well as chapters entitled: "The family as *communio personarum*[15]" and "Attempts at theological interpretation." The co-authors of the work are: Rev. Jerzy Chmiel, Fr. Andrzej Bober SJ, Rev. Jerzy Bajda, Teresa Kukolowicz, Wanda Poltawska, Jan Klys, Fr. Karol Meissner OSB, Bishop Stanislaw Smolenski, Rev. Tadeusz Pieronek, Cardinal Franciszek Macharski, Bishop Jozef Rozwadowski. The editor in charge of the effort: Bishop Stanislaw Smolenski.

Theology of the Family. Introduction [Karol Wojtyla]: Totus Tuus ego sum et omnia mea Tua sunt.[16]

This is not the first time a work is undertaken under the title of "theology." And furthermore, this is not the first time we intend to speak of the family. But this is probably the first time in Poland that we feel the need of a synthesis under the title *The Theology of the Family*. This does not mean that there were no Polish-language theological works about the family, and especially works written from the point of view of faith and a Christian outlook on the world, above all from a position of Catholic ethics. But it seems that despite the existence of many such works in the past, there is a need for a new theological synthesis on the subject of the family. We are led to this undertaking by many circumstances and experiences in the dimension of our own society, here in Poland, and by the inspiration of the Universal Church.

At this point, we could make reference to the vast number of publications on the subject of the family, which illuminate various aspects of the reality of the family in Poland and in the contemporary world. Most often, these tend to state the crisis of the family, or at least to emphasize the changes which it is undergoing. This is the common denominator of the writings on this subject.

The Second Vatican Council, too, saw the necessity of taking up this matter, and did so in the pastoral constitution "On the Church in the

---

[15] Communion of persons
[16] I am totally Yours, and all that I have is Yours.

Contemporary World." The second part of this document carries a meaningful title: "Some of the more burning (or rather — pressing) issues." And first among those issues is contained in a chapter entitled: "Increasing the dignity of marriage and the family" ...

February 21 — Warsaw, Main Council of the Polish Episcopate * February 23 — Defense of a doctoral thesis by Rev. Zbigniew Majchrzyk: *The Problem of Alienation Among Polish Marxists*; reviewer — K. Wojtyla.

February 24 — At the chapel of the Daughters of Charity at the Helclow Home for the aged:

> I must tell you that although I visit this house only occasionally and say Mass here only from time to time, I am often with you in my thoughts and my heart. And you make this easy for me, because we maintain regular correspondence: the residents of the Helclow House write to me, and I answer them. And sometimes we make use of other means, for example the recording of greetings on a tape recorder, so that we can hear each other and communicate, and feel that we are united by one spirit, namely the Spirit of Christ, the Spirit of Love.

Same day — 1:00 p.m., Pradnik Czerwony, chapel of the Albertine Sisters, conclusion of a course for women active in parish ministries * 4:30 p.m., chapel of the Daughters of Charity at 8 Warszawska Street in Krakow, Mass and sermon — on the occasion of a forty-hour devotion. (Congregation of the Daughters of Charity)

February 26 — 6:00 p.m., residence chapel, closing of the process of Mother Urszula Ledochowska * February 27 — Mogilany, Ash Wednesday:

> Ash Wednesday is a day when the Church sprinkles ashes on the heads of its children, and reminds us of the words which defined the fate and history of man ever since the first fall: "Remember man, you are dust and to dust you will return." The Church is very courageous in constantly reminding us of this. And every person who faces up to this truth every year is also very courageous ... This is a truth about the body of man and about all of matter; about all the bodies which make up the visible world of which we are a part. This world will pass away, this world is subject to death: it arose from dust and it will return to dust, just as man will along with it.

February 28 — 6:00 p.m., residence chapel, a decision about the cult of Queen Jadwiga.

March 2 — Pcim:

> We are celebrating this great jubilee in the Church, beginning with the parish, then through the diocese, i.e. the Church of Krakow to which your parish belongs as to a great family and community. I thank you for always remembering your bishop here, for praying for him, for joining with him spiritually and forming this unity of faith, hope and love.

March 3 — St. Kazimierz Church in Krakow, blessing of a memorial plaque dedicated to Rev. J. Mac, the builder of the church and the parish,:

> **The Church is constantly being built, it is being built on a broader scope than the scope of the lifetime of a single person, even of the longest lifetime. It is being built by means of this living bond with Jesus Christ. It is being built because of the fact that He can act within us, that He can speak to our mind, to our heart, to our conscience. This is the essence of building.**

Same day — the church in Rybna:

> **[The Holy Year in the community of the parish, the diocese; this year — a pilgrimage to the Cathedral, and next year] the Holy Father invites all Christians to Rome ... we are also invited. I don't know to what extent we will be able to make it happen, but even if we cannot do it physically, we will still try to express, with all our hearts and souls, our moral unity with the Holy Father in the community of the Universal Church. It has been our tradition, we have it in our blood — the Church in Poland has always, through the entire 1000 years, been very strongly tied to the Apostolic See.**

Same day — in Oswiecim {Auschwitz}:

> **By the tradition of celebrating the Holy Year [Jesus Christ, the Lord of time, of millennia, of centuries, of months and hours, living among us with a mystical life] wants to mark, in a special way, His place among the generations of humanity, particularly among the individual generations of Christians in the Church ... Perhaps we remember how during the previous Holy Year we marked the presence of Jesus Christ in our Catholic and Polish life by the sign of the Cross. I remember a great celebration of the Holy Year in Krakow, when the Cracovians gathered on Wawel Hill around their unforgettable Metropolitan Archbishop Prince Cardinal Adam Stefan Sapieha, who was close to death at that time. And under his guidance they raised up a large cross, to be carried through the streets of Krakow. Even then, the authorities did not allow this solemn procession: the cross could not be carried beyond Wawel Hill. Nevertheless, the Cracovians set off from the Cathedral, from Wawel Hill, and singing hymns in honor of the cross, they poured out to the streets of the city ... This was in 1950; that generation, which is still living and is also present here today, remembers that time when we came out of the horrible way of the cross which was the Nazi occupation, and that is why that sign of the cross became for us a particular expression of our age ... This cross remains in our lives. It remains at the crossroads[17], it remains in our houses, our apartments; it remains wherever people want it to remain and are ready to defend it. And sometimes they defend it at the peril of their lives, as it happened in Nowa Huta over a dozen years ago, when the inhabitants and parishioners defended a cross planted in the ground as a sign that a church was to rise there. And when there was an attempt to remove the cross, so that the church would not rise, the people resisted and today the church is rising, and is already under roof.**

---

[17] Reference to many roadside shrines in rural Poland.

March 5 — 18th session of the Main Committee of the Synod. Presentation and discussion of proposed schemas: liturgical renewal in the Archdiocese of Krakow; dissemination of the Word of God; diocesan structures — pastoral ministry, Christian charity in the Archdiocese; the vocation of lay people — family, upbringing; about the priesthood; religious orders in the life of the Archdiocese; particular dangers threatening the Church of Krakow; religious freedom; ministry to tourists; the culture of recreation; the cult of the Sacred Heart of Jesus; the veneration of the Blessed Mother in the Krakow Archdiocese. (From the minutes)

March 7 — Participated in the celebrations in honor of St. Thomas Aquinas at the Basilica of the Dominican Fathers in Krakow on the 700th anniversary of his death.

> **[Through the glorification of truth and of those who proclaim it] man's deepest need is satisfied, a need closely connected with his spiritual, reasoning nature. It is the need to seek truth, to strive for it, to learn it, to find it, to proclaim it and to remain in it. We can admire the work of St. Thomas Aquinas as a magnificent work of academic technique, a brilliant academic method. But these are all means to an end. The essence of the matter lies in the magnificent revelation of humanity that turns toward God. A humanity hungry for truth and finding it in its own work, in its own cognitive efforts, but, above all, through the agency of that divine light in which St. Thomas and all of us participate as a result of our faith.**

March 9 — 5:00 p.m., Przeciszow, concelebrated Mass with sermon during the celebrations of the Holy Year * March 10 -10:00 a.m., Zielonki, celebrations of the Holy Year, Mass with sermon * March 12 — Presentation entitled *Personal Structure of Self-Determination* as part of the 17th Philosophical Week at KUL[18] (March 11-14: "Relevance of Thomism, on the 700th Anniversary of the Death of St. Thomas") * March 13-14 — Participated in funeral ceremonies for the late Cardinal Boleslaw Kominek in Wroclaw * March 15 — Meeting of the Council of the Pontifical Department of Theology in Krakow. The dean of the Department read a letter from His Excellency the Grand Chancellor to the Council of the Department, with an attached copy of a letter dated February 18, 1974, addressed to the Premier of the government, in the matter of the Department, with reference to the 600th anniversary of the birth of Queen Jadwiga. Similar letters were sent to: the Chairman of the Council of State, the Minister of Higher Education, Arts, Science and Technology; the President of PAN[19], the Senate of PAN and the President of the Krakow chapter of PAN; the Rector and Senate of the Jagiellonian University, the chairman of the

---

[18] Catholic University of Lublin.
[19] Polish academy of Arts and Sciences.

City Council in Krakow and the "wojewoda" {governor} of Krakow. A separate letter was sent to Vice-Premier Jozef Tejchma.

In the portion of the session devoted to organizational matters, the Grand Chancellor read and commented upon a "pro memoria" letter to the Council of the Department concerning the filling of vacant chairs, and the possibility of earning a Master's degree during the basic studies in philosophy and theology; he also spoke of the need to maintain contacts with academic circles in Krakow. (From the minutes of the Council)

March 16 — Luborzyca, about the dangers to the family and the youth:

> **Let us have foresight, let us be watchful. We want ... to turn our eyes again toward Jesus Christ, our Savior; we want to look at the Cross and draw inspiration from it: that is so simple, but so shattering.**
> **Just think ... let each of you think: how valuable man must be, how high his price is, if God throws His own Son into the scale of the salvation of man's soul. And He wishes that this Son live in His Church through the Cross, that he continue to reveal Himself to us through the Cross and, through the Cross, bear witness to God's infinite love which encompasses every person, which lifts up and saves every person.**

March 17 — Ciezkowice:

> **Nowadays, when the choice [whether to live with Christ or without Him or against Him] stands before us so clearly, when the agenda of life without God is so prominent and insistent, the Holy Year is a special occasion for us to choose Christ, to renew our covenant with Him, to reunite ourselves with Him to the very core of our human essence. Could there be anything more magnificent for man than the unification with God, than life with God?**

Same day — 5:00 p.m. in Zarki:

> **The roots of sin ... not only remain in the human soul, but also in interpersonal relations, in social life ... That is why in our battle with sin, in our struggles against sin, we go not only to the human soul, to the conscience, as we did during the retreat; we also turn our attention to our whole life in society, and to everything [within it] which is a threat to the Kingdom of Christ, which runs counter to the holiness of God and which runs counter to the reconciliation of man with God.**

March 18 — 8:00 a.m., Wawel Cathedral, Mass for the late Cardinal B. Kominek * 10:00 a.m., Krakow, 3 Franciszkanska Street, meeting of the Episcopate's Committee for Catholic Education. Discussions concerned, among others, the state of the scientific cadres in Poland for the academic year 1972/73, the organization of the Departments of Theology, their statutes, agreements of cooperation between the Seminaries, the matter of theological publishers and preliminary proceedings in conjunction with the Congress of the Polish

Theologians in 1976. Also considered were the uniformity of higher education in all seminaries and the aligning of their academic systems, as well as further preparation of new scientific cadres. The most important event of the year, proclaimed the Cardinal, was the creation of the Educational Council. (From the Committee's minutes)

March 19[20] — At the Church of St. Joseph:

> **St. Joseph was a husband in whom God placed the greatest trust. God entrusted him not only with the Mother of His Son, but also entrusted him, in some measure, with His own Fatherhood ... St. Joseph was to be a substitute for God the Father Himself to this Son of God, the Child of Mary, the Son of Mary. The majesty of Divine Fatherhood came to rest upon this humble worker. All of this testifies to his greatness; his greatness was from God, and in the human sphere he was a humble and quiet man.**

Same day — 5:00 p.m., at the church in Igolomia:

> **Following the call of the Holy Father, we are celebrating the Holy Year on this Polish land, in the Krakow Archdiocese. Each day, the People of God gather in a different parish to participate in the great Jubilee of Jesus Christ together with their parish community ... It is good that in today's celebration you also remember ... a man whom our entire country wishes to be beatified, raised to the honors of the altar, because he gave example of such holiness, such a moving example of the love of God and neighbor, an example which is so needed by contemporary man ... I am thinking of the Servant of God Brother Albert, who came into the world here in Igolomia, whose life is a special manifestation of holiness in the almost 600-year history of your parish.**

March 20 — He applies to the Sacred Congregation for Catholic Education with a request that the Department of Theology in Krakow be given the title of "Pontifical." The conferment of this title *"properly emphasizes the establishment of the canonical structure of the Department of Theology of the Jagiellonian University in Krakow and, at the same time, questions the idea of moving this department to Warsaw by the power of a unilateral act of the state."* The title was conferred by the power of a decree issued on May 2, 1974 * On the same day — 5:00 p.m., Lazany, Holy Year celebrations, a Mass with sermon * March 21 — 10:00 a.m., residence, a session organized by the Pontifical Department of Theology in Krakow at the request of the Sisters of the Sacred Heart for the 50th anniversary of the death of the Servant of God Rev. Bishop Jozef Pelczar * Same day — 7:00 p.m., St. Anne's Church, concelebrated Mass and sermon for the 50th anniversary of the death of Bishop J. Pelczar * 8:15 p.m., Church of Our Lady of Lourdes, conclusion of a retreat for students * March 22 — 5:00

---

[20] March 19 is the Feast of St. Joseph.

p.m., Gronkow, Mass with sermon — Holy Year * March 23 — 8:15 p.m., Krakow, St. Anne's Church, conclusion of an academic retreat * March 24 — 11:00 a.m., Gorka Koscielnicka, Holy Year celebrations * 5:00 p.m., Swiatniki, Mass with sermon — Holy Year * March 25 — Annunciation, 9:00 am Wawel Cathedral, celebrations of the 40th anniversary of the priesthood of the class of 1934, and a pilgrimage of nuns to the Cathedral on the occasion of the Holy Year: "The mystery of the Incarnation: the beginning of the mystery of Redemption that brought equilibrium to the spiritual world of man; the mystery that balanced out sin from the very beginning; from the first parents through all time, through our sad time, until the end of time."

March 26 — 10:00 a.m., Warsaw, Main Council of the Polish Episcopate * March 27-28 — Warsaw, 141st plenary conference of the Polish Episcopate * March 29 — Departs for Rome for the meeting of the Secretariat of the Council of the Synod of Bishops * March 31 — Rome, St. Stanislaw Church, concelebrated Mass, sermon for the 600th anniversary of Queen Jadwiga.

April 4 — 12:00 noon, Vatican, an audience with Pope Paul VI * April 5 — 12:00 noon, Vatican, Pope Paul VI's audience for the Secretariat of the Council of the Synod of Bishops * April 6 — Departs for Poland * April 7 — 10:00 a.m., Wawel Cathedral, Pontifical High Mass, blessing of palms * 5:00 p.m., Wawel Cathedral, on the occasion of the Holy Year, a pilgrimage of the academic youth to the Cathedral:

> I invited you to the cathedral to fulfill ... the will of the Holy Father, so that we could gather in this particular community which is the university community of Krakow gathered around its bishop in the Cathedral of Wawel. We are gathered here; and I express my great joy that I can be united with you so visibly, united through your chaplains, united by these walls of the Wawel Cathedral, and above all, united by your living, Christian academic community.
>
> The Church has great hope in you, the young generation, you who are seeking reconciliation with God and with man, because, you can bring a living leaven, an evangelical ferment into this young, university community to which you belong, a ferment that can raise the whole loaf and make it a nourishing bread. And we need this nourishing bread, so that we would not die from hunger in the midst of all of our technology, in the midst of our orientation towards consumption ... Man can be fed only by people who are themselves fed by God, Jesus Christ.

Same day — 7:30 p.m., St. Joseph's Church, Mass, sermon for the beginning of a retreat for lawyers * April 8 — 5:00 p.m., Sucha Beskidzka, celebrations of the Holy Year * April 9 — 7:30 p.m., Church of the Felician Sisters, concelebrated Mass, sermon during a retreat of physicians * April 10 — 6:00 p.m., Zator, celebrations of the Holy Year * April 11 — Wawel Cathedral, Holy Thursday — concelebrated Mass with the pastors of the diocese, blessing of oils.

> I unite with you, dear Brothers in priesthood, in a special way; this day is our day. It reminds us of the founding of the sacrament which defines our calling and our place among the People of God, the sacrament which speaks to us about our ministry, about our task; the sacrament which is inscribed on our souls by an indelible mark, and inscribed in our lives by our daily priestly labor.

Same day — 9:30 p.m., residence chapel, Holy Hour with the seminarians * April 12 — 11:00 a.m., the Franciscan church, Stations of the Cross with the seminarians * April 13 — Residence, Easter greetings * April 14 — Mistrzejowice, Mass of the Resurrection:

> [Of the loneliness of Christ in the Garden, before His judges, on the cross] This morning — the loneliness of Resurrection. There is a singular, unique greatness in this. A supernatural greatness: this road could only be walked alone by Jesus Christ, the Son of God. No man could walk this road with Him. He had to walk this road alone so as to show it to us, so that He could remain our guide and leader on this road for all time. For although we have many leaders, lords, kings, temporal authorities here on earth, we have no leader on that road which leads through man's death. There, everyone abandons man — only Christ remains. And He is the sole guide through the most difficult passage facing each one of us: the passage from life to death and from death to life, to eternity ... (After His passage from death to life, Our Lord sought out everyone He had taught, and told them to be His witnesses; just as He does with us.) And we tried to be with Him in the ancient Wawel Cathedral, and in so many parishes, and in so many churches, and also here, in your new parish being formed around a church which is to rise here. It is my heartfelt wish for you that the construction may begin, and I earnestly pray that this matter might get underway. Because in all these places, in all these communities, and here in this parish, too, we want to be witnesses to Jesus Christ ... we want to bear witness to Him in our times in which we live; in these new conditions, in these new circumstances of life, in this modern city being formed here, near this huge industrial complex, but at the same time within the environs of ancient royal Krakow, not far from Wawel, we want to bear witness to Jesus Christ ...
> It gives me joy that this morning I can sing with you the Alleluia of Christ's Resurrection again: here, in this heroic Mistrzejowice which has been so tenaciously and so patiently developing its parish community and the building of its church.

Same day — 10:00 a.m., Wawel Cathedral, High Mass with sermon, a Holy Year pilgrimage of the Krakow parishes * April 15 — The Church of the Norbertine Sisters:

> Formerly, the Holy Year was an individual devotion ... Presently, however, we try above all to experience the communion. The communion of each parish which, each in its own way, carries the mystery of Jesus Christ within it. [In the case of this parish, it is Emmaus.] Emmaus ... is the symbol of all those people who walk with Christ and with whom Christ walks,

but who do not recognize Him for some time ... On the other hand, Emmaus is also the symbol of that joyous moment of recognition, when man realizes that Christ exists, that we walk with Him ... Not long ago, a book was published under the title *The Nameless Speak of Prayer.* I must admit I read that book voraciously, because it describes a variety of break-throughs, a variety of encounters with Christ who walks with the various nameless people ... who write about how He walked with them and how they encountered Him. These are the contemporary reincarnations of the Emmaus from the Gospel of St. Luke.

Same day — 4:00 p.m., he departs for Litomierzyce in Czechoslovakia * April 16 — 10:00 a.m., Litomierzyce, funeral of Cardinal Stefan Trochta. Local government officials did not give per-mission for Cardinal Wojtyla to celebrate Mass. He approached the altar rail along with the other faithful to receive Holy Communion. Despite the order of the local authorities — he spoke at the coffin of the Cardinal. Same day — 10:00 p.m., Vienna — the nunciature[21], private concelebrated Mass * April 17 — 5:00 p.m., Rome, Angelicum. Inauguration of the Congress for the 700th anniversary of St. Thomas Aquinas, participated in the Congress.

> As a philosopher, the Metropolitan Archbishop of Krakow ... partici-pates actively in the great congress in honor of St. Thomas Aquinas, orga-nized by the Dominican Order in 1974 (on the 700th anniversary of the death of St. Thomas) in Rome and Naples. Together with a large group of Poles, we take part in the deliberations, and (having traveled from Rome to Naples with the participants of the congress) also in a Mass concele-brated by one hundred and several score priests under the leadership of Cardinal Wojtyla. During his beautiful sermon (a comparison of St. Thomas the Apostle with St. Thomas Aquinas), delivered in fluent Italian, I began to realize two strange things: that the torch of faith and deep philo-sophical reflection is being passed to Poland in some to way, and that Cardinal Karol Wojtyla is the man who fulfills all the conditions to become a future Pope. At that time I was so overcome with emotion that I told my wife about this, and right after Mass I found the Cardinal in a cloister adjacent to the church, I stopped him as he was passing, and I told him, with full conviction, what I was thinking. He looked very gravely and deeply into my eyes — and said nothing. (Stefan Swiezawski, "TP", 47/1978)

April 21 — Italy, a pilgrimage to places closely related with St. Thomas: Fossanuova, Aquino, Roccasecca, Naples * April 23 — 9:00 a.m., Naples, a presentation during the Congress organized on the occa-sion of the 700th anniversary of the death of St. Thomas Aquinas: *"The Personal Structure of Self-Determination"* (the text also exists in the Polish version entitled: *Osobowa struktura samostanowienia*) * 4:00 p.m., Naples, concelebrated Mass at the Marian Shrine of Madonna del'Arco * April 24 — Rome * April 25 — Rome, a visit to the

---

[21] Vatican diplomatic mission.

Salesian University * April 26 — return to Warsaw and Krakow * April 27 — Krakow, 7:00 a.m., residence chapel, private concelebrated Mass * 7:00 p.m., Gniezno, procession of St. Wojciech {Adalbert}, parting remarks * April 28 — 9:30 a.m., Gniezno, Pontifical High Mass, procession of St. Wojciech * Same day — 5:00 p.m., An address at a symposium "The Laity in the Mission of the Church" in Gdansk-Oliwa (the cathedral):

[The word apostle] speaks of the fact that man who has encountered the revelation of God's truth and love in Jesus Christ, receives a mission from Christ through that encounter. Man cannot be merely a listener to that truth, he cannot even be only a very incisive analyst or theoretician of that truth. God's truth and love which has been revealed in Jesus Christ is a great good, and it demands to be shared, carried from place to place, propagated ...

To be an apostle means to be sent ..., but sent merely on the strength of an external mandate or an order? ... To be sent, above all, by the force of interior conviction, by the power of that truth which illuminates everything for us; by the power of the love which is the greatest good of man ...

[Marriage] constitutes a particular entry into the world. Because marriage continues to create the human world anew. And it is through humans that this world is the world. For if there were no humans in the entire masterpiece of creation, the world would not be the world; the world exists through people ...

To be an apostle means ... to reveal God's thought to the world. To reveal it not with words, but to reveal it with one's existence ...

We must recognize the fact that almost every parish in Poland has peripheral members who are more or less distant. That there are a great many people tied to the Church in name only, but departing from it in some way in practice and de facto. [That is why a parish is a missionary unit], and its missionary character can be guaranteed only by lay people. That means people who can meet with people. The ones who are closer with the ones farther out, the ones standing at the center with those on the periphery; and they can contribute to gathering together around one common center. That center is Jesus Christ living in the Church ...

At the moment when Our Lord told the Apostles: "Go forth into the whole world...", we may say that they were very immature. Our Lord said this very soon after the day of the great disappointment that they had caused Him. But He judged that they were ready; they received everything that they could have received — they looked, they saw, they heard, they were baptized by the baptism of the Spirit. And He also told them: "Go forth, you will be My witnesses!"

April 29 — 6:00 p.m., Wawel Cathedral, an address for the beginning of the novena to St. Stanislaw the Bishop:

We know that the cult of St. Stanislaw in Poland has its royal traditions. The procession from Wawel to Skalka, which for so many centuries has gone through the streets of Krakow, was a royal procession. The Kings of Poland walked in this procession, following the holy remains of St. Stanislaw, in commemoration of an event which took place in 1079 ... when their ancestor, the King of Poland, killed the Bishop of Krakow. The death of the bishop, his martyrdom, and the penance of the king became the foundation of the spiritual history of our nation. Jadwiga is present in this heritage ... Quite likely she, too, participated in such processions. In any case, this year we want her to participate in spirit ...

Polish culture is Christian to its deepest roots. It cannot be torn away from Christianity without being damaged. This must be remembered by those who create culture today. As Christians, we have a constitutional right to actively take advantage of cultural values; we have the right to shape them according to our convictions. We must reach into the great world of history, to the inspirations that flow from Stanislaw and from Jadwiga, and from so many other figures, so that with a heroic spirit we may shape Polish life, Polish culture, as the extension of its thousand-year heritage.

April 30 — Bolechowice, during silver jubilee of the pastor and priests of the year 1949 — concelebrated Mass and a homily:

The priesthood is a great mystery, one closely connected with the mystery of God who created us, who as the Creator continually receives homage from His creation. The priest, the priesthood, express that homage. And the priesthood is connected with God who redeemed us. Redeemed, that means He gave Himself as a sacrifice. And in that sacrifice of Himself He expressed the infinite love that God has for man and for all of creation. And He always wants to express the love with which man reciprocates the love of God ...

We remember those years well; for all of us, the beginning of our calling to the priesthood is connected with the period of German occupation, a very difficult period in the life of the nation and the Church; it is connected with memories of the magnificent person of Prince Cardinal Adam Stefan Sapieha, who fulfilled his priestly mission till the end: the mission of a bishop and a Pole. These are the beginnings of your calling, and also our common calling; the beginnings of the road to the priesthood which 25 years ago was crowned by the ordination received at the hands of our unforgettable Shepherd ... I thank you with all my soul! If I may say so, I thank you in the name of our departed Shepherd, and I thank you in my own name!

May 1 — Sermon in Metkow, consecration of the church:

Today we are experiencing an unusual celebration of the Holy Year. Allow me to begin with myself. I thank you for inviting me to this celebration; I wish to tell you that it is an extraordinary celebration for me. I realized that in its full scope when I saw the walls of this church, which I know so well from the first years of my priesthood, when in the years 1948/49 I was working as a vicar in the parish of Niegowic. There I came to know this church, these wooden walls which have lasted 300 years. I remember well this spacious, light interior, where for so many generations Jesus Christ has lived with His people in the parish of Niegowic. This church was the stage of many meetings with Christ the Lord: meetings of the whole parish, and of individuals, and my own; all of this remains in my memory. I saw in my mind's eye the months spent here in priestly ministry at the side of the venerable pastor, departed for so many years, the late Msgr. Kazimierz Buzala. You, the inhabitants of Niegowic, know this well, because he was a pastor and dean here for many years.

[At that time, for the 50th anniversary of the pastor's ordination to the priesthood, the parishioners of Niegowic began to build a new masonry church which had been planned for a long time.] And so this old Church of Niegowic has lived through, as I have, the last year of service there. Because a church, be it a masonry or a wooden one, a cathedral or a humble chapel in the missions, fulfills a particular service to the People of God in all places.

From that moment, this venerable landmark became no longer necessary in Niegowic. But it became necessary for you. The efforts of many years to move it to this part of the parish of Babice have borne fruit today. I feel great joy that I can be with you today ... My joy is enormous, first of all because of the memories of this church from Niegowic. Secondly, because of this meeting at a new place, where it has been moved to fulfill its role anew by serving the People of God in Metkow ...

My wish for you, old church from Niegowic, is that you may provide new service here in Metkow, that you may serve through many more years and decades, and more centuries. My wish for you is that you stand with the People of God alongside Christ, that you lead to Christ all those who enter here.

It is a good thing that these wooden walls, that these beams of the old church are still sturdy enough, strong enough to hold up a new community of the People of God at a new location. It is a great joy to us. Your presence here in such great numbers is an expression of that joy, as is the presence of so many priests from various parts of the Archdiocese, who treat the matter of the new church in Metkow as a common matter of the entire Archdiocese, because that it how it should be treated. That is how we should treat every case of new church construction or moving a church to a new location, because this is one common cause, a cause that concerns not only the bishop, but all of the priests and faithful of the Church of Krakow. It is good that the state authorities understood the significance of this matter and that, after so many years, they finally granted permission to move the church from Niegowic to Metkow ... And you, ancient temple, may you serve these People of God just as you served the parish of Niegowic for so many centuries. Bring us closer to Our Lord, bring us closer to Our Lady of Jasna Gora, bring us closer to St. Joseph ... May your path ... be always straight and smooth, may it lead to Jesus, to Mary, to Joseph — and to this temple, which is a great gift for you in the Holy Year, in the year of the great Jubilee of Jesus Christ. Amen.

May 1-2 — Trzebnica, meeting of the Episcopate's Committee for Pastoral Ministry, presided over by Bishop W. Miziolek. A discussion about the pastoral program and matters pertaining to it. The Krakow region (represented by Rev. Franciszek Macharski) presented its pastoral program for the years 1974/75, the apostolic mission of lay Catholics in the parish. A program for the Holy Year. Prof. Andrzej Swiecicki reported on work pertaining to labor law — a discussion followed. Holy Mass at the tomb of St. Jadwiga. Second day — the spirit and methodology of the work of the Committee. Cooperation with the Pastoral Institute in Wroclaw (Rev. Rector Jozef Majka). Presentation by Bishop Ignacy Tokarczuk: *Principles and Direction of capitalist and socialist humanism.* Discussion. (From the minutes of the Committee)

May 2 — 10:30 a.m., residence, conference of priests — heads of deaneries regarding the celebrations of the Feast of St. Stanislaw, the sacral architecture and the youth ministry * May 3[22] — 11:00 a.m., Jasna Gora, concelebrated High Mass; 7:00 p.m., summit, evening service, sermon:

> Jesus Christ on the Cross. His arms spread wide. Wide. They do not close. They cannot close. They must be spread wide, because every person must find refuge in them, must find his humanity, his dignity, the dignity of the child of God which he carries in his soul and in his life's calling. Every person can find his freedom, the truth about himself[23] in these arms of Christ. The arms of Christ cannot close, they must remain open, because new people, new generations, come all the time.
>
> Every 25 years we must announce a Holy Year, so that everyone can become reconciled with God through Jesus Christ, and thus find the ultimate sense of their earthly pilgrimage, of their life ... A true reconciliation among people, especially in this society of ours, which is so overwhelmingly Catholic, must be based on respect for the thousand-year heritage which we all carry within us like a treasure, and we wish this treasure to be respected.
>
> We know that this treasure cannot be replaced by anything, and we are fearful that people, especially the youth, who have this treasure taken away from them, will suffer a terrible loss, a damage that cannot be subsequently repaired or made up. We are fearful, and we admit this openly, because we look at reality and that reality confirms our conviction of the great threat to our Christian traditions, to the ethical traditions of our Polish nation.
>
> We say all of this before this altar today, because this is our offering, we come here with it as with bread and wine. With this we look into the motherly eyes which once, on Calvary, saw the suffering of the Son, and then saw His Resurrection, and this is the totality of the great Mystery by which Jesus Christ, the Son of God, reconciled us, people, with His Father, and we remain and continue to live in that reconciliation.
>
> We pray at Jasna Gora to Mary, the Queen of Poland, that this Holy Year bring about the reconciliation of all people, especially of our countrymen, that they may find themselves in Jesus Christ, that they affirm their spiritual freedom, that they overcome all fears and intimidations, that they proclaim the God who from the Cross proclaimed man, the man of all times, the man whom He embraced in all his truth, and united with His Father.
>
> And that is the deep content of our prayer here before You, Mother of God, Queen of Poland, You, who have so loved the kingdom of Your Son on our Polish land.

May 4 — At the Mariacki Basilica, Mass for graduating secondary school students:

---

[22] See Glossary.
[23] In Polish, all of the pronouns in this paragraph are gender-neutral.

> My dear friends, here you stand today, on the eve of your final exam, young men and women about to graduate. Each of you represents a great value. I don't know what kind of grades you will receive. Maybe you will get grades of excellent, maybe good, maybe satisfactory — I don't know. But I want to tell you that each of you represents a great value. I want to tell you this from Jesus Christ, who, by his life, paid the price for each of you, of each person, to the end, who has affirmed it to the end, affirmed it with His word, affirmed it with His sacrifice: His Body and Blood.

Same day — 7:00 p.m., celebration of the laying the cornerstone for the new Church of the Immaculate Conception of Our Lady being constructed in Krakow at Azory. The Cardinal was the main celebrant during Mass, after the Gospel the Cardinal performed the act of laying the cornerstone, a Holy Relic from The Grotto of the Annunciation in the Holy Land, that was blessed by Pope Paul VI. After the celebrations, at the cloister of the Reformed-Franciscans, the Cardinal met with the clergy, the builders of the church, the parish representatives. Supper was served afterwards. From the sermon:

> This Jesus Christ [the cornerstone] is with you. He lives in your souls through faith. And His life in your souls gives Jesus Christ a certain right of citizenship. Let us consider: there was a man who has the wondrous right to citizenship in ever new nations, in ever new peoples and generations ... At the same time, your rights as citizens are the consequence of His citizenship here at Azory ...
> Jesus Christ is the cornerstone. What kind of structure rises upon Him? A very unusual one; it is a structure which He builds within us, and which we, through Him, build within ourselves ... A structure of reconciliation with God.

May 5 — 8:00 a.m., residence chapel, Mass and sermon for *Tygodnik Powszechny* * Oswiecim, opening remarks for the 75th anniversary of the Salesian Fathers in Poland * 5:00 p.m., Brzezie, consecration of the church, Mass and sermon * May 6 — 11:00 a.m., outdoor Mass * May 8 — 8:00 a.m., Wawel, a pilgrimage of priests from the diocese of Plock with Bishop Bogdan Sikorski — welcome; 1:00 p.m., at the residence, farewell to the pilgrimage * Same day — Wawel Cathedral, the third plenary meeting of the Pastoral Synod of the Krakow Archdiocese. Participants of the meeting: auxiliary bishops, the Metropolitan Chapter, members of the synodal committees, superiors of the theological seminaries, superiors of religious orders, deans, representatives of study teams, invited representatives of neighboring dioceses: Czestochowa, Katowice, Kielce, Tarnow — in total, 1300 people. Cardinal Wojtyla presided, delivered opening remarks, preaches a homily during Mass.

> Introduction: [About the study teams:] ...we need teams that will study the teachings of the Second Vatican Council ... consider them in the light of the realities of our Church in Krakow and its needs. Those studies are

to lead to concrete, mature resolutions ... primarily of a pastoral nature, because our Synod is pastoral in character ... Today's plenary meeting ... is to bring together the two major themes that define the work of the Synod ... the activity of the study teams [that is one of the themes, the other is] the inauguration, the first word on the subject of the concluding resolutions of the Synod ...

Homily: Today, even as the Synod speaks of itself, it ceases to speak of itself and expresses a concern ... Because a Synod's purpose is to express that concern which we have inherited from the Good Shepherd. We have inherited it organically, because we are grafted into Him: each of us ... through Baptism, then the graft is strengthened through Confirmation ... The Good Shepherd sees the wolf ... St. Stanislaw saw the wolf in his times and took up the struggle with it, commensurate with his times. Let us not delude ourselves; the wolf of our times is drawing near to the flock. Our wolf is probably much more dangerous, much more experienced. That is why we must rediscover the legacy of St. Stanislaw within the community, and thus rediscover the legacy of the Good Shepherd.

May 8 — An appeal to the priests of the Krakow Archdiocese:

Dear Brother Priests!

The Holy Year which we are celebrating forces us to broach a subject which is undoubtedly the most painful one among all of the wounds of the Church and of Catholic society in Poland. This concerns the matter of termination of pregnancies, or the killing of unborn children in the wombs of their mothers. This is connected with a fear for the future of the entire nation, which over the past several years has lost millions of its sons and daughters in violation of the Fifth Commandment of God. This is also connected with a concern for human souls and Christian consciences which are not only subject to the terrible perils of mortal sin, but also to the danger of moral insensitivity.

Motivated by these concerns, which are of the utmost gravity, the Polish Episcopate has appealed to the government of our country in 1971 with an appropriate memorial, whose content we all know very well.

But the greatness of this cause requires something more from us than a mere reminder. Together with our parish communities we must take up action which will confirm that we not only preach and judge the Christian conscience of unfortunate mothers and fathers, but we also want to help them. And that is why together with you, Dear Brother Priests, I wish to declare a readiness to take care of children which are endangered in the wombs of their mothers. We take up pastoral and educational care through the entire work of the family ministry and family counseling. Nevertheless, in many cases what is needed is material help. Providing adequate material means might be an effective way to help many mothers faced with the temptation to terminate a pregnancy. This has been confirmed by the experience of persons who are actively involved in the care of families. I am personally acquainted with people who have saved the lives of many endangered unborn children because at a critical moment they offered material help to the mothers. We also know that in many countries there are social funds dedicated to this cause.

I turn to you, Dear Brother Priests, for material help in this matter. At the same time I ask you to go and find families which can take in a mother with child or a child alone for a certain time (on a paid basis, if necessary).

Further information is available from family counseling centers at the churches, especially at the Mariacki Church in Krakow, and the Department of Family Ministry in the Curia.

In any event, the love of God and neighbor, the love of Christ, prompts us to make haste to confront this matter ourselves and as a Catholic society. This appeal of mine is only the beginning of this great cause. I ask that you consider it in your congregations and meetings of priests, carefully reading the aforementioned memorial of the Episcopate. May the Most Blessed Mother obtain for you the spirit of wisdom and heroism in this difficult matter.

+ Karol Cardinal

Krakow, May 8, 1974.

Appeal

To the Faithful of the Archdiocese of Krakow
in the Defense of the Life of the Unborn
Dear Brothers and Sisters!

The Holy Year which we are celebrating forces us to broach a subject which is undoubtedly the most painful one among all of the wounds of the Church and of Catholic society in Poland. This concerns the matter of termination of pregnancies, or the killing of unborn children in the wombs of their mothers. This is connected with a fear for the future of the entire nation, which over the past several years has lost millions of its sons and daughters ... Motivated by these concerns, which are of the utmost gravity, the Polish Episcopate has appealed to the government of our country in 1971 with an appropriate memorial.

The Church will always protect the inviolability of life, it will protect every conceived child. Life is a gift from God and we are to guard it solicitously. But we know of circumstances where a conceived human being becomes a source of many difficulties for some families or single mothers. That is why we hasten with aid to the needy, so as to prevent the tragedy of infanticide. Difficulties of a material or health nature must not be allowed to drive a mother to the killing of conceived life.

Let us save every conceived child!

I declare that we will provide immediate aid to all that need aid, guaranteeing confidentiality. Further information is available from family counseling centers at the churches, especially at the Mariacki Church in Krakow, and the Department of Family Ministry in the Curia.

I summon, but also entreat, all doctors and workers of the health services to save the lives of unborn children, in accordance with your calling, your oath, and your Christian conscience.

I appeal to families and Houses of Religious Sisters that can accept a mother and child, or a child alone for a certain period of time (on a paid basis, if necessary) — to register at the centers of Family Ministry. Let us be mindful of the words of Christ: "Whosoever receives such a child in my name, receives me."

I appeal most ardently to everyone to cooperate in the work of saving the lives of unborn children, to provide material assistance and to create a healthy atmosphere. Every mother, from the moment of conception, should be surrounded by the kindness of us all, especially of the older generation from the circle of her immediate family and friends. This is also a task for the study teams.

At the same time, I ask everyone to extend particular care to families with many children. I entrust their fate to you, and I ask your support for them, both moral and material. We should show them respect and gratitude for the effort of bringing up numerous progeny, which is the deciding factor in the future of our nation.

May the Most Blessed Mother obtain for you the spirit of wisdom and heroism in this difficult matter.

+ Karol Cardinal

Krakow, May 8, 1974.

At the order of H. E. Cardinal Karol Wojtyla, the Department of Family Ministry, whose charter is primarily the care of families, appealed to the Congregation of the Sisters of the Holy Family of Nazareth to provide care for single mothers, in cooperation with the Department. Taking into consideration the fact that one of the goals of the Congregation is the care of families, the superiors of the Congregation agreed, in spite of great difficulties with accommodation facilities. On November 4, 1974, the first expectant single mother was accepted into the house of the Sisters of the Holy Family of Nazareth at 13 Warszawska Street. Until October 1978, that is, the time of the election of Cardinal Wojtyla to the Chair of Peter, 98 single mothers had passed through the house.

The response of the society of Krakow to the Cardinal's pastoral letter was very vital. The parishes, the Department of Family Ministry, the Centers of Family Counseling received many persons who offered money or gifts in the form of clothing, layettes, washing machines, electric sewing machines, etc.

At first, there were great financial difficulties. The Cardinal instructed the Charity Department to dedicate a portion of the funds coming from charitable contributions to S.O.S (that was the name of the fund dedicated to the saving of the unborn). Funds also started to come in from the priests.

The Cardinal, realizing the difficult housing situation of the Sisters of the Holy Family of Nazareth, ordered the administration of the Curia to make arrangements to purchase a house which would be dedicated as the Home of the Single Mother. The house was purchased and was opened on Sept. 28, 1978.

Today, in 1980, there exists an appropriately furnished house with a chapel for 10 expectant women (at 39 Przybyszewskiego Street). Its director is Sister Cherubina Bokota, of the Sisters of the Holy Family of Nazareth. Medical, nursing and educational care is provided for the expectant mothers. They are being prepared for childbirth by attending the "birthing classes" conducted here by a midwife. Each mother is obligated to earn 600 zl. a month towards her upkeep (she usually remains in our care for 3 to 4 months). Any shortfall in the funds necessary for the upkeep and administrative matters is covered by the Department of Family Ministry from the offerings of priests and the faithful. From the beginning, we have maintained a chronicle of the fate of each girl, from the moment she enters our house until she leaves it, with a notation of her further fortunes. The Department of Family Ministry and the director of the house remain in close contact with the {female} gynecologist, the Adoption Center, and the hospital where the residents of the house give birth. Help is also extended to the mothers of families with multiple children, in cases where the father is opposed to the birth of another child and wants the wife to terminate the pregnancy.

The social need for this kind of care is growing; consequently, a Home for the Mother and Child will be opened in the near future. It will also be under the care of the Sisters of the Holy Family of Nazareth. (Maria Nieniewska, Archdiocesan instructor of the Archdiocese of Krakow).

May 9 — 9:00 a.m., residence chapel, concelebrated Mass with the Council of Priests, sermon, a meeting of the Council of Priests * May 10 — Czestochowa, Oswiecim, Krakow, the arrival of Cardinal Franjo Seper * May 11 — 11:00 a.m., residence, 142nd conference of the Polish Episcopate, a session dedicated to contemporary theology * The arrival of Bishop Emil De Smedt * 6:00 p.m., Wawel Cathedral; during a service in honor of Blessed Queen Jadwiga, in the presence of Cardinal Wyszynski, Cardinal Seper, Bishop De Smedt of Brugge, Polish bishops, representatives of the departments of theology from all of Poland, he spoke of the canonical character of the cult of Queen Jadwiga, as one recognized by the bishops and dating back to the times before the constitution *Caelestis Jerusalem* of 1634 by Pope Urban VIII, and announces the filing of a petition to the Apostolic See for the confirmation of Queen Jadwiga's sainthood per viam cultus * May 12 — Skalka, during observances of the Feast of St. Stanislaw, a welcome of the Primate of Poland, Archbishop Baraniak, all Polish bishops, Cardinal Seper, Bishop De Smedt and other bishops — celebrants:

We stand here today in front of this altar in order to offer the Most Holy Sacrifice under the direction of the living bishops present here among us. But most of all, under the spiritual leadership of the bishop who once gave up his life here. And because he gave up his life, he lives — after 900 years he lives and gathers the People of God around his memory, around his sainthood, around his witness.

Same day — 6:30 p.m., residence, Main Council of the Polish Episcopate * May 13 — 10:00 a.m., Krakow, 3 Franciszkanska Street, III meeting of the Educational Council of the Polish Episcopate. At the beginning of the session, a meeting with Cardinal Franjo Seper, Prefect of the Congregation for the Doctrine of the Faith. Cardinal Wojtyla introduces all members of the Council to the visitor, then invites him to ask questions. His questions pertained to the workings of the Council and to the doctrinal situation in Poland. Later during the meeting (without Cardinal Seper present), discussions centered on the matter of the nomination of professors, details of the Council's regulations regarding nominations of independent academic workers, the matter of "Collectanea Theologica" and the international character of this publication, and the matter of raising the level of competence of lecturers at Higher Theological Seminaries. This last point of discussion was introduced by Cardinal Wojtyla. An outline of problems to be discussed at the Congress of Polish Theology was presented. The meeting adjourned at 5:30 p.m. (From the minutes of the Commitee) * Same day —

6:00 p.m., Bienczyce, Holy Year celebrations, service in honor of Our Lady of Fatima, Eucharistic procession.

May 14-16 — Meeting of the Episcopate's Committee for Catholic Education — with the participation of chairmen of the professors' sections. A report on the sections' yearly activities. The matter of establishing a separate patristics[24] section is brought up. In his summary, the Cardinal points out the imbalance in the activities in various areas of theology (sections); he suggests that the number of academic workers in certain disciplines be increased sufficiently to "allow them to get away from just teaching without doing academic research." A lively discussion of the topics for the next Congress of Theologians followed. In his summary, the Cardinal formulated the theme of the Congress: "Theology — the Study of God." The Congress will take place in Krakow. In the afternoon — a discussion on the proposal to create a uniform basic program of higher education for the majority of seminaries; in the evening (only members of the Committee with the invited Bishop Tadeusz Etter), a discussion on the matter of academic publications * May 16 -10:15 a.m. conclusion of the meeting.

May 16 — 9:00 a.m., The Dominican cloister, unveiling of a memorial plaque for the 25th anniversary of the death of Fr. Jacek Woroniecki. During a session in honor of Fr. Jacek Woroniecki:

> I think that he was one of those who helped us, and continue to help us to believe in our own strengths. For there are many tensions in our Polish Catholicism. On the one hand, we have this feeling that we occupy a special place in the Church and the world, that we have contributed to the history of Christianity in a special way ... but, on the other hand, we sometimes have a feeling of inferiority, as if we were of a lesser value, as if on the margin, which begins at our western border. If, on the one hand, we are attracted by the West ... sometimes we feel repulsed by it ... During the last Congress of St. Thomas for the 700th anniversary of his death, which took place in Rome and Naples after Easter, we constituted a very well-defined group of Poles from Poland and from beyond Poland. I think we have demonstrated a very mature approach to the thought of St. Thomas in its historical aspect and in its contemporary meaning, in its contemporary mission. We have also realized that we have done much, and continue to do much so that this magnificent and irreplaceable fabric of the Thomist thought find its contemporary meaning in various fields — that it be convincing. We even felt that perhaps we have done and are doing more in this regard than other Western centers, perhaps more traditional in their approach to the thought of St. Thomas and thereby less fresh (I apologize for saying so — I am sharing my experiences and thoughts which have been shaped during the Congress).

May 18 — 5:00 p.m., Polanka Wielka, Holy Year celebrations *

---

[24] Study of the (writings of) the Fathers of the Church.

May 19 — Wawel Cathedral, ordination of new priests:

> **As you stand here ... I cannot help but remember what I think of your class. About that class of priestly ordinations which, according to our information ... is the largest, in terms of the number of new priests, of all the classes which have passed through our Seminary, all of the classes which our Archdiocese has produced ... You came to the Seminary in the year of 1968 ... In that year, 1968, the Archdiocese of Krakow was being visited by Our Lady of Jasna Gora. And many times, as I looked at you studying here in such a great number, I thought that it was she who brought you to the Seminary in such numbers ... And today, in 1974, in the Holy Year, she brings you to ordination.**

Same day — in Nowy Targ, during the ordination of priests from this region:

> **When we stand here before this altar, where in a moment, together with the bishop, you will conduct your first Eucharistic Service as ordained priests ... we must see before the eyes of our soul the parish baptismal font, because that is where you were born as sons, sons of men and adopted sons of God, so that today, following the example of the One Eternal Son, the adopted sons of God might take on the robes of His priesthood.**

May 20 — Meeting of the Committee for the Apostolate of the Laity. Deliberations on the topic of further works of the Committee; third draft of a directory about dialogue; a document about the councils. * May 21 — 7:30 a.m., residence chapel, concelebrated Mass with sermon — delegation of Polonia with Msgr. Stanislaw Sypek * May 23 — 3:00 p.m., residence, a visit by Cardinal Paul Gouyon * 5:30 p.m., train station, the arrival of a pilgrimage from Milan * An interview granted by Cardinal Wojtyla to *Przewodnik Katolicki* [Catholic Guide] on the subject of the rights and duties of a Catholic in the work of the post-conciliar renewal (*Przewodnik Katolicki* 1974, no. 21, dated May 23) * May 24 — 9:00 a.m., Wawel Cathedral, concelebrated Mass with Bishop Bernard Citterio at the tomb of St. Stanislaw, sermon for the pilgrims from Milan * Same day — meeting of the Council of the Pontifical Department of Theology in Krakow. Among others, a proposed agreement of cooperation with the Theological Seminary in Przemysl, proposed memorandum to the authorities in the matter of the Department. "Cardinal Karol Wojtyla was asked to take over the chair of moral and general theology." (From the minutes of the Council of the Department) * 5:00 p.m., residence, a visit of Cardinal Giovanni Colombo with the pilgrimage from Milan * May 25 — Jasna Gora, a meeting with a pilgrimage of priests and faithful from Milan (about 500 people) under the leadership of Cardinal Colombo. At 11:00 a.m., at the Chapel of Our Lady, Cardinal Wojtyla preached a sermon to them * Same day — 5:00 p.m., Bodzentyn (Diocese of Kielce), visitation by the image of Our Lady, in the presence of the Bishop of Kielce — reminiscence about Bodzentyn's belonging to the great Krakow Diocese since the year 1000, and its being a favorite place of the bishops Krakow:

> **Mary came to lead us into the future. May this future be in agreement with the past, with the whole millennium. May this future be in agreement with that great moment when the fulness of time was upon us. For it continues to come upon us. Because God sent His only-begotten Son, born of a woman, and He continues to send Him, so that He may be among us, so that we may all continue to exist in the fullness of time.**

May 26 — Piekary Slaskie, during a pilgrimage of men, on the topic of the pastoral synod of the Diocese of Katowice; about the ties of Silesia with Krakow:

> **I am grateful to your representative, that he greeted me as one of you. That he reminded me of the years of physical labor through which Divine Providence and the Mother of God prepared me for the priesthood and the bishop's office. I truly value those years, and I see my vocation as a priest, bishop and cardinal as a continuation of these invaluable experiences ...**
>
> **At the beginning we mentioned our dearly departed brother, a Silesian, Cardinal Boleslaw Kominek, who sat in this spot as recently as last year. He came from the Silesian land, the son of a miner. He graduated from the Jagiellonian University and went to Wroclaw. He went to reclaim our Wroclaw of the Piast dynasty for Poland and for the Church, after so many centuries ... Allow me to recall also the memory of one other cardinal who was our guest several times. I am referring to Cardinal Stefan Trochta, a cardinal of the fraternal Czech nation, who was inducted into the College of Cardinals at the same time as Cardinal Kominek, and like him, departed after a year. We always remember our brothers across our southern border, across the Carpathians, because it was from them, by their agency, that we received the faith. And today our wish for them is that through the testament of their faith, life and death, they may maintain the Church, the presence of Christ and Mary in their nation, just as we do in ours ...**
>
> **We wish to point out [to the state authorities] the tremendous threat to family life; first of all in the area of propagation of life. We are afraid that it may so happen in our country that more lives are terminated than propagated. That would lead to incalculable and disastrous consequences ...**
>
> **[On the reform of education:] Upbringing must not be a method of spiritually tearing children away from their parents! It must not be a method of creating differences, conflicts and collisions in this fundamental community, i.e. a family. So we say very plainly: this concerns us very greatly! ...**
>
> **[On the matter of building churches in new settlements] And we ask about this in the name of the true meaning of the word: socialist. Is this word intended to mean the respect of the rights of working people, or something else?**

Same day — 5:00 p.m., Zywiec-Sporysz, Holy Year celebrations * May 28 — 8:00 a.m., Wisniowa, concelebrated Mass, sermon, get-together of priests ordained in 1969 * Same day — Krakow,

Theological Seminary (Manifestu Lipcowego Street), visit with seminarians from the same class.

May 30 — Dlugoszyn, Sacrament of Confirmation:

> First, together with your pastor and all of you, I wish to thank God for giving us a day without rain, because if it had rained, which is quite a common, almost everyday occurrence in this month, it would have been impossible to hold this service of the Holy Year in your small, although honored, chapel ...
>
> [Joy at the community arising in Dlugoszyn near Szczakowa, joy at the presence of the priest at that chapel:] It is your joy, it corresponds to your faith, your convictions; but it is also my joy as a bishop, to whom Our Lord has entrusted the responsibility for many parishes, many towns, many thousands of Christians, and among all of them also your town, your community, Dlugoszyn ...
>
> Our meeting today is a source of great emotion for me. I can tell you, I will admit that many observances of the Holy Year which take place in magnificent churches ... are not the source of such great personal experiences and emotions as this one here today ... Just like this, standing here under the open sky, standing at the steps of the chapel, because this chapel obviously cannot accommodate us. But, at the same time, this deep emotion is associated with a deep pain. For I think to myself: for how many years, 12 or 14, you know it best, has the Cardinal Bishop, the Metropolitan Curia, petitioned {the authorities} in the matter of Dlugoszyn? ... It seems to me that if you were asking that a cinema or a cafe be built here, that facility would long be standing here ... That is a source of great pain to me, and that is a common feeling, that is not my private pain. It is our common pain, because we see a lack of understanding of our needs in all of this ...
>
> [Commenting on the plan to demolish a building which had been slated for religious education:] We might be able to stand under the open sky, as we do now, but it would be difficult to teach religion to small children in classrooms under the open sky. And I think that for our thousand years of fidelity to Poland, to our Homeland, for the suffering during the occupation ... for all the hard work of the Catholics here, we deserve that our children have a place to learn religion. And we expect that this place will be found here ... And if there is no such place here, then the meaning of that decision is unequivocal: it is an act of injustice towards the citizens who believe, an act that is in conflict with the guarantees of our constitution! ... I regret that I have to say all of this during my first visit here in Dlugoszyn. But I cannot be silent, because I am your bishop, and if I left here without saying this, you could say that you do not have a bishop ...
>
> This celebration of the Holy Year is being experienced by the entire community of the Church of Krakow; today it is also being experienced by your small but important community. Just as each person is important in a family, so also in the great family of the Church of God, and in particular in our Church of Krakow, each community is important, each parish is important; and the smaller it is and the more difficult its life, the more important it is.
>
> And that is why I skip many parishes, because I cannot come to all of them for the observances of the Jubilee Year. But I come to you, because you have many difficulties and many needs, and you need great faith and

heroism to be able to remain and endure in this Christian community which derives from Christ Himself, through His Apostles, through us, the apostolic successors, through our holy faith. During today's observances, we pray for this from the depths of our souls. Tell all the inhabitants here that we pray for them also. For those that are close and for those that are far. We skip no one — all of them have been redeemed by the Blood of Our Lord. He wants to lead all of them to the Father, in the Holy Spirit.

May 31 — Rakowicki cemetery in Krakow, a funeral of Prof. Adam Bochnak, a long time professor of art history at the Jagiellonian University (died May 28). Cardinal Wojtyla celebrated Mass and led the funeral.

May — Wawel Cathedral, ordination of deacons:

[This diaconate is temporary, not permanent] Nevertheless, what is to remain of this diaconate for the rest of your future life, your life in the priesthood, is the basic thought of our Master and Redeemer Jesus Christ: the awareness of service ... In order to redeem, one must serve. To bring about the good of the People of God — one must serve. To build the Church — one must serve ... It is our common calling, yours and mine.

June 1 — 5:30 p.m., Chrzanow-Koscielec, Mass with sermon, Holy Year celebrations * 9:00 p.m., Trzebinia, a visit to the sick during the retreat, sermon, celebrations of the Holy Year * June 2 — The cathedral in Kielce, Pentecost, conclusion of the visitation of the image of Our Lady of Jasna Gora in the Diocese of Kielce, in the presence of the Bishop of Kielce and many other bishops:

[On the effects of the Descent of the Holy Spirit, on the courage of the previously fearful Apostles:] Let us think what the fruit of the action of the Holy Spirit was, what kind of fundamental change, what revolution it was. In those days there was no charter of the rights of man, there was no constitution that guarantees freedom of religion and conscience, there was no declaration of the Second Vatican Council on religious freedom — there was none of this ... The Apostles had nothing to fall back on — these documents were not in place. Today we have them. All of the development of man's awareness, all of the progress of man's history, all of the domestic and international jurisprudence is behind us. We just need to draw the appropriate conclusions. But it is not sufficient to draw conclusions, if we lack the strength of the spirit and the readiness to bear witness.

June 3 — At the Church of the Sisters of the Holy Spirit in Krakow:

Our Lord said that new things must be drawn out from the old. There are rich deposits of religiousness, Christianity, faith, hope and love hidden in us — we must ensure that new elements grow from these deposits, from these layers; that, in this fashion, we mature in the awareness of the Church; that this Church, which plays such a huge role in the life of our Homeland, might also be our spiritual homeland.

June 4 — 9:00 a.m., Main Committee of the Diocesan Synod * 6:00 p.m., the Mariacki Basilica, Mass, introductory remarks, blessing of the

Oswiecim {Auschwitz} Banner * June 5 — 3:00 p.m., Brzeszcze, concelebrated Mass, reunion of priests ordained in 1973 * Same day — 4:00 p.m., church in Rajsk:

> [Your chapel] remember, is a former stable of the manor. I want to share with you the impressions which I remember from my former wanderings around Rome ... Many times I would visit the old Roman Forum. I was struck by the fact that the first Christian temples arose in the old pagan temples. And certainly many of them arose in a private homes ... And there are surely temples which arose in stables. Because the Christians, taking advantage of the freedom which they gained after three centuries of persecution, created houses of God wherever they could, taking advantage of whatever was in place ... You formed your parish by taking advantage of what was in place. You may want to consider that you are not the first to have done something like this; that the Christians of 2000 years ago, of 17 centuries ago, did the same. And had it been necessary for their community, they would have entered a stable and invited Our Lord into that stable. And something like that is nothing new for Him, either, because, after all, He was born in a stable here on earth.

June 6 — 8:00 p.m., Krakow, Church of the Salesian Fathers, Holy Year celebrations * June 7 — A session of the Council of the Pontifical Department of Theology in Krakow. Public defense of the doctoral thesis by Rev. Edward Staniek and Rev. Marian Jakubiec * June 8 — Celebrations of the Feast of the Holy Trinity in Mszana Dolna:

> Take a close look at the sign of the cross which you make, which others make. In this gesture there is some sort of embrace: I embrace my forehead, my torso, my shoulders. And the words which I say while doing that testify that in this gesture, God embraces me — because God embraces everything. Unembraceable by all of creation, He embraces all of creation. Unembraceable by human thought, by the human heart, by human will — He embraces all of man.

June 9 — Kalwaria Zebrzydowska, participated in the 4th Men's Day attended by men from the archdiocese. In the sermon he directed their thoughts to the cross erected by the academic youth on the "drozki,"[25] and to the mystery of the Holy Trinity.

June 10 — 10:00 a.m., Zakopane — "Ksiezowka," concelebrated Mass, sermon during a reunion of priests ordained in 1972 * Same day — 2:00 p.m., Wadowice, rectory, 50th anniversary of Rev. Gabryl and his colleagues' high school graduation * 6:00 p.m., Roj (Diocese of Katowice), concelebrated Mass, sermon during a reunion of priests ordained in the same year as the Cardinal * June 11 — 7:00 a.m., Jejkowice (Diocese of Katowice), concelebrated Mass, sermon during a reunion of priests ordained in the same year as the Cardinal * 12:00

---

[25] Literally "little paths", paths with Stations of the Cross.

noon, Zywiec-Zablocie, concelebrated Mass, sermon, reunion of priests ordained in 1964 * 6:00 p.m., Lipnica Mala, reunion of priests ordained in 1967 * 9:00 p.m., Zakopane — "Ksiezowka," reunion of priests ordained in 1970.

June 13 — Krakow, Corpus Christi celebrations. Procession, sermons at the four altars.

Sermon 1: The reform of education and upbringing, no matter how useful it might be, if it is to conform to principles of equality, brotherhood, social justice — must respect our social reality: thirty plus million Catholic Christians. And this matter cannot be treated as a peripheral matter, because we are not from the periphery! ... It is not the periphery that is building our contemporary Homeland! The nation is building it! The society is building it! That society, in the vast majority a Catholic society, cannot be treated as the periphery in any area ...

[On the construction of new churches:] I ask about the civic equality — is it within the program of civic equality, within the program of the socialist system, that people stand under the open sky for years on end, because they have no church or even a room for religious education? I ask, what program is that part of? I ask, whether the central principle of our system, i.e. the will of the working people is respected in all of this? And I ask about that, because I also belong to the working people! Not only because of my past, when I was a laborer, but also because of my present. The work of a bishop is hard work — I will say no more ... Let us go on ... and let us pray at all of the altars along the route of the procession of Corpus Christi. We will pray for various causes of our city, our Homeland, our Church. Here we will pray for the entire nation, for those, who wield authority in it, that they may wield it in a spirit of freedom, equality and brotherhood. We will pray for the Church in Poland, for the entire People of God, for the Episcopate, for the Cardinal Primate: Our Father...

Sermon 2 [in front of the Church of St. Peter and St. Paul]: Each of those matters [the construction of churches] is our common cause. And that is why here today, in this great community of the faithful People of God in Krakow, we will pray for the intention of church construction, we will pray for the freedom to organize and open facilities for religious education, we will pray that the needs of the faithful in our city, in the Archdiocese and in Poland be truly satisfied : Our Father....

Sermon 3 [altar near the Nowodworski Lyceum[26]]: At the third stop of the procession of Corpus Christi, let us unite spiritually with all those who are suffering. And there are many of them: in hospitals, and in homes; and there are many kinds of suffering: physical and spiritual ... Let us pray for our university youth, our high school youth, working youth, all the youth — that they be healthy physically and morally ... Let us pray for the conscience of the youth, as they are often commanded or at least induced to compromise their consciences.

Sermon 4 [altar in front of the Theological Seminary]: First, it is with great joy that I want to proclaim before God and man that this year, as never before, the Krakow Seminary is giving the Church 44 new priests;

---

[26] Secondary school

they have been already ordained and in the next few weeks will go into pastoral ministry. This also allows us to think of the missions, and this year three priests of our Archdiocese will leave to work in Africa.

Same day — 5:00 p.m., at the Church of Corpus Christi:

"Every one who acknowledges me before men, I also will acknowledge before my Father." It is necessary, my children, that this proclamation go with you, that you take it with you on vacation, where the proclamation of faith will be tested ... Every Sunday will be such a test ... And every day will be such a test — every morning and every evening ... You must proclaim your faith and not be afraid. We have a sacred right to that and we can be proud of it! Nobody ever was nor ever will be greater than Jesus Christ, no genius of humanity, no statesman, no great historical personage! Let us look into the entirety of His truth, that simple, human, deep, humble and so very Divine truth. We certainly have someone to be proud of! ... God-the-Man, who stood at a workbench for 30 years, is not afraid of any times, any reforms which are being instituted under the motto of labor, of human labor.

June 14-15 — Scientific session organized by the Institute of Contemporary Thought at the Pontifical Department of Theology: "Catholicism — Romanticism — Zygmunt Krasinski" (lectures by: Pawel Hertz, Zygmunt Kubiak, Ewa Bienkowska, Bohdan Cywinski, Henryk Krzeczkowski).

The session was organized under the aegis of the Cardinal, at the bishop's residence on Franciszkanska Street, with his active participation. Inaugurating the session and greeting the assembled as host of the Bishop's Palace, Cardinal Karol Wojtyla stated at the outset that this is the first symposium held at that place that is devoted to the history of literature. Although there were earlier initiatives for meetings and discussions on important cultural issues, at no time previously was there discussion of the work and views of prominent poets. So if today one wishes to speak of the third — the most controversial — of the great bards of Polish Romanticism[27], it is primarily because we encounter issues in his literary work that are still very relevant to us. The issues raised for the first time so lucidly in the works of Krasinski are still relevant in the contemporary world, and there is nothing to lead us to believe that they will be solved or moved to the periphery of life in the near future.[28] (Znak, 244/1974, p. 1239)

June 15 — 6:00 p.m., Stroza, Holy Year celebrations * June 16 — 11:30 a.m., Gorenice, Holy Year celebrations * June 17 — In the morning, at the chapel on Franciszkanska Street — Holy Mass to which the Cardinal invited the Higher Catechetic Institute on the occasion of the end of the school year. In the afternoon, at the convent of the Ursuline Sisters, the Cardinal presented diplomas to the H.C.I. graduates. (From the chronicles of the Ursuline Sisters) * Same day — 10:00 a.m., residence

---

[27] Zygmunt Krasinski; the others were Adam Mickiewicz and Juliusz Slowacki

[28] Krasinski's 1840's drama *The Undivine Comedy* was a prophetic description of a totalitarian state with decidedly Communist overtones..

chapel, the "sending" of newly-ordained priests * 6:00 p.m., Suchedniow (Diocese of Sandomierz), a service for the intention of the beatification of the Servant of God Queen Jadwiga, homily * June 18 — 11:00 a.m., Warsaw, Main Council of the Polish Episcopate * June 19-20 — 11:00 a.m., Warsaw, 143 plenary conference of the Polish Episcopate * June 21 — 8:00 a.m., Wawel Cathedral, concelebrated Mass for the 10th anniversary of the ordination to the priesthood of the class of 1964 * Same day — at the Church of the Jesuits, on the Feast of the Most Sacred Heart of Jesus:

> **Today we honor Love and thank God for Love ... We wish to give thanks for every good deed, even if only a cup of water handed to a thirsty person ... For all the people who live in truth; for all the people who have the courage and fortitude to uphold their convictions, for all the people who have the interior spiritual freedom of the children of God ... Today we wish to give thanks to Jesus Christ for all goodness, for the goodness which comes at a price ... On this day we also wish to make reparations for all kinds of evil ... There are many kinds of evil which are tolerated and even promoted in our country. We say this here with pain, because we do not turn away from the responsibility for such evil. For the evil which is present in our marriages and families, for the thousands of beings conceived and unborn, whose lives had been taken away before they came into the world; for all the frivolously contracted and frivolously broken marriages; for all the children deprived of their own parents, lost, doomed to an orphan's lot, to life in orphanages — and for many, many other social evils.**

June 23 — 9:00 a.m., Lipnica Wielka, Holy Year celebrations, procession * 5:30 p.m., Nowe Bystre — Holy Year * June 24 — 12:00 noon, Orawka, Holy Year celebrations * 5:00 p.m., residence, a meeting with the department of moral theology.

June 25 — expanded meeting of the Council of the Pontifical Department of Theology in Krakow (at the residence at 3 Franciszkanska Street) with the bishops from Czestochowa: Stefan Barela and Tadeusz Szwagrzyk, faculty members of the Seminaries associated with the Department by agreements of cooperation: Czestochowa, Silesia, Tarnow, Theological Institute of the Missionary Fathers, seminaries of the Pauline Fathers, the Salesians, the Congregation of the Resurrection. The topic of the discussion and of the presentations was the cooperation between the institutes. The Cardinal, as Grand Chancellor, presented an overall summation. (From the minutes of the Council) * 7:00 p.m., Wawel Cathedral, at the sarcophagus of Queen Jadwiga, sermon and prayers of participants of the nationwide catechetic course (Queen Jadwiga's 600th anniversary) * June 26 — 1:00 p.m., Silesian seminary, conclusion of a catechetic course, singing of *Te Deum* * On this day he designates new places within the territory of the Archdiocese of Krakow where pilgrims can obtain the indulgence of the Holy Year. These places are: the Cross atop Giewont {a peak in the Tatra Mountains}, a Chapel of the Holy Cross at the monastery of the Albertine Sisters at Kalatowki, the parish Church of the Holy Family in Zakopane * June 28 -11:00 a.m., Warsaw, departure for Rome * June 30 — 6:00 p.m., Rome, St. Peter's Basilica, participated in the 11th anniversary of the pontificate of Pope Paul VI and the consecration of Bishop Andrzej Deskur.

July 2 — Returns to Krakow * July 4 — he adds the Chapel of Our Lady of Jaworzyna at Wiktorowki to the list of pilgrimage sites of the Holy Year * 8:00 a.m., Wawel Cathedral, Mass with sermon, pilgrimage of sextons * 4:00 p.m., he departs for Kalwaria * July 5 — 7:00 a.m., Kalwaria Zebrzydowska, Mass * July 7 — 8:30 a.m., Ciechanowiec (Diocese of Drohiczyn on the Bug River), conclusion of the visitation of Our Lady, sermon * 6:00 p.m., Piotrkow Trybunalski, Pontifical Mass, beginning of visitation * July 8 — Rokiciny, convent of the Ursuline Sisters. "Today at 8:30 p.m. Cardinal Karol Wojtyla showed up, he visited with our Rev. Canon and friends, he stayed for supper, at 9:40 p.m. he visited Sister Emilia Podlesiecka, who was recuperating after a car accident." July 9- Aug. 4 — Vacation * July 20 — 7:00 a.m., Residence chapel, Mass for the late Bishop Piotr Kalwa * 2:00 p.m., Lublin, the funeral of Bishop Piotr Kalwa * July 28 — Fiszor — greetings and best wishes for the Primate * July 28-August 4 — Rajgrodzkie Lake.

August 5 — Jasna Gora, Chapel of Our Lady, 50th anniversary of the Primate's ordination to the priesthood, remarks at the beginning of Mass (celebrated by Bishop Lucjan Bernacki):

> **Here, at Jasna Gora, here, before this image of which the young sing that it captures all hearts, here your heart was captured 50 years ago on the day when you celebrated your first Mass, the inaugural Mass of your priesthood. It was not the day following, but three days after your ordination.**

August 9 — 7:00 a.m., Zawoja-Wilczna, private Mass * August 11 — 11:00 a.m., Makow Podhalanski, celebrations of the Holy Year — Holy Year indulgence for the deanery of Makow, concelebrated Mass, sermon * 4:00-9:00 p.m., Rdzawka, Olszowka, Wielka Polana,[29] visits to "Oasis" {charismatic} groups.

August 12 — 6:00 p.m., Rzyki, visit of an "Oasis" * August 14 — Mistrzejowice, Feast of Blessed Maximilian Kolbe:

> **As we recall all of this today, the entire history of this parish commu-**

---

[29] All names of towns

nity becomes in our eyes a special attribute of the glory of Blessed Maximilian Kolbe, our countryman, the saint of our times; a particular ray of light which he shines upon his beloved native land, a particular link in the chain which, through the mystery of the Communion of Saints, connects him with the pilgrim Church, the militant Church, the Church which is winning its right to exist on this earth, in this city of Kraków, in Nowa Huta, in Mistrzejowice.

All of this, this entire history is very vital and convincing. If someone should wish to study the mystery of the Church, the reality of the Church, it is sufficient to look at that totality, to delve into it, and we will find everything in it. We will find Christ and His Eucharist. We will find a profession of faith that is prepared for anything and which was known in the language of early Christians as "martyrium." We will find the Communion of Saints, and the person of a Blessed, and the People of God, and the priesthood. All of this together — an "Oasis" of the Living Church, all of this during the few years of the history of Mistrzejowice, which is so closely connected with the person of our countryman, Blessed Maximilian.

Same day — Kalwaria Zebrzydowska. He participated in the service for the youth on the Mountain of the Crucifixion on the occasion of the Feast of the Assumption; Mass and homily. On the next day — solemn High Mass and a sermon for a large number of pilgrims.

August 15 — Ludzmierz, a pilgrimage for the Holy Year. In his sermon, he spoke, among other topics, of Blessed Maximilian Kolbe:

Each August 14th, we will walk to that image on our knees! Even if there are any number of locks on the place where our saintly Pole was born. For it was padlocked yesterday, so that Poles and Christians could not enter there, and could not offer the Sacrifice of the Holy Mass, as has been the tradition of whole generations. From the first years of Christianity, during times of persecution, Christians have always gone to the graves of their martyrs to pray, to offer the Sacrifice of Christ. For us, such a place is Auschwitz — the concentration camp — the cell of Blessed Maximilian Kolbe, the saint of our times ... But that is a digression. That is not what I had intended to speak about. This news has just reached me, and I could not refrain from expressing my indignation — as a Pole and as a bishop — at what happened in Auschwitz yesterday ...

This Holy Year is a year of Providence; it demands from us much spiritual mobilization so that we do not allow ourselves to be removed from the sources of life and holiness. Because that would mean death! Just as an infant cannot be removed from a mother's breast, because that would mean death! ...

[On the Feast of the Assumption] let us pray ardently that our life be a good pilgrimage towards God, towards eternity, towards heaven. Because heaven ... stands at the extension of earth; heaven begins on earth; heaven is the ultimate stage of the maturity of our communion with God, our unity with God, which begins here ...

We are pilgrims on earth. This is also important here in the Podhale region. As your bishop, I wish to point out that here, too, in this region, so traditionally religious, so Christian despite its faults, we see the encroachment of various manifestations of practical materialism: and people who have been so closely connected with Our Lady of Ludzmierz are allowing the image of the Blessed Virgin Assumed into Heaven to be obscured by temporal goods, temporal interests, temporal cares — and only the temporal. The manifestations here are not yet severe, but you should be warned of them. Because St. Paul the Apostle writes to Timothy — as if he were writing to me — be urgent in season; so I am warning you as your bishop.

Same day — 4:00 p.m., Niegowic, concelebrated Mass, sermon, procession on the 25th anniversary of the construction of the new church * Same day — At the Mariacki Basilica in the evening, during the first Mass of the newly-consecrated Bishop Andrzej Deskur, in the presence of his family and bishops from Gniezno, Wloclawek, Tarnow, Czestochowa, about a special affinity of Poles for this feast[30], and especially for the observance of this feast in the churches:

> We look at this triptych, at the masterpiece of Wit Stwosz[31] and we see it ... in various ways ... We look at the masterpiece of Wit Stwosz from bottom to top, and we hear the Magnificat of Mary Assumed into Heaven, which resounds in the vertical dimension of the altar ...
> [We greet the new bishop, a member of our diocese, and we rejoice together with his family.] We share this joy with all his contemporaries on his road to the priesthood, because he traveled this road together with us. At first, in the period of the occupation, when we all had to study in secret, and then later, during the first post-war years [and the studies abroad, after which he remained in Rome and became a close collaborator of Pope Paul VI in the pioneer work in the sphere of mass media.]
> [Another interpretation of the altar of Wit Stwosz: from top to bottom.] She, who lives forever with the Holy Trinity is also united with us, she lives among the Apostles ... We have the deep faith and the unshaken confidence that Mary is with us ... with the People of God in Krakow, and in Podhale ... that she is with the Church, with the Apostles; she will be with you, dear Brother, Bishop Andrew ... she will be with you! — And she will be with Peter! — She will be with Peter! ...

August 16 — 9:00 a.m., Czestochowa, Main Council of the Polish Episcopate * August 17 — 8:30 p.m., Kalwaria Zebrzydowska, Mass and sermon, night vigil of the youth * August 18 — Tylmanowa and Brzegi.

> The Cardinal together with Bishop Tadeusz Blaszkiewicz and Bishop Piotr Bednarczyk participated in a day of inter-"Oasis" communion in Tylmanowa and Brzegi.
> In Tylmanowa the guests participated in an "hour of unity." The Cardinal stated that "the movement of the Living Church is the pupil in the eye of the Polish Episcopate."
> In Brzegi, the bishops were joined by Bishop Deskur. On the outskirts of the village the Cardinal blessed a cross of the Holy Year erected by the "Oasis" groups. The guests were greeted at the site of the blessing by the

---

[30] The Assumption of the Blessed Virgin Mary, August 15.
[31] A magnificent polychrome wooden carving on the Gothic altar of the Mariacki Church. The central group depicts the scene of Mary falling asleep among the Apostles prior to her Assumption.

participants and by local gorale.[32] The bishops participated in the "hour of witness." The Cardinal, sitting on the steps of the rectory, sang songs along with everyone else, and since it was already late evening, he delivered a short address in which he invited the "Oasis" groups to his diocese, so that they would become active in the Podhale and Spisz regions.[33]

August 19 — 7:00 a.m., residence chapel, Mass for the intention of the late Dr. Janina Wiadrowska * August 20 — He issues a statement regarding the demolition by a bulldozer of a catechetic room by the chapel in Raclawice Olkuskie-Szklary and the closing of the place of martyrdom of Blessed Fr. Maximilian Kolbe to the pilgrims * August 21 — Kalwaria Zebrzydowska, on the Octave of the Assumption, to the youth of the Liturgical Service of the Altar ("Oasis"):

> [At the moment of the Annunciation, Mary describes herself as one who serves:] The service of motherhood is always a service of the body, but at the same time a service of the soul; it is a service of the whole person, a service that is unique and incomparable. Nobody comes so close to a person, no one serves all of humanity to the same extent as a mother ...
>
> There are many ways of serving God. The idea of "service," of a "servant" entails something that people find humiliating, something they do not always accept. Man does not want to "serve," man wants to dominate. And that is why service is often unpalatable to man, he rejects service. And if he does serve, it is because he must, because he has no choice. The service of the altar could be treated in this same way; every priestly vocation could be treated in this way. But we must not! We must not! We must not — for the good of the human heart, and for the good of that great cause, which we call the service of God.

August 22 — Raclawice Okulskie — Szklary, after the demolition by the bulldozers of an addition of the catechetic room by the chapel:

> I come to you here and I celebrate this Most Sacred Sacrifice of the Mass at the place designated for religious education, so that everything that you have suffered, everything that has befallen you — and there are also bruises on your bodies, maybe someone is still in the hospital — may be offered up in sacrifice. [A request to the parishioners to lay down their sufferings on a temporary altar and to offer them to God in conjunction with the Sacrifice of the Cross, by which Christ] redeemed the whole world, all of humanity — all the people, both those who are with Him, and those who are against Him — Christ embraced all of them with His love, with His Redemption, with His Cross. For this is what God is like — He makes no distinctions, He is the Father of all and He wishes to redeem all equally ... I have come to you in this spirit [of reconciliation]. I have come because I feel that it is my duty as a bishop to be with you in difficult moments; to be here and to bring Jesus Christ among you, the One Eternal Priest, who always offers up everything that His children, His followers, experience, everything that they suffer, as a sacrifice to His Heavenly Father.

---

[32] Mountain folk living in the region.
[33] Quote unattributed

August 22. In Kalwaria Zebrzydowska, a Holy Year pilgrimage of the Archdiocese of Krakow:

> This Shrine of Kalwaria is so eloquent. Dear pilgrims, I will admit to you that I like to come here very much; maybe "like" is not the right word: I feel the need to come here, because here the deepest truths of our faith are discovered anew. It is here that the human and divine dimensions of reconciliation are discovered. The Sacrifice of Christ is discovered here and, at the bottom of it all, the love of the Father ... This Kalwaria builds man up ...
>
> [About the events in Szklary:] I speak of this because I told the parishioners in Szklary that I am going to Kalwaria and that I would take all of their sufferings, all of their efforts for the restitution of their loss, and present them to the Blessed Mother. So, I am fulfilling that promise, made not only in my word, but in my heart, because this belongs to the duties of a priest, and especially a bishop.

August 22 — Rdzawka, a visit at a retreat of an "Oasis" group * August 23-24 — Rzaska, Cardinal's private retreat * August 24 — 5:30 p.m., Collegiate Church of St. Anne in Krakow, Holy Mass during which he blessed the marriage of Zofia Gorzanowska and Stanislaw Mitkowski:

> Dear newlyweds, honorable parents and all the witnesses of this sacrament. St. Paul called it a great sacrament. We continually experience the greatness of this sacrament. We experience it because the Church is eternally married to Christ. The Church, our Mother, is the Bride of Christ, and receives from Christ, Her Divine Bridegroom, all of Her life, Her spiritual fertility. The fact that we all live the life of God, as children of God, is the fruit of the eternal marriage of Christ and His Church. And that is why marriage is a great sacrament. It is, as it were, the prototype of all the sacraments, the Church continually lives through that sacrament; the Church is this sacrament. And that is why the Church celebrates each Sacrament of Marriage entered into by newlyweds, as you are doing today, with special tenderness . The Church sees, and quite rightly, a great human cause in this sacrament; an important and responsible decision of two young people. A decision on which so much depends in your own lives, in the lives of your family, in the life of society, of the nation, of the state, of humanity. This decision must not be belittled because it is so individual, and because it is made by only two people. Everything depends on that decision. And that is why we are so happy that your decision, and the human love that stands behind that decision, are accompanied by the grace of Christ. That through the sacrament you are taking that love and that decision directly to the Heart of God-the Man, which is the very source of life and holiness. This fills us with great hope. Together with you we build on that, but primarily it is you who build the whole good, human, Christian, happy future of your marriage and your family which begins with this marriage. My dear newlyweds! The Church has really told you everything in today's Liturgy of the Word. So concise, yet so rich in content. And it has expressed all our wishes. We could not express better ones, these are the best. So let me just repeat what we have heard, what you have heard, a moment ago. Christ says: "Remain in my love." What more could

we wish you? That is our wish for you, knowing that it is what you wish most for yourselves. Christ wishes this for you, you wish it and expect it from Christ. Remain in His love! Love is the source of peace. But love is also connected with trials, and that is why Christ also said: "I give you a new commandment, that you should love one another." Accept this commandment! It is the condition for remaining in His love. Therefore, in order to be faithful to the Liturgy of the Word which the Church gives you to ponder during your marriage ceremony today, I wish to make reference to the words from the Old Testament: on your road together, may you mature together. I once read somewhere in a book the words of an engaged couple, where the man says to his betrothed: "We will grow old together." This surprised me, but it is so real, and so promising. And this is what the Sacrament of Marriage expresses, contains, promises: until death do us part. And that is everything that the Church wishes for you today in the words of the liturgy. All of this is confirmed in the second sentence of the Gospel reading, where Christ says, "May your joy be full." And this is the wish of the Church for you, the wish of the People of God gathered here, the wish of your parents, of course, and my wish as a priest and bishop who is fully aware of the greatness of this moment which we are experiencing here with you. Amen. (Transcribed from an audio tape)

After the Mass, he came to the residence of the bride's parents, disregarding discrete protests of his chaplain, Fr. Stanislaw Dziwisz, and reminders that he {Wojtyla} was expected outside Krakow, and will be late. After exchanging words of good wishes with the newlyweds, family, and the witnesses, he departed, but he did not decline the invitation to visit the wedding reception, even if for the shortest time. (According to an account by Jozef Mitkowski)

August 25 — Bialy Pradnik, Krakow. 25th anniversary of the approval of the Congregation of the Sisters of the Most Sacred Soul of Jesus:

> The beginnings of your congregation are humble and difficult. But we trust that this is how the works of God begin: there is no easy road, no easy beginning. Often these works begin as if on a rocky road, and in some respects the measure of difficulty is also a measure of victory ... It was already over the Infant of Nazareth that these words were spoken: "He is given as a sign which will be opposed by many." And that is how it was, and that is how it is.

Same day — 4:00 p.m., Rybitwy, celebrations of the Holy Year * August 26 — 11:00 a.m., Czestochowa, Pontifical High Mass * August 27 — 7:00 a.m., Wroclaw, Chapel of the Theological Seminary, Wroclaw Days of Recollection — a presentation: *"Lay Apostolate as Participation in the Basic Functions of the Church"* * August 28- 11:00 a.m., Wawel Cathedral, Mass for the late Eugeniusz Kwiatkowski * 3:00 p.m., the Rakowicki cemetery, funeral of Eugeniusz Kwiatkowski.

September 1 — 11:00 a.m., Wislica, 50th anniversary of the revival of the collegiate church and the Chapter in Wislica, in the presence of the Bishop of Kielce, the auxiliary bishops and the Metropolitan Chapter; a review of the history of the collegiate church in Wislica since the 9th century, before the christening of Poland, to today's celebrations:

> **All of us …, and I as the successor of the bishops of Krakow who were your shepherds for so many centuries, as the successor of Gedeon-Gedko, as the successor of Blessed Wincenty Kadlubek and so many others, wish, first of all, to honor and pay homage to your great past, not only of the last 50 years, but of so many centuries.**

Same day — 5:00 p.m., Zakrzow, celebrations of the Holy Year * September 2 — 5:00 p.m., Krakow-Krowodrza, Mass with sermon in a catechetic facility, a get-together * September 3 — Wroclaw cathedral, he attends a funeral of Bishop Andrzej Wronka, Vicar-general of the Wroclaw Archdiocese:

> **The soul … of a priest, the soul of a bishop, always remains in this one current, at this one point which is the central point of his activity: the fulfilling of the duties of his vocation … When he could no longer serve the people, when he could not visit the people, he would receive everyone, he rejoiced even in this service, he grew close to his people. The mission of a bishop is universal, and the suffering of a bishop is universal, too.**

September 3-5 — Gniczno. Cathedral, bishops' retreat, concelebrated Mass by the tomb of St. Wojciech {Adalbert} * September 5 — 6:30 p.m., Gniezno, a pilgrimage for the Holy Year to the tomb of St. Wojciech * September 6 — 4:00 p.m., Main Council of the Polish Episcopate * September 7 — 11:00 a.m., Szczecin, 144th plenary conference of the Polish Episcopate, 5:00 p.m., Szczecin, chapel, concelebrated Mass with the Primate of Poland * September 8 — 11:00 a.m. Szczecin, St. James's Cathedral, concelebrated Mass for the 850th anniversary of the baptism of Western Pomerania {Pomorze} * September 10 — Mnikow — blessing of a chapel * 10:00 a.m., Krakow, St. Florian's Church, a retreat for the ailing, Mass with sermon * 1:00 p.m., 4 Manifestu Lipcowego Street, 25th anniversary of the Minor Theological Seminary, closed at the present time * September 11 — 11:00 a.m., residence, a conference of the priests of the archdiocese regarding church construction * September 12 — 10:00 a.m., residence, a conference of priests — heads of deaneries, dedicated to the discussion of the pastoral program for the upcoming year and the 600th anniversary of the birth of Blessed Jadwiga * September 13 — 10:30 a.m., residence, a meeting with priests involved in the "Oasis" {charismatic} movement * 1:00 p.m., Rakowice, the funeral of Prof. Eugeniusz Brzezicki * September 14 — Meeting of the Metropolitan Curia, with the participation of all members. The participants present work plans for the years 1974/75 * 5:00 p.m., Stara Wies, celebrations of the Holy Year * September 15 — Skalka, during the unveiling of the memorial plaque of the First Regiment of motorized artillery:

> You did well ... in choosing Skalka as the spiritual meeting place of all of your comrades-at-arms, of all your colleagues from the front lines of 1939 and subsequent years of the war, until 1945. This is a place of deserving Poles. Our wish, along with yours, is to add to the names of all the great, deserving Poles — deserving, above all, because of their battles of the spirit — that great silent army of Poles who earned honor on various battlefields. We will not mention any names; they are displayed upon the tombs of the deserving. But to these names of the deserving we will simply add: The First Regiment of Motorized Artillery.

The same day — in Mogila, a pilgrimage for the Holy Year:

> At the beginning of Mass, during the act of penitence, your young cantors have sung a shattering litany of transgressions for us. When the Cross is torn out of the human soul, man is deprived of his last support. You cannot take the Cross away from man with impunity; that carries a high price; its cost is the subsequent moral collapse of society, an increasing percentage of murder of conceived life, growing collapse of social and family ties, growing social ills: drunkenness and shoddy work. Why did the workers of Nowa Huta defend the Cross? Because they know best that no great labor, no great effort and exertion of man, of the nation, of society, can be undertaken without the Cross.

The same day — in Staniatki, on the 50th anniversary of the coronation of the image of Our Lady of Staniatki:

> In the next few days I will have to leave Krakow for an extended period of time. I am going to Rome for the Synod of Bishops, which by the decision of the Holy Father is to concern itself with just one topic: the evangelization of the contemporary world ... And I admit to you, it is my great joy that my last meeting before my departure — my last meeting with the People of God of the Krakow Archdiocese, whose Archbishop I am by the will of Jesus Christ and the Holy Father, is here in this place ... The heart [of Mary] becomes more eloquent than all of the words of teachers, priests, bishops, the successors of the Apostles. That heart speaks a language that is most understandable, the most convincing, the most authentic. And it is a language which this heart has learned from the Son of God Himself. First, when He was carried beneath it, having been conceived as a child, before coming into the world. Then, when that Mother's heart looked upon the Her Son's agony on the Cross, as is depicted in the image of Staniatki.

September 16 — 5:30 p.m., residence chapel, Mass for the intention of Jerzy G. * September 17 — 9:00 a.m., Silesian Seminary, inaugural address during the congress of moral theologians * 5:00 p.m., he departs for Warsaw (later to Frankfurt and Rome).

September 18 — 12:00 noon, Frankfurt, Munich, a visit to Cardinal Julius Dopfner * September 19 — 8:00 a.m., Dachau, Chapel of the Carmelite Sisters, concelebrated Mass with Cardinal Dopfner and Msgr. Lubowiecki, sermon, a visit of the camp * September 20 —

Frankfurt * September 21 — 7:00 a.m., Frankfurt, cathedral, 50ᵗʰ anniversary of Rev. Lubowiecki's ordination to the priesthood, concelebrated Mass with sermon * September 22 — 8:00 a.m., Frankfurt, Sankt Georgen, private concelebrated Mass, a meeting with the Jesuits, departure for Rome * September 23 — He did not participate in the plenary session of the Council for the Laity because he attends the Synod of Bishops. He submitted his remarks in writing. Both the session and the remarks which he submitted concerned the future of the Council. The Cardinal emphasized the need to re-fashion the Council in such a manner that it would be more representative of the laity (he did not believe that it was necessary to establish a separate congregation for the laity) * September 24 — Rome, auditorium of the Synod, pre-synodal meeting (*relatores*-the presenters), Congregation pro Institutione Catholica — a get-together * September 25 — Deliberations of the Congregation pro Institutione Catholica * September 27-October 26 — Rome, third ordinary session of the Synod of Bishops on the topic of: "Evangelization of the Contemporary World". Cardinal Wojtyla participated as one of the three members of the Conference of the Polish Episcopate. Cardinal Wojtyla is the presenter of the doctrinal works of the Synod * September 27 — 11:00 a.m., the Sistine Chapel, the Synod began; a homily by the Holy Father — 5:00 p.m., in the auditorium, the Synod * September 29 — 11:00 a.m., Rome, Consilium de Laicis * September 30 — 5:00 p.m., Rome, a meeting of the Secretariat and the presenters of the Synod * October 3 — 12:00 noon, an audience with Consilium de Laicis * 6:00 p.m., a conclusion of Consilium * October 6 — Monte Livata, Sacro Specchio in Subiaco * October 8 — After 9:00 a.m., Cardinal Wojtyla, as the presenter of the second part of the schema on the evangelization in the contemporary world, dealing with matters of theology, presented a report in which he discussed certain theological issues related to pastoral practices. It was a reflection "on the theological dimension of evangelization itself, as well as on the methods of theological presentation of these issues." In the chapter entitled *Certainty of Faith*:

> Faith possesses singular anthropological dimensions: it plays a fundamental role in the life and self-education of the human person, and in the life and culture of every society. Through faith, the human spirit is protected from banishment to "alienation," and directed to its interior, finds itself ... In faith, man finds himself thanks to the communion with God that faith provides. Indeed, according to the testimony of many, true human culture is not possible in isolation from God ... In the contemporary world, evangelization is subject to much sharper resistance than was the case previously, and that both in the intellectual, ideological and the moral sphere, as well as in the entire idea of human existence. In certain parts of the world, the forces of "anti-evangelization" have grown to such

an extent, and the opposition has become so open, that the Gospel of Jesus Christ must truly manifest itself as the "sign of resistance." (In the discussion of the relation between eternal salvation and the development of man): The emphasis on eternal salvation in contemporary evangelization is very closely related to the efforts towards the true development of man, which the Church has always considered an integral part of its mission and activities on earth ... That is why matters of eternal salvation cannot be separated from those of the development of man, neither in the activities of the entire Church, nor in the lives of individual Christians, because both of these areas were most intimately united in the sphere of creation and that of salvation.

Same day — about 1:30 p.m., a press conference in the Vatican Sala Stampa. Bishop Fernandez and Bishop Thiandoum participated in it along with Cardinal Wojtyla, there were about 200 reporters. Cardinal Wojtyla gave a synopsis of the morning deliberations in the auditorium, and answered questions that were posed to him (among others R. Laurentin's) * One more press conference for the representatives of diplomatic missions accredited by the Apostolic See. He gave an interview (together with Bishop Enrico Bartoletti) for Italian Radio and Television on the topic of the works of the Synod. (More information: *L'Osservatore Romano* October 17, 1974, p. 2) * Same day — an interview for Radio Vatican on the report introducing the second part of the deliberations of the Synod on the matter of theological issues related to evangelization:

[The concept of] "the world" in my report has three aspects. First of all, it is the world in which evangelization is performed; second, the world which, through evangelization, acquires a new fuller sense; and finally, the world which is also set in opposition to the Gospel, as if it were the only dimension of the existence of man and his exclusive goal.

October 11 — 7:00 p.m., Conference for the diplomatic corps * October 13 — 11:00 a.m., a press conference for Centro Romano di Incontri Sacerdotali (CRIS), via Marcantonio Colonna 27 * 2:00 p.m., Vatican. A dinner at the Holy Father's with the Primate and Bishop Frantisek Tomasek.

Same day — about 7:00 p.m., Cardinal Wojtyla delivered a lecture in Italian at CRIS on the topic of Evangelization and the Interior Man *(L'Evangelisation et l'homme interieur* — published in "Omnis Terra," no. 118, fevrier 1976 and again in "Omnis Terra," no. 323, mai 1996). This lecture was also published (1975) in Italian under the same title: *L'Evangelizzazione e l'uomo interiore.*

To Cardinal K. Wojtyla, the true object of evangelization, speaking in the language of St. Paul, is to "strengthen the inner man with the help of the faith and love of Christ" (Eph. 3:16-17). This is needed by Christians living in an indifferent and consumer society, so that they can resist everything that turns them into "a man of the flesh" (Cor. 2:14). This is also needed by all people — including non-believers — who live in conditions of persecution, limited religious freedom, oppression and spiritual indoctrination, which under the pretenses of human liberation, progress and social justice strip human existence of all transcendental perspective. This "interior strengthening" is by no means a flight from responsibility that a human and a Christian has to the world. It is but an appropriate response to the challenge thrown down by technical progress and materialistic ideology. (Rev. Dr. Adam Kubis)

October 14 — 11:00 a.m., Cardinal Wojtyla presented a synthesis of the discussions of the Fathers of the Synod on the second part of the schema and his own report. The synthesis was penned by Fr. Domenico Grasso, professor at Gregorianum. However, the presenter added his own observations, in which he {Wojtyla} stressed that the most important thing for the further work of the Synod of Bishops is to remember the sources of evangelization, and that:

> the entire theology of evangelization arose not from teaching, but from a mandate (mandato). This mandate from Jesus Christ, which imposes and reveals the saving will of God, is expressed thus: "Go therefore, and make disciples of all nations ... proclaim the Good News to all creation" (Mt. 28:19; Mk. 16:15). So we are not concerned here with only some description of the experiences of evangelization or with a theological analysis of evangelization, but with the faithful fulfillment of Christ's mandate — both through the pastoral practice and through theology. Those are the specifics of evangelization that I tried to show in my presentation.

Among the issues which became particularly noticeable during the Synodal discussions, Cardinal K. Wojtyla mentioned: indigenousness, i.e. the mutual conformance between the Gospel and the life and native cultures of various countries or continents (Africa); the topic of the great non-Christian religions (the Middle East, Asia); the topic of liberation in the theological, moral and social sense (Latin America); the topic of secularization and the dangers of secularism (Western Europe, North America); the topic of formalistic atheism or the total negation of the Gospel and religion in the individual and social life of people.

October 16 — The Vatican Radio, an address about the 600th anniversary of the birth of Queen Jadwiga:

> It is a providential coincidence that this year [in which we celebrated the 600th anniversary of the birth of Queen Jadwiga] Wroclaw celebrates the 800th anniversary of the birth of St. Jadwiga, Duchess of Silesia, whose tomb is in Trzebnica ... She was the mother of Prince Henry the Pious, whom she gave courage for his war with the Tatars. In this war, Henry died in the battle of Legnica, but the Tatar hordes retreated eastwards and Poland and all of Europe were saved ... [Jadwiga Angevin[34] was given the name of the recently canonized Jadwiga of Silesia] Maybe her calling, her

mission, was already written in that name in some way. In any case, it is significant that Jadwiga chose the day of October 16, 1384 for the day of her coronation ... And the entire accomplishment of her life consisted in initiating, through her marriage with Jagiello, the union with Lithuania, which extended the boundaries of the united country to the east, and thereby the boundaries of the Church and of Christianity.

October 17 — about 2:00 p.m., Cardinal Wojtyla spoke as the last speaker during the Synod. It was the 17th general congregation. These remarks, which he delivered from the presiding chair which he occupied on that day, have not been recorded in any of the Synodal reports which appeared in print. The remarks deserve to be noted, however, because the Cardinal spoke out decidedly in support of independence and full freedom of religious education conducted by the Church. The only thing that can bind the bishops in this regard is the "Instructions for Catechesis" of the Apostolic See. (Rev. Adam Kubis) * October 20 — the Vatican Radio, a speech about the Synod of Bishops on the subject of evangelization:

> In preparing the synthesis, the editor [Cardinal Wojtyla] was assisted first of all by Fr. Dominik Grasso, a Jesuit, a professor of the Gregorian University, who was the special secretary of that part, and by a team of assistants ... [It was the basis for work in language groups, after which there was a plenary meeting.] Each of these reports represents a valuable document in its own right, testifying as to what is attracting the particular attention of the bishops of the whole world ... Personally, I felt that the report of the French group ("A") was especially lucid and precise, but others also contained many valuable elements.

For most of the year 1974 the Cardinal had solicited the Congregation for Catholic Education for approval of the statute and ratio studiorum for the Pontifical Department of Theology in Krakow. The Apostolic See approved it on October 21, 1974.

October 22 — 9:00 a.m., the Cardinal read (alternating with Cardinal Joseph Cordeiro) the draft of the closing document of the 1974 Synod of Bishops. Before the reading, Cardinal Wojtyla gave the reasons why the preparation of the text was not easy: the complexity of the issues, the lack of full clarification of the position {of the Synod} regarding certain issues, the difficulty of creating a single document from two different proposals, the short time available. The presenters, in deciding to submit the text to the evaluation of the Fathers of the Synod, realize that the text needs many changes and improvements. In the voting, which took place after the intermission, the first part of the draft, which formed about 44% of the whole, was accepted (143 aye, 47 nay), but the following three parts were rejected. As a result, the Synod withdrew the document. (The accepted first part corresponded in

---

[34] Later to become Queen Jadwiga.

essence with the synthesis which Cardinal K. Wojtyla presented to the Synodal assembly on October 14, 1974.) (Rev. Adam Kubis)

The same day — before noon, during the 20th General Congregation the outcome of the vote for the members of the Council of the Secretariat of the Synod of Bishops was given. Cardinal Wojtyla was elected as one of the three representatives of Europe: 115 votes out of 192 cast. This gave him second place. Archbishop Roger Etchegaray was first (140); third, Cardinal Juliusz Dopfner (53).

October 23 — about 10:00 a.m., after some initial announcements, Bishop E. Bartoletti, the chairman of a special committee to study the issue of " the woman in society and in the Church," presented a report on the work of the committee. Cardinal K. Wojtyla spoke in a discussion on this report:

> Studies concerning the woman should, first of all, take the fact that she is a human person (persona umana) as their starting point. In the changes which are sweeping the world, the role of the woman is especially important. Special attention must be paid to the process of secularization, which can be observed in a variety of forms. In this process, the human person is often perceived as valuable and important, but that is not always the case, especially with regard to women. Catholic teaching contains many elements which place the position of women in the appropriate perspective. We must allow these to become known, emphasizing particularly those realizations of femininity (realizzazione della feminilita) which we recognize in the Virgin Mary.

Same day — 12:00 noon, Cardinal Wojtyla answered (in Italian) questions demanding an explanation of the genesis of the rejected draft. The conclusion he drew is important, because the Synod undertook its implementation:

> As we know, the purpose of the Synod of Bishops is to offer advice and assistance to the Holy Father. Therefore the solution to this situation might be to convey to him the entire material in its varied complexity and richness. The Synod itself could work out a text that would function as a message and a document at the same time. After all, much can be said in just a few words. Given its resources and time frame, the Synod is not in a position to work out something that would be similar to the document of the Vatican Council. Besides, that is not its purpose. The persons who had worked on the document that was rejected, are able to prepare such a "message-document."

October 23 — Conference at the Pontifical Institute of Church Studies in Rome: personal reflections about the 1974 Synod.

> What I intend to say has a rather personal character, although, of course, it concerns an event that has quite a large scope and affects the entire Church. But I intend to look at the events of the Synod through the prism of my own experiences ...

[The topic of "evangelization" chosen by the Holy Father and considered in its broad implications: the entire Church is in statu missionis — it is a topic that is pastoral, but carries theological issues with it. The preparation of the Synod: in 1973 a "Questionnaire" was sent to all of the Episcopal Conferences. On the basis of the replies, an "instrumentum laboris" was gradually prepared, in which the theological topics were brought out. At this point, the Holy Father recommended that Cardinal Wojtyla work out a report on the second part, which took up just those theological issues, hence an attempt at a synthesis: an outline of the theology of evangelization. He first prepared this himself, then submitted it for review to Fr. Domenico Grasso, a theologian, a professor of Gregorianum, the main author of the aforementioned "instrumentum laboris." At the Synod: discussion of this document.] It seems to me that this certain duality in the approach to the issue of the theology of evangelization — one more synthetic, the other more analytic — was, after all, necessary ... It is a theology which creates and is created in conjunction with the life of the Church. At this point I think we are on the same wavelength as was the Vatican Council ... When [at the Synod] the bishops from the various parts of the world come to the plenary sessions and share their experiences, it becomes immediately apparent how different the conditions of the life of the Church and of evangelization are: they are different on different continents and in the different so-called worlds ... There is the First World, there is the Second World, there is the Third World. This is very important for us, because until now, in many statements, both oral and written — it was as if our reality did not exist. We would say in the past: "The Church of Silence." I often asked myself, is the "Church of Silence" the one that is silent, or the one about which we are silent? Our experience has shown that in order to stop the silence about our Church, our Church has to stop being silent. Thank God that the Vatican Council and the Synods, especially this last one, helped us a great deal in this, and we could speak with a full sense of responsibility and with complete sincerity. Thanks to that, this Church stopped being the "Church of Silence."

[The different problems of the various continents: the drive to indigenous practices in Africa, "liberation" in South America, secularization in Western Europe, contacts with the great non-Christian religions in Asia, the issue of religious freedom in our world: a whole geography of problems.] This is not a geography of theological problems or even pastoral problems; it is the geography of the conditions surrounding pastoral problems ...

[In our world, the Marxist idea of "alienation" — religion is supposed to somehow dehumanize man. The war against religion was declared in the name of this thesis.]

If the basic issue in our world is the issue of freedom of religion and freedom of conscience, then it is so in this specific meaning: as the right of a person, affirmed by a person. I am not alienated by my faith, I am enriched by my faith. Nobody from the outside has the right to tell me that it is any different. And nobody from the outside has the right, in the name of his conviction, in the name of his thesis, to handicap me because of this ... A Synod has a somewhat different character than a Council, because these different conditions typical of the various continents and the various worlds come into prominence at a Synod, the different conditions in which the Church lives and realizes itself through evangelization. That is the source of the special richness of this Synod. This is the third Synod in which I have participated and I think that this one is the richest and the fullest in terms of mutual enrichment through the exchange of experiences. I was not surprised, then, that the Holy Father came to the auditorium almost every day and listened to everything very carefully.

[The main theological problems sensu stricto: the problem of salvation and the tendency towards pneumatology] ... That is why, when I considered the ultimate issue of evangelization — de salute — I thought that it could be formulated in this fashion: de salute et promotione humana. It is in the spirit of the teachings of Christ, that Christians on their way to eternal salvation are obliged to shape the face of the earth, to make human life more humane ... [The true meaning of progress, Marcel's "to be more" as opposed to "to have more."]

There is an organic union between the Holy Spirit, Jesus Christ, and the Church.

[About ecumenism, local Churches, especially as emphasized by episcopates in Africa:] The bishops are aware of the regularity that, in some way, the Church, Christianity, always delineates the shape of the culture of a given people. We know this well from our own experience ... That is why when we were discussing this topic (our group consisted of Frenchmen, Blacks and one Pole), I said: I must accept your position on the basis of our own history. Our Polish history is also a sort of drive to the indigenous, where we were witnesses to the rise of a Polish Church within the Universal Church. [On "liberation" as a theological problem — the liberation brought by Christ is liberation from sin — the problem is how to carry it over into the social, economic and political order:] It seems to me that all social, economic or political structures that oppress man are, in a way, derived from sin. [But there is also the problem of the entity which does not want to abolish the structures which would liberate other entities:] We know that this is the tragedy of power in the history of man and in the history of contemporary humanity, of various nations — that power becomes an end in itself — that it is possessed and desired for the purpose of dominating others, and not primarily for the purpose of liberating them. [About this problem — in Latin America.] [The last theological problem] is the problem of the hierarchical and charismatic vision of the Church ... Evangelization simply demands that all of the resources of the Church be mobilized, that all of its charismatic forces be released (the role of the laity) ...

These are, as can be seen, very personal reflections. In any case, these are the matters which are particularly important to me in this magnificent reality, in this historic event, i.e. the Synod. The preparation of a closing document turned out to be unfeasible, first because of lack of time, but mainly because of the richness which the Synod brought in all of its statements.

October 24 — about 5:00 p.m., after a short presentation by Cardinal Cordeiro (in English), Cardinal Wojtyla read an outline of a "message-document" (Nuntii-Documenti) of the Fathers of the Synod for the conclusion of their work. The text was prepared by a special committee whose members included the two aforementioned main presenters of the 1974 Synod of Bishops. It was the first editorial draft, which was to be changed or modified after discussion and according to the suggestions of the Fathers. (Rev. Adam Kubis) * October 25 — about 6:00 p.m., after an address by Fr. W. Weber, Cardinal Cordeiro considered the changes to the final document suggested by the Fathers. Only those which truly served to improve the text were accepted. The improved text of the declaration of the Fathers of the Synod for the conclusion of the 1974 Synod, which was then submitted to a vote, was read by Cardinal Wojtyla. Of 193 votes cast, 182 were affirmative, 11 negative. At the very beginning of this declaration, the Fathers of the Synod stated:

> **The inexhaustible riches discovered by us in our exchange of experiences were difficult to close into one formula without disturbing their integrity. Being so much the richer after this experience, we preferred to offer the undisturbed fruits of our communion to the Holy Father with hope and simplicity, awaiting new encouragement from him ... In this our declaration we merely intend to elaborate on certain basic recommendations and important suggestions for the purpose of deepening this work which we have begun.**

As far as the deliberations in smaller groups which discussed both the first and the second part of the working schema on the subject of evangelization in the contemporary world, Cardinal Wojtyla participated in the work of the French group "B" (Circulus minor gallicus B). Apart from this, Cardinal Wojtyla participated (as presenter) in numerous sessions organized outside general congregations by the cardinals — chairmen delegate and Bishop W. Rubin, Secretary General of the Synod. He participated in the works of a group appointed to prepare a draft of the final document rejected by the Synod (members of the group: Cardinal Cordeiro, Cardinal Wojtyla, Bishop D'Souza, Bishop Lorscheider, Bishop Descamps, Bishop Rubin, Msgr. Delhay, Msgr. Farhat and Rev. Dr. Kubis). Two sessions were held: on October 20, from 8:45 a.m. to 2:00 p.m., and on October 21. Cardinal Wojtyla was present at the latter session until about 12:30 a.m. (October 22). He spoke more about it in his intervention of October 23. (Rev. Adam Kubis).

October 27 — 11:00 a.m., visit to the shrine of St. Paul of the Cross, Monte Argentario * October 30 — 6:30 p.m., Rome, Church of Our Lady in Trastevere, concelebrated Mass, parting remarks, a prayer for the beatification of the Servant of God, Stanislaw Hozjusz * October 31 — 11:00 a.m., an audience with the Holy Father Paul VI.* On the same day — together with Bishop Jerzy Ablewicz, Bishop Bronislaw Dabrowski and Prelate Edward Lubowiecki — at a dinner in the new (dedicated in December 1973) house of the Marian Fathers (Rome, via Corsica, 1). Fragment of Cardinal Wojtyla's speech:

As far as I know, the Servant of God, Stanislaw Papczynski, intended this religious order to be a Marian order as well as a penitentiary {expiatory} order. The times gave it a more apostolic and pastoral character. But we know very well that any apostolate, any pastoral ministry that is not deeply rooted in penance and conversion, in metanoia, cannot survive, cannot, first of all, work fruitfully. I think, therefore, that it is both from the very beginnings of your religious family and from its history, even its historical tensions and conflicts, that you can draw a lot for the future of this congregation, this spiritual community and for its growth and development.

I say this in the context of the event which we are experiencing, at least I am, today. We have found ourselves in a new house. A new house was built at an old place. I think that this means something. The place is as old as your congregation, your spiritual family is old. But this house is as new as the same congregation, the same religious order, the same spiritual family is new. This new house testifies to your vitality, freshness and looking to the future.

November 1 — 7:00 a.m. Rome, concelebrated Mass at the tomb of St. Peter, on the anniversary of ordination * Same day — early in the evening, he and seven Polish priests from the Diocese of Krakow arrive at San Giovanni Rotondo. He is first welcomed at the clinic by the city syndic {legal advisor} and the leadership of the "Work of Padre Pio". He responds in a few warm words to the syndic's welcoming remarks. He spends the night at the "Vittoria" hotel. He is accompanied by: Bishop A. Deskur, Rev. E. Lubowiecki, Rev. Prof. I. Rozycki, Rev. A. Kubis, Rev. S. Dziwisz * He concelebrated the first Mass of the day in the crypt of Padre Pio and preaches a short homily. After this Mass, a moment of prayers at the tomb of Padre Pio, then a second Mass in the new church. During the second Mass Bishop Andrzej Deskur delivered a homily, emphasizing the fact that the Cardinal of Krakow came to San Giovanni to remember his ordination, but also to remind himself that he {Wojtyla} was here as a young priest to visit Padre Pio. After the Mass, in the sacristy of the church, the Cardinal wrote these words in the visitors' book: "I commend myself with the entire Archdiocese of Krakow, and with all people who call upon the Servant of God, Padre Pio, to your memory. + Karol Cardinal Wojtyla, Archbishop of Krakow, on the 28th anniversary of my first Mass, and 26 years since my visit to San Giovanni Rotondo to see Padre Pio". After a simple breakfast in the refectory of the cloister, he visited all the places that were associated with Padre Pio — the cell, choir loft, chapel, small church, the hallways. In the afternoon he went to the Mountain of St. Michael the Archangel and concelebrated a third Mass there in the chapel-grotto in the rock. Homily during the Mass celebrated in the crypt of Padre Pio:

We find ourselves at the altar of God to celebrate the mystery of Death and Resurrection. We celebrate it every day, but today, when we remember all the deceased, it has a special meaning.

Yesterday we remembered all the Saints, today we remember all of the deceased, because the deceased must be, must become saints, participating in the death and resurrection of Our Lord Jesus Christ.

There is a special meaning, there is a special depth in the fact that we celebrate this Eucharist in the vicinity of the tomb of Padre Pio, who proclaimed the Passion, Death and Resurrection of Our Lord Jesus Christ throughout his entire life. We hope that during this Holy Sacrifice, during our prayer together, he will be also praying with us.

November 3 — Homily during Mass celebrated in the old church:

We, priests and bishops from Poland, all of us from the Diocese of Krakow, have received permission to concelebrate a Sunday Holy Mass in this old church. This old church remains in my memory as the place where I met the Servant of God, Padre Pio. After almost 27 years I can still see him in my mind's eye, I feel his presence, I hear his words, I remember the Mass he said at the side altar, the confessional where he heard the confessions of women, the sacristy, the main altar before which we now stand and where, after celebrating his Mass, he distributed Holy Communion.

All this gives us occasion for reflection, and also allows us to better understand the sentence which is the guiding thought of today's liturgy: "A living person is the glory of God." After almost 27 years, I see how this truth — a living person is the glory of God — has integrated itself into the life of man.[35]

Having behind me a month of work at the Synod of Bishops, where the topic was the evangelization of the contemporary world, I also think that this truth is a basic truth of evangelization in yesterday's and in today's world. What should we pray for during this Holy Sacrifice which we celebrate, and in which you, my beloved Brothers and Sisters, participate here in this old church still so full of Padre Pio's presence? We should pray that evangelization should be fulfilled in all of us, in each of us. For it to be fulfilled, each of us must become the living person who is the glory of God. Amen. (On the basis of "La Casa Sollievo della Sofferenza," no. 20 bk. 16, October 3, 1978, and "Voce di Padre Pio," no. 12, 1978, compiled by Fr. Andrzej Zebik OFM Cap. Texts of homilies in Italian were also printed there.)

November 4 — 7:00 p.m., Rome, Polish College, name-day supper * November 5 — 10:00 a.m., the Sistine Chapel, Pontifical High Mass for deceased cardinals * 3:00 p.m., Rome. Hospice of St. Stanislaw, a meeting with the priests — rectors of Polish missions * November 6 — Rome — Chapel of the Albertine Sisters. Sermon * 11:00 a.m., continuation of the meeting with the rectors * Same day — he wrote a preface to the book by Mieczyslaw Kotlarczyk *The Art of the Living Word* (Rome 1975). He reminisces about his ties with the author: "I knew [Kotlarczyk] already in the late twenties and early thirties of this century." November 8 — The Vatican Radio, German section. Conversation with Cardinal Wojtyla * On the same day — departure for

---

[35] Unclear whether he meant "a man" meaning presumably Padre Pio, or "man" meaning mankind.

Warsaw * In Rome Cardinal Wojtyla granted an interview to "Mundo Cristiano": Catholics in Poland. (Print. 1974, no. 143) * November 10 — 9:00 a.m., Wieclawice, celebrations of the Holy Year * Same day — 12:00 noon, the Mariacki Basilica, on the 200th anniversary of the death of Rev. Stanislaw Konarski, concelebrated Mass and concluding remarks:

> **The youth ... seek the truth, because they know that only through the truth, through the complete truth, can we become complete people. Complete in the scope of this world, and mature for unity with God in eternity...**

November 11 — 6:00 p.m., Theological Seminary, the first meeting with the seminarians after the return {from Rome} * November 13 — 8:00 p.m., Church of the Jesuits, concelebrated Mass, sermon during the celebration of the Feast of St. Stanislaw Kostka, blessing of books and lecture notes, a meeting with the university youth * November 16 — 6:00 p.m., Chrzanow-Rospontowa, celebrations of the Holy Year * November 17 — 8:00 a.m., Szczakowa, celebrations of the Holy Year, "youth" Mass, sermon, Eucharistic procession * Same day — 4:00 p.m., Krakow, the Church of St. Barbara, Holy Year, concluding remarks * November 18 — 9:00 a.m., Wawel Cathedral, a welcome of a pilgrimage of charity workers of the Archdiocese of Krakow * The same day — a letter from the Cardinal to the Episcopal Conference regarding the Committee for the Apostolate of the Laity: "It would be appropriate for the academic youth ministry to delegate [i.e. present candidates] new members, i.e. an academic chaplain and a student ..." (Archives of the Secretariat of the Conference of the Polish Episcopate) * November 19 — 8:00 a.m., residence, visit of a bishop from Burundi * 5:00 p.m., Poznan, cathedral, inauguration of the Pontifical Department of Theology, Mass, parting remarks * Jasna Gora, a speech to the pilgrims on the occasion of the Holy Year:

> **Is it not a miracle of Grace that you, dear brothers and sisters, coming here from such diverse places, from parts of Poland so distant from one another, still form a unity? For the most part, you don't even know one another's names or surnames, yet you form a unity? By what power? It is the gift of unity in the Holy Spirit that produces this unity that you represent here. May it be so in every parish, in every Christian community.**

November 20-December 1 — Committee for the Apostolate of the Laity. Text of the Directory handed over to the subcommittee. Acceptance of a directive pertaining to pastoral parish councils. Sacrament of Confirmation: text for the Pastoral Committee as a supplement to the pastoral directive. International ministry: report on the participation in an ecumenical consultation on the subject of the formation of apostolates of lay people in Assisi in September 1974 and at the European Forum in London in August 1974. Meeting with representatives of foreign centers of lay Catholics.

November 12-24 — Participation in a symposium dedicated to St. Bonaventure (on the 700th anniversary of his death). He presided at a concelebrated Mass in St. Francis Basilica in Krakow and delivered a sermon:

> **Although the Franciscan Order has divided into many branches, these divisions came about as the result of a search for the authentic ideal lived by St. Francis, so they do not reflect negatively on the Order. The jubilee observances in honor of St. Bonaventure indicate that the Franciscans did not cease to be one family.**

November 22 — 10:00 a.m., Theological Seminary, regional conference * November 23 — 27th meeting of the Main Committee of the Synod of the Archdiocese of Krakow. After listening to the report given by the chairman of the committee, the Cardinal reminds that the starting point of the Synod is the notion of the local Church, and that the character of the Synod (it is not limited to purely canonical structures) is pastoral — because it is an active auto-realization of the Church of Krakow. He evaluates a preliminary document by Rev. Msgr. Eugeniusz Florkowski — "this text is very fundamental and important" — considers in detail the documents prepared so far — detailed schemas. As to the pastoral councils — the studies conducted by Fr. Niward Karsznia indicate that the councils should be formed by evolution, not administratively (peremptorily on the part of the clergy or members of the council!) The Synod is, after all, a large pastoral council — a diocesan one.

November 24 — 10:00 a.m., Wawel Cathedral, concelebrated Mass, sermon, pilgrimage for the Holy Year * 12:00 noon, Parish of the Good Shepherd, consecration of the church, Mass with sermon * November 25 — 11:00 a.m., Warsaw, Main Council of the Polish Episcopate * November 26-27 — 10:00 a.m., Warsaw, 145th plenary conference of the Polish Episcopate * November 26 — 6:30 p.m., at the Church of All Saints in Warsaw, he talked about the 600th anniversary and the beatification process of Queen Jadwiga:

> **[The person of Queen Jadwiga in light of the Synodal topic: evangelization and the history of her continuing cult, and the efforts made to bring about her beatification per viam cultus:] When on February 17 of this year we announced a pilgrimage of secondary-school youth to the Wawel Cathedral for the anniversary of Queen Jadwiga's birth, not only was the whole cathedral tightly packed with the youth, but just as many people stood outside. This means that Jadwiga is still fulfilling her mission, that she evangelizes. She did not stop doing that upon her death, but continues to do it, especially in our time ... There are many dimensions of**

evangelization. There is the dimension which was the lot of Queen Jadwiga, the Lady of Wawel, the mother of peoples; and there is a dimension that is more humble, discrete, everyday, ordinary. One arises from the other.

November 28 — 10:00 a.m., Zakopane, regional conference * November 29 — 10:00 a.m., Biala, regional conference * November 30 — 11:00 a.m., residence, Committee for the Apostolate of the Laity.

December 1 — 8:00 a.m., Wawel Cathedral, a solemn Mass for priests deceased in 1974, sermon * December 2 — 9:00 a.m., Wadowice, regional conference * 7:30 p.m., Krakow, a Mass at a private residence * December 3 — 10:00 a.m., Theological Seminary, regional conference of the deaneries of the immediate vicinity of Krakow * December 4 — 10:00 a.m., Oswiecim, regional conference of the deaneries of the immediate vicinity of Krakow * December 5 — 3:30 p.m., residence, visit of the ambassador of Spain * 7:00 p.m., Theological Seminary, a St. Nicholas evening.

December 8 — In Maniowy:

> The Holy Year, as you have heard, is being celebrated under the motto of renewal and reconciliation. I think that you need renewal very much at this moment, when your parish is faced with a new situation (relocation of the village because of the damming up of the Dunajec River) ... It is particularly in such situations, critical ones, that people need a lot of unity, mutual understanding, forbearance, patience. So they would not get in one another's way, but help one another — these are the fruits of the Gospel, the fruits of Redemption.

Same day — 5:45 p.m., he consecrated the first new chapel in the parish Church of the Reformed Franciscans under construction at Azory in Krakow. He celebrated Mass and preached a sermon * December 9 — 2:00 p.m., Biezanow, a conference about the Synod of Bishops * December 10 — 11:00 a.m., residence, a meeting with hospital chaplains * 4:00 p.m., the Administrative Council of the Archdiocese * Same day — 8:00 p.m., St. Anne's Church, reflections on the 1974 Synod of Bishops to academic youth:

> [The Synod] provides us with a look at the Church ... And this is the great value of this Synod. If is enough for me to remember the row of armchairs in which I was seated, and to remember who was sitting next to me in the nearest seats, and at once we see the universality of this gathering. And so in the first four chairs in the row where I was sitting, the first seat was taken by the Bishop of Berlin, Cardinal Bengsch, next was the archbishop from Indonesia, Cardinal Darmojuwono, I was the third, next to me the cardinal from Brazil, from Porto Alegre, and the last in the row was the cardinal from the Philippines, from Cebu. So in this one row we have a small cross-section of the whole world. And, of course, in the entire auditorium of the Synod we could see the whole world, or at least the whole Church in today's world. This is already a very rich and enriching experience.

Maybe this is our specific, Polish, Christian contribution of the Second World to the work of the Synod, to the cause of evangelization. We have a sharpened vision — especially we Poles — of the truth about man, his dignity and his truth. We tried to tell this to the Synod, to the Church, to our brother bishops in a way that is appropriate for bishops, but also in a way that is appropriate for the sons of this nation, which by tapping its thousand-year tradition of Christianity and the Gospel, carries within it in a particular way the leaven of man's dignity, the leaven of man's freedom, which comes from the Gospel.

December 12 — 8:00 p.m., Church of Our Lady of Lourdes; concelebrated Mass, sermon, academic *Oplatek*[36] * December 13 — 12:00 noon, residence, Council of the Pontifical Department of Theology * On this day — the funeral of Rev. Msgr. Adam Gorkiewicz, a 90 year-old priest, pastor of the St. Szczepan Parish in Krakow.

As Bishop of the Church of Krakow, and in the name of all my predecessors, I wish to thank him for everything that he built as a priest, for all his service as a vicar, pastor and dean ... I wish to thank him for all of this in the human way. Because we cannot apply God's measure to our gratitude. That only God can do, that is His purview.

Same day — 8:00 p.m., Jesuit Basilica in Krakow, sermon preached during *Oplatek* for the conclusion of a retreat for students: "If we rise up, if we continue to rise up, it is because this is God's will, flowing from the mystery of Incarnation, along with our good will."

December 15 — 10:00 a.m., Lodz, cathedral, a sermon during the conclusion of the visitation of Our Lady of Jasna Gora:

No words of elation can express the gratitude which is due to Our Blessed Mother for the response of faith that was given during these months by so many human souls in the land of Lodz ... Mary passed among you quietly and discreetly ... and by her passing she helped you to be renewed and united ... During the time of visitation of Our Lady of Jasna Gora, the diocese ... tried to work with her on the realization of the Kingdom of God in your families ... There is not in Poland — I would even say, in Europe, in our world — a more pressing task than this.

Same day — 7:00 p.m., the Mariacki Basilica, on the sixth anniversary of the coronation of the image of Our Lady and for the conclusion of the jubilee services in Krakow: "Years go by, centuries go by, millennia go by, generations pass by, jubilees pass by, but 'Jesus Christ today is the same as yesterday', we are all in Him, we are all from Him." December 17 — 4:00 p.m., residence, seminar in moral theology * Same day — an address on the occasion of conferring a doctorate honoris causa of the Jagiellonian University to Mr. Edward Piszek, Vice-president of the Kosciuszko Foundation in the U.S.A.:

---

[36] See Glossary.

I express my great joy and sincere congratulations that the representative of our countrymen overseas has been awarded the honor of doctor honoris causa of the Jagiellonian University. I trust that it will serve to strengthen the bonds not only with his person, with his family, but also between the entire American Polonia and the old Country.

I express my joy at being able to host Mrs. Edward Piszek, his wife and his entire family in my home. In memory of this meeting, which is not our first, I wish to present to him this folk carving, a so-called "swiatek."[37] It is a simple gift, but so characteristic.

December 18 — 8:00 p.m., Church of the Dominicans, academic *Oplatek*[38] * December 19 — 8:00 p.m., St. Szczepan Church, academic *Oplatek* * December 19 — 7:00 a.m., residence chapel, Mass with sermon, *Oplatek* for the Higher Catechetic Institute * 1:00 p.m., residence, a third meeting of the Committee of Experts of the Provincial Synod. Cardinal Wojtyla presided. The Committee came to the conclusion that convoking a Provincial Synod is possible and appropriate. It was decided that a Coordinating Committee for the Provincial Synod be appointed. The committee was made up of the current experts of the committee and two representatives of every diocese familiar with the pastoral environment and its problems (in March of 1977 two more members were added to the committee.) * December 22 — A visit in the monastery of the cloistered Sisters of St. Clare at Grodzka Street. A note in the visitors' book: *"In the Holy Year with a blessing for the Sisters in the spirit of renewal and reconciliation. +Karol Cardinal Wojtyla, the Metropolitan of Krakow"* * 4:00 p.m.., residence, *Oplatek* for teachers * December 23 — 11:00 a.m., residence, presentation of awards * December 24 — 8:00 a.m., Wawel Cathedral, Advent morning service {roraty} * 11:00 a.m. — 1:00 p.m., residence, greetings * Same day — at the Krowodrza settlement, "Pasterka" {midnight Mass}:

Our presence here today, and not only today, but a constant and persevering presence, has its own importance. It is important with respect to our times. My dear brothers and sisters, as long as I have been a bishop, each year I have celebrated Midnight Mass under the open sky! Only the place changes. It began in Nowa Huta — Bienczyce, then came Mistrzejowice, then Wzgorza Krzeslawickie, then Azory, and now comes Krowodrza. Every year I celebrate Midnight Mass under the open sky, and everywhere it is attended by these contemporary shepherds, the first to proclaim Jesus Christ.

We proclaim His presence among us, we proclaim that we are His Church — and by this common proclamation we demand the rights of a citizen for the new-born Christ! Just as once Mary and Joseph went to register themselves and Jesus in the registry of citizens of their country, so we come here, so that He, Jesus Christ, would be registered in the register of

---

[37] Wooden figure of a saint.
[38] See Glossary.

the citizens of our country, and that He be given, and with Him we also, a roof over our heads.

December 25 — At the Wawel Cathedral:

Today, when our Holy Father Pope Paul VI began, in accordance with the rhythm of the years, this Holy Year in Rome, we present to him the entire achievement of the Holy Year in our Homeland, and, in particular, in the Krakow Archdiocese. We do this in a spirit of apostolic unity, and also in a spirit of filial trust which all of us bishops, and with us all the priests and the entire People of God, place in the successor of St. Peter, calling him Father — our Holy Father.

We are all embraced by time, subject to its pulse, its passage. When Jesus Christ, the Son of God Himself, became Man, He became subject to time, became subject to history, just as each one of us.

December 26. Wzgorza Krzeslawickie:

In this period [of Christmas] we look especially for all those places which bring to us the living memory of the birth of Our Lord. And we know that it was a birth in poverty and in the cold ... That is what the Gospel teaches us, this is the tradition of 2000 years, and that is how we see it with our contemporary eyes.

For where is Our Lord born, if not in the poverty and cold here, at Wzgorza Krzeslawickie? Is this not a truth which is not only written in the Gospel, but experienced by all of us? But primarily by all of you ... who remain here year after year, in fair weather and foul, in sun and rain, so that in this poverty you can continue to receive Christ who is being born: He is being born in your souls. His birth still continues; His birth is extended by your faithfulness, by your perseverance, by your witness.

That is why I come to you with particular emotion at the time of Christmas, because your witness is particularly telling at that time. We meet with Jesus Christ in the stable of Bethlehem, as it were, anew and in real life; just as it was there, so it is here. And although we do not meet at midnight of Christmas Day, on Christmas Eve or at Midnight Mass, nevertheless today's meeting has the same significance, and perhaps an even greater one, because then, during Midnight Mass, the moon was shining, it was cold but clear, whereas today it is raining. And the testament of your faith in Jesus Christ, in the mystery of His birth, is even more powerful and more convincing.

December 27 — 1:00 p.m., Chapel of the Daughters of Divine Charity, *Oplatek*[39] for the Sisters * December 28 — 6:00 p.m., Chapel of the Discalced Carmelites, *Oplatek* for the cloistered nuns * December 29 — 10:00 a.m., residence, a reunion * 12:15 p.m., residence chapel, Mass with sermon for colleagues from his senior class of secondary school * 5:00 p.m., Zakopane, *Oplatek* with the priests, sermon * December 31 — 6:00 p.m., St. Szczepan Church, Mass for the end of the old year; Midnight — Franciscan Basilica, concelebrated

---

[39] See Glossary.

Mass: " It is ... a jubilee year for the great Franciscan family — the 750th anniversary of the death of St. Francis of Assisi ... we ask that our own times may produce our own St. Francis, or our own Franciscan saints, so they, too, would shape the spirituality of our era."

1975

January 1-6 — Zakopane-Jaszczurowka, ski trip * January 6 — a solemn Mass with a sermon at the Wawel Cathedral, attended by representatives of the parishes and churches in Krakow. After the Mass, New Year greetings were exchanged as is the annual tradition. From the sermon:

> **My wish for you is that the revelation that reached the Three Wise Men might reach every person residing in our city ... I have the entire Church of Krakow in mind ... our entire homeland and all of mankind ... It is a wish that is extremely timely in this day and age, because I know that there is a struggle within these people between light and darkness, between the star and Herod ... We certainly live in an age of a struggle between faith and unbelief ... Unbelief uses various means, it has its own agenda. Its resources are quite vast. Often these means are used to bring pressure on a person. His position in society is made dependent on whether he is a believer, or an atheist ... It is necessary to wish everyone here, that they emerge victorious from such a test of faith ... whatever the cost may be.**

January 7 — 11:00 a.m., residence, a meeting with the co-authors of *Theology of the Family*. They were a circle of theologians, moralists and other specialists from Krakow who co-operated with the Archbishop. Among them were: Bishop Stanislaw Smolenski, Rev. Msgr. Juliusz Turowicz, Fr. Karol Meissner OSB, Dr. Wanda Poltawska and others * January 8 — 9:00 a.m., a private concelebrated Mass at the residence chapel * January 8-9 — Krakow, No. 3 Franciszkanska Street, a meeting of the Committee of the Episcopate for Pastoral Ministry. The report by Cardinal Wojtyla entitled *Polish Pastoral Ministry in Light of the 4th Synod of Bishops Dedicated to Evangelization of the Contemporary World*: the geography of the problems of the Church in Poland is in many respects similar to that of the Churches in other countries and on other continents. For example, the similarities with the Church in Latin America are "a tradition of a homogenous Catholic society coupled with a certain 'folk' character and the problem of social justice and the struggle for human rights." The Cardinal spoke of the difficulties that a Western European encounters when he tries to understand Eastern Europe. As a result, there is often a fascination with Marxism as an idea and a program. Mention is also made of the crisis of the authority of the Church in the West, its disposition to consumption, liberalism and secularism: "All of these tendencies are fundamentally reflected in Poland."

"The Church in Poland continues to preserve its credibility ... in an existential sense ... we must do everything in our power to consolidate this basis of evangelization in our homeland" ... Most urgent tasks: "to cleanse folk religiousness from the blemishes that appear during its vital development;" the matter of "non-practicing Catholics;" a clearer portrayal of the positive elements of Christianity; post baptismal catechumenate; small parish communities; a complete pastoral ministry including the youth; the laity; pastoral ministry in the Holy Spirit (prayer, contemplation); Marian devotion; bearing witness with one's life. (On the basis of the minutes). A discussion follows; the participants ask that the report be delivered to all of the bishops at the next Episcopal Conference. In the afternoon — reports by Fr. J. Majka, *Contemporary Polish Religiousness*, and Bishop W. Miziolek, *Changes in Religiousness*. A discussion ensues. Other current matters. (From the minutes of the Committee)

January 10 — 7:00 p.m., at the collegiate Church of St. Florian in Krakow, the Cardinal celebrated a Mass for the repose of the soul of the late Fr. Wladyslaw Bukowinski who died in Karaganda. Thirty people gathered at the rectory after the Mass. An address was given by Prof. Adam Vetulani, a former member of the Academic Circle of the Kresy Region,[1] an organization that the deceased was involved with during his studies at the Jagiellonian University. The Professor thanked the Cardinal for celebrating the Mass and for his participation in the gathering. (Jan Iwaszkiewicz) * January 11 — 8:00 p.m., *Oplatek*[2] at the Club of Catholic Intellectuals * January 12 — 9:00 a.m., at the Ursuline Sisters, a Mass and an *Oplatek* for teachers:

> **In its program of the evangelization of the contemporary world, the Synod places primary emphasis on life in the Spirit. This means the interior life, prayer and contemplation; the understanding of theology as a deepening of the Gospel, of Revelation, of the mystery; as the initiation of human thought and human will into the reality of God, into Divine order. The Synod also emphasizes catechesis.**

The same day — 12 noon, at the Wawel, *Oplatek* for the academic choir * 3:00 p.m., at the residence, *Oplatek* for "oasis" {charismatic} groups * 5:30 p.m., at Lagiewniki: "Once again we celebrated a traditional *Oplatek*, organized by Sister Klawera Wolska at the 'Zrodlo'[3] and attended by His Eminence Cardinal Karol Wojtyla, who honored us with his presence. The Cardinal came with his chaplain Father Stanislaw Dziwisz." (From the chronicles of the Congregation of the Sisters of Our Lady of Mercy) * The same day — 7:00 p.m., the residence chapel, Mass with sermon, and *Oplatek* for physicians * January 13 — A consultation meeting at his residence on plans for church construction * 3:30 p.m. — the Synodal Marian Group * January 14 — Warsaw,

---

[1] Eastern Poland, formerly USSR, now Ukraine.
[2] See Glossary
[3] Youth Center run by Our Lady of Mercy Sisters.

the Main Council of the Polish Episcopate * January 15 — Krakow, the monastery of the Pauline Fathers at Skalka. Sermon for university students (the Feast of St. Paul the Hermit) * January 15-16 — Warsaw, 145th Plenary Conference of the Polish Episcopate * January 15 — A document signed by the Cardinal Primate, that "in accordance with a motion by the Main Council, the 145th Plenary Conference of the Polish Episcopate appointed Your Eminence Chairman of the Committee for the Apostolate of the Laity. Thanking you for your acceptance of the duty to chair this committee, I trust..." Attached to the letter is a list of the members of the committee and a remark, that "the Committee, with membership as per the attached list, will begin its activity on January 15, 1975." The make-up of the Committee: the Chairman, Bishop Lech Kaczmarek, Bishop Jan Pietraszko and Bishop Boleslaw Pylak; Rev. Franciszek Macharski, Rev. Tadeusz Federowicz, Rev. Eugeniusz Weron, Prof. Czeslaw Strzeszewski, Prof. Stefan Swiezawski, Mr. Kazimierz Czaplinski, Dr. Halina Wistuba, Barbara Klys, M.A., Jan Klys, M.A., Ms. Katarzyna Lopuska. Added to the aforementioned list were: Editor Jerzy Turowicz, Rev. Jan Sobcza, Mr. Jozef Hejnosz, and Marek Kosmicki, M.A. (From the archives of the Secretariat of the Polish Episcopate.)

There were also three letters signed on the same day by Bishop Bronislaw Dabrowski, whose content was almost identical: " I wish to notify you, that in accordance with a motion by the Main Council, the 145th Conference of the Polish Episcopate appointed Your Eminence Chairman of the Committee for Catholic Education; member of the Committee for Polish Institutions in Rome; member of the Committee for Pastoral Ministry.

January 16 — Warsaw, private morning Masses at the Chapel of the Ursuline Sisters * January 17 — At the meeting of the Council of the Pontifical Department of Theology, the Cardinal formulated the final evaluation of materials to be sent to the state authorities in the matter of lifting the law of 1954 and compensating the Department of Theology for the wrongs committed against it. The memorial was signed by the members of the Council of the Pontifical Department of Theology and sent to the Apostolic See, to Cardinal Garrone, to Archbishop Poggi, to the Episcopal Conference, to the ordinary bishops of the Metropolitan See of Krakow, to the rectors of the seminaries, to the Premier, to the Chairman of the National Council, to the Senate of the Jagiellonian University, to the rectors of institutions of higher learning in Krakow, and to the First Secretary of the Central Committee of PZPR.[4] The Cardinal stated that he sent a letter to the editorial offices of "Collectanea Theologica" regarding the matter of restoring this periodical to its former status. The Cardinal also requested that three priests (Rev. Marian Finke, Rev. Antoni Witkowiak, and Rev. Marian Kowalewski from Poznan) be admitted to exams to qualify them for assistant professorship. (From the minutes of the Departmental Council) * The same day — 7:00 p.m., Mass with sermon at the Church of Our Lady of Lourdes. *Oplatek* with charity workers * January 18 — 11:00 a.m., Mass with sermon at St. Anne's Church for the late Prof. Jerzy Gierula; at 1:00 p.m., the funeral of Prof. J. Gierula at Rakowice * 4:00 p.m., *Oplatek* for artists at his residence * 7:00 p.m., residence chapel, Mass with sermon for his friends from the *Srodowisko*[5]. Singing of carols * January 19 — 9:15 a.m., Mass with sermon at the residence chapel, also, *Oplatek*[6] for the Institute of the Family * at 12:00 noon, at the Church of the Franciscan Fathers, *Oplatek* for the blind * 4:00 p.m., Mass with sermon at the residence chapel, also, *Oplatek* for nurses * at 7:00 p.m., at the residence chapel — a concelebrated Mass with a sermon, also, *Oplatek* for lawyers * January 19-26 — The central religious services for the Ecumenical Week, celebrated at the Basilica of the Dominican Fathers in Krakow. The services were inaugurated by Bishop S. Smolenski, and concluded by Cardinal Wojtyla * January 20 — 9:00 a.m., a sermon at the Dominican Fathers' during the days of recollection for the those on retreat and for missionaries from religious orders:

> **The Polish Episcopate has not lost its awareness of the civil rights in Poland ... During the last few years, we have on many occasions demanded the integral respect for the principles of religious freedom, so that we could indeed speak of the true normalization of relations between the Church and the State ... From a realistic point of view, we are obliged to remind the authorities of these rights, to move these matters forward as much as we can. But this is the actual reality: the reality is made up of parishes and the lay people in the parishes ... Here, there is always something new in relation to the situation in the world ... What we need ... is the gift of unity with the Holy Spirit, the gift of unity between the priests and the lay people.**

The same day — at 4:00 p.m., at his residence, a seminar of moral theologians * January 21 — 5:00 p.m., Witkowice, a concelebrated Mass with a sermon, *Oplatek* with priests of the class of 1974 * January 22 — 2:30 p.m., *Oplatek* with the Musical Institute and organists, at 10 Sw. Marka Street in Krakow * Same day — 5:00 p.m., at the Theological Seminary, a concelebrated Mass with a sermon during a

---

[4] Polish United Workers Party, the formal name of the Polish Communist Party.
[5] See Glossary.
[6] See Glossary.

retreat for graduating secondary school students * January 23 — The funeral of Prof. Kazimierz Wyka: Church of the Norbertine Sisters — Mass at the casket, and the funeral at the cemetery at Salwator * The same day — 5:00 p.m., a concelebrated Mass with a sermon in Komorowice and *Oplatek* with priests of the class of 1971 * January 25 — At the Church of the Dominican Fathers, a speech at an *Oplatek* for former members of the legions:

> **Dear ladies and gentlemen, you have gathered together here, at this *Oplatek*. The tradition of *Oplatek* grows out of the history of the Polish soul. It is an expression of the soul's bond with Christ ; with Christ who was born, with Christ who is continually reborn {in us} and with Christ who has thus become a witness of our historical identity, the historical identity of our Polish soul through the ages. It is precisely at the sharing of an *oplatek* that we most realize this fact. This is a family gathering. You are soldiers. Surely you were often deprived of such a gathering in the circle of your own family. But you know how valuable, how necessary such gatherings are. Moreover, as former soldiers, you make up your own specific family, which has its own history, its admirable merits; and which should continue to meet as a Polish family of soldiers, a family of legionnaires. Therefore, my Dear Gentlemen, as I share this Christmas wafer with you, I extend to you my sincere wishes; that the blessing of God always accompany you, each one of you individually and all of your loved ones, your wives, daughters, nieces and nephews, all those who are here with us today. My wish is that the blessing of God accompany you and your families, and, above all, that this blessing of God never leave our native land, that it continue to force its way to us even through the clouds and fog which hide the little hand of the Child to whom we sing, and to whom we ardently pray: "Raise your hand, oh Child of God, and bless our precious homeland; support her strength with your strength, grant her welfare and good providence."[7] This blessing is my wish for our homeland, and for all the new generations growing up in it.**

January 26 — 8:00 p.m., Mass with sermon in the home of the sick * 1:00 p.m., Mass with sermon on the Feast of the Conversion of St. Paul, at the Church of the Missionary Fathers at Stradom. * The same day — 7:00 p.m., at the Dominican Basilica in Krakow, conclusion of an octave of prayers for unity among Christians.

> **The need for unity among the Churches arises from action, from evangelization … Such awareness arose during the Synod of Bishops; a Synod that was dedicated to the evangelization of the contemporary world. This is at least how I, your Bishop, experienced this meeting with the representatives of the World Council of Churches, a meeting which took place within the framework of the Synod.**

January 27 — 5:00 p.m., celebrations in honor of St. Aniela {Angela}, the foundress of the Ursuline Sisters. The Cardinal celebrat-

---

[7] Words of a Polish Christmas carol.

ed Mass at the chapel of the Sisters, and then attends an evening of Christmas carols at the Higher Catechetical Institute * The same day — the Cardinal appointed a diocesan organizing committee for the upcoming Holy Year pilgrimage to Rome * January 28 — 10 a.m., at his residence, a conference of priests — heads of deaneries; the Cardinal presented the deans with extensive information on the topic of the last Synod of Bishops. The matter of the Holy Year jubilee pilgrimage to Rome was also discussed * 6:30 p.m., at the residence chapel, a Mass for the intention of his family * January 29 — 4:00 p.m., Frydrychowice, a concelebrated Mass with a sermon, *Oplatek* with priests of the class of 1973 * January 30 — 11:00 a.m., residence, a meeting with the bishops of the Metropolitan See of Krakow * 6:00 p.m., residence chapel, Mass with sermon, Baptism * January 31 — Zakopane.

February 2 — 7:00 a.m., residence chapel, a private Mass * The same day — 3:00 p.m., the 30th session of the Main Committee of the Pastoral Synod of the Archdiocese of Krakow. The Cardinal calls attention to the contrast between the Krakow synod and the synods organized according to the regulations of the codex. The value of the inductive method of the synod. The work within the synodal groups: we should not overestimate this work, but the reality has considerably exceeded expectations — a few hundred groups have been formed. The groups are mobilizing the Laity. A discussion on the status of the work of the synod. A summation by the Cardinal. From a speech delivered during the session:

> **Through this Synod we wish to spark interest in the Second Vatican Council among the wider circles of the clergy and Catholic society, to create the awareness that the Council is coming down to them, becoming their property. Through the pastoral Synod we also want to arrive at certain resolutions, prepare certain documents ... which will define the reality of the Church of Krakow and ... give direction to the life of that Church ... into the future ... We want to get to know this reality thoroughly ...**
>
> **This is what the special genius of the Second Vatican Council consisted in; it was such a good Council ad intra because it was and wanted to be very ad extra: it wanted to portray the Church in the world, it wanted to portray this world — not to be afraid of these contacts, not to be afraid of confrontation, but to illuminate it. This reasoning also relates to our synod and its purposes.**

The same day — the beginning of the visitation of the parish of Pleszow, a visit to the parish church, the chapel, and the religious education center in Krzeslawice. The visitation was cut short due to the freezing weather * The same day — at 8:00 p.m., pastoral visit at the Theological Seminary * February 2 — 7:00 a.m., a Mass at the bed of a sick woman * The same day — 11:00 a.m., at the Redemptorist Fathers in Krakow-Podgorze, a {concelebrated}Mass for the workers of the local transit system:

> I am happy to be able to preside over this Eucharistic Sacrifice ... and thereby, as it were, to take into my hands, into our priestly hands, all of your human toil, ... so that, by this action, the value of your toil, which frequently goes unnoticed, which is often forgotten, may be recognized as worthy in the eyes of God.

The same day — 6:00 p.m., residence, an *Oplatek* for academic workers * February 2 — Wzgorza Krzeslawickie, Mass and homily, blessing of church bells:

> The entire militant atheism uses all the means at its disposal for one sole purpose: to extinguish the Light that was lit in the temple in Jerusalem on the day of the Presentation of Our Lord Jesus Christ by His Mother and St. Joseph; the Light that was lit more than a thousand years ago, on the day of Poland's Christening, and is continually being lit on the day of the baptism of every person living in this native, Polish land ... During this recent period, when certain changes to the constitution of our country are being announced, the Polish Episcopate is once again warning those responsible for such changes, that these changes should not be based on the premises of militant atheism. That these changes do not lead to even greater discrimination against those citizens who are believers. And that these changes do not divide the nation into a group of the privileged and a vast mass of second-class citizens. Second-class citizens solely because they are believers! I spoke about these matters at the Wawel Cathedral during Christmas celebrations. I spoke about these matters at the Wawel Cathedral during the observances of the Feast of the Epiphany. And today, I speak about them for the third time ... I do not speak alone. The entire Polish Episcopate is speaking about it, because this is why the Holy Spirit selected us as shepherds, as bishops of the Church in Poland, so that we would be on guard to defend the inviolable rights of the People of God! ... Before this Mass, at the conclusion of this Christmas season,[8] on the Feast of the Presentation of Our Lord {Candlemas}, I had the great privilege to bless these bells. They ... will sound the signal that there is a living Church here; that there is a living community of the People of God here, a community which still does not have its temple, does not have a roof over its head, only this poor covering, a community that stands in the cold and the rain, today in the cold. But the community wants its temple! And no principle of atheism can be used to justify the denial of the right of hardworking citizens to have a temple ... Yesterday, I began the visitation of the parish in Pleszow. It is a parish where this great yearning of the People of God has begun, the yearning of those living at Wzgorza Krzeslawickie and those at Stoki, who are a part of our gathering today. I visited the parish church in Pleszow, the chapel, and the religious education center in Krzeslawice. And today, as I consecrate your bells, I am beginning the visitation of your community. I am beginning the visitation and, at the same time, I am interrupting it, postponing it until a more practical time, until the time before Easter, when it will be warmer, I hope, and easier to carry out these visitations and to meet with all of the People of God belonging to this community.

---

[8] In Poland, the Christmas season is observed from December 24 to the Feast of Presentation of the Lord or Candlemas on February 2.

February 3-14 — Regional conferences of priests took place at six locations in the archdiocese, all of them under the leadership of Cardinal Wojtyla (with the participation of the bishops). There were reports and discussions on the issue of the apostolic formation of the youth. * February 3 — 7:00 a.m., residence chapel, a private requiem Mass * The same day — 11:00 a.m., a regional conference in Biala * February 4 — A speech during the regional conference in Zakopane, "the matter of the Laity in the ministry to the working youth" (the "Oasis"):

> This is a phenomenon of our times, this great ... community of the youth which transcends national and continental boundaries ...
> What is needed is an elitist movement, what is needed are groups. I mentioned "Oasis" groups as an example ... they may have a different character, but they are always needed as a leaven, not in isolation, not as an escape ... There is a need for secular apostles among our youth. What struck me the most during our discussion today was the number of statements about this, that these young people are moving in this direction, that they are apostles to their own milieu, even though this comes to them with great difficulty ... What we need are people, who will have the courage to be free ... who will have the courage to accept personally, in their milieu, professionally, socially the truth expressed in the document of the Second Vatican Council entitled "On Religious Freedom." ... On Sunday, I had a meeting with the academic workers of Krakow. People from various centers were present, including quite a large group of young people. They were able to take a decisive stand on this issue.

February 5 — 11:00 a.m., Krakow, a regional conference of the deaneries in the immediate vicinity of Krakow * 6:00 p.m., residence chapel, a concelebrated Mass with a sermon, Baptism * February 6 — 11:00 a.m., a regional conference in Wadowice * February 7 — 6:00 p.m., a private Mass at the residence chapel.

February 8-9 — In the main hall of the Franciscan monastery in Krakow, the first nationwide academic session of doctors and theologians. The main topic: specific aspects of the problem of termination of pregnancy; presenters: Assistant Prof. Dr. Tomasz Cieszynski, Assistant Prof. Dr. Maria Rybakowa, Assistant Prof. Dr. Wlodzimierz Fijalkowski, Dr. Wanda Poltawska, Bishop Stanislaw Smolenski, Rev. Kazimierz Gorny. Cardinal Wojtyla delivered the opening speech:

> The initiative for this session came from the Family Study Group, which is associated with the Pontifical Department of Theology. Due to its pastoral character, the Study Group is also associated with the Department of the Apostolate of Families in the Krakow Archdiocese. Since this initiative ... seems to be particularly appropriate at this time ... for the entire Church in Poland, and for our entire Catholic society, ... we sent notification about it to all of the dioceses, ... to the heads of institutions of higher learning, universities and seminaries. The first addressees of our under-

taking are the lecturers of pastoral medicine ... We invited many doctors, especially doctors of gynecology ... as well as many colleagues who are moral theologians ... The issue of the termination of pregnancy is a social burden, a burden which we all feel, and which has existed long before today. It has a lengthy history behind it. Its effects are pronounced. We must not look at this solely through the eyes of the specialists. We must look at this as Christians, and as Poles. The work of this session is intended to produce scientific material; may it also increase our awareness of this issue, the awareness which seems to be more and more vague in ever-widening circles ... Despite its national scope ... our initiative is modest ... But I trust that it is also of great weight ... We will attempt to approach this issue in a manner that is the most objective.

February 9 — 12:00 noon, a concelebrated Mass with a sermon at the Italian Chapel, in the Church of the Franciscan Fathers * February 10 — 11:00 a.m., a speech during the regional conference in Krakow (pastoral ministry among the youth): "Especially today, against the background of such disorientation, confusion of notions, opinions, ideas, and values — our youth is searching instinctively and spontaneously for definitive values and principles, which means in practice that they are searching for demands to be placed on them." * The same day — 11:00 a.m., the funeral of Sister Emeryka, the elder Sister (the highest superior) of the Albertine Sisters.

He himself led the funeral procession. He did not say a word, but only stood in silence at the open grave. Practically all of the priests had already left, and only the Cardinal remained with us. He stood together with us in silence. At the time, this was more meaningful than any words that could have been spoken. (The Albertine Sisters)

February 11 — 6:30 p.m., a concelebrated Mass at the parish Church of Our Lady of Lourdes; sermon:

That quiet, that humble handmaiden of God, the Mother of the Son of God, is also the Mother of a great struggle ... Our life is such a struggle ... it is the battle between light and darkness ... between faith and unbelief ... the parish is the place, where you will find support in this struggle.

February 12-16 — Canonical visitation of the parish in Czyzyny * February 13 — 4:00 p.m., visit to the religious education center in Leg * February 14 — 10:00 a.m., a regional conference in Oswiecim * February 16 — On the first Sunday of Lent, a pastoral letter written by the Cardinal was read in all of the churches of the archdiocese. The topic of the letter: "Remember the sabbath day, to keep it holy." This was his third Lenten letter in a row dedicated to the Ten Commandments * Cardinal Wojtyla delivered an announcement on the matter of public dances organized for the youth during Lent * The same day — Czyzyny, episcopal visitation. The blessing of married couples: "In today's civilization a certain devaluation of the meaning of words can be observed, even of those words which bind two people together. That is why you, Christian spouses, should constantly renew in yourself the power of these sacramental words." * February 16 — The conclusion of the visitation in Czyzyny:

> **A parish is like a large family composed of many families ... Do not deprive yourselves ... of the merit of giving life and raising your own children ... There can not exist a Christian and human upbringing without the collaboration of three elements ... the collaboration between the family, the school, and the Church.**

February 17-21 — Archbishop Luigi Poggi visited the Archdiocese of Krakow. He is the Chairman of the delegation of the Apostolic See to seek working contacts with the Polish government * February 17 — 10:00 a.m., Warsaw, a conference at the Cardinal Primate's residence * February 18-19 — Krakow, residence, a session on history * February 18 — 6:30 p.m., residence chapel, Mass for the repose of the soul of Irena Vetulani, homily * February 18-19 — Krakow, at the monastery of the Dominican Fathers, a symposium under Cardinal Wojtyla's patronage dedicated to the discussion of the program of works and publications to be undertaken in the next few years within the framework of *The Atlas of Christianity in Poland* * February 19 — in the evening, at his residence, a meeting with *Tygodnik Powszechny* * February 20 — Krakow, the Archbishop's chapel. Holy Mass for the repose of the soul of the late Sister Emeryka Gaca, the Superior of the Albertine Sisters * 3:00 p.m., residence, a seminar of moral theologians.

February 21 — Krakow, a session discussing the articles to be included in a joint publication. The articles were to appear first in the "Roczniki Filozoficzne KUL,"[9] and then later in German translation. The group publication was conceived as a voice in the discussion between Marxism on the one hand, and the verbal personalism of certain German moral theologians on the other. The authors participating in the publication: Cardinal Karol Wojtyla, Rev. Assistant Prof. Tadeusz Styczen, Rev. Dr. Zbigniew Majchrzyk, and Rev. Mgr. Andrzej Szostek. (The publication appeared in "Roczniki Filozoficzne KUL," No. 24 (1976), book 2, under the title *The Person, Subject and Community*, and then in the German translation in *Der Streit um den Menschen. Personaler Anspruch des Sittlichen*, Kerelaer 1979 (Verlag Butzon-Bercker). The first part contains the work by Cardinal Wojtyla: Person: *Subjekt und Gemeinschaft* pp. 11-68, translated by Jorg Splett. The German publication was ready for print before October 16, 1978.)

---

[9] Philosophic Annals of the Catholic University of Lublin.

February 21-23 — Visitation of the parish of Wola Duchacka *
February 24 — Krakow, Franciszkanska Street, a meeting of the
Episcopate's Committee for Catholic Education. The committee
deliberated on the organization of church studies and the organization
of academic schools in Poland, after the decrees of the Apostolic See
issued in 1974, and on the draft of a communique from the Episcopate
concerning the state of affairs in this area. Further in the discussion: on
the character of higher studies in the seminaries — the problem of regulation and promotion of the academic cadres in Poland. The organization of the Congress of Theologians in 1976. The matter of giving specialized profile to the academic and diocesan annals published in
Poland. The discussion on each respective topic is opened by the
Cardinal: "We should form strong centers — academic workshops with
a fully qualified cadre of professors." (From the minutes of the Committee)
* The same day — 7:30 p.m., residence chapel, a Mass for Prof.
Kazimierz Wyka * February 26 — 12:00 noon, Warsaw, a meeting with
Archbishop Poggi, the Cardinal Primate, and Bishop Dabrowski * 4:00
p.m., departure for Fribourg in Switzerland * February 27 — 7:00 a.m.,
Fribourg, Polish Mission, a concelebrated Mass * 4:00 p.m., visit with
Cardinal Charles Journet * On the same day — he delivered a lecture
entitled *Participation or Alienation?*[10] (in the Polish version:
Uczestnictwo czy alienacja?). The lecture was prepared for the
International Colloquium of Phenomenology in Fribourg whose topic
was: *Soi et autrui — la crise de l'irreductible dans l'homme*). The col-
loquium was held from January 24 to January 28, 1975. Cardinal
Wojtyla went to Fribourg a month later and delivered his lecture on
February 27 at the Department of Philosophy of the university there.
(Cf. Analecta Husserliana 6/1977, pp. 61-73. The correct sequence of these
events was established by Rev. Michal Jagosz) * February 28 — 8:00 a.m.,
Fribourg, Polish Mission, concelebrated Mass * 12:00 noon, a visit
with Bishop Peter Mamie; at 4:00 p.m., a visit at the Dominican
Fathers.'

March 1 — 8:00 a.m., Fribourg, Polish Mission, a concelebrated
Mass * 12:00 noon, Berne, Switzerland, the national synod * 4:00 p.m.,
departure for Rome.

March 3-8 — The Cardinal participated in the first meeting of the
new Council of the Secretariat of the Synod of Bishops in Rome. The
Council was preparing a synthesis of the material of the synod, for the
purpose of turning it over to the Holy Father, Paul VI. This was in
accordance with the decision of the 1974 Synod * March 6 — 5 p.m.,

---

[10] Title given in English in the original text.

Rome, the Church of St. Stanislaw. Holy Hour * March 7 — 7:00 a.m., Rome, concelebrated Mass with sermon, at the chapel of the Felician Sisters * On the same day the Vatican Radio broadcast Cardinal Wojtyla's speech: The Holy Year in Poland * March 8 — 7:00 a.m., Rome, chapel of the Sisters at the Polish College, a concelebrated Mass with Msgr. Lubowiecki * The same day — 12:00 noon, an audience with the Holy Father, Paul VI * March 9 — 7:00 a.m., Rome, chapel of the Polish College, concelebrated Mass * Return to Poland via Vienna, a visit at the Congregation of the Resurrection in Vienna * March 10 — 7:00 a.m., Warsaw, chapel of the Ursuline Sisters, a private concelebrated Mass * 11:00 a.m., the Main Council of the Polish Episcopate in Warsaw * 7:00 p.m., Club of Catholic Intellectuals, a conference pertaining to the Synod of 1974 * March 11-12 — Warsaw, the 147th plenary conference of the Polish Episcopate * March 13 — 3:00 p.m., at his residence, a visit of Rev. Prof. Burkhardt Neinheuser OSB from Rome * March 14 — 11:00 a.m., Krakow, Committee for Religious Vocations * March 14-16 — Canonical visitation in Balin * March 15 — 8:30 p.m., residence chapel, concelebrated Mass with sermon * A meeting "pod Lipkami" (Szwedzka Street). "Lipki" was the home of Mrs. Szkocka (presently of Mr. & Mrs. Pozniak), with whom the Cardinal was associated during the German occupation. He always went there at Christmastime to sing carols. This year he could not visit them during the Christmas season, so he visited the house of Mr. & Mrs. Pozniak during Lent * March 17 — 7:00 a.m., Zakopane, chapel of the Ursuline Sisters, private Mass * 4:00 p.m., the arrival in Krakow of Archbishop Luigi Poggi together with Msgr. Julius Paetz * March 18 — The Cardinal and Archbishop Poggi visit in succession: the Theological Seminary, the Department of Theology, and the parishes of: Mistrzejowice, the Good Shepherd, and Krowodrza * March 19 — 7:00 a.m., Church of St. Joseph (the Bernardine Sisters), concelebrated Mass with sermon * 9:00 a.m., residence chapel, a Mass for nuns celebrated by Archbishop Poggi * 12:00 noon, residence, a meeting of Archbishop Poggi with male religious orders * The same day — the Cardinal spends the afternoon with Archbishop Poggi in Tyniec. They visit the monastery and talk with the monks. The Cardinal drinks black coffee with lemon (a migraine?) to the astonishment of the Vatican dignitary.

March 20 — 7:00 a.m., residence chapel, private concelebrated Mass * 7:30 a.m., residence chapel, a private Mass celebrated by Archbishop Poggi * 10:00 a.m., residence, a meeting of the workers of the Curia with Archbishop L. Poggi * 2:00 p.m., a visit to the concentration camp in Oswiecim {Auschwitz} with Archbishop Luigi Poggi * The same day — 7:00 p.m., Nowa Huta — Bienczyce, a farewell to Archbishop L. Poggi:

The day before yesterday, we visited a few places [where churches are being built or where there are difficulties connected with this] ... our visitor saw all of this with his own eyes; he wanted to see it for himself. He spoke at all of these places, and emphasized that citizens who are believers have a right to a church, that this is a human right and a civic right, clearly arising from the freedom of worship and the freedom of religious life. He spoke of these things ... in the same way that I have spoken of them, for so many years. In our discussions, we brought up a series of matters that are the most urgent in the life of the Archdiocese of Krakow. The most important of these matters dealt with the problem of the ancient Department of Theology ... a Department that was liquidated. I also talked about this many times before, and I do so again today. We discussed ... the basic problems in the life of the Church, which are connected with the building of churches, with the teaching of the truths of faith ... with the freedom of the centers of religious education, with the ever more painful matter of censorship, which does not hesitate to strike down even papal documents. We mentioned the unsettled ... matter of the central procession of Corpus Christi, which ... cannot proceed along its traditional route, from the Cathedral to the Main Market Square. Of course, we also talked about all of the brighter sides of our lives ... the pain accompanying the birth of the Church of Our Lady Queen of Poland in Nowa Huta has an epochal significance ... because they {the authorities} wanted to build a new city without God ... without a new church ... it was then stated in the words of the Polish people: you must not, in the name of the interests of the working class, fight with religion ... Who builds these churches, who goes in patient, persevering delegations to the authorities ... who, if not the Polish worker? ... Because for the worker in Poland, religion is a good, it is the light, it is the way, it is the truth, and it is life ... There cannot be a just society, if man's rights to a spiritual life are not respected to the end, to the very roots. And these rights are expressed succinctly in the freedom of religion and the freedom of conscience ... The Church in the contemporary world fights ... for man ... everywhere, in every political system, on every continent, in every cultural and civilizational milieu ... The mission of Archbishop Poggi ... is, in some way, a portion of this mission ... In the last thirty years, the Polish Episcopate ... has not faltered in its faithful service to the People of God ... to the entire Polish nation ... We have not discriminated against anyone, but we have defended our believers from discrimination ... Please tell the Holy Father, Paul VI ... that we are building on Him, on St. Peter.

March 21 — 8:00 a.m., the departure of L. Poggi * 4:45 p.m., the parish of Rakowice, Stations of the Cross and a sermon for the youth * 8:00 p.m., residence chapel, Mass with sermon for the *Srodowisko*[11] * March 22-24 — Visitation of the parish of Byczyna * March 25 — 7:30 p.m., the Church of St. Joseph (Bernardine Sisters), a concelebrated Mass with a sermon during a retreat for lawyers * March 26 — 4:00 p.m., Wawel Cathedral, Officium (this was the Office of Holy Thursday also called "Tenebrae" celebrated on Wednesday in anticipation of

---

[11] See Glossary.

Holy Thursday) * The same day — 7:30 p.m., Church of the Felician Sisters, Mass and closing remarks during a retreat for physicians * March 27 — Holy Thursday, Wawel Cathedral, Mass of the Holy Cross concelebrated with bishops and 120 priests, homily:

> **As the Bishop of the Church of Krakow, I extend sincere greetings to all of you gathered here ... to the entire community of the People of God, of this Church, for whom this Cathedral is its mother and, moreover, for whom, in accordance with our ancient tradition, this church is the mother of all churches, ... parishes, ... and communities that are located within the Metropolitan See of the Church of Krakow.**

5:00 p.m., the Cathedral, Mass of the Last Supper * 9:00 p.m., Church of St. Joseph, Holy Hour devotion with the clerics of the Seminary of Krakow * March 28 — 10:00 a.m., Wawel, Officium {Holy Office service} * 12:00 noon, Church of the Franciscan Fathers, Stations of the Cross together with the Krakow Seminary * 5:00 p.m., Wawel Cathedral, the liturgy of Good Friday * March 29 — 8:00 a.m., Wawel Cathedral, Officium {Morning Prayer} * 11:00 a.m. to 1:00 p.m., residence, Easter greetings * 5:00 p.m., Wawel Cathedral, the liturgy of the Paschal eve, Resurrection Mass, and closing remarks * March 30 — Easter, 6:30 a.m., in Nowa Huta — Bienczyce:

> **Yesterday evening I performed the Paschal celebrations ... and then I led the procession of the Resurrection at Wawel Cathedral. We walked out of the Wawel Cathedral, upon this ancient swatch of land representing the life and greatness of our Homeland, singing: "A happy day has now arrived for us." Today, early in the morning, I come to Nowa Huta, in order to proclaim with you this same truth to our city and to our times, upon the site of this new church. [The truth about eternal life, which conquers death] flows from age to age ... it passes from the old Wawel to Nowa Huta[12], from generation to generation. It is necessary that this truth be passed on forever, because it is the hope of humanity.**

The same day — 10 a.m., Wawel Cathedral, concelebrated Mass with sermon * 3:00 p.m., Cathedral, vespers * 5:00 p.m., Krakow, Mass with sermon for an ill woman at her home at 1/3 Bracka Street * March 31 — 11:00 a.m., Krakow, Church of the Most Holy Savior in Krakow, "Emmaus:"

> **[The two people speaking with Our Lord] represented man, who comes from the world; who comes full of doubt ... they represented people to whom it seems that the power of evil ... the power of the temporal world ... the power of material things in all their historical manifestations surpasses, crushes man ... Emmaus is an encounter with Christ, who in His "today," as the Risen One, as the Glorified One, forever is, forever acts ... This encounter lifts man up, it shows him another dimension of reality ...**

---

[12] "Nowa Huta" means New Steel Mill.

in which good is ultimately victorious ... It is worthwhile to dedicate your-self to good, it is worthwhile to toil and struggle in its name, it is worthwhile even to apparently lose in its name. This is extremely important to man who wants to be victorious ... but too often he wants to be a false victor, to win only temporal victories.

Same day — 5:00 p.m., Smolensk Street, Mass in the home of an ill woman (Danuta Rybicka)

April 1 — 4:00 p.m., residence, Easter repast for those involved in family ministry, a homily * April 3 — A pilgrimage to Jasna Gora commemorating the 30th anniversary of the publication of *Tygodnik Powszechny*. A homily:

Individuals and communities as a whole are confronted by many anxieties. A particular anxiety that is on our consciences, one that we struggle with, is that of the path to follow: the path that I have traveled so far, and the one that I will yet travel; the path to my vocation and of the work which God has placed before me, the work He continues to place before me, and how I am to accomplish that work. This sort of anxiety is good. It is a creative anxiety. It is good and creative for each of us, and it is also good and creative for the community, given that it is something that the community feels. I surmise that this is the reason why you have come here, having just such a feeling of anxiety ... Christ is the answer to the many fears and anxieties of man ... If you have tied your calling, the creative calling of your community, to Him, to His truth, to His Gospel, to His Church, then He remains one and the same. And His identity has been, will be, and should be, the basis of your own identity. An inner identity in relation to your self, to your community; and an external identity in relation to the Church, to the Catholic society in Poland, a society which has been looking to you and is still looking to you, a society which has placed its trust in you and will continue to do so ... I am aware that the Primate, in writing his Easter letter to the editor of *Tygodnik Powszechny*, expressed his great joy, a joy which is also your own, that we continue still to exist, that we have survived ... I would like to complement the greetings of the Primate, by wishing you ... the good fortune to grow into one with the new generation of literati and with our Catholic society. In addition, I hope that you shall have many new vocations to your profession, writers, journalists, people dedicated to social issues. After all, there is such a vast scale of possibilities and needs within the apostolate of the the Laity, in the apostolate of the laity. I must confess to you that this has always been my deepest concern for *Tygodnik Powszechny* and for *Znak*, that there would be others to continue their work. And today I express this concern in the form of a greeting. Gaude Mater Polonia, prole fecunda nobili.

In the Chapel of the Rosary, Cardinal Wojtyla's conversation with the editorial staff of *Tygodnik Powszechny*:

How was it from the beginning? Well, Mr. Turowicz came to me and said: "The thirtieth anniversary of *Tygodnik Powszechny* is approaching" That's very nice, I said, but what of it? The thirtieth is not, after all, such an important anniversary. Do you really intend for this anniversary to be identified with this other thirtieth anniversary?[13] Well, it's not really all that simultaneous. And he replied in this manner: "But, we would like to go to Jasna Gora." I find this to be very interesting, that you would like to go to Jasna Gora for your thirtieth anniversary. And he added: "But we would also want you, Reverend Cardinal, to accompany us there." And I said, this is becoming even more interesting for me, but why should I go there, too, for what sins am I to repent? Well, we talked like this for some time before the truth finally came out. Mr. Turowicz confided in me that, at this moment, the entire milieu, particularly *Tygodnik Powszechny*, felt a deep need to take a look at itself, to take a look at itself from within, a look that would be illuminated from above. And this is precisely why they would like to go on a pilgrimage to Jasna Gora. And then, and this is absolutely true, I felt ashamed and I conceded. I said that I would certainly enjoy being with you at Jasna Gora under these circumstances, and in this situation. Well, as you can see, I am here ...

I believe that this whole thing revolves around the two visions of the Church. This is to say, our own vision and one that is forced on us from the outside. According to the one forced on us from the outside, the Church is, roughly speaking, an institution based on a cult. According to our own vision, the Church is the People of God. Of course, it is the Mystical Body of Christ, and it has a mission. A mission, at whose center, undoubtedly, there is a cult, but the cult is only the center. From the center, there evolves an entire series of domains of life, activity, and responsibility ...

I am unable to list from memory all of the memorials that the authorities of the Polish People's Republic received from the Episcopal Conference within the last four years. In any case, these were memorials that referred to one major issue. They were intended to show that the normalization of relations between the Church and the State cannot be a strictly formal and diplomatic measure; that this is not just an arrangement between the authorities of the State and the highest authorities of the Church. Normalization must signify the normalization of the social life of Catholic society. And this life is still not normal ...

One of the memorials was on the matter of Christian culture in Poland ... The issues raised there were ones that were extremely important to us. In my opinion, the problem of Christian culture, of its rights, of the shape it takes in Poland, is a simple emanation, a consequence of the principles of religious freedom ...

There cannot exist some sort of ghetto in this domain [the domain of culture]. Unfortunately, what we clearly see is that there is a ghetto in our culture, a specific Catholic ghetto, whose borders it is not permissible to cross. Eventually, you are able, in the sphere of this ghetto, to add or remove some things. But, with regard to these additional positions ... there were also interventions in the matter of the organizations of the youth, especially organizations of university students. When our youth was being organized or, more precisely, being united into one association, one of a socialist nature, the existing youth organizations were given a uniform character. We protested against this action very vigorously, claiming that the action went against all of the premises of democracy, that it was an expression of a tendency towards totalitarianism. And, above all, what was

---

[13] Of the Communist government.

most important for us, was that it aimed at the principle of the freedom of conscience of the youth. If one type of organization is forced upon the entire youth, a type that has a clear "socialist" nature (and it is very clear that in our circumstances, "socialist" means one that is based on the Marxist doctrine), then, a conflict of conscience arises for every believing student or young person, for every young Pole ...

Then there was the well-known matter, one that doesn't need to be addressed in detail because it was so well-publicized, the matter of the reform of education and upbringing. There was a series of interventions in this matter; the last of these was in the form of a declaration on the subject of the Christian upbringing of the youth in Poland ... Maybe it would be worthwhile to recall an action which became particularly prominent, namely the campaign of building churches and, conversely, the campaign by the authorities to repress this action of building churches ... We are witnessing the evolution of a very characteristic attitude in our society, that when this society expresses the desire to have a church and stands firmly by this decision ...

Our national, political and social life is completely in contradiction with article 69 of our Constitution, which guarantees equal rights to all citizens ...

What is the political representation of Catholics in Poland, the political representation of this large percentage of the population, of this majority? I do not mean the state authorities, the central or the local ones, but even in the parliament ...

And if you, ladies and gentlemen, are wondering what the mission of the Church is, then I believe that the mission of the Church is, among others, to prevent our countrymen from becoming accustomed to what is an injustice. The mission of the Church is supernatural; it is eschatological. The mission of the Church is at the same time very deeply humanistic, deeply social, and it might be said, very temporal. It might be said so. One is closely interwoven into the context of the other, because man is a unified whole. Man, who is supposed to be ultimately redeemed by his eternal meeting with his Creator, by his union with God, this man, here on earth, is also a citizen and a worker in one or another category, in one or another occupation. And this man, here, in these earthly dimensions, in these temporal surroundings, must be also, and I will not say, redeemed, because this is still not a redemption, but he must be somehow defended, rescued ...

Now, in order to somehow tie all of this in with *Tygodnik*, I believe that what I have prattled about is what unites us very closely. I believe it and I feel it. After all, we live in close proximity. And neighbors know about each other. Maybe we are not always united quite as openly and clearly, because we know that you have the problem of censorship constantly hovering over you. This censorship allows for the shaping of your publication only to the extent that it has determined. Nevertheless, if people think with originality, if they think independently, then they feel what they feel. And this can always be felt and heard.

It would be difficult for me to run on too long on these matters, since we have already engaged in similar discussions on numerous occasions at 3 Franciszkanska Street. We have held these discussions for long hours, and what we have discussed during those countless hours cannot be reduced to just a few minutes of talk.

April 4 — 9:00 a.m., Zakopane, at the Ursuline Sisters * April 5, 11:00 a.m., residence, a symposium — a study on modern thought dedicated to Prof. A. Kepinski (cf. *Znak* 254) * April 5-7 — Visitation of the parish of Plaza; including Bolecin on April 5 — meeting with the youth, Mass with sermon * April 6 — Bolecin, at the building designated for religious instruction:

> This place is the property of your church community, it is your building, your home ... However, it cannot be used for worship, because of its present design. And you, quite rightly, have attempted for many years to obtain permission to establish your house of God in this place ... It is indeed amazing that the efforts which you have made for the last 14 years and which the Metropolitan Curia in Krakow has presented to the appropriate authorities of the province for the last 14 years ... have not brought any results ... And one must be amazed because all of you ... are, after all, citizens, and more than that, citizens who, through their hard work, have contributed immensely to augmenting the wealth of our nation. You live here in an industrial area. The people who live here are people of hard work, work which they gladly give to their Homeland. This is, after all, an important part of our Christian and Polish spirit, which constantly reminds us: work and pray, and it does not separate these two exhortations ... We need prayer in the same way that we need food, drink and a suitable environment. We need a house of prayer ... in the same way that we need stores, restaurants ... and even our own homes. This is our logic, and ... we cannot understand why this matter has not been taken care of for 14 years. How can working people be treated in this way ... I am continually making efforts in these matters, and so is the entire Metropolitan Curia ... in various places ... even in Krakow itself, there were and there are a number of such places ... The efforts to obtain permission for the construction of temples, churches and chapels are the daily bread of your bishop ... It is up to you ... to present these matters very firmly; you have a right to do this ... Experience teaches us, after all, that a firm position taken by society is the only thing that leads to the settlement of these matters pertaining to the construction of places of worship in our Homeland, and particularly in our archdiocese.

The same day — in Plaza, the blessing of young married couples:

> Today, when I participated with you in the Holy Mass, I reminded myself that nearly a year ago I placed my hands on one of your contemporaries, a son of your parish, and I conferred upon him ... the Sacrament of the Holy Orders through which he entered onto the road of his calling ... I am telling you this in order to tell you, ... all of the young married couples assembled here, that your life is also a calling from God.

April 7 — On the occasion of the visitation of the parish of Plaza, he visited the Daughters of Charity of St. Vincent de Paul. Following this, he went to visit the sick at the Institution — he talked with them and blessed them. (Congregation of the Daughters of Charity) * April 8 — 4:00 p.m., Kroscienko, a concelebrated Mass on the 25th anniversary of the priesthood of priests from Krakow and Czestochowa * April 9 —

10:00 a.m., Warsaw, a meeting of the Main Council of the Polish Episcopate * April 10 — 10:00 a.m., residence chapel, concelebrated Mass with priests ordained in 1974, homily * 4:00 p.m., residence, meeting of the Synodal Mission Team * 7:00 p.m., Easter repast at the Club of Catholic Intellectuals * April 11-13 — Canonical visitation of the parish of Chelmek * April 14 — 11:00 a.m., a concelebrated Mass on the 40th anniversary of the ordination to the priesthood of priests from the class of 1935 * 7:00 p.m., Theological Seminary, closing remarks during the observances of the 25th anniversary of Rev. Rector's ordination to the priesthood * April 15 — 6:00 p.m., Church of the Sisters of the Sacred Heart, a concelebrated Mass on the 81st anniversary of the founding of the congregation with prayers for the beatification of Bishop J. Pelczar, a meeting with the Sisters * April 16 — 10:00 a.m., residence, a council of priests * April 17 — 11:00 a.m., Zakopane — "Ksiezowka", a concelebrated Mass with a sermon on the 10th anniversary of priesthood * 6:00 p.m., Bronowice Male, Confirmation, Mass with sermon * April 18 — 1:00 p.m., residence, Council of the Department of Theology * 8:00 p.m., Church of the Franciscans, a meeting with those involved in academic apostolate * April 19-21— Visitation of the parish of Babice (including: April 20, 1:30 p.m. — Rozkochow; 3:00 p.m. — Kwaczala; April 21 — Jankowice) * April 20 — On the 12th Worldwide Day of Prayer for Vocations, a papal proclamation was read at the churches of the Archdiocese of Krakow. The proclamation was preceded by a short address by Cardinal Wojtyla * April 22 — 5:00 p.m., residence chapel, Mass for the repose of the soul of the late Prof. J. Gierula * 6:00 p.m., residence, a seminar in moral theology * April 23 — 6:30 p.m., residence chapel, meditation with deacons on the Feast of St. Wojciech {St. Adalbert} * 7:15 p.m., Church of St. Wojciech, Mass with sermon * April 24 — residence, a conference of priests — heads of deaneries in the Archdiocese of Krakow. The subject of the deliberations was: the method of organizing the congregations of the deaneries; matters regarding the Krakow Synod; the celebrations honoring the main patrons of Poland * The same day — 4:00 p.m., a sermon during the funeral of Rev. Pastor Marian Laczek in Biezanow:

> **I will never forget this day, ... when he came to me for the first time with the idea that, similarly ... to other special ministries, a ministry for sextons and sacristans should be formed. He came to me, not only to present his suggestions ... but also to say: I will undertake this task ... He was a pastor and a priest with all of his soul.**

The same day — 7:30 p.m., residence chapel, Mass with sermon for the late Jerzy Ciesielski * April 25 — 10:00 a.m., residence, a meeting of the apostolate of the youth * 3:00 p.m., residence, a pastoral session regarding the matter of termination of pregnancy * 7:00 p.m., residence chapel, private Mass * April 26 — The Higher Catechetical Institute was invited by Reverend Cardinal to his residence for a Mass at 7:00 a.m., afterwards, there was a meeting. (Chronicle of the Ursuline Sisters) * The same day — 6:00 p.m., Gniezno, celebrations of the jubilee of the 875th anniversary of the establishment of that Metropolitan See. The Cardinal presided over the solemn vespers and led a procession with the relics of the Patron Saints of Poland along the streets of the city. At the end of the procession he delivered a speech. In his sermon he spoke about the Synod of Bishops dedicated to evangelization. April 27 — Gniezno, 9:00 a.m., a concelebrated Mass at the cathedral and a procession * April 28 — 7:00 a.m., Krakow, residence chapel, a private Mass * 1:00 p.m., residence, a meeting of the preparatory committee of the Congress of Theologians in 1976 * The same day — Wawel Cathedral, the beginning of a novena to St. Stanislaw:

> After the conclusion of the celebrations in Gniezno, today we are inaugurating the preparations to the celebration of our patronal feast here in Krakow ... in accordance with the tradition of this day, we begin a preparatory eight-day liturgical service ... During this year, we will be reflecting on the martyrdom of our countrymen, and particularly those of Polish priests, who suffered in concentration camps during the last, horrible world war.

April 30-May 2 — Archbishop Jozef Schroffner, the Secretary of the Roman Congregation pro Institutione Catholica was visiting Krakow * April 30 — 6:00 p.m., the Mariacki Basilica, a Mass with the participation of Archbishop Schroffner, for graduating secondary school students. The sermon: "Our entire humanity is always fulfilled in the presence of God ... this cannot be seen from the outside, this cannot be qualified in categories of our profession. Our entire humanity is known only to Him ... for whom ... every one of us is transparent." * The same day — 7:30 p.m., residence, a meeting with the rectors of theological seminaries with the participation of Archbishop Schroffner. Afterwards, there was a visit to the Theological Seminary and a meeting with the representatives of the Committee for Catholic Education, the Educational Council and the Dean's Office of the Department of Theology * The same day — 6:00 p.m., Wawel Cathedral, a concelebrated Mass with Archbishop Schroffner.

May 1-2 — A visitation of the parish of Spytkowice * May 2 — 12:00 noon, in the company of Archbishop Schroffner, a visit of the concentration camp — museum in Oswiecim {Auschwitz} * The same day — 4:00 p.m., residence of the Bishop Ordinary of Czestochowa, a session of the Committee of the Episcopate for Pastoral Ministry. Reports: Rev. J. Majka, *The Issue of Catechesis of Adults against the*

Background of Modern Religious Reality; Bishop W. Pluta *The Pastoral Aspect of the New Rite of the Sacrament of Penance.* Matters regarding the program of sermons. (From the minutes of the Committee) *
May 3[14] — 11:00 a.m., Jasna Gora, a concelebrated Mass (a sermon by the Cardinal Primate) * 7:00 p.m., Jasna Gora, a sermon during the Pontifical High Mass celebrated by the bishops of Czestochowa on the occasion of the 50th anniversary of the Archdiocese of Czestochowa:

> **The fate of a disinherited person is horrible. There are various types of human, social and economic disinheritance; there are people who are dying of hunger, there are social classes that are disadvantaged, there are nations doomed to extermination ... but the most horrible disinheritance of man is to take God away from him ... We are living in times of a struggle between Christ's law of God's inheritance ... and the horrible temptation to disinherit ... Mary with all of her motherhood was placed in the heart of this spiritual struggle; the struggle within man and for man ... Fifty years ago, the Queen of Poland became the Mother and the Patroness of the Church of the Diocese of Czestochowa ... We wish this church ... on its fiftieth anniversary, that it not only pray along with the entire Church of Poland for justice and peace, as we are doing at this moment, but that it strive with all of its strength to establish the indispensable conditions necessary for achieving this justice and peace.**

May 4 — 10:00 a.m., a concelebrated Mass at the cathedral, closing remarks * The same day — Cardinal Wojtyla's address was read in the churches of the archdiocese before the celebrations in honor of St. Stanislaw. It concerned the 4th plenary session of the Krakow Synod and the procession to Skalka * May 4-5 — Canonical visitation in Zagorze * May 6 — 12:00 noon, Theological Seminary, examination for a Master's degree in theology * 3:00 p.m., residence, a seminar in moral theology * May 7-15 — On the anniversary of the 150th birthday of the Servant of God Maria Aniela Truszkowska, the foundress of the Congregation of the Felician Sisters — a novena of prayer for her beatification was held at the Church of the Immaculate Heart of Mary on Smolensk Street in Krakow. During the novena Cardinal Wojtyla and the bishops of Krakow visited the tomb of the Servant of God * May 7 — 6:00 p.m., Mietustwo, the 25th anniversary of Rev. Pastor Stefan Kajdas's ordination to the priesthood * May 8 — The Feast of the Ascension; in the afternoon, at the Wawel Cathedral — a plenary meeting of the Krakow Synod, chaired by Cardinal Wojtyla, who delivered the opening speech. The Cardinal's decree concerning the creation of pastoral parish councils in the Archdiocese of Krakow was read. The Cardinal concelebrated Mass at the tomb of St. Stanislaw and delivered a homily. Over 1300 people participated in the meeting, including rep-

---

[14] See Glossary.

resentatives from neighboring dioceses. The subject of the meeting dealt with the work of the synodal committees on the preparation of final documents. The main topic of discussion: the transmission of faith within a family. From his speech at the plenary assembly: "The conclusions we are intending to reach must be the result of the collaboration of the entire People of God in the Archdiocese of Krakow; they must be representative of the entire community..." From the homily:

> We see that [the work of the synod] is general, that it is gradual. It cannot be anything else. The task that we have put before us is a serious one. It requires us to plumb the depths of and to strengthen our faith, to find the basis of our faith, to find the basis of our belonging to Christ in His threefold mission, a mission which is ours also. This Christ who left us and ascended into heaven; this is how he will come back to us, this is how he comes back to us ... he comes back to us by the power of His Spirit ...
>
> In its work, the Synod has been dealing with the matter of family ... We have been expending a great deal of effort on this matter for years. We are working together with lay people, because this is, above all, their calling, their sacrament ... The Krakow Synod has also concerned itself with the matter of parishes ... Thus, our synod, too, moves in the direction of the strengthening of the community, for there is strength in unity ... This is, at the same time, an evangelical truth, one that is confirmed by the entire mission of Christ, and we are confirming it constantly ... Together with my concelebrants, I now wish to deposit all of this great labor of the synod on the altar of our patron, St. Stanislaw. It is in his name that we have taken up this labor through the grace of God. We have done this, so that, together with him, we might look up to the heavens.

May 9 — 9:00 a.m., a meeting of the Council of Priests, a concelebrated Mass at the residence chapel * A liturgical celebration in honor of St. Stanislaw. At 4:40 p.m., Wawel Cathedral, ordination to the diaconate of seminarians of the Theological Seminary in Krakow. From his sermon: "They are supposed to be, above all, servants. This is expressed in this first and basic degree of the ordination, which is conferred not as something passing but something that marks the deacon with a permanent imprint. It is the charism of service — and the office of service." * May 10 — 12:00 noon, Kalwaria Zebrzydowska * 5:00 p.m., residence chapel, Mass with sermon, Holy Baptism * May 11 — During the celebrations in honor of St. Stanislaw, at Skalka in Krakow:

> We are standing here in a historic year ... 975 years from the time when ... the Metropolitan See of Gniezno was established. In that same year, the Diocese of Krakow was canonically established within the Metropolitan See of Gniezno, as were the Diocese of Wroclaw and the Diocese of Kolobrzeg ... We remember the 600th anniversary of the Metropolitan See of Lvov ..., the founding fifty years ago of the Metropolitan See of Krakow, composed of the dioceses of Tarnow, Kielce, Katowice and Czestochowa ... I would like to specifically emphasize ... the presence of the ancient, practically 600-year-old Department of Theology

of the Jagiellonian University. We continue to call the Department by this name, because we are basing it on the heritage of our great Blessed Queen Jadwiga, on her legacy. St. Stanislaw (..) becomes the patron of our times in a very special, relevant way. For he gave an expression to the truth that the nation can not live and develop without the law of God.

The same day — at 6:00 p.m., a visitation in Nawojowa Gora (the parish of Rudawa):

Every person, every family builds its own house. It is not surprising that your Christian community ... desires to build some kind of a house, in which you would be able to feel like a family of God, gathered around your Savior. And you have been making these efforts for years ... to the secular authorities, who, guided by their own law, wish to control the permissions for all types of construction, especially of church structures. We are not questioning their laws, ... we only believe that these laws should be applied in consideration of the real social and personal needs of every citizen, without exception and without difference ... I must admit, that as the bishop of the Church of Krakow, as its ordinary, I am in a difficult situation. The needs continue to increase, but the way to settle these matters ... is very slow, very sluggish, causing great delays, so that the number of letters that we send yearly to the local and provincial authorities continues to grow. New needs keep arising at a faster rate than the old ones are being settled. Of course this does not mean that we can forego the pursuit of our rights ... We are doing this very patiently ... we must not become disillusioned, quite to the contrary, we must constantly remind the authorities of our rights as citizens ... And let us remember that we are doing this together, as a collective effort, ... The bishop is always on your side ... You have a just basis for your efforts. As we stand here today, on this beautiful day in May, among these blossoming trees, I can say it is a pleasure to participate in this Holy Mass. Nonetheless, the weather is not always like this ... on some occasions it is freezing, at others times the wind and the rain are slashing down ... I know this very well from personal experience. If you were asked, I am sure that you would reply that the bishops of Poland, and particularly the Bishop of Krakow, is quite accustomed to celebrating Mass under the open sky. It is difficult for me to even remember the time when I last celebrated Christmas Midnight Mass under a roof. As long as I have been a bishop, I have celebrated this Mass "at a Bethlehem," always somewhere under the open sky. Moreover, it was difficult to choose where I should go first. There are so many places in the Krakow region that are like the stable in Bethlehem that it would be impossible for me to attend all of them at the same hour on the same night ... There is a distance of at least 9 kilometers from Nawojowa Gora to the parish church in Rudawa ... and the road there is very busy because it serves as a thoroughfare to Katowice. There are many accidents on this road, and one even affected your pastor last year. This alone gives you sufficient reason and a right to seek permission to build a church here ... A priest has been with you here for the past year ... in spite of the fact that there are not adequate conditions for a ministry. Even though the conditions are very difficult for him, he accepted the will of his bishop immediately, without a word of complaint, ... and he is here with you.

May 12 — 6:00 p.m., Mydlniki, the blessing of the construction of the church, Mass with sermon * May 13 — 6:00 p.m., Mistrzejowice, the blessing of the site for the church, a concelebrated Mass with a sermon * May 16 — 6:00 p.m., Church of the Felician Sisters, a concelebrated Mass with a sermon for the 150th anniversary of the congregation. Also, prayers for the beatification of the Servant of God Aniela Truszkowska * May 17 — 12:00 noon, Kalwaria Zebrzydowska * 6:00 p.m., Krakow, Church of St. Szczepan, the blessing of the new building (parish house), Mass with sermon * 8:30 p.m., the Dominican Church, the rock opera *Jesus Christ Superstar* * May 18, 9:00 a.m., Wawel, ordination of priests: "The priests, who are being ordained today, are — according to my deepest conviction — the fruit of the prayer of the Church of Krakow together with Mary, the Mother of Christ, in the year of her visitations." * 12:00 noon, Theological Seminary, a traditional celebration of farewell to the newly-ordained priests * The same day — 4:30 p.m., ordination of priests in Milowka, a homily * May 19 — 8:00 a.m., Milowka, concelebrated Mass with sermon, get-together with priests of the class of 1966 * May 19 — Celebrations in honor of Our Lady Mother of the Church, the jubilee of the 800th anniversary of the religious order of the Sisters of the Holy Spirit. On the same day — a solemn Mass at the Mariacki Basilica at 5:00 p.m., then a visit of an exhibit pertaining to the jubilee at the church on Szpitalna Street. (The Cardinal participated in the celebrations of the jubilee until about 9:00 p.m.). From the sermon:

> **I believe that the members of the Polish Episcopate acted with deep theological justification, when, during the Second Vatican Council, ... they asked the Holy Father to pronounce Mary the Mother of the Church. And then to make the Monday after Pentecost the Feast of the Mother of the Church. There is a deep logic of faith at work here, there is the experience of our history of salvation, our own Polish history of salvation, which may and probably should serve the history of salvation of other nations and peoples around the world ... upon which the Holy Spirit descends ... This calling, which your Sisters have realized throughout the ages here in Krakow, at the Holy Spirit Square, near Szpitalna Street, is nothing other than an expression of spiritual motherhood: of a motherhood of the spirit.**

May 20 — A meeting of the Committee for Catholic Education, together with the chairmen of the sections. The Cardinal: there arose a need for closer collaboration between the Committee and the sections. Perhaps it is necessary to investigate more closely and modify the organization and the regulations pertaining to the sections. The matter of the Congress of Theologians — information presented by the committee preparing the Congress. During lunch, discussion of the issue of giving direction to scholarly research and of the conditions of the same in the diocese. In the afternoon, a meeting of the members of the Committee. The matter of the Catholic institutions of higher learning in Bialystok and Olsztyn; the Congress; the 10th anniversary of the Second Vatican Council; the task of the Committee for Catholic Education in the sphere of "doctrina fidei". The Committee asked the Cardinal to prepare a report on the subject of threats to morality and faith in Poland. (From the minutes of the Committee) * The same day — 8:30 p.m., Church of Our Lady of Lourdes, a Mass with sermon for graduates of institutions of higher education * May 21 — 11:00 a.m., residence, the 4th meeting of the Educational Council of the Polish Episcopate. A discussion on the proposed rules and regulations of the Council. An animated discussion on "what should the Educational Council do, when the Qualifying Committee is not sending its replies (as is the case with KUL and ATK)? Everyone agreed that only the decision of the school is valid for the Educational Council." Those who spoke several times during the discussion were: Cardinal Wojtyla, Bishop Rechowicz and Bishop Wojcik, Rev. Prof. Stepien, Rev. Prof. Zurowski, Rev. Prof. Olejnik, Rev. Prof. Majka, Rev. Prof. Darowski, Rev. Prof. Jaworski, Father Jankowski and others. Matters dealing with the preparations for the Congress of Polish Theologians were also discussed. (From the minutes of the Council) * The same day — 6:00 p.m., Gaj, a concelebrated Mass with sermon during the meeting of priests of the class of 1973 * May 22 — 7:30 a.m., Pewel Slemienska, a concelebrated Mass with sermon * Pewel Mala, a get-together with the priests of the class of 1972 * The same day — 12:00 noon, St. Anne's Church in Krakow, the ceremonial promotion of 10 doctors from the Pontifical Department of Theology * The same day — 7:30 p.m., residence, a meeting with *Tygodnik Powszechny* * May 23 — 7:30 a.m., residence chapel, a private concelebrated Mass * 11:00 a.m., the residence, a session of bishops, at 8:00 p.m. a meeting with the editorial staff * The same day — the Cardinal handed texts of the agreements for the Seminaries of Czestochowa, Silesia, and Tarnow, and the Theological Institute of the Missionary Fathers, that were approved by the Apostolic See on March 3, 1975. The agreements regarded academic collaboration between the schools mentioned above and the Pontifical Department of Theology in Krakow.

May 24 — The Committee for the Apostolate of the Laity. A Directory on dialogue — the text was accepted but was not intended for dissemination: the impossibility of formulating a more precise theological and philosophical definition of dialogue. The documents popularizing the issue — a turn towards the formation to dialogue. Preparation of the statutes of the Committee (it had operated under internal procedural rules) * The same day — 6:00 p.m., Church of St. Stanislaw Kostka at Debniki, blessing of stained glass windows, concelebrated Mass with sermon * May 25 — 9:30 a.m., Piekary Slaskie, a pilgrimage of men and male youth on the occasion of the 50th anniversary of the establishment of the Diocese of Katowice:

> **It is you ... who shaped this wonderful, noble custom not only here in Silesia, but spread it over the entire Polish countryside: the words of the greeting: May God speed you. May God bless your work. All of your work is in the name of God ... The Church of the People of God residing in Silesia has a specific profile, a specific religious and social profile ... one which is the union of prayer and work ... When we are in Piekary, we come to realize that one cannot fight with religion in the name of the working class, or in the name of its interests and needs! One cannot not undertake a program of propagating atheism in the name of the truth of the Silesian coal miner, in the name of the truth of the society which, through its hard work, is building the greater good of our Homeland ... I said exactly the same thing when I was in Nowa Huta ... It is necessary to keep demanding that churches be built ... that people should not have to stand under the open sky in both summer and winter, in all kinds of bad weather ... that the principle of religious freedom be respected; that parents should have complete liberty, without any outside pressure, to raise their children and their youth in the truths of the faith that have accomplished so much here ... that no one should suffer because of their religious beliefs, that you not be threatened with dismissal from work, regardless of whether you are a miner or a manager ... that you not be forced to work on Sundays.**

The same day — 5:30 p.m., Skalka, Mass with sermon for the Family of the Rosary * The same day — the Cardinal's address on the preparation of children and the youth for the summer vacations and on the procession of Corpus Christi was read in the churches of the diocese * May 27 — 9:00 a.m., Theological Seminary, the visit of Cardinal Sebastian Baggio, the Prefect of the Sacred Congregation for Bishops * 6:00 p.m., Mogila, participation in May liturgical services, sermon * May 28 — 7:00 a.m., residence chapel, a concelebrated Mass with Cardinal Baggio, farewell to the guest * May 28-30 — Canonical visitation of the parish of Zarki * May 29 — Corpus Christi, a procession from Wawel through the streets of Krakow:

> **[Sermon at the first altar:] I am overjoyed that we are standing here together with such a large number of representatives of the Catholic society of our city ... and that I could put this cape on for today's celebration, a cape that was given to me by the Holy Father, Paul VI, along with a letter which he sent last year, for the 600th anniversary of the birth of our Blessed Queen Jadwiga ... Sadly, I must state that when we are denied the use of this traditional processional route from the Cathedral to the Mariacki Basilica, a route which is one of the elements of our Polish and Christian heritage, I am inclined to think that such actions do not work in favor of the process of normalization of relations between the Church and the State ... We pause and carefully consider the 69th article [of the Constitution], which clearly guarantees the equality of all the citizens of this country, regardless of race, origin, or creed ... The power of authority lies**

in the preservation of all the rights of citizens, the rights of all citizens without exception ...

[At the 2nd altar:] We call for healthy principles of law and morality for the Polish family ...

[At the 3rd altar:] We pray that Roman Catholic parents not encounter various obstacles as they seek to exercise their right to bring their children up in accordance with their own beliefs. We pray that a program of atheistic upbringing may not be forced upon them, that their children not be corrupted, especially in the area of sexual education ... that our youth possess the knowledge, the spirit to discern what is true from what is false; what is good from what is bad ...

[At the 4th altar:] In a spirit of particular solidarity with all the parishes and neighborhoods of Krakow, where churches do not exist, where we pray under the open sky, and where priests tirelessly perform their service under this open sky, let us ask Christ for new vocations to the priesthood for our archdiocese ... and for the entire Church. Let us ask Christ for the strength to hold on, for the resoluteness for all those, who go in delegations, in order to obtain the valuable permissions to build churches, permissions for which many churches and communities wait for many years.

May 31 — 11:00 a.m., residence, a session with auxiliary bishops * The same day — Fr. Jan Piatek (from Kielce) defends his doctoral dissertation in Rome. The title: *La Formazione della persone umana all'amore allo luce del pensiero filosofico del Card. Karol Wojtyla*. The promoter: Fr. Feliks Bednarski.

June 1 — 11:00 a.m., Plock, a concelebrated Mass with sermon on the 900th anniversary of the Diocese of Plock * The same day — an address by Cardinal Wojtyla before the pilgrimage of men and male youth to Kalwaria Zebrzydowska was read in the whole archdiocese * June 2 — 6:00 p.m., Church of St. Mark in Krakow, benediction of lectors, a concelebrated Mass with sermon * June 3 — 5:00 p.m., residence, a seminar in moral theology * June 5 — 2:00 p.m., Kalwaria Zebrzydowska * 8:00 p.m., Kalwaria, the Chapel of the Mother of God, a private Mass * June 6 — 7:00 a.m., Church of the Sisters of the Visitation in Krakow, a concelebrated Mass with sermon * At the Jesuit Fathers,' the Feast of the Sacred Heart of Jesus, a concelebrated Mass with sermon, and a Eucharistic procession.

We gather here today in the spirit of making reparations, in the spirit of repentance ... The matter is not that we sin, but that ... we do not make reparations for our sins, that we do not repent, that we take our sins lightly, that our society fosters a callousness of conscience.

June 7-9 — A canonical visitation of the parish of Gron * June 8 — 11:00 a.m., the pilgrimage of men to Kalwaria Zebrzydowska. Sermon:

This pilgrimage has its precedents. During the post-war years, it was a pilgrimage of male youth, at the time, members of the organization of Catholic Young Men. Later, this organization was forcibly liquidated by the authorities. Even though the organization was banned, neither the men who grew up in it, nor the young men who were their sons, had ceased to exist ... And after many years, during the time of the Millennium, they decided once again to return to the Cross that they had erected many years ago on the hilltop of Kalwaria. They had erected it as an eternal token of remembrance. And now, the men and male youth from the Archdiocese of Krakow have been coming here for the past few years during the observances of Corpus Christi on a pilgrimage to Kalwaria Zebrzydowska ... We would like ... to pray about, to think through this basic matter, the one that the Synod of the Archdiocese of Krakow presented to all of us: the family passes the faith on ... The times we are living in today do not facilitate the transmittal of faith ... This is the reality that the Polish Catholic family finds itself in. Stuck in this reality, the family must ... tell itself: we must take the responsibility for passing our faith on ... We cannot rely on the help of the state, nor on the help of institutions, nor on the help of the schools. We must rely on God, on ourselves and on our Church. We are capable of accomplishing this. Above all, we really want to accomplish this ... You must remember ... that fatherhood is, first and foremost, caring for the mother ... There is no excuse for leaving her alone in her motherhood ... the family transmits life ... The faith of the family must not break down at this most basic level of family life ... Meanwhile, we are witnessing the rise of a great social insensitivity with regard to this issue in Poland. More and more often we hear that it is "only a medical procedure." And it has been accepted as such even in the consciousness of the older generations. A few days ago, I had such a conversation with a young woman, a young mother who was speaking of her mother-in-law ... She had to defend her right to motherhood before a representative of the older generation ... The older a child is, the more it needs the faith of its parents, especially the faith of its father.

June 10 — 10:00 a.m., Krakow, Wzgorza Krzeslawickie, a concelebrated Mass with a sermon during a meeting with priests of the class of 1974 * The same day — 6:00 p.m., Podlesie, a concelebrated Mass during a meeting of priests of the class of 1942 * June 11 — 10:00 a.m., Polanka Wielka — on the occasion of the 12th anniversary of the priesthood (of the class of 1963):

> Through His Son, through the Holy Spirit, God the Father entrusted us with His truth and His life as His gift to the entire human family. We are the sons of God's great trust. We may not fully realize the magnitude of this trust in our daily lives ... Our life as priests, as bishops, is a human life ... It is necessary that we become particularly aware of this during such meetings ... The greatness of Him, who placed His trust in us, and the greatness of what He entrusted to us ... Once we are aware of this, we will be protected from everything that might threaten us, from a depreciation of our calling, from it becoming routine ... We should always be aware of how great He who called us is, and how great is what we have been called to.

June 13-14 — An International colloquium in Paris. The Cardinal sent his lecture *Subjectivity and the Irreducible* {sic} *in Man*[15] * June

---

[15] Title is in English in the original.

13-15 — Visitation of the parish of Odrowaz, including visits to the chapels in Dzial, Pieniazkowice and Zaluczne, consecration of a new part of the cemetery in the parish of Odrowaz * June 15-16 — Visitation of the parish of Rogoznik * June 16 — 10:00 a.m., Wielka Polana, a visit to an "Oasis" {charismatic} group * June 17 — 6:30 p.m., Krakow — Plaszow, a concelebrated Mass with a sermon, a farewell ceremony for Rev. Wincenty Turek SCJ * June 18 — 4:00 p.m., the 36th Meeting of the Main Committee of the Synod of the Archdiocese of Krakow. The Cardinal sums up the accomplishments and the progress that the Synod has made to date. Remaining to be done: a division of editorial work on further detailed issues. The Cardinal asks about the work on the catechism of the Synod and of the Vatican Council. (From the minutes) * 6:30 p.m., residence chapel, a Mass for the repose of the soul of the late Archbishop E. Baziak * June 19 — 8:00 p.m., residence chapel, a Mass for the repose of the soul of the late J. Vetulani * June 20 — 2:00 p.m., Kalwaria Zebrzydowska, prayers * June 21 — 10:00 a.m., residence chapel, a Mass for the repose of the soul of the late Stanislaw Golubiew * June 22 — 10:00 a.m., Pieniezno, ordination of ten priests of the Society of the Divine Word, a homily * The same day — 6:00 p.m., Gdansk, the Parish of the Resurrection of Our Lord, a social get-together, concelebrated Mass with sermon * The same day — Cardinal Wojtyla's address on the occasion of the 900th anniversary of the abbey in Tyniec was read in the archdiocese * June 23 — 9:00 a.m., Gdansk, the Parish of the Resurrection of Our Lord, concelebrated Mass * June 24 — Szaflary, celebrations of the 40th anniversary of the local pastor's ordination to the priesthood (in the presence of priests of Diocesis Luceoriensis):

> Today ... when we consider the testimony of John the Baptist anew, we desire to reach out to wherever this testimony is being fulfilled and confirmed. And it is being confirmed ... all over the world, at every longitude and latitude; wherever man lives, wherever people created by God and redeemed by Jesus Christ live. In all those places, there lives the truth that St. John the Baptist proclaimed on the Jordan river ... in all those places, the reality of the Lamb of God is fulfilled ... In all those places, where man discovers the reality of God who created him and redeemed him, even if this realization comes without the help of priests, in all those places there is the People of God, in all those places there is the Church, and in all those places, the eternal Mystery of Love fulfills itself, a Mystery whose symbol is the Lamb of God, the symbol that came about during the paschal celebration of the Old Covenant, and through the words of St. John the Baptist on the Jordan river.

The same day — 4:00 p.m., residence, receives a delegation from Krowodrza * June 25 — 10:00 a.m., Warsaw, the Main Council of the Polish Episcopate * 7:30 p.m., officiates at the marriage of Anna Owoc and Eugeniusz Wysocki at the Church of the Sisters of the Visitation in Warsaw. The Sisters could not believe, that "the Cardinal, himself, would honor their church with his presence" — and yet, they prepared the chasuble — a gift of the Queen, Louise Maria Gonzaga. The Cardinal delivered a speech, and afterwards visited the home of Mr. and Mrs. Owoc (cf. October 7, 1951) * June 26 — 10:00 a.m., Warsaw, the plenary conference of the Polish Episcopate * January 27 — 7:00 a.m., Warsaw, the Chapel of the Ursuline Sisters, a concelebrated Mass for the repose of the soul of the late Bishop Franciszek Jedwabski * June 28 — 10:00 a.m., Krakow, residence chapel, Mass with sermon for candidates for the first year of theological studies * June 29 — 10:30 a.m., Tyniec, celebrations on the occasion of the 900th anniversary of the abbey. Sermon:

> The founding of Tyniec some nine hundred years ago is not an isolated incident in the history of Polish church life, or even in the history of Polish religious life. It is a complex event, reaching deeply into the history of the nation, into the history of the Polish spirit; reaching into the course of that destiny towards which our entire history was directed, and towards which it continues to direct itself today.
>
> The speech during lunch:
>
> We wish you strength, which must be measured and qualified in various ways, because it is needed in various ways. We also wish you that you may be numerous, that you remain very Benedictine, that you remain very biblical and liturgical, that you remain very Polish; and finally, that you remain very ecclesiastical and universal, in accordance with the principles of your Benedictine order.

The same day — 7:00 p.m., Krakow, Church of St. Peter and St. Paul, a Mass for the intention of the Holy Father:

> We, the citizens of Krakow, gathered together here today; we, the representatives of the Church of Krakow, unite in a special way with the successor of St. Peter, with the Holy Father, Paul VI ... This, our spiritual union with the Apostolic See, with the Holy Father, takes on a particular meaning this year because this is, as you know, the Holy Year in Rome. Last year we celebrated the Holy Year outside of Rome, we celebrated it in the respective parishes and communities of the Church of Krakow. This year, ... pilgrims from around the world are gathering at the thresholds of the Apostolic See ... Today, we, who are unable to make our way to Rome on a pilgrimage ... join together with the Holy Father in a spiritual way ... and He assured us that this spiritual union with him and with the pilgrims of the Holy Year can be and is the basis for receiving the indulgence of the jubilee ... The prayers of the entire Church flow today with Peter and for Peter.

The same day — Cardinal Wojtyla's address on the occasion of the 12th anniversary of the election of the Holy Father, Paul VI, was read in the archdiocese.

July 1 — 11:00 a.m., the Rakowicki cemetery, a funeral of the Mother Provincial of the Daughters of Divine Charity * July 2 — 9:00 a.m., Jasna Gora, pilgrimage of teachers.

The true value and greatness of man is the inviolable foundation of the process of upbringing in the family and in school ... [Thoughts on the mystery of the Visitation.] The upbringing of man begins in the womb of the mother ... We know well, it is our painful Polish experience, how much evil can be brought about in the upbringing of man by introducing falsehood into this first, fundamental situation of parenting ... Because to bring up means to love: to love from the first moment of existence. Only then can you love till the end, if you love from the beginning.

Same day — 1:00 p.m., A visit to the ailing Bishop Franciszek Jop * Myslachowice, blessing of a corner stone, concelebrated Mass and sermon * July 3 — Residence chapel, Mass (and homily) for the late Mother Provincial of the Daughters of Divine Charity * July 4 — 9:00 a.m., Wawel Cathedral, anniversary of consecration, Mass and sermon for the sextons of the Archdiocese of Krakow * Same day — 2:00 p.m., visit to the "Oasis" {charismatic} groups in Olszowka, Rdzawka and Rokiciny * July 5-8 — Bachledowka, retreat * July 8 — 9:00 a.m., Kalwaria Zebrzydowska, Mass * Same day — 4:00 p.m., Zywiec-Zblocie, funeral of the late Msgr. Stanislaw Slonka, concelebrated Mass and sermon * July 9-22 — Beskid Niski, vacation * July 23 — 7:00 a.m.,Warsaw, Chapel of the Ursuline Sisters, private Mass * July 24-30 — Vacation, Lake Wierzchowo (Diocese of Koszalin), private Masses and sermons * July 31 — 8:00 a.m., Fiszor, (Archdiocese of Warsaw), concelebrated Mass with the Primate during vacation.

August 1 — Called to serve in the new Congregation for Sacraments and Divine Worship (from the very beginning of its existence), he participated in the works on the reform of the liturgy of the ordination and became involved in the matter of canceling the requirement to observe the feasts of certain saints. In connection with this matter, he raises the issue of the Polish liturgical calendar — such that would take Polish traditions into account. He participated in the preparation of the reform of liturgy, among others, the introduction of the use of the vernacular. He remained member of the Congregation until the time of his election to the See of St. Peter * In Fiszor — greetings and best wishes for the Primate.

August 1-9 — Beskid Niski, private Masses during vacation * August 10 — 10:00 a.m., Lewiczyn, (Archdiocese of Warsaw), coronation of the image of Our Lady, High Mass, the coronation was performed by the Primate * August 11-12 — 7:00 a.m., residence chapel, private Masses * August 13 — Rdzawka, conclusion of the "Oasis" retreat, concelebrated Mass and sermon:

> I think that the fruits of your retreat should be judged by the degree to which you lose yourselves in Christ and, at the same time, by the degree to which you open your eyes and your hearts as a result of that ... My heart overflows with gratitude to you, my brother priests, who ever more frequently undertake the pastoral ministry to the "Oasis" communities. I can tell you from my own experience that not only do you serve Christ and the youth in this fashion, but you also shape your own spirituality in the best possible way.

August 14 — 7:00 a.m., residence chapel, concelebrated Mass with Rev. Gustav Jooss * 12:00 noon, a visit to "Oasis" groups in Rzyki, Kroscienko, Trybsz * August 15 — 7:00 a.m., Brzegi, concelebrated Mass and sermon for an "Oasis" group * Same day — 11:00 a.m., Ludzmierz, High Mass and sermon, procession * Same day — 7:30 p.m., the Mariacki Church in Krakow. In the presence of Cardinal Humber Medeiros, the Archbishop of Boston.

> Our dear and distinguished guest has learned ... the text of the Mass in our Polish language, so that he could concelebrate it with the Polish priests. He probably does that also in his own archdiocese, because there are many Poles or persons of Polish origin there. I had opportunity to see that six years ago, when I visited the United States and was also received in Boston ... Keeping in mind the mystery of today's feast[16], we ardently pray that every person could cross the threshold of eternity ... the threshold of heaven. But, at the same time, we pray that every person could cross the threshold into the temporal world, the threshold to life on earth, to existence, to humanity. And this begins with the moment of conception.

August 16 — 7:00 a.m., Wawel Cathedral, concelebrated Mass with Archbishop Medeiros * Same day — 7:00 p.m., Slupsk, Mass and sermon * August 17 — Kolobrzeg, concelebrated Mass, concluding remarks during the celebrations of the 975th anniversary of the diocese * August 18 — 7:00 a.m., Koszalin, cathedral, concelebrated Mass with bishop ordinary and priests, sermon * August 19 — 7:00 a.m., Lublin, Chapel of the Ursuline Sisters, private concelebrated Mass * 10:00 a.m., opening remarks before a series of lectures for clergy at KUL[17] (August 19-21): "Lay Catholics in the Parish":

> Theology is a study that has certain characteristics of service: it serves the mission, the pastoral mission in the broad sense of that term. Therefore, it is most appropriate that today, in various parts of the world, and also in Poland, there is a call for a greater bond with pastoral ministry, and for a bond between pastoral ministry and theology ... To acknowledge the role of the apostolate of the laity, to create an appropriate place in your parish for it, to give it the proper conditions, to set it free, that means to fully

---

[16] August 15 is the Feast of the Assumption of the Blessed Virgin.
[17] Catholic University of Lublin.

understand your pastoral mission and to realize it in the fullest sense of the word.

August 20. Kalwaria Zebrzydowska — he concelebrated a Holy Mass with the Rector of the Krakow Seminary and the newly ordained priests of the diocese, delivered a sermon and, after the Mass, blessed the crosses made and brought by the pilgrims.

August 23 — 3:00 p.m., residence, an audience for Germans * 4:00 p.m., residence, the arrival of Cardinal Paul Zoungrana and Bishop Wladyslaw Rubin, a visit to Nowa Huta * August 24 — 11:00 a.m., Przeczyca (Diocese of Tarnow), re-coronation of the statue of Our Lady, sermon. Cardinal Wojtyla presided over the coronation, assisted by Cardinal Zoungrana and Bishop Jerzy Ablewicz. The Mass was also concelebrated by Bishop Wladyslaw Rubin and Bishop Ignacy Tokarczuk * Same day — 7:00 p.m.:

> Cardinal Wojtyla organized a meeting of the community of Krakow with the dignitary of the African Church at the Mariacki Basilica, where he ceremoniously greeted his guest and introduced him to those present. The Mass was concelebrated by Cardinal Zoungrana with Msgr. Safar from Egypt and with Rev. Jan Zajac, the diocesan missionary chaplain. Also present were Bishop Wladyslaw Rubin, Bishop Jerzy Ablewicz, Bishop Julian Groblicki and other Church dignitaries. The Mariacki Basilica could not accommodate everyone who wished to take part in this meeting. The meeting was concluded by an agape at the Mariacki parsonage. ("Notificationes")

From the sermon at the Mariacki Basilica:

> We have gathered in great numbers to meet with him. I consider this a historic visit; indeed it is without precedent. For the first time, Poland, and specifically Krakow, is hosting within its walls ... a cardinal who represents the Church of the Black Lands of Africa. The missionary Church, which is presently becoming the particular hope of the Universal Church, because missionary activities bring such abundant fruit.

August 25 — 8:00 a.m., Wawel Cathedral, concelebrated Mass with Cardinal Zoungrana * Same day — 5:00 p.m., Ligota, concelebrated Mass and sermon, blessing of the tabernacle, reunion with priests ordained in 1968 * August 26 — 11:00 a.m., Jasna Gora, Pontifical High Mass, (the Primate gave the sermon) * Same day — 4:00 p.m., residence, a meeting with Sisters Superior * 6:00 p.m., residence chapel, Mass, christening * August 28 — 10:00 a.m., Wroclaw, a presentation during Days of Pastoral Ministry * 12:00 noon, seminary chapel, private Mass * August 29-30 — 11:00 a.m., coronation of the miraculous image of Our Lady in Jodlowka near Jaroslaw (Diocese of Przemysl). The coronation was performed by Cardinal Wojtyla, who presided during a solemn concelebrated Mass. The sermon was preached by Bishop Jerzy Ablewicz from Tarnow. After the Mass, a short address by Cardinal Wojtyla. (Synopsis of the address: *Kronika Diecezji Przemyskiej*[18] 1975, bk. 5 and 6, p. 122) * Same day — an appeal from Cardinal Wojtyla to mothers and young women before their pilgrimage to Kalwaria was read in the churches of the archdiocese.

September 1 — Church of the Norbertine Sisters in Krakow, Feast of Blessed Bronislawa:

> **Bronislawa became a chosen daughter of the Heavenly Father ... Here on earth, near Wawel, in the district where the Parish of the Most Holy Redeemer had conducted its activities for a long time ... she accepted it with the full depth of her soul, she fulfilled it and left it to us as her heritage.[19]**

September 2 — 6:00 p.m., Krakow, Krowoderskie settlement {subdivision}, a sermon for the beginning of the school year and catechesis at the Parish of Blessed Queen Jadwiga. Blessing of the Cross. "Catechesis, teaching religion and studying religion is your duty, but it is also your right ... it is our sacred right as citizens, that our children may study religion." * September 3 — 7:00 a.m., Kalwaria Zebrzydowska, concelebrated Mass with sermon during a retreat of organists, social get-together * Same day — 12:00 noon, residence, a visit from Cardinal Franz Konig and Bishop Franz Jachym * September 4 — Warsaw, Main Council of the Polish Episcopate * September 5-6 — Lomza, plenary conference of the Polish Episcopate * September 5 — 7:00 a.m., Lomza, 50th anniversary of the diocese, Theological Seminary, private concelebrated Mass * September 6 — On the eve of the coronation of the statue of Our Lady of Sejny, at 6:00 p.m. — inauguration of the celebration. He said: "the 50th anniversary of the Diocese of Lomza, a century and a half of the Diocese of Sejny will find its final expression in the coronation of the statue of Our Lady of Sejny, for which you have prepared for a long time." * September 7 — 11:00 a.m., Sejny, coronation of the statue of Our Lady. The coronation was performed by the Primate, Cardinal Wojtyla presided over the concelebrated Holy Mass * Same day — An appeal from the Cardinal was read in the churches of the Archdiocese of Krakow for the beginning of a new year of catechesis. Commending the children and the youth to Jesus Christ and to the care of the Blessed Mother, the Cardinal challenged them to come nearer to the light through catechesis, and urged all teachers, parents and religious instructors to seriously take to heart the work of catechesis in the archdiocese. At the beginning of the new year of catechesis the Cardinal also issued a letter to the youth, in which he said: "Let your catechesis become not only a school of thought, a

---

[18] Chronicles of the Diocese of Przemysl.
[19] antecedent unclear.

school of faith, of Christian awareness, but also a school of character and will, a school of Christian life, a school of true love". ("Notificationes") * September 8 — 10:00 a.m., Krakow, Church of the Norbertine Sisters, a catechetic course * 5:00 p.m., Gdow — blessing of a polychrome, concelebrated Mass, sermon * September 9 — 10:00 a.m., Theological Seminary of Krakow, a cathechetic course * 6:00 p.m., residence chapel, blessing of a marriage, Mass * September 10 — 9:00 a.m., Silesian Theological Seminary, conference of priests-rectors, a presentation entitled *Priesthood and Celibacy* * 10:00 a.m., Theological Seminary of Krakow, a cathechetic course * September 11 — 2:00 p.m., Silesian Theological Seminary, conclusion of the conference of priests — rectors * 4:00 p.m., Theological Seminary of Krakow, a cathechetic course * September 12 — 4:00 p.m., residence, a visit from Bishop Alexander Fernandes of New Delhi and Bishop James Sangu of Mbeya (Tanzania) * September 13 — 8:00 a.m., Wawel Cathedral, concelebrated Mass with Bishop Fernandes and Bishop Sangu * 12:00 noon, he presided during a meeting of all officials of the metropolitan Curia. During the meeting, a proposal made by Cardinal Wojtyla regarding the regionalization of the Archdiocese of Krakow was discussed, and a plan of pastoral activities of specific committees for the near future was presented. ("Notificationes") * 4:00 p.m., residence, a gathering of the laity with Bishop Fernandes and Bishop Sangu * September 14 — 8:00 a.m., Bujakow, consecration of a church, sermon * Same day — 12:00 noon, Church of the Cistercians in Nowa Huta-Mogila, Feast of the Triumph of the Cross:

> We have guests ... who came here to join our pilgrimage from very far ... India. That is the country of our chief celebrant. My ties with him go back to the time of our cooperation during the Second Vatican Council, when we were preparing the constitution on the Church in the modern world together. We are also connected by our work at the Synods ... Our guest from another continent ... — Bishop Sangu from Tanzania. He and I, too, are joined by the bonds of our collaboration, especially during last year's Synod of Bishops ... This is then an unusual pilgrimage ... And that is why our thoughts today rise to the Cross of Christ in its universal scope ... The world turns, but the Cross stands still. And we can see how this turning world, with its momentum, converges upon the Cross from all directions.

Same day — 4:00 p.m., Trzebinia-Bujakow, consecration of the church under the title of St. Peter and St. Paul.

> I express great joy at what you have accomplished here together with your zealous pastor for the 650th anniversary of your parish ... What a splendid sight, when you entered here in such numbers ... When we filled the great expanse of this church, shoulder to shoulder. How splendid, when this whole church raises its voice in song ... May this temple always remind

you of the calling of man, which transcends earth ... may it serve to exalt man in Christ, in His Cross.

September 15 — 7:00 a.m., residence chapel, concelebrated Mass with the guests from India and Tanzania * 11:00 a.m., residence, meeting in the matter of church construction * On the same day he announces the division of the Archdiocese into four regions *"entrusted to the special care of the auxiliary bishops."* Each bishop auxiliary is also entrusted with *"the care for the particular departments of work in the Archdiocese* * September 16 — "At the residence of the Cardinal, the dean priests gathered for their third conference of the year. The topic of the deliberations was the matter of regionalization of the archdiocese and current pastoral matters." ("Notificationes") * September 17 — 4:00 p.m., residence, a conference with the Department of Catechesis on the ministry of the youth * September 18 — 9:00 a.m., Jasna Gora, he led the liturgy (the Primate gave the homily) during the celebrations of the 600th anniversary of the Archdiocese of Lwow. Day of prayers for the canonization of Blessed Jakub Strzemie and the beatification of the Servant of God Archbishop Jozef Bilczewski * Same day — 6:00 p.m., residence, a conference with the Department of Family Ministry and Health Services * September 19 — 11:00 a.m., Letownia, blessing of a cornerstone for a new church, Mass and sermon * 12:00 noon, departure for East Germany * September 20 — 7:00 a.m., Gorlitz (Bishop Bernhard Huhn), private concelebration * 9:00 a.m., Budziszyn * 11:00 a.m., Crostwitz (Chruscice) * 12:00 noon, Dresden (Bishop Gerhart Schaffran) * 1:00 p.m., Naumburg * 4:00 p.m., Erfurt * September 21 — 9:00 a.m., Erfurt, diocesan pilgrimage * 2:00 p.m., Erfurt, concelebrated service, get-together * September 22 — 7:00 a.m., Erfurt, cathedral, a concelebrated Mass for the seminarians * A visit at the Theological Seminary * A visit to Cardinal Alfred Bengsch * September 23 — 7:30 p.m., Krakow, residence chapel, Mass for the intention of M. and E. Wislocki (20th wedding anniversary) * September 24 — 6:00 p.m., Przemysl, sermon at the cathedral for the 600th anniversary of the existence of the church, opening of the *Sacrosong*:[20]

> O Church of Przemysl, glorify your Lord through this sacred song: Sacrosong 1975 ... There is a close connection between art and beauty and work; and what you wish to express in today's composition, in this music for the Mass now being performed, also shows a close connection between art and work. This was expressed particularly well by Cyprian Kamil Norwid in his work "Promethidion,"[21] and what he wrote there is constantly being proven and realized in the life of generations. I think that it

---

[20] Festival of sacred song
[21] "Beauty is there to enrapture us to work-work, so that we might be raised from the dead" Cyprian Kamil Norwid (1821-1883), *Promethidion*.

is well that the Church of Przemysl, which over the course of six centuries has left so much evidence of a Polish, Christian spirit, is now, on this jubilee, contributing this effort and this struggle of our time ... a struggle for the right to be human, to be Christian, in full truth and full freedom.

Same day in the evening — at the Church of the Salesian Fathers in Przemysl, Cardinal Wojtyla celebrated a Mass for the conclusion of the 7th Sacrosong Festival and participated in a solemn final concert. He gives a short speech * September 25 — 1:30 p.m., Krakow, 3 Franciszkanska Street, in connection with the preparations to the Third Symposium of the Bishops of Europe, a discussion meeting under the leadership of Cardinal Wojtyla concerning the subject matter of the symposium. Meeting participants are bishops delegated to the symposium (J. Ablewicz, K. Majdanski, S. Smolenski; absent: Bishop I. Jez and Bishop J. Stroba) and two theologians: S. Nagy and A. Kubis. The meeting began with a dinner * 4:00 p.m., residence, gathering of the Marian Group * 6:00 p.m., Krakow-Lagiewniki, concelebrated Mass, sermon, a reunion of priests ordained in 1969 * September 26 — 1:00 p.m., residence, meeting of the Council of the Pontifical Department of Theology * September 26-29 — Canonical visitation of the parish of Dabrowa Narodowa (including a visit to a center of religious education in Wysoki Brzeg on September 27) * September 27 — Wawel Cathedral, 6:00 p.m., a golden jubilee of Msgr. Stanislaw Czartoryski, Msgr. Kazimierz Figlewicz and Msgr. Eugeniusz Florkowski:

> **It seems to me ... that you have added a new chapter to the ancient history of the Metropolitan Chapter of Krakow, which has such an extraordinary past, which over the course of centuries has earned the right to be called seminarium episcoporum ... All of us assembled here, and I in particular, are convinced that we owe much, a large part of our lives, our vocations, to your priestly prayers.**

September 28 — A pastoral letter from Cardinal Wojtyla before the beginning of the 31st Week of Mercy was read in all the churches of the archdiocese * September 30 — 7:00 a.m., residence chapel, Mass for the late Jan Dultz * 5:00 p.m., residence, seminar in moral theology.

October 1 — Theological Seminary, concelebrated Mass, sermon for the inauguration of the new {school} year * Same day — Inwald, a reunion of priests ordained in 1971 * October 2 — 12:00 noon, Theological Seminary, Council of the Pontifical Department of Theology * 8:30 p.m., residence chapel, Mass for the late Prof. Jozef Chojnacki * October 3 — 6:00 a.m., Carmelite Sisters of St. Theresa of the Infant Jesus, 100th anniversary of founding:

> **More and more, we understand her wondrous charism in the Church of the previous and current century. This charism is tied closely to God's**

economy, in which all that is great, that is the greatest, is small and hidden. And conversely, all that is the smallest, is great, powerful. This is what is expressed in the spiritual path of St. Theresa of the Infant Jesus.

October 3-6 — Visitation of the parish of Jelen * October 6 — 7:00 a.m., residence chapel, Mass for the late Jan D. * Same day — At the residence, the 13th scientific seminar for liturgy instructors at institutes of theology in Poland. The meeting was opened by Cardinal Wojtyla. During the seminar (conducted on October 6-7), four presentations were made on the topic of the liturgy of the Eucharist * October 7 — Cardinal Wojtyla, the Primate of Poland[22] and the Archbishop of Poznan left for Rome for the symposium of European bishops dedicated to the subject: "A Bishop in the Service of the Faith." The Cardinal was one of the main editors, and presented the theological foundations of the matter which was the topic of the symposium. ("Notificationes") * October 7 — 8:00 a.m., Vienna, nunciature, private concelebrated Mass * October 8-10 — Rome, Polish College, private concelebrated Mass * October 10 — 10:00 a.m., Rome, consultation of the Laity * Same day — at Ciampino airport in Rome, he welcomed a group of pilgrims (94 persons) from the Archdiocese of Krakow as part of a larger national pilgrimage for the Holy Year from Poland * October 11 — 12:00 noon, an audience of the Polish pilgrimage with Pope Paul VI * Same day — in the evening, he led a solemn concelebrated Mass at the Basilica of St. John Lateran on the occasion of the visit of the Polish pilgrimage. The sermon is preached by the Primate * October 12 — 9:00 a.m., participated in the canonization of Blessed Oliver Plunkett * Same day in the evening — the pilgrims from Krakow together with Cardinal Wojtyla, Bishop Smolenski and Bishop W. Rubin were received by the Parish of Our Lady of Czestochowa in Rome. The church in this parish was built to commemorate the 1000th anniversary of Christianity in Poland. The Cardinal presided over the concelebrated Mass * October 13 — 8:00 a.m., Rome, Polish College, concelebrated Mass * October 14 — 8:00 a.m., the Carmelite church, Mass with sermon for the pilgrims from Krakow * October 14-18 — Rome, the Third Symposium of the Bishops of Europe on the topic: "A Bishop in the Service of the Faith," organized by the Council of the Conference of the Bishops of Europe. Cardinal Wojtyla led the delegation of the Polish Episcopate (6 bishops and 2 theologians). He presented one of the three main lectures, illustrating the theological aspects of the issue * October 15 — 9:00 a.m., Cardinal Wojtyla delivered his lecture, entitled The Bishop in the Service of the Faith. *The Theological Basis of the Issue.*

---

[22] Stefan Cardinal Wyszynski

Chapters of the lecture:

"Evangelical meaning of service (diakonia) in the Church"

The Second Vatican Council has a similar understanding of the service of a bishop, the diakonia, which in its fundamental and essential meaning is nothing other than the service of faith. A very meaningful expression of this is found in Art. 24 of the constitution *Lumen Gentium,* which speaks of the bishop's *ministerium (i.e.diakonia)*; Art. 25 and Art. 26 impose upon the bishop the obligation to proclaim God's Word and to sanctify the faithful, and finally Art. 27 precisely defines this service as an authority which the bishops personally wield in the name of Jesus Christ. Thus, in the opinion of the Second Vatican Council, "invested with a sacred power, the holders of this office are, in fact, dedicated to promoting the interests of their brethren." (*Lumen Gentium*, no. 18).

... The text of the constitution very appropriately unites the service performed by the bishops with that of the priests into one whole. We must not for a moment lose sight of the truth *that all of the bishop's service of the faith is done* above all *with the help of priests* ...

"Faith as both source and object of the bishop's service"

Everything that has been said up to now clearly indicates that faith is first of all the source of the bishop's service, in order to become, in turn, the object and the goal of that service. In this aspect one can again see the similarity between the mission of a bishop and that of the Apostles. Just as the Apostle, as for example, St. Paul, whom we continually invoke (cf. 2 Cor. 4:13; 2 Tim. 1:12), so also the bishop must first of all believe in Christ deeply and strongly, so that he may serve the People of God. He must not only believe with the Faith of the Church, as any other Christian, but he must also define his mission as a bishop, from its foundations, in the faith. This *self-definition of the bishop in faith*, faith as the content of his consciousness and his basic existential position of a person, a Christian, who has been consecrated, *forms the essential foundation of the bishop's service,* which, as indicated by *Lumen Gentium* (Art. 21), is in its totality a service of faith. We mention this only briefly, because it is clear to everyone that a bishop's office may rightfully arise only from faith; it is in faith that it finds its inexhaustible source.

... In becoming the servant of faith in all men, the bishop is always guided by the keen awareness that faith is the starting point and the *basic condition of salvation extended to humanity by the Father through Jesus Christ* as part of the eternal Plan. A bishop strives with all his might for the realization of that Plan. The bishop's service of faith flows from love, which makes the bishop a man for others, a man for everyone, in small measure similar to Christ. "The bishop's service of faith in the community of the People of God, which he, having been appointed by Christ, is to lead ..."

... As was rightly pointed out by one of our theologians, a bishop must understand and realize his position in the Church "in communione." It is not a one-way position. A bishop (similarly to priests and deacons) is tied to his People by the communion of Christ's gift, and his "own gift" is formed on the background of this community.

The bishop's service of faith is realized by the totality of his life and service. Although the teaching Magisterium is of particular importance here, and we will later speak about it separately, we must stress that bishops serve the faith through the entire scope of their office and their activities. This is closely connected with the existential nature of faith which is so clearly emphasized by Vatican II. Faith is not only what we believe, it also shapes the life of the Christian within the community of the Church. This life continually emanates from Christ the Priest, the Prophet and King, and it also defines the place of everyone within that community. "To believe", in light of the teachings of the Council, means not only to accept as true what God has revealed and what the Church gives us to believe, but *"to believe" means much more: to share in the mission of the Church* which is defined by the mission of Christ Himself.

And the bishop is the first servant in his Church of the faith understood in this way.

The faith of a bishop is closely tied to the faith of his Church. And if we can say that the faith of a bishop finds support and reinforcement in the People of God whom he leads, then by the same token his entire mission, his office and charism are aimed at awakening, molding, deepening and strengthening the faith of the People who form his Church. In this service, the bishop, just as every priest, is chosen by Christ from among the people and appointed by Christ to serve the people (Heb. 5:1) ...

"The meaning of the bishop's magisterium for the faith of the Church. Preaching and teaching."

... "Among the more important duties of bishops that of preaching the Gospel has pride of place. For the bishops are heralds of the faith (fidei praecones), who draw new disciples to Christ; they are authentic teachers (doctores), that is, teachers endowed with the authority of Christ, who preach the faith to the people assigned to them, the faith which is destined to inform their thinking and direct their conduct." One of our theologians, on the basis of these words of the constitution *Lumen Gentium*, formulates the very appropriate statement, corresponding to the apostolic tradition, that within the three tasks of the bishop's office, that of teacher, priest, and pastor, we must adhere to the *principle of the primacy of the Word of God,* the Word preached by the bishop by way of living kerygma. This statement is based, among others, on the fact that the cited text (*Lumen Gentium,* no. 25) describes bishops first as "fidei praecones" (heralds of the faith), and only second as "doctores" (teachers). Therefore, the theologian concludes, we must accept that *preaching takes precedence over teaching.*

We wish to pursue this thought further in this presentation, making use of valuable suggestions and appropriate expressions that have been provided to us. However, we must not overlook something that is the deepest characteristic of the office and mission of the bishop, and which has a fundamental significance for his preaching. The bishop's *"Magisterium,"* both the solemn and the everyday teaching, carries within itself a specific responsibility for the truth of the revealed Word, which is a requisite of the *objective certainty of the Church's faith.* Therefore, this same text (*Lumen Gentium* no. 25) which puts the living preaching of the Gospel ("fidei praecones") before teaching ("doctores"), is nonetheless almost entirely devoted to a bishop's teaching, and the characteristics it should possess to ensure the certainty of faith ...

... let us hasten to state (in accordance with the point made earlier) that in the entirety of the Church's life, and especially in a bishop's service of faith, we must definitely accept the primacy of the preaching of the Gospel, kerygma, over mere authoritarian teaching. Kerygma has a missionary meaning; through it, the bishops (and with them the priests and deacons) draw new disciples to Christ, they call people to faith or they strengthen the faith. With regard to the content, preaching should not be concerned with lecturing on dogma, but with the *Gospel as a message with the mystery of Christ at its center.* The goal of preaching is above all to show man the ways of salvation and the ways of fulfilling God's plan in Christ.

We must agree that the "magisterium," taken to mean "to impart knowledge" or to "lecture" on it, is supposed to be at the service of preaching the Gospel, and that in this, the bishop's primary service of faith is realized. We must also agree that the preaching must make faith pertinent and fruitful for the listeners by taking into account the broad scope of human experience, by addressing the authentic questions posed by contemporary man. However, the main force of preaching lies in such propagation of the faith that man *surrenders to the action of the Spirit of God Himself.* And then the bishop, as well as any other herald of the faith (praeco fidei), becomes a more direct and effective servant of that faith, the faith which is the center of his entire mission ...

"The bishop's service of faith in both dimensions of the Church, 'ad intra' and 'ad extra'"

... The bishop's service of faith, in preaching and in magisterium, as well as in the entire priestly and pastoral ministry, must be comprehensible in both dimensions of the realization of the Church, "ad intra" and "ad extra." It must be appropriate to the mission of the Church both with regard to the "household members of the faith" (Gal. 6:10) and to those who for whatever reason and in whatever sense find themselves "on the outside." Therefore, the bishop must live in the fullness of the mystery of the faith, and at the same time, in the fullness of its openness. By his teaching and his service, which is to say, by the totality of his activities as a bishop, he must enhance the credibility of the Church, of the Gospel, of his own mission, in the eyes of the critical and difficult people of our generation on the European continent, where certainly some indicator[23] has moved past the hour of historical climax. And besides, the whole historical complexity of this continent, the division between East and West, have reached a peak today, towards the end of the second millennium of Christianity, in a way that is totally new and different from the traditional currents of history. A Europe drawing the world into the sphere of its influence becomes a Europe drawn into gigantic global processes. Within these jolts to civilization, to political systems, to mentalities, the bishops together with Peter gathered around Christ, just as in that boat on the Sea of Galilee, must do everything to show, as one of our theologians said, *that the Gospel alone has the power to give full meaning to human life and to ensure its salvation ...*

(Fragments quoted from the text published in "Ateneum Kaplanskie" {Priests' Atheneum} 406 (1976) 223-240.)

October 15 — about 5:30 p.m., Cardinal Wojtyla read questions that were topics of the discussions in groups (circuli minores) as a result of his lecture, he summed up the reports presented by the group leaders, led the discussion and responded to the questions. It was noted that the Cardinal spoke with the questioners in their respective native languages (Italian, French, German, English). The Cardinal participated in

---

[23] Alternate translation: hand of the clock.

the works of the *circulus minor Gallicus* — 2[24] (Rev. Adam Kubis) *
October 17 — 7:00 a.m., Cardinal Wojtyla lead the concelebrated Mass
of the European bishops and other participants of the Symposium, during which he delivered a homily * 6:00 p.m., speaking during a discussion, Cardinal Wojtyla defines three tasks emerging for the future from
the activities of the Third Symposium of the European Bishops. In his
opinion: It is important to deepen the contacts and the exchange of
experiences between Eastern and Western Europe. Mutual understanding is essential, particularly as it had already been suggested by Bishop
E. De Smedt; cooperation should be initiated, based on the documentation of the Helsinki conference (1975) and on the teachings of the
Church as expressed in the documents of the Second Vatican Council,
to guarantee the fundamental human rights, especially the freedom of
religion and conscience; in Europe closer cooperation between the
Magisterium and the theologians is recommended (Rev. Adam Kubis)
* Same day — Friday, 6:00 a.m., two airplanes with pilgrims from the
Archdiocese of Krakow (about 210 people) departed for Rome from the
airport in Balice near Krakow. This pilgrimage was organized on the
invitation of Cardinal Colombo, the Archbishop of Milan. The jubilee
pilgrimage from Krakow was led by Cardinal Wojtyla, Bishop
Groblicki and Bishop Smolenski. The Cardinal was already in Rome,
participating in the Third Symposium of the European Bishops. The
pilgrimage started from Assisi (Zofia Hajnos) * October 18 — 12:00
noon, Rome, Symposium of the European Bishops, an audience with
Paul VI * Same day — the Cardinal was waiting for the pilgrims in
front of St. Peter's Basilica in Rome. He led them into the church
through the Porta Santa. They all prayed in the chapel where the Pieta
by Michelangelo is. (Zofia Hajnos) * October 19 — 9:00 a.m., Rome,
Basilica of St. Peter, participation in the beatification of Maria Teresa
Ledochowska * Rome, the Basilica of the Twelve Apostles, concelebrated Mass after the beatification of Maria Teresa Ledochowska.
Sermon to the Polish pilgrims for the Holy Year:

> **Today, at St. Peter's Square ... we were but a small portion of the pil-
> grims of this mission Sunday. Because we are a portion of the People of God
> who walk as pilgrims on this earth. And as a portion of that people, we
> rejoiced, we rejoice, and we will continue to rejoice that the harvest of the
> centuries has given forth another blessed one with a Polish name ... Due to
> historical circumstances, this blessed woman, who had a Polish name, could
> not live in an independent Polish state. However, the Kingdom of Christ
> knows no boundaries. This day, ... which by the will of the Holy Father was
> marked by four missionaries from various nations being raised to the hon-
> ors of the altar, confirms this truth: "Some shall sow, so others may reap."**

---

[24] Second French-language sub-group.

October 20 — 11:00 a.m., private audience with Pope Paul VI *
3:00 p.m., Consilium de Laicis * 7:00 p.m., at a church in the EUR district, Cardinal Wojtyla celebrated a Mass for the pilgrims; in the homily he remembered St. John of Kanty; Holy Communion was distributed under two forms.[25] (Zofia Hajnos) * October 20 — A communique by Cardinal Wojtyla informing the community of the status of church construction in the archdiocese was read in the churches of the archdiocese * October 21 — 4:00 p.m., Bologna, human rights conference: *"I diritti della persona umana (alla luce del Concilio Vaticano II)"* * After the death of Jerzy Braun, founder and chairman of "Unia":

Karol Cardinal Wojtyla
Archbishop Metropolitan of Krakow   **Rome, October 21, 1975**

Dear Madam,

Please accept my most sincere condolences upon the death of your husband, Dr. Jerzy Braun. We all watched His life full of sacrifice, His service to the cause of the Church and the country at the price of great suffering, we followed His untiring creative efforts and achievements for the benefit of the Polish Catholic culture here and abroad. Now that he has already departed, we wish to express our deep esteem and respect for his person, and ask God for the eternal light for him and a rest after the labors of life in Christ the Lord.

A planned trip to Bologna makes it impossible for me to participate in the funeral.

/-/ + Karol Cardinal Wojtyla

(The document was made available by Mr. Czeslaw Domaradzki)

* August 22 — General audience; thanks to the efforts of the Cardinal, the pilgrims from Krakow were seated in the best section (Zofia Hajnos) * October 23 — 8:00 a.m., Bologna, residence chapel of the Cardinal, private concelebrated Mass * October 24 — 2:00 a.m., return to Krakow with the second group of the Pilgrimage of the Holy Year from the Archiocese of Krakow * 6:00 a.m., on the invitation of the Cardinal, the pilgrims participate in a Mass at the residence chapel on Franciszkanska Street for the intention of Cardinal Colombo and in thanksgiving for the pilgrimage. Communion under two forms. (Zofia Hajnos) * October 26 — 10:30 a.m., Borek Falecki, 50th anniversary of the Parish of Our Lady of Victory. Consecration of the church.

I consider this history to be also my own. Although I was never, strictly speaking, a parishioner here, I was connected with Borek Falecki, with the great workplace here, and with this parish during the worst period of the German occupation. And I myself know best how much I owe to this old barrack which was the temple of the People of God of your communi-

---

[25] Bread and wine

ty. It was here that we met during the occupation, so that later we could look into one another's eyes with a clear conscience, when we were at the workplace, in the factory halls, by the lime kilns, in the quarry, and by all of the other machinery that produced soda, caustic and the other products of Solvay. These are our common memories ... And that is why ... today I come here with the deepest emotion, and with the deepest emotion I consecrate this altar and this church ... After all, this church is also a great workplace, a workplace where people are being molded. And there is no doubt that because of this, the industrial workplace ... also gains. Guided by this awareness, in the period between the wars, concurrent with the growth of the settlement here, an effort was undertaken to form a parish here and to build a church ... What we observed here together, what we experienced together, what we accomplished together, was the expression of a fundamental social justice. A workplace was created, a settlement was built, and simultaneously, a parish and a church, because the people of faith, the citizens, the workers, demanded that. And they did not meet any obstacles ... Unfortunately, what we can say about Borek Falecki of the prewar years, we cannot say about many other districts ... of contemporary Krakow in today's reality. This is what I remind you of in my communique, read in all of the churches of Krakow and of the whole archdiocese today ... That is why I speak here to the people who are the agents of social justice: in the name of social justice, in the name of that justice exemplified by Borek Falecki, I appeal to those who are and wish to be the agents of social justice, that the people who have stood under the open sky for years ... may receive permission at least for a barrack, for any kind of roof over their heads. If it was possible to give this to people in those times which are often criticized as being unjust, why can they not receive the same in times which lay claim to social justice ... I myself have worked physically here at this place, and I know how hard, how great, and how necessary this labor is. In the name of the hard labor of Catholics, citizens of the city of Krakow and of the archdiocese, I cry out to the people who direct this labor, who manage this labor, who build our contemporary society upon this labor, that the needs of the Catholic society, the need for church construction, be considered and fully honored, just as they were in the past.

Same day, 3:30 p.m., inauguration of the academic year at the Pontifical Department of Theology. Closing remarks, after the inaugural lecture by Prof. Adam Vetulani:

At the time when the Jagiellonian University was celebrating the 600th anniversary of its foundation by King Casimir ... at that time, Professor, you said that you had one more wish: to help in the rebuilding of the Department of Theology. This was over 10 years ago ... Today, on this occasion, I wish to particularly thank you, Professor, for those words addressed to me, which I still remember exactly, and for all of the consequences of those words, which you undertook and continue to undertake from year to year, and which you again expressed today.

Same day — in the evening, at 6:00 p.m., St. Anne's Church, a word of thank-you to all participants before the blessing at the end of the Mass:

> First of all I wish to thank the Apostolic See that in the shortest possible time after the dissolution of the Department of Theology at the Jagiellonian University, its existence has been approved in Krakow. This fact ... gives us the basis to continue and develop the magnificent heritage of the centuries, the heritage of Blessed Queen Jadwiga, the heritage of our Homeland and of the Church, in these new conditions.

October 27 — 7:00 a.m., residence chapel, concelebrated Mass and sermon to the seminarians drafted into the army * October 28 — First conference of the Coordinating Committee of the Krakow Provincial Synod — 50th anniversary of the establishment of the Krakow Metropolitan See, of the bull *Vixdum Poloniae unitas*. The Cardinal presided. He spoke of informing a larger circle of individuals, both clergy and laity, about the Synod and its goals, of establishing contacts between the Synod and some key centers in the particular dioceses. At the beginning, the Cardinal discussed the prepared text on the subject of "Initial issues" (Based on the minutes) * Same day, 8:00 p.m., Church of Our Lady of Lourdes, Mass with sermon for the inauguration of the academic year * October 29 — 1:30 p.m., residence, 25th anniversary of professional activity of Director Tadeusz Nowak * Same day — 4:00 p.m., participated in a colloquium for the admission to assistant professorship of Rev. Dr. Jerzy Chmiel * October 30 — 3:00 p.m., Kalwaria Zebrzydowska * October 31 — 5:00 p.m., Boleslaw, visitation of Our Lady (for the second time — on the occasion of the regaining of the parish church), Mass and sermon.

November 1 — Canonical visitation of the parish of Waksmund * November 2 — 11:00 a.m., Chapel at the Rakowicki cemetery, Mass and sermon * 12:00 noon, residence chapel, concelebrated Mass * 5:00 p.m., Cathedral, Mass, funeral procession * November 3 — 6:00 p.m., Theological Seminary, Mass and sermon, "agape"[26] * November 4 — 11:00 a.m., name-day, greetings from: religious sisters, priests, *Tygodnik Powszechny*, the Curia, children and others * 7:30 p.m., residence chapel, concelebrated Mass with the priests from the academic ministry, greetings from the students * November 5 — 10:00 a.m., Oltarzew, a theological symposium — *Responsibility for the World,* organized by the Higher Theological Seminary of the Pallotine Fathers on the 40th anniversary of the death of Sister Faustina, 1:00 p.m. — lecture, 6:00 p.m. — at the church in Oltarzew, concelebrated Mass and sermon * November 6 — Krakow, residence, Editorial Team of the Synod * Same day — 6:00 p.m., the Mariacki Church, Holy Mass with sermon and exequies for Wincenty Witos[27] on the 30th anniversary of his death:

---

[26] Christian supper; in early Christian times a communal meal of the congregation.
[27] Prime Minister of Poland in the 1930's, leader of the Polish Populist Party.

Surely many of us present here today remember his funeral, here at this ancient Mariacki Basilica of Krakow. We remember it from that day, tightly packed with a great throng of faithful countrymen. We remember how the Metropolitan Archbishop of Krakow, a Cardinal and a prince, bent over his coffin, the coffin of this great Polish peasant. We remember how the then President of Poland stood next to that coffin ... [Witos] was faithful to the whole truth of the soul of the Polish people. And that truth which is an integral part of the Polish people included, and still includes, a deep faith in God. This peasant and statesman who died 30 years ago had that faith throughout his whole life. And he not only took it with him to his grave, but he also left it as a testament at the threshold of that age which was then, 30 years ago, beginning. A testament of faith in God is a testament of man's strength ... Because the greatness of man comes from God and is expressed in the fact that man responds to God, communes with God, plays out the entire drama of his life before God, and returns to God when his earthly remains are laid in a coffin, and with that coffin in the ground.

Same day — 7:30 p.m., residence, greetings from "Oasis" {charismatic} groups * November 7 — 5:30 p.m., Zator, Mass with sermon, blessing of the home of the Sisters of the Resurrection * November 8 — 9:00 a.m., Rakowicki cemetery, a funeral of Prof. Wojciech Modelski * 3:00 p.m., residence, session of physicians * 8:00 p.m., residence chapel, Mass and sermon for physicians * November 9 — 11:00 a.m., the Cathedral of Kielce, sermon for the 50th anniversary of Bishop Jan Jaroszewicz's ordination to the priesthood.

We place a wreath on the head of the honoree, and a staff in remembrance of he cross into his hand. Because the cross is our strength, our support. The cross is also a signpost, it points the way and leads us, leads us from every evil into good, from the temporal to the eternal, from sin and weakness to grace.

Same day — residence, a session of physicians * 5:00 p.m., Mass at the Church of St. Peter and St. Paul for the 100th anniversary of the Ursuline Sisters in Krakow, later he participated in an agape with the sisters and the former students at the Ursuline Sisters' house at 9 Bohaterow Stalingradu Street * November 10 — 10:00 a.m., regional congregation: Threats to the Christian Family. From a conference during the congregation (32 typed pages):

Let us try to outline the broad scope of the issue of the family ... it turns out that a burning issue in conjugal love is, first of all, the connection between marital abstinence and the ethical means of birth control. It should be noted that the Second Vatican Council did not say everything in this regard, leaving the last word to the Holy Father, who expressed it in the encyclical *Humanae vitae*, in accordance with the position taken by the Council. *Humanae vitae* should then be considered a continuation of Chapter I of Part II of *Gaudium et spes*. These are the selected topics which undoubtedly lie at the center of the ethical difficulties of marriage and the contemporary family.

Developments in the world, and especially in Europe, indicate that this center is moving ever farther. Namely, in the 10 years after the Council, we witnessed many protests, from many directions, against the encyclical *Humanae vitae*, and also attempts at legalization of the termination of pregnancy. This brought unfortunate results ...

As far as the Polish context ... From the point of view of the situation of marriage and the family, the last 30 years[28] can be divided into three phases. The first was approximately from 1945 to 1956, the second to 1970, and the third after 1970 ...

This was the approximate profile of the second phase, 1956-1970. Even before the end of this period, we observed a subtle change in orientation, at least on the part of the controlling elements. We noticed, first, a lessening of pressure towards abortion and the appearance in the press of a new phenomenon, namely expressions in favor of larger families ...

At once there arose the concern, which still remains, whether these manifestations of sound judgment were not too late ...

The third phase, the shortest one, began in some respects before 1970 and has lasted until the present. How is it characterized?

We can notice some changes that favor larger families, not with one child or two, but ... with the introduction of certain resolutions of a social and legislative nature to help families, especially those with the lowest incomes. But these are really minimal improvements. The law legalizing abortion is still in effect. And while it is in effect, the basis for the action of a whole series of institutions and persons who dispose of unborn Polish lives in any manner they choose is also in effect ...

We have also observed new phenomena on the ideological front. There are attempts to create a path towards a so-called socialistic family. There is a new subject in the schools which was initially called "Preparation to life in the socialistic family." Currently, this title has been retired. Now, there is talk of "upbringing to life in the family," without the addition of "socialistic," but the true intent may be assumed to have remained as before ... We only need to recall the whole program of secular pre-marital instruction, civil marriage ceremonies, secular funerals, ceremonies of bestowing of names, etc. We should add that all of this is accompanied by a weakening of moral principles and a practical demoralization. One follows upon the other. The introduction of divorces was the first step towards secularization, the legalization of abortion and birth control propaganda was the second step, and today, what is contained within the subject called "the upbringing of the family" contains all of the foregoing. The educational program itself is relatively neutral, but the auxiliary materials for the teachers, which are to be used in this work, are unequivocal ...

The position of the Church during this period has been unequivocal. Unequivocal, i.e. directed towards the defense of the law of God, and so also the law of nature and a properly understood human law concerning marriage and the family. It has been directed towards defending fundamental values that are not only Christian but also human, because these two go hand in hand in the life of a marriage and a family. It has been directed towards an open and overt struggle against everything that is simply a crime or a sin.

The Church in Poland took an unequivocal stance in relation to the

---

[28] Postwar Communist rule.

encyclical *Humanae vitae*, this is undoubtedly a difficult issue, but what proved to be most dangerous in this difficult issue were the stances which were somewhat ambiguous.

One other thing should be added concerning the activity of the Church in Poland, especially that of the Episcopal Conference, for 20 years we have sought contact with the health services, and particularly with the world of physicians ...

The family ministry in the Archdiocese of Krakow. The guiding principles are these: we need an ever fuller and more mature coordination of pastoral work with the apostolic involvement of the laity. I would place this as the *first principle* ...

The second principle: our activity in this regard must be universal, it cannot be merely elitist ...

The third principle: our entire activity, and the coordination of this activity between the priests and the lay people, must be based on a very thorough knowledge, on a program of education in the facts of life. It is necessary to combine the pastoral activities, the apostolate of the laity with a program of thorough education in the facts of life, with an understanding of the essence of the matter, with a vision of marriage, with a vision of the ethos of Christian marriage ... And that is why, when I was forming the Department of the Family Ministry and all of its activities, I saw the need to base this activity on an academic and educational body, which I named the Institute of the Family, this is the uniqueness of the Krakow model of operation. The task of this body is to educate, to conduct discussions with priests and with the lay people. This is a new element in the sphere of doctrine and it is being followed by a new element in the sphere of pastoral ministry.

Finally, the *fourth principle*, which is in some sense a sub-point of the third: education in the facts of life, as is emphasized by Paul VI in *Humanae vitae*, cannot have a solely bio-medical character; it must lead us to a mature view of the faith and of Christian morality. Or, simply put, to a fuller realization of the sacramental nature of marriage ...

Now I also wish to speak about the several forms of activity in the family ministry ... We have advanced various methods of *preparation for marriage* ...

The *second form* of action is the ministry to existing marriages and families ...

The *third form* of the ministry to marriages and families in the archdiocese is counseling ...

And finally the *fourth form* of action, this could be called the most social form, is the effort aimed at the shaping of public opinion.

November 11- 10:00 a.m., regional conference of deaneries of the areas in the immediate vicinity of Krakow (Bishop Albin Malysiak's region) * Same day — 3:00 p.m., Niedzwiedz, funeral of Rev. Wladyslaw Bedek, concelebrated Mass, sermon * Same day — choir "Organum" * 7:30 p.m., Mass and sermon for the *Srodowisko*[29] * November 13 — Seminar with Rev. Prof. Josef Ziegler, professor of

---

[29] See Glossary.

moral theology at the Department of Theology of the university in Mainz * Same day — 8:00 p.m., celebration of the Feast of St. Stanislaw Kostka at the Basilica of the Sacred Heart of Jesus in Krakow; the church was filled with the youth who gathered for prayer, according to the tradition of this day. Cardinal Wojtyla concelebrated Mass with the academic chaplains, preached the sermon, and blessed the textbooks and lecture notes as the tools of the students' work * November 14 — 10:00 a.m., Oswiecim, regional conference (Bishop Stanislaw Smolenski's region) * 4:00 p.m., residence, during a meeting of the Council of the Pontifical Department of Theology the Cardinal was soliciting for the creation of the Historical Institute at the Pontifical Department of Theology as an institution of scientific research and study. (From the minutes of the Council of the Department)

Middle of November — the Committee of the Episcopate for Catholic Education begins its activities (appointed on November 27, 1974).

November 15 — Gdansk, 50th anniversary of the Diocese of Gdansk; 5:00 p.m., Gdansk-Oliwa, sermon * 6:00 p.m., Church of Our Lady of the Rosary at Przymorze (Gdansk):

> Here is Mary in her image of Jasna Gora, visiting individual communities of the People of God ... gathering us about her and instructing us by her example, given in Bethlehem, that we are to seek a shelter for God whom we have received into our hearts ... And often we begin with a little stable, with a catechetic classroom, with some sort of canopy. That is the history of the creation and construction of churches, unfortunately not enough of them, over the past 30 years ... Your church has its own special page in history ... we admire it; on this page ... we read the record of your effort, all of the efforts made by your bishop, your priests, the whole community of the people of the sea ... We rejoice that your patient quest has been rewarded with such a magnificent result ... By building it at a historic moment, you have attained a particular achievement in the 50-year history of the Church of Gdansk.

November 16 — 10:00 a.m., Gdansk, Church of the Sacred Heart of Jesus, for the 50th anniversary of the Church of Gdansk, to the academic youth:

> Such a conscious choosing of Christ, affirmed by the experience of generations, by the experience of people to whom living in Christ brought fruit, bountiful fruit, allowed them to rejoice in an abundance of humanity, allowed them to enrich human life, just such a shaping of our Christianity is the challenge of our time, the necessity of our time. In these times, on Polish soil and on the soil of Gdansk, ... the idea of freedom of religion, freedom of conscience acquires particular importance, a special meaning ... We must state clearly that the freedom of conscience and the freedom of religion can be realized in our society only by people who are conscious of their faith.

Same day — 4:30 p.m., Oliwa, cathedral, sermon for school-age youth and blessing of a museum open in the old Cistercian Monastery * November 17 — 8:00 a.m., Gdansk, chapel of the Theological Seminary, concelebrated Mass, sermon * Same day — Warsaw, seminar in ethics * November 18 — 10:00 a.m., Warsaw, Main Council of the Polish Episcopate * November 19-20 — 10:00 a.m., Warsaw, 150th plenary conference of the Polish Episcopate * November 21 — 2:00 p.m., Krakow, residence, conference of bishops * 6:00 p.m., Wola Duchacka, laying of the corner stone of the church:

> This cornerstone, blessed by the Holy Father, unites your church and your community with the great, universal oneness of the Church, which is led by the successor of Peter, our Holy Father Paul VI ... Faith in the Risen Christ is a particular heritage of your parish community, because the Risen Christ is the main patron of your parish ... At the time when you were immersed in death, a political death, having lost the independence of your homeland, the independence of this country with such glorious historical past, the thoughts and hearts of Poles turned, through faith, to Christ immersed in death, who broke the bonds of death and rose on the third day ... It is not difficult for Poles, for Catholics in Poland, to build churches, but it is more difficult to obtain permissions to build, as attested by the review, conducted yesterday by the Conference of the Polish Episcopate, of this year's permissions for construction of churches. It turns out that of all the applications for permission to build churches or chapels, submitted by the diocesan and archdiocesan curiae, only 6 percent were granted.

November 22 — 11:00 a.m., residence, session of the Curia * 6:00 p.m., Convent of the Carmelite Sisters on Wesola Street (in Krakow), concelebrated Mass for the 250th anniversary * November 23, 10:00 a.m., Wawel Cathedral, Feast of Christ the King:

> According to our custom, representatives of parishes who were visited by the bishop in the past year come to the Cathedral on this day ... The Kingdom of God is continually being built, it is being built on the path of life of man and of humanity, and the building of this Kingdom does not take place without hard struggle ... And that is why all of us who live in this era must with ever greater zeal, the zeal of faith and the strength of grace, realize the Kingdom of God which has been given to us as a gift in Christ. We must contribute to it in all respects, in our personal life, in our family life, in the upbringing of the youth, in the work of our parish communities, in the work of our archdiocese and in the work of so many other Churches. Today, more than ever, we must concern ourselves with this Kingdom of God within us and among us, as a right of man, and also as a right of Christ, His right to citizenship among the people, among society, among the families, among the youth, in all of our nation. He earned this right with the price of His blood, with the price of truth, with the price of life which He gives us.

Same day — 8:00 p.m., departure for Rome via Vienna * November 24-28 — Cardinal Wojtyla participated in the meeting of the Council of the Secretariat of the Bishops, joins the minor committee, which during its deliberations on November 26-27 worked out a second edition of a document on the topic of catechesis, as recommended to the Council of the Secretariat by the experts. (Rev. Adam Kubis) * November 28 — 12:00 noon, an audience with Pope Paul VI * November 30 — 8:00 a.m., Rome, concelebrated Mass with sermon at the titular Church of St. Caesarius.

December 1 — 4:00 p.m., arrived in Milan on the invitation of Cardinal Giovanni Colombo * 9:00 p.m., Ambrosianum, conference and a lecture: *The Rights of a Human Person in Light of the Latest Synod of Bishops* * December 2 — Milan, cathedral, concelebrated Mass at the tomb of St. Charles * 12:00 noon, Lonigo (in the vicinity of Verona), a visit to the tomb of the Servant of God Hadrian Osmolowski, a Polish Bernardine monk * December 3 — 7:00 a.m., Rome, chapel of the Polish College, concelebrated Mass and sermon * 12:00 noon, meeting with Archbishop L. Poggi * December 4 — Rome, Chapel of the Sisters of the Holy Family of Nazareth, concele- brated Mass, sermon * December 5 — 10:00 a.m., arrival of the Primate {Wyszynski} and the Episcopate * 12:00 noon, meeting with Archbishop Giovanni Benelli at the Polish Institute * December 6 — 7:00 a.m., Rome, Chapel of the Missionary Sisters of St. Peter Claver, concelebrated Mass by the tomb of the Blessed Maria Teresa Ledochowska * 10:00 a.m., St. Peter's Basilica, pilgrimage of the Polish Episcopate in the Holy Year * 12:00 noon, an audience of the Polish Episcopate with Pope Paul VI * a meeting with Cardinal Jean Villot * a meeting with Cardinal Franjo Seper * December 7 — 5:30 p.m., Rome, Chapel of the Felician Sisters, concelebrated Mass, ser- mon * Angelicum, a visit * December 8 — 10:00 a.m., Basilica of St. Peter, participated in a solemn ceremony of the dedication of all mat- ters of the Church to the Blessed Mother, conducted by the Holy Father Paul VI * 5:00 p.m., Basilica of Santa Maria Maggiore, the Holy Father's act of dedication to Mary * December 9 — 10:00 a.m., Basilica of St. Peter, an act of dedication on the occasion of the Holy Year * Return to Krakow * December 10 — 7:00 a.m., residence chapel, concelebrated private Mass * 12:00 noon, session of bishops * December 11 — 1:00 p.m., Kalwaria Zebrzydowska * December 12 — 12:00 noon, residence, Council of the Pontifical Department of Theology, examination of Rev. Dr. Waclaw Swierzawski for admission to assistant professorship * December 12-31 — visitation of the parish of Nowa Huta-Mogila * December 13 — 8:30 p.m., Church of the Jesuits, *Oplatek*[30] with university students * December 15 — Session

---

[30] See Glossary.

of the Council of Priests * Session of the Family Institute * Same day — Krakow-Azory, blessing of the Church of the Immaculate Conception of Our Lady (under construction):

It is necessary that churches rise quickly in Krakow, because Krakow is growing very quickly. Take your parish as an example. During the last visitation which I held here in 1962 — there was no opportunity for another visitation later because of construction. This was a small parish on the periphery, numbering 2000, at most 3000, souls. And now, as I have said, a gigantic parish. And so it is all over Krakow. Our city is growing very rapidly. Nowa Huta has sprung up, as we know; it is itself a large city of 200 thousand inhabitants today, which is just slightly less than all of Krakow before the war. There, in Nowa Huta, we needed to follow the expansion of the city with the expansion of church construction. We know how much effort that took, how many sacrifices, how difficult it was to convince the authorities that this church, the church in Nowa Huta, has the right of citizenship in the society. From the perspective of time, I think that perhaps all of these sufferings were unnecessary. I think that our authorities could have spared us these sufferings and surely their power would not have been diminished. Nevertheless, since those churches in Nowa Huta had to win their right to existence at the cost of such sacrifices, we see a sign of the times in that, and we take up this sign of the times. And this sign of the times challenges our living faith. We know that at one time, churches were constructed from the generosity of human hearts, that huge churches were built in small Krakow. And we know that today, the faith of the entire society is required to build even small churches; small in external dimensions, small in capacity. But large because of the faith and the human spirit that brought about their construction ... As the Bishop of the Church of Krakow I continue to maintain that we must keep up with the growth of the city, that we have too few temples ... No one can use the old city as an argument in this case. This argument about the old city, where there are many churches, merely indicates how it should be, how it was in the days of generosity for the cause of God, how neither room, materials nor time were spared to build the temples then. But we in our time have more modest aspirations. And even those aspirations, claims, petitions, which are realistic enough, we must present to the authorities consistently and repeatedly. And sometimes it seems to us that those that listen to us and read our documents do not understand what we say and why, although we say it very clearly. For example, we say such an obvious thing: if Krakow is growing, if new subdivisions and settlements are being built, and if these districts have tens of thousands of inhabitants, then let us adopt a principle that in each new settlement a site will be reserved for a church, for a pastoral center. We ask that this be considered, respected. We feel that we have the right and the duty to present this matter in this way, and we do not understand why it is not respected ... I am greatly concerned, this is not the first time I speak of it here, about the neighboring settlement of Krowodrza, which is also a parish of ten-and-several thousand, and which meets in a small catechetic classroom. So I speak of this to the representatives of the working people: look at the conditions in which these priests work. Can those who so glorify work, look with a clear conscience at the working conditions of these priests? And after all, this work is beneficial work, it aims to bring people up, to strengthen their morality as individuals and as members of the society. What I say here is not to cloud this solemn occasion, but to tell you how this bishop, who is your guest today, experiences the issues of church construction in Krakow ... What I am saying to you here, I have said and written many times in my letters to the authorities, because I feel that this is my right, and that this is their duty. And if at this moment I wish to thank anyone, it would be all of those upright people who, regardless of the consequences, do not hesitate to support the initiatives, the claims, the petitions of the bishop, the pastors and priests regarding the construction of churches, and who tirelessly go in delegation to various authorities ... Once again, I wish to express my gratitude here today to those delegations, and to say to all those who do this in Krakow and in the Archdiocese, that you have an inviolable right as citizens to do this, and you cannot be, well, let us say, subjected to any harassment because of this. It is your inviolable right as citizens.

December 17 — In Poznan, participated in a colloquium for the admission to assistant professorship of Rev. Marian Finke and Rev. Antoni Witkowiak. In his opening remarks he stated that the newly opened Catholic theological institution in Poznan needs qualified academicians. The ancient Department of Theology in Krakow has always offered its assistance * Same day — 8:00 p.m., the Dominican Church, *Oplatek* for university students * December 18 — Visitation of the parish of Nowa Huta-Mogila, a meeting with nurses, speech, *Oplatek* * 8:00 p.m., Church of St. Szczepan {Stephen}, Mass and sermon, *Oplatek* with university students * December 19 — Nowa Huta-Mogila. Sermon with a blessing of married couples: "The testament of faith given by the parents must always be solid, without a doubt, so that this testament would have the power to educate. So that it would influence the Christian formation of these people whom God gave you as your children." * Same day — 8:00 p.m., Church of Our Lady of Lourdes, Mass with sermon, academic *Oplatek* * December 20 — 6:00 a.m., Nowa Huta-Mogila, Holy Communion at the hospital * 12:00 noon, residence, session of the Curia * 4:00 p.m., Nowa Huta, acceptance of candidates for altar boys * December 21 — Nowa Huta-Mogila, Holy Communion, and visit to the sick at the hospital, *Oplatek* with the schola * Same day — *Oplatek* for the academic youth:

> If it weren't for Christmas ... all we would have is the awareness of our species, which is where every kind of materialism is propelling us: we are the human species. This day, this Holy Night brought us a new awareness: an awareness of family. We are a family, because we have a Father, His Son is among us.

December 22 — 10:00 a.m., Wawel Cathedral, funeral of Msgr. Edward Lubowiecki, who died November 12, 1975, in Frankfurt on

---

[31] See Glossary.

Main:

> The deceased will remain in our memory most closely tied to the great person who will never be forgotten by Krakow, Poland and the Church, Prince Cardinal Adam Stefan Sapieha, Metropolitan Archbishop of Krakow ... There were few priests who so understood the spirit of Cardinal Sapieha and could incorporate this spirit into their lives so well ... And we know that what was closest to the heart of Prince Archbishop, was the matter of man, especially of man who is the most needy. And that matter has always been written most tellingly into the broad context of the life of the Church and the nation.

Same day — Nowa Huta-Mogila, *Oplatek* with the "Oasis" {charismatic} groups * December 23 — 12:00 noon, residence, session of bishops * December 24 — Greetings, *Oplatek* (among others at 11:30 a.m., *Tygodnik Powszechny*) * 4:00 p.m., Wawel Cathedral, matins of Christmas * 6:00 p.m., residence chapel, reading of Martyrology * For "wigilia"[32] he invited to his table the seminarians of the fifth year who stayed at the Seminary for Christmas, and the superiors of the Seminary * 12:00 midnight, Krakow, Krowodrza settlement, "Pasterka" {midnight Mass}:

> I extend my greetings to all the inhabitants of this settlement ... without exception. That means not only to those who are present, who came here, because those who come, will already find. But also to those who did not come, for whatever reasons. Whether because they do not expect to find, or because they have lost, or because they are afraid, whatever the reason may be why they did not come, my wish to all without exception is that they may find. That they may find Christ, because He is the Savior of the world.

December 25 — 10:00 a.m., Wawel Cathedral, concelebrated Mass:

> But allow me ... in my first words to turn to those who are not present, but are close to my heart. To those who would be here serving, helping in the sacred rites, but are prevented from doing so by the fact that they have been plucked from their studies, from their preparation to the priesthood in the theological seminary, and drafted into military service. Of course, it is an honorable thing for every Pole to serve his Homeland, but these circumstances are painful. For they were drafted during the course of their studies, which is not done to other students ... Not long ago, there was a front-page article in a political journal in Poland, an article in which the author wonders what it is that might be the "will of individuals" in our Homeland. Or rather, he did not wonder. He immediately found a ready answer. We would wish that this author might stroll across the Polish land, especially on Christmas Eve, especially on Christmas Day. And that he might hear how individuals, that means the people[33], sing the hymn "We

---

[32] The traditional Christmas Eve supper, the central observance of the Polish Christmas tradition.

yearn for God" everywhere. Christianity, religion, love of Christ, of the mystery of Bethlehem, of the mystery of Calvary and the Last Supper, love of the Blessed Mother, of the Holy Family, these are the constructive elements of the will of the people. And there should be no illusions that these are merely elements of folklore.

On the same day — Nowa Huta — *Oplatek* with the academic youth.

December 26 — 8:00 a.m., Chapel of the Daughters of Divine Mercy, concelebrated Mass, sermon, Baptism * Same day — 12:00 noon, Church of St. Szczepan {Stephen}, sermon during the Sacrament of Baptism:

> In a sense, the Feast of St. Stephen is a celebration of the first Christian community, the one which arose immediately after the Resurrection and departure of Our Lord ... Stephen was a man of that community ... he belonged to the group of disciples which was, in some sense, the second generation ... I mention this community because I know that your young marriage began in a community of the academic ministry. I know that your marriage and this christening are considered by your community to be an event of their own; we have with us here the academic chaplain, who was your chaplain for so many years. The community transmits faith ... In our times it is necessary that families, and every person within a family, find support in a broader community, one that serves the faith and helps to mold the life of God within human beings.

Sermon during Mass:

> This right of a citizen, of a believing person, of a Christian, to bear witness to Christ is defined by our concept of the freedom of expression. And that means both written and spoken expression ... Freedom of expression. And also the freedom of action that is consistent with that expression, a freedom which shows respect for man. Because if man is deprived of the freedom of expression, if that expression is somehow controlled and fitted to preconceived ideas, then man is, in effect, not respected. Then, life becomes inhumane: from the points of view of both citizenship and humanity ... Today, such realities are obviously at odds with the idea of the civil rights and human rights. It is unacceptable. It is not acceptable that when a bishop preaches a sermon, the same sermon cannot be printed even in our own *Diocesan News*, in *Notificationes*. That government censorship is applied to all utterances by the Church, even to those made by the Head of the Church, even when he speaks on matters of faith and morals, his texts are deleted ... A bishop cannot, a priest cannot, a Christian cannot, cease to bear witness ... And I mentioned the seminarians because they are being drafted into the military during their studies and in the course of their service bear a very singular witness to their faith. They must struggle much to be able to pray, to be able to pray. This is the same story: it would be permissible for you to turn to God within the depths of your soul, as long as no one could see it. But he replies: I am a believer in Christ, I am to be

---

33 Same word as used in "People's Republic"

a priest in the future, I will not hide the fact that I pray. And they pray. Even in spite of various difficulties about which I would rather not speak, of which I would prefer not to speak ... There is a growing problem for us in Poland, of bearing witness; bearing witness by our life as a society, by our culture. Do we, Christians, people of faith, do we see ourselves mentioned in the daily press? But we have a right to that; we make up the nation, we should see ourselves in the daily press; our lives, the truth about us. What can we say when the only socio-cultural periodical in Krakow cannot for many years get permission to raise its circulation from 40 to 50 thousand. I am speaking of *Tygodnik Powszechny*. And this in a society, in a nation, which has 34 million citizens; I will not say how many of those 34 million are Catholics, but we know well that the vast majority of that 34 million is made up of baptized persons. This is also a matter of bearing witness. Witness can be borne in the press, television and radio; we wish to bear this witness with a feeling of freedom, that is with a feeling that it is respected, that in the great totality of Polish life, of Polish communications media, the press, television, radio, books, there is a proportional space for us, people of faith ... We have earned this freedom by so many years of captivity, partitions, a horrible occupation. We have not betrayed Christ or Poland!

Same day — 5:00 p.m., Mass at the home of Mr. & Mrs. Miesowicz, final remarks * December 27 — 6:30 p.m., residence chapel, Mass and sermon for the 20th wedding anniversary of S. and L. Abrahamowicz * December 28 — 10:00 a.m., 650th anniversary of the parish, Mass and sermon, Sacrament of Confirmation * 6:00 p.m., Warsaw cathedral, unveiling of a memorial plaque for Wincenty Witos.[34] The unveiling was performed by the Primate {Wyszynski} * December 29 — 11:00 a.m., residence, session of bishops * 4:00 p.m., Myslenice, concelebrated Mass, *Oplatek*[35] with priests ordained in 1971 * December 30 — 3:00 p.m., residence, editorial teams of the Synod * 6:00 p.m., residence chapel, private Mass * December 31 — 8:00 a.m., Mass and sermon at Mr. & Mrs. Poltawski's * 12:00 noon, residence, session of the Curia * 6:00 p.m., Nowa Huta-Mogila, vespers for the end of the old year and the visitation, sermon and a New Year's Eve meeting with the academic youth * 12:00 midnight, Church of the Franciscans, Mass and sermon.

In the years of 1974 and 1975 he publishes a number of articles that were a continuation of his considerations in *Love and Responsibility*, and his pronouncements on the topic of the encyclical *Humanae vitae*. The articles are: "Family as communio personarum," in *Ateneum Kaplanskie* 83/1974, pp. 347-361; "Parenthood and communio personarum," in *Ateneum Kaplanskie* 84/1975; "On the meaning of betrothed

---

[34] Prime Minister of Poland in the 1930's, leader of the Polish Populist Party.
[35] See Glossary.

love," *Roczniki Filozoficzne* {Philosophical Annals} KUL 22/1974, b.
2, pp. 162-174; "Pastoral contemplations on the family," *Rocznik Nauk
Spolecznych* {Annals of the Social Sciences} 3/1975, pp. 58-76.

Excerpts from the article "Parenthood and communio personarum":

"Man is the only creature on earth whom God wanted for man himself," and at the same time, man "cannot discover who he truly is except in the selfless giving of himself." Both of these quotes are taken from the documents of the Second Vatican Council. These two expressions from the Second Vatican Council form a unified whole, in which the first expression cannot be understood (because it cannot be realized) without the second; nor the second without the first ... In the communion of persons, this self-fulfillment is realized by the mutual gift of oneself to the other, a gift which is selfless in nature. Man, as a person, is capable of such a gift ... because a person is capable of self-possession, and only those who fully possess themselves can give themselves. Such a gift is unselfish and that is why it truly deserves to be called a gift ... The entire tradition of Christian thought postulates a dimension of human action and existence that is above the merely useful, above the utilitarian. This is at the core of the Gospel's teaching on love and grace. In the final analysis, grace is ... a selfless gift from God to man, who manifests this dimension of existence and action above the utilitarian, which is proper to the world of human persons. And so, too, in inter-personal relations, "the selfless gift of oneself" (i.e. of the person) stands at the foundation of the entire rule of love, its entire authenticity ... Status naturae creatae, lapsae et redemptae demand a detailed theological synthesis, a detailed theology of the flesh, as it were, in the interest of a proper and adequate interpretation of this basic reality, the reality of the community of marriage, i.e. the specific *communio personarum* which is ultimately shaped by the Sacrament of Matrimony. The theological dimension of the matter determines its ethical dimension ... A man and a woman, uniting themselves in such a close communion of life and calling, in which the mutual gift of self is expressed in bodily union arising from the differences between the sexes, cannot in any way violate the profound laws which govern the unity of persons, which establish the conditions for their true communion. For these are objective laws, more profound than any somatic or emotional reactions ... Moreover, we know that the conjugal union is fulfilled in parenthood ... Marriage as communio personarum is, by its nature, open to these new persons, and through them achieves its appropriate fullness. ("Ateneum Kaplanskie," 83, pp. 354-355 and 359-361)

An article "The person: subject and community," written in the
years 1974 — 1975, is published in Roczniki Filozoficzne 24/1976, bk.
2, pp. 5 — 39. The author analyzes the various dimensions of personal
community: "I — you," "us". It is an extension of the deliberations
from the last chapter of the book *Person and Act*, entitled *An outline of
the theory of participation*. He concludes that alienation is the antithesis of the participation he discusses here:

In noticing the differences in communal relations of the type "I — you"

versus "us" ... we conclude ... that the person as an individual remains the basis of analogy between them ... In each of these dimensions, participation is connected with transcendence, and thus is rooted in the person as the subject, and in the drive within that person towards self-realization, towards self-fulfillment. Man as a person fulfills himself through personal relations of the type "I — you," and through a relation to the common good which allows him to exist and act together with others as "us" ... And participation conceived in this way, as the characteristic of a person through which this person maintains identity in a social community, seems to be the condition of a true *communio personarum* ... Alienation is the opposite of participation ... Alienation contributes to the state ... in which man is deprived in some respect of the ability to fulfill himself in the community ... Alienation ... can occur ... in both dimensions of the community ... Alienation as the antithesis of participation ... not so much "dehumanizes" man as an individual, but strikes at the person as a subject. (pp. 34-38)

The thoughts in this article have been expanded in a lecture presented in 1977 in Mainz, and also in a presentation delivered in Fribourg in 1975 and in contemplations on the topic of the role of "praxis" and culture (a lecture presented in Genoa in 1976 and Milan in 1977). (Compiled by Rev. Andrzej Szostek).

1976

January 1-6 — Zakopane-Jaszczurowka, ski trip with Father M. Jaworski. He lived and said Masses at the chapel of the Ursuline Sisters at 7 a.m. * January 4 — Recreation with the sisters, celebration of the chaplain's anniversary * January 6 — Departure in the afternoon * Same day — 6 p.m., celebration of the Feast of the Epiphany at the Wawel Cathedral.

> And in this we are all gathered here today, in this we are all united: joy at our faith, joy at reaching Bethlehem, joy at Christ's coming. A joy attained perhaps by a loss in the temporal sphere which we call a career. In this way we are able to repay Him for what He has paid on our account ... Because in fact, as stated in the "Instructions" recently studied by our society, Poland has attained a certain level of prestige in the world. And do you know why? Because the entire world is watching, to what extent Poland is a country, a republic, respecting the convictions of each individual, respecting his interior truth, his conscience, his religion. And to what extent we, Poles, a nation, a society, are able to uphold this respect by our attitude, to uphold it as an inheritance, a deposit, a milieu, a climate, in which man is only human. So my wish to you, my country of Poland, is that you may continue to enjoy this prestige ... Accept, o my country, these wishes from the Bishop of Krakow, the guardian of Wawel, the guardian of the nation's memories, spokesman for the great tradition, spokesman for all history, successor to St. Stanislaw.

January 7 — 5:00 p.m., concelebrated Mass, sermon and *Oplatek*[1] for the gardeners * 8 p.m., residence, Christmas carols * January 8 — Krakow, residence, second meeting of the Committee to coordinate the Provincial Synod. Approval of the texts *Information About Preliminary Work of the 1st Synod of the Krakow Province and The Subject Matter of the Work of the 1st Synod of the Krakow Province as Presented by the Committee of Experts*. Appointment of a subcommittee to deal with the matter of statutes * 4 p.m., residence, meeting of a Marian group * 7 p.m., residence chapel, concelebrated Mass, Christmas carols with an "Oasis" group * January 9 — 10 a.m., Warsaw, Main Council of the Polish Episcopate * January 10 — 10:30 a.m., meeting of the Committee for the Apostolate of the Laity. Appointment of a subcommittee to edit a document on the education to dialogue. Worldwide conference of the laity (Rome, October 7-15, 1975), participants present reports. A document on the subject of Confirmation. Preparation of the Forum (Belgium). The Theological Institute of the Society of the Apostolate of the Laity — as a center of documentation. Possibility of a retreat (days of recollection) for the centers, a meeting with those

---

[1] See Glossary.

invited on the topic of the apostolic aspects of Sacrosong[2] * Same day — 4:00 p.m., Oplatek for legionnaires at the Dominican Fathers:

I am happy that Poland, particularly the Church in Poland, continues to be the guardian of the great tradition, of the significant facts in the history of our nation, which make up the life of our country, particularly in this century. I have this year's events at Jasna Gora and in Warsaw in mind, those events which allowed us to introduce memories of the Eaglets of Lwow,[3] memories of the unknown soldier, and of many other public heroes who did so much for the regaining and maintaining of independence, into the treasury of our history, the history of both the Church and our nation. The Church in Poland wishes to continue to serve the history of the nation in all eras, not only in the obscure past, but also in the heated, contemporary period of the 20th century. And that is what I want to tell all of you gathered here, to confess before you, to respond to the words which we have just heard. Man lives sustained by truth. A nation lives sustained by truth, and we all have the duty to contribute, to lend a hand, so that we may live sustained by truth day by day, the truth about ourselves, the truth about our national realities, both in the past and today. This is a matter of extreme importance for the molding of new generations. Our observations have taught us that the new generations, the youngest ones, are distancing themselves from everything that has been prepared, and they are searching only for the truth about the history of their nation, the truth about their own past. We must all contribute to this, we must help to pass the truth of our nation's history along, to pass it down to the younger generations, and we must make sure that this be the real truth.

Same day — 8 p.m., H. E. Cardinal Karol Wojtyla honored with his presence the traditional "Oplatek" at "Zrodlo."[4] The archpastor was very interested in this type of apostolic work, in which he saw a very positive influence on the youth. He prayed that as many as possible of these "sources" emerge throughout Poland. (From the chronicle of the Sisters of Our Lady of Mercy.) * Same day — 11:30 a.m., singing of Christmas carols at the home of Mr. and Mrs. J. J. * January 11 — 9 a.m., second day of deliberations of the Committee for the Apostolate of the Laity, a homily delivered at the Archbishop's chapel.

The Theophany of Christ, the Revelation of God in Man, the revelation of the Son, one in being with the Father, united in person with man. This is the ultimate, this is the last word; this is the maximum approach to humanity.

Same day — 5 p.m., he led the celebration of the 100th anniversary of the Sisters of the Holy Family of Nazareth at the Basilica of the Dominican Fathers in Krakow * 8 p.m., *Oplatek*, Christmas carols at the Club of Catholic Intellectuals * January 12 — 10 a.m., regional conference (Krakow region) * 7 p.m., residence chapel, Mass for Prof. J. Gierula * 8 p.m., residence, Study Group * A letter dated on this day

---

[2] Festival of sacred song.
[3] Groups of children who fought alongside soldiers to defend the city of Lwow against Ukrainians at the end of WW I.
[4] Youth Center run by Our Lady of Mercy Sisters.

from Cardinal Wojtyla to all the bishops of the Krakow Metropolitan See informing them of the Synod's work and inviting them to the meeting on January 28th * January 13 — Krakow, 3 Franciszkanska Street, meeting of the Committee of the Episcopate for Pastoral Ministry. Lectures: Rev. Rector Jozef Majka, *Conditions of Evangelization in Poland Today*; Rev. Hilary Jastak, *Religiousness and the Pastoral Problems in Large Cities — taking Gdynia as an Example*; Rev. J. Pawlik — information on the pastoral care of Polish workers in the German Democratic Republic and Czechoslovakia; Bishop Pawel Socha, *Religiousness and the Pastoral Problems in Medium-Sized Cities in Poland*; Rev. Jozef Tischner, *Religious and Moral Problems in Rural Areas*. The discussion was summed up by Cardinal Wojtyla * On the same day he sent a letter to the priests of the archdiocese with a clear explanation concerning two areas of the youth ministry in the Archdiocese of Krakow: the ministry for youth liturgy, and the ministry for the youth, both male and female, on a broader scale * January 14 — Second day of the deliberations of the Committee of the Episcopate for Pastoral Ministry. A presentation by Cardinal Wojtyla: *Evangelization as a Topic of Pastoral Ministry in Poland*:

> It has probably never been the case in the land of Poland before, that anti-evangelization should become a program as clearly formulated, and implemented with such an expenditure of resources as currently ... We do not intend to take up evangelization as a counteraction to anti-evangelization, as in anti-anti-evangelization ... For the Church, anti-evangelization is more of a call than a challenge, more a call from God than a challenge from man (or Satan). As the key to its mission, the Church in Poland has rightly chosen ... the mystery of the Mother of God.

Further, he spoke in greater detail about the program of pastoral ministry. During the discussion there is a proposal to appoint a sub-committee for long-range and perspective planning. (From the minutes) * Same day — 5 p.m., Kozy, Confirmation, concelebrated Mass, homily * January 15 — 3 p.m., residence, meeting with Ms. Winowska, ministry for teachers * 4 p.m., a meeting before the regional conference * 7 p.m., Skalka, Feast of St. Paul, the first hermit, the feast of the Pauline order, meeting with students and seminarians, participation in an *Oplatek* until late in the evening. From the homily:

> What does it mean to be a hermit? ... Let us not think that the dominant element in the calling of a hermit, in the calling of St. Paul the first hermit, is the scorn of the world. This would not be a foundation that we might call deeply evangelical. The dominant characteristic, the essence of this calling, is the love of God above everything else. Above everything that ties man to the world, to the temporal, to the earth, to the family, to the country, even, in a way, to himself. This is a specific charisma, a specific vocation. The Lord God did give people such vocations and continues to do

so today.

For what purpose did God give people such vocations? ... If there could be a one-word answer to this question, it would be the word, witness. The Church and the world need people who bear radical witness. Not all people can live in such a way, and not all people can bear such witness. But these people are needed, those who are able to bear such radical witness. What is expressed in such witness? The perspective of man's vocation in general. Because, ultimately, none of us was created for this world. We know well that there is an end to life on earth. We cannot plant our roots in the worldly life for eternity. We also know well that we cannot truly fulfill ourselves on this earth. Each person's life, no matter how successful, is, in the temporal dimension, unfinished.

January 16-18 — Visitation of the parish of Nowa Huta — Ruszcza * January 17 — Participated in an academic symposium organized on the occasion of the 50th anniversary of Msgr. Eugeniusz Florkowski's academic work. In his speech, he stated that Msgr. Florkowski is a symbol of the unbroken continuity of the Department of Theology in Krakow. Even though in 1954 the continuity was shaken, the attitude of the Monsignor contributed to maintaining the continuity. (From the minutes of the Council of the Department) * 4:00 p.m., Nowa Huta — Ruszcza, participated in a religion lesson for pre-school students * 7:30 p.m., residence chapel, Mass with sermon, *Oplatek* for physicians * January 18 — Krakow — the Basilica of the Dominican Fathers. Sermon on the 100th anniversary of the establishment of the Congregation of the Sisters of the Holy Family of Nazareth * January 19 — 9:00 a.m., Krakow, at the Dominican Fathers, introduction and lecture at a conference of missionaries and retreat masters * 12:00 noon, Theological Seminary, participated in a retreat for graduating secondary school students * Same day — 5:30 p.m., Rajcza, concelebrated Mass, sermon, *Oplatek* with priests ordained in 1974 * January 20 — 12:00 noon, Rakowice Cemetery, funeral of Jacek Macharski * 3:00 p.m., residence, meeting of the Administrative Council * January 21 — 2:30 p.m., Ciecina, he led the funeral of the pastor, Rev. Canon Jan Bryndza, who died in an automobile accident on January 17. From the sermon:

> For me, this particular characteristic of the dearly departed Rev. Canon Jan Bryndza became particularly apparent when I was here several years ago on an episcopal visitation. At that time, as I was experiencing this visitation with him, I also experienced his personality, I got to know him in connection with my whole experience of the parish. And I thought that this pastor had grown close, in a very special way, to the community of this parish, the parish of Ciecina. He had grown very close.

Same day — 4:00 p.m., Brzeszcze, *Oplatek*[5] with the priests ordained in 1975 * 7:30 p.m., residence, meeting in connection with the

Committee for Catholic Education * That day he sent an appeal to the priests in connection with the 25ᵗʰ anniversary of the death of Cardinal Adam Stefan Sapieha. Remembering this great shepherd of the Metropolitan See of Krakow, he announced the celebration of the anniversary within the archdiocese * January 22 — 4:00 p.m., Wola Justowska, concelebrated Mass, homily, *Oplatek* with priests of the class of 1972 * 7 p.m., residence, seminar in moral theology * January 23 — 1:00 p.m., residence, session with bishops * 6 p.m., residence chapel, Mass with homily, *Oplatek* for nurses * January 24 — 12:00 noon, session of the Curia * 4 p.m., *Oplatek* with a group of artists * 6:00 p.m., residence chapel, Mass with homily for the colleagues of Father Kacz from the ministry for the sick, *Oplatek* * January 25 — 10:00 a.m., residence chapel, Mass with homily, *Oplatek* for the Family Ministry group * 12:00 noon, Silesian Seminary, *Oplatek* with the disabled * 1:00 p.m., Church of the Missionary Fathers at Stradom in Krakow under the appellation of the Conversion of St. Paul:

> **One cannot measure the development of man, one cannot measure the progress of human civilization in strictly material categories, by numbers only. One has to measure them in terms of the conversion of humanity. Our world will be better, our society will be better, our town will be better, each family will be better, in proportion to the number of converted people, those converted and those being converted to goodness, to truth, simply, to God. The greater the number of those with a deep moral sensibility, the greater the number of good people, people with a deep and honest conscience, the better the world.**

3:00 p.m., residence chapel, Mass with homily, *Oplatek* with teachers * 7:00 p.m., Basilica of the Dominican Fathers in Krakow, conclusion of an octave of prayers for the unification of Christians, concelebrated Mass, homily, agape:

> **Poland has never been the stage of religious wars. Despite many disputes, sometimes even very sharp ones, despite the differences of opinion, Poles managed to maintain peace in this regard. And this probably grew from the same root from which the Second Vatican Council derived its contemporary ecumenical stand, namely, from the respect for religious freedom, principally, the respect for the spiritual freedom of each individual. We Poles have always possessed, or so it seems, maybe we are a bit too presumptuous in this respect, maybe we evaluate ourselves falsely, but it seems that we have always had a great love of freedom. And despite the one-sided nature of this love, despite the tragic liberum veto,[6] which cost us, among others, our independence, we seemed to have always understood this truth, that each individual has his dignity. That his dignity is connected with his awareness, his conscience, his freedom. And that it is impermissible to encroach upon this interior sphere, to break him, to force him to do some-**

---

6 The 17ᵗʰ and 18ᵗʰ century principle in the Polish parliament that a single vote (veto) could prevent enactment of laws.

thing that is against his convictions, his understanding, his self-determination. This matter belongs somehow to our spiritual patrimony, to our Polish heritage ... We Poles remained, for the most part, Catholics ... maintaining, I claim, in our Catholicism, in the Catholic Church, an attitude of internal strength, of our identity, of our spiritual resistance, thanks to which our nation survived, but at the same time we respected the beliefs of others ... We read in the press about the predicted changes to the constitution ... The matter of the constitution is always a fundamental matter for the well being of the people and the nation ... Several weeks ago when the commission that was to make amendments or changes to the existing constitution had been set up, the Conference of the Polish Episcopate, fully aware of its responsibility, sent an appropriate comprehensive memorial to this commission ... For, in light of what the Constitution of a country is, each word in it has, can and should have a proper and exact meaning. The Constitution cannot contain internal inconsistencies. Neither can it create such situations in which the Polish nation, the Catholic society, the Catholic Church, believing Catholics, and all Christians would find themselves as if thrown overboard; as if they were second-class citizens, for whom decisions are made, who cannot in any way make decisions about this common good, which is our Homeland, our country. Therefore, we are obliged to read all of the proposed changes with great discernment, and we will do so, especially those that pertain to things that most concern us. Namely, about the ideological foundations. In this domain there can be no inconsistency between what is found in the Constitution, and what constitutes the nation, the society. There can be no inconsistency between the Constitution and that which forms our spiritual heritage. After all, "Polishness", the Polish character are a kind of possession, a kind of spiritual inheritance ... I mention this in the context of my reflections on ecumenical matters ... It is appropriate specifically with respect to these two matters: prayers for unity among Christians, striving for unity among Christians, the ecumenical movement and the freedom of religion, meaning respect for the rights of individuals, not concessions (!) made by some group for the people of faith, but respect for the rights of individuals (!), for the rights of the human spirit, because these two realities grow from the same root.

January 26 — 4:00 p.m., Zawoja, concelebrated Mass, *Oplatek*[7] with priests from the class of 1973 * January 27 — 10:00 a.m., at the residence, he presides at a conference of priests — heads of deaneries of the Archdiocese of Krakow. Issues discussed included pastoral ministry during the Holy Year and its continuation, the preparations for the celebrations of the 600th anniversary of the shrine at Jasna Gora, problems associated with the planned changes to legislation at the country's highest levels, the 25th anniversary of Cardinal Adam Stefan Sapieha's death, activities of the Council of Priests * 5:00 p.m., on the Feast of St. Angela Merici he celebrated Mass at the Chapel of the Ursuline Sisters. Then, a jubilee celebration (100th anniversary of the convent) which

---

[7] See Glossary.

included singing of Christmas carols at the convent refectory and an expanded artistic program featuring some of the former students from Bursa Akademicka {a student dormitory in Krakow} who participated many times in closed retreats led by the Cardinal in the 1950's; later — an agape. (From the chronicles of the Ursuline Convent) * January 28 — 10:30 a.m., residence, conference of the bishops of the Metropolitan See of Krakow, *Oplatek* * 3:00 p.m., a visit from the Consul of the United States * 5:00 p.m., Mass with homily for the alumnae of a nursing course, *Oplatek*, singing of Christmas carols by the "little choir" * January 29 — he participated in the Council of the Pontifical Department of Theology, during which Rev. Dr. Tadeusz Pieronek presented his dissertation in the field of canon law to qualify himself for assistant professorship. In his address, the Cardinal expressed his happiness at the increase in the number of independent academic workers, something he had always fostered. (From the minutes of the Council of the Department) * January 29 — 4:00 p.m., funeral of Fr. Stanislaw Zadlo (90 years old) in Sicniawa:

> It was already at the very beginning of my ministry as a bishop that I met Fr. Zadlo. I participated in the golden jubilee of his priesthood in Rajcza; most of my contacts with him go back to the time when he was dean of the great deanery of Zywiec, before the recent divisions. And throughout all these meetings, the person of the deceased Monsignor remained deep in my memory and in my heart ... I remember several conversations that I had with him when he was dean. He was always very concerned, always mindful of all his brother priests in the deanery and of everyone, even in the most distant parishes ... What always struck me about the deceased was a sense of sobriety, objectivity, soundness of judgment, together with a great sense of peace and serenity of spirit. He was a man of insight, understanding and intelligence. He always had a passion for books, reading, reflection ... This morning we spoke of him with Bishop Julian Groblicki, and we recalled this event, which took place in Rajcza in November of 1966, during the time of the Millennium celebrations in the Zywiec deanery. After the conclusion of the Mass, we walked outside where a cross had been erected to commemorate the one thousand years of Christianity in Poland. This cross had been blessed; later we kissed this sign of our redemption. We remember how our late pastor from Rajcza, who is resting here today, knelt to embrace the cross; he grasped the cross in his arms and held it for a long time. His action was exceptional. This certainly was not just some external gesture, it flowed from the depth of his soul. From the depth which the crucified Christ formed by his divine and human mystery since the moment of baptism.

Same day — 7:30 p.m., Borek Falecki, religious education room, *Oplatek* with former employees of Solvay * January 30 — at 3 p.m., residence, visit of the French Consul * 7:30 p.m., Theological Seminary, a Christmastime pastoral visit * Same day — he orders that prayers for the intention of the Homeland be said in all churches of the archdiocese. This directive came about as a result of the proposed changes in the text of the Constitution of the Polish People's Republic * January 31 — 12 noon, a session of bishops * 7 p.m., residence, *Oplatek* for academics.

February 1-2 — A visit of the parish of Pleszow * February 1 — 12 noon, Lubocza, blessing of the Candlemas candles * 7 p.m., residence chapel, concelebrated Mass, homily, *Oplatek* for lawyers * February 2 — 10:45 a.m., Krzeslawice * 5:00 p.m., Wzgorza Krzeslawickie, blessing of candles * 8 p.m., residence chapel, Mass and singing of Christmas carols with the *Srodowisko*[8] * February 3-5 — residence chapel, private Masses * February 4 — 1 p.m. , residence chapel, the swearing in of pastors * February 5-6 — Zakopane-Jaszczurowka, the Ursuline Sisters. He arrived, unannounced, with Rev. T. Styczen. Skiing * February 7 — Krakow, residence, symposium on the topic of sobriety. Opening address of the working session:

> I would like to share with you, ladies and gentlemen, my position on this matter and to tell you with what feeling I undertake this work, because, ultimately, it is the bishop who undertakes this ministry. So, my position is the following: we must not abandon any area of the Church's mission in Poland, in the Polish pastoral ministry, dealing with faith and morality, regardless of how difficult that area might be. We must not abandon this. For example, a very difficult area is that of family life, of the responsibility for life, of chastity within marriage and prior to marriage. This is undoubtedly a difficult area. The facts which are accumulating, the facts which are controlled, not all, but certainly a large number of them, are decidedly against us, meaning against the Gospels, against the Church and against the pastoral ministry. But we continue to go out and confront this issue and this area of Polish life; we face it and we don't say or think that this is a lost cause. We must never write anything off as a loss, because this would mean being unfaithful to Christ. Perhaps we do not accomplish all that much, but the fact remains that we exist, that we speak the truth; from the practical point of view we have certain tools, certain means of action like the family ministry ... However, when it comes to the ministry of sobriety, I have a feeling as a bishop, that this area is left neglected. Which is to say that the means which we have employed thus far are not sufficient, are out of proportion ... We do not want to abandon this area, one of the more difficult areas of Polish life, because in so doing we would be unfaithful to the Gospels and to Christ. Instead, we must confront it. Perhaps this matter seems difficult and hopeless, just as other spheres {aspects} of our Polish lives do. All the same, we must undertake them and in such a way that we will be convinced that what we are doing is serious, that it is effective. It is well-known that counteracting addictions and habits of a person is very difficult. But the Church and, above all, the priests must consciously do everything in this area that can be done under the given conditions.

February 7-8 — At the Dominican monastery — Second academic

---

[8] See Glossary.

session for Polish physicians and theologians (Krakow) on the topic: "Special Aspects of the Problem of Birth Control." Lectures by Cardinal Wojtyla — *Personalistic Concept of Man*; Rev. Dr. Karol Meissner, Rev. Dr. Stanislaw Nowak, Bishop Stanislaw Smolenski, Prof. Dr. Paul Chauchard, Dr. Wanda Poltawska * February 7 — opening address by Cardinal Wojtyla:

> Both of these issues [relating to the topic of the current session and that of May 8-9, 1975] belong to the broader area of Catholic ethics of married and family life. Catholic, meaning conforming to the norms embodied in the Revelation and in God's laws taught by the Church. [The list of participants of this session] points out the direction of our work. Since we are dealing with the people who strive to reveal the principles of Catholic ethics in the areas of married life and family life to others, and to advise others in light of these principles ... this session will concentrate on how to address these matters even better, how to present them more clearly, how to give more effective counsel in this sphere ... Last year's academic session of our Institute has greatly encouraged its organizers to participate in today's meeting.

Same day — 8 p.m., concelebrated Mass for the participants of the session * February 8 — 1 p.m., Mass for the participants of the session, homily:

> It is my wish that this entire, enormous and invisible workshop, which you brought here today, become an altar, just as moments ago this table standing here, our workbench, became an altar. Such is the unity of human and divine matters in Jesus Christ.

The same day — a lecture: *Personalistic Idea of an Individual.*

> 1. Introduction from the point of view of the Magisterium[9] ... The matter of the appropriate relationship between love and fertility in marriage was one of the topics undertaken by the Second Vatican Council ... This subject was discussed in a more precise detail in the 1968 encyclical by the present pope, Paul VI, *Humanae vitae* ...
>
> The idea of man as a person must be presented and expounded in close relation to this topic ... ever since my time at the university, I have been involved in work on the issue of man as a person ... I do not [however] intend to present or expound my "personalistic idea," but to reveal the truth about man as a person which lies at the foundation of the Church's teaching on the subject of marriage.
>
> 2. Man and woman, as persons united by the covenant of marriage (Personalistic character of the gift of one's self and of the received gift).
>
> 3. The true realization of who one is as a person and the internal orderliness of married life:
>
> The negative stand of the Church on contraception is founded on the conviction that an indissoluble relationship exists between the twofold purpose of marital relations, namely, the strengthening of unity and the role of parenthood.

[9] The Church's teaching.

The same day — the Cardinal's proclamation about respectful observance of Lent was read in all the churches of the archdiocese. He made an appeal to the youth, parents and educators that there would be no dance parties organized during Lent * February 9-15 — Zakopane-Jaszczurowka, private Mass at the Chapel of the Ursuline Sisters, and preparation of the Vatican retreat. Solitary ski trips, among others to Poronin. Fr. T. Styczen joins him on February 12 * February 16 — 12 noon, residence, session of the Curia * February 17 — 10 a.m., Warsaw, Main Council of the Polish Episcopate * February 18-19 — 10 a.m., Warsaw, 151st plenary conference of the Polish Episcopate * February 20-25 — Krakow, residence, before noon, preparations for the Vatican retreat * February 20 — 2 p.m., residence, visit of Prof. J. Pieper * 5 p.m., residence chapel, Mass for the intention of the Rybicki family * 6 p.m., residence, seminar in moral theology * February 21 — 4 p.m., residence chapel, wedding, Mass with homily.

February 21 — A letter from the Cardinal to the custodian of the shrine in Kalwaria Zebrzydowska:

> **I would like to turn to you with a special request. This year, the Holy Father entrusted me with the task of conducting the Lenten retreat at the Roman Curia from March 7 to 14. The time frame is relatively short which does not give me too much time for preparation, as I only received the invitation on February 14. In connection with this, I turn to Fr. Gwardian with a request for prayers at the feet of the Mother of God in Kalwaria, both during the time of preparation and the retreat itself. I thank everyone in advance for their prayers at the Shrine and I extend fraternal greetings to all. Karol Cardinal Wojtyla.**

February 23 — 10 a.m., Silesian Seminary, regional conference * February 24-Mar 4 — Regional pastoral congregations dedicated to the issues of the ministry of sobriety were held in five regions of the archdiocese. At the first congregation in Krakow, the Cardinal said, among others, that "the activity to promote sobriety is mandated by the mission of the Church, whose role is to serve man and his nation; it is mandated by the civic mission of pastoral work. We undertake this subject so that we would not be tempted to leave it at the periphery of our attention because it is difficult, thankless and unattractive." * February 24 — 8:30 a.m., the residence, meetings of the Committee for Seminaries and the Committee for Education * 7:30 p.m., meeting with *Tygodnik Powszechny* * February 25 — 1:00 p.m., Chapel of the Daughters of Charity (Warszawska Street), concelebrated Mass, sermon, meeting with the youth ministry and the liturgical ministry * Same day — he sent a letter to the Council of the Pontifical department of Theology in the matter of the Congress of Polish Theologians in Krakow — Mogila (Sept. 14-16, 1976). He asked for help in organizing the congress. He proposed the establishment of a Department of Philosophy at the Pontifical Department of Theology in Krakow. For several years he had wanted to establish cooperation with the Department of Philosophy of the Jesuit Fathers; when his efforts did not produce results, he decided to establish a separate one, indicating the need for it in Krakow. He was concerned above all with the education of the large numbers of clergy in southern Poland. (From the minutes of the Council of the Department) * February 26-28 — Zakopane-Jaszczurowka, the Ursuline Sisters, preparation of the Vatican retreat * February 29 — 7:30 a.m., Theological Seminary (at 4 Manifestu Lipcowego Street), concelebrated Mass, sermon, visit * 12:30 p.m., Theological Seminary (at 8 Podzamcze Street), lunch, visit * 5:30 p.m., at W. P., Mass with sermon.

March 1 — 12:00 noon, residence, a session of the bishops * 4:00 p.m., departure for Rome via Warsaw * March 2-6 — Rome, Polish College, concelebrated Masses, preparation for a retreat * March 6 — Mentorella * March 7 — 10:30 a.m., St. Peter's Basilica, 100th anniversary of the birth of the Servant of God, Pius XII * 6:30 p.m., Chapel of St. Mathilda, beginning of the Vatican retreat, opening sermon * March 8-12, — 7:00 a.m., San Carlo Chapel, concelebrated Masses at 9:00 a.m., 11:00 a.m., 5:00 p.m., St. Mathilda's Chapel, conferences, 6:00 p.m. — meditations * March 13 — 9:00 a.m., St. Mathilda's Chapel, conference for the conclusion of the retreat * 12:00 noon, an audience with the Holy Father Paul VI. (The Polish text of the Vatican retreat was published under the title *Znak, ktoremu sprzeciwiac sie beda,*[10] Pallottinum, Poznan — Warsaw 1976, II edition Paris 1980.) * March 14-16 — Polish College, private concelebrated Mass * March 14 — Mentorella * March 16 — Return to Krakow * March 17 — Residence chapel, private concelebrated Mass * Same day — 12:00 noon, residence, session of bishops * March 18 — Residence chapel, private concelebrated Mass * March 19 — 7:00 a.m., Krakow, St. Joseph's Church, Feast of St. Joseph:

> **A home is not just a dwelling, a place where people live. A home is a climate ... It was with good reason that the Son of God spent 30 years of his life in the privacy of his home. By that He wanted to show that a home is a source of strength, a fundamental strength of man ... Today, on the Feast of St. Joseph, let us pray ardently for all Polish homes. Let us pray that this Polish home would not break apart, but come together. Because all of the successes which we express in statistics will mean nothing if the Polish home falls apart. Because man is not for industry, but industry for man. St. Joseph was also a man of labor, but his mission established a proper order in this respect.**

---

[10] "A sign which will be opposed"; in English it was published as *Sign of Contradiction.*

A letter of the same date to the priests of the archdiocese on the issue of the Synod of the Archdiocese: the significance of the Synod's study teams in the work of the Synod, and an appeal to the pastors of parishes which do not yet have study teams, to establish them * March 20-21 — Canonical visitation of the parish of Strumiany * March 22-24 — Residence chapel, private Masses * March 24 — Residence, a session of bishops * 4:00 p.m., seminar in moral theology * March 25 — 11:00 a.m., residence, session of the Curia * March 26 — Warsaw, a meeting with the Primate, departure for Rome, participation in the works of the Roman Congregation pro Institutione Catholica * March 27 — Rome, Polish College, concelebrated Mass * March 27 — 5:00 p.m., Gregorianum, *Introduzione del punto di visita di una fenomenologia dell'azione*: introduction to the discussion during the session on the topic "I gradi dell'essere nella fenomenologia e nella metafisica classica" * March 28 — 10:00 a.m., Mass at the Church of St. Stanislaw:

> **There are two major dimensions of this truth: the human dimension and the national dimension ... This awareness has been our inspiration and continues to be our inspiration. It has been our inspiration in the recent months, when the Polish Episcopate spoke up repeatedly in the matter, well known around the world, of changes to the Constitution of our country. The Episcopate presented memoranda, spoke through the bishops from the pulpits. And it all flowed from one source: from our awareness of the heritage that we, people, we Poles, share with Jesus Christ. Man must not be diminished! A Pole must not be diminished! Because there is some measure of man and of a Pole that has been established once and for all by God, when He gave us His Son.**

* On the same day — 5:00 p.m., Gregorianum — he delivered a lecture.

March 29 — 7:00 a.m., Chapel of the Polish College, private concelebrated Mass, later a meeting with Cardinal Seper, Cardinal Garrone and Archbishop Poggi * March 30 — Congregation pro Institutione Catholica — a visit with Cardinal Garrone, the Secretariat of the State — a visit with Cardinal Villot * March 31 — 7:00 a.m., Chapel of the Albertine Sisters, concelebrated Mass, sermon on the day of prayers for the beatification of Brother Albert * Congregation pro Institutione Catholica * Archbishop Agostino Casaroli.

April 1 — Chapel of the Polish College, concelebrated Mass * 11:00 a.m., at Bishop Rubin's * 5:00 p.m., St. Stanislaw's Church, Holy Hour * 6:00 p.m., Angelicum, "Incontri culturali," lecture * April 2 — Return to Krakow * April 3-4 — Canonical visitation of the parish of Krzczonow * April 3 — Rome, the Vatican Radio broadcast his statement: The current tasks of the Church in Poland * April 6-11 —

Visitation at Wzgorza Krzeslawickie * April 7 — 5:00 p.m., Church of the Holy Cross, concelebrated Mass, sermon for the conclusion of a retreat for artists * April 8 — 9:00 a.m., the Rakowicki cemetery, requiem Mass and funeral of Olgierd Piekarski * April 12 — 7:30 p.m., Church of St. Joseph, concelebrated Mass, retreat for lawyers * April 13 — 7:00 a.m., Zakopane, Chapel of the Ursuline Sisters, Mass * April 14 — 4:00 p.m., Wawel Cathedral, Tenebrae * 7:30 p.m., Church of the Felician Sisters, concelebrated Mass, sermon for the conclusion of a retreat for physicians * April 15 — Holy Thursday, Wawel Cathedral, concelebrated Mass with the bishops and over 100 diocesan and religious priests, blessing of the Holy Chrism; homily, after the homily a renewal of vows by the priests * Same day — 5:00 p.m., Wawel Cathedral, Mass of the Last Supper of Our Lord * Same day — pastoral and canonical visitation at Wzgorza Krzeslawickie, where there was no church building, only a canopy over the altar. "Cold, slush, mud. His Eminence the Cardinal arrived here with all the seminarians of the Krakow Seminary on Holy Thursday. The purpose of this visit was the Adoration of the Blessed Sacrament. This adoration left an overwhelming impression." (Rev. Jakub Gil) * April 16 — 8:00 a.m., Wawel Cathedral, Tenebrae, Prayer of the Hours * 11:00 a.m., Church of the Franciscans, Stations of the Cross with the seminarians of the Theological Seminary * 5:00 p.m., Wawel Cathedral, Liturgy of Good Friday * April 17 — 8:00 a.m., Wawel Cathedral, Tenebrae * 11:00 a.m. — 1:00 p.m., residence, Easter greetings from the sisters, priests, Metropolitan Chapter, employees of the Curia. A response to the Easter greetings sent by Bishop Groblicki on behalf of the clergy of the Archdiocese of Krakow, with reference to the retreat he had preached at the Vatican:

We remember the Easter of 1946 ... when we could finally enter the Cathedral, and we could bring a great statesman of our country and of our Church, our beloved Prince Archbishop, attired in the red robes of a Cardinal, into this Cathedral. All of Krakow remembers that day; I myself was still a seminarian and I had no idea that after a number of years I would inherit this bishop's seat and this Metropolitan See from him ... I thank you for reminding us of this great figure who continues to illuminate our paths, the life of our Archdiocese, especially the life of priests; because that was the special secret of the Prince Cardinal, his closeness to the priests. I remember how, at the funeral, the Primate, in his long eulogy about the deceased, posed this question to the priests: "Tell me, why did you love him so much? For what did you love him so much?" And we all carry this within us; I also carry some part of this love which the clergy of Krakow and the Archdiocese felt for the Prince Cardinal Adam Stefan Sapieha; this love will remain in our souls forever. And that is what we want to express on the 25th anniversary of his death ...

Regarding my retreat at the Vatican for the Holy Father and his closest co-workers, I treated it first of all as a service, a very honorable one, but at the same time, I must admit, a very strenuous ... service. It arose from the providential circumstance which causes the Church in Poland to be not only closely tied with the Apostolic See, but also to be, to a certain extent, particularly necessary to the Apostolic See. Necessary because of its situation, of its difficult experiences and of the witness that, under the care of Our Blessed Mother it bears, thank God, in the midst of those experiences. So I tried to convey all of this there as best I could, and to express it. And I think that it bore fruit, it hit the mark. After all, you as priests or retreat masters know when our word reaches our listeners and when it does not. I think that what I said during this retreat, did reach my audience, that it was somehow necessary ... As I say this, I see before me the figure of the Holy Father, by now so tired, so worn down by life, by the experiences of the Church, even to some degree sickly, his legs especially are giving him trouble ... But when I speak of the Holy Father in this context, I must add that ... towards the end of March certain events took place which deeply shook public opinion within the Church. The Holy Father was painfully offended, personally offended, by a French publicist; this offense undoubtedly came about as a result of the last document of the Aposolic See, by the congregation Doctrina Fidei, *Personae Humanae*[11].

Yesterday, the thought came to me while I was praying with the seminarians at the Church of the Franciscans, during the Way of the Cross, to offer this Way of the Cross for the intention of the Holy Father, in unity with him, and to notify him of this. And yesterday I sent such a telegram to the Apostolic See ... Since we have, in our history, entered deeply into the experiences of Good Friday, therefore the Sunday of the Resurrection comes to life within us, in Poland as a nation. And I think that this helps, that this has really helped us ... to deal with all of these actions relating to the Constitution of our country which we felt were a danger to us, a danger to our Polish character, to Poland, to the nation and its undeniable rights, as well as to the human person and its undeniable rights. And we, the Polish Episcopate, did everything we could to represent these matters ... from the point of view of bishops and shepherds, the teachers of truth. I feel that these our efforts achieved certain results, certain, but incomplete. That is why this matter is still before us ... It is good that we can draw support in this matter from ... this mystery of Easter, in which the human rights of man and nation are contained.

5:00 p.m., Wawel Cathedral, Resurrection Mass: "... And Poland has risen from the dead. And she carries within herself the strength which flows from this faith, which is shared like inspiration not only by the spirits of the great leaders and poets who rest here, but by the entire Polish nation." * April 18 — 6:00 a.m., Easter Sunday, Nowa Huta — Wzgorza Krzeslawickie:

We feel the need to go forth with the Blessed Sacrament, in which Christ is truly present, to go forth into the roads and streets ... So that we might proclaim the great truth of the Gospel, of the Good News, to all of the houses and streets, and to the great industrial complex which stretches out below, and to all of Nowa Huta, which is a new city of people of faith.

---

[11] Personae Humanae: the title of the document in English is *Declaration on Certain Problems of Sexual Ethics*.

10:00 a.m., Feast of the Resurrection of Our Lord, Wawel Cathedral:

> I remember a conversation which I had here at Wawel, at the residence of the state authorities, over a dozen years ago. The matter concerned the construction of a church in Nowa Huta-Bienczyce. The person with whom I was speaking, a high representative of the government, directed the conversation towards man's longing to live beyond the bounds of death; a longing to life, a longing to prolong life, a feeling of the insufficiency of that life which is bounded by the limits of birth and death. This, he said, is an inner truth of man. But, after all, this longing can be fulfilled only to the extent that man remains in the memory of others ... This is what he said; I must say that we conducted this conversation with a great mutual respect for each other's outlook on life and for each other's convictions.

On the same day — he confers the "Pro Ecclesia et Pontifice" distinction upon the choir of Wawel Cathedral. Entry in the chronicle:

> **Krakow, Wawel, April 18, 1976. The Feast of the Resurrection of Our Lord.**
>
> Sincere congratulations to the Choir of Wawel Cathedral on the occasion of receiving the "Pro Ecclesia et Pontifice" distinction which I had the honor to confer today, wishing you further years in the service of God and the Church through the love of church music in its unique beauty.
>
> **Karol Cardinal Wojtyla**
> **Metropolitan of Krakow**

signed also: Bishop Julian Groblicki, Rev. Bogdan Niemczewski (Dean of the Chapter), Rev. Eugeniusz Florkowski, Rev. Kazimierz Figlewicz, Rev. Franciszek Walancik, Rev. Czeslaw Obtulowicz, Rev. Jozef Szczotkowski, Rev. Teofil Kurowski.

April 19 — Easter Monday, 10:00 a.m., Szczyrk, Mass and sermon, Sacrament of Confirmation:

> The efforts undertaken by the various communities and parishes of our Archdiocese to obtain permission to build new churches now number around 100 ... And one of the reasons I come here today is to bear special witness to the importance of this matter, before you, and before the state authorities, before the authorities of Bielsko, so that everyone may understand that this is our common cause which unites us as believers in the Risen Christ ... It was not possible to hide the truth that Christ rose from the dead. We had to make it known, we had to proclaim it, we had to bear witness to it!

April 20 — 8:00 a.m., Zakopane, the Ursuline Sisters, private Mass * April 21 — 6:30 p.m., residence chapel, Mass on the wedding anniversary of Mr. & Mrs. Hennel * April 22 — 10:00 a.m., residence, a meeting with members of the youth ministry and the ministry of the liturgical service of the altar * 4:00 p.m., residence, meeting with the synodal Marian team * 7:00 p.m., meeting with the editoral team of *Tygodnik Powszechny* * April 23 — 7:00 a.m., Church of St. Wojciech

{Adalbert}, Mass with sermon on the eve of the Feast of St. Wojciech * 10:30 a.m., residence, meeting of priests before the celebrations in honor of St. Stanislaw * 6:30 p.m., Zakopane — "Ksiezowka", concelebrated Mass on the 10th anniversary of priesthood * April 24 — 7:00 a.m., residence chapel, Mass for the late J. Gierula and J. Ciesielski * Same day — 7:00 p.m., Gniezno, vespers, procession, sermon * April 25 — 9:30 a.m., Gniezno, Pontifical Mass, procession * 7:00 p.m., Opole, a visit with Bishop Franciszek Jop * April 26 — 10:00 a.m., sermon at the Church of the Bernardine Fathers in Krakow on the occasion of the 750th anniversary of the death of St. Francis of Assisi, for the beginning of a symposium:

> I think that we must pray very hard for a St. Francis of our times. Maybe not just for one, maybe for very many. We live in an age in which the Second Vatican Council has revealed the depth and width of the dimension of the People of God. So perhaps it is necessary in our democratic times that Francis should become the profile of us all: of the entire Church in Poland ...
>
> A word for the beginning of deliberations: Now I want to express my wishes as a bishop: I wish you, esteemed brothers and sisters, that the content of this academic symposium have a pastoral meaning and effect. That it may help us to recreate, in these our times, the wondrous mystery of St. Francis. To gain the world's attention anew, as he did in his lifetime, and as he continues to do in many subsequent generations and epochs. To convince the world of the truth of the Gospel, and to testify that only He who was the center of St. Francis's life carries with Him the secret of true and everlasting love of the world and of man. We wish you these fruits in your souls and in your work. The fruits which are awaited by the Church in our Homeland and by the entire Universal Church.

* Participation in the Franciscan symposium * Same day — 4:30 p.m., residence, meeting of the Council of the Pontifical Department of Theology * April 27 — Warsaw, Main Council of the Polish Episcopate * April 28-29 — Warsaw, 152nd plenary conference of the Polish Episcopate * April 30 — 9:15 a.m., Krakow, residence, participated (as a reviewer) in the defense of a doctoral thesis by Rev. Franciszek Plonka * 2:00 p.m., Zywiec, sermon to graduating secondary-school students:

> Man matures also, and above all, to friendship with God ... You have gone in groups to Jasna Gora, because that is such a well-proven trail of Polish hearts ... I wish to emphasize this here in a special way, because in the past the youth of Zywiec, specifically those graduating from secondary school, have been able, at the time of graduation, to defend their right to this pilgrimage ... Seek out the friendship with Christ through His Mother.

Same day — 7:30 p.m., Krakow, the Mariacki Basilica, sermon to graduating secondary-school students:

> **At this moment, you should feel a deep sense of indebtedness. You have taken on multiple debts ... I will pray together with you ... so that you may realize your indebtedness and have the willingness and the ability to repay this debt which you have, that you may have the ability to reciprocate and pass along the goodness which you carry within you and which you have inherited from people, from your parents, from your Homeland, from the Church, from Jesus Christ, from God Himself.**

Same day — 8:30 p.m., Club of Catholic Intellectuals, "swiecone" {Easter social}, greetings.

May 1-2 — Visitation of the parish of Pawlikowice. During the visitation (on the 25th anniversary of the parish), to married couples:

> **Yes, it has been 70 years since you started to organize the community of St. Michael here, at this place, the community which, from the very beginning, has undertaken the task of evangelical service, of working for the youth ... As the Bishop of Krakow I wish to express my great joy that your congregation has found its place here, within the Archdiocese of Krakow.**
>
> **[Sermon to children and the youth:] We are nourished by the Word of God, just as people, a family, gathering around a table, at a meal, is also nourished by words. People share good human words with one another.**

Same day — a pastoral letter before the celebrations in honor of St. Stanislaw.

May 3[12] — 11:00 a.m., Jasna Gora, concelebrated Mass * There — 4:00 - 5:40 p.m., a meeting of the subcommittee (Committee for Pastoral Ministry), on the matter of a long range, strategic pastoral program — Cardinal Wojtyla, Bishop Stroba and Bishop Tokarczuk, Rev. Rector Majka, Rev. Dr. Kocylowski, Rev. Bijak; Bishop Miziolek was absent due to illness. Lecture prepared by Rev. Majka. In the discussion, Cardinal Wojtyla underscores the importance of the issue relating to the structure of the parish. (From the minutes of the Committee) * 7:00 p.m., participated in the Holy Mass * May 4 — 7:00 a.m., Jasna Gora, Chapel of Our Lady, concelebrated Mass, sermon * 9:00 a.m., residence of the bishop, meeting of the Episcopate's Committee for Pastoral Ministry. Report from the meeting of the subcommittee (May 3, 1976). Discussion of the declaration by the Congregation for the Doctrine of the Faith of December 29, 1975 — Bishop S. Smolenski. Lecture on the state of education in Poland — Bishop J. Stroba. The attitude of the mass media towards the subject of sex and sexuality (Bishop J. Jez); Rev. Prof. J. Chowanczak — situation among the youth,

---

[12] See Glossary.

pastoral aspects. In the discussion, Cardinal Wojtyla stated that there is no overt opposition here in Poland, as is the case in the West, to *Humanae vitae*, but we must consider whether there is covert opposition. There is a need for the Church to expound the issue, to prepare a letter, to provide moral theologians, priests, laity with full information ... A decision was made to send a memorandum to the government, to issue a pastoral letter on the moral danger threatening our society, to discuss the declaration of the Congregation at the annual convention of moral theologians, to develop pastoral aides, to organize catechetic courses on this matter, to remind society about excommunication for abortions. Further in the meeting, matters pertaining to the pastoral and preaching programs were discussed. * Same day — in Libiaz, he spoke at the coffin of the late Rev. Kazimierz Pajak, vicar of the parish there (near Chrzanow) * May 5 — 10:00 a.m., residence, a conference of priests — heads of deaneries of the Archdiocese of Krakow. The subjects of the discussion were the Krakow Synod, celebrations in honor of St. Stanislaw, observances of the 25th anniversary of Cardinal Sapieha's death, sobriety, parish pastoral councils, the youth ministry * 6:30 p.m., residence chapel, private Mass * 7:30 p.m., residence, session on the subject of the conference of the World Council of Churches in Nairobi * May 6 — 3:00 p.m., Kalwaria Zebrzydowska, "little paths"[13] * May 7 — Unveiled the monument of Prince Cardinal Adam Stefan Sapieha, with wide participation by the clergy and the community of Krakow. The ceremony began with a Mass at the Franciscan Basilica, which he concelebrated with Bishop S. Smolenski and Bishop J. Pietraszko. A bronze sculpture was placed in the church yard near the Franciscan Basilica.

> **Today we fulfill our obligation to history by unveiling a monument to a great son of the Polish nation, a hero of the dark night of the occupation, a benefactor of the poor, Prince Cardinal Adam Stefan Sapieha, on the 25th anniversary of his death ... The artist of the monument is the late sculptor August Zamoyski ... Several years ago, he came to me with the proposal to sculpt the figure of the late Prince Cardinal ... But he admitted to me from the outset that he wished to express a single leading idea in this work. That idea was prayer ... After all, he was a great son of his Homeland; firm in difficult moments, courageous beyond any norms, an exceptional son of his Homeland, an exceptional statesman of history and of Poland.**

May 8 — Feast of St. Stanislaw. In the morning, at Wawel Cathedral, by the tomb of St. Stanislaw, he ordained the alumni of the Krakow Seminary to the diaconate * 11:00 a.m., auditorium of the Seminary, an open session of the Pontifical Department of Theology in honor of Cardinal Sapieha * 4:30 p.m., 5th plenary meeting of the

---

[13] A local form of devotion, consisting of Stations of the Cross along pathways in the park.

Pastoral Synod of the Archdiocese of Krakow. As in previous meetings, the representatives of the Archdiocese of Gniezno participated. Main topic: participation of the Church of Krakow in the universal mission of Christ: six reports. An outline of the subject of the participation in the priestly mission of Christ was also presented. Cardinal Wojtyla presides, delivered an inaugural address and a homily during Mass.

From the address:

In order to provide some clear organizing principles for the concluding activities of the Synod, activities which are to lead to the final documents, we have chosen ... this truth and this vision: the vision of Christ who fulfills His mission within the People of God, with their active participation.

From the homily:

Jesus Christ, Priest, Prophet, and King; He is the Good Shepherd who told us that He was the Good Shepherd, and in parables, He told us why He was ...

We are grateful that 900 years ago He shared the secret of the Good Shepherd with the Bishop of the Church of Krakow, Stanislaw ... above all, that He allowed Stanislaw to lay down his life for his sheep. [Through the Synod] we wish to take up the pastoral concern of Jesus Christ, a concern which is always the same, yet always new ... always going forth to meet the needs of new times ...

I wish to thank you for that portion of your lives which you sacrifice for the Synod ... I wish ... to ask that you persist in your efforts ... That you continue to shape this new life of the Church of Krakow, which is indispensable in these times in which the Universal Church of Christ has also begun to seek its new shape. This new shape is not different, but it is new. It is new while maintaining its essential identity. And what is more: it is the shape of the future ... The path to the future is always the path of life. We also want to live, despite all obstacles, despite all attempts, so it seems, against that life. We want to live the authentic, Christian, Polish life, that life which was begun by the Baptism of Poland in Gniezno. That life, which was affirmed and strengthened in a particular way by St. Stanislaw's sacrifice.

May 9 — 8:30 a.m., Wawel Cathedral, laying of a wreath at the tomb of Tadeusz Kosciuszko by an American delegation * Same day — main celebrations in honor of St. Stanislaw, the Bishop of Krakow; a procession from Wawel to Skalka with a delegation of the Episcopate of the United States: Archbishop of Cincinnati Joseph L. Bernardin, President of the National Conference of Catholic Bishops in the U.S.A.; Bishop James S. Rausch, Secretary General of the U.S. Episcopate, along with accompanying clergy and representatives of American Polonia, as well as Bishop Wladyslaw Rubin, Secretary General of the Synod of Bishops; Archbishop Luigi Poggi, representative of the Apostolic See. Cardinal Wojtyla delivered a speech of welcome at Skalka. The homily was delivered by the Primate. From the welcome: "Today, with these relics, the Church of Krakow brings together its distant and not so distant past" * Same day — a communique to the Archdiocese on the celebrations, planned for May 16 in Lipnica Murowana, in honor of the Blessed Maria Teresa Ledochowska * May 10 — 12:00 noon, a farewell to the guests from the United States (J. L. Bernardin, J. S. Rausch) * 2:30 p.m., residence, a meeting with speakers for the Congress of Theologians.

May 11 — Krakow, Franciszkanska Street, meeting of the Committee for Catholic Education with the chairmen of the professors' sections; reports by the chairmen of the sections, extensive discussion, a short report by Rev. Marian Jaworski on the upcoming Congress of Theologians (to be held at the Cistercian Abbey in Mogila). In the afternoon a meeting of the Committee in closed session. In summarizing the discussion on the reception of the Second Vatican Council in Poland, the Cardinal said: The pessimistic report by the speaker (Rev. B. Inlender) had a positive result because of the discussion it provoked. The degree to which the teachings of the Vatican Council were accepted is still an open matter. On the matter of post-seminary studies: it would be appropriate to study the matter and bring some order — but not too much — because each particular situation is colored by its own needs. (From the minutes of the Committee) * May 12 — Residence, a meeting of the Educational Council of the Polish Episcopate. Discussions concerned "the functioning of the regulations in the matter of evaluating admissions of Ph.D.'s to assistant professorship by the Educational Council, and the conferment of titles of ordinary and extraordinary professors." Further discussions on the issues relating to the Second Congress of Polish Theologians to be held Sept. 14-16, 1976. "The Cardinal analyzed the text of the regulations, paying particular attention to its main resolutions" (the regulations were approved at the 151st plenary conference of the Polish Episcopate on February 18, 1976) * 8:00 p.m., residence, the Editorial Committee of the Polish Theological Society.

May 13 — Warsaw, 11:00 a.m., Niepokalanow, he participated in a conference of major superiors of the religious orders of men * 6:00 p.m., a visit to Laski[14] * May 14 — Warsaw, a meeting of the delegation of the Polish Episcopate before the Eucharistic Congress in Philadelphia * 3:00 p.m., a meeting with the representatives of the National Conference of Catholic Bishops in the U.S.A.; issues relating to Polonia * May 15 — 11:00 a.m., Krakow, residence, session of bishops * 3:30 p.m., residence, a visit by Prof. Rene * Same day — 6:00 p.m., Tarnow, concelebrated Mass, sermon during the celebrations of

---

[14] An institution for the blind.

Blessed Maria Teresa Ledochowska * May 16 — 7:00 a.m., residence chapel, private concelebrated Mass * 11:00 a.m., Lipnica Murowana, introductory remarks during the nationwide celebrations in honor of Blessed Maria Teresa Ledochowska * 8:00 p.m., Krakow, "day of song" organized by the youth of the Parish of the Most Sacred Savior * May 17 — 7:30 p.m., residence chapel, Mass and sermon, First Holy Communion of Tadeusz Kakol * May 18 — residence, plenary meeting of the Council of Priests of the Archdiocese of Krakow. It was begun with a concelebrated Mass in the chapel. The topic of the discussion was the issue of coexistence and cooperation * 4:00 p.m., residence, Curia session of bishops * May 19 — Trzebinia, during the main celebrations of the 75th anniversary of the Society of the Divine Savior {Salvatorian Fathers and Brothers} in Poland, the Cardinal concelebrated Mass with the priests of the Trzebinia deanery and the Salvatorians. The sermon was delivered by the Primate {Wyszynski} * Same day — 5:30 p.m., Zakopane — "Ksiezowka," concelebrated Mass with priests of the class of 1973 * May 20 —10:00 a.m., residence, meeting with members of the academic ministry * 3:00 p.m., session of bishops * 6:00 p.m., meeting with E. Piszek (from American Polonia) * May 21-22 — Lublin, KUL, he participated in a meeting of the Council of the International Federation of Catholic Universities (FIUC) and in a conference of rectors of the European Catholic Universities, during which he delivered a comprehensive presentation on the situation of the Catholic Church in Poland, with special focus on the state of higher Catholic education * May 22 — 5:00 p.m., Naleczow, concelebrated Mass at the Salvatorian Fathers * May 23 — 9:00 a.m., Wawel, ordination to the priesthood, homily:

> The priesthood is a great mystery of God. The Son of God brought it down to earth; and while keeping it within Himself, He simultaneously shares it with people. He shares it in the Holy Spirit. This is a special gift of the Holy Spirit to man, to the Church: the calling to the priesthood.

Same day — 12:00 noon, Theological Seminary, a farewell ceremony for the new priests * May 23-24 — Visitation in Orawka. Homily for the youth:

> It is well that you pray. Remember that you must continue to learn to pray anew, you must keep learning it, and most important, you must remain in prayer and not allow prayer to be snatched away from you in your life ... For example, today, during this solemn service, I was thinking how much of God's Word was proclaimed, most of all within the liturgy ... This is the great change which has come about in the ten years since the Vatican Council, that the participants in the Mass not only listen to, but also proclaim the Word of God. We must listen in such a way, that the Word of God reaches our souls.

May 24 — 6:00 p.m., Lekawica near Zywiec, concelebrated Mass with priests ordained in 1972, sermon * May 25 — 5:30 p.m., Brzeszcze, concelebrated Mass, sermon, procession on the 100th anniversary of the parish * May 26-27 — Visitation of the parish of Frydman * May 28-29 — Residence, 9:00 a.m., sessions of the Curia * May 28 — 6:00 p.m., at the main liturgical center of the Archdiocese at St. Mark's Church, he performed a solemn benediction of the lectors and coordinators of liturgy, he also presided over the ceremony of acceptance to the various scholae. The benediction was performed during the Mass concelebrated by the Cardinal and the priests from those churches and parishes of Krakow, whose youth participated in the annual Masses along with their parents * Same day — meeting of the Main Committee of the Krakow Synod at Cardinal Wojtyla's residence * May 29-30 — Visitation of the parish of Lopuszna * May 30 — 9:00 a.m., Piekary Slaskie, sermon during the pilgrimage of men:

> **The entire Church in Poland is aware of the fact that the apostolate of the laity should be realized in our homeland, and that it is, in fact, being realized ... If people are being degraded because they are believers and profess Christ, and attend church; if people are barred from academic promotion, that is a scandal! Because science must serve the truth! And we have the right to demand from this place that the Constitution be observed! That the bill of human rights, signed by the government of our country, be respected! The right of civic freedom. It is not permissible to create, under whatever appellation, conditions under which there is a group that is privileged because it claims to embrace atheism, be it out of conviction, or maybe even against its own conscience. And there is a society that has made many contributions, a hard-working, generous society, well-tested in historical crises, which is handicapped because it does not embrace atheism, because human dignity and conscience do not allow it ... The Conference of the Polish Episcopate has long maintained the position that a full and consistent respect for the principle of civic equality, for the principles of the freedom of conscience and the freedom of religion is a fundamental condition of the normalization of relations between the Church and the state. And this is the principle which we place at the foundation of this great cause, a cause of both the Universal Church and the Church in Poland, namely, the cause of the apostolate of the laity. This apostolate has its social dimension. It begins in the family and is expressed in the parish. But it must reach everywhere. It must reach the university, it must also reach the coal mine, it must reach the school and the workplace. We must not create the fiction that all of these are secular, meaning atheistic, institutions, when they are full of the people of faith! Man is at stake here! Man must be respected!**

May 30 — At the bishop's palace before noon, he received a group of former students of the clandestine University, they presented him with a copy of a book *Ne cedat Academia,* containing the history of the clandestine University, and a medal for the 600th anniversary of the Jagiellonian University. Present were: Irena Bajerowa, Maria

Bobrownicka, Janina Garycka, Franciszek Kleszcz, Halina and Tadeusz Kwiatkowski, Danuta Michalowska, Ewa Radlinska, Tadeusz Ulewicz. (Maria Bobrownicka) * Same day —1:00 p.m., Kalwaria Zebrzydowska, "little paths"[15] * Same day — Mass and sermon, Baptism, First Holy Communion of the childern of the *Srodowisko*[16].

June 1 — 10:00 a.m., Krakow, the residence. Third meeting of the Coordinating Committee of the Provincial Synod. Acceptance of the proposal of the statutes and regulations of the Synod. From the statutes (for the full text, see *Notificationes* no. 5 — 6, 1977):

1. The purpose of the Synod ... is to undertake a common activity aimed at the deepening of faith and the revitalization of religious life through the inspirations of the Second Vatican Council, and to do so in all the dioceses of the Metropolitan See.

2. The Synod realizes its purpose through the exchange of information and experiences among the dioceses of the Metropolitan See, and by undertaking common activities according to the guidelines established by the Synod and these statutes.

3. Synod participants, with the right to cast votes, shall be the ordinary bishops and auxiliary bishops of the dioceses. Participants in an advisory capacity shall be the clergy (in observance of Canons 286, par. 3-4), and Catholic lay persons called up by their respective ordinaries, after consultation with the Coordinating Committee of the Synod.

4. The activities of the Provincial Synod shall be directed by the Metropolitan Archbishop of Krakow, in collegial unity with the bishops of the Metropolitan See, based on the work of the Coordinating Committee, Synodal Consulting Teams and the Plenary Assembly of the Synod.

Same day — 4:00 p.m., seminar in moral theology * 6:30 p.m., St. Florian's Church, concelebrated Mass, sermon, meeting with the priests ordained in 1970 * June 2 — 12:00 noon, Theological Seminary (Department of Theology), conclusion of the seminar in patristics[17], concelebrated Mass, sermon * Same day — 5:00 p.m., Makow Podhalanski, during a reunion of priests ordained in 1974:

A priest must radiate joy in his vocation. Such joy has an apostolic meaning, because people are so sad today ... For it is also our calling not to be "of this world" while being in this world, being in the heart of this world, in the fire of all of our problems ... May we not be defeated by the world. May we maintain our initial ardor.

June 3 — 6:00 p.m., Dobczyce, Confirmation:

To bear witness means to profess your faith in such a way that every-one could tell: this is a Christian! Regardless of circumstances ... Sometimes, it is easy for me to do something, when everyone else does the same ... Maybe here, in this parish, everyone does the same ... But maybe

---

[15] A local form of devotion, consisting of Stations of the Cross along pathways in the park.
[16] See Glossary.
[17] Study of the Fathers of the Church.

later you will go someplace ... and there, it will be different than here, in Dobczyce. There, this is not spoken of, there is silence; nobody knows if you are a believer or a nonbeliever, everyone acts the same, somehow neutrally. You are to profess your faith, which means you must always remember that you have been confirmed, that you have been strengthened ... You have been strengthened so that you may be a witness, and not a coward ... Pray for this, because fear often descends on man, and the human spirit, which rises up to God in exalted moments like this one, sometimes hides from God, flees from God, in moments of weakness, in moments of difficulty. Pray that you might always have the strength which is necessary to profess your faith before people.

June 4 — 11:00 a.m., meeting of the Committee for the Apostolate of the Laity. Preparation of a meeting on the topic of apostolic formation (December 4-5, 1976). Discussion on the first draft of the document on formation to Confirmation; discussion on the current state of the apostolate (10th anniversary of the Committee); reports on the Forum (July 1976) in Belgium. Meeting on the issue of the apostolic formation with the invited members of the "Swiatlo i Zycie" {Light and Life} movement * Same day — 6:00 p.m., Ryczow, Confirmation, Mass and sermon * June 5 — 10:00 a.m., residence, opening remarks and sending off of the new priests to their pastoral assignments * June 5-8 — Visitation of the parish of Nowa Biala and the parish of Krempachy * June 6 — 10:00 a.m., Wawel Cathedral, Feast of Pentecost, concelebrated Mass, homily; Cardinal Wojtyla led the renewal of the prayer of the Holy Father Paul VI, of December 8, 1975, to Mary, Mother of the Church, in which the Holy Father dedicated the world to the Blessed Mother * Same day — Kroscienko:

> On the eve of the Feast of Pentecost, on the Feast of Pentecost itself, and on the Feast of Mary, Mother of the Church, a Central Mother "Oasis" {C.O.M.} was held in Kroscienko. It was a prayerful meeting of the diakonia of the movement from all of Poland combined with the acceptance of the mission, receiving of the blessing and of the symbols of the unity of the movement, primarily the formation materials and the candle. In 1973, the Cardinal participated in the C.O.M. on the Feast of Mary, Mother of the Church. This time, it was on the very day of the Feast of Pentecost.
>
> A new, larger chapel under the appellation of Christ the Servant was prepared on Kopia Gorka. During his visit in Kroscienko, Cardinal Wojtyla consecrated the chapel, then he met with the participants of the C.O.M., acquainted himself with the current program of the movement and gave a speech. He spoke of the Church of the Pentecost and of how a man of faith filled with the gifts of the Holy Spirit is an "oasis" in today's world. On the other hand, in light of the growing illegal actions by the authorities, he assured us of the legality of the activities of the "Oasis" retreats, and assured us that the Episcopate will continue to defend that legality.[18]

---

[18] Quote unattributed.

June 8-9 — Visitation of the parish of Lapsze Wyzne * June 9 — Visitation of the parish of Lapsze Nizne * June 10 — 10:00 a.m., Kalwaria Zebrzydowska, "little paths"[19] * June 11 — 7:00 a.m., Przcmysl, chapel at the bishop's residence, private Mass * 10:00 a.m., Main Council of thc Polish Episcopate * June 12 — 10:00 a.m., Przemysl, plenary conference of the Polish Episcopate * June 13 — 600th anniversary jubilee of the Diocese of Przemysl. Cardinal Wojtyla led the solemn concelebrated Mass in front of the cathedral basilica. (Detailed report: "Chronicle of the Przemysl Diocese" 1976, bk. 4, from p. 87) * Same day — Cardinal's appeal before the Feast of Corpus Christi was read in the churches of the archdiocese * June 14 — Krakow, 12:00 noon, residence, meeting of the bishops * 5:00 p.m., residence chapel, concelebrated Mass, reunion of priests ordained in 1946/47 * June 15 — 9:00 a.m., residence chapel, concelebrated Mass, sermon, reunion of pricsts ordaincd in 1945/46 * 3:00 p.m., residence, a visit from Bishop Ernest Tewes from Munich * 4:00 p.m., Council of the Pontifical Department of Theology * 6:00 p.m., Wawel Cathedral, Pontifical Mass for the repose of the soul of Archbishop E. Baziak * June 16 — 8:00 p.m., Kalwaria Zebrzydowska, Chapel of Our Lady, Mass * June 17 — Feast of Corpus Christi. The Cardinal celebrated Mass at the Wawel courtyard, afterwards led a Eucharistic procession through the city streets. He delivered sermons at each of the four altars on the route of the procession:

> **Sermon 1: We live in an age of those who profess the faith ... Today we must also record these contemporary Acta Martyrum, to document those who profess, so that we might encourage one another, so that we know about one another. So that any wrong committed against anyone because of his convictions, because of his faith and conscience, becomes our common cause. Often they hold it against me, that I speak about these matters. But how could I not speak of them? How could I not write about them? And how could I not intervene in them? Every such matter, of each child, each mother, each one of us, whether simple or educated, university professor or university student, every such matter is our common cause. And I, the bishop, must be the first servant of this cause ...**
> **Sermon 2: As we continue this procession, let us pray for all of our brothers living in the districts and suburbs where there is no church ... so that the authorities of our city may understand that serious issues of citizenship are involved here. That the issue here is the respect for real social needs ... Although our procession today will not be able to go to the Market Square, I myself and the priests of Krakow do not rest in our efforts to bring this situation, which is a sign of nothing other than discrimination against the people of faith, to an end ...**

---

[19] A local form of devotion, consisting of Stations of the Cross along pathways in the park.

Sermon 3: It would be better if the agents of censorship did not prey on Church texts, on Catholic publications, but paid more attention to the essential morality, an important foundation of social good ... Materialism alone, consumption alone, is not capable of shaping a strong man and a strong society ... The responsibility for everything that lowers morals, that undermines, that weakens the spirit, this responsibility must be considered in the social dimension, in the dimension of today and tomorrow ...

Sermon 4: The bishops of Poland are continually serving their Homeland and are continually expressing this ... They are also expressing this at present, when we are faced with this important matter of the people who work the land, who feed us, so that their rights, their land, might be respected. We get our inspiration for all of this from the mystery of the Bread.

June 17-18 — Visitation of the parish of Podszkle * June 18 — 1:00 p.m., Trzebinia, a visit with the sick during their retreat * 4:00 p.m., residence, session of the bishops * June 19-23 — Visitation of the parish of Maniowy * June 20 — In an appeal directed to the clergy and the faithful of Krakow, the Cardinal reminded about the 25th anniversary of the dedication of Poland to the Sacred Heart of Jesus, and announced that the jubilee service will be celebrated at the Basilica of the Sacred Heart of Jesus in Krakow. A separate appeal was directed to the men and male youth before their annual pilgrimage to the shrine of Kalwaria Zebrzydowska * June 24-25 — 11:00 a.m., residence, session * June 24 — Chapel of the Ursuline Sisters, he delivered a short lecture on the topic of the Diocesan Higher Catechetic Institute on its 25th anniversary * Same day — Kalwaria Zebrzydowska, Mass * June 25 — 1:00 p.m., residence, Council of the Pontifical Department of Theology * Same day — on the Feast of the Most Sacred Heart of Jesus, concelebrated Mass with the priests of Krakow at the Basilica of the Sacred Heart of Jesus in Krakow. After the Mass, he led a Eucharistic procession outside the Basilica. Sermon * June 26 — 10:00 a.m., residence chapel, Mass with sermon on the occasion of the acceptance of seminarians to the first year of studies * 1:00 p.m., residence, session of the Curia * 6:00 p.m., Church of the Sisters of the Sacred Heart, Mass and sermon * June 27 — Kalwaria Zebrzydowska, a pilgrimage of men and male youth of the Archdiocese of Krakow under the motto: "Sunday in the life of a family:"

It is not enough to tear oneself away from work. It is not enough to get on a bus and go somewhere, and maybe there to tip some number of steins, to cloud ones senses, to commit sin and then to come back and to reenter the same workplace, it is not enough ... Man must transcend himself, he must open himself to the One whose image and likeness he is, if he is not to lose himself, to negate himself. Perhaps they will write about me somewhere when I say this, but this whole program of laicization, secularization, is also a program of negating man! Man truly finds himself when he reveres the mystery of the world, the mystery of creation. When he reveres the mystery of his own humanity ... when he reveres the name of God. When he opens himself to God, when he communes with God ... We must do everything to ensure that Sunday remains the day of the Lord, a holy day, among our families. That it remains so for fathers and mothers, for the youth, and for children ... Today when we are alarmed at the phenomenon of the decline of social and individual morality, we see a variety of causes. But there is one that is beyond any doubt: there is no reverence for man ... there is no reverence for the day of the Lord.

Same day — 3:00 p.m., a visit with "Oasis" groups * 6:00 p.m., Wroblowice, blessing of the rectory, Mass, final remarks * June 28 — 12:00 noon, residence, the *Srodowisko*[20] * 8:00 p.m., Mass and sermon for the *Srodowisko* * June 29 — A day of retreat at Kalwaria Zebrzydowska * Same day — in the evening, at the Church of St. Peter and St. Paul, he presides over the Holy Mass and led prayers for the intention of the Holy Father Paul VI on the 13th anniversary of his coronation.

July 1-20 — Vacation * July 21 — 7:00 a.m., residence chapel, private Mass.

July 22 — Jasna Gora, 11:15 a.m., he celebrated the Eucharist with Bishop Deskur at the Chapel of Our Lady. In his speech, he stressed that the purpose of his coming to Jasna Gora was to ask the Blessed Mother to bless the work of the Eucharistic Congress to be held in the United States, where he was going as the delegate of the Polish Episcopate. He also asked the Blessed Mother for a blessing for himself as a participant in the celebrations of the 200th anniversary of independence of the United States. After the Mass the Cardinal met with a delegation of the faithful from Nowa Huta * July 23 — 8:00 a.m., Fiszor, concelebrated Mass with the Primate {Wyszynski} and Bishop A. Deskur * 1:00 p.m., Warsaw, departure for USA * 7:00 p.m., New York, a welcome at the airport.

July 23 — September 11 — In the United States as a leader of the delegation of the Polish Episcopate for the 41st Eucharistic Congress in Philadelphia, and also to visit Polonia[21] in the USA and Canada.

July 24 —7:30 a.m., Boston, St. Adalbert's Church, concelebrated Mass * 12:00 noon, Harvard * 3:00 p.m., departure for Pomfret * July 25 — 7:30 a.m., Pomfret, concelebrated Mass with Rev. Stanislaw Dziwisz, return to Boston * 7:00 p.m., Boston, a visit with Cardinal Medeiros * July 26 — 8:00 a.m., Boston, St. Adalbert's Church, concelebrated Mass * 12:00 noon, Harvard, Palmer House * 6:00 p.m., a gathering at Mr. and Mrs. Houthakker's * July 27 — 8:00 a.m. Boston,

---

[20] See Glossary.
[21] Community of Poles outside of Poland.

St. Adalbert's Church, concelebrated Mass * 12:00 noon, Harvard, a lecture: *Participation or Alienation*, at the student pastoral center, supper with the Dean of the Divinity School * July 28 — 8:30 a.m., Boston, collegiate church, Mass * Same day — Harvard, a tour of the library at the Ukrainian Institute, lunch with Secretary John T. Dunlop * Departure for Washington {DC}, a visit with Cardinal William Baum * July 29 — 8:30 a.m., Washington, concelebrated Mass at a parish church, later a concelebrated Mass at the residence of Cardinal Baum * 3:00 p.m.,Washington, Catholic University, interview reception * Same day — 7:30 p.m., Catholic University of America in Washington, Department of Philosophy, lecture. The topic of the lecture was: *L'autoteleologia dell'uomo e la transcendenza della persona nell'atto.* This lecture was mailed earlier for the 6th International Congress of Philosophy, Arezzo-Siena, organized by Facolta di Lettere (Siena) and Facolta di Maggistri (Arezzo), in Arezzo June 1-5, 1976. In the USA Cardinal Wojtyla delivered this lecture in English *(The Transcendence of the Person in Act and Man's Auto-Teleology)* * July 30 — 8:00 a.m., a farewell to Cardinal Baum * 10:00 a.m., Prof. McLean, OMI * 12:30 p.m., French chapel, (Fr. Deroquois), private concelebrated Mass, later a reception at Fr. Deroquois's center * July 31- 6:45 a.m.,Washington, French chapel, private concelebrated Mass * 10:30 a.m., Philadelphia, St. Adalbert's Parish, a meeting with the Committee * A meeting of the delegation of Polish bishops * 6:00 p.m., Philadelphia, Theological Seminary.

August 1-8 — Philadelphia. Eucharistic Congress * August 1 — Philadelphia, 9:00 a.m., St. Charles's Seminary, concelebrated Mass with the Polish bishops * 12:00 noon, Cathedral, inauguration of the Congress * 7:00 p.m., Eucharistic procession * August 2, Philadelphia, Congress, liturgical preparation * 1:00 p.m., St. Adalbert's Church, concelebrated Mass, sermon * 6:00 p.m., reception and a performance at the parish hall * August 3 — Philadelphia, Eucharistic Congress, 4:00 p.m., a reception at Cardinal Krol's * 5:00 p.m.,Veterans Stadium, led a concelebrated Mass (Cardinal Knox, Cardinal Krol, Cardinal Rugambwa, Archbishop Benelli, Archbishop Jadot), he delivered a homily "The Eucharist and a Hunger for Freedom" * August 4 — Philadelphia, Congress, a day of vocations to the priesthood and religious life * 9:00 a.m., Doylestown (American Czestochowa {Shrine}), led a concelebrated Mass, sermon * 3:00 p.m. , a conference with the clergy * 8:00 p.m., Philadelphia, Academy of Music, a concert of Polish music * August 5 — Philadelphia, Congress, topic of the day: "The Eucharist and a Hunger for Truth," prayer for saints * 10:45 a.m., Passaic, Our Lady of the Rosary Parish, led a concelebrated Mass, delivered the opening and concluding remarks on the site of the death of the Servant of God Archbishop Jan Cieplak * 8:00 p.m., Philadelphia, participated in an ecumenical service * August 6 — 7:00 a.m., Philadelphia, Church of the Redemptorist Fathers, led a concelebrated Mass at the tomb of Blessed John Neumann (televised). Congress: "The Eucharist and a Hunger for Understanding" — youth day * 9:00 p.m., concelebrated Marian Mass, Archbishop Fulton Sheen: "Mary — the Lord's Tabernacle" * August 7 — Philadelphia, Congress: "The Eucharist and a Hunger for Peace" * 10:30 a.m., a reception for the Polish delegation at Cardinal Krol's * 1:00 p.m.,Veterans Stadium, a concelebrated Mass for Polonia (homily by Cardinal Krol, parting remarks by Bishop Ablewicz) * 4:00 p.m., a get-together with Polonia, "dozynki"[22] * August 8 — Philadelphia, Congress: "The Eucharist and a Hunger for Jesus" * 11:00 a.m., at the Sisters of the Holy Family of Nazareth, concelebrated Mass, sermon * 4:00 p.m., Statio Orbis, broadcast of a speech by the Holy Father * Participation in a concelebrated Mass for the conclusion of the Congress * 8:00 p.m., a meeting with Polonia.

August 9 — 8:00 a.m., departure from Philadelphia * 12:00 noon, Baltimore, new cathedral, meeting with Cardinal Lawrence Shehan * Old cathedral, meeting with Archbishop William Borders, meeting with Polonia * 4:00 p.m., Washington, National Conference of Catholic Bishops in the USA (Cardinal Baum) * Our Lady's Shrine (the Marian Shrine[23]), led a concelebrated Mass, delivered a sermon * August 10 — 8:00 a.m.,Washington, St. Joseph's home, interview * 12:00 noon, St. Matthew's Cathedral, led a concelebrated Mass with the participation of Cardinal Baum (opening remarks) and Bishop W. Rubin (sermon) * August 10 — 2:00 p.m., meeting with Polonia (Rev. Philip Majka), an address * 4:00 p.m., a visit with the Polish Ambassador[24] * August 11-13 — at the Polish Theological Seminary in Orchard Lake[25] a symposium on the issue: *What can Polonia do for Poland, and what can Poland do for Polonia?* * August 11 — 8:00 a.m., Orchard Lake, Seminary chapel, concelebrated Mass, introductory remarks * 11:00 a.m., a conference on the situation of Polonia and the Polish Apostolate * 6:00 p.m., a hall in Detroit, a meeting with women's organization supporting the Orchard Lake Seminary, parting remarks * August 12 — Orchard Lake, a second conference with representatives of the U.S. Polonia. The Cardinal makes an introductory presentation regarding the situation of the Church in Poland * 4:00 p.m., Detroit, St. Adalbert's Church, concelebrated Mass with the delegation of Polish bishops, con-

---

[22] Fall harvest festival, a long-time rural tradition in Poland often observed by Polish communities abroad.
[23] National Shrine (now the Basilica) of the Immaculate Conception.
[24] Witold Trompczynski.
[25] Near Detroit, Michigan.

cluding remarks * 8:00 p.m., a Polonian banquet (parting address by Bishop Artur Krawczak) * August 13 — 7:30 a.m., Orchard Lake, Seminary chapel, concelebrated Mass * 9:00 a.m., a third conference of the Polish bishops with the representatives of the Orchard Lake Seminary, resolutions * 3:00 p.m., radio press conference * 7:00 p.m., departure for Boston to Msgr. Stanislaw Sypek * August 14 — 8:00 a.m., Boston, Chapel of the Discalced Carmelite Sisters, concelebrated Mass, sermon * 12:00 noon, lunch, Bishop Slowakiewicz, National Church[26] * 3:00 p.m., Blue Hall * 6:00 p.m., St. Adalbert's Parish, supper with Cardinal Medeiros * August 15 — 10:00 a.m., Boston, at the Polish Sisters, led concelebrated Mass with Cardinal Medeiros, closing remarks * 3:00 p.m., St. Adalbert's Church, welcome, procession, he led a concelebrated Mass, sermon in Polish * 5:30 p.m., a banquet with Polonia * August 16 — Boston, St. Adalbert's Church, concelebrated Mass * 10:00 a.m. Plymouth * 11:00 a.m., at the grave of Cardinal Richard Cushing * 2:00 p.m., a visit at the St. Sebastian Brothers, lunch, visited at Prof. Dziewanowski and at Brother Rafal's mother * 6:00 p.m., Boston, farewell at Cardinal Medeiros' * August 17 — 8:00 a.m., departure for Buffalo * 10:00 a.m., a ceremonial welcome at the airport (Bishop Head, Bishop Ablewicz, Bishop Rubin, Rev. Kazmierczak of Polonia), press conference * 5:00 p.m., Buffalo, St. Casimir's Parish, led a concelebrated Mass with the entire delegation of the Polish Episcopate, concluding remarks * 7:30 p.m., banquet with the Polish community * August 18 — 9:00 a.m., Buffalo, St. Casimir's Church, blessing of the statue of the Blessed Mother, concelebrated Mass, sermon * Niagara Falls * 1:00 p.m., Canada * 3:00 p.m., London {Ontario}, a visit with Bishop Gerald Carter, Chairman of the Canadian Episcopate * 5:00 p.m., Hamilton, meeting at St. Stanislaw Parish * August 19 — 10:00 a.m., Hamilton, St. Stanislaw parish hall, meeting with the clergy and representatives of Polonia * 1:00 p.m., departure for Toronto * Toronto, 4:30 p.m., Cathedral, meeting with Archbishop Philip Pocock and others, concelebrated Mass, sermon; present were bishops from the East[27] * 9:00 p.m., St. Casimir's Parish, Credit Union, reception * August 20 — 8:00 a.m., Hamilton, concelebrated Mass at the convent * 10:00 a.m., Hamilton, cathedral, concelebrated Mass with the ordinary bishop * 11:00 a.m., Port Credit, an address during the welcome: departure for Chicago * 3:00 p.m., Chicago, reception at Cardinal John Cody's * Tour of the Holy Family of Nazareth Hospital * 6:00 p.m., Lake Michigan * 10:00 p.m., the Congregation of the Resurrection, tour of the school * August 21 — 8:00 a.m., Chicago,

---

[26] Polish National Catholic Church is not part of the Roman Catholic Church.

[27] "The East" was typically a euphemism for the Soviet Union, but in this context the term may refer to the Eastern Rite of the Church.

Five Holy Martyrs Parish * Radio station studio * 11:00 a.m., Mausoleum of Polonia * 1:00 p.m., dinner with Polish clergy and Cardinal Cody, speech * 4:00 p.m., Polish Roman-Catholic Union * 5:00 p.m., St. Jadwiga's {Hedwig} Church (of the Congregation of the Resurrection), concelebrated Mass, sermon, meeting with Polonia from the Veterans' Club, with Bishop Alfred Abramowicz * August 21 — An appeal to the archdiocese in connection with the beginning of a new school year, and a new year of catechesis bears this date. In this appeal, among others: "In our times, catechesis is the fundamental profession of faith ..." The Cardinal also directed a letter to the youth, in which the main focus is the mystery of the Eucharist, which relates to the 41st Eucharistic Congress * August 22 — 11:00 a.m., Chicago, Church of the Five Holy Martyrs, concelebrated Mass, sermon, blessing of the stained glass windows * 3:00 p.m., Hotel Hilton, meeting with the Polish American Congress * 6:00 p.m., banquet with Polonia, speech, Cardinal Cody present * August 23 — 8:00 a.m., departure for Stevens Point {Wisconsin} * 9:30 a.m., welcome * 11:00 a.m., meeting with farmers * 1:00 p.m., a visit with Polonia, first post of the Felician Sisters * 3:00 p.m., Stevens Point University, lecture in English: *Science in Poland* * 6:00 p.m., concelebrated Mass with bishop ordinary, sermon * August 24 — 7:00 a.m., Stevens Point, St. Joseph's Church, concelebrated Mass, sermon * 9:00 a.m., a visit to homes for the aged and sick * 10:30 a.m., departure for Boston * 2:00 p.m., Boston * 6:00 p.m., Pomfret * August 25-27 — Pomfret, rest, private concelebrated Masses * August 27 — evening, return to Boston * August 28 — 9:30 a.m., departure for San Francisco, welcome at the airport by Polonia * 1:00 p.m., visit with Archbishop Joseph Mc Gucken, tour of the city * 3:00 p.m., Chapel of the Mission of the Polish Apostolate, concelebrated Mass, sermon addressed to Polonia * 9:30 p.m., departure for Los Angeles * August 29 — 11:30 a.m., Los Angeles, Our Lady of the Rosary Parish, concelebrated Mass, sermon, meeting with Polonia from San Diego, press conference, meeting with the local Polish community * 5:00 p.m., concelebrated Mass, sermon, meal with the clergy and the parishioners, speech * August 30 — 7:30 a.m., Los Angeles, Our Lady of the Rosary Parish, private concelebrated Mass, conversations with the clergy * 10:00 a.m., City Hall (City Council), reception; he was handed the keys of the city * 12:00 noon., tour of the city: cathedral, old town, mausoleum, *The Crucifixion* (by Styka)[28], Mexican neighborhood * 3:00 p.m., departure for Great Falls, 8:00 p.m., arrival, welcome * August 31 — Great Falls — Geyser, at

---

[28] Adam Styka, 20th C. Polish painter.

Msgr. Jozef Gluszek's (priest of the Krakow Archdiocese) * 9:00 a.m., visit to the chapel * 10:00 a.m., Geyser, church and rectory, meeting with Polish priests (Msgr. Kochan), 1:00 p.m., group meal * 3:00 p.m., Stanford, chapel * 7:30 p.m., Geyser, concelebrated Mass, meeting with the parishioners.

September 1 — 7:00 a.m., departure for Billings and Chicago (Bishop Abramowicz, Rev. Bednarz, Rev. Peszkowski, Rev. Wincenciak) * 2:00 p.m., Cincinnati, visit with the President of the Episcopal Conference of the USA, Archbishop L. Bernardin * September 2 — 7:30 a.m., Cincinnati, chapel at the cathedral, private concelebrated Mass * 9:30 a.m., conversation with Archbishop J. L. Bernardin, dinner, departure for Detroit * 6:00 p.m., Detroit, visit with Cardinal John Dearden (Bishop Krawczak, Rev. Ziemba, Rev. Peszkowski) * September 3 — 9:00 a.m., Orchard Lake, Polish Seminary, welcome * 10:00 a.m., Seminary chapel, concelebrated Mass with the superiors and professors, sermon * 3:00 p.m., conversations with the faculty * 4:00 p.m., press conference, an interview with the Cardinal before his departure from the United States conducted by Stanislaw Krajewski, a reporter of "Dziennik Polski" from Detroit * 6:00 p.m., Rosary Hour * September 4 — 7:00 a.m., Orchard Lake, private concelebrated Mass * He sends letters to the American bishops and to the American Polonia thanking them for their hospitality * 11:00 a.m., New York, airport, welcome by Cardinal Cody, Rev. Rojek; Polonia * 1:00 p.m., residence of Cardinal Terence Cooke * 3:00 p.m., reception at the veterans facility, speech * 7:00 p.m., Polish Institute of Arts and Sciences * 8:00 p.m., Kosciuszko Foundation * September 5 — 10:00 a.m., New York, St. Patrick's Cathedral, concelebrated Mass, sermon (English and Polish) * Meeting with the Polish community, farewell to Cardinal Cody * 5:00 p.m., St. Stanislaw Kostka Church, a visit with Msgr. Rojek * 8:30 p.m., departure * September 6 — 11:00 a.m., Rome, Polish College, private concelebrated Mass * 5:00 p.m., a visit with Bishop Deskur * 7:00 p.m., a visit with Bishop Rubin * September 7 — 7:00 a.m., Rome, Polish College, private concelebrated Mass * 2:00 p.m., at Bishop Deskur's with Archbishop Poggi * 7:00 p.m., meeting at Bishop Rubin's * September 8 — 7:00 a.m., Rome, Polish College, private concelebrated Mass * 10:00 a.m., departure for Genoa * 1:00 p.m., Genoa, inaugural lecture at the Congress of Philosophy, dedicated to the issue "Teoria e prassi". Title of the lecture: *Teoria — praxis: un tema umano e cristiano* * September 9 — 9:00 a.m., Genoa, Congress of Philosophy * 11:00 a.m., Chapel of the Jesuits, private concelebrated Mass * 2:00 p.m., at Cardinal Giuseppe Siri's, Congress * September 10 — 9:00 a.m., Genoa, deliberations of the Congress, * 12:00 noon, private concelebrated Mass * September

11 — 8:00 a.m., departure for Warsaw * 7:00 p.m., Krakow, residence chapel, private concelebrated Mass.

After the conclusion of the Eucharistic Congress in Philadelphia — a conversation with the spokesman for the Polish Episcopate, Rev. Alojzy Orszulik (Sodalis, November, pp. 235-237).

September 12 — Pilgrimage of women and girls to Kalwaria Zebrzydowska, at 11:00 a.m., Cardinal Wojtyla concelebrated a Holy Mass together with the clergy of the youth apostolate and delivered a sermon on the theme of the pilgrimage: "Sunday in the life of the family." From the sermon:

> May you be the heart of the family of families: the parish, the nation, the Church, may you be the heart. This is what I want to pray for with you. And I wish to tell you that this is what constitutes your Eucharistic mission. A woman is the heart, she gathers those closest to her around herself, she forms the community. She gathers them at table, she gathers them at prayer, she gathers them in conversation, she gathers them around herself. Today, the observance of Sunday is threatened in various ways. It is threatened as a day of rest, because the so-called social-action activities[29] are often organized on that day. But, most of all, it is in danger as a day of the Eucharist, because there are attempts to give a secular character to this day. But this is the Day of the Lord!

September 13 — 11:00 a.m., residence, meeting of the bishops * 6:00 p.m., Mistrzejowice, concelebrated Mass, sermon dedicated to the late Rev. Jozef Kurzeja, first pastor and builder of the new parish:

> We feel in our human way that he did not just depart, that he was not just buried. We feel, in our human way, as I have said, that he ... was incorporated like a cornerstone into the building of this church, into the building of this community which is the living Church in Mistrzejowice: like a cornerstone. And this is the most magnificent thing that can be said about him ... We thank Christ Our Lord for this priest, for his witness ...
>
> I know his secret. I can even repeat his words, because one never forgets such words. Those were words he spoke to me in 1970, when he came to ask me, as his superior, as his bishop, to allow him to begin pastoral work in the catechetic outpost here in Mistrzejowice, where at the time, as you well remember, there was nothing except this roadside canopy which was the beginning of the history of your community, your parish ... He knew what he was asking for. He knew that this matter would cost him dearly ... he even added in jest: if I have to suffer for this cause, even if I have to go to prison, it will only do me good ... I remember his words and I will not forget them till the end of my life. Because these words, uttered in jest at the time, indicated the price of his sacrifice.

September 14-16 — Mogila, 3rd Congress of Polish Theologians: "Theology: the Study of God" * September 14 — 9:00 a.m., Basilica

---

[29] Supposedly "voluntary" community service work which the authorities required to be performed as a condition of keeping a job, a desirable place to live, etc.

of the Triumph of the Cross in Mogila: "From this greatest wisdom of the Cross we may gain the greatest truth about God". * 6:00 p.m., Mogila, the Cistercians, concelebrated Mass, sermon * September 15 — 8:00 a.m., Wawel, procession with the participation of the Sisters of the Holy Family of Nazareth, Mass and sermon * September 16 — 8:00 a.m., Wawel Cathedral, concelebrated Mass on the occasion of the Congress of Polish Theologians: "We must ... in a very special way bring attention to Blessed Queen Jadwiga, whom with increasing conviction we call the Mother of Polish theologians." * Same day — 3:00 p.m., conclusion of the Congress, closing remarks * 4:00 p.m., meeting of philosophers: Rev. McLean, Rev. Klosak, Rev. Jaworski, Fr. Skrzydlewski OP, Fr. Kloczowski OP, and others. The organizational matters of the upcoming symposium of philosophers (August 1978) were discussed, as well as cooperation between Polish philosophers and the world organization of Catholic philosophers, whose secretary is Rev. McLean, matters of publications and other issues * September 17 — 6:00 p.m., Lublin, cathedral, 8th Festival of Religious Song, Sacrosong 76, sermon during concelebrated Mass:

> **Since I have been connected with this magnificent movement from the beginning ... I wish to join with all of you in offering to God in this Holy Mass everything that makes up this year's Sacrosong ... and, above all, this deep inspiration and this noble effort, in times which do not favor it, and which even oppose it, to bear witness to God and to man in this manner.**

Same day — 7:00 p.m., Lublin, St. Michael's Church, Sacrosong * September 18 — 9:00 a.m., Tarnow, convention of priests-rectors, speech * 6:30 p.m., Krakow, visit at the Sisters of the Holy Family of Nazareth * September 19 — A penitential pilgrimage of the community of Krakow to the Shrine of Christ's Cross in Mogila, with the participation of a pilgrimage of American Polonia * 12:00 noon., he led a concelebrated Mass with the pastors of the parishes of Krakow. From the sermon:

> **This fundamental love, love for a human being who is conceived, who is carried beneath the heart of a mother, who is to be born: this is a fundamental love! The entire existence of the nation depends on it ... It is the obligation of the government to create conditions in which the nation can develop ... And when we, the bishops of Poland, continue to express this in various ways, it is because we are guided by the love of our Homeland, and because we are guided by the love of God! ... who is the source of all love ... This is not merely a "sermon", this is a confession of faith! I share here what every Pole, every Polish bishop carries in the depths of his soul, being fully aware of the deep responsibility for the common good which is our Homeland, Christian for a thousand years, for each person in it, each child in it, for everything that constitutes this Homeland and makes up its future.**

Same day — Residence, a visit by Rev. Stanislaw Sypek with a group of pilgrims from the USA * 7:15 p.m., the Mariacki Basilica, he led a celebration on the 50th anniversary of the death of the Servant of God, Fr. Pawel Smolikowski from the Congregation of the Resurrection; concelebrated Mass with 40 priests from the Congregation of the Resurrection * September 20-25 — Zakopane-Jaszczurowka, house of the Ursuline Sisters, private retreat * September 25 — 5:00 p.m., Mydlniki, at a church construction site * 5:30 p.m., Rzaska, Confirmation, Mass and sermon * 8:30 p.m., Tyniec, meeting with Pax Christi — *Znak* * September 26 — 8:30 a.m., Zakrzowek, consecration of an altar and blessing of the Church of the Society of the Divine Savior {Salvatorian Fathers}, concelebrated Mass, sermon * Same day — 11:00 a.m.-3:00 p.m., at the parish administered by the Reformed Franciscans in Krakow — Bronowice Wielkie, he led diocesan jubilee celebrations commemorating the 750th anniversary of the death of St. Francis. They were combined with the ceremony of the laying of a cornerstone for a new church — a monument of the Franciscan Year. Representatives of the Franciscan religious orders of men and women from the archdiocese participated together with the clergy, parishioners of Bronowice, and residents of Krakow. During the concelebrated Mass celebrated at the site of the church under construction, the Cardinal blessed and laid a cornerstone (it came from Alwernia Mountain). From the sermon:

Our 20th century, at its mid-point, or rather in its final quarter, is a time of particular struggle of faith with unbelief. That is why these times require a multitude of people like St. Francis, and a multitude of us to whom Christ must say: "Support my Church" ... We must thank God that there are many people who heed this call ... And just as Francis went before the Sultan, so also they do not hesitate to go before the representatives of authority, with all of the respect that authorities deserve, but also with the great firmness of our Christian character, and they say: we need a church in Bronowice, we need a church at Azory, we need a church at Wzgorza Krzeslawickie, we need a church at Krowodrza, I will not list all of them. But I thank God that there are so many who repeat this with me. As a bishop who worked on the documents of the Second Vatican Council, especially on the document on the apostolate of the laity, I see that both the message contained in these documents and the teachings of the Council are being fulfilled in this. We must be receptive to the voice of Christ. We must hear the various ways in which He speaks to us: to the bishops, to the priests, to the religious orders, to the laity, to parents, to the youth, to children; to engineers, to scientists, to physicians, to all of us without exception: "Support my Church!"

Same day — 4:30 p.m., Kaniow, 100th anniversary of the parish, Confirmation: "There is power in community. It is the power of a temporal order. It is also a power of the People of God in their quest for God ... The parish is such a community ..." * September 27 — 12:00

noon, residence, meeting of the committee for the division of parishes, conference on the issue of departmental studies — formatio permanens * September 28-29 — Funeral of Bishop Franciszek Jop in Opole * September 28 — Cardinal Wojtyla led the funeral procession to the Opole cathedral. Sermon:

> We have, in a very special way, experienced his firmness, his uncompromising stance combined with great prudence, his evangelical strength of spirit, in the difficult 4-year period, during which he administered the Krakow Archdiocese as capitular vicar. We all know that these were the most difficult times, times of, speaking most tactfully, the absence of the Primate,[30] the absence of so many other bishops removed from their sees, times of particular responsibility. And all of us who lived through those times with him in Krakow and in the Archdiocese, are certain that we had a providential bishop. There was so much prudence, but also so much heroism in his behavior. A simplicity and straightforwardness which served the Church and bore witness before all.

September 29 — Residence, the Secretariat of the Synod of the Archdiocese of Krakow * September 30 — Residence at Franciszkanska Street in Krakow, conference of priests — heads of deaneries. On the agenda, among others, Cardinal Wojtyla's comments on the 41st Eucharistic Congress and his visit to Polish centers in the USA; the matter of the 154th plenary session of the Episcopal Conference; archdiocesan matters concerning theology, the Theological Seminary, the Archdiocesan Synod, catechesis, family apostolate, youth apostolate, charity apostolate and administrative matters * 6:00 p.m., residence, a meeting with Prof. Maria Dluska * 6:30 p.m., residence chapel, Mass for the repose of the soul of the late Zofia Twardoszowa.

In September (date unavailable), a short visit to Bachledowka (a few hours).

October 1 — Krakow, he led a funeral of Prof. Adam Vetulani. Sermon during the funeral Mass at the university Church of St. Anne:

> We wish to thank him for his great love of his Homeland, of its history, its past. For his great love of the nation's culture, of this university. This love, combined with knowledge, with science, was manifest in his work, his publications and seminars. This love of the past was so necessary in these times, when the past, history, forms for us a special basis of our identity. And this is what Poles strive for most strenuously, that our identity not be lost, not be erased, that we not allow it to disappear ... The Church of Krakow is grateful to him because at the time when the Jagiellonian University was diminished by what had been its integral part, namely the Department of Theology, Prof. Vetulani did everything he could to ensure

---

[30] Stefan Cardinal Wyszynski had been imprisoned by the Communist government.

that this ancient Department of Theology, which had been excluded from the University, might nevertheless remain true to itself. As I stand by his coffin, I wish to thank him for providing me with his support and witness in those difficult days and those difficult years. For that, the Church of Krakow thanks him.

Same day — 6:00 p.m., Theological Seminary, chapel, service for the beginning of the new academic new year, an act of devotion to the Blessed Mother, meeting * October 2 — He responds to the letter of invitation to participate in the Second International Congress of Church Universities and Departments organized by the Sacred Congregation for Catholic Education. In his letter, he introduces the members of the Polish delegation. The Congress was held this year in November (Dyduch, op. cit., p. 77) * 11:00 a.m., residence, conference of bishops * October 2-3 — Canonical visitation in Podstolice * October 3 — 12:00 noon, Basilica of the Franciscans in Krakow, sermon for the 750th anniversary of the death of St. Francis of Assisi:

> The person of the blessed, not yet according to the canons of the Church, but certainly according to our deep-seated feelings and the opinion of the faithful, Servant of God, Brother Albert, is a special fruit of this Franciscan holiness in our times ... The lay spirituality, the spirituality of creation which St. Francis possessed, must be balanced by the spirituality of God, the spirituality of the Creator. Only when we are filled to the core with admiration for the Creator, as he was, can we truly understand creation. Otherwise, we will be merely users of creation, and we will devastate it. We will use up and devastate our own humanity.

Same day — Cardinal Wojtyla's appeal for the opening of the 32nd Week of Mercy was read in the churches of the Archdiocese. Its content related to the motto of the Week, "The Holy Mass as the Source of Mercy" * October 4 — 2:00 p.m., residence, Council of the Pontifical Department of Theology * 6:00 p.m., Theological Seminary (4 Manifestu Lipcowego Street), concelebrated Mass, sermon * 8:00 p.m., Church of the Franciscans, Oratorio of St. Francis * October 5 — 10:00 a.m., residence, Council of the Pastoral Department (includes departments of the Curia directly involved in pastoral ministry) * 4:00 p.m., conversations with the deacons * October 6 — 1:00 p.m., conversations with the deacons * 6:30 p.m., residence chapel, Mass for the repose of the soul of the late Dr. Janina Biernacka * deacons * October 7 — 7:00 p.m., Kalwaria Zebrzydowska, private Mass * October 8 — 7:00 a.m., residence chapel, private Mass * 5:00 p.m., residence, session of the Curia * session of bishops * October 9 — 8:00 p.m., St. Anne's Church, Mass for the souls of the late Jerzy, Katarzyna and Piotr Ciesielski * October 10 — 10:00 a.m., inauguration of the academic year 1976/77 at St. Anne's collegiate church in Krakow:

It seems that there are more and more sad people on earth today, that there are more and more sad people in Poland and in Krakow. And this sadness results from the lack of an answer or from the avoidance of an answer. But most of all, from the lack of questions, from the avoidance of questions about the most essential matters. A person who does pose this question: What must I do to attain eternal life? And who does not accept the answer of Jesus Christ, departs into sadness ... I am thinking now of this enormous work of the university and the academic ministry ... Therefore it is my wish, as bishop of the Church of Krakow, for whom this work, these questions and these answers are the fundamental message of my episcopal ministry, it is my wish to inaugurate all of this here at this altar. And to receive from you all of the questions with which you come to begin your studies, in whatever field or specialty; this whole hunger for the truth, this whole longing for freedom, because truth goes hand in hand with the freedom of man.

Same day — 6:00 p.m., Wroclaw, the Dominican Fathers, sermon on the occasion of the 750th anniversary of the arrival of the Dominican Order in Poland and in Krakow * October 11 — 8:00 a.m., Wroclaw, cathedral, concelebrated Mass, sermon, inauguration of the academic year at the Pontifical Department of Theology and at the Major Theological Seminary * 11:00 a.m., the auditorium of the Theological Seminary, speech * October 12 — 1:00 p.m., Krakow, residence chapel, ceremony of swearing in of new pastors, speech * 3:00 p.m., residence, Administrative Council * 6:30 p.m., residence chapel, Mass and sermon, wedding * October 13 — Residence, various meetings * 8:00 p.m., academic ministry at the Dominican Fathers', inaugural lecture "The Idea of a Person" * October 14 — 3:00 p.m., residence, meeting with the academic ministry * 4:00 p.m., residence, the Marian team * 8:00 p.m., Our Lady of Lourdes Parish, inauguration of the academic year, concelebrated Mass, sermon, meeting with the students * October 15 — 11:00 a.m., residence, a meeting with the delegation of the Polish Episcopate to the Eucharistic Congress in the USA and a visit by Polonia * Same day — 6:00 p.m., on the eve of the unveiling of the Monument of Grunwald[31] at Jan Matejko Square in Krakow, Cardinal Wojtyla celebrated Mass in the Cathedral at the tomb of the victor of Grunwald, King Wladyslaw Jagiello and his wife, Blessed Queen Jadwiga. He delivered a speech before the final blessing. The sermon during the Mass was preached by the curator of the Cathedral, Msgr. Figlewicz, a witness of the unveiling of the monument in 1910 * October 16 — 11:00 a.m., residence, session of the bishops * Session of the Curia * October 16-23 — Canonical visitation of the pastoral center under the appellation of Blessed Queen Jadwiga at Krowodrza *

---

[31] A victory by the forces of the Polish-Lithuanian Commonwealth, under the command of King Jagiello, over the Knights of the Teutonic Order in 1410. The trophies of this victory were removed from Wawel Castle by the Nazi invaders in 1939.

October 17 — Day of Prayers for the building of new churches: Cardinal Wojtyla's communique was read, informing the Catholic community of the pressing need for building new churches in the rapidly growing city of Krakow and in the Archdiocese, and of the efforts undertaken in this matter * October 18 — Wroclaw, the Cardinal presides over the inaugural concelebrated Mass for "the opening of theological sciences" and delivered a homily * October 20 — Lublin, KUL, 9:00 a.m., Collegiate church, concelebrated Mass, sermon, lecture for the 12th Ecclesiological Week (October 20 — 23, The Church in the Community") * Same day — 5:00 p.m., Bachledowka, concelebrated Mass for the conclusion of the retreat for priests involved in the youth ministry * October 23 — 12:00 noon, residence, session of the bishops * October 24 — 9:00 a.m., Jasna Gora, concelebrated Mass, sermon for the apostolate of sobriety from all of Poland:

> We would like this pilgrimage of ours, this common prayer of our society, offered up with so much faith, with so much pastoral and apostolic ardor, to become a means of regaining vision for many. For we know that the matter of returning to sobriety is, first of all, a matter of *conversion*, and a difficult conversion. Social conditions must be created for this conversion. We, who are gathered here, wish to consider what other social conditions in the life of the country, the nation, the Church, must be created to allow people to revert to sobriety, but we know well that ultimately this must be a *conversion*. That is why the great majority of us present here are the clergy, and those of our brothers and sisters who came with us, are people who wish to undertake with us the great task of converting our entire nation to sobriety.

Same day — 5:00 p.m., Krakow, the collegiate Church of St. Anne, inauguration of the academic year 1976/77 at the Pontifical Department of Theology:

> As we begin this new academic year at the Pontifical Department of Theology in Krakow, we reiterate our demands to the national authorities. These demands are aimed at ensuring that what has been so closely united in the history of the nation and the Church also gain recognition from the state, just as it has been for 557 years.

October 25 — 11:00 a.m., residence, a session connected with his participation in the meeting of the Congregation pro Institutione Catholica * 5:00 p.m., Szklary, reunion of priests ordained in 1971, concelebrated Mass, sermon, Confirmation * October 26 — Krakow, residence, fourth meeting of the Coordinating Committee of the Synod of the Province of Krakow. The Cardinal emphasized the need to appoint consulting teams — theological and sociological teams that would prepare theological and sociological descriptions of the Metropolitan See. In the area of pastoral ministry: a catechetic team and a team to research the participation of the laity in catechesis, teams of pastors, youth teams and the youth ministry teams from among the laity, a team of the apostolate of families. Other teams would handle the matter of the formation and the life of the clergy — also a team for further education at the Pontifical Department of Theology — perhaps continuing education; also a team formed from among the Councils of Priests. Because of the importance of Marian spirituality in Poland, there should be a Marian team, and one for the cult of the Sacred Heart of Jesus. After extended discussions, 15 such teams were constituted. (From the minutes) * Same day — 5:00 p.m., Rudawa, reunion of priests ordained in 1975, concelebrated Mass, sermon * 8:00 p.m., meeting with the professors of the Jagiellonian University * October 27 — Reunion of the secondary-school graduates of the class of 1924 * October 28 — 10:30 a.m., residence chapel, concelebrated Mass of priests ordained in 1928, sermon * 3:00 p.m., residence, delegation of Pax Romana (Felix Marti — President, Marek Skwarnicki — Vice-president, Eric Sottas — Secretary General) * October 29 — Kalwaria Zebrzydowska * 6:00 p.m., residence, Sisters of the Holy Family of Nazareth * October 30 — 11:00 a.m., residence, session of bishops * 12:00 noon, session of the Curia * 2:00 p.m., residence chapel, wedding, Mass and sermon * October 30-31 — Canonical visitation of the parish of Raciborowice.

November 1 — Brzegi. In 1975 the Metropolitan Archbishop of Krakow delegated the pastoral ministry in the parish of Brzegi to the National Apostolate of Liturgical Service. They undertook the task of the renewal of the parish of Brzegi by paying special attention to liturgical matters and by connecting all aspects of parish life with liturgy. The renewal of the parish was also fostered by evangelizing retreats that resulted in the creation of apostolic groups. The Cardinal came to become familiar with this renewal process and to meet the local parishioners, in connection with the 25th anniversary of the building of the church. First he led the Eucharistic sacrifice and preached a homily connecting the Feast of All Saints {November 1} with the principles of Church renewal promulgated by the Vatican Council. In his homily he brought out the fact that today, together with the residents of Brzegi, he is celebrating the 30th anniversary of his ordination to the priesthood. After the Mass he met with the formation and apostolic groups of the parish and with Fr. Blachnicki and his co-workers. (An account provided by Fr. F. Blachnicki) From the sermon:

> **Jesus Christ, the holiest of saints, wants to make saints of us ... Because if we are to enter the community of All Saints, if He is to lead us to that community, He must continue to make us saints: day after day, week after week and year after year. Let us try to realize this fully, so that we may fully participate in the Sacrifice ... I experience this especially**

deeply today, because today 30 years has passed since the day when I was ordained to the priesthood. And the passing years make one understand better and experience ever more deeply this gift of God which one has received, so that one may become more holy, and, in cooperation with Jesus Christ, help others to become holy.

Same day — 3:30 p.m., the Rakowicki cemetery, Church of the Resurrection of Our Lord, Mass and sermon, procession, prayers for the dead. From the sermon:

May the doors of this chapel be opened, so that we may go forth to the four corners of the world, in the direction of all of the graves among which the living wander, and tell our departed that we are united with them ... through the faith which tells us to trust that we will find ourselves in God, who is the fullness of life, of eternal life.

Same day — 5:00 p.m., sermon at the Dominican Basilica for the conclusion of a Rosary service: "We will ask by thanking, because this is the most proper order of our prayer." * November 2 — 7:00 a.m., residence chapel, two concelebrated Masses * 5:00 p.m., Wawel Cathedral, third solemn Mass, procession to the royal tombs * November 3 — 11:00 a.m., residence, audiences * 1:00 p.m., students from Stevens Point * 3:00 p.m., seminar in moral theology * 7:00 p.m., Theological Seminary, an evening in honor of St. Charles Borromeo * November 4 — 11:00 a.m., residence, name-day greetings, among others from *Tygodnik Powszechny*, from the bishops of Tarnow, from the youth of the "Oasis" movement * 7:30 p.m., residence chapel, concelebrated Mass, sermon, university youth * November 5 — 7:30 p.m., residence chapel, Mass for the late Andrzej * November 6 — 12:00 noon, Warsaw, the Ursuline Sisters, private concelebrated Mass * Same day — 5:00 p.m., cathedral in Plock, conclusion of the visitation, sermon:

When Mary visits, man opens up ... because the Mother of God herself comes, and she brings God with her ... She is the living witness of God Incarnate, because she carried Him in her womb, and she brings Him in the same way ... in this wondrous ritual of our Polish faith and piety which is the visitation of the image of Jasna Gora ... This is attested to by this magnificent gathering of the Church of Plock, not only in this ancient cathedral, but in a wide area around the cathedral, because the cathedral itself could not accommodate all of the participants. This is the great prayer of the Polish soul: stay with us, Mother of Life, Mother of the Word, Mother of God, stay!

November 7 — Lodz, visit * 12:30 p.m., Ostrow Wielkopolski, Pontifical Mass for the beginning of the visitation of the image of Our Lady in the Archdiocese of Poznan * November 8 — 3:00 p.m., Krakow, residence, KUL's seminar in ethics * 5:30 p.m., meeting regarding the session: St. Stanislaw in Literature * 8:00 p.m., residence, a meeting with the editorial staff of *Tygodnik Powszechny* * November

9 — Participated in a pilgrimage of the archdiocesan priests — four auxiliary bishops and about 700 priests — to Kalwaria Zebrzydowska. He had encouraged them to participate by sending a letter:

> **Dear Brother Priests. By this letter I wish to invite all of you on a pilgrimage to our shrine in Kalwaria Zebrzydowska. The last time we went there was at the threshold of the Holy Year, on November 5, 1973. The Holy Year, the great jubilee of Our Lord Jesus Christ, bore fruits both in our own Church, where we celebrated it mainly in 1974, and in the Universal Church in 1975. We feel the need to express our gratitude for these fruits. It is right to do this in the same place where we started. And that is why I invite you to the shrine of Our Lady of Kalwaria on November 9 of this year. I invite all priests, both diocesan and religious. All of us make up one Priesthood. Together we undertake the priestly service and the pastoral responsibility. The pilgrimage, whose main purpose is thanksgiving, will also serve to contemplate certain particularly significant areas and matters of our priestly and pastoral responsibilities. We contemplate these matters in a number of circumstances. But we can do that most fully on our knees, in common prayer, united in the sacramental bond with Christ, and, at the same time, before His Mother.**

Same day — 9:00 a.m., Kalwaria Zebrzydowska, conference during the pilgrimage of priests:

> **What I have said makes us aware that, together with the entire nation and the entire Church in Poland, because these two realities, the Church and the nation, have become very deeply intertwined. We find ourselves in a time of a great trial. These times are a trial for everyone: for our brothers, our sisters, the laity; they are also a time of trial for us. A trial always strives to reveal some weakness, to take advantage of a weakness. Perhaps the lack of prudence, lack of courage, lack of firmness, causes some to stumble ... I think that this is not only a trial of our Homeland, not only a trial of the Church in Poland. Today, it is clearly a trial that is universal in scope ... The whole world is going through some kind of a great trial, which comes down to the affirmation or negation of God. Sometimes I get the impression that I am saving a drowning man, who, contrary to proverbial wisdom, does not grasp at any straw, but sinks ever lower, ever deeper. This in spite of all efforts to extricate him, to save him from drowning. And sometimes we reflect: Why? Because these failures sometimes befall priests, whom we do not expect to be subject to this; even they are touched by failure. Surely the causes are hidden very deeply, and even the penetrating eye of the spiritual director or bishop cannot fully discern them ...**
>
> **We come to Kalwaria to create a community near Mary, so that, at her side, we may live through our problems, joys and uncertainties, and lay our thanksgiving and our pleas for forgiveness at her feet. Our reasons for joy and thanksgiving are the numerous priestly vocations, the increasing participation of the youth in the Church, the development of theological studies in Krakow, the initiatives of various priests in creating new pastoral outposts; for some, this becomes a labor of a lifetime, as it was in the case of the late Fr. Jozef Kurzeja.**
>
> **There are also reasons for sadness and for asking forgiveness, such as:**

breakdowns of priests, machinatio contra legitimam auctoritatem Ecclesiae. We are going through a trial of faith and a trial of the priesthood against the background of the program of secularization.

We come to the Blessed Mother to ask her for light and strength, for the ability to realize our priesthood, the spirit of poverty, the spirit of unity and community.

After the conference he concelebrated Mass together with 800 priests (homily — Bishop Jan Pietraszko), after the Mass, before the Blessed Sacrament, a solemn act of dedication of the entire community of priests in the Archdiocese to the Blessed Mother * Same day — 4:00 p.m., residence, conference on matters of the ministry of sobriety * 8:00 p.m., conference regarding the Committee for matters of Education and the Department {of Theology} * November 10 — 1:00 p.m., residence chapel, nomination of pastors, a study group of the theology of the family * November 10-14 — Visitation of the parish of Mistrzejowice. To the married couples during visitation: "As a bishop visiting the parish, I feel this need to renew the awareness and the grace of this Sacrament in the married couples." * November 11 — 1:00 p.m., St. Anne's Church, conferment of doctorates * November 13 — 11:00 a.m., residence, session of bishops * November 14 — 12:00 noon, Biskupice, Mass with sermon * Same day — he blessed and laid the cornerstone for the new Church of Blessed Maximilian Maria Kolbe in Nowa Huta — Mistrzejowice. The corner stone comes from the foundation of the Vatican Basilica. This was the high point of the canonical visitation of the newly founded parish in Nowa Huta. (*Notificationes*) * November 15 — 10:30 a.m., he participated in a celebration of the 50th anniversary of the founding of the Seminary of Czestochowa in Krakow, concelebrated Mass, commemorative meeting, final address * Same day — a meeting in the matter of Kanonicza Street, negotiations with the city authorities regarding the renovation of the historical buildings on this street, owned by the Cathedral Chapter; also — the Synodal team * November 16 — 10:00 a.m., Warsaw, Main Council of the Polish Episcopate * 7:00 p.m., subcommittee for the preparation of a pastoral plan * November 17-18 — Warsaw, 156th plenary session of the Episcopal Conference of Poland * November 18 — 7:00 p.m., Warsaw, (meeting with) the bishops * November 19 — 10:00 a.m., Warsaw, session of ordinary bishops * 8:00 p.m., Krakow, a synodal team * November 20 — 11:00 a.m., residence, session of bishops, session of the Curia * 5:30 p.m., Theological Seminary (8 Podzamcze Street), consecration of the altar in the chapel, concelebrated Mass, sermon * November 21 — Wawel Cathedral, renewal of the act of dedication of Poland to the Most Sacred Heart of Jesus, with the participation of the archdiocesan youth confirmed this year:

The world in which you live and in which you will live is most in need of a heart ... That is why, today, we wish that all of these paths that you walk now and will walk in the future be rooted in the Sacred Heart of Jesus.

Same day — 1:00 p.m., departure for Rome via Vienna * November 22-December 3 — In Rome, Second International Congress of Universities and Departments of Church Studies, organized by the Congregation for Catholic Education. Cardinal Wojtyla, as a member of this organization, was also chairman of the 14-man Polish delegation to the Congress. (*Notificationes*) * November 22 — 8:00 a.m., Rome, Congregation pro Sacramentis et Cultu Divino * November 23-December 2 — Rome, deliberations of the Congress of Catholic Education * December 23 — In Krakow, an annual Mass for the beatification of the Servant of God, Brother Albert was celebrated. The Cardinal could not be with them in person, but he sent a letter to the participants of the Mass, expressing his spiritual unity with them * November 23 — 12:00 noon, St. Peter's Basilica, concelebrated Mass * November 24 — Rome, meeting with Cardinal Sergio Pignedoli, Bishop Deskur, Bishop Rubin * November 25 — Rome, Chapel of the Ursuline Sisters, concelebrated Mass, sermon, meeting with Archbishop Poggi, meeting of the Polish delegation * November 26 — 1:30 p.m., Chapel of the Sisters of the Holy Family of Nazareth, concelebrated Mass, sermon for the conclusion of the retreat * Same day — a program on the Vatican Radio, *Academic Church Studies in Poland*. Cardinal Wojtyla's remarks as president of the delegation for church studies in Poland:

It must be emphasized that one of the most significant events after the regaining of independence by the Polish state was the founding of the first Catholic University in Poland in Lublin in 1918. To this day, this University is the most important center of learning, extending its influence not only within the country but also in the international arena; to mention only the contacts between Lublin and Louvain. The Episcopal Conference is convinced, and is supported in this conviction by the Apostolic See, that the following academic centers are necessary for Catholic education: Krakow, Lublin, Warsaw, Wroclaw, Poznan, five academic centers which are indispensable to the Church in fulfilling its mission.

November 27 — 7:00 a.m., Rome, Chapel of the Albertine Sisters, concelebrated Mass, sermon, meeting with Msgr. Francesco Marchisano * November 28 — St. Stanislaw's Church, sermon during a concelebrated Mass with the delegates for the International Congress of Rectors of Church Universities:

After all, the patronage of St. Stanislaw is closely connected with the oldest Polish university in Krakow, is closely connected with the person of Blessed Queen Jadwiga, who was instrumental in founding the oldest

Department of Theology at the oldest university almost 600 years ago. The year of 1397 is a most significant date for all of us theologians and representatives of Catholic studies in Poland, both when we are in our Homeland and when we are in Rome.

November 28 — An appeal from Cardinal Wojtyla was read in the churches of the archdiocese; he reminded in it that the defense of the faith and its enrichment are the fundamental goals of the pastoral Synod of the Archdiocese — in connection with the letter of the Episcopate "Call to Prayer in Defense of the Holy Faith in our Homeland". (*Notificationes*) * November 29 — 7:15 a.m., Rome, Chapel of the Felician Sisters, concelebrated Mass, sermon * 1:00 p.m., an audience with Pope Paul VI, together with Rev. Prof. M. Jaworski, Rev. Prof. T. Pieronek; presentation to the Holy Father of the last volume of the annual "Analecta Cracoviensa" dedicated to the memory of Blessed Queen Jadwiga * Meeting with Prof. Lazatti and Dr. Brasco of the Sacro Cuore University in Milan * November 30 — 7:15 a.m., St. Peter's Basilica, concelebrated Mass with Bishop Deskur * Meeting with Cardinal Garrone and Bishop Deskur.

December 1 — 7:15 a.m., Chapel of the Sisters of the Resurrection, concelebrated Mass, sermon * 1:00 p.m., St. Stanislaw hospice, dinner * 3:00 p.m., visit at the Embassy of the Polish Peoples Republic * 6:00 p.m., Secretariat of State * December 2 — Visit at Archbishop Casaroli's, at Mr. and Mrs. Habicht's * During his visit in Rome he answers (in writing) the questions prepared by Renzo Giacomelli of the Vatican Radio for an interview on the subject of *Evangelizzazione e la promozione umana* * December 3 — Departure for Warsaw, return to Krakow * December 4 — 10:00 a.m., Wawel Cathedral, concelebrated Mass at the coffin of Msgr. Dr. Bogdan Niemczewski:

> He always carried within him a great sense of the dignity of man, the dignity of a Christian, the dignity of a priest ... He was ... a great support for me as a bishop, as a bishop of the Church of Krakow, at various stages and at various times.

December 4-5 — Residence, Committee for the Apostolate of the Laity * December 5 — 9:30 a.m., residence chapel, concelebrated Mass * Same day — The seat of the Metropolitan Archbishop of Krakow. In the second day of meetings of the Committee of the Episcopate for the Apostolate of the Laity, the "Light & Life" movement was presented in the context of the discussions on the activity of lay people in the sphere of formation. Cardinal Wojtyla invited Rev. F. Blachnicki and his coworkers to this meeting. The Cardinal delivered two speeches — an introductory one and a concluding one; he also took part in the discussion. In his introductory speech, the Cardinal outlined

Kalendarium

the state of the apostolate of the laity in Poland after the liquidation {by the authorities} of Catholic organizations and associations. Secondly, he pointed out that in this situation we are now dealing with the "Light & Life movement," which is not an organization, but possesses certain organizational forms. The Committee should consider "to what extent this can serve as a pattern, to what extent the entire apostolate of the laity, and, particularly, groups of lay Catholics in Poland, can be guided along similar, if not identical, lines." In his concluding speech, the Cardinal concentrated on the fundamental structure of the movement in relation to Church structures: the movement began in the parish and returned to the parish with fully formed lay apostles. He also emphasized the need for working out "a pragmatic way of coming together of the parish and the movement." "As a Committee of the Episcopate ... we feel the need to advance this process, we are glad that this process is beginning, and displays signs of maturity." * December 6 — 3:00 p.m., the team of catechumens from the Parish of Our Lady of Lourdes * 7:00 p.m., Theological Seminary, "Mikolaj" {visit of St. Nicholas} * December 7 — The 5th Week of Biblical Studies dedicated to the issues presented by Pope Paul VI in his exhortation *Evangelii nuntiandi* — within the celebrations of the 20th anniversary of the Biblical School of KUL. The Cardinal participated in the inauguration of the Week at St. Paul's Church in Lublin. Also present were Rev. Rector Mieczyslaw Krapiec, professors, students. The Cardinal spoke during the concelebrated Mass with the professors and students of the School, underscoring the matter of the permanence and significance of the Word of the Lord to people of all times, in which they search for the unfathomable wisdom of the message of the Bible. (Rev. Jan Szlaga) * December 8 — 3:00 p.m., Skawica, concelebrated Mass, concluding remarks for the 25th anniversary of the parish * December 9-14 — Visitation of the parish of Zakopane * December 10 — 8:00 a.m., a meeting with representatives of the religious orders of women in Zakopane. Mass and homily at the Chapel of the Carmelite Sisters at 8 Koscielna Street.

We must look to the light which Christ has brought to us, we must see the horizons which He revealed for us, we must go to them, giving much of ourselves. The calling to religious life is a calling to selfless love, a calling to sacrifice, for others and to others.

On December 10, Pope Paul VI carried out a reorganization of the Council for the Laity, establishing in its place the Pontifical Council for the Laity *(Pontificium Consilium pro Laicis)*. Its members were mostly the lay faithful. Cardinal Wojtyla did not become its member.

December 15 — 1:00 p.m., reunion of priests ordained in 1976 *

6:00 p.m., residence chapel, Mass for the late Jerzy Braun * December 16 — Residence chapel, concelebrated Mass with the Council of Priests, meeting of the Council * Religious Seminary in Krakow. Scientific symposium, subject: "Contemporary Problems of Myth" * 5:00 p.m., Tarnow, cathedral, funeral of Msgr. Jan Bochenek * December 17 — 2:00 p.m., residence, committee for the division of parishes * 4:00 p.m., session of bishops * 8:00 p.m., Our Lady of Lourdes Church, Mass and sermon, "Oplatek"[32] for university students * December 18 — 12:00 noon, residence, session of the Curia * 7:30 p.m., Church of the Jesuits, concelebrated Mass, sermon, "Oplatek" for university students * December 19 — 11:00 a.m., Tarnobrzeg, monastery of the Dominican Fathers — celebration of the 300th anniversary of the image of Our Lady:

> **And this place on Polish soil was also chosen, just as Bethlehem was once chosen as the birthplace of God. And for many centuries this has been a birthplace of the children of God. It has been such a place ever since the time when, together with the Dominican Fathers, there arrived here this image, famed for its graces, this truly blessed image of Our Lady of Dzikow, Our Lady of Tarnobrzeg ... this very same Marian image, so beloved and so venerated, crowned several times.**

Tarnobrzeg, the new chapel built in the outbuildings of a former monastic compound:

> **These changes, which are taking place here in the region of Tarnobrzeg, also take place in various other regions of contemporary Poland. In connection with this, there arises the need for new churches, new chapels, new rooms or houses for religious instruction ... You have given her this utility building as a temple. We must not be surprised, we must not be shocked, because after all the Son of God chose a stable as His first temple on earth. So, all of these barns and stables, and other farm buildings where houses of God arise as necessary, have a good, evangelical genealogy.**

December 20 — Residence, 3rd meeting of the Main Committee of the Synod * 4:00 p.m., residence, a visit by the USA Consul * 8:00 p.m., Church of the Dominican Fathers * December 21 — 1:00 p.m., residence, session of bishops * 7:30 p.m., Mass for the intention of married couples of the *Srodowisko*[33] * 8:30 p.m., Church of St. Anne, "Oplatek" for university students * December 23 — 3:00 p.m., residence, session of bishops * 8:15 p.m., Cistercian Fathers in Mogila, "Oplatek" for university students * December 24 — 8:00 a.m., Wawel, "roraty"[34] * From 11:00 a.m., residence, Christmas greetings * 4:00 p.m., Wawel Cathedral, Matins of Christmas * 6:00 p.m., Theological

---

[32] See Glossary
[33] See Glossary.
[34] Mass at dawn during Advent, a traditional Polish devotion.

Seminary, "Wigilia" supper, singing of carols * 12:00 midnight, "Pasterka" Mass at Wzgorza Krzeslawickie

> In the stable, the Son of God took on the citizenship of the inhabitants of the earth ... And so I accept Him together with you, dear brothers and sisters, parishioners of Wzgorza Krzeslawickie and Stoki, so I accept Him with you, I, the Bishop of the Church of Krakow. Not in the Wawel Cathedral, but here. This is the place of His birth and the hope that He is born for the future shines from here.

December 25 — 9:00 a.m., residence chapel, Mass for the workers of Solvay and their families * 10:00 a.m., Wawel Cathedral, Christmas Day:

> He was born in order to help me, a human being, to become human. To give me the power to become human. Because to be truly human means to become a son of God ... The mystery of Jesus Christ, God born in Bethlehem of the Virgin Mary, has shaped our souls, our history, our culture, our identity. This has been going on for a full thousand years ... And whichever era in Polish history we touch ... we find proof of this everywhere, while today we cannot find any acknowledgment of the same in contemporary publications, even during the time of Christmas.

The same day — 3:00 p.m., Wawel Cathedral, vespers of Christmas * December 26 — the Pontifical Department of Philosophy was founded in Krakow * On the same day — 10:30 a.m., Wegrzce, blessing of a Catholic home, Mass with sermon * 12:00 noon — the Feast of St. Stephen at the parish of St. Stephen:

> The Church in Poland, when the need arises, calls for acts flowing from faith. And when people are wronged, suffering, the Church wants to assist them. It comes with help as the Church, not from any political motives! But from motives of Christian charity, Christian solidarity! That is how it was in 1970, after the events on the seacoast, that is how it was also in this difficult year ... St. Stephen, full of faith..., is a figure for our times, because our times demand from us, the followers of Christ, a conscious faith, a faith that lives through good deeds, a courageous faith ... Our faith must be full, it must become full. It must not be subject to diminishment, conformism, compromises. It must not become overly private ...
> In these mass media, for example on television, it is possible to tell unheard-of tales about what the Pope agreed to in connection with the review of the concordat in Italy. But there is no time available for us to objectively state the truth of this matter. It takes a very mature faith for Catholics, after hearing such news on television, not to pose questions such as: Is it true, that the Holy Father has agreed to divorces?

December 27 — 6:30 p.m., residence chapel, Mass with sermon for the Sisters of the Holy Family of Nazareth * December 28 — 6:30 p.m., residence chapel, Mass with sermon for Daughters of Divine Charity * December 29 — 6:30 p.m., residence chapel, Mass with sermon for the Sisters of the Sacred Heart of Jesus * December 30 — 6:30 p.m.,

Sisters of St. Claire, Mass with sermon. Common meal in the refectory. The Sisters presented a little theatrical scene entitled "St. Francis and the Wolf" * December 31 — 11:00 a.m., residence, session of bishops, session of the Curia * Same day — 12:00 noon, the Cardinal celebrated Mass at the Chapel of the Ursuline Sisters in Krakow for the opening of the provincial chapter of the Ursuline Sisters of the Roman Union. The sisters renewed their vows during the Mass. Later, dinner at the convent refectory. Then the Cardinal delivered a lecture in the hall of the congregation and blessed new crosses for all sisters of the province. (From the chronicles of the Ursuline Sisters) * 7:00 p.m., concelebrated Mass, sermon for the end of the year at Krowodrza:

> And when another year ends in the history of the nation, in the history of our Homeland, in the history of Poland, every Pole asks himself: have we lost anything from the magnificent heritage of the nation, from the independence of the spirit? ... One cannot be a frivolous Pole: our geographical position is a difficult one. This places a particular responsibility upon every Pole, and even more so in times like the present. In this regard, we must say that the year just past has not been an easy one. We had to struggle for the fundamental truths in order to answer these questions: what is the nation? what is the state? And that in the very first months of the year. We had to keep reminding that it is the nation, not anything else, which is the essence of the existence of the state. This nation, which through so many struggles, on the fronts of so many wars, through so much suffering, has earned the right to be a nation that is fully free and independent! We must be very vigilant Poles, so that we do not squander our difficult but so valuable heritage, so that others never squander it for us. As this year is ending, we must pray especially for those who are suffering. Indeed, the Polish Episcopate has, since the end of June of this year, petitioned, demanded, that people who stood up in defense of their rights to their own life, to existence, to reasonable material conditions, not be punished. We must continue to ask God that our Homeland be a country of true freedom, of respect for the rights of citizens and a country of true justice.

The same day — midnight, at the Basilica of the Franciscan Fathers, concelebrated Mass, sermon for the end of the year.

1977

January 1 — Zakopane-Jaszczurowka, house of the Ursuline Sisters. Cardinal Wojtyla arrived with Rev. Marian Jaworski about 10:30 a.m. (they could not enter the house, the sisters were at breakfast), skiing outings with Rev. Stanislaw Nagy * January 5 — Evening, singing of Christmas carols with the Sisters * January 6 — In the afternoon, departure for Krakow. (According to an account by the Ursuline Sisters) * January 6 — Feast of the Epiphany, 6:00 p.m., Wawel Cathedral, concelebrated Mass, homily:

We do not find ourselves in what we read, in what is being written and broadcast in the mass media. Just as if Poland were an atheistic country. Everyone has the right to speak and be heard on the radio or television, but the sick can never hear a Holy Mass on the radio or television ... All of these disquieting phenomena related to the process of secularization, laicization, all of them stem from a fundamental lack: the lack of the worship of God. A man who does not respect God eventually will not respect man.

Same day — 8:00 p.m., Christmas carols at the residence of the Janik family * January 7 — Meeting with the ordinary bishops of the Krakow Metropolitan See. During the meeting, the bishops expressed their opinion in the matter of the synodal consulting teams, accepting their makeup and adding some new members * 5:00 p.m., residence chapel, concelebrated Mass, greetings and *Oplatek*[1] for gardeners * 7:00 p.m., residence, preparatory session on the subject: Premarital chastity (for February 5 and 6) * January 8 — 12:00 noon, residence, session of bishops * 7:00 p.m., residence chapel, *Oplatek* with the Club of Catholic Intellectuals * Christmas carols at J.J. * January 9 — 9:00 a.m., Chapel of the Ursuline Sisters, concelebrated Mass, sermon, *Oplatek*, singing of carols at the Higher Catechetic Institute * Same day — 4:00 p.m., Lagiewniki, a gathering of the youth and recently married couples at the "Source" {*Zrodlo*} for the traditional *Oplatek*. (From the chronicles of the convent) * 6:00 p.m., residence, *Oplatek* of academic workers * January 10 — 2:00 p.m., departure for Zakopane * January 11 — Zakopane — "Ksiezowka", a meeting of the Committee of the Episcopate for Pastoral Ministry. Presentations: *Practical Meaning of the Exhortation "Evangelii nuntiandi (December 8, 1975) by Paul VI in the Polish Reality* — Bishop I. Tokarczuk; *The Most Important Challenges and Pastoral Issues of the Present Time* — Rev. Rector J. Majka * January 12 — Second day of meetings of the Committee; discussion on a presentation from the day before. Presentation by Rev. A. Bardecki, *Pastoral Counteraction to the Secularization of Our*

[1] See Glossary.

Society. The presentation and discussion became the basis for the preparation of a pastoral letter * January 13 — Third day of meetings of the Committee; issues of pastoral programs, communiques and others. At 5:00 p.m. — adjournment of the meetings. Each day the meetings would start with a concelebrated Mass led by Cardinal Wojtyla, the homily was preached by Rev. Rector Franciszek Macharski. (From the minutes of the Committee) * January 14 — 2:30 p.m., residence, meeting of the Metropolitan chapter on the matter of Kanonicza Street * 4:00 p.m., session of bishops * 7:30 p.m., residence chapel, Mass and sermon, Christmas carols, the *Srodowisko*[2] * January 15 — 11:00 a.m., residence, session of the bishops and the Curia * 5:00 p.m., the Dominican Church, veterans' *Oplatek* * 7:00 p.m., residence chapel, Mass and sermon, *Oplatek* with physicians * January 16 — 9:00 a.m., residence chapel, Mass and sermon, *Oplatek* with the Institute of the Family * 11:15 a.m., the Franciscan Church, Christmas and New Year's wishes for the blind * 2:30 p.m., residence, Christmas and New Year's wishes for the Study Group for Young Children * 7:00 p.m., residence chapel, concelebrated Mass, sermon, *Oplatek* for lawyers * January 17 — Residence, 5th meeting of the Coordinating Committee of the Krakow Metropolitan Synod. The Cardinal pointed out that the first task was to begin the activities of the synodal consulting teams. He pointed out the tasks of the respective teams. He discussed the subject of the work of the various teams and declared the current year as a time dedicated to the exchange of information, and the next (1978) — to working out the practical solutions and proposals of final decisions. The study teams may meet at the residence of the Archbishop in Krakow or any other place, but they must notify the secretariat of the Synod. In the second part of the meeting, information was exchanged regarding the synods of the Katowice, Krakow and Czestochowa dioceses. The proceedings were concluded with a prayer and dinner. (From the minutes) * 8:30 p.m., Christmas carols at the home of Mr. and Mrs. Buchholz * January 18 — 7:00 a.m., residence chapel, concelebrated Mass, sermon on the anniversary of the nomination to the post of archbishop * 5:30 p.m., residence, the Secretariat of the Synod of the Krakow Archdiocese * January 19 — 3:00 p.m., residence, a get-together with the seminarians * 5:00 p.m., Skawina, parish church, concelebrated Mass, sermon, *Oplatek* with priests of the class of 1973 * January 20 — 6:00 p.m., residence chapel, *Oplatek* with the "Oasis" groups * January 21 — 2:30 p.m., residence, Council of the Pontifical Department of Theology * 4:00 p.m., session of Bishops' * 6:00 p.m.,

---

[2] See Glossary.

a get-together with the seminarians * January 22 — 3:00 p.m., residence, a get-together with the seminarians * 4:00 p.m., *Oplatek* with the artists * Same day — 9:30 p.m., Jasna Gora, symposium and days of prayer for poets, writers and composers connected with the preparations for the 600th anniversary of Jasna Gora, the Cardinal led the singing of the Jasna Gora Pledge * January 23 — 8:00 a.m., Jasna Gora, Mass at the Chapel of Our Lady, homily for the Polish artists, poets and composers in the chapel of the miraculous image of Our Lady:

> To understand man, one must delve into the depth of the mystery; to understand a nation, one must come to its shrine. We always come here with hope and trust. And it is well that when we come here, we hear most often the Gospel reading which we also heard today. The Gospel which recalls Cana of Galilee, an event that seems insignificant, but which says so much about concern. The concern of the newlyweds, the concern of the hosts of the wedding feast for bread and wine for the wedding guests. And amid that concern, the words of Mary: "Son, they have no wine." ...
>
> Today, Poles have various needs, the nation has various needs, a nation which, after a thousand years of difficult existence, is still seeking its identity, seeking to establish it and safeguard it. Poles have various needs. These needs are made known in dramatic ways.
>
> Among these needs is the need for inspiration which lies at the base of the nation's culture, a culture which is Polish and Christian. Polish and Christian! The history of the nation, the identity of the nation are connected with it. "Man does not live by bread alone, but by every word that proceeds from the mouth of God." ...
>
> There is also a thanksgiving in this plea. We give thanks that some are inspired, that still, despite all the created situations, despite the whole system, Polish culture, Polish arts are expressed in religious forms and draw upon religious inspiration.
>
> The greatest works by Poles of our time are works whose inspiration is Christian, religious. There is a great need for such inspiration. So we give thanks for that, but we also ask that we might never lack for this inspiration, and that Polish culture, art, literature, poetry, music, sculpture, theater, that all of them, drawing upon Christian inspiration, continue the magnificent and authentic traditions of Polish culture.

Same day — 11:00 a.m., Krakow, Sisters of the Holy Family of Nazareth, a get-together with the "Oasis" families * 1:00 p.m., Church of the Missionary Fathers at Stradom, the Feast of the Conversion of St. Paul; sermon:

> This is also a kind of reflection of the mystery of Paul. Where there is a lot of rejection, there are also a lot of conversions ... There, Christ becomes the spokesman of the most basic issues and the most basic rights of man.

Same day — 3:00 p.m., residence, Mass, *Oplatek*[3] for teachers * 7:00 p.m., Church of the Dominican Fathers, concelebrated Mass, sermon during the Ecumenical Week * January 24 — 9:00 a.m., Chapter house of the Dominicans, inaugural meeting of missionaries and retreat masters * 4:00 p.m., Slemien, concelebrated Mass, sermon, *Oplatek* with priests of the class of 1974 * January 25 — 4:00 p.m., Komorowice, concelebrated Mass, sermon, *Oplatek* with priests of the class of 1975 * January 26 — 4:00 p.m., Krzeszow, concelebrated Mass, sermon, *Oplatek* with priests of the class of 1976 * January 27 — 10:00 a.m., residence, symposium on the topic: "Diocesan Structures in Light of Canon Law" * 4:30 p.m., Chapel of the Ursulines, concelebrated Mass, sermon, singing of carols at the Higher Catechetic Institute * January 28 — 11:00 a.m., residence, session of bishops * 3:00 p.m., residence, session of the Curia * January 29 — 7:00 p.m., residence chapel, concelebrated Mass, sermon, installation of Rev. Witold Kacz * January 30 — Residence chapel, Mass with sermon, *Oplatek* with the Family Ministry * 1:00 p.m., Silesian Seminary, *Oplatek* for the disabled * 3:00 p.m., residence chapel, Mass with sermon * 6:00 p.m., Theological Seminary, *koleda*[4] * January 31 — 10:00 a.m., residence, Synod of the Province, Committee of Theology * 5:00 p.m., Jaworzno, concelebrated Mass, sermon, *Oplatek* with priests of the class of 1972.

February 1 — At the residence, presided over the conference of priests — heads of deaneries, discussion of matters regarding the Synod of Bishops * 5:00 p.m., residence, *koleda* for children from Pedzichow * 6:30 p.m, Church of the Discalced Carmelites, concelebrated Mass at the tomb of Brother Albert, homily relating to the announcement about the heroism of his virtues:

> **Every year we would meet here, at the Carmelite Church, to pray that he be raised to the honors of the altar ... I myself have witnessed conversations with people who have authority in these matters in the Sacred Congregation of the Apostolic See, who are charged with matters of beatification of servants of God; with people — as I have indicated — who have the authority, who often told me that they have rarely come across a person so heroic ... When we consider the person of Brother Albert, we cannot escape the impression that he expressed his own time, but was also ahead of his time. Because of that, he is a man of our time. And so we feel that our times, especially in our land, demand a saint of his spiritual profile. I repeat: this is how we feel, this is our impression.**

February 2 — 12:00 noon., Targanice, funeral of Rev. Canon Stefan Wojtylka * Same day — the Feast of the Purification of Our Lady

---

[3] See Glossary.
[4] See Glossary.

{CandleMass}, 5:00 p.m., Bielsko-Biala, Zlote Lany neighborhood, Chapel of the Daughters of Divine Charity, Mass, homily:

> We have appeared before the authorities, first in Katowice, presently in Bielsko-Biala, with a petition for the permission to build an appropriate structure which would be used in our ministry ... Fortunately, thanks to the decisive courage and steadfastness of the inhabitants of Zlote Lany, especially the owners of an appropriate house, there is a center of religious instruction there. Nevertheless, in light of the needs of the district which is growing so rapidly ... this is insufficient ... These people of faith ... who have contributed so much to society, people who toil at various kinds of hard work, deserve a pastoral center ... I wanted to be here personally tonight, and to personally speak of what we know anyway, about the whole situation of Catholic society in this part of the great city of Bielsko-Biala, and of our rightful efforts ... As we undertake them, we follow a lawful, administrative path. The respect ... for our rights as citizens, for our convictions as people of faith, demands that our petitions and pleas be honored within a reasonable time.

Same day — 5:00 p.m., Bielsko-Biala, parish church, concelebrated Mass, homily:

> The Christmas season[5] is a joyful time. We express this joy in Christmas carols ... We experience this period as a period of the great Visitation ... This explains the other great custom, which we call *koleda*. and which is the visiting of Christian families by their pastors ... In these visits of the priests we see some trace of the great Visitation of God who became man ... God, who comes to us as a Child and as the Light.

February 3 — 7:00 a.m., residence chapel, Mass for the repose of the soul of the late K. Dobrzycki * 1:00 p.m., Chapel of the Daughters of Charity, a gathering with high school seniors on retreat * Same day — 10:30 p.m., Zakopane — Jaszczurowka * February 4 — Went skiing * February 4 — 7:00 p.m., Nowa Huta — Mogila, retreat for the members of the liturgical service of the altar ("Oasis" groups), inauguration:

> Father prior mentioned here that I gladly visit "Oasis" groups, the youth gathering for retreats. Indeed, I do that very gladly. And always, the conversations which I have with the participants of such retreats confirm that it is a joyful experience for them ... Sometimes I would ponder how these young people, young men and women, go to the "Oasis" groups and undertake quite a demanding program. And I would think, that perhaps it was too hard, that it was too much, that it might discourage them. But quite the contrary ... And so, my dear young people, do not be afraid to lose your souls to the Gospel. Dedicate your time and effort, even your rest, to this Gospel. Do not be afraid that this is lost time, that you will not rest. This is exactly when you will rest the most, because man must rest with his whole being, both physical and spiritual, so that he may rest in truth and return having found himself.

---

[5] In Poland, it is observed until February 2.

February 5 — 10:00 a.m., residence, meeting of the representatives of the pastoral councils from 27 parishes * 12:00 noon, session of bishops * February 5-6 — Chapter house of the Dominican monastery, a scientific session of the Family Institute on the topic: "Premarital chastity". Lectures: Bishop Stanislaw Smolenski, Rev. Dr. Salezy Kafel, Rev. Dr. Niward Karsznia, Dr. Maria Lijowska, Cardinal Wojtyla *(Problems Concerning the Maturing of a Person — Anthropological and Theological Aspects)*, Dr. Wanda Poltawska, Prof. Gottfried Roth, Rev. Franciszek Slomka, Dr. Ryszard Rudzinski. Introductory remarks by Cardinal Wojtyla:

> **We wish to look at the entire issue, not in an academic fashion, of course, not only theoretically ... The subject matter we have chosen coincides, but certainly not by mere coincidence, with the last document of the Apostolic See, issued in the spring of last year, Persona Humana ...**
>
> **[Homily at the Mass for participants of the symposium:] "Blessed are the pure of heart, for they shall see God."**
>
> **[Lecture:] What does it mean, that man matures as a person? ... The essential spiritual structures of humanity manifest themselves ever more fully, but remain completely unique. They form the subjective "I" of each of us ... They manifest themselves, on the one hand, as cognition, awareness, and on the other, and dependent on the former, as freedom and responsibility ... To some extent, responsibility is the main proof of the personal maturity of man. The entire process of maturing as a person has also a relational character. Man matures as a person through relations with other persons and, at the same time, matures to such relations. We find the proof of the personal maturity of each individual in how he coexists and interacts with others ... We must consider the matter of premarital chastity in the context of the truth about the maturing of man as presented above ...**
>
> **[Further parts of the lecture:] Indispensable theological elements in the interpretation of the maturing of man. Maturing and upbringing. Responsibility to one's conscience and to God.**

February 7 — 1:00 p.m., residence, a visit by Prof. Dr. Roth and Dir. Jaroszewski * 3:30 p.m., meeting with the Catechetic Department * February 8 — 10:00 a.m., Warsaw, residence of the Primate, Main Council of the Polish Episcopate * 8:00 p.m., meeting of educators * February 9 — 10:00 a.m., Warsaw, plenary conference of the Polish Episcopate, meetings in the afternoon * February 10 — 10:00 a.m., plenary session of the Episcopal Conference. Return to Krakow * February 11 —11:00 a.m. Theological Seminary (Manifestu Lipcowego Street), get-together with the graduating secondary-school students (retreat) * 12:00 noon, Theological Seminary (Podzamcze Street), a retreat gathering with the graduating secondary-school students * Same day — 6:30 p.m., Our Lady of Lourdes Parish, patronal feast. Concelebrated Mass, homily:

The entire Church is nothing other than a great community of people, who in some mysterious, but at the same time real and visible way — although it is a profoundly spiritual and interior way — unite with Christ for the purpose of creating a new world, a truly magnificent world ... No civilization, no achievements of technology, no matter how spectacular, can create such a world if man lacks holiness.

February 12 — 12:00 noon, residence chapel, institution of Rev. Canon Franciszek Macharski (appointed capitular canon on January 11, 1977) * 12:30 p.m., residence, session of the Curia * February 12-13 — Visitation of the parish of Wieclawice * February 14 — 10:00 a.m.,Wadowice, regional conference (Bishop Jan Pietraszko's region) * 6:00 p.m., residence chapel, Mass and sermon for the sisters who completed a nursing course * February 15 — 10:00 a.m., Theological Seminary, regional conference, the city of Krakow * 1:00 p.m., residence, a meeting with Bishop Wesoly * 5:30 p.m., residence chapel, private Mass * February 16 — 10:00 a.m., Theological Seminary, regional conference, deaneries in the immediate vicinity of Krakow (Bishop Albin Malysiak's region) * 4:00 p.m., Mietustwo, a visit to a retreat * 6:00 p.m., Trybsz, a visit to a retreat * February 17 — 10:00 a.m., Zakopane, regional conference, southern deaneries (Bishop Julian Groblicki's region) * 7:00 p.m., "Ksiezowka", a visit to a retreat for priests who are chaplains of "Oasis" groups * February 18 — 6:30 a.m., Zakopane, Chapel of the Ursuline Sisters, private Mass * 10:00 a.m., Oswiecim, regional conference, western deaneries (Bishop Stanislaw Smolenski's region) * 6:00 p.m., residence, session of bishops * February 18 — 8:00 p.m., Krakow, Church of the Bernardine Fathers, meeting with the youth * February 19-20 — Visitation of the parish of Michalowice * February 20 — 4:00 p.m., residence, kinder-ball * February 21 — 3:00 p.m., residence, a conference of bishops: Catechetic Department, youth ministry * 6:30 p.m., residence chapel, private Mass * February 22 — 4:30 p.m., Cardinal Wojtyla celebrated Mass at the Chapel of the Daughters of Charity (in Krakow, at 8 Warszawska Street) for the Forty-Hour Devotion, and preached a sermon:

During a forty-hour devotion, even the number of hours is significant. This forty-hour devotion is especially significant on the threshold of a 40-day fast {Lent}. We satisfy the deepest longing of our soul when, at the outset of Lent, in the last days before Ash Wednesday, we gaze at the Blessed Sacrament. We receive the Sacrament frequently, daily. Although we participate in the Eucharistic Sacrifice every day, we must also open our thoughts and our hearts, so that this mystery may radiate within us. The Eucharist must be made an object of contemplation. Then its full richness speaks to us, and it is an abundant richness. The truth as simple as bread and as nourishing as bread speaks to us in a special way — the truth about love, which is forever expressed in this Bread. Because this Bread is the sacrament of sacrifice, a sacrament of death — a death through which God expressed His love for us. He so loved the world that He gave it His only-begotten Son so that those who believe in Him shall not perish, but shall attain life everlasting. This Bread is a sacrament of love. This very love of God which was expressed in the death of Jesus Christ. And that is why we do well to spend time contemplating this mystery. We do well to contemplate the Eucharist, not only to receive it, not only to celebrate it, not only to participate in it, but also to contemplate it. For when we ponder this love which is expressed in the Sacrament of Bread, then love is ignited within us, love is renewed within us. Therefore, these are not hours spent in idleness, when we isolate ourselves from our work, but these are moments, hours, when we undertake something that constitutes the deepest meaning of all of our work. For no matter how numerous our activities, our ministries, however numerous our concerns, our exertions — if there is no love, everything becomes meaningless. When we devote our time to ponder the mystery of love, to allow it to radiate in our hearts, we are preparing ourselves in the best possible way for any kind of service, for any activity, for any charitable work. And so it is good that you, Daughters of Charity of St. Vincent de Paul and St. Louise de Marillac, you whose particular calling is just this kind of work, set time aside to contemplate the Eucharist. It is good that you invite other people, who are dear to you, into your community, so that they may drink with you from this same source. May love, dear Sisters, be renewed in your hearts, and may the renewal of love bring about the strengthening of your vocation, your calling of service within the Church. May this great, unique love, expressed by Christ in the Eucharist, turn into a myriad of small but meaningful acts of charity in your lives, in your works, in your service, so that you may continue to earn the name which the Church gave you, calling you daughters of charity.

Same day — residence, a conference with the representatives of the Benno-Verlag publishing house * February 23 — Ash Wednesday, 8:00 a.m., Wawel Cathedral, Mass and sermon, blessing of the ashes, sprinkling of heads with ashes * 1:00 p.m., residence, post-regional conference * 3:00 p.m., conference of bishops * 5:00 p.m., seminar in moral theology * February 24 — 3:00 p.m., residence, philosophy seminar (ethics) * February 25 — 7:00 a.m., residence chapel, Mass with sermon for the Daughters of Divine Charity (Provincial Chapter) * 2:00 p.m., residence, session of bishops * February 25-27 — Zakopane (he stayed at Jaszczurowka), establishment of new parishes in Zakopane * February 26-27 — Canonical visitation of Zakopane — Krzeptowki, Pallottine Fathers (skiing) * February 28 — 5:30 p.m., Krakow, Church of St. Peter and St. Paul, concelebrated Mass, sermon, lectors, acolytes (with the Theological Seminary) * Residence, a conference in the matter of Benno-Verlag publishing house * February 28 (or earlier) appointment of a Committee for the Apostolate of Sobriety in the Archdiocese of Krakow under the leadership of Rev. Franciszek Skupien.

March 1 — 1:00 p.m., residence, Committee of the Provincial Synod dealing with the matter of the Department of Theology * 6:30

p.m., residence chapel, private Mass * March 2 — 10:30 a.m., residence, a meeting of priests on the issue of church construction * 12:00 noon, meeting of the team dealing with "inter-diocesan structures" of the Provincial Synod * 3:00 p.m., session of bishops * 7:00 p.m., residence chapel, private Mass * March 3 — 11:00 a.m., residence chapel, private Mass * Departure for Rome via Warsaw * March 4-14 — Rome, Polish College, private concelebrated Masses * March 6 — 3:00 p.m., Rome, Botteghe Oscure, meeting with Bishop Rubin and Bishop Wesoly * March 7-15 — Rome, Cardinal Wojtyla, in place of the absent Cardinal Seper, presided over the third meeting of the Council of the Secretariat of the Synod of Bishops, which prepared the works of the synod: *Instrumentum laboris, Calendarium, Panorama* and other matters. (Rev. Adam Kubis) * March 12 — 1:00 p.m., Polish College, a meeting with Archbishop Bernardin * March 13 — Rome, St. Stanislaw's Church, concelebrated Mass, sermon, a get-together with the Polonia[6] of Rome * March 14 — Rome, a meeting with Bishop Deskur * March 15 — 4:00 p.m., Rome, the Academy (Teologica Romana?), concelebrated Mass, sermon, a get-together * March 16 — 10:00 a.m., Congregatio pro Episcopis at Cardinal Baggio's, with Bishop Rubin * 1:00 p.m., Congregatio pro Institutione Catholica at Cardinal Garrone's and Archbishop Antonio Javierre's * 8:00 p.m., at the home of Mr. & Mrs. Habicht * March 17 — 12:00 noon, Rome, Polish Hospice, departure for Milan via Florence * March 18 — 12:00 noon, Milan, Catholic University Sacro Cuore, university chapel, concelebrated Mass and sermon * 3:00 p.m., auditorium, a meeting with students on the topic of the Church in Poland * 5:00 p.m., lecture *Il problema del costituirsi della cultura attraverso la praxis umana* (Polish translation: *Roczniki Filozoficzne* {Philosophical Annals} 27/1979, bk. 1) Fragments:

> Culture grows primarily within an entity which is capable of deciding for itself. Its fundamental thrust is not so much "production" of human works, but, first of all, a "creation" of the self which, in turn, radiates upon the world of produced works ... For by his actions man not only performs deeds, but also becomes himself through them, fulfills himself in them ... The fact that man — any man and every man, and therefore all of us — becomes more human through this, determines that culture is constituted by means of human praxis ... Alongside societies and individuals who have an abundance of resources, there are societies and individuals who suffer from their lack. Of course, we have to strive for an equitable distribution of goods ... The question arises, however, if the danger is not greater where the abundance of resources, the abundance of what man "has," eclipses who man "is," who he should be. This is a crucial, haunting question about

---

[6] A Polish community outside of Poland.

the future of culture in the world around the Atlantic ... At the same time, the selfless interior communion with truth, goodness and beauty is a source of the praxis through which one's humanity radiates to the outside world. The power of this radiance makes man's actions and works possible, actions and works through which he expresses himself most fully ... Culture constitutes itself through human praxis, provided that man does not become a slave of actions, of producing works, but can find it in his heart to delight in, to admire reality.

After the lecture, a meeting with professors * March 19 — 7:00 a.m., Milan, cathedral, concelebrated Mass at the relics of St. Charles * A visit and a meal with Cardinal Colombo * 1:00 p.m., return to Poland with Bishop B. Dabrowski and to Krakow with Bishop J. Pietraszko * March 20-21 — Canonical visitation of the parish of Bialy Dunajec and the rectorate of Bedkowice * March 22 — Dziekanowice, concelebrated Mass and a homily at the funeral of Rev. Jozef Pedziwiatr:

Whenever a priest departs from this world, I, the Bishop of the Church of Krakow, must recall the words of the Vatican Council which say that a priest represents the person of a bishop among the People of God, among the communities, among the liturgical gatherings, especially during Mass ... This bond ... had another basis in the past, in our youth. I wish to thank your departed pastor, that living in the same milieu as I did, attending the same secondary school, he entered the life of the priesthood before me. None of us knows, how much, on the path of his priestly vocation, he owes to those who entered that path before him and walked it alongside. Let God Himself be the judge of that and reward that ... May the priests who are among us show the path to the priesthood to new priests. Just as once another priest showed the path to the priesthood to his colleague.

March 23 — 5:00 p.m., Krakow, Church of the Holy Cross, Mass with sermon for the conclusion of a retreat for artists * March 24 — 12:00 noon, residence, a visit of priests — professors from Erfurt {Germany} * 6:00 p.m., residence chapel, Mass and sermon for graduates of a nursing school * March 25 — 12:00 noon, residence, Theological Committee of the Provincial Synod * 2:30 p.m., session of bishops * 7:00 p.m., residence chapel, Mass with sermon, ordination to the diaconate of Brother Marian Marcin Wojtowicz, an Albertine (by education an engineer, one of the *srodowisko*[7], participant in vacations and gatherings).

We have attempted to perform the episcopal service of ordaining deacons by keeping in mind the Servant of God Brother Albert, by being aware of his image, his example, his holiness — the Gray Brother. For the first time, a deacon is entering the ranks of his spiritual sons, one who, we hope, will soon be a priest. This is not contrary to Brother Albert's thinking, nor is it against his rule. This was foreseen by him, and is only now

---

[7] See Glossary.

being realized for the first time.

March 26 — 11:00 a.m., residence, session of the Curia * 3:00 p.m., residence, a visit of the French Consul * March 26-29 — Visitation of the parish of Zielonki * March 27 — The Dominican Basilica, conclusion of an academic retreat, opening of an exhibit dedicated to Pier Giorgio Frassati.

> **In the generation with which I had very close contacts, in my student days, the memory of [this person] was extremely vivid. He was considered a model; on mountain hikes, climbing trips, on winter ski outings, we thought that he might have done the same, that this was part of his road to sanctification, that he found God in all of this ... Each of us must break something within himself, break through some sort of shell — each of us, and here I also speak of myself — in order to see man, in order to be concerned with man, in order to understand man's situation, his suffering, his difficulties. That is what he did: Pier Giorgio Frassati ... Go and see what a man of the eight beatitudes looked like ... Let us all rekindle a desire in ourselves to become people of the eight beatitudes. In this there are riches, in this there is maturity. In this there is the fullness which Christ realizes in us.**

Same day — Zielonki, visitation. Sermon to older married couples:

> **Such perseverance is the result of God's grace, so we ask God for His blessing. It is also the result of the good, noble, human will. And so we ask people to persevere ...**
> **[Blessing of young married couples:] You must have great faith in God in order to be equal to the duties of the community of marriage, especially in the sphere of transmitting life. How delicate are these duties, how much human desire struggles here with true love, which means true responsibility — how deep a faith in God is required to be equal to all of this ... God has said: "Thou shalt not kill!" If you believe in God, you will believe in the person who has been conceived, who is already alive, who is carried by a woman beneath her heart.**

Same day — Tonic (a town belonging to the parish of Zielonki), Mass for the ailing near the historic statue of St. Stanislaw: "When St. Stanislaw came eye to eye with the danger of life, when he had to bear witness to the truth, thereby emulating Our Lord Jesus, this inner power of the spirit gave him strength — the power of the Holy Spirit. May ... the very same power of the Holy Spirit give you comfort and strength in your suffering." * Same day — Pawlikowice, visitation. Sermon to the youth and children: "The family of the children of God, the family of the Church, the parish family always meets at a common meal, at the family table ... We feast on the Word of the Lord ... And most of all we feast on the Body of Christ." * March 29 — Departure for Rome for a session of the Congregatio pro Institutione Catholica * 12:00 noon, Vatican, Bishop Deskur's chapel, concelebrated Mass * 5:00 p.m., Basilica of St. Peter, Capella Papalis, Mass * March 30 — 7:00 a.m.,

Rome, Chapel of the Norbertine Sisters, concelebrated Mass, sermon *
12:00 noon, meeting with Bishop Deskur, Bishop Rubin and Bishop
Wesoly * 7:30 p.m., Archbishop Poggi, Msgr. Faustino Sainz * March
31 — 7:00 a.m., Rome, chapel of the Polish College, concelebrated
Mass * 10:15 a.m., Vatican, an audience with Pope Paul VI *
Archbishop Casaroli * Congregatio pro Causis Sanctorum *
Congregatio pro Institutione Catholica * A visit at Mr. & Mrs. Habicht
* On the same date: a letter from M. A. Krapiec, Rector of KUL[8], to the
Department of University and Pedagogical Research and Studies with-
in the Ministry of Science, Higher Education and Technology in
Warsaw: a petition for the approval of the resolution by the Senate of
KUL of December 10, 1976 (previously, a motion based on the resolu-
tion by the College of Christian Philosophy of November 11, 1976), to
grant Cardinal Karol Wojtyla the title of Honorary Professor of KUL (a
title provided for by the constitution of KUL). The documents of KUL
show no record of any response from the Ministry. (Rev. Andrzej Szostek)

April 1 — 7:00 a.m., Rome, chapel at the Polish College, concelebrated Mass * 10:00 a.m., departure for Warsaw * 1:00 p.m., Warsaw,
a visit with Bishop B. Dabrowski * 2:00 p.m., a visit with the Primate
* Return to Krakow * April 2 — 11:00 a.m., Krakow, residence, session of bishops * 12:00 noon, session of the Curia * 4:30 p.m., beginning of the visitation of the parish of Raclawice Olkuskie * 9:00 p.m.,
Krakow, Church of St. Szczepan, the conclusion of an "evangelizing
retreat" * April 2-3 — Visitation of the parish of Raclawice (Szklary) *
April 3 — Szklary, as part of the visitation of the parish of Raclawice
Olkuskie, blessing of the church organ, blessing of families: "And
because you have come here in such great numbers, ... the best thing
we can do is to have each family gather together and stand ... around
the chapel. I will then be able to see each family in its entirety and bless
it. Let this be a special visitation of all the families." He said that this
was the third stage of the visitation. He had been here towards the end
of October 1976 (Confirmation), and before: "I remember well that
Sunday in August when I was here for the first time. It is good that we
no longer recall that. It is good that peace has returned ... We are trying to forget everything which hurt us." * April 4 — 2:00 p.m., residence, Council of the Pontifical Department of Theology * 7:30 p.m.,
Church of St. Joseph, concelebrated Mass, introductory remarks during
a retreat for lawyers * April 5 — 6:30 p.m., residence chapel, private
Mass * April 6 — 1:00 p.m., Salvatorian cemetery, funeral of Barbara
Kudlinska * 5:00 p.m., cathedral, Tenebrae * 7:30 p.m., Church of the
Felician Sisters, concelebrated Mass, final remarks during a retreat for

---

[8] Catholic University of Lublin.

physicians * April 7 — 10:00 a.m., Holy Thursday, Wawel Cathedral, concelebrated Missa Chrismatis:

> **All of us also, dear brother priests, all of us bishops, who have already been chosen despite all our unworthiness, in full awareness of this unworthiness, we wish to prepare ourselves so that He could come to us, so that He may come through us; through our words, through our service, through our sufferings and trials.**

Same day — 2:00 p.m., residence, agape with the bishops, superiors of religious orders * April 8-25 — Illness * April 8 — 3:00 p.m., Holy Communion * April 9 — 1:00 p.m., Holy Communion * April 10 — Easter Sunday, residence chapel, concelebrated Mass, sermon * April 11-18 — Residence chapel, private Masses at noon * April 14 — 7:00 p.m., Mass and sermon for the 25th wedding anniversary of Mr. & Mrs. Janik * April 16 — Sends a letter to the participants of the 6th plenary meeting of the Pastoral Synod of the Archdiocese of Krakow. 457 people invited by the Archbishop participated in the meeting, 200 persons were eligible to vote. Proposals of the first two documents were put to the vote: *Preaching the Word of God* and *Transmittal and Growth of Faith in the Family.* Cardinal Wojtyla was absent due to illness. The meeting was held at the monastery of the Cistercian Fathers in Nowa Huta-Mogila. The letter: Welcome of the participants; participation — in addition to those eligible under canon law — the laity and the diocesan and religious clergy, whose presence (by the approval of the Holy See: letter of April 22, 1975) "reflects both the canonical principles and the post- conciliar, pastoral character of the Synod"; the responsible task facing the gathering: "the concluding phase". Expression of thanks for the preparation of the meeting * April 19 — 10:00 a.m., Krakow, residence. 6th meeting of the Coordinating Committee of the Krakow Metropolitan Synod. Reports of the consulting teams, summed up by the Cardinal. The focal point is the exchange of information. There is a need to add new members to the teams — to broaden the creative, not the technical, activities of the secretariat. (From the minutes) * 6:00 p.m., Rzaska, Albertine Sisters — convalescence * April 19-25 — Rzaska, Chapel of the Albertine Sisters, private Masses * April 26 — 10:00 a.m., residence chapel, private Mass * 12:00 noon, a visit of Cardinal Joseph Hoffner and Bishop Desiderio Collino from Argentina * April 27 — 11:00 a.m., residence, Bishop Bednorz * 1:00 p.m., residence, apostolate of the liturgical service of the altar[9] * 5:30 p.m., Chrzanow, Sacrament of Confirmation, concelebrated Mass and sermon * April 28 — 12:00 noon, residence, the youth ministry * 2:00 p.m., Tarnow, at Bishop Ablewicz's * 6:00 p.m., Wawel Cathedral, the beginning of a

---

[9] lectors, acolytes (altar servers).

novena to St. Stanislaw, Mass and sermon * April 29 — 2:00 p.m., residence, session of bishops * Same day — 7:00 p.m., the Mariacki Basilica, sermon to graduating secondary-school students:

> **What will you, as a person, make of your life? What will you elicit from all of the talents and the potential which you are carrying within you? That is the question posed to us by the Eucharist ... I ask myself this question together with you, and I admit this to you. It is the most essential question for each person, and also for entire societies, communities, nations, for the Church ... That is why we unite prayer with Sacrifice and Sacrifice with prayer ... So that each of us would pass the examination of maturity in the scope of his entire life. We pray for this grace for one another. As your bishop and shepherd, I pray for this in your name ... that it may be granted to each of you to the fullest extent possible. Believe me, what I say is not mere rhetoric. I say this from the depth of my heart — this is what I feel! I came here with this feeling. With this feeling I stand at this altar ... I would like ... to turn to the Mother, to whose maternal care God the Father entrusted His own Son, that she may — do not be afraid of this word, I am not exaggerating — take possession of each of you — like a mother.**

April 30 — 11:00 a.m., residence, session of the Curia * 1:00 p.m., visit of a Vicar General from Berlin * April 30-May 2 — visitation of the parish of Morawica.

May 2 — 8:00 a.m., Wawel Cathedral, concelebrated Mass with priests celebrating the 40th anniversary of their ordination to the priesthood, homily * Same day, funeral of Rev. Msgr. Andrzej Bajer, pastor of the Parish of the Good Shepherd in Krakow:

> **When he would come to the Curia, when he would come to see me, ever since I was a bishop, I always felt that this man brought something special within him. I always felt that he did not come alone; he always came with his parish. And he never came in his own matters. I became convinced that he had no matters of his own ... And whenever I came here, be it for Confirmation, or a visitation, when I saw and heard your pastor, I always got the impression that he was so very much like you ... Often, in my thoughts and in my heart, I traverse this royal, splendid, rapidly growing city of ours, and I reflect. I reflect on this: I do not know if I have grown to the same level of concern shown by your pastor; but I reflect upon it, I reflect and I look into the hearts, the consciences of my brother priests — I reflect. Because we have to build the Church of the future. After so many centuries of history with the Good Shepherd in our land, in our city, we cannot allow the disappearance of His signs, disappearance of the life which He gave us, because "a Good Shepherd lays down his soul for his sheep." Your pastor took up this task. He prepared your parish for the future at the providential moment when it began to grow rapidly; he ... found the means to build a new church.**

May 3[10] — 11:00 a.m., Jasna Gora, concelebrated High Mass upon

---

[10] See Glossary.

the ramparts (the so-called "summit") of Jasna Gora * Main Council of the Polish Episcopate * 7:00 p.m., Mass and sermon:

> The promises of Jasna Gora form the program of the life of the nation. The program of a nation — and of society, of the young generation — who wish to live their lives according to these promises ... We, the Polish bishops, try to be faithful to this program of the life of the nation ... also when we, as in the recent months, appeal to the authorities in the matter of the workers, the people of labor, in matters of their existence, asking for amnesty for them. All of this is the legacy of the promises of Jasna Gora ... These promises are a special asset of the nation and ... of man in Poland: a Christian, a believer, and, I must say, also the non-believer. Because we respect all people, including those who honestly, according to their own convictions, do not believe. That is a matter of their own conscience, a matter of their own inner responsibility. But this matter absolutely cannot be the content of a political program or the content of a program of the upbringing of our children ... It is good that we will be renewing our promises of Jasna Gora on the Feast of St. Stanislaw ... Stanislaw built the foundations of moral order ... and defended man in the name of that order. He told the king many times: "you may not." Not because he did not respect the king, but because moral order, social justice, righteous behavior are the foundations of authority.

May 4-5 — 7:00 a.m., Jasna Gora, Chapel of Our Lady, concelebrated Mass, 158th plenary conference of the Polish Episcopate * May 6 — 11:00 a.m., Krakow, residence, conference of bishops * 3:00 p.m., Kalwaria Zebrzydowska * 8:00 p.m., Chapel of Our Lady, Mass, sermon * May 7 — 9:00 a.m., Wawel Cathedral, ordination of deacons:

> All of this has been written by you yourselves on those pages, on which you asked me, your bishop, in your own words, for ordination to the diaconate ... I must admit that I took your petitions, all these pages, with me to Jasna Gora, where the Conference of the Polish Episcopate was held since May 3, during observances of the Feast of Our Lady Queen of Poland. I thought to myself: there I will be able to read them in solitude. I thought to myself: let all of this lie here for a few days, in the presence of the Mother of God. And then yesterday, late in the evening, I spoke with you about what you wrote. Remember it well. This is the same truth: the Church lives, the Church owes its vitality to the work of the Spirit, whom we have thanks to the Crucified and Risen Christ. In our Homeland ... the Church owes its vitality, unusual in the scope of history, to the work of the Spirit as expressed in the person of Stanislaw, the Bishop of Krakow ... The Church hopes to owe its continued vitality to you.

Same day — 7th plenary meeting of the Pastoral Synod of the Archdiocese of Krakow (at Wawel Cathedral). The topic: participation of the Church of Krakow in the priestly mission of Jesus Christ (six reports), and reports on the functioning of parish councils. Cardinal Wojtyla presided at the meeting, delivered an inaugural speech and preaches a homily during Mass.

> [Inaugural address:] The Synod ... is supposed to transplant the

renewal of the Church, begun by the Second Vatican Council, into the life of the Church of Krakow. This involves ... more than becoming familiar with the content of the Council documents. This involves the process of renewal of the Church.

[Homily about St. Stanislaw:] It was necessary that such a priest should stand at the beginning of our history, 900 years ago, upon the Wawel hill. It was necessary that by the price of his death, suffered during the celebration of the Eucharistic Sacrifice, something should begin to unite and come together in the history of our nation, in the history of the Polish spirit ...

Today, although the sword of a king does not fall upon the heads of bishops or priests, as it did 900 years ago, there emerge other divisions, produced by contemporary methods and reaching much more deeply into the awareness of contemporary man. There are attempts to separate what is human from what is holy. Just as once, it took the sacrifice of Stanislaw, so today it takes many conscious efforts on our part, apostolic and pastoral efforts, to prevent this division. And if such division should occur ... then there is an even greater need for people, communities, who have a deepened awareness of participation in the royal priesthood of Christ, who will become a new leaven — just as once, centuries ago ... it was necessary for Bishop Stanislaw to stand before the altar, to suffer a martyr's death.

Same day — 7:30 p.m., residence, visit of Bishop Carter and guests from Canada, supper * May 8[11] — 7:00 a.m., residence chapel, concelebrated private Mass * 9:00 a.m., procession from Wawel to Skalka with the participation of guests from Canada and the Polish Episcopate (the procession was led by Bishop Rakotondrasoa of Madagascar), participation in a concelebrated Mass led by Bishop Carter, introductory remarks: "We are the same Catholic nation, the same People of God, the royal priesthood, made so by Christ, through the service of His great bishops: Wojciech {Adalbert} in Gniezno, and Stanislaw in Krakow." * Same day — 5:00 p.m., Polish-Canadian conference * May 9 — With Primate Wyszynski and Bishop Carter, farewell to the guests * May 19 — Krakow, Franciszkanska Street, 23rd meeting of the Committee for Catholic Education with the chairmen of the sections. Since the sections had been active for 20 years, the Cardinal asked the chairmen for more extensive reports, so that the Committee could draw conclusions for the future. A proposal (accepted-moved by Mrs. Jasinska-Wojtkowska) to create a section of instructors of religious literature at Theological Seminaries. A proposal to publish a document on the state of Catholic education in Poland. In the afternoon: a discussion that was not on the original agenda (the Cardinal, Bishop Oblak, Bishop Wojcik, Rev. Prof. Zurowski, Rev. Prof. Jaworski, Rev. Prof. Majka, Rev. Prof. Inlender, Rev. Prof. Peter; and Fr. Przybylski) on the work of the sections; the issue of new regulations; later a meeting of the members of

---

[11] May 8th is the Feast of St. Stanislaw, Bishop & Martyr, Bishop of Krakow, early 11th C.

the committee only: Issues facing the Committee following the Congress of Catholic Institutes of Higher Learning in Rome (November 23-December 4, 1976) — the issue of implementing the memorial by the Committee for Education, and the matter of a study group of Marxism at KUL and other departments — suggestion by the Cardinal that the Grand Chancellor, Bishop Pylak, be asked to create such a study group at KUL. (From the minutes) * May 11 — 9:00 a.m., residence, meeting of the Educational Council of the Episcopate.

In his introductory remarks, the Cardinal made reference to last year's Second International Congress of Catholic Institutes of Higher Learning in Rome. All such institutions in Poland were represented either as members or in the role of observers (ATK) ... Rome confirmed the correctness of this form of Catholic institutes that is guaranteed in Poland by the Educational Council of the Episcopate. As he summarized the discussion on the proposed new statutes, Cardinal Wojtyla stated, "The discussion proved that ... the Council is concerned with more than just the promotion of cadres. In the future, the Council should become the body representing Catholic scholarship in Poland ... In a way, the Educational Council fulfills the role of a Central Qualifying Committee. [What is required] is that the process of creating academic cadres remain in the Church's own hands." (From the minutes)

Same day — 4:00 p.m., Kalwaria Zebrzydowska * May 12 — 2:30 p.m., residence, session of bishops * 6:00 p.m., Bestwina, Sacrament of Confirmation, Mass and sermon * May 13 — Presented a nomination to the post of ordinary professor to Rev. Boleslaw Przybyszewski. In his address the Cardinal emphasized the vitality of the Department. (From the minutes of the Council of the Department) * May 13-14 — Visitation of the parish of Poreba Zegoty * May 14 — 11:00 a.m., residence, session of bishops * May 15 — 12:00 noon, consecration of the church in Nowa Huta — Bienczyce.

We were witnesses to an act of great importance performed by the Metropolitan Archbishop of Krakow, Karol Cardinal Wojtyla — the pastor on the seat of St. Stanislaw. The chronicles and history of the Church will record that from the first years of his service as bishop, he involved himself fully in matters of adequate organization of religious life and of building churches in Nowa Huta ...

[Thousands of the faithful participated, in pouring rain, in the celebrations of the consecration. The Church in Nowa Huta, a socialist city, whose history from the very beginning has been marked with dramatic events, grew into a symbol of the invincible faith of the Polish people and the fidelity of the workers.]

...Who participated in the consecration? First of all, the local parishioners. Other people came from old Krakow and other corners of Poland, both spontaneously and as invited guests ... There were also groups from the German Democratic Republic, who had, as part of the noted Aktion Suhnezeichen, made a significant contribution of labor to the building effort. Many groups came from Austria, a pilgrimage from Burgenland, a group from the Diocese of St. Polten which was particularly connected with the building effort (the diocese had donated a tabernacle in the shape of the cosmos, in which a piece of moon rock was set, a gift of Pope Paul VI), a group from Linz, and a group from Vienna. Catholics in groups of various sizes came to Nowa Huta from Czechoslovakia, Hungary, Yugoslavia. A numerous group of guests from the Federal Republic of Germany, among them Bishop Paderborn, Fr. Paul Northus and delegates of the international organization "Pax Christi," to whom the building effort owes much. Two monsignors from France as the official representatives of the Archbishop of Paris, F. Marty, a group from Belgium, one from Holland (a set of bells was the gift of the Dutch to the church), a guest from Japan, a Portuguese group which was associated with this church. There were also representatives of the faithful from England, Canada, USA, Finland and Italy ...

... some concise information about the church. Permission for its construction was granted on October 13, 1967. Early the following morning, after saying Mass, Cardinal Wojtyla went to the church site and removed the first symbolic piece of earth with a pickax to make room for the foundations of the new temple. Construction lasted 10 years. The cornerstone, from the ruins of the walls of Constantine's Basilica of St. Peter in Rome, was presented to the Church of Nowa Huta by Pope Paul VI. The unusual architecture of the church, in the shape of an ark, the interior decoration and other details relating to it were designed by a Krakow architect Wojciech Pietrzyk... (*Tygodnik Powszeczhny*, 22 May 1977)

Cardinal Wojtyla's sermon:

We want this temple, which has a Mother as its patroness, to be our mother. We also want this temple, whose patroness is the Queen of Poland, to reign over us. Most of all, however, we long for the Mother. We feel such a strong need for her presence at this turn of history where mankind now finds itself, where Europe and our Homeland found themselves ... This city is not a city of people who belong to no one. Of people, to whom one may do whatever one wants, who may be manipulated according to the laws or rules of production and consumption. This city is a city of the children of God ... This temple was necessary so that this could be expressed, that it could be emphasized ... We still have among us those who ... began to build it with their suffering. We pay them the highest respect ... Was it not possible — is it still not possible — to take any other path as we continue to struggle to build other houses of God which are so necessary in Poland? ... Let us hope that in this our Homeland, which has a Christian and humanitarian past, these two orders — light and the Gospel, and the respect for human rights — come together more effectively in the future.

May 17 — 9:00 a.m., residence chapel, concelebrated Mass with the Council of Priests, sermon, meeting of the Council of Priests * 4:30 p.m., a get-together with the editorial teams of *Tygodnik Powszechny* and *Znak* * Same day — 7:00 p.m., Skotniki, Sacrament of Confirmation, Mass and sermon * May 18 — 10:00 a.m., residence, conference of priests — heads of deaneries * 6:00 p.m., Strumiany, concelebrated Mass, sermon, reunion with priests ordained in 1973 * May 19 — Visitation in Dabrowa Szlachecka * May 21 — 11:00 a.m., residence, session of bishops * 3:30 p.m., Krakow, 10 St. Mark Street, a visit at the Catechetic Study Group * 5:30 p.m., Marcyporeba, blessing of an altar, Sacrament of Confirmation, concelebrated Mass, sermon, reunion of priests ordained in 1976 * May 22 — 9:00 a.m., Wawel Cathedral, ordination of priests: "Social unity is very necessary for the Church, it is necessary for the nation and for humanity. The Church, especially in Poland, is striving for it." * Same day — 5:00 p.m., he ordained two priests in Poronin:

> **A priest is taken from among the people ... — it is necessary then, that the People of God, the parishioners, the families of all of Podhale[12], of the whole Archdiocese, of all of Poland, provide these men. Christ does not take them away, but summons them. And when He calls, it means we must follow — we must give. Because this gift is repaid a thousand-fold.**

May 23 — 6:00 p.m., Oswiecim, concelebrated Mass, sermon, reunion of the priests on the fifth anniversary of ordination. From the sermon:

> **The very fact of ordination unites the entire priesthood and the individual years of the priesthood with the bishop. It is well ... that we meet ... to speak of these matters among ourselves, to ponder them, to pray over them together, because after all we are brothers.**

May 24 — 6:00 p.m., Czernichow, sermon during a reunion of priests ordained in 1974 (instead of a visitation, which had been planned for April 17, but did not take place because of the Cardinal's illness):

> **You know well that it is my custom to talk with each seminarian during his stay at the seminary. And often, to my question "what brought you to the seminary," I hear the answer that it was these times, times of a great struggle between good and evil, times of the great struggle between Mary and Satan, that draw many ... into the priesthood, so that they might participate in this great battle fully, decisively, in a well-defined manner ... I will say even more: this battle runs through the heart of each one of us. A priestly ordination, a priestly vocation, do not free us from the battle ... All of this convinces us to turn our hearts and our minds to the Mother of God, Succor of priests.**

May 25 — 5:00 p.m., residence, presided over a session of the Archdiocesan Committee for Sobriety * May 26 — 3:30 p.m., residence, the Marian Team * 6:00 p.m., Chyzne, concelebrated Mass, sermon, reunion of priests ordained in 1970 * May 27 — 12:00 noon., residence, the Council of the Pontifical Department of Theology, the Cardinal participated in a colloquium examining Rev. Dr. Kazimierz Hota for admission to assistant professorship * 7:00 p.m., at the home

---

[12] A region in the Carpathian Mountains in the south of Poland.

of Mr. & Mrs. Grygiel * May 28 — 11:00 p.m., residence, a session of bishops * May 28-29 — Visitation of the parish of Kamien * May 29 — Piekary Slaskie, a pilgrimage of men, sermon:

> It is well that today, here on the hill of Piekary, we remind ourselves of everything by which man himself can become the destroyer of his greatness. It is well that mention is made, among others, of the vice of drunkenness. Because man, to whom Jesus Christ has given the gift of the Holy Spirit, must be worthy of his humanity. He must not tatter it and drag it through the mud! He must not debase himself, deprive himself of his senses, and especially the one that says the most about man: the sense of responsibility ...
>
> I began my greeting with the words: Praise be Lord Jesus Christ. And I wish to end with your Silesian greeting. But in order for it to be Silesian, I will tell you about a small event of which I was a witness and a participant several days ago. I was strolling in the little forest of Bielany. I think that many Silesians know where Bielany is, on magnificently wooded hills above the Vistula, where there is a Church of the Camaldolese Fathers. And all of a sudden I hear shouting coming from the woods. I think to myself: What, are the Tartars attacking Krakow again? It turns out that it was a group of schoolchildren — possibly grade 8, I think — boys and girls. When they saw me walking in my cassock, they said to me: Godspeed! I answered: Godspeed! I thought to myself, now I know where these "Tatars" came from (applause). But I must say, I was quite impressed. Everyone who passed me, your sons and daughters, said to me: Godspeed! So today I want to reciprocate, here at Piekary, at the feet of Our Lady — so I say to you: ... Godspeed![13]

May 30 — 7:00 a.m., Chapel of the Theological Seminary (Manifestu Lipcowego Street), Mass with sermon * May 31 — 4:00 p.m., residence, a visit of the French consul * 6:00 p.m., Toporzysko, concelebrated Mass, sermon, reunion of priests ordained in 1966.

June 1 — 7:30 a.m., residence chapel, wedding, Mass with sermon * 11:00 a.m., visit of Archbishop L. Poggi * 3:00 p.m., residence, a visit of Prof. Wojciech Bartel * 7:00 p.m., at the home of Mr. & Mrs. Turowski — the synodal team * June 2 — 2:00 p.m., Trzebinia, a visit to the sick during their retreat (with Archbishop L. Poggi) * June 3 — 4:00 p.m., Zarki, funeral of Rev. Canon Jan Mroz, concelebrated Mass and sermon (with Archbishop L. Poggi) * June 4 — 11:00 a.m., residence, session of bishops * 2:00 p.m., a farewell to Archbishop L. Poggi * June 4-5 — Visitation of the parish of Pobiednik Maly * June 5 — Kalwaria Zebrzydowska, participation in the 9th Men's Day. The Archbishop presided over the Holy Mass concelebrated with the newly ordained priests of the Archdiocese of Krakow, he hands awards for the reciters. Sermon based on the words of Jesus Christ: "Go forth and

---

[13] Free translation of a traditional Silesian greeting, literally "May God grant you good fortune."

teach all the nations....," discussion of the issue of catechesis:

> **We must defend our nation against the imposition of atheism, wherever it occurs: in schools, in offices, in the military ... The state does not have the right to impose atheism, because authority comes from the nation. We must defend ourselves against the various manifestations of this forcible secularization.**

June 6 — 1:00 p.m., residence chapel, swearing in of 16 new pastors * 4:00 p.m., Trzebinia, a meeting with former prisoners of Rawicz[14] * 7:00 p.m., Bronow, Diocese of Katowice, concelebrated Mass, sermon, blessing of the Stations of the Cross, reunion of priests ordained in the same year as the Cardinal * June 7 — 8:30 a.m., Bronow, concelebrated Mass, sermon * 11:00 a.m., Gilowice, concelebrated Mass, sermon, reunion of priests ordained in 1963 * 2:00 p.m., Kalwaria Zebrzydowska, "drozki"[15] * 6:00 p.m., residence, a visit of Rev. Prof. McLean * 7:30 p.m., residence chapel, Mass for the late Jan Wilk * June 8 — 10:00 a.m., Board of the International Ecumenical Circle for the ministry to the speech and hearing impaired of Christian denomination * 1:30 p.m., the Rakowicki cemetery, funeral of Prof. Stefan Myczkowski * June 8-9 — Visitation in Nowa Wies Szlachecka * June 9 — Krakow, Mass at Wawel and a procession for the Feast of Corpus Christi. Sermons by each of the four altars.

> **[First altar]: The proof must be forthcoming, that human rights, citizens' rights, are being respected. Because this matter is compounding! It is compounding all over the world, it is compounding in our society. The awareness of human rights keeps growing. These rights are undeniable!**
>
> **[Second altar:] We must bend over every mother in Poland who has conceived a new human, a new Pole: we must bend over her with respect, and not with a doctor's lancet! (..) The nation must not put itself to death. It was put to death often enough by others in the course of its distant and recent history ... Forgive me, but I could not refrain from saying that in this great hour of sincerity, which is for us the procession of Corpus Christi.**
>
> **[Third altar:] (At this altar, the first part of the meditation was dedicated to the issues of children and the youth:) And we ask all of our educators to conform to the principles of the freedom of religion, and not to some other secret directives ... (Speaking about the university youth, he made reference to the events of May 15th:) Everyone was glad that this day, which was memorable because of the consecration of the church in Nowa Huta — Bienczyce, also began and ended peaceably in old Krakow. However, we must be aware of the significance of the fact that the university youth of Krakow, having gathered at the foot of Wawel hill in the evening, sang "Jeszcze Polska nie zginela"[16] — not surprising, after all it depends on them, but they also sang the hymn "God save Poland." Now this is very telling.**

---

[14] A political prison run by the Communist government.
[15] Literally "the pathways," a local form of devotion consisting of Stations of the Cross along pathways in the park.
[16] The Polish National Anthem.

And it is also significant that these young people made a choice. On this day they chose reflection, quiet, and not the noise of the annual Juvenalia.[17] This is very significant. It attests to the fact that the young people — and there are tens of thousands of students in Krakow — that they are capable of thinking about fundamental matters: for example, about the great mystery of human death, which sometimes befalls a young person. And that they are capable of thinking also of such fundamental matters as social justice and peace, as human rights, the rights of a human person, the rights of the nation, the responsibility for the great heritage of our nation ...

I also wish to say a few words about the Catholic press in Krakow, which has made special contributions here. I am thinking of *"Tygodnik Powszechny"* and the monthly *"Znak,"* which have been published in Krakow for the entire 30-year period.[18] In recent years the Episcopal Conference has felt the need to proclaim that these few — as if Mohicans — Catholic publications, press, book publishers, organizations, Clubs of Catholic Intellectuals, are a special asset of the Church, entries on its balance sheet. I speak of this here to tell those who serve the written word, who serve the good of the Homeland and the Church by means of this written word, of our solidarity with them, to tell them that we consider their cause our common cause.

[Fourth Altar:] I ask forgiveness from Our Lord that — at least seemingly — I did not speak of Him. But it only seems that way. I spoke of our matters ... I spoke of them so that we might all understand that He, living in the Sacrament of the Eucharist, lives our human life — the life of each and every one of us, of various generations and eras.

June 10 — Warsaw, Main Council of the Polish Episcopate * June 11 — 10:00 a.m., Krakow, residence, distribution of parish assignments to the newly ordained * 11:00 a.m., distribution of parish assignments to priests * June 11-13 — Visitation in Raba Wyzna * June 13 — Rokiciny.

The visit of Cardinal Wojtyla in our house in Rokiciny, as part of the canonical visitation of the parish of Raba Wyzna. At 7:45 a.m. we gathered at the welcoming gate in the park. The Cardinal was welcomed in the name of the convent by our Sister Superior, and subsequently by delegations of children, the youth and parents. In procession, singing "Pod Twa Obrone, Ojcze na niebie,"[19] we went to the chapel, where the Cardinal celebrated Holy Mass with our pastor, Rev. Waclaw Heczko and Rev. Stanislaw Dziwisz, the Cardinal's chaplain. In his address, the Cardinal made reference to the observances of the 100th anniversary of the Ursuline Sisters in Krakow, he spoke of the work and the contributions of the order. After the Mass, during which almost everyone received Holy Communion, the Cardinal was visibly moved by the prayerful mood of the people. Going out into the sacristy, he whispered under his breath, "Incredible, incredible." Breakfast with the priests was in the refectory; Dr. Jezierski and his family were also present. The Cardinal was interested in the work we were doing in religious instruction, and this was related by Sr. Iwona Dudzinska. After breakfast, the Cardinal visited the apartment of the chaplain, then

---

[17] A festival of university students, a tradition dating back to medieval times.

[18] Of Communist rule.

[19] "Unto Your protection, O Father in Heaven".

he went to visit the sick, who had been gathered in the home of Mr. & Mrs. Majchrowicz. At 1:00 p.m. we went by van to the cemetery, where the Cardinal also arrived. Together we prayed a decade of the rosary for the intention of the departed, then the Cardinal, together with the priests accompanying him, stopped at individual graves, blessed the new ones, including our new tomb. (From the chronicle of the Ursuline Sisters in Rokiciny Podhalanskie).

June 13 — Raba Wyzna, Rev. Msgr. Jozef Polonski's 50th anniversary of service as a pastor (during visitation):

This is the source of the deep spiritual culture which we feel so clearly in this parish. The hours spent in the confessional, the building of pastoral ministry from its very foundations, because ministry means, first of all, concern for the life of souls ... This venerable pastor of yours knows that this is where he must fulfill his duty, and for 50 years he has been fulfilling it.

June 14 — 3:00 p.m., residence, session * 4:00 p.m., conferences on translocations * June 15 — 3:00 p.m., Warsaw, a meeting with Prof. McLean * Warsaw — Tarchomin, Main Council of the Polish Episcopate * June 16 — 10:00 a.m., Warsaw, a conference of ordinary bishops * June 17 — 9:00 a.m., Krakow, Church of the Sisters of the Sacred Heart, solemn Mass, sermon:

The theology of the Divine Heart is part of the program of a life of faith ... The theology of the Divine Heart ... is not mainly an agent of deepening knowledge through the contemplation of God and self. It is above all a program of action: Have heart!

Same day — 1:30 p.m., residence, a dinner with the Superior General of the Conventual Franciscans * June 17 — 7:00 p.m., Basilica of the Jesuits. Feast of the Most Sacred Heart of Jesus, concelebrated Mass, procession, an act of reparation. From the sermon:

Today I spoke with a worker who told me how, in the workers' dormitories, the administration has been ordered to tear down all holy pictures and throw them in the trash! This "little" atheism, this administrative one, this primitive one, is directed against the human person ...
As we worship the heart of the God-the-Man, we think of how much the human heart has been uplifted. How much the greatness of man has been brought forth.

June 18 — 7:00 a.m., Kalwaria Zebrzydowska * 9:00 a.m., residence, session in the matter of Nowa Huta — Bienczyce * 11:00 a.m., residence, session of bishops and the Curia * June 18-20 — Visitation of the parish of Zawoja * June 21 — 7:00 a.m., Warsaw, Chapel of the Ursuline Sisters, private concelebrated Mass, departure for Mainz * 11:00 a.m., Mainz, airport, welcome (Cardinal Herman Volk, university representative Jozef Greniuk) * 8:00 p.m., Mainz, a hall by the Cathedral, conference on the topic: *To Be a Christian in Light of*

Vatican II, a meeting with the metropolitan chapter * June 22 — 7:00 a.m., Mainz, residence chapel, concelebrated Mass with Cardinal Volk, the Rev. Rector of KUL, Rev. Dean of the Pontifical Department of Theology * June 22 — 11:00 a.m., Maria Laach, Benedictine Abbey, visit * 1:00 p.m., Bonn, a visit at the Secretariat of the Episcopate * 3:00 p.m., Cologne, a visit with Cardinal Joseph Hoffner, President of the Conference of the German Episcopate * Neviges, sightseeing * June 23 — 7:00 a.m., Mainz, residence chapel of Cardinal Volk, private concelebrated Mass * 11:00 a.m., on the occasion of the 500th anniversary of its foundation, the Johann Gutenberg University in Mainz, bestowed a doctorate honoris causa on Cardinal Wojtyla. The ceremony was held on June 23 with the participation of Cardinal Herman Volk. The welcoming address was delivered by Prof. Dr. Ludger Schenke, Dean of the Department of Theology, and laudatio by Rev. Prof. Jozef Ziegler. Cardinal Wojtyla gave his doctoral lecture on the topic: *Subject and Community (Thoughts on the Topic of Contemporary Struggle for Man).* Participating in the solemn ceremony, among others: Rev. Prof. Marian Jaworski, Rev. Dr. Franciszek Macharski and Rev. Prof. Albert Krapiec. *(Notificationes)* * June 24 — 7:00 a.m., Mainz, residence chapel of Cardinal Volk, private concelebrated Mass * 10:00 a.m., departure for Warsaw, from Warsaw — departure for Olsztyn * June 25 — 7:00 a.m., Olsztyn, Cathedral, Fourth National Mariological and Marian Congress * Same day — Gietrzwald, blessing of the stations of the rosary * June 26 — 9:00 a.m., Krakow, the Dominican Basilica, concelebrated Mass for the end of the academic year, sermon:

> **We need both perseverance and the virtue of long-range thinking. The most important thing is this: once we put our hand to the plow, we cannot look back. If the cause to which you gave your heart and your conscience, is just, then we cannot be satisfied with outbursts, merely temporary manifestations of activity. We must serve this cause with perseverance, calmly, faithfully. This is very important for us Poles, and perhaps even more important for the young people, because the young are so ardent.**

Same day — 12:00 noon, Wadowice, jubilee of the 50th anniversary of Rev. Msgr. Dean Edward Zacher's priesthood.

> **I must admit that when I come to this church, every corner in it, every spot, has special meaning for me ... When I came into the church today, I had to look at one spot that will always remain in my memory. It is the space between the pew and the first altar ... I myself stood on that spot on the day I received the Sacrament of Confirmation from the hands of the great Metropolitan Archbishop of Krakow, Prince Cardinal Adam Stefan Sapieha. I remember this spot, I will not forget it till the end of my life. This was in senior high school, probably shortly before graduation ... And the Rev. Monsignor was our high-school catechist, he taught us religion at the Marcin Wadowita Secondary School, beginning with the 3rd grade of high**

school.[20] I remember, since the juncture of the years 1932/33, until graduation ... How many times were we together at Leskowiec! ... I must say, it
is impossible to overestimate how much of the true and deep devotion to
the Blessed Mother I learned in that Sodality ... And I wish to thank you,
my dear Rev. Monsignor, ... that you have arranged for my inaugural
Masses at this church in Wadowice so many times: first when I became a
priest, then a bishop, then archbishop, then cardinal. At each of these inau-
gurations, I always had the opportunity to meet with the parish to which I
owe my spiritual birth and development ... Man ages in only one aspect —
the soul must always remain young. I will never forget my old professor, a
venerable professor in Rome, who would say to me: Only now do I really
feel like a child ... And this wreath of fresh leaves symbolizes this spiritual
youth, this childhood, which is not only the beginning but also the end of
our spiritual pilgrimage.

Same day — 5:00 p.m., Lodygowice, blessing of the cornerstone
for the new church: "For the past few years we have again been able to
rejoice in the fact that the heritage of the People of God on this Polish
soil, which expresses itself in the construction of new temples, is strong
and is still growing." June 27 — 10:00 a.m., residence, session and conferences * 6:00 p.m., Bibice, blessing of the chapel, Mass and sermon
* June 28 — 10:00 a.m., residence, a get-together with the staff of
Tygodnik Powszechny * Before noon, a meeting with major superiors of
the religious orders of women in the Archdiocese on the subject of education of the sisters * June 29 — 8:00 a.m., the clinic, 27 Kopernika
Street, visit to Bishop Jan Pietraszko and Prof. Wladyslaw Krol * 11:00
a.m., residence chapel, a meeting with the candidates for the first year
of theology * 7:00 p.m., Church of St. Peter and St. Paul, concelebrated Mass, sermon, gathering. From the sermon:

In this Church we find ourselves anew. Let us love this Church, let us
build this Church! Because each of us is supposed to build this Church in
a spirit of unity with the Apostles, in unity with the bishops and priests. (..)
Not long ago, a very simple person said to me: What would we do without
you? The answer must be: And what would we do without you?

June 30 — 11:00 a.m., residence, session of bishops.

July 1 — 10:00 a.m., departure for Paris * 3:00 p.m., Paris, Polish
Theological Seminary, visit * 8:30 p.m., Paris, Center of the Pallotine
Fathers "Centre du Dialogue," lecture: *The Church in Poland on the
900th Anniversary of the Death of Bishop Stanislaw*, followed by a live-
ly discussion * July 2 — 1:00 p.m., Paris, visit to the Archbishop of
Paris, Cardinal Francois Marty * 6:00 p.m., Polish church, Sacrament
of Confirmation of several adults, concelebrated Mass, sermon * July 3
— Paris-Osny, at Bishop Andre Rousset's * 11:00 a.m., concelebrated

---

[20] In those days, secondary school had 8 grades.

Mass * Sermon during the Convention of Polish Catholics: about 4000 participants. Such conventions have been organized by the Pallotines every year since 1947 * 8:00 p.m., gathering at the Polish "ognisko"[21] *(Fr. M. Kolbe Foyer)* for the Polish youth in Paris. He signed a visitors' book: *I fully confirm what has been written above* (the entry made by Beata and Slawomir Kuchalski about the values and the role played by Foyer). *I would like to add a word about Teresa S[kawinska] who prepared herself for Foyer at St. Anne's Parish in Krakow. My heartfelt wishes for God's blessings upon Sister Maria* (Sister Maria de la Croix from the order of St. Clothilde, family name — Wanda Horszowska) *and all the residents* (Teresa Skawinska, *On rozda milosc* {He Will Give Away Love}, ed. Polish Catholic Mission in France, Paris 1997, p. 186) * July 4 — 7:00 a.m., Paris, Theological Seminary, concelebrated Mass, return to Warsaw and Krakow * July 5 — Krakow, various meetings * 9:00 p.m., Kalwaria Zebrzydowska, beginning of a private retreat * July 6-8 — Kalwaria, from 7:00 a.m., Mass, retreat * July 9 — 7:00 a.m., Kalwaria Zebrzydowska, concelebrated Mass, sermon for the "Oasis" groups for the conclusion of a retreat * July 10-29 — Vacation, private Masses, sermons three times * July 14 — On the occasion of the visitation in Bystra Krakowska, he met with the Daughters of Charity working in this parish (Congregation of the Daughters of Charity)

July 29 — 7:00 a.m., Zawoja-Wilczna, private Mass, return to Krakow * July 30 — 12:00 noon, Warsaw, a visit with the Primate to extend name-day wishes * July 31-August 6 — Vacation. Jezioro Biale in the Notec Virgin Forest, private Masses. Five days of camping in tents near the village of Biala (20 km away from Czarnkow on the Notec River). Kayak outings on the lake.

> **At one point, 5 kayaks came out from behind the islands, floating down the middle of the lake towards Mezyk. In the last kayak was a single gentleman in a grey cap, wearing a sports shirt. He left the others and directed his kayak towards me, coming within 8 meters. He greeted me in a resounding, pleasant voice, saying, "Good day, sir" — not knowing that I am a priest. My God! I didn't know that this was the Cardinal, it never entered my mind that I could meet such a distinguished personage on a lake in the middle of the virgin forest. (Rev. E. Klemczak)**

On his way back, by car via Poznan — a visit at the hospital where seriously ill Archbishop Antoni Baraniak was staying.

August 7 — 11:30 a.m., Laczany, blessing of the church, sermon * 6:00 p.m., Zakopane — Olcza, Witkewicz chapel, wedding of Katarzyna Piotrowska and Andrzej Zaleski, Mass and sermon * August

---

[21] Literally, "the hearth" or "home fire," a Polish community center.

8 — 7:30 a.m., Zawoja, private Mass * August 9 — Vacation * August 10 — 8:00 a.m., Wielka Polana, a visit of the "Oasis" groups * 12:00 noon, Krakow, residence chapel, private Mass * Wola Radziszowska, Polana Juszczynska, Bystra, Harkabuz, a visit to the "Oasis" groups * August 11 — 8:00 a.m., Nowy Targ, retreat for the sick * Rabka, a visit to Bishop Pietraszko * 12:30 p.m., Rdzawka, a community day of the "Oasis" groups of the Archdiocese of Krakow, concelebrated Mass, sermon, get-together * 4:00 p.m., Czorsztyn, at Bishop Andrzej's * 6:00 p.m., Trybsz, visit to an "Oasis" group * August 12 — 12:00 noon, residence, a pilgrimage from Aachen with Bishop Jozef Buchkremer * 3:00 p.m., Jasna Gorka (Slemienska), a visit to young people on retreat * 6:00 p.m., Kamcsznica, visit at the "Oasis" group * Zywiec, a visit * August 13 — 10:00 a.m., Miedzybrodzie Bialskie, visit to the ailing, at the health spa * Same day — 12:00 noon, Wilkowice, sermon at the funeral of Rev. Canon Adolf Bascik:

> He is also remembered by the parishioners of the parish from which I come, where, at one time, he was a vicar, as a great confessor. Certainly, he was a great confessor, because his heart was sensitive to the needs of man, sensitive to human suffering. And sin is always a suffering of the human soul, a pain of the human conscience. That is why it is important that, at the moment of confessing our sins, there be on the other side of the confessional screen a man who is sensitive, who can sympathize. Just like the priest of whom St. Paul writes in the letter to the Hebrews: one who can sympathize. Fr. Bascik was faithful and tireless in his battle for the faith, in his pastoral work. He went through many parishes and was always ready to undertake work in new areas. One might say he had a facility for changing these areas, the front lines of his spiritual battles, meaning his pastoral duties, continuing his work at ever new locations. Maybe this was because he did not become overly attached to material things. And he even complained about it — as a bishop I know this, because I often had talks with him on this subject — that as a pastor he also had to administer and manage, but he wanted to devote as much time as possible to his priestly duties, to the ministry of the word and the sacraments ...
>
> We can say about your pastor that he not so much died as perished, perished in an accident. This is also a symptom of our times: priests perish in accidents; they perish because life, the demands of pastoral duties, requires them to hurry, to use modern, rapid means of transportation. Maybe it was too late for your pastor to be riding a motorcycle, and it was on this motorcycle that he met his death. But this is a symptom of our times, and a symbol of our struggle, our zeal — to be on time, to be everywhere, to serve everyone.

August 14 — Wola Filipowska, sermon during the blessing of the cornerstone:

> The undertaking of the initiative to build a church here, the continual striving towards that goal, and everything that has been achieved in that regard to date, is proof of a particular strength of spirit. The priestly spirit and the Christian spirit of all the members of the Christian community

which has rallied and united around this church. Because the idea of building a church here, in this part of the ancient parish of Tenczynek — a church that is so necessary — grew in you, in your community led by your pastor, from the soil of the living faith. Although the times in which we live do not favor the idea of building churches, although we all know how many obstacles there are on the road to this goal — still, your living faith, inspired by the sacrifice of Blessed Maximilian Kolbe, impelled you to undertake this initiative and not to rest, until you have accomplished your goal. In this respect, Wola Filipowska is an exception and becomes an example. In a relatively short time, you have received permission from the authorities to build the church, and that is always the primary step.

Nevertheless, all of us who saw how you were struggling to obtain this permission, know that it was accomplished by no other means but by the strength of the collective will, flowing from your living faith ... And that is a great achievement. And this is also an example. In these difficult times, when the road to the construction of churches, which are so necessary, is barred by so many obstacles, we need examples like this ...

It is a good thing that in this particular case, the authorities followed the spirit of the Gospel. If for no other reason, the permission was granted because of our steadfastness, our persistence. We rejoice greatly in every permission; we feel that every such permission for church construction is a positive contribution to the normalization of relations between Church and state in Poland. All of us, we bishops first of all, and with us the entire Catholic society, await and truly desire this normalization. We truly desire a true normalization. We feel that a permission for the building of a church is a true contribution to that cause.

The same day — 5:00 p.m., Bystra Krakowska, blessing of a cornerstone:

A new Christian community is being formed here, a new parish of the Archdiocese of Krakow. At the same time, a new church will rise, appropriate to the needs of this community. The new church will rise in place of the chapel which you had until now, an inadequate one, but one to which your community owes much ...

Just as the first community of Christ's disciples had their home in Jerusalem, in this very Upper Room[22] which I mentioned — so through the ages, all of the communities of Christ's disciples, which are born of His Blood, which are nourished by His Body, which establish kinship with His Mother — all of them seek a home for themselves, an upper room, a roof over their heads ...

This important social issue, the establishing of a new parish, the construction of a church for this parish, found understanding with the authorities who make decisions about such things. Everywhere, at each location, I stress the fact that the understanding of these fundamental issues such as the creation of new parishes and the construction of churches which the Catholic society needs, is a real contribution to the cause of normalization of relations between the Church and the state in Poland. And this is a fundamental matter for the social life in our Homeland. So when I express my satisfaction that this matter found understanding here in Bystra, I am also

---

[22] The room where Jesus and the Apostles had the Last Supper.

thinking of all the similar cases in the province of Bielsko which are still waiting for resolution: and there are many of them. And I must tell you that they are very serious. Your community is relatively small, not among the largest. There are parishes that are growing rapidly, such as the one within the city of Bielsko itself, in the district called Zlote Lany,[23] where there is a burning need for a new church, where it is necessary to create appropriate social conditions for that Christian community. And there are many such places. The Metropolitan Curia of Krakow has submitted a large number of petitions for church construction to the authorities of the Province of Bielsko. If I remember correctly, there are about 30 of them. Several of them have been resolved this year, but I would have to say that the most important ones, the ones that represent tens of thousands of needy, believing citizens, have not been resolved yet.

I am also thinking of one other case, which might be called symbolic, that is, the construction of a church in Oswiecim {Auschwitz}. Several years, six years, have gone by since the beatification of Fr. Maximilian Kolbe — today we observe his feast, because it was on August 14, on the eve of the Feast of the Assumption of the Blessed Mother, that he gave up his life in the starvation bunker for his fellow man — but the matter of the construction of the church, which is sponsored by the former prisoners of the camp from Poland and from all over the world, is still waiting to be resolved. So I bring this up, because the day and the circumstances demand it.

August 15 — 8:00 a.m., Zakopane — Olcza, nationwide community day of the "Oasis" groups. On this day he visited "Oasis" groups in Olcza and Chocholow * Same day — 11:30 a.m., Ludzmierz, an anniversary of the coronation.[24] High Mass, homily:

We remember that it was a rainy day [the day of the coronation]. Until noon, it rained buckets, as it can do in Podhale,[25] but in the afternoon it stopped. The celebration took place outside. All of us still have it before our eyes and carry it in our hearts. And those young ones, who were born later, were told about it. Today, when I came here, the weather was uncertain, and the pastor wanted to celebrate the High Mass inside the church. But I said that we should go outside — as it was during the coronation. So, my dear brothers and sisters, if you get drenched, please remember that it is not the fault of your pastor, but mine. Because the pastor tends to his flock and wants to keep it dry — but the bishop is not that kind... But, my dear people, I must tell you that although, as you well know, it rained and even poured on the morning of the coronation of Our Lady here in Ludzmierz, where Fr. Leonard Haredzinski serves as your pastor, it poured even harder the following year in Rychwald, which is your pastor's home town. So I can understand why he is so afraid of the rain, because in his home town, in Rychwald, it really did rain buckets during the coronation itself; and, after all, this did not happen here in Ludzmierz.

This is what I mean to say — after the coronation in Rychwald, which took place a year after the one in Ludzmierz — as we were walking to the rectory with the Cardinal Primate, and when we were even complaining a

[23] "Golden Fields"
[24] of the Icon of Our Lady of Ludzmierz
[25] Podhale—a region in the Carpathian Mountains in the south of Poland.

bit about the downpour, the Cardinal Primate said: "Rain is a sign of God's grace. May God's grace flow as abundantly on our souls, as today's rain drenched us, washed over us during this coronation." I think that this is the best wish that can be offered to Ludzmierz and to any shrine, every year on the anniversary of the coronation. And so, this is my wish for you here, on the Feast of the Assumption: may the rain of God's grace fall abundantly on your souls. You know what rain means to the fertility of the earth — without it, nothing can bear fruit. And so without God's grace nothing can bear fruit in the human soul: no goodness, no truth, no holiness. For that you need grace ...

That is why when we were debating where to celebrate this Mass, in the church or outside, I was strongly supported by the Rev. Monsignor from Poronin. For this year in Poronin, at the end of May, during the ordination of priests, the sky was pitch black; we were just waiting for it to start pouring. But not a drop fell — the ordination took place. And if later there were a few drops, and then many more drops, this was also a symbol of grace flowing upon souls. I speak about this ordination in Poronin not without reason. For by praying with you to Our Lady of Ludzmierz today, I would like to obtain the grace of many vocations to the priesthood and to religious life from the land of Podhale. It just seems to me, as your bishop, that in the past there were more of these vocations from here.

The retreats of the Living Church, the retreats of "Oasis" groups, are a legal form of pastoral work of the Church. So it is difficult to understand the various harassments that are being used in attempts to cripple this work. And this is aimed especially at the farmers, at our hospitable "gorale,"[26] whether here in Podhale, or in Orawa, or in the foothills of the Beskidy Mountains, as I had occasion to see not far from here, in Harkabuz. These people are being threatened. For what? For being of service to Catholic youth, for offering them shelter, for that? At the least, this is very strange. And various excuses are being thought up! Picayune faults are found in order to frighten this farmer, this hospitable "goral," so that he would be afraid, so that he would give in to them! Fortunately, the farmers do not give in. We must state with satisfaction that through all of July and so far in August, not one "Oasis" retreat in Podhale was dissolved, all of them have been completed successfully. And rightly so, because, as citizens, we have a right to such things and this is also in accordance with our Christian conscience. Our Christian conscience tells us, people of faith, that no one has the right to interfere in our prayer, in a retreat, in a group prayer. If anyone interferes, even if by creating difficulties for those who extend hospitality to those who pray, that person commits an act of lawlessness! I declare that openly here, in Ludzmierz. This has also been declared in Krakow, in Tarnow, and in Warsaw, everywhere our stance on this matter is in agreement ...

And so I call to you, Our Lady of Ludzmierz, Queen of Podhale, guard that light in young souls, guard that inspiration which allows the youth, young men and women, to find the way of their entire lives: towards the altar, towards the service of God, towards the evangelical mission. I ask this of you, Our Lady of Ludzmierz, in a very special way.

Same day — 7:15 p.m., Krakow, the Mariacki Church, concele-

---

[26] Mountain folk in particular the Podhale region.

brated Mass with Cardinal Cook of New York, a word of introduction, sermon * August 16 — Residence, a visit by Cardinal Cook * 4:00 p.m., visit by Cardinal Mario Nasalli Rocca * August 17 — He stayed at the Kalwaria Shrine in the company of Cardinal Nasalli Rocca. The Cardinals participated in a jamboree of the youth on the occasion of the Feast of the Assumption. The Cardinal celebrated Mass and preached a sermon:

> I must admit to you that I greatly enjoy to visit "Oasis" groups, their retreats, to meet with them. I greatly enjoy listening to what you call testimonies, and indeed that is what they are. These testimonies reveal the whole value, the depth of experience which you gain from these retreats in these "Oasis" groups. And one becomes aware of how deeply the Holy Spirit works within your young souls, the Spirit who was given to the Church by Lord Jesus for all time. And how readily you accept this work of the Holy Spirit, how you hunger for it, how you are responsive to it. This is the freshness of the youth, of young souls. That they are responsive to the work of the Holy Spirit, of God Himself. That they are responsive to goodness, to truth, to beauty: and all of this is from God. All of this is accomplished within us, through Jesus Christ, by the Holy Spirit.
>
> So it is a good thing that we can come together with all of this here today, and crown it all, as it were, at the feet of the Blessed Mother. I would even say that we want to take all of this, this entire spiritual achievement of our vacation, and place it as a crown upon the head of the Mother of God in a very sincere albeit inexpressible manner. To place it on her head as a new crown, for she is crowned by everything that flows from the spiritual merits of the death and resurrection of Jesus Christ, her Son ...
>
> You bring a great achievement here. Prayer was the main content of your retreat. It was a school of prayer, you were learning how to pray. I will tell you: when I listened to you pray, I was also learning from you how to pray with all this freshness, with all the spiritual depth, with all of the openness of your hearts to God. And I ask one thing of you today: that you maintain this great achievement of prayer, of the school of prayer, through the following days and weeks, through the whole year and your entire lives.

August 18 — 11:00 a.m., Poznan, Cathedral, funeral of the late Archbishop Antoni Baraniak, concelebrated Mass * August 19 — 10:00 a.m., residence, a meeting on the issue of the pastoral care of the American Polonia * Same day — 7:30 p.m., Kalwaria Zebrzydowska, participation in the rites of "the Funeral of the Blessed Virgin", Mass, sermon:

> "And lead us not into temptation, but deliver us from evil!" This is how Our Lord commanded us to pray — to speak to the Father in this way. This last plea is particularly significant in light of man's experience and his struggle with evil on this earth ... We must be on guard against temptation, we must ally ourselves with the Immaculate Mother, the Refuge of sinners, so that she may support us, in her maternal way, in our battle with temptation. It is good if a rosary is entwined in our hands. It is good if we wear scapulars on our breast. All of these are signs of our continual plea: "Lead

us not into temptation," in which we seek the support of the Blessed Mother.

My dear brothers and sisters, many are the temptations aimed at man, which lead him to sin. There are especially many of them in the contemporary world. The most dangerous among these temptations is the one that says that "there is no sin," the one which does not want to call sin a sin ...

The temptation to which we are particularly exposed in our times is called atheism. Man is told: There is no God! The first humans were told: "You shall be as gods!" But contemporary man is told: There is no God! And everything is being done, whole systems are created, whole agendas, to tear man away from God, to distance him from God. To tear out, to uproot God from man's heart and mind ...

Many are the evils which threaten man on this earth. There is the evil which touches mostly the body, the evil which paralyzes our physical powers. There is the evil that comes from the elements of nature: fires, cataclysms, floods. We hear much about them: hurricanes, collapsed mines. We read about them all the time. And quite rightly Christ tells us to pray to the Father: "Deliver us from evil", from every evil. And quite rightly we sing in our Supplications: "From wind, hunger, fire, war..."[27], from every evil. But especially dangerous is the evil that comes from man. That is why, as I said at the beginning, Our Lord combined both of these matters into one plea: "And lead us not into temptation, but deliver us from evil!" Because, as we are taught by the Apostles, in particular by St. James, temptation gives birth to sin. And sin produces death: the death of the soul. And this is the evil which we must fear most. That is how Our Lord taught us: "Of this you must be fearful...!" ...

We must look at our entire life from the perspective of this closing plea. We must plead with humility! As I speak to you here, I am reminded of St. Paul, who also proclaimed the Gospel as we bishops do. I am reminded of St. Bernard, whose feast day is tomorrow, and of the words which were spoken by these saints: "so that in preaching to others, I myself would not be rejected."

August 20 — 11:00 a.m., residence, session of the Curia * Same day — 2:00 p.m., Chrzanow, sermon during the funeral of the late Msgr. Jan Wolny:

He was always characterized by a great inner peace, a stability of the spirit and a stability of heart. In relations with other priests, both his contemporaries and the younger ones, he exuded particular serenity which is not a random trait of character but the fruit of a true love of neighbor. The way that the departed Monsignor interacted with people showed that he was a man who knew how to see people in their proper scope, how to notice them, how to experience them in their own individuality. Without exception, in all his interactions, including those with his bishop, he knew how to maintain a proper sense of measure. There was something about him that he acquired through the years of his work with the youth because pastoral interaction with the youth shapes a particular spiritual attitude within us. It is the attitude of love: a trusting love, a love that expects, but also a pru-

---

[27] Words from a traditional prayer and hymn: Holy God, Holy Mighty One, Holy Immortal One.

dent love, one that can find the answer and provide guidance. In the past he had been an educator of students in secondary schools; later he was also and educator of priests. Many priests, primarily young ones, came to visit this ever older pastor of Chrzanow. He was always able to find a common language with them, he always brought unity; he knew how to bring unity.

At the beginning of the Holy Mass, we pray for the gift of unity in the Holy Spirit. We greet each other recalling this gift. Our dearly departed possessed this gift: he knew how to unite people. Around him all tensions disappeared; people became a community. That is how priests felt around him, those whose superior he was in the parish as the pastor, and in the deanery as the dean. And his parishioners always felt that they were a community around him.

August 21 — 8:00 a.m., Radom, parish church, Mass and sermon * Same day — 11:00 a.m., Blotnica, (Diocese of Sandomierz), coronation of the image of Our Lady of Consolation. Co-celebrants — Bishop Piotr Golebiowski, apostolic administrator of the Diocese of Sandomierz, Archbishop Henryk Gulbinowicz, Bishop Bronislaw Dabrowski. About 20 bishops participated. Pontifical Mass at the grand coronation plaza. In his homily on the topic of the family, the Cardinal mentions Rev. Karol Skorkowski, who was the last bishop of Krakow (1828 — 1851) before the times of Cardinal Dunajewski (1879). In the interim, Krakow only had an Apostolic Administrator. Skorkowski came from the region of Blotnica, he was a rector and a professor of the Jagiellonian University. The celebrations, under the motto "Our Lady of Consolation — Hope of the Family," lasted from August 20 to 21. (Stanislaw M. Chmielewski) * August 22 — 7:00 a.m., residence chapel, Mass for the intention of Dr. J. Wiadrowska * 12:00 noon, Bachledowka, retreat for the youth, a visit * 2:00 p.m., Mietustwo, a visit with the youth during their retreat * August 23 — 11:00 a.m., residence, session of the Curia * August 24 — 11:00 a.m., residence, session of the Curia * Same day — 7:00 p.m., Podwawelskie settlement, the small Church of St. Bartholomew, Mass and sermon, Eucharistic procession. From the sermon:

For this is the particular legacy of the Apostles, of St. Bartholomew, faith and love. Faith, meaning the acceptance of the truth contained in the Gospel, and the love of that Gospel. The proof of this love is in the words which they said, all twelve of them, when, after the departure of Christ, after His Ascension, they were called before the Jewish Council and forbidden to proclaim the Gospel. They said then: "We must heed God more than men." ... This is the proof of the faith and love of the Gospel, when we heed "God more than men" in the various aspects of our lives. Today, in this particular era in the history of man, of humanity, of Europe, of our Homeland, we need such people, such Christians, who can "heed God more than men" ...

And a second thought: ... this Church to which we belong, is not only the Church of Christ, but also the Church of the Apostles. It is Christ's because it is Apostolic. For it was on this one Foundation, which was Jesus Christ, that the Apostles continued to build, thus becoming the foundations of many Churches within the unity of the Church, through all time. And in each era, the Church returns to this foundation: it continues to return to the Apostles, because in this way the Church returns to Christ, its very first foundation. This foundation is very important. But not only the foundation. If a building ended at the foundation, it would not be a building. The Church, however, is a building and a constant process of building. We are continually building on this foundation. This Apostolic foundation is not static. It is dynamic, it is creative, it continually creates the Church. For with every generation, no, with every person, the Church begins anew and is rebuilt as if from the beginning. In each generation and in each person. When I was coming here, I was greatly touched by the fact that parents, fathers and mothers, were bringing their children in their arms, sometimes very small ones, of a few months. That moved me very deeply, almost to tears. Because this little one, through Baptism, begins to create, begins to build the Church within itself, or rather, the Church begins to build itself in the child. This Church of the interior, spiritual, fundamental dimension. This is the Church that is being built on the foundation of Christ and the Apostles, built within each of us since birth, since Baptism. And later, everything will depend on how this structure will develop internally ...

And if, on the occasion of today's observance, there is anything that I can wish you as a Catholic society, as a community, then it must certainly be a wish that your community finally receive permission of the authorities for the expansion of your temple. This beautiful, historical Chapel of St. Bartholomew is not, of course, adequate for so large a community, several thousand strong, as lives in this neighborhood ...

Only where faith is strong, aware, alive, where the love of the Gospel is ardent, I would say, uncompromising, where this love of the Gospel is expressed in an attitude similar to that of the Apostles — "We must heed God more than men" — only there, and always there, can we accomplish a visible structure.

* On the same day — He sends an article to Vita e Pensiero entitled "Una frontiera per l'Europa dove?"

August 25 — Residence, session of the Curia * Same day — 6:00 p.m., Morawica, Mass and sermon, consecration of the altar:

We know from the Old Testament that altars arose at the places of special encounters with God. That is how God commanded Abraham, Jacob and the other patriarchs to build altars, just as He did to the prophets of the Old Covenant. In the New Testament, Jesus Christ became the living altar ...

I am glad that this consecrated altar remains here as the last word of our meeting, of this visitation. For it bears witness to that encounter. It bears witness not only to our encounter of a bishop with the parish, and the parish with the bishop. but it also bears witness to that encounter with the Living God which you experienced here at this church, in this parish.

August 26 — 9:00 a.m., Jasna Gora, Chapel of Our Lady, concele-

brated Mass for the intention of Primate Wyszynski * 11:00 a.m., Jasna
Gora, summit, the promises of Jasna Gora, sermon:

> **Her image unites us, and that is why we venerate it so.** It united us
> back then, when they wanted not only to erase the name of Poland from
> the map of Europe, but to uproot that man whose name was "a Pole," who
> sings Bogurodzica[28] in the language of his forefathers, who feels his whole
> spiritual heritage, the heritage of culture, history, and nation. And, at the
> same time, the heritage of faith and hope.
>
> They came here, across the borders, from all the partitions, here they
> would meet ...
>
> She also became the Mother of those who had to leave our land ...
>
> They went forth from Wielkopolska, and from the so-called Kingdom,
> which remained under czarist occupation, and from Galicia, where there
> was great poverty. They went forth, and their entire heritage, their spiritu-
> al heritage, was contained in this image. Today, wherever you go to visit our
> compatriots overseas both across the Atlantic and the Pacific, as in
> Australia, everywhere this image proclaims that we are one! That is why
> the presence here today of the Cardinal Archbishop of Chicago together
> with a bishop and priests of Polish descent is so important. They came here
> to join our six-year preparation and our six-year thanksgiving for the six
> centuries of Mary's presence in the image of Jasna Gora, thereby her pres-
> ence in our nation. All Poles must give thanks, no matter where they are!
> Whether in Poland or abroad! ...
>
> In the year of 1977 we must call for help, as in the time of St. Adalbert:
> "Hear our voices! Fill the thoughts of men." Because we are threatened
> with a void, if the whole program of atheism should be realized; we are
> threatened with a void in our thoughts and in our hearts! These are the
> most frequent and most justified words on the lips of an apostle and a mis-
> sionary: "Fill the thoughts...", because only God can fill them.
>
> The human heart is restless until it can rest in Him. And the human
> mind, the human spirit, remains in a void, if He does not fill it! ...
>
> That is why we continue to remind, we continue to warn, that atheism
> should not be imposed in our schools, in our pre-schools; that they stop
> imposing atheism in our whole Polish life! We remind, because we are like
> the Confederates of Bar[29], "we are aides-de-camp of Christ, servants of
> Mary!" And today we say even more: captives of Mary; we are not
> ashamed to say that. This is the fullness of our freedom and our dignity.
> "We are aides-de-camp of Christ," let her make use of our services. Just as
> she used those of Fr. Kordecki[30] or Andrzej Kmicic[31] in the defense of
> Polish nation, in the defense of the spiritual heritage of Poles, in the defense
> of Polish nationality and Christianity! May she make use of our services:
> We are aides-de-camp of Christ, servants of Mary.

Same day — 2:00 p.m., to Krakow via Oswiecim with Cardinal
Cody, Bishop Alfred Abramowicz and a delegation of priests from
Chicago * August 27 — Residence, Cardinal Cody, a tour of Wawel,
Nowa Huta, Mistrzejowice and Wzgorza Krzeslawickie * 5:00 p.m.,

---

[28] A hymn of medieval knights dating back to the 13th-14th century, a battle hymn and de facto the
first Polish National Anthem.

[29] An uprising against the partitioning powers in the late 18th century.

[30] Prior of the abbey of Jasna Gora, military commander of the defense against the Swedish seige in 1656.

[31] A fictional figure from the novel *The Deluge* by Henryk Sienkiewicz about the Swedish invasion.

concelebrated Mass with Bishop Abramowicz in Nowa Huta —
Bienczyce. From the sermon:

> I am here for the first time since the day I consecrated your church; I
> am glad to see that today, with weather better than it was then (pouring
> rain), the church is tightly packed, especially with children, who have
> already begun their religious instruction here. This gathering around the
> altar of your church has an enormous significance. For hidden behind it
> are so many great causes, and, above all, so many threads of our history
> meet here, are expressed here. You too, inhabitants of Nowa Huta, are for
> the most part immigrants. You left your towns, your villages, you parishes,
> and you found your way here, to this huge workplace which promises a
> greater future for our country, and also for your families, for your chil-
> dren, for the new generations. And having come here from various parts of
> Poland, you gave expression to your faith — your living faith. This temple
> is a symbol of just that. Built not only from inanimate stones — and there
> are supposedly 5 million of them — but built primarily from living stones,
> many of them drenched in blood!
>
> My dear brothers and sisters, our coming together here today obligates
> us. We meet here through the faith, which is our common heritage. These
> our guests, Americans of Polish descent, came here in pilgrimage. Guided
> by their faith, they came to the cradle of their faith — and that is Poland,
> our Homeland ... They came into this church; many guests from overseas
> come to this church. But I say to you, my dear friends, I say to you: let us
> build the Church! Because it is never finished, because we must continue
> to build it, this Church made of living stones must be continually built year
> by year, day by day.

Same day — Wzgorza Krzeslawickie, sermon in the open air in the
presence of Cardinal Cody:

> When I came in, I saw priests at the altar, the priests who came here
> with the Cardinal: these are American priests, but all of them of Polish
> descent and all of them speak Polish; they came to visit the old country. I
> asked them if any one of them in Chicago, in America, had a parish like
> yours, a church like yours? Everyone admitted that they didn't have one
> like this. So, you see, we have something that they can envy us, just this
> canopy, where the wind blows from every direction ... But envy is a bad
> feeling, so they do not envy us. If there is anything that they might envy us,
> it is the fact that here, under the open sky and this decrepit canopy, we do
> perform the service of the Lord after all: this is something for which they
> could envy us.

August 28 — A tour of Obidowa, Klikuszowa with the guests from
Chicago * 11:00 a.m., Nowy Targ, a meeting of Cardinal Cody, Bishop
Abramowicz and the delegation of the Archdiocese of Chicago with the
community of Podhale:

> And now I wish to remind all of us assembled here of the Fourth
> Commandment. This Commandment says "Honor your father and moth-
> er, so that you may have a long and prosperous life." It is often remembered
> in this longer version, although the first words are the most important:

"Honor your father and mother..."

My dear brothers and sisters, why do I remind us of this Commandment? Because today's celebration is taking place in the spirit of that Commandment. Who are these, who have come here as our guests? We hear their names: they are Poles, children of Polish soil, Polish families, Polish grandparents, great-grandparents. Some of them are in Poland for the first time; all of them were born in America, but their fathers, their grandfathers, their great-grandfathers were born here, in Poland, in the region of Skalne Podhale. And leaving from here, from this hard land, from this rocky, infertile soil, they took in their hearts a great love and a great longing ...

And as they were departing from this region, these our brothers, fathers, forefathers, took with them hard hands, hands ready for work. For work which would create better conditions of life for them, for their families, but also for their relatives in Poland. And in their hearts they took a great treasure — the treasure of faith. They carried this treasure across the oceans, and found it on the other side! There are churches, parishes, priests, bishops there, too; the same Church of Christ ...

The love of parents, which God Himself enjoins on us in the Fourth Commandment, goes further. It encompasses grandparents and great-grandparents, and the whole community which we call the Homeland. We could say that these our brothers and sisters across the ocean, in the United States, in Chicago, have a new homeland. But they also have the old homeland, in Poland, here, on Skalne Podhale.

Same day — a tour of Glodowka, Morskie Oko, Zakopane with the delegation from Chicago * August 29 — "Ksiezowka", farewell to the guests * 12:00 noon, Krakow, Theological Seminary, catechetic course * On the same day — at the Church of the Salesian Fathers at Debniki — the funeral of Rev. Jozef Matlak SDB, former pastor of St. Stanislaw Kostka parish. Cardinal Wojtyla led the funeral procession and, in his eulogy, emphasized the fact that the deceased was a person very close to his heart * 5:00 p.m., departure for Wroclaw for the Nationwide Pastoral Days. Lecture: *The Spiritual Structures of the Church and the Community of the People of God* * August 30 — 7:30 a.m., Wroclaw, Theological Seminary, concelebrated Mass * 10:00 a.m., lecture: *Redemptive Mission of the Church and the Community of the People of God* * 4:00 p.m., a visit in Gliwice, Katowice, Jaworzno * September 1 — Krakow, Theological Seminary, consultative catechetic course for the priests.

September 1 — 7:00 p.m., Church of the Norbertine Sisters, concelebrated Mass, sermon * September 2 — 11:00 a.m., residence, talks * September 3 — 3:00 p.m., meeting with the Dean's Office of the Pontifical Department of Theology in Krakow * 6:00 p.m., departure for Siedlce * September 4 — Koden on the Bug River, celebrations of the 50th anniversary of the return of the miraculous image of Our Lady of Koden. Before the Mass, in the Basilica of Koden, Cardinal Wojtyla blessed a memorial tablet with the following inscription: To the memory of the Heroic Uniates[32], the Martyrs of Podlasie, who at this place got their inspiration and strength to defend their faith in unity with the Catholic Church. On the 50th anniversary of the return of the miraculous image of Our Lady from banishment to Koden, September 4, 1977". (Rev. Zdzislaw Mlynarski). Sermon:

> 50 years ago, the first bishop of the re-established Diocese of Podlasie in the reborn Republic of Poland, solemnly brought Our Lady of Koden back, after a captivity of more than 100 years, to the same place from which she had been banished.
>
> The pilgrims, with the bishop at their head, came from Siedlce to Koden on foot. They gave thanks for its [the image's] return. Because this return symbolizes unity — the unity of the Church. For she was banished from here, taken away, at a time when this unity was under severe attack. She was removed from here simply so she would not be the symbol of that unity for which our brothers shed their martyrs' blood ...
>
> Accept the word of the Archbishop of Krakow, who wishes to speak to you in place of the absent Primate of Poland. I also want this ministry of the word to be a prayer for his quick return to health and to all of his tasks, particularly the task of preaching the word, which he has fulfilled so often and so gladly for so many years for the People of God upon Polish soil ...
>
> 50 years ago, when Our Lady of Koden was returning here from her peculiar banishment, Adam Stefan Sapieha, the Prince Archbishop of Krakow and the direct descendant of Mikolaj Sapieha of Koden, whom we recall today in a special way, celebrated the Most Holy Eucharistic Sacrifice here, in his own name and in the name of the People of God of the Diocese of Siedlce ...
>
> Christ wanted His Mother to be with them [the apostles]. He wanted her to be with them at the moment when, through the inspiration of the Holy Spirit, they would become His Church; when they would set out from the Upper Room of Pentecost into the whole world to proclaim the Gospel to all of creation ... He wanted them to take the memory of her presence, her living image with them. He wanted her, the Mother, to unite all the Apostles ...
>
> He wanted them to be united by the image of her, to whom humanity and the Church owe His existence: the Word which was made Flesh and dwelt among us. And so the mystery of the Upper Room lives through generations and centuries. When Mikolaj Sapieha brought the image of the Blessed Mother from the Gregorian chapel of Pope Urban VIII here, to the region of Podlasie, a wondrous process began: Mary unites the People of God. And we are in a region where this process of uniting the People of God had a particular, historical meaning. It was here that the meeting of the separated Churches — the Western Church and the Eastern Church — took place. It was here that their coming together, their union, was accomplished. This was at the end of the 16th century.

Same day — 6:00 p.m., Warsaw, a visit with the Primate *
September 5 — 10:00 a.m., Krakow, the Czestochowa Seminary, at a

---

[32] Catholics of the Eastern rite, converts from the Orthodox Church, who were persecuted for their faith by the Tsarist authorities.

meeting of national representatives of pastoral ministry, he presented an introductory lecture entitled *Responsibility for the Church*:

It says in the program: the fundamental[33] lecture — I would say that it is not so much the fundamental lecture, but rather a fundamental issue. And it is undoubtedly a fundamental issue for all the pastoral programs which the committee is so busily preparing — and for all the programs of preaching, and for all the activities of the Church. It is a fundamental issue not only for this year, for which we are to prepare ourselves here in the course of our meeting, but a fundamental issue that continues in all areas of the life and activity of the Church everywhere. Certainly, in a special way in Poland. Here I wish to bring this fundamental issue to your attention. To show it at least in outline, to delineate its dimensions. To bring it to your attention and to place it at the basis of our deliberations for the next year, 1977/78 — because the new program begins from the first Sunday of Advent — and to show the significance of the responsibility for the Church within the context of that program ... The issue of responsibility for the Church lies at the very center of what we call the implementation of the Vatican Council or the Council's program of renewal ...

The whole richness of what is contained in the constitution Lumen gentium and in the pastoral constitution Gaudium et spes can be reduced to a very simple formula. Namely: We are the Church.

We are the Church — this means the necessity to overcome a certain traditional division into the teaching Church and the listening Church. In some way, into the Church in the active sense and the Church in the passive sense ...

Of course, "we," but not as the exclusive and ultimate subject. This would be a terrible error of horizontalism, which is often committed in practice. The Council indicated: We in Christ are the Church ... We are the Church to the extent that we participate in His mission, in the threefold mission of Prophet, Priest and King. The participation of the entire People of God in triplici munere Christi is one of the cornerstones of the Magisterium[34] of the Second Vatican Council on the Church ...

The threefold participation — in triplici munere Christi — is also the basis of the Christian calling. And so, recently, a great development of the study of the calling can be observed; the word "calling" is now being given an ever wider scope in pastoral ministry and homiletics, whereas before it was a term of a fairly restricted meaning.

The responsibilities of all who belong to the People of God vary; the responsibility of the pope is different from the responsibility of a bishop or a priest, a lay person, a religious, a university professor, a father of a family, etc. Nevertheless, it is an integrated responsibility; variegated, but at the same time a responsibility in solido ...

We cannot express the essence of the Church in terms of a community, in terms of the People of God, without stating that the Church is the Body of Christ. We must therefore look at the Head. But, neither can we express the essence of the Church as the Body if we look only at the Head, without indicating that it is also an authentic community of the People of God ...

---

[33] Literally, "main lecture," but in Polish the word is the same as "fundamental", which is used as a word play in the next phrase.
[34] Official teaching.

We need to introduce one other supplementary concept which is also found in Lumen gentium, but is greatly expanded in the pastoral constitution Gaudium et spes. In Church studies, in the doctrinal constitution, the "we" of the Church is already being expanded beyond those who are members of the Church, beyond those who are baptized, in a sense, to all people living in the world, especially in the contemporary world. We could adopt the principle that all those who truly identify with the cause of man, who participate in making the world more human — this is how the Council expresses it — they also participate in the mission of salvation, they also create conditions for the coming of the Kingdom — even if they do not formally belong to the Church, still — as we read in Lumen gentium — they are in some way aligned with the Church ... This matter is connected with the issue of the responsibility for the Church ...

The Church is an asset to all people. All are in Christ, all are redeemed. All, at least potentially, belong to His Mystical Body. All are in Christ, therefore the responsibility for the Church extends beyond the boundaries of the Church. Perhaps this is a paradoxical principle, especially in a country where we are witnesses to a battle against the Church, led from outside the Church. But we must not forget that even in Poland, there are many people who are outside the Church, who cannot find their own place in it, but who still consider it to be a true good — and what is more, are convinced that the Church is an authentic good of the Polish nation. Perhaps they do not see it as the good of all of humanity, perhaps they view humanity through the nation — but in some way they want the good of this Church, too. A good understood very essentially — they want the Church to be able to fulfill its mission. They see that only the Church can fulfill the mission to which others are merely pretenders ...

This is not only a sociological aspect, nor, heaven forbid, only a political one. It is very definitely a doctrinal aspect.

What does responsibility mean? ... It appears that in light of philosophical analyses, this phenomenon of responsibility is the key factor in the revelation of the reality of man as a person, in finding his identity. (I am thinking here first of all of the late work by Prof. Ingarden, from the very last period of his life) ...

The phenomenon of responsibility, the experience of responsibility, is what testifies to the fact that man is a very individual subject. Responsibility has many shapes, which Prof. Ingarden also points out. I remember that we talked about this shortly before his death. Certainly there exists a responsibility "to," meaning that there is some authority to which we are responsible. This authority is both outside of us and within us; it is a responsibility "to." But there is an earlier direction of responsibility, which is a responsibility "for." We are always responsible "for someone," "for something," and we are also responsible "to someone." In this case we say: "for" the Church ...

We are responsible to God, we are responsible to our own conscience, therefore to ourselves, for something. In this case for the Church. We are responsible to our own conscience for the Church ...

Responsibility in terms of an object, in terms of that something for which we are responsible, always implies a value. I am responsible when I am aware of value. I am responsible to the extent of the value that I impute, given that I impute a value ...

The deciding factor in creating the responsibility for the Church is the growth of awareness in all dimensions: the awareness of the community, the group, the society, and personal awareness — this is most important, but always within the community — the awareness that the Church represents a value, and what kind of value ...

And now this awakening and development of the awareness that the Church represents a value, and what kind of value — well, we know what great horizons open up to us here — in practice comes down to what we call (in our partly pastoral and partly technical language) apostleship, ministry, testimony, Christian life; it ultimately comes down to that process. Indeed, the process of our responsibility for the Church, the responsibility understood in this manner, lies at the very heart of the intentions of Vatican II, as a Council which issues its Magisterium, and at the very center of implementing Vatican II as a renewal of the Church ...

I think that each one of us — bishop, pastor, priest — who is connected with a pastoral workplace, should adopt this as a certain criterion of his mission, his calling, his activity: to what extent do I experience the Church as a value? What kind of value does it represent to me? And what do I do to help others to experience the Church as a value, so that, as a result of such experience, the responsibility for the Church may grow. Because, my dear fellow priests, it must grow organically. It may not grow only formally. It is not sufficient to repeat a thousand times: you are responsible for the Church. We must cause them to experience the Church as a value. We must reveal to them that the Church represents value to them. We must help them to find themselves in situations where they can experience the value of the Church ...

The responsibility for the Church is always the responsibility of a specific priest, bishop, sister, lay person, father of a family — it is a personal responsibility. And this, too, falls into line with the teachings of Vatican II.

It must be added here immediately, that this responsibility of a Christian cannot be replaced by anything. And this again is a very important element in pastoral work, in all the pastoral programs in Poland, that every person, every Christian in Poland, and to some extent every person in Poland — because it is especially in Poland that this responsibility for the Church from without the Church has deep roots; it is difficult to explain this in a few words — anyway, we must try to help each of them to realize that his or her responsibility for the Church is unique, irreplaceable ...

Therefore, everything that is contained in the idea of responsibility for the Church is, in a sense, the total sum of all these responsibilities — of everyone, of all who make up the "we" of the People of God in Poland. Of course, as I have said, the individual responsibilities vary. The overall responsibility is the sum and also somehow the resultant. The life of the Church in Poland as a whole, the Church in the world as a whole, is the resultant of the extent of the responsibility for the Church undertaken by the "we" of the entire People of God, or rather of those responsibilities undertaken by each Christian "I" in this great "we" of the People of God ...

Now a more detailed observation. Today in pastoral work — also in ecclesiology, but primarily in pastoral work — we make use of sociology, we conduct surveys ... various surveys which are conducted in Poland very intensively, and, we must add, are conducted on both sides ...

I know that before permission was finally granted for the construction of the church in Nowa Huta, the church where there will be a concelebrated Mass today, various surveys were conducted to gauge the awareness and attitude of the inhabitants of Nowa Huta. And only when the results of these surveys did not validate their assumed schema, they said — well, go ahead and build. They said this with anger, but they said it ...

What do these surveys indicate? It seems to me, that they indicate, more or less, there are sociologists present, they will correct me and criticize me when necessary. They indicate in general that, first of all, there is a majority of believers in our nation and an insignificant minority of people who describe themselves as atheists. The ratios vary depending on the milieu where the surveys are conducted, but the overall results are similar. But what is apparent from all these surveys and studies is that the quality of faith varies greatly ...

A small group within this majority of believers in Poland is made up of Catholics who are fully responsible for the Church ...

This is not bad, because we know that a very aware, decisive minority can still accomplish its goals ...

These are the facts. But we cannot stop at the criteria of sociology or social psychology. If, as it appears to us, it is definite that of the majority of believers in Poland, only a small group exhibits a full responsibility for the Church — that is, fully experiences the value of the Church — then we must work towards getting the rest of that majority to the same state. And this is the sense of our ministry.

Same day — Kaniow, concelebrated Mass, a gathering of priests ordained in 1975 * September 6 — Krakow, 11:00 a.m., Department of Charity, meeting with the representatives of the deaneries * 12:00 noon, Seminary of Czestochowa, conclusion of the pastoral symposium * 4:00 p.m., residence, a meeting of the editorial teams of the Synod of the Archdiocese of Krakow * September 7 — 10:30 a.m., meeting of a Coordinating Committee of the Provincial Synod. Discussion on the results of the activities of the Theological Committee of the Synod; discussion on the character of the document to be prepared by the committee; the Cardinal took part in these discussions. The Cardinal presented the matter of the final document of the Synod. Every team will be responsible for one chapter. The Document prepared by the Theological Committee will be theoretical, subsequent chapters will be practical in nature. After a detailed summation and a discussion of the achievements, the Cardinal concluded that the matter of the final document is still open, and needs further analysis and proposals. (From the minutes) * 1:00 p.m., residence, a visit of the Superior General of the Missionaries of Our Lady of La Salette * 5:00 p.m., residence chapel, a wedding. An account by H. J. as to how this wedding came about:

The first time I saw Father Cardinal (this is what he was called by all of us young people, and that is how we addressed him in our many encounters) was on the day before his name-day in the year 1973. As a new student, unfamiliar with the city, together with the Academic Jesuit Community, otherwise known as WAJ,[35] I went to Franciszkanska Street,

---

[35] The initials in Polish of "Academic Jesuit Community".

to the chapel at the palace of the archbishop. The Mass and the short sermon preached by Father Cardinal remained in my memory forever ... Then
there were subsequent meetings, *Oplatek, swiecone*[36], When I was singing in
the schola, at get-togethers in the refectory I would sit very close to Father
Cardinal, on his left. Every year we met several or perhaps over a dozen
times, either on Kopernika Street (the Jesuit center for the academic ministry in Krakow), at Wawel, at Skalka, or in his home, in his apartment on
the upper floor on Franciszkanska Street, which was always noisy because
of passing streetcars ... After one such meeting for prayer and song, in
November of 1975, I walked my future wife from Franciszkanska Street to
her dormitory for the first time. In 1977 I began my last semester of studies. Encouraged by the permission of the chaplain, Rev. Stanislaw Dziwisz,
I decided to seek a private audience with Father Cardinal. It was definitely
on a Tuesday, a beautiful day in May. Around noon, in a one-on-one conversation, I mustered up the courage to ask him to officiate at our marriage.
To this day I cannot explain why I did this and where this idea came from.
The friendly atmosphere of our talk gave me confidence and moved me. I
fell to my knees, thanking him for his consent, and he, with a gesture so
characteristic of him, asked me to get up ... On September 7, 1977 we were
married, receiving a blessing from his hands at the chapel on
Franciszkanska Street. The musical ensemble and the schola, in which I
sang for so many years, also participated in this ceremony ... Later, we
would often visit Father Cardinal, whether on the occasion of the tenth
anniversary of his ministry as a Cardinal, or for Christmas. We would also
meet outside Krakow, in small towns whose parishes he visited. Every such
meeting was a great experience for us. He became a patron for our group,
a patron who was very personal, but also very social, because he noticed
hundreds of young people like us, with our problems and joys ... At the end
of September 1978, between one conclave and the next, on the anniversary
of our marriage, we visited Father Cardinal for the last time in Krakow, not
knowing that in a month we would hear the news on the radio which shook
us and left us with mixed emotions in our hearts ... (II. J. Cieszyn)

Same day — 7:00 p.m., Bienczyce * September 8 — Day off *
September 9 — 3:00 p.m., session of bishops * September 10 — 1:00
p.m., departure for Warsaw (there, a meeting with Rev. McLean), later
to Olsztyn * September 11 — 11:00 a.m., Gietrzwald, celebrations of
the 100th anniversary of the apparition of Our Lady, sermon * 4:00
p.m., Warsaw, a visit with the Primate * September 11 — Kalwaria
Zebrzydowska, participation in the 5th Day of Women only through a
letter directed to the participants; at the time, the Cardinal was participating in the jubilee celebrations in Gietrzwald. In the letter he greeted
the women and girls congregated at the Kalwaria shrine, he reassured
them that he would be with them in spirit. Bishop S. Smolenski came
in place of the Cardinal * September 12 — 12:00 noon, Gliwice,
Church of St. Bartholomew, funeral of Barbara Paszkowska, concelebrated Mass, sermon * 6:00 p.m., residence, meeting of the authors of

---

[36] *Oplatek*: Christmas social (see Glossary); Swiecone: Easter social.

a book in honor of Cardinal Sapieha * September 13 — Jasna Gora, Chapel of Our Lady, a pilgrimage of actors, literary men and women, Catholic writers; concelebrated Mass. Homily:

> It seems to me, that if we are to serve the image of Jasna Gora in a particular way, with the pen, with literature, we must above all concentrate on the second part of the event in Cana of Galilee, which expresses the mediation of Mary between Christ and us, between Christ and man, between Christ and the people who participated in the wedding feast at Cana, and between Christ and the people who have participated in the history of Jasna Gora for six centuries. Because this is the continuation of that earlier event.
>
> [He led the singing of the promises of Jasna Gora:] And although most often the people who come here are simple folk, with simple matters, ordinary matters, these simple and ordinary matters have their greatness. And when the people who come here are writers, creators of contemporary Polish culture, their matters are also close to the Heart of the Blessed Mother. And her Heart should open up to these matters, in return for the opening of our hearts. May all of this, then, all of this that fills our day today, which forms the culmination of the day, find its place here. From all corners of the Polish land, from the whole world, from all of the secret recesses of Polish hearts, may our calls to our Mother meet here at this place, and may she — as always — hear them. May she hear our calls.

September 14 — 12:00 noon, Krakow, a visit after the funeral of B. Paszkowska * 4:00 p.m., departure for Warsaw * September 15 — Warsaw, meeting of the delegation for the Synod of Bishops * September 16 — 7:00 a.m., residence chapel, Mass and sermon for first-year students of the Theological Seminary * 3:00 p.m., residence, session of bishops * 4:00 p.m., session on the issue of the 1978 jubilee * September 17 — Day off * 5:00 p.m., Lgota, blessing of a cornerstone:

> When we travel across our Polish land, we see many buildings, many temples from various centuries. All of them bear witness to the history of our nation. The issue of building a church is always a social issue. So we must state with satisfaction that the authorities have presently understood the social significance of the matter of building the church in Lgota, and have given their permission for it ...
>
> The Church is built on living people. And your church here is being built the same way. It is being built as our common cause, the cause of the bishop and the People of God. That is why for a number of years we continued to present a petition to the authorities to obtain permission to build a house of the Lord that was larger than this old, beautiful chapel which you were using until now. And when we received official permission in 1974, a priest came here, and he, as you yourselves admitted in your words of welcome, became the soul of your community and the soul of your building effort. But he has not and does not undertake this task by himself ...
>
> I have personal recollections of that wayside chapel, which is still standing, because it is beautiful. I remember the visitation in 1973, the visitation of the parish of Ploki, which fell on a very wintry November day. I

remember how we prayed together, of course not in the chapel, but beside it, under the open sky.

September 18 — Nowa Huta-Mogila, 12:00 noon, celebration of the Triumph of the Cross. Sermon:

> Not long ago I had an article from the Krakow press in my hand, in which the author was trying to convince us that there is freedom of religion and freedom of conscience in Poland. And that everything that is happening here is in line with the teachings of the Second Vatican Council. But, at the same time, the author of the article claims that the right to freedom does not in any way abolish the right of the state to a one-sided engagement in the ideological sense. This is a truly dialectic argument. And we can perceive such articles only in terms of dialectic argument! After all, what is the state, if not the homeland of people? But, if everything that forms the content of teaching in schools, everything that forms the content of cultural life in publications, in the press, in television programs, does not suit the majority of the society, their convictions, their faith! Can we then say, that this is a just situation? ...
>
> The great heritage of the Cross and of the Mother standing beneath the Cross is absent, eliminated, from our contemporary culture ...
>
> As if they wanted to show us that indeed, we are valued as tools of production, but do not count as creators of what our Homeland truly is, as creators of the history of contemporary Poland. These are matters about which I speak with the greatest pain ...
>
> Dear brother! Dear sister! Brethren in Christ, do not deprive your daily life of what gives this life its fullest, deepest value! Do what is necessary to be able to look at this Cross daily, and have it look at you. Do you think this has no meaning? This shapes your entire life! And this is particularly necessary in our Catholic homes today, when this Sign is absent from our classrooms, hospitals and other institutions and offices, where the majority are Catholics. We must return the Cross to its rightful place in our Polish life, in all areas which are open to us.

Same day — 5:00 p.m., Halcnow, Mass and sermon, Sacrament of Confirmation, blessing of the interior of the church:

> When I was confirming the youth, I addressed each boy and each girl with these words: Receive the gift of the Holy Spirit. And I waited for each of them to answer me: Amen. This "Amen" has a great meaning, even though it is a tiny word. It signifies affirmation. Just as if you said in Polish: Yes, I agree, I accept ...
>
> After anointing them with the Holy Chrism, I said to each of the confirmands: Peace be with you! And again each of you answered: And with your spirit. So that the unity which the Holy Spirit fosters in young souls, the unity of faith, would be a visible unity ...
>
> When I was anointing the foreheads of your children, these young parishioners, with Holy Chrism, then the older sponsors of confirmation placed their hands on the shoulders of the young people. By this you wanted to show the community of faith which passes from generation to generation, from parents to children and grandchildren. All of the many generations that have already passed through the life of this parish were given expression today in this sign of the hands placed on the shoulders of con-

firmed boys and girls.

September 19 — In the afternoon he met with a group of Catholic intellectuals in Tyniec * Same day — 5:30 p.m., residence chapel, Mass and sermon for the *Srodowisko*[37] * 7:30 p.m., residence, meeting with the editorial staff of *Tygodnik Powszechny* * September 20 — 10:00 a.m., Czestochowa Seminary, participation in a convention of priests who are rectors, speech * September 21 — Residence, meeting with Bishop Dabrowski * 11:00 a.m., Czestochowa Seminary, conclusion of the convention, speech * 4:00 p.m, residence, Marian team * 5:00 p.m., meeting with Bishop Dabrowski * September 22 — 7:00 a.m., residence chapel, concelebrated Mass with Bishop Dabrowski * 10:00 a.m., residence, conference of priests — heads of deaneries * 5:00 p.m., residence, a visit of E. Piszek * September 23 — 12:00 noon and 3:00 p.m., residence, session of bishops * September 24 — Meeting of the Committee for the Apostolate of the Laity * September 26 — 1:00 p.m., residence, committee for matters of construction * 4:00 p.m., Synod of the Province * 6:00 p.m., Wawel Cathedral, 80th anniversary of the birth of Pope Paul VI:

> We are gathered here today to greet with him the great, distinguished point in human life. An 80th birthday is such a point: great and distinguished.
> And this point does not mean rest for him. It means more toil. Because, at the moment, he is a providential leader for the Church — he feels that and we all feel that. We know that he must continue to be the servant of the servants of God, that he must continue to fulfill Christ's admonition: "Feed my lambs, feed my sheep" — that he must continue to be a father. And because we feel that way, because he undertakes that wish of Christ, we particularly want to be together with him ...
> [Our Lord] ... declared, addressing Simon, to whom He had earlier given the name of Peter: "Thou art a rock, and upon this rock I will build my Church. And whatever you shall bind on earth shall be bound in Heaven!" So spoke Christ, the Eternal Shepherd, and later, after He had fulfilled the act of redeeming our souls, He simply said to Peter: "Feed my lambs, feed my sheep." But before that, He asked Peter three times: "Do you love me?" I am certain that today, the successor of Peter, Paul VI, is reliving especially deeply everything that transpired between Jesus Christ, the Eternal Shepherd, and Peter, and which continues to transpire on the basis of the Apostolic succession, the succession of Peter, between Jesus Christ and him, the successor of Peter, Paul VI ...
> Even though he does so every day, it is particularly today that Paul VI, the successor of Peter, probably thinks of himself as a servant. Servus servorum Dei, the servant of the servants of God — this is most proper title which Peter could have assumed through his successors. Because the Lord Himself, the Eternal Shepherd, said this of Himself at the Last Supper, at

[37] See Glossary.

the moment of the Eucharist, as He was washing the feet of the Apostles, that is what He said of Himself. And so, he who is at the pinnacle of the visible Church thinks of himself in the same way that the Lord and Master did: the servant of the servants of God ...

A family rests on a father. If it has a father, it is a family. The father is the one who ties the family members into that unity whose name is family. The Church is a family, it considers itself a family, and in today's liturgy, in the words of the responsorial psalm, the Church thanks the Eternal Shepherd that it has a Father. The Church can sing: "I shall not want," as long as it has what is most important. As long as it has a Father who is a sign of unity, who unites all of us, who causes the Church, that family of God, to reveal itself and to reaffirm itself as a family — because it has a Father.

September 27 — 1:00 p.m., residence, session before the regional conference * September 28 — 8:00 a.m., Cathedral, took part in a Mass on the 19th anniversary of the consecration * 11:00 a.m., residence, session of bishops * 3:00 p.m., residence, a meeting of the Council of the Pontifical Department of Theology * 4:00 p.m., visit of Archbishop Aurelio Sabattani and Msgr. Charles Lefebvre (dean of the Rota) * 6:00 p.m., residence chapel, concelebrated Mass * September 29 — 7:00 a.m., departure for Rome via Warsaw * 12:00 noon — 1:00 p.m., Laski, meeting with the Primate, Bishop Dabrowski and Prof. Zdzislaw Lapinski; visit to the institution for the blind * 7:00 p.m., Warsaw, nunciature[38] (the house of the nunciature), meeting with Archbishop Sabattini, Msgr. Ch. Lefebvre and Bishop Dabrowski * September 30-Oct. 29 — Sixth ordinary session of the Synod of Bishops in Rome. Topic: An appropriate way to conduct catechesis in our times, especially catechesis of children and young people. During the work sessions of the Synod, Cardinal Wojtyla participated in the Italian language group * September 30 — Warsaw, 7:30 a.m., departure * 11:00 a.m., Rome, Polish College, private concelebrated Mass * 5:00 p.m., session of the Synod of Bishops with the participation of Pope Paul VI.

October 1-12 — 7:00 a.m., Rome, Polish College, private concelebrated Masses * October 1 — Rome, session of the Synod and the Holy Father, 3:00 p.m., a meeting of the Polish team * October 3 — In his intervention at the Synod, Cardinal Wojtyla presented some of the Polish experiences, feeling that they might become helpful to all in the process of catechesis. He said:

Public schools have been removed from any influence of the Church. Of course, this can also happen elsewhere and is related to the fundamental right to freedom of religion. For this reason, the Church must be very watchful here: because the freedom in the sphere of religious instruction testifies to the true freedom of religion allowed by a given political system.

---

[38] Vatican diplomatic mission..

[The lack of such freedom] is an implementation of a program of atheism. Atheism is imposed as a new state religion, it pervades the whole system of education, it alone has exclusive access to the media of mass communication. In this way, an anti-catechesis atmosphere is created in the life of society, which violates freedom of religion and freedom of conscience, and indirectly all other rights of the human person, especially in nations with a long Catholic tradition. The bishops feel that this form of secularization of the school and of public life is contrary to justice, and violates the rights of Catholics who support the public schools with their own labor and effort. In this situation, the people of God see catechesis as a fundamental activity of the Church. (Rev. Adam Kubis)

October 4 — 9:00 a.m. and 5:00 p.m., sessions of the Synod * 1:30 p.m., Polish Institute, a meeting with Msgr. F. Maczynski * 8:00 p.m., meeting of the teams * On this day the Vatican Radio broadcast Cardinal Wojtyla's conference: The Issue of Catechesis at the Synod of Bishops * October 5 — 9:00 a.m. and 5:00 p.m., sessions of the Synod * October 6 — 9:00 a.m., session of the Synod with Pope Paul VI in attendance * 1:00 p.m., a visit to Bishop A. Deskur with Archbishop L. Poggi * 5:00 p.m., St. Stanislaw's Church, Holy Hour for the priests, meeting at the parish hall * October 7 — 9:00 a.m., a talk with the secretary of the "Urbanianum" * 3:00 p.m., an interview for the TV of the Federal Republic of Germany * 5:00 p.m., session of the Synod, circuli minores * 8:00 p.m., a visit to Rev. Dr. R. Karpinski * October 8 — 9:00 a.m., session of the Synod, the Italian-language group * 3:00 p.m., a dinner at Cardinal Villot's * 8:00 p.m., a meeting of the Polish group * October 9 — 9:00 a.m., Rome, the Basilica of St. Peter, canonization (of Blessed Charbel Makhlont) * 5:00 p.m., Church of St. Stanislaw, concelebrated Mass of the Polish bishops with the participation of Archbishop L. Poggi. Homily:

In Poland this Sunday is a day of prayers for the intention of the Cardinal Primate. We are impelled to these prayers, to this day of prayer, primarily by the state of his health, which in recent times has caused concern to the whole Church in Poland and to all of Polish society. Although we can now think of this concern as something that belongs to the past, and this on the basis of the declarations by physicians, particularly by Prof. Lapinski, who performed the last surgery and the one before that. But we feel the need for prayer all the more ... When we gather here to unite with the entire Church in Poland and to commend the person of the Primate to God in a special way, to plead and to give thanks. The Blessed Mother, Our Lady of Jasna Gora should be present in our thanksgiving in a very special and extraordinary way. We asked all people in Poland to do this today. We know that this Primate of the Millennium has, to use a colloquial human term, "wagered" on Mary in a particular, extraordinary, charismatic way. He confessed to her a mystery, the same mystery spoken of by St. Luke the Evangelist. She keeps all these words in her heart, and the power of her maternal heart is such that all who join with her, who unite with her, who pray with her, who believe with her, who love with her — all of them can also keep these words, which she guards in her heart, can keep them regardless of how strongly these words are contradicted, how strongly their truth is denied, how much they are ridiculed, criticized. The Primate of Poland sensed that Mary possesses such strength. And so today, as we participate in the prayers of the entire Church in Poland, which the Cardinal Primate commends to God through Our Lady of Jasna Gora — giving thanks and also pleading, we want to pray with deep conviction, out of the need for unity among the bishops, out of the need for unity among the entire clergy, in the entire Church, in the entire society! We pray that the charisma which he has shown may continue to serve our Homeland, our nation and the Church in Poland.

Same day — 7:00 p.m., at Bishop Rubin's, a meeting of the Polish bishops with Archbishop Poggi * October 10 — 9:00 a.m. and 5:00 p.m, sessions of the Synod, circulo minore * October 10 — 9:00 a.m., session of the Synod (reports) * 1:00 p.m., Hospice of St. Stanislaw, bishops from Canada * 5:00 p.m., session of the Synod, later, at Msgr. Paetz's * October 12 — 9:00 a.m. and 5:00 p.m., sessions of the Synod * October 13 — 7:15 a.m., Chapel of the Congregation of the Resurrection, concelebrated Mass, sermon * 9:00 a.m., session * 1:00 p.m., Collegio San Girolamo (Croats), dinner * 7:00 p.m., Polish College, Bishop Edward Materski's name-day * October 14 -7:30 p.m., Polish College, private concelebrated Mass * Vatican Radio * 1:00 p.m., Palazzo San Carlo, a meeting with Cardinal Francois Marty and French bishops * 3:00 p.m., Genzano, a visit * 7:30 p.m., Polish Institute, Bishop Valerians Zondaks, Bishop Liudas Povilonis, Archbishop Poggi and Polish bishops * October 15 — 9:00 a.m., session of the Synod, reports of the various language groups * 2:30 p.m., Gelunstadt * 3:00 p.m., O.W. and S. * 5:00 p.m., the Franciscans, Chapel of Blessed Maximilian Kolbe. Homily:

> Catechesis cannot be a merely intellectual exercise. It is not similar to the teaching of any other subject, of any other area of knowledge. It is connected with the entire existence of man, both the Christian and the one who is the subject of catechesis. And this is an existence in Christ. Catechesis achieves its full dimension when the witness of life goes hand in hand with the word. Both of these — the Word of God and the witness of life — are incorporated into the order of the sacraments, because it is in this order, through the sacraments, that we meet with the work of the Living God.

Same day — a reception at Cardinal Nasalli Rocca's * 8:30 p.m., meeting of the Polish group * October 16 — 7:30 a.m., Chapel of the Felician Sisters, concelebrated Mass, sermon * 10:00 a.m., Basilica of St. Peter, 80th birthday of Pope Paul VI * Arnult Gebhard — Msgr. from Bamberg * October 17 — 7:00 a.m., chapel at the Polish College, private concelebrated Mass * 1:00 p.m., Hospice of St. Stanislaw, invited were the chairmen of the Synod * The Vatican Radio broadcast an interview with Cardinal Wojtyla: The Synod of Bishops on Catechesis

* October 18 — 8:00 a.m. and 5:00 p.m., sessions of the Synod. Cardinal Wojtyla spoke during discussion on the reports of the various groups. In his opinion:

> Catechesis should introduce the youth into the mystery of Christ not only by means of intellectual acceptance, but also through an affinity of lifestyle. Those in whom the mystery of Christ brought forth the greatest fruits of salvation, the saints, were the best catechists. We must also put stronger emphasis on the connection between the catechesis of children and the calling to the priesthood or to other forms of life dedicated to God. The grace of a vocation often has its beginning in catechesis. It follows from this that the personal example of the catechist — priest or sister — is very important.

Same day — 1:30 p.m., Hospice of St. Stanislaw, bishops from the USA, Australia, Scotland, Cardinal Cordeiro * 7:00 p.m., at Msgr. Bogumil Lewandowski's — editors * October 19 — Dies recollection-is {days of recollection} * 1:30 p.m., Polish Institute, Cardinal Seper, Archbishop Franc Franic, Archbishop Maksym Hermaniuk, Bishop Ceslaus Sipovic, Bishop Janez Jenko * 7:00 p.m., at Mr. Tolentino's, representatives of the Catholic University of Milan * October 19 — An interview granted to the German section of the Vatican Radio * October 20 — Feast of St. John of Kanty, patron of the Polish College, 7:00 a.m., chapel of the College, solemn concelebrated Mass, parting remarks * 1:30 p.m., meeting with the bishops and other guests * 7:00 p.m., General House of Canons Regular of the Lateran * A program on the topic of the Synod of Bishops on the Vatican Radio:

> Catechesis has always been born from faith; from faith which seeks an appropriate maturity, and thereby seeks on the basis of the maturity of some, the catechists, to increase the maturity of others — the subjects of catechesis. It is a fundamental process of the life of the Church, as the great community of the believing People of God. It is a dynamic process, not least because the catechists also learn much from the catechized. This fundamental process in the history of Christianity, and in the life of the contemporary Church, goes hand in hand with another process. This is the process of the birth, shaping and development of theology. In some respect, catechesis and theology grow from the same root. Both tend towards the same goal, although this happens on different wavelengths, as it were.
>
> One might say that, on average, catechesis does not reach quite as far as theology. But, at the same time, catechesis always contains theology within it, a theology which awaits its full form, its universal development. From another point of view, we could say that catechesis in all its forms, even catechesis of pre-school children, always waits for the fullness of theology, for the fullest possible understanding of the whole content of the faith ...
>
> And even though not everything that theology works out will be effectively incorporated into catechesis, theology still does well to act as the servant (ancilla) of catechesis. It stands then at the very center of the life of the Church, in the dynamic current of the maturing of the faith of the bap-

tized. This is its glory. This was the position in which theology was already placed by the Apostles, especially Paul and John, and then by the ancient Fathers, Doctors of the Church. From this position, theology, combined with the Magisterium, and with the sense of faith of the entire People of God, will become incorporated into the life of the Church, through which the Church continually strives to enrich the faith ...

October 21 — Polish College * 1:00 p.m., Hospice of St. Stanislaw, bishops of German-speaking nations * 5:00 p.m., session of the Synod, proposals * 8:00 p.m., at Archbishop Poggi's and Bishop Deskur's * October 22 — 12:00 noon, session of the Synod, manifestatio sententiarum * 1:00 p.m., at Bishop Deskur's, Archbishop Jerome Hamer, Bishop Edouard Gagnon * 7:00 p.m., Parish of St. Pius V, Sacrament of Confirmation, Mass and sermon * October 23 — 7:00 a.m., Seminario Romano, concelebrated Mass, sermon * Monte Circeo * Hospice of St. Stanislaw, a conference for the sisters, concelebrated Mass, final remarks * Msgr. Marian Oles * October 24 — 7:00 a.m., Chapel of the Albertine Sisters, concelebrated Mass, sermon * 9:00 a.m. and 5:00 p.m., sessions of the Synod — proposals * Same day — announcement of the election results to the Council of the Secretariat of the Synod of Bishops. Cardinal Wojtyla became a member, along with Cardinal Hoffner and Archbishop Etchegaray * Same day — Cardinal Wojtyla rose to speak about the exposé delivered by Bishop Deskur on the activities of the Pontifical Council for Social Communications, stating that the issue of the role of those media — especially in the countries where the authorities use the media as a means of control, rather than to inform — is a pastoral problem worthy of deeper consideration. (Rev. Adam Kubis) * 1:00 p.m., Polish College, a dinner with the Italian cardinals and bishops * 7:30 p.m., at the Congregation of the Resurrection * October 25 — 7:00 a.m., Polish College, private concelebrated Mass * 5:00 p.m., session *manifestatio sententiarum* * 8:00 p.m., meeting of the Polish team * In the Vatican Radio: The Right to Catechesis and the Duty to Catechize * October 26 — 9:00 a.m., "Urbanianum" University, led a mission symposium * 1:00 p.m., Cardinal Sergio Pignedoli * 7:00 p.m., at Bishop Deskur's, Cardinal George B. Hume, Archbishop Derek Worlock * October 27 — 7:00 a.m., Chapel of the Grey Ursuline Sisters, concelebrated Mass, sermon * 9:00 a.m., session of the Synod * 1:00 p.m., at the Jesuit College del Gesu * 4:30 p.m., Pontifical Institute of Church Studies, Rome, Piazza B. Cairoli, 117, a lecture about the Synod together with Bishop Stroba and Bishop Materski * with bishops S. and B. * 7:00 p.m., Collegio Teutonico, Cardinal Hoffner, Cardinal Volk, Archbishop Etchegaray * October 28 — 31 — Chapel of the Polish College, private concelebrated Mass * October 28 — 1:00 p.m., at Rev. Tadeusz

Rakoczy's * October 29 — 9:00 a.m., Vatican, audience hall, final session of the Synod, farewell to Pope Paul VI * During the Synod Cardinal Wojtyla submitted in writing his statements on the following subjects: *L'importanza della catechesi per i genitori dei bambini catechizzati, Il movimento "Luce et Vita" come strumento del rinnovamento post-conciliare in Polonia, Il inodo dei Vescovi su bambini piu piccoli. La catechesi della prima eta, Sulla formazione dei catechisti* * 2:00 p.m., Mentorella, Marian shrine * October 30 — 9:30 a.m., Rome, Basilica of St. Peter, beatification of Mutius Maria Viaux and Michael Cordero (school brothers) * Monte Circeo * October 31 — 1:30 p.m., at Bishop Deskur's, Archbishop Casaroli and Archbishop Poggi, Bishop Metody Stratiew.

November 1 — 7:30 a.m., St. Peter's Basilica, concelebrated Mass *ad limina*[39] * Departure for Loretto, at the Sisters of the Holy Family of Nazareth * November 2 — 6:30 a.m., Loreto, Basilica of Our Lady, concelebrated Mass * 7:00 a.m., concelebrated Mass * 10:00 a.m., cemetery of Polish soldiers, concelebrated Mass with Archbishop Loris Capovilla and Bishop Edward Kisiel * 1:00 p.m., dinner, meeting at the Sisters of the Holy Family of Nazareth * 7:30 p.m., return to Rome * November 3 — Sisters' chapel at the Polish College, concelebrated Mass, sermon * Vatican — 10:00 a.m., audience with the Holy Father * at Bishop Deskur's * Mentorella * November 4 — 7:00 a.m., church at Mentorella, Mass * Dies recollectionis {days of recollection} * 7:15 p.m., Cardinal Wojtyla's name-day gathering * November 6 — 7:00 a.m., Church of St. Caesarius in Palatio, concelebrated Mass, sermon * Meeting with Bishop Deskur * 8:00 p.m., evening service * November 7 — 7:30 a.m., St. Peter's Basilica, by the tomb of St. Peter (ad limina) * 11:15 a.m., Congregatio pro Doctrina Fidei, at Cardinal Seper' s * 12:00 noon, Congregatio pro Episcopis, at Cardinal Sebastiano Baggio's * 1:30 p.m., at Bishop Deskur's; Cardinal Garrone, Archbishop Javierre, Msgr. Francesco Marchisano, Msgr. Flaminio Cerruti, Rev. Dr. Nowak * 5:00 p.m., Gregorianum University, a doctorate of Rev. Stanislaw Slabon * 7:30 p.m., supper, among others, Cardinal Seper, Archbishop Hamer, Bishop Groblicki * November 8 — 7:00 a.m., Chapel of the Polish College, private concelebrated Mass * Fiumicino, welcome of Primate Wyszynski * 1:00 p.m., Polish Institute, dinner * 4:00 p.m., Hospice of St. Stanislaw, meeting of the rectors of the mission, opening address * 7:00 p.m., Polish Institute, meeting with the Primate * November 9 — 7:00 a.m., Polish College, private concelebrated Mass * 11:00 a.m., at Archbishop Giuseppe

---

[39] "At the threshold," the tradition of bishops periodically visiting the "Apostolic thresholds" of Rome.

Caprio's * 12:00 noon, Sacred Congregation for the Sacraments and Divine Worship, at Cardinal James Knox's * 1:30 p.m., Istituto Orientale with Archbishop Gulbinowicz * 4:00 p.m, Hospice of St. Stanislaw, a conference of the rectors of the missions * 5:00 p.m., Polish Institute, meeting of the ordinary bishops with the participation of the Primate * November 10 — 7:00 a.m., Chapel of the Sisters of the Holy Family of Nazareth, concelebrated Mass * 9:30 a.m., Hospice of St. Stanislaw, meeting of the rectors of the Polish missions * 1:00 p.m., at the Felician Sisters, dinner for Polish bishops * 5:00 p.m., Church of St. Stanislaw, rectors of Polish missions, the Primate, Bishop Dabrowski * 7:00 p.m., Hospice of St. Stanislaw, reception * November 11 — 7:00 a.m., Polish College, private concelebrated Mass * 11:30 a.m., Consilium pro Laicis * 12:00 noon, Commissio pro Migratione et Turismo * Delegation * 1:30 p.m., at Bishop Deskur's: Bishop Martin, Fr. Roberto Tucci SJ * 5:00 p.m., Polish Institute, Main Council of the Polish Episcopate * November 12 — 7:00 a.m., Chapel of the Ursuline Sisters, concelebrated Mass, sermon * 10:50 a.m., at Cardinal Villot's * 11:30 a.m., an audience of the bishops with the Holy Father * 1:30 p.m., Polish College, doctoral dinner of Rev. M. * At Prof. Faber's: Mr. Sieniewicz, Mr. Solka, Msgr. Langman, Rev. Rector Biffi, Rector Later, Bishop Wosinski * 7:00 p.m., Genzano, Sisters of the Sacred Heart * November 13 — 10:00 a.m., Rome, Main Council of the Polish Episcopate * 1:00 p.m., Angelicum * 3:00 p.m., at Bishop Deskur's * 6:00 p.m., Church of St. Andrew at Quirinal, concelebrated Mass, sermon on the Feast of St. Stanislaw Kostka[40] * 8:00 p.m., General House of the Basilian Fathers * November 14 — 7:00 a.m., Polish College, private concelebrated Mass * 10:00 a.m.-1:00 p.m.,Congregation pro Causis Sanctorum, Cardinal Corrado Bafile, Archbishop Giuseppe Casoria, Msgr. Pietro Frutaz, Cardinal Garrone, Bishop Deskur, Cardinal Wright, Bishop D. * 1:30 p.m., Istituto Gemelli, Bishop Tokarczuk, Bishop Groblicki * 7:00 p.m., St. Stanislaw Hospice, with Archbishop Gleeson (Adelaide) and the Superior General of the Society of Christ, Bishop Rubin, Bishop Wesoly * November 15 — 7:00 a.m., Chapel of the Polish College, private concelebrated Mass * 10:00 a.m., departure for Warsaw and Krakow * November 16 — 7:00 a.m., Krakow, residence chapel, private concelebrated Mass * 12:00 noon, residence, session of bishops and the Curia * November 17 — 9:00 a.m., St. Anne's Church, concelebrated Mass for the late Prof. J. Chojnacka * 12:00 noon, the Rakowicki cemetery, funeral of the late Prof. J. Chojnacka * November

---

[40] The tomb of St. Stanislaw Kostka is in this church.

18 — 1:30 p.m., 25th anniversary of Rev. Chancellor Msgr. Mikolaj Kuczkowski * 3:00 p.m., residence, session of the Curia * 7:30 p.m., residence chapel, Mass for the intention of J. Ciesielski and the deceased of the *Srodowisko*[41] * November 19 — Rev. Dean of the Pontifical Department of Theology in Krakow * 6:00 p.m., Italian TV * 7:00 p.m., Theological Seminary, supper (25th anniversary of Rev. Canon Mieczyslaw Mackowski) * November 20 — 10:00 a.m., Feast of Christ the King, Wawel Cathedral, concelebrated Mass, sermon to the parishioners visited and confirmed this year. From the sermon:

> When Christ came into the world, the people of Israel called Him a king. They thought, however, of a different kingdom, a temporal kingdom which would gain greatness and glory only for this people — only for Israel. That is why Christ rejected the title of that kind of king. And this was later brought up as His transgression. Indeed, when He was crucified, there was a sign above His head: King of the Jews. As if those who did the crucifying wanted to erase Christ the King. But Christ knew that when He was being crucified, when He gave Himself up on the cross as a sacrifice for the sins of the world, when He gave Himself up to the Father, He gained that Kingdom which His Father gave Him from eternity, which His Father had intended for Him and gave Him in such a miraculous way. That is why, as He was hanging on the cross, He said to one of those hanging next to Him: "This day you will be with me in paradise." He shares His kingdom which He gained on the cross, which He won for every person, for all ...
>
> Just as once upon the cross of Calvary, so today on the cross of human history, on the cross of the history of our nation, the Kingdom of Christ is being erased — the Kingdom of Grace and Truth, the Kingdom of Love and Life. Man is stripped of the right of citizenship in this Kingdom, he is being shown a different dimension of existence and reigning: beyond the mystery of the cross and the resurrection of Christ, beyond the scope of His Kingdom ...
>
> He was asked, first of all, if He was a king. His answer to the question of the Roman governor and procurator was: "I was born and came into the world so that I might witness to the Truth." His Kingdom is, above all, a Kingdom of Truth. It is the truth about God; about God, who is the Father, about God, who loves ...
>
> We come here to express our willingness to bear witness to the same Truth with Him. That is why, my dear brothers and sisters, my dear brother priests, dear parents, and especially you, dear young people, dear boys and girls — that is why it is so very important to get to know this Truth which Christ has brought — to get to know it through catechesis.

Same day — 4:00 p.m., Nawojowa Gora, Mass with sermon, Confirmation * November 21 — 6:30 a.m., residence chapel, concelebrated Mass, sermon for the Sisters of the Presentation * 11:00 a.m., Warsaw, arrival of Cardinal Volk * 3:00 p.m., Lublin, KUL, lecture: *From Evangelization to Catechesis* at the catechetic symposium on the

---

[41] See Glossary.

topic "Catechesis at the Fifth Synod of Bishops" * 6:00 p.m., KUL, lecture by Cardinal Volk * November 22 — A visit to Jasna Gora with Carinal Volk * 4:00 p.m., Krakow, a visit by Cardinal Volk * November 23 — 10:00 a.m., Czestochowa Seminary, regional conference of the deaneries in the immediate vicinity of Krakow * 7:00 p.m., residence, a visit by Cardinal Volk * November 24 — 7:30 a.m., residence chapel, concelebrated Mass with Cardinal Volk and Archbishop Gulbinowicz * 9:00 a.m., a tour of the city with Cardinal Volk and Archbishop Gulbinowicz * 12:00 noon, extraordinary meeting of the Council of the Pontifical Department of Theology in the auditorium of the Seminary at 8 Podzamcze Street, Cardinal Wojtyla welcomed Cardinal Herman Volk of Mainz, and informed the guest of the academic and didactic activities of the Department and the scope of its work. (From the minutes of the Department) * Same day — 3:00 p.m., Oswiecim {Auschwitz}, tour of the camp with Cardinal Volk and a service by the Cross *

Fragment of a letter dated November 24, 1977, written by Cardinal Wojtyla, the Metropolitan of Krakow, to the widow of the late Stanislaw Bukowski:

"I met him within the framework of the clandestine movement which based its work on Christian philosophy of life, I will say more — on Christian social teaching. This was the position of "Unia" which, in its conspiratorial work, attempted to draw manifold conclusions from the social teaching of the Church, rightly assuming that the Polish Catholicism requires that the social, economic and cultural life of the nation be built precisely according to this teaching."

(The above document was made available by Mr. Czeslaw Domaradzki)

* November 25 — 8:00 a.m., Cardinal Volk's departure * 10:00 a.m., Theological Seminary, regional conference (Krakow) * 2:30 p.m., residence, Theological Committee of the Provincial Synod * 4:00 p.m., residence, session of bishops * 7:30 p.m., Church of St. Anne's, concelebrated Mass for the professors of the Department of Theology of the Jagiellonian University and others * November 26 — 9:00 a.m., St. John's Church, Mass and sermon for the celebration of the 350th anniversary of the Presentation Sisters and 400th anniversary of the image of Our Lady of St. John * 1:00 p.m., took part in an anniversary meeting * 2:00 p.m., left for Bialystok via Warsaw * November 27 — 7:00 a.m., Bialystok, Parish of St. Roch, Chapel of the Missionary Sisters of St. Roch, Mass and sermon * Same day — Bialystok, 11:30 a.m., participated in the celebrations of the 50th anniversary of the coronation of the image of Our Lady of Mercy (20 bishops), blessed the Chapel of Our Lady of Mercy in the procathedral, delivered a sermon during the concelebrated Mass lead by Archbishop Henryk

Gulbinowicz. Sermon:

> "O Holy Maid, who Czestochowa's shrine dost guard and on the Pointed Gateway[42] shine!" And although we stand here and although we regard with joy this image blessed just now, which is a copy, our thoughts fly to the same place as the thoughts of the poet: "Meanwhile, bear off my yearning soul..."[43]
>
> Or rather, our thoughts are both there and here. We express our great joy that there, too, the 50th anniversary of the coronation of the Blessed Mother in her image of Ostra Brama was observed by our brothers, that this great anniversary was commemorated by a proper ceremony both there and here. It is indeed a great anniversary ...
>
> The invocation of the Homeland[44] turns immediately to the Blessed Mother: "Who defends Jasna[45] Czestochowa and shines in the Pointed Gate."
>
> We must remember the depth of suffering from which these words flowed, the depth of the soul that spawned them: they flowed from the depth of the soul of Adam Mickiewicz, who was banished from his Homeland, Lithuania, who, before leaving his Homeland, attended a morning Mass before the image of the Mother of Ostra Brama, his face buried in his hands, his soul steeped in prayer. And that is how he went into banishment, this great son of his Homeland. Many others went in the same way. Those that remained made countless sacrifices, endured humiliations and sufferings. Many times they took up armed struggle, so that finally the day might come on July 2, 1927, when a crown from the Holy Father Pius XI was placed on the head of Our Lady of Ostra Brama, which was also the crown of the People of God, the crown of our history, the crown of Poland and Lithuania ...
>
> Very often, justice without mercy is unjust. Justice without mercy is often an injustice, it does not build equality, it often creates new inequities, it divides people anew, separates them into layers, into the privileged and the dispossessed, into first and second or even third-class. Such is justice by itself. Man is not accommodated within the dimensions of justice, within the boundaries of justice. The whole truth about man calls for the equality which is found in mercy, it calls for the Mother of Mercy. The whole truth about man calls for the equality which is found in God's Mercy: when Christ bends over us, when His Mother bends over us, that expresses the image and likeness of God. In the name of our unfathomable equality with God, which we have attained in Jesus Christ, God bends over us: He is merciful to us.

November 28 — 11:00 p.m., Krakow, residence, an audience * 5:30 p.m., residence, Committee for the Pontifical Department of Theology

---

[42] A Shrine in Vilnius with a miraculous image of the Virgin Mary, known as Our Lady of Ostra Brama in Polish and Ausras Vartai in Lithuanian. It is also known as Our Lady of Mercy and Our Lady of the Dawn of the Gate. In Polish history it was second in importance only to the Black Madonna of Czestochowa. At the time Wojtyla spoke these words, Vilnius was in the Lithuanian Socialist Republic, part of the Soviet Union.

[43] The two quotes are from the national verse epic *Pan Tadeusz* by Adam Mickiewicz, which laments the occupation of Lithuania (a part of Polish Lithuanian Commonwealth prior to the partitions) by Russians. Mickiewicz's 19th century denunciations of Russians were often used in the 1960's & 70's as coded protests against the Communists.

[44] in the epic by Mickiewicz

[45] Jasna means bright, echoed by "shines" in the next phrase. Reference to the location of the abbey in Czestochowa, Jasna Gora, which means "Bright Mount."

* Synod of the Province * November 29 — 11:00 a.m., Zakopanc, regional conference * 2:00 p.m., Kalatowki, at the ruins left by a fire of the home of the Albertine Brothers, * 8:00 p.m., Kalatowki, Chapel of the Albertine Sisters, Mass for the intention of the colleagues * November 30 — 10:00 a.m., Wadowice, Chapel of Our Lady of Perpetual Help, private Mass * 3:00 p.m., Krakow, residence, a meeting with the Dean of the Pontifical Department of Theology * 7:00 p.m., meeting with the superiors of Theological Seminaries.

December 1 — 10:00 a.m., Oswiecim, regional conference * 4:00 p.m., residence, a meeting with the bishops * December 2 — 7:00 a.m., at the Franciscans' * 1:00 p.m., meeting of the Council of the Pontifical Department of Theology. At an open session of the Council (3 Franciszkanska Street) he introduced the participants to the issues of the 5th Synod of Bishops in Rome. He presented the reasons for its convocation, its purpose, character and scope of activities pertaining to the catechesis of the world. (From the minutes of the Council of the Department) * 4:00 p.m., Residence, meeting of philosophers * 6:30 p.m., residence chapel, private Mass (parents and children) * December 3 — meeting of the Committee for the Apostolate of the Laity. The Committee in relation to the issue of Christian culture in Poland; discussion on the Sacrament of Confirmation; addition of two members to the Committee "by election"; the matter of the delegation to the Forum VII 78 in Luxembourg was discussed with those invited (almost all dioceses), on the topic of engaging the arts in catechesis * December 3 — 3:00 p.m., the Mogila Abbey, 8th Plenary Meeting of the Pastoral Synod of the Krakow Archdiocese.

> In particular I wish to thank all those present today, who came here to express their position and to cast votes — votum deliberatum — in the matters which are the topic of today's plenary meeting. These matters are defined in four documents and projects prepared for today's meeting ... They are defined by the following titles: "Catechesis," "The Mission of Theology in Shaping the Life of the Faith of the Church of Krakow," "Religious Institutes in the Service of the Church of Krakow," "The Missionary Activities of the Church of Krakow" ...
>
> According to the thematic concept of our Synod, all of these are to express the participation of the Church of Krakow, and of the People of God who make up this Church, in the prophetic mission of Jesus Christ ...
>
> Our Synod is based on many, very many study groups, its work is based on a broad spectrum of Catholic society, both clergy and laity. In this way, our Synod wishes not only to proclaim what is contained in the Magisterium of the Second Vatican Council, but, by its very method of work, the Synod wishes to bring this Magisterium[46] of the Council to life.

---

[46] Official teaching.

And therefore every thought, every suggestion, every reservation, every correction, leading up to the preparation of the documents, and later to their approval, brings great value to this cause. It is an expression of our common, community responsibility for the Church.

December 4 — 9:00 a.m., residence chapel, concelebrated Mass, sermon * Residence, meeting of the Committee for the Apostolate of the Laity on the topic "Lay People in Catechesis," with the participation of representatives of lay Catholics from all Polish dioceses * December 5 — 7:00 a.m., Church of the Bernardine Sisters, Mass in honor of St. Joseph * 11:00 a.m., residence, an audience * 1:00 p.m., residence, visit of the Dean of KUL, Fr. A. Krapiec * Same day — Tyniec, 3:00 p.m., celebrated a funeral Mass for the late Felicja Zurowska, delivered a eulogy, led the coffin to the local cemetery. Remained there, praying the rosary until the grave is completely covered, all were very surprised by his actions especially the family of the deceased, from Sweden: "In our place even the priest never stayed that long, and here the Cardinal?" * December 6 — 5:00 p.m., the Mariacki Church, concelebrated Mass for the late Rev. Wladyslaw Galat * December 7 — 3:00 p.m., Lublin, KUL, meeting with the Rector and others * December 8 — 7:30 a.m., Lublin, chapel of the boarding school, concelebrated Mass * The collegiate church of KUL, celebration of the conferment of the doctorate honoris causa upon Cardinal John Krol {of Philadelphia}, sermon during concelebrated Mass, final remarks * December 9 — 10:00 a.m., Krakow, residence, a visit of Cardinal Krol, a meeting during a meal. The Cardinal presented the guest with the relics of St. John of Kanty * 7:00 p.m., St. Anne's Church, service with a sermon at the relics of St. John of Kanty * December 10 — 11:00 a.m., residence, session with the bishops before the visitation * December 10-12 — Visitation of the parish of Dobczyce * December 12 — 6:00 p.m., departure for Warsaw, Main Council of the Polish Episcopate * December 14-15 — Warsaw, plenary conference of the Polish Episcopate * December 14 — 7:30 a.m., Niepokalanow, concelebrated Mass, sermon, symposium * Warsaw, meeting with the bishops and Msgr. Tadeusz Fedorowicz * December 16 — 11:00 a.m., Krakow, residence, a visit by Bishop W. Rubin * 1:00 p.m., meeting of the Council of the Pontifical Department of Theology: the Cardinal informed about the upcoming 900th anniversary of St. Stanislaw's death; about the Papal audience, during which, for the first time, he talked at length about the Department of Theology in Krakow; about the academic contacts of our Department with those of Louvain, Erfurt, Leipzig and Washington {DC}; extended his greetings to the Council and the entire Department for Christmas and the New Year.

(From the minutes of the Council) * 3:00 p.m., residence, session of bishops * Same day — 7:00 p.m., Nowa Huta — Mogila, homily during retreat * 8:00 p.m., Church of Our Lady of Lourdes, Mass, sermon, academic *Oplatek*[47] * December 17 — 6:30 a.m., residence chapel, private Mass * 11:00 a.m., residence, session of bishops and the Curia * 5:00 p.m., meeting with the Secretariat of the Provincial Synod * 7:00 p.m., Basilica of the Jesuits, concelebrated Mass, sermon, academic *Oplatek* * 9:00 p.m., Church of the Redemptorist Fathers, conclusion of a retreat, sermon, academic *Oplatek* * December 18 — 11:00 a.m., Cisiec, filial church, consecration of the altar, Mass with sermon:

I come to your community in Cisiec in order to consecrate a new altar. I don't have to tell you, dear brothers and sisters, that I come here with deep emotion. Just as I came here five years ago, when your church rose here in 48 hours, without formal permission, but based on the greatest need — a social need, and also a need of Christian souls and hearts. It must be said that our meeting then, my coming here 5 years ago, was full of dramatic tension. We were under pressure. And yet, under that pressure, together, we were able, thanks to God's Providence, thanks to the mediation of Mary, the Seat of Wisdom, we were able to maintain calm, balance, dignity, determination. Today I come to you without this tension. After 5 years, the external situation has changed. It has changed to the extent that your church, your community has become a social fact that cannot be changed now. And the expression of your maturity is everything that you have done to furnish your temple.

A very significant part of the consecration of an altar is the sealing of holy relics within it. The relics of a saint are placed within the mensa. Here, within this mensa,[48] the relics of Blessed Maximilian Kolbe should be placed for he became a great inspiration for your community in the building of this church ...

We do not have relics of Blessed Maximilian. You know well that, after he had been starved to death, his body was incinerated in the ovens of the crematorium of the camp in Auschwitz. There is not even a fragment of bone. And so, St. Stanislaw comes to your altar. We should not say that he comes "in place of" Blessed Maximilian. This bishop and martyr, a bishop of the Church of Krakow ... comes here, to rest in your altar in his relics.

Same day — 4:00 p.m., Myslenice, parish church, blessing of the church bells, homily:

It was a great voice calling in the wilderness, the voice of the predecessor of Christ ...

A bell is just such a voice. We might say it is only a voice. That is the essence of a bell, to give voice, to produce sound, to resound, so that God may speak through this sound. The bell is also the voice of the calling Christ ...

The bells sound, their voice calls out, Christ calls out through them in particularly important moments of human life — of the life of every

---

[47] See Glossary
[48] Altar slab

Christian: it accompanies man on his last voyage. On that voyage, which is a passage from this life into eternity, or rather a passage from this life to new life. Because death is also a birth of man for God, a birth for eternity.

Same day — 8:00 p.m., Krakow, Church of the Missionaries of Our Lady of La Salette, concelebrated Mass, sermon for the 75th anniversary:

Mary of the second Advent and the third Advent — the advent of all humanity and the advent of every person — is the Mary standing at the foot of the Cross, and the one to whom, from the height of the Cross, Christ gave His disciple for a son. And with him, Christ gives every man — the whole Church and all of humanity. Mary of the second and the third Advent is Mary, our Mother, Mother of the Church, Mother of every person. And so we understand that this Mary of our Advent, the Advent of every man, the Mary of the Advent of all of humanity, can — and sometimes must — shed tears. And so we understand that among the various private apparitions which have occurred in the history of the Church, the apparition of Our Lady of La Salette is particularly close to our idea of the motherhood of Mary, the Mother of Man, the Mother of the human family, the Mother of the Church. We know well that a mother who loves, often weeps. Had there been no images of Mary weeping among these private apparitions of the Mother of our Advent, confirmed by the Church, we would not have a full image of Her maternal love. A mother who loves, often weeps. She weeps when her child is threatened by some great danger ...

The weeping Mother of La Salette is the one who calls to penance. She calls to conversion. By her tears the true Mary of Advent continues the mission of Christ's predecessor, John the Baptist from the River Jordan, who said: "Repent! The Kingdom of God is nigh" ...

As we turn our thoughts to Mary, the Mother of the Church, we are aware that this Church, the Mystical Body of Christ, the Church of which Mary is the Mother, finds itself, in our times, in the midst of great difficulties. In times of that great negation of God, of Christ's Gospel, of man's supernatural calling — the Church's situation is perhaps more difficult than ever before — at least it seems so to us. It could be, that there were situations as difficult or, in their own way, even more difficult in the past, but to us this one seems to be particularly hard.

And so we turn to the Mother of the Church. We understand Her maternal tears and we trust that these tears, that her weeping, are a special way of obtaining the Grace of God, and Grace is the greatest strength of the Church.

December 19 — 9:00 a.m., residence chapel, concelebrated Mass, sermon, meeting with the Council of Priests * 8:00 p.m., Church of the Dominicans, academic *Oplatek*[49] * December 20 — 1:00 p.m., residence chapel, nominations of pastors * 7:00 p.m., residence chapel, Mass and sermon, academic *Oplatek* — St. Anne's apostolate * December 21 — 7:00 a.m., residence chapel, Mass and sermon, *Oplatek* for the Higher Catechetic Institute * 3:00 p.m., residence, ses-

---

[49] See Glossary.

sion of the bishops * 7:00 p.m., residence, meeting with *Tygodnik Powszechny* * December 22 — 1:00 p.m., the Rakowicki cemetery, funeral of the late Prof. Jan Gwiazdomorski * 5:00 p.m., residence chapel, concelebrated Mass, sermon, wedding of Prof. Wojciech M. Bartel * December 23 — 4:00 p.m., Wieliczka, funeral of the late Rev. Dean Wladyslaw Grohs.

> **This was a man who was deeply connected with the history of his nation. He had a great sense of history. I think that perhaps this led him, years ago, to suggest that he take on the pastorate in Wieliczka. Certainly, the historical character of your city, of this parish, the history of the Wieliczka salt mines, the tradition of Blessed Kinga, the connections with the Krakow Academy — all of this drew this man, who felt a very profound bond with his Homeland, with its history, with the very difficult history of Poland.**
>
> **The more so that he himself participated in this difficult history in a most dramatic moment, during World War II, during the horrible occupation, when he was a prisoner in concentration camps. First in Auschwitz, then in Mauthausen. Before he was sent to the camp, he was a chaplain of the Home Army.[50] He felt that as a priest, he had to make a priestly contribution to the great task of fighting for the independence of his Homeland. And we know that such courage had a high price. He was sent to the camp because of his priestly service, because of his concern for children who were receiving their first Holy Communion. He wanted to prepare for them a meal appropriate to the solemn occasion. That was all it took in those terrible days of contempt, and especially contempt for our nation, to condemn a man, a priest, to the concentration camp.**

Same day — 8:00 p.m., Nowa Huta — Mogila, *Oplatek* for university students * December 24 — 8:00 a.m. , "Roraty" {morning Advent devotions} * 11:00 a.m.-1:00 p.m., residence, holiday wishes presented by various groups * 4:00 p.m., Cathedral, Matins * 6:00 p.m., residence chapel, Martyrologium, (5th year seminarians), residence, "wigilia"[51] with the 5th year seminarians and Superiors of the Seminary * 12:00 midnight, the *Pasterka* {Midnight} Mass at Wzgorza Krzeslawickie in Krakow, sermon:

> **And although He was born in isolation, very soon people appeared around Him. This is the most wondrous mystery which is contained in the Mystery of Christmas ... We must say that your community, the community of inhabitants and Christians of Nowa Huta, from Wzgorza Krzeslawickie and the slopes of Grebalow, has a fairly long history behind it. Through this history you relate to Christmas night. Every year, the Midnight Mass was a particularly telling, particularly exalted, particularly sincere coming together of the People of God of this parish in the process of its creation. I often participated in these gatherings. For I feel that on the night of Christmas, when the Son of God is being born in a stable, the**

---

[50] The underground resistance against the German occupation.
[51] Christmas Eve supper, the central observance of the Polish Christmas tradition.

Bishop of the Church of Krakow must leave Wawel Cathedral and be in places where Christ is homeless. So I was here with you many times, and I saw how, just like the shepherds of Bethlehem, you gathered here year after year for Midnight Mass at Wzgorza. I saw how the community of the People of God was evolving here ... Today I come with a somewhat lighter heart and with joy that I can offer my congratulations on the successful completion of the first step towards gaining a roof over the heads of your community. We are grateful for that to God, to the new-born God, to Christ of Bethlehem ... We are grateful to people who, through their perseverance, created such a compelling social fact here that it became the foundation for the decision of the authorities. And I also expressed my gratitude to the authorities, emphasizing that whenever they act to meet the real needs of Catholic society, their decision is appreciated by that society. I expressed this in my own name, but I am sure that I spoke in your name also ... I can already see with the eyes of my soul the structure whose construction you will be beginning. First you will start with a pastoral center, where there will be rooms for religious instruction, where the priests will live; later there will be a church, for this center only makes sense if the church is the ultimate goal ... The altar of Jesus Christ, in His Church, is the sign of everlasting life. I rejoice that I can bless this altar here today, even if only this provisional one, under this temporary canopy. I rejoice in the fact that this altar will some day stand in the church of your parish at Wzgorza Krzeslawickie.

December 25 — 8:00 a.m., residence chapel, second Mass, sermon * 10:00 a.m., Wawel Cathedral, concelebrated Pontifical High Mass, sermon * 3:00 p.m., Cathedral, vespers * December 26 — 10:00 a.m., residence chapel, Mass and sermon for the 25th wedding anniversary of Barbara and Gabriel Turowski * 12:00 noon, Church of St. Szczepan {Stephen}, sermon:

In these times, when mass media have become such an important factor in the dissemination of ideas, the Church everywhere, all over the world, turns to these media. The Church states that there must not be situations in which these media are used one-sidedly. They are being used, in large part, against the beliefs and convictions of the majority of society. These media must be accessible to all. The Church also has something worthwhile to say, by means of Mass media, to Poland and Poles of the second half of the 20th century. Of course, we value whatever we have in this regard. Once before, in the sermon for Corpus Christi, I emphasized how we cherish the fact that the weekly *Tygodnik Powszechny*, the monthly *Znak* and other publications are published in Krakow.[52] This is something of value for Krakow and for all of Poland. But we must say that in the scope of our whole country, the means at our disposal are inadequate and incommensurate.

And so, in the name of St. Stephen, considering the development of the situation in the cultural sphere, we turn our attention to the mass media, to these methods of dissemination of ideas. Just as we turn our careful attention to the activities of schools and institutions of learning. We con-

---

[52] See June 9, 1977

tinue to emphasize that the school, which is the property of the nation, which exists only because the nation supports it, cannot serve those ends, cannot proclaim those theories, which are contrary to the convictions of the vast majority of Poles — that is, contrary to the convictions of the people of faith. It must not in any way contribute to the erosion of that heritage of faith, of morality, to which we owe our identity for the past thousand years! Often we are approached with the statement that there is a decadence, a decline of morality. The Church could help us with that. In that case, the Church first needs all the means which are necessary for the Church to fulfill its mission in our age — the age of progress, the age of mass media, the age of social and cultural advancement:[53] give us the means! You cannot set tasks before the Church and, at the same time, prevent it from fulfilling these tasks.

Same day — 4:00 p.m., residence, a visit by Bishop W. Rubin * 7:00 p.m., at the residence of Mr. & Mrs. Turowski * December 27 — 11:00 a.m., residence, an audience * 5:30 p.m., residence, a session of bishops * December 28 — 11:00 a.m., Church of the Norbertine Sisters at Salwator, funeral of the late Rev. Msgr. Juliusz Malysiak:

The dearly departed Msgr. Juliusz Malysiak, to whom we bid farewell today after an exceptionally long life of over 90 years, was, for the most significant part of his life, a catechist. A catechist in various schools, mostly in Krakow, in elementary schools and secondary schools, general and trade schools ...
As we bid him farewell, I wish to state that he was as if a living illustration of that historical truth which was brought out in the past year by the Synod of Bishops, and which I tried to emphasize at the Synod. Catechesis in Poland, catechesis in Krakow, has undergone a transformation. It ceased to be a part of the school program, it was removed from schools. The school is being subjected ever more frequently to the process of secularization. We must struggle and be vigilant that this school not become a place of conversion of our children to atheism, because this would be contrary both to our consciences and to the fundamental rights of man and the nation. But, at the same time, the catechesis which went from the schools to the parishes, to the churches, to the centers of religious instruction, is still a living and telling reality in Poland and in Krakow ...
However, if this form of catechesis, despite all difficulties, despite all opposition, has earned a strong place in the awareness of our society, it is thanks to the catechists of the previous generation, the post-war generation, who led religious instruction in the schools. By their service, by their work, they made the study of religion, catechesis, something which was indispensable, something which could not be treated as a second-rank issue, even though all kinds of methods were forcefully employed to create such a perception. This is the contribution of that generation; a generation that is slowly passing away. The dearly departed Msgr. Juliusz Malysiak is one of the magnificent representatives of that generation.

Same day — 7:00 p.m., at Mr. & Mrs. Janik's * December 29 —

[53] A Marxist catch-phrase meaning the supposed material advancement of underprivileged.

11:00 a.m., residence, an audience * 6:30 p.m., residence chapel, Mass for the family P. * December 30 — 11:00 a.m., Prokocim * December 31 — 7:00 a.m., Church of St. Joseph * 11:00 a.m., residence, session of the bishops and the Curia * 5:00 p.m., sermon for the end of the Old Year in the Krowodrza neighborhood:

> **When we consider the words ... of our ancient Polish carol: "He who was scorned, is covered in glory..." we must unite spiritually with all those, around the world, who are suffering scorn, and with all who are victims of whatever persecutions and discriminations. Be it racial discrimination, or class discrimination, the underprivileged poor in relation to the rich, or whole systems that make some groups underprivileged in relation to others. Or finally, if this should be a greatly underprivileged status of some because of their convictions or religion.**
>
> **With what pain, but at the same time with what solidarity, especially at this time of Christmas, when the Holy Family sets the example, must we think of all those who cannot pray freely, who cannot freely congregate in temples; whose right to religious freedom is limited or totally denied. We must realize that there are many forms of this scorn for Jesus Christ; and that from year to year and from age to age, in so many ways, Jesus Christ is always on the side of the scorned, the underprivileged, the discriminated against. "He who was scorned" — we sing — "is covered in glory!" ...**
>
> **"God is born, earthly power quakes with fear."[54] It appears that today's world, a world fascinated by its own accomplishments, wants to reverse this. It would like to sing: The world is born, God quakes with fear! It is good that this ancient Polish carol reminds us of the appropriate perspective: "God is born, earthly power quakes with fear!"**
>
> **You have received permission to build a church. It was a joyous day, it was a turning point in the history of your growing Christian community, of this parish that is being formed here.**
>
> **And — as you can well imagine — this is also a great joy for me. This joy comes from the responsibility for the Church of Krakow, of which I am the bishop.**

Same day — 8:00 p.m., a visit to the ailing Msgr. Mieczyslaw Satora on the eve of his name-day.

---

[54] Words of a Polish Christmas carol.

1978

January 1 {midnight from December 31, 1977 to January 1, 1978}, the Franciscan Basilica in Krakow — Holy Mass with sermon and greetings for the New Year * 10:00 a.m., Zakopane, arrival with Rev. Jaworski * 5:00 p.m., a sermon at the parish church:

> The Son of God was immediately willing to take up all of the sufferings that accompany the motherhood of a human mother. He was also willing to support all motherhood that is despised, unwanted, derided ... It is possible to destroy a defenseless person, one who is not yet born, by "scientific methods". But this is a disgrace for science.

January 2-6 — 7:00 a.m., Zakopane-Jaszczurowka, a Mass. Afterwards, skiing. * January 5 — Singing of Christmas carols * January 6 — departure in the afternoon * 6:00 p.m., Wawel, the Feast of the Epiphany, a concelebrated Mass and a sermon:

> He revealed God within man. Not *to* man, but *within* man, so as to show man his own humanity anew. He revealed God and He revealed man.

January 7 — 12:00 noon, residence, a session of bishops * 2:00 p.m., visit of Fr. J. Loew * 3:00 p.m., 10 Sw. Marka {St. Mark's} Street, *Oplatek* for the study group of lay catechists * 6:00 p.m., in Katowice, he visited ailing Bishop Juliusz Bieniek * January 8 — 9:00 a.m., Krakow, the Ursuline Sisters, a meeting with teachers, a concelebrated Mass, *Oplatek*, and homily:

> God entrusted people to people, a person to a person. This is why a person can participate in the growth of the soul of another person ... This is the most wonderful part of a calling, whether it is that of a priest, or that of a teacher; the calling of an educator.
> [An outline of the collaboration between priests and teachers:] We always feel that we have established a very close rapport with the community of teachers ... As a bishop, I experience this during practically every visitation, because I meet teachers on virtually every one of my visitations ... A large majority of teachers as well as a large majority of pastors feel united in a common cause ... This common cause is the cause of Christian upbringing. For we cannot see any convincing arguments that would make us give up this great heritage.

The same day — Lagiewniki, *Oplatek* at the *Zrodlo*[1] {Source} — a meeting room for the youth run by the Sisters of Our Lady of Mercy * The same day, the church in Liszki, consecration of the altar:

> After all, Bishop Stanislaw Rospond, a man very much alive in our memory, came from Liszki. I have many fond memories of him, since I received my nomination and consecration as bishop in the year of his

---

[1] Youth center run by the Sisters of Our Lady of Mercy.

death. I was, at first, an auxiliary bishop of Krakow, just as he was until the end of his life.

The same day — 7:00 p.m., residence, *Oplatek* for scholars followed by singing of carols * January 9 — 10:30 a.m., residence, 3 Franciszkanska Street, the 7th assembly of the Coordinating Committee of the 1st Synod of the Province of Krakow. The committee is supposed to prepare material for the meeting of the bishops of the Metropolitan See of Krakow (it will take place on January 27, 1978). An attempt at a theological synthesis (text prepared by Rev. Prof. Stanislaw Nagy). The Cardinal asks the Committee for its opinion on the matter of passing this text on to the bishops of the Metropolitan See. There is a discussion on the matter and motions are made. There is also a discussion on the text prepared by Rev. Prof. Tadeusz Pieronek, "A Proposal by the Secretariat in the Matter of the Final Document of the Synod." A motion is made for the participation of the Cardinal in the meetings of each of the consulting groups. Rev. Prof. Marian Jaworski provides information regarding the work of the Committee for the Department of Theology. In addition, motions were made concerning the material that will be presented to the bishops of the Metropolitan See. (From the minutes) * 5:00 p.m., residence chapel, concelebrated Mass with sermon. Afterwards, *Oplatek* for gardeners * 7:00 p.m., the Silesian Seminary, the festivities surrounding the arrival of St. Nicholas * January 10-12 — Zakopane, "Ksiezowka," session of the Committee of the Episcopate for Pastoral Ministry.

January 10 — Meeting of the Committee of the Episcopate for Pastoral Ministry. At 10:30 a.m., Reverend Cardinal Wojtyla's report: *Pastoral Implications of the Fifth Synod of Bishops in Rome.* In the introduction — the connection between catechesis and pastoral ministry: a panorama of the Church in the world — the diversity of situations; a detailed discussion of the proclamation of the Fathers of the Synod to the People of God. A report by Bishop Stroba, *Practical Applications of the Results of the Roman Synod in Poland*; discussion * January 11 — The second day of deliberations of the Committee of the Episcopate for Pastoral Ministry. A lecture by Prof. Jerzy Kloczowski, *The Influence of Christianity in Shaping the Culture of the Nation through the Centuries.* A report by Rev. Nieweglowski, *Current Pastoral Possibilities of Shaping Christian Culture.* Discussion. * January 12 — The third day of deliberations of the Committee of the Episcopate for Pastoral Ministry was dedicated to the pastoral program. Discussions, reports. The work was finished at 2:00 p.m. * The same day — 3:00 p.m. in Zakopane, a session with the movement "Swiatlo-Zycie" {Light-Life} * January 13 — Participation in the funeral of the

Mother General of the Sisters of the Holy Spirit — Mother Redempta Sledzinska * 10:00 a.m., the Cardinal celebrated the Mass and led the funeral procession from the main gates of the Rakowicki cemetery (12:30 p.m.). He delivered a homily dedicated to the deceased, whom he knew since 1963. From the homily:

> **The calling to the religious life, just as the calling to priesthood, is a social act. But it is also a deep mystery. It begins with the words of Jesus Christ. It begins with the encounter of a young girl's human soul with her Betrothed. Love begins to take shape during this encounter. It is a love that transcends all the love that life may offer to someone — whether to a woman or a man.**

The same day — 5:30 p.m., Parish of Our Lady of Lourdes, *Oplatek* with the parish charity team * 8:15 p.m., the Church of the Most Holy Redeemer, a Mass with sermon. Also, *Oplatek* for university students * January 14 — 11:00 a.m., residence, a session of bishops and the Curia * 7:30 p.m., residence chapel, a Mass with a sermon, followed by *Oplatek* with physicians * The same day — a review of a treatise by Dr. Jerzy Galkowski (KUL), submitted in partial fulfilment of the requirements for admission to assistant professorship, *Labor and the Individual:. An attempt at the Philosophical Analysis of Labor.* The Cardinal presented his remarks and review in a private letter to the author of the work, dated June14, 1977. The Cardinal received this more than three hundred page text in April of that year, and, as he wrote in his letter, he was unable to read the text until June of that year. From his review:

> **Insofar as I was able to form my opinion on the basis of two readings somewhat separated in time, I feel that the treatise *Labor and the Individual* is an interesting and successful work, and fulfills the requirements for works presented to qualify for admission to assistant professorship ... The author sees the goal of his treatise on the subject of labor in arguing for what our epoch is demanding — namely, for the full humanization of labor, technology and civilization ... As to the type of academic work that this treatise is, it does not have a primarily analytical character, though we do find analytical texts throughout it ... As a whole, it is more of an attempt at a synthesis, ordering various treatments (even partial ones) and various approaches to the topic, while at the same time searching for the essence of labor — for what constitutes it. Basically, the author is developing his own thought, offering his opinion on the ideas of others along the way ... This is the character of the work; quite original. The author has avoided compilations or juxtapositions.**

Jerzy Galkowski's examination colloquium for admission to assistant professorship took place on March 3, 1979.

January 15 — 9:00 a.m., a homily at the Sunday Study Group of the Theology of Marriage and the Family. The topic — manhood:

A man is called to become a bridegroom ... He must always remember that in becoming a bridegroom he is a "friend of the Divine Bridegroom" ... A man must be a servant ... A woman in marriage is the servant of life ... Manhood, which has its natural tendencies towards domination, must be balanced with readiness to serve ... An apostle means one who is sent ... A man can be sent in many ways ... This type of apostleship may be expressed in various ways, but it is expressed specifically in a great responsibility for the people who, together with him, form a family.

The same day — 7:00 p.m., residence chapel, a concelebrated Mass, sermon, *Oplatek* for lawyers. From the sermon:

It is because man is the greatest asset of the Homeland, the nation, and also the Church ... Man who is guided by conscience, man who loves true freedom, man ready to make sacrifices, living not only for consumption, one who is not merely utilitarian, but man living by principles, living in truth, capable of love. This is the kind of man we pray for by the stable of Bethlehem. This is our wish for one another. These wishes are also demanding. But ... I would say that they should never be easy. To wish someone something means also to demand.

January 16 — 11:00 a.m., residence, audiences * 6:00 p.m., chapter house of the Dominicans, *Oplatek* for war veterans, homily. * 8:00 p.m., at 4 Plac Wolnosci,[2] in accordance with the annual tradition he participated in the singing of Christmas carols together with members of the former "Chorek"[3] from the Church of St. Florian and Church of St. Catherine * January 17 — 3:00 p.m., residence, a visit of Bohdan Cywinski * 7:30 p.m., Theological Seminary, singing of carols * January 18 — 7:00 a.m., residence chapel, a concelebrated Mass. Closing remarks on the 14th anniversary of his nomination as archbishop * 1:00 p.m., residence, a celebratory lunch in connection with the anniversary * 3:00 p.m., the Committee organizing the celebrations in honor of St. Stanislaw * January 19 — Warsaw, General Council of the Polish Episcopate * Gives a written interview to Patrice Canette from "Le Pelerin" magazine * January 20 — Katowice, at the funeral of Archbishop Juliusz Bieniek. The sermon: "He possessed this deep conviction that 'he was taken from among the people and put in place for the people'." * January 21 — 11:00 a.m., residence, session of bishops and the Curia * 4:00 p.m., residence, *Oplatek* for artists * 6:00 p.m., at the residence of Prof. Mr. & Mrs. Janik, singing of Christmas carols * 8:00 p.m., *Oplatek* at the Club of Catholic Intellectuals * 9:00 p.m., residence, *Oplatek* with the Institute headed by Msgr. Kacz * January 22 — 11:15 a.m., the Silesian Seminary, *Oplatek* with invalids (ministry to the sick), a sermon * 12:00 noon, Chapel of the Ursuline Sisters, a catechetical symposium of the Higher Catechetic Institute. The

---

[2] Freedom Square
[3] Little Choir also see Glossary *Srodowisko*.

Cardinal delivered a short lecture on the matter of the Synod of Bishops and on the important role of the symposiums organized by the Higher Catechetic Institute. (From the chronicle of the Ursuline Sisters) * 3:00 p.m., to teachers during *Oplatek*:

> **The school, which is in the bosom of the nation, cannot stop being a school for the nation ... And because this nation is made up of baptized people, the alliance between the Church and the school cannot be broken. To do so would create something false, something forced, something unreal. This is why this alliance between the Church and the school remains, although not in an official form ... The fruits of this alliance are bountiful ... One of them is the presence here, today, of all of you. If I dared to invite you here today — as I do successively in each of the regions of the Archdiocese — and if my invitation has met with such a warm response, as shown by your presence, then this is proof that an alliance exists between the people who shape the school, and the Church ... After we have shared the Christmas wafer together, let us sing some carols. I believe that once we start to sing carols, the whole city of Krakow will hear us.**

The same day — 6:00 p.m., residence, *Oplatek* for nurses, a homily. * 7:00 p.m., the Dominican Basilica, the conclusion of the octave of prayer for unity among Christians, concelebrated Mass, sermon, ecumenical meeting. From the sermon: "If in the minds of believers, of people, this faith assumed various shapes and forms throughout the ages, it is necessary to seek the paths to the rediscovery of the common faith. Just this action of seeking already brings us closer; it prevents us from being strangers." * January 23 — 9:00 a.m., Dominican chapter house, a sermon for the opening of a session for religious retreat masters * 2:00 p.m., residence, a conference on economic matters * 5:00 p.m., Libiaz, concelebrated Mass, sermon, and *Oplatek* with priests ordained in 1974 * January 24 — 4:30 p.m., Komorowice, *Oplatek* with priests ordained in 1977 * 7:00 p.m., Kalwaria Zebrzydowska, a sermon to graduating secondary school students participating in a retreat, singing of the promises of Jasna Gora * January 25 — Church of the Missionary Fathers in Krakow at Stradom, the observances of Feast of the Conversion of St. Paul: "Paul shows us Christ, One who never fails us. Paul shows us Christ, who is not only the mystery of man's life in his personal calling, but also the mystery of the community of humankind." * The same day — 4:30 p.m., Rabka — Zaryte, *Oplatek* with priests ordained in 1971 * January 26 — 10:00 a.m., residence, a conference of priests who are heads of deaneries * 4:30 p.m., Zebrzydowice, *Oplatek* with priests ordained in 1976 * 7:30 p.m., Krakow, Borek Falecki, *Oplatek* with former work colleagues * January 27 — Krakow, a meeting of the bishops of the Metropolitan See of Krakow, for the purpose of acquainting them with the work of the Coordinating Committee of the Synod of the Krakow Province,

Oplatek * 4:00 p.m., a session * 4:30 p.m., a visit of the Ambassador of the United States * 5:30 p.m., Chapel of the Ursuline Sisters, a Mass and singing of carols at the Higher Catechetic Institute * January 28 — the wedding of Piotr and Marta:

> ... I cannot forget to mention today, that twenty five years ago I blessed your parents ... I retrace again the trail of those days and years, which your parents and many other people have lived ... You will be slowly traveling this same trail, too ... Once, in a book written by a Polish author — an excellent author — I read an interesting sentence ... There was a certain phrase there, one that seemed strange coming from the mouth of a young person, from the mouth of a young man who is engaged. He is saying these words to his intended lifelong companion — who is also young, just like Marta is in relation to you at this time. He says to her: "From now on, we will grow old together." It is important to think about love with some perspective.

January 30 — 12:00 noon, residence, Theological Committee of the Provincial Synod * 5:00 p.m., Radziechowice, *Oplatek* with priests ordained in 1975 * 8:00 p.m., Ujsoly, the visitation of young people participating in a training course * January 31 — 4:00 p.m., Zywiec, *Oplatek* of the "Oasis" group * 6:00 p.m., Lodygowice Gorne, *Oplatek* with priests ordained in 1972.

February 1 — 5:00 p.m., Bolechowice, *Oplatek* with priests ordained in 1973 * February 2 — Free time in Zakopane * The same day -7:00 p.m., at the Church of the Redemptorist Fathers in Krakow, concelebrated Mass and homily to the workers of the MPK {city transit authority}:

> We rejoice that you are here today ... that you have come here openly, in your uniforms, with your banners: that you value this so highly. We rejoice in this, we see this as an act of courage on your part. We also see in you a need to be yourselves, which is a basic condition of our humanity ... My wish to you is that the pay you receive for your work be commensurate with your work, and, above all, that this pay meets the material needs of the families of which you are the mothers and fathers, the educators, and for which you are responsible. May God bless you in your personal lives.

February 4 — 11:00 a.m., residence, session of bishops and the Curia * February 4-5 — Canonical visitation of the parish of Bestwina * February 6 — 10:00 p.m., he arrived at Jaszczurowka, sick with influenza * February 6-14 — Zakopane-Jaszczurowka, private Masses * February 8 — Ash Wednesday, marking of the heads of the faithful with ashes * February 14 — He returns to Krakow, still sick; convalescence until the 28th of February * February 15 — Krakow, on Franciszkanska Street, a meeting of the Committee for Catholic Education. In his opening statement, Cardinal Wojtyla points out that the most important matters are the issues connected with the realization of academic cooperation — today — on the affiliation or aggregation of religious studies to their maternal institutions in Rome. There was also discussion on the matters of modernizing the program of study for priests (the Cardinal spoke in this discussion), and of organizing a Marian year. The Cardinal gave a short account of the five years of activity of the Educational Council, and announced that a special report on this topic would be forthcoming.

Matters of Catholic scholarship in Poland. A report of the chairman of the Educational Council of the Episcopate and the Committee for Catholic Education, for the five-year period 1973 — 1978 (typescript by Cardinal Wojtyla):

> The Commission for Catholic Education in Poland separated itself, prior to 1977, from the former Committee for Higher Education and Seminaries, in which the Committee initially functioned, for a time, as a separate sub-committee. The Committee gradually worked out its mission, and prepared the elements necessary for appointing the Educational Council. Its main mission was and continues to be the implementation of the right of the Church in Poland to determine the program of its own education, meaning Catholic education. The Episcopal Conference recognized that it was inappropriate that essential matters of Catholic education should be decided primarily by a secular authority, and an atheistic one at that ... The Conference saw a danger in the fact that promotions of independent Catholic academic workers at existing academic institutions were decided by the state authorities, often on the basis of criteria that were not academic, but political ...
>
> The tasks ... which the Educational Council set for itself in this period, in close collaboration with the Committee for Catholic Education, ... were first and foremost 1) the establishment of Catholic academic institutions in appropriate numbers, and obtaining for them full academic status ... The first concern here is for the institutions that are purely ecclesiastical: the Pontifical Departments of Theology in Krakow, Wroclaw, Poznan, and Warsaw ... All of these institutions attained their full rights (in a canonical sense) ... According to the laws of the Church, full academic rights include the right to enter into agreements on academic collaboration with the major theological seminaries ... Connected with this is a second basic task that we set for ourselves in the activities of the past five years — namely, the strengthening of the academic programs of study at major theological seminaries throughout Poland ...
>
> The implementation of this second task is still only partially complete ... The Educational Council has taken the position that since it serves the Episcopate in caring for the entirety of Catholic education matters in Poland, it should have some influence in making sure that the nominations and promotions, especially of professors, be handled "iuris publici in foro ecclesiastico". Otherwise, what remains for them (when it comes to the professors of ATK) is only a "forum civile" — and only in this forum will they be "publici iuris". This matter has not been brought to its conclusion ... We still have much to do. We have carried a certain tradition from the past, a tradition developed by the theological departments of government universities. However, this tradition belongs to the past. We cannot mix the

state's authentic respect and recognition for theology and academic degrees in theology ... with a tactic of one-sided dependence. Under these conditions, we must keep reminding, and we must decidedly take the position that an academic degree in theology ... is first of all an asset of the Church, and not an asset of the state. I believe that if we were united on this position, the state authorities would stop tormenting us by instituting various tactics designed to make us dependent. The means necessary for this unity will be found within the structure of the Educational Council, as far as we understand it.

I must confess with a certain sense of sadness, that the institutions which are dependent on the state ..., although within the Council of the Committee they come in contact with and collaborate with schools that are purely ecclesiastical, in their official behavior they very deliberately ignore the ecclesiastical schools ... When Masters or doctors from the Department in Krakow go abroad to study, every Catholic university in the world recognizes their degrees of licentiate or doctorate ... every one, with the exception of the Catholic University of Lublin ... in Poland. The Committee is addressing this issue ... by regular contacts with so-called professors' sections ... This form of teaming and team effort of people who are involved in various fields of study was established after 1956 (in connection with the dissolution of the Polish Theological Society); it has become well-accepted ... There are about 20 sections.

The Educational Council and the Committee for Education are, in a particular way, patrons of the Congress of Polish Theologians. The last Congress, in 1976, was on the topic: "Theology — the Study of God." The previous one, in 1971: "Theology and Anthropology" ... More and more frequently, our Catholic scholars participate in congresses and sessions abroad, often as highly sought-after speakers. Besides one-time speaking engagements, there are invitations to become "visiting professors" ... This indicates a move from the passive participation in centers of Catholic scholarship outside of Poland, to a creative contribution ... We must strive to cease being those who merely make use of the contributions of others, and to become those who contribute, who are reckoned with, etc ...

Our ambition, after all, stems not from some kind of "fight for the marketplace," but rather from a sense of our right to a more equitable and many-sided exchange of such goods as theological ideas, philosophical ones, historical, canonical, Biblical, etc. We must, and we do, consider our fundamental and most important task to be the work of Catholic scholarship for the Church in Poland and for Polish Christian culture as a fundamental value of our nation. We must ensure that Catholic scholarship fulfills its tasks in relation to pastoral work, in relation to the intellectual and moral demands of Polish society ... Today, these demands have greatly increased ...

In the last five years, we have initiated collaboration with FIUC (Federation International des Universitees Catholiques) ... For the time being, besides KUL and ATK, only PWT[4] Krakow has accepted the invitation to collaborate. Other institutions are still considering.

The main source and foundation of our participation in academic activities is still Congregatio pro Institutione Catholica at the Holy See. We

---

[4] Pontifical Department of Theology.

maintain constant and systematic contact with this center.

February 17 — Nowa Huta-Mogila, the Cistercian Fathers, a congregation of the deanery of Krakow VI * 1:00 p.m., the Council of the Pontifical Department of Theology * February 18 — 11:00 a.m., residence, session of bishops and the Curia * February 21 — Residence, a meeting with the editorial staff of *Tygodnik Powszechny* * February 23-24 — 11:00 a.m., audiences * February 25 — 11:00 a.m., residence, session of bishops and the Curia * 1:00 p.m., the Salvatorian cemetery, Mass and sermon, the funeral of Mieczyslaw Kotlarczyk.

March 1 — 10:00 a.m., residence, meeting of the Consulting Team of the Provincial Synod, "the youth" * March 4 — 11:00 a.m., residence, session of bishops and the Curia * March 4-5 — Visitation of the parish of Rybarzowice * March 6 — The cathedral in Wroclaw, funeral of Archbishop Jozef Marek. The sermon:

> **And he stood before us, straight and strong, full of promise, and full of spiritual, moral and physical health ... God's plan, however, was different. When a person puts himself at God's disposal, when he gives himself totally — and this is how it should be on the day of consecration as a bishop — then he leaves the decision-making to God Himself. He leaves it up to God how He will accept his human calling, his sacrifice of self. And it frequently happens that God accepts this offering of self as the beginning of a great, long-term work for the Church, for society, and for the nation. But sometimes it so happens that God accepts this offering in a different way. This is precisely what happened in this instance ... And if God accepts the offering in this way, it means that ... this kind of fulfillment of the sacrifice was necessary. We do not always know why.**

March 7 — Warsaw, the Main Council of the Polish Episcopate * March 8-9 — Warsaw, plenary conference of the Polish Episcopate * March 10 — Departure for Rome with Bishop W. Rubin * March 11 — Rest * March 12 — Rome, Polish College * March 12 — 10:00 a.m., Church of St. Stanislaw in Rome, concelebrated Mass and speech on the occasion of the 30th anniversary of the death of Servant of God Rev. Jan Balicki: "In these our times, very special times, the Church on Polish soil is struggling to discern the sense of humanity, the sense of human life and human calling. Saints throw the greatest light on life. That is why the Church in Poland is praying for saints from Poland." * The same day — 1:00 p.m., at Bishop A. Deskur's residence at the Vatican, a visit with priests from Krakow * March 14-15 — 10:15 a.m., Rome, he participated in the sessions of the Congregation for Catholic Education. The materials regarding the reform of the Church academic legislation submitted by Catholic universities and bishops were discussed during the plenary session * March 16 — 9:00 a.m., the Mathilda chapel, participation in the celebrations associated with the presentation of the pallium to Cardinal Tomasek * March 17 — 10:00 a.m., departure for Warsaw * 6:00 p.m., arrival in Krakow * March 18 — 11:00 a.m., residence, a session of bishops and the Curia * March 18-19 — Visitation of the parish of Trzebunia * March 20 — 7:30 p.m., Church of St. Joseph, concelebrated Mass, sermon during a retreat for lawyers * March 22 — Wednesday of Holy Week, Mass at the Church of the Felician Sisters; closing remarks at the conclusion of a retreat for physicians, get-together * March 23 — Holy Thursday, 1:00 p.m., residence, a meal with the Chapter and the Curia * Wawel Cathedral, during the Mass of the Holy Oils:

> Today we come here, we priests, with great emotion. Holy Thursday is our feast. You found each of us in a special way; You called us by name; You summoned us to give up other aspirations and goals that stand before us in our life on earth, in order that we may give ourselves up totally to Your service and to the service of Your Church; to the service of redemption. In choosing the priesthood, we also chose celibacy, a life in a pure state, so that we could serve the People of God and the cause of redemption without any distractions or divisions in loyalty.

March 24 — 11:00 a.m., the Franciscan Church, Stations of the Cross with the superiors and seminarians of the Theological Seminary * March 25 — 11:00 a.m.-1:00 p.m., residence, exchanging greetings with: sisters, *Tygodnik Powszechny*, bishops, the Chapter, priests, workers of the Curia * 8:00 p.m., Theological Seminary, Easter repast * March 26 — Wawel Cathedral, on the day of the Lord's Resurrection:

> We must proclaim the truth about the Resurrection, because it is the truth of our times. We must do this because everything that we create in such a hurry, in such overwork, in such an atmosphere of haste, in such a time of distress — all of this will lose its sense, if we do not measure it against the Resurrection of Our Lord Jesus. So, in today's celebration, let us immerse ourselves in Resurrection, bring it into our lives, into all of our activities, into our work. Above all, into the upbringing of new generations. That they may live in the perspective of eternal life ... That they not lose faith in God, because what will then become of the human heart?

The same day -12:30 p.m., Church of the Congregation of the Resurrection, consecration of a statue from Lwow; homily * March 27 — 9:00 a.m., Zator, blessing of the bells, Mass with sermon, meeting with the parish pastoral council * 12:00 noon, the Church of the Most Holy Redeemer in Krakow, a *odpust*, a procession, and a meal. From the sermon:

> This is exactly the meaning of the mystery of Emmaus: that Christ walks with every man. Even with one who does not recognize Him ... We must give Christ the freedom to walk with every man, openly and everywhere, because He can tell us much, openly and everywhere, also in our times.

March 29 — 4:00 p.m., Wadowice, the funeral of Anna Silkowska * 8:00 p.m., residence, a meeting with Italian priests * March 30 — 2:00 p.m., a consistory of the Evangelical Church with the bishop from Magdeburg * March 31 — Zakopane, a day of recollection.

April 1 — Bachledowka, the Cardinal was supposed to lead the retreat of priests on the occasion of their tenth anniversary of priesthood (from March 19, in fact), but Fr. Nowak served as his replacement. The Cardinal came to the retreat on April 1st for its conclusion. He delivered a homily, and then, in a cordial, family-like atmosphere, he participated in lunch. * April 3-5 — Residence, numerous visits and audiences * April 4-12 — Talked with 3rd-year clerics at his residence * April 5 — 12:00 noon, residence, the Committee for Vocations * 8:00 p.m., a conference of the "Oasis" ministry * April 6 — 4:00 p.m., residence, a meeting on the matter of the Church and culture. It was probably for this session that he prepared a presentation entitled "The Church and the Issues of Culture in Poland" * April 7 — 2:00 p.m., residence, the Theological Committee of the Provincial Synod * April 7-9 — Visitation of the parish of Sulkowice * April 8 — 11:00 a.m., residence, session of the Consulting Group of the "Apostolate of the Laity" of the Provincial Synod * The archbishop's chapel, Easter wishes to the co-workers of the Department of Family Ministry:

> The words: He is not here, He is not where they have laid Him, He is risen, are only the first words of the truth of Easter. The subsequent words of this truth come from Jesus Christ Himself, because a Risen Christ does not leave his followers, the immediate ones and those, like us, who are somewhat removed, with a mere event, with just the fact of an empty grave. He comes to them, this is the most remarkable. When He comes in this way, He always comes as the One who ultimately says: you will be my witnesses (see Jn. 20:22; Acts 1:8). And hence, our Easter gatherings are of an inherently different climate, and I would also have to say, of a different weight. Everything that we experience at Christmas Eve gatherings, is only a premonition, only a prelude to what should take place during our Easter gatherings ...
>
> I would like to extend my most sincere greetings to all of you present here today, who represent the witness that marriages and families in the Church of Krakow would like to bear to the Risen Christ. Because this is what it is all about ... It is a mission, it is one of the missions which result from the mystery of the Resurrection and from the entire mystery of Christ. It is one of the missions which Christ included in His call: You will be my witnesses ...
>
> Often I have heard these words: well, pastors and priests prepare themselves for the priesthood for six years in a seminary; there are novitiates and postulates where one can prepare to the religious life, but there are no comparable institutions for preparing for the married life. And yet, this is no less a calling, one which has its own important and difficult specifics. I believe that everything that the family ministry, the Institute of the Family work on, is equivalent to a theological seminary. It is also equiv-

alent to the novitiates and postulates in religious orders. Perhaps it is not fully adequate, but it is a real equivalent.

April 11 — 1:00 p.m., the Committee of the Provincial Synod for charity * April 12 — 1:00 p.m., the vicar's house at the Mariacki Basilica, a course for sisters on the youth ministry * 4:00 p.m., residence, the Committee for the Apostolate of Sobriety * 6:00 p.m., St. Anne's Church, the 20th anniversary of KIK {Club of Catholic Intellectuals}, concelebrated Mass and sermon:

> It is quite difficult — carrying this name: Catholic — to desire anything else other than to have Christ make use of us. To desire that He make use of us in the most essential matters, those that are eternally established between Him and the Father; among the Father, Him, and all of us collectively, and each of us individually. Among the Father, the Son, our nation, its present generation, the Catholic intellectuals, and all of the Polish intellectuals as a social group, including the intellectual youth as a new generation of this social group ... And allow me to state at the end, that in fulfilling this task, the Club of Catholic Intellectuals is closely connected with the Catholic Church in Poland, that it is part of the assets of the Church. The Catholic Church in Poland, and particularly the Episcopate, wishes not only to hold on to this asset, but also to build it up and let it flourish ... [The text was printed in *Tygodnik Powszechny* 18/1978]

April 13 — 3:30 p.m., residence, Marian team * April 14 — Zakopane — Jaszczurowka, a day of recreation, skiing until 7:00 p.m. * April 15 — Departure from Zakopane * April 15-19 — Residence, three visits of third-year seminarians * April 15 — 2:30 p.m., residence, meeting on the matter of a cultural center * 4:00 p.m., individual conversations with second-year seminarians * April 15-16 — Visitation of the parish of Krzywaczka * April 16 — Krzywaczka, a sermon to married couples:

> Let us pray that there will never be a shortage of people in Poland — people that only marriages can give to Poland. But if marriages are to give people to the nation, no method of destroying people before they are even born can be introduced in marriages; the number of children cannot be restricted to a minimum. The Polish family must produce new people, and the Polish state must create conditions for these people to be born.

April 16-17 — Kielce, participation in the main celebrations of the jubilee commemorating the 250th anniversary of the Theological Seminary. On the first day, at a Mass at 5:00 p.m., he preaches a homily; on the second day, a presentation during a commemorative meeting in the auditorium. The homily:

> In his speech at the beginning, the Bishop, your archpastor, called the Kielce Seminary "a special forge of Catholic thought." Surely, it was such a forge, and it still is. It is a place of scholarship. For this reason the seminary depends on a group of superiors and professors who by their own

labors, by their personal research and studies, find the light which they then pass along to their students, the seminarians, sharing this light of Divine and human wisdom. They pass it on so that this forge of Catholic thought keeps working, so that it keeps functioning here at its core and in all other centers: in places where there is a need for Catholic thought, where there is a need for the light of theology, where there is a need for a grain of truth. Such a forge of thought is of great importance. This seminary, as a center of scholarship, has a great significance ...

The Seminary operates not only within the human intellect, but also within the heart and will of every young man; on the soil of that young humanity which carries a seed of God's calling within it. That is, after all, where the name comes from: a seminary is a place of seeds, a planting ground, as it were. This planting ground hides within itself seeds that are particularly important to the People of God, seeds of God's calling, of Christ's priesthood ...

This Seminary of yours has a history that is longer than that of the diocese, but it is also a difficult history ...

In the period after the January Insurrection {1863}, the Seminary was closed, dissolved for a number of years. That is because those who founded this Seminary, its superiors, professors, seminarians, were also Poles, and thus understood that since they had been taken from among the people and put in the service of the people, they were therefore obliged to keep their faith to the people. They kept this faith even in the face of numerous persecutions ...

This Seminary endured many tests and trials in the form of visitations forced upon it by the czarist authorities. But it did not give in. We can say today, that during the hardships of the 19th century, the Seminary in Kielce, as well as other seminaries, were able to work out an awareness of the Church in the service of the nation. But in order to serve the nation, the Church must have its proper freedom and independence. And these experiences and historical lessons, like the ones that the Seminary in Kielce experienced in the last century, have helped us very much and continue to help us in our century ...

There is a saying that is widely used, one that even the Second Vatican Council borrowed, that a Seminary is the pupil of the bishop's eye ... If we want to say that something is very dear to a person, we say: he guards it like the pupil of his eye ... Because the eye is something through which we see. Our ability to see depends on our sight. So we protect our eyes in order that we may look, in order that we may see. The seminary is the pupil of the eye, the pupil through which bishops, and not only bishops, but the whole Church, looks at its future. If the seminary is alive, if it attracts vocations, if those vocations mature there, if priests come from the seminary, if Christ is the Gate for the sheep at this seminary, then the bishop and the Church and the People of God can look through the Seminary into the future. They can see their future. When it is not like this — they fear for their future.

There are such churches, dioceses, and bishops in the world, who must fear for their future, because they see empty seminaries.

April 18 — Krakow, 10:00 a.m., residence, a conference of priests — heads of deaneries * April 19 — 10:30 a.m., residence, the Committee of the Provincial Synod for matters of Special Ministry *

April 20 — 10:00 a.m., the Pontifical Department of Theology, a philosophical symposium * April 21 — 10:00 a.m., residence, the Committee of the Provincial Synod for Mass Media * 6:00 p.m., Church of Our Lady of Lourdes, concelebrated Mass, sermon for the conclusion of an academic evangelizing retreat, agape. From the sermon:

> **Evangelization is accomplished within the Church. The intensity of the evangelization within the Church determines how strongly it shines to the outside, into the world ... No doubt this retreat has provided you with the gifts of the Holy Spirit, so that, enlivened with the energy, the strength and the light of the Gospel, you may go evangelize our Polish world.**

April 22 — 10:00 a.m., residence, a visit of Adrian Mungandu, the bishop from Livingstone (Zambia) * April 22-23 — Gniezno, celebrations in honor of St. Wojciech {Adalbert} * April 24 — 11:00 a.m., Krakow, residence, a meeting in matters of construction works * 5:00 p.m., the 15th anniversary of the catechetic center in Bory * Dabrowa Narodowa — the Stale settlement (Jaworzno) — sermon * April 26-28 — The Cardinal Metropolitan Archbishop of Krakow, Chairman of the Committee of the Episcopate for Christian Education, organized a nationwide symposium on the topic of new interpretations of dogma, with the participation of philosophers and theologians from university centers of theology in the country * April 26 — 12:00 noon, residence, meeting with priests involved in youth ministry and the liturgical service ministry * 8:15 p.m., Theological Seminary, a visit with the 1st year seminarians * April 27 — 3:00 p.m., Wroclaw, the 30th anniversary of the Theological Seminary * April 28 — 10:00 a.m., Wroclaw, he presided over the session "Faith and Science" * April 28-May 2 — Visitation of the parish of Jelesnia.

May 2 — 7:30 p.m., the Mariacki Basilica in Krakow, a Mass and sermon for graduating secondary school students:

> **The Church of Krakow considers this meeting to be very important, and personally, I also feel this way, because it expresses a particular sacrifice, a particular gift: a gift of a living person, a gift of a young Polish man, a young Polish woman, a young Christian. It is a gift which is now beginning to bear fruit, which is now maturing. But, at the same time, it is a gift which is still to express itself ... There is a great need for mature Polish men and women. There is a great need for people of knowledge and character.**

May 3[5] — 10:00 a.m., at Jasna Gora:

> **The Millennial act of surrendering Poland into the maternal bondage of Mary is a call to all Poles — to all without exception — that they should be responsible. To be responsible means to be guided by truth. Not to**

---

[1] See Glossary.

diminish, not to cut down any of the history of our nation, or the Polish *raison d'etat*, or our sense of being a person and a Pole; not to cut all of this down to fit some prepared formulas: because not everything fits there. To be responsible means to be a person who is free, and one who draws this freedom from God.

May 4-5 — 11:00 a.m., Jasna Gora, 163rd Plenary conference of the Polish Episcopate * May 4 — 7:00 p.m., Main Council of the Polish Episcopate * May 4 — The makeup of the Educational Council of the Polish Episcopate: Karol Cardinal Wojtyla (Chairman), Bishop Marian Rechowicz (Deputy Chairman), Rev. Marian Jaworski (Secretary), Rev. Adam Kubis (Deputy Secretary). Members: Professors: Bishop Alfons Nossol, Bishop Wincenty Urban, Bishop Walenty Wojcik, Rev. Marian Finke, Rev. Eugeniusz Florkowski, Rev. Wladyslaw Hladowski, Fr. Augustyn Jankowski, Fr. Andrzej Krupa, Rev. Stanislaw Lach, Rev. Stanislaw Olejnik, Rev. Pawel Palka, Mr. Czeslaw Strzeszewski, Mr. Stefan Swiezawski. Contributors to the Council include the rectors and deans of the schools as well as the twenty professors' sections at the Committee for Catholic Education. Those who were dropped from the initial make-up of the Educational Council (the period of 1973 to 1978) include: Rev. Prof. Antoni Slomkowski, Rev. Prof. Wincenty Granat and Rev. Prof. Ignacy Rozycki. Those who took their place were: Bishop Nossol, Rev. Prof. Finke, and Rev. Prof. Hladowski * May 5 — 2:30 p.m., Czestochowa, at the Albertine Brothers * May 6 — 11:00 a.m., Krakow, residence, a session of bishops with the Rector of the Theological Seminary and the Curia * 4:00 p.m., a conversation with the seminarians prior to their ordination * May 7 — 9:00 a.m., a pilgrimage to Szczepanow with the holy relics of St. Stanislaw; 12:00 noon, in Szczepanow, national celebrations in honor of St. Stanislaw, a concelebrated Mass, closing remarks * May 8 — 12:30 p.m., residence, a visit of the youth from Gdansk * May 8 — The abbey of the Cistercian Fathers in Mogila, 9th plenary session of the Pastoral Synod of the Archdiocese of Krakow. 413 people participated. The Cardinal chaired the session. Opening address:

> Today, we can submit to the vote ... three further editions of documents: "The Eucharist, the Source and Culmination of Christian life," "Baptism and Confirmation as Sacraments Leading into Christian Sanctity" ... "The Participation of a Christian in Christ's Suffering and in His Victory Over Death — the Sacrament of Anointing the Sick." These three projects belong to the second series of synodal documents, those connected with the participation in the priestly mission of Christ.

In the evening, at Wawel Cathedral — he concelebrated a Mass with Archbishop Ablewicz and Msgr. Franco Biffi, Rector of the Lateran University, during which he delivered a sermon:

The Church permits us and orders us to look at St. Stanislaw through the parable of the Good Shepherd ... A shepherd is one who cares, who is concerned. There are several types of concern. There is concern that is full of sadness and depression. But the concern of a good shepherd flows from love ... it creates good, it protects from evil ... A person of our times is very deeply concerned, and has much reason to be anxious. A modern person living in Poland is very anxious, and often succumbs to depression ... The most profound sickness of our society is ... a deep sense of frustration. This is exactly why we need the parable of the Good Shepherd; so that we may know how to cross all of the thresholds of our contemporary frustrations: so that we may be able to be creative in our concerns. The Good Shepherd is concerned in a good, creative way ...

What is supposed to become of the Synod of the Archdiocese of Krakow after its conclusion on May 8, 1979? I believe that the work of the Synod, undertaken with such enthusiasm, that this community of creative concern, the community united in the Heart of the Good Shepherd, cannot be reversed ...

"A good shepherd lays down his life for his sheep." Stanislaw from Szczepanow charted the historical roads of Poles for many centuries ahead. It is no wonder that in this century we are returning to his person, richer by a whole new era, richer by new historical experiences. And how many of these experiences there were in our time. ...

When I entered the Wawel Cathedral today, when I found myself in front of the tomb of St. Stanislaw, I was approached by a group representing former prisoners of Oswiecim {Auschwitz}, of other concentration camps, and by representatives of the Home Army.[6] These are people whom we should honor in a special way, because they fought and because of what they fought for; because they suffered, and because of what they suffered for. They presented me with this vestment in which I am celebrating the Most Holy Sacrifice. May God reward you! May God reward you for the gift of this vestment! And more importantly, may God reward you because you fought and because you suffered ... The fight and the suffering of St. Stanislaw of Szczepanow, the holy bishop ... his victory under the sword, took place in most difficult times and continues to be the source of hope for ever new victories. And it is so whenever a sword is hanging over us: in different times, in different moments of history.

May 10 — 10:00 a.m., residence, meeting of the Council of Priests * 3:00 p.m., residence, meeting of the Synod of the Archdiocese * May 11 — 7:00 a.m., Lublin — Poczekajka, Chapel of the Grey Ursuline Sisters, private Mass * 11:00 a.m., meeting on philosophical matters * 1:00 p.m., a meeting with the priests studying in Krakow * 2:00 p.m., participation in celebrations in honor of Rev. Rector W. Granat * 4:00 p.m., Lublin, auditorium of KUL, presentation of an award named after Rev. Radziszewski; closing remarks * May 12 — Kalwaria Zebrzydowska, free time * May 14 — 9:00 a.m., Skalka, celebrations in honor of St. Stanislaw, procession, opening remarks:

---

[6] The underground resistance forces fighting the German occupation.

> During his lifetime, all of the concerns, thoughts, and responsibilities that were particularly important in those times, piled up on his pastoral head. And from the time of his martyrdom, our history, the spiritual history of our nation, is piling up on his martyred head ... We want to learn from him, under the maternal protection of the Mother of God, to take responsibility for the Church; for the Church in Poland, sanctified by the martyr's blood of St. Wojciech {Adalbert}, of St. Stanislaw, of all the saints whom we summon in our annual procession from Wawel to Skalka.

The same day — 5:00 p.m., residence, pilgrims from Muenster * 6:00 p.m., Committee for Catholic Education * 8:00 p.m., Theological Seminary, discussion on the eve of ordination (seminarians of the 6th year) * May 15 — The Monday of Pentecost, Wawel Cathedral, ordination of priests:

> This is how we are receiving you today, at the Wawel Cathedral, in its center, in the midst of the People of God, in the midst of the priesthood of Krakow, ... during the celebrations in honor of Mary, the Mother of the Church. This has its own significance: she was at the birth of the Church in the Upper Room. She is here today at the birth of the Church of Krakow ... together with your ordinations. She is with each of you, just as she was with all of the Apostles in the Upper Room in Jerusalem.

The same day — 4:00 p.m., departure for Rome via Warsaw * May 16-19 — Rome, session of the Council of the General Secretariat of the Synod of Bishops, a series of meetings (with Cardinal Villot, Archbishop Poggi, Bishop Rubin) * May 19 — 12:00 noon, at the Vatican, an audience with the Holy Father, Paul VI * 4:00 p.m., Polish College * May 20 — 8:00 a.m., departure for Milan * 12:00 noon, departure for Warsaw * 2:30 p.m., Warsaw, a visit with the Primate * 3:30 p.m., Laski, with Msgr. T. Fedorowicz * May 21 — 9:00 a.m., Poznan, the conclusion of the peregrination of the copy of the image of Our Lady of Czestochowa * 11:00 a.m., Poznan, Pontifical Mass * May 22 — 8:00 p.m., Jachowka, reunion of priests ordained in the same year as Cardinal Wojtyla * May 23 — 7:30 a.m., Jachowka, concelebrated Mass and sermon during the reunion * 11:30 a.m., Kety, St. John's Chapel, a reunion of priests ordained in 1972 * 4:00 p.m., Kalwaria Zebrzydowska, a pilgrimage * May 24 — 10:30 a.m., residence, a meeting with the academic apostolate * 5:00 p.m., arrival of Archbishop L. Poggi * On May 24, the Cardinal received the work by Sister Stanislawa Manowarda OSU — a report and a photo album dealing with the history of the images of the Blessed Mother in Poland. The authoress died on December 6, 1973. The work was found and copied by her blind sister, Janina Manowarda, a former teacher in Katowice, who still lived there.

> **Highly Esteemed Madam!**
> With great emotion, I accepted your gift in the form of a type-written

script "The Queen of Poland and Her Nation" along with the album of photographs, the fruit of many years of work and tireless research by Sister Stanislawa Manowarda, an Ursuline. I cordially thank you and your brothers and sisters for sharing with me such a very interesting item. We will try to make use of it for the honor of Our Blessed Mother, our Beloved Lady of Czestochowa.

In addition to my sincere thanks, I am sending you my heartfelt wishes that Mary Immaculate protect you and your brothers and sisters. I commend the soul of the deceased to God the Supreme Goodness, and I bless you from my heart.

+ Karol Cardinal Wojtyla

May 25 — 9:00 a.m., Feast of Corpus Christi in Krakow, with the participation of Archbishop Luigi Poggi. Sermon during the procession:

1st altar: The Church is building itself on the Eucharist; it is building itself on the mystery of the Body of Christ ... we would like to pray together with our guest that the legal status of the Church in Poland become clearly and appropriately defined. Because, after all, being such a large community, a community that is almost as big as the whole nation, we cannot be outside the law ... The definition of the legal status of the Church is at the same time the definition of our place, of all our rights: everything that springs from the idea of the right of religious freedom, a right that has been recognized all over the world, that has been stated in international documents — it is not necessary for me to enumerate them ...

[2nd altar: the sermon of Archbishop Luigi Poggi.]

3rd altar: Now that God has come to live with man, the earth that is inhabited by people is an earth on which the desire for justice and peace is constantly being reborn. And let not any "thinker," clinging to any given outlook on the world, think that only he, on the basis of some kind of monopoly, knows this matter and can resolve it to its conclusion. Our prayer with the Holy Father for justice and peace in the modern world, for justice and peace in our Polish land, is a prayer for man: for each and every person ...

4th altar: We lift up our eyes. The towers of Wawel appear before us. Wawel means our past — the past that is still present in our hearts, in our present time, in our reality. We pray for our Homeland, as we look at its entire past. It is a great and difficult past: a past which squeezed out the tears from the eyes of entire generations. Whole generations shed blood, wore shackles! Our Homeland is so much more precious to us, because it was bought at the price of so many generations. We will never tear ourselves away from our past! We will not allow that it be torn from our souls! For it is part of our identity today. We want our youth to learn the whole truth about the history of our nation. We want the heritage of our Polish culture, without any deviations, to be passed on to new generations of Poles! A nation lives by the truth about itself. It has a right to the truth about itself! And it has a right to seek and learn this truth. Above all, it has the right to expect it from those who are its educators; from those who head kindergartens, schools, and universities. This is the basic message of our prayer for our Homeland. The soul of a young Pole must not be bent and warped because, uprooted from this deep, thousand-year-old soil, he stops seeing who he is and easily becomes prey to his weaknesses. And there are many weaknesses. We fear for our future, when we see how our various weaknesses have gained the status of civic rights in our community. Various weaknesses whose consequences are sometimes irreversible and incalculable. That is why, here, on this spot we offer a prayer to Heaven for the future of our Homeland, because we love it! Because we love it! This is our great love! And may no one dare to make us give an accounting of our love for our Homeland, for Poland! May no one even dare...! [shouts of "May he live long", "May he live long" and applause] I am including all Poles without exception in this prayer for our Homeland. I am not separating nor excluding anyone. May everyone know, that we are embracing everyone in this prayer for our Homeland.

The same day — 5:00 p.m., observances of the Feast of Corpus Christi at the settlement named for the 30th Anniversary of the Polish People's Republic (at Azory) in Krakow. Participating in the observances was Archbishop Luigi Poggi:

The Lord Jesus wants to fulfill His mission through your community, through your church, through your growing parish. In today's celebrations, we will be thanking Him for this. We will be thanking Him for all the good inspiration, for all the firmness that you showed ... for this entire Christian climate that you were able to create in this neighborhood ... We will be asking Our Lord to make sure that the further matters associated with the construction of the church, with the building of a community within and around this church, continue to be resolved through the Mystery of the Body of Christ ...

The homily delivered by Archbishop Poggi — translated by Cardinal Wojtyla:

He is thankful that I bring him here, to this parish, for the second time. He remembers that the last time he was here, was a few years ago in the winter ... He thanks you ... for your perseverance in striving to reach your goal. He also addresses the representatives of the authorities and likewise thanks them for understanding the need and granting the proper permissions.

May 26 — 9:00 a.m., residence, L. Poggi * 1:00 p.m., residence, meeting of the Council of the Pontifical Department of Theology: the Cardinal discussed the matter of obtaining academic degrees, a matter which had been on his mind for a long time now. He presented a proposal to institute the obtaining of a master's degree as part of completing the basic course of theological studies. He asked for such arrangement of the courses, especially the seminars, that this could be achieved. He pointed out the necessity to educate the clergy within the scope of the specialization offered by the licentiate program. (From the minutes of the Departmental Council) * The same day — 2:00 p.m., in Trzebinia, the Reverend Cardinal visited the sick who are staying at a retreat house:

The Cardinal appeared unexpectedly during the afternoon liturgical service. He prayed for a moment and talked with the sick, then he visited with us. Extending his greetings to each one of us individually, the Cardinal asked about our work in Trzebinia, about our studies, and about our vacations. We told him about the procession of Corpus Christi, one in which all of the sick participated. The Cardinal, referring to the service in Krakow, promised that next year the procession will go to the Main Market Square. A little while later, he departed. (According to an account by Jadwiga Wielgut, a student and member of the group taking care of the sick during the retreat)

The same day — 3:00 p.m., Oswiecim, visiting the grounds of the concentration camp with Cardinal W. Baum from Washington * 5:30 p.m., Oswiecim — a prayer near the Cross * May 27 — At the residence and at Wawel, the visit of Cardinal W. Baum * 7:15 p.m., the Mariacki Basilica, a concelebrated Mass with Cardinal Baum, opening remarks * May 28 — 9:00 a.m., Piekary Slaskie, a pilgrimage of men, and a sermon during the High Mass:

> The word *odpoczac* {to rest} — as was etymologically proven by our great poet Cyprian Kamil Norwid in such a wonderful manner — means to start from the beginning ... Man must find himself, must rebuild himself, must retrieve himself ... Man is the image of the living God! — God created man in His own image. Man, then, recovers himself, finds himself again, when he delves into this image, when he reacquaints himself with his own godliness! ... Polish children are saying it, the Polish youth is saying it, and so are mothers and wives: Sunday belongs to us! ... Man, who has been created for work, has also been created for *humanity*! ... Man is called to love — he must not exclude himself from it ... if he does not take up this calling to love, *his life is wasted*. Let us ask, are there not too many lives being wasted in our Homeland? Let us ask, are the new generations of Poles not threatened by the danger of frustration? by the feeling of the absurdity of life and work?

May 28-29 — A canonical visitation of the parish of Zarzecze * May 29-30 — 3:00 p.m., residence, a session "St. Stanislaw in Polish Literature." * May 29 — 8:00 p.m., visit of Archbishop Franjo Kuharic of Zagreb * May 30 — 7:00 a.m., Mass for the repose of the soul of the late Marek Wiadrowski * 10:00 a.m., residence, the editors of "Glas Koncila" and "Druzina"; Archbishop Kuharic * 1:30 p.m., lunch with the guests * May 31 — 11:00 a.m., Wzgorza Krzeslawickie, a concelebrated Mass, sermon, and a meeting with priests ordained in 1974 * The same day — 6:00 p.m., Bialy Dunajec, concelebrated Mass and sermon for the conclusion of a liturgical service for the month of May * 8:00 p.m., same place — a social gathering of priests ordained in 1975.

June 1 — 6:00 p.m., Kalwaria Zebrzydowska, a private pilgrimage * June 2 — 12:00 noon, residence, an audience for the Philosophical Institute from Louvain * The same day — the Feast of the Sacred Heart of Jesus, at the Sisters of the Sacred Heart in Krakow:

You can say that Christ comes into the hearts of people, just as they are: He does not throw anyone "overboard" — He accepts everyone ... A person who has a "grudge" against God, who makes God "absent" in the world — very often, makes God absent because of his own sins — a person who creates a whole system of sin, making God nonexistent in the world, in himself — would that this person see, through this one Heart, that God is Love.

The same day — at the Basilica of the Jesuit Fathers in Krakow:

We come here to make reparations for the programmed rejection of God. This rejection expresses itself in various forms, and, particularly, in the forms well known in our Polish arena, namely in atheism and secularization ... We call out to all of our countrymen, who are under the influence of this process: stop in your tracks. Do not destroy the deepest substance of your humanity, of your spirituality! Do not depart from Christ! Do not accept as truth the lies about God! Man's experience is too long, a Christian experience of a Pole is too long, to allow so easy a parting with God, the Father of Jesus Christ, so easy a parting with Jesus Christ Himself, and with His Sacred Heart!

June 3 — 5:30 p.m., Suchedniow, the 5th anniversary of the visitation of the image of Our Lady of Jasna Gora; blessing of the image of Our Lady of Czestochowa; sermon:

Our Lady of Jasna Gora undertook a gigantic effort of concentrating all the Poles who live in our contemporary Homeland into one spiritual family: this is the explanation for the peregrination ... And although this is occurring over time, it is realizing one program: the program of concentration, joining, unification, formation of one family ... we are here, on this earth, as one family. This is what the word "Poland" means ... Man must be strong ... To be strong, he must meet the gaze of his Mother ... may this gaze ... help everyone to find themselves, to find their dignity, to lift themselves up, to trust ... to rebuild their spirit ... to counteract the poisons of the spirit!

June 4 — 11:00 a.m., Kalwaria Zebrzydowska, a pilgrimage of men and the youth from the Archdiocese of Krakow; concelebrated Mass, sermon:

And in this very world, in these contemporary times, a new, spontaneous and, I would say, passionate search for "a faithful witness" begins. Jesus Christ is this witness ... It is in Your name that we come here to Kalwaria ... All of this is a manifestation of our times: this great cry to Christ, the faithful witness.

The same day — 4:00 p.m., Krakow — Lagiewniki, he enters the new church, Confirmation, and a sermon * 6:00 p.m., Plaszow, the 50th anniversary of the Congregation of the Sacred Heart in Poland and the 100th anniversary of the foundation of the order: "The hunger for the Heart grows even more in our times and the need for your service and your calling grows along with it." * June 5 — 5:00 p.m., Godziszka, concelebrated Mass, sermon, and a meeting with the priests ordained in 1963 * June 6 — 1:00 p.m., residence, Committee of the Provincial Synod for matters of religious orders * 4:00 p.m., a visit of an archbishop from Zaire * 10:00 p.m., a meeting with the editorial team of *Tygodnik Powszechny* * June 7 — 10:30 a.m., Krakow, residence, the 10th meeting of the Coordinating Committee of the Synod of the Province of Krakow. Cardinal Wojtyla's reflections on the matter of meetings with the consulting teams (the Cardinal has participated in eight such meetings since January). A discussion on the topic of the concluding document — summed up by the Cardinal. Information about the activities of the groups. The groups announce the schedule for the presentation of their conspectus documents. (The subjects: Youth, Marriage and Family; Apostolate of Charity; Religious Orders in Pastoral Work; Apostolate of the the Laity; Formation for the Priesthood; Life and Service of Priests; The Liturgy; Christological and Mariological Inspirations; Interdiocesan Structures). (From the minutes) * The same day — 3:00 p.m., residence, consultations on a philosophical session and on the Institute of Philosophy * 7:00 p.m., Kalwaria Zebrzydowska, Chapel of the Blessed Mother, a Mass of thanksgiving * June 8 — The 25th meeting of the Committee for the Apostolate of the Laity * The issue of an institution (an agency) in the Committee for Christian Culture; acceptance of the document on Confirmation; "Report on the State of the Apostolate of the Laity in Poland." * June 9 — from 2:30 p.m., free time * June 10 — 11:00 a.m., residence, the handing out of parish assignments * 12:00 noon, meeting with priests — heads of deaneries * June 10-12 — Visitation of the parish of Lekawica, near Zywiec * June 11 — 6:00 p.m., Stadniki, celebrations of the 100th anniversary of the Order of the Sacred Heart, a concelebrated Mass and a sermon:

> **A person who feels like a sinner is already on the road to sanctity ... he looks for a place where he could ask for the forgiveness of his sins. And then, he must meet with the Sacred Heart of Jesus ... There is an enormous need for these two mysteries, which are one. The Polish heart is in great need of: "The Heart of Jesus, forgiveness of our sins" ... I am saying this as a bishop and a shepherd of souls, in the name of all the bishops, those who are present here as well as those who are not. Because we deeply feel our sins! We deeply feel the growing sins of our nation. Along with this, we deeply feel the need to pray for the forgiveness of our sins. This is our episcopal social need for your service, for your mission on Polish soil.**

June 13 — Warsaw, Main Council of the Polish Episcopate * June 14-15 — Warsaw, 164th plenary conference of the Polish Episcopate * June 15 — 4:00 p.m., Warsaw, Primate's chapel, a liturgical service to the Most Sacred Heart of Jesus, adoration of the Blessed Sacrament * After June 15 — Bachledowka; the Cardinal delivered a speech (conference) during a meeting with the young people of the "Oasis" charismatic movement, and participated in an agape * June 16 — 3:30 p.m., Krakow, residence, Council of the Pontifical Department of Theology * 7:30 p.m., a hospital visit to Msgr. Juliusz Turowicz * June 17-18 — Visitation of the parish of Pietrzykowice * June 18 — 6:00 p.m., Ciecina, blessing of a cornerstone, concelebrated Mass and sermon * 8:00 p.m., Ujsoly, an apostolic retreat * June 19 — 10:00 a.m., Kameśznica, a social gathering of priests ordained in 1967, concelebrated Mass and sermon * 12:00 noon, Kameśznica, a visit to an "Oasis" group * 5:30 p.m., residence, a delegation of graduates from the secondary school of the Piarist Fathers, from the years 1927-1939 * June 20 — Departure for Milan via Warsaw * June 21-25 — The Cardinal participated in a congress, organized on the occasion of the 10th anniversary of the encyclical *Humanae Vitae*, by the International Center of Family Research (CISF) in Milan. He delivered a lecture *Matrimonio ed Amore* for the opening of the congress (The essential fragments of the lecture appeared in "Famiglia Cristiana" No. 43, October 29, 1978) * June 21 — 8:00 p.m., Milan, a meeting at the Sons of Divine Providence * June 22 — Vienna, a visit with Cardinal Konig * 4:00 p.m., Gaubitsch, a visit with Rev. Boleslaw Sadus, a priest from the Archdiocese of Krakow working in Austria * 6:00 p.m., Gaubitsch, a children concert * 7:00 p.m., Mass with sermon, and a meeting with parishioners * June 23 — Departure for Krakow * June 24 — 4:00 p.m., Kielce * 7:00 p.m., Gostyn (Archdiocese of Poznan) * June 25 — 9:00 a.m., main celebrations of the 50th anniversary of the coronation of Our Lady of Swietogora, in Gostyn on Swieta Gora, at the Congregation of St. Philip:

> **This shrine ... is a place of reflection ... It connects each person with the Lady of this place in a very special way ... For the truth about man can be learned only in this reflection before Mary and in reflection before God.**

Same day — 6:00 p.m., Sieradz, at the Grey Ursuline Sisters * June 26-28 — Kalwaria Zebrzydowska, retreat "ad imaginem BMV" * June 29 — 1:00 p.m., Kalwaria Zebrzydowska, Mass with sermon to candidates for the first year at the seminary, handing out of "suscepta" (documents of acceptance into the ranks of seminarians) * Same day — 7:00 p.m., Church of St. Peter and St. Paul in Krakow:

> **For his triple denial, [St. Peter] paid with a triple declaration of love ... [St. Paul] was a man of great elan. An Apostle of God, a pilgrim of the Gospel, which he carried to the entire then-known world. A builder of the Church from its very foundations ... The deaths of both Apostles, Peter and Paul, were a crowning of their lives. They were not only an end, but also a beginning — and, above all, a fulfillment. Everything that their lives were, was expressed in their deaths ... The Church remembers this today**

... Today we turn to the Holy Father, Paul VI, the successor of Peter. We turn to him in a special, personal way, because this is demanded by his office and by his person. There were many reasons, over the last few days, to think of his person. There was the day of June 24th, his name-day, because the name that he received at baptism is that of John the Baptist; also June 21st, the anniversary of his election to the Chair of Peter, 15 years ago, in 1963; and then, there is today, the Feast of St. Peter and St. Paul, and tomorrow, the anniversary of his coronation to the Chair of Peter. During these days our thoughts and hearts turn to the Holy Father in a most personal way, because he is a living person. A person known to us, very close. And he is also connected with us in a very personal way, not only because of the office which he holds, but because of who he is. In particular, we bishops, who maintain close contact with him, have special reason to celebrate — together with our Church, with the entire Archdiocese of Krakow — the anniversary of the election of Paul VI to the Chair of Peter ... to pray for Paul VI. I am notifying the Holy Father of our group prayer, because this is an expression of the unity which all the Churches and all Christians maintain with Peter and his successors. We pray ... that in these difficult times, the Lord be with him.

June 30 — An appeal to the parishes of the Archdiocese in the matter of vacation-time retreats for young people. The Cardinal explains the essence of the "Oasis" retreats which are held in parishes in the mountains and foothills, and emphasizes the legality of these retreats from the point of view of the Episcopal Conference and the point of view of the constitution of the Polish People's Republic. The appeal was issued in connection with the action by the authorities against the participants of the "Oasis" retreats and against the owners of the houses in which the participants were lodging. This appeal is but one of the manifestations, over many years, of the Cardinal's attempts to gain legal recognition for the activities of the "Oasis" movement.

July 1 — 2:00 p.m., residence, Mr. and Mrs. Kitchener and Piszek (John) * 5:00 p.m., Wola Radziszowska, Brody (Little Tomb of Our Lady), Kalwaria Zebrzydowska, visit of "Oasis"{charismatic} groups * July 2 — 9:00 a.m., Feast of the Visitation of Our Lady, Jasna Gora, pilgrimage of teachers and educators * 10:00 a.m., Chapel of Our Lady, sermon, meeting with the pilgrims from Skalka:

We come here ... so that in this special community ... we may join in the mystery of the Visitation, join in that special exchange of words, feelings, joy, but also an exchange of responsibility ... so that we may share with Our Lady of Jasna Gora our responsibility as Catholic educators, our responsibility to the Church and to the nation. For this is a place where, through Mary, a most wondrous unification of these two threads of our history took place ... Jasna Gora is the national shrine of Poles ... If the school is to remain faithful to the family and the Homeland, to the family and the nation ... it must pass along the entire heritage of the culture and history of our nation. And this is an authentic heritage. For a thousand years we have lived our own life — not a borrowed one ... We must strive to let young people ... learn the entire truth of the history of their nation, so that they can experience the fullness — without trimming, without bias — of Polish culture, Polish literature, Polish music and of everything in which the Polish Christian spirit has expressed itself over the centuries ... We, teachers, must especially remember that man's deepest hunger is the hunger for truth.

Same day, 4:00 p.m., Nowe Bystre, Mietustwo, visit of the apostolic retreats * Harkabuz, visit of "Oasis" groups * July 3 — 1:30 p.m., Rdzawka, Olszowka I, II, visit of "Oasis" groups * 4:00 p.m., Rabka I, II, visit of the apostolic retreats * July 4 — 8:30 a.m., Wawel, Mass and sermon for the sextons of the Archdiocese of Krakow, prayer before the Cross * 11:00 a.m., residence, a visit by Prof. Jerzy Szablowski * 3:00 p.m., Nowa Wies, vacation — retreat of the sick — a visit * 5:00 p.m., Krzeszow, visit of the "Oasis" * July 6-7 — til 2:00 p.m., free time * July 7 — 2:00 p.m., Wielka Polana, Polany Suszynskie, Trybsz, Frydman, visit of "Oasis" groups * July 8 — 3:00 p.m., Miedzybrodzie Bialskie, visit at the retreat for the sick * 5:00 p.m., Miedzybrodzie, visit at the apostolic retreat * July 9 — 9:00 a.m., Sucha, Rdzawka, Trybsz, visit of the apostolic retreats * Same day — Snozka Mountain Kluszkowce, the Cardinal arrived for a day of meeting with the "Oasis" community. In his homily he broadly elaborated on the words: "Gift of unity in the Holy Spirit." He explained each one of these words in relation to the Lord, the human person, and the Church * July 9 — 4:00 p.m., beginning of vacation till July 21 * July 22 — 9:00 a.m., residence, session * 11:00 a.m., Wola Justowska * July 23-30 — Vacation, Lake Krepsko * July 31 — 10:00 a.m., meeting with the Primate (Fiszor), a speech on the occasion of the Primate's name-day * 7:00 p.m., return to Krakow * August 2-8 — Vacation * August 6 — 9:40 p.m., the Holy Father Paul VI died * August 8 — 5:00 p.m., return to Krakow * August 8 — Letter to Rev. Andrzej Szostek. Cardinal Wojtyla sent a copy of this letter to the Department of Philosophy at KUL, asking that it be treated as a review, that he had undertaken earlier. And this is what has happened; the text was read during the defense of the doctoral thesis, *Philosophical Aspects of a Discussion on Generally Important Norms in Contemporary Theology.* The defense took place on September 20, 1978.

Letter — review:

I read the text you sent me with great interest — although in some haste (because of the well-know circumstances).

I think that this is a very useful work. It deals with the very crux of today's problems, it provides critical information about them, it gets to the core of theological concepts according to the criteria of philosophy (ethics), it ties together and unifies what is happening "in the market place" of the West (esp. in Germany) with what we are doing here in Poland.

It is certainly the fruit of a great effort, of extensive reading, and, above all, a clear passion for research (and a digger's instinct). It is written in a lively style, it is interesting, it is suitable for publication and for reading.

I am merely noting my impressions from a quick reading. Personally, I have no doubts that the work fulfills all the requirements of a doctoral thesis. But let the specialists take it apart and let them judge you on all the details. That is their right and your right.

There is a great condensation of thought, of erudition, of formulations in this work. Perhaps it could be somewhat "thinned out," maybe more numerous subtitles would help in that regard. As far as Chapter 3: it seems to me that the conclusions and suggestions are appropriate; I agree with them. Should they be presented in yet another light, with regard to the "partners in the discussion"? — something to be considered.

In the immediate future — contrary to my expectations — there will be no opportunity to discuss this. I would gladly discuss this later, because I myself have learned much, much, from this treatise. Ars longa, vita brevis.

I send my sincere greetings — and I wish you God's blessings. Give my regards to Tadeusz when you see him.

August 10 — 11:00 a.m., residence, the Katholikentag matter * 6:00 p.m., Wawel Cathedral, concelebrated Mass for Paul VI * August 11 — Departure for Warsaw, then for Rome, with the Primate and the government delegation * 3:00 p.m., Rome, at the bodily remains of Paul VI * August 12 — 11:00 a.m., Rome, congregation of cardinals * 6:00 p.m., Pope's funeral, concelebrated Mass by the cardinals * August 13 — Ducale Auditorium, the College of Cardinals receives delegations of the governments * 6:00 p.m., St. Peter's Basilica, Mass concelebrated by the cardinals for the soul of Paul VI, under the leadership of Cardinal Giuseppe Siri, procession to the grave, prayer * August 14 — 11:00 a.m., congregation of cardinals * 6:00 p.m., St. Peter's Basilica, concelebrated Mass by the cardinals for Paul VI * August 15 — 9:00 a.m., departure with Bishop Deskur: Lagi di Vien, at Msgr. Walerian Meysztowicz's * August 16-24 — Rome: August 16 — 11:00 a.m., congregation of cardinals; 6:00 p.m., Polish Institute, visit at Primate Wyszynski's * August 18 — 9:40 a.m., St. Peter's Basilica, funeral of Cardinal Paul Yu Pin * August 19 — Speech at the congregation of cardinals * August 21 — Vatican Radio, speech, *My Meetings with Paul VI*:

The first of these meetings took place during the first session of the Vatican Council, when the Holy Father Paul VI was still a cardinal, ... the Archbishop of Milan. I turned to him in a very particular matter. As the then capitular vicar of the Archdiocese of Krakow, I presented to him the plea of the Parish of St. Florian — through its pastor — for a gift of church bells. This was to be a symbol, a sign of the unity and ties between Churches. Cardinal Montini understood this immediately, and began talking of his personal recollections of Poland, where he had lived as a worker of the nunciature in Warsaw. He had been a witness to the return of the bells which had been taken away during the First World War, and then brought to a large field. Representatives of various parishes came there to try to recognize their bells. The church bells were indeed offered by the parish of Seregno ...

I remember particularly well ... the meeting before my elevation to the College of Cardinals. It was in April of 1967. I will never forget what the Pope said then, in connection with the preparation of the document which, a year later, appeared as the encyclical *Humanae vitae*. Since I was a member of a special committee, but could not participate in its meeting — in June of 1966 — I sent my opinion to the Holy Father in writing. The Pope immediately began a discussion on that topic ... And I understood then the gravity of the problem that Paul VI faced as the highest teacher and shepherd of the Church. Our audiences were of various natures. Most of them were private, when I was talking to the Holy Father alone. But there were also group audiences. A number of times I participated in those audiences which Paul VI held for the Council of the Laity. I participated in this council in the role of an advisor. Other audiences were those for the Council of the General Secretariat of the Synod of Bishops. And finally, group audiences for the Polish bishops. I remember with particular emotion the audience in November of 1973, when, together with the Cardinal Primate and the new Metropolitan Archbishop of Wroclaw, and the resident bishops of Opole, Gorzow, Szczecin, Koszalin, Gdansk and Warmia, we gave thanks for the definitive establishment of a regular Church hierarchy on the Polish western and northern territories ... During the 15-year pontificate, there were three visits *ad limina*: 1967/68, 1972, and 1977. I always admired how well the Holy Father was prepared for his audiences ... It was most moving when he himself began speaking about Church matters — sometimes also about the Church in Italy, in Rome itself; when, what he said took on the dimension of a personal reflection ... Those who participated in this conversation felt particularly obligated for being part of this truly Paulist sollicitudo omnium Ecclesiarum ... He was a very warm person — many times he would prolong an audience, even though he was notified that the time was up ... He never refused to receive accompanying priests, although I tried never to take advantage of this. Of course, I remember most vividly that exceptional meeting with Paul VI to which he invited me during Lent of 1976. It was a retreat ... On the last day he thanked me, receiving me in private audience ... We could say much about the gifts we received from him, at various meetings with him. I will mention just one, a particularly significant one: it was during the Vatican Council. The Holy Father was very interested in the matter of the church in Nowa Huta. I remember, as I was telling him about how those parishioners attended Holy Mass ..., he, listening to what I was saying to him in Italian, interrupted me in Polish: "*mroz*[7] — yes, I remember that from the time when I had a better knowledge of your language." The finale of these talks was that Paul VI personally blessed the cornerstone for the church in Nowa Huta ... The last time I saw Paul VI was on May 19 of this year. It was an audience of the Council of the General Secretariat of the Synod of Bishops ... And now is the very last meeting. On the 11th of August, Bishop Andrzej Deskur drove me straight from the airport to the Basilica. I knelt, I prayed and I looked into that face which I had seen so many times in our conversations. Eyes

[7] freezing

which had been so alive, are now closed. He rests in the center of the Basilica in front of the altar of St. Peter ... I no longer speak with him, I can no longer speak with him about any of those matters of which we had spoken in the past. He is in another dimension. He looks at a different Face. Death remains the place of greatest concentration in the state of which I have seen him on this earth.

* Cardinal Wojtyla sent a letter (in French) to the participants of the Congress of Philosophy (held in Krakow from August 23 to August 25) whose topic was: *La person humaine dans la philosophie contemporaine (Human person in contemporary philosophy)* expressing regret that he could not participate in the congress.

August 24 — 10:00 a.m., selection of rooms for the conclave * August 25 — 9:30 a.m., St. Peter's Basilica, concelebrated Mass pro eligendo summo Pontifice * 4:30 p.m., beginning of the conclave, Veni Creator * August 26 — 6:00 p.m., election of John Paul I * August 27 — 9:00 p.m., Sistine Chapel, concelebrated Mass with the Holy Father * 11:00 a.m., opening of the conclave * 6:00 p.m., Polish College, meeting with the Primate * August 29 — Ad mare * August 30 — 11:00 a.m., an audience of the College of Cardinals with John Paul I, individual audiences.

August — Cardinal Wojtyla sent a lecture entitled "The Mystery of Life — the Mystery of Love" to be read during "Pastoral Days" in Wroclaw.

September 1 — Turin (at Archbishop Anastasio Ballestrero's), a visit of the Shroud of Turin * September 2 — 7:15 a.m., present at a Mass at the Polish Chapel in Rome * 12:00 noon, Rome, Polish College, postulator of the case of the founder of Opus Dei * 5:00 p.m., recording for Vatican Radio * 6:00 p.m., Church of St. Stanislaw, Mass for the intention of John Paul I, sermon by the Primate * 8:00 p.m., Villa Stritch, reception for the 25th anniversary of the consecration of Cardinal Krol * September 3 — 5:45 p.m., plaza in front of the Basilica, inauguration of the pontificate of John Paul I, homage * September 4 — 4:00 p.m., Embassy of the Polish People's Republic, with the Primate and Bishop Dabrowski * On the Vatican Radio. A word after the election of the Holy Father John Paul I * September 5 — Rome, farewell at the airport * 2:00 p.m., welcome in Warsaw. In Warsaw, directly from the airport he went to Antoni Golubiew. After the recent tragic death of their (second) son, the Golubiews were staying with their daughter. The Cardinal had a long private conversation with Mr. Antoni Golubiew * September 6 — 7:00 a.m., Krakow, residence chapel, Mass * September 6-8 — residence * September 9 — An excursion with Rev. Styczen. On his return trip the Cardinal visited

Rev. Kazimierz Pietka, who was recovering from a very serious accident, in the hospital in Makow Podhalanski, * 5:00 p.m., Zawoja * 9:00 p.m., Kalwaria Zebrzydowska, beginning of the pilgrimage of women and the youth * September 10 — Anniversary of the coronation of the miraculous image of Our Lady of Stara Wies (Jesuit Fathers), Diocese of Przemysl. Cardinal Wojtyla led the solemn concelebrated Mass (sermon: Bishop Jerzy Ablewicz from Tarnow). In his speech after the Mass, the Cardinal refers to the election of John Paul I. Same day in the afternoon — Cardinal Wojtyla in the company of Bishop Ablewicz visited the Mother House of the Little Sisters Servants in Stara Wies and a historical wooden church in nearby Blizne * Same day — 4:30 p.m., Tarnow, Cathedral Plaza, observances of the Feast of St. Stanislaw * September 11-13 — Krakow, residence, daily audiences from 11:00 a.m. * September 13 — Cardinal Wojtyla sends a meditation entitled: "Wir wollen einem jeden helfen das Geheimnis des Menschen zu losen. Gedanken uber das Priestertum" for the 85th Deutscher Katholikentag which was held from September 16 to 17 in Freiburg.

* September 14 — 6:30 p.m., residence chapel, Mass with sermon for the first year students of the Seminary * September 15 — 2:00 p.m., Olsztyn, funeral of Bishop Jozef Drzazga. Sermon:

> On these lands — we remember it well — there were many attempts to raise the Cross of Jesus Christ. There were those times, in the distant past, when this was done with the help of the sword ... This method was opposed by the Servant of God, Queen Jadwiga ... and also at the Council in Constance, by the great chancellor of the Jagiellonian University, Pawel Wlodkowic ... When several score years ago Poland returned to these lands of Warmia and Mazury, to this diocese, when Polish bishops and priests came here again, maybe a distant cause, and perhaps a deep justification of this historical process, was just in this truth about the raising of the cross in the hearts of people: by the method of the blessed queen of Wawel, and by the teaching of Pawel Wlodkowic ... We must recall this, as we stand by the coffin of the first ordinary bishop, after so many years, of the Diocese of Warmia.

September 16 — 11:00 a.m., Krakow, residence, session of bishops, Curia, Catechetic Department * 4:00 p.m., St. Mark's Church, inauguration of the Catechetic Study Group of the Laity * September 17 — 8:30 a.m., Roczyny near Andrychow, blessing of the cornerstone for a new church:

> Together with you, I thank God for this beautiful day, on which we can see the beauty of this landscape, of these mountains of which I have grown so fond ever since childhood. Together with you I thank God for the beauty of this day, which we particularly owe to Jesus Christ, our Savior, because this is His day, the Lord's Day.
> O Christ, the cornerstone of God's structure on earth which is to last for all eternity, O Christ, You cornerstone, accept this our offering and take

it to the Father. But also remain with us! Because that is the reason we place You, symbolized by this cornerstone, in the foundation of our structure, so that You would remain with us and always be the foundation of our life! Buildings are inanimate, stones are inanimate, bricks are inanimate — but people are alive!

Same day — 12:00 noon, Mogila, sermon during the celebration of the Triumph of the Cross:

We all realize that the Papacy, although it is a great office, is also a very great cross. And on August 29, John Paul I accepted not only the highest office in the Church — he also accepted a cross: the cross of the whole Church! And the cross of the whole Church is also measured by time ... So the Pope took up the cross of contemporary man. The cross of all these tensions, all these dangers. We still dread, we cannot even imagine, what another war would mean! We live with this great danger. He took up the cross of all the tensions and dangers which arise from various injustices: the violation of human rights, the enslavement of nations, new forms of colonial exploitation; from all these various wrongs done to man, to peoples, to nations, wrongs which can be righted only in the spirit of Christ's Cross. Because they can be righted only through justice and love, not through any other political or economic programs.

Same day — 4:00 p.m., Katowice, visit to Bishop Bednorz * 6:00 p.m., Czestochowa, Cathedral, sermon for the inauguration of the 10th Festival of Religious Song, Sacrosong '78. Last presence of the Cardinal in Czestochowa before he was elected pope:

I still have before my eyes the first Sacrosong in Lodz in 1969, to which I dared come.

I remember the situation perfectly, and it was even worse than today — the church wired up in various ways, equipped with all that is part of modern music.

I rejoice in the fact that it has been is almost 10 years since that first Sacrosong, that in the course of this decade Fr. Jan Palusinski and all his collaborators from all over Poland: composers, authors, singers, orchestras, conductors, soloists, choirs (forgive me if I have forgotten to mention someone), and of course priests and bishops — travel from city to city, from diocese to diocese. And we must add the judges — after all, Sacrosong is a contest which evaluates creativity ... I am glad that this Sacrosong takes place in the cathedral, not only at Jasna Gora but in the cathedral of Czestochowa, where the Holy Family is the patron.

And here I come to the crux of the matter. The family. The climate of the family is necessary for the birth, the creation of any kind of goodness. For man to develop creativity, to become a creator, requires the climate of a family. I will use here a quote from the poet Norwid, who, even if not one of the three great Bards of the 19th century, is certainly a prophet of our century. He wrote: "Beauty is there, to enrapture us to work; work — so that we might be raised from the dead."

We must be enraptured! We must create a community of the enraptured! We must create a climate of enrapture! This is dearest to the family. In a true family, modeled after the Holy Family, this climate exists. There is rapture over the first smile of a baby, over the first words of a child, over man.

We need this rapture, so that the lives of man, of society, of the nation may be filled with beauty. That beauty which is the foundation and the wellspring of culture.

Culture cannot be created by administrative means! Administrative means can only be used to destroy culture. This is very important, and this must be remembered in our times.

We need rapture over everything that is in man. And if there is a dimension in man which we call holy (and there is!) then this cannot be lied about, this cannot be eliminated by administrative methods, by saying that this is the shape of contemporary culture. The secular shape.

I think that many pioneers of secularism are ashamed of this development in these matters.

Even if there was just one person in all of Poland who had within him that dimension of the holy, then for that one person this holy dimension is a civic right within Polish society and Polish culture. But what if there are millions of such people! And if these millions inherit the traditions of so many generations — of the whole millennium? ...

It is indeed shameful that despite 10 years of Sacrosong, even the name itself is forbidden — in Polish mass media, in the Polish press, the Polish radio ...

Once, and it was almost 200 years ago, Adam Mickiewicz wrote about group singing. He wrote: "O common song, you arc of covenant between the older and the newer years."

I wish to express a wish on the 10th anniversary of Sacrosong: may it also become a kind of "ark of the covenant" between the entire past of Polish Christian history, and its present and future. And may no one be fearful that he has to be this "ark of the covenant" — or, if we prefer a more contemporary language, a bridge — let no one be fearful that this happens so unofficially, at the margins. What is important, is that "in you the people deposit the arms of their knights."

September 24 — At Sacrosong in Czestochowa, the second prize in the song category was a song with words by Andrzej Jawien,[8] *This moment of an entire life* (music by Edward Bury, performed by Anna Wielgus and Tadeusz Chudzikowski and a schola from Bedzin). The donor of the award was Msgr. Kazimierz Cubas, pastor of St. Lambert's Parish in Radom * September 18 — 7:00 p.m., residence chapel, Mass for the late Stanislaw Zachorowski and Wojciech Golubiew, homily * September 19 — Departure for Fulda via Warsaw * September 20 — 9:00 a.m., Warsaw, visit at the residence of the Primate * 10:30 a.m., airport, official farewell * 1:00 p.m./12:00 Frankfurt, welcome, Cardinal Herman Volk, Bishop Edward Schick * 2:00 p.m.-1:00 p.m. Fulda, Cathedral, at the tomb of St. Boniface * dinner at the residence of Bishop Schick, after dinner, the first meeting with the Conference of the German Episcopate, speech * September 21 — 7:30 a.m., Fulda, St. Michael's Church from the 9th century, concelebrated Mass with the

---

[8] Pen name of Karol Wojtyla.

German bishops * 9:00 a.m., Fulda, participation in a meeting of the Conference of the German Episcopate, speech * 1:00 p.m., dinner * 3:30 p.m., Hall of the Institute of Theology, a conference for priests of the Diocese of Fulda, with a discussion. The title of the conference for the priests: Priestly Ministry (Duszpasterz Polski Zagr. 1979, pp. 55-62) * 6:00 p.m., Cathedral, liturgical service for the conclusion of the conference (speech by the Primate) * 8:00 p.m., a visit at the Bishop of Fulda, E. Schick * September 22 — 7:30 a.m., Fulda, Cathedral, concelebrated Mass at the tomb of St. Boniface, sermon:

> ...may today's meeting at the tomb of St. Boniface confirm the fruits of the apostolic mission of the Church in our nations, may it serve to renew the spirit of the Gospel, to strengthen us in truth, in love, in the healing of wounds of long ago and of the recent past. As we stand by this milestone of the march of the Gospel in the first Millennium, we ask the Eternal King of Ages, the Savior of our souls, that — as we come closer to the juncture between the second and the third Millennium of Christianity — new paths may be opened to this march; that the hearts of all men, all nations, all races, may mature and receive life, which is more powerful than death.

Same day — 9:00 a.m., departure for Cologne * 12:15 p.m., Cologne, reception, dinner (among others, Cardinals Hoffner, Volk) * 1:00 p.m., speech to the representatives of the Episcopate, clergy and laity * 3:00 p.m., Cologne, Church of the Dominicans, at the tomb of St. Albert the Great * Church of the Franciscans, the tomb of Duns Scotus and Kolping * 6:50 p.m., Cologne, Cathedral, concelebrated Mass (he is the main celebrant) with Cardinal Hoffner, Cardinal Volk and the bishops * 8:00 p.m., a visit with Vicar General — Msgr. Norbert Felhoff * September 23 — 11:15 a.m., Neviges, concelebrated Mass for Polonia, final remarks (sermon by the Primate) * September 23 — 3:00 p.m., Essen, visit at Bishop Hengsbach's, tour of the 9th century cathedral, museum * 4:30 p.m., flight Dusseldorf — Munich * 6:30 p.m., Munich, cathedral, word of welcome by Bishop Tewes, Mass, prayer at the tomb of Cardinal J. Dopfner * 8:00 p.m., supper * September 24 — The Primate and the bishops in Dachau * 9:30 a.m., Munich, cathedral, Pontifical Mass with sermon * 6:00 p.m., Mainz, welcome by Cardinal Volk in front of the Cathedral, led the concelebrated Mass (among others with Cardinal Volk), opening remarks, prayer at the tomb of Bishop Ketteler * 8:00 p.m., Theological Seminary, supper * September 25 — 6:45 a.m., Mainz, residence of the bishop, residence chapel, private concelebrated Mass * 10:00 a.m., Bonn, visit at the nunciature * 11:00 a.m., Cologne, visit at the Embassy of the Polish People's Republic * 12:00 noon, participated in a press conference * 1:00 p.m., departure * 5:40 p.m., arrival at

Okecie,[9] welcome * September 26 — 12:00 noon, Czerna, concelebrated Mass, sermon, meeting with priests ordained in 1966 * 5:00 p.m., Chrzanow, concelebrated Mass, sermon during a reunion of priests ordained in 1977 * September 27 — 12:00 noon, Krakow, residence, a meeting of the ministry for liturgical service * 2:00 p.m., Bachledowka. During a deanery retreat for youth chaplains, in the afternoon he delivered a speech and took part in a fireside chat in the refectory * 5:00 p.m., Chrzanow — Koscielec, concelebrated Mass, sermon during a reunion of priests ordained in 1973 * September 28 — Krakow, residence, meeting of the moderators of the "Light and Life" movement in the archdiocese. The Cardinal came in for a few minutes. He was waiting for a car to take him away. When Rev. Chowaniec spoke on the matters of families within the "movement," the Cardinal interrupted, stating: "The "Oasis" youth is getting married, there should not be a gap in their formation — from the youth or student groups they should move directly into "Oasis" circles for married couples. And that is why this issue needs special attention." At this point it was the Cardinal who was interrupted — he had to leave * September 28 — 10:00 a.m., Kalwaria Zebrzydowska * 6:00 p.m., Wawel Cathedral, celebrations of St. Wenceslaus. Homily:

> **I come here to honor him [St. Wenceslaus] on the day which marks 20 years since my consecration as a bishop. I am very grateful to all who came here to pray with me today ... St. Wenceslaus was a saint whose sainthood arose from a conflict. St. Stanislaw was a saint whose sainthood arose from a conflict. But the Gospel is the word of peace. In a most wondrous way, the holy martyrs, following the example of Christ, become the sources of spiritual unity. They unite where previously there was division. The Church of our times, the Church of Krakow of our time, must also unite.**

Same day — 7:30 p.m., the opening of the Wawel Cathedral Museum * Night of September 28/29 — Death of Pope John Paul I * September 29 — 10:00 a.m., 3 Franciszkanska Street, meeting of the Council of the Pontifical Department of Theology. In answer to the words of Rev. Dean M. Jaworski, the Cardinal stated that "although at times life surprises us, we must accept everything in a spirit of deep faith." He reminded that the institution should concentrate its efforts on coming forth to meet the needs of the southern regions of Poland. He indicated the need for the enlargement of the Department in the near future, the need to establish communication with the institutions developing in the area. He pointed out that the fact of including the Pontifical Department of Theology in the International Federation of Studies strengthens its rank in the world, but also poses very serious challenges.

---

[9] Airport in Warsaw.

He expressed a wish that the Department accept challenges and realize them under the patronage of the Seat of Wisdom and St. John of Kanty, in communion with the Church. (From the minutes of the Council) * September 29-October 1 — Canonical visitation of the parish of the Divine Providence at Zlote Lany in Bielsko-Biala.

October 1 — 7:00 p.m., the Mariacki Basilica, Mass and sermon for the late Pope John Paul I:

> I still have him before my eyes, I see his face, as he rises and turns toward the approaching cardinal-kamerling. To the question — do you accept? — he responds: I accept. And then immediately his name: John Paul. And then a great joy: first, the joy of the College of Cardinals ... then the joy of Rome that same evening: Habemus Papam! And the next day the joy of the Romans, of the pilgrims, of the visitors: spontaneous, indescribable joy! And the joy of John Paul himself, who was a joyous man, he smiled easily, he opened himself easily to people, he was simple and humble. And he won everyone over by this. And we felt that by this he won the heart of his Master, who selected him, who summoned him and called him ... We took joy in his freshness, in his originality ... And when our thoughts and emotions follow the deceased Pope with all of their human inadequacy and helplessness, we recall something that we Poles cannot forget: he entered the Papacy on the day of Our Lady of Jasna Gora. And that is the source of our great hope in his death.

October 2 — 10:00 a.m., Warsaw, Main Council of the Polish Episcopate (at the seat of the Primate's Institute in Choszczowka) * October 3 — 7:30 a.m., departure for Rome * 11:00 a.m., prayer at the coffin of John Paul I * 11:30 a.m., Chapel of the Polish College, private concelebrated Mass * October 4 — 7:15 a.m., Polish College, chapel, sacrum participatio * 4:00 p.m., funeral of John Paul I, Mass concelebrated by the cardinals (1st) (led by Cardinal Carlo Confalonieri) * 7:00 p.m., at Bishop Deskur's with Archbishop Stroba and Rev. Stanislaw Dziwisz * October 5 — 7:15 a.m., Chapel of the Polish College, participation in a Mass * 11:00 a.m., Apostolic Palace, congregation of cardinals * 1:00 p.m., Bishop Rubin, Bishop Wesoly, Bishop Gurda, Mr. Turowicz and Mr. Skwarnicki * Same day — 5:00 p.m., St. Peter's Basilica, Mass concelebrated by the cardinals (2nd) (led by Cardinal Giuseppe Siri) * October 6 — 7:15 a.m., Chapel of the Polish College, participated in a Mass * 11:00 a.m., Apostolic Palace, congregation of cardinals * 5:00 p.m., St. Peter's Basilica, Mass concelebrated by the cardinals (3rd), later — at the Primate's * October 7 — 7:15 a.m., Chapel of the Polish College, private concelebrated Mass * 9:00 a.m., an excursion to Mentorella * October 8 — 7:15 a.m., Polish College, concelebrated Mass, sermon * 10:00 a.m., St. Stanislaw's Church, homily during a Mass for John Paul I, celebrated by the Primate:

> The Apostolic See is in mourning again. It is living through the nine

days of mourning, praying for the soul of the dearly departed John Paul I every day. The whole Church mourns, the Church in Poland mourns. We pray in the Polish cathedrals, in the Polish shrines, in Polish temples in our land. And today we pray here, in Rome, in the Church of St. Stanislaw, within the hospice, as was intended by its great founder, Cardinal Stanislaw Hozjusz — that this place form a special bond for us with the Holy See, that here we share its joys and sorrows.

Christ says of Himself, that He is the cornerstone. The cornerstone of the edifice. The Church is a vineyard and at the same time an edifice. Not long ago, Pope John Paul I was called into that vineyard, so that the words once spoken to Peter: "Thou art Rock" could be fulfilled in him. For the Church is at once a vineyard and an edifice. It needs a foundation. So John Paul I was summoned to become the new foundation of that edifice of the Church — the Kingdom of God on earth. This happened on the day of August 26th of this year. Six weeks ago. This happened on the Feast of Our Lady of Jasna Gora in our Polish land.

When we think about this wondrous way in which Pope John Paul was called, we must return to that first call, the call directed to Simon, whom Our Lord gave the name of Peter; to that definitive call after the Resurrection, when Christ asked him three times: "Do you love me?" And Peter answered three times: "Yes, Lord, you know that I love you." And Christ asked: "Do you love me more than these?"

Through the text of John's Gospel we can still feel the trembling of this Apostle's heart, when he answered, "Lord, You know everything, You know that I love You!" This question was so difficult, so very demanding. And of all the Apostles, it was quite possibly Simon Peter who best understood how this question exceeds the scope of a human. That is why he trembled when answering. When he answered, "Lord, You know that I love You," he was giving himself up to the love of Him who was asking the question.

As I look back, from the perspective of these past six weeks, at the event which took place on August 26th in the Sistine Chapel, I think that a conversation similar to that of Christ with Simon Peter must have occurred at that moment. The succession of Peter, the call to the office of the Papacy, always carries in itself a call to the highest love, to a very special love. And always, when Christ says to a man, "Come, follow me," He asks him as He asked Simon: "Do you love me more than the others do?" Then the heart of the man must tremble. The heart of Simon trembled, and the heart of Albino Luciani trembled before he took the name of John Paul I. A human heart must tremble, because there is also a demand in this question: You must love! You must love more than the others do, if the entire flock of sheep is to be entrusted to you, if the charge "Feed my lambs, feed my sheep" is to reach the scope which it reaches in the calling and mission of Peter.

The text of St. John's Gospel continues. Christ utters some enigmatic words. He says them to Peter: "When you were young, you girded yourself and walked where you would. But when you are old ... another will gird you and carry you where you do not wish to go." Mysterious, enigmatic words.... The Evangelist adds that by these words Christ foretold by what kind of death Peter would glorify God.

Hence, in this call, directed to Peter by Christ after His Resurrection, Christ's command "Come follow me" has a double meaning. It is a call to service, and a call to die.

In the case of Pope John Paul I, both of these calls from John's Gospel have already been fulfilled. We know already by what manner of death he would glorify God. Now this death is behind us.

Christ said to Peter: "When you grow old..." In our terms, in human terms — John Paul I did not grow old. A month of pontificate. But this month had to be sufficient. It had to be sufficient not on the scale of human calculations, not on the scale of human time, not on the scale of human history. It had to be sufficient on the scale of those fundamental words of Christ: "Do you love me?"

This month of pontificate had to be sufficient as a time of love.

And looking at the man who, on August 26th, took the name of John Paul I, and looking at all of his days — the 33 days of his pontificate — we think that it was sufficient. Because love has a different reckoning, obeys different laws. In a sense, with regard to love, the laws of time are suspended, as are the laws of this world, the laws of material things. Love can be fulfilled in a short time. Sometimes in one action — one action suffices. It may come to pass, as the Scripture says: "In a short time he lived through much time..." Certainly the love which John Paul I expressed to Christ on August 26th and then through the 33 days of his pontificate, did not find expression in documents which guide the thinking of the Church and of all humanity. It did not find expression in pastoral work, in apostolic voyages. It was not given to him to celebrate even one Mass at the tomb of St. Peter. All of this was lacking. But, in a sense, love does not need any of this. It can be expressed without this. And Our Lord, conversing with Peter at the beginning of the first pontificate asked about nothing except love: "Do you love me?" This is the only question through which we are to examine every pontificate and every human life.

Certainly, the history of the Church will not have many facts to enter under the name of John Paul I. From a human perspective — and history is a human perspective — this will be a simple pontificate, devoid of great documents and great events. From a human point of view (and history is subject to the laws of human points of view) this pontificate will be in the shadow of John and Paul. But today we understand a little better why he chose those names. Maybe because even then he knew that he would remain in the shadow of these two names, these two great pontificates: of John and of Paul. That is history. Also the history of the Church.

But the Book of Life is written according to other laws. We do not know what words will be used to record the 33-day pontificate of John Paul in the Book of Life. We can only assume, on the basis of what we have heard, of what we have felt — that the answer given to Christ's question "Do you love me?" was particularly ardent. We can even suppose that it was so ardent, that the human heart did not survive it. Because the love of God is greater than a human heart. And sometimes it is expressed by a person's death.

It is the month of October. The entire Church is entwined in the rosary. The rosary is being prayed by many different people. Our countrymen pray it. We also pray it. We wish to entwine the person of John Paul I in this rosary, the person so dear to us, who left us a few days ago, leaving the Church in mourning. As we mourn him, we seek consolation by passing the beads of the rosary through our fingers, and the mysteries of the Holy Rosary through our thoughts. The entire Church, and especially the Church of Poland, bids farewell to this Pope elected on the day of Our

Lady of Jasna Gora, by praying the rosary.

Christ speaks to us in today's liturgy of the word. These are words taken from His address in the Upper Room. Words directed to the Apostles. Christ says: "You did not choose me, but I chose you, that you may go and bring forth fruit." In this Eucharistic prayer, in this Eucharistic Sacrifice, we wish to thank Christ that, by his life, by his short pontificate, His servant John Paul I, so clearly expressed the truth of these words to the world: "You did not choose me, but I chose you." And following these words of Christ, we wish that they might be fulfilled to the end. That you go and bring forth fruit, and that the fruit may continue.

In this Holy Sacrifice let us pray that the fruit of the 33-day pontificate of John Paul I continue.

Same day — 1:00 p.m., Genzano, at Bishop Rubin's and Sisters of the Sacred Heart * Castel Gandolfo, tour * Polish College, rosary * October 9 — 10:00 a.m., Committee "pro laicis" * 11:00 a.m., Apostolic Palace, congregation of cardinals * 1:00 p.m., at Bishop Deskur's with Cardinal Nasalli Rocca, Archbishop Poggi, Bishop Rubin and Bishop Wesoly * October 11 — 11:00 a.m., congregation of cardinals * 1:00 p.m., at bishop Deskur's with Cardinal Cody, Bishop Rubin and others * October 12 — 11:00 a.m., congregation of cardinals * *Ad mare* * October 13 — 10:00 a.m., congregation of cardinals, lottery of rooms for the conclave * Bishop Deskur's illness * meeting with the Primate * visit to Bishop Deskur in the hospital * at Bishop Rubin's * * Polish College, with the Primate, Bishop Rubin and Bishop Dabrowski * October 14 — 7:15 a.m., Polish College, concelebrated Mass for the intention of Bishop Deskur * 10:00 a.m., St. Peter's Basilica, Mass "De Spiritu Sancto" concelebrated by the cardinals * 3:00 p.m., the Gemelli clinic, with Bishop Deskur * 4:30 p.m., Veni Creator, beginning of the conclave * October 15 — 7:00 a.m., concelebrated Mass, conclave * October 16, 7:00 a.m., concelebrated Mass, conclave.

Last entry in the "Chronicle of the Bishop's Activities" of the Metropolitan Archbishop of Krakow, dispatched to Krakow from Rome, entered after the election:

"About 5:15 p.m. — John Paul II".

GLOSSARY

Koleda: Literally — Christmas carol. Also used to mean a pastoral visit of a parish pastor or other priest at a parishioner's home during the Christmas season, which is traditionally observed from Christmas Day until February 2.

May 3rd: The anniversary of the Polish Constitution of 1791, the first constitution in Europe, modeled after that of the United States and used as one of the guiding principles of the French Revolution. This day was the Polish National Holiday before World War II, but its observance was banned by the Communist government (it substituted July 22, the date a provisional Communist committee declared itself the government in 1945, its successor subsequently recognized by the Western powers). Since the 1960s, the Church had declared May 3rd the Feast of Our Lady Queen of Poland, so that a religious celebration could be observed where the civil one was banned.

Odpust: A parish celebration in honor of its patron saint. It is a spiritual celebration whereby one has the opportunity to participate in a solemn celebration of the Eucharist, hear a well prepared homily, and obtain the plenary indulgence. It is also a day of parish social festivities. It is translated at times as "kermess."

Oplatek: 1. A form of bread (white wafer made from flour and water, same as the Communion host, but not consecrated) that the Polish people and other people of that region use in the ceremony of "breaking bread" at Christmastime. This is done within the family at the first observance of Christmas, the Christmas Eve dinner ("Wigilia"). Subsequently, the wafer is shared with friends and acquaintances at visits and get-togethers during the Christmas season (which in Poland is observed traditionally from Christmas Day until February 2).

2. A social gathering during the Christmas season in January (and occasionally in late December), usually in a public place, at which the wafer is shared with one's friends, amid the exchange of good wishes for the Christmas season and the New Year.

Srodowisko: {It has several meanings in English: environment, circle, milieu, inner place.} It is a name adopted by a group of people with whom Karol Wojtyla, as a young parish priest at St. Florian's Parish in Krakow, first became acquainted during his ministry to university students. He would accompany them on vacation excursions of mountaineering and kayaking. He maintained friendship, contact and collaboration with them through his years as Archbishop and Cardinal, until his election to the Papacy. He would meet with them periodically for prayer, holiday celebrations and discussion. For Fr. Boniecki's descriptions of this group, see *Introduction*, p. 20-21, and *Kalendarium* entry for June 17, 1967.

GRADES RECEIVED BY KAROL WOJTYLA
at Marcin Wadowita Secondary School in Wadowice
Compiled from surviving documents and shared with the author of "Kalendarium"
by Dr. Gustaw Studnicki (2 Slowackiego Street, 34-100 Wadowice)

School Year	31/2		32/3		33/4		34/5		35/6		36/7		37/8	
Class	II		III		IV		VA		VIA		VII		VIII	
# on Class Roster	44		44		48		25		23		45		36	
Deportment	5	5	5	5	5	5	5	5	5	5	5	5	5	
Religion	5	5	5	5	5	5*	5	5	5	5	5	5	5	
Polish	5	5*	5	5	4	5	5	5	5	5	5	5	5	
Latin	-	-	-	-	4	5	5	5	5	5	5	5	5	
Greek	-	-	-	-	-	-	5	5	5	5	5	5	5	
German	5	5	5	5	5	5	5	5	5	5	5	5	5	
History	5	5	-	-	5	5	5	5	5	5	5	5	4	
Geography	5	5	5	5	-	-	5	5	5	5	-	-	-	
Natural Science	5	5	5	5	5	5	-	-	-	-	-	-	-	
Physics / Chemistry	-	-	-	-	-	-	-	-	-	-	5	5	4	
Mathematics	5	5	5	5	5	5	5	5	5	5	5	5	5	
Intro to Philosophy	-	-	-	-	-	-	-	-	-	-	-	-	5	
Hygienics	-	-	-	-	-	-	-	-	-	-	5	5	-	
Drawing	5	5	5	5	-	-	-	-	-	-	-	-	-	
Singing / Music	5	5	5	5	-	-	-	-	-	-	-	-	-	
Shop	5	5	5	5	-	-	-	-	-	-	-	-	-	
Physical Education	5	5	5	5	5	5	5	5	5	5	5	5	5	
Drawing (elective)	-	-	-	-	5	5	-	-	-	-	-	-	-	
Absent (class hrs)	-	15	30	51	12	14	-	1	4	3¹	-	10	6	
Grade Average	5		5		5		5		5		5		5	

* Denotes a remark made in the grade book: "Exhibits special predilection."

¹ "School days,"rather than "class hours."

Grade 5 denotes the highest grade possible.

Bartlomiej Wojtyla
Anna Chudecka of Czaniec (wife)

Franciszka
b. 03.25.1823
Walenty Kowalczyk
Community Councilor

Stanislaw
b. 04.01.1830
Julianna Madeja

Franciszek
iudex comunitatis
Franciszka Galuszka

Marianna
Mateusz Ciezki

Jozef
b. 01.15.1845

Maciej
01.01.1852 - 09.23.1923
Anna Przeczek (1st)
Maria Zalewska (2nd)

Jan

Pawel

Franciszek
Cantor, Parish of Czaniec
d. 1968

Karol
07.18.1879 - 02.18.1941
Emilia Kaczorowska

Stefania

Adelajda

Edmund
08.23.1906-04.12.1932

(daughter)
died at birth

Karol Jozef
b. 05.18.1920
John Paul II

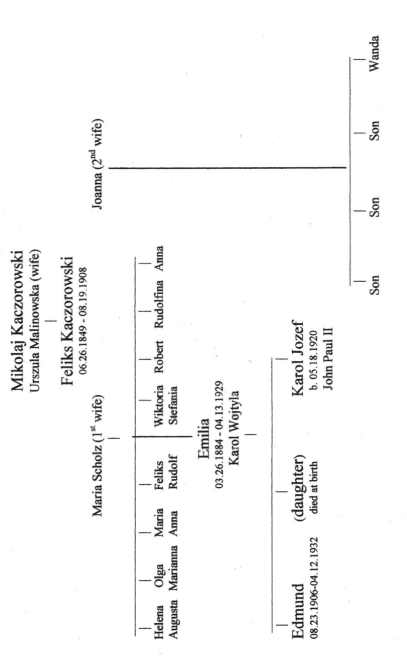

The Bibliography of Karol Wojtyla

Compiled by Zofia Skwarnicka

The Bibliography of Cardinal Karol Wojtyla[1] lists his works published before October 16, 1978. This same date is used to bind the scope of the second part of the bibliography which contains a list of publications written about the author and about his major academic and pastoral work.

The bibliography includes all books written by Karol Wojtyla, writings published in collective works, introductions and prefaces written for works of other authors, academic and popular articles; fragments of larger works published separately in periodicals, literary works published anonymously or under pseudonyms, appeals, pastoral letters, speeches, sermons and homilies. Official documents, related to the administration of the diocese, are not included.

The first part of the bibliography lists works by the author and is organized chronologically by date of publication. Within a given calendar year, the first entries are descriptions of works published as separate books, followed by works published in other publications or collective works, then works published in periodicals, arranged in alphabetical order by title of periodical, ending with works edited by the Cardinal. The second part of the bibliography lists works about the author and is organized in a somewhat different manner. Works of a general nature, biographic works and bibliographic materials are listed separately from analyses and reviews of Karol Wojtyla's individual works. Within each of these sections, the entries are chronological.

This bibliographer took care to record the full titles of all publications faithfully, maintaining their wording and punctuation. An ellipsis at the beginning or within an entry indicates the omission of Karol Wojtyla's name, if his name is part of the title assigned by the publisher. All explanations by this bibliographer are enclosed in square brackets, to distinguish them from the text in parentheses, which contains an integral part of the particular title.[2]

The common bibliographic practice of abbreviating titles of period-

---

[1] Althouth other bibliographies of Karol Wojtyla's works have been published since his election as Pope John Paul II (a noteworthy publication in this regard is *Karol Wojtyla negli scritti Bibliografia* by Fr. Wiktor Gramatowski and Zofia Wilinska), nonetheless, I have included in this publication the bibliography prepared by Zofia Skwarnicka. Its value lies in the descriptive quality of entries. They contain additional information for the English speaking reader. Some original entries in Polish were abbreviated, but the English translation reflects original entries, as they appeared in the original publication of *Kalendarium. zycia Karola Wojtyly*. {Note made by the editor. Cf. Introduction p. 13}

[2] In this bibliography, as in the main body of this book, notes and explanations of the translator are enclosed in curly braces {…}, and all subsequent footnotes are supplied by the translator.

icals has not been used here. This should make it easier for the reader to give proper citations of Karol Wojtyla's works, reducing the number of errors which otherwise occur frequently.

I wish to thank everyone who helped me gather the data for this bibliography, particularly Sister Emilia Ehrlich, thanks to whom the list was augmented by over a dozen entries of the Cardinal's works published abroad, and difficult to obtain in Poland. All entries taken from other bibliographies, which I did not compile through direct examination, are indicated by an asterisk next to the entry number.

Zofia Skwarnicka

PUBLICATIONS
From 1946 through October 16, 1978

1946

1. "Piesn o Bogu ukrytym" {Song about the hidden God}. Poetry Parts 1 — 2. *Glos Karmelu* (1946) Vol. 15 no. 1 / 2 pp. 23-26, no. 3, pp. 25-28. Published anonymously.

1949

2. "Mission de France". *Tygodnik Powszechny* (1949) Vol. 5, no. 9, pp. 1-2.

3. "Apostol" (O Janie Tyranowskim) {The Apostle (About Jan Tyranowski)}. *Tygodnik Powszechny* (1949), Vol. 5, no. 35 pp. 8-9.

1950

4. "Zagadnienia wiary w dzielach sw. Jana od Krzyza" {Issues of faith in the works of St. John of the Cross}. *Ateneum Kaplanskie* (1950) Vol. 42, no. 52, notebook 1 pp. 24-42, notebook 2 pp. 103-104.

5. "Questio de fide apud S. Joannem a Cruce". *Collectanea Theologica* (1950) Vol. 21, pp. 418-468.

6. [Pseudonym] Jawien, Andrzej: "Piesn o blasku wodu" {Song of the brightness of water}. [Poetry] *Tygodnik Powszechny* (1950) Vol. 6, no. 19 p. 1. {Poems:}

"Nad studnia w Sychem" {By the well at Sichem}; "Gdy otworzysz oczy w glebi fali…. {When you open your eyes in the depths of the waves…}; "Slowa niewiasty u studni, które wypowiedziala odchodzac" {The words of the woman at the well, which she spoke when leaving}; "Pozniejsze rozpamie-tywanie spotkania" {Later reminiscences of the meeting}; "Rozmowy, które prowadzil w niej On i ludzie ze sciany wieczoru" {Conversations led within her by Him and the people from the evening wall}; "Samarytanka" {The Samaritan woman}; "Rozwazanie ponowne" {Meditation anew}; "Piesn o blasku wody" {Song of the brightness of water}.

7. [Pseudonym] Jawien, Andrzej: " Matka". {Mother.} [Poetry] *Tygodnik Powszechny* (1950) Vol. 6, no. 50, p. 1. {Poems:}

   Part 1. "Pierwsza chwila uwielbionego ciala" {The first moment of the adored body}; "Zdumienie nad Jednorodzonym" {Amazement at the Only Begotten Son}; "Skupienie dojrzale" {Mature concentration}; Part 2. "Prosba Jana" {John's plea}; "Przestrzen, która w Tobie zostala" {The space that remained in You}; Part 3. "Otwarcie piesni" {The song's opening}; "Objeta nowym czasem" {She is embraced by a new time}.

1951

8. "Tajemnica i czlowiek" {Mystery and man}. *Tygodnik Powszechny* (1951) Vol. 7, no. 51/52 pp. 1-2.

9. O humanizmie sw. Jana od Krzyza {On the humanism of St. John of the Cross}. *Znak* (1951) Vol. 6 no. 1 pp. 6-20.

1952

10. [Pseudonym] Jasien, Piotr: "O teatrze slowa" {On the theater of the word}. *Tygodnik Powszechny* (1952) Vol. 8 no. 11 pp. 4-5.

11. "Instykt, milosc, malzenstwo" {Instinct, love, marriage}. *Tygodnik Powszechny* (1952) Vol. 8 no. 42 pp. 1-2, 11.

12. "Katechumenat XX wieku" {The Catechumenate in the 20th century}. *Znak* (1952) Vol. 7 no. 4 pp. 287-296.

13. [Pseudonym] Jawien, Andrzej: "Mysl jest przestrzenia dziwna" {Thought is a strange space}. [Poetry] Parts I-IV. *Tygodnik Powszechny* (1952) Vol. 9 no. 42 p. 5. {Poems:} I. 1. "Opor stawiany wyrazom przez mysl" {Opposition to words by thought}. 2. "Dawna rozmowa z której teraz niektóre zdania zapamietane wyrywan" {An old conversation from which I pluck certain remembered sentences}. 3. "Opor stawiany myslom przez wyrazy" {Opposition to thoughts by words}. II. "Jakub" {Jacob}. III. 1. "Przestrzen potrzebna kroplom wiosennego deszczu" {The space required by the drops of a spring rain}. 2. "Blad" {Error}. 3. "Ciezar wlasciwy" {Specific gravity}. IV. "Dla towarzyszow drogi" {To my travelling companions}.

1953

14. "Religijne przezywanie czystosci" {The religious experience of chastity}. *Tygodnik Powszechny* (1953) Vol. 9 no. 6 pp. 1-2.

15. "System etyczny Maxa Schelera jako srodek do opracowania

etyki chrzescijanskiej" {Max Scheler's ethical system as a means of formulating a Christian ethic}. *Polonia Sacra* (1953/1954) Vol. 6 bk 2/4 pp. 143-161.

1955

16. "W sprawie liturgii Wielkiej Soboty" {In the matter of the liturgy of Holy Saturday}. *Ruch Biblijny i Liturgiczny* (1955) no. 1 pp. 40-47.

1957

17. "Ewangeliczna zasada nasladowania. Nauka zródel objawienia a system filozoficzny Maxa Schelera" {The evangelical principle of imitation. The study of sources of revelation and the philosophical system of Max Scheler}. *Ateneum Kaplanskie* (1957) Vol. 49 55 bk. 1 pp. 51-67.

18. [Pseudonym] Ksiadz {Priest}: List do redakcji w sprawie campingu {A letter to the editor on the matter of camping}. *Homo Dei* (1957) Vol. 26 no. 3 pp. 420-423.

19. "Zagadnienie woli w analizie aktu etycznego" {The issue of free will in the analysis of an ethical act}. *Roczniki Filozoficzne* (1955/1957) Vol. 5 bk. 1 pp. 111-135. Abstract, p. 158.

20. "Problem oderwania przezycia od aktu na tle pogladów Kanta i Schelera" {The problem of separation of experience from action in light of the thinking of Kant and Scheler}. *Roczniki Filozoficzne* (1955/1957) Vol. 5 bk. 3 pp. 113-140. Abstract, pp. 171-172.

21. "W poszukiwaniu podstaw perfekcjoryzmu w etyce" {In search of the basis for perfectionism in ethics}. *Roczniki Filozoficzne* (1955/1957) Vol. 5 bk. 4 pp. 303-317. Abstract, p. 331.

22. "Traktat o pokucie w Dekrecie Gracjana w swietle rekopisu gdanskiego Mar. F. 275" {Treatise on penance in the Decree of Gratian in light of the Gdansk manuscript Mar. F. 275}. *Roczniki Teologiczno-Kanoniczne* (1957) Vol. 4 bk. 1 pp. 31-71. Summary pp. 198-199.

23. "Moralnosc a etyka" {Morality and Ethics}. "Elementarz Etyczny" {Ethical Primer}. *Tygodnik Powszechny* (1957) Vol. 11 no. 9 p. 3.

24. "Problem etyki naukowej" {The issue of academic ethics}. "Elementarz Etyczny" {Ethical Primer}. *Tygodnik*

Powszechny (1957) Vol. 11 no. 10 p. 3.

25. "O pochodzeniu norm moralnych" {On the origin of moral standards}. "Elementarz Etyczny". *Tygodnik Powszechny* (1957) Vol. 11 no. 11 pp. 3, 11.

26. "Realizm w etyce" {Realism in ethics}. "Elementarz Etyczny". *Tygodnik Powszechny* (1957) Vol. 11 no. 12 p. 7.

27. "Natura i doskonalosc" {Nature and perfection}. "Elementarz Etyczny". *Tygodnik Powszechny* (1957) Vol. 11 no. 13 p. 11.

28. [Pseudonym.] Jawien, Andrzej: "Dramat slowa i gestu" {The drama of word and gesture}. *Tygodnik Powszechny* (1957) Vol. 11 no. 14 p. 5.

29. "Znaczenie powinnosci" {The meaning of obligation}. "Elementarz Etyczny". *Tygodnik Powszechny* (1957) Vol. 11 no. 16 p. 11.

30. "Prawo natury" {Natural law}. "Elementarz Etyczny". *Tygodnik Powszechny* (1957) Vol. 11 no. 28 p. 7.

31. "Humanizm a cel czlowieka" {Humanism and mankind's purpose}. "Elementarz Etyczny". *Tygodnik Powszechny* (1957) Vol. 11 no. 31 p. 7.

32. "Problem prawdy i milosierdzia" {The issue of truth and mercy}. "Elementarz Etyczny". *Tygodnik Powszechny* (1957) Vol. 11 no. 33 p. 11.

33. "Problem bezinteresownosci" {The issue of altruism}. "Elementarz Etyczny". *Tygodnik Powszechny* (1957) Vol. 11, no. 34 p. 7.

34. "Wlasciwa interpretacja nauki o szczesciu" {The proper interpretation of the teaching on happiness}. "Elementarz Etyczny". *Tygodnik Powszechny* (1957) Vol. 11 no. 36 p. 11.

35. "Stosunek do przyjemnosci" {Attitude to pleasure}. "Elementarz Etyczny". *Tygodnik Powszechny* (1957) Vol. 11 no. 38 p. 7.

36. "Wartosci" {Values}. "Elementarz Etyczny". *Tygodnik Powszechny* (1957) Vol. 11 no. 39 p. 11.

37. "Co to jest asceza?" {What is an ascetic practice?} "Elementarz Etyczny". *Tygodnik Powszechny* (1957) Vol. 11 no. 40 p. 7.

38. "Idea i pokora" {Idea and humility}. "Elementarz Etyczny". *Tygodnik Powszechny* (1957) Vol. 11 no. 41 p. 7.

39. "Widzenie Boga" {Seeing God}. "Elementarz Etyczny". *Tygodnik Powszechny* (1957) Vol. 11 no. 43 p. 7.

40. [Pseudonym] Jawien, Andrzej: "Kamieniolom" {The stone quarry}. [Poetry] *Znak* (1957) Vol. 9 no. 6 pp. 559-563.

41. "Mysli o malzenstwie" {Thoughts on marriage}. *Znak* (1957) Vol. 9 no. 7 pp. 595-604. Abstract p. 717.

1958

42. "Propedeutyka sakramentu malzenstwa". W: *Rola kobiety w Kosciele.* {Propaedeutics of the sacrament of marriage. In: *The role of women in the Church.*} Lublin 1958 pp. 87-92.

43. "Propedeutyka sakramentu malzenstwa. Kryzys instytucji i kryzys sakramentu." {Propaedeutics of the sacrament of marriage. The crisis of the institution and the crisis of the sacrament.} *Ateneum Kaplanskie* (1958) Vol. 50, no. 56, notebook 1 pp. 20-33.

44. "O kierowniczej lub sluzebnej roli rozumu w etyce. Na tle pogladów Tomasza z Akwinu, Hume'a i Kanta". {On the guiding role of reason in ethics. In light of the views of Thomas Aquinas, Hume and Kant.} *Roczniki Filozoficzne* (1958) Vol. 6, bk. 2 pp. 13-31. Abstract p. 144.

45. "Kamien wegielny etyki spolecznej" {The cornerstone of social ethics}. "Elementarz Etyczny" {Ethical Primer}. *Tygodnik Powszechny* (1958) Vol. 12, no. 1 p. 7.

46. "Spawiedliwosc a milosc" {Justice and love}. "Elementarz Etyczny". *Tygodnik Powszechny* (1958) Vol. 12, no. 2 p. 7.

47. [Pseud.] Jawien, Andrzej: "Rapsody tysiaclecia" {Rhapsodies of the Millennium}. *Tygodnik Powszechny* (1958) Vol. 12, no. 3 p. 5.

48. "Problem walki" {The problem of struggle}. "Elementarz Etyczny". *Tygodnik Powszechny* (1958) Vol. 12, no. 3 p. 7.

49. "Etyka niezalezna w swietle idei sprawiedliwosci" {Independent ethics in light of the concept of justice}. "Elementarz Etyczny". *Tygodnik Powszechny* (1958) Vol. 12, no. 6, p. 7.

50. "Profile Cyrenejczyka" {Profiles of the man from Cyrene[3]}. [Poetry]. *Tygodnik Powszechny* (1958) Vol. 12, no. 13 p. 4.

---

[3] According to the gospel accounts, Simon of Cyrene was a bystander pressed by the Roman soldiers to help Jesus carry His cross on the way to His crucifixion.

{Poems:}

Part I. "Zanim jeszcze potrafilem rozrózniac wiele profilów" {Before I could distinguish many profiles}. Part II. "Teraz juz zaczynam rozrózniac poszczególne profile" {Now I begin to distinguish individual profiles}. 1. "Melancholik" {Melancholic}. 2. "Schizotymik" {Schizothymic}. 3. "Niewidomi" {The blind}. 4. "Aktor" {Actor} 5. "Dziewczyna zawiedziona w milosci" {The girl disappointed in love}. 6. "Dzieci" {Children}. 7. "Mysli czlowieka" {Man's[4] thoughts}. 8. "Rysopis czlowieka" {A man's description} 9. "Robotnik z fabryki samochodów" {The worker from the automobile factory}. 10. "Robotnik z fabryki broni" {The worker from the arms factory}. 11. "Magdalena". 12. "Czlowiek emocji" (A man of emotion}. 13. "Czlowiek intelektu" {A man of intellect}. 14. "Czlowiek woli" {A man of free will}. Part III. "Szymon z Cyreny" {Simon of Cyrene}.

51. "Boze Narodzenie 1958" {Christmas 1958}. *Tygodnik Powszechny* (1958) Vol. 12, no. 52 pp. 1-2.

52. [Review:] Bednarski, Felix: *Przedmiot etyki w swietle zasad sw. Tomasza z* Akwinu {The subject of ethics in light of the principles of St. Thomas Aquinas}. Lublin 1956. *Roczniki Filozoficzne* (1958) Vol. 6, no. 2 pp. 133-136.

53. [Review:] Znamierowski, Czeslaw: *Zasady i kierunki etyki* {Principles and directions in ethics}. Warsaw 1957. *Zeszyty Naukowe Katolickiego Uniwersytetu Lubelskiego* {Academic Workbooks of the Catholic University of Lublin} (1958) no. 1, pp. 76-78.

54. [Editor:] *Roczniki Filozoficzne* {Philosophical Annals} Towarzystwo Naukowe Katolickiego Uniwersytetu Lubelskiego {Academic Society of the Catholic University of Lublin}, Lublin. Vol. 6 (1958) through Vol. 20 (1972). Co-editor of several publications dedicated to works in the field of ethics.

1959

55. *Ocena mozliwosci zbudowania etyki chrzescijanskiej przy zalozeniach systemu Maxa Schelera* {An assessment of the possibility of establishing Christian ethics on the foundations of the system of Max Scheler}, Lublin 1959, 135 pages. In: *Towarzystwo Naukowe Katolickiego Uniwersytetu Lubelskiego,*

---

[4] In items 7, 8, 12, 13, 14, *czlowiek* in Polish translated as "man" is gender-neutral, as in "human"

Rozprawy Wydzialu Filozoficznego {Academic Society of the Catholic University of Lublin, Dissertations of the Department of Philosophy}, Vol. 5.

56. [Pseudonym] Jawien, Andrzej: "Matka" {Mother}. [Poetry]. *W: Matka Boska w poezji polskiej, Anthology* {In: The Blessed Mother in Polish poetry.} Vol. 2. Lublin 1959, pp. 237-241. (Part I, Part III. Reprint from *Tygodnik Powszech*ny, see entry 7.)

57. "Czym powinna byc teologia moralna?" {What should be the nature of moral theology?} *Ateneum Kaplanskie* (1959) Vol. 51, no. 53, notebook. 1/3 pp. 97-104.

58. "Milosc i odpowiedzialnosc" {Love and Responsibility}. *Ateneum Kaplanskie* (1959) Vol. 51, no. 59, notebook 2, pp. 163-172.

59. "O metafizycznej i fenomenologicznej podstawie normy moralnej. (W oparciu o koncepcje sw. Tomasza z Akwinu oraz Maxa Schelera.)" {Of the metaphysical and phenomenological basis of moral standards. (On the basis of concepts of St. Thomas Aquinas and Max Scheler.)} *Roczniki Teologiczno-Kanoniczne* (1950{?}) Vol. 6, no. 1/2 pp. 99-124.

60. "Le traité de 'Penitentia' de Gratien dan l'abrégé de Gdansk Mar. F. 275". *Studia Gratiana* (1959) Vol. 7, pp. 357-390.

61. "Mysli o Niepokalanym Poczeciu" {Thoughts on the Immaculate Conception}. *Tygodnik Powszechny* (1959) Vol. 13 no. 49 pp. 1, 3.

62. "Natura ludzka jako podstawa formacji etycznej" {Human nature as the basis of ethical formation}. *Znak* (1959) Vol. 11, no. 6 pp. 693-697. Abstract pp. 822-823.

1960

63. *Milosc i odpowiedzialnosc. Studium Etyczne* {Love and Responsibility, An Ethical Study} Lublin: Towarzystwo Naukowe Katolickiegu Uniwersytetu Lubelskiego {Academic Society of Catholic University of Lublin} 1960, 246 pp. (2nd Edition, see entry 77; 3rd Edition, see entry 137)

64. * *Consilia et Vota Episcoporum ac Praelatorum.* Polonia. 32. Exc.-mi P. D. Caroli Wojtyla Episcopi tit. Ombitani, Auxiliaris Cracoviensis. In: *Acta et Documenta Concilio Oecumenico Vaticano II apparando.* (Series antepraeparatoria). Vol. 2 pars. 2. Typis Polyglottis Vaticanis 1960 pp. 741-

748.

65. "Swiety Józef" {St. Joseph}. *Tygodnik Powszechny* (1960) Vol. 14, no. 12, pp. 1-2.

66. "Wychowanie milosci" {The upbringing of love}. *Tygodnik Powszechny* (1960) Vol. 14, no. 21, p. 1.

67. "Rozwazania o królestwie" {Meditations on the kingdom}. *Tygodnik Powszechny* (1960) Vol. 14, no. 44, pp. 1-2.

68. "Niektóre uwagi o zyciu wspólczesnej mlodziezy i mlodej inteligencji" {Various comments on the life of contemporary youth and young intellectuals}. (Summary of a lecture.) *Zeszyty Naukowe KUL* {Academic Workbooks of KUL} (1960) Vol. 3, no. 3, pp. 117-119.

69. "Milosc i odpowiedzialnosc" {Love and Responsibility}. *Znak* (1960) Vol. 12, no. 5, pp. 561-614. Abstract pp. 708-716.

70. [Pseudonym] Jawien, Andrzej: *Przed sklepem jubilera. Medytacja o sakramencie malzenstwa, przechodzaca chwilami w dramat* {The Jeweler's shop. A meditation on the sacrament of marriage, turning at times into drama.} [Poetry]. *Znak* 1960 Vol. 12, no. 12, pp. 1564-1607.

I. "Sygnaly" {Signals}. II. "Oblubieniec" {The bridegroom}. III. "Dzieci" {Children}.

1961

71. "Program wykladów nauk spolecznych w seminariach i instytutach teologicznych w Polsce"{Program of social science courses in seminaries and theological institutes in Poland}. *Roczniki Teologiczno-Kanoniczne* (1961) Vol. 8, no. 3, pp. 65-66.

(Summary of a lecture delivered at the 20th Convention of Deans and Professors of Theological Institutes … in Poland, Lublin, Catholic University of Lublin, Sept. 9-11, 1958.)

72. [Pseudonym] Jawien, Andrzej: "Dziady i dwudziestolecie" { 'Forefathers Eve[5]' and the 20th anniversary}. *Tygodnik Powszechny* (1961) Vol. 15, no. 40, p. 6.

73. "Mysli o laikacie" {Thoughts about the laity}. *Tygodnik Powszechny* (1961) Vol. 15, no. 44, pp. 1, 4.

74. "Nauczal z lodzi" {He taught from a boat}. (Sermon).

---

[5] A 19th century drama by the poet Adam Mickiewicz

Tygodnik Powszechny (1961) Vol. 15, no. 49, p. 1.

75. "Personalizm tomistyczny" {Thomistic personalism}. *Znak* (1961) Vol. 13 no. 5 pp. 664-675.

76. "Uwagi o zyciu wewnetrzym mlodej inteligencji" {Comments on the interior life of young intellectuals}. *Znak* (1961) Vol. 13, no. 6 pp. 761-769. Abstract pp. 994-995.

1962

77. *Milosc i odpowiedzalnosc. Studium Etyczne* {Love and Responsibility. An ethical study}. 2nd Edition, revised and augmented. Kraków: Wydawnictwo *Znak* 1962, 313 pages. Bibliography of 80 entries.

78. "Problem 'uswiadomienia' z punktu widzenia teologii {The problem of 'becoming aware'[6] from a theological point of view}. *Ateneum Kaplanskie* (1962) Vol. 54, no. 64, notebook 1 pp. 1-5.

79. "Kazanie..." {Sermon given by His Excellency Bishop {Wojtyla}... at the funeral of the Metropolitan Archbishop Eugeniusz Baziak, in the Metropolitan Basilica at Wawel Castle, on June 18, 1962 (excerpts)}. *Notificationes e Curia Metropolitana Cracoviensi* (1962) no. 7 pp. 194-198.

80. "Odezwa do duchowienstwa..." {A message to the clergy and faithful of the Krakow Archdiocese [about Archbishop E. Baziak]}. *Notificationes e Curia Metropolitana Cracoviensi* (1962) no. 7 pp. 199-200.

81. "Pismo..." {A letter of His Eminence Bishop {Wojtyla} on the occasion of the 350th anniversary of the death of Father Piotr Skarga}. *Notificationes e Curia Metropolitana Cracoviensi* (1962) no. 11 pp. 317-318.

82. "Przemowienie..." {A speech by His Excellency Bishop {Wojtyla}... delivered at Wawel Cathedral after the Holy Mass celebrated by Bishop Julian Groblicki, in the evening of Oct. 5, 1962, before departure for Rome for the General Council}. *Notificationes e Curia Metropolitana Cracoviensi* (1962) no. 12 pp. 357-362.

83. "List Pasterski..." {Pastoral letter of His Eminence Bishop {Wojtyla} from the first session of the Second Vatican Council, November 5, 1962.} *Notificationes e Curia*

---

6 Usually a euphemism for sexual education.

Metropolitana Cracoviensi (1962) no. 12 pp. 362-364.

84. "Wladza i krzyz" {Authority and the cross}. Excerpts [of a speech at the funeral of Archbishop Eugeniusz Baziak]. *Tygodnik Powszechny* (1962) Vol. 16 no. 26 pp. 1-2.

85. List Ks. Biskupa... {A letter from Bishop {Wojtyla} ... to Tygodnik Powszechny [from Rome, from a session of the Vatican Council]}. *Tygodnik Powszechny* (1962) Vol. 16, no. 46, p. 3.

86. List papieski... {Papal letter ...} [Excerpts]. *Tygodnik Powszechny* (1962) Vol. 16, no. 47 p. 9.

87. Przemawiaja Biskupi Polscy... {Polish bishops speak}[Excerpts of a speech by ... at the Vatican Council]. *Tygodnik Powszechny* (1962) Vol. 16, no. 48, p. 2.

88. Kazanie Ks. Biskupa... {A sermon by Bishop ...} [at a Mass on the occasion of the beginning of the academic year 1961/1962 at KUL]. *Zeszyty Naukowe Katolickiego Uniwersytetu Lubelskiego* (1962) Vol. 5, no. 1, pp. 137-141.

89. [Review:] Kalinowski, Jerzy: *Teoria poznania praktycznego* {Theory of practical Cognition}. Lublin 1960. *Roczniki Filozoficzne* (1962) Vol. 10, no. 2 pp. 153-156.

1963

90. [Introduction to:] Turowicz, Jerzy: *Chrzescijanin w dzisiejszym swiecie* {The Christian in today's world}. Krakow: Wydawnictwo Znak (1963) pp. 5-10.

91. "Opiekun doskonaly" {The perfect protector}. [About St. Joseph]. *Przewodnik Katolicki* (1963) no. 17, p. 209.

92. "Wypowiedz..." {Statement of His Eminence Bishop {Wojtyla}... on the Vatican Radio [Nov. 24, 1962 on the subject of the first session of Vatican II]}. *Notificationes e Curia Metropolitana Cracoviensi* (1963) no. 1/2 pp. 23-26.

93. "List Pasterski..." {Pastoral letter of His Eminence Bishop {Wojtyla}... from Rome [on the occasion of the Feast of St. Stanislaw Kostka]}. *Notificationes e Curia Metropolitana Cracoviensi* (1963) no. 1/2 pp. 15-16.

94. "Odezwa..." {A message of His Eminence the Bishop urging prayers for unity of Christians (May 5, 1963)}. *Notificationes e Curia Metropolitana Cracoviensi* (1963) no. 3/4 pp. 87-88. The same: *Tygodnik Powszechny* (1963) no. 3 p. 7.

95. "Odezwa..." {A message of His Eminence Bishop {Wojtyla}on the occasion of ordination to subdiaconate at the Archdiocesan Theological Seminary (Jan. 1, 1963)}. *Notificationes e Curia Metropolitana Cracoviensi* (1963) no. 3/4 pp. 88-89.

96. "Odezwa..." {A message of His Eminence the Bishop for the 1963 Lenten Season}. *Notificationes e Curia Metropolitana Cracoviensi* (1963) no. 5/6 pp. 144-147.

97. "J.Eks. Biskup... do Kaplanow Archidiecezji Krakowskiej" {His Eminence the Bishop to the priests of the Krakow Archdiocese. [A letter of March 2, 1963 on the subject of Marian Days]}. *Notificationes e Curia Metropolitana Cracoviensi* (1963) no. 5/6 pp. 147-148.

98. "Odezwa..." {A message of His Eminence the Bishop for the beginning of the 8th Year of the Great Novena}. *Notificationes e Curia Metropolitana Cracoviensi* (1963) no. 7/8 pp. 207-210.

99. "Z kazan..." {From the sermons of His Eminence Bishop {Wojtyla} given after his return from the first session of the Second Vatican Council}. *Notificationes e Curia Metropolitana Cracoviensi* (1963) no. 5/6 pp. 211-220.

100. "Modlitwy..." {Prayers of the priests of the Krakow Archdiocese at Jasna Gora {Czestochowa} (April 1963). An address given by the Bishop on April 23, 1963. (Excerpts).} *Notificationes e Curia Metropolitana Cracoviensi* (1963) no. 9/10 pp. 268-274.

101. "Odezwa..." {A message of the Bishop to the clergy and the faithful of the Krakow Archdiocese [on the subject of the coronation of the statue of Our Lady of Ludzmierz].} *Notificationes e Curia Metropolitana Cracoviensi* (1963) no. 11/12 pp. 285-287.

102. "List Wielkopostny" ...{A Lenten letter of ...} *Tygodnik Powszechny* (1963) no. 11 p. 1.

103. "Sens dziesieciolecia" {The meaning of the decade}. Pastoral letter of .... [concerning the Great Novena]. *Tygodnik Powszechny* (1963) no. 20 p. 1.

104. "Dwaj powstancy" {Two freedom fighters}. [Fr. Rafal Kalinowski and Br. Albert (Adam) Chmielowski]. *Tygodnik Powszechny* (1963) no. 33 pp. 1-2.

105. "Matka Boska Ludzmierska" {Our Lady of Ludzmierz}.

(Fragment of the pastoral letter). *Tygodnik Powszechny* (1963) no. 34 p. 1.

106. "Msza sw. Papieza Jana" {The Mass of Pope John}. *Znak* (1963) Vol. 15, no. 7/8 pp. 765-769.

107. [Cryptonym:] A. J.: "Kosciól"{The Church}. (Excerpts) [Poetry]. *Znak* (1963) Vol. 15, no. 11, pp. 1376-1382. {Poems:} [1.] "Pasterze i zródla" {Shepherds and sources}: "Sciana" {The wall}, "Przepasc" {The chasm}, "Murzyn" {The black man}, "Posadzka" {The floor}, "Krypta"{The crypt}, "Synodus", "Ewangelie" {The Gospels}, "Zródla i rece" {Sources and hands}, "Dwa miasta" {Two cities} (epilog). [2.] "Narodziny wyznawców" {The Birth of believers}: 1. ("Mysli biskupa udzielajacego sakramentu bierzmowania w pewnej podgórskiej wsi" {Thoughts of a bishop administering the Sacrament of Confirmation in a certain village in the foothills}). 2. ("Mysli czlowieka przyjmujacego sakrament bierzmowania w pewnej podgórskiej wsi" {Thoughts of a person receiving the Sacrament of Confirmation in a certain village in the foothills}).

1964

108. "Na 600-lecie Uniwersytetu Jagiellonskiego" {For the 600th anniversary of Jagiellonian University}. (Radio interview October 19). *Duszpasterz Polski Zagranica* {Polish Priest Abroad}(1964) Vol. 15, no. 2, pp. 134-137.

109. "Na kanwie Dni Maryjnych"{On the background of Marian Days}. *Homo Dei* (1964) Vol. 33, no. 3, pp. 135-139.

110. "O godnosci osoby ludzkiej" {On the dignity of the human person}. A speech of the Metropolitan Archbishop on Vatican Radio, October 19, 1964. *Notificationes e Curia Metropolitana Cracoviensi* (1964) no. 12 pp. 287-289.

111. "Lud Bozy" {The People of God}. *Przewodnik Katolicki* (1964) no. 7 p. 65.

112. "Skarb wielki" {The great treasure}. [Fragment of an oration during the ingress {entry into the cathedral for the assumption of the office of Archbishop}]. *Przewodnik Katolicki* (1964) no. 15 pp. 139-140.

113. "Kosciol wobec wspolczesnego swiata" {The Church in relation to the contemporary world}. *Przewodnik Katolicki* (1964) no. 44 pp. 401-402.

114. "Wypowiedz Ks. Biskupa..." {Statement of Bishop ... on Vatican Radio on the role of the laity in the Church (November 25, 1963)}. *Notificationes e Curia Metropolitana Cracoviensi* (1964) no. 1/2 pp. 27-30.

115. "List Pasterski..." {Pastoral letter of the Metropolitan Archbishop for the First Sunday of Lent in 1964}. *Notificationes e Curia Metropolitana Cracoviensi* (1964) no. 3/4 pp. 33-36.

116. "Do wszystkich kaplanów Archidiecezji Krakowskiej" {To all the priests of the Krakow Archdiocese}. *Notificationes e Curia Metropolitana Cracoviensi* (1964) no. 3/4 pp. 66-74.

    (Reflections on the pilgrimage to the Holy Land after the first session of the Second Vatican Council.)

117. "Przemowienie..." {An address given by the Metropolitan Archbishop during the ingress[7] (Excerpts).} *Notificationes e Curia Metropolitana Cracoviensi* (1964) no. 5/6 pp. 102-105.

118. "List do duchowienstwa..." {Letter to the clergy on the occasion of the ingress. (Excerpts)}. *Notificationes e Curia Metropolitana Cracoviensi* (1964) no. 5/6 pp. 97-101.

119. "List do duchowienstwa..." {Letter to the clergy on the 600th anniversary of the consecration of Wawel Cathedral}. *Notificationes e Curia Metropolitana Cracoviensi* (1964) no. 5/6 pp. 102-105[8].

120. "Problematyka drugiej sesji II Soboru Watykanskiego" {Questions from the Second Session of the Second Vatican Council}. From the sermons of the Metropolitan Archbishop after his return from the Council session. *Notificationes e Curia Metropolitana Cracoviensi* (1964) no. 7 pp. 145-160.

121. "List pasterski Ks. Arcybiskupa Metropolity na 200 rocznice beatyfikacji Bl. Wincentego Kadlubka" {Pastoral letter by the Metropolitan Archbishop for the 200th anniversary of the beatification of Bl. Wincenty Kadlubek}. *Notificationes e Curia Metropolitana Cracoviensi* (1964) no. 8/9 pp. 200-202.

122. "Przemowienie Ks. Metropolity w Katedrze Wawelskiej w dniu wyjazdu na III sesje soborowa 10 IX 64 r." {An address given by the Metropolitan Archbishop in Wawel Cathedral on the day of departure for the third session of the Council —

---

[7] Entry into the cathedral for the assumption of the office of Archbishop.
[8] Sic. Note duplication of page nos. with entry 117.

September 10, 1964}. *Notificationes e Curia Metropolitana Cracoviensi* (1964) no. 8/9 pp. 200-202.

123. "List Ks. Metropolity na uroczystosc sw. Jana Kantego w 1964 r." {Letter of the Metropolitan Archbishop for the Feast of St. John of Kety in 1964}. *Notificationes e Curia Metropolitana Cracoviensi* (1964) no. 12 pp. 273-276.

124. "Listy z Soboru: Do duchowienstwa" {Letters from the Vatican Council: To the clergy}. *Notificationes e Curia Metropolitana Cracoviensi* (1964) no. 12 pp. 280-282.

125. "Kosciól wobec wspólczesnego swiata" {The Church in relation to the contemporary world}. Speech of the Metropolitan Archbishop on Vatican Radio, Sep. 28, 1964. *Notificationes e Curia Metropolitana Cracoviensi* (1964) no. 12 pp. 282-284.

126. "List Pasterski Ks. Arcybiskupa ...[w zwiazku z nominacja na ordynariusza krakowskiego i ingrsem] "{Pastoral letter of Archbishop ... [in connection with his nomination as Archbishop Ordinary and his ingress]}. *Tygodnik Powszechny* (1964) Vol. 18, no. 10, p. 1.

127. "O soborze" {About the Council}. (Excerpts of sermons). *Tygodnik Powszechny* (1964) Vol. 18 no. 11 pp. 1-2.

128. "Kazanie ...w Katedrze Wawelskiej" {Sermon by ... in Wawel Cathedral during the ingress [entry into the cathedral for the assumption of the office of Archbishop]}. *Tygodnik Powszechny* (1964) Vol. 18, no. 12, p. 3.

129. "Kazanie na 600-lecie Uniwersytetu Jagiellonskiego w kosciele swietej Anny w Krakowie" {Sermon for the 600th anniversary of Jagiellonian University in the Church of St. Anne in Krakow}. (Excerpts). *Tygodnik Powszechny* (1964) Vol. 18, no. 21, p. 3.

130. "Na 200 rocznice beatyfikacji blogoslawionego Wincentego Kadlubka" {On the 200th anniversary of the beatification of Blessed Wincenty Kadlubek}. [Pastoral letter of August 23, 1964]. *Tygodnik Powszechny* (1964) Vol. 18, no. 36, pp. 3-4.

131. "List pasterski z Soboru" {Pastoral letter from the Vatican Council [of November 8 1964]}. *Tygodnik Powszechny* (1964) Vol. 18, no. 48, p. 1.

132. "Kosciól w swiecie wspólczesnym" {The Church in the contemporary world}. (Speech broadcast on the Vatican Radio on

---

[9] Duplicate of 131?

September 28 1964). *Tygodnik Powszechny* (1964) Vol. 18, no. 43 pp. 1-2.

133. "List pasterski z Soboru" {Pastoral letter from the Vatican Council}. *Tygodnik Powszechny* (1964) Vol. 18, no. 48, p. 1.[9]

134. "Czlowiek jest osoba" {A human being is a person}. [Speech broadcast on the Vatican Radio during the third session of the Vatican Council.] *Tygodnik Powszechny* (1964) Vol. 18, no. 52, p. 2.

135. "Chrzescijanin a kultura" {The Christian and the culture}. *Znak* (1964) Vol. 16, no. 10, pp. 1153-1157.

136. [Cryptonym:] A. J.: "Rozwazania o ojcostwie" {Meditations on fatherhood}. *Znak* (1964) Vol. 16, no. 5, pp. 610-613.

1965

137. *Milosc i odpowiedzialnosc. Studium Etyczne* {Love and Responsibility. An ethical study}. 3rd Edition, London: "Veritas" 1965, 279 pages. *Biblioteka Polska*. [Blue Series, Vol. 17]. (1st Ed., see entry 58; 2nd Ed., see entry 77.)

138. *Amour et responsibilité. Étude de morale sexuelle.* (Trad. du polonais par Thérese Sas. Revu par Marie-Andrée Bouchaud-Kalinowska. Préf. de Henri de Lubac.) Paris: Soc. d'Éditions Internationales 1965, 285 pages.

139. Introduction to: Malej, Witold: *Ks. W. M. Zaleski, Delegat apostolski Indii Wschodniej, arcybiskup Teb, patriarcha Antiochii* {Rev. W. M. Zaleski. Apostolic Delegate to the East Indies, Archbishop of Thebes, Patriarch of Antioch}. Rome 1965 pp. 7-8.

140. "Idea ludu Bozego i swietosci Kosciola a poslannictwo swieckich" {The concept of the People of God and the holiness of the Church in relation to the mission of the laity}. *Ateneum Kaplanskie* (1965) Vol. 57, no. 68, notebook 5/6 pp. 307-315.

141. *Ecclesia Mater, Mater Ecclesiae.* Fragment wykladu ... na temat: 'Idea ludu Bozego i swietosci Kosciola a poslannictwo swieckich' {*Ecclesia Mater, Mater Ecclesiae.* Excerpt of a lecture on the subject of 'the Concept of the People of God and the holiness of the Church in relation to the mission of the laity'}. *Kierunki* (1965) no. 37, p. 8.

142. "Przemowienie radiowe Ksiedza Arcybiskupa ...Metropolity Krakowskiego. Naswietlenie deklaracji o wolnosci religijnej." {Radio address of ... Metropolitan Archbishop of Krakow.

Explanation of the declaration on religious freedom}. *Notificationes e Curia Metropolitana Cracoviensi* (1965) no. 11/12 pp. 269-271.

143. "Sobór a praca teologów" {The Vatican Council and the work of theologians}. An Address given by the Metropolitan Archbishop on Vatican Radio, February 12, 1965. *Notificationes e Curia Metropolitana Cracoviensi* (1965) no. 3/4 pp. 87-88.

144. "Wymowa Oswiecimia" {The eloquence of Auschwitz}. Address of the Metropolitan Archbishop on Vatican Radio on the 20th anniversary of the liberation of the concentration camp in Auschwitz (February 18, 1965). *Notificationes e Curia Metropolitana Cracoviensi* (1965) no. 3/4 pp. 81-83.

145. "Odezwa Ks. Metropolity w XX rocznice wyzwolenia obozu oswiecimskiego" {Message of the Metropolitan Archbishop on the 20th anniversary of the liberation of the concentration camp at Auschwitz (January 27, 1945 - January 27, 1965)}. *Notificationes e Curia Metropolitana Cracoviensi* (1965) no. 5 pp. 113-114.

146. "Odezwa Ks. Metropolity do duchowienstwa" {Message of the Metropolitan Archbishop to the clergy [on the occasion of the feast honoring St. Stanislaw Bishop and Martyr]}. *Notificationes e Curia Metropolitana Cracoviensi* (1965) no. 5 pp. 114-115.

147. "List pasterski Ks. Arcybiskupa Metropolity na 200 rocznice ustanowienia swieta Najsw. Serca Pana Jezusa" {Pastoral letter of the Metropolitan Archbishop on the 200th anniversary of the establishment of the Feast of the Most Sacred Heart of Jesus}. *Notificationes e Curia Metropolitana Cracoviensi* (1965) no. 9/10 pp. 218-220.

148. "List Ks. Metropolity Krakowskiego do wiernych Archidiecezji Krakowskiej" {Letter of Metropolitan Archbishop to the faithful of the Krakow Archdiocese [in the matter of dedication of the Archdiocese to the Blessed Mother in Wawel Cathedral].} *Notificationes e Curia Metropolitana Cracoviensi* (1965) no. 9/10 pp. 220-223.

149. "List Ks. Metropolity do kaplanow Archidiecezji Krakowskiej..." {Letter of Metropolitan Archbishop to the priests of the Archdiocese [in the matter of dedication of the Archdiocese to the Blessed Mother].} *Notificationes e Curia Metropolitana Cracoviensi* (1965) no. 9/10 pp. 224-225.

150. "Przemowienie Ks. Metropolity przed wyjazdem na IV Sesje Soboru" {Address given by the Metropolitan Archbishop before his departure for the fourth session of the Vatican Council}. *Notificationes e Curia Metropolitana Cracoviensi* (1965) no. 9/10 pp. 234-237.

151. "Sobór a praca teologów" {The Vatican Council and the work of theologians}. *Przewodnik Katolicki* (1965) no. 9, p. 75.

152. "W dwudziestolecie oswobodzenia obozu koncentracyjnego w Oswiecimiu" {On the 20th anniversary of the liberation of the concentration camp in Auschwitz}. *Przewodnik Katolicki* (1965) no. 14, p. 124.

153. "Zagadnienie katolickiej etyki seksualnej" {The issue of Catholic sexual ethics}. Reflections and postulates. *Roczniki Filozoficzne* (1965) Vol. 13, bk. 2 pp. 5-25. With abstract.

154. "Millenium a Sobór" {The Millenium and the Vatican Council}. Letter to the editor of *Tygodnik Powszechny*. *Tygodnik Powszechny* (1965) Vol. 19, no. 13, p. 1.

155. "Do redakcji 'Tygodnika Powszechnego'" {To the editors of 'Tygodnik Powszechny'. [in connection with the 20th anniversary of the publication].} *Tygodnik Powszechny* (1965) Vol. 19, no. 13, p. 1.

156. "Sobór od wewnatrz" {The Vatican Council from within}. Letter to the editor of *Tygodnik Powszechny*. *Tygodnik Powszechny* (1965) Vol. 19 no. 16 pp. 1, 3.

157. "Sobór a praca teologów" {The Vatican Council and the work of theologians}. [Address on Vatican Radio, February 12, 1965]. *Tygodnik Powszechny* (1965) Vol. 19, no. 9, p. 1.

158 [Cryptonym:] A. J.: "Wedrówka do miejsc swietych" {Voyage to holy places}. [Poetry]. *Znak* (1965) Vol. 17 no. 6 pp. 773-777.

1966

159. "Osoba i czyn w aspekcie swiadomosci" {Person and Act in the aspect of consciousness}. (An excerpt from the study "Person and Act"). In: *Pastori et Magistro*, Lublin 1966 pp. 293-305. With abstract.

160. "Vaticanum II a praca teologów" {Vatican II and the work of theologians}. *Collectanea Theologica* (1966) Vol. 36, fasc. 1/4 pp. 8-14.

161. W poczuciu odpowiedzialnosci {In the sense of responsibili-

ty}. Excerpt of a sermon. *Kierunki* (1966) no. 20, p. 3.

162. "List...na srebrny jubileusz *Naszej Przeszlosci"* {Letter from ... for the silver anniversary of *Nasza Przeszlosc* {Our Past}}. *Nasza Przeszlosc* (1966) vol. 25 pp. 5-6.

163. "Przemowienie radiowe ... *"Communio Ecclesiarum* czyli o uroczystosci tysiaclecia Kosciola w Polsce na tle zblizenia Kosciolów na Soborze'" {(Vatican) Radio address of the Metropolitan Archbishop of Krakow entitled: *Communio Ecclesiarum*, or on the observance of the Millennium of the Church in Poland, in light of the drawing together of Churches at the Vatican Council}. *Notificationes e Curia Metropolitana Cracoviensi* (1966) no. 1/2 pp. 35-37.

164. "Przemowienie radiowe 'Stworzenie a odkupienie'" {(Vatican) Radio address by the Metropolitan Archbishop of Krakow entitled: Creation and salvation}. (Schema XIII). *Notificationes e Curia Metropolitana Cracoviensi* (1966) no. 3/4 pp. 59-62.

165. *"Sacrum Poloniae Millenium"*. {Pastoral letter for the first Sunday of Lent}. *Notificationes e Curia Metropolitana Cracoviensi* (1966) no. 3/4 pp. 62-64.

166. "Kazanie wygloszone..." {Sermon given at Wawel Cathedral on Holy Saturday}. *Notificationes e Curia Metropolitana Cracoviensi* (1966) no. 3/4 pp. 64-66.

167. "List pasterski do duchowienstwa i wiernych" {Pastoral letter to the clergy and faithful of the Archdiocese for Easter Sunday 1966}. *Notificationes e Curia Metropolitana Cracoviensi* (1966) no. 3/4 pp. 66-68.

168. "Powitanie Obrazu Matki Boskiej Czestochowskiej..." {Welcome of the Image of Our Lady of Czestochowa by the Metropolitan Archbishop of Krakow at Wawel Cathedral on May 6, 1966}. *Notificationes e Curia Metropolitana Cracoviensi* (1966) no. 5/6, pp. 101-102.

169. "Powitanie uczestnikow sesji naukowej..."{Welcome of participants to the academic session [on the millenium of Christianity in Poland at Wawel Cathedral on May 7, 1966] by the Metropolitan Archbishop of Krakow}. *Notificationes e Curia Metropolitana Cracoviensi* (1966) no. 5/6 pp. 102-104.

170. "Adam Stefan Kardynal Sapieha Metropolita Krakowski oraz duchowienstwo archidiecezji w okresie ciemnej nocy okupacji" {Cardinal Adam Stefan Sapieha, Metropolitan

Archbishop of Krakow and the clergy of the Archdiocese during the dark night of the occupation}. *Notificationes e Curia Metropolitana Cracoviensi* (1966) no. 5/6 pp. 122-126.

171. "Pozegnanie Obrazu Matki Boskiej Czestochowskiej..." {Farewell to the Image of Our Lady of Czestochowa by the Metropolitan Archbishop of Krakow at Wawel Cathedral on May 8, 1966}. *Notificationes e Curia Metropolitana Cracoviensi* (1966) no. 3/4 pp. 126-127.

172. "Odezwa J.E. Ksiedza Arcybiskupa Metropolity Krakowskiego do kaplanow z okazji Tygodnia Milosierdzia" {Message from His Eminence the Metropolitan Archbishop of Krakow to the priests on the occasion of the Week of Mercy}. *Notificationes e Curia Metropolitana Cracoviensi* (1966) no. 7/10, p. 245.

173. "Slowo wstepne ..." {Introductory remarks ...at an academic session of the Polish Theological Society in Krakow on April 26, 1966}. *Ruch Biblijny* Vol. 19, no. 2, p. 66.

174. "Religijne przezycie Millenium" {The religious experience of the Millenium}. Letter to the editor. *Tygodnik Powszechny* (1966) Vol. 20, no. 19 p. 1.

175. "Logika wewnetrzna Vaticanum II (a zarazem próba uporzadkowania dokumentów soborowych celem ich przedstawienia)" {The internal logic of Vatican II (and also an attempt to organize the Council documents for the purpose of presenting them)}. *Wroclawskie Wiadomosci Koscielne* {Wroclaw Church News} (1966) Vol. 21, no. 7 pp. 159-163.

176. " Przemowienie wygloszone ..." {An address given at an assembly in the Archbishop's Theological Seminary in Wroclaw, on the occasion of its 400th anniversary, April 24, 1966}. *Wroclawskie Wiadomosci Koscielne* (1966) Vol. 21 pp. 233-239.

177. [Cryptonym:] A. J.: "Wigilia Wielkanocna 1966" {Easter Vigil 1966}. [Poetry]. *Znak* (1966) Vol. 18, no. 4, pp. 435-444. {Poems:} I. "Inwokacja" {Invocation}. II. "Opowiesc o drzewie zranionym" {Tale of the wounded tree}. III. "Spojenia" {Couplings}. IV. "Rozwój jezyka" {The development of language}. V. "Echo pierworodnego placzu" {Echo of the first-born weeping}. VI. "Obrzed" {The rite}. VII. "Wigilia Wielkanocna" 1966 {Easter Vigil}.

1967

178. "Humanista. Bp. Michal Klepacz (1893-1967) {The humanist. Bishop Michal Klepacz}. In: *W nurcie zagadnien posoborowych* {Within the mainstream of questions after the Vatican Council}. [Vol. 1]. Warsaw 1967 pp. 451-454.

179. "Duchowosc pasyjna i duchowosc paschalna" {Passion spirituality and Paschal spirituality}. On the 100th anniversary of the canonization of St. John of the Cross 1867-1967. *Ateneum Kaplanskie* Vol. 59 no. 70 notebook 5/6 pp. 258-264.

180. "Wychowanie do sluzby Kosciolowi" {Formation for service to the Church}. *Ateneum Kaplanskie* Vol. 59 no. 70, notebook 3/4 pp. 220-225.

181. "Kazanie ... w uroczystosc Chrystusa Krola" {Sermon by His Eminence the Metropolitan Archbishop in Wawel Cathedral on the Feast of Christ the King, Oct. 30, 1966}. *Notificationes e Curia Metropolitana Cracoviensi* (1967) no. 3/4 pp. 85-87.

182. "List pasterski..." {Pastoral letter for the first Sunday of Lent 1967}. *Notificationes e Curia Metropolitana Cracoviensi (1967) no. 3/4 pp. 87-90.*

183. "List ... {Letter of the Metropolitan Archbishop to the priests of the Archdiocese on the occasion of Holy Thursday}. *Notificationes e Curia Metropolitana Cracoviensi* (1967) no. 3/4 p. 90.

184. "Stulecie urodzin..." {The 100th anniversary of the birth of Prince Cardinal Adam Sapieha. Speech by ... Metropolitan Archbishop of Krakow}. Radio Vaticana, May 12, 1967. *Notificationes e Curia Metropolitana Cracoviensi* (1967) no. 5/6 pp. 94-96.

185. "Kazanie..." {Sermon by Archbishop ... at Skalka} in Krakow, May 14, 1967 [for the Feast of St. Stanislaw Bishop and Martyr]. *Notificationes e Curia Metropolitana Cracoviensi* (1967) no. 5/6 pp. 96-100.

186. "Consilium de Laicis." Address by ... Metropolitan Archbishop of Krakow.} Radio Vaticana, April 24, 1967. *Notificationes e Curia Metropolitana Cracoviensi* (1967) no. 5/6 pp. 107-110.

187. "Kazanie..." {Sermon by the Metropolitan Archbishop of Krakow at the coffin of Bishop Michal Klepacz,} Cathedral of Lodz, January 31, 1967. *Notificationes e Curia Metropolitana*

Cracoviensi (1967) no. 5/6 pp. 110-116.

188. "Kazanie powitalne..."{Welcoming sermon by His Eminence Cardinal ... delivered in front of Wawel Cathedral upon his return from Rome, July 9, 1967}. *Notificationes e Curia Metropolitana Cracoviensi* (1967) no. 7/9 p. 127.

189. "Kazanie..."{Sermon by His Eminence the Cardinal during the ingress, July 9, 1967}. *Notificationes e Curia Metropolitana Cracoviensi* (1967) no. 7/9 pp. 129-132.

190. Kazanie... {Sermon by H. Em. Cardinal ... delivered in the Basilica of Our Lady over the coffin of Msgr. Dr. Ferdynand Machay on August 3, 1967}. *Notificationes e Curia Metropolitana Cracoviensi* (1967) no. 7/9 pp. 196-202.

191. *Concilium de Laicis. Przewodnik Katolicki* (1967) no. 22 pp. 193-194.

192. "Stulecie urodzin Ksiecia Kardynala Adama Stefana Sapiehy" {The centenary of the birth of Prince Cardinal Adam Stefan Sapieha}. *Przewodnik Katolicki* (1967) no. 23 p. 204.

193. "Sp. Ks. Biskup Michal Klepacz" {The dearly departed Bishop Michal Klepacz}. (Excerpts from the sermon by ... delivered at the funeral, January 31, 1967.) *Przewodnik Katolicki* (1967) no. 28 p. 251.

194. "Kazanie zalobne..." {Funeral sermon by ... over the coffin of Bishop Michal Klepacz}. *Wiadomosci Diecezji Lódzkiej* {Newsletter of the Diocese of Lodz} (1967) Vol. 41 no. 2 pp. 36-49.

195. "Etyka a teologia moralna"{Ethics and moral theology}. *Znak* (1967) Vol. 19 no. 9 pp. 1077-1082.

1968

196. "Osoba i czyn na tle dynamizmu czlowieka" {Person and Act against the background of the dynamics of man}. In: *O Bogu i czlowieku* {Of God and man}. Vol. 1. Warsaw 1968 pp. 201-226.

197. General introduction to: *Sobór watykanski II. Konstytucje, dekrety, deklaracje* {The Second Vatican Council. Constitutions, decrees, declarations}. Polish text. Poznan 1968 pp. 9-23.

198. General introduction to: *Sobór watykanski II. Konstytucje, dekrety, deklaracje* {The Second Vatican Council.

Constitutions, decrees, declarations}. Latin-Polish text. Poznan 1968 pp. 9-23.

199. "Znaczenie konstytucji *Dei Verbum* w teologii" {The meaning of the constitution "Dei Verbum" in theology} In: *Idee przewodnie soborowej Konstytucji o Bozym Objawieniu* {Guiding concepts in the Council's Constitution on Divine Revelation}. Krakow 1968 pp. 7-11.

200. "Problem malzenstw mieszanych na Synodzie Biskupów" {The problem of mixed marriages at the Synod of Bishops}. *Ateneum Kaplanskie* (1968) Vol. 60, no. 71, notebook 3 / 4, pp. 187-190.

201. "Apostolstwo swieckich" {The apostolate of the laity}. Excerpt from a speech. *Ateneum Kaplanskie* (1968) Vol. 60, no. 71, notebook 5 pp. 274-280.

202. "Znaczenie Konstytucji Pastoralnej dla teologów" {The meaning of the Pastoral Constitution for Theologians}. *Collectanea Theologica* (1968) Vol. 38 fasc. 1 pp. 5-18. With abstract.

203. "Na 700-lecie Blogoslawionej Salomei" {On the 700th anniversary of Blessed Salomea}. *Notificationes e Curia Metropolitana Cracoviensi* (1968) no. 11/12 pp. 263-264.

204. "Przemowienie..." {Address by Cardinal {Wojtyla} ... for the 50th anniversary of KUL [Catholic University of Lublin]. Vatican Radio, October 19, 1968}. *Notificationes e Curia Metropolitana Cracoviensi* (1968) no. 11/12 pp. 261-263.

205. "Homilia..." {[Homily delivered during a Mass on February 18, 1968 at the Church of St. Caesar in Rome on the occasion of ingress]}. *Notificationes e Curia Metropolitana Cracoviensi* (1968) no. 3/5 pp. 38-40.

206. "Osoba i czyn. Refleksywne funkcjonowanie swiadomosci i jej emocjonalizacja" {Person and Act. The reflexive functioning of consciousness and its emotionalization}. Excerpt. *Studia Theologica Varsoviensia* (1968) Vol. 6 no. 1 pp. 101-119. With abstract.

207. "List..." {Letter of ... to the editors of *Tygodnik Powszechny* on the occasion of the 1000th issue of its publication. *Tygodnik Powszechny* (1968) Vol. 22, no. 17, p. 1.

208. "Uniwersytet katolicki: koncepcje i zadania" {The Catholic University: Concepts and mission}. *Zeszyty Naukowe Katolickiego Uniwersytetu Lubelskiego* {Academic Workbooks

of the Catholic University of Lublin} (1968) Vol. 11 no. 3/4 pp. 13-16.

1969

209. *Osoba i Czyn {Person and Act}.* Krakow: Polskie Towarzystwo Teologiczne {Polish Theological Society} 1969, 325 pgs.

210. *Komentarz teologiczno-duszpasterski do "Humanae Vitae" {A theological-pastoral commentary on "Humanae Vitae"}.* Rome: Centralny Osrodek Duszpasterstwa Emigracji {Central Office for the Ministry to ...Émigrés} 1969, 104 pgs.

211. * Proemio. In: *Introduzione all'Enciclica Humanae Vitae.* Tipografia Polyglotta Vaticana (1969) pp. 5-9.

212. *Miejsce zakonów i kleru w swiecie wspólczesnym {The role of religious orders and clergy in the contemporary world}.* Address at a Council symposium for generals of male religious orders. Krakow 1969, 11 pgs.

213. *Amor y responsibilidad.* Estudio moral sexual. Pref. De Henri de Lubac. Trad. Del fraces por Juan Antonio Segarra. Madrid: Edit. Razion y Fe 1969, 347 pgs. *Coleccion Psicologia, Medicina Pastoral,* vol. 70.

214. *Amore e Responsabilita.* Studio di morale sessuale. Pref. Alla ed italiana del Giovanni Colombo. Trad.: A. Berti Milanoli. Torino: Marietti 1969, 287 pages. La Vela. Collana Maior, 23.

215. "Problem teorii moralnosci" {The problem of the theory of morality}. In: *W nurcie zagadnien posoborowych* {In the mainstream of Postconciliar questions}. Vol. 3. Warsaw 1969 pp. 217-250.

216. "Nauka encykliki *Humanae Vitae* o milosci" {Teachings of the encyclical Humanae Vitae about love}. (Textual analysis). *Analecta Cracoviensis* (1969) Vol. 1 pp. 341-356. With abstract.

217. "Slowo wstepne" {Introductory note}. *Analecta Cracoviensis* (1969) Vol. 1 pp. 5-8. Same note in French, pp. 7-8.

218. "Il *boom* affettivo". *Corriere della Sera* (1969), from Nov. 4.

219. *...zeby On przyszedl...* {...that He may come...} (From the sermon by H. Em. Cardinal {Wojtyla} ... delivered at Piekary Slaskie during a pilgrimage of men and boys on May 26, 1968). *Duszpasterz Polski Zagranica* (1969) Vol. 20, no. 4 pp. 216-217.

220. "Crisis in morality". The Vatican speaks out on love and sex. *The Hartford Courant* (1969) no. 82, Sep. 29 {Entry in English in the original.}

221. "Wprowadzenie do encykliki *Humanae Vitae*" {Introduction to the Encyclical "Humanae Vitae"}. *Notificationes e Curia Metropolitana Cracoviensi* (1969) no. 1/4 pp. 1-3.

222. "Do kaplanów Archidiecezji Krakowskiej" {To the priests of the Krakow Archdiocese}. Krakow, January 18, 1969. [A letter on the subject of the Priests' Council]. *Notificationes e Curia Metropolitana Cracoviensi* (1969) no. 5/7 pp. 108-112.

223. "La verita dell'enciclica *Humanae Vitae*", *L'Osservatore Romano* (1969) Vol. 109 no. 4 pp. 1-2.

224. "Na dwudziesta rocznice gnieznienskiego ingresu Prymasa Polski" {On the 20th anniversary of the ingress of the Primate of Poland in Gniezno}. *Przewodnik Katolicki* (1969) no. 5 pp. 42-43.

225. "Kardynal ... o swojej podrózy do Kanady i USA" {Cardinal ... about his trip to Canada and the USA}. Statement on Vatican Radio. *Przewodnik Katolicki* (1969) no. 49 pp. 1-2.

226. "Problem doswiadczenia w etyce" {The problem of experience in ethics}. *Roczniki Filozoficzne* (1969) Vol. 17 bk. 2 pp. 5-24. With abstract.

227. "Experiences de nos grands seminaires: l'obeissance et l'esprit de dependance". *Seminarium* (1969) no. 1.

228. "Osoba i czyn. Refkeksywne funkcjonowanie swiadomosci i jej emocjonalizacja" {Person and Act. The reflexive functioning of consciousness and its emotionalization}. *Studia Theologica Varsoviensia* (1969) Vol. 6 no. 1 pp. 101-119. With abstract.[10]

229. "Z pobytu Kardynala ... w Rzymie" {From the trip of Cardinal... in Rome}. Interview conducted by Alojzy Orszulik. Excerpt. *Tygodnik Powszechny* (1969) Vol. 23 no. 2 p. 3.

230. "Wypowiedz ..." {Statement by ... at the Synod, Sep. 15, 1969}. *Tygodnik Powszechny* (1969) Vol. 23 no. 43 p. 5.

231. "... o swoim pobycie w Ameryce" {... on his trip to America}. Interview by Tomasz Rostworowski. *Tygodnik Powszechny* (1969) Vol. 23 no. 46 p. 5.

---

[10] Duplicate of 206.

1970

232. "Introduction" In: Thomas Aquinas, St.: *Summa Theologicae.* Vol. 18: *Justice.* London 1970 pp. 7-9.

233. "Introduzione al testo polacco del Cardinale ... In: Malej, W.: *Ladislao Michele Zaleski. Delegato Apostolico delle Indie Orientali, Archivescovo di Tebe - Patriarce di Antiocha.* Roma 1970 pp. 9-11.

234. "Wspomnienie of ksiedzu profesorze Wladyslawie Wichrze"{Reminiscences of Rev. Prof. Wladyslaw Wicher}. *Analecta Cracoviensa* (1970) vol. 2 pp. 7-13. Same text also in French, pp. 15-22.

235. "Synod Biskupów. Zebranie nadzwyczajne, Rzym 1969" {The Synod of Bishops. Extraordinary session, Rome 1969}. *Analecta Cracoviensa* (1970) vol. 2 pp. 131-156. With abstract.

236. "Notatki na marginesie Konstytucji *Gaudium et Spes*" {Sidenotes to the Constitution *Gaudium et Spes*}. *Ateneum Kaplanskie* (1970) Vol. 62, no. 2, notebook 1, pp. 3-6.

237. 'List ...' {Letter of Cardinal {Wojtyla}. ... to the Canadian Episcopate. (Comments on the meaning of visits by Polish bishops among Canadian Polonia)}. *Duszpasterz Polski Zagranica* (1970) Vol. 21 no. 2 pp. 127-129.

238. "List do kaplanow ... " {Letter to priests. For the conclusion of the pastoral visit in Canada}. *Duszpasterz Polski Zagranica* (1970) Vol. 21 no. 2 pp. 129-131.

239. "List do Mlodziezy ..." {Letter to young people. For the conclusion of the pastoral visit in Canada}. *Duszpasterz Polski Zagranica* (1970) Vol. 21 no. 2 pp. 131-133.

240. "Dziennik podrozy Kardynala" {Travel Journal of Cardinal {Wojtyla}. ... to Polish-Canadian centers in Canada}. *Duszpasterz Polski Zagranica* (1970) Vol. 21 no. 2 pp. 134-140.

241. "List Kardynala do rodakow ..." {Letter of the Cardinal ... to his countrymen in the United States of America}. *Duszpasterz Polski Zagranica* (1970) Vol. 21 no. 3 pp. 201-202.

242. "Dziennik podrozy Kardynala..." {Travel Journal of Cardinal {Wojtyla}. ... in the United States}. *Duszpasterz Polski Zagranica* (1970) Vol. 21 no. 3 pp. 203-209.

243. "Przemowienie ..." {Address of Cardinal {Wojtyla}... to the Holy Father on behalf of a pilgrimage of priests [to Rome on the 25th anniversary of the liberation of concentration camps]}. *Duszpasterz Polski Zagranica* (1970) Vol. 21 no. 5 pp. 353-354.

244. List do Duchowienstwa I Wiernych ... {Letter of ... to the Clergy and Faithful of the Archdiocese of Krakow in connection with the nomination of two auxiliary bishops}. *Notificationes e Curia Metropolitana Cracoviensi* (1970) no. 1/3 pp. 63-64.

245. "Konferencja o Synodzie ..." {A presentation on the Synod delivered at St. Anne Church in Krakow on November 27, 1969}. *Notificationes e Curia Metropolitana Cracoviensi* (1970) no. 1/3 pp. 64-69.

246. "Kazanie ..." {Sermon by ... at Wawel Cathedral on the Feast of the Three Kings (1970) during a Mass attended by faithful from parishes of the Archdiocese and by clergy and members of religious orders}. *Notificationes e Curia Metropolitana Cracoviensi* (1970) no. 1/3 pp. 69-73.

247. "Kazanie ..." {Sermon delivered at Wawel Cathedral during the consecration of bishops, April 5, 1970}. *Notificationes e Curia Metropolitana Cracoviensi* (1970) no. 4/6 pp. 111-113.

248. "Ostatnie slowo nalezy do milosci" {Love has the last word}. (From a homily delivered by ... at the Polish church of St. Stanislaw in Rome, Mar. 23, 1979). *Przewodnik Katolicki* (1970) no. 11 p. 89.

249. "Osoba ludzka a prawo naturalne" {The human person and natural law}. *Roczniki Filozoficzne* {Philosophical Annals} (1970) Vol. 18 bk. 2 pp. 53-59. With abstract.

250. "Wielki Post 1970" {Lent of 1970}. Pastoral letter. Tygodnik Powszechny (1970) Vol. 24 no. 10 p. 1.

251. "List do *Tygodnika Powszechnego* ..." {Letter to *Tygodnik Powszechny* in connection with the 25th anniversary of the publication}. *Tygodnik Powszechny* (1970) Vol. 24 no. 16 pp. 1-2.

252. "Kazanie ..." {Sermon delivered at the Basilica of St. Peter}. *Tygodnik Powszechny* (1970) Vol. 24 no. 28 p. 1-2.

253. "Wspomnienie o Jerzym Ciesielskim" {Reminiscence of Jerzy Ciesielski}. *Tygodnik Powszechny* (1970) Vol. 24 no. 51/52 p. 2.

1971

254. Introduction. In: *Teologia a antropologia* {Theology and Anthropology}. Kongres teologów polskich {Congress of Polish Theologians} Sep. 21-23, 1971. Krakow 1973 p. 1.

255. "Teologia i teologowie w Kosciele posoborowym" {Theology and theologians in the postconciliar Church} In: *Teologia a antropologia* {Theology and Anthropology}. Kongres teologów polskich Sep. 21-23, 1971. Krakow 1973 pp. 27-42.

256. Introduction to: Miazek, Bonifacy: *Slowa na pustyni* {Words in the desert}. An anthology of contemporary poetry by priests. London 1971 pp. 5-6.

257. *Dyrektorium Apostolstwa Swieckich w Polsce* {A directory of the Apostolate of the Laity in Poland}. *Kronika Diecezji Przemyskiej* {Chronicle of the Diocese of Przemysl} (1971) Vol. 57 pp. 73-78.

258. The same: *Oredownik Diecezji Chelminskiej* {Orator of the Diocese of Chelm} (1975) Vol. 26 pp. 117-129.

259. "List Gratulacyjny..." {Congratulatory letter to Rev. Alfons Schletz, the editor of *Nasza Przeszlosc* {Our Past}, on the 25th anniversary of the publication}. *Nasza Przeszlosc* 1971 vol. 36 pp. 8-9.

260. "Slowo na Boze Narodzenie 1970" {A word for Christmas 1970}. *Notificationes e Curia Metropolitana Cracoviensi* (1971) no. 1/2 p. 31.

261. "Slowo do kaplanów na dzien Wielkiego Czwartku" {A word to the priests for Holy Thursday. Krakow, March 11, 1971}. *Notificationes e Curia Metropolitana Cracoviensi* (1971) no. 5/6 pp. 140-141.

262. "Do Duchowienstwa ..." {To the clergy of the Krakow Archdiocese [in the matter of the Priests' Council]}. *Notificationes e Curia Metropolitana Cracoviensi* (1971) no. 7/9 pp. 193-194.

263. "Przemowienie w Radio Watykanskim..." {Address on Vatican Radio, October 5, 1971 [about Fr. Maksymilian Kolbe]}. *Notificationes e Curia Metropolitana Cracoviensi* (1971) no. 10/12 pp. 242-244.

264. "Konferencja Prasowa ..." {Press conference, Rome, October 14, 1971 [about Fr. Maksymilian Kolbe]}. *Notificationes e Curia Metropolitana Cracoviensi* (1971) no. 10/12 pp. 248-

250.

265. "Po zakonczeniu Synodu Biskupow ..." {After the conclusion of the Synod of Bishops. Speech on Vatican Radio, November 10, 1971}. *Notificationes e Curia Metropolitana Cracoviensi* (1971) no. 10/12 pp. 274-276.

266. "Pragne odpowiedziec na pytanie *Przewodnika Katolickiego...*" {I wish to respond to the question of *Przewodnik Katolicki* ... [Rights and duties of a Catholic in the work of postconciliar renewal]. *Przewodnik Katolicki* (1971) no. 21 pp. 185-186.

267. "Wklad nauki polskiej do badan nad antykiem chrzescijanskim" {The contribution of Polish scholarship to studies of Christian antiquity}. *Studia Theologica Varsoviensis* (1971) Vol. 9 bk. 1 pp. 21-50.

268. "Znak naszej epoki" {The sign of our times}. *Tygodnik Powszechny* (1971) Vol. 25 no. 42 p. 1.

269. "Udzial biskupów polskich w Soborze Wtykanskim II" {Participation of Polish bishops in the Second Vatican Council}. *Wiadomosci Archidiecezji Warszawskiej* {Newsletter of the Archdiocese of Warsaw} (1971) Vol. 53 no. 5 pp. 40-46.

270. "Znaczenie Kardynala Wyszynskiego dla wspólczesnego Kosciola" {The significance of Card. Wyszynski for the contemporary Church}. *Zeszyty Naukowe Katolickiego Uniwersytetu Lubelskiego* (1971) Vol. 14 no. 3 pp. 19-37. With abstract.

271. "List ..." {Letter to Ms. Hanna Malewska, editor in chief of the monthly *Znak* [on the occasion of the 25th anniversary of the publication]}. *Znak* (1971) Vol. 23 no. 2/3 pp. 141-144.

272. "Mysli o uczestnictwie" {Thoughts about participation}. Excerpt from the book "Person and Act." *Znak* (1971) Vol. 23 no. 2.3 pp. 209-225.

1972

273. *U podstaw odnowy {Sources of Renewal}.* A study on the implementation of the Second Vatican Council. Krakow: Polskie Towarzystwo Teologiczne 1972, 366 pgs.

274. "Swiadomosc Kosciola wedle Vaticanum II" {Awareness of the Church according to the Second Vatican Council} In: *W nurcie zagadnien posoborowych.* {In the mainstream of

Postconciliar questions}. Vol. 5: *Jan XXIII I jego Dzielo* {John XXIII and His Work}. Warsaw 1972 pp. 255-309.

275. "Przemowienie ..." {Address given by the Director of the Committee for Catholic Education [at the start of the 8th Congress of Polish Biblical Scholars, June 26, 1970]} In: *Wspólczesna biblistyka polska (1945-1971)* {Contemporary Polish Biblical Scholarship}. Warsaw 1972 pp. 23-26.

276. "List Ks. Kardynala ..." {Letter of Cardinal {Wojtyla} ... to the Editorial Director of *Znak* cited in: Rendu, Charles; Rendu Elizabeth: *Czy Kosciól nas oszukal?* {Did the Church betray us?} Krakow 1972 p. 5.

277. "Dlaczego beatyfikacja Ojca Maksymiliana" {Why the beatification of Father Maximilian} In: *W nurcie zagadnien posoborowych* {In the mainstream of Postconciliar questions}. Vol. 6: Blogoslawiony Maksymilian wsród nas {Blessed Maximilian among us} Warsaw 1972 pp. 204-210. Contains: "Message to priests prior to the beatification of Fr. Maximilian Kolbe" (Vatican) Radio address on October 5, 1971]; Press conference [Rome, October 14, 1971].

278. Introduction to: *Homilie i godziny biblijne* {Homilies and Bible hours}. Krakow 1972 pp. 5-6.

279. "Komentarz teologiczno-duszpasterski..." {Theological-pastoral commentary to the act of dedication from Jasna Gora on the day of May 3, 1966}. *Ateneum Kaplanskie* (1972) Vol. 64, no. 79, notebook. 1/2 pp. 5-21.

280. *Il sacerdoto — le aspettative della Chiesa.* Roma 1972 Cris. Documenti 6.

281. "List Pasterski ..." {Pastoral letter in connection with the 900th anniversary of St. Stanislaw's death}. *Notificationes e Curia Metropolitana Cracoviensi* (1972) no. 4/5 pp. 102-104.

282. "Przemowienie ..." {Speech delivered for the opening of the Synod of the Archdiocese of Krakow, May 8, 1972 at Wawel Cathedral}. *Notificationes e Curia Metropolitana Cracoviensi* (1972) no. 6/8 pp. 142-143.

283. "Przemowienie ..." {Speech delivered during the opening of the Pastoral Synod of the Archdiocese of Krakow on May 8, 1972 in Wawel Cathedral}. *Notificationes e Curia Metropolitana Cracoviensi* (1972) no. 4/5 pp. 153-158.

284. "Uroczystosc ..." {The Feast of Bl. Maximilian Maria {Kolbe}, on the first anniversary of the beatification in

Auschwitz. Notification and invitation [along with] commentary}. *Notificationes e Curia Metropolitana Cracoviensi* (1972) no. 9/10 pp. 173-175.

285. "Slowo wygloszone ..." {Remarks spoken during a meeting of directors of Synodal study groups on October 10, 1972 in Krakow}. *Notificationes e Curia Metropolitana Cracoviensi* (1972) no. 11/12 pp. 243-252.

286. "Slowo o Kongresie Eucharystycznym w Australii" {A word about the Eucharistic Congress in Australia}. *Notificationes e Curia Metropolitana Cracoviensi* (1972) no. 11/12 p. 266.

287. *"Oddanie Bogarodzicy w swietle nauki Soboru"* {Dedication to the Mother of God in light of the teachings of the Vatican Council}. *Przewodnik Katolicki* (1972) no. 26 p. 226.

288. "List do Redaktora..." {Letter to the editor on the occasion of the 25th anniversary of the publication}. *Ruch Biblijny i Liturgiczny* {Biblical and Liturgical Movement} (1972) Vol. 25 no. 1 p. 1.

289. "O Synodzie Biskupów" {About the Synod of Bishops}. *Tygodnik Powszechny* (1972) Vol. 26 no. 10 pp. 1, 5.

290. "List Pasterski..." {Pastoral letter [about the 900th anniversary of St. Stanislaw Bishop and Martyr]}. *Tygodnik Powszechny* (1972) Vol. 26 no. 16 p. 1.

291. "Fragment przemowienia..." {Excerpt of a speech for the opening of the Synod of the Krakow Archdiocese}. *Tygodnik Powszechny* (1972) Vol. 26 no. 21 p. 1.

292. "W pierwsza rocznice beatifykacji Ojca Maximiliana Kolbego" {On the first anniversary of the beatification of Fr. Maximilian Kolbe}. *Tygodnik Powszechny* (1972) Vol. 26 no. 39 p. 1.

1973

293. "Objawienie Trójcy Swietej a swiadomosc zbawienia w swietle nauki Vaticanum II" {The revelation of the Holy Trinity and the awareness of salvation in light of the teachings of the Second Vatican Council}. In: *Z zagadnien kultury chrzescijanskiej* {On the issues of Christian culture}. Lublin 1973 pp. 11-19. Excerpt of the work *U podstaw odnowy {Sources of Renewal}*, see entry 273.

294. "Slowa powitania..." {Words of welcome spoken by Cardinal {Wojtyla} ... for the beginning of the observance [of the first

anniversary of beatification of Bl. Maksymilian Kolbe at Auschwitz on Oct. 15, 1972]}. *Duszpasterz Polski Zagranica* (1973) Vol. 24, no.1. pp. 6-8.

295. "Sytuacja prawna Wydzialu Teologicznego w Krakowie" {The legal status of the Department of Theology in Krakow}. (A letter from the Cardinal ... to the priests). *Duszpasterz Polski Zagranica* (1973) Vol. 24 no. 3 pp. 250-254.

296. "Swiadomosc Kosciola wedle Vaticanum II" {Awareness of the Church according to the Second Vatican Council}. *Duszpasterz Polski Zagranica* (1973) Vol. 24 no. 3 pp. 255-309.

297. "Inspiracja Maryjna Vaticanum II" {The Marian inspiration of the Second Vatican Council}. *Duszpasterz Polski Zagranica* (1973) Vol. 24, no. 4, pp. 344-355.

298. "List Ks. Kardynala..." {Letter of the Cardinal ... to Poles in Australia for the end of his visit}. *Duszpasterz Polski Zagranica* (1973) Vol. 24, no. 4, pp. 398-400.

299. "Prawo do chrzescijanskiego wychowania mlodego pokolenia" {The right to Christian upbringing of the young generation}. [Sermon delivered May 5, 1973 in Wieruszow on the occasion of the 300th anniversary of the death of Fr. A. Kordecki {The Prior who led the defense of the fortress of Czestochowa against the Swedish invasion in 1656.}]. *Duszpasterz Polski Zagranica* (1973) Vol. 24, no. 5, pp. 461-462.

300. "Sprawy katechetyczne i wychowawcze w zwiazku z ostatnia uchwala sejmowa o wychowaniu mlodziezy" {Catechetical and educational issues in connection with the latest parliamentary resolution concerning the upbringing of young people}. Speech by the Cardinal ... to the priests assembled at a regional conference in Bielsko-Biala, May 17, 1973. *Duszpasterz Polski Zagranica* (1973) Vol. 24, no. 5, pp. 463-465.

301. "O poszanowaniu przekonan wierzacych obywateli" {On the respecting of the convictions of believing citizens}. Sermon delivered by H. Em. Card. ... during the Corpus Christi procession in Krakow on June 21, 1973. *Duszpasterz Polski Zagranica* (1973) Vol. 24, no. 6, pp. 465-466.

302. "Wychowanie religijne. Sprawy katechetyczne i wychowawcze w zwiazku z uchwala sejmowa o wychowaniu mlodziezy"

{Religious education. Catechetical and educational issues in connection with the parliamentary enactment concerning the upbringing of young people}. Excerpt of a lecture delivered on May 18, 1973 at a conference of priests of Krakow Deaneries. *Duszpasterz Polski Zagranica* (1973) Vol. 24, no. 6, pp. 575-579.

303. "Kongres Eucharystyczny w Melbourne oraz odwiedziny Polonii australijskiej (luty 1973)" {The Eucharistic Congress in Melbourne and the visit to Australian Polonia (February 1973)}. [Travel Journal]. *Notificationes e Curia Metropolitana Cracoviensi* (1973) no. 4/5 pp. 109-132.

304. "Przemowienie..." {Address given for the beginning of the second year of activity of the Pastoral Synod of the Krakow Archdiocese. Wawel Cathedral, May 8, 1973}. *Notificationes e Curia Metropolitana Cracoviensi* (1973) no. 6/7 pp. 141-148.

305. "Fragmenty z listu pasterskiego..." {Excerpts from a pastoral letter on the occasion of the 900th anniversary of the ascension of Stanislaw Szczepanowski to the diocesan see of Krakow}. *Przewodnik Katolicki* (1973) no. 19. p. 176.

306. "Sluzebnosc kaplanstwa" {Priesthood as service}. *Studia Pelplinskie* (1973) vol. 3 pp. 47-55.

307. "Przed Kongresem Eucharystycznym w Australii" {Before the Eucharistic Congress in Australia}. *Tygodnik Powszechny* (1973) Vol. 27 no. 5 p. 1.

308. "Kazanie..." {Sermon delivered at the funeral of Hanna Chrzanowska, May 2, 1973}. *Tygodnik Powszechny* (1973) Vol. 27 no. 25 p. 3.

309. "Ewangelie odczytac calym zyciem" {To interpret the Gospel with your whole life}. From a sermon for the conclusion of the 750th anniversary of the Polish Dominicans. *W Drodze* (1973) no. 3 / 4, pp. 91-95.

310. [Editor] *Z zagadnien kultury chrzescijanskiej* {On the issues of Christian culture}. Editorial committee Karol Wojtyla et al. Lublin: Towarzystwo Naukowe KUL (1973), 664 pgs. 13 tables, bibliography.

1974

311. "Wielki znak nadziei" {A great sign of hope} In: *Blogoslawiony Maksymilian Maria Kolbe* {Blessed Maria Maximillian Kolbe}. Niepokalanów 1974 pp. 44-50.

312. "Na otwarcie Kongresu Maryjnego" {For the opening of the

Marian Congress}. In: *Blogoslawiony Maksymilian Maria Kolbe*. Niepokalanów 1974 pp. 62-66.

313. "W pierwsza rocznice beatyfikacji Ojca Maksymiliana Maria Kolbe" {On the first anniversary of the beatification of Fr. Maria Maximillian Kolbe}. In: *Blogoslawiony Maksymilian Maria Kolbe*. Niepokalanów 1974 pp. 97-99.

314. "Slowo Powitalne..." {Word of welcome during nationwide observance in honor of Bl. Maximilian Kolbe}. In: *Blogoslawiony Maksymilian Maria Kolbe*. Niepokalanów 1974 pp. 101-102.

315. Introduction to: Wyszynski, Stefan: *Sursum corda*. [A selection of speeches]. Poznan 1974 pp. 5-6.

316. "Udzial swieckich w zyciu parafii" {Participation of lay people in the life of the parish}. In: *Dei Virtus*. Wroclaw 1974 pp. 81-88.

317. "Od Przewodniczacego Rady Naukowej..." {From the Director of the Academic Council of the Polish Episcopate, Karol Cardinal Wojtyla}. In: *Dzieje teologii katolickiej w Polsce* T. 1: *Sredniowiecze* {History of Catholic Theology in Poland. Vol 1: Middle Ages.} Lublin 1974 pp. XI-XIV.

318. "The Personal Structure of Self-Determination" {Original title in English}. In: *Tomaso d'Aquino nel suo VII centenario*. Congresso Internationale Roma-Napoli 17-24 aprile 1974. Roma 1974 pp. 379-390.

319. "Wypowiedz wstepna..." {Opening remarks during a discussion of *Osoba i Czyn [Person and Act]* at Catholic University of Lublin, December 16, 1970. *Analecta Cracoviensis* (1973-1974) Vol. 5/6 pp. 53-55.

320. " Slowo koncowe..." {Closing remarks [after the discussion of the book *Osoba i Czyn*]}. *Analecta Cracoviensis* (1973-1974) Vol. 5/6 pp. 243-263.

321. "La struttura generale dell autodecisione". *Aspreans* (1974) Vol. 4 pp. 337-346.

322. "Rodzina jako *communio personarum* Próba interpretacji teologicznej" {The family as *communio personarum* An attempt at a theological interpretation.} Excerpt of a work. *Ateneum Kaplanskie* (1974) Vol. 66, no. 83, notebook 3 pp. 347-361.

323. "L'evangelizzazione e l'uomo interiore". Cris (1974) Vol. 19 pp. 1-15.

324. "L' évangelisation du monde contemporain" Rapport du Card. Wojtyla, Archev findpat Íque de Cracovie, sur la IIᵉ partie (théologique) du theme Synode (8 octobre). *Documentation Catholique* (1974) Vol. 71 pp. 966-969.

325. "List Metropolity Krakowskiego..." {Letter from the Metropolitan Archbishop of Krakow, Card. ... to former prisoners of the concentration camp in Auschwitz and other concentration camps}. *Duszpasterz Polski Zagranica* (1974) Vol. 25 no. 1 pp. 19-20.

326. "600-lecie urodzin Królowej Jadwigi" {The 600ᵗʰ anniversary of the birth of Queen Jadwiga}. Sermon of Card. ... delivered in the Marian Basilica on February 1, 1974. *Duszpasterz Polski Zagranica* (1974) Vol. 25 no. 2 pp. 306-310.

327. "Deklaracja Ks. Metropolity...w sprawie kultu Krolowej Jadwigi" {Declaration by the Metropolitan Archbishop ... in the matter of the cult of Queen Jadwiga}. *Duszpasterz Polski Zagranica* (1974) Vol. 25 no. 2 pp. 319-320.

328. Rinnovamento ed evangelizzazione conclusi gli interventi sulla seconda parte del tema sinodale". La sinesi del cardinale Wojtyla. *L'Osservatore Romano* (1974) Vol. 114 no. 237 pp. 1, 6.

329. "L'evangelizzazione del mondo contemporaneo". *L'Osservatore Romano* (1974) Vol. 114 No. 232 pp. 1-2, no. 233 p. 5.

330. "600 Rocznica urodzin Blogoslawionej Królowej Jadwigi" {The 600ᵗʰ anniversary of the birth of Blessed Queen Jadwiga}. (Excerpts). *Notificationes e Curia Metropolitana Cracoviensi* (1974) no. 1/2 pp. 6-8.

331. "Slowo wstepne wygloszone na rozpoczecie III zebrania plenarnego..." {Introductory remarks at the opening of the 3rd plenary session of the Pastoral Synod of the Archdiocese of Krakow, May 8, 1974 at Wawel Cathedral}. *Notificationes e Curia Metropolitana Cracoviensi* (1974) no. 5/6 pp. 74-76.

332. "Kazanie wygloszone w Katedrze Wawelskiej..." {Sermon delivered in Wawel Cathedral at a Mass during the 3rd plenary session of the Pastoral Synod of the Archdiocese of Krakow, May 8, 1974}. *Notificationes e Curia Metropolitana Cracoviensi* (1974) no. 5/6 pp. 97-100.

333. "Kazanie wygloszone w Katedrze Wawelskiej..." {Sermon delivered at Wawel Cathedral during a service in honor of Blessed Queen Jadwiga, May 11, 1974}. *Notificationes e*

Curia Metropolitana Cracoviensi (1974) no. 5/6 pp. 100-104.

334. "Refleksje na marginesie Synodu — 1974" {Reflections on the margins of the Synod}. (Lecture delivered at the Papal Institute of Church Studies in Rome, Oct. 23, 1974). *Notificationes e Curia Metropolitana Cracoviensi* (1974) no. 9/10 pp. 224-236.

335. "O znaczeniu milosci oblubienczej" {On the meaning of spousal love}. Inspired by the discussion between Karol Meissner and Andrzej Szostek). *Roczniki Filozoficzne KUL* (1974) Vol. 22 bk. 2 pp. 162-174.

336. "Blogoslawiona Królowa Jadwiga" {Blessed Queen Jadwiga}. Sermon delivered at Wawel Cathedral on May 11, 1974. *Tygodnik Powszechny* (1974) Vol. 28 no. 23, p. 1.

337. "Ewangelizacja w swiecie Wspólczesnym" {Evangelization in the contemporary world}. *Tygodnik Powszechny* (1974) Vol. 28 no. 51/52 pp. 1, 10-11.

1975

338. Introduction to: Grzybek, Stanislaw; Kudasicwicz, Józef; Olszanski, Tadeusz: *Biblia na co dzien* {The Bible for every day}. Commentary to the Gospels. Krakow 1975 pp. 5-6.

339. Introduction to: *Katolicy swieccy w parafii* {Catholic lay people in the parish}. Krakow 1975 pp. 1-6.

340. Allocution by ... in: Mantesu-Bonamy, H. M.: *La doctrine mariale de Pere Kolbe.* Paris 1975 pp. 11-15.

341. Foreword in: Kotlarczyk, Mieczyslaw: *Sztuka zywego slowa* {The art of the living word}. Rome 1975 pp. 7-9.

342. Introduction to: *Biskup Pelczar* {Bishop Pelczar}. (Materials from the academic session dedicated to the life and works of the Servant of God J. S. Pelczar, Krakow 1974). Rome 1975 pp. 7-9. Also participation in the discussion, same, pp. 103-104; An address for the conclusion of the academic session, same, pp. 109-111.

343. "Rodzicielstwo a communio personarum" {Parenthood and *communio personarum*}. *Ateneum Kaplanskie* (1975) Vol. 67 no. 84, notebook 1 pp. 17-31.

344. "Perspektywy czlowieka — integralny rozwój a eschatologia" {Humanity's perspectives — integral development and eschatology}. Colloquium Salutis. *Wroclawskie Studia Teologiczne* {Wroclaw Theological Studies} (1975) Vol. 7 pp. 133-145,

with abstract.

345. "List do posla Janusza Zablockiego dyrektora OdiSS" {Letter to member of parliament Janusz Zablocki, director of ODiSS} [Center of Documentation and Social Studies]. *Chrzescijanin w Swiecie* {The Christian in the World} (1975) no. 4 pp. 11-12.

346. * *L'evangelizzazione al'uomo interiore.* Roma 1975 *Cris. Documenti* 19. See also entry 358.

347. "Refleksje na marginesie Synodu — 1974" {Reflections on the Synod}. *Duszpasterz Polski Zagranica* (1975) Vol. 26 no. 1 pp. 26-38.

348. "Pamietaj, abys dzien swiety swiecil" {Remember to keep holy the Sabbath Day} [Words of the 3rd Commandment]. *Duszpasterz Polski Zagranica* (1975) Vol. 26 no. 2 pp. 143-146.

349. "Sluzebnosc kaplanstwa" {Priesthood as service}. *Duszpasterz Polski Zagranica* (1975) Vol. 26 no. 4 pp. 389-398.

350. "Slowa Ks. Metropolity..." {Words spoken by Metropolitan Archbishop Card. ... at the coffin of Msgr. Marian Laczek, Dean of Podgórze and Pastor at Krakow-Biezanów, April 24, 1975}. *Notificationes e Curia Metropolitana Cracoviensi* (1975) no. 4/4 pp. 46-49.

351. "Rocznice Kosciola Krakowskiego" {Anniversaries of the Church in Krakow}. *Notificationes e Curia Metropolitana Cracoviensi* (1975) no. 5/7 pp. 53-56.

352. "Przemowienie wygloszone na otwarcie IV zebrania plenarnego..." {Speech delivered for the opening of the fourth plenary session of the Pastoral Synod of the Archdiocese of Krakow, on May 8, 1975}. *Notificationes e Curia Metropolitana Cracoviensi* (1975) no. 5/7 pp. 58-60.

353. "Homilia wygloszona w Katedrze Wawelskiej ..." {Homily delivered at Wawel Cathedral during the fourth plenary session of the Pastoral Synod of the Archdiocese of Krakow, on May 8, 1975}. *Notificationes e Curia Metropolitana Cracoviensi* (1975) no. 5/7 pp. 87-92.

354. "Homilia na swieto Matki Kosciola wygloszona..." {Homily for the Feast of Mary Mother of the Church delivered at the Mariacki Basilica on April 19, 1975}. *Notificationes e Curia Metropolitana Cracoviensi* (1975) no. 8/10 pp. 169-171.

355. "Przemowienie..." {Speech by the Metropolitan Archbishop

Card. ... delivered at the Basilica of the Twelve Apostles in Rome, after the beatification of M. Teresa Ledochowska on October 19, 1975}. *Notificationes e Curia Metropolitana Cracoviensi* (1975) no. 11/12 pp. 205-207. See also entry 389.

356. "W sluzbie ewangelizacji" {In the service of evangelization}. [Letter to the editor on the occasion of the 80th anniversary of the publication]. *Przewodnik Katolicki* (1975) no. 20 pp. 8-9.

357. "Rozwazania pastoralne o rodzinie" {Pastoral meditations on the family}. *Roczniki Nauk Spolecznych* {Annals of Social Studies} (1975) Vol. 3 pp. 58-76. With abstract.

358. "L'evangelizzazione al'uomo interiore". *Scripta Theologica* (1975) Vol. 7 pp. 335-352.

359. "Do *Tygodnika Powszechnego*" {To *Tygodnik Powszechny*}. [30th anniversary of the publication]. *Tygodnik Powszechny* (1975) Vol. 29 no. 13 p. 1.

360. "Slowo Pasterskie..." {Pastoral remarks [delivered at Jasna Gora on Apr. 3 1975 on the occasion of the 30th anniversary of *"Tygodnik Powszechny"*]}. *Tygodnik Powszechny* (1975) Vol. 29 no. 15 p. 1.

361. "Jestesmy uczniami Chrystusa" {We are the disciples of Christ}. Homily delivered at Wawel Cathedral on May 8, 1975. *Tygodnik Powszechny* (1975) Vol. 29 no. 22 pp. 1-2.

362. "Odezwa Metropolity Krakowskiego — 31 Tydzien Milosierdzia" {Message of the Metropolitan Archbishop of Krakow — for the 31st Week of Mercy}. *Tygodnik Powszechny* (1975) Vol. 29 no. 40 p. 1.

363. "Po beatyfikcji Marii Teresy Ledóchowskiej" {After the beatification of Maria Teresa Ledochowska}. Sermon delivered at the Basilica of the Twelve Apostles in Rome, Oct. 19, 1975. *Tygodnik Powszechny* (1975) Vol. 29 no. 47 pp. 1-2. See also entry 355.

364. "Ewangelizacja wspólczesnego swiata" {Evangelization of the contemporary world}. Theological report by ... at the Synod of Bishops 1974. Translated by Apolonius Zynel. *Znak* (1975) Vol. 27 no. 4/5 pp. 415-439.

365. [Pseudonym] Gruda, Stanislaw Andrzej: "Rozwazania o smierci" {Meditations on death}. [Poetry]. *Znak* (1975) Vol. 27 no. 3 pp. 271-276. {Poems:} I. "Mysli o dojrzewaniu" {Thoughts on maturing}. II. "Mysterium Paschale" III. "Bojazn, która lezy w poczatku" (The fear which lies at the

origin}. IV. "Nadzieja, która siega poza kres" {The hope which reaches beyond the end}.

366. "Teologiczne aspekty ewangelizacji" {Theological aspects of evangelization}. [Report by Card. Karol Wojtyla at the Synod of Bishops in 1974]. *Zycie i Mysl* {Life and Thought} (1975) Vol. 25 no. 8 pp. 101-107. Translated from *"L'Osservatore Romano"* (1974) no. 232.

367. "Podsumowanie dyskusji plenarnej..." {Summary of the plenary discussion [at the Synod of Bishops in 1974]}. *Zycie i Mysl* (1975) Vol. 25 no. 8 pp. 175-176. Translated from *"L'Osservatore Romano"* (1974) no. 232.

1976

368. *Znak, któremu sprzeciwiac sie beda {The Sign of Contradiction}.* Retreat at the Vatican. Rome — Vatican, the Apostolic See March 5-12, 1976. Poznan - Warsaw. "Pallotinum" 1976, 152 pages (4 pages unnumbered).

369. Introduction. *Analecta Cracoviensis* Vol. 8, (1976) pp. 5-6.

370. Introduction to: *Swieta Malgorzata Maria* {Saint Margaret Mary}. Warsaw 1976.

371. "Ewangelizacja wspólczesnego swiata" {Evanglizing the contemporary world}. Theological report by Card. Karol Wojtyla at the Synod of Bishops 1974. Translated by Apolonius Zynel. In: *W nurcie zagadnien posoborowych* {In the mainstream of Postconciliar questions} Vol. 8: *Chrzescijanstwo zywych* {Christianity of the living}. Warsaw 1976 pp. 59-83.

See also entries 364, 366.

372. "Inspiracja Maryjna Vaticanum II" {The Marian inspiration of the Second Vatican Council}. In: *W kierunku prawdy* {Towards the truth}. Warsaw 1976 pp. 112-121.

373. "Teologiczne podstawy duszpasterkiej misji kaplana" {The theological basis of the pastoral mission of the priest}. In: *Osobowosc kaplana* {The personality of the priest}. Wroclaw 1976 pp. 55-69.

374. Introduction to: Bednarski, Feliks: *Wychowanie mlodziezy dorastajacej* {The upbringing of adolescents}. Rome 1976 pp. 5-6.

375. "Special contribution to the debate: The intentional act — the human act that is, act and experience". *Analecta Husserliana* (1976) vol. 5 *The crisis of culture* pp. 269-280. {This entry in

English in the original}.

376. "Biskup — sluga wiary. Podstawy teologiczne" {The bishop — a servant of faith. Theological basis}. *Ateneum Kaplanskie* (1976) Vol. 68 no. 87 notebook 2 pp. 223-240. {See entry 380.}

377. "Il coraggio di confessare la fede". Discorsi presso quattro altari la domenica procedente il Corpus Domini 1976. *Cris. Documenti* 4 (1977) no. 34 pp. 5-13.

378. Wyznanie wiary dzisiaj {Profession of faith today. Sermon by Cardinal {Wojtyla}. ... during the *Corpus Christi* procession in Krakow, Jun. 17, 1976}. *Duszpasterz Polski Zagranica* (1976) Vol. 27 no. 4 pp. 428-434.

379. "Dwudziestopieciolecie smierci s.p. Ksiecia Kardynala Adama Stefana Sapiehy Metropolity Krakowskiego" {The 25th anniversary of the death of Prince Cardinal Adam Stefan Sapieha, Metropolitan Archbishop of Krakow}. Speech by the Cardinal ... at the unveiling of a monument of Prince Cardinal Metropolitan Archbishop Adam Stefan Sapieha at the Basilica of the Franciscan Fathers in Krakow on May 8, 1976. *Duszpasterz Polski Zagranica* (1976) Vol. 27 no. 4 pp. 438-440.

See also entry 382.

380. "Bishops as servants of the Faith". The Problem and its Theological Foundations. *The Irish Theological Quarterly* (1976) Vol. 43 pp. 260-273 {Entry in English in the original. See entry 376.}

381. "W zwiazku z 25-ta rocznica smierci s.p. Ksiecia Kardynala Adama Stefana Sapiehy Metropolity Krakowskiego" {In connection with the 25th anniversary of the death of Prince Cardinal Adam Stefan Sapieha, Metropolitan Archbishop of Krakow}. *Notificationes e Curia Metropolitana Cracoviensi* (1976) no. 1/2 pp. 40-41.

A pastoral letter from Jan. 21 1976.

382. "Dwudziestopieciolecie smierci s.p. Ksiecia Kardynala Adama Stefana Sapiehy Metropolity Krakowskiego" {The 25th anniversary of the death of Prince Cardinal Adam Stefan Sapieha, Metropolitan Archbishop of Krakow}. Speech by the Cardinal ... delivered at the unveiling of a monument of Prince Cardinal Metropolitan Archbishop Adam Stefan Sapieha at the basilica of the Franciscan Fathers in Krakow on May 8, 1976. *Notificationes e Curia Metropolitana Cracoviensi* (1976) no.

9/10 pp. 187-189. See also entry 379.

383. "Osoba: podmiot i wspólnota" {The person: subject and community}. *Roczniki Filozoficzne* (1976) vol. 24 bk. 2 pp. 5-39.

384. "Teoria e prassi nella filosofia della persona umana". *Sapienza* (1976) Vol. 29 bk. 4 pp. 377-384.

385. "Rozwazania Drogi Krzyzowej" {Meditations of the Way of the Cross}. [Traversed during the Lenten retreat in the Vatican in 1976]. *Tygodnik Powszechny* (1976) Vol. 30, no. 15 pp. 1-2.

386. "Wywiad dla *Tygodnika Powszechnego*" {Interview with *"Tygodnik Powszechny"* [on the topic of the Eucharistic Congress in Philadelphia and ministry to Polonia]. Interview by Andrzej Bardecki}. *Tygodnik Powszechny* (1976) Vol. 30 no. 45 pp. 1, 4.

387. "Znak, któremu sprzeciwiac sie beda" {Sign of Contradiction}. Vatican Retreat, March 5-12, 1976. Excerpt. *Znak* (1976) Vol. 28 no. 10 pp. 1315-1363.

1977

388. * *Segno di contraddizione*. Meditazioni. Milano: *Vita e pensiero* 1977.

389. "Po beatyfikacji Marii Teresy Ledóchowskiej" {After the beatification of Maria Teresa Ledochowska. (Sermon delivered at the Basilica of the Twelve Apostles in Rome, October 19, 1975.} In: *W nurcie zagadnien posoborowych* {In the mainstream of Postconciliar questions}. Vol. 9: *Maria Teresa Ledóchowska i misje* {Maria Teresa Ledóchowska and the mission}. Warsaw 1977, pp. 93-95. See also entry 355.

390. "Przemowienie w Lipnicy Murowanej..." {Address in Lipnica Murowana [May 16, 1976, on the occasion of the Feast of the Blessed Maria Teresa Ledochowska]}. In: *W nurcie zagadnien posoborowych* Vol. 9: *Maria Teresa Ledóchowska i misje*. Warsaw 1977 pp. 139-141.

391. "Das Problem der Erfahrung in der Ethik". In: W *700-lecie smierci sw. Tomasza z Akwinu* {On the 700th anniversary of the death of St. Thomas Aquinas}. Lublin 1977, pp. 267-288.

392. Introduction to: Drazek, Cz.: *Poslugacz tredowatych* {Servant of lepers}. Krakow 1977, pp. 5-6.

393. "Participation or Alienation?" *Analecta Husserliana* (1977) Vol. 6 pp. 61-73. {Title in English in the original}.

394. "Kazanie wygloszone w Kosciele OO. Bernardynow z okazji 750 rocznicy smierci sw. Franciszka z Asyzu" {Sermon delivered at the Church of the Bernadine Fathers on the occasion of the 750th anniversary of the death of St. Francis of Assisi, April 26, 1976}. *Ateneum Kaplanskie* (1977) Vol.70, no. 88, notebook 1, pp. 5-7.

395. "Slowo wygloszone na rozpoczecie sympozjum naukowego z okazji 750 rocznicy smierci sw. Franciszka z Asyzu" {Remarks delivered for the beginning of an academic symposium on the occasion of the 750th anniversary of the death of St. Francis of Assisi, April 26, 1976}. *Ateneum Kaplanskie* (1977) Vol. 70, no. 88 notebook 1 pp. 7-9.

396. "Teologia kaplanstwa" {Theology of the priesthood}. *Czestochowskie Studia Teologiczne* (1977) vol. 5 pp. 7-18.

397. "List Kardynala..." {Letter of Cardinal (Wojtyla). ... to the Polonia of the United States and Canada}. *Duszpasterz Polski Zagranica* Vol. 28 no. 1 pp. 81-82.

398. "Aktualnosc sw. Szczepana jako swiadka i obroncy wiary" {The relevance of St. Stephen as a witness and defender of the Faith}. Sermon of Card. ... in the Parish of St. Stephen in Krakow, Dec. 26, 1976 {the Feast of St. Stephen}. *Duszpasterz Polski Zagranica* Vol. 28 no. 2 pp. 165-169.

399. "Brat Albert, nasladowca sw. Franciszka z Asyzu" {Brother Albert, imitator of St. Francis of Assisi}. (Sermon of the Cardinal... at the grave of Servant of God Brother Albert, Feb. 1, 1977). *Duszpasterz Polski Zagranica* Vol. 28 no. 2 pp. 170-173.

400. "Konsekracja Kosciola w Nowej Hucie" {Dedication of the Church in Nowa Huta}. Sermon by the Cardinal... May 15, 1977. *Duszpasterz Polski Zagranica* Vol. 28 no. 4 pp. 394-399.

401. "Person: Ich und Gemeinschaft". *Klerusblatt* (1977) Vol. 57 no. 9 pp. 189-192.

402. "S.p. Ks. Infulat Bogdan Niemczewski" {The late Rev. Msgr. Bogdan Niemczewski}. Sermon delivered at Wawel Cathedral at a funeral on December 4, 1976. *Notificationes e Curia Metropolitana Cracoviensi* (1977) no. 1/2 pp. 81-94.

403. "List Wielkopostny o piatym przykazaniu Bozym" {Lenten letter about the Fifth Commandment}. *Notificationes e Curia Metropolitana Cracoviensi* (1977) no. 5/6 pp. 145-148.

404. "List do uczestnikow..." {Letter to the participants [of the 6th plenary session of the Pastoral Synod of the Archdiocese of

Krakow]. Krakow, April 16, 1977}. *Notificationes e Curia Metropolitana Cracoviensi* (1977) no. 7/7 pp. 192-193.

405. "Przemowienie inauguracyjne na otwarcie VII plenarnego zebrania..." {Speech for the inauguration of 6th plenary session of the Pastoral Synod of the Archdiocese of Krakow [May 7, 1977]}. *Notificationes e Curia Metropolitana Cracoviensi* (1977) no. 7/8 pp. 211-214.

406. "Homilia w czasie Mszy sw...." {Homily during a Mass [about St. Stanislaw Bishop and Martyr, and the priestly mission of the People of God, delivered May 8, 1977]}. *Notificationes e Curia Metropolitana Cracoviensi* (1977) no. 7/8 pp. 233-235.

407. "Kazanie na 50-lecie proboszczowania..." {Sermon for the 50th anniversary of service as a pastor by Rev. Msgr. Józef Polanski in Raba Wyzna (Jun. 13, 1977)}. *Notificationes e Curia Metropolitana Cracoviensi* (1977) no. 9/10 pp. 304-307.

408. "S.p. Ks. pralat Andrzej Bajer" {The late Rev. Msgr. Anrzej Bajer}. Sermon delivered at a funeral, May 2, 1977. *Notificationes e Curia Metropolitana Cracoviensi* (1977) no. 9/10 pp. 304-307.

409. "Slowo wygloszone podczas pogrzebu..." {Words during the funeral of Rev. Józef Pedziwiatr, March 22, 1977 in Dziekanowice}. *Notificationes e Curia Metropolitana Cracoviensi* (1977) no. 9/10 pp. 308-309.

410. "Il problema del constituirsi della cultura attraverso la 'Praxis' umana". *Rivista di Filosofia Neoscolastica.* (1977) An. 19 fasc. 3 pp. 513-524.

411. "... o katechizacji" {... about catechization [Excerpts]. Homily delivered at Kalwaria Zebrzydowska during the annual pilgrimage of men, June 5, 1977}. *Tygodnik Powszechny* (1977) Vol. 31 no. 30 p. 1.

412. Odezwa Metropolity Krakowskiego..." {Message of the Metropolitan Archbishop [on the occasion of the 80th anniversary of the birth of Holy Father Paul VI]}. *Tygodnik Powszechny* (1977) Vol. 31 no. 39 p. 1.

413. "Glosy w dyskusji na V Sesje Synodu Biskupow..." {Participation in the discussion at the fifth session of the Synod of Bishops in Rome, 1977}. *Zycie i Mysl* {Life and Thoughts} (1977) Vol. 28 pp. 51, 163, 179-180.

1978

414. "The Eucharist and Man's Hunger for Freedom". Homily given at the 41st International Eucharistic Congress in Philadelphia on August 3, 1976. Boston, Daughters of St. Paul 1979. {Entire entry in English in original.}

415. *Amore e responsibilita.* Proemio di Card. C. Colombo. Roma: Marietti 1978, p. 287.

416. Introduction to: *Milosc, malzenstwo, rodzina* {Love, marriage, family}. Collective work edited by F. Adamski. Krakow 1978 pp. 5-7.

417. "Signum magnum". Fragments. *Communio* (1978) Vol. 3 bk. 4 pp. 92-95.

418. "Travail et sens de l'homme". *Documentation Catholique* (1978) Vol. 75 pp. 911-913.

419. "Wizerunek Ostrobramskiej Matki Milosierdzia" {The Image of the Mother of Mercy of Ostra Brama}. *Duszpasterz Polski Zagranica* (1978) Vol. 29 no. 3 pp. 273-278.

420. La visione antropologice della *Humanae Vitae".* *Lateranum N. S.* (1978) An. 44 no. 1 pp. 125-145.

421. "Slowo Ksiedza Kardynala Metropolity ..." {Remarks by the Cardinal Metropolitan Archbishop [for the 8th plenary session of the Pastoral Synod of the Archdiocese of Krakow]}. *Notificationes e Curia Metropolitana Cracoviensi* (1978) no. 7/8 pp. 192-194.

422. "Kazanie w czasie pogrzebu..." {Sermon during the funeral of Rev. Msgr. Jan Wolny in Chrzanów, August 20, 1977}. *Notificationes e Curia Metropolitana Cracoviensi* (1978) no. 7/8 pp. 244-249.

423. "Slowo na otwarcie IX Zebrania Plenarnego" {Remarks for the opening of the 9th Plenary Session of the Synod of the Archdiocese of Krakow}. *Notificationes e Curia Metropolitana Cracoviensi* (1978) no. 9/10 pp. 252-254.

424. "Homilia" {Homily [delivered May 8, 1978 at Wawel Cathedral]}. *Notificationes e Curia Metropolitana Cracoviensi* (1978) no. 9/10 pp. 271-274.

425. "La sainteté sacerdotale comme carte d'identité". *Seminarium* (1978) no. 2 pp. 167-181.

426. "Christ sein im Lichte des Vaticanum II". *Trierer*

Theologische Zeitschrift (1978) Vol. 87 bk. 2 pp. 87-97.

427. "Na jublileusz sióstr Prezentek" {On the anniversary of the Sisters of the Presentation}. *Tygodnik Powszechny* (1978) Vol. 32 no. 1.

428. "List na Wielki Post 1978 (o VI przykazaniu Bozym)" {Letter for Lent 1978 (about the Sixth Commandment)}. *Tygodnik Powszechny* (1978) Vol. 32 no. 9 pp. 1, 7.

429. "Homilia wygloszona..." {Homily given April 12, 1978 at the Church of St. Anne in Krakow (for the 20th anniversary of the Club of Catholic Intellectuals)}. *Tygodnik Powszechny* (1978) Vol. 32 no. 18 p. 1.

430. "W sprawie uroczystosci sw. Stanislawa" {Regarding the Feast of St. Stanislaw}. *Tygodnik Powszechny* (1978) Vol. 32 no. 19 p. 1.

431. "Pasterz Kosciola Powszechnego" {The Shepherd of the Universal Church}. Homily given during a Requiem Mass for the repose of the soul of Holy Father Paul VI at Wawel Cathedral. *Tygodnik Powszechny* (1978) Vol. 32 no. 34 pp. 1, 8.

432. "Komunikat Kardynalow Polskich..." {Communiqué of the Polish Cardinals [after the election of Pope John Paul I]}. *Tygodnik Powszechny* (1978) Vol. 32, no. 36, p. 1. [Co-author].

433. "Slowo Pasterskie..." {Pastoral remarks to the Archdiocese of Krakow after the election of Pope John Paul I}. *Tygodnik Powszechny* (1978) Vol. 32 no. 38 p. 1.

434. "Homilia wygloszona w Bazylice Mariackiej..." {Homily delivered at the Mariacki Basilica during a Mass for the intention of Pope John Paul I, Oct. 1, 1978}. *Tygodnik Powszechny* (1978) Vol. 32 no. 41 pp. 1-2.

435. "Wypowiedz w ankiecie ..." {Statement in the survey "The living tradition of the European university." } *Zeszyty Naukowe Katolickiego Uniwersytetu Lubelskiego* (1978) Vol. 21 no. 2 pp. 51-53.

SIGNIFICANT WORKS ABOUT WOJTYLA

General

436. "Nowy Biskup sufragan..." {The new auxiliary bishop of Krakow}. Kronika Religijna {Religious Chronicle}. *Tygodnik Powszechny* 1958 Vol. 12 no. 33 p. 7.

437. Susul, Jacek: "Ingres dn. 8 III 1964 r." {The ingress of March 8, 1964}. *Tygodnik Powszechny* (1964) Vol. 18, no. 11, pp. 1-2.

438. Schletz, Alfons: "Kardynal Karol Wojtyla". Biographic sketch and bibliography of work 1949-1967. *Nasza Przeszlosc* (1967) Vol. 27, pp. 7-28, with photo.

439. Slipko, Tadeusz: "Wojtyla, Karol" In: *Enciclopedia Filosofica* Vol. 6, Firenze 1967 pp. 1152-1152.

440. "Metropolita Karol Wojtyla kardynalem" {Metropolitan Archbishop Karol Wojtyla becomes a Cardinal}. *Tygodnik Powszechny* (1967) Vol. 21 no. 23 p. 1.

441. Susul, Jacek: "Powrót na Wawel po otrzymaniu godnosci kardynala" {Return to Wawel after receiving the rank of Cardinal}. *Tygodnik Powszechny* (1967) Vol. 21 no. 30 pp. 1, 6.

442. Turowicz, Jerzy: "W Rzymie na konsystorzu (w czasie którego Arcybiskup Karol Wojtyla zostal kreowany kardynalem" {In Rome at the consistory (during which Archbishop Karol Wojtyla was created Cardinal)}. *Tygodnik Powszechny* (1967) Vol. 21, no. 30, p. 5.

Signed with the cryptogram J. T.

443. Górski, Tadeusz: "W piedziesieciolecie urodzin Ks. Kardynala Karola Wojtyly" {On the 50th birthday of Card. Karol Wojtyla}. *Kierunki* (1970) Vol. 15 no. 21 p. 4.

444. "25-lecie kaplanstwa Ks. Kardynala Wojtyla Wojtyly" {The 25th anniversary of the priesthood of Cardinal Karol Wojtyla}. *Tygodnik Powszechny* (1971) Vol. 25 no. 47 p. 1.

445. "Sprawozdanie z uroczystej Rady Profesorskiej w Krakowie … {Report from the solemn Council of Professors in Krakow on the 25th anniversary of the ordination and academic activity of Cardinal Karol Wojtyla, Metropolitan Archbishop of Krakow}. [November 21 1971]. *Analecta Cracoviensis* (1971) Vol. 3 pp. 439-440.

446. *Logos i ethos. Rozprawy teologiczne* {Logos and ethos. Philosophical deliberations}. Krakow: Polskie Towarzystwo Teologiczne 1971, 410 pgs.

A collective work dedicated to Cardinal Karol Wojtyla on the 25th anniversary of his ordination to the priesthood.

447. Jaworski, Marian: "Slowo Wstepne. Biografia naukowa Karola Wojtyly" (Introduction. An academic biography of

Karol Wojtyla}. In: *Logos i ethos*. Krakow 1971 pp. 9-18.

448. Styczen, Tadeusz: "Bibliografia wazniejszych prac Kard. K. Wojtyly" {A bibliography of the more significant works of Card. K. Wojtyla}. In: *Logos i ethos*. Krakow 1971 pp. 29-30. Contains 60 bibliographic entries.

449. Szteinke, Anselm: "Podróz kardynala Wojtyly do Australii" {The voyage of Card. Wojtyla to Australia}. (February 8-29, 1973). *Nasza Przeszlosc* (1973) Vol. 39 pp. 252-259.

450. "Diariusz z podrózy ks. Kardynala Wojtyly na Kongres Eucharystyczny w Melbourne oraz na Nowej Gwinei i Nowa Zelandii" {Diary of Cardinal Wojtyla's voyage to the Eucharistic Congress in Melbourne and to New Guinea and New Zealand}. *Notificationes e Curia Metropolitana Cracoviensi* (1973) pp. 109-132.

451. Pasquale, O.: "Il Congresso Internationale Tomaso d'Aquino nel suo VII Centenario, impresione — storia — doctrina." *Asprina* (1974) Vol. 4, pp. 497-505.

452. Turowicz, Jerzy: "Biskupi polscy u Polonii amerykanskiej" {Polish Bishops with American Polonia}. *Tygodnik Powszechny* (1976) Vol. 30 no. 42 pp. 1-3.

453. * Ziegler, J. G.: *Laudatio fur Karol Wojtyla anlasslich seiner Ehrenpromotion durch den Fachberiech Katolische Theologie der Johannes Gutenberg-Universitat in Mainz am 23 Juni 1977.*

454. Rhode, G.: "Polnische Ethik und Moraltheologie haben uns etwas zu sagen". Erzbischof von Krakau wurde Mainzer Ehrendoktor. *Kulturpolitische Korespondenz* 10 Juli, 1977 pp. 15-16.

455. Kochler, H.: "The dialectical Conception of Self-Determination. Reflections on the systematic Approach of Cardinal Karol Wojtyla". {Original title in English} *Analecta Husserliana* 1977 Vol. 6 pp. 75-80.

456. "Delegacja Episkopatu Polsiego za Oceanem" {Delegation of the Polish Episcopate Overseas}. *Duszpasterz Polski Zagranica* (1977) Vol. 28 no. 1 pp. 74-80.

457. "Doktorat honoris causa Ksiedza Kardinala Karola Wojtyly"

{The doctorate honoris causa of Card. Karol Wojtyla}. *Notificationes e Curia Metropolitana Cracoviensi* (1977) no. 9/10 pp. 237-238.

458. Póltawski, Andrzej: "Ethical Action and Consciousness. Philosophical and Psychiatric Perspectives". {Title in English in the original}. *Analecta Husserliana* (1978) Vol. 7 pp. 115-150.

Analyses of individual works.

Milosc i odpowiedzalnosc {Love and Responsibility} Lublin 1960; Ed. 2: Krakow 1962.

459. Witek, Stanislaw: "Milosc i odpowiedzialnosc" {Love and Responsibility}. *Ateneum Kaplanskie* (1961) vol. 63 pp. 284-288.

460. Rev. Faytt, Tytus: *Homo Dei* (1961) no. 3 pp. 277-279.

461. Rev. Kakol, Jerzy: *Wiez* (1961) no. 1 pp. 124-129.

462. Rostworowski, S[tanislaw] J[an]: "Prawdziwy sens milosci" {The true meaning of love}. *Za i Przeciw* (1961) no. 9 p. 4.

463. Bednarski, Feliks: "Bp. K. Wojtyla, 'Milosc i odpowiedzialnosc'. *Duszpasterz Polski Zagranica* (1962) no. 2 pp. 205-208.

464. Bortnowska, Halina: "Miara milosci" {The measure of love}. *Znak* (1963) Vol. 15 no. 4 pp. 401-420.

465. Olcjnik, Stanislaw: *'Milosc i odpowiedzialnosc'. Ateneum Kaplanskie* (1963) Vol. 55, no. 66, notebook. 1 pp. 84-92.

466. Meissner, Karol: "Prawo do osoby — problem etyki zycia seksulanego" {The right to a person — the problem of the ethics of sexual life}. *Roczniki Filozoficzne* (1974) Vol. 22 bk. 2 pp. 151-158.

467. Szostek, Andrzej: "Wolnosc osoby i jej konsekwencje" {Personal freedom and its consequences}. Comments on the article by Karol Meissner {entry 466}. *Roczniki Filozoficzne* (1974) vol. 22 bk. 2 pp. 158-161.

468. Piatek, J.: *Persona e amore nel pensiero filosofico del card. Karol Wojtyla.* Roma 1976.

Ocena mozliwosci zbudowania etyki chrzescijanskiej przy zalozeniach Systemu Maxa Schelera {An Assessment of the Possibility of Building Christian Ethics on the foundations of the

System of Max Scheler}. Lublin 1959.

469. Rev. Urmanowicz, Walenty: *Ateneum Kaplanskie* (1961) vol.
     63 bk. 3 pp. 279-284.

470. Keller, Józef: "Zwodnicze rozwazanie zle postawionego prob-
     lemu" {The false consideration of an ill-posed problem}.
     Studia Filozoficzne (1961) vol. 5, book 1, pp. 201-203.

471. Strózewski, Wladyslaw: "Ksiazki o etyce" {Books on ethics}.
     Znak (1961) no. 2, pp. 265-275.

Osoba i Czyn {Person and Act} Krakow 1969.

472. Bardecki, Andrzej: "Solidarnosc i sprzeciw" {Solidarity and
     opposition}. *Homo Dei* (1970) Vol. 39, no. 2, pp. 132-137.

473. Szpor, Romuald: "Studium osoby ludzkiej" {A study of the
     human person}. *Kierunki* (1970) Vol. 15, no. 21, p. 4.

474. Kuc, Leszek: "Tajemniczy swiat osoby" {The mysterious
     world of the person}. *Tygodnik Powszechny* (1970) Vol. 24, no.
     21, pp. 1-2.

475. Trzebuchowski, Pawel: "Byc i dzialac" {To be and to act}.
     Zycie i Mysl (1970) Vol. 19, no. 6, pp. 142-144.

476. Trzebuchowski, Andrzej: "Czyn a swiadomosc" {Act and
     awareness}. In: *Logos i Ethos* Krakow 1971 pp. 83-113.

477. Jaworski, Marian: "Z problematyki osoby w twórczosci kar-
     dynala Wojtyly" {On the problem of the person in the works
     by Cardinal Wojtyla}. *Analecta Cracoviensis* (1971) Vol. 3
     pp. 440-446.

478. Smolenski, Stanislaw: "Norma personalistyczna"{The per-
     sonalistic norm}. *Analecta Cracoviensis* (1971) Vol. 3 pp.
     311-320.

479. Pilus, Henryk: "Próba wspólczesnej tomistycznej teorii osoby
     ludzkiej" {An attempt at a contemporary Thomistic theory of
     the human person}. *Czlowiek i Swiatopoglad* (1971) no. 4 pp.
     91-98.

480. Rev. Kalinowski, Jerzy: *Revue Philosophique de Louvain*
     (1971) no. 69 pp. 602-603.

481. Stepien, Antoni B[azyli]: "Kilka uwag o swiadomosci" (W

zwiazku z ksiazka Kard. K. Wojtyly *Osoba i Czyn* {Several comments about conciousness (In reference to the book by Cardinal Wojtyla *Person and Act*} *Roczniki Filozoficzne* (1971) Vol. 19 bk. 1 pp. 129-130.

482. Grygiel, Stanislaw: "Czyn objawienem osoby?" {Act as the revelation of a person?} *Znak* (1971) Vol. 23 no. 2/3 pp. 200-208.

483. Zdybicka, Zofia Józefa: "O konieczna dla etyki filozofie czlowieka" {The philosophy of man required for ethics}. (A discussion of the book by Card. K. Wojtyla *Person and Act*). *Znak* (1971) Vol. 23 no. 4 pp. 400-511.

484. Pilus, Henryk: "Teoria osoby w klamrach metodologii"{A theory of the individual in the grasp of a methodology}. *Czlowiek i Swiatopoglad* (1972) no. 2 pp. 223-228.

485. Styczen, Tadeusz: "O metodzie antropologii filozoficznej. Na marginesie *Osoby i Czynu* K. Wojtyly oraz *Ksiazeczki o Czlowieku* R. Ingardena" {On the method of philosophical anthropology. Notes about *Person and Act* by K. Wojtyla and *The Little Book About Man* by R. Ingarden}. *Roczniki Filozoficzne* (1973) Vol. 21, bk. 2, pp. 105-114.

486. Lekiewicz, Zdzislaw: "Czyn osoby i rzeczywistosc" {A person's act and reality}. *Studia Filozoficzne* (1973) no. 5 pp. 263-268.

487. Gogacz, Mieczyslaw: "Hermeneutyka czynu. Sformulowanie kierunku rozwazan nad ksiazka K. Wojtyly *Osoba i Czyn*" {Hermeneutics of act. Formulation of the line of discussion on K. Wojtyla's book *Person and Act*} In: *Wokól problemu osoby* {Around the question of the person}. Warszawa 1974 pp. 106-122.

488. "Dyskusja nad dzielem Kardynala Wojtyly *Osoba i Czyn* {Discussion on the work of Cardinal Karol Wojtyla *Person and Act* on December 16, 1970 at the Catholic University of Lublin}. *Analecta Cracoviensis* (1973/1974) Vol. 5/6 pp. 49-272. For the contents of the discussion, see entries 319, 320, 489-509.

489. Szostek, Andrzej: "Wprowadzenie do dyskusji..." {Introduction [to the discussion on the work of Card. Karol Wojtyla "Person and Act"]. *Analecta Cracoviensis* (1973 /1974) Vol. 5/6 pp. 49-51.

490. Krapiec, Albert Mieczyslaw: "Ksiazka Kardynala Karola Wojtyly mongrafia osoby jako podmiotu moralnosci" {The

book by Card. Karol Wojtyla as a monograph of the person as the subject of morality}. *Analecta Cracoviensis* (1973/1974) Vol. 5/6 pp. 57-61.

491. Kalinowski, Jerzy: "Metafizyka i fenomenologia osoby ludzkiej. Pytania wywolane przez *Osobe i Czyn* {Metaphysics and phenomenology of the human person. Questions brought up by *Person and Act*}. *Analecta Cracoviensis* (1973/1974) Vol. 5/6, pp. 63-71.

492. Karminski, Stanislaw: "Jak filozofowac o czlowieku?" {How to philosophize about man?}. *Analecta Cracoviensis* (1973 /1974) Vol. 5/6, pp. 73-79.

493. Klosak, Kazimierz: "Teoria doswiadczenia czlowieka w ujeciu Kardynala Karola Wojtyly" {The theory of human experience as seen by Card. Karol Wojtyla}. *Analecta Cracoviensis* (1973/1974) Vol. 5/6 pp. 81-84.

494. Tischner, Józef: "Metodologiczna strona dziela *Osoba i Czyn*" {The methodological aspect of the work *"Person and Act"*}. *Analecta Cracoviensis* 1973/1974 Vol. 5/6 pp. 85-89.

495. Jaworski, Marian: "Koncepcja antropologii filozoficznej w ujeciu Kardynala Karola Wojtyly". (Próba odczytania w oparciu o studium *Osoba i Czyn*) {The concept of philosphical anthropology as approached by Card. Karol Wojtyla. (An attempt at interpretation based on the study *Person and Act)*}. *Analecta Cracoviensis* (1973/1974) Vol. 5/6 pp. 91-106.

496. Styczen, Tadeusz: "Metoda antropologii filozoficznej w *Osobie i Czynie*" Kardynala Karola Wojtyly {The method of philosophical anthropology in *Person and Act* by Card. Karol Wojtyla}. *Analecta Cracoviensis* (1973/1974) Vol. 5/6 pp. 107-115.

497. Forycki, Roman: "Antropologia w ujeciu Kardynala Karola Wojtyly" {Anthropology as seen by Card. Karol Wojtyla}. (On the basis of the book *Person and Act* Krakow 1969) *Analecta Cracoviensis* (1973/1974) Vol. 5/6, pp. 117-124.

498. Gogacz, Mieczyslaw: "Hermeneutyka *Osoby i Czynu* {The Hermeneutics of *Person and Act*} (A review of the book by Card. Karol Wojtyla). *Analecta Cracoviensis* (1973/1974) Vol. 5/6 pp. 125-138.

499. Grygiel, Stanislaw: "Hermeneutyka czynu oraz nowy model swiadomosci" {Hermeneutics of action and the new model of awareness}. *Analecta Cracoviensis* (1973/1974) Vol . 5/6 pp.

139-151.

500. Stepien, Antoni B[azyli]: Fenomenologia tomizujaca w ksi-azce *"Osoba i Czyn"* {Thomistic Phenomenology in the book "Person and Act"}. *Analecta Cracoviensis* 1973/1974 Vol. 5 /6 pp. 153-157.

501. Póltawski, Andrzej: "Czlowiek a swiadomosc" {Man and awareness}. (In connection with the book of Card. Karol Wojtyla "Person and Act"). *Analecta Cracoviensis* 1973/1974 Vol. 5/6 pp. 159-175.

502. Galkowski, Jerzy W.: "Natura, osoba, wolnosc" {Nature, the person, freedom}. *Analecta Cracoviensis* 1973/1974 Vol. 5/6 pp. 177-182.

503. Kuc, Leszek: "Uczestnictwo w czlowieczenstwie "innych"? - {Participation in the humanity of "others"?}. *Analecta Cracoviensis* (1973/1974) Vol. 5/6 pp. 183-190.

504. Wojciechowski, Tadeusz: "Jednosc duchowo-cielesna czlowieka w ksiazce *Osoba i Czyn"* {The unity of spirit and body in the book *Person and Act*}. *Analecta Cracoviensis* (1973/1974) Vol. 5/6 pp. 191-199.

505. Zdybicka, Zofia Józefa: "Praktyczne aspekty dociekan przed-stawionych w dziele *Osoba i Czyn"* {Practical aspects of inquiries presented in the work *Person and Act*}. *Analecta Cracoviensis* (1973/1974) Vol. 5/6, pp. 201-205.

506. Stroba, Jerzy: "Refleksje duszpasterskie" {Pastoral reflec-tions}. *Analecta Cracoviensis* (1973/1974) Vol. 5/6 pp. 207-209.

507. Kukolowicz, Teresa: "*Osoba i Czyn* a wychowanie w rodzinie" {*Person and Act* and family upbringing}. *Analecta Cracoviensis* (1973/1974) Vol. 5/6 pp. 211-221.

508. Póltawska, Wanda: "Koncepcje samoposiadania — podstawa psychoterapii obiektywizujacej" {Concepts of self-possesion — the basis of objectivist psychotherapy}. (In light of the book by Card. Karol Wojtyla *Person and Act*). *Analecta Cracoviensis* 1973/1974 Vol. 5/6 pp. 223-241.

509. Szostek, Andrzej: "Discussion sur l'ouvrage du Cardinal Karol Wojtyla intitule *Osoba i Czyn* (La personne et son agir; *Person und Tat*). Resume: Andrzej Szostek. *Analecta Cracoviensis* 1973/1974 Vol. 5/6 pp. 265-272.

U podstaw odnowy. Studium o realizacji Vaticanum II {Sources of

Renewal. A study of the implementation of the Second Vatican Council}. Krakow 1972.

510. Rev. Kubis, Adam: *Ruch Biblijny i Liturgiczny* (1972) Vol. 25, no. 4/5, pp. 299-300.

511. Rev. Kubis, Adam: *Tygodnik Powszechny* (1972) Vol. 26 no. 45 p. 2.

512. Cywinski, Bogdan: "Rzecz o wzbogaceniu wiary" {A work about enriching the faith}. (Review of a book by K. Wojtyla *Sources of Renewal*). *Znak* (1973) Vol. 25 no. 228 pp. 778-787.

513. Nagy, Stanislaw: "Program ocalenia." (W zwiazku z ksiazka *"U podstaw odnowy"*) {A program of salvation (In connection with the book *Sources of Renewal*)}. *Tygodnik Powszechny* 1976 Vol. 30 no. 13.

514. Rev. Polkowski, Andrzej, *Zycie i Mysl* (1973) no. 6, pp. 130-132.

Znak, ktoremu sprzeciwiac sie beda. Rekolekcje w Watykanie. {Sign of Contradiction}. The retreat in the Vatican}. Poznan 1976.

515. Grygiel, Stanislaw: *Doswiadczenie i swiadectwo* {Experience and testimony}. *Tygodnik Powszechny* (1977) Vol. 31 no. 32 pp. 1, 6.

Index of Persons and Places

Please Note: Geographical names of places without a reference to a country refer to Poland

A

Aachen (Germany) 536, 763
Ablewicz, Jerzy, Bishop 290, 309, 315, 317, 343, 380, 453, 570, 618, 661, 662, 665, 715, 716, 749, 815, 829
Abraham, Patriarch 241
Abrahamowicz Family 133
Abrahamowicz, Stanislaw and Lidia 684
Abramczuk, Olga 182
Abramowicz, Alfred, Bishop 717, 718, 771, 772
Adalbert, see St. Adalbert
Adam (First man) 241
Adam-Albert, see Brother Albert
Adamowicz, Helena 87
Adamski, Jan 127
Adamski, F. 889
Adelaide (Australia) 521, 789
Africa 511, 601, 613, 616, 661
A. J. (Andrzej Jawien) Karol Wojtyla's pen name 861, 863, 865
Albertine Brothers 186, 284, 793, 815
Albertine Sisters 23, 176, 191, 192, 201, 202, 216, 224, 235, 257, 283, 284, 290, 301, 378, 387, 392, 419, 442, 457, 470, 489, 558, 620, 637, 638, 698, 749, 787, 793
Albrecht, Archduke 35
Aleksandrowicz, Monika 505
Alexander of Hales 104, 106
Alwernia 273
Ambassador (United States) 806
America 101, 439, 772, 773 (see also United States)
American Czestochowa (Doylestown, PA USA) 376
American Delegation 705
American Polonia 349
Amsterdam (Holland) 114
Andruskiewicz, Janusz 146
Andrychow 52, 53, 332, 362, 829
Andrzej (no last name) 727
Andrzej (Bishop) 763
Andrzej K. (from Srodowisko) 218
Andrzejewski, Jerzy 57
Angelicum (University, Rome) 112, 698, 789

Angevin, (Jadwiga, Blessed Hedwig) 614
Annas 265
Annecy, France 404
Antigone 72
Antoniewicz, Stanislaw 509
Antoniszczak, John 219
Apostolic See 740
Aquinas (see St. Thomas Aquinas)
Aquino (Italy) 584
Arabian Peninsula 523
Arezzo (Italy) 714
Argentina 749
Ariccia (Italy) 246
Arimethea (Holy Land) 224
Ashfield (Australia) 509
Asia 335, 613
Assisi (Italy) 114, 376, 622, 670
Athens (Greece) 64, 224
ATK (Academy of Catholic Theology, Warsaw) 653, 753, 807, 808
Atlantic 746
Augustinian Sisters 218, 301, 481
Augustow 143
Augustowski Canal 143
Auschwitz (see Oswiecim) 80, 88, 173, 258, 263, 281, 308, 365, 409, 441, 450, 454, 464, 477, 478, 484, 485, 540, 560, 578, 599, 640, 648, 765, 791, 797, 816
Auschwitz-Birkenau 487
Australia 498, 499, 500, 501, 503, 507, 509, 511, 513, 515, 516, 517, 518, 520, 521, 522, 524, 525, 531, 532, 538, 786
Austria 753, 823
Austrian Authorities 352
Azory 320, 413, 414, 491, 563, 589, 625, 721, 819

B

B., Mr. and Mrs. 498
Babia Gora 137
Babica 560
Babinski (Professor) 49
Bachledowka 298, 327, 367, 403, 440, 477, 478, 544, 545, 659, 811, 822

936 *Kalendarium*

Parents, Karol Wojtyla and Emilia Kaczorowska, at their wedding, 1904. Karol is wearing his uniform as a noncommissioned officer in the Austrian-Hungarian army.

Karol with his mother, Emilia, 1920.

Karol in his first year of life.

The Wojtyla family's parish church in Wadowice, Poland. Karol was baptized here and later served as an altar boy.

Interior of church: The baptismal font where Karol was baptized.

The Wojtyla family.

Karol as a young boy
with his father.

The young
Wojtyla at his
First Holy
Communion.

The House in Wadowice where Karol was born: then, 2 Rynek St.; presently, 7 Koscielna St., Apt. 4.

Karol (*1st on left in top row*) among his school friends.

Karol *(2nd from left in 1st row)* among a group of altar boys flanking Fr. Figlewicz, the local pastor in Wadowice.

Karol's class trip to historical salt mines in Wieliczka in 1930, which Karol's father attended *(4th person from the right, 2nd row)* as one of the chaperones.

As a boy, Karol *(holding the ball)* enjoyed playing soccer with his friends.

Karol as a schoolboy in his uniform.

From the summer of 1938, Karol Wojtyla lived with his father in a basement apartment of this house at 10 Tyniecka St., Krakow, Poland.

Jan Tyranowski *(2nd from left, 1st row),* known as the Apostle of Debnica Youth, introduced the young Wojtyla to the world of Christian mysticism.

Karol performs in Nizynski's play, *Moon Cavalier*, during a local festival in Krakow at the courtyard of Nowodworskie Collegium.

High School graduation portrait of Karol, Wadowice, 1938.

The young Wojtyla strolls with his aunt and godmother, Maria Anna Wiadrowska.

During the German occupation of World War II, Karol Wojtyla as a laborer in the Solvay quarries.

Nr 5

Kraków, dnia czerwca 19 39 *r.*

PODKOMISJA DLA MAGISTERJUM

z f i l o l o g i i   p o l s k i e j

PROTOKÓŁ EGZAMINU

z gramatyki opisowej współczesnej polszczyzny

Nr	Data	Imię i nazwisko	Wynik	Podpis egzaminatora	Uwaga
45	11/VI	Truszkiewicz Zyta	niedost.		I
46	11	S.Urszula Walczyńska Wiktoria	dostat.		I
47	12/VI	Wojtyła Karol	dobry		I
48	"	Zając Irena	dostat.		I
49	"	Zarębska Antonina	dobry		I
50	"	Zbijewska Krystyna	dobry		I
51	20/VI	Dobrowolski W.	niedost.		

Przewodniczący Podkomisji:

Kraków, dnia 30 marca 1939 r.

The 1939 report of Karol Wojtyla's examination on Polish grammar from the Jagiellonian University.

UNIWERSYTET JAGIELLOŃSKI

Rok akademicki 193*9* /*80*

Dnia _____/_____19__

2 ? ? 1939

KARTA INDYWIDUALNA DLA SŁUCHACZY SZKÓŁ WYŻSZYCH

(Wypełnia k a ż d y student i wolny słuchacz na początku roku akad. Absolwenci, magistranci, doktoranci itp. tej karty nie wypełniają).

1. Nazwisko	*Wojtyła*	Imię	*Karol Józef*	
2. Nr albumu	*264 6*	3. Student czy ~~wolny słuchacz~~	*Student*	

I Obecne studia wyższe:		III. Wykształcenie średnie ogólnokształcące:		
1. Wydział (oddział, studium)	*filozoficzny*	Posiada świadectwa	1. dojrza-łości	typu	*neoklas.*
				wydane w roku	*1938*
2. Sekcję	*humanistyczną*		2. ukoń-czenia klas	typu	
				wydane w roku	
3. Przedmiot główny	*Filolog. polska*		wydane przez szkołę	w miejscowości	*Wadowice*
				w powiecie	"
4. Rok studiów (kurs)	*drugi*			w województwie	*Kraków*
				za granicą (kraj)	

II. Poprzednie studia wyższe:			IV. Cechy osobiste kandydata:	
(Wypełnia słuchacz, który przed zgłoszeniem się na dany wydział uczęszczał do jakiejkolwiek szkoły wyższej).			1. Płeć (męska, żeńska)	*męska*
1. Poprzednio był immatrykulowany	A. W tej samej szkole	1. Na wydziale i sekcji	*filozof.* *humanist.*	2. Data urodzenia	*18.V. 1920*
		w roku	*1938*	3. Miejsce urodzenia (miejscowość, powiat, województwo)	*Wadowice, pow. Wado- wice, woj. Kraków*
		2. Na wydziale i sekcji		4. Narodowość	*polska*
		w roku		5. Język ojczysty	*polski*
	B. W innej szkole	w szkole (nazwa)		6. Wyznanie	*rzym.-kat.*
		w miejscowości		7. Stan cywilny	*wolny*
		za granicą (kraj)		8. Zdolność do służby woj-skowej (kategoria)	*A*
		na wydziale i sekcji		9. Stopień wojskowy	w rezerwie	
		w roku			w służbie czyn.	
2. Posiada dyplom	Rodzaj dyplomu (podać bliższe określenie, np. lekarz, dr medyc., ma-gister filoz., inżynier chemik itd.)			10. Główne środki utrzy-mania (od rodziny, z własnych zarobków czy ze stypendium)	*od rodziny*
	uzyskany	w roku		10. Miejsce stałego za-mieszkania rodziców lub opiekunów (dla sierót) własne	miejscowość	*Kraków*
		na wydziale			miasto czy wieś	*miasto*
		w szkole (nazwa)			powiat	*Kraków*
		w miejscowości			województwo	"
		za granicą (kraj)			za granicą (kraj)	
				12. Obecny adres słuchacza	*Kraków, Tyniecka 10. Dęb?*
				13. Przynależność państw.	*polska*

The 1939 student record of Karol Wojtyla at the Jagiellonian University
(front).

14. Zawód i stanowisko w zawodzie ojca — żyjącego lub nieżyjącego
(Należy wpisać kreską pionową w odpowiedniej rubryce. Za podstawę określenia zawodu ojca należy przyjąć zajęcie, będące głównym źródłem jego dochodów)

Rolnictwo	1. Właściciele i dzierżawcy powyżej 50 ha		**Służba publiczna**	19. Urzędnicy i pracownicy umysłowi administracji państwowej, samorządowej i innych związków prawno-publicznych
	2. Właściciele i dzierżawcy powyżej 15—50 ha			
	3. Właściciele i dzierżawcy powyżej 5—15 ha			20. Profesorowie i nauczyciele szkół publicznych, państwowych i samorządowych
	4. Właściciele i dzierżawcy do 5 ha			
Przemysł i górnictwo	5. Pracownicy umysłowi			21. Niżsi funkcjonariusze i pracownicy fizyczni administracji państwowej, samorządowej i innych związków prawno-publicznych
	6. Robotnicy			
	7. Przedsiębiorcy więksi (wykupiono świadectwo przemysłowe od I—VII kategorii)			
	8. Przedsiębiorcy mniejsi, rzemieślnicy samodzielni (nienajemni)			22. Oficerowie wojska, K. O. P., policji, straży granicznej i więziennej
	9. Pracownicy umysłowi			
	10. Rzemieślnicy najemni, robotnicy i chałupnicy			23. Podoficerowie i szeregowcy wojska, K. O. P., policji, straży granicznej i więziennej
Handel i ubezpieczenia prywatne	11. Przedsiębiorcy więksi (wykupujący świad. przemysłowe I lub II kategorii)			
	12. Przedsiębiorcy mniejsi, drobni sprzedawcy			24. Profesorowie i nauczyciele szkół prywatnych
	13. Pracownicy umysłowi			
	14. Robotnicy i służba			25. Duchowni
Komunikacja i transport (przedsiębiorstwa państwowe, samorządowe i prywatne) łącznie z kolejami państw. i samorządowymi oraz pocztą	15. Przedsiębiorcy		**Inne zawody**	26. Wolne zawody (wolno praktykujący lekarze, adwokaci itp.)
	16. Samodzielni szoferzy, furmani, przewoźnicy itp. (nienajemni)			27. Emeryci, ~~inwalidzi i rentierzy~~ ╱
	17. Urzędnicy i pracownicy umysłowi			28. Służba domowa
	18. Niżsi funkcjonariusze, robotnicy i służba			29. Inne zawody: a) samodzielni (nienajemni): b) » (najemni): 1) pracownicy umysłowi 2) pracownicy fizyczni (wyrobnicy):

Czy pracuje w zawodzie, czy jest bezrobotny *emeryt*
(bezrobotnych kwalifikuje się według ostatniego zajęcia)

Imiona rodziców wzgl. opiekuna:
Karol i śp. Emilia

Zawód rodziców wzgl. opiekuna: (podać dokładnie rodzaj i miejsce zatrudnienia):
emeryt. porucznik W. P.

Kraków, dnia *3. listopada.* 193*9*

Karol Wojtyła
podpis studenta

His 1939 student record at the Jagiellonian University
(back).

Wykaz not egzaminacyjnych w tajnym nauczaniu w latach 1941-1945.

I. rok studiów.

	Logika II	Meta-fizyka I	teoria pozna.	Kosmo logia	Historia Kościoła cz. I	Apolo getyka cz. I	Wstęp ogólny do Pisma św.	Język grecki	Herm neutyka
Baziński Andrzej	1	2	3	2	3	2	2 zalb. 2 kan. edb.		1
Borowy Kazimierz	2	1	1	2	2	2	1 zalb. 13 kan.	1	1
Majda Władysław	1	1	2	1	1	2	1	2	1
Sidełko Jan	2	3	4	3	3	4	2 zalb. 3 kan. mkr.	2	3
Suder Kazimierz	2	1	1	3	3	2	2 kan. zalb. 2 zalb.	3	2
Targosz Karol	2	1	1	2	1	2	2 kan. zalb. 2	2	2
Wojtyła Karol	2	1	2	2	2	1	2 zalb. 1 kan.	1	1
Konieczny Franciszek		3		2	2	3	3 zalb. 3 kan. zalb.	3	3
Kościelny Stanisław	4	2	3	3 4	2	2	3 zalb. 3	2	3
Wilczyński Ryszard	3	2	3	3	2	1 2	1	2
Starowieyski Stanisław					2				

II. rok studiów.

	Psycholog.	Historia filozofii	Je przyrodni Kosmolna	Wstęp do NT proг. i dyd	Historia Kościoła	Apologetyk. o św. II o Kościele
Baziński Andrzej	3	3	3	4	3	2 2
Borowy Kazimierz	2	2	2	1	2	2
Majda Władysław	2	2	1	1	1	3
Sidełko Jan	3		2		2	3
Suder Kazimierz	3	3	2	2	4 3	3
Targosz Karol	2	1	1	2	1	2
Wojtyła Karol	3	2	1		1	1
Konieczny Franciszek					1	3
Kościelny Stanisław						
Wilczyński Ryszard	2					

Objaśnienie not eminenter = 1, valde bene = 2, bene = 3, sufficienter = 4.

Kraków 26/VI 1945

Karol Wojtyla's academic transcript from the underground university, 1941-45 *(front)*.

Uzupełnienie wyjaśniające do poprzednich not

V K/Borowy, historia kanonu : eminenter

L K. Suder, kosmogonia biblijna : valde bene

J Sidełko. De principiis : valde bene : wstęp szcz. księgi historyczne.
+ kosmog. biblijna · sufficienter; wstęp do ewang. syn. bene

Fr Konieczny, fundamentalna (o Kościele) : bene, Hist. Kościoła " eminen.

Kraków 29/5 1945.

His academic transcript from the underground university, 1941-45
(back).

D. Uwaga: Nazwisko i imię winno być napisane czytelnie.

Należy podawać dokładny adres zamieszkania — zgłaszać bezzwłocznie w kwesturze zmiany adresu. Kto obowiązku tego nie dopełni, naraża się na to, że sprawy dotyczące jego osoby a w szczególności sprawy dyscyplinarne z powodu niemożności odszukania będą załatwiane zaocznie.

Rok szkolny 193 *l/3 ?* **KARTA WPISOWA DLA DZIEKANATU** Rok studiów: _1/_

Nazwisko:		Imię:		Jest studentem		Wydział
Wojtyła		*Karol*		wolnym /	zwyczajnym	*filozoficzny*

Miejsce urodzenia	*Wadowice*	Dzień, miesiąc i rok urodzenia	*18 / V*	Religia	Język	Narodowość	Przynależność państwowa	Mieszkanie w Krakowie
Powiat	*Wadowice*		*19 20*	*rzym.-kat.*	*polski*	*polska*	*Polska*	Ul. *Tyniecka*
Województwo	*Kraków*							L. domu: *10.*

Imię i zatrudnienie rodziców lub opiekuna *Karol i śp. Emilia – ojciec por. emeryt. porucznik im. 4. P.*

Miejsce zamieszkania rodziców lub opiekuna *Kraków, ul. Tyniecka 10. (Dębniki)*

Stosunek do służby wojskowej *kategoria „A" – do służby wojskowej dotychczas nie powoływany*

Zakład naukowy, w którym student przebywał w poprzednim roku szkolnym *Gimnazjum Państwowe im. M. Wadowity, Wadowicach*

Wykaz wykładów na które student zamierza uczęszczać.

Try-mestr	Tytuł wykładu, ćwiczeń lub seminariów (należy wpisać w porządku trymestralnym)	Ilość godzin tygodniowo	Nazwisko wykładającego	Wykonane ćwiczenia i zdane kollokwia lub egzaminy	Uwaga
I	*Zasady polskiej etymologii*	4	*Prof. s.h.t. Nitsch*	✓	
I	*Elementy polskiej fonetyki opis z ćwicz.*	3	*Docent dr. H. Gaertnerówna*	✓	
I	*Ćwiczenia porównawcze o jęz. polskiego*	3	*Legł. mgr. K. Urbańczyk*	✓	
I	*Teatr i dramat w Polsce od poł. XIX w.*	2	*Prof. dr. St. Pigoń*	✓	
I	*Literatura wiosny ludów*	1	— " —		
I	*analiza wybranych utworów*	1	— " —		
I	*Seminarium dla młodszych*	2	— " —	✓	
I	*Analiza treści dramatu*	2	*Prof. dr. L. Kołaczkowski*		
I	*Powieść pamiętnik i korespon. Brzozowskiego*	2	— " —		
I	*Literatura polskiego średniowiecza*	3	*Doc. dr. I. Kamykowski*	✓	
I	*Ćwiczenia z Wierszy Staropolskich*	2	— " —		
~~I~~	~~Ćwiczenia prosem. z hist. literatury pol.~~	~~2~~	~~lektor dr. K. Wyka~~		
I	*Interpretacja dramatów i gryzeika*	3	*Lektor. dr. t. Dobrowolska*	✓	
II	*Historia i geografia pol. system. Jęz.*	4	*Prof. dr. K. Nitsch*	✓	
~~II~~	~~Wybrane partie z polskiej fonetyki~~	~~1~~	~~Docent dr. H. Gaertnerówna~~		
II	*Teatr i dramat w Polsce od poł. XIX w.*	2	*Prof. dr. St. Pigoń*	✓	
II	*Literatura wiosny ludów*	1	— " —		
II	*Analiza wybranych utworów*	1	— " —		
II	*Seminarium dla młodszych*	2	— " —		
II	*Humor, komizm, ironia i ich rola literackiej*	2	*Prof. dr. St. Kołaczkowski*	✓	
II	*Dramat i dobra naturalizmu i liryki polskiej*	2	— " —		✓
~~II~~	~~Dzieje powieści angielskiej~~	~~2~~	~~Doc. dr. Kamykowski~~		
II	*Ćwiczenia z literatury staropolskiej*	2	— " —	✓	
II	*Ćwiczenia prosem. z hist. literatury pol.*	**1**	*lektor. dr. K. Wyka*	✓	

No.	Course	Hrs	Instructor	✓
1	*[illegible]*	2	*[illegible]*	
2	*[illegible] z gramatyki [...]*	2	Doc. d. T. Milewski	✓
3	Interpretacja [...]	3	Lektor dr. A. Dobrowolski	✓
4	*[illegible] geografji [...]*	4	Prof. z dr. K. Nitsch	✓
5	*[illegible]*	2	Prof. z dr. S. Pigoń	✓
6	Literatura *[illegible]* ludów	1	— " —	✓
7	Analiza wybranych wzorów	1	— " —	✓
8	Seminarium dla *[illegible]*	2	— " —	✓
~~9~~	~~*[illegible]*~~	~~3~~	Prof. z dr. K. Nitsch	
10	*[illegible]*	2		
11	*[illegible]*	3	Doc. dr. T. Kłapyszewski	
12	*[illegible]*	2	— " —	
13	*[illegible]*	2	dlgi. dr. K. Łyka	✓
14	Interpretacja najnowszej [...]	6	Lektor dr. A. Dobrowolski	
1	Ćwiczenia bibliograficzne	2	Asyst. dr. Spytkowski	✓
1	Kurs wn. jęz. rosyjsk.	2	Lektor dr. Bednarek	✓
1	Interpretacja liryki współcz.	2	Lektor dr. Dobrowolski	✓
II	Wstęp do literatury	4	Asyst. dr. Spytkowski	✓
II	Kurs wn. jęz. rosyjsk.	2	Lektor dr. Bednarek	✓
I	Interpretacja liryki	2	Lektor dr. Dobrowolski	✓
II	Charakterystyka tych wzorów	2	Prof. dr. M. Nitsch	✓
II	Kurs wn. jęz. rosyjsk.	2	Lektor dr. Bednarek	✓
III	Wstęp do literatury	4	Asyst. dr. Spytkowski	✓

Zgodność indeksu z rodowodami sprawdzono:

Kraków, dnia 31 9 193...

[signature]
Sekretarz Dziekanatu.

[signature]
Dziekan.

His enrollment record from the 1939-40 academic year *(back)*.

Uwaga: Kartę należy wypełniać starannie i czytelnie.

Należy podawać dokładnie adres zamieszkania — zgłaszać bezzwłocznie w kwesturze zmiany adresu. Kto obowiązku tego nie dopełni, naraża się na to, że sprawy dotyczące jego osoby a w szczególności sprawy dyscyplinarne z powodu niemożności odszukania będą załatwione zaocznie.

Rok szkolny 194*4./5* **Karta wpisowa dla Dziekanatu** Rok studiów: *3.*,

Nazwisko: *Wojtyła*	Imię: *Karol Józef (2-ie)*	Jest studentem ~~wolnym~~ zwyczajnym	Wydział *teologiczny*

Miejsce urodzenia *Wadowice*	Dzień, miesiąc i rok urodzenia *18. V 1920.*	Religia *rzym. kat.*	Język *polski*	Narodowość *polska*	Przynależność państwowa *polska*	Mieszkanie w Krakowie
Powiat *Wadowice*						Ul. *Franciszkańska*
Województwo *Kraków*						L. domu: *3.*

Imię i zatrudnienie rodziców lub opiekuna	*Nie żyją* + *Karol emer. porucz. W. P.* + *Emilia*
Miejsce zamieszkania rodziców lub opiekuna	
Stosunek do służby wojskowej	*kleryk zarejestrowany (nr. zaświadczenia 687.)*
Zakład naukowy, w którym student przebywał w poprzednim roku szkolnym	

Wykaz wykładów, na które student zamierza uczęszczać

Trymestr	Tytuł wykładu, ćwiczeń lub seminariów (należy wpisać w porządku trymestralnym)	Ilość godzin tygodniowo	Nazwisko wykładającego	Wykonane ćwiczenia i zdane kollokwia lub egzaminy	Uwaga
I, II	De Sacramentis in genere et de Sacr. Eucharistiae in specie	5	ks. dr. Ing. Florkowski	religijne	✓
I, II	Wstęp szczeg. do Ewang. synopt.	3	ks. dr. Eug. Król	religijne	✓
I, II	Virtutes theolog.; I,II,III Prae. Dec.	4		religijne	✓
I, II	Liturgika	2		religijne	✓
I, II	Katechetyka	2		b. dobre	✓
II, III	Wstęp szczeg. do Ksiąg dydakt. i pror. St. Test.	2	ks. dr. Eug. Król	religijne	✓
III	Poenitentia	4	ks. dr. W. Wicher	religijne	
II, III	Exegesis Evangelii	5	ks. dr. Józef Kaczmarek	religijne	✓
I, II	De Deo Uno et Trino	6	ks. dr. Ign. Różycki	religijne	✓
II	Proseminarium	1	ks. dr. Ign. Różycki		
I, II, III	Patrologia	2	ks. dr. Jan Michalski	religijne	✓
II	Sztuka kościelna	2	ks. dr. T. J. Kruszyński	religijne	
III	Konserwacja zabytków	1	ks. dr. T. J. Kruszyński		
I, II	Język hebrajski	2	O. Eforian Głodź O. P.		
	Wstęp do St. T. ks. hist. i krn			religijne	✓
	Logika			b. dobre	✓
	Metafizyka			~~b. dobre~~	religijne ✓
	Teoria poznania			b. dobre	✓
	Kosmologia			b. dobre	✓
	Hist. Kościoła cz. I			b. dobre	✓
	Apologetyka			~~b. dobre~~	religijne ✓
	Wstęp szczeg. do Pisma św.			b. dobre	✓
	nowik. tekst }				
	kan.			~~b. dobre~~	religijne

Karol Wojtyla's enrollment record from the 1944-45 academic year *(front)*.

Język grecki			~~b. dobra~~	religijne
Hermeneutyka			~~b. dobra~~	religijne
Psychologia			~~dostateczna~~	dobre
Historia filozofii			b. dobre	✓
Moralna			~~b. dobra~~	religijne
Hist. Kościoła m. ½			~~b. dobra~~	religijne
Apologetyka			~~statut~~	religijne

Zgodność indeksu z rodowodami sprawdzono :

Kraków, dnia .... 194....

....
Sekretarz Dziekanatu   Dziekan

His enrollment record from the 1944-45 academic year *(back)*.

Young Fr. Wojtyla with the Marians at their house in Rome, 1948.

Książęco-Metropolitalne   R.szk. 1944/45.

Seminarium Duchowne   R.studiów III.

  w Krakowie

                    P R O T O K O Ł
                    - - - - - - - - - - - - - - - -

  z egzaminu z Teologii Moralnej / De Poenitentia / złożonego w dniu
  4.czerwca,1945.r-

  1) Baziński Andrzej   *valde bene* ⊿
  2) Borowy Kazimierz   *eminenter* ⊿
  3) Sidełko Jan   *bene* ⊿
  4) Suder Kazimierz   *valde bene* ⊿
  5) Targosz Karol   *eminenter* ⊿
  6) Wojtyła Karol   *eminenter* ⊿
  7) Junak Ludwik C.R.   *bene* ⊿

    Komisja Egzaminacyjna   Egzaminator

    Kraków,4.VI.1945.

Results of Karol Wojtyla's examination on moral theology
from the seminary in Krakow.

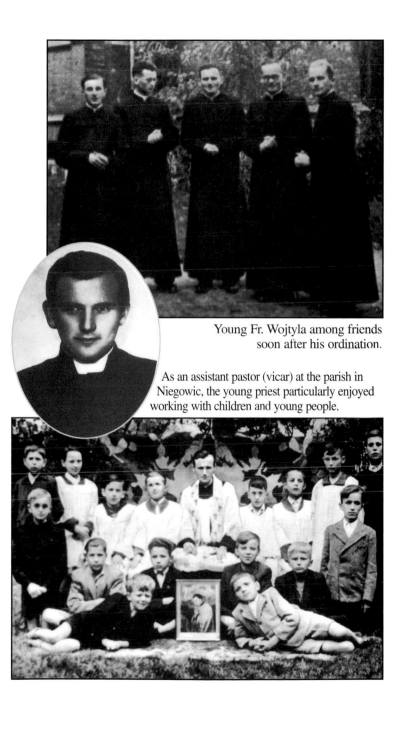

Young Fr. Wojtyla among friends
soon after his ordination.

As an assistant pastor (vicar) at the parish in
Niegowic, the young priest particularly enjoyed
working with children and young people.

L.384/45

U M O W A

o pracę, zawarta w Krakowie dnia 15 października   194 5 r.

między Dziekanem Wydziału **Teologicznego**   Uniwersytetu Jagielloń-

skiego działającym w imieniu Skarbu Państwa, jako pracodawcy a Pan em

W O J T Y Ł Ą   Karolem   jako pracownikiem.-

1).Pan **W O J T Y Ł A   Karol**   zwany w dalszej treści niniej

szej umowy pracownikiem, przyjmuje na siebie od dnia **1 listopada**

_____ **194 5** r.do dnia **31 sierpnia**   **194 6** r.obowiązki **kontr.**

młodszego asystenta   przy Seminarium dogmatyki szczegóło-

wej i hist.dogmatów Uniw.Jagioll.w wymiarze **15** godzin tygodniowo.

2).Pracownik otrzymywać będzie wynagrodzenie ustalone rozporządze-
niem Ministra W.R.i O.P.z dnia 15 grudnia 1936 r.o wynagrodzeniu za-
stępców profesorów, kontraktowych pomocniczych sił naukowych i za godziny zlecone w państwowych szkołach akademickich, oraz przewidziany
dodatek naukowy po myśli dekretu z dnia 6.VI.1945 (Dz.Z.Nr 25 poz.
152),, które to wynagrodzenie wypłacane mu będzie do miesiąc z góry.-

3).W razie podróży służbowej lub delegacji, zleconych przez władze
akademickie, pracownik otrzymywać będzie należności według norm,prze-
widzianych dla funkcjonariusza państwowego,pobierającego uposażenie
grupy

4).W razie niemożności pełnienia obowiązków wskutek powołania do
pełnienia czynności sędziego przysięgłego,ławnika sądu pracy, albo
innych obowiązków obywatelskich, nałożonych przepisami prawa publicz-
nego, albo też wskutek wykluczenia od zajęć przez władzę sanitarną,
dla zapobieżenia rozwleczenia choroby zaraźliwej, pracownik zachowuje
przez okres trzech miesięcy prawo do wynagrodzenia, zmniejszonego o
kwoty, otrzymane ze Skarbu Państwa z tytułu powołania do pełnienia wy
żej wymienionych obowiązków, albo też wykluczenia od zajęć przez władze sanitarne.W razie powołania do ćwiczeń wojskowych rezerwy będzie
pracownik otrzymywał wynagrodzenie, określone w punkcie 2, bez potrą-
ceń.Ze wszystkich wymienionych wyżej wyp adkach niemożności pełnienia obowiązków prawo do wynagrodzenia gaśnie przed upływem trzech miesięcy, jeżeli w ciągu tych trzech miesięcy umowa niniejsza ulegnie
rozwiązaniu wskutek upływu czasu, na który ją zawarto. W razie powołania do czynnej służby wojskowej na 5 miesięcy w myśl art.62 ustawy
z dnia 23 maja 1924 r.o powszechnym obowiązku wojskowym, oraz w razie
powołania do służby wojskowej na skutek mobilizacji lub częściowego
uzupełnienia wojska do stopy wojennej, przestanie pracownik otrzymywać
wynikające z niniejszej umowy wynagrodzenie z końcem miesiąca, w którym nastąpiło wcielenie.-

5).Pracownik zobowiązuje się ściśle stosować do ustaw i innych
przepisów, regulaminów i instrukcji, obowiązujących personel nauczy-
cielski szkół akademickich, względnie pomocnicze siły naukowe tych
szkół, oraz do wszelkich zarządzeń władz akademickich.-

Karol Wojtyla's 1945 contract *(front)* to work as a teaching assistant
in the Theology Department, the Jagiellonian University.

6).W razie uchybienia warunkom umowy, mogą być nałożone na pracownika kary pieniężne do wysokości 10% wynagrodzenia,niezależnie od możności stosowania innych rygorów.

7).Rozwiązanie stosunku pracy z niniejszej umowy następuje:

a) wskutek upływu czasu, na który umowę zawarto,
b) w razie przejścia pracownika do służby o charakterze publiczno-prawnym, z dniem poprzedzającym dzień od którego będzie przysługiwało pracownikowi uposażenie służbowe na podstawie nominacji.-

c)w razie powołania pracownika do odbycia obowiązkowej służby wojskowej z dniem wcielenia,
d) z chwilą śmierci pracownika.

Umowa nie ulega rozwiązaniu z powodu powołania pracownika do służby wojskowej na skutek mobilizacji lub częściowego uzupełnienia wojska do stopy wojennej, względnie z powodu powołania do pięciomiesięcznej obowiązującej służby czynnej w wojsku stałym, o ile stosunek pracy do chwili powołania trwał co najmniej rok.-

Po upływie trzech miesięcy niepełnienia obowiązków z powodu choroby lub nieszczęśliwego wypadku może Dziekan Wydziału **Teologicznego** U.J.uznać umowę za rozwiązaną.-

Umowa niniejsza może być każdej chwili rozwiązana przed upływem czasu, na jaki została zawarta.-W tym wypadku rozwiązanie stosunku pracy następuje po wypowiedzeniu umowy przez pracodawcę lub pracownika.Wypowiedzenie dokonane być winno na piśmie najpóźniej na 6 tygodni naprzód na koniec miesiąca.-

W razie popełnienia przez pracownika zaniedbania lub czynu, który będź to podpada pod powszechnie obowiązujące ustawy karne i ścigany ma być w drodze karno-sądowej, bądź też stanowiłby,jeśliby się go dopuścił profesor etatowy, względnie takaż pomocnicza siła naukowa występek służbowy w rozumieniu odnośnych ustaw i przepisów, służyć będzie Dziekanatowi Wydz. **Teologicznego** U.J.prawo jednostronnego uznania niniejszej umowy za rozwiązaną natychmiast. Decyzja ta,która winna być umotywowana i doręczona na piśmie,powoduje rozwiązanie stosunku pracy z chwilą jej doręczenia i wstrzymanie z tą chwilą określonego w punkcie 2 wynagrodzenia.Pracownikowi będzie służyło prawo odwołania się od tej decyzji w ciągu 14 dni od dnia następującego.po dniu doręczenia do Ministerstwa.Orzeczenie Ministerstwa jest ostateczne. Odwołanie nie ma w żadnym wypadku mocy wstrzymującej, a tylko w razie uchylenia decyzji przez Ministerstwo będzie pracownikowi służyło prawo żądania przywrócenia go do pełnienia obowiązków na warunkach niniejszej umowy, przy czym wynagrodzenie, jakie należałoby się od chwili zwolnienia, winno być dodatkowo wypłacone. Poza tym zrzeka się pracownik prawa podnoszenia z powodu wyżej unormowanego jednostronnego natychmiastowego rozwiązania umowy jakichkolwiek zarzutów, względnie żądania jakiegokolwiek odszkodowania.

8).W razie rozwiązania stosunku pracy pracownik będzie obowiązany zwrócić otrzymane zaliczki i uregulować zaciągnięte względem pracodawcy (Skarbu Państwa) zobowiązania pieniężne i inne.

9).Dla wszystkich sporów, jakie mogą wyniknąć z niniejszej umowy, będą w I instancji kompetentne sądy przedmiotowo-właściwe,mające siedzibę w Krakowie.

Kraków, dnia **15 październ.** 1945r.

K.Ż.ks.Jan Krzemieniecki
podpis pracodawcy *dziekan*

Karol Wojtyła
podpis pracownika.

Zanotowano
na odwrocie b.dział.
a/a 27/X45

His 1945 contract *(back)*
with the university.

UNIWERSYTET JAGIELLOŃSKI W KRAKOWIE
WYDZIAŁ TEOLOGICZNY

L. 284/48

DYPLOM
MAGISTRA TEOLOGII

Ks. Karol W O J T Y Ł A,

urodzony dnia 18 maja 1920 _____ roku w Wadowicach, wojew.krakowskie

odbył przepisane studia XX filozoficzno-teologiczne (tajne) w Seminarium Duchownym Krakowskim w latach 1942 - 1945, które na podstawie uchwały Rady Wydziału Teologicznego Uniwersytetu Jagiellońskiego z dnia 16.II. 1945 r. zaliczono do studiów uniwersyteckich, na Wydziale Teologicznym U.J.w latach 1945-1945/46, oraz w Instytucie "Angelicum" w Rzymie w r.1946/47

od roku akad. _ _ _ _ do roku akad. _____ i zdał następujące egzaminy:

z filozofii chrześcijańskiej i historii filozofii . . . z wynikiem bardzo dobrym

z nauk biblijnych Nowego Zakonu . . . . z wynikiem celującym

z nauk biblijnych Starego Zakonu. . . . . . z wynikiem celującym

z historii Kościoła katolickiego . . . . z wynikiem celującym

z teologii fundamentalnej (apologetyki) . . . . z wynikiem celującym

z teologii dogmatycznej . . . . z wynikiem celującym

z teologii moralnej ogólnej i szczegółowej . . . z wynikiem celującym

z prawa kanonicznego . . . . z wynikiem celującym

z teologii pastoralnej z liturgiką i homiletyką . . z wynikiem celującym

z pedagogiki, katechetyki i metodyki . . . . . z wynikiem bardzo dobrym

oraz przedstawił z wynikiem bardzo dobrym _____ pracę magisterską na temat "Pojęcie środka zjednoczenia duszy z Bogiem w nauce św.Jana od Krzyża".

Wobec tego Rada Wydziału Teologicznego Uniwersytetu Jagiellońskiego na wniosek Komisji Egzaminacyjnej nadaje Księdzu K a r o l o w i W O J T Y L E _____ stopień

MAGISTRA TEOLOGII

jako dowód zakończenia studiów uniwersyteckich

W Krakowie dnia 24 listopada _____ 1948 r.

REKTOR

DZIEKAN

Do Dziekanatu Wydziału Teologicznego
Uniwersytetu Jagiellońskiego
w Krakowie

Podpisany, załączając rozprawę et.
„De fide apud S. Joannem a Cruce", prosi o
dopuszczenie do egzaminu doktorskiego.
Rozprawa została wypracowana podczas
studiów na rzymskim Uniwersytecie Pa-
pieskim „Angelicum", wreszcie, była na-
wet tam broniona w letniej serii egza-
minów roku bieżącego. Niemniej zapoczst-
kowanie powyższej pracy miały miejsce
już w czasie studiów na Wydziale Teologicznym U.J. w Krakowie. Na tym też Wydziale podpisany posiada stopień magisterski,
którego dokument załącza, jak również
dokumenta stwierdzające wyniki uzyskane
w „Angelicum"

ks. Karol Wojtyła
(Niegowić k. Bochni)

Karol Wojtyla's petition to the Theology Department,
the Jagiellonian University, requesting a credit transfer from Rome
and admission to his final doctoral examination, 1948.

Q. F. F. F. Q. S.

SUMMIS AUSPICIIS

SERENISSIMAE REIPUBLICAE POLONORUM

NOS

ALEXIUS KLAWEK

S. THEOLOGIAE DR. STUDII BIBLICI VETERIS TESTAMENTI PROFESSOR P O.
h. t. UNIVERSITATIS IAGELLONICAE RECTORIS VICEM GERENS

IOSEPHUS KACZMARCZYK

S. THEOLOGIAE DR. STUDII BIBLICI NOVI TESTAMENTI PROFESSOR P O.
h. t. ORDINIS FACULTATIS THEOLOGIAE DECANUS VICEM GERENS

ET

LADISLAUS WICHER

S. THEOLOGIAE DR. THEOLOGIAE MORALIS PROFESSOR P. O.
PROMOTOR RITE CONSTITUTUS

IN

VIRUM CLARISSIMUM

CAROLUM WOJTYŁA

ORIUNDUM WADOWICE

POSTQUAM DISSERTATIONE t. t. „DOCTRINA DE FIDE APUD S. IOANNEM DE CRUCE"

CONSCRIPTA ET EXAMINIBUS LEGITIMIS LAUDABILEM IN UNIVERSA S. THEOLOGIA DOCTRINAM PROBAVIT

DOCTORIS S. THEOLOGIAE

NOMEN ET HONORES IURA ET PRIVILEGIA CONTULIMUS IN EIUSQUE REI EIDEM HASCE LITTERAS UNIVERSITATIS SIGILLO
SANCIENDAS CURAVIMUS

DATUM CRACOVIAE, DIE XVI MENSIS DECEMBRIS ANNO MCMXLVIII

ALEXIUS KLAWEK

IOSEPHUS KACZMARCZYK   LADISLAUS WICHER

CRACOVIAE 1949 — TYPIS UNIVERSITATIS IAGELLONICAE

Karol Wojtyla's Doctorate in Theology
from the Jagiellonian University.

7722/58

E.mo Card. Stefano Wyszynski
Arcivescovo di Gniezno e Varsavia
       Varsavia

Copia

Mi reco a doverosa premura di portare a cono_
scenza di Vostra Eccellenza Rev.ma la seguente
comunicazione, qui recentemente pervenuta dalla
S. Congregazione Concistoriale, la quale modifica
in parte quanto avevo avuto l'onore di parteci_
parLe con la precedente lettera N°5725/58 in data
10 luglio c.a.:

"Essendo stato soppresso il titolo vescovile
di Antigona che era uno di quelli che dovevano
essere depennati dopo la morte del titolare –
infatti la sede vescovile di Antigona non è pubblica
ta sull'Annuario Pontificio del 1958 – questa S. Con
gregazione ha assegnato il titolo vescovile di
Ombi a Mons. Carlo Wojtyla nel Luglio scorso
promosso all'Episcopato e deputato ausiliare di
S. E. Mons. Eugenio Baziak, Arcivescovo di Leopoli
dei Latini."

Sarò grato all'Em. V. se di tanto vorrà infor_
mare l'interessato.

Profitto ....

7722/58

Letter from the Vatican Secretariat of State to the Primate of Poland,
Cardinal Stefan Wyszynski, explaining how a mistake was made
in giving bishop nominee, Karol Wojtyla, his titular diocese.

Nr S.30/160/16/54/pfn.

P r o t o k ó ł IV
-------------- /

z posiedzenia poszerzonego Senatu Uniwersytetu Jagiellońskiego w dniu 19 stycznia 1954 r. /dalszy ciąg posiedzenia
z dnia 18.I.1954 r./.

O b e c n i : Rektor Prof.dr Teodor MARCHLEWSKI, Prorektorzy:
prof.dr Kazimierz LEPSZY, prof.dr Jan MOSZEW, prof.dr Mieczysław
KLIMASZEWSKI. Dziekani: Ks.prof.dr Tadeusz KRUSZYŃSKI, prof.dr Stanisław
SMRECZYŃSKI. Prodziekani: Ks.prof.dr Władysław WICHER, prof.dr Karol
OSTROWSKI, prof.dr Jan SAFAREWICZ, prof.dr Adam BOCHNAK, prof.dr Bro-
nisław ŚREDNIAWA, prof.dr Zygmunt GRODZIŃSKI. Kier.Studium Języków Obcych
dr Vilim FRANCIC. Delegat pom.sił nauk. mgr Danuta KUNISZ.

Z a p r o s z e n i :

Prof.dr Kazimierz Przybyłowski	-	do punktu	II/1, 2, 6,	
" dr Konstanty Grzybowski	-	" "	II/1,	
" dr Stefan Grzybowski	-	" "	II/1, 6,	
" dr Adam Vetulani	-	" "	II/2,	
" dr Władysław Wolter	-	" "	II/3,	
" dr Michał Patkaniowski	-	" "	II/3,	
" dr Wojsław Mole	-	" "	II/4, 5,	
" dr Tadeusz Dobrowolski	-	" "	II/4,	
" dr Karol Estreicher	-	" "	II/5,	
" dr Jan Dąbrowski	-	" "	II/7,	
" dr Roman Grodecki	-	" "	II/7, 8, 9,	
" dr Sylwiusz Mikucki	-	" "	II/8,	
" dr Kazimierz Dobrowolski	-	" "	II/9,	
" dr Józef Szaflarski	-	" "	II/10, 11,	
" dr Roman Wojtusiak	-	-	II/10, 11.	

N i e o b e c n i : dr Bolesław Drobner, dr Stefan Białas,
prof.dr Antoni Walas, prof.dr Witold Taszycki, prof.dr Feliks Polak,
płk.Cynkin, mgr Dawid Erdstein, mgr Jan Bugajski, mgr Jerzy Skórnicki,
prof.dr Władysław Madyda, dr Witold Zakrzewski, Delegaci organizacji
młodzieżowych.

Protokołował: Kierownik Sekretariatu Stanisław Brzykczyk.

I. Sprawa wniosków o przyznanie tytułów naukowych pracownikom nauki
Wydziału Teologicznego.

Rektor Marchlewski oświadcza, że wobec wątpliwości, czy przepisy
Centralnej Komisji Kwalifikacyjnej odnoszą się do prac.nauk.Wydziału
Teologicznego - zastosuje się dawną procedurę.

Prodziekan Wydziału Teologicznego U.J. ks.dr Władysław Wicher
odczytuje i uzasadnia kolejno wnioski Wydziału Teologicznego
w sprawie nadania:

./.

1954 record *(front)* granting Karol Wojtyla the title of assistant professor
in the Theology Department, the Jagiellonian University.

1/ Ks.dr Tadeuszowi Kruszyńskiemu - tytułu naukowego
profesora nadzwyczajnego.

Uchwalono jednogłośnie.

2/ Ks.dr Teofilowi Długoszowi - tytułu naukowego
profesora nadzwyczajnego.

Uchwalono jednogłośnie.

3/ Ks.dr Marianowi Michalskiemu - tytułu naukowego
profesora nadzwyczajnego.

Uchwalono jednogłośnie.

4/ Ks.dr Ignacemu Różyckiemu - tytułu naukowego
profesora nadzwyczajnego.

Uchwalono jednogłośnie.

5/ Ks.dr Aleksandrowi Usowiczowi - tytułu naukowego
profesora nadzwyczajnego.

Uchwalono jednogłośnie.

6/ Ks.dr Eugeniuszowi Florkowskiemu - tytułu naukowego
docenta.

Uchwalono jednogłośnie.

7/ Ks.dr Piotrowi Boberowi - tytułu naukowego
docenta.

Uchwalono jedno głośnie.

8/ Ks.dr Eugeniuszowi Wyczawskiemu - tytułu naukowego
docenta.

Uchwalono jednogłośnie

9/ Ks.dr Kazimierzowi Kłósakowi - tytułu naukowego docenta,

Uchwalono jednogłośnie.

10/ Ks.dr Władysławowi Smerece - tytułu naukowego docenta.

Uchwalono jednogłośnie.

11/ Ks.dr Stanisławowi Grzybkowi - tytułu naukowego docenta.

Uchwalono jednogłośnie.

12/ Ks.dr K. Wojtyle - tytułu naukowego docenta.

Uchwalono jednogłośnie.

1954 record *(back)* granting him the title of assistant professor
of Theology.

Karol Wojtyla's *(3rd from the right)*
10th high school reunion.

Karol Wojtyla is flanked by his former high school teachers in the market square of Wadowice: To the left are Professors Szeliski, Panczakiewicz, and Gebhardt. To the right are Professors Jach and Forys.
(Photo by Zbigniew Silkowski.)

As a passionate outdoorsman, Karol Wojtyla enjoys hiking and bicycling, among other activities.

Życiorys

Urodziłem się 18. V 1920 w Wadowicach (woj. Kraków) jako syn Karola Wojtyły i zmarłej śp. Emilii Kaczorowskiej. Do szkoły powszechnej jak też do gimnazjum ogólnokształcącego (typ. neo-klas.) uczęszczałem w miejscu urodzenia. Tam też złożyłem w maju 1938 r. egzamin dojrzałości, a korzystając z uzyskanego mi odroczenia służby wojsk., rozpocząłem studia na Wydz. humanist. U.J. w Krakowie (filologia polska). Wojna 1939 r. przeszkodziła mi w kontynuacji tych studiów, a warunki życia w pracie okupacji spowodowały, że w latach 1940 – 44 pracowałem jako robotnik fizyczny w zakładach „Solvay" w Borku Fałęckim k. Krakowa. Ta praca uchroniła mnie od wywozu na roboty do Niemiec, a równocześnie umożliwiła mi nawiązanie od października 1942 r. kontaktu z tajnym nauczaniem na Wydz. Teolog. U.J. w Krakowie. W ten sposób pierwsze dwa lata studiów teolog. odbyłem pracując jako robotnik. W sierpniu 1944 r. wobec szybkiego odwrotu okupanta udało ca mi zebrać tajnych studentów teologii w Seminarium Duch. Metropol. w Krakowie, gdzie też po wyzwoleniu mogłem kontynuować swe studia do r. 1946 na Wydz. Teolog. U.J. We wrześniu – dzienniku i listopadzie tego roku na poszczeg. ostatniego rocznika studiów otrzymałem wyższe święcenia (święcenia kapłańskie 1 XI. 1946), po nich zaś wyjechałem na życzenie Księcia Kardynała Adama Stefana Sapiehy, Arcybiskupa Krakowskiego, i na podstawie wydanego przez M.S.Z. paszportu udałem się na dalsze studia teolog. do Rzymu. Studiowałem w latach 1946-48 w uniwersytecie „Angelicum", po powrocie zaś przedstawiłem na Wydziale Teolog. U.J. w Krakowie rozprawę pt. „Zagadnienie wiary w dziełach św. Jana od Krzyża" jako pracę doktorską. Na jej podstawie zostałem promowany w grudniu 1948. r. uzyskując tytuł doktora św. Teologii na Uniw. Jag. w Krakowie. Równocześnie od 30. VII. 1948. do 17. VIII. 1949. przybywałem w parafii: Niegowić /k. Bochni spełniając w niej funkcję wikariusza, od dnia zaś 17. VIII. 1949. zostałem przeniesiony na takie samo stanowisko do parafii św. Floriana w Krakowie, na którym przebywam do chwili obecnej.

ks. Karol Wojtyła

Kraków, 8. IV. 1957.

Autobiography *(back)* written in April of 1957.

As an auxiliary bishop of Krakow, Karol Wojtyla makes a pastoral visit to the Chocholow Valley in the Tatra Mountains, June of 1961.

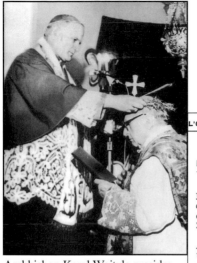

Archbishop Karol Wojtyla presides at the liturgy to celebrate Msgr. Edward Zacher's jubilee of priesthood. Msgr. Zacher was his religion teacher and the longtime pastor in Wadowice.

Official notice in *L'Osservatore Romano* of Karol Wojtyla's nomination as titular bishop of the diocese of Antigona.

L'OSSERVATORE ROMANO — 31 Agosto 1958 —

Provvista di Chiese

La Santità di Nostro Signore Si è benignamente degnata di promuovere:

alla Chiesa titolare Vescovile di Leptis magna il Reverendissimo Sacerdote Guglielmo Pluta, della diocesi di Katowice, parroco a Katowice-Zaleza;

alla Chiesa titolare Vescovile di Antigona il Reverendissimo Sacerdote Dr. Carlo Wojtyla, dell'arcidiocesi di Cracovia, professore di teologia morale all'Università Cattolica di Lublino, deputandolo in pari tempo *Ausiliare* di Sua Eccellenza Reverendissima Monsignor Eugenio Baziak, Arcivescovo di Leopoli dei Latini ed Amministratore Apostolico di Cracovia;

Cardinal Karol Wojtyla flanked by colleagues and friends in the courtyard of the Archbishop's Residence in Krakow, 1969. To the left are: S. Necek, Fr. A. Rajda, Z. Nowotarska, S. Wozniak, W. Pallner, and Fr. F. Gabryl. To the right are: J. Krupska and Auxiliary Bishop Julian Groblicki.

Receiving a cardinal's hat from
Pope Paul VI on June 28, 1967.

On one of his frequent trips
to Rome.

Signing a document for laying
a cornerstone at a church in Pradnik
Bialy in Krakow, May 22, 1972.

+ Drodzy Państwo Młodzi,

    Dziękując za wiadomość o Waszym ślubie,
przesyłam serdeczne życzenia błogosławieństwa
Bożego na dzień Sakramentu oraz na całą dro-
gę życia, która się w tym dniu rozpoczyna

+ ław. Karol Wojtyła

Jan Paweł pp. II
30. 9. 1980.,

WPaństwo
Hanna z d.Pokornowska i Stanisław GRZESIEKOWIE
P o z n a ń
Gwardii Ludowej 53 m.4

In a letter, Cardinal Wojtyla sends best wishes on a friend's wedding day – a proof of faithful remembrance of his old friends.

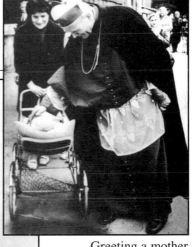

Greeting a mother and her baby.

Visiting the elderly in a nursing home run by the Albertine Sisters, Krakow.

The Cardinal blesses
the faithful with the
relics of St. Stanislaus,
Bishop and Martyr,
on his feast day in
Skalka, Krakow.

He greets Zywiec
residents.

Visiting an exhibit in the cathedral museum, Krakow, 1978.

The Cardinal enjoys winter sports.

Preaching to the faithful in Nowa Huta.

Cardinal Karol Wojtyla joins in blessing with Pope Paul VI.

Cardinal Wojtyla officiates in the enthronement of the image of Our Lady in Smardzewice, August. 27, 1972, with Cardinal Wyszynski, Primate of Poland.

As Archbishop of Krakow, Karol Wojtyla
performs his pastoral duties.

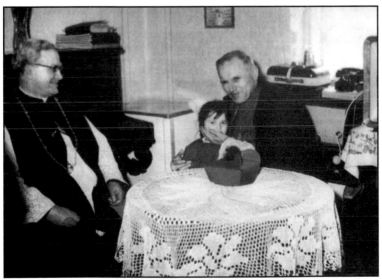

During a pastoral visit, the Cardinal embraces a child
while Msgr. Teofil Kurowski looks on.

Cardinal Wojtyla is joined by Cardinals Wyszynski and Kominek
in a procession on St. Stanislaus's feast day, Skalka, Krakow.

Cardinal Wojtyla speaks in the Podhale region during a 1977
visit from Cardinal Patrick Cody, Archbishop of Chicago.

In Nowy Targ, Cardinal Wojtyla enjoys a musical performance with Cardinal Patrick Cody and Bishop Alfred Abramowicz of Chicago, August 28, 1977.

Cardinal Wojtyla lights a bonfire in the Tatra Mountains in Chocholow, along with Bishop Abramowicz, August of 1977.

In Auschwitz, Cardinal Wojtyla and Cardinal John Krol, Archbishop of Philadelphia, pay their respects at the death cell of Maximilian Kolbe.

Cardinal Wojtyla at a ceremony in the Auschwitz Concentration Camp after the beatification of Maximilian Maria Kolbe.

Cardinal Wojtyla preaches
at Jasna Gora Monastery in Czestochowa.

Children gather as Cardinal Wojtyla and Cardinal John Krol, Archbishop
of Philadelphia, visit the construction site of a new church.

The Jagiellonian University
(Collegium Novum) in Krakow.

Senate Room
at the Jagiellonian University in Krakow.

Archbishop's
Residence in
Krakow at 3
Franciszkanska St.

The courtyard of
the Archbishop's
Residence in
Krakow.

Reception Room in the Archbishop's Residence.

Celebration
of St. Stanislaus's
Jubilee
in Szczepanow,
August 28, 1977.

Cardinal
Wojtyla's
audience with
the newly
elected Pope
John Paul I,
August 30,
1978.

Karol Wojtyla enjoys
natural beauty in the mountains.

Newly elected Pope John
Paul II acknowledges
the crowd in St. Peter's,
October 16, 1978.

In an audience with the
Poles, the newly elected
Pope embraces Cardinal
Wyszynski, Primate of
Poland.